IMPORTANT

HERE IS YOUR REGISTRATION CODE TO ACCESS MCGRAW-HILL PREMIUM CONTENT AND MCGRAW-HILL ONLINE RESOURCES

For key premium online resources you need THIS CODE to gain access. Once the code is entered, you will be able to use the web resources for the length of your course.

Access is provided only if you have purchased a new book.

If the registration code is missing from this book, the registration screen on our website, and within your WebCT or Blackboard course will tell you how to obtain your new code. Your registration code can be used only once to establish access. It is not transferable

To gain access to these online resources

1. USE your web browser to go to: **www.mhhe.com/messier4e**

2. CLICK on "First Time User"

3. ENTER the Registration Code printed on the tear-off bookmark on the right

4. After you have entered your registration code, click on "Register"

5. FOLLOW the instructions to setup your personal UserID and Password

6. WRITE your UserID and Password down for future reference. Keep it in a safe place.

If your course is using WebCT or Blackboard, you'll be able to use this code to access the McGraw-Hill content within your instructor's online course.

To gain access to the McGraw-Hill content in your instructor's WebCT or Blackboard course simply log into the course with the user ID and Password provided by your instructor. Enter the registration code exactly as it appears to the right when prompted by the system. You will only need to use this code the first time you click on McGraw-Hill content.

These instructions are specifically for student access. Instructors are not required to register via the above instructions.

Thank you, and welcome to your McGraw-Hill/Irwin Online Resources.

Messier, Glover, Prawitt
Auditing and Assurance Services, 4/E
0-07-310319-5

REGISTRATION CODE

JMBB-DTED-1M39-UAR5-IMKT

AUDITING & ASSURANCE SERVICES
A SYSTEMATIC APPROACH

AUDITING & ASSURANCE SERVICES
A SYSTEMATIC APPROACH

Fourth Edition

William F. Messier, Jr.
Deloitte & Touche Professor
School of Accountancy
Georgia State University

Steven M. Glover
PricewaterhouseCoopers Research Fellow
Marriott School of Management
Brigham Young University

Douglas F. Prawitt
Deloitte Research Fellow
Marriott School of Management
Brigham Young University

McGraw-Hill Irwin

Boston   Burr Ridge, IL   Dubuque, IA   Madison, WI   New York   San Francisco   St. Louis
Bangkok   Bogotá   Caracas   Kuala Lumpur   Lisbon   London   Madrid   Mexico City
Milan   Montreal   New Delhi   Santiago   Seoul   Singapore   Sydney   Taipei   Toronto

McGraw-Hill
Irwin

AUDITING & ASSURANCE SERVICES: A SYSTEMATIC APPROACH

Published by McGraw-Hill/Irwin, a business unit of The McGraw-Hill Companies, Inc., 1221 Avenue of the Americas, New York, NY, 10020. Copyright © 2006, 2003, 2000, 1997 by The McGraw-Hill Companies, Inc. All rights reserved. No part of this publication may be reproduced or distributed in any form or by any means, or stored in a database or retrieval system, without the prior written consent of The McGraw-Hill Companies, Inc., including, but not limited to, in any network or other electronic storage or transmission, or broadcast for distance learning.

Some ancillaries, including electronic and print components, may not be available to customers outside the United States.

This book is printed on acid-free paper.

1 2 3 4 5 6 7 8 9 0 VNH/VNH 0 9 8 7 6 5 4

ISBN 0-07-294623-7

Editorial director: *Brent Gordon*
Publisher: *Stewart Mattson*
Sponsoring editor: *Steve DeLancey*
Developmental editor I: *Kelly Odom*
Marketing manager: *Marc Chernoff*
Media producer: *Victor Chiu*
Project manager: *Jim Labeots*
Senior production supervisor: *Michael R. McCormick*
Coordinator freelance design: *Artemio Ortiz Jr.*
Supplement producer: *Matthew Perry*
Senior digital content specialist: *Brian Nacik*
Cover design: *Artemio Ortiz Jr.*
Interior design: *Artemio Ortiz Jr.*
Typeface: *10/12 New Aster*
Compositor: *Cenveo*
Printer: *Von Hoffmann Corporation*

Library of Congress Cataloging-in-Publication Data

Messier, William F.
    Auditing & assurance services : a systematic approach / William F. Messier, Steven Glover, Douglas Prawitt.—4th ed.
        p.   cm.
    Includes bibliographical references and index.
    ISBN 0-07-294623-7 (alk. paper)
    1. Auditing. I. Glover, Steven M., 1963–   II. Prawitt, Douglas F.   III. Title.
HF5667.M46 2006
657′.45—dc22   2004056944

www.mhhe.com

This book is dedicated to Teddie, Stacy, Mark, Bob, Brandon, and Zachary.
—William F. Messier, Jr.

This book is dedicated to Tina, Jessica, Andrew, Jennifer, Anna, Wayne, and Penny.
—Steven M. Glover

This book is dedicated to Meryll, Nathan, Matthew, Natalie, Emily, AnnaLisa, Lileah, George, and Diana.
—Douglas F. Prawitt

About the Authors

Professor William F. Messier, Jr. is the Deloitte & Touche Professor at the School of Accountancy, Georgia State University. He holds a Professor II at the Institute for Accounting & Auditing, Norwegian School of Economics and Business Administration and he is a visiting faculty member at SDA Bocconi in Milan, Italy. Professor Messier holds a BBA from Siena College, an MS from Clarkson University, and an MBA and DBA from Indiana University. He is a CPA in Florida and has taught at the Universities of Florida and Michigan. Professor Messier is Editor of *Auditing: A Journal of Practice & Theory* and is associate Editor of the *Journal of Accounting Literature*. Professor Messier serves on the AICPA's Auditing Standards Board as Chair of the AICPA's International Auditing Standards Subcommittee. He was formerly Chairperson of the Auditing Section of the American Accounting Association. He has authored or coauthored over 50 articles in accounting, decision science, and computer science journals.

Professor Steven M. Glover is an Associate Professor of Accounting and PricewaterhouseCoopers Research Fellow at the Marriott School of Management, Brigham Young University. Professor Glover is a CPA in Utah and holds a PhD and BS from the University of Washington and an AA in Business from BYU – Idaho. He is a CPA and previously worked as a senior auditor for KPMG LLP and a director in the national office of PricewaterhouseCoopers LLP. Professor Glover sits on the board of advisors for two technology companies and actively consults with public companies and public accounting firms. Professor Glover is on the editorial boards of *Auditing: A Journal of Practice & Theory* and *Accounting Horizons*. He has authored or coauthored over 25 articles and books primarily focused in the areas of auditor decision making, audit education, and audit practice.

Professor Douglas F. Prawitt is a Professor of Accounting and Deloitte Research Fellow at the Marriott School of Management, Brigham Young University. Professor Prawitt is a CPA in Utah and holds a PhD from the University of Arizona, and BS and MAcc degrees from Brigham Young University. He has consulted extensively with several prestigious companies and international and local public accounting firms. Over the past three years he has worked with the Committee of Sponsoring Organizations (COSO) and PricewaterhouseCoopers on the COSO *Enterprise Risk Management Framework* project, which builds on the COSO *Internal Control Integrated Framework*. Professor Prawitt has served in several positions with the American Accounting Association, and is on the editorial boards of *Auditing: A Journal of Practice & Theory* and *Accounting Horizons*. He has authored or coauthored over 25 articles and books, primarily in the areas of auditor judgment and decision making, audit education, and audit practice.

In the wake of corporate scandals, significant changes have occurred and will continue to evolve within the auditing profession.

The 4th edition of *Auditing & Assurance Services: A Systematic Approach* has been revised to respond to this changing environment. Chapter concepts and topics acknowledge past fraudulent events and fully integrate material on Sarbanes/Oxley, the PCAOB, and the Audit of Internal Control over Financial Reporting.

Among all of this change, the 4th edition of *Auditing & Assurance Services* holds true to its fundamental values:

Student Engagement. The authors believe students are best served by understanding the basic concepts that underlie the audit process and how to apply those concepts to various audit and assurance services. The primary purpose for an auditing text is to facilitate student learning, and this text is written accordingly. The text is intended to be accessible to students through straightforward writing and through the use of engaging, relevant real-world examples, illustrations, and analogies. Additionally, the case for EarthWear Clothiers, a mail-order retailer, has been updated and integrated throughout the book and Online Learning Center.

A Systematic Approach. The text continues to take a systematic approach to the audit process by first introducing the three underlying concepts: audit risk, materiality, and evidence. These concepts are then applied to each major business process and related account balances using a risk-based approach. The text has been revised to include the risk assessment process proposed by the Auditing Standards Board and adopted by the International Auditing and Assurance Standards Board. The assessment of control risk is then described, followed by discussion of the nature, timing, and extent of evidence necessary to reach the appropriate level of detection risk.

Decision Making. In covering these important concepts and their applications, the book focuses on critical judgments and decision-making processes followed by auditors. Much of auditing practice involves the application of auditor judgment. If a student understands these basic concepts and how to apply them to an audit engagement, he or she will be more effective in today's dynamic audit environment.

Current in Times of Change

EarthWear Case.

The EarthWear Clothiers integrated case is based on a real-world company and is used to demonstrate important auditing concepts throughout the book. The company's 2005 Annual Report is bound into the book following Chapter 1, where the case is introduced. A home page for the company contains extensive information on EarthWear, and a home page for the company's auditors, Willis & Adams, CPAs, contains extensive audit-related information (mhhe.com/messier4e). The website will contain an assignment that allows students to perform risk analysis for EarthWear, including assessment of the five internal control components. Additionally, numerous problems and Internet assignments related to EarthWear are found throughout the text.

Expanded Student Supplement Package.

NEW! ACL™ audit software is packaged with every new copy of the 4th edition. Basic *ACL* assignments are found on the text Online Learning Center (mhhe.com/messier4e) for each chapter of the text. These assignments will allow students to test controls, perform audit sampling, and conduct other analysis. Some chapters will lend themselves better to *ACL*, depending on content, but every chapter will offer at least 1–2 assignments.

NEW! The Study Guide/Casebook, developed by Helen Roybark of Radford University, consists of two parts: Section I includes a detailed case study entitled "Townsend Office Supplies and Equipment, Inc.," and Section II includes a unit for each chapter in the textbook. Each chapter unit in Section II includes a chapter summary, true/false questions, multiple-choice questions, short essay questions, a crossword puzzle to test terminology, and a case activity for Townsend, Inc. Solutions are included.

Problem Material.

The end-of-chapter materials contain review questions, multiple-choice questions from CPA examinations, problems, Internet assignments, and discussion cases.

- Review questions allow students to quickly test their knowledge of the learning objectives for each chapter and provide a basis for meaningful in-class discussion.
- Multiple-choice questions provide a sound basis for testing understanding of the chapter material.
- Problems are drawn from the CPA and CIA examinations and require relatively in-depth application of chapter material.
- Internet assignments involve solving problems related to the EarthWear case and accessing various types of accounting and industry information online.
- Discussion cases are based on real-world examples and require the student to research solutions using various information sources.
- *ACL* *ACL* assignments are located on the text Online Learning Center (mhhe.com/messier4e).

Chapter 1:

- Provides an overview of the recent events that are powerfully reshaping the profession.
- A new introduction to auditing and auditors allows students to develop an intuitive understanding of the demand for assurance and the characteristics of audits and auditors.
- The overview of the audit process and of fundamental auditing concepts (audit risk, materiality, and evidence) has been moved from Chapter 2 to Chapter 1 to give immediacy to the central focus of the text and to pique student interest.
- The chapter uses plain language, clear illustrations, and intuitive analogies to make a compelling case for auditing as a dynamic, challenging, and valuable service to society.

Chapter 2:

- Restructured to help students understand the context in which financial statement auditing takes place.
- Provides a high-level model of business (including governance, objectives, strategy, business processes, transactions, risk management, and control) as the primary context for the financial statement audit.
- Explains the responsibilities, standards, and key organizations affecting the auditor's work environment.
- Offers an overview of the various types of assurance services and assurance providers in the broader world of auditors and auditing.
- Gives an overview of the new CPA Exam.

Chapter 3:

- The chapter has been revised to present the risk assessment process before introducing the discussion of materiality.

- The discussion of the auditor's risk assessment process has been substantially revised based on standards proposed by the ASB and adopted by the IAASB.
- Expanded coverage of fraud.
- The description for establishing and evaluating materiality has been revised to better reflect current audit practice and to be clearer to students.
- New real world cases (Tyco and Nortel) included to illustrate concepts.

Chapter 4:

- Chapter 4 has been revised in accordance with the new standard on audit evidence proposed by the ASB and adopted by the IAASB.
- The chapter presents the new categories for management assertions and types of audit evidence.
- Expanded coverage of audit documentation requirements by the PCAOB.
- For simplicity and to better reflect current practice, rather than elaborate on both "assertions" and "audit objectives," the text now focuses only on assertions.

Chapter 5:

- The discussion of the audit planning process has been revised and updated.
- The discussion of analytical procedures has been substantially revised to better reflect current audit practice.
- To help students better understand the various testing methods, we introduce two conceptual aids: the "Audit Testing Hierarchy" and "Assurance Buckets."

Chapter 6:

- Updated for recent changes in internal controls.
- Presents a base for assessing internal control for financial statement audits and audits of internal control over financial reporting.

Chapter 7:

- This is a new chapter containing a detailed presentation of audits of internal control over financial reporting based on the PCAOB's Auditing Standard No. 2.

Chapter 8:

- Before getting into the statistical terms and technical concepts, we now illustrate the fundamental concepts of sampling in a nontechnical, intuitive, and interactive manner using straightforward illustrations and analogies.
- The discussion of attributes sampling has been simplified and updated to better reflect current practice.

Chapter 9:

- The discussion of monetary unit sampling has been simplified and updated to better reflect practice.
- Classical variables sampling now begins with a review of the theory of sampling distributions.

Chapters 10–16:

- The business process chapters (cycles) have been updated to reflect the changes made in Chapters 3–5 for the auditor's risk assessment process, management assertions, and types of evidence.

- Several new real world cases have been inserted to illustrate concepts.

Chapter 17:

- Added completion procedures and communications associated with an audit of internal controls over financial reporting.
- New working paper with archiving and retention requirements outlined.

Chapter 18:

- Updated to include reports for an integrated audit and the audit of internal controls over financial reporting.

Chapter 19:

- Clarified discussion of fundamental ethical and moral theories.
- Updated to reflect new independence rules imposed by the SEC and PCAOB after the Sarbanes-Oxley Act of 2002.
- Reorganized presentation for enhanced clarity.

Chapter 20:

- New Advanced Module provides an in-depth look at an actual trial where auditors are convicted on fraud charges.
- Some of the historical cases are now covered on the book's website (mhhe.com/messier4e).
- General updating to reflect new auditor liability cases (e.g., Andersen and Enron) as well as the new requirements and liability under Sarbanes Oxley.

Chapter 21:

- New section on internal auditing and the Institute of Internal Auditors.

For Instructors...

Instructor's Resource CD-ROM (ISBN 0072946245): Contains all essential course supplements including:

- Solutions Manual, revised by William F. Messier, Jr., Steven M. Glover, and Douglas F. Prawitt
- Instructor's Manual, revised by Jane Kapral of Boston University
- Test Bank Word files, revised by Mark Taylor of Creighton University
- Computerized Test Bank by Brownstone
- PowerPoint Presentations, prepared by Jon A. Booker, Charles W. Caldwell, and Susan C. Galbreath

Online Learning Center (OLC): mhhe.com/messier4e

The Instructor Edition of the Auditing & Assurance Services, 4e OLC is password-protected and another convenient place for instructors to access essential course supplements. Additional resources include: Links to Professional Resources, Sample Syllabi, Text Updates, and Solutions to *ACL* assignments.

For Students...

Study Guide/Casebook for use with Auditing & Assurance Services: A Systematic Approach, 4e **(ISBN 0073024899):** developed by Helen Roybark of Radford University. New to the 4th edition, this companion resource offers students the opportunity to practice chapter material, reinforce key terms, and complete activities relating to the case study, "Townsend Office Supplies and Equipment, Inc."

Online Learning Center (OLC): mhhe.com/messier4e

The Student Edition of the Auditing & Assurance Services, 4e OLC contains tools designed to enhance students' learning experience: Chapter Learning Objectives, Relevant Accounting and Auditing Pronouncements by Chapter, Multiple-Choice Quizzes, Key Term Flash Cards, PowerPoint Presentations, Auditing Web Links, and text updates. Should the instructor choose to integrate *ACL* into his or her course, assignment material, which requires students to use the software issued for free with their text, is located on the OLC. The home pages for EarthWear Clothiers and Willis & Adams, CPAs are also located here.

Acknowledgments

First and foremost, we thank our families for their continuous support. We would like to acknowledge the American Institute of Certified Public Accountants for permission to quote from auditing standards, the Code of Professional Conduct, the Uniform CPA Examination, and the *Journal of Accountancy*. We would also like to thank ACL Services, Ltd. for granting permission to distribute the educational version of *ACL* software with our textbook.

We have received extensive feedback from users and nonusers of the 3rd edition. Our market research includes surveys and in-depth reviews; the valuable feedback provided by these processes helped us develop and enhance the 4th edition text. Thank you to the following colleagues for their invaluable advice:

Jeff Austin,
Southern Methodist University

Duane M. Brandon,
Auburn University

James Crockett,
University of Southern Mississippi

Mary Curtis,
University of North Texas

Frank Daroca,
Loyola Marymount University

Todd DeZoort,
University of Alabama – Tuscaloosa

William Dilla,
Iowa State University

Robert Ekew,
Purdue University

Charles Holley,
Virginia Commonwealth University

Pam Legner,
College of DuPage (IL)

Ralph Licastro,
Pennsylvania State University – University Park

Robert McCabe,
California State University – Fullerton

Robert Minnear,
Emory University

Vincent Owhoso,
Bentley College

John Rigsby,
Mississippi State University

Sandra Roberson,
Furman University

Helen Roybark,
Radford University

Brian Shapiro,
University of Minnesota – Minneapolis

Scott Vandervelde,
University of South Carolina

Glen Van Whye,
Pacific Lutheran University

George Young,
Florida Atlantic University

Dave S. Baglia,
Grove City College

Brief Table of Contents

Table of Contents

6 Internal Control in a Financial Statement Audit — 218

AUDITING & ASSURANCE SERVICES
A SYSTEMATIC APPROACH

Part I

INTRODUCTION TO FINANCIAL STATEMENT AUDITING

CHAPTER 1

LEARNING OBJECTIVES

Upon completion of this chapter you will

[1] Understand why studying auditing can be valuable to you and why it is different from studying accounting.

[2] Understand why there is a demand for auditing and assurance.

[3] Understand intuitively the demand for auditing and the desired characteristics of auditors and audit services through an analogy to a house inspector and a house inspection service.

[4] Understand the relationships among auditing, attestation, and assurance services.

[5] Understand the basic definition and three fundamental concepts of a financial statement audit.

[6] Understand why on most audit engagements an auditor tests only a sample of transactions that occurred.

[7] Understand the basic financial statement auditing process and the phases in which an audit is carried out.

[8] Understand why auditing demands logic, reasoning, and resourcefulness from auditors.

RELEVANT ACCOUNTING AND AUDITING PRONOUNCEMENTS

AU 110, Responsibilities and Functions of the Independent Auditor
AU 150, Auditing Standards
AU 310, Establishing an Understanding with the Client
AU 311, Planning and Supervision
AU 312, Audit Risk and Materiality in Conducting an Audit

AU 315, Communications between Predecessor and Successor Auditors
AU 319, Consideration of Internal Control in a Financial Statement Audit
AU 326, Evidential Matter

An Introduction to Assurance and Financial Statement Auditing

The last few years have been tremendously eventful for the accounting profession and particularly for auditors. These events have brought challenges but also tremendous opportunity and growth. Never has the demand for capable accountants and auditors of high integrity been greater. How did the current state of affairs come about? The stock market bubble of the late 1990s, fueled in part by speculation regarding the future of "dotcom" companies, led to the creation of unprecedented paper wealth. The frenzied financial markets led to the notion of a "new economy" and seemed to create a selfish attitude in corporate America of "get all you can get—however you can get it."

The stock market bubble burst in spring 2000, and by fall 2001, it was revealed that top executives at Enron, the Houston, Texas, energy giant, had been deceiving investors by fraudulently overstating the company's profitability. In hindsight, it appears that Arthur Andersen, the public accounting firm that audited Enron's financial statements, may have lacked sufficient objectivity in evaluating Enron's accounting methods. The lack of independence allegedly arose because Andersen served as both the internal and external auditor and the fact that Andersen was paid tens of millions of dollars in separate consulting fees amounting to more than the fee for the external audit itself. Regardless of the cause, Andersen failed to report the vast extent of Enron's improper accounting.

In August 2002, Andersen officially stopped providing audits of public companies and began to dismantle its business. Andersen's collapse was a result of the firm's loss of reputation through a long string of audit failures and of the firm's indictment and subsequent conviction on federal charges of obstruction of justice. Ironically, for most of Andersen's 89 years of existence it had a reputation for taking tough stands against clients that wanted to adopt aggressive financial reporting strategies. To be sure, there were many partners and employees at Andersen who were highly ethical and competent—but the firm's reputation was so severely damaged that the firm's clients switched to other firms.

The Enron accounting fraud was not the largest in recent history, but it is perhaps the most infamous because it led to the demise of Arthur Andersen and triggered enormous outrage among investors, creditors, regulators, and government officials. In fact, the Enron fraud was just one of the first in a long string of high-profile accounting frauds reported in recent years. Some of America's and Europe's most well-respected companies have reported massive frauds, including WorldCom (now MCI), Xerox, HealthSouth, Ahold, Parmalat, SunBeam, Waste Management, Adelphia, Global Crossing, Qwest, and Tyco.

The widespread nature of the frauds and scandals caused investors to doubt the integrity of the nation's financial reporting system. Public outcry over the scandals and accounting frauds also put enormous pressure on Congress to restore public trust in the marketplace through legislation. In July 2002, Congress passed the *Sarbanes-Oxley Public Company Accounting Reform and Investor Protection Act*, the most significant legislation related to financial statement audits of public companies since the Securities Acts of 1933 and 1934. One of the most significant components of the 2002 legislation for auditors was the formation of the *Public Company Accounting Oversight Board*, which took from the accounting profession authority for establishing standards for the audits of public companies. The Sarbanes-Oxley Act has several other important implications for auditors of public companies, including banning the provision of most consulting services by auditors to their audit clients.

While the scandals, public scrutiny, government reforms, and new regulated process for establishing auditing standards have certainly been painful for accountants and auditors, the events of the last few years have also been a powerful reminder of just how critical the roles of accounting and auditing are in our society. In fact, the increased emphasis on auditing is so great that auditing firms are finding it difficult to staff enough people to keep up with the demand for their services. We believe the events of the last few years have provided a much-needed wake-up call, and that as the profession returns to its roots of competence, integrity, and objectivity it will be stronger and more valued than ever.

In a time when the amount of information available for decision makers via electronic databases, the Internet, and other sources is rapidly expanding, there is a need for information to be reliable, credible, relevant, and timely. Reliable information is necessary if managers, investors, creditors, and regulatory agencies are to make informed decisions. Auditing and assurance services can help ensure that information is reliable, credible, relevant, and timely. In fact, auditing provides a useful framework or "toolbox" for improving the reliability of information used by decision makers. Learning this framework makes the study of auditing valuable to future accountants and business decision makers.

The following examples present situations where auditing enters into economic transactions and increases the reliability and credibility of an entity's financial statements:

> Sara Thompson, a local community activist, has been operating a not-for-profit center that provides assistance to abused women and their children. She has financed most of her operations from private contributions. Ms. Thompson has applied to the State Health and Human Services Department requesting a large grant to expand her two shelters to accommodate more women. In completing the grant application, Ms. Thompson discovered that the state's laws for government grants require that recipients have their financial statements audited prior to the final granting of funds. Ms. Thompson hired a CPA to audit the center's financial statements. Based on the center's activities, the intended use of the funds, and the auditor's report, the grant was approved.

> Conway Computer Company has been a successful wholesaler of computer peripheral products such as disk drives and tape backup systems. The company was started by George and Jimmy Steinbuker five years ago. Two years ago, a venture capital firm provided needed capital for expansion by acquiring 40 percent of the company. Conway Computer has been very successful, with revenues and profits increasing by 25 percent in each of the last two years. The Steinbuker brothers and the venture capital firm are considering taking the company public through a stock sale. They have contacted a number of underwriters about the public offering. The underwriters have informed the company that the company's financial statements will need to be audited by a reputable public accounting firm before a registration statement can be filed with the Securities and Exchange Commission. The company hired a major public accounting firm. Subsequently, the company successfully sold stock to the public.

These situations show the importance of auditing to both private and public enterprise. By adding the audit function to each situation, the users of the financial statements have reasonable assurance that the financial statements do not contain material misstatements or omissions. Auditors can also provide valuable assurance for operating information, information systems reliability and security, and an entity's internal control. Consider the following example:

EarthWear EarthWear Clothiers has been a successful mail-order retailer of high-quality clothing for outdoor sports. Over the last few years the company has expanded sales through its Internet site. EarthWear's common stock is listed and traded on NASDAQ. Securities laws enacted in 2002 now require company officials to certify that they have properly designed, implemented, and tested internal control over their accounting and reporting information systems. EarthWear's public accounting firm, Willis & Adams, will examine the design and documentation of EarthWear's internal control and conduct independent tests to verify that EarthWear's system is operating effectively. Willis & Adams will then issue a report to the public expressing its opinion on management's assertion that EarthWear's internal control is well designed and operating effectively. In this way, stockholders, creditors, and other stakeholders can have increased confidence in the financial reports issued by EarthWear's management.

Most readers of an introductory auditing text initially have little understanding of what auditing and assurance services entail. Thus, this chapter starts by comparing auditing to other well-known forms of assurance to provide an intuitive understanding of the role auditing and assurance play in economic transactions. This part of the chapter is then summarized by analyzing in general terms why there is a demand for auditing and assurance services. Auditing, attest, and assurance services are then defined, and an overview of the auditing process is provided. 🌎

The Study of Auditing

[LO 1]   You will find that the study of auditing is different from any of the other accounting courses you have taken in college, and for good reason. Most other accounting courses focus on learning the rules, techniques, and computations required to prepare and analyze financial information. Auditing focuses on learning the analytical and logical skills necessary to evaluate the relevance and reliability of the systems and processes responsible for recording and summarizing that information, as well as of the information itself. As such, you will find the study of auditing to be more conceptual in nature than your other accounting courses. Learning auditing essentially helps you understand how to gather and assess evidence so you can evaluate assertions made by others.

This text is filled with the tools and techniques used by financial statement auditors. You'll find that the "tool kit" used by auditors consists of a coherent logical framework, filled with tools and techniques useful for analyzing financial data and gathering evidence in a variety of settings from small business to consulting and even executive decision making. An important implication is that learning this framework makes the study of auditing valuable to future accountants and business decision makers, whether or not they plan to become auditors!

While we are convinced the concepts and techniques covered in this book will be useful to you regardless of your career path, our experience is that students frequently fall into the trap of defining auditing in terms of memorized lists of rules, tools, and techniques. The study of auditing and the related rules, tools, and techniques will make a lot more sense to you if you can first build up your intuition of why audits are needed, what an auditor does, and what are the necessary characteristics of audits and auditors.

Reliable information is important for managers, investors, creditors, and regulatory agencies to make informed decisions. Auditing helps ensure that information is reliable, credible, relevant, and timely. In fact, you will find that the concepts behind financial statement auditing provide a framework or tool kit that can be used for improving the reliability of information for decision makers of all kinds.

The Demand for Auditing and Assurance[1]

≋ **[LO 2]**   An important question a student might ask is, "Why do entities request an audit?" Some might offer the answer that audits are required by law. While this answer is true in certain circumstances, it is far too simplistic. Audits are often utilized in situations where they are not required by law, and audits were in demand long before securities laws required them. In fact, evidence shows that some forms of accounting and auditing existed in Greece as early as 500 BC.[2] However, the development of the corporate form of business and the expanding world economy over the last 200 years have given rise to an explosion in the demand for the assurance provided by auditors. One research study showed that in 1926, several years prior to any laws requiring audits in the United States, 82 percent of the companies on the New York Stock Exchange were audited by independent auditors.[3]

Principals and Agents

Until the late 18th and early 19th centuries, most organizations were relatively small and were owned and operated as sole proprietorships or partnerships. The birth of modern accounting and auditing occurred during the industrial revolution, when companies needed to raise capital to finance expansion.[4] Securities exchange markets exist so that companies can raise the investment capital necessary to expand to new markets, to finance expensive research, and to fund the buildings, technology, and equipment necessary to deliver a product to market. A capital market allows a public company to sell small pieces of ownership (i.e., stocks) or to disaggregate borrowed funds into small loans (i.e., bonds) so that vast amounts of capital can be raised from a wide variety of investors and creditors. A *public company* is a company that sells its stocks or bonds to the public, giving the public a valid interest in the proper use of, or stewardship over, the company's resources. Thus, the growth of the modern corporation led to the prevalence of absentee owners (stockholders) and the use of professional managers who ran the corporation on a day-to-day basis. In this setting, the managers served as *agents* for the stockholders (referred to as *principals*) and fulfilled a *stewardship* function by managing the corporation's assets.

---

[1]See G. L. Sundem, R. E. Dukes, and J. A. Elliott, *The Value of Information and Audits* (New York: Coopers & Lybrand, 1996), for a more detailed discussion of the demand for accounting information and auditing.

[2]G. J. Costouros, "Auditing in the Athenian State of the Golden Age (500–300 BC)," *The Accounting Historian Journal* (Spring 1978), pp. 41–50.

[3]G. J. Benston, "The Value of the SEC's Accounting Disclosure Requirements," *The Accounting Review* (July 1969), pp. 515–532.

[4]Also see M. Chatfield, *A History of Accounting Thought* (Hinsdale, IL.: Dryden Press, 1974), for a discussion of the historical development of accounting and auditing.

Accounting and auditing play an important role in this principal-agent relationship. We'll first explain the roles of accounting and auditing from a theoretical perspective. Then we'll use an analogy involving a house inspector to illustrate the concepts. First, it is important to understand that the relationship between an owner and manager often results in information asymmetry between the two parties. *Information asymmetry* means that the manager generally has more information about the "true" financial position and results of operations of the entity than does the absentee owner. Second, because their goals may not coincide, there is a natural *conflict of interest* between the manager and the absentee owner. If both parties seek to maximize their self-interest, the manager will not always act in the best interest of the owner. For example, the risk exists that a manager may follow the example of Tyco's former CEO Dennis Kozlowski, who is accused of spending Tyco funds on excessive personal benefits such as $6,000 shower curtains. Or the manager might follow the example of Andrew Fastow, the former CFO of Enron, who pleaded guilty to manipulating the reported earnings of Enron in order to inflate the price of the company's stock so that he and the other parties involved could earn larger bonuses and sell their stock holdings at artificially high prices. The owner can attempt to protect himself or herself against the possibility of such activities by reducing the manager's compensation by the amount of perks that the owner expects the manager to consume. In an attempt to minimize the reduction in compensation, the manager may agree to some type of monitoring provisions in his or her employment contract. For example, the two parties may agree that the manager will periodically report on how well he or she has managed the owner's assets. The reporting of this financial information to the owner follows agreed-upon accounting principles. Thus, the role of accounting information is to hold the manager accountable to the owner—hence the origin of the word "accounting."

The Role of Auditing

Of course, accounting doesn't solve the problem by itself. Because the manager is responsible for reporting on the results of his or her own actions, which the absentee owner cannot directly observe, the manager is in a position to manipulate the reports. The owner protects against this possibility by again assuming that the manager will manipulate the reports to his or her benefit and by reducing the manager's compensation accordingly. It is at this point that the demand for auditing arises. If the manager is honest, it may very well be in the manager's self-interest to hire an auditor to monitor his or her activities. Note that as the amount of capital and the number of potential owners increase, the potential savings through reduced cost of capital also increase. The auditor's role is to determine whether the reports prepared by the manager conform to the contract's provisions. Thus, the auditor's verification of the financial information adds credibility to the report and reduces information risk, potentially benefiting both the owner and the manager. While auditing is only one possible form of additional monitoring, the extensive presence of auditing in such situations suggests that auditing is a cost-effective monitoring device. Figure 1–1 provides an overview of this agency relationship.

While the setting we've outlined is very simple, it does realistically portray the initial development of auditing. An understanding of the basic

FIGURE 1–1	**Overview of the Principal–Agent Relationship Leading to the Demand for Auditing**

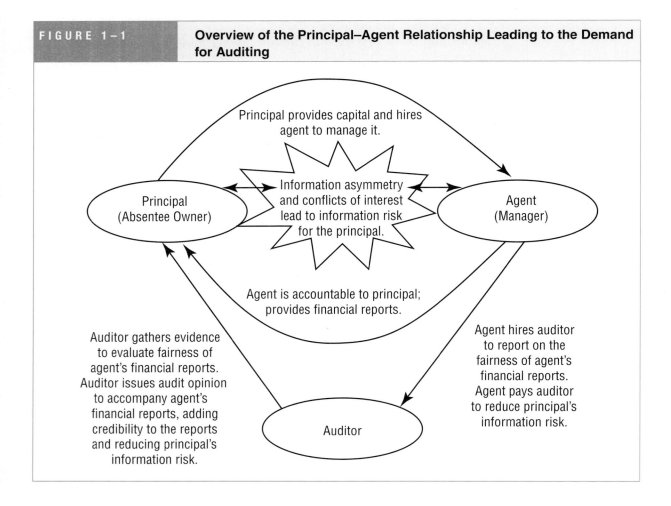

owner-manager relationship is a powerful conceptual tool that can be extrapolated to much more complex employment and other contractual arrangements, and these same ideas apply to other relationships that involve the entity. For example, how can a debt holder prevent management from taking the borrowed funds and using them for its own purposes? One way is to place restrictive covenants in the debt agreement that must be complied with by the entity and its management. Again, this arrangement gives rise to a demand for auditing.

The purpose of this discussion is to demonstrate why there is a demand for auditing services in a free market. While regulations such as the Securities Acts of 1933 and 1934 account for some of the demand, they cannot account for all of it. Auditing is demanded because it plays a valuable role in monitoring the contractual relationships between the entity and its stockholders, managers, employees, and debt holders. Certified public accountants have been asked to provide audit services because of their traditional reputation of competence, independence, objectivity, and concern for the public interest.

An Assurance Analogy: The Case of the House Inspector

❧ [LO 3]   Before we discuss financial statement auditors further, let's first consider another situation that often involves an "auditor" or assurance provider as an analogy: buying an older home. This analogy will illustrate the theoretical concepts we just covered and will help you further develop your understanding of what auditors do and what characteristics must be present in an auditor and in an audit. In the purchase of an existing house, *information asymmetry* usually is present because the seller typically has more information about the house than does the buyer. There is also a natural *conflict of interest* between the buyer and the seller. Sellers generally prefer a higher selling price to a lower one, and may be motivated to overstate the positive characteristics and to understate or remain silent about the negative characteristics of the property they have for sale.

Seller Assertions, Information Asymmetry, and Inspector Characteristics

To support the asking price, sellers typically provide declarations or *assertions* about their property. For instance, the seller of an older home might assert that the roof is watertight, that the foundation is sound, that there is no rot or pest damage, and that the plumbing and electrical systems are in good working order. Similarly, the seller of a used car might assert that the car has never been in an accident; that the brakes, engine, and transmission are all in good working order; and that the car has received regular oil changes and tune-ups. Fortunately, many sellers are honest and forthcoming, but this obviously is not always the case. The problem is that the buyer often does not know if she or he is dealing with an honest seller or if the seller has the necessary expertise to evaluate all the structural or mechanical aspects of the property. Lacking the necessary expertise to validate the seller's assertions, the buyer can logically reduce information asymmetry by hiring a house inspector. Before moving on, imagine for a moment that you are buying an existing house and are wisely considering hiring an inspector. Test your intuition—what characteristics would you like your inspector to possess? In Table 1–1 we have listed several characteristics we think would be desirable. Of course, many of the characteristics we would find desirable in a house inspector are also desirable in a financial statement auditor.

Desired Characteristics of the House Inspection Service

Now that you have identified some of the characteristics of a good inspector, consider the key characteristics of the service he or she will provide. Are some of the seller's assertions more important than others? For instance, you are probably not equally concerned with the assertion that there is no structural rot and the assertion that the lightbulbs in the bathroom are relatively new. Would you be willing to pay the inspector to evaluate both? Further, depending on what you are willing to pay, the inspection could theoretically range from driving past the house to taking the home entirely apart, board by board. How thorough do you want the inspector to be? Do you want the inspector to issue a "pass-fail" grade or would you like more details, such as costs of necessary repairs? As you can see, there are a lot of factors to take into account in deciding on the nature and extent of the assurance service

TABLE 1–1	Important Characteristics of House Inspectors and Inspections

Desirable Characteristics of House *Inspectors*
- Competent—they possess the required training, expertise, and experience to evaluate the property for sale.
- Objective—they have no reason to side with the seller; they are independent of the seller's influence.
- Honest—they will conduct themselves with integrity, and they will share all of their findings with the buyer.
- Skeptical—they will not simply take the seller's assertions at face value; they will conduct their own analysis and testing.
- Responsible and/or liable—they should stand behind their assessment with a guarante and/or be subject to litigation if they fail to act with due care.

Desirable Characteristics of a House Inspection *Service*
- Timely—the results of the service are reported in time to benefit the decision maker.
- Reasonably priced—the costs of the services must not exceed the benefits. For this to occur the service provider will likely need to focus attention on the most important and risky assertions and likely can't provide absolute assurance.
- Complete—the service addresses all of the most important and risky assertions made by the seller.
- Effective—the service provides some degree of certainty that it will uncover significant risks or problems.
- Systematic and reliable—the service is based on a systematic process, and the conclusions are based on reliable evidence. In other words, another comparable inspector would likely find similar things and come to similar conclusions.
- Informative—the service provides a sense for how likely mechanical or structural failure is in the near future and provides an estimate of the cost to repair known defects or failures.

you want to buy. In Table 1–1 we have listed what we think are desirable characteristics of a house inspection service.

Table 1–1 actually contains concepts that are fundamental to most forms of inspection (and all financial statement audits). Certainly home inspections and other assurance services must be focused on the assertions that are most important, and they must be conducted in a timely and cost-effective manner. Some assertions are more important than others because of their potential risk or cost. For example, a house inspector should recognize the signs that indicate an increased risk for a leaky roof. If those signs are present she or he should investigate further, because damage caused by a leaky roof can be very expensive to repair. Similarly, an auto mechanic should be able to recognize the signs of a failing transmission and alert the prospective buyer to the potential for trouble. At the same time, just because the seller of a used car asserts that she or he recently lubricated the door hinges doesn't mean it would be wise to pay the mechanic to validate this assertion.

Relating the House Inspection Analogy to Financial Statement Auditing

Now that we have discussed some of the basic characteristics of inspectors and their services, let's consider how these relate to financial statement auditors. As noted previously, the demand for the assurance provided by a house inspector comes from information asymmetry and conflicts of interest between the buyer and the seller. One important difference between our house inspector example and financial statement auditing is that the buyer of a home typically hires the inspector. In other words, the buyer identifies and hires the inspector rather than using someone that the seller recommends—presumably because by hiring an inspector directly, they increase the likelihood of objectivity and independence.

However, as was discussed previously, there are some important differences in most financial statement audit settings that shift the model so that the companies selling stocks or bonds to the public typically hire and pay the auditor, rather than the other way around. To raise capital in the marketplace, companies often sell many small parcels of stocks and bonds to small investors. Suppose a financial statement audit of a given company would cost $500,000. Under such circumstances, it obviously doesn't make sense for each individual investor to pay for an audit. Instead, the company hires and pays for the auditor because a reputable independent auditor's opinion can provide assurance to thousands of potential investors. In addition, recall from our previous discussion that the initial demand for auditing comes not from the principal but from the agent. By purchasing the assurance provided by an audit, the company can sell its stocks and bonds to prospective owners and creditors at more favorable prices, significantly reducing the cost of capital. In fact, studies indicate that audits save companies billions of dollars in costs of obtaining capital.

Understanding that the seller of stocks and bonds typically hires the auditor, consider just how crucial a strong reputation is to an independent auditor. Four large, international accounting firms dominate the audits of large companies, auditing over 95% of the revenue produced by all such companies in the United States. One reason these firms dominate this space is because they have well-known names and strong reputations. Entities who buy assurance from these firms know that potential investors and creditors will recognize the auditing firm's name and reputation and know that they will therefore face reduced information risk.

The fact that the entity being audited typically hires the auditor also highlights just how important the attitude of objectivity and independence is to the investing public. In fact, as the preface to this chapter indicates, Arthur Andersen (the fifth of the former five large, international accounting firms) failed in 2002 essentially because the firm lost its reputation as a high-quality, objective auditor whose opinion could be relied upon by investors and creditors. Later in the book we will discuss some recent changes enacted to strengthen the independence of financial statement auditors, including prohibiting auditors from providing most kinds of consulting services to their public audit clients.

Management Assertions and Financial Statements

We've seen that home sellers might make a number of different assertions about which a home buyer might want independent assurance. What assertions does a seller of stocks or bonds make? Some of the most important assertions entities make to investors are implicit in the entities' financial statements. At the end of this chapter you will find a set of financial statements for EarthWear, a hypothetical seller of high-quality outdoor clothing. EarthWear is a publicly traded company, which means that its stock is available for purchase to the general public and its securities are traded on public securities exchanges. Let's consider what assertions EarthWear, as a seller of securities to the public, makes to potential investors when it publishes its financial statements. For example, EarthWear lists the asset account "cash" on its balance sheet and indicates that the account's year-end balance was $48.9 million. What specific assertions is the company making about cash? An obvious answer is that it is asserting the cash really exists. While that answer is true, EarthWear is also implicitly asserting that the cash amount is fairly and accurately recorded, that all cash is included, and that the cash is not restricted or otherwise pledged. Of course, because EarthWear is publicly traded, the company must report in accordance with generally accepted accounting principles (GAAP); this assertion is also implicit for each account in the financial statements.

Obviously, information asymmetry exists between the managers of Earth-Wear and potential investors. The interests of EarthWear managers and investors may also conflict. For example, if managers are overly optimistic, they may intentionally or unintentionally overstate the company's assets and future prospects (by understating the allowance for doubtful accounts or overstating the cash balance, for example).

If you were asked to audit EarthWear, how would you go about collecting evidence for the cash account? The process is logical and intuitive. First, you would carefully consider the most important assertions the company is making about the account, and then you would decide what evidence you would need to substantiate the truthfulness of each important assertion. To ensure the cash exists, you might call the bank, look at bank statements, or send a letter to the bank requesting confirmation of the balance. To ensure the cash hasn't been pledged or restricted, you might review the minutes of key management meetings to look for discussions on this issue. Once you are finished auditing the important assertions relating to the accounts contained in the company's financial statements, you will need to report your findings to the company's shareholders and to the investing public because EarthWear is publicly traded.

Instead of EarthWear's auditor, imagine you are a prospective investor in EarthWear. As an investor, would the reputation of the company's auditor matter to you? What if the lead partner on the audit were related to Earth-Wear's president? Would it be comforting to know that the audit firm used a well-recognized audit approach to gather sufficient, competent evidence? What form of report would you expect? Refer back to Table 1–1, and you will see that these questions lead to answers quite similar to those relating to house inspectors and the house inspection service.

We hope the analogy of house inspectors and auditors as "information inspectors" has helped you understand the basic intuition behind the necessary characteristics of auditors and auditing and why auditing is in demand, even when it is not required by law. We will refer back to this analogy occasionally throughout the book to remind you of this basic intuition. Before you memorize lists of standards, techniques, or concepts, we encourage you to consider how the information relates to your basic understanding of important characteristics of "information inspectors" and the services they offer. Remember—keep the big picture in mind!

Auditing, Attest, and Assurance Services Defined

❧ **[LO 4]**   The professional literature refers to three general types of services that provide assurance: auditing, attest, and assurance services. Many times these terms are used interchangeably because, at a general level, they encompass the same process: *the evaluation of evidence to determine the correspondence of some information to a set of criteria, and the issuance of a report to indicate the degree of correspondence.*

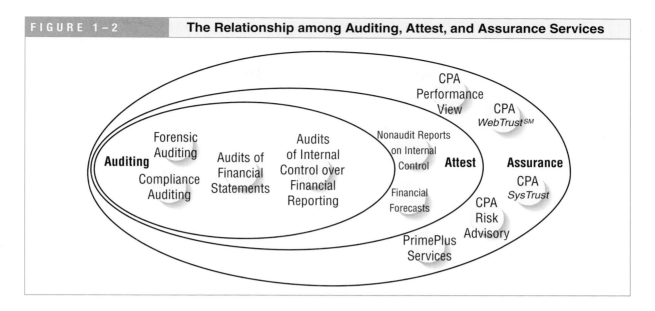

FIGURE 1–2   **The Relationship among Auditing, Attest, and Assurance Services**

In this section, these services are presented from the most detailed (auditing) to the most general (assurance). This presentation is consistent with their historical development. Figure 1–2 shows the relationship among auditing, attest, and assurance services. Auditing services are a subset of attest services, which, in turn, are a subset of assurance services. The remainder of this section defines and discusses each of these forms of services.

Auditing

The Committee on Basic Auditing Concepts provided the following general definition of auditing:

> **Auditing** is a systematic process of objectively obtaining and evaluating evidence regarding assertions about economic actions and events to ascertain the degree of correspondence between those assertions and established criteria and communicating the results to interested users.[5]

A number of phrases in this definition deserve attention. The phrase "systematic process" implies that there should be a well-planned and thorough approach for conducting an audit. This plan involves "objectively obtaining and evaluating evidence." Two activities are involved here. The auditor must *objectively search for* and *evaluate* the relevance and validity of evidence. While the type, quantity, and reliability of evidence may vary between audits, the process of obtaining and evaluating evidence makes up most of the auditor's activities on an audit.

As our analogy between house inspection and auditing illustrates, the evidence gathered by the auditor must relate to "assertions about economic actions and events." The auditor compares the evidence gathered to assertions

---

[5]American Accounting Association, Committee on Basic Auditing Concepts, "A Statement of Basic Auditing Concepts" (Sarasota, FL: AAA, 1973).

about economic activity in order to assess "the degree of correspondence between those assertions and established criteria." While numerous sets of criteria are available for measuring the degree of correspondence in various settings, generally accepted accounting principles (GAAP) are normally used for preparing financial statements.

The last important phrase, "communicating the results to interested users," is concerned with the type of report the auditor provides to the intended users. The communication will vary depending on the type and purpose of the audit. In the case of financial statement audits, very specific types of reports are prescribed by auditing standards to communicate the auditor's findings. For other types of audits, the content and form of the reports vary with the circumstances and the intended users.

Attestation

Auditors have a reputation for independence and objectivity. As a result, over the years various users requested that auditors provide attestation on information beyond traditional historical financial information, but traditional auditing standards prohibited auditors from providing such services. The profession responded to this demand for services by issuing a separate set of attestation standards beginning in the 1980s.

Attestation standards provide the following definition for attest services:

> **Attest** services occur when a practitioner is engaged to issue or does issue a report on subject matter, or an assertion about subject matter, that is the responsibility of another party.

This definition is broader than the one previously discussed for auditing because it is not limited to economic events or actions. Subject matter in the case of attest services can take many forms, including prospective information, analyses, systems and processes, and behavior. However, the auditor's role is similar: He or she must determine the correspondence of the subject matter against criteria that are suitable and available to users. To accomplish this, the auditor obtains and evaluates evidence in order to provide reasonable support for the report. Note that financial statement auditing is a specialized form of an attest service.

Assurance

The accounting profession, through the work of the Special Committee on Assurance Services,[6] extended auditing and attest services to include *assurance services*. Extending auditors' activities to assurance services allows the auditor to report not only on the reliability and credibility of information but also on the *relevance* and *timeliness* of that information. Assurance services are defined as follows:

> **Assurance services** are independent professional services that improve the quality of information, or its context, for decision makers.

This definition captures a number of important concepts. First, the definition focuses on decision making. Making good decisions requires quality information, which can be financial or nonfinancial. Second, it relates to

---

[6]See the AICPA's home page (www.aicpa.org) for the report of the Special Committee on Assurance Services.

TABLE 1–2		Relationships among Auditing, Attest, and Assurance Services
Service	Value Added to Information Reported on	Definition of Service
Auditing	Reliability Credibility	A report on an examination of a client's financial statements (and for a public client, the entity's system of internal control over financial reporting)
Attest	Reliability Credibility	A report on subject matter, or an assertion about subject matter that is the responsibility of another party
Assurance	Reliability Credibility Relevance Timeliness	Professional services that improve the quality of information, or its context, for decision makers

improving the quality of information or its context. An assurance service engagement can improve quality through increasing confidence in the information's reliability and relevance. Context can be improved by clarifying the format and background with which the information is presented. Third, the definition includes independence. With assurance services, independence relates only to the quality or context of the information, and does not necessarily include consideration of other relationships that may exist between the assurance provider and the client. Last, the definition includes the term *professional services,* which encompasses the application of professional judgment. To summarize, assurance services can capture information, improve its quality, and enhance its usefulness for decision makers.

Table 1–2 summarizes the relationships among auditing, attest, and assurance services. Note that the definitions included in Table 1–2 progress from very specific for auditing services to very general for assurance services. This text focuses primarily on one type of auditing—financial statement auditing— because it represents the major assurance service offered by most public accounting firms. However, in many instances, the approach, concepts, methods, and techniques used for financial statement audits also apply to attest and assurance service engagements. While this text focuses primarily on financial statement auditing, Chapters 2 and 21 describe various examples of audit, attest, and assurance services commonly offered by auditors.

Fundamental Concepts in Conducting a Financial Statement Audit

[LO 5] Figure 1–3 presents a simplified overview of the audit function for a financial statement audit. The auditor gathers evidence about the business transactions that have occurred (economic activity and events) and about management (the preparer of the report). The auditor uses this evidence to compare the assertions contained in the financial statements to the criteria chosen by the user. The auditor's report communicates to the user the degree of correspondence between the assertions and the criteria.

The conceptual and procedural details of a financial statement audit build on three fundamental concepts: audit risk, materiality, and evidence

| FIGURE 1-3 | An Overview of the Financial Statement Audit Process |

relating to management assertions. The auditor's assessments of audit risk and materiality influence the type and amount of audit work to be performed (referred to as the *scope* of the audit). In establishing the scope of the audit, the auditor must make decisions about the nature, timing, and extent of evidence to be gathered in order to evaluate management's assertions. This section briefly discusses each of these concepts. Chapters 2 through 4 cover these concepts in greater depth.

Audit Risk

The first major concept involved in auditing is *audit risk*.

> **Audit risk** is the risk that the auditor may unknowingly fail to appropriately modify his or her opinion on financial statements that are materially misstated.[7]

The auditor's standard report states that the audit provides only reasonable assurance that the financial statements do not contain material misstatements. The term *reasonable assurance* implies some risk that a material misstatement could be present in the financial statements and the auditor will fail to detect it. In conducting an audit, the auditor decides what level of audit risk he or she is willing to accept and plans the audit to achieve that level of audit risk. The auditor controls the level of audit risk

---

[7]AU 312, Audit Risk and Materiality in Conducting an Audit.

by the effectiveness and extent of the audit work conducted. The more effective and extensive the audit work (and the more costly the audit), the less the risk that a misstatement will go undetected and that the auditor will issue an inappropriate report. However, the concept of reasonable assurance means that an auditor could conduct an audit in accordance with professional auditing standards and issue a clean opinion, and the financial statements might still contain material misstatements. Just as a house inspector cannot absolutely guarantee the absence of problems without taking apart a house board by board, due to cost considerations and the sheer impossibility of investigating every facet of an entity's financial statements, the risk that an auditor will mistakenly issue a clean opinion on financial statements that are in fact materially misstated cannot be driven to zero. Even careful and competent auditors can only offer reasonable, rather than absolute, assurance.

Materiality

The second major concept involved in auditing is materiality. The auditor's consideration of materiality is a matter of *professional judgment* and is affected by what the auditor perceives as the view of a reasonable person who is relying on the financial statements. The Financial Accounting Standards Board has provided the following definition of materiality:

> **Materiality** is the magnitude of an omission or misstatement of accounting information that, in the light of surrounding circumstances, makes it probable that the judgment of a reasonable person relying on the information would have been changed or influenced by the omission or misstatement.[8]

The focus of this definition is on the users of the financial statements. In planning the engagement, the auditor assesses the magnitude of a misstatement that may affect the users' decisions. This assessment helps the auditor determine the nature, timing, and extent of audit procedures. Relating the concept of materiality to our house inspector analogy is rather intuitive—a house inspector will not validate the remaining life on lightbulbs or thoroughly test every cabinet hinge or drawer glide. These items are not critical to the buyer's decision.

A common rule of thumb is that total (aggregated) misstatements of more than about 3 to 5 percent of net income before tax would cause financial statements to be materially misstated. While other factors must be considered in determining materiality, suppose the auditor decides that the financial statements of a client will be materially misstated if total misstatements exceed $400,000. In planning audit tests for particular account balances or classes of transactions, the auditor will design tests to be precise enough to detect misstatements that are substantially smaller than overall materiality. Continuing our example, in planning the audit of inventory, the auditor may design inventory audit procedures that will identify any misstatement greater than $150,000. When audit testing is complete for all

---

[8]Financial Accounting Standards Board, Statement of Financial Accounting Concepts No. 2, "Qualitative Characteristics of Accounting Information" (CON2). This definition is also included in AU 312, Audit Risk and Materiality in the Conduct of an Audit.

accounts, the auditor will issue a clean audit opinion only if total unadjusted misstatements are less than overall materiality of $400,000.

As we shall see later in this chapter, the wording of the auditor's standard audit report includes the phrase "the financial statements present fairly *in all material respects.*" This is the manner in which the auditor communicates the notion of materiality to the users of the auditor's report. Keep in mind, as we explained in connection with the concept of audit risk, there can be no absolute guarantee that the auditor will uncover *all* material misstatements. The auditor can only provide *reasonable assurance* that all material misstatements are detected, and the auditor provides no assurance that immaterial misstatements will be detected.

Evidence Regarding Management Assertions

The third major concept involved in auditing is *evidence regarding management's assertions.* Most of the auditor's work in arriving at an opinion on the financial statements consists of obtaining and evaluating evidence. Chapter 2 contains more detail about the specific assertions relevant to financial statement auditing. Evidence that assists the auditor in evaluating management's financial statement assertions consists of the underlying accounting data and any corroborating information available to the auditor.[9]

As illustrated earlier in our discussion about EarthWear, management's assertions are used as a framework to guide the collection of audit evidence. The assertions, in conjunction with the assessment of materiality and audit risk, are used by the auditor to determine the nature, timing, and extent of evidence to be gathered. Once the auditor has obtained sufficient competent evidence that the management assertions can be relied upon for each significant account, reasonable assurance is provided that the financial statements are fairly presented.

In obtaining and evaluating evidence, the auditor is concerned with the relevance and reliability of the evidence. *Relevance* refers to whether the evidence relates to the specific management assertion being tested. *Reliability* refers to the diagnosticity of the evidence. In other words, can a particular type of evidence be relied upon to signal the true state of the management assertion being examined?

The auditor seldom has the luxury of obtaining completely convincing evidence about the true state of a particular assertion. In most situations, the auditor obtains only enough evidence to be persuaded that the assertion is fairly stated. Additionally, for many parts of an audit, the auditor examines only a sample of the transactions processed during the period.

Sampling: Inferences Based on Limited Observations

[LO 6] You might ask why the auditor relies on concepts such as audit risk and materiality in designing an audit. Why not test all transactions that occurred during the period so that audit risk can be driven to zero, even for immaterial misstatements? The main reason is the cost and feasibility of such an audit. In a small business, the auditor might be able to examine all transactions that occurred during the period and still issue the audit report

---

[9]AU 326, Evidential Matter.

in a reasonable amount of time. However, it is unlikely that the owner of the business could afford to pay for such an extensive audit. For a large organization, the sheer volume of transactions, which might well reach into the millions, prevents the auditor from examining every transaction. Thus, just as with a house inspector, there is a trade-off between the exactness or precision of the audit and its cost.

To deal with this problem, the auditor uses (1) his or her knowledge about the transactions and/or (2) a sampling approach to examine the transactions. Many times the auditor is aware of items in an account balance that are likely to contain misstatements based on previous audits or knowledge of the industry. For example, the auditor's prior knowledge may indicate that transactions with certain types of customers or large dollar account items are likely to contain misstatements. The auditor can use this knowledge to specifically select those transactions or account items (e.g., specific accounts receivable) for examination. When the auditor has no special knowledge about which particular transactions or items may be misstated, he or she uses sampling procedures that increase the likelihood of obtaining a sample *representative* of the population of transactions or account items. In such cases, the auditor uses the laws of probability to make inferences about potential misstatements in total based on examining a sample of transactions or items.

The size of a sample is a function of materiality and acceptable audit risk for the account or assertion being examined. There is an *inverse* relationship between sample size and materiality and between sample size and acceptable audit risk. For example, if an auditor assesses materiality for an account to be a small amount, a larger sample will be needed than if materiality were a larger amount. This occurs because the auditor must gather more evidence (a larger sample) to have a reasonable likelihood of detecting smaller errors. You can think of materiality as the "fineness of the auditor's filter." A lower materiality amount requires the auditor to use a finer filter in order to detect smaller errors, and it takes more work to create a finer filter. Similarly, as the amount of audit risk the auditor is willing to accept decreases for a given materiality amount, the sample size necessary to test the management assertion under examination becomes greater. This occurs because the auditor must gather more evidence in order to further reduce the amount of uncertainty or risk associated with the test.

The Audit Process

[LO 7]   This section provides an overview of how auditors go about the process of auditing financial statements and then presents the major phases that the auditor performs during a financial statement audit. Later chapters provide detailed coverage of the process and the phases of the audit.

Overview of the Financial Statement Auditing Process

Consider the auditor's job from a logical perspective. The end product of a financial statement auditor's work is an audit opinion indicating whether or not the client's financial statements are free of material misstatement. What might an auditor do, from a conceptual perspective, to obtain the information needed to develop and support that opinion? The auditor must first obtain a thorough understanding of the client, its business, and its industry.

The auditor must understand the risks the client faces, how it is dealing with those risks, and what remaining risks are most likely to result in a material misstatement in the financial statements. Armed with this understanding, the auditor plans procedures that will produce evidence helpful in developing and supporting an opinion on the financial statements.

To understand this process intuitively, consider what financial statements are made of. From your financial accounting courses, you know that accounting systems capture, record, and summarize individual transactions. Entities, of course, must design and implement controls to ensure that those transactions are captured, recorded, and summarized appropriately. These individual transactions are grouped and summarized into various account balances, and finally, financial statements are formed by organizing meaningful collections of those account balances. We have just identified three stages in the accounting process that take place in the preparation of financial statements: *internal controls* are implemented to ensure appropriate capturing and recording of *individual transactions,* which are then collected into ending *account balances*. This summary might seem like an oversimplification, but at a high level it will help you understand the stages of a client's accounting process on which auditors focus to collect evidence and issue an audit opinion.

Keep in mind that the auditor's job ultimately is to express an opinion on *whether the financial statements are fairly stated*. It makes sense, then, that the auditor can design procedures to collect *direct* information about the ending account balances that make up the financial statements. For example, an auditor might confirm the ending balance of the cash account by contacting the client's bank or the auditor might physically examine individual inventory items that make up the ending balance for the inventory account. But remember—account balances are made up of *individual transactions* that occurred over the past year (or beyond). If the auditor designs procedures to test whether the transactions were actually captured and handled properly, the auditor can obtain *indirect* information about whether the ending account balances are likely to be fairly stated. This information is clearly one step removed from the ending account balances themselves. But we can even back up one more step. If the auditor designs procedures to test whether the entity's *internal control* over financial transactions is effective, the auditor can obtain additional *indirect* information regarding whether the account balances are fairly stated. Be sure to follow the logic in this last step: If controls are effective, then the transactions will probably be captured and summarized properly, which means in turn that the account balances are likely to be free of material misstatement. Thus, information about internal control is even more indirect than information about transactions, but it is useful information nonetheless! In fact, while it is indirect, evidence about internal control is usually a relatively cost-effective form of audit evidence.

In summary, the auditor can collect evidence in each of three different stages in a client's accounting system to help determine whether the financial statements are fairly stated: (1) the *internal control* put in place by the client to ensure proper handling of transactions (e.g., evaluate and test the controls); (2) the *transactions* that affect each account balance (e.g., examine a sample of the transactions that happened during the period);

and (3) the ending *account balances* themselves (e.g., examine a sample of the items that make up an ending account balance at year-end). Evidence that relates directly to ending account balances is usually the highest-quality, but also the costliest, evidence. Thus, an auditor will usually rely on a combination of evidence from all three stages in forming an audit opinion regarding the fairness of the financial statements. On which of these three areas it is best to focus depends on the circumstances, and this is generally left to the auditor's discretion. Chapter 4 addresses the types of procedures and types of evidence available to the auditor in more detail.

Major Phases of the Audit

The audit process can be broken down into a number of audit phases (see Figure 1–4). While the figure suggests that these phases are sequential, they are cumulative and interrelated in nature. Phases may include audit procedures designed for one purpose that may provide evidence for other purposes, and sometimes audit procedures accomplish purposes in various phases. Figure 1–4 points out the specific chapters where each of these phases is discussed in detail.

Client Acceptance/Continuance and Establishing Engagement Terms

Professional standards require that public accounting firms establish policies and procedures for deciding whether to accept new clients and to retain current clients. The purpose of such policies is to minimize the likelihood that an auditor will be associated with clients who lack integrity. If an auditor is associated with a client who lacks integrity, the risk increases that material misstatements may exist and not be detected by the auditor. This can lead to lawsuits brought by users of the financial statements (see Exhibit 1–1).[10] For a prospective new client, auditors are required

EXHIBIT 1–1	**Recent Litigation Settlements by Auditors**	
Auditors	*Company Audited*	*Settlement Amount*
Ernst & Young	Cendant	$335 million
Andersen	Waste Management	75 million
Andersen	Sunbeam	110 million
PricewaterhouseCoopers	Microstrategy	51 million
Ernst & Young	Savings & Loans*	400 million
Deloitte	YBM Magnex International	76 million
KPMG	Rite Aid	125 million

*Various Savings & Loans, including Lincoln and Silverado.

Source: M. Maremont, "KPMG, Former Auditor of L&H, May Draw Investor Ire," *The Wall Street Journal* (January 18, 2001); N. Harris, "Andersen to Pay $110 Million to Settle Sunbeam Accounting-Fraud Lawsuit," *The Wall Street Journal* (May 2, 2001); J. Weil, "Pricewaterhouse Agrees to Settle Microstrategy Suit for $51 Million," *The Wall Street Journal* (May 10, 2001); securities, stanford.edu/news-arhive/2002; and www.philly.com/mld/inquirer.

---

[10]See Z. Palmrose, "Litigation and Independent Auditors: The Role of Business Failure and Management Fraud," *Auditing: A Journal of Practice & Theory* (Spring 1987), pp. 90–103, for a discussion of the impact of management fraud on litigation against auditors.

FIGURE 1–4

Major Phases of an Audit

Client acceptance/
continuance
and establishing
engagement terms
(Chapter 5)

Preplanning
(Chapter 5)

Establish materiality
and assess risks
(Chapter 3)

Plan the audit
(Chapters 3 and 5)

Consider and audit internal
control (Chapters 6 and 7)

Audit business processes
and related accounts
(e.g., revenue generation)
(Chapters 10–16)

Complete the audit
(Chapter 17)

Evaluate results and issue
audit report (Chapters 2 and 18)

to confer with the predecessor auditor and frequently conduct background checks on top management. The knowledge that the auditor gathers during the acceptance/continuance process provides valuable understanding of the entity and its environment, thus helping the auditor assess risk and plan the audit. Once the acceptance/continuance decision has been made, the auditor establishes an understanding with the client regarding the services to be performed and the terms of the engagement. Such terms would include, for example, the responsibilities of each party, the assistance to be provided by client personnel and internal auditors, the timing of the engagement, and the expected audit fees.

Preplanning   There are generally three preplanning activities: (1) updating an understanding of an existing client or gaining a deeper understanding of a new client and its environment beyond that obtained during the acceptance/continuance process, (2) determining the audit engagement team requirements, and (3) ensuring the independence of the audit team and audit firm.

The auditor starts by updating or deepening his or her understanding of the entity and its environment. The auditor's understanding of the entity and its environment should include information on each of the following categories:

- Industry, regulatory, and other external factors.
- Nature of the entity, including the entity's application of accounting policies.
- Objectives and strategies and related business risks, including the entity's risk assessment process.
- Measurement and review of the entity's financial performance.
- Internal control.

Because the understanding of the entity and its environment is used to assess the risk of material misstatement and to set the scope of the audit, the auditor should perform risk assessment procedures to support that understanding (e.g., inquiring of personnel, reading business plans and strategies).

The engagement partner or manager ensures that the audit team is composed of team members who have the appropriate audit and industry experience for the engagement. The partner or manager also determines whether the audit will require IT or other types of specialists (e.g., actuaries or appraisers).

The independence of the auditor from the client in terms of freedom from prohibited relationships that might threaten the auditor's objectivity must also be established up front. Chapter 5 addresses the preplanning phase of the audit process in more detail.

Assess Risks and Establish Materiality   In order to plan the audit properly, the audit team must make a preliminary assessment of the client's business risks and determine materiality. The audit team relies on these judgments to then assess risk relating to the likelihood of material misstatements in the financial statements. Chapter 3 discusses both of these concepts.

Plan the Audit   Proper planning is important to ensure that the audit is conducted in an effective and efficient manner. In developing the audit plan, the auditor should be guided by (1) the procedures performed to gain and document an understanding of the entity and (2) the results of the risk assessment process. As part of the planning process, the auditor may conduct preliminary analytical procedures (such as ratio analysis) to identify specific transactions or account balances that should receive special attention due to an increased risk of material misstatement. In many instances, audit planning will include a preliminary assessment of the entity's internal control system. This assessment of internal controls will be in greater depth if the client is a public company, because for public companies the auditor is required to audit both the company's internal control over financial reporting and the company's financial statements. The auditor should prepare a written audit plan that sets forth, in reasonable detail, the nature, extent, and timing of the audit work. Chapters 3 and 5 cover the issues that are involved in this phase of the audit.

Consider and Audit Internal Control   Internal control is designed and effected by an entity's board of directors, management, and other personnel to provide reasonable assurance regarding the achievement of objectives in the following categories: (1) reliability of financial reporting, (2) effectiveness and efficiency of operations, and (3) compliance with applicable laws and regulations (AU 319). When obtaining an understanding of the entity and its environment, the auditor should gain an understanding of internal control. Chapter 6 provides detailed coverage of internal control in a financial statement audit. Chapter 7 covers the audit of internal control for public companies. Later chapters apply the process of considering internal control in the context of various business processes; for example, Chapter 10 covers the revenue process.

Audit Business Processes and Related Accounts   The auditor typically assesses the risk of material misstatement by examining the entity's business processes or accounting cycles (e.g., production and distribution process or sales and postsales services). The auditor then determines the audit procedures that are necessary to reduce the risk of material misstatement to a low level for the financial statement accounts affected by a particular business process. Individual audit procedures are directed toward specific assertions in the account balances that are likely to be misstated. For example, if the auditor is concerned about the possibility of obsolete inventory, the auditor could conduct lower-of-cost-or-market tests to determine if the inventory on hand is properly valued. On most engagements, actually conducting the planned audit tests comprises most of the time spent on a financial statement audit or an audit of internal control over financial reporting. For public company clients, the audit of internal control is done in an integrated way with the financial statement audit. Chapter 7 offers detailed coverage of the audit of internal control for public company clients.

Complete the Audit   After the auditor is done testing the account balances, the sufficiency of the evidence gathered needs to be evaluated. The auditor must obtain sufficient competent evidence in order to reach and justify a conclusion on the fairness of the financial statements. In this phase, the auditor also assesses the possibility of contingent liabilities, such as lawsuits, and searches for any events subsequent to the balance sheet date that may impact the financial statements. Chapter 17 covers each of these issues in detail.

Evaluate Results and Issue the Report   The final phase in the audit process is choosing the appropriate audit report to issue. The auditor's goal at the completion of the audit is to ensure that the risk of material misstatement is reduced to an acceptable level such that the overall financial statements are highly likely to be fairly stated. At the completion of the audit work, the auditor determines if the preliminary assessments of risks were appropriate in light of the evidence collected and whether sufficient evidence was obtained. The auditor then aggregates the total uncorrected misstatements that were detected and determines if they cause the financial statements to be materially misstated. If the uncorrected misstatements do not cause the financial statements to be materially misstated, the auditor issues an unqualified (i.e., "clean") report. If the audit client is a public company, the auditor is also required to report on the effectiveness of the company's system of internal control over financial reporting. Chapters 2, 7, and 18 cover the auditor's report options. An overview of audit reporting is covered early in the text so that you will have a better understanding of how the results of the evidence-gathering process affect the auditor's choice of audit reports.

Conclusion

[LO 8]   You can see from this chapter that a good financial statement auditor needs to understand not only accounting but also the concepts and techniques of gathering and evaluating evidence to assess management's financial statement assertions. An auditor needs a deep understanding of business in general as well as of the specific industries in which his or her clients operate. This is why professionals with auditing experience frequently have attractive opportunities to move into other areas of business and management. Chief executive officers (CEOs), chief financial officers (CFOs), and controllers are commonly former auditors.

This chapter is designed to help you develop an intuitive understanding of basic auditing concepts. You will understand and appreciate the details of the auditing process much more fully if you have a good grasp of the underlying concepts—why financial statement auditing is in demand, what it is, and the basic process by which it is carried out.

Keep in mind that auditing is a fundamentally logical process of thinking and reasoning—don't be hesitant to exercise your reasoning skills! You will benefit much more from your reading of this text if you study it with a reasoning, inquisitive approach, rather than merely attempting to memorize details. As you learn new auditing concepts, take some time to understand the underlying logic and how the concepts interrelate with other concepts. As you learn about auditing procedures, ask yourself how and why the procedure might yield relevant evidence, and try to think of other ways you might obtain useful evidence.

Being a good auditor sometimes requires imagination and innovation. For example, an auditor was faced with figuring out how to verify a client's assertion regarding the existence of inventory. The problem was that the "inventory" consisted of thousands of head of cattle on a ranch covering hundreds of square miles. There was no standard procedure manual for the auditor to refer to—he simply had to figure out an effective and efficient way to obtain persuasive evidence that the cattle existed in the numbers asserted by the ranch's management.

In the end, the auditor decided to charter a small airplane to fly high over the ranch and take photos—one per fifty square acres. The auditor was able to obtain a count of the cattle from the photos. He also evaluated veterinary records to see if the number of required annual vaccinations approximated the number of cattle counted in the photos. Finally, he did some calculations based on average bovine birth and death rates, taking into account recorded purchases and sales of the livestock during the year. Using this combination of procedures, the auditor was able to obtain persuasive evidence supporting management's assertion regarding inventory (and got an airplane ride in the process).

We hope this example helps illustrate why you will need to approach the study of auditing differently from that of most other accounting courses. As you learn the concepts and techniques of auditing, you are acquiring the tools to become an effective financial statement auditor, a conceptual tool kit that will be useful to you in many different settings and contexts.

KEY TERMS

Assurance. Independent professional services that improve the quality of information, or its context, for decision makers. Encompasses attest services and financial statement audits.

Attest. A service when a practitioner is engaged to issue or does issue a report on subject matter, or an assertion about subject matter, that is the responsibility of another party. Encompasses financial statement audits.

Audit risk. The risk that the auditor may unknowingly fail to appropriately modify his or her opinion on financial statements that are materially misstated.

Auditing. A systematic process of (1) objectively obtaining and evaluating evidence regarding assertions about economic actions and events to ascertain the degree of correspondence between those assertions and established criteria and (2) communicating the results to interested users.

Evidential matter. Accounting data and all corroborating information that support the amounts included in the financial statements.

Financial statement assertions. Expressed or implied representations by management that are reflected in the financial statement components.

Fraud. Intentional misstatements that can be classified as fraudulent financial reporting and misappropriation of assets.

Information asymmetry. The concept that the manager generally has more information about the true financial position and results of operations of the entity than the absentee owner does.

✓**Materiality.** The magnitude of an omission or misstatement of accounting information that, in light of surrounding circumstances, makes it probable that the judgment of a reasonable person relying on the information would have been changed or influenced.

Misstatement. An instance where a financial statement assertion is not in accordance with the criteria against which it is audited (e.g., GAAP). Misstatements may be classified as fraud (intentional), other illegal acts such as noncompliance with laws and regulations (intentional or unintentional), and errors (unintentional).

Reasonable assurance. The possibility that, while an auditor can provide some assurance, a material misstatement could be present in the financial statements without the auditor detecting it.

Risk of material misstatement. The risk that the entity's financial statements will contain a material misstatement whether caused by error or fraud.

www.mhhe.com/ messier4e	Visit the book's Online Learning Center for a multiple-choice quiz that will allow you to assess your understanding of chapter concepts.

REVIEW QUESTIONS

[LO 1]   1-1   Why is studying auditing different from studying other accounting topics? How might understanding auditing concepts prove useful for consultants, business managers, and so forth?

[2]   1-2   Discuss why there is a demand for auditing services in a free-market economy. What evidence suggests that auditing would be demanded even if it were not required by government regulation?

[2]   1-3   What is meant by the statement, "The agency relationship between absentee owners and managers produces a natural conflict of interest"?

[3]   1-4   Why is independence such an important standard for auditors? How does independence relate to the agency relationship between owners and managers?

[4]   1-5   Define *auditing*, *attest*, and *assurance services*. Provide two examples of each type of service.

[4]   1-6   The Committee on Basic Auditing Concepts has provided a widely cited definition of auditing. What does the phrase "systematic process" mean in this definition?

[5]   1-7   Define *materiality* and *audit risk*. How are these concepts reflected in the auditor's report?

[6]   1-8   Briefly describe why on most audit engagements an auditor tests only a sample of transactions that occurred.

[7]   1-9   What are the major phases of an audit?

[7]   1-10   The auditor's understanding of the entity and its environment should include knowledge of which categories of information?

[8]   1-11   Briefly discuss why auditors must often exercise creativity and innovation in auditing financial statements. Give an example different from the one offered in the text.

MULTIPLE-CHOICE QUESTIONS

[LO 2,3,4]   1-12   An independent audit aids in the communication of economic data because the audit
  a. Confirms the exact accuracy of management's financial representations.
  b. Lends credibility to the financial statements.
  c. Guarantees that financial data are fairly presented.
  d. Assures the readers of financial statements that any fraudulent activity has been corrected.

[2,3,4]   1-13   Which of the following best describes the reason why an independent auditor reports on financial statements?
  a. Management fraud may exist, and it is more likely to be detected by independent auditors than by internal auditors.
  b. Different interests may exist between the entity preparing the statements and the persons using the statements, and thus outside credibility is needed.
  c. A misstatement of account balances may exist, and all misstatements are generally corrected as a result of the independent auditor's work.
  d. An entity may have a poorly designed internal control system.

[4]   1-14   Which of the following best describes relationships among auditing, attest, and assurance services?
  a. Attest is a type of auditing service.
  b. Auditing and attest services represent two distinctly different types of services.
  c. Auditing is a type of assurance service.
  d. Assurance is a type of attest service.

[4]   1-15   Which of the following can be called an assurance service?
  a. Performance measurement.
  b. Tax planning.
  c. Personal financial planning.
  d. Systems design and implementation.

[5,7]   1-16   What is the ultimate reason why the auditor obtains an understanding of the entity and its environment?
  a. To determine the audit fee.
  b. To decide which facts about the entity to include in the audit report.
  c. To plan the audit and determine the scope of audit procedures to be performed.
  d. To limit audit risk to an appropriately low level.

[7]   1-17   Which of the following is not a condition that potentially increases the entity's business risk?

a. The entity's information system is not adequate to handle its volume of sales transactions.

b. The entity's competitors have introduced major changes to their production processes, whereas the client has not.

c. The entity has made major changes to the lines of reporting within the organization.

d. The external auditor does not possess a sufficient understanding of the entity and its environment to conduct an effective audit.

[5,7]   1-18   Prior to beginning the field work on a new audit engagement in which a CPA does *not* possess expertise in the industry in which the client operates, the CPA should

a. Reduce audit risk by lowering the preliminary levels of materiality.

b. Gather more evidence about the client's internal control to compensate for the lack of industry expertise.

c. Engage financial experts who are familiar with the nature of the industry to accompany the auditor while doing audit work.

d. Obtain a knowledge of matters that relate to the nature of the entity's business.

[2,3,7]   1-19   Which of the following, if material, would be fraud?

a. Mistakes in the application of accounting principles.

b. Clerical mistakes in the accounting data underlying the financial statements.

c. Management appropriation of entity assets for personal use.

d. Misinterpretations of facts that existed when the financial statements were prepared.

PROBLEMS

[1,2,3]   1-20   You recently attended your five-year college reunion. At the main reception, you encountered an old friend, Lee Beagle, who recently graduated from law school and is now practicing with a large law firm in town. When you told him that you were a CPA and employed by a regional CPA firm, he made the following statement and snickered. "You know, if the securities acts had not been passed by Congress in the 1930s, no one would be interested in having an audit performed. You auditors are just creatures of regulation." Since you did not wish to cause a scene at the reunion, you let his comment pass. You and Lee agreed to have lunch the following week to talk over old times. However, you were still unhappy with Lee's comment.

Required:
In preparation for your luncheon with Lee, draft a memo that highlights your thoughts about why auditors are not "creatures of regulation." Cite any relevant evidence of a demand for auditing services outside of legal and regulatory requirements in your memo. Focus on the value that auditing provides.

[2,3]   1-21   Greenbloom Garden Centers is a small, privately held corporation that has two stores in Orlando, Florida. The Greenbloom family owns 100 percent of the company's stock, and family members manage the operations. Sales at the company's stores have been growing rapidly, and there appears to be a market for the company's sales concept—providing bulk garden equipment and supplies at low prices. The controller prepares the company's financial statements, which are not audited. The company has no debt but is considering expanding to other cities in Florida. Such expansion may require long-term borrowings and is likely to reduce the family's day-to-day control of the operations. The family does not intend to sell stock in the company.

Required:
Discuss the factors that may make an audit necessary and potentially valuable for the company. Be sure to consider the concept of information risk.

[3,5]   1-22   Sheri Shannon was recently hired by the CPA firm of Honson & Hansen. Within two weeks, Sheri was sent to the first-year staff training course. The instructor asked her to prepare answers for the following questions:
a. How is evidence defined?
b. How does evidence relate to assertions and to the audit report?
c. What characteristics of evidence should an auditor be concerned with when searching for and evaluating evidence?

[7]   1-23   The audit process described in Figure 1–4 started with the auditor obtaining and supporting an understanding of the entity and its environment and ended with the issuance of an audit report.

Required:
Briefly describe the intervening steps in this process.

[7]   1-24   John Josephs, an audit manager for Tip, Acanoe, & Tylerto, was asked to speak at a dinner meeting of the local Small Business Administration Association. The president of the association has suggested that he talk about the various phases of the audit process. John has asked you, his trusted assistant, to prepare an outline for his speech. He suggests that you answer the following:
a. List and describe the various phases of an audit.
b. Describe how audit procedures designed for one purpose might provide evidence for other purposes. Give an example.
c. One of the phases involves understanding an entity's internal control. Why might the members of the association be particularly interested in the work conducted by auditors in this phase of the audit?

DISCUSSION CASE

[1,3,5,8]   1-25   In a report, the General Accounting Office (GAO) gave the following results based on an examination of 39 failed banks:[11]

---

[11]US General Accounting Office, *Failed Banks: Accounting and Auditing Reforms Urgently Needed* (GAO/AFMD-91-43) (April 1991).

The early warning system provided by bank call reports* is seriously flawed. The 39 failed banks' call reports did not provide the regulators with advance warning of the true magnitude of the deterioration in the banks' financial condition. As a result of the asset valuations FDIC prepared after these banks failed, loss reserves increased from $2.1 billion to $9.4 billion. A major portion of the $7.3 billion deterioration in asset values was not previously reported because deficiencies in GAAP allowed bank management to unduly delay the recognition of losses and mask the need for early regulatory intervention that could have minimized losses to the Bank Insurance Fund.

The key to successful bank regulation is knowing what banks are really worth. The 39 bank failures are expected to cost the fund $8.9 billion. Large banks present a major threat to the solvency of the Bank Insurance Fund and need closer scrutiny.

The corporate governance system upon which successful regulation depends is seriously flawed. Of the 39 banks, 33 had serious internal control problems that regulators cited as contributing significantly to their failure. Had these problems been corrected, the banks might not have failed or their failure could have been less expensive to the fund.

Many of the 39 failed banks did not obtain an independent audit in their last year prior to failure. Without an audit, a troubled institution's management can more easily conceal its financial difficulties.

Audits would enhance both the corporate governance and regulatory functions. In addition, the roles of both management and the auditors would be strengthened if they were required to assume responsibility for assessing and reporting on the condition of internal control, a significant cause of bank failures.

Required:
a. How do you think the GAO conducted its review of these failed banks? What types of documents do you think it examined, and what types of criteria do you think it used to determine that the banks' failure could have been prevented or the losses minimized?
b. Indicate how audits by external auditors could have prevented or limited the losses incurred by the Bank Insurance Fund.

INTERNET ASSIGNMENTS

[1,8]   1-26   Using an Internet browser, identify five Internet sites that contain accounting or auditing resources. For each site identified, prepare a brief summary of the types of information that are available. For example, the PCAOB's home page (www.pcaobus.org) contains extensive information on the organization's activities.

[1,3,7]   1-27   EarthWear Clothiers makes high-quality clothing for outdoor sports and sells most of its products through mail order. Use the Internet to obtain information about the mail-order retail industry.

---

*A call report is a Quarterly Consolidated Report of Condition and Income submitted by management to bank regulators. It consists of unaudited financial information that is required to be prepared in accordance with federal regulatory requirements, which are generally consistent with GAAP.

[1,3,7]   1-28   Visit EarthWear Clothiers' home page (www.mhhe.com/earthwear) and list the types of information contained there.

[1,3,7]   1-29   Willis & Adams are the auditors of EarthWear. Visit Willis & Adams's home page (www.mhhe.com/willisandadams) and list the types of information contained there.

| www.mhhe.com/ messier4e | Visit the book's Online Learning Center for problem material to be completed using the *ACL* software packaged with your new text. |

EarthWear

2 0 0 5

COMPANY HISTORY AND OPERATIONS EarthWear Clothiers was founded in Boise, Idaho, by James Williams and Calvin Rogers in 1973 to make high-quality clothing for outdoor sports, such as hiking, skiing, fly-fishing, and whitewater kayaking. Over the years, the company's product lines have grown to include casual clothing, accessories, shoes, and soft luggage. EarthWear offers its products through three retailing options: catalogs, retail outlets, and its website.

The company strives to provide excellent, high-quality products at reasonable prices. EarthWear has a commitment to excellence in customer service and an unconditional guarantee. The company is also conscious of its environmental responsibilities. All company facilities are insulated, recycle, and conserve power. The company continuously monitors the environmental impact of its products. The company believes that many of its customers share this concern for the environment.

The company offers its products principally through regular mailings of its monthly catalogs in the United States, Europe, and Japan. EarthWear has ten U.S. outlet stores, four in the U.K., two in Germany, and two in Japan. The company also offers its products over the Internet (www.mhhe.com/earthwear). During 2005, the Company expanded its global presence by launching sites in France, Italy, Ireland, and several eastern European countries. Currently, revenue from catalog sales, retail outlets, and the website are 74 percent, 5 percent, and 21 percent, respectively. Management expects that Internet sales will grow significantly in the future, perhaps replacing catalogs as the major source of sales.

EarthWear was incorporated in Idaho in 1975 and became a Delaware corporation in 1986 when it went public.

COMPANY

HISTORY AND BACKGROUND

COMPANY GROWTH STRATEGY EarthWear's growth strategy has three elements. First, the company attempts to increase sales by expanding its customer base and by increasing sales to existing customers through improved product offerings. Second, the company seeks to generate additional sales by targeted mailings of special issues of its catalogs and by offering its products through its website. Third, the company is pursuing additional opportunities to expand its merchandising skills internationally.

CATALOGS AND SALES OPERATIONS During 2005 the company mailed 12 issues of its regular monthly catalog with an average of 75 pages per issue from its U.S. operations. Worldwide, the company mailed approximately 160 million full-price catalogs. EarthWear views each catalog issue as a unique opportunity to communicate with its customers. Products are described in visual and editorial detail, and the company uses such techniques as background stories and distinctive covers to stimulate the readers' interest.

Each issue of the regular catalog offers certain basic product lines for men and women. The regular catalog also offers seasonal merchandise. In addition, EarthWear mails two end-of-season clearance catalogs. The company mails its catalogs to prospective customers who are identified based on lists of magazine subscribers and lists of households meeting certain demographic criteria. In addition, the company identifies prospective new customers through its national advertising campaign.

In 1991 the company introduced its first business specialty catalog, which offered its products to groups and companies for corporate incentive programs. EarthWear's embroidery capabilities allow for the design and monogram of unique logos or emblems for groups and companies. In 2005 the company mailed five issues of its corporate sales catalogs.

The international business segment includes operations in Japan, Germany, and the United Kingdom, and various Internet sites. Catalogs mailed in those countries are written in the local languages and denominated in local currencies. In the spring of 2005, EarthWear launched local websites in each of these countries in their respective languages and currencies.

CUSTOMER DATABASE A principal factor in the company's success has been the development of its own list of active customers. At the end of 2005 the company's mailing list consisted of about 21.1 million persons, approximately 7 million of whom were viewed as customers because they had made at least one purchase from the company within the last 24 months. The company routinely updates and refines the database before mailing catalogs to monitor customer interest as reflected in criteria such as the regency, frequency, dollar amount, and product type of purchases.

EarthWear believes that its customer database has desirable demographic characteristics and is well suited to the products offered in the company's catalogs. A survey conducted by the company in the United States during 2004 indicated that approximately 50 percent of its customers were in the 35–54 age group and had median incomes of $62,000.

The company advertises nationally to build its reputation and to attract new customers. In 2005 this advertising campaign appeared in about 40 national magazines, as well as on five national cable television networks. In addition, the company advertises in approximately 75 national, regional, and local publications in Canada, the United Kingdom, Germany, and Japan. EarthWear also advertises on a number of Internet search engines and websites.

PRODUCT DEVELOPMENT
EarthWear concentrates on clothing and other products that are aimed at customers interested in outdoor activities. The company products are styled and quality crafted to meet the changing tastes of the company's customers rather than to mimic the changing fads of the fashion world. At the same time, the company seeks to maintain customer interest by developing new products,

improving existing core products, and reinforcing its value positioning.

The company continues to incorporate innovations in fabric, construction, and detail that add value and excitement and differentiate EarthWear from the competition. In order to ensure that products are manufactured to the company's quality standards at reasonable prices, product managers, designers, and quality assurance specialists develop the company's own products.

EarthWear deals directly with its suppliers and seeks to avoid intermediaries. All goods are produced by independent manufacturers except for most of its soft luggage, which is assembled at the company's facilities. During 2005 the company purchased merchandise from approximately 300 domestic and foreign manufacturers. One manufacturer and one intermediary accounted for about 14 and 29 percent of the company's received merchandise, respectively, in 2005. In 2005 about 80 percent of the company's merchandise was imported, mainly from Asia, Central America, Mexico, and Central America. The company will continue to take advantage of worldwide sourcing without sacrificing customer service or quality standards.

ORDER ENTRY, FULFILLMENT, AND DELIVERY EarthWear has toll-free telephone numbers that customers can call 24 hours a day, seven days a week (except Christmas Day) to place orders or to request a catalog. Approximately 90 percent of catalog orders are placed by telephone. Telephone calls are answered by the company's well-trained sales representatives, who utilize online computer terminals to enter customer orders and to retrieve information about product characteristics and availability. The company's three U.S. telephone centers are located in Boise, Idaho; Reston, Virginia; and Canton, Ohio. International telephone centers are located in London, England; Tokyo, Japan; and Mannheim, Germany.

The company's order entry and fulfillment system permits shipment of in-stock orders on the following day, but orders requiring monogramming or inseaming typically require one or two extra days. The company's sales representatives enter orders into an online order entry and inventory control system. Customers using the company's Internet site see color photos of the products, their availability, and prices. When ordering a product over the Internet, the customer completes a computer screen that requests information on product code, size, color, and so on. When the customer finishes shopping for products, he or she enters delivery and credit card information into a computer-based form. EarthWear provides assurance through CPA WebTrust^{SM} that the website has been evaluated and tested to meet WebTrust^{SM} principles and criteria. This assurance service is provided by the company's independent auditors, Willis & Adams, LLP.

Orders are generally shipped by United Parcel Service (UPS) at various tiered rates that depend on the total dollar value of each customer's order. Other expedited delivery services are available at additional charge. Domestically, the company utilizes two-day UPS service at standard rates, enhancing its customer service. Comparable services are offered in international markets.

MERCHANDISE LIQUIDATION Liquidations (sales of overstock and end-of-season merchandise at reduced prices) were approximately 12 percent, 11 percent, and 8 percent of net sales in 2005, 2004, and 2003, respectively. Most liquidation sales were made through catalogs and other print media. The balance was sold principally through the company's outlet retail stores.

COMPETITION The company's principal competitors are retail stores, including specialty shops, department stores, and other catalog companies. Direct competitors include Eddie Bauer, Land's End, L. L. Bean, Patagonia, and Timberland. The company may also face increased competition from other retailers as the number of television shopping channels and the variety of merchandise offered over the Internet increase. The apparel retail business in general is intensely competitive. EarthWear competes principally on the basis of merchandise value (quality and price), its established customer list, and customer service, including fast order fulfillment and its unqualified guarantee.

TRADEMARKS The company uses the trademarks of "EarthWear" and "EWC" on products and catalogs.

SEASONALITY OF BUSINESS The company's business is highly seasonal. Historically, a disproportionate amount of the company's net sales and most of its profits have been realized during the fourth quarter. If the company's sales were materially different from seasonal norms during the fourth quarter, the company's annual operating results could be materially affected. Accordingly, results for the individual quarters do not necessarily indicate results to be expected for the entire year. In 2005, 37 percent of the company's total revenue came in the fourth quarter.

EMPLOYEES The company believes that its skilled and dedicated workforce is one of its key resources. Employees are not covered by collective bargaining agreements, and the company considers its employee relations to be excellent. As a result of the highly seasonal nature of the company's business, the size of the company's workforce varies, ranging from approximately 3,500 to 5,300 individuals in 2005. During the peak winter season of 2005, approximately 2,700 of the company's 5,300 employees were temporary employees.

EXECUTIVE OFFICERS OF THE COMPANY
James G. Williams, 65, is chairman of the board and former chief executive officer. Mr. Williams was one of the two original founders of EarthWear. He stepped down as chief executive officer in December 1999.

Calvin J. Rogers, 57, is president and chief executive officer of the company. Mr. Rogers was one of the two original founders of the company. He assumed his present position in December 1999.

Dominique DeSantiago, 56, is executive vice president and chief operating officer. Mr. DeSantiago joined the company as chief operating officer in June 1991. He was promoted to vice president in October 1994. Mr. DeSantiago was previously employed by Eddie Bauer in various capacities.

Linda S. McDaniel, 45, is senior vice president of sales. She joined the company in July 1996. Ms. McDaniel served as divisional vice president, merchandising, with Patagonia between 1986 and 1990. Ms. McDaniel was the president and chief executive officer for Mountain Goat Sports from 1990 until 1996. She has been serving as a director of the company since November 1997.

James C. ("JC") Watts, 45, is senior vice president and chief financial officer. Mr. Watts joined the company in May 1996, assuming his current position. He was previously employed by Federated Department Stores.

Mary Ellen Tornesello, 47, is senior vice president of operations. Ms. Tornesello joined the company in 1994 as operations manager. She served as vice president of operations from 1995 until 1997, at which time she assumed her present position.

06

2005

Market Information The common stock of the company is listed and traded on NASDAQ under the symbol EWCC. The high and low prices of the company's common stock for 2005 were $52.50 and $21.75 per share. The closing price of the company's stock on December 31, 2005, was $40.25 per share.

Shareholders As of December 31, 2005, the number of shareholders of record of common stock of the company was 2,120. This number excludes shareholders whose stock is held in nominee or street name by brokers.

Independent Auditors The company has been audited by Willis & Adams since incorporation in 1975.

EARTHWEAR CLOTHIERS

Consolidated Statements of Operations

(In thousands, except per share data)

	For the period ended December 31		
	2005	2004	2003
Net Sales	**$ 950,484**	$ 857,885	$ 891,394
Cost of sales	**$ 546,393**	$ 472,739	490,530
Gross Profit	**$ 404,091**	$ 385,146	400,864
Selling, general, and administrative expenses	**$ 364,012**	$ 334,994	353,890
Nonrecurring charge (credit)	**-**	(1,153)	8,190
Income from operations	**40,079**	51,305	38,784
Other income (expense):			
Interest expense	**(983)**	(1,229)	(5,027)
Interest income	**1,459**	573	10
Other	**(4,798)**	(1,091)	(1,593)
Total other income (expense), net	**(4,322)**	(1,747)	6,609
Income before income taxes	**35,757**	49,559	32,175
Income tax provision	**13,230**	18,337	11,905
Net income	**$22,527**	$ 31,222	$ 20,270
Basic earnings per share	**1.15**	1.60	1.02
Diluted earnings per share	**1.14**	1.56	1.01
Basic weighted average shares outstanding	**19,531**	19,555	19,806
Diluted weighted average shares outstanding	**19,774**	20,055	19,996

CONSOLIDATED FINANCIAL STATEMENTS

07
2005

EARTHWEAR CLOTHIERS

Consolidated Balance Sheets

(In thousands)

	December 31	
Assets	**2005**	**2004**
Current Assets:		
Cash and cash equivalents	$ 48,978	$ 49,668
Receivables, net	12,875	11,539
Inventory	122,337	105,425
Prepaid advertising	11,458	10,772
Other prepaid expenses	6,315	3,780
Deferred income tax benefits	7,132	6,930
Total current assets	209,095	188,115
Property, plant, and equipment, at cost		
Land and buildings	70,918	66,804
Fixtures and equipment	67,513	66,876
Computer hardware and software	64,986	47,466
Leasehold improvements	3,010	2,894
Total property, plant, and equipment	206,426	184,040
Less accumulated depreciation and amortization	85,986	76,256
Property, plant and equipment, net	120,440	107,784
Intangibles, net	423	628
Total assets	$ 329,959	$ 296,527
Liabilities and shareholders' investment		
Current liabilities:		
Lines of credit	$ 11,011	$ 7,621
Accounts payable	62,509	48,432
Reserve for returns	5,890	5,115
Accrued liabilities	26,738	28,440
Accrued profit sharing	1,532	1,794
Income taxes payable	8,588	6,666
Total current liabilities	116,268	98,067
Deferred income taxes	9,469	5,926
Shareholders' investment:		
Common stock, 26,121 shares issued	261	261
Donated capital	5,460	5,460
Additional paid-in capital	20,740	19,311
Deferred compensation	(79)	(153)
Accumulated other comprehensive income	3,883	1,739
Retained earnings	317,907	295,380
Treasury stock, 6,546 and 6,706 shares at cost, respectively	(143,950)	(129,462)
Total shareholders' investment	204,222	192,535
Total liabilities and shareholders' investment	$ 329,959	$ 296,527

EARTHWEAR CLOTHIERS

Consolidated Statements of Stockholders' Investment

(In thousands)

09
2005

	Comprehensive Income	Common Stock	Donated Capital	Additional Paid-In Capital	Deferred Compensation	Accumulated Other Comprehensive Income	Retained Earnings	Treasury Stock	Total
Balance, December 31, 2002		$ 261	$5,460	$17,197	($681)	$569	$243,888	($108.931)	$157,763
Purchase of treasury stock								(23,112)	(23,112)
Issuance of treasury stock								1,199	1,199
Tax benefit of stock									
options exercised				349					349
Deferred compensation expense					424				424
Comprehensive income:									
Net income	$20,270						20,270		20,270
Foreign currency									
translation adjustments	733					733			733
Comprehensive income	$21,003								
Balance, December 31, 2003		$ 261	$5,460	$17,546	($257)	$1,302	$264,158	($130,844)	$157,626
Purchase of treasury stock								(2,935)	(2,935)
Issuance of treasury stock								4,317	4,317
Tax benefit of stock									
options exercised				1,765					1,765
Deferred compensation expense					103				103
Comprehensive income:									
Net income	$31,222						31,222		31,222
Foreign currency	60					60			60
translation adjustments	377					377			377
Comprehensive income	$31,659								
Balance, December 31, 2004		$ 261	$5,460	$19,311	($154)	$1,739	$295,380	($129,463)	$192,534
Purchase of treasury stock								(18,192)	(18,192)
Issuance of treasury stock								3,704	3,704
Tax benefit of stock									
options exercised				1,429					1,429
Deferred compensation expense					75				75
Comprehensive income:									
Net income	$22,527						22,527		22,527
Foreign currency									
translation adjustments	(1,151)					(1,151)			(1,151)
Unrealized gain on									
forward contracts	3,295					3,295			3,295
Comprehensive income	$24,671								
Balance, December 31, 2005		$ 261	$5,460	$20,740	($79)	$3,883	$317,907	($143,950)	$204,222

EARTHWEAR CLOTHIERS

Consolidated Statements of Cash Flows

(In thousands)

	For the period ended December 31		
Cash flows from (used for) operating activities:	**2005**	2004	2003
Net income	**$22,527**	$ 31,222	$ 20,270
Adjustments to reconcile net income to net cash flows from operating activities:			
Non-recurring charge (credit)		(1,153)	8,190
Depreciation and amortization	**$15,231**	13,465	12,175
Deferred compensation expense	**$75**	103	424
Deferred income taxes	**$3,340**	5,376	(3,866)
Loss on disposal of fixed assets	**$284**	602	381
Changes in assets and liabilities excluding the effects of divestitures:			
Receivables, net	**($1,336)**	2,165	(3,666)
Inventory	**($16,912)**	37,370	13,954
Prepaid advertising	**($686)**	3,110	(1,849)
Other prepaid expenses	**($2,534)**	1,152	(1,628)
Accounts payable	**$14,078**	(8,718)	2,716
Reserve for returns	**$775**	439	692
Accrued liabilities	**($709)**	(4,982)	4,545
Accrued profit sharing	**($262)**	328	(1,320)
Income taxes payable	**$1,923**	(2,810)	(3,834)
Tax benefit of stock options	**$1,429**	1,765	349
Other	**$2,144**	437	733
Net cash from (used for) operating activities	**$39,367**	79,871	48,269
Cash flows from (used for) investing activities:			
Cash paid for capital additions	**(28,959)**	(18,208)	(30,388)
Net cash flows used for investing activities	**(28,959)**	(18,208)	(30,388)
Cash flows from (used for) financing activities:			
Proceeds from (payment of) short-term debt	**3,390**	(17,692)	4,228
Purchases of treasury stock	**(18,192)**	(2,935)	(23,112)
Issuance of treasury stock	**3,704**	4,317	1,199
Net cash flows used for financing activities	**(11,097)**	(16,310)	(17,685)
Net increase (decrease) in cash and cash equivalents	**(690)**	45,352	197
Beginning cash and cash equivalents	**49,668**	4,317	4,120
Ending cash and cash equivalents	**$ 48,978**	$ 49,668	$ 4,317
Supplemental cash flow disclosures:			
Interest paid	**$ 987**	$ 1,229	$ 5,000
Income taxes paid	**6,278**	13,701	18,107

EARTHWEAR CLOTHIERS

Five-Year Consolidated Financial Summary (unaudited)

(In thousands, except per share data)

	For the period ended December 31				
	2005	2004	2003	2002	2001
Income statement data:					
Net Sales	950,484	857,885	891,394	821,359	503,434
Pretax Income	35,757	49,559	32,175	66,186	38,212
Percent of net sales	3.8%	5.8%	3.6%	8.1%	7.6%
Net income	22,527	31,222	20,270	41,698	22,929
Per share of common stock:					
Basic earnings per share	1.15	1.60	1.02	2.01	1.54
Diluted earnings per share	1.14	1.56	1.01	2.00	1.53
Common shares outstanding	19,531	19,555	19,806	20,703	14,599
Balance sheet data:					
Current assets	209,095	188,115	191,297	194,445	122,418
Current liabilities	116,268	98,067	133,434	118,308	65,505
PPE and intangibles	120,863	108,412	105,051	87,312	46,658
Total assets	329,959	296,527	296,347	281,757	170,121
Noncurrent liabilities	9,496	5,926	5,286	5,686	4,211
Shareholders' investment	204,222	192,535	157,627	157,763	100,405
Other data:					
Net working capital	92,827	90,048	57,863	76,136	56,913
Capital expenditures	28,959	18,208	30,388	31,348	8,316
Depreciation and amortization expense	15,231	13,465	12,175	9,833	6,101
Return on average shareholders' investment	11%	18%	13%	28%	24%
Return on average assets	7%	11%	7%	16%	15%

NET INCOME

$50,000	
$40,000	
$30,000	
$20,000	
$10,000	

2003 2004 **2005**

NET SALES

$900,000	
$800,000	
$700,000	
$600,000	
$500,000	
$400,000	

2003 2004 **2005**

NET INCOME PER SHARE

$2.00	
$1.50	
$1.00	
$0.50	

2001 2002 2003 2004 **2005**

NOTE A: SUMMARY OF SIGNIFICANT ACCOUNTING POLICIES

NATURE OF BUSINESS EarthWear markets high quality clothing for outdoor sports, casual clothing, accessories, shoes, and soft luggage. The company manages its business in three operating segments consisting of core, business-to-business, and international. The company's primary market is the United States; other markets include Canada, Europe, and Japan.

PRINCIPLES OF CONSOLIDATION The consolidated statements include the accounts of the company and its subsidiaries after elimination of intercompany accounts and transactions.

USE OF ESTIMATES The preparations of financial statements in conformity with generally accepted accounting principles requires management to make estimates and assumptions that affect the reported amounts of assets and liabilities and disclosure of contingent assets and liabilities at the date of the financial statements and the reported amounts of revenues and expenses during the reporting periods. Actual results may differ from these estimates.

REVENUE RECOGNITION The company records revenue at the time of shipment for catalog and e-commerce sales and at the point for sale for stores. The company provides a reserve for returns.

RESERVE FOR LOSSES ON CUSTOMER RETURNS At the time of sale, the company provides a reserve equal to the gross profit on projected merchandise returns, based on prior returns experience.

INVENTORY Inventory is stated at the last-in, first-out (LIFO) cost, which is lower than market. If the first-in, first-out method of accounting for inventory had been used, inventory would have been approximately $10.8 million and $13.7 million higher than reported at December 31, 2005 and 2004, respectively.

ADVERTISING The company expenses the costs of advertising for magazines, television, radio, and other media the first time the advertising takes place, except for direct-response advertising, which is capitalized and amortized over its expected period of future benefits. Direct-response advertising consists primarily of catalog production and mailing costs, which are generally amortized within three months from the date catalogs are mailed.

DEPRECIATION Depreciation expense is calculated using the straight-line method over the estimated useful lives of the assets, which are 20 to 30 years for buildings and land improvements and 5 to 10 years for leasehold improvements and furniture, fixtures, equipment, and software. The company allocates one half year of depreciation to the year of addition or retirement.

INTANGIBLES Intangible assets consist primarily of goodwill, which is amortized over 15 years on a straight-line basis.

FINANCIAL INSTRUMENTS WITH OFF-BALANCE-SHEET RISK The company uses import letters of credit to purchase foreign-sourced merchandise. The letters of credit are primarily U.S. dollar-denominated and are issued through third-party financial institutions to guarantee payment for such merchandise within the agreed-upon time periods. At December 31, 2005, the company had outstanding letters of credit of approximately $23 million, all of which had expiration dates of less than one year.

FOREIGN CURRENCY TRANSLATIONS AND TRANSACTIONS Financial statements of the foreign subsidiaries are translated into U.S. dollars in accordance with Statement of Financial Accounting Standards No. 52. Translation adjustments are recorded in accumulated other comprehensive income, which is a component of stockholders' equity.

NOTE B: STOCKHOLDERS' EQUITY

COMMON STOCK The company currently is authorized to issue 70 million shares of $0.01 par value common stock.

TREASURY STOCK The company's board of directors has authorized the purchase of a total of 12.7 million shares of the company's common stock. A total of 6.5 million and 6.7 million had been purchased as of December 31, 2005 and 2004, respectively.

STOCK AWARDS AND GRANTS The company has a restricted stock award plan. Under the provisions of the plan, a committee of the company's board may award shares of the company's common stock to its officers and key employees. Such shares vest over a 10-year period on a straight-line basis.

The granting of these awards has been recorded as deferred compensation based on the fair market value of the shares at the date of the grant. Compensation expense under these plans is recorded as shares vest.

STOCK OPTIONS The company has 3.5 million shares of common stock that may be issued pursuant to the exercise of options granted under the company's stock option plan. Options are granted at the discretion of a committee of the company's board of directors to officers and key employees of the company. No option may have an exercise price less than the fair market value per share of the common stock at the date of the grant.

NOTE C: LINES OF CREDIT

The company has unsecured domestic lines of credit with various U.S. banks totaling $150 million. There were $23.4 million amounts outstanding at December 31, 2005 compared to $20.2 million outstanding at December 31, 2004. In addition, the company has unsecured lines of credit with foreign banks totaling the equivalent of $30 million for its wholly owned subsidiaries. At December 31, 2005, $11 million was outstanding at interest rates averaging 4.6 percent, compared with $7.6 million at December 31, 2004.

NOTE D: LONG-TERM DEBT

There was no long-term debt at December 31, 2005 and 2004.

NOTE E: LEASES

The company leases store and office space and equipment under various lease arrangements. The leases are accounted for as operating leases.

NOTE F: RETIREMENT PLANS

The company has a retirement plan that covers most regular employees and provides for annual contributions at the discretion of the board of directors. Included in the plan is a 401(k) feature that allows employees to make contributions.

MANAGEMENT'S DISCUSSION AND ANALYSIS:

The year 2005 was a year during which we've seen the results of our strategic initiatives of the last two years take hold. Sales momentum picked up towards the end of the third quarter and continued strongly through our all-important holiday season, and we reported a double-digit increase in both revenue and earnings for the fourth quarter. This success enabled us to complete the year with an annual 3.2 percent increase in total revenue, but a 27.8 percent decrease in earnings, mainly due to the weakness of the first nine months. Our strong finish for the year was gratifying in the face of a difficult economy.

MANAGEMENT'S DISCUSSION AND ANALYSIS: RESULTS OF OPERATIONS FOR 2005 COMPARED TO 2004

TOTAL REVENUE INCREASED BY 3.2 PERCENT

Total revenue for the year just ended was $950.5 million, compared with $857.9 million in the prior year, an increase of 3.2 percent. Seasonally strong sales resulted in a higher level of backorders during the fourth quarter and a first-time fulfillment rate of 85 percent for the year as a whole, slightly below the prior year's rate. Overall merchandise sales growth was primarily attributable to changes in circulation, which included adding back our post-Thanksgiving catalog and our January full-price catalog, shifting the timing of our fall/winter mailings, increased page circulation and improved merchandise selection and creative presentations.

NET INCOME DECREASED Net income for 2005 was $22.5 million, down 27.8 percent from the $31.2 million earned in 2004. Diluted earnings per share for the year just ended were $1.14, compared with $1.56 per share for the prior year. The diluted weighted average number of common shares outstanding was 19.8 million for 2005 and 20.0 million for 2004.

GROSS PROFIT MARGIN Gross profit for the year just ended was $404 million, or 42.5 percent of total revenue, compared with $385 million, or 41.6 percent of total revenue, for the prior year. Liquidations were about 11 percent of net merchandise sales in 2005, compared with 12 percent in the prior year. In 2005, the cost of inventory purchases was down 2.0 percent, compared with deflation of 2.7 percent in 2004. This reduction was a result of improved sourcing. As a result, the LIFO inventory reserve was reduced by $2.8 million and $3.8 million in 2005 and 2004, respectively.

SELLING, GENERAL, AND ADMINISTRATIVE EXPENSES Selling, general and administrative (SG&A) expenses increased 9.2 percent to $364 million in 2005, compared with $334 million in the prior year. As a percentage of sales, SG&A was 38.3 percent in 2005 and 36.2 percent in the prior year. The increase in the SG&A ratio was primarily the result of higher catalog costs associated with increased page circulation, as well as higher information services expenses as we continue to invest in the Internet and upgrade systems capabilities. The cost of producing and mailing catalogs represented about 39 percent and 38 percent of total SG&A in 2005 and 2004, respectively.

CREDIT LINES AND CAPITAL EXPENDITURES Interest expense on lines of credit was down in 2005 due to lower average borrowing levels. Interest expense decreased to $1.0 million in 2005, compared to $1.2 million in 2004. We spent $29 million in cash on capital expenditures, which included $20 million for computer hardware and software. In addition, the company acquired a new airplane by exchanging two of its own aircraft in 2005. Also, we purchased about $18 million in treasury stock. No long-term debt was outstanding at year-end 2005. Depreciation and amortization expense was $15.2 million, up 13.1 percent from the prior year, mainly due to computer software. Rental expense was $10.4 million, up 3.4 percent from 2004, primarily due to additional computer hardware.

To the Stockholders

EarthWear Clothiers, Inc.

Management of EarthWear Clothiers, Inc. (the "Company") is responsible for the preparation, consistency, integrity, and fair presentation of the consolidated financial statements. The consolidated financial statements have been prepared in accordance with accounting principles generally accepted in the United States of America applied on a consistent basis and, in management's opinion, are fairly presented. The financial statements include amounts that are based on management's informed judgments and best estimates.

Management has established and maintains comprehensive systems of internal control that provide reasonable assurance as to the consistency, integrity, and reliability of the preparation and presentation of financial statements; the safeguarding of assets; the effectiveness and efficiency of operations; and compliance with applicable laws and regulations. The concept of reasonable assurance is based upon the recognition that the cost of the controls should not exceed the benefit derived. Management monitors the systems of internal control and maintains an independent internal auditing program that assesses the effectiveness of internal control. Management assessed the Company's internal control over financial reporting for financial presentations in conformity with accounting principles generally accepted in the United States of America. This assessment was based on criteria for effective internal control over financial reporting established in Internal Control — Integrated Framework issued by the Committee of Sponsoring Organizations of the Treadway Commission (the COSO Report). Based on this assessment, management believes that the Company maintained effective internal control over financial reporting for financial presentations in conformity with accounting principles generally accepted in the United States of America as of December 31, 2005.

The Board of Directors exercises its oversight role with respect to the Company's systems of internal control primarily through its Audit Committee, which is comprised solely of outside directors. The Committee oversees the Company's systems of internal control and financial reporting to assess whether their quality, integrity, and objectivity are sufficient to protect shareholders' investments.

The Company's consolidated financial statements have been audited by Willis & Adams LLP ("Willis & Adams"), independent auditors. As part of its audit, Willis & Adams considers the Company's internal control to plan the audit and determine the nature, timing, and extent of auditing procedures considered necessary to render its opinion as to the fair presentation, in all material respects, of the consolidated financial statements, which is based on independent audits made accordance with the standards of the Public Company Accounting Oversight Board (United States). Management's assertion that the Company maintained effective internal control over financial reporting for financial presentations in conformity with accounting principles generally accepted in the United States of America has been audited by Willis & Adams. Management has made available to Willis & Adams all the Company's financial records and related data, and information concerning the Company's internal control over financial reporting, and believes that all representations made to Willis & Adams during its audits were valid and appropriate.

Calvin J. Rogers

*President and Chief
Executive Officer*

James C. Watts

*Senior Vice President and
Chief Financial Officer*

To the Stockholders

EarthWear Clothiers, Inc.

We have audited management's assessment, included in the accompanying Management Report on the Financial Statements and Internal Control, that EarthWear Clothiers maintained effective internal control over financial reporting as of December 31, 2005, based on criteria established in Internal Control—Integrated Framework issued by the Committee of Sponsoring Organizations of the Treadway Commission (COSO). EarthWear Clothiers' management is responsible for maintaining effective internal control over financial reporting and for its assessment of the effectiveness of internal control over financial reporting. Our responsibility is to express an opinion on management's assessment and an opinion on the effectiveness of the company's internal control over financial reporting based on our audit.

We conducted our audit in accordance with the standards of the Public Company Accounting Oversight Board (United States). Those standards require that we plan and perform the audit to obtain reasonable assurance about whether effective internal control over financial reporting was maintained in all material respects. Our audit included obtaining an understanding of internal control over financial reporting, evaluating management's assessment, testing and evaluating the design and operating effectiveness of internal control, and performing such other procedures as we considered necessary in the circumstances. We believe that our audit provides a reasonable basis for our opinion.

A company's internal control over financial reporting is a process designed to provide reasonable assurance regarding the reliability of financial reporting and the preparation of financial statements for external purposes in accordance with generally accepted accounting principles. A company's internal control over financial reporting includes those policies and procedures that (1) pertain to the maintenance of records that, in reasonable detail, accurately and fairly reflect the transactions and dispositions of the assets of the company; (2) provide reasonable assurance that transactions are recorded as necessary to permit preparation of financial statements in accordance with generally accepted accounting principles, and that receipts and expenditures of the company are being made only in accordance with authorizations of management and directors of the company; and (3) provide reasonable assurance regarding prevention or timely detection of unauthorized acquisition, use, or disposition of the company's assets that could have a material effect on the financial statements.

Because of its inherent limitations, internal control over financial reporting may not prevent or detect misstatements. Also, projections of any evaluation of effectiveness to future periods are subject to the risk that controls may become inadequate because of changes in conditions, or that the degree of compliance with the policies or procedures may deteriorate.

In our opinion, management's assessment that EarthWear Clothiers maintained effective internal control over financial reporting as of December 31, 2005, is fairly stated, in all material respects, based on criteria established in Internal Control—Integrated Framework issued by the Committee of Sponsoring Organizations of the Treadway Commission (COSO). Also in our opinion, EarthWear Clothiers maintained, in all material respects, effective internal control over financial reporting as of December 31, 2005, based on criteria established in Internal Control—Integrated Framework issued by the Committee of Sponsoring Organizations of the Treadway Commission (COSO).

We have also audited, in accordance with the standards of the Public Company Accounting Oversight Board (United States), the consolidated financial statements of EarthWear Clothiers and our report dated February 15, 2006 expressed an unqualified opinion.

Willis & Adams

Willis & Adams, CPAs

Boise, Idaho
February 15, 2006

To the Stockholders

EarthWear Clothiers, Inc.

We have audited the consolidated balance sheets of EarthWear Clothiers as of December 31, 2005 and 2004, and the related consolidated statements of operations, stockholders' equity, and cash flows for each of the three years in the period ended December 31, 2005. These financial statements are the responsibility of the Company's management. Our responsibility is to express an opinion on these financial statements based on our audits.

We conducted our audits in accordance with the standards of the Public Company Accounting Oversight Board (United States). Those standards require that we plan and perform the audit to obtain reasonable assurance about whether the financial statements are free of material misstatement. An audit includes examining, on a test basis, evidence supporting the amounts and disclosures in the financial statements. An audit also includes assessing the accounting principles used and significant estimates made by management, as well as evaluating the overall financial statement presentation. We believe that our audits provide a reasonable basis for our opinion.

In our opinion, the consolidated financial statements referred to above present fairly, in all material respects, the financial position of the Company as of December 31, 2005 and 2004, and the results of its operations and its cash flows for each of the three years in the period ended December 31, 2005, in conformity with U.S. generally accepted accounting principles.

We also have audited, in accordance with the standards of the Public Company Accounting Oversight Board (United States), the effectiveness of EarthWear Clothiers' internal control over financial reporting as of December 31, 2005, based on criteria established in Internal Control—Integrated Framework issued by the Committee of Sponsoring Organizations of the Treadway Commission (COSO) and our report dated February 15, 2006 expressed an unqualified opinion on management's assessment that EarthWear Clothiers maintain effective internal control and an unqualified opinion that internal control was effective.

Willis & Adams

Willis & Adams, CPAs

Boise, Idaho
February 15, 2006

LEARNING OBJECTIVES

Upon completion of this chapter you will

[1] Understand the events that led up to the recent change and turmoil in the auditing profession.

[2] Recognize that auditing takes place in a context that is shaped largely by the audit client's business.

[3] Understand a high-level model of a business entity, including the elements of corporate governance, objectives, strategies, processes, controls, transactions, and financial statements.

[4] Be familiar with a five-component model of business processes (or cycles) that auditors often use in organizing the audit into manageable components.

[5] Recognize the sets of management assertions that are implicit in a business entity's financial statements.

[6] Understand that auditing standards are established by the AICPA's Auditing Standards Board (ASB) for private entities, and by the Public Company Accounting Oversight Board (PCAOB) for public companies.

[7] Be familiar with the 10 "generally accepted auditing standards" (GAAS).

[8] Understand the nature of the Statements on Auditing Standards (SAS) as interpretations of the ten GAAS.

[9] Be aware that the PCAOB adopted the ASB's SAS on an interim basis and is now issuing its own Auditing Standards (AS) that apply to the audits of public companies.

[10] Understand that auditing is a profession that places a premium on ethical behavior and that is governed by a Code of Professional Conduct.

[11] Know that management is primarily responsible for the entity's financial statements and understand the auditor's responsibility for detecting errors, material fraud, and illegal acts.

[12] Know the basic elements of audit reporting.

[13] Understand the organization and composition of public accounting firms.

[14] Be familiar with the various services offered by assurance providers.

[15] Be familiar with the different types of auditors.

[16] Identify and be familiar with the major organizations that affect the public accounting profession's environment.

RELEVANT ACCOUNTING AND AUDITING PRONOUNCEMENTS

CON2, FASB Statement of Financial Accounting Concepts No. 2, Qualitative Characteristics of Accounting Information

AT 100, Attestation Standards

AU 110, Responsibilities and Functions of the Independent Auditor

AU 150, Generally Accepted Auditing Standards

AU 316, Consideration of Fraud in a Financial Statement Audit

AU 319, Consideration of Internal Control in a Financial Statement Audit

AU 326, Evidence

AU 411, Federal GAAP Hierarchy

AU 411, The Meaning of *Present Fairly in Conformity with Generally Accepted Accounting Principles* in the Independent Auditor's Report

AU 508, Reports on Audited Financial Statements

The Financial Statement Auditing Environment

This chapter covers the context, or environment, in which auditors function. It starts by providing an overview of the events leading up to the recent turmoil in the public accounting profession. One of the most important and useful skills auditors develop is the ability to quickly understand and analyze various business models, strategies, and processes, and to identify key risks relevant to a particular client. Accordingly, the chapter introduces a high-level model of business and then offers a model of business processes that is useful for organizing an audit. The chapter then expands on the concept of management assertions introduced in Chapter 1 and introduces auditing standards, explaining how these standards are established in today's professional and regulatory environment. Ethical behavior and reputation play key roles in shaping the public accounting profession and its environment, and the chapter explains that the auditing profession is governed by a Code of Professional Conduct. Management's primary responsibility for the financial statements is then discussed, along with the auditor's responsibility to provide reasonable assurance. Because the reporting requirements shape the way auditors perform their work, the basic elements of audit reporting are then introduced to provide an initial understanding of the output of the audit process. The chapter discusses public accounting firms and the major categories of services they offer and introduces the various types of auditors other than financial statement auditors. The chapter concludes with a discussion of the other major organizations that affect the public accounting profession and its environment.

A Time of Challenge and Change for Auditors

[LO 1] The environment in which financial statement auditors work has been dramatically reshaped by the events taking place in the business world during the first few years of this new century. In fact, the profession is going through a period of almost unprecedented change. This section briefly discusses the issues and controversies that led up to the dramatic changes forced on the profession through the Sarbanes-Oxley Act in 2002 and the establishment of the Public Company Accounting Oversight Board (PCAOB) as the standard setter and regulator of public company audits. While the profession has undergone revolutionary changes, the events of the last few years have served to solidify the crucial role of accounting and auditing.

Problems and Warning Signs

During the economic boom of the late 1990s and early 2000s, accounting firms aggressively sought opportunities to market a variety of high-margin nonaudit services to their audit clients. Independence standards in force at the time allowed auditors to perform many such services, including information systems design and implementation and internal audit services, even for public company audit clients. The consulting revenue of the largest public accounting firms grew extremely quickly, until in many instances consulting revenues from audit clients greatly exceeded the fee for the external audit. Exhibit 2–1 provides a sample of audit and nonaudit fees reported in 2000.

During the same time period, in his now famous "Numbers Game" speech,[1] Arthur Levitt, chairman of the SEC, charged that many companies were involved in inappropriate earnings management and even fraud. He also accused auditors of directly or indirectly assisting management by not challenging management's actions.

A fierce public battle between the SEC and the accounting profession ensued, with the profession turning to members of Congress for support. Eventually, the SEC took several actions. In August 1999, the SEC issued Staff Accounting Bulletin (SAB) 99-*Materiality*, which guides auditors in limiting management manipulation of accounting numbers to manage earnings. The SEC also passed new rules on auditor independence in November 2000.[2] These new independence rules represented a compromise between the SEC and the profession, with most observers concluding that the profession had essentially won the battle.

An Explosion of Scandals

After the independence compromise, things began to settle down, the profession believing the worst was behind it. However, in October 2001, Enron, one of the largest public companies in the United States at the time, became the subject of an SEC investigation into its accounting practices. The

---

[1] A. Levitt, "The 'Numbers Game'" (NYU Center for Law and Business, September 28, 1998). Also see C. Loomis, "Lies, Damned Lies, and Managed Earnings," *Fortune* (August 2, 1999), pp. 74–92.

[2] See www.sec.gov/rules/final for a copy of the final rules entitled "Revision of the Commission's Auditor Independence Requirements."

EXHIBIT 2-1	A Sample Disclosure of Audit and Nonaudit Fees in the Pre-Sarbanes-Oxley Environment

Company	Auditor	Types of Fees (in millions)		
		Audit	IT	Other
J. P. Morgen Chase	PricewaterhouseCoopers	21.3	11.1	73.1
General Electric	KPMG	23.9	11.5	68.2
Waste Management	Andersen	48.0	31.0	
Sprint	Ernst & Young	2.5	12.4	51.4
Delphi Auto Systems	Deloitte	6.6	41.3	9.5
AOL Time Warner	Ernst & Young	7.9	7.2	43.8

Source: J. Well and J. A. Tannenbaum, "Big Companies Pay Audit Firms More for Other Services," *The Wall Street Journal* (April 10, 2000), pp. C1–C2.

investigation quickly uncovered massive financial deception that had been going on for several years. The company released earnings restatements for previous years, disclosing billions of dollars in overstated earnings and previously undisclosed debt obligations.

Shortly after the Enron scandal, numerous other scandals involving corporate giants (Tyco, WorldCom, Xerox, Adelphia, Ahold, etc.), brokerage firms (e.g., Merrill Lynch), stock exchanges (e.g., the New York Stock Exchange), the large public accounting firms (e.g., Arthur Andersen), and managers of mutual funds (e.g., Piper Jaffray) were uncovered. The Enron scandal alone weakened investor confidence in the stock market, but the subsequent series of scandals caused many investors to doubt the integrity of the entire system of public ownership and accountability in the United States.

Government Regulation

Under pressure to restore public confidence, congress passed the Sarbanes-Oxley Public Company Accounting Reform and Investor Protection Act in July 2002. Similar to the impact of the Securities Acts of 1933 and 1934, the Sarbanes-Oxley Act started a process of broad reform in corporate governance practices that would affect the duties and practices of public companies, financial analysts, external auditors, and securities exchange markets.

With respect to the accounting profession, the Sarbanes-Oxley Act effectively ended the profession's era of "self-regulation," creating and transferring authority to set and enforce auditing standards to the Public Company Accounting Oversight Board (discussed in more detail below). In addition, the Act mandated that the SEC impose strict independence rules, prohibiting the provision of most types of nonaudit services to public company audit clients (Chapter 19 presents a detailed discussion of the SEC's new independence rules). The Act also gave the SEC the mandate and the authority to regulate the public accounting profession in several other important ways, including the requirement for audit firms to rotate audit partners off audit engagements every five years and to provide an audit of internal control over financial reporting for public companies. The Act is extremely important in its implications for corporate governance, for the accounting profession, for managements of public companies, and for the capital markets system in the United States. Chapter 20 provides further discussion of the Sarbanes-Oxley Act.

Back to Basics

The impact of the events of the past decade, culminating in the Sarbanes-Oxley Act of 2002 and the formation of the PCAOB, cannot be overemphasized. The public accounting profession has been through a revolutionary shift from an era of apparently unsuccessful self-regulation toward governmental regulation and oversight. Most of the large firms, prohibited from providing many nonaudit services for public company audit clients, sold their consulting divisions and began to refocus their efforts once again on their core service: financial statement audits. While these changes have caused pain and turmoil, they highlight the essential importance of auditing in our economic system and have created new opportunities for auditors.

The Context of Financial Statement Auditing

[LO 2]   The first chapter explained why assurance is in demand, defined what auditing is, and laid out the phases through which financial statement auditing is carried out. This chapter is designed to help you understand the forces of change in the auditing profession as well as the overall business and regulatory *environment* in which auditing operates.

Business as the Primary Context of Auditing

The context with which an auditor is concerned on a day-to-day basis is the industry or business of his or her audit client(s). In studying subsequent chapters, you will be building your auditing tool kit. How you apply auditing tools on any particular engagement will depend greatly on the nature of the client's business. For example, if you are auditing a computer hardware manufacturer, one of your concerns will be whether your client has inventories that are not selling quickly and are becoming obsolete due to industry innovation. Such inventory might not be properly valued on the client's financial records. If you are auditing a jeweler, on the other hand, you will probably not be overly concerned with whether the client possesses warehouses full of obsolete diamonds—the possibility of a competitor producing a "new model" of diamond is probably not a serious threat in the diamond business. However, you would be interested in inventory valuation. You may need to hire a diamond appraiser to provide objective evidence, and you would certainly want to keep up on the dynamics of the international diamond market. The point is that the context provided by the client's business greatly impacts the auditor and the audit, and is thus a primary component of the environment in which financial statement auditing is conducted. While every business is different, business organizations can be conceptualized or modeled in common ways. The next section describes the essential characteristics of a business: governance, objectives, strategies, processes, risks, controls, and reporting.

A Model of Business

[LO 3]   Business organizations exist to create value for their stakeholders. To form a business enterprise, entrepreneurs decide on an appropriate organizational form (e.g., corporation or partnership) and hire managers to manage the resources that have been made available to the enterprise through investment or lending.

Corporate Governance

Due to the way resources are invested and managed in the modern business world, a system of *corporate governance* is necessary, through which managers are overseen and supervised. Simply defined, corporate governance consists of all the people, processes, and activities in place to help ensure the proper stewardship over an entity's assets. Corporate governance is the implementation and execution of processes to ensure that those managing an entity properly utilize their time, talents, and available resources in the best interest of absentee owners. Good corporate governance creates a system that ensures proper stewardship over invested capital and faithfully reports the economic condition and performance of the enterprise. The body primarily responsible for management oversight in U.S. corporations is the *board of directors*. The *audit committee,* consisting of members of the board, oversees the internal and external auditing work done for the organization. Through this link, and through the audit of financial statements (which can be seen as a form of stewardship report), auditors play an important role in facilitating effective corporate governance.

Objectives, Strategies, Processes, Controls, Transactions, and Reports

Management, with guidance and direction from the board of directors, decides on a set of *objectives*, along with *strategies* designed to achieve those objectives. The organization then undertakes certain *processes* in order to implement its strategies. The organization must also assess and manage risks that may threaten achievement of its objectives. While the processes implemented in business organizations are as varied as the different types of businesses themselves, most business enterprises establish processes that fit in five broad *process categories*, sometimes known as *cycles*. The five categories that characterize the processes of most businesses are the *revenue process*, the *purchasing process*, the *human resource management process*, the *inventory management process*, and the *financing process*. Each process involves a variety of important transactions. The enterprise must design and implement *accounting information systems* to capture the details of those transactions and must design and implement a *system of internal control* to ensure that the transactions are handled and recorded appropriately and that its resources are protected. The accounting information system must be capable of producing financial reports, which summarize the effects of the organization's transactions on its account balances and which are used to establish management accountability to outside owners. The next section provides a brief overview of the five process categories. Auditors often rely on this process model to divide the audit of a business's financial statements into manageable pieces. Chapters 10 to 16 go into considerable detail regarding how these processes typically function and how they are used to organize an audit.

A Model of Business Processes: Five Components

[LO 4]   Figure 2–1 illustrates the five basic business processes in context with the overall business model presented in the previous section.

The Financing Process

Businesses obtain capital through borrowing or soliciting investments from owners and typically invest in assets such as land, buildings, and equipment in accordance with their strategies. As part of this process, businesses also need to repay lenders and provide a return on owner investments. These types of transactions are all part of the financing process. For example, while EarthWear tends not to rely on long-term debt financing, it primarily uses capital provided by shareholders to invest in such long-term assets as its headquarters building, retail stores, and various order and distribution centers across the United States and in Japan, Germany, and the United Kingdom.

The Purchasing Process

Businesses must acquire goods and services to support the sale of their own goods or services. For example, EarthWear must purchase inventory for sale to customers. The company must also purchase office supplies, needed services, and many other items to support its activities.

The Human Resource Management Process

Business organizations hire personnel to perform various functions in accordance with the enterprise's mission and strategy. For example, at EarthWear this process starts with the establishment of sound policies for hiring, training, evaluating, counseling, promoting, compensating, and terminating employees. The main transaction that affects the financial statement accounts in this process is a payroll transaction, which usually begins with an employee performing a job, and ends with payment being made to the employee.

The Inventory Management Process

This process varies widely between different types of businesses. Service providers (such as auditors) rarely have significant inventories to manage, since their primary resources typically consist of information, knowledge, and the time and effort of people. Manufacturers, wholesalers, and retailers, including EarthWear, all typically have significant, numerous, and often complex transactions falling in the inventory management process. While the actual purchasing of finished goods or raw materials inventories is included in the purchasing process (see above), the inventory management process for a manufacturer includes the cost accounting transactions to accumulate and allocate costs to inventory.

The Revenue Process

Businesses generate revenue through sales of goods or services to customers, and collect the proceeds of those sales in cash, either immediately or through collections on receivables. For example, EarthWear, Inc., retails

FIGURE 2-1   An Overview of Business

Management and Board of Directors

Business Objectives and Strategies

Business Processes

Information Systems and Internal Controls to Ensure Transactions are Properly Executed, Captured, and Processed

Financing process

Purchasing process

Business Transactions

Revenue process

Human resource management process

Inventory management process

Risk Assessment and Management

Corporate Governance

Performance Measurement and Assessment

External Financial Reporting

high-quality clothing for outdoor sports. To create value for its customers, employees, and owners, EarthWear must successfully process orders for, and deliver its clothing to customers. It must also collect cash on those sales, either at the point of sale or through later billing and collection of receivables. Management establishes controls to ensure that sales and collection transactions are appropriately handled and recorded.

Relating the Process Components to the Business Model

Management establishes processes in the five categories discussed above to implement the organization's strategies and achieve its objectives. Management then identifies risks, or possible threats to the achievement of established objectives (including compliance with applicable laws and regulations and reliable external reporting), and ensures that the organization's system of internal control mitigates those risks to acceptable levels. The organization's accounting information system must be capable of reliably measuring the performance of the business to assess whether objectives are being met and to comply with external reporting requirements. Financial statements represent an important output of the entity's efforts to measure the organization's performance and an important form of external reporting and accountability.

Management Assertions

[LO 5] In Chapter 1, we introduced the concept that the financial statements issued by management contain explicit and implicit assertions. Table 2–1 summarizes and explains management assertions. Take a few minutes to examine and understand these assertions—you will see over the next several chapters that this simple conceptual tool is actually quite powerful and underlies much of what auditors do. Assertions are evaluated within three categories: transactions, account balances, and presentation and disclosure. For example, management asserts among other things that *transactions* relating to inventory actually *occurred*, that they are *complete* (i.e., no valid transactions were left out), that they are classified properly (e.g., as an asset rather than an expense), and that they are recorded accurately and in the correct period. Similarly, management asserts that the inventory represented in the inventory account balance *exists*, that the entity *owns* the inventory, that the balance is *complete*, and that the inventory is properly *valued*. Finally, management asserts that the financial statements properly *classify* and *present* the inventory (e.g., inventory is appropriately listed as a current asset on the balance sheet) and that all required *disclosures* having to do with inventory (e.g., a footnote indicating that the company uses the FIFO inventory method) are included appropriately, accurately, and clearly.

Although all balance-related assertions apply to every account, the assertions are not equally important for each account. Recognizing the assertions that deserve the most emphasis depends on an understanding of the business and of the particular type of account being audited. For example, for liability accounts the completeness assertion is typically the most important assertion for two reasons. First, when all obligations are not properly included

TABLE 2–1	Summary of Management Assertions by Category

Assertions about classes of transactions and events for the period under audit:

- **Occurrence**—transactions and events that have been recorded have occurred and pertain to the entity.
- **Completeness**—all transactions and events that should have been recorded have been recorded.
- **Authorization**—all transactions and events have been properly authorized.
- **Accuracy**—amounts and other data relating to recorded transactions and events have been recorded appropriately.
- **Cutoff**—transactions and events have been recorded in the correct accounting period.
- **Classification**—transactions and events have been recorded in the proper accounts.

Assertions about account balances at the period end:

- **Existence**—assets, liabilities, and equity interests exist.
- **Rights and obligations**—the entity holds or controls the rights to assets, and liabilities are the obligations of the entity.
- **Completeness**—all assets, liabilities, and equity interests that should have been recorded have been recorded.
- **Valuation and allocation**—assets, liabilities, and equity interests are included in the financial statements at appropriate amounts and any resulting valuation or allocation adjustments are appropriately recorded.

Assertions about presentation and disclosure:

- **Occurrence and rights and obligations**—disclosed events, transactions, and other matters have occurred and pertain to the entity.
- **Completeness**—all disclosures that should have been included in the financial statements have been included.
- **Classification and understandability**—financial information is appropriately presented and described, and disclosures are clearly expressed.
- **Accuracy and valuation**—financial and other information are disclosed fairly and at appropriate amounts.

in the liability account, the result is often an overstatement of net income. Second, management is more likely to have an incentive to understate a liability than to overstate it.

Auditing Standards

≫ **[LO 6,7]**   *Auditing standards* serve as guidelines for and measures of the quality of the auditor's performance. Auditing standards help ensure that financial statement audits are conducted in a thorough and systematic way that produces reliable conclusions.

The Roles of the ASB and the PCAOB

Until recently, establishing auditing standards for all nongovernmental audits was the responsibility of the Auditing Standards Board (ASB), a committee of the American Institute of CPAs (AICPA), a private, nongovernmental professional association. However, when the U.S. Congress passed the Sarbanes-Oxley Act of 2002, it transferred the authority to set auditing standards for public company audits to the Public Company Accounting Oversight Board (PCAOB). The PCAOB is overseen by the Securities and Exchange Commission (SEC). The AICPA, the SEC, and the PCAOB are described in more detail below.

Public accounting firms that audit the financial statements of public companies are required to perform these audits in accordance with the auditing and related professional practice standards established by the PCAOB. Firms that audit the financial statements of nonpublic entities are required to comply with the auditing standards established by the AICPA's Auditing Standards Board.

As of the writing of this text, with the exception of the PCAOB requirement for an integrated audit of internal control and financial statements (see Chapter 7), the standards of the ASB and the PCAOB are very similar. This is because the PCAOB adopted the ASB's auditing standards that existed as of April 2003 on an interim basis. Because the PCAOB's auditing standards are currently very similar to those of the ASB, we describe auditing standards in terms of those promulgated by the ASB, while noting throughout the text where PCAOB standards are different (e.g., see Chapter 7). You can see the latest standards established by the PCAOB on its website (www.pcaobus.org).

The 10 Generally Accepted Auditing Standards

The ASB first issued what are known as the 10 generally accepted auditing standards (GAAS) in 1947 and has periodically modified them to meet changes in the auditor's environment. The PCAOB adopted these standards and refers to them as "the standards of the PCAOB." The generally accepted auditing standards are composed of three categories of standards: general standards (three), standards of field work (three), and standards of reporting (four). Table 2–2 contains the 10 generally accepted auditing standards.

Three General Standards

The three general standards are concerned with the auditor's qualifications and the quality of his or her work. These standards will remind you of the characteristics of a reliable house inspector listed in Chapter 1. The first general standard recognizes that an individual must have adequate training and proficiency as an auditor. This is gained through formal education, continuing education programs, and experience. It should be recognized that this training is ongoing, with a requirement on the part of the auditor to stay up to date with current accounting and auditing pronouncements.

TABLE 2–2	**Generally Accepted Auditing Standards**

General Standards:
1. The audit is to be performed by a person or persons having adequate technical training and proficiency as an auditor.
2. In all matters relating to the assignment, an independence in mental attitude is to be maintained by the auditor or auditors.
3. Due professional care is to be exercised in the planning and performance of the audit and the preparation of the report.

Standards of Field Work:
1. The work is to be adequately planned and assistants, if any, are to be properly supervised.
2. A sufficient understanding of internal control is to be obtained to plan the audit and to determine the nature, timing, and extent of tests to be performed.
3. Sufficient, competent evidential matter is to be obtained through inspection, observation, inquiries, and confirmations to afford a reasonable basis for an opinion regarding the financial statements under audit.

Standards of Reporting:
1. The report shall state whether the financial statements are presented in accordance with generally accepted accounting principles.
2. The report shall identify those circumstances in which such principles have not been consistently observed in the current period in relation to the preceding period.
3. Informative disclosures in the financial statements are to be regarded as reasonably adequate unless otherwise stated in the report.
4. The report shall contain either an expression of opinion regarding the financial statements, taken as a whole, or an assertion to the effect that an opinion cannot be expressed. When an overall opinion cannot be expressed, the reasons therefore should be stated. In all cases where an auditor's name is associated with financial statements, the report should contain a clear-cut indication of the character of the auditor's work, if any, and the degree of responsibility the auditor is taking.

Auditors should also stay current with developments in the business world that may affect their clients.

The second general standard requires that the auditor maintain an attitude of independence on an engagement. Independence precludes relationships that may impair the auditor's objectivity. A distinction is often made between *independence in fact* and *independence in appearance.* An auditor must not only be independent in fact (i.e., actually be objective) but also avoid actions that may *appear* to affect independence. If an auditor is perceived as lacking independence, users may lose confidence in the auditor's ability to report truthfully on financial statements. For example, an auditor might borrow a large sum of money from an audit client's CEO but still conduct the audit in an objective manner (i.e., be independent in fact). Third parties, however, cannot observe whether or not the auditor is acting objectively, and may question whether the auditor is really independent due to the lack of independence in appearance (and thus such loans are strictly prohibited). The AICPA's Code of Professional Conduct and the SEC's independence regulations identify actions (such as having business interests in clients or providing certain types of consulting services) that are believed to impair the auditor's appearance of independence.

Due professional care is the focus of the third general standard. In simple terms, due care means that the auditor plans and performs his or her duties with a degree of skill commonly possessed by others in the profession.

Three Standards of Field Work

The standards of field work relate to the actual conduct of the audit. These three standards provide the conceptual background for the audit process (and will remind you of some of the desirable characteristics of a house inspection service). The first standard of field work deals with planning and supervision. Proper planning leads to a more effective audit that is more likely to detect material misstatements and assists in completing the engagement in a reasonable amount of time. This standard also requires that assistants on the engagement be properly supervised.

The second standard of field work requires that the auditor gain a sufficient understanding of the auditee's internal control to plan the audit. The degree to which the auditor relies on the auditee's internal control directly affects the nature, timing, and extent of the work performed by the independent auditor. In addition, if the auditor can identify areas of weakness in a client's internal control, this information can help the auditor focus on areas where misstatements may be more likely to occur.

Sufficient, competent evidence is the focus of the third field-work standard. Most of the auditor's work involves the search for and analysis of evidence to evaluate and support management's assertions in the financial statements. The auditor uses various audit procedures to gather this evidence. For example, if the balance sheet shows an amount for accounts receivable of $1.5 million, management asserts that this amount is the net realizable value, or the amount expected to be collected from customers, for those receivables. The auditor can send confirmations to customers and examine subsequent payments by customers to gather sufficient competent evidence on the proper value of accounts receivable. While auditing standards give general guidance, the point at which the evidence for a particular management assertion is sufficient and competent is generally a matter of professional judgment on the part of the auditor.

Four Standards of Reporting

The four standards of reporting require that the auditor consider each of the following issues before rendering an audit report: (1) whether the financial statements are presented in accordance with generally accepted accounting principles, (2) whether those principles are consistently applied, (3) whether all informative disclosures have been made, and (4) what degree of responsibility the auditor is taking and the character of the auditor's work. An overview of the nature of the auditor's report is given later in this chapter and further detail is offered in Chapter 18.

Statements on Auditing Standards—Interpretations of GAAS

[LO 8,9]   Statements on Auditing Standards (SAS) are issued by the Auditing Standards Board and are considered interpretations of GAAS. The SAS receive their authority from Rule 202 of the AICPA's Code of Professional Conduct. The GAAS and the SAS are considered to be *minimum standards* of performance for auditors. (When "GAAS" is used in this text, it generally refers to the 10 GAAS *and* the SAS.) As with the 10 GAAS, the PCAOB adopted on an interim basis the ASB's Statements on Auditing Standards as constituted as of April 2003. Standards issued by the PCAOB are simply called "Auditing Standards" (AS). The AS issued by the PCAOB will add to or modify the existing body of standards adopted by the PCAOB. One notable difference between standards issued by the AICPA's ASB for private entities and those issued by the PCAOB for public companies is that the PCAOB standards are federal law. We provide additional information on the PCAOB below and in Chapter 20.

Unlike financial accounting pronouncements, which usually provide very specific rules, the ASB's SAS and the PCAOB's AS tend to be more general in nature. The auditor must apply due diligence and sound *professional judgment* given the particular circumstances of the engagement in conducting an audit. Keep in mind that the auditor *never* has sufficient evidence to "guarantee" that the financial statements do not contain material misstatements.

SAS are classified by two numbering categories: SAS and AU numbers ("AU" for Auditing Standards). The SAS numbering applies to the order in which the standards are issued by the ASB and are thus chronological, much like the FASB's Statements on Financial Accounting Standards. The SAS, many of which contain material that is relevent to more than one of the 10 GAAS, are then reorganized by topical content, closely following the structure of the 10 GAAS. The summary below shows how the SAS are reorganized into the AU codification with the numbers in parentheses representing the AU sections:

Introduction (100s)
The General Standards (200s)

The Standards of Field Work (300s)

The First, Second, and Third Standards of Reporting (400s)

The Fourth Standard of Reporting (500s)

Other Types of Reports (600s)

Special Topics (700s)

Compliance Auditing (800s)

Special Reports of the Committee on Auditing Procedures (900s)

For example, SAS No. 39, "Audit Sampling," is found under AU 350 because the AU 300s relate to the standards of field work or evidence collection and evaluation. Similarly, SAS No. 58, "Reports on Audited Financial Statements," is found in AU 508 because SAS No. 58 relates to the fourth standard of reporting. While auditors research and cite both the SAS and AU sections, the AU are more frequently used because some SAS affect several AU sections. For example, SAS No. 98, "Omnibus Statement on Auditing Standards," was reorganized into over nine AU sections. The PCAOB's AS are currently classified only by the order in which the standards are issued (e.g., AS No. 1, AS No. 2) with conforming changes made to the "interim" standards adopted from the ASB. While the PCAOB has made reference to AU sections in its public communications, it is not yet clear how the Board will organize the topics addressed in its various Auditing Standards as they are issued.

A major complication for auditors in the future will be the development of two different sets of auditing standards as the PCAOB standards diverge from those it adopted from the ASB. It is possible that there will eventually be very different sets of standards for public company audits and for non-public entity audits.

Ethics, Independence, and the Code of Professional Conduct

✿ **[LO 10]** As indicated by the second general GAAS standard, ethical behavior and independence on the part of the auditor are vital to the audit function. The demand for auditing arose from the need for a competent, independent person to monitor the contractual arrangements between principal and agent. If an auditor is incompetent or lacks independence, the parties to the contract will place little or no value on the service provided.

Ethics refers to a system or code of conduct based on moral duties and obligations that indicates how we should behave. *Professionalism* refers to the conduct, aims, or qualities that characterize or mark a profession or professional person.[3] All professions (e.g., medicine, law, and accounting) operate under some type of code of ethics or code of conduct. The 10 GAAS and the AICPA's Code of Professional Conduct establish acceptable behavior for auditors. The Code of Professional Conduct contains principles, rules of conduct, and interpretations of the rules that clarify the intent of

---

[3]S. M. Mintz, *Cases in Accounting Ethics and Professionalism*, 3d ed. (New York: McGraw-Hill, 1997).

the 10 GAAS. A major portion of the Code identifies actions that may impair auditors' independence. The AICPA's Code of Professional Conduct applies to all auditors, including those auditing public companies. Why? Because the SEC requires that the auditor signing an audit report for a public company be a CPA, and the courts have consistently held CPAs to the standards of conduct established by the Code. Further, the Code of Professional Conduct was also adopted by the PCAOB on an interim basis. Thus, the Code is an important element of the environment in which auditors work.

Auditors are frequently faced with situations that may test their professionalism, ethical character, and independence. For example, auditors' independence is tested when clients engage in *opinion shopping*—that is, when clients seek the views of other CPAs, hoping they will agree with the client's desired accounting treatment. Clients sometimes attempt to influence the auditor to go along with the desired accounting treatment by threatening to change auditors. Chapter 19 contains an in-depth discussion of professional ethics and the Code of Professional Conduct.

The Auditor's Responsibility for Errors, Fraud, and Illegal Acts

[LO 11]   Many readers of financial statements believe that auditors are ultimately responsible for the financial statements or at least that they have a responsibility to detect *all* errors, fraud, and illegal acts. This is simply not true. The financial statements are the responsibility of management (note that the assertions are called *management assertions*); the auditor's responsibility is to express an opinion on the financial statements. In fact, the Sarbanes-Oxley Act of 2002 requires that CEOs and CFOs take explicit responsibility for their company's financial statements by "certifying," among other things, that they are responsible for establishing and maintaining internal control, and that the financial statements fairly present the entity's financial conditions and operations. It is important to remember that while auditors do have important responsibilities, *management* is primarily responsible for the fairness of the company's financial statements.

Auditing standards (AU 110.02) provide the following responsibility for auditors:

> The auditor has a responsibility to plan and perform the audit to obtain reasonable assurance about whether the financial statements are free of material misstatement, whether caused by error or fraud. Because of the nature of audit evidence and the characteristics of fraud, the auditor is able to obtain reasonable, but not absolute, assurance that material misstatements are detected. The auditor has no responsibility to plan and perform the audit to obtain reasonable assurance that misstatements, whether caused by errors or fraud, that are *not material* to the financial statements will be detected.

Due professional care requires that the auditor exercise *professional skepticism*, which is an attitude that includes a questioning mind and a critical assessment of audit evidence. If the auditor fails to exercise due professional care, he or she can be held liable for civil damages and even criminal penalties. The auditor's responsibility to provide reasonable assurance with respect to errors, fraud, and illegal acts clearly shapes the auditor's environment. More information on the auditor's responsibility for errors, fraud, and illegal acts is contained in Chapters 3 and 5, and details on auditors' potential legal liability are provided in Chapter 20.

Audit Reporting

❧ **[LO 12]** The auditor's report is the main product or output of the audit. Just as the report of a house inspector communicates the inspector's findings to a prospective buyer, the audit report communicates the auditor's findings to the users of the financial statements. The audit report, also known as the audit opinion, is the culmination of a process of collecting and evaluating sufficient competent evidence concerning the fair presentation of management's assertions in the financial statements. A brief overview of audit reporting is presented here so you can understand the final output of an audit. More detail is provided in Chapter 18. Figure 2–2 gives an overview of audit reporting.

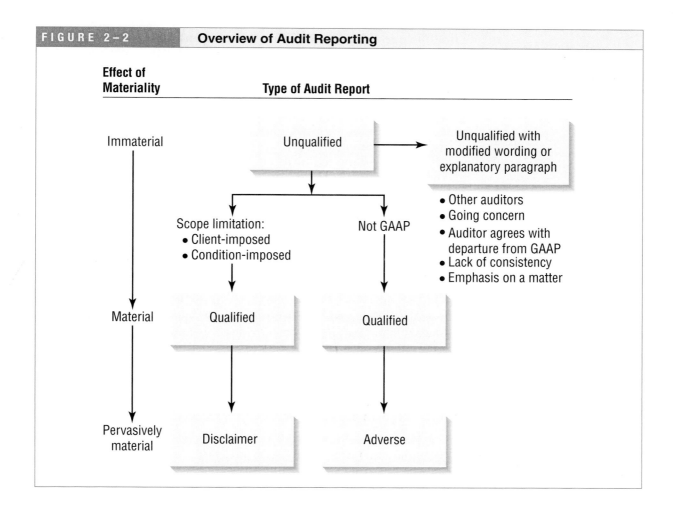

FIGURE 2–2 **Overview of Audit Reporting**

Generally
Accepted
Accounting
Principles as
Audit Criteria

In order to evaluate a set of financial statements, benchmarks or criteria must exist against which the fairness of the statements can be measured. Generally accepted accounting principles (GAAP) have, over time, become the primary criteria used to prepare financial statements, and compliance with GAAP is required for public companies. As the term implies, these principles are generally accepted by the diverse users of financial statements in the United States.

The Auditor's
Standard
Unqualified
Audit Report

The most common type of audit report issued is the "standard unqualified audit report" (i.e., a "clean" opinion), because management's assertions about the entity's financial statements are usually found to conform to generally accepted accounting principles. Such a conclusion can be expressed only when the audit was performed in accordance with generally accepted auditing standards (for nonpublic companies) or in accordance with the standards of the PCAOB (for public companies). This is not to say that entities' financial records rarely include errors or material misstatements. On the contrary, entities often have to make auditor-proposed adjustments to the financial statements, but they are typically willing to make such adjustments to receive a clean opinion. Exhibit 2–2 presents an audit report issued on EarthWear Clothier's financial statements.[4] This report covers financial statements that include balance sheets for two years and statements of income, stockholders' equity, and cash flows for three years. The audit report presented in Exhibit 2–2 is the standard type of audit opinion issued for publicly traded companies.

The report is headed with a title referring to the "Independent Registered Public Accounting Firm." This title is required for audit reports for public companies. For nonpublic entity audits, examples of acceptable report titles are "Independent Auditor's Report," or "Report of the Independent Auditor." The audit report is addressed to the individual or group that engaged the auditor. In the normal situation, the report is addressed to the entity, its board of directors, and/or the entity's stockholders.

The body of the report begins with the introductory paragraph, which indicates which financial statements are covered by the report, that the statements are the responsibility of management, and that the auditor has a responsibility to express an opinion.

The second, or scope, paragraph communicates to the users, in very general terms, what an audit entails. In addition to indicating that the audit was conducted in accordance with the standards of the PCAOB (for public companies) or generally accepted auditing standards (for nonpublic companies), it emphasizes the fact that the audit provides only reasonable assurance that the financial statements contain no material misstatements. The scope paragraph also discloses that an audit involves an examination of evidence on a test basis (i.e., using samples rather than examining entire populations), an assessment of accounting principles used and significant estimates, and an overall evaluation of financial statement presentation. Finally, the scope

---

[4]Note that because EarthWear is a publicly traded company, the audit report refers to "the standards of the Public Company Accounting Oversight Board (United States)." Audit reports for nonpublic companies refer instead to "generally accepted auditing standards."

EXHIBIT 2-2	**The Auditor's Standard Unqualified Report—Comparative Financial Statements (with explanatory paragraph)**

Title:

Addressee:

Introductory paragraph:

Scope paragraph:

Opinion paragraph:

Explanatory paragraph referring to the audit of internal control:

Name of auditor:

Date of report:

REPORT OF INDEPENDENT REGISTERED PUBLIC ACCOUNTING FIRM

To the Stockholders of EarthWear Clothiers

We have audited the consolidated balance sheets of EarthWear Clothiers as of December 31, 2005 and 2004, and the related consolidated statements of operations, stockholders' equity, and cash flows for each of the three years in the period ended December 31, 2005. These financial statements are the responsibility of the Company's management. Our responsibility is to express an opinion on these financial statements based on our audits.

We conducted our audits in accordance with the standards of the Public Company Accounting Oversight Board (United States). Those standards require that we plan and perform the audit to obtain reasonable assurance about whether the financial statements are free of material misstatement. An audit includes examining, on a test basis, evidence supporting the amounts and disclosures in the financial statements. An audit also includes assessing the accounting principles used and significant estimates made by management, as well as evaluating the overall financial statement presentation. We believe that our audits provide a reasonable basis for our opinion.

In our opinion, the consolidated financial statements referred to above present fairly, in all material respects, the financial position of the Company as of December 31, 2005 and 2004, and the results of its operations and its cash flows for each of the three years in the period ended December 31, 2005, in conformity with U.S. generally accepted accounting principles.

We also have audited, in accordance with the standards of the Public Company Accounting Oversight Board (United States), the effectiveness of EarthWear Clothiers' internal control over financial reporting as of December 31, 2005, based on criteria established in Internal Control—Integrated Framework issued by the Committee of Sponsoring Organizations of the Treadway Commission (COSO), and our report dated February 15, 2006 expressed an unqualified opinion on management's assessment that EarthWear Clothiers maintains effective internal control and an unqualified opinion that internal control was effective.

Willis & Adams
Boise, Idaho

February 15, 2006

paragraph asserts the auditor's belief that the audits performed provide a reasonable basis for the opinion to be expressed in the report.

The third paragraph contains the auditor's opinion concerning the fairness of the financial statements based on the audit evidence. Two important phrases contained in this paragraph require further explanation. First, the phrase "present fairly . . . in conformity with U.S. generally accepted accounting principles" is the wording used by the auditor to comply with the first standard of reporting. Second, the opinion paragraph also contains the phrase "in all material respects." As mentioned earlier, this phrase is included in the report to emphasize the concept of materiality. It is also important to note that auditing standards require that the opinion identify the United States as the country of origin of those accounting principles. Note that the scope paragraph indicates how the *audit* was conducted (in accordance with the standards of the PCAOB or GAAS), while the opinion paragraph indicates the auditor's opinion as to whether the financial statements are fairly presented in accordance with the *criteria against which they were audited*—GAAP.

The fourth paragraph contains explanatory language. The details of when an explanatory paragraph is required to be added to the standard unqualified audit report are discussed in Chapter 18. As shown in Exhibit 2–2, when the auditor's opinion on a public company's financial statements is presented separately from the auditor's report on internal control over financial reporting, the report must include an explanatory paragraph, briefly referring to the audit of internal control. (See Chapter 7, which discusses in detail the audit of internal control over financial reporting.)

The audit report concludes with the manual or printed signature of the CPA firm providing the audit and with the date of the report. Generally, the auditor's report is dated as of the date on which the auditor has completed all significant auditing procedures. The audit report date indicates to the user the last day of the auditor's responsibility for the review of significant events that have occurred after the date of the financial statements.

Reasons for Departures from an Unqualified Audit Report

There are three basic reasons an auditor may be unable to express an unqualified opinion (see Figure 2–2):

1. *Scope limitation.* A scope limitation results from a lack of evidence, such as an inability to conduct an audit procedure considered necessary.
2. *A departure from GAAP.* A departure from GAAP occurs when the financial statements are prepared using an accounting principle that is not in conformity with GAAP.
3. *The auditor is not independent.* The auditor must be independent of the entity being audited in order to express an opinion on the entity's financial statements.

Other Types of Audit Reports

When an auditor is unable to express an unqualified opinion, three types of audit reports other than the standard unqualified (clean) audit report are available to the auditor (see Figure 2–2):

1. *Qualified.* The auditor's opinion is qualified for either a scope limitation or a departure from GAAP with material consequences, but the *overall* financial statements present fairly. With a qualified report, the opinion paragraph is modified by the words "except for."
2. *Disclaimer.* When issuing a disclaimer, the auditor states that he or she cannot give an opinion on the financial statements because of a

lack of sufficient competent evidence to form an opinion on the overall financial statements or because of a lack of independence.

3. ***Adverse.*** The auditor's opinion states that the financial statements do not present fairly in conformity with GAAP because the departure affects the overall financial statements.

The choice of which audit report to issue on a client's financial statements depends on the condition and the materiality of the departure, as indicated in Figure 2–2.

Public Accounting Firms

[LO 13]   Very small organizations can be audited by a single auditor, operating as the sole owner of a public accounting firm. However, auditing larger business and other organizations requires significantly more resources than a single auditor can provide. Thus, public accounting firms range in size from a single proprietor to thousands of owners (or "partners") and thousands of professional and administrative staff employees. Public accounting firms typically offer a variety of professional services in addition to financial statement audits.

Organization and Composition

Public accounting firms are organized as proprietorships, general or limited liability partnerships, or corporations. Typically, local public accounting firms are organized as proprietorships, general partnerships, or corporations. Regional, national, and international accounting firms are normally structured as general or limited liability partnerships. Structuring public accounting firms as proprietorships and partnerships does not provide limited liability for the owners or partners. Thus, users can seek recourse not only against the CPA firm's assets but also against the personal assets of individual partners.

Because of the increasing cost of litigation against CPAs, public accounting firms organize as corporations when possible. However, corporations are created by individual states, and some states do not allow accounting firms to organize as corporations. Thus, because they span state boundaries, it is generally not possible for regional, national, or international firms to structure themselves as corporations. However, over the last several years, the large national and international firms have restructured themselves as limited liability partnerships (LLPs). An LLP is generally governed by the laws applicable to general partnerships. However, this organizational structure provides greater personal protection against lawsuits. Under an LLP, partners are not *personally* responsible for firm liabilities arising from *other* partners' and most employees' negligent acts.[5] The personal assets of the responsible partner(s) and the assets of the partnership itself are vulnerable to lawsuits resulting from other partners' or employees' acts.

Public accounting firms are often categorized by size. For example, the largest firms are the "Big 4" public accounting firms: Deloitte, Ernst &

---

[5]G. Simonetti, Jr., and A. R. Andrews, "Limiting Accountants' Personal Liability Won't Solve the Country's Liability Crisis!" *Journal of Accountancy* (April 1994), pp. 46–54, for an excellent discussion of organizational reform of CPA firm structure.

TABLE 2–3	**Selected Duties of Audit Team Members**

Audit Team Member	Selected Duties
Partner	• Reaching agreement with the client on the scope of the service to be provided. • Ensuring that the audit is properly planned. • Ensuring that the audit team has the required skills and experience. • Supervising the audit team and reviewing the working papers. • Signing the audit report.
Manager	• Ensuring that the audit is properly planned, including scheduling of team members. • Supervising the preparation of and approving the audit program. • Reviewing the working papers, financial statements, and audit report.
Senior/In-charge	• Assisting in the development of the audit plan. • Preparing budgets. • Assigning audit tasks to associates and directing the day-to-day performance of the audit. • Supervising and reviewing the work of the associate.
Associate/Staff	• Performing the audit procedures assigned to them. • Preparing adequate and appropriate documentation of completed work. • Informing the senior about any auditing or accounting problems encountered.

Young, KPMG, and PricewaterhouseCoopers. These large international organizations have annual global revenues ranging from $10 billion to $14 billion. As a group, the Big 4 audit about 80 percent of all publicly traded companies in the United States and over 90 percent of public companies with annual sales greater than $1 million.[6]

Following the Big 4 in size are several national firms with international affiliations. These include such firms as Grant Thornton, RSM McGladrey, and BDO Seidman. The annual revenues for these firms range from $1.8 billion to $2.4 billion. Last, there are thousands of regional and local CPA firms that have one or a few offices. These CPA firms provide audit, tax, and accounting services, generally to smaller entities.

Audits are usually conducted by teams of auditors. The typical audit team is composed of, in order of authority, a partner, a manager, one or two seniors, and several staff members. Audit teams for large international entities are typically made up of several partners and managers and many seniors and staff. The lead engagement partner has the authority and decision-making responsibility for accounting and auditing matters, including the issuance of the audit report. Table 2–3 summarizes the duties performed by each member of the audit team.

Types of Audit, Attest, and Assurance Services

≈ **[LO 14]**   Opportunities where auditors can provide auditing, attest, or assurance services arise from the need for management to be accountable to employees, shareholders, customers, and communities. In this section, examples of these types of services are briefly discussed.

---

[6]United States General Accounting Office Report to the Senate Committee on Banking, Housing, and Urban Affairs and the House Committee on Financial Services, Public Accounting Firms: Mandated Study on Consolidation and Competition, July 2003.

Audit Services

In addition to the financial statement audit, there are four major types of audits: internal control audits, compliance audits, operational audits, and forensic audits. These types of audits can be performed by public accounting firms or by other types of auditors such as internal or governmental auditors, discussed below.

Internal Control Audits

Financial statement auditors have always had the option of testing controls to obtain indirect evidence about the fairness of the financial statements on which they have been engaged to express an opinion. However, until recently auditors were generally neither required nor allowed to express an opinion on a client's system of internal control as part of a financial statement audit.[7] This changed when the Sarbanes-Oxley Act required (1) that managements of public companies assert to the effectiveness of their internal control systems and (2) that auditors of public companies attest to this management assertion. An audit of internal control is not required for private entities.

Because the objectives and work involved in performing an audit of internal control and an audit of financial statements are closely interrelated, auditing standards require an *integrated audit* of internal control and financial statements. More detailed information about the newly required internal control audit for public companies is provided in Chapter 7.

Compliance Audits

A compliance audit determines the extent to which rules, policies, laws, covenants, or government regulations are followed by the entity being audited. For example, a company may ask auditors to determine whether corporate rules and policies are being followed by departments within the organization. Another example is examination of tax returns of individuals and companies by the Internal Revenue Service for compliance with the tax laws.

Operational Audits

An operational audit involves a systematic review of part or all of an organization's activities in relation to the *efficient* and *effective* use of resources. The purpose of an operational audit is to assess performance, identify areas for improvement, and develop recommendations. Sometimes this type of audit is referred to as a *performance audit* or *management audit*. Operational audits offer different challenges than financial statement audits or compliance audits because operational audits require the auditor to identify or create objective, measurable criteria against which to assess effectiveness and efficiency. Operational auditing has increased in importance in recent years, and this trend will likely continue. An example is when entities employ auditors to assess the efficiency and effectiveness of the entity's use of information technology resources.

---

[7]Exceptions include audits of government agencies and audits of large banks complying with the Federal Depository Institution Corporation Improvement Act (FDICIA) of 1991, which, similar to the Sarbanes-Oxley requirement for all public companies, required both a management assertion as to the bank's internal control and an auditor attestation regarding that assertion.

EXHIBIT 2–3 ✗	**PricewaterhouseCoopers Issues Report on Fraudulent Activities at Lernout & Hauspie**

Lernout & Hauspie Speech Products NV (L&H), headquartered in Leper, Belgium, was a leader in speech translation software. L&H went public in late 1995 on the NASDAQ stock exchange and at one time had a market captialization of nearly $6 billion. In 2000, the high-flying company came under an SEC probe for reported revenues in Asia. Subsequently, the company filed for bankruptcy in both Belgium and the United States.

At the request of the company's new management, PricewaterhouseCoopers (PwC) was hired to conduct a forensic audit of the accounting fraud. Its audit discovered that most of the fraud occurred in L&H's Korean unit. In an effort to obtain bonuses based on sales targets, the managers of the Korean unit went to great lengths to fool L&H's auditor, KPMG. The PwC auditors reported that the Korean unit used two types of schemes to perpetrate the fraud. One involved factoring of receivables with banks to obtain cash to disguise the fact that the receivables were not valid. L&H Korea gave the banks side letters that provided that the money would be given back if the banks could not collect them. These side letters were concealed from KPMG. The second scheme arose after KPMG questioned why L&H Korea was not collecting more of its outstanding receivables. L&H Korea had its customers transfer their contracts to third parties who then took out bank loans to pay L&H Korea. L&H Korea provided the collateral for the loans. PwC reported that nearly 70 percent of the $160 million in sales booked in the Korean unit of L&H were fictitious.

Source: M. Maremont, J. Elsinger, and J. Carreyrou, "How High-Tech Dream at Lernout & Houspie Crumbled in a Scandal," *The Wall Street Journal* (December 7, 2000), pp. A1, A18; J. Carreyrou and M. Maremont, "Lernout Unit Engaged in Massive Fraud to Fool Auditors, New inquiry Concludes," *The Wall Street Journal* (April 6, 2001), p. A3; and J. Carreyrou, "Lernout Unit Booked Fictitious Sales, Says Probe," *The Wall Street Journal* (April 9, 2001), p. B2.

Forensic Audits   A forensic audit's purpose is the detection or deterrence of fraudulent activities. The use of auditors to conduct forensic audits has increased significantly. Some examples where a forensic audit might be conducted include

- Business or employee fraud.[8]
- Criminal investigations.
- Shareholder and partnership disputes.
- Business economic losses.
- Matrimonial disputes.

For example, in a business fraud engagement, an audit might involve tracing funds or asset identification and recovery. Exhibit 2–3 describes a forensic audit conducted by a major accounting firm for the board of directors of Lernout & Hauspie Speech Products NV. Some public accounting firms specialize in forensic audit services.

Attest Services   Auditors can provide numerous types of attest services. Two examples are briefly discussed here, and Chapter 21 presents more detailed information.

---

[8]See J. T. Wells, *Occupational Fraud and Abuse* (Austin, TX: Obsidian, 1997), for an excellent discussion of various types of business fraud.

Reporting on Internal Control

Though not required, private companies or other entities sometimes ask auditors to provide an attest report on management's assertions about the effectiveness of the organizations' internal control.[9] Until the Sarbanes-Oxley Act required an audit of internal control for all public companies, auditors provided this service as a separate attest service. When provided for a private entity, auditors still provide the service as a separate attest service rather than as part of an integrated audit.

Financial Forecasts and Projections

Entities often prepare prospective (forward-looking) financial information and request that auditors attest to the information. Financial *forecasts* are prospective financial statements that present *expected* financial results. Financial *projections* are prospective financial statements that present, *given hypothetical assumptions*, financial results for an entity.

In such engagements, auditors typically attest to the preparation, support for assumptions, and presentation of the prospective financial information. They do not offer assurance that the results forecasted or projected will actually be realized.

Assurance Services

Three general types of assurance services are discussed briefly. Note that the Sarbanes-Oxley Act prohibited external auditors from providing most forms of nonaudit assurance and consulting work to a public company that is also a financial statement audit client (see Chapter 19). Assurance services provided by CPAs are governed by either the attest or consulting standards. More detailed information on assurance services is contained in Chapter 21.

Risk Assessment

Organizations that manage risk well are more likely to succeed in an environment marked by ever-changing technology and globalization. Auditors can provide assurance on an entity's profile of business risks and can evaluate whether the entity has appropriate systems in place to manage those risks effectively.

Performance Measurement

Many organizations ask their auditors to provide assistance in benchmarking their business processes and performance. While traditionally this service has mainly involved financial measures, clients often seek help with measuring such leading indicators as customer satisfaction, effectiveness of employee training, and product quality. Through performance measurement services, the accountant can assist a client to understand drivers of the business and to measure their performance.

Information System Reliability and E-Commerce

More entities are becoming dependent on information technology, including e-commerce

---

[9]See W. F. Messier, Jr., and O. R. Whittington, "Auditor Attestation to Management Reports on Internal Control—Should It Be Required?" in *The Expectation Gap Standards: Progress, Implementation Issues, Research Opportunities* (AICPA, 1993), pp. 244–255.

applications, to run their businesses. As a result, it is critical that such systems be secure, available when needed, and consistently able to produce accurate information. Auditors can provide assurance on an entity's information system and its e-commerce applications. For example, the AICPA and the Canadian Institute of Chartered Accountants (CICA) have introduced a set of services known as Trust Services, including WebTrust and SysTrust. SysTrust services provide assurance that an information system is reliable. WebTrust services provide assurance on online businesses by verifying compliance with such principles as privacy, security, confidentiality, and business practices. Once an entity has received a report indicating that its online business meets the WebTrust principles and criteria, it can display the WebTrust seal on its website.

Other Nonaudit Services

In addition to the audit, attest, and assurance services discussed in this chapter public accounting firms perform three other broad categories of services.

Tax Services   Public accounting firms have tax departments that assist clients with preparing and filing tax returns, provide advice on tax and estate planning, and provide representation on tax issues before the Internal Revenue Service or tax courts.

FIGURE 2–3	Practice Mix of Services by Major International Public Accounting Firms

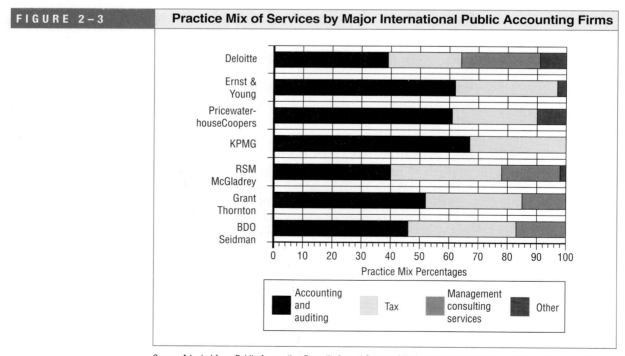

Source: Adapted from Public Accounting Report's Annual Survey of National Accounting Firms—2004 (Public Accounting Report, March 15, 2004, p. 4). Copyright 2004 by Aspen Publishers, Inc., 1185 Avenue of the Americas, New York, NY 10036. 646-728-3048. Percentages based on U.S. net revenue by practice area; firms listed in order of total U.S. net revenue.

Management Advisory Services   Management advisory services (MAS) are consulting activities that may involve providing advice and assistance concerning an entity's organization, personnel, finances, operations, systems, or other activities. Because of independence and other issues, a number of the major firms have sold their consulting practices. However, these firms' assurance practices continue to perform MAS, primarily for nonpublic or nonaudit clients. Figure 2–3 presents the practice mix of the major international firms. The Sarbanes-Oxley Act of 2002 prohibited the provision of most MAS services to public companies that are also financial statement audit clients. However, the major firms are experiencing significant growth in the areas of internal control audits and internal control consulting for nonaudit clients.

Accounting and Review Services   Public accounting firms perform a number of accounting services for their nonpublic or nonaudit clients. These services include bookkeeping, payroll processing, and preparing financial statements. When a public accounting firm provides nonaudit accounting services relating to the financial statements of companies, the services are known as compilations or reviews. These forms of services are less rigorous and provide less assurance than a financial statement audit. Accounting services are discussed in more detail in Chapter 21.

Types of Auditors

⚹ [LO 15]   A number of different types of auditors can be identified; however, they can all be classified under four headings: external auditors, internal auditors, government auditors, and forensic auditors. One important requirement for each type of auditor is independence, in some form, from the entity being audited.

External Auditors   External auditors are often referred to as *independent auditors* or *certified public accountants* (CPAs). An external auditor may practice as a sole proprietor or as a member of a CPA firm (discussed above). Such auditors are called "external" or "independent" because they are not employed by the entity being audited. In this book, the terms *external auditor, independent auditor,* and *CPA* are generally used interchangeably. External auditors audit financial statements for publicly traded and private companies, partnerships, municipalities, individuals, and other types of entities. They may also conduct compliance, operational, and forensic audits for such entities. However, federal law and auditing standards restrict the other types of audit services that an external auditor can provide for financial statement audit clients that are public companies.

The CPA certificate is regulated by state law through licensing departments in each state. The requirements for becoming a CPA vary among the states, with most states requiring at least a four-year college degree with selected courses in business and accounting. In addition, many states require professional experience before the CPA certificate is granted. All states require that an individual pass the Uniform CPA Examination monitored by the American Institute of Certified Public Accountants (see Exhibit 2–4). The AICPA has passed a resolution that those individuals applying for membership who first become eligible to take the CPA examination after the year

EXHIBIT 2-4	The Computer-Based Uniform CPA Examination

Background

The Uniform CPA Examination has a long and trusted history in the licensing of certified public accountants. To keep pace with the evolution of the accounting and business worlds—especially in the areas of technology and skills assessment—the Uniform CPA Examination has changed to ensure continued protection of the public interest in a rapidly changing world.

The examination's most visible change is its recent transition from a paper-and-pencil exam to a computer-based test (CBT). However, even more important than this new delivery method are the revisions to the examination's content. Based on recent practice analysis findings, the computer-based CPA examination incorporates increased emphasis on information technology and general business knowledge with a broadened scope in the audit area. Significantly, changes include increased skills testing; for example, research and analytical skills.

The American Institute of Certified Public Accountants (AICPA), the National Association of State Boards of Accountancy (NASBA), and Prometric, the world's leading technology-based testing company, have a signed joint agreement to deliver a computerized Uniform CPA Examination. As of April 5, 2004, the Uniform CPA Examination is delivered in a computer-based format at Prometric test centers across the United States.

Examination Content

Length   The revised CPA examination has four sections and a total length of 14 hours. Three sections, Auditing and Attestation, Financial Accounting and Reporting, and Regulation cover much of the content contained in the paper-based CPA examination. The fourth section, Business Environment and Concepts (BEC), covers knowledge of the general business environment and business concepts.

Each exam section contains five units called "testlets." A testlet is comprised of either a group of approximately 25 multiple-choice questions (MCQs) or one complete case study known as a simulation. Simulations provide a set of facts and require candidates to complete related tasks and access authoritative literature. At launch, each exam section except BEC contained three MCQ testlets and two simulations. BEC initially contained five MCQ testlets; simulations will be added to BEC at a later date.

Sections
- Auditing and Attestation (4.5 hours). Covers knowledge of auditing procedures, generally accepted auditing standards, and other standards related to attest engagements and the skills needed to apply that knowledge in those engagements.
- Financial Accounting and Reporting (4 hours). Covers knowledge of generally accepted accounting principles for business enterprises, not-for-profit organizations, and governmental entities and the skills needed to apply that knowledge.
- Regulation (3 hours). Covers knowledge of federal taxation, ethics, professional and legal responsibilities, and business law and the skills needed to apply that knowledge.
- Business Environment and Concepts (2.5 hours). Covers knowledge of general business environment and business concepts that candidates need to know in order to understand the underlying business reasons for and accounting implications of business transactions and the skills needed to apply that knowledge.

Source: Adapted from AICPA/NASBA Briefing, July 18, 2003. Visit www.cpa-exam.org for examination information and links to NASBA and Boards of Accountancy.

2000 must obtain 150 semester credit hours of education at an accredited college or university, including a bachelor's degree or its equivalent. More than 40 states now mandate the 150-hour requirement.[10]

Internal Auditors

Auditors employed by individual companies, partnerships, government agencies, individuals, and other entities are called internal auditors.[11] In major corporations, internal audit staffs may be very large, and the director of internal auditing (sometimes called the chief audit executive, or CAE) is usually a major job title within the entity.

The Institute of Internal Auditors (IIA) is the primary organization supporting internal auditors. Its mission is to be "the primary international professional association, organized on a worldwide basis, dedicated to the promotion and development of the practice of internal auditing." The IIA has developed a set of standards to be followed by internal auditors and has established a certification program. An individual meeting the certification requirements established by the IIA, which include passing a uniform written examination, can become a certified internal auditor (CIA).[12] Many internal auditors also have a CPA certificate.

The IIA defines internal auditing as "an independent, objective assurance and consulting activity designed to add value and improve an organization's operations. It helps an organization accomplish its objectives by bringing a systematic, disciplined approach to evaluate and improve the effectiveness of risk management, control, and governance processes."

Internal auditors may conduct financial, internal control, compliance, operational, and forensic audits within their organizations (see previous section). They in some cases may assist the external auditors with the annual financial statement audit. Internal auditors may also be involved in assurance and consulting engagements for their entities. Chapter 21 offers more detail on the IIA and the internal auditing profession.

Government Auditors

Government auditors are employed by federal, state, and local agencies. They generally can be considered a subset of the broader category of internal auditors. At the federal level, two agencies use auditors extensively: the Government Accountability Office (GAO) and the Internal Revenue Service (IRS). The GAO is under the direction of the Comptroller General of the United States and is responsible to Congress. GAO auditors conduct audits of activities, financial transactions, and accounts of the federal government. They also assist Congress by performing special audits, surveys, and investigations. The majority of the audits conducted by GAO auditors are compliance and operational audits.

---

[10]The National Association of State Boards of Accountancy (NASBA) maintains a listing of the CPA Licensure Requirements by state, as well as links to individual state boards of accountancy. See www.nasba.org.

[11]See R. L. Ratliff, W. A. Wallace, J. K. Loebbecke, and W. G. McFarland, *Internal Auditing: Principles and Techniques*, 2d ed. (Altamonte Springs, FL: The Institute of Internal Auditors, 1996); D. Galloway, *Internal Auditing: A Guide for the New Auditor* (Altamonte Springs, FL: The Institute of Internal Auditors, 1996), for a detailed discussion of internal auditing.

[12]See the IIA's home page (www.theiia.org) for more information on the IIA and the certified internal auditor program.

The IRS is part of the U.S. Treasury Department. The main activity of IRS auditors is examining and auditing the books and records of organizations and individuals to determine their federal tax liability. IRS audits are typically compliance audits, ensuring that individuals and organizations are complying with federal tax laws.

Two other federal agencies that conduct audits are the Army Audit Agency and the Federal Bureau of Investigation (FBI). FBI auditors, for example, frequently audit for fraud in government agencies and organizations subject to federal laws. Last, most state and local governments have auditing agencies that perform functions similar to GAO and IRS auditors but at the state level.

Forensic Auditors

Forensic auditors are employed by corporations, government agencies, public accounting firms, and consulting and investigative services firms.[13] They are trained in detecting, investigating, and deterring fraud and white-collar crime (see the discussion of forensic auditing above). Some examples of situations where forensic auditors have been involved include

- Reconstructing incomplete accounting records to settle an insurance claim over inventory valuation.
- Probing money-laundering activities by reconstructing cash transactions.
- Investigating and documenting embezzlement and negotiating insurance settlements.

The Association of Certified Fraud Examiners (ACFE) is the primary organization supporting forensic auditors. The ACFE is a 25,000-member professional organization dedicated to educating certified fraud examiners (CFEs), who are trained in the specialized aspects of detecting, investigating, and deterring fraud and white-collar crime.

The ACFE offers a certification program for individuals wanting to become CFEs. Individuals interested in becoming a CFE must pass the Uniform CFE Examination.[14] CFEs come from various professional backgrounds, including auditors, accountants, fraud investigators, loss prevention specialists, attorneys, educators, and criminologists. CFEs gather evidence, take statements, write reports, and assist in investigating fraud in its varied forms.

Organizations That Affect the Public Accounting Profession

[LO 16]   A number of organizations affect the practice of auditing by independent auditors. Figure 2–4 provides a representation of the relationship of these organizations to a financial statement audit. The following subsections discuss the activities of five of these organizations.

---

[13]See J. T. Wells, *Fraud Examination: Investigative and Audit Procedures* (New York: Quorum Press, 1992), for a detailed discussion of forensic auditors.

[14]See the Association of Certified Fraud Examiners home page (www.acfe.org) for more information on the association and the CFE program.

FIGURE 2-4 **Organizations Affecting the Financial Statement Audit**

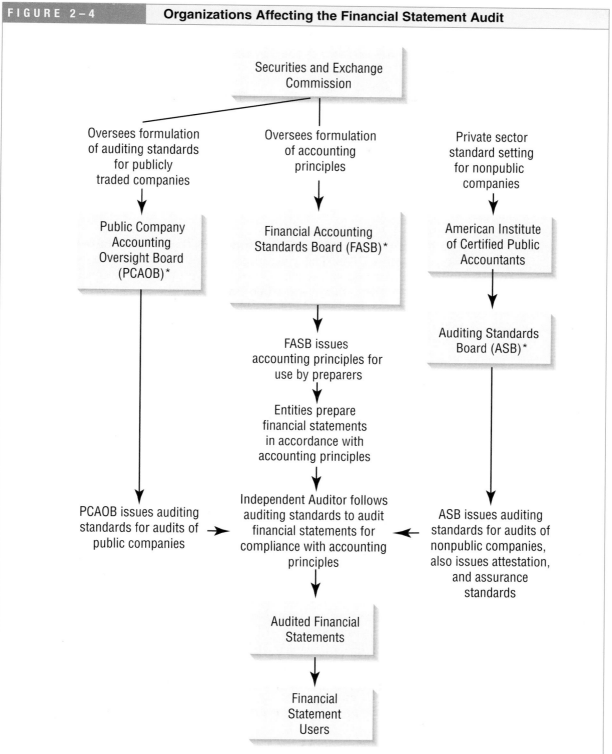

Securities and Exchange Commission

Oversees formulation of auditing standards for publicly traded companies

Oversees formulation of accounting principles

Private sector standard setting for nonpublic companies

Public Company Accounting Oversight Board (PCAOB)*

Financial Accounting Standards Board (FASB)*

American Institute of Certified Public Accountants

Auditing Standards Board (ASB)*

FASB issues accounting principles for use by preparers

Entities prepare financial statements in accordance with accounting principles

PCAOB issues auditing standards for audits of public companies

Independent Auditor follows auditing standards to audit financial statements for compliance with accounting principles

ASB issues auditing standards for audits of nonpublic companies, also issues attestation, and assurance standards

Audited Financial Statements

Financial Statement Users

* The Governmental Accounting Standards Board (GASB) issues accounting standards, and the Government Accountability Office (GAO—formerly known as the General Accounting Office) issues auditing standards, for governmental entities.

TABLE 2–4	Rules and Standards Issued by the AICPA
	• Bylaws • Code of Professional Conduct • Statements on Auditing Standards for Nonpublic Entities • Statements on Standards for Attestation Engagements • Statements on Standards for Accounting and Review Services • Statements on Quality Control Standards • Standards for Performing and Reporting on Peer Reviews • Statements on Standards for Consulting Services • Statements on Standards for Tax Services

American Institute of Certified Public Accountants (AICPA)

The AICPA performs a number of functions that directly bear on the activities of member CPAs. The most important of these functions is the promulgation of rules and standards that guide audit practice and related services provided to nonpublicly traded companies and other entities such as universities. Table 2–4 lists the types of rules and standards issued by various boards and committees within the AICPA.

- *Bylaws.* The bylaws establish the rules and regulations that govern the activities of the AICPA. The bylaws include issues such as admission, retention, and termination of membership; organization; financial management; and other activities.

- *Code of Professional Conduct.* The code was adopted by the membership of the AICPA to guide all members in the performance of their professional responsibilities. It is composed of two major sections: "Principles" and "Rules of Conduct." The code is covered in detail in Chapter 19.

- *Auditing standards.* The Auditing Standards Board (ASB) is responsible for establishing generally accepted auditing standards and issuing pronouncements on auditing matters for nonpublic entities (i.e. SAS).

- *Attestation standards.* The AICPA has authorized the ASB, the Accounting and Review Services Committee, and the Management Advisory Services Executive Committee to issue *Statements on Standards for Attestation Engagements* for services for nonpublic entities beyond audits of historical financial statements. Attestation standards are covered in Chapter 21.

- *Compilation and review standards.* The AICPA's Accounting and Review Services Committee is responsible for issuing pronouncements related to the conduct of compilation and review services for nonpublic entities. These standards are referred to as *Statements on Standards for Accounting and Review Services* (SSARS). SSARS are covered in Chapter 21.

- *Quality control and peer review standards.* CPA firms should maintain a system of quality control that ensures that a firm's practice meets professional standards. AICPA member accountants may be associated with public accounting firms involved in providing auditing and attest services only if the firm participates in one of two

AICPA practice-monitoring programs. In addition, firms that audit public companies are subject to inspection by the PCAOB. Quality control is covered in Chapter 19.

- ***Standards for consulting services and tax practice.*** *Statements on Standards for Consulting Services* are issued by the AICPA's Management Advisory Services Executive Committee. *Statements on Standards for Tax Services* emphasize the practitioner's responsibilities when involved with tax engagements.

In addition to its standard-setting role, the AICPA supports accounting and auditing research, produces a number of important publications, and provides a wide range of continuing education programs. For example, the AICPA publishes the *Journal of Accountancy, The Tax Advisor,* Auditing Research Monographs, Auditing Practice Releases, and Industry Audit and Accounting Guides. The AICPA is responsible for preparing and grading the Uniform CPA Examination, and plays an important role in administering the CPA certification in conjunction with the individual State Boards of Accountancy.

Securities and Exchange Commission (SEC)

The Securities and Exchange Commission (SEC) is a government agency that administers the Securities Act of 1933, the Securities Exchange Act of 1934, and the Sarbanes-Oxley Act of 2002, among others. The Securities Act of 1933 regulates disclosure of material information in a registration statement for an initial public offering of securities. *S forms,* which are used for issuing the securities, contain the audited financial statements of the registrant. The Securities Exchange Act of 1934 regulates ongoing reporting by companies whose securities are listed and traded on a stock exchange or that possess assets greater than $1 million and equity securities held by 500 or more persons. The most common documents encountered by auditors under the Securities Exchange Act of 1934 are the *10K, 10Q,* and *8K.* The 10K and 10Q are, respectively, the annual and quarterly reports, which include the financial statements that are filed with the SEC by a publicly traded entity. An 8K is filed whenever a significant event occurs that may be of interest to investors (such as sale of a division).

Because the SEC has responsibility and authority to oversee the establishment of accounting and auditing standards, the FASB, ASB, and PCAOB work closely with the SEC when formulating such standards.

Public Company Accounting Oversight Board (PCAOB)

The Public Company Accounting Oversight Board describes itself as "a private-sector, nonprofit corporation, created by the Sarbanes-Oxley Act of 2002, to oversee the auditors of public companies in order to protect the interests of investors and further the public interest in the preparation of informative, fair, and independent audit reports." While the board is a private-sector, nonprofit corporation, it is in reality a quasi-governmental regulatory agency overseen by the SEC. The Sarbanes-Oxley Act of 2002 essentially transferred authority for standard setting, inspection, investigation, and enforcement for public company audits from the profession (as represented by the AICPA) to the PCAOB. All public accounting firms providing audits for public companies are required to register with, pay fees to, and follow the rules and standards of the PCAOB. As of August 2004 the board had approved the registration of over 1,000 public accounting firms.[15] The PCAOB's stated goal is to ensure that the financial statements of public companies are audited in accordance with high standards of quality, independence, and ethics.

The PCAOB conducts a continuing program of regular "inspections" to assess the degree of compliance of registered public accounting firms with the Sarbanes-Oxley Act, PCAOB and SEC rules, and professional standards, in connection with the performance of public company audits and the issuance of audit reports. The PCAOB also has broad investigative and disciplinary authority over public company audit firms.

The PCAOB also has authority to impose sanctions designed to deter a possible recurrence of rule violations and to enhance the quality and reliability of future audits. The sanctions can range from revoking a firm's registration or barring a person from participating in audits of public companies to monetary penalties and requirements for remedial measures.

Financial Accounting Standards Board (FASB)

The Financial Accounting Standards Board (FASB) is a privately funded body whose mission is to establish standards for financial accounting and reporting. You should already be familiar with the operations of the FASB from your financial accounting classes. The Statements of Financial Accounting Standards (SFAS) and interpretations issued by the FASB are recognized as GAAP by the PCAOB and by the AICPA's Code of Professional Conduct.

An important group within the FASB is the Emerging Issues Task Force (EITF). The EITF was established by the FASB to meet accountants' needs for timely guidance on accounting practices and methods and to limit the number of issues requiring formal pronouncements from the FASB. See the FASB's website (www.fasb.org) for more information on the FASB's activities.

Conclusion

Chapter 1 introduced the concept of assurance and discussed the basics of financial statement auditing. This chapter explains the broader context in which financial statement auditing takes place. To fully understand auditing, you must be aware of the factors that shape the auditing environment, including the general business environment, clients' businesses and industries, and the standards, legal responsibilities, codes of conduct, and reporting requirements that guide the financial statement auditor's work. You must also understand the nature of public accounting firms within which auditors organize themselves to conduct audits of organizations of various sizes, and you must be aware of the outside professional, regulatory, and standard-setting bodies that directly impact how auditing is done. This chapter provides an introduction to the complex and ever-changing environment in which financial statement auditing is performed.

---

[15]See the PCAOB's website (www.pcaobus.org) for a list of registered accounting firms and other information about the PCAOB.

KEY TERMS

Assertions. Expressed or implied representations by management that are reflected in the financial statement components. The three sets of assertions relate to ending account balances, transactions, and presentation and disclosure.

Audit committee. A committee consisting of members of the board of directors, charged with overseeing the entity's system of internal control over financial reporting, internal and external auditors, and the financial reporting process. Typically must be independent of management.

Board of directors. Persons elected by the stockholders of a corporation to oversee management and to direct the affairs of the corporation.

Business processes. Processes implemented by management to achieve entity objectives. Business processes are typically organized into the following categories: revenue, purchasing, human resource management, inventory management, and financing processes.

Corporate governance. The oversight mechanisms in place to help ensure the proper stewardship over an entity's assets. Management and the board of directors play primary roles, and the independent auditor plays a key facilitating role.

Ethics. A system or code of conduct based on moral duties and obligations that indicates how an individual should behave.

Generally accepted accounting principles (GAAP). Accounting principles that are generally accepted for the preparation of financial statements in the United States. GAAP standards are currently issued primarily by the FASB, with oversight and influence by the SEC.

Generally accepted auditing standards (GAAS). Ten broad statements regarding the conduct of financial statement auditing.

Illegal acts. Violations of laws or government regulations.

Independence. A state of objectivity in fact and in appearance, including the absence of any significant conflicts of interest.

Management advisory services. Consulting services that may provide advice and assistance concerning an entity's organization, personnel, finances, operations, systems, or other activities.

Public accounting firm. An organization created to provide professional accounting-related services, including auditing. Usually formed as a proprietorship or as a form of partnership.

Reporting. The end product of the auditor's work, indicating the auditing standards followed, and expressing an opinion as to whether an entity's financial statements are fairly presented in accordance with agreed-upon criteria (e.g., GAAP).

Standards of the PCAOB. Standards regarding the conduct of financial statement auditing for public companies. Currently consist primarily of standards and statements established by the AICPA's Auditing Standards Board, as these statements and standards were adopted by the PCAOB in 2003 on an interim basis.

Statements on Auditing Standards (SAS). Statements issued by the AICPA's Auditing Standards Board, considered as interpretations of the 10 GAAS statements.

Unqualified audit report. A clean audit report, indicating the auditor's opinion that a client's financial statements are fairly presented in accordance with agreed-upon criteria (e.g., GAAP).

www.mhhe.com/messier4e	Visit the book's Online Learning Center for a multiple-choice quiz that will allow you to assess your understanding of chapter concepts.

REVIEW QUESTIONS

[LO 1] 2-1 Briefly discuss the key events that led up to the Sarbanes-Oxley Act of 2002 and the creation of the PCAOB.

[1] 2-2 Discuss how the events that have so dramatically affected auditors and the public accounting profession since the Enron scandal may in some senses be "healthy" for the profession.

[3] 2-3 Briefly discuss the essential components of the high-level model of business offered in the chapter. Why might understanding the characteristics of a client's business in each of these areas be important for a financial statement auditor?

[3,4] 2-4 What roles do information systems and systems of internal control play in the high-level model of business discussed in the chapter, and why might it be important for an auditor to understand these roles?

[5] 2-5 How might the three categories of management assertions provide a powerful tool for the financial statement auditor?

[7] 2-6 List the three categories of GAAS. Discuss why the GAAS and the SAS are considered minimum standards of performance for auditors.

[10] 2-7 Why is independence such an important standard for auditors? How does auditor independence relate to the agency relationship between owners and managers?

[11] 2-8 Compare and contrast management's responsibility for the entity's financial statements with the auditor's responsibilities for detecting errors and fraud in the financial statements.

[12] 2-9 Identify the elements of the auditor's standard unqualified report.

[14] 2-10 Give one example each of compliance, operational, and forensic audits.

[15] 2-11 List the various types of auditors.

[16] 2-12 The AICPA performs a number of functions that directly bear on independent auditors of nonpublic entities, including promulgation of rules and standards. List five types of standards issued by the AICPA.

[16] 2-13 What kind of organization is the PCAOB, why was it formed, and what does it do?

[16] 2-14 What role does the SEC play in the establishment of accounting and auditing standards for public companies?

[16] 2-15 What are some of the common documents encountered by auditors that are required by the Securities Exchange Act of 1934? What is the purpose of each of these documents?

MULTIPLE-CHOICE QUESTIONS

[1]   2-16   Which of the following best places the events of the last several years in proper sequence?

a. SEC consternation leading to new independence requirements after a fierce public battle, increased consulting services to audit clients, Enron and other scandals, Sarbanes-Oxley Act, prohibition of most consulting work for audit clients, establishment of PCAOB.

b. Increased consulting services to audit clients, SEC consternation leading to new independence requirements after a fierce public battle, Sarbanes-Oxley Act, Enron and other scandals, prohibition of most consulting work for audit clients, establishment of PCAOB.

c. SEC consternation leading to new independence requirements after a fierce public battle, Enron and other scandals, Sarbanes-Oxley Act, increased consulting services to audit clients, prohibition of most consulting work for audit clients, establishment of PCAOB.

d. Increased consulting services to audit clients, SEC consternation leading to new independence requirements after a fierce public battle, Enron and other scandals, Sarbanes-Oxley Act, prohibition of most consulting work for audit clients, establishment of PCAOB.

[3,4]   2-17   Which of the following best describes the relationship between business objectives, strategies, processes, controls, and transactions?

a. To achieve its objectives, a business formulates strategies and implements processes, which are carried out through business transactions. The entity's information and internal control systems must be designed to ensure that the transactions are properly executed, captured, and processed.

b. To achieve its strategies, a business formulates objectives and implements processes, which are carried out through the entity's information and internal control systems. Transactions are conducted to ensure that the processes are properly executed, captured, and processed.

c. To achieve its objectives, a business formulates strategies to implement its transactions, which are carried out through business processes. The entity's information and internal control systems must be designed to ensure that the processes are properly executed, captured, and processed.

d. To achieve its business processes, a business formulates objectives, which are carried out through the entity's strategies. The entity's information and internal control systems must be designed to ensure that the entity's strategies are properly executed, captured, and processed.

[6]   2-18   Which of the following is correct regarding the types of audits over which the AICPA's Auditing Standards Board and the PCAOB, respectively, have standard-setting authority?

	ASB	*PCAOB*
a.	Nonpublic company audits	Nonpublic company audits
b.	Public company audits	Public company audits
c.	Nonpublic company audits	Public company audits
d.	Public company audits	Nonpublic company audits

[7]   2-19   Which of the following best describes the general character of the three generally accepted auditing standards classified as standards of field work?

    a. The competence, independence, and professional care of persons performing the audit.

    b. Criteria for the content of the auditor's report on financial statements and related footnote disclosures.

    c. Criteria for audit planning and evidence gathering.

    d. The need to maintain an independence of mental attitude in all matters relating to the audit.

[11]   2-20   Which of the following statements best describes management's and the external auditor's respective levels of responsibility for a public company's financial statements?

    a. Management and the external auditor share equal responsibility for the fairness of the entity's financial statements in accordance with GAAP.

    b. Neither management nor the external auditor has significant responsibility for the fairness of the entity's financial statements in accordance with GAAP.

    c. Management has the primary responsibility to ensure that the company's financial statements are prepared in accordance with GAAP, and the auditor provides reasonable assurance that the statements are free of material misstatement.

    d. Management has the primary responsibility to ensure that the company's financial statements are prepared in accordance with GAAP, and the auditor provides a guarantee that the statements are free of material misstatement.

[12]   2-21   Which of the following statements best describes what is meant by an unqualified audit opinion?

    a. Issuance of an unqualified auditor's report indicates that in the auditor's opinion the client's financial statements are not fairly enough presented in accordance with agreed-upon criteria to qualify for a clean opinion.

    b. Issuance of an unqualified auditor's report indicates that the auditor is not qualified to express an opinion that the client's financial statements are fairly presented in accordance with agreed-upon criteria.

    c. Issuance of an unqualified auditor's report indicates that the auditor is expressing different opinions on each of the basic financial statements regarding whether the client's financial statements are fairly presented in accordance with agreed-upon criteria.

    d. Issuance of a standard unqualified auditor's report indicates that in the auditor's opinion the client's financial statements are fairly presented in accordance with agreed-upon criteria, with no need for the inclusion of qualifying phrases.

[12]   2-22   The auditing standards used to guide the conduct of the audit are

    a. Implicitly referred to in the opening paragraph of the auditor's standard report.

    b. Explicitly referred to in the opening paragraph of the auditor's standard report.

    c. Implicitly referred to in the scope paragraph of the auditor's standard report.

    d. Explicitly referred to in the scope paragraph of the auditor's standard report.

    e. Implicitly referred to in the opinion paragraph of the auditor's standard report.

    f. Explicitly referred to in the opinion paragraph of the auditor's standard report.

[12] 2-23 A client has used an inappropriate method of accounting for its pension liability on the balance sheet. The resulting misstatement is moderately material. The auditor is unable to convince the client to alter its accounting treatment. The rest of the financial statements are fairly stated in the auditor's opinion. Which kind of audit report would an auditor most likely issue under these circumstances?

    a. Standard unqualified opinion.

    b. Unqualified opinion with an explanatory paragraph.

    c. Qualified opinion due to scope limitation.

    d. Qualified opinion due to departure from GAAP.

    e. Adverse opinion.

    f. Disclaimer of opinion.

[16] 2-24 The Public Company Accounting Oversight Board

    a. Is a quasi-governmental organization that has legal authority to set auditing standards for audits of public companies.

    b. Is a quasi-governmental organization that has legal authority to set accounting standards for public companies.

    c. Is a quasi-governmental organization that has a policy to ignore public comment and input in the process of setting auditing standards.

    d. Is a quasi-governmental organization that is independent of the SEC in setting auditing standards.

[15] 2-25 Which of the following is not a part of the role of internal auditors?

    a. Assisting the external auditors.

    b. Providing reports on the reliability of financial statements to investors and creditors.

    c. Consulting activities.

    d. Operational audits.

[14] 2-26 Operational auditing is oriented primarily toward

    a. Future improvements to accomplish the goals of management.

    b. The accuracy of data reflected in management's financial records.

    c. Verification that an entity's financial statements are fairly presented.

    d. Past protection provided by existing internal control.

[14] 2-27 Which of the following would be considered part of a consulting services engagement?

    I. Expressing an opinion about the reliability of a client's financial statements.

    II. Reviewing and commenting on a client-prepared business plan.

    a. I only.

    b. II only.

    c. Both I and II.

    d. Neither I nor II.

PROBLEMS

[7]   2-28   Dale Boucher, the owner of a small electronics firm, asked Sally Jones, CPA, to conduct an audit of the company's records. Boucher told Jones that the audit was to be completed in time to submit audited financial statements to a bank as part of a loan application. Jones immediately accepted the engagement and agreed to provide an auditor's report within one month. Boucher agreed to pay Jones her normal audit fee plus a percentage of the loan if it was granted.

Jones hired two recent accounting graduates to conduct the audit and spent several hours telling them exactly what to do. She told the new hires not to spend time reviewing the internal control but to concentrate on proving the mathematical accuracy of the general and subsidiary ledgers and summarizing the data in the accounting records that supported Boucher's financial statements. The new hires followed Jones's instructions and after two weeks gave Jones the financial statements excluding footnotes. Jones reviewed the statements and prepared an unqualified auditor's report. The report did not refer to generally accepted accounting principles, and no audit procedures were conducted to verify the year-to-year application of such principles.

Required:
Briefly describe each of the generally accepted auditing standards and indicate how the action(s) of Jones resulted in a failure to comply with *each* generally accepted auditing standard.
(AICPA, adapted)

[7]   2-29   Terri Harrison, CPA, has discussed various reporting considerations with three of her audit clients. The three clients presented the following situations and asked how they would affect the audit report.

a. A client has changed its depreciation method on its machinery from straight line to double declining balance. Both Harrison and the client agree that the new depreciation method better reflects the usage of the machinery in the manufacturing process. The client agrees with Harrison that the change is material but claims that it needs disclosure only in the "Summary of Significant Accounting Policies" footnote to the financial statements, not in Harrison's report.

b. A client has a loan agreement that restricts the amount of cash dividends that can be paid and requires the maintenance of a particular current ratio. The client is in compliance with the terms of the agreement, and it is not likely that there will be a violation in the foreseeable future. The client believes there is no need to mention the restriction in the financial statements because such mention might mislead the readers.

c. During the year, a client correctly accounted for the acquisition of a majority-owned domestic subsidiary but did not properly present the minority interest in retained earnings or net income of the subsidiary in the consolidated financial statements. The client agrees with Harrison that the minority interest presented in the consolidated financial statements is materially misstated but takes the position that the minority shareholders of the subsidiary should look to that subsidiary's financial statements for information concerning their interest therein.

Required:
Each of the situations presented relates to one of the four generally accepted auditing standards of reporting. Identify and describe the applicable, generally accepted auditing standard of reporting in each situation, and discuss how the particular client situation relates to the standard.

(AICPA, adapted)

[12]   2-30   The auditor's standard report consists of an introductory paragraph describing the financial statements and management and auditor responsibilities, a scope paragraph describing the nature of the examination, and an opinion paragraph expressing the auditor's opinion. In some circumstances the auditor's standard report is modified by adding one or more separate explanatory paragraphs and/or modifying the wording of one or more of the paragraphs included in the report.

For this question, assume the auditor is independent and has expressed an unqualified opinion on the prior year's financial statements. For the current year, only single-year (not comparative) statements are presented.

Required:
Identify the circumstances necessitating modification of the auditor's standard report. For each circumstance, indicate the type of opinion that would be appropriate.

[14,15]   2-31   Audits can be categorized into five types: (1) financial statement audits, (2) audits of internal control, (3) compliance audits, (4) operational audits, and (5) forensic audits.

Required:
For each of the following descriptions, indicate which type of audit (financial statement audit, compliance audit, operational audit, or forensic audit) best characterizes the nature of the audit being conducted. Also indicate which type of auditor (external auditor, internal auditor, government auditor, or forensic auditor) is likely to perform the audit engagement.

a. Evaluate the policies and procedures of the Food and Drug Administration in terms of bringing new drugs to market.

b. Determine the fair presentation of Ajax Chemical's balance sheet, income statement, and statement of cash flows.

c. Review the payment procedures of the Accounts Payable Department for a large manufacturer.

d. Examine the financial records of a division of a corporation to determine if any accounting irregularities have occurred.

e. Evaluate the feasibility of forecasted rental income for a planned low-income public housing project.

f. Evaluate a company's Computer Services Department in terms of the efficient and effective use of corporate resources.

g. Audit the partnership tax return of a real estate development company.

h. Investigate the possibility of payroll fraud in a labor union pension fund.

DISCUSSION CASE

[2,7,14]   2-32   **Part I: Merry-Go-Round** (MGR), a clothing retailer located primarily in shopping malls, was founded in 1968.[16] By the early 1990s, the company had gone public and had expanded to approximately 1,500 stores, 15,000 employees, and $1 billion in annual sales. The company's locations in malls targeted the youth and teen market. The company was listed by *Forbes* magazine as one of the top 25 companies in the late 1980s. However, in the early 1990s, the company faced many challenges. One of its cofounders died, and the other left to pursue unrelated business interests. The company faced stiff competition from other retailers (e.g., The Gap and Banana Republic), fashion trends changed, and mall traffic declined. Sales fell, and experts speculated that MGR failed to anticipate key industry trends and lost sight of its customer market. To try to regain its strong position, the company acquired Chess King, Inc., a struggling chain of men's clothing stores located in malls, in 1993.

The company's sales continued to fall, and later in 1993, it brought back one of its cofounders to manage the company and wrote down a significant amount of inventory. However, this inventory write-down caused the company to violate loan covenants. Facing bankruptcy, the company, based on the advice of its newly hired law firm Swidler and Berlin, hired turnaround specialists from Ernst and Young (E&Y) to help overcome the financial crisis and develop a long-term business plan. However, the company's decline continued, and it filed for Chapter 11 reorganization in 1994. In 1996, the remaining assets were sold for pennies on the dollar.

Subsequently, a group of 9,000 creditors (including former employees and stockholders) began litigation against parties it deemed responsible for their losses. These parties included E&Y, which the creditors sued for $4 billion in punitive and compensatory damages (E&Y's fees from MGR totaled $4.5 million).

The lawsuit alleged that E&Y's incompetence was the main cause of MGR's decline and demise. The lawsuit alleged in part that

- The turnaround team did not act fast enough.
- The leader of the team took an eight-day vacation at a critical point during the engagement.
- The cost-cutting strategy called for only $11 million in annual savings, despite the fact that the company was projected to lose up to $200 million in 1994.

---

[16]The following articles were sources for the information in the case: E. MacDonald, "Ernst & Young Will Pay $185 Million to Settle Claims of Merry-Go-Round," *The Wall Street Journal*, April 29, 1999, and E. McDonald and S. J. Paltrow, "Merry-Go-Round: Ernst & Young Advised the Client, but Not about Everything—It Didn't Reveal Business Ties Alleged to Pose Conflict with Its Consulting Job—Settlement for $185 Million," *The Wall Street Journal*, August 8, 1999, p. A1.

- While store closings were key to MGR's survival, by 1995 only 230 of 1,434 stores had been closed and MGR still operated two stores in some malls.
- The turnaround team included inexperienced personnel—a retired consultant, a partner with little experience in the United States and with retail firms, and two recent college graduates.
- E&Y charged exorbitant hourly rates and charged unreasonable expenses (e.g., charges included reimbursement for a dinner for three of the consultants totaling in excess of $200).
- E&Y denied any wrongdoing but in April 1999 agreed to pay $185 million to settle with the injured parties.

Required:

a. Although this was not an audit engagement for E&Y, some of the allegations against the firm can be framed in terms of the 10 generally accepted auditing standards. Which of the 10 GAAS was E&Y alleged to have violated?

b. Should there be specific professional standards for CPAs who consult? Given that non-CPAs who consult do not have formal professional standards, describe the advantages and disadvantages that result from such standards.

[10]   2-33   **Part II: Merry-Go-Round.** Additional charges made against E&Y include the following (recall that MGR hired Ernst and Young for turnaround consulting services):

- E&Y had a close relationship with Rouse Co., one of MGR's primary landlords (E&Y was soliciting business from Rouse and provided significant tax services).
- Swidler (the law firm that recommended E&Y to MGR) and E&Y had participated in at least 12 different business arrangements, some of which resulted in Swidler receiving significant fees from E&Y.
- E&Y did not disclose either of these relationships to MGR.

Required:

a. Do you think that E&Y acted unethically given it had these relationships?

b. How could these relationships have affected E&Y's advice to MGR? In other words, refer to the charges above and speculate as to whether any of the charges against E&Y may have stemmed from the relationships described above.

To assist you in answering this question, consider the articles about MGR in footnote 16.

INTERNET ASSIGNMENTS

[16]   2-34   a. Go to the AICPA's website (www.aicpa.org). Find the AICPA's mission statement (currently under the link "About the AICPA"). Read and briefly summarize the AICPA's mission as described in its mission statement.

b. Go to the Security and Exchange Commission's website (www. SEC.gov). Find the SEC's description of its mission (currently under the "What We Do" link under the heading "About the SEC"). Read the material under the link "Introduction," describing the SEC's primary mission and purpose. Write a paragraph summarizing the SEC's mission and purpose.

c. Go to the SEC's website (www.SEC.gov). Read the material under the link "Creation of the SEC," describing the SEC's creation in the 1930s. Write a paragraph summarizing when and why the SEC was formed. What were the triggering events leading up to the SEC's formation?

d. Go to the Public Company Accounting Oversight Board's website (www.pcaobus.org). Find and briefly summarize the PCAOB's description of its standard-setting process (currently under the "Standards" link along the left-hand side of the page). Identify the section of the Sarbanes-Oxley Act of 2002 that empowers the PCAOB to set auditing standards for the audits of public companies.

[2,12] 2-35 Many companies post their financial statements and auditor's report on their home pages. Use one of the Internet search engines to do the following:

a. Visit Intel's (www.intel.com) and Microsoft's (www.microsoft.com) home pages and review their financial statements, including their auditors' reports.

b. Search the Web for the home page of a non-U.S. company and review its financial statements, including its auditor's report. For example, BMW's home page (www.bmw.com) allows a visitor to download the financial statements as a .pdf file. The auditor's report on BMW's financial statements is based on German auditing standards.

c. Compare the standard U.S. audit report with the audit report for the non-U.S. company (e.g., BMW). Note that in some cases, non-U.S.-based companies' reports use a U.S. audit report (for example, DaimlerChrysler's home page: www.daimlerchrysler.de).

d. Visit the SEC's website (www.sec.gov), and find the link for EdgarScan. Find, download, and print the auditor's report for a U.S. company of your choice. Identify what type of audit report it is (e.g., standard unqualified, qualified for scope limitation, disclaimer, adverse, etc.)

[14,15] 2-36 Visit the GAO's home page (www.gao.gov) and search for a recently completed audit. Prepare a summary of the GAO audit that includes background on the issue and the GAO's findings and recommendations.

www.mhhe.com/ messier4e	Visit the book's Online Learning Center for problem material to be completed using the *ACL* software packaged with your new text.

BASIC AUDITING CONCEPTS: RISK ASSESSMENT, MATERIALITY, AND EVIDENCE

LEARNING OBJECTIVES

Upon completion of this chapter you will

[1] Understand the concept of audit risk.

[2] Learn the form and components of the audit risk model.

[3] Understand how to use the audit risk model.

[4] Understand the auditor's risk assessment process.

[5] Identify the factors that determine the auditor's assessment of the risk of material misstatement.

[6] Learn how to respond to the results of the risk assessments.

[7] Learn how to evaluate the results of the audit tests.

[8] Understand the documentation requirements for risk assessments and responses.

[9] Learn the auditor's communication requirements to management and the audit committee.

[10] Learn the limitations of the audit risk model.

[11] Understand the concept of materiality.

[12] Identify the steps to applying materiality in an audit.

[13] Apply the materiality steps to an example (EarthWear).

RELEVANT ACCOUNTING AND AUDITING PRONOUNCEMENTS

CON2, FASB Statement of Financial Accounting Concepts No. 2, Qualitative Characteristics of Accounting Information

AU 311, Planning and Supervision

AU 312, Audit Risk and Materiality in Conducting an Audit

AU 316, Consideration of Fraud in a Financial Statement Audit

AU 317, Illegal Acts

AU 333, Management Representations

AU 339, Audit Documentation

AU 350, Audit Sampling

AU 380, Communications with Audit Committees

AICPA Auditing Standards Board, Exposure Draft, "Understanding the Entity and Its Environment and Assessing the Risks of Material Misstatement"

AICPA Auditing Standards Board, Exposure Draft, "Performing Audit Procedures in Response to Assessed Risks and Evaluating the Audit Evidence Obtained"

SEC Staff Accounting Bulletin No. 99, Materiality

Risk Assessment and Materiality

The three fundamental concepts that underlie the conduct of a financial statement audit were briefly discussed in Chapter 1. This chapter provides detailed coverage of two of those concepts: *audit risk* and *materiality*.

The wording of the auditor's report recognizes both of these concepts. First, the scope paragraph states that the auditor obtains "reasonable assurance" that the financial statements are free of material misstatements. The term *reasonable assurance* informs the reader that there is some level of risk that the audit did not detect *all* material misstatements. Second, the opinion paragraph states that the financial statements present fairly, "in all material respects." This phrase communicates to third parties that the audit report is limited to *material* information. Financial statements are materially misstated if they contain errors or fraud that causes them not to present fairly in conformity with GAAP.

Audit risk and materiality significantly impact the auditor's evidence decisions. The auditor considers both concepts in planning the nature, timing, and extent, of audit procedures and in evaluating the results of those procedures. The audit risk model serves as a framework for assessing audit risk. The auditor follows a risk assessment process to identify the risk of material misstatement in the financial statement accounts. The risk of material misstatement is composed of two components of the audit risk model: inherent risk and control risk. The risk of material misstatement is used to determine the acceptable level of detection risk and to plan the auditing procedures to be performed. The auditor restricts audit risk at the account balance level in such a way that, at the end of the engagement, he or she can express an opinion on the financial statements, taken as a whole, at an acceptable level of audit risk. The auditor considers materiality from a reasonable user perspective and follows a three-step process in applying materiality on an audit. The auditor must recognize that there is an inverse relationship between audit risk and materiality, and between the desired level of audit risk and the amount of audit evidence the auditor must collect. 🌏

Audit Risk

[LO 1]   Risk is the first fundamental concept that underlies the audit process. An auditor engaged to perform a financial statement audit faces two types of risk: *audit risk* and *engagement risk*. They are defined as follows:

> **Audit risk** is the risk that the auditor may unknowingly fail to appropriately modify the opinion on financial statements that are materially misstated.

> **Engagement risk** is the auditor's exposure to loss or injury to professional practice from litigation, adverse publicity, or other events arising in connection with financial statements audited and reported on.

In simple terms, audit risk is the risk that an auditor will issue an unqualified opinion on materially misstated financial statements. The auditor should perform the audit to reduce audit risk to a sufficiently low level that is, in the auditor's professional judgment, appropriate for expressing an opinion on the financial statements. In doing so, the auditor needs to consider audit risk at the financial statement level and at the account balance or class of transactions level. In considering audit risk at the overall financial statement level, the auditor considers risks of material misstatement that relate *pervasively* to the financial statements and potentially affect many assertions. Such risks often relate to the entity's control environment and may be relevant to the auditor's consideration of the risks of material misstatement arising from fraud (e.g., management override of internal control). The auditor also considers audit risk at the individual account balance or class of transactions level because such consideration directly assists the auditor to plan the appropriate audit procedures for those accounts or transactions. Audit risk is discussed extensively throughout the remainder of this section.

Engagement risk relates to an auditor's exposure to financial loss and damage to his or her professional reputation. For example, an auditor may conduct an audit in accordance with auditing standards and still be sued by the client or a third party. Although the auditor has complied with professional standards and may ultimately win the lawsuit, his or her professional reputation may be damaged in the process by the negative publicity.

Engagement risk cannot be directly controlled by the auditor, although some control can be exercised through the careful acceptance and continuance of clients. Audit risk, on the other hand, can be directly controlled by the scope (nature, timing, and extent) of the auditor's test procedures. As the next section demonstrates, the *audit risk model* provides a framework for auditors to follow.

The Audit Risk Model

[LO 2]   Auditing standards do not provide specific guidance on what is an acceptable level of audit risk. The determination of audit risk and the use of the audit risk model involve considerable judgment on the part of the auditor. The audit risk model assists the auditor in determining the scope of auditing procedures for a particular account balance or class of transactions.

The audit risk model, at the *account balance* or *class of transactions* level, can be specified as

$$AR = IR \times CR \times DR$$

where

> AR = Audit risk (the risk that the auditor may fail to modify the opinion on materially misstated financial statements)
>
> IR = Inherent risk (the susceptibility of an assertion to material misstatements, assuming no related controls)
>
> CR = Control risk (the risk that material misstatements that could occur in an assertion will not be prevented or detected on a timely basis by the internal controls)
>
> DR = Detection risk (the risk that the auditor will not detect a material misstatement that exists in an assertion)

Detection risk can be divided further into analytical procedures risk (*APR*) and substantive tests of details risk (*TDR*). *Analytical procedures risk* is the risk that substantive analytical procedures will fail to detect material misstatements, while *tests of details risk* is the allowable risk for failing to detect a material misstatement that is not detected by internal controls or substantive analytical procedures. In discussing the audit risk model in the remainder of this text, detection risk will not be divided for ease of presentation.

Detection risk results from two uncertainties that are a function of the effectiveness of an audit procedure and of its application by the auditor. The first uncertainty, referred to as *sampling risk*, relates to the fact that, in many instances, the auditor does not examine 100 percent of the account balance or class of transactions. Because the auditor examines only a subset of the population, the sample drawn may not represent the population, and the auditor may thus draw the wrong conclusion on the fairness of the account balance.

The second uncertainty is called *nonsampling risk* and can occur because the auditor used an inappropriate audit procedure, failed to detect a misstatement when applying an appropriate audit procedure, or misinterpreted the audit results. Nonsampling risk may be present even when the auditor examines 100 percent of the population. Nonsampling risk can be reduced to a negligible level through adequate planning, proper assignment of audit staff, supervision and review of the audit work performed, and supervision and conduct of a firm's audit practice in accordance with appropriate quality control standards.

At the account balance or class of transaction level, audit risk consists of

1. The risk that the balance or class and related assertions contain misstatements that could be material to the financial statements when aggregated with misstatements in other balances or classes (inherent risk and control risk).
2. The risk that the auditor will not detect such misstatements (detection risk).

From the auditor's perspective, inherent risk and control risk differ from detection risk in that inherent risk and control risk exist independently of the audit. In other words, the levels of inherent risk and control risk are functions of the entity and its environment. The auditor has little control over these risks. Sometimes the combination of inherent risk and control risk is referred to as *auditee risk*. Detection risk, on the other hand, can be controlled by the auditor through the scope of the audit procedures performed. Detection risk has an inverse relationship to inherent risk and control risk. For example, if an entity's inherent risk and control risk are judged to be high, the auditor sets a lower level of detection risk in order to meet the planned level of audit risk. Conversely, if inherent risk and control risk are low, detection risk is set at a higher level.

The auditor's assessment of audit risk and its component risks (*IR, CR,* and *DR*) is a matter of professional judgment. At the completion of the audit, the *actual* level of audit risk is *not* known with certainty by the auditor. If the auditor assesses the *achieved* audit risk as being less than or equal to the *planned* level of audit risk, an unqualified report can be issued. If the assessment of the achieved level of audit risk is greater than the planned level, the auditor should either conduct additional audit work or qualify the audit report.

Use of the Audit Risk Model

The audit risk model expresses the general relationship of audit risk and the components of the model. The model is not intended to be a precise formula that includes all factors influencing the assessment of audit risk. However, auditors may find the model useful when planning risk levels for audit procedures. The discussion that follows concerning the audit risk model is limited to its use as an audit planning tool. Three steps are involved in the auditor's use of the audit risk model at the account balance or class of transaction level:

❂ **[LO 3]**

1. Setting a planned level of audit risk.
2. Assessing inherent risk and control risk.
3. Solving the audit risk equation for the appropriate level of detection risk.

In applying the audit risk model in this manner, the auditor determines or assesses each component of the model using either quantitative or qualitative terms. In Step 1, the auditor sets audit risk for each account balance or class of transaction in such a way that, at the completion of the engagement, an opinion can be issued on the financial statements at an acceptable level of audit risk. Step 2 requires that the auditor assess inherent risk and control risk. The auditor may assess inherent risk and control risk in combination (auditee risk) or separately. To assess these two components, the auditor assesses the entity's business risks and the risk of material misstatement due to error or fraud. Figure 3–1 shows the relationship of the assessment of the entity's business risks and risk of material misstatement to inherent risk and control risk. These assessments are described in detail in the next two sections of the chapter. In Step 3, the auditor determines the appropriate level of detection risk by solving the audit risk model as follows:

$$AR = IR \times CR \times DR$$

$$DR = \frac{AR}{IR \times CR}$$

The auditor uses this level of detection risk to design the audit procedures that will reduce audit risk to an acceptable level. However, it is not

FIGURE 3–1 The Relationship of the Entity's Business Risks to the Audit Risk Model

appropriate for an auditor to rely completely on his or her assessments of inherent risk and control risk to the exclusion of performing substantive procedures of account balances where material misstatements could exist. Auditing standards include this caveat because of the imprecision that may occur in assessing inherent risk and control risk.

Consider the following numerical example:

> Suppose that the auditor has determined that the planned audit risk for the accounts receivable balance can be set at .05 based on the significance of the account to the financial statements. By establishing a relatively low level of audit risk, the auditor is reducing the possibility that the account may contain a material misstatement. Assume further that the auditor assesses inherent risk for accounts receivable to be .80. After evaluating the internal control over the revenue process, the auditor assesses control risk to be .60. Substituting the values for *AR*, *IR*, and *CR* into the equation indicates that the auditor should set *DR* at approximately .10 [$DR = .05/(.80 \times .60)$] for testing the accounts receivable balance. Thus, the auditor establishes the scope of the audit for accounts receivable so that there is only a 10 percent chance that a material misstatement, if present, is not detected.

A public accounting firm may find it more appropriate to use qualitative terms to implement the audit risk model. For example, audit risk might be classified into three categories, *very low, low,* and *moderate*. It is not likely that an audit planned in accordance with auditing standards would consider a high level of audit risk. The remaining component of the audit risk model may be classified into categories such as *low, moderate,* or *high*. This method of using the model is identical to that followed when using the numerical values. Audit risk would be set using one of the category choices. Similarly, the auditor would assess the appropriate category for inherent risk and control risk. The various combinations of the components would be used to determine the level of detection risk. Following are three examples of the use of a nonquantitative approach to the audit risk model.

Example	AR	IR	CR	DR
1	Very low	High	High	Low
2	Low	Low	High	Moderate
3	Moderate	High	Low	Moderate

In Example 1, the auditor has determined that a very low level of audit risk is appropriate for this account because of its importance to the financial statement. Assume further that the auditor has assessed inherent risk and control risk as high. A high assessment for these components indicates that there is a high risk that a material misstatement occurred and was not prevented or detected by the internal control system. Given a low level of audit risk and high assessments for inherent and control risk, the auditor would set detection risk as low. A low assessment for detection risk implies that the auditor will conduct a more detailed investigation of this account than if the assessment of detection risk were high.

The Auditor's Risk Assessment Process

[LO 4]
Management's Strategies, Objectives, and Business Risks

Strategies are the operational approaches used by management to achieve objectives. For example, managers of companies pursue strategies, such as being the low-cost or high-quality provider of a product, to achieve their business objectives. Typical business objectives include growth in market share, first-rate reputation, desirable workplace atmosphere, and excellent service. Business risks are threats to management's ability to achieve its objectives, and these risks result from significant conditions, events, circumstances, and actions or inactions that may adversely affect management's ability to execute its strategies and to achieve its objectives. Business activities, strategies, objectives, and the business environment are ever-changing, and the dynamic and complex nature of business causes business risks. For example, risks arise from the development of a new product because the product may fail or because flaws in the product may result in lawsuits or damage to the company's reputation. Management is responsible for identifying such risks and responding to them. Usually, management develops approaches to address business risks by implementing a risk assessment process.

Business Risks and the Risk of Material Misstatement

Business risk is a broader concept than the risk of materially misstated financial statements. However, most business risks have the potential to affect the financial statements either immediately or in the long run. Auditors need to identify business risks and understand the potential misstatements that may result. For example, an audit client selling goods or services in a declining industry with a shrinking customer base faces pressure to maintain historical profit margins, which increases the risk of misstatement associated with the valuation of assets such as receivables. However, the same risk may also have longer-term implications to the company's overall health if the economy remains depressed. In such a case, the auditor would consider the likelihood that the client will not remain financially viable and whether the going concern assumption is still appropriate.

The auditor should obtain an understanding of the management's objectives and strategies and the related business risks that may result in material misstatement of the financial statements. A thorough understanding of business risks increases the likelihood of identifying material misstatements in the financial statements. The remaining sections discuss the auditor's risk assessment process.

Understanding the Entity and Its Environment

Figure 1–4 presented an overview of the audit process. This process starts by obtaining an understanding of the entity and its environment, including internal control. Obtaining an understanding of the entity and its environment is a continuous, dynamic process of gathering, updating, and analyzing information throughout the audit. The goal of this step in the process is to assess the business risks faced by the entity. Based on the auditor's understanding of the entity's business risks and how those risks are controlled or not controlled, the auditor assesses the risk of material misstatement at the assertion level. Figure 3–2 provides an overview of the auditor's assessments of business risks and the risk of material misstatement (i.e., the auditor's risk assessment process). Unless otherwise stated in the text, the risk of material misstatement refers to misstatements caused by *error* or *fraud*.

Business risks include any external and internal factors, pressures, and forces that bear on the entity's ability to survive and be profitable. The auditor's understanding of the entity and its environment includes knowledge about the following categories:

- Industry, regulatory, and other external factors.
- Nature of the entity.
- Objectives and strategies, and related business risks.
- Measurement and review of the entity's financial performance.
- Internal control.

Industry, Regulatory, and Other External Factors
The auditor should obtain an understanding of industry, regulatory, and other external factors that are relevant to the audit client. Obtaining an understanding of these factors assists the auditor in identifying risks of material misstatements. Some industries are subject to risks of material misstatement as a result of unique accounting estimates. For example, a property and casualty insurance company needs to establish loss reserves based on historical data that may be subject to misstatement. Table 3–1 presents examples of industry, regulatory, and other external factors that should be considered by the auditor.

FIGURE 3–2

An Overview of the Auditor's Assessment of Business Risks and the Risk of Material Misstatements

Perform risk assessment procedures to obtain an understanding of the entity and its environment, including internal control.

Identify *business risks* that may result in material misstatements in the financial statements.

Evaluate the entity's responses to those *business risks* and obtain evidence of their implementation.

Assess the risk of material misstatement at the assertion level and determine the audit procedures that are necessary based on that risk assessment.

TABLE 3–1

Industry, Regulatory, and Other External Factors

Industry conditions:
- The market and competition, including demand, capacity, and price competition.
- Cyclical or seasonal activity.
- Product technology relating to the entity's products.
- Energy supply and cost.

Regulatory environment:
- Accounting principles and industry specific practices.
- Regulatory framework for a regulated industry.
- Legislation and regulation that significantly affect the entity's operations.
  - Regulatory requirements.
  - Direct supervisory activities.
- Taxation.
- Government policies currently affecting the conduct of the entity's business.
  - Monetary, including foreign exchange controls.
  - Fiscal.
  - Financial incentives (e.g., government aid programs).
  - Tariffs and trade restrictions.
- Environmental requirements affecting the industry and the entity's business.

Other external factors:
- General level of economic activity (e.g., recession, growth).
- Interest rates and availability of financing.
- Inflation and currency revaluation.

Nature of the Entity

The nature of an entity refers to the client's operations, its ownership, the types of investments it is making and plans to make, and the way the entity is structured and how it is financed. An understanding of the nature of an entity gives the auditor a better idea of what to expect in the financial statements. For example, an entity with a complex structure may give rise to a risk of material misstatement as a result of the accounting for investments in joint ventures, subsidiaries, equity investments, or special-purpose entities. The auditor also obtains an understanding of the entity's application of accounting policies including accounting practices common to the industry. Table 3–2 presents examples of client

---

TABLE 3–2	Examples of Client Characteristics That Auditors Should Consider

Business operations:
- Nature of revenue sources (e.g., manufacturer, wholesaler, banking, insurance, or other financial services, technology products, and services).
- Products or services and markets (e.g., major customers and contracts, terms of payment, profit margins, market share, competitors, exports, pricing policies, reputation of products, warranties, order book, trends, marketing strategy and objectives, and manufacturing processes).
- Conduct of operations (e.g., stages and methods of production, business segments, delivery of products and services, and details of declining or expanding operations).
- Alliances, joint ventures, and outsourcing activities.
- Involvement in e-business, including Internet sales and marketing activities.
- Geographic dispersion and industry segmentation.
- Location of production facilities, warehouses, and offices.
- Key customers.
- Important suppliers of goods and services (e.g., long-term contracts, stability of supply, terms of payment, imports, and methods of delivery, such as just in time).
- Employment (e.g., by location, supply, wage levels, union contracts, pension and other postemployment benefits, stock option or incentive bonus arrangements, and government regulation related to employment matters).
- Research and development activities and expenditures.
- Transactions with related parties.

Investments:
- Acquisitions, mergers, or disposals of business activities.
- Investments and dispositions of securities and loans.
- Capital investment activities, including investments in plant and equipment and technology, and any recent or planned changes.
- Investments in nonconsolidated entities, including partnerships, joint ventures, and special-purpose entities.

Financing:
- Group structure—major subsidiaries and associated entities, including consolidated and nonconsolidated structures.
- Debt structure, including covenants, restrictions, guarantees, and off-balance-sheet financing arrangements.
- Leasing of property, plant, or equipment for use in the business.
- Beneficial owners (local and foreign business reputation and experience).
- Related parties.
- Use of derivative financial instruments.

Financial reporting:
- Accounting principles and industry specific practices.
- Revenue recognition practices.
- Accounting for fair values.
- Inventories.
- Foreign currency assets, liabilities, and transactions.
- Industry-specific significant categories (e.g., loans and investments for banks, accounts receivable and inventory for manufacturers, research and development for pharmaceuticals).
- Accounting for unusual or complex transactions including those in controversial or emerging areas.
- Financial statement presentation and disclosure.

TABLE 3–3	Examples of Matters That the Auditor Considers When Developing an Understanding of the Entity's Objectives and Strategies

- Existence of objectives relating to the following:
  — Industry developments.
  — New products and services.
  — Expansion of the business.
  — New accounting requirements.
  — Regulatory requirements.
  — Current and prospective financing requirements.
  — Use of IT.
- Effects of implementing a strategy, particularly any effects that will lead to new accounting requirements.

characteristics that the auditor should consider in identifying and evaluating business risks.

Objectives, Strategies, and Related Business Risks   As discussed above, the auditor must identify and understand the entity's objectives and strategies to achieve its objectives and the business risks associated with those objectives and strategies. Typically, management implements a *risk assessment process* to identify and control business risks that arise from industry, economic, regulatory, or other factors. The auditor should obtain an understanding of this process, including how management identifies risks, estimates the significance of the risks, assesses the likelihood of their occurrence, and decides upon actions to manage them. Table 3–3 provides examples of matters the auditor considers when developing an understanding of the entity's objectives and strategies.

Measurement and Review of the Entity's Financial Performance
Internally generated information used by management to measure and review the entity's financial performance may include key performance indicators (KPIs); budgets; variance analysis; segment information and divisional, departmental, or other level performance reports; and comparisons of an entity's performance with that of competitors. External parties (e.g., analysts and credit rating agencies) may also measure and review the entity's financial performance. Internal measures provide management with information about progress toward meeting the entity's objectives. Thus, a deviation in the performance measures may indicate a risk of misstatement in the related financial statement information. When the auditor intends to make use of the performance measures for the purpose of the audit, the auditor should consider whether the information provided is reliable and trustworthy and whether it is sufficiently detailed or precise. Both internal and external information is useful to the auditor's understanding of the entity and its environment. Table 3–4 presents examples of information the auditor might use to develop an understanding of the entity's measurement and review system.

TABLE 3-4	Examples of Matters That the Auditor Might Consider When Developing an Understanding of the Entity's Measurement and Review of Performance

- Key ratios and operating statistics.
- Key performance indicators.
- Employee performance measures and incentive compensation policies.
- Trends.
- Use of forecasts, budgets, and variance analysis.
- Analyst reports and credit rating reports.
- Competitor analysis.
- Period-on-period financial performance (revenue growth, profitability, and leverage).

Internal Control   Internal control is the label given to the entity's policies and procedures designed to provide reasonable assurance about the achievement of the entity's objectives with regard to reliability of financial reporting, effectiveness and efficiency of operations, and compliance with applicable laws and regulations. Internal control is implemented by the client's board of directors, management, and other personnel. Because of the significance of internal control to the financial statement audit, we cover it in great detail in Chapter 6. To provide you with an introduction to the concept of internal control, here are several examples of policies and procedures that may be a part of a company's internal control:

- Active and qualified board of directors and audit committee with members independent from the company.
- Effective risk assessment process (e.g., adequate insurance, disaster recovery plans, and industry forecast and analysis).
- Competent and objective internal audit staff.
- Proper computer controls (e.g., passwords and firewalls are used to restrict unauthorized access, sales order software requires a valid credit card before processing the sale).
- Proper authorization of transactions (e.g., a supervisor must approve all purchases over $5,000, only the vice president or president can sign checks).
- Proper segregation of duties (e.g., the person receiving customer payment does not have access to the accounting records).
- Procedures to ensure assets exist (e.g., inventory counts, matching a loading dock receiving report to an invoice for payment).
- Procedures to ensure all valid transactions are recorded (e.g., purchase orders are sequentially numbered, and numbers missing or skipped in the accounting journals are accounted for as void or unused).
- Monitoring of controls (e.g., supervisor observes the procedures at the loading dock to ensure control procedures are properly followed).

The auditor should understand and assess the effectiveness of internal control. The auditor should use the understanding of internal control to identify types of potential misstatements; consider factors that affect the risks of material misstatement; and design appropriate audit procedures.

Auditor's Risk Assessment Procedures

The auditor obtains an understanding of the entity and its environment by performing the following risk assessment procedures: inquiries of management and others, analytical procedures, and observation and inspection.

Inquiries of Management and Others
The auditor obtains information about the entity and its environment through inquiry of management, individuals responsible for financial reporting, and other personnel within the entity. Making inquiries of others *within* the entity may be useful in providing the auditor with a perspective different from that of management and those responsible for financial reporting. Depending on the circumstances, the auditor might make inquiries of

- Internal audit personnel.
- Production, marketing, sales, and other personnel.
- Employees with different levels of authority.
- Employees involved in initiating, processing, or recording complex or unusual transactions.
- In-house legal counsel.
- The board of directors or audit committee.

For example, inquiries directed to internal audit personnel might relate to their activities concerning the design and operating effectiveness of the entity's internal controls. The auditor might also inquire of the in-house legal counsel about issues such as litigation, compliance with laws and regulations, and the meaning of contract terms. The auditor might also inquire of others *outside* the entity. For example, the auditor may consider it is appropriate to make inquiries of customers, suppliers, or valuation specialists. Fraud is typically perpetrated by a relatively small number of people in top management and/or the entity's financial reporting department. Discussions with people outside those areas may provide information that will assist the auditor in uncovering the fraud. For example, customers may report that they received large quantities of unordered products from the audit client just before year-end. This would be an indicator of overstated revenues.

Analytical Procedures
As discussed later in Chapter 5, auditing standards require that the auditor conduct analytical procedures in planning the audit. Such preliminary analytical procedures assist the auditor in understanding the entity and its environment and in identifying areas that may represent specific risks relevant to the audit. Analytical procedures can be helpful in identifying the existence of unusual transactions or events and amounts, ratios, and trends that might have implications for audit planning. In performing analytical procedures for planning purposes, the auditor should develop expectations about plausible relationships that are expected to exist, based on the understanding of the entity

and its environment. However, the results of such high-level analytical procedures provide only a broad initial indication about whether a material misstatement may exist.

Observation and Inspection   Observation and inspection include audit procedures such as

- Observation of entity activities and operations.
- Review or inspection of documents, records, and controls manuals.
- Visits to the entity's premises and plant facilities.
- Reviewing written business plans and strategies.
- Tracing transactions through the information system relevant to financial reporting (walkthroughs).

The auditor uses other audit procedures as appropriate, such as reading about industry developments and trends, reading the current year's interim financial statements, and reviewing regulatory or financial publications. The nature, timing, and extent of the auditor's risk assessment procedures depend on the circumstances of the engagement, such as the size and complexity of the entity.

Table 3–5 presents sources where the auditor can obtain information for developing an understanding of the entity and its environment. As discussed in Chapter 4, information obtained or derived from sources external to the entity generally can be deemed reliable in the absence of evidence to the contrary. Support for information obtained from sources within the entity may require a more in-depth assessment of the reliability of the information source, its credibility, and the relationship of the information to information obtained from other sources. Inquiries are an important source of evidence, but they generally provide stronger evidence when integrated with other procedures or similar inquiries made of multiple people.

TABLE 3–5	Sources of Information for Understanding the Entity and Its Environment

- Cumulative knowledge and experience obtained from prior audits, including the nature and cause of misstatements and accounts affected.
- Procedures performed in client acceptance and continuance process.
- Knowledge obtained from performing interim procedures.
- Consulting, tax, or other engagements performed for the entity.
- Communications with predecessor auditors including review of predecessor auditor working papers.
- Published annual reports and interim reports to shareholders, if applicable.
- Discussions with management.
- Minutes of board of director and/or audit committee meetings.
- Entity's business/strategic plans, budgets, or other documentation.
- Reports prepared by analysts, banks, underwriters, rating agencies, and the like.
- Individuals knowledgeable about the industry, such as the engagement team members for clients in a similar business/industry.
- Audit firm—generated industry guidance, databases, and practice aids, where applicable.
- Government statistics.
- Economic and financial journals.
- Industry or trade journals.
- Client press releases, publications, and brochures.
- Internal audit reports.

Identifying Business Risks

Entities generally face a broad array of business risks that may affect their operations, financial reporting, and compliance with laws and regulations. During the process of obtaining an understanding of the entity and its environment, the auditor should identify the business risks faced by the entity. Some examples of conditions and events that may indicate the existence of business risks are

- Significant changes in the entity such as large acquisitions, reorganizations, or other unusual events.
- Significant changes in the industry in which the entity operates.
- Significant new products or services or significant new lines of business.
- New locations.
- Significant changes in the IT environment.
- Operations in areas with unstable economies.
- High degree of complex regulation.

Once risks that may result in material misstatements in the financial statements are identified, the auditor should evaluate the entity's response to those risks and obtain evidence that those responses have been implemented. For example, the auditor should obtain information on the entity's risk assessment process and whether it is operating effectively. If the entity's response to the identified risk is adequate, the risk of material misstatement may be reduced. However, if the entity's response to the identified risk is inadequate, the auditor's assessment of the risk of material misstatement may increase. If the entity does not respond adequately to business risks, the auditor will have to develop tests to determine if any misstatements are present in the related account balances or class of transactions.

Assessing the Risk of Material Misstatement Due to Error or Fraud

[LO 5]   Based on knowledge of the entity and its environment, the auditor should assess the risk of material misstatement at the assertion level and determine the audit procedures that are necessary based on that risk assessment (see Figure 3–2).

To assess the risk of material misstatement, the auditor

- Identifies risks by considering the entity and its environment, including controls that relate to the risks, and by relating these risks to the classes of transactions and account balances in the financial statements.
- Relates the identified risks to what can go wrong at the assertion level.
- Considers whether the risks are of a magnitude that could result in a material misstatement of the financial statements.
- Considers the likelihood that the risks will result in a material misstatement of the financial statements.

The auditor uses information gathered by performing risk assessment procedures to obtain an understanding of the entity and its environment, including the audit evidence obtained in evaluating the design of controls and determining whether they have been implemented, as audit evidence to support the risk assessment. When the risk assessment is based on an expectation that controls are operating effectively, the auditor is required to perform tests of controls to obtain evidence that the controls are operating effectively (discussed in Chapter 6).

The auditor determines whether the identified risks of material misstatement relate to specific classes of transactions or account balances and related assertions or whether they relate more pervasively to the financial statements as a whole and potentially affect many assertions. Risks at the financial statement level may derive from inadequate general computer controls (e.g., lack of security and restricted access) or inappropriate ethical tone set by management (e.g., excessive pressure to meet financial goals). The risks that arise from a weak overall control environment such as management's lack of competence or integrity may have a more pervasive effect on the financial statements and may require the auditor to issue a qualified or adverse opinion or resign from the engagement. The following subsections focus primarily on assessing the risk of material misstatement due to fraud, sometimes referred to as the fraud risk assessment.

Types of Misstatements[1]

A misstatement of the financial statements may consist of any of the following:

- A difference between the amount, classification, or presentation of a reported financial statement element, account, or item and the amount, classification, or presentation that would have been reported under generally accepted accounting principles.
- The omission of a financial statement element, account, or item.
- A financial statement disclosure that is not presented in accordance with generally accepted accounting principles.
- The omission of information required to be disclosed in accordance with generally accepted accounting principles.

Misstatements in the financial statements can result from error or fraud. *Errors* are unintentional misstatements or omissions of amounts or disclosures and may involve

- Mistakes in gathering or processing data from which financial statements are prepared.
- Unreasonable accounting estimates arising from oversight or misinterpretation of facts.
- Mistakes in the application of accounting principles relating to amount, classification, manner of presentation, or disclosure.

---

[1]See A. Eilifsen and W. F. Messier, Jr., "Auditor Detection of Misstatements: A Review and Integration of Empirical Research," *Journal of Accounting Literature* 2000 (19), pp. 1–43 for a detailed review of research studies that have examined auditor-detected misstatements.

Fraud, from the auditor's perspective, involves intentional misstatements that can be classified into two types: (1) misstatements arising from fraudulent financial reporting and (2) misstatements arising from misappropriation of assets. Thus, the primary distinction between errors and fraud is whether the misstatement was intentional or unintentional. Unfortunately, it is often difficult to determine intent. For example, suppose the auditor detects a misstatement in an account that requires an estimate, such as bad debt expense; it may be difficult to determine whether the misstatement was intentional.

Misstatements arising from fraudulent financial reporting are intentional misstatements or omissions of amounts or disclosures in financial statements intended to deceive financial statement users. Fraudulent financial reporting may involve acts such as the following:

- Manipulation, falsification, or alteration of accounting records or supporting documents from which financial statements are prepared.
- Misrepresentation in, or intentional omission from, the financial statements of events, transactions, or other significant information.
- Intentional misapplication of accounting principles relating to amounts, classification, manner of presentation, or disclosure.

Misstatements arising from misappropriation of assets (sometimes referred to as *defalcation*) involve the theft of an entity's assets where the theft causes the financial statements to be misstated. Examples of misappropriation include

- Embezzling cash received.
- Stealing assets.
- Causing the entity to pay for goods or services not received.

Misappropriation of assets may be accompanied by false or misleading records or documents, possibly created by circumventing controls, and may involve one or more individuals among management, employees, or third parties.

Conditions Indicative of Material Misstatement Due to Fraud

Three conditions are generally present when material misstatements due to fraud occur:

1. Management or other employees have an *incentive* or are under *pressure* that provides a reason to commit fraud.
2. Circumstances exist that provide an *opportunity* for a fraud to be carried out.
3. Those involved are able to *rationalize* committing a fraudulent act. Some individuals possess an *attitude,* character, or set of ethical values that allow them to knowingly and intentionally commit a dishonest act. Even honest individuals can commit fraud in an environment where sufficient pressure is being exerted on them. The greater the incentive or pressure, the more likely an individual will be able to rationalize the acceptability of committing fraud.

Withholding evidence or misrepresenting information through falsified documentation, including forgery, may conceal fraud. For example, management may manipulate accounting records by recording unsupported journal entries. Fraud also may be concealed through collusion among management, employees, or third parties. For example, through collusion, false evidence that control activities have been effectively performed may be presented to the auditor by more than one individual within the entity.

Management has the ability to perpetrate fraud because it is in a position to directly or indirectly manipulate the accounting records and prepare fraudulent financial reports. In most cases, fraudulent financial reporting also involves some management override of controls. For example, management may manipulate accounting estimates that are normally made and approved by others, leading to misstated financial results.

Because of the characteristics of fraud, particularly those involving concealment through collusion; withheld, misrepresented, or falsified documentation; and the ability of management to override or instruct others to override controls, an auditor may unknowingly rely on audit evidence that appears to be valid, but in fact is false and fraudulent.

The Fraud Risk Identification Process

Figure 3–3 presents a diagram of the fraud risk identification process. The first part of the process is the inputs—the sources of information used to identify risks. Within this first part of the process the auditor should perform

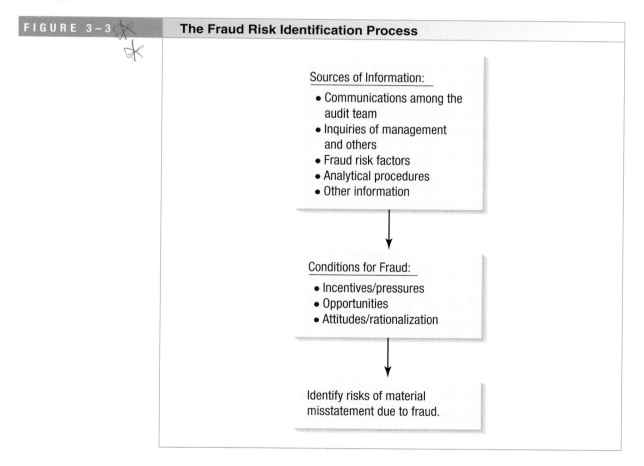

FIGURE 3–3   The Fraud Risk Identification Process

the following steps to obtain information to identify the risks of material misstatement due to fraud:

- Discussion among the audit team members regarding the risks of material misstatement due to fraud.
- Inquire of management and others about their views on the risks of fraud and how it is addressed.
- Consider any unusual or unexpected relationships that have been identified in performing analytical procedures in planning the audit.
- Understand the client's period-end closing process and investigate unexpected period-end adjustments.
- Consider whether one or more fraud risk factors exist that should be considered in evaluating the risk of material misstatement due to fraud.
- Consider any other information that might indicate the possibility of fraud.

The second part of the process is consideration of this information in terms of the presence of the three conditions for fraud: incentives/pressures, opportunities, and attitudes/rationalizations. The last part of the process considers the identified risks of material misstatement due to fraud and how the auditor responds to the presence of such risks. The following sections provide more detail on this process.

Discussion among the Audit Team

In planning the audit, the engagement partner or manager should communicate with members of the audit team regarding the potential for material misstatement due to fraud. The engagement partner or manager should determine which audit team members should be included in the communication, how it should occur, and the extent of the communication. The objectives of this communication are to

- Share their insights about the entity and its environment and the entity's business risks.
- Provide an opportunity for the team members to discuss how and where the entity might be susceptible to fraud.
- Emphasize the importance of maintaining the proper state of mind (referred to as *professional skepticism*) throughout the audit regarding the potential for material misstatement due to fraud.

The discussions among engagement team members should include a consideration of the known external and internal influences that might create incentives/pressures for management or others to commit fraud and the opportunities to do so. Engagement team members should be encouraged to communicate and share information obtained throughout the audit that may affect the assessment of risks of material misstatement or the auditor's responses to those risks.

The auditor should conduct the audit with professional skepticism. Professional skepticism is an attitude that includes a questioning mind and a critical assessment of audit evidence. The auditor should conduct the engagement assuming there is a possibility that a material misstatement due to fraud could be present, regardless of any prior beliefs or past experience with the entity and regardless of the auditor's belief about management's honesty and integrity.

Inquiries of Management and Others

Inquiry of management is an important source of evidence. Some of the inquiry would take place when the auditor obtains an understanding of the entity and its environment. The auditor should inquire about management's knowledge of fraud within the entity. The auditor should also understand the programs and controls that management has established to mitigate specific risk factors and how well management monitors those programs and controls.

The entity's audit committee (see Chapter 5 for a detailed discussion of the audit committee) should assume an active role in oversight of the assessment of the risk of fraud and the policies and procedures management has established. The auditor should obtain an understanding of how the audit committee exercises its oversight activities, including direct inquiry of audit committee members. When the entity has an internal audit function, the auditor also should inquire of internal audit personnel about their assessment of the risk of fraud, including whether management has satisfactorily responded to internal audit findings during the year.

The auditor should also consider inquiries from others within the entity and third parties. For example, the auditor should consider making inquiries of personnel within the entity, such as operating personnel not directly involved in the financial reporting process; employees with different levels of authority within the entity; and employees involved in initiating, processing, or recording complex or unusual transactions. The auditor also may consider making inquiries of third parties, such as vendors, customers, or regulators. Situations have arisen where the auditors failed to detect a massive financial accounting fraud. After the fraud was exposed, people who knew or were suspicious of wrong doing said that they would have told the auditors about the illegal activities, but "the auditor never asked." It can be uncomfortable to inquire about potentially fraudulent activities; however, it is much more uncomfortable to fail to detect a material fraud.

Fraud Risk Factors

As indicated earlier in this chapter, fraud risk factors related to fraudulent financial reporting and misappropriation of assets can be classified among the three conditions generally present when fraud exists:

- An *incentive/pressure* to perpetrate fraud.
- An *opportunity* to carry out the fraud.
- An *attitude/rationalization* to justify the fraudulent action.

Fraudulent Financial Reporting   Tables 3–6 to 3–8 present the risk factors related to each category of conditions for the potential for fraudulent financial reporting. Table 3–6 contains numerous risk factors that, if present, may suggest that management and others have incentives to manipulate financial reporting. For example, the entity may be facing increased competition that results in declining profit margins. Similarly, in the high-technology

TABLE 3–6	Risk Factors Relating to Incentives/Pressures

a. Financial stability or profitability is threatened by economic, industry, or entity operating conditions, such as (or as indicated by)
- High degree of competition or market saturation, accompanied by declining margins.
- High vulnerability to rapid changes, such as changes in technology, product obsolescence, or interest rates.
- Significant declines in customer demand and increasing business failures in either the industry or overall economy.
- Operating losses making the threat of bankruptcy, foreclosure, or hostile takeover imminent.
- Recurring negative cash flows from operations or an inability to generate cash flows from operations while reporting earnings and earnings growth.
- Rapid growth or unusual profitability, especially compared with that of other companies in the same industry.
- New accounting, statutory, or regulatory requirements.

b. Excessive pressure exists for management to meet requirements or expectations of third parties due to
- Profitability or trend level expectations of investment analysts, institutional investors, significant creditors, or other external parties (particularly expectations that are unduly aggressive or unrealistic) including expectations created by management in, for example, overly optimistic press releases or annual report messages.
- Need to obtain additional debt or equity financing to stay competitive—including financing of major research and development or capital expenditures.
- Marginal ability to meet exchange listing requirements or debt repayment or other debt covenant requirements.
- Perceived or real adverse effects of reporting poor financial results on significant pending transactions, such as business combinations or contract awards.

c. Management or the board of directors' personal financial situation is threatened by the entity's financial performance arising from the following:
- Significant financial interests in the entity.
- Significant portions of their compensation (e.g., bonuses, stock options) being contingent upon achieving aggressive targets for stock price, operating results, financial position, or cash flow.
- Personal guarantees of significant debts of the entity.

d. There is excessive pressure on management or operating personnel to meet financial targets set up by the board of directors or management, including sales or profitability incentive goals.

sector, rapid changes in technology can affect the profitability and the fair market value of products. Entities that have recurring operating losses and negative cash flow from operations may face bankruptcy, foreclosure, or takeover. In each of these situations, management may have incentives to manipulate reported earnings. Management (or the board of directors) may also be facing pressures to maintain the entity's reported earnings to meet analysts' forecasts because their bonuses or personal wealth is tied to the entity's stock price (see Exhibit 3–1).

Management must also have the opportunity to commit the fraud. Table 3–7 lists the opportunities that may be available to management or the board of directors to perpetuate fraudulent financial reporting. For example, assets, liabilities, revenues, or expenses may be based on subjective estimates that may be difficult for the auditor to corroborate. Two examples of such situations are the recognition of income on long-term contracts when the percentage of completion method is used and establishing the amount of loan loss reserves for a financial institution. Another opportunity for fraudulent financial reporting is when a single person or small group dominates management. Dominance by one individual may lead to processing accounting transactions that are not consistent with the entity's controls.

EXHIBIT 3–1	**Nortel Networks Terminates CEO, CFO, and Controller**

On April 28, 2004, Nortel Networks fired its CEO, CFO, and controller "with cause." The SEC had been looking into Nortel's use of reserve accounts and trying to determine if Nortel released those reserves back into earnings for legitimate reasons. Speculation suggests that Nortel's problems may have arisen as employees sought ways to participate in a bonus program tied to Nortel's 2003 turnaround after years of heavy losses. Known within the company as the "Return to Profitability" bonus program, Nortel paid out $300 million in employee bonuses in 2003, with approximately $80 million paid to senior executives. One analyst stated that management was too aggressive with accounting accruals in order to show profitability and receive bonuses.

Sources: Nortel Networks, News Release. Nortel Networks Announces William Owens as New President and CEO (www.nortelnetworks.com), and M. Heinzl, D. Solomon, and J. S. Lublin, "Nortel Board Fires CEO and Others," *The Wall Street Journal* (April 29, 2004), pp. A3, A6.

Risk factors reflective of attitudes/rationalizations by board members, management, or employees may allow them to engage in and/or justify fraudulent financial reporting. Table 3–8 lists a number of attitudes or rationalizations that may be used to justify fraudulent financial reporting. For example, the entity may have weak ethical standards for management

TABLE 3–7	**Risk Factors Relating to Opportunities**

a. The nature of the industry or the entity's operations provide opportunities to engage in fraudulent financial reporting due to
  - Significant related-party transactions not in the ordinary course of business or with related entities not audited or audited by another firm.
  - A strong financial presence or ability to dominate a certain industry sector that allows the entity to dictate terms or conditions to suppliers or customers that may result in inappropriate or non-arm's-length transactions.
  - Assets, liabilities, revenues, or expenses based on significant estimates that involve subjective judgments or uncertainties that are difficult to corroborate.
  - Significant, unusual, or highly complex transactions, especially those close to year-end that pose difficult "substance over form" questions.
  - Significant operations located or conducted across international borders where differing business environments and cultures exist.
  - Significant bank accounts or subsidiary or branch operations in tax-haven jurisdictions for which there appears to be no clear business justification.

b. There is ineffective monitoring of management due to
  - Domination of management by a single person or small group (in a non-owner-managed business) without compensating controls.
  - Ineffective board of director or audit committee oversight over the financial reporting process and internal control.

c. There is a complex or unstable organizational structure as evidenced by—
  - Difficulty in determining the organization or individuals that have controlling interest in the entity.
  - Overly complex organizational structure involving unusual legal entities or managerial lines of authority.
  - High turnover of senior management, counsel, or board members.

d. Internal control components are deficient due to
  - Inadequate monitoring of controls, including automated controls and controls over interim financial reporting (where external reporting is required).
  - High turnover rates or employment of ineffective accounting, internal audit, or information technology staff.
  - Ineffective accounting and information systems including situations involving reportable conditions.

TABLE 3-8	Risk Factors Relating to Attitudes/Rationalizations

- Ineffective communication implementation, support, and enforcement of the entity's values or ethical standards by management, or the communication of inappropriate values or ethical standards.
- Nonfinancial management's excessive participation in, or preoccupation with, the selection of accounting principles or the determination of significant estimates.
- Known history of violations of securities laws or other laws and regulations, or claims against the entity, its senior management, or board members alleging fraud or violations of laws and regulations.
- Excessive interest by management in maintaining or increasing the entity's stock price or earnings trend.
- A practice by management of committing to analysts, creditors, and other third parties to achieve aggressive or unrealistic forecasts.
- Management failing to correct known reportable conditions on a timely basis.
- An interest by management in pursuing inappropriate means to minimize reported earnings for tax-motivated reasons.
- Recurring attempts by management to justify marginal or inappropriate accounting on the basis of materiality.
- The relationship between management and the current or predecessor auditor is strained as exhibited by
  — Frequent disputes with the current or predecessor auditor on accounting, auditing, or reporting matters.
  — Unreasonable demands on the auditor such as unreasonable time constraints regarding the completion of the audit or the issuance of the auditor's reports.
  — Formal or informal restrictions on the auditor that inappropriately limit access to people or information or the ability to communicate effectively with the board of directors or audit committee.
  — Domineering management behavior in dealing with the auditor, especially involving attempts to influence the scope of the auditor's work.

behavior or poor communication channels for reporting such behavior. Management may fail to correct known reportable conditions or use inappropriate accounting. Lastly, management may have strained relationships with its predecessor and current auditors.

Misappropriation of Assets

Risk factors that relate to misstatements arising from misappropriation of assets also are classified along the three conditions generally present when fraud exists: incentives/pressures, opportunities, and attitudes/rationalizations. Some of the risk factors related to misstatements arising from fraudulent financial reporting also may be present when misstatements arising from misappropriation of assets exist (see Exhibit 3–2). Tables 3–9 to 3–11 present the risk factors related to each category of conditions for the potential of misappropriation of assets. Table 3–9 presents incentives or pressures that might lead to misappropriated assets. For example, an employee may have financial problems that create an incentive to misappropriate the cash. Similarly, there may be adverse relations between the entity and employees due to anticipated employee layoffs.

Table 3–10 presents a list of risk factors for the opportunity to misappropriate assets. For example, in order for the employee who has financial problems to misappropriate cash, he or she must have access to the cash. This is likely to occur only when there is inadequate segregation of duties or poor oversight by personnel responsible for the asset. An important factor listed in Table 3–10 is the lack of a policy requiring a mandatory vacation for personnel responsible for key control activities. If an individual has misappropriated assets and there is no mandatory vacation policy, he or she can continue to cover the shortage. With a mandatory vacation policy, another

EXHIBIT 3–2

TYCO: Misappropriation of Assets on a Grand Scale

TYCO International, Ltd., is a diversified manufacturing and service company. Throughout most of the 1990s and early 2000, TYCO grew rapidly through acquisitions. Its stock was a leading performer and its executives were some of the highest paid in the U.S.

Behind the scenes, however, TYCO's management (L. Dennis Kozlowski, chief executive officer; Mark H. Swartz, chief financial officer; and Mark A. Belnick, chief corporate counsel) was bilking the company of millions of dollars. The company said the improper conduct of its former management has damaged Tyco's reputation and credibility with investors, lenders, and others. While the amount of money improperly diverted by Tyco's senior executives is small in comparison with Tyco's total revenues and profits, it is very large by any other relevant comparison.

The company said that this pattern of improper and illegal activity occurred for at least five years prior to its discovery in June 2002 and that this activity was concealed from the board and its relevant committees. Three of the schemes used by the three executives to misappropriate assets included:

- **Relocation Programs.** Under the program, Mr. Kozlowski improperly borrowed approximately $61,690,628 in nonqualifying relocation loans to purchase real estate and other properties, Mr. Swartz borrowed approximately $33,097,925, and Mr. Belnick borrowed approximately $14,635,597.
- **The "TyCom Bonus" Misappropriation.** Mr. Kozlowski caused Tyco to pay a special, unapproved bonus to 51 employees who had relocation loans with the company to forgive the relocation loans totaling $56,415,037, and to pay compensation sufficient to discharge all of the tax liability due as a result of the forgiveness of those loans. The total gross wages paid by the company in this mortgage forgiveness program were $95,962,000, of which amount Mr. Kozlowski received $32,976,000 and Mr. Swartz received $16,611,000.
- **The Key Employee Loan (KEL) Program.** This program allowed certain executive officers to borrow money for purposes other than the payment of taxes due upon the vesting of restricted shares, or borrow in excess of the maximum amount they were permitted under the program. By the end of 2001, Mr. Kozlowski had taken over 200 KEL loans and his total borrowings over that time exceeded $250 million. Approximately 90% of Mr. Kozlowski's KEL loans were nonprogram loans, which he used to fund his personal lifestyle, including speculating in real estate, acquisition of antiques and furnishings for his properties, and the purchase and maintenance of his yacht. Mr. Swartz also borrowed millions in nonprogram loans. Like Mr. Kozlowski, Mr. Swartz used those unauthorized loans to purchase, develop, and speculate in real estate; to fund investments in various business ventures and partnerships; and for miscellaneous personal uses having nothing to do with the ownership of Tyco stock.

Sources: TYCO Press Release "TYCO files Form 8-K Report on Improper Conduct of Former Management" (September 17, 2002); Securities and Exchange Commission, Accounting and Auditing Enforcement Release No. 1627, "TYCO Former Executives L. Dennis Kozlowski, Mark H. Swartz and Mark A. Belnick Sued for Fraud"; and *Securities and Exchange Commission v. L. Dennis Kozlowski, Mark H. Swartz and Mark A. Belnick,* Complaint (September 11, 2002).

TABLE 3–9

Risk Factors Relating to Incentives/Pressures

a. Personal financial obligations may create pressure for management or employees with access to cash or other assets susceptible to theft to misappropriate those assets.

b. Adverse relationships between the entity and employees with access to cash or other assets susceptible to theft may motivate those employees to misappropriate those assets. For example, adverse relationships may be created by
- Known or anticipated future employee layoffs.
- Recent or anticipated changes to employee compensation or benefit plans.
- Promotions, compensation, or other rewards inconsistent with expectations.

TABLE 3–10	**Risk Factors Relating to Opportunities**

    a. Certain characteristics or circumstances may increase the susceptibility of assets to misappropriation. For example, opportunities to misappropriate assets increase when there are
- Large amounts of cash on hand or processed.
- Inventory items small in size, of high value, or in high demand.
- Easily convertible assets, such as bearer bonds, diamonds, or computer chips.
- Fixed assets that are small in size, marketable, or lacking observable identification of ownership.

    b. Inadequate internal control over assets may increase the susceptibility of misappropriation of those assets. For example, misappropriation of assets may exist because there is a(n)
- Inadequate segregation of duties or independent checks.
- Inadequate management oversight of employees responsible for assets (for example, inadequate supervision or monitoring of remote locations).
- Inadequate job applicant screening procedures relating to employees with access to assets.
- Inadequate record keeping with respect to assets.
- Inadequate system of authorization and approval of transactions (for example, in purchasing).
- Inadequate physical safeguards over cash, investments, inventory, or fixed assets.
- Lack of complete and timely reconciliation of assets.
- Lack of timely and appropriate documentation for transactions (for example, credits for merchandise returns).
- Lack of mandatory vacations for employees performing key control functions.
- Lack of management understanding of information technology, which allows information technology employees to perpetrate a misappropriation.
- Inadequate access controls over automated records.

TABLE 3–11	**Risk Factors Relating to Attitudes/Rationalizations**

- Disregard for the need for monitoring or reducing risks related to misappropriations of assets.
- Disregard for internal control over misappropriation of assets by overriding existing controls or by failing to correct known internal control deficiencies.
- Behavior indicating displeasure or dissatisfaction with the company or its treatment of the employee.
- Changes in behavior or lifestyle that may indicate assets have been misappropriated.

person would perform those duties and there would be a possibility that the misappropriation would be detected.

Table 3–11 lists risk factors that may be reflective of employee attitudes/rationalizations that allow them to justify misappropriating assets. For example, an employee who has access to assets susceptible to misappropriation may have a change in behavior or lifestyle that may indicate he or she has misappropriated assets.

The Auditor's Response to the Results of the Risk Assessments

    [LO 6]   Based on the assessment of the entity's business risks and the risk of material misstatement due to error or fraud, the auditor should decide what responses to take given the risk assessment. The main consideration for the auditor based on the assessed level of the risks of material misstatement is the nature, timing, and extent of audit procedures. The auditor should first determine overall responses to address the risks of material misstatement at the financial statement level. The assessment of the risks of material misstatement at the financial statement level is generally affected by the auditor's assessment of the control environment. If the entity's control environment is effective, the auditor can have more confidence in other aspects of internal control and the reliability of audit evidence generated internally within the entity.

The auditor next has to consider how to respond to the risks of misstatement at the assertion level. Figure 3–4 shows the relationship of the assessment of the risk of material misstatement to the design and performance of audit procedures. A distinction is made between high-risk and low-risk assertions. For *high-risk* assertions, the auditor should consider how material misstatements may occur and design and perform *extended* audit

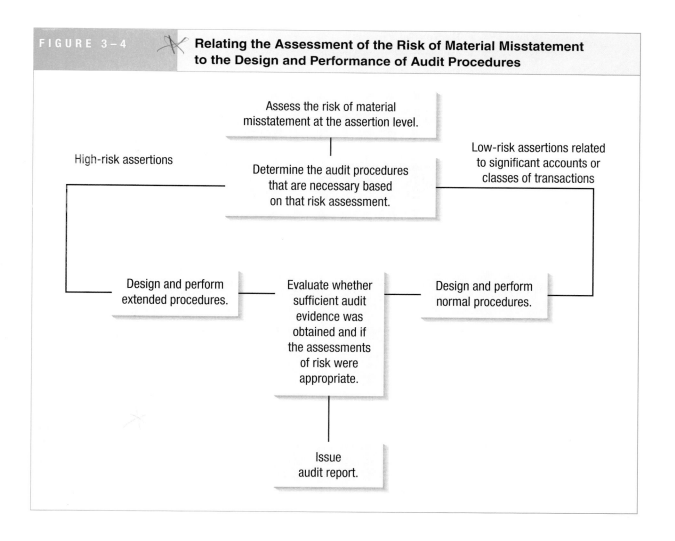

FIGURE 3–4   Relating the Assessment of the Risk of Material Misstatement to the Design and Performance of Audit Procedures

procedures to specifically address the potential misstatements. Examples of the types of items that may require extended audit procedures include:

- Assertions identified with fraud risk factors.
- Nonroutine or unsystematically processed transactions.
- Significant accounting estimates and judgments.
- Highly complex transactions.
- Application of new accounting standards.
- Revenue recognition in certain industries or for certain types of transactions.
- Industry specific issues.

For *low-risk* assertions, the auditor may not require procedures of an extended nature. Usually, low-risk assertions relate to routine processing of significant transactions whose characteristics often allow highly automated processing by IT with little or no manual intervention. Such transactions are likely to be

- Recurring.
- Objectively measurable.
- Processed in a similar way.

If the risk factor assessment indicates that fraud might be present, the auditor might respond as follows:

- Increase professional skepticism by questioning and critically assessing audit evidence.
- Assign more experienced auditors who have the knowledge, skill, and ability commensurate with the increased risk of the engagement.
- Consider management's selection and application of significant accounting policies, particularly those related to recognizing revenue, valuing assets, or capitalizing versus expensing.
- Modify the nature, timing, and extent of audit procedures to obtain more reliable evidence and use increased sample sizes or more extensive analytical procedures.

Evaluation of Audit Test Results

[LO 7]   At the completion of the financial statement audit, the auditor should consider whether the accumulated results of audit procedures affect the assessments of the entity's business risks and the risk of material misstatement due to error or fraud. The auditor should aggregate the total uncorrected misstatements that were detected and determine if they cause the financial statements to be materially misstated. If the auditor concludes that the total misstatements cause the financial statements to be materially misstated, the auditor should request management to eliminate the material misstatement. If management does not eliminate the material misstatement, the auditor should issue a qualified or adverse opinion. On the other hand, if the uncorrected total misstatements do not cause the financial statements to be materially misstated, the auditor should issue an unqualified or "clean" report.

If the auditor has determined that the misstatement is or may be the result of fraud, and either has determined that the effect could be material to the financial statements or has been unable to evaluate whether the effect is material, the auditor should

- Attempt to obtain audit evidence to determine whether, in fact, material fraud has occurred and, if so, its effect.
- Consider the implications for other aspects of the audit.
- Discuss the matter and the approach to further investigation with an appropriate level of management that is at least one level above those involved in committing the fraud and with senior management.
- If appropriate, suggest that the client consult with legal counsel.

If the results of the audit tests indicate a significant risk of fraud, the auditor should consider withdrawing from the engagement and communicating the reasons for withdrawal to the audit committee or others with equivalent authority and responsibility.

Documentation of the Auditor's Risk Assessment and Response

[LO 8] The auditor has extensive documentation requirements for understanding the entity and its environment, the consideration of fraud, and responding to assessed risks. The auditor should document the risk of material misstatement for all material accounts and classes of transactions in terms of the related assertions. The level of risk may be described quantitatively or nonquantitatively (high, medium, or low). Exhibit 3–3 shows the use of a questionnaire to document the nature of the entity. Other areas that require documentation include the following:

- The nature and results of the communication among engagement personnel that occurred in planning the audit regarding the risks of material misstatement due to fraud.
- The steps performed in obtaining knowledge about the entity's business and its environment. The documentation should include
  - *a.* The risks identified.
  - *b.* An evaluation of management's response to such risks.
  - *c.* The auditor's assessment of the risk of error or fraud after considering the entity's response.
- The nature, timing, and extent of the procedures performed in response to the risks of material misstatement due to fraud and the results of that work.
- Fraud risks or other conditions that caused the auditor to believe that additional audit procedures or other responses were required to address such risks or other conditions.
- The nature of the communications about fraud made to management, the audit committee, and others.

EXHIBIT 3–3

A Partial Questionnaire for Documenting the Understanding of EarthWear Clothiers and Its Environment

CLIENT NAME: EARTHWEAR CLOTHIERS
Entity and Environment Category: Nature of the Entity
Year ended: December 31, 2005

Completed by: _____
Reviewed by: _____

Risk Factors	*Description/Response*	*Any Remaining Risk*
What are the entity's major sources of revenue, including the nature of its products and/or services?	EarthWear Clothiers generates revenue mainly through the sale of high-quality clothing for outdoor sports, such as hiking, skiing, fly-fishing, and white-water kayaking. The company's product lines also include casual clothes, accessories, shoes, and soft luggage. These sales are made mainly through the company's toll-free number and over its Internet websites. In 2005, Internet sales accounted for 21 percent of total revenue.	No. The company uses conservative methods to record revenue and provides an adequate reserve for returned merchandise.
Who are the entity's key customers?	The company's key customers are the 21.5 million persons on its mailing list, approximately 7 million of whom are viewed as "current customers" because they have purchased from the company in the last 24 months. Market research as of January 2004 indicates that approximately 50 percent of customers are in the 35–54 age group and had a median income of $62,000. Almost two-thirds are in professional or managerial positions.	No.
Who are the entity's key suppliers?	During 2005, the company had purchase orders for merchandise from about 300 domestic and foreign manufacturers, including intermediaries (agents). One manufacturer and one intermediary accounted for about 14 and 29 percent of the company's received merchandise dollars, respectively, in 2005. In 2005, about 80 percent of the merchandise was imported, mainly from Asia, Central America, Mexico, South America, and Europe. The remaining 20 percent was made in the United States. The company will continue to take advantage of worldwide sourcing without sacrificing customer service or quality standards.	Yes. The company would be subject to some risk in finding alternative sourcing if this manufacturer and/or intermediary experiences prolonged work stoppages or economic problems. The availability and cost of certain foreign products may be affected by United States and other countries' trade policies, economic events, and the value of the U.S. dollar relative to foreign currencies.
What is the entity's organizational structure?	The company has a well-developed organizational structure with clear lines of authority among the various operating departments and staff functions. The organizational structure is appropriate for EarthWear's activities.	No.
Where are its major locations?	Boise, Idaho, is the main corporate location. EarthWear also has phone and distribution centers in the United Kingdom, Germany, and Japan. During 2005, EarthWear expanded its global Internet presence by launching sites in France, Italy, Ireland, and several eastern European countries.	Yes. France and Italy have restrictive trade laws where local companies get a certain degree of protection from the government when their markets are threatened. Political instability in the eastern European countries could affect EarthWear's sales activities in these countries.

(continued)

EXHIBIT 3-3	**(Continued)**	
Risk Factors	*Description/Response*	*Any Remaining Risk*
What are the entity's major assets?	The major assets of the company are inventory; property, plant, and equipment; and its customer mailing list.	No.
What are the entity's major liabilities?	The company has no long-term debt. However, it maintains a line of credit for financing purchases during the peak purchasing season.	No. The company has adequate cash flow to meet its current obligations.
What are the entity's financial characteristics including financing sources and current and prospective financial condition?	The company uses its line of credit to meet its normal financing activities. Overall the company's financial condition is good.	No.
Are there any potential related parties?	No.	No.
Are there any individually significant events and transactions such as acquisitions or disposals of subsidiaries, businesses, or product lines during the year?	The expansion of the company's Internet presence to France, Italy, Ireland, and several eastern European countries.	Yes. Restrictive trade laws and the potential for political instability in the eastern European countries.
Does the entity have any major uncertainties or contingencies?	No.	No.

Communications about Fraud to Management, the Audit Committee, and Others

[LO 9] Whenever the auditor has found evidence that a fraud may exist, that matter should be brought to the attention of an appropriate level of management. Fraud involving senior management and fraud that causes a material misstatement of the financial statements should be reported directly to the audit committee of the board of directors. In addition, the auditor should reach an understanding with the audit committee regarding the expected nature and extent of communications about misappropriations perpetrated by lower-level employees.

The disclosure of fraud to parties other than the client's senior management and its audit committee ordinarily is not part of the auditor's responsibility and ordinarily would be precluded by the auditor's ethical or legal obligations of confidentiality. The auditor should recognize, however, that in the following circumstances a duty to disclose outside the entity may exist:

- To comply with certain legal and regulatory requirements.
- To a successor auditor when the successor makes inquiries in accordance with AU 315, Communications between Predecessor and Successor Auditors.
- In response to a subpoena.
- To a funding agency or other specified agency in accordance with requirements for the audits of entities that receive governmental financial assistance.

Figure 3–5 presents on overview of the auditor's requirements for fraud.

FIGURE 3-5

Key Requirements Summary For SAS 99—Consideration of Fraud in a Financial Statement Audit

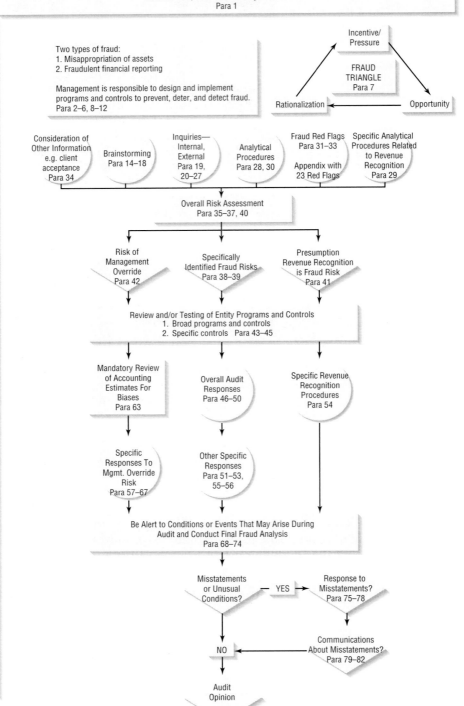

AUDITOR RESPONSIBILITY-Plan and perform audit to obtain reasonable assurance the financial statements are free of material misstatement, whether caused by fraud or error.
Para 1

Two types of fraud:
1. Misappropriation of assets
2. Fraudulent financial reporting

Management is responsible to design and implement programs and controls to prevent, deter, and detect fraud.
Para 2–6, 8–12

Incentive/Pressure

FRAUD TRIANGLE
Para 7

Rationalization ← → Opportunity

PROFESSIONAL SKEPTICISM ——Para 13

PROFESSIONAL SKEPTICISM——>MINDSET THAT FRAUD IS POSSIBILITY REGARDLESS OF PAST EXPERIENCE<——

Consideration of Other Information e.g. client acceptance Para 34

Brainstorming Para 14–18

Inquiries—Internal, External Para 19, 20–27

Analytical Procedures Para 28, 30

Fraud Red Flags Para 31–33
Appendix with 23 Red Flags

Specific Analytical Procedures Related to Revenue Recognition Para 29

Overall Risk Assessment
Para 35–37, 40

Risk of Management Override Para 42

Specifically Identified Fraud Risks Para 38–39

Presumption Revenue Recognition is Fraud Risk Para 41

Review and/or Testing of Entity Programs and Controls
1. Broad programs and controls
2. Specific controls   Para 43–45

Mandatory Review of Accounting Estimates For Biases Para 63

Overall Audit Responses Para 46–50

Specific Revenue Recognition Procedures Para 54

Specific Responses To Mgmt. Override Risk Para 57–67

Other Specific Responses Para 51–53, 55–56

Be Alert to Conditions or Events That May Arise During Audit and Conduct Final Fraud Analysis
Para 68–74

Misstatements or Unusual Conditions?

— YES →

Response to Misstatements? Para 75–78

NO

Communications About Misstatements? Para 79–82

Audit Opinion

Limitations of the Audit Risk Model

[LO 10]   Auditing standards provide for the use of the audit risk model as a way of ensuring that the risk of issuing materially misstated financial statements is kept to an acceptably low level. However, this model has a number of limitations that must be considered by auditors and their firms.[2]

The audit risk model is a planning tool. If an auditor uses the model to *revise* an audit plan or to *evaluate* audit results, the *actual* level of audit risk may be greater than the audit risk indicated by the formula. This may occur because the model assumes that the components (*IR*, *CR*, and *DR*) are *independent* of one another as indicated by the multiplicative form of the model. However, in practice, the risk of a material misstatement (*IR*) occurring may be a function of the client's internal controls (*CR*). Thus, inherent risk may depend on control risk. In practice, some public accounting firms make a *combined risk assessment* for *IR* and *CR*.

Other limitations may also be present. Because the auditor *assesses* inherent risk and control risk, such assessments may be higher or lower than the *actual* inherent risk and control risk that exist for the client. Such differences can affect the determination of detection risk and the achieved audit risk. The audit risk model also does not specifically consider the possibility of auditor error.

The point of this discussion is to alert the reader to the possible limitations of the audit risk model. The model, however, does serve as an important tool that auditors can use for planning an audit engagement.

Materiality

[LO 11]   The auditor's consideration of materiality on an audit is a matter of *professional judgment*. As discussed in Chapter 2, materiality is assessed in terms of the potential effect of a misstatement on decisions made by a reasonable user of the financial statements. This focus arises from the FASB's Statement of Financial Accounting Concepts No. 2, "Qualitative Characteristics of Accounting Information," which provides the following definition:

> **Materiality** is the magnitude of an omission or misstatement of accounting information that, in the light of surrounding circumstances, makes it probable that the judgment of a reasonable person relying on the information would have been changed or influenced by the omission or misstatement.

This definition in the accounting literature is equivalent to the courts' determination of materiality in interpreting the federal securities laws. For example, the U.S. Supreme Court stated that a fact is material if there is "a substantial likelihood that the . . . fact would have been viewed by the

---

[2]See B. E. Cushing and J. K. Loebbecke, "Analytical Approaches to Audit Risk: A Survey and Analysis," *Auditing: A Journal of Practice and Theory* (Fall 1983), pp. 23–41; W. R. Kinney, Jr., "A Note on Compounding Probabilities in Auditing," *Auditing: A Journal of Practice and Theory* (Spring 1983), pp. 13–22; and W. R. Kinney, Jr., "Achieved Audit Risk and the Audit Outcome Space," *Auditing: A Journal of Practice and Theory* (Suppl. 1989), pp. 67–84, for more detailed discussions of the limitations of the audit risk model.

reasonable investor as having significantly altered the 'total mix' of information made available."[3] Both of these perspectives require that the auditor assess the amount of misstatement that could affect a reasonable user's decisions.

Professional standards provide little specific guidance on how to assess what is material to a reasonable user. As a result, the AICPA and auditing firms have developed policies and procedures to assist auditors in establishing materiality. The following sections present an approach to assessing materiality. The presentation is based on the general approach provided by auditing standards and to some extent on the more specific policies and procedures suggested by the AICPA.[4] While the policies and procedures of individual CPA firms may differ in some respects, the approach presented here provides the reader with a basic framework for understanding the consideration of materiality in an audit.

In establishing materiality for an audit, the auditor should consider both quantitative and qualitative aspects of the engagement. Although materiality may be planned and implemented using a quantitative approach, the qualitative aspects of misstatements of small amounts may also materially affect the users of financial statements. For example, a client may illegally pay a commissioned agent to secure a sales contract. While the amount of the illegal payment may be immaterial to the financial statements, the disclosure of the illegal act may result in loss of the contract and substantial penalties that may be material. The next section presents an approach to applying materiality, which is then followed by an example.

Steps in Applying Materiality

[LO 12]

Figure 3–6 presents the three major steps in the application of materiality to an audit. Steps 1 and 2 are normally performed early in the engagement as part of planning the audit (see Figure 1–6 in Chapter 1). Step 3 is performed usually just prior to, or when the auditor evaluates the evidence at the completion of the audit to determine if it supports the fair presentation of the financial statements (again, refer to Figure 1–6).

Step 1: Establish a Preliminary Judgment about Materiality   The auditor should establish a preliminary judgment about materiality. While auditing standards do not require that the auditor quantify and document this judgment, it is common to document at least a range in practice, and we believe that such an approach offers benefits to public accounting firms and their personnel. By quantifying materiality, the audit team is better able to plan the scope of the audit and evaluate the results of the audit tests.

The preliminary judgment about materiality is the maximum amount by which the auditor believes the financial statements could be misstated and still *not* affect the decisions of reasonable users. Materiality, however, is a relative, not an absolute, concept. For example, $5,000 might be considered highly material for a small sole proprietorship, but this amount would clearly be immaterial for a large multinational corporation. Thus, the

---

[3]*TSC Industries* v. *Northway, Inc.*, 426 U.S. 438, 449 (1976).

[4]American Institute of Certified Public Accountants, Audit Guide, *Audit Sampling* (New York: AICPA, 2001).

FIGURE 3-6

Steps in Applying Materiality on an Audit

Step 1 — Establish a preliminary judgment about materiality.

Step 2 — Determine tolerable misstatement.

Step 3 — Estimate likely misstatements and compare totals to the preliminary judgment about materiality.

relative size of the company being audited affects the preliminary judgment about materiality.

In specifying materiality, an auditor should establish a base (or bases) that, when multiplied by a percentage factor, determines the initial quantitative judgment about materiality. The following quantitative bases are used for establishing materiality:

- Total assets.
- Total revenues.
- Net income before taxes.
- Net income from continuing operations.
- Gross profit.
- Average of three years' net income before taxes.

The resulting materiality amount can then be adjusted for any qualitative factors that may be relevant to the engagement (refer to Table 3–12).

Total assets, total revenues, or some form of net income are frequently used by auditors when establishing materiality. When net income before taxes is relatively stable, predictable, and representative of the entity's size, a rule of thumb to determine overall financial statement materiality that is commonly used in practice is 3 to 5 percent of net income before taxes. In determining where in the range to establish materiality, the auditor would generally use a percentage at the lower end of the range if any of the following factors are present:

- First-year engagement.
- Known material weaknesses in controls.
- Significant management turnover.

TABLE 3–12	**Qualitative Factors That May Affect Establishing and Evaluating Materiality**

Establishing the preliminary judgment about materiality (Step 1):
- Material misstatements in prior years.
- Potential for fraud or illegal acts.
- Small amounts may violate covenants in a loan agreement.
- Small amounts may affect the trend in earnings.
- Small amounts may cause entity to miss forecasted revenue or earnings.

Evaluating the materiality of unadjusted misstatements (Step 3):
- Whether the misstatement masks a change in earnings or trends.
- Whether the misstatement hides a failure to meet analysts' consensus expectations.
- Whether the misstatement changes a loss into income or vice versa.
- Whether the misstatement concerns a segment or other portion of the business that has been portrayed as playing a significant role in the operations or profitability of the entity.
- Whether the misstatement affects compliance with regulatory requirements.
- Whether the misstatement affects compliance with loan covenants or other contractual requirements.
- Whether the misstatement increases management's compensation.
- Whether the misstatement involves the concealment of an unlawful transaction.
- Whether the misstatement may result in a significant positive or negative market reaction.
- Whether small intentional misstatements are part of actions to "manage" earnings.

- Unusually high market pressures.
- Higher than normal fraud risk.
- Higher than normal risk of bankruptcy in the near term.

This amount is often referred to as *planning materiality*. Auditors may also decide to use a lower amount because of qualitative factors such as those listed in Table 3–12 and to allow for some aggregation of potential misstatements across accounts.

If current year pretax income is not stable, predictable, or representative of an entity's size, auditors might use an average of the previous year's income or another base. An advantage of using other bases such as total assets or total revenues is that for many companies these factors are more stable from year to year than net income before taxes. Difficulties arise in using net income as a base when the entity is close to breaking even or experiencing a loss. For example, suppose that an entity has net income before taxes of $3,000,000 one year and the auditor decides that 5 percent of that amount, $150,000, would be material. The scope of the audit in that year would be based on a preliminary judgment about materiality of $150,000. Suppose, in the following year, the entity's net income before taxes falls to $250,000 due to a temporary decrease in sales prices for its products. If the auditor uses the 5 percent factor, the preliminary judgment about materiality would be $12,500 ($250,000 × .05), and a much more extensive audit would be required. Thus, with fluctuating net income, using another base may be more feasible.

Current accounting and auditing standards do *not* provide any specific materiality guidelines for a number of reasons. First, it is difficult, if not impossible, to assess what is material to the diverse groups of users (such as investors, creditors, employees, and government agencies) that rely on financial statements. Second, auditors are unable to agree among themselves on what is material. Finally, some auditors seem reluctant to quantify materiality due

EXHIBIT 3–4

Worksheet for Calculating the Preliminary Judgment about Materiality (Planning Materiality)

Client: *EarthWear Clothiers*
Balance sheet date: *December 31, 2005*
Identify base amount:
    Base amount: $950,484,000 (the greater of total assets or total revenues)
Calculating planning materiality:
    $826,000 + [650,484,000 × .00145] = $1,769,000 (rounded)
    (Planning   (Excess)   (Factor)   (Preliminary judgment
    Materiality)   about materiality)
Use the following table to determine the percentage and additional amount to be used to calculate planning materiality.

Materiality Table*

Larger of Total Revenues or Total Assets Is:

Over	But not Over	Planning Materiality Is:	+	Factor	×	Excess Over
$ 0	$ 30 thousand	$ 0	+	.0593	×	$ 0
30 thousand	100 thousand	1,780	+	.0312	×	30 thousand
100 thousand	300 thousand	3,960	+	.0215	×	100 thousand
300 thousand	1 million	8,260	+	.0145	×	300 thousand
1 million	3 million	18,400	+	.00995	×	1 million
3 million	10 million	38,300	+	.00674	×	3 million
10 million	30 million	85,500	+	.00461	×	10 million
30 million	100 million	178,000	+	.00312	×	30 million
100 million	300 million	396,000	+	.00215	×	100 million
300 million	1 billion	826,000	+	.00145	×	300 million
1 billion	3 billion	1,840,000	+	.000995	×	1 billion
3 billion	10 billion	3,830,000	+	.000674	×	3 billion
10 billion	30 billion	8,550,000	+	.000461	×	10 billion
30 billion	100 billion	17,800,000	+	.000312	×	30 billion
100 billion	300 billion	39,600,000	+	.000215	×	100 billion
300 billion	. . .	82,600,000	+	.000148	×	300 billion

*The amounts used in this table are taken from Appendix C of the AICPA's Audit Guide, *Audit Sampling* (New York: AICPA, 2001.)

to litigation. As a result, some CPA firms provide general guidelines that allow their auditors considerable leeway in establishing materiality, while other firms provide detailed quantitative guidelines. Exhibit 3–4 provides an example of a materiality worksheet that can be used for establishing a preliminary judgment about materiality. This worksheet is adopted from the materiality worksheet included in the AICPA audit guide.[5]

This worksheet has two bases: total assets and total revenues. The auditor first enters the larger of total assets or total revenues in the worksheet. The amount of planning materiality is selected from the materiality table and then adjusted by the appropriate percentage factor. The materiality table contains a set of percentages that decrease as the size of the entity increases. This calculation results in the initial quantitative estimate of planning materiality. This amount may then be increased or decreased based on qualitative factors that are relevant to the audit (see Table 3–12). For example, planning materiality may be increased based on favorable qualitative factors, such as

---

[5]AICPA, Audit Guide, *Audit Sampling* (New York: AICPA, 2001).

past audit history (few misstatements in prior years, low potential for fraud or illegal acts, no possibility of violating debt covenants), strong financial condition, or sound economic conditions in the entity's industry. Conversely, unfavorable qualitative factors, such as numerous misstatements in prior years, depressed industry conditions, or high possibility of violating debt covenants, may result in a decrease in planning materiality.

Step 2: Determine Tolerable Misstatement   Step 2 involves determining tolerable misstatement based on planning materiality. Tolerable misstatement is the amount of planning materiality that is allocated to an account or class of transactions. An *account balance* represents an individual line item on the financial statements, such as accounts receivable or inventory. A *class of transactions* refers to a type of transaction processed by the client's accounting system, such as revenue or purchase transactions. The purpose of allocating a portion of the preliminary judgment about materiality is to plan the scope of audit procedures for the individual account balance or class of transactions. Because of the many factors involved, there is no required or optimal method for allocating materiality to an account balance or class of transactions. The process can be done judgmentally or using some formal quantitative approach.[6]

As with overall materiality, there are qualitative factors that must be considered in determining tolerable misstatement. Examples of qualitative factors auditors would consider when determining tolerable misstatement for an account include the size and complexity of the account, the importance of changes in the account to key performance indicators, debt covenants, and meeting published forecasts or estimates. In conjunction with qualitative factors, common computational benchmarks used in practice to determine tolerable misstatement are 2 to 15 percent of the account (but never greater than materiality) or 50 to 75 percent of preliminary or planning materiality. Obviously, these approaches result in an allocation of combined tolerable misstatement that is greater than materiality. There are a number of reasons why allocating combined tolerable misstatement greater than materiality makes sense from an audit planning perspective:

- Not all accounts will be misstated by the full amount of their tolerable misstatement allocation.
- Audits of the individual accounts are conducted simultaneously. In other words, for all but the smallest of audit clients, the audit team will be made up of several auditors who are testing different accounts at the same time. If accounts were audited sequentially, unadjusted misstatements observed during testing would count against materiality and theoretically the auditor could carry the unused portion of materiality to the next account and so forth. The simple benchmarks such as 50 to 75 percent of materiality have proven to be a useful way to determine tolerable misstatement for planning purposes.

---

[6]For an example of a quantitative approach to allocating the preliminary judgment about materiality, see G. R. Zuber, R. K. Elliott, W. R. Kinney, Jr., and J. J. Leisenring, "Using Materiality in Audit Planning," *Journal of Accountancy* (March 1983), pp. 42–55.

- Materiality as a percentage of large accounts, such as inventory, accounts receivable, revenues, or plant, property and equipment, is often a very small fraction of the account (less than 2 percent). By using a tolerable misstatement percentage that is considerably less than materiality, the scope of planned auditor procedures will be sufficiently precise to identify significant misstatements.

- When control weaknesses or misstatements are identified in an account, the auditors typically perform additional procedures in that, and related, accounts. Thus, the actual testing will often achieve a much smaller margin for misstatement than planned tolerable misstatement.

- Overall financial statement materiality serves as a "safety net." If individual unadjusted misstatements are less than tolerable misstatement, but aggregate to an amount greater than materiality, then the auditor cannot accept the financial statements as presented fairly in accordance with GAAP. If this occurs, (1) the audit client needs to make adjustments to decrease the unadjusted misstatements below materiality, (2) the auditor needs to perform more testing, and/or (3) the auditor will issue a qualified or adverse opinion.

Taken together, these points suggest that it would be inefficient for the auditor to simply subdivide materiality proportionally to each account because this would result in unnecessarily low tolerable misstatement levels. The lower the tolerable misstatement, the more extensive the required audit testing. In the extreme, if tolerable misstatement were very small or zero, the auditor would have to test every transaction making up an account. Let's relate this concept back to the house inspector example in Chapter 1. Just imagine how a house inspector's investigation would differ if she or he were asked to identify all potential damages greater than $2 versus a "tolerable damage" threshold of $2,000. Certainly the additional costs of testing to a level of $2 would exceed the benefits to the potential homeowner. Similarly, auditors are engaged to provide reasonable assurance that the financial statements are presented fairly in accordance with GAAP. Auditing standards recognize that an auditor works within economic limits, and for the audit opinion to be economically useful, it must be formed within a reasonable length of time at reasonable costs. Thus, the auditor and users of the financial statements must allow a reasonable margin for error in the underlying accounts.

Step 3: Estimate Likely Misstatements and Compare Totals to the Preliminary Judgment about Materiality

Step 3 is completed near the end of the audit, when the auditor evaluates all the evidence that has been gathered. Based on the results of the audit procedures conducted, the auditor aggregates misstatements from each account or class of transactions. The aggregate amount includes known misstatements and projections based on the sample data collected. It should also include consideration of the effect of misstatements not adjusted in the prior period because they were judged to be immaterial. The auditor compares this aggregate misstatement (referred to as *likely misstatement*) to the preliminary judgment about materiality. If the auditor's judgment about materiality at the planning stage (Step 1) was based on the same information available at the evaluation stage (Step 3), materiality for planning and evaluation would be the same. However, the auditor may identify factors or items during the course of the audit that cause a revision to the preliminary judgment about materiality. Thus, the preliminary judgment about materiality may differ from the materiality judgment used in evaluating the audit findings. When this occurs, the auditor should carefully document the reasons for revising the preliminary judgment about materiality.

When the likely misstatements are less than the preliminary judgment about materiality, the auditor can conclude that the financial statements are fairly presented. Conversely, when the likely misstatements are greater than the planned judgment about materiality, the auditor should request that the client adjust the financial statements. If the client refuses to adjust the financial statements for the likely misstatements, the auditor should issue a qualified or adverse opinion because the financial statements do not present fairly in conformity with GAAP.

An Example
❧ [LO 13]

In this example, the three steps for applying materiality are discussed using financial information for EarthWear Clothiers for the year ended December 31, 2005. This financial information is taken from the case illustration included in Chapter 1.

Step 1: Determine the Preliminary Judgment about Materiality

Exhibit 3–4 presents the calculations used to estimate the preliminary judgment about materiality for EarthWear Clothiers. Because EarthWear's total revenues are larger than its total assets, the $950,484,000 of revenues is used for the base amount. Using the materiality table in Exhibit 3–4, the preliminary judgment about materiality is $1,769,000 (rounded). This amount is determined by taking the planning materiality of $826,000 (the amount for over $300 million but not over $1 billion) and adding $943,000 to it. The $943,000 was determined by taking the excess over 300 million ($650.5 million) and multiplying it by .00145 (650.5 million × .00145). To determine the final amount for materiality, the auditor should consider whether any qualitative factors are relevant for the engagement (see Table 3–12). In our example, assume that the auditor has determined that none of the qualitative factors are relevant and that the $1,769,000 will be used for the preliminary judgment about materiality. This is the amount that is allocated to the specific accounts or classes of transactions in Step 2.

Step 2: Determine Tolerable Misstatement

Public accounting firms use a number of different approaches to accomplish this step. In our example, for simplicity of presentation, we assume that EarthWear's auditors allocate 50 percent of preliminary materiality to each account as tolerable misstatement. Therefore, tolerable misstatement is $885,000 (rounded, $1,769,000 × .50).

Step 3: Estimate the Likely Misstatement and Compare to Materiality

The allocated amounts of materiality (tolerable misstatement) are also used for determining the fair presentation of the individual accounts after completion of the audit work. Auditing standards require

EXHIBIT 3–5	**Example Working Paper for Estimating Likely Misstatements**

EARTHWEAR CLOTHIERS
Schedule of Proposed Adjusting Entries
12/31/05

Workpaper Ref.	Proposed Adjusting Entry	Assets	Liabilities	Equity	Revenues	Expenses
N10	Payroll expense					75,000
	Bonuses					140,000
	Accrued liabilities		215,000			
	To accrue payroll through 12/31 and recognize 2005 bonuses.					
F20	Cost of sales					312,500
	Inventory	(312,500)				
	To adjust ending inventory based on sample results.					
F22	Inventory	227,450				
	Accounts payable		227,450			
	To record inventory in transit at 12/31.					
R15	Accounts receivable	79,850				
	Sales				79,850	
	To record sales cutoff errors at 12/31.					
	Total	(5,200)	442,450		79,850	527,500

Tolerable Misstatement = $885,000 (50 percent of preliminary materiality)
Conclusion: Based on the above analysis, the account balances for EarthWear Clothiers are fairly stated in accordance with GAAP.

that the auditor document the nature and effect of aggregated misstatements. Exhibit 3–5 presents an example of a working paper that can be used to aggregate the effects of misstatements identified during the audit. Assume that during the course of the audit the auditor identified four misstatements. The misstatements are compared to the tolerable misstatement allocated to each account. For example, the first misstatement indicates an error in the accrual of payroll expense and bonuses. The total misstatement of accrued payroll is $215,000. The second entry is based on the results of a statistical sampling application for inventory. The statistical results indicated a projected misstatement plus an allowance for sampling risk of $312,500. In this example, no error is larger than the tolerable misstatement amount of $885,000, and the total of the misstatements is also less than overall financial statement materiality. Before making a final decision, the auditor should consider further possible misstatements that may be due to sampling and misstatements that carry forward from the prior year. The auditor should document his or her conclusion as to whether the aggregated misstatements cause the financial statements to be materially misstated (see Exhibit 3–5). If one of the entries were in excess of the tolerable misstatement for an account balance, or if the aggregated misstatements were greater than materiality the client would have to adjust the financial statements or the auditor would have to issue a qualified or adverse opinion.

KEY TERMS

Analytical procedures. Evaluations of financial information made by a study of plausible relationships among both financial and nonfinancial data.

Analytical procedures risk. The risk that substantive analytical procedures and other relevant substantive tests will fail to detect material misstatements.

Audit procedures. Specific acts performed as the auditor gathers evidence to determine if specific audit objectives are being met.

Audit risk. The risk that the auditor may fail to modify the opinion on materially misstated financial statements.

Business risks. Risks resulting from significant conditions, events, circumstances, actions or inactions that may adversely affect the entity's ability to execute its strategies and to achieve its objectives.

Control risk. The risk that material misstatements that could occur will not be prevented or detected by internal controls.

Detection risk. The risk that the auditor will not detect a material misstatement that exists in the financial statements.

Engagement risk. The risk that the auditor's exposure to loss or injury to professional practice from litigation, adverse publicity, or other events arising in connection with financial statements audited and reported on.

Errors. Unintentional misstatements or omissions of amounts or disclosures.

Expected misstatement. The amount of misstatement that the auditor believes exists in the population.

Fraud. Intentional misstatements that can be classified as fraudulent financial reporting and misappropriation of assets.

Inherent risk. The susceptibility of an assertion to material misstatement, assuming no related controls.

Materiality. The magnitude of an omission or misstatement of accounting information that, in light of surrounding circumstances, makes it probable that the judgment of a reasonable person relying on the information would have been changed or influenced.

Professional skepticism. An attitude that includes a questioning mind and a critical assessment of audit evidence. The auditor should not assume that management is either honest or dishonest.

Risk assessment. The identification, analysis, and management of risks relevant to the preparation of financial statements that are fairly presented in conformity with GAAP.

Tests of details risk. The allowable risk for failing to detect material misstatement that is not detected by internal controls, analytical procedures, or other relevant substantive tests.

Tolerable misstatement. The amount of the preliminary judgment about materiality that is allocated to a financial statement account.

www.mhhe.com/
messier4e

Visit the book's Online Learning Center for a multiple-choice quiz that will allow you to assess your understanding of chapter concepts.

REVIEW QUESTIONS

[LO 1]	3-1	Distinguish between audit risk and engagement risk.
[1,2]	3-2	How do inherent risk and control risk differ from detection risk?
[4]	3-3	Distinguish between sampling and nonsampling risk.
[4,5]	3-4	In understanding the entity and its environment, the auditor gathers knowledge about what categories of information?
[4,5]	3-5	Give three examples of conditions and events that may indicate the existence of business risks.
[4,5]	3-6	Distinguish between errors and fraud. Give three examples of each.
[10]	3-7	What are some limitations of the audit risk model?
[11,12]	3-8	Why is it important for CPA firms to develop policies and procedures for establishing materiality?
[12]	3-9	List and describe the three major steps in applying materiality to an audit.
[12,13]	3-10	Discuss why total assets or revenues might be better bases for determining materiality than net income before taxes.
[12,13]	3-11	Give three examples of qualitative factors that might affect the preliminary judgment about materiality.
[12,13]	3-12	List four qualitative factors that the auditor should consider when evaluating the unadjusted misstatements detected during the audit.

MULTIPLE-CHOICE QUESTIONS

[1,11] 3-13 Which of the following elements underlies the application of generally accepted auditing standards, particularly the standards of field work and reporting?
a. Internal control.
b. Corroborating evidence.
c. Quality control.
d. Materiality and relative risk.

[1] 3-14 The existence of audit risk is recognized by the statement in the auditor's standard report that the auditor
a. Obtains reasonable assurance about whether the financial statements are free of material misstatement.
b. Assesses the accounting principles used and also evaluates the overall financial statement presentation.
c. Realizes that some matters, either individually or in the aggregate, are important while other matters are not important.
d. Is responsible for expressing an opinion on the financial statements, which are the responsibility of management.

[1,2] 3-15 Auditee risk refers to a combination of which two components of the audit risk model?
a. Audit risk and inherent risk.
b. Audit risk and control risk.
c. Inherent risk and control risk.
d. Control risk and detection risk.

[4,5] 3-16 When is a duty to disclose fraud to parties other than the client's senior management and its audit committee most likely to exist?

a. When the amount is material.

b. When the fraud results from misappropriation of assets rather than fraudulent financial reporting.

c. In response to inquiries from a successor auditor.

d. When a line manager rather than a lower-level employee commits the fraudulent act.

[4,5] 3-17 Which of the following is least likely to indicate a material misstatement in the financial statements?

a. A significant contingent liability was omitted from the accounting process.

b. Manufacturing expenses were classified as selling expenses.

c. The company did not provide a footnote to disclose information related to its capital leases.

d. The company wrote off a significant amount of inventory after discovering that it had been stolen.

[4,5] 3-18 Which of the following is a misappropriation of assets?

a. Classifying inventory held for resale as supplies.

b. Investing cash and earning a 3 percent rate of return as opposed to paying off a loan with an interest rate of 7 percent.

c. An employee of a stereo dealer steals 12 CD players.

d. Management estimates bad debt expense as 2 percent of sales when it actually expects bad debts equal to 10 percent of sales.

[5,7] 3-19 Which of the following is an example of fraudulent financial reporting?

a. Company management falsifies inventory count tags, thereby overstating ending inventory and understating cost of sales.

b. An employee diverts customer payments to his personal use, concealing his actions by debiting an expense account, thus overstating expenses.

c. An employee steals inventory, and the shrinkage is recorded as a cost of goods sold.

d. An employee borrows small tools from the company and neglects to return them; the cost is reported as a miscellaneous operating expense.

[5,7] 3-20 Auditing standards require auditors to make certain inquiries of management regarding fraud. Which of the following inquiries is required?

a. Whether management has ever intentionally violated the securities laws.

b. Whether management has any knowledge of fraud that has been perpetrated on or within the entity.

c. Management's attitudes toward regulatory authorities.

d. Management's attitudes toward internal control and the financial reporting process.

[12,13] 3-21 In considering materiality for planning purposes, an auditor believes that misstatements aggregating $10,000 would have a material effect on an entity's income statement but that misstatements would have to aggregate $20,000 to materially affect the balance sheet. Ordinarily, it would be appropriate to design auditing procedures that would be expected to detect misstatements that aggregate

a. $10,000.

b. $15,000.

c. $20,000.

d. $30,000.

[3,12]   3-22   As lower acceptable levels of both audit risk and materiality are established, the auditor should plan more work on individual accounts to

a. Find smaller errors.

b. Find larger errors.

c. Increase the tolerable misstatements in the accounts.

d. Decrease the risk of overreliance.

PROBLEMS

[1,2,3,11]   3-23   The auditor should consider materiality and audit risk when planning and performing an examination of financial statements in accordance with generally accepted auditing standards. Materiality and audit risk should also be considered together in determining the nature, timing, and extent of auditing procedures and in evaluating the results of those procedures.

Required:

a. 1. Define *audit risk*.

   2. Describe its components of inherent risk, control risk, and detection risk.

   3. Explain how these components are interrelated.

b. 1. Define *materiality*.

   2. Discuss the factors affecting its determination.

   3. Describe the relationship between materiality for planning purposes and materiality for evaluation purposes.

(AICPA, adapted)

[1,2,3]   3-24   The CPA firm of Koch & Tabbs uses a quantitative approach to implementing the audit risk model. Calculate detection risk for each of the following hypothetical clients.

Client No.	Audit Risk	Inherent Risk	Control Risk	Detection Risk
1	5%	40%	50%	
2	5%	60%	80%	
3	10%	50%	25%	
4	10%	80%	50%	

[1,2,3]   3-25   The CPA firm of Petersen & Pauley uses a qualitative approach to implementing the audit risk model. Audit risk is categorized using three terms: very low, low, and moderate. Inherent risk and detection risk are categorized using three terms: low, moderate, and high. Control risk is categorized using four terms: very low, low, moderate, and high. Calculate detection risk for each of the following hypothetical clients.

Client No.	Audit Risk	Inherent Risk	Control Risk	Detection Risk
1	Moderate	High	Low	
2	Very low	Low	Very low	
3	Low	Moderate	High	
4	Very low	High	Moderate	

[1,2,3] 3-26 When planning a financial statement audit, a CPA must understand audit risk and its components.

Required:

For each illustration, select the component of audit risk that is most directly illustrated. The components of audit risk may be used once, more than once, or not at all.

Components of Audit Risk:

a. Engagement risk
b. Control risk
c. Detection risk
d. Inherent risk

Illustration	Component of Audit Risk
1. A client fails to discover employee fraud on a timely basis because bank accounts are not reconciled monthly.	
2. Cash is more susceptible to theft than an inventory of coal.	
3. Confirmation of receivables by an auditor fails to detect a material misstatement.	
4. Disbursements have occurred without proper approval.	
5. There is inadequate segregation of duties.	
6. A necessary substantive audit procedure is omitted.	
7. Notes receivable are susceptible to material misstatement, assuming there are no related internal controls.	
8. Technological developments make a major product obsolete.	
9. An auditor complies with GAAS on an audit engagement, but the shareholders sue the auditor for issuing misleading financial statements.	
10. XYZ Company, a client, lacks sufficient working capital to continue operations.	

[3,4,5] 3-27 For each of the following situations, explain how risk of material misstatement should be assessed and what effect that assessment will have on detection risk.

a. Johnson, Inc., is a fast-growing trucking company operating in the southeastern part of the United States. The company is publicly held, but Ivan Johnson and his sons control 55 percent of the stock. Mr. Johnson is chairman of the board and CEO. He personally makes all major decisions with little consultation with the board of directors. Most of the directors, however, are either members of the Johnson family or long-standing friends. The board basically rubber-stamps Mr. Johnson's decisions.

b. Close-Moor Stores has experienced slower sales during the last year. There is a new vice president of finance and a new controller. Mr. Musiciak, president of the company, has a reputation for hard-nosed business tactics, and he is always concerned with meeting forecast earnings.

c. MaxiWrite Corporation is one of several companies engaged in the manufacture of high-speed, high-capacity disk drives. The industry is very competitive and subject to quick changes in technology. MaxiWrite's operating results would place the company in the second quartile in terms of profitability and financial position. The company has never been the leader in the industry, with its products typically slightly behind the industry leader's in terms of performance.

d. The First National Bank of Pond City has been your client for the past two years. During that period you have had numerous arguments with the president and the controller over a number of accounting issues. The major issue has related to the bank's reserve for loan losses and the value of collateral. Your prior audits have indicated that a significant adjustment is required each year to the loan loss reserves.

[4,5] 3-28 Sandy Pitts is auditing Hofmeister Hardware Company, a fast-growing retail hardware chain in the Atlanta area. While Pitts has previously worked on this engagement, this is her first year as the audit manager. As she planned the engagement, Pitts identified a number of risk factors (such as strong interest in maintaining the company's earnings and stock price, unrealistic forecasts, and high dependence on debt financing for expansion) that indicated that fraud might exist.

Required:

a. How should Pitts respond to the possibility of fraud at the planning stage? What is the required documentation for identified risk factors?

b. If Pitts had evidence that suggested that fraud existed, what would be her communication responsibilities to management, the audit committee, and others?

[12,13] 3-29 Calculate the preliminary judgment about materiality (PJM) for each of the following hypothetical clients using Exhibit 3–4:

Client No.	Total Assets	Total Revenues	PJM
1	$5.45 million	$2.34 million	
2	30.75 million	72.3 million	
3	475 million	2 billion	
4	97 billion	4 billion	

DISCUSSION CASES

[4,5,6,12] 3-30 **Merry-Go-Round (MGR).**   Refer to the information about Merry-Go-Round (MGR) in Problems 2–32 and 2–33. Assume that you are MGR's auditor for the year ended December 31, 1995. Consider who is likely to be using MGR's financial statements and why they are using them.

Required:[7]

a. Would you recommend setting materiality and audit risk relatively high or low? Describe your reasoning for each recommendation.

b. Which of MGR's accounts have the highest likelihood of being misstated? Why? Is your answer based on factors that are related more closely to inherent risk or control risk?

---

[7]Refer to the following articles for more information on MGR: J. Martin and T. Eiben, "The Man Who Boogied Away a Billion," *Fortune*, 12/23/96, pp. 89–100, and E. McDonald and S. J. Paltrow, "Merry-Go-Round: Ernst & Young Advised the Client, but Not about Everything" *The Wall Street Journal*, August 10, 1999, p. A1.

c. What is the risk that MGR's financial statements are misstated because of fraud? In your answer, consider the two types of fraud and include reasons why each type of fraud is or is not likely to be present for MGR. Which accounts are most susceptible to fraud?

d. Is engagement risk high or low for the 12/31/95 audit? Why?

e. Is the client's business risk high or low for the 12/31/95 audit? Why?

[4,5,6]   3-31   **Cendant Corporation (Cendant).**   On December 17, 1997, CUC International merged with HFS Incorporated to form Cendant. Cendant operates primarily in three business segments—alliance marketing, travel, and real estate services. Cendant franchises include Century 21, Coldwell Banker, Avis, Days Inn, and Ramada Inn. Cendant, headquartered in Stamford, CT, and Parsippany, NJ, has nearly 40,000 employees, operates in over 100 countries, and makes more than 100 million customer contacts annually.

In April 1998, Cendant issued a press release stating that CUC had committed a massive accounting fraud. The press release stated that 1997 earnings were overstated by as much as $115 million. Cendant's audit committee hired Arthur Andersen (AA) to investigate the fraud. AA's report, issued in August 1998, revealed that CUC's chief executive officer (CEO) and chief operating officer (COO) created a culture that accepted fraudulent accounting activities and failed to implement appropriate controls and procedures that might have deterred or detected the fraud. Additional details from AA's report are summarized below (Source: C. J. Loomis, "Lies, Damned Lies, and Managed Earnings," *Fortune,* August 2, 1999, pp. 74–92):

- In the three years 1995–97, CUC's operating income before taxes was improperly inflated by $500 million, which was more than one-third of its reported pretax income for those years.
- Though many of the improprieties occurred in CUC's biggest subsidiary, Comp-U-Card, they reached to 16 others as well. No fewer than 20 employees participated in the wrongdoing.
- Several CUC employees who were interviewed said they understood that the purpose of inflating earnings was to meet "analysts' expectations."
- In the first three quarters of each of the affected years, CUC put out unaudited financial statements that headquarters deliberately falsified, mostly by "adjusting" CompU-Card's revenues upward and its expenses downward. These favorable "adjustments" grew: They were $31 million in 1995, $87 million in 1976, and $176 million in 1997.
- At the end of each year, before its outside auditors, Ernst & Young (EY), came in to make their annual review, CUC undid those improprieties (which would almost certainly have been discovered in the audit process) and instead created the earnings it needed mainly by plucking them from cookie-jar reserves.
- In most cases, the explanations that CUC gave EY for these reserve infusions satisfied the accounting firm, which in general did not display impressive detective skills. On one occasion, EY could not find justification for $25 million transferred from a reserve and let it pass as "immaterial."

- In one particularly colorful incident, CUC used a merger reserve it had established in 1997 to swallow up $597,000 of private airplane expenses that its CEO, Walter Forbes, had paid in 1995 and 1996, and for which he had requested reimbursement. Had these expenses not been allocated to the reserve, they would have turned up where they should have: in operating costs.

Required:
a. Discuss the fraud in terms of the three conditions for fraud.
b. From the information given, speculate about signs of potential fraud that EY perhaps should have recognized.

INTERNET ASSIGNMENTS

Note: The company in the following case will serve as an example throughout the textbook. The company will be used directly in some chapters as an illustration of the material being presented. It will also be utilized in some chapter problem assignments.

[4,5,11,12]   3-32   Don Jones is the senior in charge of the audit of Calabro Paging Services. Jones's firm, Abbott & Johnson, LLP, has audited Calabro for 10 years. Calabro's unaudited statements are shown here for the year ended December 31, 2005.

General Information: Calabro Paging Services

Calabro Paging Services is a business services company that uses wireless communications technology to develop solutions for business and organizational problems. The company owns and operates paging systems; manufactures, leases, and sells pagers; and provides commercial paging services in 12 major metropolitan areas in the southeastern part of the United States. The company emphasizes its systems, reliability, solution-oriented marketing, and high level of customer service. The company provides high-quality, low-cost service to the marketplace.

Calabro was founded 15 years ago, when Ronald Calabro purchased a local paging company in Tampa, Florida. The company expanded by building paging systems in major metropolitan areas. Calabro Paging Services went public 10 years ago, and its stock is traded on the NASDAQ stock exchange. Five years ago, the day-to-day operations of the company were turned over to the founder's son, Matthew Calabro, who has served as chief executive officer since that time. Ronald Calabro continues to serve as chairman of the board.

As of 2005, the company has built and still operates 12 paging systems, with the last system constructed in 2000. In recent years the company has focused on internal growth rather than geographic expansion, and its compound annual subscriber growth rate has been 20 percent. The company improved its earnings during this period and used its excess cash provided by operations to reduce its debt burden to approximately $3.5 million at December 31, 2005.

Company Operations

Calabro offers a variety of pagers to its subscribers. Subscribers may lease a pager from the company or purchase a pager and pay only an access fee for the company paging system. Each subscriber enters into a service contract with the company, which provides for the payment of the access fee and the purchase or lease of one or more pagers. The company's contracts with customers with large numbers of pagers are typically for three- to five-year terms, while contracts for smaller quantities are typically for one-year terms with annual renewal. The combined lease and access fee of a single leased pager currently ranges from approximately $5.00 to $40.00 per month, depending upon the type of pager and optional features selected. The company charges a monthly access fee for service to each customer-owned pager. Volume discounts on access fees and lease costs are typically offered to large-unit-volume subscribers. Comparable to prior years, approximately 82 percent of the company's pages in service at December 31, 2005, were leased from the company, and approximately 18 percent were owned by subscribers.

Required:

a. Determine the preliminary judgment about materiality for Calabro Paging Services using the worksheet included in Exhibit 3–4.

b. Use the Internet to gather information on the paging industry, including information on the factors that are used in assessing client business risk. Note that many paging companies are owned by larger telecommunications companies that are better financed than Calabro Paging Services.

c. Draft a memo describing Calabro Paging Services' client business risk.

CALABRO PAGING SERVICES

CP5

Year Ended December 31,

	2005	2004	2003	2002	2001
	(Dollars in thousands, except per share amounts)				
At end of period:					
Pagers in service	145,872	130,400	117,514	98,718	80,364
Operating data:					
Revenues	$20,742	$18,289	$17,465	$15,452	$12,526
Operating income (loss)	2,663	1,801	1,510	762	(452)
Income (loss) before extraordinary item	1,535	1,710	774	210	(500)
Net income (loss)	1,535	1,710	1,279	385	(500)
Net income (loss) per share:					
Before extraordinary item	.38	.42	.19	.05	(.13)
Net income (loss)	.38	.42	.32	.10	(.13)
Balance sheet data:					
Total assets	$29,611	$27,465	$25,934	$23,850	$23,244
Long-term debt, including current maturities	3,890	3,539	4,859	4,599	4,842
Total liabilities	9,564	8,116	8,187	7,631	7,424
Total stockholders' equity	19,851	19,349	17,747	16,219	15,821
Other data:					
Earnings before taxes, other income (expense), depreciation, and amortization	$7,203	$5,776	$5,164	$3,988	$2,316

CALABRO PAGING SERVICES
Consolidated Balance Sheet
Assets

	December 31,	
	2005	*2004*
Current assets:		
Cash and cash equivalents	$ 516,709	$ 128,018
Trade accounts receivable, less allowance for doubtful accounts of $135,300 and $110,800 as of December 31, 2005 and 2004, respectively	3,582,600	3,389,775
Inventories	864,963	820,048
Other current assets	2,074,265	1,782,123
	$ 7,038,537	$ 6,119,964
Property, plant, and equipment:		
Land	2,383,800	2,043,222
Buildings	7,154,400	6,129,670
Pagers	19,207,010	17,000,432
Communications equipment	9,737,543	8,799,951
Office equipment	1,347,489	1,269,904
	$ 39,830,242	$ 35,243,179
Less accumulated depreciation	(19,645,924)	(16,138,402)
	$ 20,184,318	$ 19,104,777
Other assets, net of accumulated amortization of $1,935,600 and $1,427,800 as of December 31, 2005 and 2004, respectively	2,388,415	2,240,735
Total	$ 29,611,270	$ 27,465,476

Liabilities and Stockholders' Equity

	2005	2004
Current liabilities:		
Accounts payable	$ 621,390	$ 664,128
Other accrued expenses and liabilities	5,052,073	3,913,809
Current maturities of long-term obligations and capital lease obligations	424,061	398,864
	$ 6,097,524	$ 4,976,801
Long-term debt, less current maturities	3,466,346	3,139,673
Deferred tax liability	196,785	—
Commitments		
Stockholders' equity:		
Common stock, $0.01 par value, 10,000,000 authorized, 4,182,800 and 4,116,200 issued	41,828	41,162
Additional paid-in capital	19,903,523	19,769,264
Retained earnings (deficit)	1,090,185	(235,420)
Less treasury stock at cost	(1,184,921)	(226,004)
	$19,850,615	$19,349,002
Total	$29,611,270	$27,465,476

CALABRO PAGING SERVICES
Consolidated Statement of Operations

	Year Ended December 31,	
	2005	*2004*
Revenues:		
Pager lease and access fees	$18,753,376	$16,434,978
Pager and paging equipment sales	1,989,024	1,854,421
	$20,742,400	$18,289,399
Cost of sales and services:		
Pager lease and access fees	$ 4,974,121	$ 4,634,203
Pager and paging equipment sales	932,812	1,058,337
	$ 5,906,933	$ 5,692,540
Expenses:		
Sales and marketing	$ 4,245,273	$ 3,749,794
General and administrative	3,980,880	3,371,291
Depreciation and amortization	3,946,001	3,674,623
	$12,172,154	$10,795,708
Operating income	$ 2,663,313	$ 1,801,151
Other income (expense):		
Interest and other income	$ 42,585	$ 105,590
Gain on sale of assets	—	106,185
Interest expense	(284,623)	(302,455)
	$ (242,038)	$ (90,680)
Income before income taxes	$ 2,421,275	$ 1,710,471
Provision for income taxes	886,530	—
Net income	$ 1,534,745	$ 1,710,471
Net income per share	.38	.42

CALABRO PAGING SERVICES
Consolidated Statement of Retained Earnings

Balance at December 31, 2003	**$(1,945,891)**
Net income	1,710,471
Balance at December 31, 2004	**$ (235,429)**
Net income	1,535,745
Less dividends	209,140
Balance at December 31, 2005	**$ 1,090,185**

3-33 Auditors are required to obtain and support an understanding of the entity and its environment in order to identify business risks. Much of the information needed to identify the risks can be obtained from the company's annual report, 10K, and proxy materials. Many companies publish these documents on their website. Additionally, industry information on these companies can be obtained from websites such as Yahoo (http://yahoo.marketguide. com).

a. In groups (of two or three members) complete the questionnaire (except for the business process section) for a real world company assigned by your instructor.* There may be some questions asked on the questionnaire that you will be unable to answer. If you cannot answer a question, respond "information not available."

b. The measurement and performance section asks for information on the entity's key performance indicators (KPIs). Identify what you think the KPIs are for the company assigned, and how does the company compare to its industry averages and major competitors. Prepare tables for this data and a memo of your analyses.

Risk Response Table

Business Risks	Audit Area Affected	Assertion	Response

ACL

www.mhhe.com/ messier4e	Visit the book's Online Learning Center for problem material to be completed using the *ACL* software packaged with your new text.

---

*A Word version of the questionnaire is available from your instructor or from the book's website (www.mhhe.com/messier4e). EarthWear may also be used for the example company. Much of the necessary information is contained at the websites for EarthWear and its auditors.

CHAPTER 4

LEARNING OBJECTIVES

Upon completion of this chapter you will

[1] Understand the relationship between audit evidence and the auditor's report.

[2] Know management assertions about classes of transactions and events for the period under audit, assertions about account balances at the period end, and assertions about presentation and disclosure.

[3] Define audit procedures and understand their relationship to assertions.

[4] Learn the basic concepts of audit evidence.

[5] Identify and define the audit procedures used for obtaining audit evidence.

[6] Understand the reliability of the types of evidence.

[7] Understand the objectives of audit documentation.

[8] Develop an understanding of the content, types, organization, and ownership of audit documentation.

RELEVANT ACCOUNTING AND AUDITING PRONOUNCEMENTS

CON2, FASB Statement of Financial Accounting Concepts No. 2, "Qualitative Characteristics of Accounting Information"

AU 311, Planning and Supervision

AU 312, Audit Risk and Materiality in Conducting an Audit

AU 316, Consideration of Fraud in a Financial Statement Audit

AU 319, Consideration of Internal Control in a Financial Statement Audit

AU 326, Evidential Matter

AU 329, Analytical Procedures

AU 330, The Confirmation Process

AU 339, Audit Documentation

AICPA Auditing Standards Board, Exposure Draft, "Audit Evidence"

AICPA Auditing Standards Board, Exposure Draft, "Performing Audit Procedures in Response to Assessed Risks and Evaluating the Audit Evidence Obtained"

PCAOB Auditing Standard No. 3, Audit Documentation (AS 3)

Audit Evidence and Audit Documentation

This chapter covers the third important concept underlying the entire audit process: *audit evidence*. Audit evidence is all the information used by the auditor in arriving at the conclusions on which the audit opinion is based, and includes the information contained in the accounting records underlying the financial statements and other information. In Chapter 1, we indicated that auditing is essentially a set of conceptual tools that guide an auditor in collecting and evaluating evidence regarding others' assertions, and we assured you that these conceptual tools are extremely useful in a variety of settings. We encourage you to keep this perspective in mind as you study Chapter 4. While this chapter does contain some lists you will likely want to commit to memory (e.g., management assertions and characteristics of audit evidence), remember that these are not just lists—they constitute powerful conceptual tools that can help you in almost *any* setting that requires you to collect and evaluate evidence. Understanding the nature and characteristics of evidence is fundamental to effective auditing, and is a key part of the conceptual tool kit we hope to help you acquire as you go through this book.

On a typical audit most of the auditor's work involves obtaining and evaluating evidence using procedures such as inspection of records and confirmations to test the fair presentation of the financial statements. To perform this task effectively and efficiently, an auditor must thoroughly understand the important aspects of audit evidence. This includes understanding how audit evidence relates to financial statement assertions and the auditor's report, the sufficiency and competency of evidence, types of audit procedures, and the documentation of evidence in the working papers. Each of these topics is covered in this chapter.

The Relationship of Audit Evidence to the Audit Report

✻ [LO 1]   The standard on audit evidence (AU 326), provides the basic framework for the auditor's understanding of evidence and its use to support the auditor's opinion on the financial statements. In reaching an opinion on the financial statements, the auditor gathers evidence by conducting audit procedures to test management assertions. The evidence gathered from the audit procedures is used to determine the fairness of the financial statements and the type of audit report to be issued. Figure 4–1 presents an overview of the relationships among the financial statements, management assertions about components of the financial statements, audit procedures, and the audit report. More specifically, there is a top-down relationship from the financial statements to the audit procedures. The financial statements reflect management's assertions about the various financial statement components. The auditor conducts audit procedures to gather evidence regarding whether each relevant management assertion is being supported. The application of audit procedures provides the evidence that supports the auditor's report.

Auditors typically divide financial statements into components or segments in order to manage the audit. A component can be a financial statement account or a business process. As indicated in Chapter 2, the basic processes of most businesses are the *revenue process*, the *purchasing process*, the *human resource management process*, the *inventory management process*, and the *financing process*. Sometimes business processes are referred to as transaction cycles (e.g., the revenue cycle). Each process involves a variety of important

FIGURE 4–1	An Overview of the Relationships among the Financial Statements, Management Assertions, Audit Procedures, and the Audit Report

transactions. Business processes support functions such as sales and postsales services, materials acquisition, production and distribution, human resource management, and treasury management. This text focuses on business processes and their related transactions and financial statement accounts. Examining business processes and their related accounts allows the auditor to gather evidence by examining the processing of related transactions through the information system from their origin to their ultimate disposition in the accounting journals and ledgers. Later chapters in this text cover each of the major business processes that auditors typically encounter on an engagement.

The following two sections expand the discussion of management assertions and audit procedures.

Management Assertions

✥ [LO 2]   Management is responsible for the fair presentation of the financial statements. Assertions are expressed or implied representations by management that are reflected in the financial statement components. For example, when the balance sheet contains a line item for accounts receivable of $5 million, management asserts that those receivables exist and have a net realizable value of $5 million. Management also asserts that the accounts receivable balance arose from selling goods or services on credit in the normal course of business. In general, the assertions relate to the requirements of generally accepted accounting principles.

Management assertions fall into the following categories:

- Assertions about classes of transactions and events for the period under audit.
- Assertions about account balances at the period end.
- Assertions about presentation and disclosure.

Table 4–1 summarizes each assertion by category.

TABLE 4–1	**Summary of Management Assertions by Category**

Assertions about classes of transactions and events for the period under audit:
- **Occurrence**—transactions and events that have been recorded have occurred and pertain to the entity (sometimes referred to as validity).
- **Completeness**—all transactions and events that should have been recorded have been recorded.
- **Authorization**—all transactions and events have been properly authorized.
- **Accuracy**—amounts and other data relating to recorded transactions and events have been recorded appropriately.
- **Cutoff**—transactions and events have been recorded in the correct accounting period.
- **Classification**—transactions and events have been recorded in the proper accounts.

Assertions about account balances at the period end:
- **Existence**—assets, liabilities, and equity interests exist.
- **Rights and obligations**—the entity holds or controls the rights to assets, and liabilities are the obligations of the entity.
- **Completeness**—all assets, liabilities and equity interests that should have been recorded have been recorded.
- **Valuation and allocation**—assets, liabilities, and equity interests are included in the financial statements at appropriate amounts, and any resulting valuation or allocation adjustments are appropriately recorded.

Assertions about presentation and disclosure:
- **Occurrence and rights and obligations**—disclosed events, transactions, and other matters have occurred and pertain to the entity.
- **Completeness**—all disclosures that should have been included in the financial statements have been included.
- **Classification and understandability**—financial information is appropriately presented and described, and disclosures are clearly expressed.
- **Accuracy and valuation**—financial and other information are disclosed fairly and at appropriate amounts.

Assertions about
Classes of
Transactions and
Events during the
Period

Occurrence   The occurrence assertion relates to whether all recorded transactions and events have occurred and pertain to the entity. For example, management asserts that all revenue transactions recorded during the period were valid transactions. Occurrence is sometimes also referred to as validity.

Completeness   The completeness assertion relates to whether all transactions and events that occurred during the period have been recorded. For example, if a client fails to record a valid revenue transaction, the revenue account will be understated. Note that the auditor's concern with the completeness assertion is opposite the concern for occurrence. Failure to meet the completeness assertion results in an understatement in the related account, while invalid recorded amounts result in an overstatement in the related account.

Authorization   The authorization assertion relates to whether all transactions have been properly authorized. For example, the purchase of a material amount of plant and equipment should be approved by the board of directors.

Accuracy   The accuracy assertion addresses whether amounts and other data relating to recorded transactions and events have been recorded appropriately. Generally accepted accounting principles establish the appropriate method for recording a transaction or event. For example, the amount recorded for the cost of a new machine includes its purchase price plus all reasonable costs to install it.

Cutoff   The cutoff assertion relates to whether transactions and events have been recorded in the correct accounting period. The auditor's procedures must ensure that transactions occurring near year-end are recorded in the financial statements in the proper period. For example, the auditor may want to test proper cutoff of revenue transactions at December 31, 2005. The auditor can examine a sample of shipping documents and sales invoices for a few days before and after year-end to test whether the sales transactions are recorded in the proper period. The objective is to determine that all 2005 sales and no 2006 sales have been recorded in 2005. Thus, the auditor examines the shipping documents to ensure that no 2006 sales have been recorded in 2005 and that no 2005 sales are recorded in 2006.

Classification   The classification assertion is concerned with whether transactions and events have been recorded in the proper accounts. For example, management asserts that all direct cost transactions related to inventory have been properly classified in either inventory or part of cost of sales.

Assertions about
Account Balances
at the Period End

Existence   The assertion about existence addresses whether assets, liabilities, and equity interests exist at the date of the financial statements. For example, management asserts that inventory shown on the balance sheet exists and is available for sale.

Rights and Obligations

The assertions about rights and obligations address whether the entity holds or controls the rights to assets, and that liabilities are the obligations of the entity. For example, management asserts that the entity has legal title or rights of ownership to the inventory shown on the balance sheet. Similarly, amounts capitalized for leases reflect assertions that the entity has rights to leased property and that the corresponding lease liability represents an obligation of the entity.

Completeness

The assertion about completeness addresses whether all assets, liabilities and equity interests that should have been recorded have been recorded. For example, management implicitly asserts that the amount shown for accounts payable on the balance sheet includes all such liabilities as of the balance sheet date.

Valuation and Allocation

Assertions about valuation or allocation address whether assets, liabilities, and equity interests are included in the financial statements at appropriate amounts and any resulting valuation or allocation adjustments are appropriately recorded. For example, management asserts that inventory is carried at the lower of cost or market value on the balance sheet. Similarly, management asserts that the cost of property, plant, and equipment is systematically allocated to appropriate accounting periods by recognizing depreciation expense.

Assertions about Presentation and Disclosure

This category of assertions relates to presentation of information in the financial statements and disclosures in the footnotes that are directly related to a specific transaction or account balance (e.g., disclosure related to property and equipment) and those that apply to the financial statements in general (e.g., the footnote for the summary of significant accounting policies).

Occurrence and Rights and Obligations

The assertions about occurrence and rights and obligations address whether disclosed events, transactions, and other matters have occurred and pertain to the entity. For example, when management presents capitalized lease transactions on the balance sheet as leased assets, the related liabilities as long-term debt, and the related footnote, it is asserting that a lease transaction occurred, it has a right to the leased asset, and it owes the related lease obligation to the lessor. In addition, there is a footnote disclosure that provides additional information on the lease such as future payments.

Completeness

The completeness assertion relates to whether all disclosures that should have been included in the financial statements have been included. Therefore, management asserts that no material disclosures have been omitted from the footnotes and other disclosures accompanying the financial statements.

Classification and Understandability

The assertions related to classification and understandability address whether the financial information is appropriately presented and described and disclosures are clearly expressed. For example, management asserts that the portion of long-term debt shown as a current liability will mature in the current year. Similarly, management asserts, through footnote disclosure, that all major restrictions on the entity resulting from debt covenants are disclosed.

Accuracy and Valuation   The accuracy and valuation assertions address whether financial and other information are disclosed fairly and at appropriate amounts. For example, when management discloses the fair value of financial instruments, it is asserting that these financial instruments are properly valued in accordance with GAAP. In addition, management may disclose in a footnote other information related to financial instruments.

Before we discuss important characteristics of evidence available to the auditor, pause for a moment to consider the usefulness of the sets of management assertions we have just discussed. The assertions collectively provide a road map for the auditor in determining what evidence to collect regarding various transactions, account balances, and required financial statement disclosures. They also guide the auditor in designing audit procedures to collect the needed evidence, as well as assisting the auditor in evaluating the competence and sufficiency of the evidence. For example, once the auditor is comfortable that he or she has enough good-quality evidence relating to each balance-related assertion for the accounts payable account, the auditor can rest assured that no important aspect of that account has been neglected. The management assertions help the auditor focus his or her attention on all the various aspects of transactions, account balances, and required disclosures that need to be considered—they help the auditor ensure that "all the bases are covered." As such, the three sets of management assertions constitute a powerful conceptual tool in the auditor's tool kit.

Audit Procedures

[LO 3]   Audit procedures are specific acts performed by the auditor to gather evidence to determine if specific assertions are being met. Audit procedures are performed to

- Obtain an understanding of the entity and its environment, including its internal control in order to assess the risks of material misstatement at the financial statement and assertion levels. Such audit procedures are referred to as *risk assessment procedures*. These procedures were discussed in Chapter 3.
- Test the operating effectiveness of controls in preventing, or detecting and correcting, material misstatements at the assertion level. Audit procedures performed for this purpose are referred to as *tests of controls*. Tests of controls are discussed in Chapters 5 and 6.
- Detect material misstatements at the assertion level. Such audit procedures are referred to as *substantive procedures*. Substantive

TABLE 4–2	Management Assertions and Illustrative Audit Procedures
Management Assertions about the Accounts Receivable Component of the Financial Statements	**Sample Audit Procedures for Accounts Receivable**
Existence	Confirm accounts receivable.
Rights and obligations	Inquire of management whether receivables have been sold.
Completeness	Agree total of accounts receivable subsidiary ledger to accounts receivable control account.
Valuation or allocation	Trace selected accounts from the aged trial balance to the subsidiary accounts receivable records for proper amount and aging.
	Test the adequacy of the allowance for doubtful accounts.
Assertions about presentation and disclosure	Examine listing of accounts receivable for amounts due from affiliates, officers, directors, or other related parties.

procedures include tests of details of transactions, account balances, and disclosures and substantive analytical procedures. Substantive procedures are discussed in detail in Chapter 5 and in each business process chapter.

A set of audit procedures prepared to test assertions for a component of the financial statements is usually referred to as an *audit program*. Table 4–2 illustrates an audit procedure for each assertion related to the audit of accounts receivable. The reader should note that there is *not* a one-to-one relationship between assertion and audit procedures. In some instances more than one audit procedure is required to test an assertion. Conversely, in some cases an audit procedure provides evidence for more than one assertion. Note that the assertions do not change whether information is processed manually or electronically. However, the methods of applying audit procedures may be influenced by the method of information processing. Examples of audit procedures used to test various account balances will be presented in later chapters.

The Concepts of Audit Evidence

[LO 4]   Audit evidence is all the information used by the auditor in arriving at the conclusions on which the audit opinion is based, and includes the information contained in the accounting records underlying the financial statements and other information. A solid understanding of the characteristics of evidence is obviously an important conceptual tool for auditors as well as for professionals in a variety of other settings. The following concepts of audit evidence are important to understanding the conduct of the audit:

- The nature of audit evidence.
- The competence of audit evidence.
- The sufficiency of audit evidence.
- The evaluation of audit evidence.

The Nature of Audit Evidence

The nature of audit evidence includes accounting records and other available information. Accounting records include the records of initial entries and supporting records, such as checks and records of electronic fund transfers; invoices; contracts; the general and subsidiary ledgers, journal entries and other adjustments to the financial statements that are not reflected in formal journal entries; and records such as work sheets and spreadsheets supporting cost allocations, computations, reconciliations and disclosures. Many times these entries in the accounting records are initiated, recorded, processed, and reported in electronic form. Other information that the auditor may use as audit evidence includes minutes of meetings; confirmations from third parties; analysts' reports; benchmarking data about competitors; controls manuals; information obtained by the auditor from such audit procedures as inquiry, observation, and inspection; and other information developed by, or available to, the auditor.

For some entities, accounting records and other information may be available only in electronic form.[1] Thus, source documents such as purchase orders, bills of lading, invoices, and checks are replaced with electronic messages or electronic images. Two common examples are Electronic Data Interchange (EDI) and image-processing systems.[2] A client that uses EDI may process sales or purchase transactions electronically. For example, the client's EDI system can contact a vendor electronically when supplies of a part run low. The vendor will then ship the goods to the client and send an invoice electronically. The client can authorize its bank to make an electronic payment directly to the vendor's bank account. In an image-processing system, documents are scanned and converted to electronic images to facilitate storage and reference, and the source documents may not be retained after conversion. In such systems, electronic evidence may exist at only a certain point in time and may not be retrievable later. This may require the auditor to select sample items several times during the year rather than at year-end.

The Competence of Audit Evidence

Competence is a measure of the *quality* of audit evidence. Evidence, regardless of its form, is considered competent when it provides information that is both *relevant* and *reliable*.

Relevance   The competence of evidence depends on its relevance to the assertion being tested. If the auditor relies on evidence that is unrelated to the assertion, he or she may reach an incorrect conclusion about the assertion. For example, suppose the auditor wants to check the completeness assertion for recording sales transactions; that is, are all goods shipped to customers recorded in the sales journal? A normal audit procedure for testing this assertion is to trace a sample of shipping documents (such as bills

---

[1]The AICPA's Audit Practice Release, *The Information Technology Age: Evidential Matter in the Electronic Environment* (AICPA 1997), provides nonauthoritative implementation guidance about electronic evidence and its impact on the audit. See also A. L. Williamson, "The Implications of Electronic Evidence," *Journal of Accountancy* (February 1997), pp. 69–71.

[2]The AICPA's Audit Practice Release, *Audit Implications of Electronic Document Management* (AICPA 1997), discusses the issues faced by auditors when a client uses electronic document management that includes image-processing systems. Discussion of such issues is beyond the scope of this text.

of lading) to the related sales invoices and entries in the sales journal. If the auditor samples the population of sales invoices issued during the period, the evidence would not relate to the completeness assertion (that is, the auditor would not detect shipments made that are not billed or recorded). The auditor should check the log of prenumbered bills of lading, after ascertaining that such documents were issued for all customer shipments. Any conclusion based on the population of sales invoices would not be based on evidence relevant to testing the completeness assertion.

Reliability   The *reliability* or validity of evidence refers to whether a particular type of evidence can be relied upon to signal the true state of an assertion. Because of varied circumstances on audit engagements, it is difficult to generalize about the reliability of various types of evidence. However, the reliability of evidence is influenced by its source and by its nature and is dependent on the individual circumstances under which it is obtained.

- ***Independent source of the evidence.*** Evidence obtained directly by the auditor from an independent source outside the entity is usually viewed as more reliable than evidence obtained solely from within the entity. Thus, a confirmation of the client's bank balance received directly by the auditor would be viewed as more reliable than examination of the cash receipts journal and cash balance as recorded in the general ledger. Additionally, evidence that is obtained from the client, but that has been subjected to verification by an independent source, is viewed as more reliable than evidence obtained solely from within the entity. For example, a canceled check held by the client would be more reliable than a duplicate copy of the check because the canceled check would be endorsed by the payee and cleared through the bank—that is, verified by an independent source.
- ***Effectiveness of internal control.*** A major objective of a client's internal control is to generate reliable information to assist management decision making. As part of the audit, the effectiveness of the client's internal control is assessed. When the auditor assesses the client's internal control as effective (that is, low control risk), evidence generated by that accounting system is viewed as reliable. Conversely, if internal control is assessed as ineffective (that is, high control risk), the evidence from the accounting system would not be considered reliable. Thus, the more effective the client's internal control, the more assurance it provides about the reliability of audit evidence.
- ***Auditor's direct personal knowledge.*** Evidence obtained directly by the auditor (e.g., observation of the performance of a control) is generally considered to be more reliable than evidence obtained indirectly or by inference (e.g., inquiry about the performance of a control). For example, an auditor's physical inspection of a client's inventory is considered to be relatively reliable because the auditor has direct personal knowledge regarding the inventory. There are, of course, exceptions to this general rule. For example, if an auditor examined an inventory composed of diamonds or specialty computer chips, the auditor may lack the competence to assess the

validity and valuation of such inventory items. In such cases, the auditor may need the skill and knowledge of a specialist to assist with the inventory audit.

- *Documentary evidence.* Audit evidence is more reliable when it exists in documentary form, whether paper, electronic, or other medium. Thus, a written record of a board of directors meeting is more reliable than a subsequent oral representation of the matters discussed.
- *Original documents.* Audit evidence provided by original documents is more reliable than audit evidence provided by photocopies or facsimiles. An auditor's examination of an original, signed copy of a lease agreement is more reliable than a photocopy.

The Sufficiency of Audit Evidence

Sufficiency is the measure of the *quantity* of audit evidence. The quantity of audit evidence needed is affected by the risk of misstatement and by the quality of the audit evidence gathered. Thus, the greater the risk of misstatement, the more audit evidence is likely to be required to meet the audit test. And the higher the quality of the evidence, the less evidence that may be required to meet the audit test. Accordingly, there is an inverse relationship between the sufficiency and competence of audit evidence.

In most instances, the auditor relies on evidence that is *persuasive* rather than *convincing* in forming an opinion on a set of financial statements. This occurs for two reasons. First, because an audit must be completed in a reasonable amount of time and at a reasonable cost, the auditor examines only a sample of the transactions that compose the account balance or class of transactions. Thus, the auditor reaches a conclusion about the account or class based on a subset of the available evidence.

Second, due to the nature of evidence, auditors must often rely on evidence that is not perfectly reliable. As discussed in the next section, the types of audit evidence have different degrees of reliability, and even highly reliable evidence has weaknesses. For example, an auditor can physically examine inventory, but such evidence will not ensure that obsolescence is not a problem. Therefore, the nature of the evidence obtained by the auditor seldom provides absolute assurance about an assertion.

The *amount* of audit evidence is determined by the auditor's professional judgment and is affected by the risk of material misstatement for the account balance or class of transactions and is affected by the risk of material misstatement. For example, when the risk of material misstatement is high, the auditor has to collect more evidence than if the risk of material misstatement is low. Determining the sufficiency of evidence is one of the more critical decisions the auditor faces on an engagement.

The Evaluation of Audit Evidence

The ability to evaluate evidence appropriately is another important skill an auditor must develop. Proper evaluation of evidence requires that the auditor understand the types of evidence that are available and their relative reliability or diagnosticity. The auditor must be capable of assessing when a sufficient amount of competent evidence has been obtained in order to determine whether the fairness of management's assertions can be supported.

In evaluating evidence, an auditor should be *thorough* in searching for evidence and *unbiased* in its evaluation. For example, suppose an auditor decides to mail accounts receivable confirmations to 50 customers. Suppose further that the client has a total of 5000 customer accounts receivable. In auditing the 50 customers, the auditor must gather sufficient evidence on *each* of the 50 accounts. In evaluating evidence, the auditor must remain objective and must not allow the evaluation of the evidence to be biased by other considerations. For example, in evaluating a client's response to an audit inquiry, the auditor must not allow any personal factors (e.g., likeable former auditor) to influence the evaluation of the client's response.

Audit Procedures for Obtaining Audit Evidence

✖ **[LO 5]** In conducting audit procedures, the auditor examines various types of audit evidence. For discussion purposes, evidence is categorized into the following types:

- Inspection of records or documents.
- Inspection of tangible assets.
- Reperformance.
- Recalculation.
- Scanning.
- Inquiry.
- Observation.
- Confirmation.
- Analytical procedures.

Inspection of Records or Documents

Inspection consists of examining internal or external records or documents that are in paper form, electronic form, or other media. On most audit engagements, inspection of records or documents makes up the bulk of the evidence gathered by the auditor. Two issues are important in discussing inspection of records or documents: the reliability of such evidence and its relationship to specific assertions.

Reliability of Records or Documents A previous section noted the independence of the source of evidence as a factor that affected the reliability of audit evidence. In particular, evidence obtained from a source outside the entity was generally considered more reliable than evidence obtained solely from within the entity. Typically a distinction is made between internal and external documents. *Internal documents* are generated and maintained within the entity; that is, these documents have not been seen by any party outside the client's organization. Examples include duplicate copies of sales invoices and shipping documents, materials requisition forms, and worksheets for overhead cost allocation. *External documents* are of two forms: documents originating within the entity but circulated to independent sources outside the entity and documents generated outside the entity but included in the client's accounting records. Examples of the first include remittance advices returned with cash receipts from customers and payroll checks, while examples of the second include bank statements and vendors' invoices.

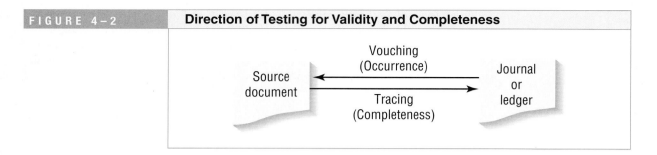

In general, such external documentary evidence is viewed as more reliable than internal evidence because a third party either initiated or reviewed it. This difference in reliability between internal and external documents is, however, relative. Internal documents generated by good internal controls are likely to be highly reliable. Conversely, external documents may be manipulated or withheld by client personnel. If this is likely on an engagement, the auditor would discount the reliability of the external documents in the client's possession. In such a situation, the auditor would also discount the reliability of the internal documents. In summary, determining the reliability of documentary evidence involves a good deal of auditor judgment.

Documentary Evidence Related to Assertions   The second issue concerning records or documents relates directly to the occurrence and completeness assertions and to the *direction of testing* taken when documentary evidence is examined. Figure 4–2 presents an overview of this relationship.

The direction of testing between the accounting records and source documents (such as sales invoices or shipping documents) is important when testing the occurrence and completeness assertions. *Vouching* refers to first selecting an item for testing from the accounting journals or ledgers and then examining the underlying source document. Thus, the direction of testing is from the journals or ledgers back to the source documents. This approach provides evidence that items included in the accounting records have *occurred* (or are valid transactions). For example, an auditor may want to examine a sample of sales transactions from the sales journal to ensure that sales are not fictitious. If adequate source documents exist for each sales transaction selected from the sales journal, the auditor can conclude that each sale was valid. *Tracing* refers to first selecting an accounting transaction (a source document) and then following it into the journal or ledger. The direction of testing in this case is from the source documents to the journals or ledgers. Testing in this direction ensures that transactions that occurred are recorded (*completeness*) in the accounting records. For example, if the auditor selects a sample of shipping documents and traces them to the related sales invoices and then to the sales journal, he or she would have evidence on the completeness of sales.

Inspection of Tangible Assets

Inspection of tangible assets consists of physical examination of the assets. Inspection is a relatively reliable type of evidence that involves the auditor inspecting or counting a *tangible asset*. An audit engagement includes many situations in which the auditor physically examines an entity's assets. Some examples might be counting cash on hand, examining inventory or marketable securities, and examining tangible fixed assets. This type of evidence primarily provides assurance that the asset exists. In some instances, such as examining inventory, physical examination may provide evidence on valuation by identifying obsolete or slow-moving items. However, physical examination provides little or no assurance on the rights and obligations assertions.

Reperformance

Reperformance is the auditor's independent execution of procedures or controls that were originally performed as part of the entity's internal control, either manually or through the use of computer-assisted audit techniques (CAATs). For example, the auditor may reperform the aging of accounts receivable. Because the auditor creates this type of evidence, it is normally viewed as highly reliable.

Recalculation

Recalculation consists of checking the mathematical accuracy of documents or records. Recalculation can be formed through the use of information technology (e.g., by obtaining an electronic file from the entity and using CAATs to check the accuracy of the summarization of the file). Specific examples of this type procedure include recalculation of depreciation expense on fixed assets and recalculation of accrued interest. Recalculation also includes footing, crossfooting, reconciling subsidiary ledgers to account balances, and testing postings from journals to ledgers. Because the auditor creates this type of evidence, it is normally viewed as highly reliable.

Scanning

Scanning is the review of accounting data to identify significant or unusual items. This includes the identification of anomalous individual items within account balances or other client data through the scanning or analysis of entries in transaction listings, subsidiary ledgers, general ledger control accounts, adjusting entries, suspense accounts, reconciliations, and other detailed reports. Scanning includes searching for large and unusual items in the accounting records (e.g., nonstandard journal entries), as well as reviewing transaction data (e.g., expense accounts, adjusting journal entries) for indications of errors that have occurred. It might be used in conjunction with analytical procedures but also as a stand-alone procedure. Scanning can be performed either manually or through the use of CAATs.

Inquiry

Inquiry consists of seeking information of knowledgeable persons (both financial and nonfinancial) throughout the entity or outside the entity. Inquiry is an important audit procedure that is used extensively throughout the audit and often is complementary to performing other audit procedures. For example, much of the audit work conducted to understand the entity and its environment including internal control involves inquiry.

Inquiries may range from formal written inquiries to informal oral inquiries. Evaluating responses to inquiries is an integral part of the inquiry process. Table 4–3 provides guidance for conducting and evaluating inquiries.

Responses to inquiries may provide the auditor with information not previously possessed or with corroborative audit evidence. Alternatively,

TABLE 4-3	**Techniques for Conducting and Evaluating Inquiries**
	In conducting inquiry, the auditor should • Consider the knowledge, objectivity, experience, responsibility, and qualifications of the individual to be questioned. • Ask clear, concise, and relevant questions. • Use open or closed questions appropriately. • Listen actively and effectively. • Consider the reactions and responses and ask follow-up questions. • Evaluate the response.

responses might provide information that differs significantly from other information that the auditor has obtained, for example, information regarding the possibility of management override of controls. The reliability of audit evidence obtained from responses to inquiries is also affected by the training, knowledge, and experience of the auditor performing the inquiry, because the auditor analyzes and assesses responses while performing the inquiry and refines subsequent inquiries according to the circumstances. In some cases, the nature of the response may be so significant that the auditor requests a written representation from the source.

Inquiry alone ordinarily does not provide sufficient audit evidence, and the auditor will gather additional corroborative evidence to support the response. For example, inquiry will not provide sufficient competent audit evidence for testing the operating effectiveness of controls. Additionally, when inquiring about management intent, the information available to support management's intent may be limited. In this case, understanding management's past history of carrying out its stated intentions may provide relevant information about management's intent.

Observation

Observation consists of looking at a process or procedure being performed by others. The actions being observed typically do not leave an audit trail that can be tested by examining records or documents. Examples include observation of the counting of inventories by the entity's personnel and observation of the performance of control activities. Observation provides audit evidence about the performance of a process or procedure but is limited to the point in time at which the observation takes place. It is also limited by the fact that the client personnel may act differently when the auditor is not observing them. Observation is generally not considered very reliable and generally requires additional corroboration by the auditor. Corroborating evidence includes data or documents from the accounting records and other documentary information (e.g., contracts and written confirmations).

Students often confuse the technical auditing definition of the term *observation* with the common usage of the word. As a result, students will use the term *observation* to describe such audit procedures as inspection of tangible assets or documents and records. However, as we discussed above, "observation" in the auditing sense consists of looking at a *process or procedure being performed by others*. Technical terms or jargon serve an important role in the efficient communication of professionals, and you will want to develop the proper vocabulary. Just as technical accounting terms such as revenue and income are not used interchangeably by professional accountants, professional auditors do not use "observation" and "inspection" interchangeably.

Confirmation

Confirmation is a specific type of inquiry. It is the process of obtaining a representation of information or of an existing condition directly from a third party. Confirmations also are used to obtain audit evidence about the absence of certain conditions, for example, the absence of a "side agreement" that may influence revenue recognition.

The reliability of evidence obtained through confirmations is directly affected by factors such as

- The form of the confirmation.
- Prior experience with the entity.
- The nature of the information being confirmed.
- The intended respondent.

Confirmations are used extensively on audits; they generally provide reliable evidence for the existence assertion and, in testing certain financial statement components (such as accounts payable), can provide evidence about the completeness assertion. Evidence about other assertions can also be obtained through the use of confirmations. For example, an auditor can send a confirmation to a consignee to verify that a client's inventory has been consigned. The returned confirmation provides evidence that the client owns the inventory (rights and obligations assertion). Table 4–4 lists selected amounts and information confirmed by auditors. Accounts receivable, accounts payable, and bank confirmations are discussed in more detail in later chapters.

Analytical Procedures

Analytical procedures are an important type of evidence on an audit. They consist of evaluations of financial information made by a study of plausible relationships among both financial and nonfinancial data (AU 329). For example, the current-year accounts receivable balance can be compared to the prior-year balance after adjusting for any increase or decrease in sales and other economic factors. Similarly, the auditor might compare the current-year gross margin percentage to the gross margin percentage for the previous five years. The auditor makes such comparisons either to identify accounts that may contain material misstatements and require

TABLE 4–4	**Amounts and Information Frequently Confirmed by Auditors**	
	Amounts or Information Confirmed	*Source of Confirmation*
	Cash balance	Bank
	Accounts receivable	Individual customers
	Inventory on consignment	Consignee
	Accounts payable	Individual vendors
	Bonds payable	Bondholders/trustee
	Common stock outstanding	Registrar/transfer agent
	Insurance coverage	Insurance company
	Collateral for loan	Creditor

more investigation or as a reasonableness test of the account balance. Analytical procedures are an effective and efficient form of evidence.

The reliability of analytical procedures is a function of (1) the availability and reliability of the data used in the calculations, (2) the plausibility and predictability of the relationship being tested, and (3) the precision of the expectation and the rigor of the investigation. Because of the importance of this type of evidence in auditing, analytical procedures are covered in greater detail in Chapter 5.

Reliability of the Types of Evidence

[LO 6]   Table 4–5 presents a hierarchy of the reliability of the types of evidence. Inspection of tangible assets, reperformance, and recalculation are generally considered of high reliability because the auditor has direct knowledge about them. Documentation, scanning, confirmation, and analytical procedures are generally considered to be of medium reliability. The reliability of inspection of records and documents depends primarily on whether a document is internal or external, and the reliability of confirmation is affected by the four factors listed previously. The reliability of analytical procedures may be affected by the availability and reliability of the data. Finally, observation and inquiry are generally low-reliability types of evidence because both require further corroboration by the auditor.

The reader should understand, however, that the levels of reliability shown in Table 4–5 are general guidelines. The reliability of the types of evidence may vary considerably across entities, and it may be subject to a number of exceptions. For example, in some circumstances, confirmations may be viewed as a highly reliable source of evidence. This may be true when a confirmation is sent to an independent third party who is highly qualified to respond to the auditor's request for information. Inquiries of client personnel or management provide another example. Audit research has shown that, in certain situations, inquiries of client personnel or management are relatively effective in detecting material misstatement.[3]

---

[3]See A. Eilifsen and W. F. Messier, Jr., "Auditor Detection of Misstatements: A Review and Integration of Empirical Research," *Journal of Accounting Literature* 2000 (19), pp. 1–43, for a detailed review of research studies that have examined auditor-detected misstatements.

TABLE 4–5	**Hierarchy of the Reliability of Types of Evidence**	
	Level of Reliability	*Type of Evidence*
	High	Inspection of tangible assets
		Reperformance
		Recalculation
	Medium	Inspection of records and documents
		Scanning
		Confirmation
		Analytical procedures
	Low	Inquiry
		Observation

Audit Documentation

Objectives of Audit Documentation

⚜ [LO 7]

Audit documentation is the auditor's principal record of the work performed and the basis for the conclusions in the auditor's report. Audit documentation also facilitates the planning, performance, and supervision of the engagement and provides the basis for the review of the quality of the work by providing the reviewer with written documentation of the evidence supporting the auditor's significant conclusions (AS 3 and AU 339).

You can think of audit documentation as the "story" of the audit. It should allow the reader to easily understand the issues and risks, the assertions tested, the audit procedures performed to gather evidence, the findings, and the conclusion. The basic characteristics of good audit documentation are similar to good documentation in other fields (e.g., medical and legal research).

Audit documentation is also referred to as working papers or the audit file. Auditing standards (AS 3 and AU 339) stipulate that working papers have two functions: (1) to provide support for the auditor's report and (2) to aid in the conduct and supervision of the audit. The form and content of the working papers are a function of the circumstances of the specific engagement.

While some working papers may be prepared in hard-copy format, audit software is normally used to prepare and store them.

Support for the Audit Report   When the engagement is complete, the auditor must decide on the appropriate type of report to issue. The basis for this decision rests in the audit evidence gathered and the conclusions reached and documented in the working papers. The working papers also document that the scope of the audit was adequate for the report issued. Information on the correspondence of the financial statements with GAAP is also included in the working papers.

Conduct and Supervision of the Audit   The working papers contain the audit evidence that documents the auditor's compliance with auditing standards. In particular, working papers document the auditor's compliance with the standards of field work. The planning of the engagement, along with the execution of the audit plan, is contained in the working papers. The working papers are also the focal point for reviewing the work of subordinates and quality control reviewers.

Content of Audit Documentation

⚜ [LO 8]

Audit documentation is the principal record of auditing procedures applied, evidence obtained, and conclusions reached by the auditor in the engagement. Because audit documentation provides the principal support for the representations in the auditor's report, it should

- Demonstrate how the audit complied with auditing and related professional practice standards.
- Support the basis for the auditor's conclusions concerning every material financial statement assertion.
- Demonstrate that the underlying accounting records agreed or reconciled with the financial statements.

Audit documentation should include a written audit program (or set of audit programs) for the engagement. The audit program should set forth in reasonable detail the auditing procedures that the auditor believed necessary to accomplish the objectives of the audit. Audit documentation should be sufficient to show that standards of field work have been followed.

Audit documentation should enable a reviewer with relevant knowledge and experience to

- Understand the nature, timing, extent, and results of the procedures performed, evidence obtained, and conclusions reached.
- Determine who performed the work and the date such work was completed, as well as the person who reviewed the work and the date of such review.

The auditor should consider the following factors when determining the nature and extent of the documentation for a particular audit area or auditing procedure:

- Risk of material misstatement associated with the assertion, account, or class of transactions.
- Extent of judgment involved in performing the work and evaluating the results.
- Significance of the evidence obtained to the assertion being tested.
- Nature and extent of exceptions identified.
- The need to document a conclusion or the basis for a conclusion not readily determinable from the documentation of the work performed (AU 339.07).

PCAOB Auditing Standard No. 3 (AS 3) requires a more stringent standard for audit documentation than the standard issued by the ASB (AU 339). AS 3 contains specific documentation requirements for audits of public companies for significant findings or issues, actions taken to address them (including additional evidence obtained), and the basis for the conclusions reached. Examples of significant findings or issues are shown in Table 4–6. Additionally, the auditor must identify all significant findings or issues in an

TABLE 4–6	**Examples of Significant Findings or Issues That Require Documentation under PCAOB Auditing Standard No. 3**

- Significant matters involving the selection, application, and consistency of accounting principles, including related disclosures (e.g., accounting for complex or unusual transactions, accounting estimates, and uncertainties as well as related management assumptions).
- Results of auditing procedures that indicate a need for significant modification of planned auditing procedures or the existence of material misstatements or omissions in the financial statements or the existence of significant deficiencies in internal control over financial reporting.
- Audit adjustments and the ultimate resolution of these items.
- Disagreements among members of the engagement team or with others consulted on the engagement about conclusions reached on significant accounting or auditing matters.
- Significant findings or issues identified during the review of quarterly financial information.
- Circumstances that cause significant difficulty in applying auditing procedures.
- Significant changes in the assessed level of audit risk for particular audit areas and the auditor's response to those changes.
- Any other matters that could result in modification of the auditor's report.

TABLE 4-7	**Documentation Requirements for Items Tested**

The identification of the items tested may be satisfied by indicating the source from which the items were selected and the specific selection criteria:

- If an audit sample is selected from a population of documents, the documentation should include identifying characteristics (e.g., the specific check numbers of the items included in the sample).
- If all items over a specific dollar amount are selected from a population of documents, the documentation need describe only the scope and the identification of the population (e.g., all checks over $10,000 from the July cash disbursements journal).
- If a systematic sample is selected from a population of documents, the documentation need only provide an identification of the source of the documents and an indication of the starting point and the sampling interval (e.g., a systematic sample of sales invoices was selected from the sales journal for the period from January 1 to October 1, starting with invoice number 375 and selecting every 50th invoice).

engagement completion memorandum. This memorandum should be specific enough for a reviewer to gain a thorough understanding of the significant findings or issues.

When documenting the extent of auditing procedures that involve inspection of documents or confirmation of balances, the audit documentation should include an identification of the items tested and, where appropriate, abstracts or copies of documents such as significant contracts or agreements. Table 4–7 presents the documentation requirements for items tested by the auditor.

Most public accounting firms maintain audit documentation in two types of files: permanent and current. *Permanent files* contain historical data about the client that are of continuing relevance to the audit. *Current files*, on the other hand, include information and data related specifically to the current year's engagement. Table 4–8 contains examples of the types of information included in each type of file.

Examples of Audit Documentation
❧ [LO 8]

Audit documentation comes in a variety of types. The more common audit documentation includes the audit plan and programs, working trial balance, account analysis and listings, audit memoranda, and adjusting and reclassification entries.

TABLE 4-8	**Examples of Information Included in Permanent and Current Files**

Permanent File:
Copies of, or excerpts from, the corporate charter.
Chart of accounts.
Organizational chart.
Accounting manual.
Copies of important contracts (pension contracts, union contracts, leases, etc.).
Documentation of internal control (e.g., flowcharts).
Terms of stock and bond issues.
Prior years' analytical procedure results.

Current File:
Copy of financial statements and auditor's report.
Audit plan and audit programs.
Copies of, or excerpts from, minutes of important committee meetings.
Working trial balance.
Adjusting and reclassification journal entries.
Working papers supporting financial statement accounts.

EXHIBIT 4–1	An Example of a Partial Working Trial Balance

EARTHWEAR CLOTHIERS
Partial Working Trial Balance
December 31, 2005

Account Description	W/P Ref.	Balance 12/31/04	Balance 12/31/05	Adjustments DR	CR	Adjusted T/B	Reclassification DR	CR	Financial Statements
Cash and cash equivalents	C lead	$ 49,668	$ 48,978						
Receivables	E lead	11,539	12,875						
Inventory	F lead	105,425	122,337						
Prepaid advertising	G lead	10,772	11,458						

Audit Plan and Programs   The audit plan contains the strategy to be followed by the auditor in conducting the audit. This document outlines the auditor's understanding of the client and the potential audit risks. It contains the basic framework for how the audit resources (budgeted audit hours) are to be allocated to various parts of the engagement. The audit programs contain the audit procedures that will be conducted by the auditor. Generally, each business process and account balance has a separate audit program.

Working Trial Balance   The working trial balance links the amounts in the financial statements to the audit working papers. Exhibit 4–1 illustrates a partial working trial balance for EarthWear Clothiers. In addition to a column for account name, the trial balance contains columns for working paper references, the prior year's balances, the unadjusted current-year balances, and columns for adjusting and reclassification entries. The last column would agree to the amounts contained in the financial statements after combining common account balances. A lead schedule is then used to show the detailed general ledger accounts that make up a financial statement category (cash, accounts receivable, and so on). For example, the trial balance would contain only one line for "cash and cash equivalents" and the "C lead" schedule would list all general ledger cash accounts. This approach is described in more detail later in the chapter.

Account Analysis and Listings   Account analysis working papers generally include the *activity* in a particular account for the period. For example, Exhibit 4–2 shows the analysis of legal and audit expense for EarthWear Clothiers for the year ended December 31, 2005. Listings represent a schedule of items remaining in the ending balance of an account and are often called *trial balances*. For example, the auditor may obtain a listing of all amounts owed to vendors that make up the accounts payable balance as of the end of the year. This listing would represent a trial balance of unpaid vendors' invoices.

EXHIBIT 4-2	**Example of an Account Analysis Working Paper**

EARTHWEAR CLOTHIERS
Analysis of Legal and Audit Expense
12/31/05

T20
GMP
2/4/06

Date	Payee	Amount	Explanation
Feb. 1	Katz & Fritz	$ 28,500.00**V**	For services related to a patent infringement suit by Gough Mfg. Co. Lawsuit was dismissed.
April 10	Willis & Adams	950,000.00**V**	Annual audit fee.
Oct. 1	Katz & Fritz	26,200.00**V**	Legal fee for patent infringement suit against Weshant, Inc.
Oct. 20	Smoothe, Sylk, Fiels, Goode & Associates	2,100.00**V**	Legal services for a purchase contract with McDonald Merchandise, Inc.
		1,006,800.00	
		F T/B	

Tick Mark Legend

V = Examined payees' bills for amount and description.
F = Footed.
T/B = Agreed to trial balance.

Conclusion: Based on the audit work performed, EarthWear's legal and audit expense account is not materially misstated.

Audit Memoranda   Much of the auditor's work is documented in written memoranda. These include discussions of items such as internal controls, inventory observation, errors identified, and problems encountered during the audit.

Adjusting and Reclassification Entries   The audit documentation should also include the adjusting and reclassification entries identified by the auditor or client. Adjusting entries are made to correct misstatements in the client's records. For example, if the auditor discovered that certain inventory items were improperly valued, an adjusting entry would be proposed to correct the dollar misstatement. Adjusting entries are posted in both the client's records and the working trial balance.

Reclassification entries are made to properly present information on the financial statements. A reclassification entry affects income statement accounts or balance sheet accounts, but not both. For example, a reclassification entry might be necessary to present as a current liability the current portion of long-term debt.

Format of Audit Documentation

[LO 8]

Audit documentation may be prepared in both hard copy and electronically. Many auditors now use personal computers and have electronic documentation programs. Whether the documentation is prepared manually or electronically, the manner in which it is formatted usually contains three general characteristics.

Heading   All audit documentation should have a proper heading. The heading should include the name of the client, the title of the working paper, and the client's year-end date. Exhibit 4–2 shows a working paper with a proper heading.

Indexing and Cross-Referencing   The audit documents must be organized so that members of the audit team or firm can find relevant audit evidence. Some firms use a lettering system; other firms use some type of numbering system. For example, the general working papers may be labeled "A," internal control systems working papers "B," cash working papers "C," and so on. When the auditor performs audit work on one working paper and supporting information is obtained from another working paper, the auditor cross-references (it can be "linked" in audit software) the information on each working paper. This process of indexing and cross-referencing provides a trail from the financial statements to the individual audit documents that a reviewer can easily follow. Indexing and cross-referencing are discussed further in the next section.

Tick Marks   Auditors use tick marks to document work performed. Tick marks are simply notations that are made by the auditor near, or next to, an item or amount on an audit document. The tick mark symbol is typically explained or defined at the bottom of the audit document, although many firms use a standard set of tick marks. Exhibit 4–2 shows some examples of tick marks. In this example of documentation, the tick mark "V" indicates that the auditor examined the bills sent to the client by the payee for proper amount and description.

Many public accounting firms document their conclusions about an individual account or component of the financial statements. Exhibit 4–2 shows an example of how an auditor might document a conclusion about an individual account.

Organization of Audit Documentation ❧ [LO 8]

The audit documentation needs to be organized so that any member of the audit team (and others) can find the audit evidence that supports each financial statement account. While no specific guidelines dictate how this should be accomplished, the following discussion presents a general approach that should assist in understanding the organization of audit documentation.

The financial statements contain the accounts and amounts covered by the auditor's report. These accounts come from the working trial balance, which summarizes the general ledger accounts contained on each lead schedule. Each lead schedule includes the general ledger accounts that make up the financial statement account. Different types of audit documentation (account analysis, listings, confirmations, and so on) are then used to support each of the general ledger accounts. Each of these audit documents is indexed, and all important amounts are cross-referenced between audit documents.

Figure 4–3 presents an example of how audit documents could be organized to support the cash account. Note that the $15,000 shown on the balance sheet agrees to the working trial balance. The "A lead" schedule in turn contains the three general ledger accounts that are included in the

FIGURE 4–3   **An Example of the Organization of Audit Documents**

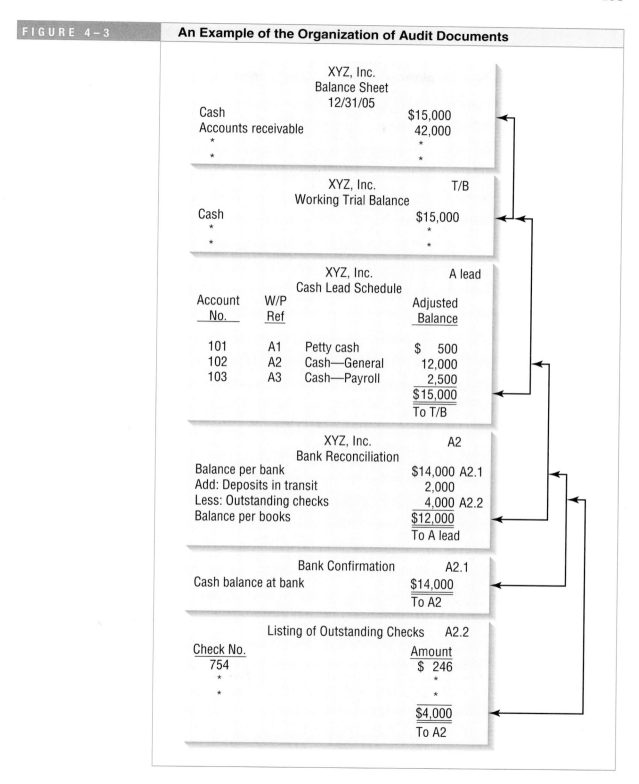

$15,000 balance. Audit documents then support each of the general ledger accounts. For example, the audit documents indexed "A2" provide the audit evidence supporting the general cash balance of $12,000. Also note that each important amount is cross-referenced. For example, the balance per bank of $14,000 on "A2" is referenced to "A2.1" and the cash balance on "A2.1" is referenced back to "A2."

Ownership of Audit Documentation

✿ [LO 8]

Audit documentation is the property of the auditor. This includes not only audit documents prepared by the auditor but also audit documents prepared by the client at the request of the auditor. The auditor should retain audit documents for a reasonable period of time in order to meet the needs of his or her practice and legal record retention requirements. Some firms microfiche audit documents, while other firms destroy them after a predetermined period.

Although the auditor owns the audit documents, they cannot be shown, except under certain circumstances, to anyone without the client's consent. Chapter 19 discusses the auditor's ethical considerations concerning the confidentiality of audit documentation.

Audit Document Archiving and Retention

Legal and auditing standards have long required auditors to retain their audit files for a number of years after an audit report is filed. However, the events leading up to the Sarbanes-Oxley Act focused the spotlight on the practice of archiving and retaining audit documentation. Exhibit 4–3 describes Arthur Andersen's federal indictment and conviction on obstruction of justice charges for deletions and alterations of audit documentation related to the Enron audit. The indictment and conviction ultimately led to the failure of Arthur Andersen. In the wake of the Enron-Andersen scandal, the Sarbanes-Oxley Act imposed new guidelines for audit file archiving and retention.

Sarbanes and the PCAOB's standard (AS 3) require that audit documentation be retained for seven years from the date of completion of the engagement, as indicated by the date of the auditor's report (or the date that fieldwork is substantially completed), unless a longer period of time is required by law (e.g., pending or threatened lawsuit, investigation, or subpoena). All documents that "form the basis of the audit or review" are required to be retained under the Sarbanes regulations. Prior to Sarbanes, public accounting firms would not typically include in their workpapers documentation that was inconsistent with the final conclusion of the audit team regarding a matter, nor would they include all internal correspondence leading up to a final decision. AS 3 requires that any document created, sent, or received, including documents that are inconsistent with a final conclusion, be included in the audit files for all significant matters. This includes any correspondence between engagement teams and national technical accounting or auditing experts in a public accounting firm's national office. AS 3 requires such document retention to facilitate any subsequent investigations, proceedings, and litigation.

Some states (e.g., New York and California) have adopted similar archiving and retention policies for all audits, including audits of nonpublic companies.

EXHIBIT 4–3	The Wholesale Destruction of Documents and the Indictment of Arthur Andersen

On March 14, 2002, a federal grand jury indicted Arthur Andersen, initiating the first criminal charge in the Enron bankruptcy. The one-count indictment, alleging obstruction of justice, read that for a one-month span in October and early November 2001, "Andersen . . . did knowingly, intentionally, and corruptly persuade" employees to "alter, destroy, mutilate, and conceal." The indictment charged that Arthur Andersen employees "were instructed by Andersen partners and others to destroy immediately documentation relating to Enron and told to work overtime if necessary to accomplish the destruction." The indictment also called the destruction an "unparalleled initiative to shred physical documentation and delete computer files. Tons of paper relating to the Enron audit was promptly shredded as part of the orchestrated document destruction. The shredder at the Andersen office at the Enron building was used virtually constantly and, to handle the overload, dozens of large trunks filled with Enron documents were sent to Andersen's main Houston office to be shredded."

In November 2001, the SEC served Andersen with the anticipated subpoena relating to its work for Enron. In response, members of the Andersen team on the Enron audit were alerted finally that there could be "no more shredding" because the firm had been "officially served" for documents. During the trial, the only major issue of dispute between the government and defense was whether anyone at Arthur Andersen acted with intent to impede the regulatory proceeding prior to being "officially served." The fate of Arthur Andersen hung on this single issue. Arthur Andersen's specialists on securities regulation maintained that the firm never considered the possibility of a federal inquiry in fall 2001 at a time others in the firm were destroying documents related to Enron.

Meanwhile, the government established that Andersen could be found guilty of obstruction of justice charges for document alteration and destruction before any official proceedings were brought against Anderson so long as it could be established that there was a reasonable possibility of an investigation or lawsuit. The government was able to point to various sources of information that were known to Andersen before the destruction began that suggested litigation against Andersen was imminent, including:

- Numerous articles appearing in major publications in late summer 2001 that questioned Enron's accounting.
- The opening of the SEC's informal and formal inquiries into Enron's accounting.
- Enron announced its first loss as well as a restatement to previously filed financial statements, and the stock price plummeted.
- Andersen received the allegations of Sherron Watkins, an Enron employee, regarding possible fraud and other improprieties at Enron.

In June 2002, the federal jury convicted Arthur Andersen of obstruction of justice after 10 days of deliberation. Ironically, in interviews, jurors said that they reached their decision because an Arthur Andersen lawyer had ordered critical deletions to an internal memorandum, rather than because of the firm's wholesale destruction of Enron-related documents (*New York Times*, June 15, 2002).

KEY TERMS

Accounting records. The records of initial entries and supporting records, such as checks and records of electronic fund transfers; invoices; contracts; the general and subsidiary ledgers, journal entries, and other adjustments to the financial statements that are not reflected in formal journal entries; and records such as work sheets and spreadsheets supporting cost allocations, computations, reconciliations, and disclosures.

Analytical procedures. Evaluations of financial information made by a study of plausible relationships among both financial and nonfinancial data.

Assertions. Expressed or implied representations by management that are reflected in the financial statement components.

Audit documentation (workpapers). The auditor's principal record of the work performed and the basis for the conclusions in the auditor's report. It also facilitates the planning, performance, and supervision of the engagement and provides the basis for the review of the quality of the work by providing the reviewer with written documentation of the evidence supporting the auditor's significant conclusions.

Audit evidence. All the information used by the auditor in arriving at the conclusions on which the audit opinion is based, and includes the information contained in the accounting records underlying the financial statements and other information.

Audit procedures. Specific acts performed as the auditor gathers evidence to determine if specific assertions are being met.

Confirmation. The process of obtaining and evaluating direct communication from a third party in response to a request for information about a particular item affecting financial statement assertions.

Inquiry. Seeking information of knowledgeable persons, both financial and nonfinancial, throughout the entity or outside the entity.

Inspection of records and documents. Examination of internal or external records or documents that are in paper form, electronic form, or other media.

Inspection of tangible assets. Physical examination of the tangible assets.

Observation. Process of watching a process or procedure being performed by others.

Other information. Audit evidence that includes minutes of meetings; confirmations from third parties; analysts' reports; benchmarking data about competitors; controls manuals; information obtained by the auditor from such audit procedures as inquiry, observation, and inspection; and other information developed by, or available to, the auditor.

Recalculation. Determination of the mathematical accuracy of documents or records.

Relevance of evidence. Whether evidence relates to assertions being tested.

Reliability of evidence. The diagnosticity of evidence; that is, whether the type of evidence can be relied on to signal the true state of the assertion.

Reperformance. The auditor's independent execution of procedures or controls that were originally performed as part of the entity's internal control, either manually or through the use of computer assisted audit techniques.

Scanning. Reviewing accounting data to identify significant or unusual items; including the identification of anomalous individual items within account balances or other client data through the scanning or analysis of entries in transaction listings, subsidiary ledgers, general ledger control accounts, adjusting entries, suspense accounts, reconciliations, and other detailed reports.

REVIEW QUESTIONS

[LO 1] 4-1 Explain why the auditor divides the financial statements into components or segments in order to test management's assertions.

[1] 4-2 How do management assertions relate to the financial statements?

[2] 4-3 List and define the assertions about classes of transactions and events for the period under audit.

[2] 4-4 List and define the assertions about account balances at the period end.

[4] 4-5 Define audit evidence. Give three examples of corroborating evidence.

[4] 4-6 Explain why in most instances audit evidence is persuasive rather than convincing.

[5] 4-7 List and define the audit procedures for obtaining audit evidence.

[5,6] 4-8 In a situation that uses inspection of records and documents as a type of evidence, distinguish between vouching and tracing in terms of the direction of testing and the assertions being tested.

[5,6] 4-9 Why is it necessary to obtain corroborating evidence for inquiry and for observation?

[6] 4-10 Discuss the relative reliability of the different types of audit procedures.

[8] 4-11 Why are indexing and cross-referencing important to the documentation of audit working papers?

MULTIPLE-CHOICE QUESTIONS

[2,3] 4-12 Which of the following procedures would an auditor most likely rely on to verify management's assertion of completeness?
a. Reviewing standard bank confirmations for indications of kiting.
b. Comparing a sample of shipping documents to related sales invoices.
c. Observing the client's distribution of payroll checks.
d. Confirming a sample of recorded receivables by direct communication with the debtors.

[2,5,6] 4-13 In testing the existence assertion for an asset, an auditor ordinarily works from the
a. Financial statements to the potentially unrecorded items.
b. Potentially unrecorded items to the financial statements.
c. Accounting records to the supporting evidence.
d. Supporting evidence to the accounting records.

[4,5] 4-14 Which of the following statements concerning audit evidence is correct?
a. To be competent, audit evidence should be either persuasive or relevant but need *not* be both.
b. The measure of the validity of audit evidence lies in the auditor's judgment.
c. The difficulty and expense of obtaining audit evidence concerning an account balance is a valid basis for omitting the test.
d. A client's accounting data may be sufficient audit evidence to support the financial statements.

[5,6] 4-15 Which of the following procedures would provide the most reliable audit evidence?
  a. Inquiries of the client's internal audit staff held in private.
  b. Inspection of prenumbered client purchase orders filed in the vouchers payable department.
  c. Analytical procedures performed by the auditor on the entity's trial balance.
  d. Inspection of bank statements obtained directly from the client's financial institution.

[5,6] 4-16 Which of the following types of audit evidence is the *least* persuasive?
  a. Prenumbered purchase order forms.
  b. Bank statements obtained from the client.
  c. Test counts of inventory performed by the auditor.
  d. Correspondence from the client's attorney about litigation.

[5,6] 4-17 Audit evidence can come in different forms with different degrees of persuasiveness. Which of the following is the *most* persuasive type of evidence?
  a. Bank statements obtained from the client.
  b. Computations made by the auditor.
  c. Prenumbered client sales invoices.
  d. Vendors' invoices.

[6] 4-18 An auditor would be *least* likely to use confirmations in connection with the examination of
  a. Inventory.
  b. Refundable income taxes.
  c. Long-term debt.
  d. Stockholders' equity.

[8] 4-19 The current file of the auditor's working papers should generally include
  a. A flowchart of the accounting system.
  b. Organization charts.
  c. A copy of the financial statements.
  d. Copies of bond and note indentures.

[8] 4-20 The permanent file section of the working papers that is kept for each audit client most likely contains
  a. Review notes pertaining to questions and comments regarding the audit work performed.
  b. A schedule of time spent on the engagement by each individual auditor.
  c. Correspondence with the client's legal counsel concerning pending litigation.
  d. Narrative descriptions of the client's accounting system and control procedures.

[8] 4-21 An audit document that reflects the major components of an amount reported in the financial statements is referred to as a(n)
  a. Lead schedule.
  b. Supporting schedule.
  c. Audit control account.
  d. Working trial balance.

PROBLEMS

[2] 4-22 Management makes assertions about components of the financial statements. Match the management assertions shown in the following left-hand column with the proper description of the assertion shown in the right-hand column.

Management Assertion	Description
a. Existence b. Rights and obligations c. Completeness d. Valuation or allocation e. Assertions about presentation and disclosure	1. The accounts and transactions that should be included are included; thus, the financial statements are complete. 2. Assets, liabilities, equity revenues, and expenses are appropriately valued and are allocated to the proper accounting period. 3. Amounts shown in the financial statements are properly presented and disclosed. 4. The assets are the rights of the entity, and the liabilities are its obligations. 5. The assets and liabilities exist, and the recorded transactions have occurred.

[5] 4-23 For each of the following specific audit procedures, indicate the type of audit procedure it represents: (1) inspection of records or documents, (2) inspection of tangible assets, (3) reperformance, (4) recalculation, (5) scanning, (6) inquiry, (7) observation, (8) confirmation, and (9) analytical procedures.

a. Sending a written request to the client's customers requesting that they report the amount owed to the client.

b. Examining large sales invoices for a period of two days before and after year-end to determine if sales are recorded in the proper period.

c. Agreeing the total of the accounts receivable subsidiary ledger to the accounts receivable general ledger account.

d. Discussing the adequacy of the allowance for doubtful accounts with the credit manager.

e. Comparing the current-year gross profit percentage with the gross profit percentage for the last four years.

f. Examining a new plastic extrusion machine to ensure that this major acquisition was received.

g. Watching the client's warehouse personnel count the raw materials inventory.

h. Performing test counts of the warehouse personnel's count of the raw material.

i. Obtaining a letter from the client's attorney indicating that there were no lawsuits in progress against the client.

j. Tracing the prices used by the client's billing program for pricing sales invoices to the client's approved price list.

k. Review the general ledger for unusual adjusting entries.

[2,5] 4-24 For each of the audit procedures listed in Problem 4-23, identify the category (assertions about classes of transactions and events or

assertions about account balances) and the primary assertion being tested.

[1,4] 4-25   a. The first generally accepted auditing standard of field work requires, in part, that "the work is to be adequately planned." An effective tool that aids the auditor in adequately planning the work is an audit program.

Required:

Describe an audit program and the purposes it serves.

b. Auditors frequently refer to "standards" and "procedures." *Standards* are measures of the quality of the auditor's performance. Standards specifically refer to the 10 generally accepted auditing standards. *Procedures* relate to acts that the auditor performs while trying to gather evidence. Procedures specifically refer to the methods or techniques the auditor uses in conducting the examination.

Required:

List at least eight different types of procedures an auditor would use in examining financial statements. For example, a type of procedure an auditor would use frequently is the observation of activities and conditions. Do not discuss specific accounts.

(AICPA, adapted)

[5,6] 4-26   Evidence comes in various types and has different degrees of reliability. Following are some statements that compare various types of evidence.

a. A bank confirmation versus observation of the segregation of duties between cash receipts and recording payment in the accounts receivable subsidiary ledger.

b. An auditor's recalculation of depreciation versus examination of raw material requisitions.

c. A bank statement included in the client's records versus shipping documents.

d. Physical examination of common stock certificates versus physical examination of inventory components for a personal computer.

Required:

For each situation, indicate whether the first or second type of evidence is more reliable. Provide a rationale for your choice.

[5,6] 4-27   Inspection of records and documents relates to the auditor's examination of client accounting records and other information. One issue that affects the reliability of documentary evidence is whether the documents are *internal* or *external*. Following are examples of documentary evidence:

1. Duplicate copies of sales invoices.
2. Purchase orders.
3. Bank statements.
4. Remittance advices.
5. Vendors' invoices.
6. Materials requisition forms.
7. Overhead cost allocation sheets.

 8. Shipping documents.
 9. Payroll checks.
 10. Long-term debt agreements.

Required:
a. Classify each document as internal or external evidence.
b. Classify each document as to its reliability (high, moderate, or low).

[5,6]   4-28   The confirmation process is defined as the process of obtaining and evaluating a direct communication from a third party in response to a request for information about a particular item affecting financial statement assertions.

Required:
a. List and describe the factors that affect the reliability of confirmations.
b. Refer back to EarthWear Clothiers' financial statements included in Chapter 1. Identify any information on EarthWear's financial statements that might be verified through the use of confirmations.

[7,8]   4-29   Audit documentation is the auditor's record of work performed and conclusions reached on an audit engagement.

Required:
a. What are the purposes of audit documentation?
b. List and describe the various types of audit documents.
c. What factors affect the auditor's judgment about the nature and extent of audit documentation for a particular engagement?

DISCUSSION CASES

[4,5,6]   4-30   **Part I.** Lernout & Hauspie (L & H) was the world's leading provider of speech and language technology products, solutions, and services to businesses and individuals worldwide. Both Microsoft and Intel invested millions in L & H. However, accounting scandals and fraud allegations sent the company's stock crashing, and forced the firm to seek bankruptcy protection in Belgium and the United States. The following selected information pertains to L & H's sales and accounts receivable:
• Consolidated revenue increased 184 percent from the 1997 fiscal year to the 1998 fiscal year.
• Revenue in South Korea, which has a reputation as a difficult market for foreign companies to enter, increased from $97,000 in the first quarter of 1999 to approximately $59 million in the first quarter of 2000.
• In the second quarter of 2000, sales grew by 104 percent but accounts receivable grew by 128 percent.
• Average days outstanding increased from 138 days in 1998 to 160 days for the six-month period ended June 30, 2000.

Required:
a. Based on the above information, which assertion(s) for sales should the auditor be most concerned with? Why?
b. Based on the above information, which assertion(s) for accounts receivable should the auditor be most concerned with? Why?

c. What audit evidence should the auditor gather to verify the assertion(s) for sales and accounts receivable? Be specific as to how each type of evidence relates to the assertions you mentioned in parts *a* and *b* of this question.

Part II. L & H's auditor did not confirm accounts receivable from customers in South Korea. However, *The Wall Street Journal* contacted 18 of L & H's South Korean customers and learned the following:

- Three out of 18 customers listed by L & H stated that they were not L & H customers.
- Three others indicated that their purchases from L & H were smaller than those reported by L & H.

Required:

a. If L & H's auditor had confirmed these receivables and received such responses, what additional evidence could they have gathered to try to obtain an accurate figure for sales to and accounts receivable from customers in South Korea?

b. If you were L & H's auditor and you had received such responses from South Korean customers, how likely would you be to use inquiry of the client as an audit procedure? Why?

Sources: M. Maremont, J. Eisinger, and J. Carreyrou, "How High-Tech Dream at Lernout & Hauspie Crumbled in a Scandal," *The Wall Street Journal* (December 7, 2000), pp. A1, A18; J. Carreyrou and M. Maremont, "Lernout Unit Engaged in Massive Fraud to Fool Auditors, New Inquiry Concludes," *The Wall Street Journal* (April 6, 2001), p. A3; and J. Carreyrou, "Lernout Unit Booked Fictitious Sales, Says Probe," *The Wall Street Journal* (April 9, 2001), p. B2.

[4,5,6]   4-31   Bentley Bros. Book Company publishes more than 250 fiction and nonfiction titles. Most of the company's books are written by Southern authors and typically focus on subjects popular in the region. The company sells most of its books to major retail stores such as Waldenbooks and B. Dalton.

Your firm was just selected as the new auditors for Bentley Bros., and you have been appointed as the audit manager for the engagement based on your prior industry experience. The prior auditors were removed because the client felt that it was not receiving adequate service. The prior auditors have indicated to you that the change in auditors did not result from any disagreements over accounting or auditing issues.

Your preliminary review of the company's financial statements indicates that the allowance for return of unsold books represents an important account (that is, high risk) because it may contain material misstatements. Consistent with industry practice, retailers are allowed to return unsold books for full credit. You know from your prior experience with other book publishers that the return rate for individual book titles can range from 30 to 50 percent. The client develops its allowance for return of unsold books based on internally generated records; that is, it maintains detailed records of all book returns by title.

Required:

a. Discuss how you would assess the reliability of the client's records for developing the allowance for return of unsold books.

b. Discuss how you would determine the return rate for relatively new titles.

c. Consider whether any external evidence can be obtained that would provide additional evidence on the reasonableness of the account.

INTERNET ASSIGNMENTS

[4,5,6]   4-32   Use one of the Internet browsers to search for the following terms:
- Electronic data interchange (EDI)
- Image-processing systems

Prepare a memo describing EDI and image-processing systems. Discuss the implications of each for the auditor's consideration of audit evidence.

| www.mhhe.com/ messier4e | Visit the book's Online Learning Center for problem material to be completed using the *ACL* software packaged with your new text. |

Part III

PLANNING THE AUDIT, AND UNDERSTANDING AND AUDITING INTERNAL CONTROL

CHAPTER 5

LEARNING OBJECTIVES

Upon completion of this chapter you will

[1] Understand the auditor's requirements for client acceptance and continuance.

[2] Know what is required to establish the terms of an engagement.

[3] Know the types of information that are included in an engagement letter.

[4] Understand how the work of the internal auditors can assist in the performance of the audit.

[5] Know the responsibilities of the audit committee and how it relates to the external auditors.

[6] Understand the steps that are involved in preplanning.

[7] Identify the steps that are performed in planning an audit engagement.

[8] Know the types of audit tests.

[9] Learn the purposes and types of analytical procedures.

[10] Understand the audit testing hierarchy.

[11] Identify financial ratios that are useful as analytical procedures.

RELEVANT ACCOUNTING AND AUDITING PRONOUNCEMENTS

FAS 57, Related Party Disclosures

AU 310, Establishing an Understanding with the Client

AU 311, Planning and Supervision

AU 312, Audit Risk and Materiality in Conducting an Audit

AU 315, Communications between Predecessor and Successor Auditors

AU 316, Consideration of Fraud in a Financial Statement Audit

AU 317, Illegal Acts

AU 319, Consideration of Internal Control in a Financial Statement Audit

AU 322, The Auditor's Consideration of the Internal Audit Function in an Audit of Financial Statements

AU 329, Analytical Procedures

AU 334, Related Parties

AU 336, Using the Work of a Specialist

AU 339, Audit Documentation

AU 350, Audit Sampling

AU 380, Communication with Audit Committees

QC 10, System of Quality Control for a CPA Firm's Accounting and Auditing Practice

QC 90, Establishing Quality Control Policies and Procedures

Audit Planning and Types of Audit Tests

Major Phases of an Audit

Client acceptance/
continuance and establishing
engagement terms
(Chapter 5)

Preplanning
(Chapter 5)

Establish materiality
and assess risks
(Chapter 3)

Plan the audit
(Chapters 3 and 5)

Consider and audit
internal control
(Chapters 6 and 7)

Audit business processes
and related accounts
(e.g., revenue generation)
(Chapters 10–16)

Complete the audit
(Chapter 17)

Evaluate results and
issue audit report
(Chapters 2 and 18)

The first standard of fieldwork requires that the audit be properly planned. If the audit is not properly planned, the auditor may issue an incorrect audit report or conduct an inefficient audit. The audit starts with the initial appointment or reappointment of the auditor by the client. Next, the auditor performs a number of activities that go into developing an overall audit strategy.

This chapter covers the following phases of the audit identified in Figure 1–4 (page **22**):

- Client acceptance and continuance.
- Establishing the terms of the engagement.
- Preplanning activities.
- Assessing risks and establishing materiality.
- Planning the audit.

It then reviews the major types of audit tests and covers analytical procedures. Analytical procedures are required to be performed as part of the planning of the audit and as part of wrapping up the audit. They are also often useful for providing substantive audit evidence during the conduct of the audit of business processes and related accounts. The *Advanced Module* presents ratios that are useful for financial statement analysis. 🌐

Client Acceptance and Continuance

☙ **[LO 1]**   The first phase of the audit process that relates to audit planning is client acceptance and continuance (see Figure 5–1). The extent of effort that goes into evaluating a new client is normally much greater than the decision to continue an existing client. With a continuing client the auditor possesses extensive knowledge about the entity and its environment.

Prospective Client
Acceptance

Public accounting firms should investigate a prospective client prior to accepting an engagement.[1] Table 5–1 lists procedures that a firm might conduct to evaluate a prospective client. Performance of such procedures would normally be documented in a memo or by completion of a client acceptance questionnaire or checklist.

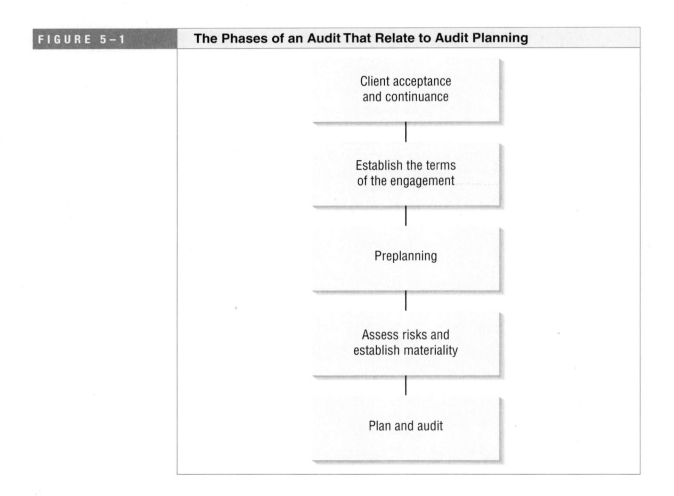

FIGURE 5–1	The Phases of an Audit That Relate to Audit Planning

Client acceptance
and continuance

Establish the terms
of the engagement

Preplanning

Assess risks and
establish materiality

Plan and audit

---

[1]See H. F. Huss and F. A. Jacobs, "Risk Containment: Exploring Auditor Decisions in the Engagement Process," *Auditing: A Journal of Practice and Theory* (Fall 1991), pp. 16–32, for a description of the client acceptance process of the Big 4 firms.

TABLE 5–1	Procedures for Evaluating a Prospective Client

1. Obtain and review available financial information (annual reports, interim financial statements, income tax returns, etc.).
2. Inquire of third parties about any information concerning the integrity of the prospective client and its management. (Such inquiries should be directed to the prospective client's bankers and attorneys, credit agencies, and other members of the business community who may have such knowledge.)
3. Communicate with the predecessor auditor as required by auditing standards (AU 315) about whether there were any disagreements about accounting principles, audit procedures, or similar significant matters.
4. Consider whether the prospective client has any circumstances that will require special attention or that may represent unusual business or audit risks, such as litigation or going-concern problems.
5. Determine if the firm is independent of the client and able to provide the desired service.
6. Determine if the firm has the necessary technical skills and knowledge of the industry to complete the engagement.
7. Determine if acceptance of the client would violate any applicable regulatory agency requirements or the Code of Professional Conduct.

When the prospective client has previously been audited, auditing standards (AU 315) require that the successor auditor make certain inquiries of the predecessor auditor before accepting the engagement. The successor auditor should request permission of the prospective client before contacting the predecessor auditor. Because the Code of Professional Conduct does not allow an auditor to disclose confidential client information without the client's consent, the prospective client must authorize the predecessor auditor to respond to the successor's requests for information. The successor auditor's communications with the predecessor auditor should include questions related to the integrity of management; disagreements with management over accounting and auditing issues; communications with the audit committee or an equivalent group regarding fraud, illegal acts, and internal-control-related matters; and the predecessor's understanding of the reason for the change in auditors. Such inquiries of the predecessor auditor may help the successor auditor determine whether to accept the engagement. The predecessor auditor should respond fully to the successor's requests unless an unusual circumstance (such as a lawsuit) exists. If the predecessor's response is limited, the successor auditor must be informed that the response is limited.

In the unusual case where the prospective client refuses to permit the predecessor to respond, the successor auditor should have reservations about accepting the client. Such a situation should raise serious questions about management's motivations and integrity.

After accepting the engagement, the successor auditor may need information on beginning balances and consistent application of GAAP in order to issue an unqualified report. The successor auditor should request that the client authorize the predecessor auditor to permit a review of his or her working papers. In most instances, the predecessor auditor will allow the successor auditor to make copies of any working papers of continuing interest (for example, details of selected balance sheet accounts).

If the client has not previously been audited, the public accounting firm should complete all the procedures listed in Table 5–1, except for the communication with the predecessor auditor. The auditor should review the prospective client's financial information and carefully assess management integrity by communicating with the entity's bankers and attorneys, as well as other members of the business community. In some cases, the public accounting firm may hire an investigative agency to check on management's background.

Continuing Client Retention

Public accounting firms need to evaluate periodically whether to retain their current clients. This evaluation may take place at or near the completion of an audit or when some significant event occurs. Conflicts over accounting and auditing issues or disputes over fees may lead a public accounting firm to disassociate itself from a client. The additional work required for public company audits brought on by the Sarbanes-Oxley Act resulted in many smaller public clients shifting from the Big 4 international public accounting firms to national and regional public accounting firms.

Establishing the Terms of the Engagement

[LO 2] The auditor and the client must agree on the terms of the engagement, including the type, scope, and timing of the engagement. This understanding reduces the risk that either party may misinterpret what is expected or required of the other party. The terms of the engagement, which are documented in the engagement letter, should include the objectives of the engagement, management's responsibilities, the auditor's responsibilities, and the limitations of the engagement. In establishing the terms of the engagement,[2] three topics must be discussed: (1) the engagement letter, (2) the internal auditors, and (3) the audit committee.

The Engagement Letter

[LO 3] An *engagement letter* formalizes the arrangement reached between the auditor and the client. This letter serves as a contract, outlining the responsibilities of both parties and preventing misunderstandings between the two parties. While an engagement letter is not required by auditing standards, good audit practice dictates that firms use such letters with their clients in order to avoid misunderstandings. Exhibit 5–1 shows a sample engagement letter for EarthWear.

In addition to the items mentioned in the sample engagement letter in Exhibit 5–1, the engagement letter may include

- Arrangements involving the use of specialists or internal auditors.
- Any limitation of the liability of the auditor or client, such as indemnification to the auditor for liability arising from knowing misrepresentations to the auditor by management. (Note that regulatory bodies, such as the SEC, may restrict or prohibit such liability-limiting arrangements.)
- Additional services to be provided relating to regulatory requirements.
- Arrangements regarding other services (e.g., assurance, tax, or consulting services).

Internal Auditors

[LO 4] When the client has internal auditors, the auditor may request their assistance in conducting the audit. The decision process the auditor follows is outlined in Figure 5–2 (AU 322). The major issue for the independent auditor is

---

[2]See K. M. Gibson, K. Pany, and S. H. Smith, "Do We Understand Each Other?" *Journal of Accountancy* (January 1998), pp. 53–59, for more discussion of the importance of establishing terms for the engagement.

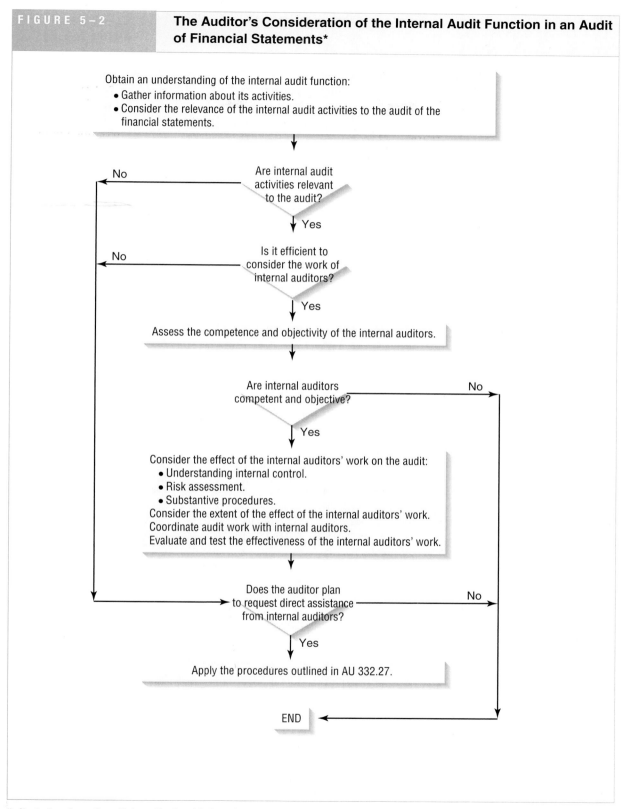

Obtain an understanding of the internal audit function:
- Gather information about its activities.
- Consider the relevance of the internal audit activities to the audit of the financial statements.

Are internal audit activities relevant to the audit? — No → / Yes

Is it efficient to consider the work of internal auditors? — No → / Yes

Assess the competence and objectivity of the internal auditors.

Are internal auditors competent and objective? — No → / Yes

Consider the effect of the internal auditors' work on the audit:
- Understanding internal control.
- Risk assessment.
- Substantive procedures.

Consider the extent of the effect of the internal auditors' work.
Coordinate audit work with internal auditors.
Evaluate and test the effectiveness of the internal auditors' work.

Does the auditor plan to request direct assistance from internal auditors? — No → / Yes

Apply the procedures outlined in AU 332.27.

END

*In Chapter 7 we discuss the auditor's consideration of the internal audit function in an audit of internal control over financial reporting.

EXHIBIT 5-1   **A Sample Engagement Letter—EarthWear Clothiers**

Williams & Adams, P.C.
Boise, Idaho

April 1, 2005

Mr. Calvin J. Rogers
EarthWear Clothiers
P.O. Box 787
Boise, Idaho 83845

Dear Mr. Rogers:

The purpose of this letter is to confirm our understanding of the terms of our engagement as independent accountants of EarthWear Clothiers (the "Company").

Services and Related Report

We will audit the financial statements of the Company at December 31, 2005, and for the year then ending. We will also audit management's assertion about the effectiveness of internal control over financial reporting at December 31, 2005. Upon completion of our audits, we will provide you with our audit report on the financial statements and internal control. If, for any reasons caused by you or relating to the affairs of the Company, we are unable to complete the audits, we may decline to issue a report as a result of this engagement.

In conjunction with the annual audit, we will perform reviews of the Company's unaudited quarterly financial statements and related data for each of the first three quarters in the year ending December 31, 2005, before the Form 10-Q is filed. These reviews will be conducted in accordance with standards established by the Public Company Accounting Oversight Board (United States), and are substantially less in scope than audits. Accordingly, a review may not reveal material modifications necessary to make the quarterly financial information conform with generally accepted accounting principles. We will communicate to you for your consideration any matters that come to our attention as a result of the review that we believe may require material modifications to the quarterly financial information to make it conform with generally accepted accounting principles.

Our Responsibilities and Limitations

The objective of the audits is the expression of opinions on the financial statements and internal controls. We will be responsible for performing the audit in accordance with standards established by the Public Company Accounting Oversight Board (United States). These standards require that we plan and perform the audit to obtain reasonable assurance about whether the financial statements are free of material misstatement. The audit will include examining, on a test basis, evidence supporting the amounts and disclosures in the financial statements, assessing accounting principles used and significant estimates made by management, and evaluating the overall financial statement presentation.

The objective of our audit of internal control over financial reporting is to express an opinion on management's assessment and an opinion on the effectiveness of the company's internal control over financial reporting based on our audit. We will be responsible for performing the audit of internal control over financial reporting in accordance with the standards of the Public Company Accounting Oversight Board (United States). Those standards require that we plan and perform the audit to obtain reasonable assurance about whether effective internal control over financial reporting was maintained in all material respects. Our audit includes obtaining an understanding of internal control over financial reporting, evaluating management's assessment, testing and evaluating the design and operating effectiveness of internal control, and performing such other procedures as we consider necessary in the circumstances.

We will design our audit to obtain reasonable, but not absolute, assurance of detecting errors or fraud that would have a material effect on the financial statements as well as other illegal acts having a direct and material effect on financial statement amounts. Our audit will not include a detailed audit of transactions, such as would be necessary to disclose errors or fraud that did not cause a material misstatement of the financial statements. It is important to recognize that there are inherent limitations in the auditing process. Audits are based on the concept of selective testing of the data underlying the financial statements, which involves judgment regarding the areas to be tested, and the nature, timing, extent, and results of the tests to be performed. Audits are, therefore, subject to the limitation that material errors or fraud or other illegal acts having a direct and material financial statement impact, if they exist, may not be detected. Because of the characteristics of fraud, particularly those involving concealment through collusion and falsified documentation (including forgery), an audit designed and executed in accordance with standards established by the Public Company Accounting Oversight Board (United States) may not detect a material fraud. Further, while effective internal control reduces the likelihood that errors, fraud, or other illegal acts will occur and remain undetected, it does not eliminate that possibility. For these reasons we cannot ensure that errors, fraud, or other illegal acts, if present, will be detected. However, we will communicate to you, as appropriate, any illegal act, material errors, or evidence that fraud may exist identified during our audit.

Management's Responsibilities

The financial statements are the responsibility of the management of the Company. In this regard, management is responsible for properly recording transactions in the accounting records and for establishing and maintaining internal control sufficient to permit the preparation of financial statements in conformity with generally accepted accounting principles. Management is responsible for adjusting the financial statements to correct material misstatements and for affirming to us that the effects of any uncorrected misstatements aggregated by us during the current engagement and pertaining to the year ending December 31, 2005, are immaterial, both individually and in the aggregate, to the financial statements taken as a whole. Management also is responsible for identifying and ensuring that the Company complies with the laws and regulations applicable to its activities.

Management is also responsible for maintaining effective internal control over financial reporting and for its assessment of the effectiveness of internal control over financial reporting. Management must accept responsibility for the effectiveness of the entity's internal control over financial reporting; evaluate the effectiveness of the entity's internal control over financial reporting using suitable control criteria; support its evaluation with sufficient evidence, including documentation; and present a written assessment of the effectiveness of the entity's internal control over financial reporting as of the end of the entity's most recent fiscal year.

Management is responsible for making available to us, on a timely basis, all of the Company's original accounting records and related information and company personnel to whom we may direct inquiries. As required by standards established by the Public Company Accounting Oversight Board (United States), we will make specific inquiries of management and others about the representations embodied in the financial statements and the effectiveness of internal control over financial reporting. Standards established by the Public Company Accounting Oversight Board (United States) also require that we obtain written representations covering audited financial statements from certain members of management. The results of our audit tests, the responses to our inquiries, and the written representations, comprise the evidential matter we intend to rely upon in forming our opinion on the financial statements.

Other Documents

Standards established by the Public Company Accounting Oversight Board (United States) require that we read any annual report that contains our audit report. The purpose of this procedure is to consider whether other information in the annual report, including the manner of its presentation, is materially inconsistent with information appearing in the financial statements. We assume no obligation to perform procedures to corroborate such other information as part of our audit.

With regard to electronic filings, such as in connection with the SEC's Electronic Data Gathering, Analysis, and Retrieval ("EDGAR") system, you agree that, before filing any document in electronic format with the SEC with which we are associated, you will advise us of the proposed filing on a timely basis. We will provide you with a signed copy of our report(s) and consent(s). These manually signed documents will serve to authorize the use of our name prior to any electronic transmission by you. For our files, you will provide us with a complete copy of the document as accepted by EDGAR.

The Company may wish to include our report on these financial statements in a registration statement to be filed under the Securities Act of 1933 or in some other securities offering. You agree that the aforementioned audit report, or reference to our Firm, will not be included in any such offering without our prior permission or consent. Any agreement to perform work in connection with an offering, including an agreement to provide permission or consent, will be a separate engagement.

Timing and Fees

Completion of our work is subject to, among other things, (1) appropriate cooperation from the Company's personnel, including timely preparation of necessary schedules, (2) timely responses to our inquiries, and (3) timely communication of all significant accounting and financial reporting matters. When and if for any reason the Company is unable to provide such schedules, information, and assistance, Willis & Adams and the Company will mutually revise the fee to reflect additional services, if any, required of us to complete the audit.

Our fee estimates are based on the time required by the individuals assigned to the engagement. Individual hourly rates vary according to the degree of responsibility involved and experience and skill required. We estimate our fees for this integrated audit of internal control and financial statements will be $950,000, exclusive of out-of-pocket expenses. This estimate takes into account the agreed-upon level of preparation and assistance from company personnel; we will advise management should this not be provided or should any other circumstances arise which may cause actual time to exceed that estimate. Invoices rendered are due and payable upon receipt.

(continues)

EXHIBIT 5–1	A Sample Engagement Letter (continued)

This engagement letter reflects the entire agreement between us relating to the services covered by this letter. It replaces and supersedes any previous proposals, correspondence, and understandings, whether written or oral. The agreements of the Company and Willis & Adams contained in this engagement letter shall survive the completion or termination of this engagement.

If you have any questions, please contact us. If the services outlined herein are in accordance with your requirements and if the above terms are acceptable to you, please have one copy of this letter signed in the space provided below and return it to us.

Very truly yours,

Willis & Adams

M. J. Willis

M. J. Willis, Partner

APPROVED:

By _Calvin J. Rogers_ Chief Executive Officer

Date   April 3, 2005

---

assessing the *competence* and *objectivity* of the internal auditors and the effect of their work on the audit. Table 5–2 presents factors that the auditor should consider when assessing the competence and objectivity of the internal auditors. In Chapter 7 we discuss the effect the Sarbanes-Oxley Act has had on the use and assessment of internal auditors for the audit of internal control over financial reporting.

The internal auditors' work may affect the nature, timing, and extent of the audit procedures performed by the independent auditor. For example, as

TABLE 5–2	Factors for Assessing the Competence and Objectivity of Internal Auditors

Competence
- Educational level and professional experience.
- Professional certification and continuing education.
- Audit policies, procedures, and checklists.
- Practices regarding their assignments.
- The supervision and review of their audit activities.
- The quality of their working paper documentation, reports, and recommendations.
- Evaluation of their performance.

Objectivity
- The organizational status of the internal auditor responsible for the internal audit function (for example, the internal auditor reports to an officer of sufficient status to ensure that the audit coverage is broad and the internal auditor has access to the board of directors or the audit committee).
- Policies to maintain internal auditors' objectivity about the areas audited (for example, internal auditors are prohibited from auditing areas to which they have recently been assigned or are to work upon completion of responsibilities in the internal audit function).

part of their regular work, internal auditors may review, assess, and monitor the entity's controls that are included in the accounting system. Similarly, part of their work may include confirming receivables or observing certain physical inventories. If the internal auditors are competent and objective, the independent auditor may use the internal auditors' work in these areas to reduce the scope of audit work. The materiality of the account balance or class of transactions and its related audit risk may also determine how much the independent auditor can rely on the internal auditors' work. When internal auditors provide direct assistance, the auditor should supervise, review, evaluate, and test their work.

The Audit Committee
❧ [LO 5]

An audit committee is a subcommittee of the board of directors that is responsible for the financial reporting and disclosure process. With privately held companies, there are no specific requirements for the composition of the audit committee. Under Section 301 of the Sarbanes-Oxley Act, the audit committee of a public company has the following requirements:

- Each member of the audit committee must be a member of the board of directors and shall be independent. "Independent" is defined as not receiving, other than for service on the audit committee, any consulting, advisory, or other compensatory fee and not being affiliated with the company.
- The audit committee is directly responsible for the appointment, compensation, and oversight of the work of any registered public accounting firm employed by the company.
- The audit committee must preapprove all audit and nonaudit services provided by its auditor.
- The audit committee must establish procedures for the receipt, retention, and treatment of complaints received by the company regarding accounting, internal control, and auditing.
- Each audit committee member must have the authority to engage independent counsel or other advisors, as it determines necessary to carry out its duties.

The audit committee should also interact with the internal audit function. An ideal arrangement for establishing the independence of the internal audit function is for the head of internal auditing to report either directly or indirectly to the audit committee.

The audit committee should meet with the external auditor before the engagement starts to discuss the auditor's responsibilities and significant accounting policies. It may also provide limited input into the scope of the auditor's work, such as requesting that the external auditor visit certain locations. The audit committee may also engage the external or internal auditors to conduct special investigations. The external auditor is required to make a number of important communications to the audit committee during or at the end of the engagement (AU 380). Most of the required communications are made at the completion of the engagement; Chapter 17 covers them in detail.

Preplanning

🎕 **[LO 6]** There are generally two preplanning activities: (1) determining the audit engagement team requirements and (2) ensuring the independence of the audit team and audit firm.

Determine the Audit Engagement Team Requirements

Public accounting firms need to ensure that their engagements are completed by auditors having the proper degree of technical training and proficiency given the circumstances of the clients. Factors that should be considered in determining staffing requirements include engagement size and complexity, level of risk, any special expertise, personnel availability, and timing of the work to be performed. For example, if the engagement involves a high level of risk, the firm should staff the engagement with more experienced auditors. Similarly, if the audit involves a specialized industry (banking, insurance, and so on) or if the client uses sophisticated computer processing, the firm must ensure that members of the audit team possess the requisite expertise. Generally, a time budget is prepared in order to assist with the staffing requirements and to schedule the fieldwork.

In some instances, the audit may require consulting with a specialist. Auditing standards (AU 336) define a *specialist* as a person or firm possessing special skill or knowledge in a field other than accounting or auditing. This would include individuals such as actuaries, appraisers, attorneys, engineers, and geologists. Such specialists may assist the auditor with valuation issues, determination of physical quantities, amounts derived from specialized techniques, or interpretations of regulations or agreements. For example, an auditor might consult an actuary to determine the amount of the client's pension obligations or a geologist to estimate a client's oil and gas reserves.

Assess Independence

The second general standard requires that the auditor be independent of the client in order to issue an opinion. According to the Statements on Quality Control Standards, a public accounting firm should establish policies and procedures to ensure that persons at all organizational levels within the firm maintain independence in accordance with Rule 101 of the Code of Professional Conduct (see Chapter 19). A firm should document compliance with this policy by having all personnel complete an annual independence questionnaire or report. This questionnaire requests information about the auditor's financial or business relationships with the firm's clients. Under certain circumstances, family members' financial or business relationships are attributable to the auditor. For example, if the spouse of an auditor participating in an engagement was an accounting supervisor for the client, independence would be considered impaired.

At the engagement level, the partner-in-charge should ensure that all individuals assigned to the engagement are independent of the client. This can be accomplished by reviewing the annual independence reports for each member of the audit team.

Another area of concern related to independence is unpaid client fees. If an account receivable from a client takes on the characteristics of a loan, the auditor's independence may be impaired. Many public accounting firms adopt a policy of not completing the current audit until all of the prior year's fees have been paid.

Finally, the CPA firm must be concerned when it also provides consulting services for an audit client. While the performance of consulting services does not, in and of itself, impair independence, the audit team must remain objective when evaluating client activities that were developed by their firm's consultants. For companies subject to the Sarbanes-Oxley Act (i.e., most public companies), the auditor is not permitted to provide certain types of consulting services for audit clients. See Chapter 19 for a list of these services.

In the rare instance where the auditor is not independent of the client, the type of audit opinion should be discussed during the planning stage. As pointed out in Chapter 2, a disclaimer of opinion must be issued when the auditor is not independent.

Assess Risks and Establish Materiality

Chapter 3 provided a detailed discussion of the process used to assess the client's business risks and to establish materiality. The auditor restricts audit risk at the account balance level in such a way that, at the end of the engagement, he or she can express an opinion on the financial statements, taken as a whole, at an acceptable level of audit risk. The audit risk model serves as a framework for this process. The auditor obtains an understanding of the entity and its environment. Based on this understanding, the auditor identifies those business risks that may result in material misstatements. The auditor evaluates the client's response to those business risks and ensures that those responses have been adequately implemented. Based on this information, the auditor assesses the level of risk of material misstatement of assertions in relation to financial statement accounts. The risk of material misstatement is used to determine the acceptable level of detection risk and to plan the auditing procedures to be performed. The auditor considers materiality from a reasonable user perspective and follows a three-step process in applying materiality on an audit. You should consider returning to Chapter 3 to review the important issues related to these concepts.

Planning the Audit

[LO 7] Engagement planning involves all the issues the auditor should consider in developing an overall strategy for conducting the audit. The objective of the audit plan is to conduct an effective and efficient audit. Basically, this means that the audit is to be conducted in accordance with auditing standards and that the risk of material misstatements is reduced to an acceptably low level. The audit plan should also consider how to conduct the engagement in a cost-effective manner.

When preparing the audit plan, the auditor should be guided by the results of the risk assessment procedures performed to gain the understanding of the entity. Additional steps that should be performed include

- Assess a preliminary level for control risk by account and assertion.
- Assess the possibility of illegal acts.

- Identify related parties.
- Conduct preliminary analytical procedures.
- Develop an overall audit strategy and prepare audit programs.
- Consider additional value-added services.

While these steps are listed in the order in which they are usually completed, an audit of financial statements is a cumulative and iterative process that often dictates that these steps be performed concurrently and that the results obtained from one step may result in a reassessment of results from another step.

Assess a Preliminary Level for Control Risk by Account and Assertion

Control risk is the risk that material misstatements will not be prevented or detected by internal controls. The auditor evaluates the effectiveness of internal control for preventing material misstatements in the financial statements and prepares a preliminary assessment of control risk. A preliminary assessment of control risk is necessary for the auditor to plan the nature, timing, and extent of testing. A primary concern is the extent to which information technology is used in processing accounting information. In evaluating the effect of information technology on the client's accounting systems, the auditor needs information on the following:

- The extent to which information technology (IT) is used in each significant accounting system or business process.
- The complexity of the client's computer operations.
- The organizational structure of the IT activities.
- The availability of data.
- The need for CAATs to gather data and conduct audit procedures.

The presence of complex information technology may require the use of an IT specialist. Chapter 6 covers these issues in more detail. Chapter 7 addresses the requirements for the audit of internal controls for public companies.

Assess the Possibility of Illegal Acts

The term *illegal acts* refers to violations of laws or governmental regulations. In some instances, fraud may also consist of illegal acts (see Chapter 3). Auditing standards (AU 317) distinguish between illegal acts that have *direct and material* effects on the financial statements and those that have *material but indirect* effects. The auditor should consider laws and regulations that are generally recognized as having a direct and material effect on the determination of financial statement amounts. For example, tax laws and laws and regulations that may affect the amount of revenue recognized under a government contract fall into this category. Auditing standards state that the auditor's responsibility for detecting illegal acts having a direct and material effect on the financial statements is the same as that for errors or fraud.

Other illegal acts, such as violations of the securities acts or occupational safety and health, Food and Drug Administration, environmental protection, equal employment regulations, and price-fixing or other antitrust violations, may materially but indirectly affect the financial statements. The auditor should be aware that such illegal acts may have occurred. If specific information comes to the auditor's attention that provides evidence concerning the existence of such material but indirect

TABLE 5–3	Information or Circumstances That May Indicate an Illegal Act

Unauthorized transactions, improperly recorded transactions, or transactions not recorded in a complete or timely manner.
An investigation by a government agency, an enforcement proceeding, or payment of unusual fines or penalties.
Violations of laws or regulations cited in reports of examinations by regulatory agencies.
Large payments for unspecified services to consultants, affiliates, or employees.
Sales commissions or agents' fees that appear excessive.
Large payments in cash or bank cashiers' checks.
Unexplained payments to government officials.
Failure to file tax returns or pay government duties.

illegal acts, the auditor should apply audit procedures specifically directed at determining whether illegal acts have occurred. However, an audit conducted in accordance with auditing standards provides no assurance that illegal acts will be detected or that any contingent liability that may result will be disclosed.

Table 5–3 presents some examples of specific information or circumstances that indicate the possibility of an illegal act. For example, the business world has seen a number of instances where payments of sales commissions or agent's fees were really bribes to secure contracts. When the auditor becomes aware of such a possible illegal act, he or she should obtain an understanding of the nature of the act, the circumstances in which it occurred, and sufficient other information to evaluate its effects on the financial statements. The auditor should then discuss the matter with the appropriate level of management. If management does not provide satisfactory information, the auditor should consult with the client's legal counsel and apply additional audit procedures, if necessary.

If an illegal act has occurred or is likely to have occurred, the auditor should consider its implications for other aspects of the audit, particularly the reliability of management representations. The auditor should ensure that the audit committee, or other body or person with equivalent authority and responsibility, is adequately informed about significant illegal acts. The auditor should also recognize that, under the circumstances noted previously, he or she may have a duty to notify parties outside the client.

Identify Related Parties

FASB No. 57, "Related Party Disclosures" (FAS 57), defines related parties as

> Affiliates of the enterprise; entities for which investments are accounted for by the equity method by the enterprise; trusts for the benefits of the employees, such as pension and profit-sharing trusts that are managed by or under the trusteeship of management; principal owners of the enterprise; its management; members of the immediate families of the principal owners of the enterprise and its management; and other parties with which the enterprise may deal if one party controls or can significantly influence the management or operating policies of the other to the extent that one of the transacting parties might be prevented from fully pursuing its own separate interests. Another party also is a related party if it can significantly influence the management or operating policies of the transacting parties or if it has an ownership interest in one of the transacting parties and can significantly influence the other to an extent that one or more of the transacting parties might be prevented from fully pursuing its own separate interests.

It is important that the auditor attempts to identify all related parties during the planning phase of the audit because transactions between the entity and related parties may not be "at arm's length." For example, the client may lease property from an entity owned by the chief executive officer at lease rates in excess of prevailing market rates. The auditor can identify related parties by evaluating the client's procedures for identifying related parties, requesting a list of related parties from management, and reviewing filings with the Securities and Exchange Commission and other regulatory agencies. Once related parties have been identified, audit personnel should be provided with the names so that transactions with such parties are identified and investigated. Here are some additional audit procedures that may identify transactions with related parties:

- Review the minutes of the board of directors and executive or operating committees for information about material transactions authorized or discussed at their meetings.
- Review conflict-of-interest statements obtained by the company from management.
- Review the extent and nature of business transacted with major customers, suppliers, borrowers, and lenders for indications of previously undisclosed relationships.
- Review accounting records for large, unusual, or nonrecurring transactions or balances, paying particular attention to transactions recognized at or near the end of the reporting period.
- Review confirmations of loans receivable and payable for indications of guarantees. If guarantees are identified, determine their nature and the relationships of the guarantor to the entity.

Interested readers should refer to AU 334 Related Parties, for additional guidance on searching for and reporting on related parties.

Conduct Preliminary Analytical Procedures

Analytical procedures are defined as consisting of evaluations of financial information made by a study of plausible relationships among both financial and nonfinancial data (AU 329). Auditing standards require that the auditor apply analytical procedures at the planning phase for all audits. The main objectives of preliminary analytical procedures at this point are (1) to understand the client's business and transactions and (2) to identify financial statement accounts that are likely to contain errors. By identifying where errors are likely, the auditor can allocate more resources to investigate those accounts. Suppose, for example, that an auditor computes a client's inventory turnover ratio for the last five years as follows:

$$\text{Inventory turnover} = \frac{\text{Cost of goods sold}}{\text{Inventory}}$$

The results of this analysis show the following trend, which is compared to industry data:

	2001	2002	2003	2004	2005
Client	8.9	8.8	8.5	8.0	7.9
Industry	8.8	8.7	8.8	8.6	8.6

The client's inventory turnover ratio in this case has declined steadily over the five-year period, while the industry turnover ratio shows only a minor decline over the same period. The auditor might suspect that the client's inventory contains slow-moving or obsolete inventory. The auditor would then plan additional testing for selected assertions such as valuation, completeness, and existence.

Develop an Overall Audit Strategy and Prepare Audit Programs

Once these planning steps have been completed, the auditor develops an overall audit strategy. This involves decisions about the *nature, timing,* and *extent,* of audit tests. At this stage, the auditor compiles his or her knowledge about the client's business objectives, strategies, and related business and audit risks. The auditor records how the client is managing its risks (i.e., through internal control processes) and then documents the effect of the risks and controls on the planned audit procedures. Auditors ensure they have addressed the risks they identified in their understanding–risk assessment processes by documenting the linkage from the client's business objectives and strategy to audit plans. The form of documentation varies from firm to firm, but a simple illustration using EarthWear might look as follows:

Business Objectives and Strategy	Business Risks	Account(s): (Assertions)	Audit Risks	Controls	Effect on Audit Plan
Increase market share through sales at new international locations (e.g., during the current year websites were developed for France, Italy, Ireland, and several eastern European countries)	Restrictive trade laws may affect sales tactics. Strong consumer protection laws in European countries. Political instability in less developed countries (LDCs).	*Revenue:* accuracy and valuation	Overstated due to pricing issues.	EwC has installed a special group to track compliance with local and international laws.	Observe and test group's policies and procedures (see workpaper R-11).
		Reserve for returns: completeness	Understated due to failure to properly track returns in new locations.	EwC has placed more frequent review of returns in new locations.	Extend audit work on EwC's return tracking with emphasis on new locations (see workpaper R-15).
	Foreign currency risks.	*Gains/losses from currency hedging:* valuation and accuracy	Gains/losses not properly calculated or accrued on hedging activity.	EwC has strong controls in the Treasury Department to account for hedging activities.	Increase the number of hedging contracts tested with particular emphasis on contracts in currencies from LDCs (see workpaper S-14).

The auditor's preliminary decision concerning control risk determines the level of control testing, which in turn affects the auditor's substantive tests of the account balances and transactions.

The audit strategy is normally documented in a written audit plan (AU 339). Audit programs containing specific audit procedures are also prepared. Exhibit 5–2 presents a partial audit program for substantive tests of accounts receivable. The types of audit tests are discussed later in this chapter.

EXHIBIT 5-2	A Partial Audit Program for Substantive Procedures Testing of Accounts Receivable

Audit Procedures	W/P Ref.	Completed by	Date
1. Obtain the December 31, 2005, aged accounts receivable trial balance and	_____	_____	_____
a. Foot the trial balance and agree total to accounts receivable control account.	_____	_____	_____
b. Randomly select thirty accounts from the aged trial balance; agree the information per the aged trial balance to the original sales invoice and determine if the invoice was included in the appropriate aging category.	_____	_____	_____
2. Confirm accounts receivable using a monetary-unit sampling plan. Set the desired confidence level = 90%, tolerable misstatement = $50,000, and expected misstatement = $20,000.	_____	_____	_____
a. For all responses with exceptions, follow up on the cause of the error.	_____	_____	_____
b. For all nonresponses, examine subsequent cash receipts and/or supporting documents.	_____	_____	_____
c. Summarize the statistical test results.	_____	_____	_____
d. Summarize the confirmation results.	_____	_____	_____
3. Test sales cutoff by identifying the last shipping advice for the year and examining five large sales for three days before and after year-end.	_____	_____	_____
4. Test the reasonableness of the allowance for doubtful accounts by the following:	_____	_____	_____
a. Test the reasonableness using past percentages on bad debts.	_____	_____	_____
b. For any large account in the aged trial balance greater than 90 days old, test for subsequent cash receipts.	_____	_____	_____
c. For the following financial ratios, compare the current year to the trend of the prior three years results and internal budgets:			
• Number of days outstanding in receivable.	_____	_____	_____
• Aging of receivables.	_____	_____	_____
• Write-offs as a percentage of sales.	_____	_____	_____
• Bad debt expense as a percentage of sales.	_____	_____	_____
5. Prepare a memo summarizing the tests, results, and conclusions.	_____	_____	_____

Consider Additional Value-Added Services

As part of the planning process, the auditor should look for opportunities to recommend additional value-added services. Traditionally, value-added services have included tax planning, system design and integration, and internal reporting processes. With auditors taking a more global view of the entity and its environment, there are new opportunities to provide valuable services for the client. For example, the assurance services (introduced in Chapter 2 and discussed in more detail in Chapter 21) include risk assessment, business performance measurement (benchmarking), and electronic commerce. The auditor also can provide recommendations based on the assessment of the entity's business risks. With the knowledge gathered through assessing business risks, the auditor can provide important feedback to management and the board of directors on the strengths and weaknesses of business processes, strategic planning, and emerging trends. Proper consideration of value-added services during the planning process should alert the audit team to proactively identify opportunities to improve client service. Of course, auditors who audit public companies are limited in the types of consulting services they can offer their audit clients (see Chapter 19).

Types of Audit Tests

[LO 8]   There are three general types of audit tests:

- Risk assessment procedures.
- Tests of controls.
- Substantive procedures.

Risk Assessment Procedures

Auditor risk assessment procedures are used to obtain an understanding of the entity and its environment, including its internal control. Risk assessment procedures include inquiries of management and others, analytical procedures, and observation and inspection. Such procedures are used to assess the risks of material misstatement at the financial statement and assertion levels. Risk assessment procedures were covered in depth in Chapter 3.

Tests of Controls

Tests of controls consist of procedures directed toward the evaluation of the effectiveness of the *design* and *implementation* of internal controls (AU 319). When tests of controls look at design issues, the auditor evaluates whether the control has been properly designed to prevent or detect material misstatements. Tests of controls directed toward the implementation of a control are concerned with whether the control is operating effectively at a point in time. The following audit procedures are examples of tests of controls:

- Inquiries of appropriate management, supervisory, and staff personnel.
- Inspection of documents, reports, and electronic files.
- Observation of the application of specific controls.
- Walkthroughs, which involve tracing a transaction from its origination to its inclusion in the financial statements through a combination of audit procedures including inquiry, observation, and inspection.
- Reperformance of the application of the control by the auditor.

For example, in evaluating the design of an automated IT application control and determining whether it has been implemented, the auditor may make inquiries of entity personnel and inspect relevant systems documentation, reports, or other documents. Table 5–4 provides additional examples

TABLE 5–4	Examples of Internal Controls and Tests of Controls
Internal Controls	*Test of Controls*
Create a separation of duties between the shipping function and the order entry and billing functions.	Observe and evaluate whether shipping personnel have access to the order entry or billing activities.
Credit Department personnel initial sales orders, indicating credit approval.	Inspect a sample of sales orders for presence of initials of Credit Department personnel.
Billing Department personnel account for the numerical sequence of sales invoices.	Inquire of Billing Department personnel about missing sales invoice numbers.
Agree sales invoices to shipping document and customer order for product types, price, and quantity.	Recompute the information on a sample of sales invoices.

of controls that are normally present in the processing of revenue transactions and tests of controls that the auditor might use to test the operation of the controls. While always an option, tests of controls are necessary in two circumstances for nonpublic clients. When the auditor's risk assessment includes an expectation of the operating effectiveness of controls, the auditor is required to test those controls to support the risk assessment. In addition, when substantive procedures alone do not provide sufficient appropriate audit evidence, the auditor is required to perform tests of controls to obtain audit evidence about their operating effectiveness. Tests of controls will be discussed further in Chapter 6. For public clients, tests of controls are required for all significant accounts and processes as part of the integrated audit of internal control and of financial statements. We discuss these requirements for public-company audits in Chapter 7.

Substantive Procedures

Substantive procedures detect material misstatements (that is, monetary errors) in a transaction class, account balance, and disclosure component of the financial statements. There are two categories of substantive procedures: (1) tests of details of classes of transactions, account balances, and disclosures and (2) substantive analytical procedures.

Tests of Details of Classes of Transactions, Account Balances, and Disclosures
Substantive tests of transactions test for errors or fraud in individual transactions. For example, an auditor may examine a large purchase of inventory by testing that the cost of the goods included on the vendor's invoice is properly recorded in the inventory and accounts payable accounts. This gives the auditor evidence about the occurrence, completeness, and accuracy assertions.

Tests of details of account balances and disclosures focus on the items that are contained in the financial statement account balances and disclosures. These important tests establish whether any material misstatements are included in the accounts or disclosures included in the financial statements. For example, the auditor may want to test accounts payable. To test the details of the accounts payable account, the auditor can examine a sample of the individual vendor invoices that make up the ending balance in accounts payable. In examining this documentation, the auditor is concerned with testing the existence and valuation assertions. Additionally, the auditor may send confirmations to vendors with zero balances in their accounts in order to test the completeness assertions.

Substantive Analytical Procedures   Because of the importance of substantive analytical procedures, they are discussed in more detail in the next section.

Dual-Purpose Tests

Tests of controls look for errors in the design and implementation of controls, while substantive tests of transactions are concerned with monetary misstatements. However, for some audit tests, it is difficult to determine whether the audit procedure is a test of controls or a substantive test of transactions. For example, in Table 5–5 (see page 189), the last control procedure shown is agreement of sales invoices to shipping documents and customer orders for product type, price, and quantity. The test of controls shown is to recompute the information on a sample of sales invoices. While this test primarily checks the effectiveness of the control, it also provides evidence on whether the sales invoice contains the wrong quantity, product type, or price. Dual-purpose tests can also improve the efficiency of the audit (AU 350.44).

This text discusses tests of controls within each business process when the assessment of control risk is covered. Substantive tests of transactions are discussed along with the other substantive tests when the financial statement accounts affected by the business process are discussed. You should remember, however, that in most audit situations substantive tests of transactions are conducted at the same time as tests of controls.

Substantive Analytical Procedures

Analytical Procedures

☙ [LO 9]

Auditing standards (AU 329) define analytical procedures as consisting of evaluations of financial information made by a study of plausible relationships among both financial and nonfinancial data. An important aspect of the definition of analytical procedures is that they involve a comparison of recorded values with *expectations* developed by the auditor. Analytical procedures can facilitate an effective audit by helping the auditor understand the client's business, directing attention to high-risk areas, identifying audit issues that might not be otherwise apparent, providing audit evidence, and assisting in the evaluation of audit results.

Purposes of Analytical Procedures

Analytical procedures are used for three purposes:

1. *Preliminary analytical procedures* are used to assist the auditor to better understand the business and to *plan* the nature, timing, and extent of audit procedures.
2. *Substantive analytical procedures* are used as a substantive procedure to obtain evidential matter about particular assertions related to account balances or classes of transactions.
3. *Final analytical procedures* are used as an overall review of the financial information in the final review stage of the audit.

Auditing standards require the use of analytical procedures for the first and third purposes. However, analytical procedures are also commonly used to gather substantive evidence because they are effective at detecting misstatements.[3] Analytical procedures are also relatively inexpensive tests to perform.

The purpose of the analytical procedures and the facts and circumstances will dictate the type of analytical procedure used to form an expectation and the techniques involved in investigating a significant difference. Analytical procedures may range from the use of simple trend analysis to the use of complex regression models. The discussion of analytical procedures in this chapter is limited to the following three types of analytical procedure:

1. Trend analysis—the examination of changes in an account over time.
2. Ratio analysis—the comparison, across time or to a benchmark, of relationships between financial statement accounts or between an account and nonfinancial data.
3. Reasonableness analysis—development of a model to form an expectation using financial data, nonfinancial data, or both, to test account balances or changes in account balances between accounting periods.

The use of regression analysis as an analytical procedure is covered in auditing texts devoted to statistical auditing methods.[4]

Substantive Analytical Procedures Decision Process

Figure 5–3 presents an overview of the auditor's decision process when using substantive analytical procedures to collect audit evidence. While the overall process is similar for the other two purposes of analytical procedures (i.e., preliminary and final analytical procedures), we will identify important differences as we discuss each step in the process.

Develop an Expectation
The first step in the decision process is to develop an expectation for the amount or account balance. This is the most important step in performing analytical procedures. Auditing standards require the auditor to have an expectation whenever analytical procedures are used. An expectation can be developed using any of the types of analytical procedures discussed previously using information available from a variety of sources, such as

- Financial and operating data
- Budgets and forecasts
- Industry publications
- Competitor information

---

[3]A. Eilifsen and W. F. Messier, Jr., "Auditor Detection of Misstatements: A Review and Integration of Empirical Research," *Journal of Accounting Literature 2000* (19), pp. 1–43, reviews the audit research on this issue.

[4]See A. D. Bailey, Jr., *Statistical Auditing: Review, Concepts, and Problems* (New York: Harcourt Brace Jovanovich, 1981), Chapter 10, for a detailed discussion of regression analysis applied to auditing.

| FIGURE 5-3 | **Overview of the Auditor's Decision Process for Substantive Analytical Procedures** |

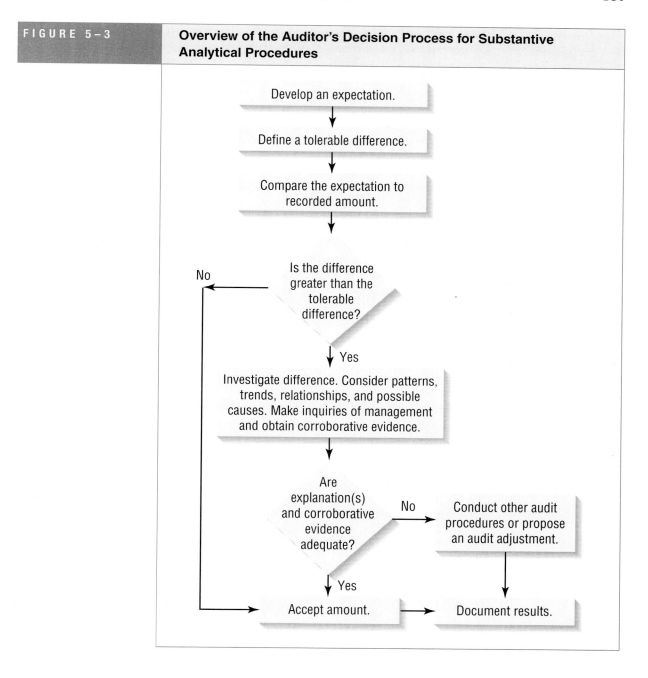

- Management's analyses
- Analyst's reports

Precision of the Expectation.   The quality of an expectation is referred to as the *precision* of the expectation. Precision is a measure of the potential effectiveness of an analytical procedure; it represents the degree of reliance that can be placed on the procedure. Precision is a measure of how closely the expectation approximates the "correct" but unknown amount. The degree of desired precision will differ with the specific purpose of the analytical procedure. The precision of the expectation is a function of the materiality and required detection risk for the assertion being tested. If the assertion being tested requires a low level of detection risk, the expectation needs to be very precise. However, the more precise the expectation, the more extensive and expensive the audit procedures used to develop the expectation, which results in a cost-benefit trade-off.

The following four factors affect the precision of analytical procedures.

Disaggregation

The more detailed the level at which an expectation is formed, the greater the precision. For example, expectations formed using monthly data will be more precise than expectations formed using annual data. Similarly, expectations formed at an individual product level will be more precise than expectations formed for all products combined.

Preliminary and final analytical procedures are often conducted at relatively high levels of aggregation. However, analytical procedures conducted to provide substantive evidence normally cannot be performed at aggregated levels (e.g., annual data, total revenues). Misstatements are difficult to detect when analyzing data at aggregate levels, due to offsetting trends or activities that can mask risks and misstatements. Examples later in the chapter illustrate this concept.

The Plausibility and Predictability of the Relationship Being Studied

As indicated previously, analytical procedures involve the study of plausible relationships among financial and nonfinancial data. The primary concern with plausibility is simply whether the relationship used to test the assertion makes sense. For example, it is usually plausible to expect that an increase in sales should lead to an increase in accounts receivable. Many factors influence the predictability of relationships among financial and nonfinancial data. For example, income statement items tend to be more predictable than balance sheet items because income statement accounts involve transactions over a period of time, whereas balance sheet accounts represent amounts at a specific point in time. Similarly, if the client operates in a static industry, the relationships are likely to be more predictable than they are for a client that operates in a dynamic industry that is rapidly changing and growing. The more plausible and predictable the relationship, the more precise the expectation can be.

Data Reliability

The ability to develop precise expectations is influenced by the reliability of the available data. The reliability of data for developing expectations depends on the three factors discussed in Chapter 4 under the competence of audit evidence (e.g., the independence of the source of the evidence, the effectiveness of internal controls, and the auditor's direct personal knowledge). In addition, data for analytical procedures are more reliable if the data were subjected to audit in the current or prior periods and if the expectation were developed from multiple sources of data. For example, if the auditor is computing ratios based on audited data from prior periods, the data used in the computations would be considered reliable, enhancing the precision of the expectation developed by the ratios.

Type of Analytical Procedure Used to Form an Expectation

The three types of analytical procedures discussed earlier (trend, ratio, and reasonableness analysis) represent different ways to form an expectation. In general, trend analysis is the least precise method used and reasonableness analysis is the most precise. All three types are used for substantive analytical procedures, but reasonableness analysis is not commonly used for preliminary or final analytical procedures. Table 5–5 provides the definitions of the types of analytical procedures and then we present several examples.

Examples of Expectations Formed by Analytical Procedures

Proper application of analytical procedures requires that the auditor have knowledge of the client's business and industry. Without such knowledge, the auditor may be unable to develop appropriate expectations or properly evaluate the results of the procedures. The auditor can use a number of different analytical procedures to form expectations. Some common examples include the following:

Comparison of Current-Year Financial Information with Comparable Prior Period(s) after Consideration of Known Changes.   This is perhaps the most commonly used analytical procedure. The comparison of financial statement amounts can be done using absolute amounts (i.e., trend analysis) or by converting the financial statement amounts to "common-size" financial statements (ratio analysis). Exhibit 5–3 presents an example of common-size

TABLE 5–5	Definitions of the Types of Analytical Procedures Used to Form Expectations*

Trend analysis is the analysis of changes in an account over time. Simple trend analyses compare last year's account balance (the "expectation") with the current balance. Trend analysis can also encompass multiple time periods and includes comparing recorded trends with budget amounts and with competitor and industry information. The number of time periods used is a function of predictability and desired precision. The more stable the operations over time, the more predictable the relationship and the more appropriate the use of multiple periods. Generally, the more time periods used and the more disaggregated the data, the more precise the expectation. Because trend analysis relies on a single predictor (i.e., prior period information for an account balance), it does not normally yield as precise an expectation as the other two types.

Ratio analysis is the comparison, across time or to a benchmark, of relationships between financial statement accounts (e.g., return on equity) or between an account and nonfinancial data (e.g., cost per square foot or sales per item). Ratio analysis also includes "common-size" analysis, which is the conversion of financial statement amounts to percentages. Industry or competitor ratios are often used to benchmark the client's performance. The advanced module to this chapter illustrates selected financial ratios useful in analytical procedures. Ratio analysis is often more effective at identifying risks and potential misstatements than trend analysis because comparisons of relationships between accounts and operating data are more likely to identify unusual patterns than is an analysis only focused on an individual account. As with trend analysis, to gather substantive evidence effectively, ratio analysis should be performed on disaggregated data (e.g., by product, location, or month) over multiple periods where applicable.

Reasonableness analysis involves forming an expectation using a model. In many cases, a simple model may be sufficient. For example, ticket revenue can be modeled by taking average attendance by average ticket price. Similarly, depreciation expense can be modeled by taking book value divided by average useful life for a class of assets. Because it forms an explicit expectation, reasonableness analysis typically forms a more precise expectation than trend or ratio analysis. Of course the precision of an expectation formed with a reasonableness test depends on the other factors influencing precision (i.e., disaggregation, predictability and reliability).

*Regression analysis is another type of analytical procedure. Because it involves relatively complex statistical modeling in audit settings, we do not discuss it in this text. See footnote 4 for further information.

EXHIBIT 5-3

Common-Size Financial Statements for EarthWear Clothiers (in thousands)

	December 31			
	2005		2004	
Assets				
Current assets:				
Cash and cash equivalents	$ 48,978	14.84%	$ 49,668	16.75%
Receivables, net	12,875	3.90%	11,539	3.89%
Inventory	122,337	37.08%	105,425	35.55%
Prepaid advertising	11,458	3.47%	10,772	3.63%
Other prepaid expenses	6,315	1.91%	3,780	1.27%
Deferred income tax benefits	7,132	2.16%	6,930	2.34%
Total current assets	209,095	63.37%	188,115	63.44%
Property, plant, and equipment, at cost				
Land and buildings	70,918	21.49%	66,804	22.53%
Fixtures and equipment	67,513	20.46%	66,876	22.55%
Computer hardware and software	64,986	19.70%	47,466	16.01%
Leasehold improvements	3,010	0.91%	2,894	0.98%
Total property, plant, and equipment	206,426	62.56%	184,040	62.07%
Less: accumulated depreciation and amortization	85,986	−26.06%	76,256	−25.72%
Property, plant, and equipment, net	120,440	36.50%	107,784	36.35%
Intangibles, net	423	0.13%	628	0.21%
Total assets	$329,959	100.00%	$296,527	100.00%
Liabilities and shareholder's investment				
Current liabilities:				
Lines of credit	$ 11,011	3.34%	$7,621	2.57%
Accounts payable	62,509	18.94%	48,432	16.33%
Reserve for returns	5,890	1.78%	5,115	1.72%
Accrued liabilities	26,738	8.10%	28,440	9.59%
Accrued profit sharing	1,532	0.46%	1,794	0.61%
Income taxes payable	8,588	2.60%	6,666	2.25%
Total current liabilities	116,268	35.24%	98,067	33.07%
Deferred income taxes	9,469	2.87%	5,926	2.00%
Shareholders' investment:				
Common stock, 26,121 shares issued	261	0.08%	261	0.09%
Donated capital	5,460	1.65%	5,460	1.84%
Additional paid-in capital	20,740	6.29%	19,311	6.51%
Deferred compensation	(79)	−0.02%	(153)	−0.05%
Accumulated other comprehensive income	3,883	1.18%	1,739	0.59%
Retained earnings	317,907	96.35%	295,380	99.61%
Treasury stock, 6,546 and 6,706 shares at cost, respectively	(143,950)	−43.63%	(129,462)	−43.66%
Total shareholders' investment	204,222	64.76%	192,535	66.93%
Total liabilities and shareholders' investment	$329,959	100.00%	$296,527	100.00%
Net Sales	$950,484	100.00%	$857,885	100.00%
Cost of sales	546,393	57.49%	472,739	55.11%
Gross Profit	404,091	42.51%	385,146	44.89%
Selling, general and administrative expenses	364,012	38.30%	334,994	39.05%
Nonrecurring charge (credit)	—		(1,153)	−0.13%
Income from operations	40,079	4.29%	51,305	5.98%
Other income (expense):				
Interest expense	(983)	−0.10%	(1,229)	−0.14%
Interest income	1,459	0.15%	573	0.07%
Other	(4,798)	−0.50%	(1,091)	−0.13%
Total other income (expense), net	(4,322)	−0.45%	(1,747)	−0.20%
Income before income taxes	35,757	3.76%	49,559	5.78%
Income tax provision	13,230	1.39%	18,337	2.14%
Net income	$22,527	2.37%	$ 31,222	3.64%
Basic earnings per share	1.15		1.60	
Diluted earnings per share	1.14		1.56	
Basic weighted average shares outstanding	19,531		19,555	
Diluted weighted average shares outstanding	19,774		20,055	

financial statements for EarthWear for 2005 and 2004. An auditor may compare the amounts shown on this year's trial balance with the prior year's audited balances and investigate those amounts that are out of line by some predetermined cutoff percentage or absolute amount. For example, the auditor can compare the current-year inventory balance with the prior year's balance after adjusting for the change in sales during the current period. In the EarthWear example, inventory has increased in absolute amounts from $105.4 million to $122.3 million and, as a percentage of total assets, from 35.6 to 37.0 percent. Because this type of analytical procedure is typically performed on the aggregated companywide financial statements, the expectation is relatively imprecise. Thus, it is typically used for planning and final review purposes, but is not considered particularly useful for providing substantive evidence about a particular account balance or class of transactions. At planning, the auditor would investigate this increase in inventory and adjust the planned audit procedures to address risks associated with the increase. To illustrate the effect of conducting analytical procedures at aggregated companywide levels, consider what percentage change in inventory would be within tolerable limits. Recall from Chapter 3 that planning materiality for EarthWear was set at $1,769,000 and tolerable misstatement was set at $885,000, which means that only a .84 percent ($885,000 ÷ $105,425,000) unexpected change in inventory could represent a material misstatement in inventory. The observed 1.4 percent increase in inventory may be reasonable since sales are up in the current period, but this example highlights that it is difficult to obtain useful audit evidence from high-level companywide analytical procedures because the expectations are typically not sufficiently precise. In other words, whether or not the auditor observes a significant difference using a year-to-year comparison may be useful for planning purposes, but it would provide little or no audit evidence because of the imprecision of the expectation.

Comparison of Current-Year Financial Information with Budgets, Projections, and Forecasts.   This technique is usually performed using trend analysis and is similar to the previous example except that the current-year budget, projection, or forecast represents the expectation (rather than the expectation being provided by prior year data). For example, the auditor can test the fairness of advertising expense by comparing the current-year amount to the client's budget and investigating differences.

Relationships among Elements of Financial Information within the Current Period.   There are many examples of one element in the financial statements directly relating to another element. This is particularly true for the association between certain balance sheet accounts and their related income or expense accounts. In these situations, reasonableness analysis is typically used to model the association. For example, there should be a relationship between the balance for long-term debt and interest expense. The auditor can model interest expense by multiplying the average long-term debt for the period by the period's average interest rate. This estimate of interest expense can be compared to the balance of interest expense shown on the trial balance. Later in the chapter we present a comprehensive example of an interest expense reasonableness test for EarthWear Clothiers.

EXHIBIT 5–4 | **An Example of Industry Data Available from Published Sources**

SIC 5961
CTLG, ML-ORDER HSES
(No Breakdown)
(451 Establishments)

	$	%
Cash	101,474	16.6
Accounts receivable	94,139	15.4
Notes receivable	3,668	0.6
Inventory	236,570	38.7
Other current	48,292	7.9
Total current	**484,142**	**79.2**
Fixed assets	82,524	13.5
Other noncurrent	44,624	7.3
Total assets	**611,291**	**100.0**
Accounts payable	125,315	20.5
Bank loans	1,834	0.3
Notes payable	14,671	2.4
Other current	97,195	15.9
Total current	**239,015**	**39.1**
Other long-term	59,907	9.8
Deferred credits	—	—
Net worth	312,370	51.1
Total liab and net worth	**611,291**	**100.0**
Net sales	2,386,410	100.0
Gross profit	925,927	38.8
Net profit after tax	78,752	3.3
Working capital	245,127	—

RATIOS	UQ	MED	LQ
Solvency:			
Quick ratio (times)	1.6	0.8	0.3
Current ratio (times)	3.9	2.1	1.4
Curr liab to nw (%)	25.1	68.6	142.6
Curr liab to inv (%)	45.8	92.0	146.8
Total liab to nw (%)	29.7	84.1	178.9
Fixed assets to nw (%)	9.3	22.3	49.4
Efficiency:			
Collection period (days)	4.4	14.1	34.1
Sales to inv (times)	14.6	7.9	5.3
Assets to sales (%)	21.2	31.2	47.3
Sales to nwc (times)	19.6	8.6	4.4
Acct pay to sales (%)	3.8	6.2	9.3
Profitability:			
Return on sales (%)	6.9	2.9	0.6
Return on assets (%)	21.2	7.4	1.2
Return on nw (%)	47.7	17.5	4.9

Source: Dun & Bradstreet, Inc.

Comparison of the Client's Financial Information with Industry Data. The auditor can compare the client's financial ratios (receivable turnover, inventory turnover, and so on) to industry averages. The industry information can serve as a benchmark for assessing how well the client's financial position and performance compare with other companies in the industry. Robert

Morris Associates, Dun & Bradstreet, and Standard & Poor's publish this type of industry data. Exhibit 5–4 contains an extract of industry data from *Industry Norms and Key Business Ratios,* published by Dun & Bradstreet. The *Advanced Module* to this chapter illustrates several ratios used in ratio analysis.

Relationships of Financial Information to Nonfinancial Information.   The auditor may have relevant nonfinancial information available for comparison purposes or for developing estimates of the client's financial information. This might include such items as cost per employee, sales per square foot, utility expense per hour, and so on. For example, the auditor can multiply the number of pagers in service by the average billing rate to test a client's total pager-leasing revenue. Other examples include computing the average number of days a product is in inventory or developing an expectation for commission expense by multiplying commissioned sales by the average commission rate and comparing this estimate to the client's recorded commission expense.

Using nonfinancial information in analytical procedures can be an effective way to identify potential frauds because while perpetrators of fraud can manage financial numbers, it is difficult or impossible to manage nonfinancial data (e.g., square feet, days in the calendar year, number of employees).

Plotting Trends over Multiple Periods.   It can be very beneficial to plot or graph trends over several periods. Figure 5–4 provides a monthly plot of ending inventory for a three-year period. Suppose the auditor is auditing year-ending inventory for year 3 and that years 1 and 2 have been previously audited. The pattern of previously audited financial information suggests some inventory "spikes" every six months. These spikes may be due to inventory buildup around busy seasons (e.g., holidays). The star at the end of year 3 indicates the auditor's expectation based on the past trends. The auditor would investigate the cause of the large increase in ending inventory at the end of year 3. Note that the potentially problematic spikes would not have shown up at all if the auditor had just plotted year-end inventory balances rather than monthly balances! Again, using detailed data is critical in enhancing precision.

The forgoing discussion and examples have all related to the first step in the analytical procedures decision process (see Figure 5–3). The first step is the most important step in performing effective substantive analytical procedures.

Define a Tolerable Difference   The second step in the analytical procedures decision process (see Figure 5–3) is to define a tolerable difference. Since the expectation developed by the auditor will rarely be identical to the client's recorded amount, the auditor must decide the amount of difference that would require further investigation. The size of the tolerable difference depends on the significance of the account, the desired degree of reliance on the substantive analytical procedure, the level of disaggregation in the amount being tested, and the precision of the expectation. The amount of

FIGURE 5–4   **An Illustration of a Monthly Plot of Ending Inventory (in millions)**

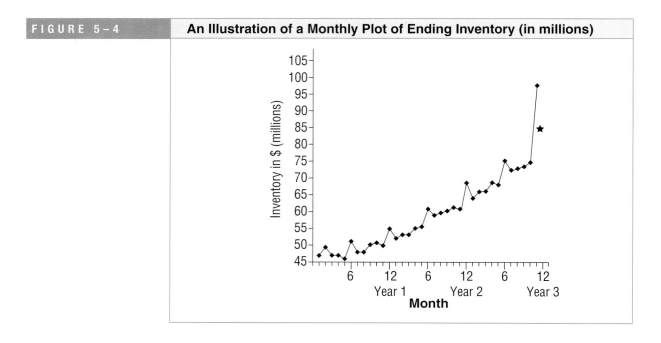

difference that can be tolerated will always be lower than planning materiality, and when testing an entire account with a substantive analytical procedure, tolerable differences will usually be equal to the account's tolerable misstatement. Auditors often use rules of thumb such as, "tolerable difference is 10 percent of the predicted amount and/or a difference less than $75,000."

Compare the Expectation to the Recorded Amount   The next step in the analytical procedures decision process (Figure 5–3) is to determine if the amount of difference between the auditor's expectation and the recorded amount exceeds the auditor's predetermined "tolerable difference." If the observed difference is less than the tolerable difference, the auditor accepts the account. If not, the auditor must investigate the difference using other audit procedures.

Investigate Differences Greater Than the Tolerable Difference
The fourth step in the analytical procedures decision process (Figure 5–3) is the investigation of significant differences and the formation of conclusions. Differences identified by substantive analytical procedures indicate an increased likelihood of misstatements. The more precise the expectation, the greater the likelihood that the difference is actually a misstatement. Inquiry of the client is frequently an important aspect of the investigation of differences. Nevertheless, client inquiry should not be the sole support for an explanation without quantification and corroboration (discussed below). There are four possible causes of significant differences—accounting

changes, economic conditions or events, error, and fraud. In most instances, the cause of an identified difference involves a legitimate accounting change or an economic condition or event. However, even when a significant difference is due to error or fraud, the client may provide a plausible, yet ultimately untrue, business explanation. Thus, the effectiveness of substantive analytical procedures in identifying material misstatements is enhanced when auditors develop potential explanations *before* obtaining the client's explanation. By doing this, the auditor is better able to exercise appropriate professional skepticism and challenge the client's explanation, if necessary.

The development of potential explanations need not be time-consuming. Auditors typically reexamine and understand the various relationships in the financial and nonfinancial data. Then, based on their previous experience with the client, other audit work performed, and discussions with other members of the audit team, they develop potential explanations for the observed difference. The independent consideration of potential explanations is more important for more significant accounts and when a higher degree of assurance is desired from substantive analytical procedures.

Explanations for significant differences observed for substantive analytical procedures must be followed up and resolved through quantification, corroboration, and evaluation.

Quantification.   It is usually not practicable to identify an explanation for the exact amount of a difference between an analytical procedure's expectation and the client's recorded amount. However, auditors should quantify the portion of the difference that can be explained. Quantification involves determining whether the explanation or error can explain the observed difference. This may require the recalculation of the expectation after considering the additional information. For example, a client may offer the explanation that the significant increase in inventory over the prior year is due to a 12 percent increase in raw materials prices. The auditor should compute the effects of the raw materials price increase and determine the extent to which the price increase explains (or does not explain) the increase in the overall inventory account.

Corroboration.   Auditors must corroborate explanations for unexpected differences by obtaining sufficient competent audit evidence linking the explanation to the difference and substantiating that the information supporting the explanation is reliable. This evidence should be of the same quality as the evidence obtained to support tests of details. Such evidence could vary from simply comparing the explanation to the auditor's knowledge from other areas, to employing other detailed tests to confirm or refute the explanation. Common corroborating procedures include examination of supporting evidence, inquiries of independent persons, and evaluating evidence obtained from other auditing procedures.

Evaluation.   The key mind-set behind effectively performing substantive analytical procedures is one of appropriate professional skepticism, combined with the desire to obtain sufficient competent audit evidence, similar to other auditing procedures. The auditor should evaluate the results of the substantive analytical procedures to conclude whether the desired level of assurance has been achieved. If the auditor obtains evidence that a misstatement exists and can be sufficiently quantified, the auditor makes note of his or her proposed adjustment to the client's financial statements. Toward the end of the audit, all such proposed adjustments are accumulated, summarized, and evaluated before being presented to the client (Chapter 17 provides further details).

If the auditor concludes that the substantive analytical procedure performed did not provide the desired level of assurance, additional substantive analytical procedures and/or tests of details should be performed to achieve the desired assurance.

The Investigation of Differences for Planning and Final Analytical Procedures

The way in which differences are investigated diverges in important ways for preliminary and final analytical procedures. At planning, the auditor is not required to obtain corroborative evidence because preliminary analytical procedures are not intended to provide substantive audit evidence regarding specific assertions. Rather, the auditor normally determines whether the planned audit procedures need to be revised in light of the results of preliminary analytical procedures. For example, to address the increased risk posed by the spike in inventory illustrated in Figure 5–4, the auditor may decide to expand the number of items tested during the observation of the year-end physical inventory count.

When conducting final analytical procedures, the auditor investigates unexpected differences by first going to the working papers to determine if sufficient competent evidence has already been gathered to explain the difference (rather than going to the client for an explanation). If the auditor cannot find sufficient evidence within the working papers, then the auditor would formulate possible explanations, conduct additional testing, and seek an explanation from the client.

Comprehensive EarthWear Example

Suppose we want to use substantive analytical procedures to test the reasonableness of interest expense reported by EarthWear Clothiers (i.e., a "reasonableness test"). Consider the following example:

EarthWear EarthWear's 2005 income statement shows $983,000 of interest expense. To conduct a substantive analytical procedure on this account, the auditor could develop an expectation using reasonableness analysis by building a model in the following manner. Obtain the ending monthly balance for the short-term line of credit from the monthly bank loan statement and calculate the average monthly ending balance. Trace the monthly loan balances to the general ledger. Determine the average interest rate for the year for the short-term line of credit based on the bank's published rate in the monthly bank loan statement. Multiply the average monthly balance previously calculated by the average interest rate, and compare the result to the recorded interest expense. Suppose that the auditor obtained the following information from EarthWear's general ledger:

Month	Balance (in thousands)
January	$ 21,500
February	18,600
March	18,100
April	17,900
May	16,100
June	15,500
July	14,200
August	20,200
September	34,500
October	28,100
November	15,200
December	11,000
Total	$230,900
Average	$ 19,240

Further, assume that interest rates recorded on the loan statements have remained stable over the year, fluctuating between 5 and 5.5 percent. If the auditor uses 5.25 percent as the average interest rate, the expectation for interest expense is $1,010,000 ($19,240,000 × 0.525).

As shown in Figure 5–3, once an expectation is developed, the next step is to determine the tolerable difference. Because interest expense is a predictable account and because the information used to form the expectation is deemed reliable, the expectation is fairly precise. Accordingly, the tolerable difference is set at 5 percent of recorded interest expense or $49,150 (.05% × $983,000). The next step is to compare the expectation of $1,010,000 to the recorded value of $983,000 to determine if the difference is greater than can be tolerated. Because the difference between the auditor's expectation and the recorded amount, $27,000, is less than the tolerable difference, the auditor would accept the interest expense account as fairly stated. However, if the difference between the recorded amount and the expectation is greater than the tolerable difference, the auditor will need to investigate the difference. In the example above, the auditor would likely carefully examine loan activity within each month to determine if there was significant variation in the balance that was not accounted for by the month-end model used to form the expectation. If the difference could still not be explained, the auditor would inquire of management about the cause of the difference. If the client provides a plausible explanation (e.g., interest expense reported in the financial statements also includes interest paid for other short-term loans that were only outstanding for a few days at a time), auditing standards require the auditor to obtain corroborating evidence. If the client's explanation and the corroborating evidence are not adequate, or if no corroborative evidence is available, the auditor will need to conduct additional audit procedures. If the explanation and evidence are adequate for resolving the difference, the auditor can accept the amount as being fairly presented.

As with other audit procedures, when analytical procedures are used to gather substantive evidence, the auditor's purpose is to evaluate one or more assertions. For example, in the interest expense example, the auditor is testing primarily the completeness and valuation assertions. The effectiveness and efficiency of substantive analytical procedures in identifying material misstatements depend on

- The nature of the assertion.
- The plausibility and predictability of the relationship.
- The availability and reliability of the data used.
- The precision of the expectation.
- The rigor and sufficiency of the investigation of observed differences (if greater than tolerable difference).

We have already discussed all but the first item in the above list.

The Nature of the Assertion   Substantive analytical procedures can be used to test all transactions and balance assertions except rights and obligations. However, they may be more effective at identifying certain types of misstatements than testing individual transactions. For example, they may be more effective at detecting omissions (completeness assertion) than providing detailed documentary evidence. The key points are that (1) some assertions are more amenable to examination through analytical procedures than others and (2) the auditor must ensure that the analytical procedure performed is appropriate for the assertion being examined.

Documentation Requirements   When a substantive analytical procedure is used as the principal substantive procedure for a significant financial statement assertion, the auditor should document all of the following:

- The expectation and how it was developed.
- Results of the comparison of the expectation to the recorded amounts or ratios developed from recorded amounts.
- Any additional auditing procedures performed in response to significant unexpected differences arising from the analytical procedure and the results of such additional procedures.

Final Analytical Procedures

The objective of analytical procedures at the overall review stage of an audit is to assist the auditor in assessing the conclusions reached and evaluating the overall financial statement presentation. This requires reviewing the trial balance, financial statements, and footnotes in order to (1) judge the adequacy of the evidence gathered to support any unusual or unexpected balances investigated during the audit and (2) determine if any other unusual balances or relationships have not been investigated.

In the first instance, competent evidence in the working papers should support any differences from the auditor's expectations. For example, the auditor can compare the audited balances from the current year with the audited balances from the prior year. If there is a material difference, the auditor's working papers should explain the difference. In the second instance, this comparison of audited values may reveal some unusual items that have not been investigated and explained. Assuming that the difference between the auditor's expectation and the recorded amount is material, the auditor will have to perform additional audit work before an audit report can be issued.

The Audit Testing Hierarchy

[LO 10] The risk-driven audit approach we have discussed so far in the text is often referred to as a "top-down" approach where the auditor obtains an understanding of the client's business objectives and strategies, identifies business and audit risks, documents an understanding of internal control, and then gathers sufficient, competent audit evidence using a combination of tests of controls, substantive analytical procedures, and tests of details to support the audit opinion (or audit opinions—remember that for public companies, the auditor performs an integrated audit and opines on both internal control and the financial statements).

Now that we have discussed evidence (Chapter 4) and introduced you to the types of audit tests (risk assessment procedures, tests of controls, substantive analytical procedures, and tests of details), you are ready to be introduced to the thought process auditors use in choosing audit tests and in what order. The overall decision approach used to gather evidence is depicted in Figure 5–5 and is referred to in later chapters as the *audit testing hierarchy*.

The audit testing hierarchy starts with tests of controls and substantive analytical procedures. Starting with controls and substantive analytical procedures is generally both more effective and more efficient than starting with tests of details.

- *Applying the audit testing hierarchy is more effective.* The auditor's understanding and testing of controls will influence the nature, timing, and extent of substantive testing and will enhance the auditor's ability to hone in on areas where misstatements are more likely to be found. If controls are highly effective, less extensive substantive procedures (i.e., substantive analytical procedures and tests of details) will need to be performed. Similarly, substantive analytical procedures can direct attention to higher-risk areas where the auditor can design and conduct focused tests of details.

- *Applying the audit testing hierarchy is more efficient.* Generally, tests of controls and substantive analytical procedures are less costly to perform than are tests of details. This is usually because tests of controls and substantive analytical procedures provide assurance on multiple transactions. In other words, by testing controls and related processes, the auditor generally gains a degree of assurance over thousands or even millions of transactions. Furthermore, substantive analytical procedures often provide evidence related to more than one assertion and often more than one balance or class of transactions. On the other hand, tests of details often only obtain assurance related to one or two specific assertions pertaining to the specific transaction(s) or balance tested.

Auditing standards require that auditors perform substantive procedures for significant account balances and classes of transactions regardless of the assessed level of control risk. In other words, assurance obtained solely from testing controls is not sufficient for significant balances and classes of transactions. Substantive procedures include substantive analytical procedures

FIGURE 5–5	**Audit Testing Hierarchy: An Evidence Decision Process for Testing Significant Balances or Classes of Transactions**

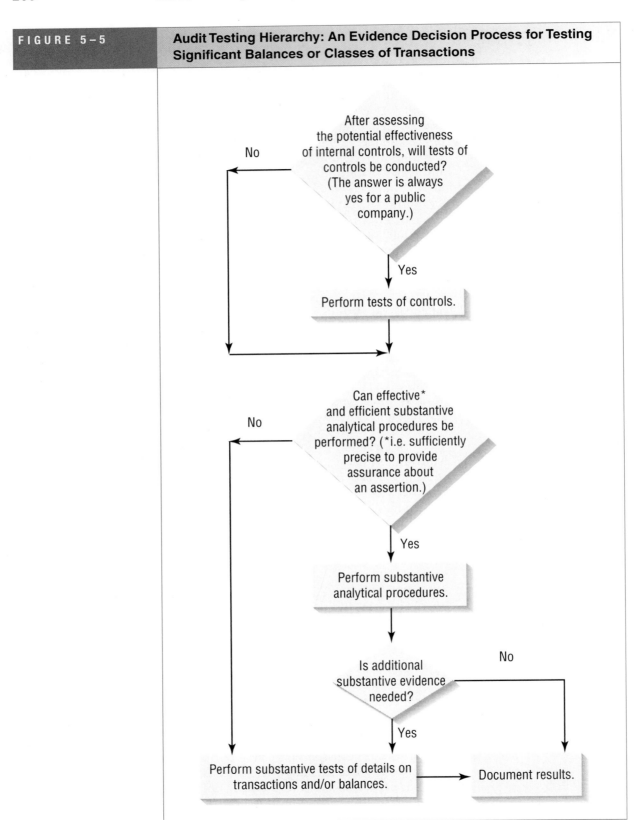

and tests of details. For this reason, Figure 5–5 depicts that either substantive analytical procedures, tests of details, or both will always be conducted for significant accounts or classes of transactions. For high-risk areas or highly material accounts, the auditors will almost always perform some tests of details in addition to tests of controls and substantive analytical procedures.

The decision process depicted in Figure 5–5 recognizes that for some assertions, tests of details may be the only form of testing used, because in some cases it is more efficient and effective to move directly to tests of details. Examples of situations where the auditor might move directly to tests of details include a low volume of large transactions (e.g., two large notes payable issued) and poor controls resulting in client data that are unreliable for use in substantive analytical procedures.

An "Assurance Bucket" Analogy

We have found that an analogy often helps students understand and visualize how an auditor decides on the proper mix of testing and evidence. Figure 5–6 illustrates what we call the "assurance bucket." The assurance bucket must be filled with sufficient evidence to obtain the level of assurance necessary to support the auditor's opinion. Following the top-down audit testing hierarchy means that auditors first begin to fill the bucket with evidence from the risk assessment procedures. In Figure 5–6, after completing risk assessment procedures, the auditor sees that the assurance bucket for a particular account and assertion is about 20 percent full. The auditor would next conduct control testing. In our example, control testing might add about another 30 percent to the bucket. How would the auditor know just how full the bucket is after testing controls? This is clearly a very subjective evaluation, and it is a matter of professional judgment.

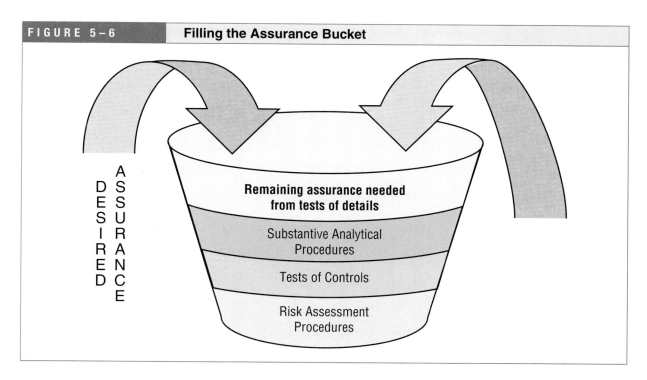

FIGURE 5–6 **Filling the Assurance Bucket**

DESIRED ASSURANCE

Remaining assurance needed from tests of details

Substantive Analytical Procedures

Tests of Controls

Risk Assessment Procedures

The auditor next performs substantive analytical procedures and adds the assurance gained from these procedures to the bucket. In Figure 5–6 the bucket is now about 70 percent full. In this illustration, the auditor would need to top off the assurance bucket with evidence obtained through tests of details.

For lower-risk, well-controlled accounts, the assurance bucket may be entirely filled with tests of controls and substantive analytical procedures. For other accounts or assertions, the bucket may be filled primarily with tests of details.

The size of the assurance bucket can vary, depending on the auditor's risk assessment and the assertion being tested. Obviously, certain assertions will be more important or present bigger risks for some accounts than for others. For instance, existence (or validity) is typically more important for accounts receivable than it is for accounts payable. After the auditor has determined the risks associated with the assertions for an account balance, she or he can determine the size of the assurance buckets (i.e., how much assurance is needed) and then begin filling the buckets by applying the audit testing hierarchy. Figure 5–7 illustrates these concepts for accounts payable. Note that the largest bucket is for the *completeness* assertion, because with liability accounts the auditor is primarily concerned with potential understatement errors. The example in Figure 5–7 also illustrates that some assertions may be filled entirely with tests of details (e.g., rights and obligations) and that others may not require any tests of details (e.g., existence). Again, these are subjective matters that require considerable professional judgment.

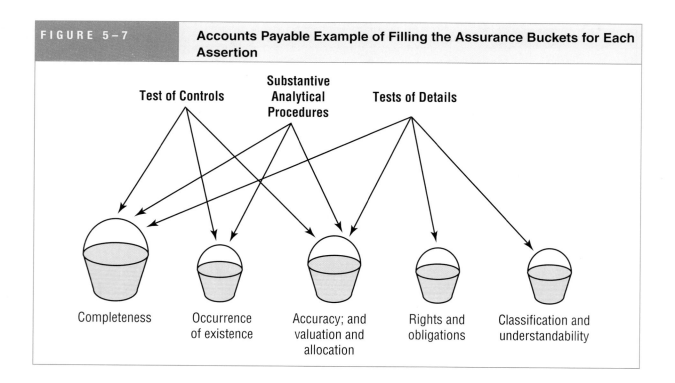

FIGURE 5–7   **Accounts Payable Example of Filling the Assurance Buckets for Each Assertion**

Advanced Module: Selected Financial Ratios

Selected Financial Ratios Useful as Analytical Procedures

❧ [LO 11] A number of financial ratios are used by auditors as analytical procedures. These ratios are broken down into four categories: short-term liquidity, activity, profitability, and coverage ratios. Although the ratios discussed apply to most entities, auditors may also use other industry-specific ratios. As follows, each ratio is calculated for EarthWear Clothiers for the year ended December 31, 2005.

A few points are worth mentioning before the financial ratios are discussed. First, in many instances, the auditor may compare the client's ratios with industry averages (see Exhibit 5–4). While the industry averages serve as useful benchmarks, certain limitations should be recognized. Because the industry ratios are averages, they may not capture operating or geographical factors that may be specific to the client. The use of different accounting principles for valuing inventory or calculating depreciation may also result in differences from industry averages for certain ratios. Finally, the industry data may not be available in sufficient detail for a particular client. For example, if the auditor was looking for industry information on a company in the paging industry (see Problem 3–32, which includes Calabro Paging Services), such ratio data are combined with the telecommunications industry data.

Second, audit research has shown that material misstatements may not significantly affect certain ratios.[5] This is particularly true for activity ratios. Third, the auditor must be careful not to evaluate a financial ratio in isolation. In certain cases, a ratio may be favorable because its components are unfavorable. If related ratios are not examined, the auditor may draw an incorrect conclusion. For example, suppose that a client's days outstanding in accounts receivable is getting larger and the inventory turnover ratio is getting smaller. The negative trend in these ratios may indicate that accounts receivable are getting older and that some inventory may be obsolete. However, both of these factors positively affect the current ratio. If the auditor calculates only the current ratio, he or she may reach an incorrect conclusion about the entity's ability to meet current obligations.

Short-Term Liquidity Ratios

Short-term liquidity ratios indicate the entity's ability to meet its current obligations. Three ratios commonly used for this purpose are the *current ratio, quick (or acid test) ratio,* and the *operating cash flow ratio.*

Current Ratio   The current ratio is calculated as follows:

$$\text{Current ratio} = \frac{\text{Current assets}}{\text{Current liabilities}} = \frac{209{,}095}{116{,}268} = 1.80$$

---

[5]See W. R. Kinney, Jr., "Attention-Directing Analytical Review Using Accounting Ratios: A Case Study," *Auditing: A Journal of Practice and Theory* (Spring 1987), pp. 59–73, for a discussion of this limitation of analytical procedures.

It includes all current assets and current liabilities and is usually considered acceptable if it is 2 to 1 or better. Generally, a high current ratio indicates an entity's ability to pay current obligations. However, if current assets include old accounts receivable or obsolete inventory, this ratio can be distorted.

Quick Ratio   The quick ratio includes only assets that are most readily convertible to cash and is calculated as follows:

$$\text{Quick ratio} = \frac{\text{Liquid assets}}{\text{Current liabilities}} = \frac{48{,}978 + 12{,}875}{116{,}268} = .53$$

Thus, inventories and prepaid items are not included in the numerator of the quick ratio. The quick ratio may provide a better picture of the entity's liquidity position if inventory contains obsolete or slow-moving items. A ratio greater than 1 generally indicates that the entity's liquid assets are sufficient to meet the cash requirements for paying current liabilities.

Operating Cash Flow Ratio   The operating cash flow ratio measures the entity's ability to cover its current liabilities with cash generated from operations and is calculated as follows:

$$\text{Operating cash flow ratio} = \frac{\text{Cash flow from operations}}{\text{Current liabilities}} = \frac{39{,}367}{116{,}268} = .34$$

The operating cash flow ratio uses the cash flows as opposed to assets to measure short-term liquidity. It provides a longer-term measure of the entity's ability to meet its current liabilities. If cash flow from operations is small or negative, the entity will likely need alternative sources of cash, such as additional borrowings or sales of assets, to meet its obligations.

Activity Ratios

Activity ratios indicate how effectively the entity's assets are managed. Only ratios related to accounts receivable and inventory are discussed here because for most wholesale, retail, or manufacturing companies these two accounts represent the assets that have high activity. Activity ratios may also be effective in helping the auditor determine if these accounts contain material misstatements.

Receivables Turnover and Days Outstanding in Accounts Receivable

These two ratios provide information on the activity and age of accounts receivable. The receivables turnover ratio and days outstanding in accounts receivable are calculated as follows:

$$\text{Receivables turnover} = \frac{\text{Credit sales}}{\text{Receivables}} = \frac{950{,}484}{12{,}875} = 73.8$$

$$\text{Days outstanding in accounts receivable} = \frac{365 \text{ days}}{\text{Receivables turnover}} = 4.94 \text{ days}$$

The receivables turnover ratio indicates how many times accounts receivable are turned over during a year. However, the days outstanding in accounts receivable may be easier to interpret because this ratio can be compared to the client's terms of trade. For example, if an entity's terms of trade are 2/10, net/30, the auditor would expect that if management was doing a good job of managing receivables, the value for this ratio would be 30 days or less. If the auditor calculates the days outstanding to be 43 days, he or she might suspect that the account contains a material amount of bad debts. Comparing the days outstanding to industry data may be helpful in detecting a slowdown in payments by customers that is affecting the entire industry. EarthWear's ratio is 4.94 days because most sales are paid in cash or by credit card.

Inventory Turnover and Days of Inventory on Hand   These activity ratios provide information on the inventory and are calculated as follows:

$$\text{Inventory turnover} = \frac{\text{Cost of goods sold}}{\text{Inventory}} = \frac{546{,}398}{122{,}337} = 4.47$$

$$\text{Days of inventory on hand} = \frac{365 \text{ days}}{\text{Inventory turnover}} = 81.6 \text{ days}$$

Inventory turnover indicates the frequency with which inventory is consumed in a year. The higher the ratio, the better the entity is at liquidating inventory. This ratio can be easily compared to industry standards. Suppose that the auditor calculates the inventory turnover to be 4.7 times a year. If the industry average is 8.2 times a year, the auditor might suspect that inventory contains obsolete or slow-moving goods. The days of inventory on hand measures how much inventory the entity has available for sale to customers.

Profitability Ratios

Profitability ratios indicate the entity's success or failure for a given period. A number of ratios measure the profitability of an entity, and each ratio should be interpreted by comparison to industry data.

Gross Profit Percentage   The gross margin percentage ratio is generally a good indicator of potential misstatements and is calculated as follows:

$$\text{Gross profit percentage} = \frac{\text{Gross profit}}{\text{Net sales}} = \frac{404{,}091}{950{,}484} = 42.5\%$$

If this ratio varies significantly from previous years or differs significantly from industry data, the entity's financial data may contain errors. Numerous errors can affect this ratio. For example, if the client has failed to record sales, the gross profit percentage will be less than in previous years. Similarly, any errors that affect the inventory account can distort this ratio. For example, if the client has omitted goods from the ending inventory, this ratio will be smaller than in previous years.

Profit Margin   The profit margin ratio is calculated as follows:

$$\text{Profit margin} = \frac{\text{Net Income}}{\text{Net sales}} = \frac{22{,}527}{950{,}484} = 2.4\%$$

While the gross profit percentage ratio measures profitability after cost of goods sold is deducted, the profit margin ratio measures the entity's profitability after all expenses are considered. Significant fluctuations in this ratio may indicate that misstatements exist in the selling, general, or administrative expense accounts.

Return on Assets   This ratio is calculated as follows:

$$\text{Return on assets} = \frac{\text{Net income}}{\text{Total assets}} = \frac{22{,}527}{329{,}959} = 6.8\%$$

This ratio indicates the return earned on the resources invested by both the stockholders and the creditors.

Return on Equity   The return on equity ratio is calculated as follows:

$$\text{Return on equity} = \frac{\text{Net income}}{\text{Stockholders' equity}} = \frac{22{,}527}{204{,}222} = 11.0\%$$

This ratio is similar to the return on assets ratio except that it shows only the return on the resources contributed by the stockholders.

Coverage Ratios

Coverage ratios provide information on the long-term solvency of the entity. These ratios give the auditor important information on the ability of the entity to continue as a going concern.

Debt to Equity   This ratio is calculated as follows:

$$\text{Debt to equity} = \frac{\text{Short-term debt} + \text{Long-term debt}}{\text{Stockholders' equity}} = \frac{(116{,}668 + 0)}{204{,}222} = .569$$

This ratio indicates what portion of the entity's capital comes from debt. The lower the ratio, the less debt pressure on the entity. If the entity's debt to equity ratio is large relative to the industry's, it may indicate that the entity is too highly leveraged and may not be able to meet its debt obligations on a long-term basis.

Times Interest Earned   This ratio is calculated as follows:

$$\text{Times interest earned} = \frac{\text{Net income} + \text{Interest expense}}{\text{Interest expense}}$$

$$= \frac{(22{,}527 + 983)}{983} = 23.9$$

The times interest earned ratio indicates the ability of current operations to pay the interest that is due on the entity's debt obligations. The more times that interest is earned, the better the entity's ability to service the interest on long-term debt.

KEY TERMS

Analytical procedures. Evaluations of financial information made by a study of plausible relationships among both financial and nonfinancial data.

Audit committee. A subcommittee of the board of directors that is responsible for the financial reporting and disclosure process.

Audit procedures. Specific acts performed as the auditor gathers evidence to determine if specific audit objectives are being met.

Dual-purpose tests. Tests of transactions that both evaluate the effectiveness of controls and detect monetary errors.

Engagement letter. A letter that formalizes the contract between the auditor and the client and outlines the responsibilities of both parties.

Illegal act. A violation of laws or government regulations.

Substantive procedures. Audit procedures performed to test material misstatements in an account balance, transaction class, or disclosure component of the financial statements.

Substantive tests of transactions. Tests to detect errors or fraud in individual transactions.

Tests of controls. Procedures that evaluate the effectiveness of the design and operation of internal controls.

Tests of details of account balances and disclosures. Substantive tests that concentrate on the details of items contained in the account balance and disclosure.

www.mhhe.com/ messier4e	Visit the book's Online Learning Center for a multiple-choice quiz that will allow you to assess your understanding of chapter concepts.

REVIEW QUESTIONS

[LO 1] 5-1 What types of inquiries about a prospective client should an auditor make to third parties?

[1] 5-2 Who is responsible for initiating the communication between the predecessor and successor auditors? What type of information should be requested from the predecessor auditor?

[2,3] 5-3 What is the purpose of an engagement letter? List the important information that the engagement letter should contain.

[4] 5-4 What factors should an external auditor use to assess the competence and objectivity of internal auditors?

[5] 5-5 What is an audit committee, and what are its responsibilities?

[6,7] 5-6 List the matters an auditor should consider when developing an overall audit plan.

[7] 5-7 Distinguish between illegal acts that are "direct and material" and those that are "material but indirect." List five circumstances that may indicate that an illegal act may have occurred.

[7] 5-8 List three audit procedures that may be used to identify transactions with related parties.

[8] 5-9 What are the three general types of audit tests? Define each type of audit test and give two examples.

[9]   5-10   What are the purposes for using preliminary analytical procedures?

[9]   5-11   When discussing the use of analytical procedures, what is meant by the "precision of the expectation"? In applying this notion to an analytical procedure, how might an auditor calculate a tolerable difference?

[9]   5-12   Significant differences between the auditor's expectation and the client's book value require explanation through quantification, corroboration, and evaluation. Explain each of these terms.

[10]   5-13   Why does the "audit testing hierarchy" begin with tests of controls and substantive analytical procedures?

[10]   5-14   Consider the "assurance bucket" analogy. Why are some of the buckets larger than others for particular assertions or accounts?

[11]   5-15   List and discuss the four categories of financial ratios that are presented in the chapter.

MULTIPLE-CHOICE QUESTIONS

[1]   5-16   Before accepting an audit engagement, a successor auditor should make specific inquiries of the predecessor auditor regarding the predecessor's
   a. Awareness of the consistency in the application of generally accepted accounting principles between periods.
   b. Evaluation of all matters of continuing accounting significance.
   c. Opinion of any subsequent events occurring since the predecessor's audit report was issued.
   d. Understanding as to the reasons for the change of auditors.

[6]   5-17   In using the work of a specialist, an understanding should exist among the auditor, the client, and the specialist as to the nature of the work to be performed by the specialist. Preferably, the understanding should be documented and would include all of the following *except*
   a. The objectives and scope of the specialist's work.
   b. The specialist's representations as to his or her relationship, if any, to the client.
   c. The specialist's understanding of the auditor's corroborative use of the specialist's findings in relation to the representations in the financial statements.
   d. A statement that the methods or assumptions to be used are *not* inconsistent with those used by the client.

[4]   5-18   Miller Retailing, Inc., maintains a staff of three full-time internal auditors who report directly to the controller. In planning to use the internal auditors to help in performing the audit, the independent auditor most likely will
   a. Place limited reliance on the work performed by the internal auditors.
   b. Decrease the extent of the tests of controls needed to support the assessed level of detection risk.
   c. Increase the extent of the procedures needed to reduce control risk to an acceptable level.
   d. Avoid using the work performed by the internal auditors.

[7] 5-19 Which of the following statements is correct concerning related-party transactions?

a. In the absence of evidence to the contrary, related-party transactions should be assumed to be outside the ordinary course of business.

b. An auditor should determine whether a particular transaction would have occurred if the parties had *not* been related.

c. An auditor should substantiate that related-party transactions were consummated on terms equivalent to those that prevail in arm's-length transactions.

d. The audit procedures directed toward identifying related-party transactions should include considering whether transactions are occurring but are *not* being given proper accounting recognition.

[7] 5-20 When planning an examination, an auditor should

a. Consider whether the extent of substantive procedures may be reduced based on the results of the internal control questionnaire.

b. Make preliminary judgments about materiality levels for audit purposes.

c. Conclude whether changes in compliance with prescribed internal controls justify reliance on them.

d. Prepare a preliminary draft of the management representation letter.

[7] 5-21 A difference of opinion regarding the results of a sample cannot be resolved between the assistant who performed the auditing procedures and the in-charge auditor. The assistant should

a. Refuse to perform any further work on the engagement.

b. Accept the judgment of the more experienced in-charge auditor.

c. Document the disagreement and ask to be disassociated from the resolution of the matter.

d. Notify the client that a serious audit problem exists.

[7] 5-22 Morris, CPA, suspects that a pervasive scheme of illegal bribes exists throughout the operations of Worldwide Import-Export, Inc., a new audit client. Morris has notified the audit committee and Worldwide's legal counsel, but neither could assist Morris in determining whether the amounts involved were material to the financial statements or whether senior management is involved in the scheme. Under these circumstances, Morris should

a. Express an unqualified opinion with a separate explanatory paragraph.

b. Disclaim an opinion on the financial statements.

c. Express an adverse opinion on the financial statements.

d. Issue a special report regarding the illegal bribes.

[7] 5-23 Which of these statements concerning illegal acts by clients is correct?

a. An auditor's responsibility to detect illegal acts that have a direct and material effect on the financial statements is the same as that for errors and fraud.

b. An audit in accordance with generally accepted auditing standards normally includes audit procedures specifically designed to detect illegal acts that have an indirect but material effect on the financial statements.

      c. An auditor considers illegal acts from the perspective of the reliability of management's representations rather than their relation to audit objectives derived from financial statement assertions.

      d. An auditor has *no* responsibility to detect illegal acts by clients that have an indirect effect on the financial statements.

[8,9]   5-24   To help plan the nature, timing, and extent of substantive procedures, preliminary analytical procedures should focus on

      (a.) Enhancing the auditor's understanding of the client's business and of events that have occurred since the last audit date.

      b. Developing plausible relationships that corroborate anticipated results with a measurable amount of precision.

      c. Applying ratio analysis to externally generated data such as published industry statistics or price indexes.

      d. Comparing recorded financial information to the results of other tests of transactions and balances.

[9]   5-25   The primary objective of final analytical procedures is to

      a. Obtain evidence from details tested to corroborate particular assertions.

      b. Identify areas that represent specific risks relevant to the audit.

      (c.) Assist the auditor in assessing the validity of the conclusions reached.

      d. Satisfy doubts when questions arise about a client's ability to continue in existence.

[9]   5-26   For all audits of financial statements made in accordance with generally accepted auditing standards, the use of analytical procedures is required to some extent

	In the Planning Stage?	As a Substantive Test?	In the Review Stage?
a.	Yes	No	Yes
b.	No	Yes	No
c.	No	Yes	Yes
d.	Yes	No	No

[10]   5-27   Trend analysis is best described by

      a. The comparison, across time or to a benchmark, of relationships between financial statement accounts or between an account and nonfinancial data.

      b. Development of a model to form an expectation using financial data, nonfinancial data, or both to test account balances or changes in account balances between accounting periods.

      (c.) The examination of changes in an account over time.

      d. The examination of ratios over time.

[10]   5-28   The assurance bucket is filled with all of the following types of evidence except

      a. Test of controls.

      b. Business risks.

      c. Substantive analytical procedures.

      d. Tests of details.

PROBLEMS

[1] 5-29 Dodd, CPA, audited Adams Company's financial statements for the year ended December 31, 2004. On November 1, 2005, Adams notified Dodd that it was changing auditors and that Dodd's services were being terminated. On November 5, 2005, Adams invited Hall, CPA, to make a proposal for an engagement to audit its financial statements for the year ended December 31, 2005.

Required:
a. What procedures concerning Dodd should Hall perform before accepting the engagement?
b. What additional procedures should Hall consider performing during the planning phase of this audit (after accepting the engagement) that would *not* be performed during the audit of a continuing client?

(AICPA, adapted)

[1] 5-30 The audit committee of the board of directors of Unicorn Corporation asked Tish & Field, CPAs, to audit Unicorn's financial statements for the year ended December 31, 2005. Tish & Field explained the need to make an inquiry of the predecessor auditor and requested permission to do so. Unicorn's management agreed and authorized the predecessor auditor to respond fully to Tish & Field's inquiries.

After a satisfactory communication with the predecessor auditor, Tish & Field drafted an engagement letter that was mailed to the audit committee of the board of directors of Unicorn Corporation. The engagement letter clearly set forth the arrangements concerning the involvement of the predecessor auditor and other matters.

Required:
a. What information should Tish & Field have obtained during its inquiry of the predecessor auditor prior to accepting the engagement?
b. What other matters would Tish & Field generally have included in the engagement letter?

(AICPA, adapted)

[2,6,7] 5-31 Parker is the in-charge auditor with administrative responsibilities for the upcoming annual audit of FGH Company, a continuing audit client. Parker will supervise two assistants on the engagement and will visit the client before the fieldwork begins.

Parker has started the planning process by listing procedures to be performed prior to the beginning of fieldwork. The list includes
1. Reviewing correspondence and permanent files.
2. Reviewing prior years' audit documentation, financial statements, and auditor's reports.
3. Discussing matters that may affect the examination with the CPA firm personnel responsible for providing audit and nonaudit services to the client.
4. Discussing with management current business developments affecting the client.

Required:
Complete Parker's list of procedures to be performed before the beginning of fieldwork.

(AICPA, adapted)

[2,3]   5-32   A CPA has been asked to audit the financial statements of a publicly held company for the first time. All preliminary verbal discussions and inquiries among the CPA, the company, the predecessor auditor, and all other necessary parties have been completed. The CPA is now preparing an engagement letter.

Required:
a. List the items that should be included in the typical engagement letter in these circumstances.
b. Describe the benefits derived from preparing an engagement letter.

(AICPA, adapted)

[5]   5-33   For many years the financial and accounting community has recognized the importance of the use of audit committees and has endorsed their formation. By now the use of audit committees has become widespread. Independent auditors have become increasingly involved with audit committees and consequently have become familiar with their nature and function.

Required:
a. Describe what an audit committee is.
b. Identify the reasons why audit committees have been formed and are currently in operation.
c. Describe the functions of an audit committee.

(AICPA, adapted)

[7]   5-34   Post, CPA, accepted an engagement to audit the financial statements of General Company, a new client. General is a publicly held retailing entity that recently replaced its operating management. In the course of applying auditing procedures, Post discovered that General's financial statements may be materially misstated due to the existence of fraud.

Required:
a. Describe Post's responsibilities regarding the circumstance described.
b. Describe Post's responsibilities to report on General's financial statements and other communications if Post is precluded from applying necessary procedures in searching for fraud.
c. Describe Post's responsibilities to report on General's financial statements and other communications if Post concludes that General's financial statements are materially affected by fraud.
d. Describe the circumstances in which Post may have a duty to disclose fraud to third parties outside General's management and its audit committee.

(AICPA, adapted)

[7,8]   5-35   Exhibit 5–2 contains a partial audit program for substantive tests of accounts receivable.

Required:

For audit procedures 1–4, identify the primary assertion being tested.

[9] 5-36 Analytical procedures consist of evaluations of financial information made by a study of plausible relationships among both financial and nonfinancial data. They range from simple comparisons to the use of complex models involving many relationships and elements of data. They compare recorded amounts, or ratios developed from recorded amounts, to expectations developed by the auditor.

Required:

a. Describe the broad purposes of analytical procedures.

b. Identify the sources of information from which an auditor develops expectations.

c. Describe the factors that influence an auditor's consideration of the reliability of data for the purpose of testing assertions.

(AICPA, adapted)

[9] 5-37 At December 31, 2005, EarthWear has $5,890,000 in a liability account labeled "Reserve for returns." The footnotes to the financial statements contain the following policy: "At the time of sale, the company provides a reserve equal to the gross profit on projected merchandise returns, based on prior returns experience." The client has indicated that returns for sales that are six months old are negligible, and gross profit percentage for the year is 42.5 percent. The client has also provided the following information on sales for the last six months of the year:

Month	Monthly Sales (000s)	Historical Return Rate
July	$ 73,300	.004
August	82,800	.006
September	93,500	.010
October	110,200	.015
November	158,200	.025
December	202,500	.032

Required:

a. Using the information given, develop an expectation for the reserve for returns account.

b. Determine a tolerable difference for your analytical procedure. Follow the suggestions in the text.

c. Compare your expectation to the book value and determine if it is greater than tolerable difference.

d. Independent of your answer in part (c), what procedures should the auditor perform if the difference between the expectation and the book value is greater than tolerable misstatement?

[8,9,11] 5-38 Arthur, CPA, is auditing the RCT Manufacturing Company as of December 31, 2005. As with all engagements, one of Arthur's initial procedures is to make overall checks of the client's financial data by reviewing significant ratios and trends so that he better understands the business and can determine where to concentrate his audit efforts.

RCT MANUFACTURING COMPANY
Condensed Balance Sheets
December 31, 2005 and 2004

	2005	2004
Assets		
Cash	$ 12,000	$ 15,000
Accounts receivable, net	93,000	50,000
Inventory	72,000	67,000
Other current assets	5,000	6,000
Plant and equipment, net of depreciation	60,000	80,000
	$242,000	$218,000
Equities		
Accounts payable	$ 38,000	$ 41,000
Federal income taxes payable	30,000	15,000
Long-term liabilities	20,000	40,000
Common stock	70,000	70,000
Retained earnings	84,000	52,000
	$242,000	$218,000

RCT MANUFACTURING COMPANY
Condensed Income Statements
Years Ended December 31, 2005 and 2004

	2005	2004
Net sales	$1,684,000	$1,250,000
Cost of goods sold	927,000	710,000
Gross margin on sales	$ 757,000	$ 540,000
Selling and administrative expenses	682,000	504,000
Income before federal income taxes	$ 75,000	$ 36,000
Income tax expense	30,000	14,400
Net income	$ 45,000	$ 21,600

The financial statements prepared by the client with audited 2004 figures and preliminary 2005 figures are presented here in condensed form.

Additional information:

- The company has only an insignificant amount of cash sales.
- The end-of-year figures are comparable to the average for each respective year.

Required:

For each year, compute the current ratio and a turnover ratio for accounts receivable. Based on these ratios, identify and discuss audit procedures that should be included in Arthur's audit of (1) accounts receivable and (2) accounts payable.

(AICPA, adapted)

DISCUSSION CASES

[7,8]   5-39   Forestcrest Woolen Mills is a closely held North Carolina company that has existed since 1920. The company manufactures high-quality woolen cloth for men's and women's outerwear. Your firm has audited Forestcrest for 15 years.

Five years ago, Forestcrest signed a consent decree with the North Carolina Environmental Protection Agency. The company had been convicted of dumping pollutants (such as bleaching and dyeing chemicals) into the local river. The consent decree provided that Forestcrest construct a water treatment facility within eight years.

You are conducting the current-year audit, and you notice that there has been virtually no activity in the water treatment facility construction account. Your discussion with the controller produces the following comment: "Because of increased competition and lower sales volume, our cash flow has decreased below normal levels. You had better talk to the president about the treatment facility."

The president (and majority shareholder) tells you the following: "Given the current cash flow levels, we had two choices: lay off people or stop work on the facility. This is a poor rural area of North Carolina with few other job opportunities for our people. I decided to stop work on the water treatment facility. I don't think that the state will fine us or close us down." When you ask the president if the company will be able to comply with the consent decree, he informs you that he is uncertain.

Required:
a. Discuss the implications of this situation for the audit and audit report.
b. Would your answer change if these events occurred in the seventh year after the signing of the consent decree?

[9]   5-40   The auditors for Weston University are conducting their audit for the fiscal year ended December 31, 2005. Specifically, the audit firm is now focusing on the audit of revenue from this season's home football games. While planning the audit of sales of football tickets, one of their newer staff people observed that, in prior years, many hours were spent auditing revenue. This staff associate pointed out that perhaps the firm could apply analytical procedures to evaluate whether it appears that the revenue account is properly stated.

The staff associate noted that information for a typical home game could be used to estimate revenues for the entire season. The home football season consisted of seven home games—one against a nationally ranked powerhouse, Bloomington University, and six games against conference opponents. One of these conference games is Weston's in-state archrival, Norwalk University. All of these games were day games except for the game against a conference opponent, Westport University.

The auditors will base their estimate on the game played against Kramer College, a conference opponent. This game is considered to be an average home game for Weston University. The following information concerning that game is available:

Total attendance   24,000 (stadium capacity is 40,000)

This attendance figure includes the 500 free seats described below, and the 24,000 figure should be used as a basis for all further calculations.

Ticket prices	
Box seats	$12 per ticket
End-zone seats	8 per ticket
Upper-deck seats	5 per ticket

At the game against Kramer College, total attendance was allocated among the different seats as follows:

Box seats	70%
End-zone seats	20%
Upper-deck seats	10%

Based on information obtained in prior year audits, the following assumptions are made to assist in estimating revenue for the other games, all:

- Attendance for the Bloomington University game was expected to be 30 percent higher than total attendance for an average game, with the mix of seats purchased expected to be the same as for a regular game; however, tickets are priced 20 percent higher than for a normal game.
- The game against Norwalk University was expected to draw 20 percent more fans than a normal game, with 75 percent of these extra fans buying box seats and the other 25 percent purchasing upper-deck seats.
- To make up for extra costs associated with the night game, ticket prices were increased by 10 percent each; however, attendance was also expected to be 5 percent lower than for a normal game, with each type of seating suffering a 5 percent decline.
- At every game 500 box seats are given away free to players' family and friends. This number is expected to be the same for all home games.

Required:
1. Based on the information above, develop an expectation for ticket revenue for the seven home football games.
2. Reported ticket revenue was $2,200,000. Is the difference between your estimate and reported ticket revenue large enough to prompt further consideration? Why or why not? If further consideration is warranted, provide possible explanations for the difference between estimated and actual football ticket revenue. What evidence could you gather to verify each of your explanations?
3. Under what conditions are substantive analytical procedures likely to be effective in a situation such as that described in this problem?

INTERNET ASSIGNMENTS

[4]   5-41   Visit the Institute of Internal Auditors (IIA) home page (www.theiia.org) and familiarize yourself with the information contained there. Search the site for information about the IIA's requirements for the objectivity and independence of internal auditors.

[7]   5-42   EarthWear Clothiers makes high-quality clothing for outdoor sports. It sells most of its products through mail order. Use the Internet to obtain information about the retail mail order industry.

[8,9,11]   5-43   Using the information from the text, EarthWear Clothiers' home page (www.mhhe.com/earthwear), and Willis & Adams's home page (www.mhhe.com/willisandadams) prepare an audit planning memo. In preparing the memo, include information on each of the following items:
- Obtain knowledge of the client's business and industry.
- Establish audit risk and materiality (refer to Chapter 3), and assess inherent risk (cite all important factors and their possible effects on the audit).
- Assess a preliminary level of control risk (limit the assessment to the control environment and order entry).
- Assess the possibility of errors, fraud, and illegal acts.
- Conduct preliminary analytical procedures, including industry data.

ACL

www.mhhe.com/ messier4e	Visit the book's Online Learning Center for problem material to be completed using the *ACL* software packaged with your new text.

LEARNING OBJECTIVES

Upon completion of this chapter you will

[1] Understand the importance of internal control to management and auditors.

[2] Know the definition of internal control.

[3] Know what controls are relevant to the audit.

[4] Identify the components of internal control.

[5] Understand the effect of information technology on internal control.

[6] Understand how to plan an audit strategy.

[7] Know how to develop an understanding of an entity's internal control.

[8] Identify the tools available for documenting the understanding of internal control.

[9] Know how to assess the level of control risk.

[10] Know the types of tests of controls.

[11] Understand audit strategies for the nature, timing, and extent of substantive procedures based on different levels of detection risk.

[12] Understand the considerations for the timing of audit procedures.

[13] Understand how to assess control risk when an entity's accounting transactions are processed by a service organization.

[14] Understand about the auditor's communication of internal control–related matters.

[15] Identify and understand general and application controls.

[16] Understand how to flowchart an accounting cycle.

RELEVANT ACCOUNTING AND AUDITING PRONOUNCEMENTS

COSO, *Internal Control—Integrated Framework* (New York: AICPA, 1992)

AU 311, Planning and Supervision

AU 312, Audit Risk and Materiality in Conducting an Audit

AU 313, Substantive Tests Prior to the Balance-Sheet Date

AU 319, Consideration of Internal Control in a Financial Statement Audit

AU 322, The Auditor's Consideration of the Internal Audit Function in an Audit of Financial Statements

AU 324, Service Organizations

AU 325, Communication of Internal Control–Related Matters Noted in an Audit

AU 329, Analytical Procedures

AU 339, Audit Documentation

AU 532, Restricting the Use of an Auditor's Report

AICPA Auditing Standards Board, Exposure Draft, "Understanding the Entity and Its Environment and Assessing the Risks of Material Misstatement"

AICPA Auditing Standards Board, Exposure Draft, "Audit Evidence"

AICPA Auditing Standards Board, Exposure Draft, "Performing Audit Procedures in Response to Assessed Risks and Evaluating the Audit Evidence Obtained"

PCAOB Auditing Standard No. 3, Audit Documentation and Amendments to Interim Auditing Standards (AS3)

Internal Control in a Financial Statement Audit

Major Phases of an Audit

Client acceptance/
continuance and establishing
engagement terms
(Chapter 5)

Preplanning
(Chapter 5)

Establish materiality
and assess risks
(Chapter 3)

Plan the audit
(Chapters 3 and 5)

Consider and audit
internal control
(Chapters 6 and 7)

Audit business processes
and related accounts
(e.g., revenue generation)
(Chapters 10–16)

Complete the audit
(Chapter 17)

Evaluate results and
issue audit report
(Chapters 2 and 18)

In Chapter 3, we noted that a major part of the auditor's understanding of the entity and its environment included knowledge about the entity's internal control. We also discussed how this preliminary assessment of control risk was used in the audit risk model to determine detection risk. In Chapter 5, we introduced you to the concepts of the assurance testing hierarchy and the "assurance bucket," which indicate that the auditor typically obtains assurance from tests of controls before substantive procedures. This chapter provides detailed coverage of the auditor's assessment of control risk. It addresses the importance of internal control and its components, as well as how evaluating internal control relates to substantive testing. Chapter 7 covers the new reporting requirements for an audit of internal control over financial reporting as required by the Sarbanes-Oxley Act of 2002. This chapter covers the COSO framework, basic concepts that apply to auditing internal control, and how the auditor's consideration of a client's internal control impacts the financial statement audit. This chapter also discusses the timing of audit procedures, service organizations, and the required communications of internal control–related matters. 🌐

Introduction

[LO 1]   Internal control plays an important role in how management meets its stewardship or agency responsibilities. Management has the responsibility to maintain controls that provide reasonable assurance that adequate control exists over the entity's assets and records. Proper internal control not only ensures that assets and records are safeguarded, but also creates an environment in which efficiency and effectiveness are encouraged and monitored. Management also needs a control system that generates reliable information for decision making. If the information system does not generate reliable information, management may be unable to make informed decisions about issues such as product pricing, cost of production, and profit information.

The auditor needs assurance about the reliability of the data generated by the information system in terms of how it affects the fairness of the financial statements and how well the assets and records of the entity are safeguarded. The auditor uses risk assessment procedures to obtain an understanding of the entity's internal control. The auditor uses this understanding of internal control to identify the types of potential misstatements; consider factors that affect the risk of material misstatement; and design the nature, timing, and extent of further audit procedures. As we discussed in Chapter 3, there is an inverse relationship between the reliability of internal control (achieved control risk) and the amount of substantive evidence required of the auditor. In other words, when the auditor is filling the assurance bucket for an assertion (see Figure 5–6), obtaining more controls evidence means he or she needs to obtain less substantive evidence to top it off.

As we shall see in this chapter, the auditor's understanding of internal control is a major factor in determining the overall audit strategy. The auditor's responsibilities for internal control are discussed under two major topics: (1) obtaining an understanding of internal control and (2) assessing control risk.

Internal Control

Definition of Internal Control

[LO 2]   Internal control is designed and effected by an entity's board of directors, management, and other personnel to provide reasonable assurance about the achievement of the entity's objectives in the following categories: (1) reliability of financial reporting, (2) effectiveness and efficiency of operations, and (3) compliance with applicable laws and regulations.

Internal control over the safeguarding of assets against unauthorized acquisition, use, or disposition is also important, and may include controls relating to financial reporting and operations objectives.

Controls Relevant to the Audit

[LO 3]   While an entity's internal controls address objectives in each category, not all of these objectives and their related internal controls are relevant to a financial statement audit. Generally, internal controls pertaining to the preparation of financial statements for external purposes are relevant to an audit. Controls relating to operations and compliance objectives may be relevant when they relate to data the auditor uses to apply auditing procedures. For example, the internal controls that relate to operating or production statistics may be utilized by the auditor as nonfinancial data for analytical procedures. On the other hand, some controls that relate to management's planning or operating decisions may not be relevant for audit purposes. For example, controls concerning compliance with health and safety regulations, although important to the entity, ordinarily do not relate to a financial statement audit. Similarly, an entity may rely on a sophisticated system of automated controls to provide efficient and effective operations, such as an airline's system that maintains flight schedules, but these controls would not necessarily be relevant to the audit.

Components of Internal Control

❧ [LO 4]

Internal control consists of five components:

- The control environment.
- The entity's risk assessment process.
- The information system and related business processes relevant to financial reporting and communication.
- Control procedures.
- Monitoring of controls.

Table 6–1 defines each of the components, while Figure 6–1 shows how the categories of objectives of internal control, including safeguarding of assets, relate to the five components. You can see that each of the five components impacts each of the objectives. However, as mentioned above, the auditor is mainly concerned with how the five components affect the financial reporting objective. In terms of safeguarding assets, the auditor is generally concerned with controls that are relevant to the reliability of financial reporting. For example, access controls, such as passwords, that limit access to data and programs that process transactions may be relevant to the audit. In summary, the controls relevant to the audit are those that are likely to prevent or detect material misstatements in the financial statement assertions.

TABLE 6–1   Components of Internal Control

Control environment The control environment sets the tone of an organization, influencing the control consciousness of its people. It is the foundation for effective internal control, providing discipline and structure. The control environment includes the attitudes, awareness, policies, and actions of management and the board of directors concerning the entity's internal control and its importance in the entity.

The entity's risk assessment process The process for identifying and responding to business risks and the results thereof. For financial reporting purposes, the entity's risk assessment process includes how management identifies risks relevant to the preparation of financial statements that are fairly presented in conformity with generally accepted accounting principles, estimates their significance, assesses the likelihood of their occurrence, and decides upon actions to manage them.

The entity's information system and related business processes relevant to financial reporting, and communication The information system relevant to financial reporting objectives, which includes the accounting system, consists of the procedures, whether automated or manual, and records established to initiate, record, process, and report entity transactions and to maintain accountability for the related assets, liabilities, and equity. Communication involves providing an understanding of individual roles and responsibilities pertaining to internal control over financial reporting.

Control procedures Control procedures are the policies and procedures that help ensure that management directives are carried out, for example, that necessary actions are taken to address risks to achievement of the entity's objectives. Control procedures, whether automated or manual, have various objectives and are applied at various organizational and functional levels.

Monitoring of controls A process to assess the quality of internal control performance over time. It involves assessing the design and operation of controls on a timely basis and taking necessary corrective actions.

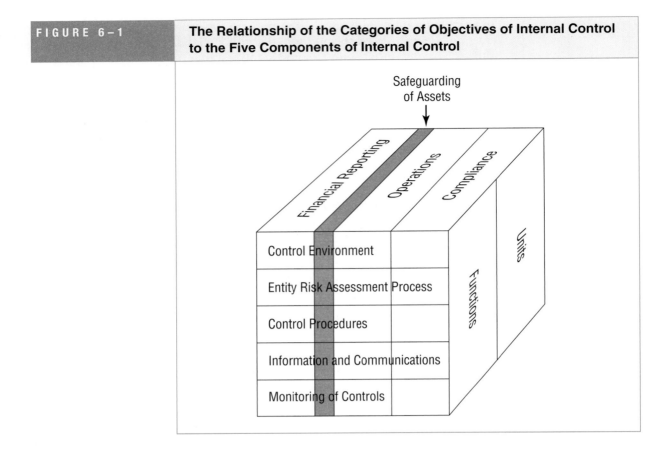

| FIGURE 6-1 | The Relationship of the Categories of Objectives of Internal Control to the Five Components of Internal Control |

The Effect of Information Technology on Internal Control

[LO 5] The extent of an entity's use of information technology (IT) can affect any of the five components of internal control. The use of IT affects the way that transactions are initiated, recorded, processed, and reported. In a manual system, an entity uses manual procedures, and information is generally recorded in a paper format. For example, individuals may manually prepare sales orders, shipping reports, and invoices on paper. Controls in such a system are manual and may include such procedures as approvals and reviews of activities, and reconciliations and follow-up of reconciling items.

On the other hand, an entity may use automated systems that share data and that are used to support all aspects of the entity's financial reporting, operations, and compliance objectives. Such information systems use automated procedures to initiate, record, process, and report transactions in electronic format. Controls in most IT systems consist of a combination of manual controls and automated controls. In such a situation, manual controls may be independent of IT. Manual controls may also use information produced by IT, or they may be limited to monitoring the functioning of IT

TABLE 6–2	Potential Benefits and Risks to an Entity's Internal Control from IT

Benefits
- Consistent application of predefined business rules and performance of complex calculations in processing large volumes of transactions or data.
- Enhancement of the timeliness, availability, and accuracy of information.
- Facilitation of additional analysis of information.
- Enhancement of the ability to monitor the performance of the entity's activities and its policies and procedures.
- Reduction in the risk that controls will be circumvented.
- Enhancement of the ability to achieve effective segregation of duties by implementing security controls in applications, databases, and operating systems.

Risks
- Reliance on systems or programs that inaccurately process data, process inaccurate data, or both.
- Unauthorized access to data that may result in destruction of data or improper changes to data, including the recording of unauthorized or nonexistent transactions or inaccurate recording of transactions.
- Unauthorized changes to data in master files.
- Unauthorized changes to systems or programs.
- Failure to make necessary changes to systems or programs.
- Inappropriate manual intervention.
- Potential loss of data.

and automated controls and to handling exceptions. An entity's mix of manual and automated controls varies with the nature and complexity of the entity's use of IT.

Table 6–2 lists the benefits and risks of using IT for an entity's internal control. The risks to internal control vary depending on the nature and characteristics of the entity's information system. For example, where multiple users may access a common database, a lack of control at a single user entry point may compromise the security of the entire database. This may result in improper changes to or destruction of data. When IT personnel or users are given, or can gain, access privileges beyond those necessary to perform their assigned duties, a breakdown in segregation of duties can occur. This may result in unauthorized transactions or changes to programs or data.

Another common challenge that increases control risk is the fact that many clients have a large variety of technological platforms, software, and hardware. Companies that have grown through merger and acquisition frequently band the legacy systems together rather than replace one or both systems. The resulting montage of servers, computers, off-the-shelf and custom-programmed software, and so on creates a complex and potentially risk-prone IT environment.

Planning an Audit Strategy

The audit risk model states that $AR = IR \times CR \times DR$. In applying the audit risk model, the auditor must assess control risk. How the auditor determines the appropriate level of CR is described in the remainder of this chapter. Figure 6–2 presents a flowchart of the auditor's decision process when considering internal control in planning an audit.

[LO 6]

As shown in Figure 6–2, the auditor's initial step is obtaining a preliminary understanding of internal control. This understanding will be developed as part of the auditor's risk assessment process using risk assessment

Flowchart of the Auditor's Consideration of Internal Control and Its Relation to Substantive Procedures

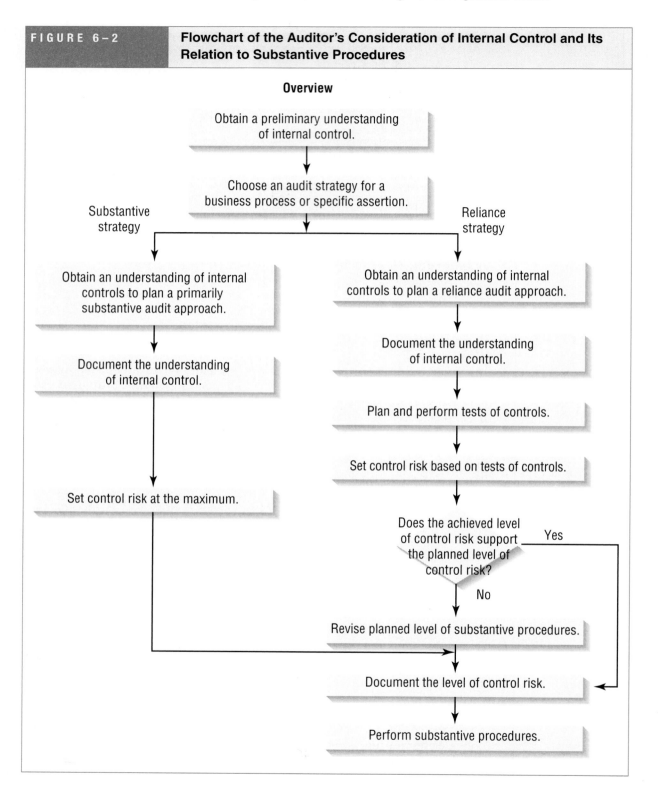

procedures. With a recurring engagement, the auditor is likely to possess substantial knowledge about the client's internal control. In that case, the auditor may be able to choose an audit strategy that includes only updating the understanding of the entity's internal control. For a new client, the auditor may delay making a judgment about an audit strategy until a more detailed understanding of internal control is obtained.

As we discussed in Chapter 3, the auditor must assess the risk of material misstatement (refer to Figure 3–1). The information gathered by performing risk assessment procedures is used to evaluate the design of controls and to determine whether they have been implemented. This audit evidence supports the risk assessment that is then used to plan the nature, timing, and extent of further audit procedures to be performed. When the auditor's risk assessment procedures suggest that the controls are operating effectively and the auditor intends to set control risk in the audit risk model at less than maximum, the auditor is required to perform tests of controls to obtain audit evidence that the controls are, in fact, operating effectively. When the auditor's risk assessment procedures indicate that the controls are not properly designed or not operating effectively, the auditor is not likely to test controls because control risk will be set at maximum. Instead the auditor will use substantive procedures to reduce the risk of material misstatement to an acceptably low level (i.e., the assurance bucket is filled almost entirely with substantive evidence).

To assist your understanding of how the auditor uses the understanding and assessment of internal control to determine the nature, timing, and extent of audit procedures, we assume that there are two audit strategies: a *substantive strategy* and a *reliance strategy*. However, there is no one audit strategy for the entire audit; rather the auditor establishes a strategy for individual business processes (such as revenue or purchasing) or by specific assertion (occurrence, completeness, and so on) within a business process. Furthermore, even when auditors are following a reliance strategy, the amount of assurance obtained by controls testing will vary from assertion to assertion. In other words, a reliance strategy just means the auditor intends to begin filling the assurance bucket with controls evidence, but the percentage of the bucket filled with controls evidence will differ between assertions. Finally, it is important to understand that auditing standards require some substantive evidence for all significant accounts and assertions. Thus, a reliance strategy reduces but does not eliminate the need to gather some substantive evidence.

Situations where the auditor may find it necessary to follow a reliance strategy include the following:

- An entity that initiates orders using electronic data interchange (EDI) for goods based on predetermined decision rules and pays the related payables based on system-generated information regarding receipt of goods. No other documentation is produced or maintained.
- An entity that provides electronic services to customers, such as an Internet service provider or a telephone company, and uses IT to log services provided to users, initiate bills for the services, process the billing transactions, and automatically record such amounts in electronic accounting records.

As we discuss in more detail in the next chapter, the Sarbanes-Oxley Act of 2002 as implemented by AS2 requires public company auditors to test and report on the design and effectiveness of public company internal controls over financial reporting. Thus, it is expected that every public company audit will follow a reliance strategy to some degree.

Substantive Strategy

Following the left-hand side of Figure 6–2, the auditor first obtains an understanding of internal control sufficient to plan a substantive audit approach. It is important to note that even when a substantive strategy is followed, the auditor is still required by auditing standards to have an understanding of the five components of internal control. A substantive audit approach means that the auditor has decided not to rely on the entity's controls and to directly audit the related financial statement accounts.

The auditor may decide to follow a substantive strategy and set control risk at the maximum for some or all assertions because of one or all of the following factors:

- The controls do not pertain to an assertion.
- The controls are assessed as ineffective.
- Testing the effectiveness of controls is inefficient.

The auditor next documents the understanding of internal control, sets control risk at the maximum, and documents the control risk assessment. Finally, substantive procedures are designed and performed based on the assessment of a maximum level of control risk. Therefore, when the auditor follows a substantive strategy, the assurance bucket is filled with some evidence from the risk assessment procedures and an extensive amount of evidence from substantive procedures (i.e., substantive analytical procedures and tests of details).

The auditor needs to be satisfied that performing only substantive procedures would be effective in restricting detection risk to an acceptable level. For example, the auditor may determine that performing only substantive procedures would be effective and more efficient than performing tests of controls for an entity that has a limited number of long-term debt transactions because corroborating evidence can be obtained by examining the loan agreements and confirming relevant information. In circumstances where the auditor is performing only substantive procedures and where the information used by the auditor to perform such substantive procedures is produced by the entity's information system, the auditor should obtain evidence about the accuracy and completeness of the information.

Reliance Strategy

Following the right-hand side of Figure 6–2, the auditor first obtains an understanding of internal control as the basis for assessing a lower level of control risk. The reliance strategy requires a more detailed understanding of internal control than the substantive strategy does because the auditor intends to rely on the controls. The auditor next documents his or her understanding of internal control and plans and performs tests of controls. Control risk is then assessed based on the results of the tests. If the achieved level of control risk does not support the planned level of control risk, the auditor

TABLE 6–3	**Assertions about Classes of Transactions and Events for the Period under Audit**

Occurrence—Transactions and events that have been recorded have occurred and pertain to the entity.
Completeness—All transactions and events that should have been recorded have been recorded.
Authorization—All transactions and events are properly authorized.
Accuracy—Amounts and other data relating to recorded transactions and events have been recorded appropriately.
Cutoff—Transactions and events have been recorded in the correct accounting period.
Classification—Transactions and events have been recorded in the proper accounts.

normally increases the planned substantive procedures and documents the revised control risk assessment. If the planned level of control risk is supported, no revisions of the planned substantive procedures are required. The level of control risk is documented, and substantive procedures are performed. The reader should remember that there may be different degrees of reliance for different business processes or assertions within a process.

From a practical standpoint, the level of control risk is normally set in terms of the assertions about classes of transactions and events for the period under audit. Table 6–3 presents the definitions of assertions related to transactions and events that were discussed in Chapter 4. Table 6–4 shows the assertions and the control procedures that are normally in place for each assertion to protect against material misstatements. For example, the use of prenumbered documents that are accounted for is a control procedure found in each business process to ensure occurrence and completeness. In a revenue process, prenumbered shipping documents that are normally accounted for provide reasonable assurance that all revenue is recorded (completeness). Similarly, reconciliation of the accounts receivable subledger to the general ledger accounts receivable account provides a control to ensure that the occurrence assertion is met. Later chapters show these control procedures for each business process.

TABLE 6–4	**Assertions about Classes of Transactions and Events and Related Control Procedures**

Assertion	Control Procedures
Occurrence	• Segregation of duties. • Prenumbered documents that are accounted for. • Daily or monthly reconciliation of subsidiary records with independent review.
Completeness	• Prenumbered documents that are accounted for. • Segregation of duties. • Daily or monthly reconciliation of subsidiary records with independent review.
Accuracy	• Internal verification of amounts and calculations. • Monthly reconciliation of subsidiary records by an independent person.
Authorization	• General and specific authorization of transactions at important control points.
Cutoff	• Procedures for prompt recording of transactions. • Internal review and verification.
Classification	• Chart of accounts. • Internal review and verification.

Obtain an Understanding of Internal Control

Overview

[LO 7]

The auditor should obtain an understanding of each of the five components of internal control in order to plan the audit. This understanding includes knowledge about the design of relevant controls and whether they have been placed in operation by the entity. This knowledge is used to

- Identify the types of potential misstatement.
- Consider factors that affect the risk of material misstatement.
- Design tests of controls.
- Design substantive procedures.

In deciding on the nature and extent of the understanding of internal control needed for the audit, the auditor should consider the complexity and sophistication of the entity's operations and systems, including the extent to which the entity relies on manual controls or on automated controls. The auditor will devote more attention to understanding internal control as the complexity and sophistication of the entity's operations and systems increase. The auditor may determine that the engagement team needs specialized skills to determine the effect of IT on the audit. An IT specialist may be either on the audit firm's staff or an outside professional. In determining whether such an IT specialist is needed on the engagement team, the following factors should be considered:

- The complexity of the entity's IT systems and controls and the manner in which they are used in conducting the entity's business.
- The significance of changes made to existing systems, or the implementation of new systems.
- The extent to which data are shared among systems.
- The extent of the entity's participation in electronic commerce.
- The entity's use of emerging technologies.
- The significance of audit evidence that is available only in electronic form.

The IT specialist can be used to inquire of the entity's IT personnel about how data and transactions are initiated, recorded, processed, and reported and how IT controls are designed; inspect systems documentation; observe the operation of IT controls; and plan and perform tests of IT controls. The auditor should have sufficient IT-related knowledge to communicate the assertions to the IT specialist, to evaluate whether the specified procedures meet the auditor's objectives, and to evaluate the results of the audit procedures completed by the IT specialist.

To properly understand a client's internal control, an auditor must understand the five components of internal control. The main difference between the reliance and substantive audit strategies, in terms of the understanding of internal control, is the extent of required knowledge about each of the components; a more in depth understanding is normally required if a reliance strategy is followed.

TABLE 6–5	Factors Affecting the Control Environment
	Communication and enforcement of integrity and ethical values.
	A commitment to competence.
	Participation of the board of directors or audit committee.
	Management's philosophy and operating style.
	Organizational structure.
	Assignment of authority and responsibility.
	Human resource policies and practices.

In addition to previous experience with a client, an auditor may use the following audit procedures to learn about internal control:

- Inquiry of appropriate management, supervisory, and staff personnel.
- Inspection of entity documents and reports.
- Observation of entity activities and operations.

Control Environment

The control environment sets the tone of an organization, influencing the control consciousness of its people. It is the foundation for all other components of internal control, providing discipline and structure. Factors that affect the control environment are shown in Table 6–5.

The importance of control to an entity is reflected in the overall attitude to, awareness of, and actions of the board of directors, management, and owners regarding control. The control environment can be thought of as an umbrella that covers the entire entity and establishes the framework for implementing the entity's accounting systems and internal controls.

Communication and Enforcement of Integrity and Ethical Values

The effectiveness of an entity's internal controls is influenced by the integrity and ethical values of the individuals who create, administer, and monitor the controls. An entity needs to establish ethical and behavioral standards that are communicated to employees and are reinforced by day-to-day practice. For example, management should remove incentives or opportunities that might lead personnel to engage in dishonest, illegal, or unethical acts. Some examples of incentives that may lead to unethical behavior are pressures to meet unrealistic performance targets and performance-dependent rewards. Examples of opportunities include an ineffective board of directors, a weak internal audit function, and insignificant penalties for improper behavior. Management can best communicate integrity and ethical behavior within an entity by example and through the use of policy statements and codes of conduct.

A Commitment to Competence

Competence is the knowledge and skills necessary to accomplish the tasks that define an individual's job. Conceptually, management must specify the competence level for a particular job and translate it into the required level of knowledge and skills. For example, an entity should have a formal or informal job description for each job. Management then must hire employees who have the appropriate competence for their jobs. Good human resource policies (discussed later in this section) help to attract and retain competent and trustworthy employees.

Participation of the Board of Directors or Audit Committee[1]

The board of directors and its audit committee significantly influence the control consciousness of the entity. As mentioned in Chapter 5, the audit committee is a subcommittee of the board of directors that is normally composed of directors who are not part of the management team. The board of directors and the audit committee must take their fiduciary responsibilities seriously and actively oversee the entity's accounting and reporting policies and procedures. Factors that affect the effectiveness of the board or audit committee include the following:

- Its independence from management.
- The experience and stature of its members.
- The extent of its involvement with and scrutiny of the entity's activities.
- The appropriateness of its actions.
- The degree to which difficult questions are raised and pursued with management.
- Its interaction with the internal and external auditors.

Management's Philosophy and Operating Style

Establishing, maintaining, and monitoring the entity's internal controls are management's responsibility. Management's philosophy and operating style can significantly affect the quality of internal control. Characteristics that may signal important information to the auditor about management's philosophy and operating style include the following:

- Management's approach to taking and monitoring business risks.
- Management's attitudes and actions toward financial reporting (conservative or aggressive selection from available alternative accounting principles and the conscientiousness and conservatism with which accounting estimates are developed).
- Management's attitudes toward information processing and accounting functions and personnel.

Organizational Structure

The organizational structure defines how authority and responsibility are delegated and monitored. It provides the framework within which an entity's activities for achieving entitywide objectives are planned, executed, controlled, and reviewed. An entity develops an organizational structure suited to its needs. Establishing a relevant organizational structure includes considering key areas of authority and responsibility and appropriate lines of reporting.

The appropriateness of an entity's organizational structure depends on its size and the nature of its activities. Factors such as the level of technology in the entity's industry and external influences such as regulation play a major role in the type of organizational structure used. For example, an entity in a high-technology industry may need an organizational structure that can

---

[1]See PricewaterhouseCoopers, *Audit Committees: Good Practices for Meeting Market Expectations* (New York: PricewaterhouseCoopers 2003), 2nd edition for a discussion of audit committees and corporate governance.

respond quickly to technological changes in the marketplace. Similarly, an entity that operates in a highly regulated industry, such as banking, may be required to maintain a very tightly controlled organizational structure in order to comply with federal or state laws.

Assignment of Authority and Responsibility

This control environment factor includes *how* authority and responsibility for operating activities are assigned and *how* reporting relationships and authorization hierarchies are established. It includes policies regarding acceptable business practices, knowledge and experience of key personnel, and resources provided for carrying out duties. It also includes policies and communications directed at ensuring that all personnel understand the entity's objectives, know how their individual actions interrelate and contribute to those objectives, and recognize how and for what they will be held accountable.

An entity can use a number of controls to meet the requirements of this control environment factor. For example, the entity can have a well specified organizational chart that indicates lines of authority and responsibility. Further, management and supervisory personnel should have job descriptions that include their control-related responsibilities.

Human Resource Policies and Procedures

The quality of internal control is a direct function of the quality of the personnel operating the system. The entity should have sound personnel policies for hiring, orienting, training, evaluating, counseling, promoting, compensating, and taking remedial action. For example, in hiring employees, standards that emphasize seeking the most qualified individuals, with emphasis on educational background, prior work experience, and evidence of integrity and ethical behavior, demonstrate an entity's commitment to employing competent and trustworthy people. Research into the causes of errors in accounting systems has shown personnel-related issues to be a major cause of error.[2]

Understanding the Control Environment

The auditor should gain sufficient knowledge about the control environment to understand management's and the board of directors' attitude, awareness, and actions concerning the control environment, considering both the substance of controls and their collective effect. This includes knowledge of the factors contained in Table 6–5. Exhibit 6–1 presents a questionnaire that includes the type of information the auditor would document about EarthWear's control environment (see Internet Assignment 6-33 for additional information).[3]

---

[2]A. Eilifsen, and W. F. Messier, Jr., "Auditor Detection of Misstatements: A Review And Integration of Empirical Research," *Journal of Accounting Literature* 2000 (19), pp. 1–43, reviews research studies that have examined the causes of auditor-detected misstatements. For example, A. Wright and R. H. Ashton, "Identifying Audit Adjustments with Attention-Directing Procedures," *The Accounting Review* (October 1989), pp. 710–728, find that approximately 55 percent of the errors detected by auditors resulted from personnel problems, insufficient accounting knowledge, and judgment errors.

[3]Exhibit 6–1 shows how the understanding of internal control can be developed and documented using a separate internal control questionnaire. Some or all of the information on the components of the entity's internal control may be captured as part of the auditor's understanding the entity and its environment (see Chapter 3).

EXHIBIT 6–1	**A Partial Questionnaire for Documenting the Auditor's Understanding of the Control Environment**

CONTROL ENVIRONMENT QUESTIONNAIRE

Client: EarthWear Clothiers		Balance Sheet Date: 12/31/2005
Completed by: SAA Date: 9/30/05		Reviewed by: DRM Date: 10/15/05

COMMUNICATION AND ENFORCEMENT OF INTEGRITY AND ETHICAL VALUES

The effectiveness of controls cannot rise above the integrity and ethical values of the people who create, administer, and monitor them. Integrity and ethical values are essential elements of the control environment, affecting the design, administration, and monitoring of other components. Integrity and ethical behavior are the product of the entity's ethical and behavioral standards, how they are communicated, and how they are reinforced in practice.

	Yes, No, N/A	Comments
Have appropriate entity policies regarding matters such as acceptable business practices, conflicts of interest, and codes of conduct been established, and are they adequately communicated?	Yes	*The permanent work papers contain a copy of EarthWear's conflict-of-interest policy.*
Does management demonstrate the appropriate "tone at the top," including explicit moral guidance about what is right or wrong?	Yes	*EarthWear's management maintains high moral and ethical standards and expects employees to act accordingly.*
Are everyday dealings with customers, suppliers, employees, and other parties based on honesty and fairness?	Yes	*EarthWear's management maintains a high degree of integrity in dealing with customers, suppliers, employees, and other parties; it requires employees and agents to act accordingly.*
Does management document or investigate deviations from established controls?	Yes	*To our knowledge, management has not attempted to override controls. Employees are encouraged to report attempts to bypass controls to appropriate individuals within the organization.*

COMMITMENT TO COMPETENCE

Competence is the knowledge and skills necessary to accomplish tasks that define the individual's job. Commitment to competence includes management's consideration of the competence levels for particular jobs and how those levels translate into requisite skills and knowledge.

Does the company maintain formal or informal job descriptions or other means of defining tasks that comprise particular jobs?	Yes	*EarthWear has formal written job descriptions for all supervisory personnel, and job duties for nonsupervisory personnel are clearly communicated.*
Does management determine to an adequate extent the knowledge and skills needed to perform particular jobs?	Yes	*The job descriptions specify the knowledge and skills needed. The Human Resources Department uses this information in hiring, training, and promotion decisions.*
Does evidence exist that employees have the requisite knowledge and skills to perform their job?	Yes	*Our prior experiences with EarthWear personnel indicate that they have the necessary knowledge and skills.*

The Entity's Risk Assessment Process

An entity's risk assessment process is its process for identifying and responding to business risks. This process includes how management identifies risks relevant to the preparation of financial statements, estimates their significance, assesses the likelihood of their occurrence, and decides upon actions to manage them. For example, the entity's risk assessment process may address how the entity identifies and analyzes significant estimates recorded in the financial statements.

This risk assessment process should consider external and internal events and circumstances that may arise and adversely affect the entity's ability to initiate, record, process, and report financial data consistent with the assertions of management in the financial statements. Once risks have been identified by management, it should consider their significance, the likelihood of their occurrence, and how they should be managed. Management should initiate plans, programs, or actions to address specific risks. In some instances, management may accept the consequences of a possible risk because of the costs to remediate or other considerations. Client business risks can arise or change due to the following circumstances:

- *Changes in the operating environment.* Changes in the regulatory or operating environment can alter competitive pressures and create significantly different risks.
- *New personnel.* New personnel may have a different focus on or understanding of internal control.
- *New or revamped information systems.* Significant and rapid changes in information systems can change the risk relating to internal control.
- *Rapid growth.* Significant and rapid expansion of operations can strain controls and increase the risk of a breakdown of controls.
- *New technology.* Incorporating new technologies into production processes or information systems may change the risk associated with internal control.
- *New business models, products, or activities.* Entering business areas or transactions with which an entity has little experience may introduce new risk associated with internal control.
- *Corporate restructurings.* Restructuring may be accompanied by staff reductions and changes in supervision and segregation of duties that may change the risk associated with internal control.
- *Expanded international operations.* The expansion or acquisition of international operations carries new and often unique risks that may impact internal control.
- *New accounting pronouncements.* Adopting new accounting principles or changing accounting principles may affect the risk involved in preparing financial statements.

Understanding The Entity's Risk Assessment Process   The auditor should obtain sufficient information about the entity's risk assessment process to understand how management considers risks relevant to financial reporting objectives and decides what to do to address those risks. For example, suppose a client operates in the oil industry, where there is always some risk of environmental damage. The auditor should obtain sufficient knowledge about how the client manages such environmental risk, because environmental accidents can result in costly litigation against the entity.

Information Systems and Communication

An information system consists of infrastructure (physical and hardware components), software, people, procedures (manual and automated), and data. The information system relevant to the financial reporting objective includes the accounting system and consists of procedures, whether automated or manual; and records established to initiate, record, process, and report an entity's transactions and to maintain accountability for the related assets and liabilities. An effective accounting system gives appropriate consideration to establishing methods and records that will

- Identify and record all valid transactions.
- Describe on a timely basis the transactions in sufficient detail to permit proper classification of transactions for financial reporting.
- Measure the value of transactions in a manner that permits recording their proper monetary value in the financial statements.
- Determine the time period in which transactions occurred to permit recording of transactions in the proper accounting period.
- Properly present the transactions and related disclosures in the financial statements.

Communication involves providing an understanding of individual roles and responsibilities pertaining to internal control over financial reporting. It includes the extent to which personnel understand how their activities in the financial reporting information system relate to the work of others and the means of reporting exceptions to an appropriate higher level within the entity. Policy manuals, accounting and reporting manuals, and memoranda communicate policies and procedures to the entity's personnel. Communications can also be made electronically, orally, or through the actions of management.

Understanding the Information System and Communications

The auditor should obtain sufficient knowledge of the information system relevant to financial reporting to understand the following:

- The classes of transactions in the entity's operations that are significant to the financial statements.
- The procedures, both automated and manual, by which transactions are initiated, recorded, processed, and reported from their occurrence to their inclusion in the financial statements.
- The related accounting records, whether electronic or manual, supporting information, computer media, and specific accounts in the financial statements that are involved in initiating, recording, processing, and reporting transactions.
- How the information system captures other events and conditions that are significant to the financial statements.
- The financial reporting process used to prepare the entity's financial statements, including significant accounting estimates and disclosures.

A well-designed information system that is operating effectively can reduce the risk of material misstatement. The auditor must learn about each business process that affects significant account balances in the financial statements. This includes understanding how transactions are initiated, how documents and records are generated, and how the documents and records flow to the general ledger and financial statements. Understanding the information system also requires knowing how IT is used to process data.

The auditor should understand the automated and manual procedures used by the entity to prepare financial statements and related disclosures. Such procedures include

- The procedures used to enter transaction totals into the general ledger.
- The procedures used to initiate, record, and process journal entries in the general ledger.
- Other procedures used to record recurring and nonrecurring adjustments to the financial statements.

In addition, the auditor should obtain sufficient knowledge of how the entity communicates financial reporting roles and responsibilities and significant matters relating to financial reporting.

Control Procedures

Control procedures are the policies and procedures that help ensure that management's directives are carried out. Control procedures may be either automated or manual. Those control procedures that are relevant to the audit include

- Performance reviews.
- Information processing controls.
- Physical controls.
- Segregation of duties.

Performance Reviews
A strong accounting system should have controls that independently check the performance of the individuals or processes in the system. Some examples include comparing actual performance with budgets, forecasts, and prior-period performance; investigating the relationship of operating and financial data followed by analysis, investigation of unexpected differences, and corrective actions; and reviewing functional or activity performance.

Information Processing Controls
A variety of controls are used to check accuracy, completeness, and authorization in the processing of transactions. The two broad categories of information systems control activities are: general controls and application controls. *General controls* relate to the overall information processing environment and include controls over data center and network operations; system software acquisition, changes, and maintenance; access security; and application system acquisition, development, and maintenance. For example, an entity's controls for developing new programs for existing accounting systems should include adequate documentation and testing before implementation.

Application controls apply to the processing of individual applications and help to ensure the occurrence (validity), completeness, and accuracy of transaction processing. Two examples are (1) the entity should have controls that ensure that each transaction that occurs in an entity's accounting system is properly authorized and (2) the entity should design documents and records so that all relevant information is captured in the accounting system.

General and application controls are covered in more detail in the *Advanced Module 1* at the end of this chapter.

Physical Controls
These controls include the physical security of assets. Physical controls include adequate safeguards, such as secured facilities, authorization for access to computer programs and data files, and periodic counting of assets such as inventory and comparison to control records.

Segregation of Duties
It is important for an entity to segregate the authorization of transactions, recording of transactions, and custody of the related assets. Independent performance of each of these functions reduces the opportunity for any one person to be in a position to both perpetrate and conceal errors or fraud in the normal course of his or her duties. For example, if an employee receives payment from customers on account and has access to the accounts receivable subsidiary ledger, it is possible for that employee to misappropriate the cash and cover the shortage in the accounting records.

Understanding Control Procedures
As the auditor learns about the other components of external control, he or she is also likely to obtain information about control procedures. For example, in examining the information system that pertains to accounts receivable, the auditor is likely to see how the entity grants credit to customers.

The extent of the auditor's understanding of control procedures is a function of the audit strategy adopted. When the auditor decides to follow a substantive strategy approach, little work is done on understanding control procedures. When a reliance strategy is followed, the auditor has to understand the control procedures that relate to assertions for which a lower level of control risk is expected. Auditors normally use walkthroughs to develop an understanding of control procedures.

Monitoring of Controls

Monitoring of controls is a process that assesses the quality of internal control performance over time. To provide reasonable assurance that an entity's objectives will be achieved, management should monitor controls to determine whether they are operating effectively.

Monitoring can be done through ongoing activities or separate evaluations. Ongoing monitoring procedures are built into the normal, recurring activities of the entity and include regular management and supervisory activities. For example, production managers at the corporate or divisional levels of an entity can monitor operations at lower levels by reviewing activity reports and questioning reported activity that differs significantly from their knowledge of the operations. In many entities, the information system produces much of the information used in monitoring. If management assumes that data used for monitoring are accurate, errors may exist in the information, potentially leading management to incorrect conclusions.

Management uses internal auditors or personnel performing similar functions to monitor the operating effectiveness of internal control. An effective internal audit function has clear lines of authority and reporting that allows for objectivity and freedom from conflicts of interest, qualified personnel, and adequate resources to enable these personnel to carry out their assigned duties.

Understanding Monitoring of Controls The auditor should know how the entity monitors the performance of internal control over financial reporting, including how corrective action is initiated.

The Effect of Entity Size on Internal Control

The size of an entity may affect how the various components of internal control are implemented. While large entities may be able to implement the components in the fashion just described, small to midsize entities may use alternative approaches that may not adversely affect their internal control. For example, a large entity may have a written code of conduct, while a small or midsize entity may not. However, a small entity may develop a culture that emphasizes integrity and ethical behavior through oral communication and the example of the owner-manager.

While the basic concepts of the five components should be present in all entities, they are likely to be less formal in a small or midsize entity than in a large entity. For example, in a small entity, the owner-manager's involvement in day-to-day activities can provide a highly effective control that identifies and monitors risks that may affect the entity. A small entity can also have effective communication channels due to its size, the fact that there are fewer levels in the organizational hierarchy, and management's greater visibility. The monitoring component can also be effective in a small to midsize entity as a result of management's close involvement in operations. For example, the owner may review all daily cash disbursements to ensure that only authorized payments are made to vendors. By being involved in day-to-day operations, management may be better able to identify variances from expectations and inaccuracies in financial data.

The Limitations of an Entity's Internal Control

An internal control system should be designed and operated to provide reasonable assurance that an entity's objectives are being achieved. The concept of reasonable assurance recognizes that the cost of an entity's internal control system should not exceed the benefits that are expected to be derived. The necessity of balancing the cost of controls with the related benefits requires considerable estimation and judgment on the part of management. The effectiveness of any internal control system is subject to certain inherent limitations, including management override of internal control, personnel errors or mistakes, and collusion. For example, in a recent survey by KPMG (see Figure 6–3), management override and collusion were reasons why fraud occurred in many companies.

Also note that fraud due to inadequate internal controls has declined in the 2003 survey. This may be attributed to the renewed interest in corporate governance and internal control in the Sarbanes-Oxley Act of 2002.

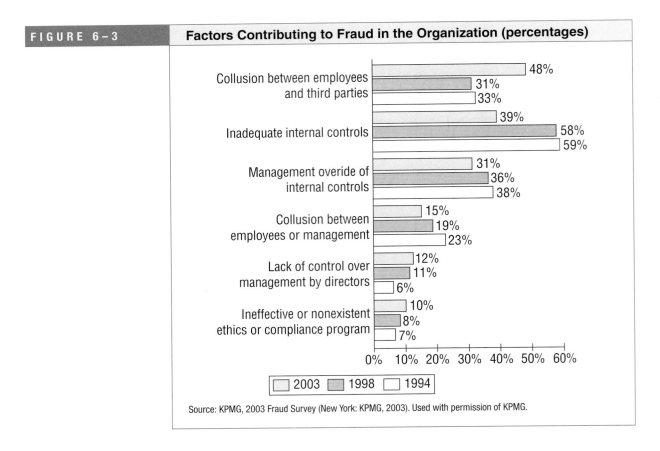

FIGURE 6-3   Factors Contributing to Fraud in the Organization (percentages)

Source: KPMG, 2003 Fraud Survey (New York: KPMG, 2003). Used with permission of KPMG.

Management Override of Internal Control   An entity's controls may be overridden by management. For example, a senior-level manager can require a lower-level employee to record entries in the accounting records that are not consistent with the substance of the transactions and that violate the entity's controls. The lower-level employee may record the transaction, even though he or she knows that it violates the entity's controls, out of fear of losing his or her job. In another example, management may enter into side agreements with customers that alter the terms and conditions of the entity's standard sales contract in ways that would preclude revenue recognition.

The auditor is particularly concerned when senior management is involved in such activities because it raises serious questions about management's integrity. Violations of control procedures by senior management, however, are often difficult to detect with normal audit procedures.

Human Errors or Mistakes   The internal control system is only as effective as the personnel who implement and perform the controls. Breakdowns in internal control can occur because of human failures such as simple errors or mistakes. For example, errors may occur in designing, maintaining, or monitoring automated controls. If IT personnel do not completely understand how a revenue system processes sales transactions, they may erroneously design changes to the system to process sales for a new line of products.

Collusion   The effectiveness of segregation of duties lies in individuals' performing only their assigned tasks or in the performance of one person being checked by another. There is always a risk that collusion between individuals will destroy the effectiveness of segregation of duties. For example, an individual who receives cash receipts from customers can collude with the one who records those receipts in the customers' records to steal cash from the entity.

Documenting the Understanding of Internal Control

⚹ [LO 8]

Auditing standards require that the auditor document the understanding of the entity's internal control components. A number of tools are available to the auditor for documenting the understanding of internal control. These include

- Copies of the entity's procedures manuals and organizational charts.
- Narrative description.
- Internal control questionnaires.
- Flowcharts.

On many engagements, auditors combine these tools to document their understanding of the components of internal control. The combination depends on the complexity of the entity's internal control system. For example, in a complex information system where a large volume of transactions occur electronically, the auditor may document the control environment, the entity's risk assessment process, and monitoring activities using a memorandum and internal control questionnaire. Documentation of the information system and communication component, as well as control procedures, may be accomplished through the use of an internal control questionnaire and a flowchart. For a small entity, documentation using a memorandum may be sufficient.

An auditor should also document his or her understanding of an entity's internal control to provide evidence that the auditor conducted the audit in conformity with GAAS.

Procedures Manuals and Organizational Charts

Many organizations prepare procedures manuals that document the entity's policies and procedures. Portions of such manuals may include documentation of the accounting systems and related control procedures. The entity's organizational chart presents the designated lines of authority and responsibility. Copies of both of these documents can help the auditor document his or her understanding of the internal control system.

Narrative Description

The understanding of internal control may be documented in a memorandum. This documentation approach is most appropriate when the entity has a simple internal control system because a narrative description will be difficult to follow and analyze for a more complex entity, such as EarthWear Clothiers.

Internal Control Questionnaires

Internal control questionnaires are one of many types of questionnaires used by auditors. Questionnaires provide

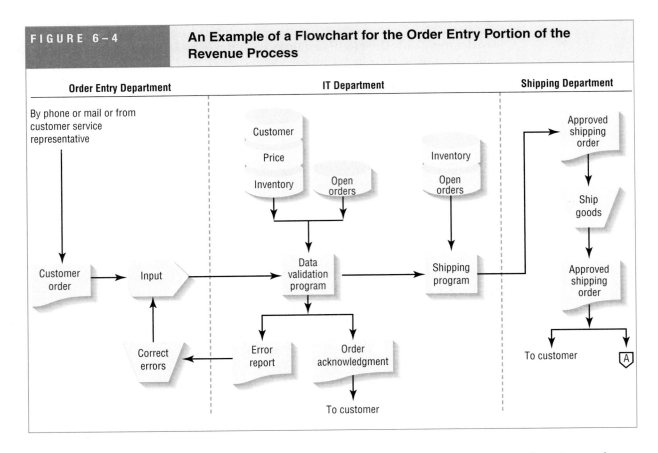

FIGURE 6–4   **An Example of a Flowchart for the Order Entry Portion of the Revenue Process**

a systematic means for the auditor to investigate areas such as internal control. An internal control questionnaire is generally used for entities with relatively complex internal control. It contains questions about the important factors or characteristics of the five internal control components. Exhibit 6–1 provides an example of the use of such questionnaires. The auditor's responses to the questions included in the internal control questionnaire provide the documentation for his or her understanding.

Flowcharts   Flowcharts provide a diagrammatic representation, or "picture," of the entity's accounting system. The flowchart outlines the configuration of the system in terms of functions, documents, processes, and reports. This documentation facilitates an auditor's analysis of the system's strengths and weaknesses. Figure 6–4 presents a simple example of a flowchart for the order entry portion of a revenue process. *Advanced Module* 2 to this chapter provides detailed coverage of flowcharting techniques. Flowcharts are used extensively in this book to represent accounting systems.

Assessing Control Risk

      ☙ **[LO 9]**   Assessing control risk is the *process* of evaluating the effectiveness of an entity's internal control in preventing or detecting material misstatements in the financial statements. As discussed earlier, the auditor can set control risk at the maximum (a substantive strategy) or at a lower level (a reliance strategy). As shown in Figure 6–2, when the auditor sets control risk at the maximum, the control risk assessment is documented and planned substantive procedures are performed. The discussion in this section focuses on the situation where the auditor plans to set control risk below the maximum. To set control risk below the maximum, the auditor must:

- Identify specific controls that will be relied upon.
- Perform tests of controls.
- Conclude on the achieved level of control risk.

Identifying Specific Controls That Will Be Relied Upon

The auditor's understanding of internal control is used to identify the controls that are likely to prevent or detect material misstatement in specific assertions. In identifying controls to be relied upon, the auditor should consider that the controls could have a pervasive effect on many assertions. For example, the conclusion that an entity's control environment is highly effective may influence the auditor's decision about the number of an entity's locations at which auditing procedures are to be performed. Alternatively, some controls only affect an individual assertion contained in a financial statement account, such as, for example, a credit check performed on a customer's order specifically related to the valuation assertion for the accounts receivable balance.

Advanced Module 1 at the end of the chapter provides a detailed discussion of the types of general and application controls. General controls are pervasive to all information systems while application controls relate to a specific business process such as sales or purchasing. It is important to note that the reliability of application controls, especially those that are automated, are affected by the reliability of the general controls. For example, if there were no general controls over program changes, it would be possible for a programmer to make inappropriate changes to controls in an information system.

Performing Tests of Controls

⚹ [LO 10]

As discussed in Chapter 5, audit procedures directed toward evaluating the effectiveness of either the *design* or the *operation* of an internal control are referred to as *tests of controls*. Tests of controls are performed in order to provide evidence to support the lower level of control risk. Tests of controls directed toward the effectiveness of the design of a control are concerned with evaluating whether that control is suitably designed to prevent material misstatements. Tests of controls directed toward operating effectiveness are concerned with assessing how the control was applied, the consistency with which it was applied during the audit period, and by whom it was applied. Procedures used as tests of controls include

- Inquiry of appropriate entity personnel.
- Inspection of documents, reports, or electronic files indicating the performance of the control.
- Observation of the application of the control.
- Walkthroughs, which involve tracing a transaction from its origination to its inclusion in the financial statements through a

combination of audit procedures including inquiry, observation, and inspection.

- Reperformance of the application of the control by the auditor.

A combination of these procedures may be necessary to evaluate the effectiveness of the design or operation of a control. The operating effectiveness of the control can be affected by whether the control is performed manually or is automated. If the control is performed manually it may be subject to human errors or mistakes. If properly designed, automated controls should operate more effectively. Because of the inherent consistency of IT processing, the auditor may be able to reduce the extent of testing of an automated control. For example, an automated application control should function consistently unless the program is changed. To test automated controls, the auditor may need to use techniques that are different from those used to test manual controls. For example, computer-assisted audit techniques may be used to test automated controls. The advanced module in Chapter 7 discusses computer-assisted audit techniques.

Concluding on the Achieved Level of Control Risk

The conclusion that results from this step is referred to as the *achieved level of control risk*. The auditor uses the achieved level of control risk and the assessed level of inherent risk to determine the acceptable level of detection risk. The level of detection risk is used to determine the nature, timing, and extent of substantive tests.

Figure 6–2 shows the decision process followed by the auditor upon completing the planned tests of controls. If the tests of controls are consistent with the auditor's planned assessment of control risk, no revision in the nature, timing, or extent of substantive procedures is necessary. On the other hand, if the tests of controls indicate that the controls are not operating as preliminarily assessed, the achieved level of control risk will have to be increased, and the nature, timing, and extent of planned substantive procedures will have to be modified.

Documenting the Achieved Level of Control Risk

Auditing standards state that the auditor should document the basis for his or her conclusions about the achieved level of control risk. For those assertions where the achieved level of control risk is set below the maximum level, the auditor should document the basis for his or her conclusion that the effectiveness of the design and operation of controls supports that assessed level. The auditor's assessment of control risk and the basis for the achieved level can be documented using a structured working paper, an internal control questionnaire, or a memorandum.

An Example

Table 6–6 presents two account balances from EarthWear Clothiers' financial statements that differ in terms of their nature, size, and complexity. The differences in these characteristics result in different levels of understanding of internal control and different control risk assessments.

In this example, inventory is a material account balance that is composed of numerous products. This account also contains significant inherent risk, and the data for this account are generated by a complex computer system. For inventory, the auditor must understand the control environment

TABLE 6–6	An Example of How Account Characteristics Affect the Auditor's Understanding of Internal Control, Control Risk Assessment, and Planned Substantive Procedures

EarthWear Account Balance	Account Characteristics	Extent of Understanding Needed to Plan the Audit	Control Risk Assessment	Planned Substantive Procedures
Inventory ($122,337,000)	• Material balance. • Numerous transactions from a large product base. • Significant inherent risk related to overstock and out-of-style products. • Complex computer processing.	• Entity control environment factors. • Risk assessment factors. • Monitoring activities. • Significant classes of transactions. • Inventory pricing policies. • Initiation, processing, and recording of transactions. • Control procedures to be relied upon.	• Tests of controls conducted on relevant controls in the purchasing and inventory cycles were consistent with the planned assessment of control risk. • Control risk is assessed to be *low.*	Substantive procedures will include • Physical examination of inventory. • Information technology–assisted audit techniques to audit the inventory compilation.
Prepaid advertising ($11,458,000)	• Significant balance. • Few transactions. • Little or no inherent risk. • Simple accounting procedures.	• Entity control environment factors. • Nature of the account balance. • Monitoring activities.	• Because there are few transactions and the procedures for amortizing advertising expenditures are simple, a substantive strategy is selected. • Control risk is assessed at the *maximum.*	• Substantive procedures will recalculate the amortization of the advertising expenditures.

factors, risk assessment factors, monitoring activities, significant classes of transactions, inventory pricing policies, the flow of transactions, and what control procedures will be relied upon. The auditor will likely use all of the audit procedures discussed to obtain an understanding of internal control for inventory. In contrast, prepaid advertising is a significant account; however, it contains few transactions. There is little or no inherent risk and the accounting records are simple, so the knowledge needed about risk assessment, the information system and communication, and monitoring is minimal. In this instance, the auditor needs only to understand the control environment factors, the nature of the account balance, and the monitoring activities. Limited knowledge of control procedures is necessary for this account. Audit procedures for the prepaid advertising account would likely be limited to recalculation of amortization of advertising.

Substantive Procedures

≋ **[LO 11]**   The last step in the decision process under either strategy is performing substantive procedures. As discussed in Chapter 5, substantive procedures include substantive analytical procedures and tests of details.

Table 6–7 presents two examples of how the nature, timing, and extent of substantive procedures may vary as a function of the detection risk level for

TABLE 6–7	Audit Strategies for the Nature, Timing, and Extent of Substantive Procedures Based on Different Levels of Detection Risk for Inventory

Low-Detection-Risk Strategy—Client 1

Nature	Audit tests for all significant audit assertions using the following types of audit procedures:
	• Physical examination (conducted at year-end).
	• Review of external documents.
	• Confirmation.
	• Reperformance.
Timing	All significant work completed at year-end.
Extent	Extensive testing of significant accounts or transactions.

High-Detection-Risk Strategy—Client 2

Nature	Corroborative audit tests using the following types of audit tests:
	• Physical examination (conducted at an interim date).
	• Analytical procedures.
	• Substantive tests of transactions and balances.
Timing	Interim and year-end.
Extent	Limited testing of accounts or transactions.

the purchasing process and inventory account. Assume that audit risk is set low for both clients but that client 1 has a high level of inherent risk and control risk while client 2 has a low level of inherent risk and control risk. The use of the audit risk model results in setting detection risk at low for client 1 and high for client 2. For client 1, the low detection risk requires that (1) more reliable types of evidence, such as confirmation and reperformance, be obtained, (2) most of the audit work be conducted at year-end, and (3) the tests be extensive (larger sample size). This is because the auditor must fill the assurance bucket almost entirely with substantive evidence. In contrast, client 2 has a high detection risk, which means that (1) less reliable types of evidence, such as analytical procedures, can be obtained, (2) most of the audit work can be conducted at an interim date, and (3) tests of the inventory account would involve a smaller sample size. Another major difference between the two strategies involves the physical examination of the inventory on hand. For the low-detection-risk strategy, physical inventory would be examined at year-end because the control risk was assessed to be high. For the high-detection-risk strategy, the auditor can examine the physical inventory at an interim date because the control risk assessment indicates little risk of material misstatement.

Timing of Audit Procedures

[LO 12]   Audit procedures may be conducted at an interim date or at year-end. Figure 6–5 presents a timeline for planning and performing a midsize to large audit for an entity such as EarthWear Clothiers with a 12/31/05 year-end. In this example, the audit is planned and preliminary analytical procedures are conducted around 5/31/05. The interim tests of controls are conducted sometime during the time frame 7/31/05 to 11/30/05. Substantive procedures are planned for the time frame 11/30/05 to 2/15/06, when the audit report is to be issued. The auditor's considerations of conducting tests of controls and substantive tests at an interim date are discussed in turn.

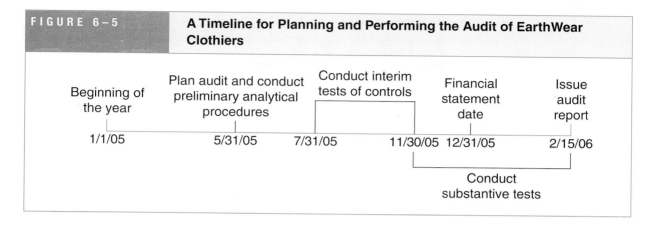

FIGURE 6–5	A Timeline for Planning and Performing the Audit of EarthWear Clothiers

Interim Tests of Controls

An auditor might test controls at an interim date because the assertion being tested may not be significant, the control has been effective in prior audits, or it may be more efficient to conduct the tests at that time. A reason why it may be more efficient to conduct interim tests of controls is that staff accountants may be less busy at the time, and it may minimize the amount of overtime needed at year-end. Additionally, if the controls are found not to be operating effectively, testing them at an interim date gives the auditor more time to reassess the control risk and modify the audit plan. It also gives the auditor time to inform management so that likely misstatements can be located and corrected before the rest of the audit is performed.

An important question the auditor must address is the need for additional audit work in the period following the interim testing period. For example, suppose the auditor examines a sample of sales transactions for the period 1/1/05 to 8/31/05. What testing, if any, should the auditor conduct for the period 9/1/05 to 12/31/05? The auditor should consider factors such as the significance of the assertion, the evaluation of the design and operation of the control, the results of tests of controls, the length of the remaining period, and the planned substantive procedures in determining the nature and extent of audit work for the remaining period. At a minimum, the auditor would inquire about the nature and extent of changes in policies, procedures, or personnel that occurred subsequent to the interim period. If significant changes have occurred, or if the results of tests of controls are unfavorable, the auditor may need to conduct additional audit procedures for the remaining period.

Interim Substantive Procedures

Conducting substantive procedures at an interim date may increase the risk that material misstatements are present in the financial statements. The auditor can control for this potential problem by considering when it is appropriate to examine an account at an interim date and by performing selected audit procedures for the period between the interim date and year-end.

The auditor should consider the following factors when substantive procedures are to be completed at an interim date:

- The control environment.
- Relevant controls.
- The objective of the substantive procedure.

- The assessed risk of material misstatement.
- The nature of the class of transactions or account balance and related assertions.
- The ability of the auditor to reduce the risk that misstatements existing at the period's end are not detected by performing appropriate substantive procedures or substantive procedures combined with tests of controls to cover the remaining period.

For example, if the entity's accounting system has control weaknesses that result in a high level of assessed control risk, it is unlikely that the auditor would conduct substantive procedures at an interim date. In this instance, the auditor has little assurance that the accounting system will generate accurate information during the remaining period. Similarly, the auditor must consider the controls followed by the entity to ensure that the account is properly analyzed and adjusted, including cutoff procedures. The auditor must have some assurance that these controls are performed both at the interim date and at year-end.

When the auditor conducts substantive procedures of an account at an interim date, some additional substantive procedures are ordinarily conducted in the remaining period. Generally, this would include comparing the year-end account balance with the interim account balance. It might also involve conducting analytical procedures or reviewing related journals and ledgers for large or unusual transactions. If misstatements are detected during interim testing, the auditor will have to revise the planned substantive procedures for the remaining period or reperform some substantive procedures at year-end.

Auditing Accounting Applications Processed by Service Organizations

[LO 13]   In some instances, a client may have some or all of its accounting transactions processed by an outside service organization. Examples of such service organizations include mortgage bankers that service mortgages for others and trust departments that invest or hold assets for employee benefit plans. More frequently, however, service organizations are IT service centers that process transactions such as payroll and the related accounting reports. Auditing standards provide guidance to the auditor when a client uses a service organization to process certain transactions.

When a client obtains services from a service organization, those services are part of an entity's information system if they affect any of the following:

- How the client's transactions are initiated.
- The accounting records, supporting information, and specific accounts in the financial statements involved in the processing and reporting of the client's transactions.
- The accounting processing involved from the initiation of the transactions to their inclusion in the financial statements, including electronic means (such as computers and electronic data interchange) used to transmit, process, maintain, and access information.
- The financial reporting process used to prepare the client's financial statements, including significant accounting estimates and disclosures.

The significance of the controls of the service organization to those of the client depends on the nature of the services provided by the service organization, primarily the nature and materiality of the transactions it processes for the user organization and the degree of interaction between its activities and those of the user organization. For example, if the client initiates transactions and the service organization executes and does the accounting processing of those transactions, there is a high degree of interaction.

Because the client's transactions are subjected to the controls of the service organization, one of the auditor's concerns is the internal control system in place at the service organization. The auditor's understanding of the client's internal control components may include controls placed in operation by the client and the service organization whose services are part of the entity's information system.

After obtaining an understanding of internal control, the auditor identifies controls that are applied by the client or the service organization that will allow an assessment of reduced control risk. The auditor may obtain evidence to support the lower assessment of control risk by testing the client's controls over the activities performed by the service organization or by tests of controls at the service organization.

Because service organizations process data for many customers, it is not uncommon for them to have an auditor issue a report on their operations. Such reports can be distributed to the auditors of a service organization's customers. There are two types of reports by a service organization's auditor. One type of report is a description of the service organization's controls and an assessment of whether they are suitably designed to achieve specified internal control objectives. The other type of report goes further by testing whether the controls provide reasonable assurance that the related control objectives were achieved during the period. An auditor may reduce control risk below the maximum only on the basis of a service auditor's report that includes tests of the controls.

Communication of Internal Control–Related Matters

[LO 14]   Standards for reporting internal control deficiencies differ for public versus private entities (referred to "nonissuers"). Under the Sarbanes-Oxley Act of 2002 management of public companies must prepare an assertion on internal control effectiveness and its registered auditors must issue an opinion on management's assertion and the effectiveness of internal control. These requirements are covered in Chapter 7. For private companies, auditing standards (AU 325) require that the auditor report to the audit committee, or to a similar level of authority when the entity does not have an audit committee, matters that are referred to as *reportable conditions*.[4] Reportable conditions

---

[4]The PCAOB adopted the terms "significant deficiency" and "material weakness" in connection with the audit of internal control over financial reporting for public companies (see Chapter 7 for definitions of these terms). The AICPA and PCAOB definitions of "material weakness" are quite similar to each other. However, the AICPA definition of a "reportable condition" is somewhat different than the PCAOB definition of a "significant deficiency." At the writing of this book, the AICPA has issued an Exposure Draft (*Reporting on an Entity's Internal Control over Financial Reporting*) proposing that the wording of the AICPA attestation standards be made consistent with PCAOB standards.

TABLE 6–8	Examples of Reportable Conditions

Deficiencies in Internal Control Design
- Inadequate overall internal control design.
- Absence of appropriate segregation of duties consistent with appropriate control objectives.
- Absence of appropriate reviews and approvals of transactions, accounting entries, or systems output.
- Inadequate procedures for appropriately assessing and applying accounting principles.
- Inadequate provisions for safeguarding assets.
- Absence of other control techniques considered appropriate for the type and level of transaction activity.
- Evidence that a system fails to provide complete and accurate output that is consistent with objectives and current needs because of design flaws.

Failures in the Operation of Internal Control
- Evidence of failure of identified controls in preventing or detecting misstatements of accounting information.
- Evidence that a system fails to provide complete and accurate output consistent with the entity's control objectives because of the misapplication of control procedures.
- Evidence of failure to safeguard assets from loss, damage, or misappropriation.
- Evidence of intentional override of internal control by those in authority to the detriment of the overall objectives of the system.
- Evidence of failure to perform tasks that are part of internal control, such as reconciliations not prepared or not prepared in a timely fashion.
- Evidence of willful wrongdoing by employees or management.
- Evidence of manipulation, falsification, or alteration of accounting records or supporting documents.
- Evidence of intentional misapplication of accounting principles.
- Evidence of misrepresentation by client personnel to the auditor.
- Evidence that employees or management lack the qualifications and training to fulfill their assigned functions.

Other
- Absence of a sufficient level of control consciousness within the organization.
- Failure to follow up and correct previously identified internal control deficiencies.
- Evidence of significant or extensive undisclosed related-party transactions.
- Evidence of undue bias or lack of objectivity by those responsible for accounting decisions.

are significant deficiencies in the design or operation of internal control that could adversely affect the organization's ability to initiate, record, process, and report financial data consistent with management's assertions. Table 6–8 presents examples of possible reportable conditions.

Reportable conditions may be identified as part of the auditor's consideration of the five components of internal control or through substantive procedures. The auditor may also identify matters that are less significant than reportable conditions. These matters may be communicated to the audit committee if the auditor chooses or if the client requests it.

Preferably, the auditor communicates reportable conditions to the audit committee in writing. The following items should be included in the report:

- A statement that the purpose of the audit was to report on the financial statements and not to provide assurance on internal control.
- A definition of reportable conditions.
- A statement of restrictions on the distribution of the report.

This information may be communicated orally; however, the auditor should document the communication in the working papers.

In some cases, the reportable condition may be of such magnitude as to be considered a *material weakness*. A material weakness in internal control is defined as

a reportable condition in which the design or operation of one or more of the specific internal control components does not reduce to a relatively low level the risk that errors or fraud in amounts that would be material in relation to the financial statements being audited may occur and not be detected within a timely period by employees in the normal course of performing their assigned functions. (AU 325.15)

The auditor may choose to separately identify reportable conditions that are material weaknesses. In reporting on such matters, the auditor is allowed to report that none of the reportable conditions were material weaknesses. However, the auditor is precluded from reporting that no reportable conditions were noted during the audit.

Advanced Module 1: Types of Controls in an IT Environment

⚹ [LO 15] There are two broad categories of information systems control procedures: general controls and application controls. *General controls* relate to the overall information processing environment and have a *pervasive* effect on the entity's computer operations. General controls are sometimes referred to as supervisory, management, or information technology controls. *Application controls* apply to the processing of specific computer applications and are part of the computer programs used in the accounting system (for example, revenues or purchasing).

General Controls

General controls include controls over:

- Data center and network operations.
- System software acquisition, change, and maintenance.
- Access security.
- Application system acquisition, development, and maintenance.

Data Center and Network Operations Controls
Data center and network operations controls include controls over computer and network operations, data preparation, work flow control, and library functions. Important controls over computer and network operations should prevent unauthorized access to the network programs, files, and systems documentation by computer operators. In advanced IT systems, traditional controls such as rotation of operator duties and mandatory vacations should be implemented. The operating systems log, which documents all program and operator activities, should be regularly reviewed to ensure that operators have not performed any unauthorized activities.

Controls over data preparation include proper entry of data into an application system and proper oversight of error correction. Controls over work flow include scheduling of application programs, proper setup for programs, and use of the correct files. The library function needs controls to ensure that (1) the correct files are provided for specific applications, (2) files are properly maintained, and (3) backup and recovery procedures exist.

Systems Software Acquisition, Change, and Maintenance Controls
Systems software are computer programs that control the computer functions and allow the application programs to run. These programs include

operating systems, library and security packages, and database management systems. For example, the operating system controls the operations of the computer and allocates computer resources among the application programs. The operating system also detects and corrects processing errors. The entity should have strong controls that ensure proper approval for purchases of new system software and adequate controls over changes and maintenance of existing systems software. Generally, an approval process similar to the one described below for application systems can accomplish this.

Access Security Controls

These general controls are concerned with (1) physical protection of computer equipment, software, and data and (2) loss of assets and information through theft or unauthorized use. Security controls include locating the computer facilities in a separate building or in a secure part of a building. They also include limiting access to the computer facilities through the use of locked doors with authorized personnel being admitted through use of a conventional key, an authorization card, or physical recognition. Control must also be enforced within the computer facility. For example, programmers must not be allowed access to the computer room; this restriction will prevent them from making unauthorized modifications to systems and application programs.

There must also be adequate protection against events such as fire and water damage, electrical problems, and sabotage. Proper construction of computer facilities can minimize the damage from such events. In order to ensure that the entity's operations are not interrupted by such events, the entity should have an operational disaster recovery plan, which may include an off-site backup location for processing critical applications.

Unauthorized access to programs or data can cause loss of assets and information. Physical control over programs and data can be maintained by a separate library function that controls access and use of files. In advanced computer systems with online, real-time database systems and telecommunications technologies, programs and data can be accessed from outside the computer facility. Access controls in advanced systems should thus include physical security over remote terminals, authorization controls that limit access only to authorized information, firewalls, user identification controls such as passwords, and data communication controls such as encryption of data. Without such controls, an unauthorized user could access the system, with a resulting loss of assets or a decrease in the reliability of data.

Application Systems Acquisition, Development, and Maintenance Controls

These controls are critical for ensuring the reliability of information processing. The ability to audit accounting systems is greatly improved if (1) the entity follows common policies and procedures for systems acquisition or development, (2) the internal and/or external auditors are involved in the acquisition or development process, and (3) proper user, system operator, and program documentation is provided for each application. For example, having internal or external auditors involved early in the design of the system can ensure that proper controls are built into the system.

The entity should establish written policies and procedures for planning, acquiring or developing, and implementing new systems. Normally, a request for a new system is submitted by the user department to the IT department or an information services committee. A feasibility study may be conducted that includes cost-benefit analysis, hardware and software needs, and the system's impact on current applications and operations. Next, the system is acquired or designed, programmed, tested, and implemented. Last, the entity should prepare good documentation, including flowcharts, file layouts, source code listings, and operator instructions. This level of documentation is necessary for the auditors to understand the accounting systems, including application controls, so that tests of controls and substantive testing can be properly planned and conducted.

The entity must also have strong controls to ensure that once programs are placed into operation, all authorized changes are made and unauthorized changes are prevented. Although not as detailed, the controls for program changes are similar to those followed for new systems development. From the auditor's perspective, the important issue here is whether changes to programs are properly authorized, tested, and implemented.

Application Controls

Application controls apply to the processing of individual accounting applications, such as sales or payroll, and help ensure the completeness and accuracy of transaction processing, authorization, and validity. Although application controls are typically discussed under the categories of input, processing, and output controls, changes in technology have blurred the distinctions among input, processing, and output. For example, many of the data validation checks that were once performed as part of production programs are now accomplished with sophisticated editing routines and intelligent data entry equipment. As a result, application controls are discussed under the following categories:

- Data capture controls.
- Data validation controls.
- Processing controls.
- Output controls.
- Error controls.

Data Capture Controls
Data capture controls must ensure that (1) all transactions are recorded in the application system, (2) transactions are recorded only once, and (3) rejected transactions are identified, controlled, corrected, and reentered into the system. Thus, data capture controls are concerned primarily with *occurrence*, *completeness*, and *accuracy* assertions. For example, checking that all transactions are recorded in the system relates to the completeness objective.

There are three ways of capturing data in an information system: (1) source documentation, (2) direct data entry, or (3) a combination of the two. When source documents are present, batch processing is an effective way of controlling data capture. Batching is simply the process of grouping similar transactions for data entry. It is important that each batch be well controlled. This can be accomplished by assigning each batch a unique number and recording it in a batch register or log. A cover sheet should also be attached to each batch with spaces for recording the batch number,

TABLE 6–9	Types of Information Used for Batch Totals	
Batch Total		*Description of Information*
Financial total		A total of some dollar field in the set of transactions (such as total sales or total amount of vouchers to be recorded).
Hash total		A total of some nonfinancial field in the batch of transactions (such as total number of units sold or total number of employee Social Security numbers).
Record count		A total of the number of transactions included in the batch.

the date, the signatures of various persons who processed the batch, and information on errors detected. To ensure complete processing of all transactions in a batch, some type of batch total should be used. Table 6–9 presents the three most common types of information used for batch totals.

Direct data entry, on the other hand, involves online processing of the data with no source documents. The combination method may involve entry of the data from source documents directly through online processing. If direct data entry or a combination of source documents and direct data entry is used, the system should create a *transaction log*. The log should contain a detailed record of each transaction, including date and time of entry, terminal and operator identification, and a unique number (such as customer order number).

Data Validation Controls   These controls can be applied at various stages, depending on the entity's IT capabilities, and are mainly concerned with the accuracy assertion. When source documents are batch processed, the data are taken from source documents and transcribed to tape or disk. The data are then validated by an edit program or by routines that are part of the production programs. When the data are entered directly into off-line storage through an intelligent terminal or directly into a validation program with subsequent (delayed or real-time) processing into the application system, each individual transaction should be subjected to a number of programmed edit checks. Table 6–10 lists common validation tests. For example, a payroll application program may have a limit test that subjects any

TABLE 6–10	Common Data Validation Controls	
Data Validation Control		*Description*
Limit test		A test to ensure that a numerical value does not exceed some predetermined value.
Range test		A check to ensure that the value in a field falls within an allowable range of values.
Sequence check		A check to determine if input data are in proper numerical or alphabetical sequence.
Existence (validity) test		A test of an ID number or code by comparison to a file or table containing valid ID numbers or codes.
Field test		A check on a field to ensure that it contains either all numeric or alphabetic characters.
Sign test		A check to ensure that the data in a field have the proper arithmetic sign.
Check-digit verification		A numeric value computed to provide assurance that the original value was not altered.

employee payroll transaction involving more than 80 hours worked to review before processing.

Some entities use *turnaround documents* to improve data accuracy. Turnaround documents are output documents from the application that are used as source documents in later processing. For example, a monthly statement sent to a customer may contain two parts; one part of the monthly statement is kept by the customer, while the other part is returned with the payment. The latter part of the statement contains encoded information that can be processed using various input devices. By using a turnaround document, the entity does not have to reenter the data, thus avoiding data capture and data validation errors.

With direct data (online) entry, accuracy can be improved by special validation routines that may be programmed to *prompt* the data entry personnel. Here the system requests the desired input data and then waits for an acceptable response before requesting the next piece of input data. In many cases, the screen displays the document format with blanks that are completed by data entry personnel. The validation routine should include a completeness test to ensure that all data items are completed before processing. Airline reservation systems and catalog retailers (like EarthWear) that take phone orders use this type of entry system. Entering data over an entity's website can be controlled in a similar manner.

Processing Controls   These are controls that ensure proper processing of transactions. In some information systems, many of the controls discussed under data validation may be performed as part of data processing. General controls play an important role in providing assurance about the quality of processing controls. If the entity has strong general controls (such as application systems acquisition, development, and maintenance controls; library controls; personnel practices; and separation of duties), it is likely that programs will be properly written and tested, correct files will be used for processing, and unauthorized access to the system will be limited. Table 6–11 presents a number of processing controls.

Output Controls   Output includes reports, checks, documents, and other printed or displayed (on terminal screens) information. Controls over output from computer systems are important application controls. The main concern here is that computer output may be distributed or displayed to unauthorized users. A number of controls should be present to minimize the

TABLE 6–11	Types of Processing Controls	
Processing Control	*Description*	
File or volume labels	Internal and external file labels should be assigned. The application program should check to ensure that the correct file is used for processing.	
Control totals	Control totals ensure the accuracy and completeness of processing. For example, run-to-run totals are control totals that reconcile two processing runs.	
Reasonableness tests	These are programmed controls that determine if the processing results are outside some predetermined value.	

unauthorized use of output. A report distribution log should contain a schedule of when reports are prepared, the names of individuals who are to receive the report, and the date of distribution. Some type of transmittal sheet indicating the intended recipients' names and addresses should be attached to each copy of the output. A release form may be part of the transmittal sheet and should be signed by the individual acknowledging receipt of the report.

The data control group should be responsible for reviewing the output for reasonableness and reconciling the control or batch totals to the output. The user departments should also review the output for completeness and accuracy because they may be the only ones with sufficient knowledge to recognize certain types of errors.

Error Controls   Errors can be identified at any point in the system. While most transaction errors should be identified by data capture and data validation controls, some errors may be identified by processing or output controls. After identification, errors must be corrected and resubmitted to the application system at the correct point in processing. For example, if a transaction is entered with an incorrect customer number, it should be rejected by a validity test. After the customer number is corrected, it should be resubmitted into the system. Errors that result from processing transactions (such as data entry errors) should be corrected and resubmitted by the data center control group. Errors that occur outside the IT department (like omitted or invalid data) should be corrected by the appropriate user department and resubmitted. This segregation of duties prevents the data center control group from processing invalid transactions.

Advanced Module 2: Flowcharting Techniques

[LO 16]   From the auditor's perspective, a flowchart is a diagrammatic representation of the entity's accounting system. The information systems literature typically discusses three types of flowcharts: document flowcharts, systems flowcharts, and program flowcharts. A document flowchart represents the flow of documents among departments in the entity. A systems flowchart extends this approach by including the processing steps, including computer processing, in the flowchart. A program flowchart illustrates the operations performed by the computer in executing a program. Flowcharts that are typically used by public accounting firms combine document and systems flowcharting techniques. Such flowcharts show the path from the origination of the transactions to their recording in the accounting journals and ledgers. While there are some general guidelines on preparing flowcharts for documenting accounting systems, the reader should understand that public accounting firms often modify these techniques to correspond with their firm's audit technologies.

Following are a number of common guidelines that are used in preparing flowcharts.

Symbols   A standard set of symbols is used to represent documents and processes. Figure 6–6 presents examples of the more commonly used symbols. Note

FIGURE 6–6	Flowcharting Symbols

Input/Output Symbols	Processing Symbols	Data Flow and Storage Symbols
Magnetic tape	Processing function	Annotation
Magnetic disk	Manual operation	Off-page connector
Diskette	Auxiliary operation	On-page connector
Online storage	Keying operation	Off-line storage
Input through online device	Decision operation	Communication link
Display		Flow arrow
Punched tape		
Transmittal tape		
Document		

that the symbols are divided into three groups: input/output symbols, processing symbols, and data flow and storage symbols.

Organization and Flow

A well-designed flowchart should start in the upper left part of the page and proceed to the lower right part of the page. When it is necessary to show the movement of a document or report back to a previous function, an on-page connector should be used. When the flowchart continues to a subsequent page, the movement of documents or reports can be handled by using an off-page connector. Flow arrows show the movement of documents, records, or information. When processes or activities cannot be fully represented by flowchart symbols, the auditor should supplement the flowchart with written comments. This can be accomplished by using the annotation symbol or just writing the comment directly on the flowchart.

A flowchart is typically designed along the lines of the entity's departments or functions. It is thus important to indicate the delineation of activities between the departments or functions. As shown in Figure 6–4, this can be accomplished by using a vertical dashed line.

KEY TERMS

Application controls. Controls that apply to the processing of specific computer applications and are part of the computer programs used in the accounting system.

Computer-assisted audit techniques. Computer programs that allow auditors to test computer files and databases.

Control environment. The tone of an organization, which reflects the overall attitude, awareness, and actions of the board of directors, management, and owners influencing the control consciousness of its people.

Control procedures. The policies and procedures that help ensure that management's directives are carried out.

Control risk. The risk that material misstatements that could occur will not be prevented or detected by internal controls.

Electronic (Internet) commerce. Business transactions between individuals and organizations that occur without paper documents, using computers and telecommunication networks.

Electronic data interchange. The transmission of business transactions over telecommunications networks.

General controls. Controls that relate to the overall information processing environment and have a pervasive effect on the entity's computer operations.

Internal control. The method by which an entity's board of directors, management, and other personnel provide reasonable assurance about the achievement of objectives in the following categories: (1) reliability of financial reporting, (2) effectiveness and efficiency of operations, and (3) compliance with applicable laws and regulations.

Material weakness. A reportable condition in which the design or operation of one or more specific internal control components does not reduce to a relatively low level the risk that errors or fraud in amounts material to the financial statements being audited might occur and not be promptly detected by employees performing their normal assigned functions.

Monitoring of controls. A process that assesses the quality of internal control performance over time.

Reliance strategy. The auditor's decision to rely on the entity's controls, test those controls, and reduce the direct tests of the financial statement accounts.

Reportable conditions. Significant deficiencies in the design or operation of internal control that could adversely affect the organization's ability to initiate, record, process, and report financial data consistent with management's assertions.

Substantive strategy. The auditor's decision not to rely on the entity's controls and to audit the related financial statement accounts by relying more on substantive procedures.

www.mhhe.com/ messier4e	Visit the book's Online Learning Center for a multiple-choice quiz that will allow you to assess your understanding of chapter concepts.

REVIEW QUESTIONS

[LO 1] 6-1 What are management's incentives for establishing and maintaining strong internal control? What are the auditor's main concerns with internal control?

[4] 6-2 Describe the five components of internal control.

[4] 6-3 What are the factors that affect the control environment?

[5] 6-4 What are the potential benefits and risks to an entity's internal control from information technology?

[6] 6-5 What are the major differences between a substantive strategy and a reliance strategy when the auditor considers internal control in planning an audit?

[7] 6-6 Why must the auditor obtain an understanding of internal control?

[7] 6-7 What is meant by the concept of reasonable assurance in terms of internal control? What are the inherent limitations of internal control?

[8] 6-8 List the tools that can document the understanding of internal control.

[8,9] 6-9 What are the requirements under auditing standards for documenting the assessed level of control risk?

[11,12] 6-10 What factors should the auditor consider when substantive procedures are to be completed at an interim date? If the auditor conducts substantive procedures at an interim date, what audit procedures would normally be completed for the remaining period?

[14] 6-11 What is the auditor's responsibility for communicating reportable conditions?

MULTIPLE-CHOICE QUESTIONS

[1] 6-12 An auditor's primary consideration regarding an entity's internal controls is whether they
   a. Prevent management override.
   b. Relate to the control environment.
   c. Reflect management's philosophy and operating style.
   d. Affect the financial statement assertions.

[1,7] 6-13 Which of the following statements about internal control is correct?
   a. A properly maintained internal control system reasonably ensures that collusion among employees cannot occur.
   b. The establishment and maintenance of internal control is an important responsibility of the internal auditor.
   c. An exceptionally strong internal control system is enough for the auditor to eliminate substantive procedures on a significant account balance.

d. The cost-benefit relationship is a primary criterion that should be considered in designing an internal control system.

[4]   6-14   Which of the following is *not* a component of an entity's internal control system?
   a. Control risk.
   b. The entity's risk assessment process.
   c. Control procedures.
   d. Control environment.

[5]   6-15   In which of the following situations would an auditor most likely use a reliance strategy?
   a. The client has been slow to update its IT system to reflect changes in billing practices.
   b. The auditor hired an IT specialist whose report to the auditor reveals that the specialist did not perform sufficient procedures to allow the auditor to properly assess the effect of the IT system on control risk.
   c. A client receives sales orders, bills customers, and receives payment based only on information generated from its IT system—no paper trail is generated.
   d. The auditor has been unable to ascertain whether all changes to a client's IT system were properly authorized.

[7]   6-16   After obtaining an understanding of an entity's internal control system, an auditor may set control risk at the maximum level for some assertions because he or she
   a. Believes the internal controls are unlikely to be effective.
   b. Determines that the pertinent internal control components are *not* well documented.
   c. Performs tests of controls to restrict detection risk to an acceptable level.
   d. Identifies internal controls that are likely to prevent material misstatements.

[7,8]   6-17   When control risk is assessed at the maximum level for all financial statement assertions, an auditor should document the auditor's:

	Understanding of the Entity's Internal Control Components	Conclusion That Control Risk Is at the Maximum Level	Basis for Concluding That Control Risk Is at the Maximum Level
a.	Yes	No	No
b.	Yes	Yes	No
c.	No	Yes	Yes
d.	Yes	Yes	Yes

[6,10]   6-18   Regardless of the assessed level of control risk, an auditor would perform some
   a. Tests of controls to determine the effectiveness of internal controls.
   b. Analytical procedures to verify the design of internal controls.
   c. Substantive procedures to restrict detection risk for significant transaction classes.

d. Dual-purpose tests to evaluate both the risk of monetary misstatement and preliminary control risk.

[9,10] 6-19 After obtaining an understanding of an entity's internal control system and assessing control risk, an auditor may

a. Perform tests of controls to verify management's assertions that are embodied in the financial statements.

b. Consider whether evidential matter is available to support a further reduction in the assessed level of control risk.

c. Apply analytical procedures as substantive procedures to validate the assessed level of control risk.

d. Evaluate whether the internal controls detected material misstatements in the financial statements.

[10] 6-20 Which of the following audit techniques would most likely provide an auditor with the most assurance about the effectiveness of the operation of an internal control?

a. Inquiry of client personnel.

b. Recomputation of the control by the auditor.

c. Observation of client personnel.

d. Confirmation with outside parties.

[10] 6-21 Evidential matter concerning proper segregation of duties ordinarily is best obtained by

a. Inspection of third-party documents containing the initials of those who applied control procedures.

b. Direct personal observation of the employee who applies control procedures.

c. Preparation of a flowchart of duties performed and available personnel.

d. Making inquiries of co-workers about the employee who applies control procedures.

[13] 6-22 Payroll Data Co. (PDC) processes payroll transactions for a retailer. Cook, CPA, is engaged to express an opinion on a description of PDC's internal controls placed in operation as of a specific date. These controls are relevant to the retailer's internal control, so Cook's report may be useful in providing the retailer's independent auditor with information necessary to plan a financial statement audit. Cook's report should

a. Contain a disclaimer of opinion on the operating effectiveness of PDC's controls.

b. State whether PDC's controls were suitably designed to achieve the retailer's objectives.

c. Identify PDC's controls relevant to specific financial statement assertions.

d. Disclose Cook's assessed level of control risk for PDC.

[14] 6-23 Which of the following statements concerning material weaknesses and reportable conditions is correct?

a. An auditor should identify and communicate material weaknesses separately from reportable conditions.

b. All material weaknesses are reportable conditions.

c. An auditor should immediately report material weaknesses and reportable conditions discovered during an audit.

d. All reportable conditions are material weaknesses.

[16]   6-24   An auditor's flowchart of a client's accounting system is a diagrammatic representation that depicts the auditor's
a. Program for tests of controls.
b. Understanding of the system.
c. Understanding of the types of fraud that are probable, given the present system.
d. Documentation of the study and evaluation of the system.

[3,6]   6-25   An auditor anticipates assessing control risk at a low level in an IT environment. Under these circumstances, on which of the following controls would the auditor initially focus?
a. Data capture controls.
b. Application controls.
c. Output controls.
d. General controls.

PROBLEMS

[2,4,6,9]   6-26   An auditor is required to obtain sufficient understanding of each component of an entity's internal control system to plan the audit of the entity's financial statements and to assess control risk for the assertions embodied in the account balance, transaction class, and disclosure components of the financial statements.

Required
a. Define internal control.
b. For what purpose should an auditor's understanding of the internal control components be used in planning an audit?
c. Why may an auditor set control risk at the maximum level for one or more assertions embodied in an account balance?
d. What are an auditor's documentation requirements concerning an entity's internal control system and the assessed level of control risk?

[4,6]   6-27   Johnson, CPA, has been engaged to audit the financial statements of Rose, Inc., a publicly held retailing company. Before assessing control risk, Johnson is required to obtain an understanding of Rose's control environment.

Required
a. Identify additional control environment factors (excluding the factor illustrated in the following example) that set the tone of an organization, influencing the control consciousness of its people.
b. For each control environment factor identified in part (a), describe the components and why each component would be of interest to the auditor.
Use the following format:

Integrity and Ethical Values

The effectiveness of controls cannot rise above the integrity and ethical values of the people who create, administer, and monitor them. Integrity and ethical values are essential elements of the control environment, affecting the design, administration, and monitoring of other components. Integrity and ethical behavior are the product of the entity's ethical and behavioral standards, how they are communicated, and how they are reinforced in practice.

[5]   6-28   Assume that you are an audit senior in charge of planning the audit of a client that your firm has audited for the previous four years. During the audit planning meeting with the manager and partner in charge of the engagement, the partner noted that the client recently adopted an IT-based accounting system to replace its manual system. The manager and partner have limited experience with IT-based accounting systems and are relying on you to help them understand the audit implications of the client's change. Consequently, they have asked you to respond to a few concerns regarding automated accounting systems.

Required

a. In previous years, the audit firm has relied heavily on substantive procedures as a source of audit evidence for this client. Given that the client now has changed its accounting system, what are some of the factors that you should consider when deciding whether to move to a reliance strategy?

b. Under what conditions should the audit firm consider hiring an IT specialist to assist in the evaluation? If the firm hires an IT specialist, what information should the auditors ask the specialist to provide?

c. How are the five components of the client's internal control affected by the client's change to an IT-based accounting system?

[8]   6-29   Auditors use various tools to document their understanding of an entity's internal control system, including narrative descriptions, internal control questionnaires, and flowcharts.

Required

a. Identify the relative strengths and weaknesses of each tool.

b. Briefly describe how the complexity of an entity's internal control system affects the use of the various tools.

[11,12]   6-30   Cook, CPA, has been engaged to audit the financial statements of General Department Stores, Inc., a continuing audit client, which is a chain of medium-sized retail stores. General's fiscal year will end on June 30, 2005, and General's management has asked Cook to issue the auditor's report by August 1, 2005. Cook will not have sufficient time to perform all of the necessary fieldwork in July 2005 but will have time to perform most of the fieldwork as of an interim date, April 30, 2005.

After the accounts are tested at the interim date, Cook will also perform substantive procedures covering the transactions of the final two months of the year. This will be necessary to extend Cook's conclusions to the balance sheet date.

Required

a. Describe the factors Cook should consider before applying principal substantive procedures to General's balance sheet accounts at April 30, 2005.

b. For accounts tested at April 30, 2005, describe how Cook should design the substantive procedures covering the balances as of June 30, 2005, and the transactions of the final two months of the year.

(AICPA, adapted)

[14]   6-31   Ken Smith, the partner in charge of the audit of Houghton Enterprises, identified the following reportable conditions during the audit of the December 31, 2005, financial statements:

1. Controls for granting credit to new customers were not adequate. In particular, the credit department did not adequately check the creditworthiness of customers with an outside credit agency.
2. There were not adequate physical safeguards over the company's inventory. No safeguards prevented employees from stealing high-value inventory parts.

Required

a. Draft the required communications to the management of Houghton Enterprises, assuming that both items are reportable conditions.
b. Assume that Smith determined that the second item was a material weakness. How would the required communication change?

DISCUSSION CASE

[4,6]   6-32   Preview Company, a diversified manufacturer, has five divisions that operate throughout the United States and Mexico. Preview has historically allowed its divisions to operate autonomously. Corporate intervention occurred only when planned results were not obtained. Corporate management has high integrity, but the board of directors and audit committee are not very active. Preview has a policy of hiring competent people. The company has a code of conduct, but there is little monitoring of compliance by employees. Management is fairly conservative in terms of accounting principles and practices, but employee compensation packages depend highly on performance. Preview Company does not have an internal audit department, and it relies on your firm to review the controls in each division.

Chip Harris is the general manager of the Fabricator Division. The Fabricator Division produces a variety of standardized parts for small appliances. Harris has been the general manager for the last seven years, and each year he has been able to improve the profitability of the division. He is compensated based largely on the division's profitability. Much of the improvement in profitability has come through aggressive cost cutting, including a substantial reduction in control procedures over inventory.

During the last year a new competitor has entered Fabricator's markets and has offered substantial price reductions in order to grab market share. Harris has responded to the competitor's actions by matching the price cuts in the hope of maintaining market share.

Harris is very concerned because he cannot see any other areas where costs can be reduced so that the division's growth and profitability can be maintained. If profitability is not maintained, his salary and bonus will be reduced.

Harris has decided that one way to make the division more profitable is to manipulate inventory because it represents a large amount of the division's balance sheet. He also knows that controls over inventory are weak. He views this inventory manipulation as a short-run solution to the profit decline due to the competitor's price cutting. Harris is certain that once the competitor stops cutting prices or goes bankrupt, the misstatements in inventory can be corrected with little impact on the bottom line.

Required

a. Evaluate the strengths and weaknesses of Preview Company's control environment.

b. What factors in Preview Company's control environment have led to and facilitated Harris's manipulation of inventory?

(Used with permission of the PricewaterhouseCoopers LLP Foundation.)

INTERNET ASSIGNMENTS

[4,7]   6-33   Go to the EarthWear Clothiers website (www.mhhe.com/earthwear), and download the EarthWear control environment questionnaire. Using the information contained in the text and Willis & Adams's workpapers, complete the remaining sections of the questionnaire.

6-34   Go to the EarthWear Clothiers website (www.mhhe.com/earthwear), and download the EarthWear internal control questionnaire that includes questions related to the remaining components of internal control. Using the information contained in the text and Willis & Adams's workpapers, complete the remaining sections of the questionnaire.

www.mhhe.com/ messier4e	Visit the book's Online Learning Center for problem material to be completed using the *ACL* software packaged with your new text.

LEARNING OBJECTIVES

Upon completion of this chapter you will

[1] Be familiar with management's responsibilities for reporting on internal control under Section 404 of the Sarbanes-Oxley Act.

[2] Understand the auditor's responsibilities for reporting on internal control under Section 404 of the Sarbanes-Oxley Act.

[3] Know the definition of internal control over financial reporting.

[4] Understand the difference between a control deficiency, a significant deficiency, and a material weakness.

[5] Understand management's assessment process.

[6] Understand the extent of management's documentation of internal control.

[7] Know the framework used by management to assess internal control.

[8] Be familiar with how auditors conduct an audit of internal control over financial reporting.

[9] Understand how the auditor can use the work of others on an audit of internal control.

[10] Know the written representations that the auditor must obtain from management.

[11] Be familiar with the auditor's documentation requirements.

[12] Know what information must be included in management's report on internal control over financial reporting.

[13] Know the various types of reports that the auditor can issue.

[14] Know the auditor's communication responsibilities on an audit of internal control over financial reporting.

[15] Understand how the audits of internal control and financial statements are integrated, and the implications of each audit for the other.

[16] Understand how to decide which locations or business units should be audited.

[17] Understand how to obtain assurance on controls at a service organization that processes transactions for the entity.

[18] Know management's and the auditor's responsibilities for controls that provide reasonable assurance for safeguarding company assets.

[19] Be familiar with computer-assisted audit techniques.

RELEVANT ACCOUNTING AND AUDITING PRONOUNCEMENTS

COSO, *Internal Control—Integrated Framework* (New York: AICPA, 1992)

COSO, *Enterprise Risk Management—Integrated Framework-Draft* (New York: AICPA, 2003)

FAS 5, Accounting for Contingencies

PCAOB Auditing Standard No. 2, An Audit of Internal Control over Financial Reporting Performed in Conjunction with an Audit of Financial Statements (AS2)

AU 322, The Auditor's Consideration of the Internal Audit Function in an Audit of Financial Statements

AU 324, Service Organizations

Auditing Internal Control over Financial Reporting in Conjunction with an Audit of Financial Statements

Major Phases of an Audit

Client acceptance/
continuance and establishing
engagement terms
(Chapter 5)

Preplanning
(Chapter 5)

Establish materiality
and assess risks
(Chapter 3)

Plan the audit
(Chapters 3 and 5)

Consider and audit
internal control
(Chapters 6 and 7)

Audit business processes
and related accounts
(e.g., revenue generation)
(Chapters 10–16)

Complete the audit
(Chapter 17)

Evaluate results and
issue audit report
(Chapters 2 and 18)

The Sarbanes-Oxley Act of 2002 was passed in response to a series of business scandals (e.g., Enron and WorldCom). A common question being asked at the time was, "Why did these companies' systems of internal control fail to prevent these frauds?" Failure of internal control over financial reporting was one of the major concerns addressed by Congress in the Sarbanes-Oxley Act, which imposes unprecedented requirements on both management and auditors of public companies. Section 404 of the Act requires that management report on the effectiveness of its internal control over financial reporting and that its auditor attest to the accuracy of management's report. Accordingly, the Public Company Accounting Oversight Board (PCAOB) adopted Auditing Standard No. 2, *An Audit of Internal Control over Financial Reporting Performed in Conjunction with an Audit of Financial Statements* (AS2), to provide guidance for the audit engagements referred to in Section 404.

This chapter covers what management must do in order to issue a report that the entity's internal control over financial reporting is effective and how the entity's auditor performs an audit of management's assertion regarding the effectiveness of internal control. The material covered in this chapter only applies to companies subject to the reporting requirements of Section 404 of the Sarbanes-Oxley Act of 2002 (i.e., most public companies).

Management Responsibilities under Section 404

[LO 1]   Section 404 of the Sarbanes-Oxley Act requires management of a publicly traded company to issue an internal control report that explicitly accepts responsibility for establishing and maintaining "adequate" internal control over financial reporting. Management must also issue an assertion as to whether internal control over financial reporting is effective as of the end of the fiscal year. Note that the Act provides no guidance on what constitutes adequate internal control. Thus, the PCAOB was left to address the issue of adequacy. Further, the assessment is to be made as of a specific point in time. Therefore, management's assessment does not cover the entire year. This has implications for the timing of both management's and the auditor's work and the handling of any control deficiencies discovered during the year. It also has implications on the use of the internal control work for financial statement audit purposes.

Management must comply with the following requirements in order for its registered public accounting firm (external auditor) to complete an audit of internal control over financial reporting:

- Accept responsibility for the effectiveness of the entity's internal control over financial reporting.
- Evaluate the effectiveness of the entity's internal control over financial reporting using suitable control criteria.
- Support its evaluation with sufficient evidence, including documentation.
- Present a written assessment of the effectiveness of the entity's internal control over financial reporting as of the end of the entity's most recent fiscal year.

Each of these steps is discussed below. Recognize, however, that the second and third bullets require substantial investment of time, energy, and money on the part of the entity.

Auditor Responsibilities under Section 404

[LO 2]   Section 404 requires that the entity's auditors audit and report on management's assertion about the effectiveness of internal control. AS2 states that the auditor must conduct an "integrated audit" of the entity's internal control over financial reporting and its financial statements. The auditor must conduct the audits of financial statements and internal control over financial reporting in an integrated way because each audit provides the auditor with information relevant to the evaluation of the results of the other audit. AS2 makes it clear that while the two audits are to be integrated, they have different objectives. The auditor's objective in an audit of internal control over financial reporting is "to express an opinion on management's assessment of the effectiveness of the company's internal control over financial reporting" (AS2, ¶4), while the objective in a financial statement audit is to express an opinion on whether the financial statements are fairly stated.

To form a basis for expressing an opinion on management's assertion regarding the effectiveness of internal control over financial reporting, the auditor must plan and perform the audit to obtain *reasonable assurance* about whether the entity maintained, in all material respects, effective internal control as of the date specified in management's assessment. Reasonable assurance in this context recognizes that no system of internal control is perfect and that there is a remote likelihood that material misstatements will not be prevented or detected on a timely basis, even if controls are, in fact, effective (AS2, ¶17). While reasonable assurance is not absolute assurance, in this context it indicates a high level of assurance.

Internal Control over Financial Reporting Defined

☞ [LO 3]   Chapter 6 presented the COSO definition of internal control. In addition to the reliability of the financial reporting objective, it also includes objectives in two other categories: (1) effectiveness and efficiency of operations and (2) compliance with laws and regulations. For purposes of both management's assessment and the audit of internal control, *internal control over financial reporting* is defined as

> A process designed by, or under the supervision of, the company's principal executive and principal financial officers, or persons performing similar functions, and effected by the company's board of directors, management, and other personnel, to provide reasonable assurance regarding the reliability of financial reporting and the preparation of financial statements for external purposes in accordance with generally accepted accounting principles and includes those policies and procedures that:
>
> (1) Pertain to the maintenance of records that, in reasonable detail, accurately and fairly reflect the transactions and dispositions of the assets of the company;
> (2) Provide reasonable assurance that transactions are recorded as necessary to permit preparation of financial statements in accordance with generally accepted accounting principles, and that receipts and expenditures of the company are being made only in accordance with authorizations of management and directors of the company; and
> (3) Provide reasonable assurance regarding prevention or timely detection of unauthorized acquisition, use or disposition of the company's assets that could have a material effect on the financial statements (AS2, ¶7).

This PCAOB definition makes it clear that the CEO and CFO are responsible for the reliability of internal control over financial reporting and the preparation of the financial statements. It is the responsibility of the board of directors and management to implement an effective internal control system. You will note that the objectives of internal control in the PCAOB's definition are much more specific than the objectives listed in the COSO definition. Items (1) and (2) relate directly to controls for initiating, authorizing, recording, processing, and reporting significant accounts and disclosures and related assertions embodied in the financial statements. Item (3) concerns controls over safeguarding of assets.

Internal Control Deficiencies Defined

Control
Deficiency

For managements and auditors to assess whether internal control over financial reporting is effective, it is necessary to define what constitutes a control deficiency and to define different levels of severity. While the

❦ **[LO 4]**   PCAOB's definitions in this area are somewhat technical, it is important that you invest the time and energy to understand them.

A *control deficiency* exists when the *design* or *operation* of a control does not allow management or employees, in the normal course of performing their assigned functions, to prevent or detect misstatements on a timely basis. A *design* deficiency exists when (1) a control necessary to meet the relevant control objective is missing or (2) an existing control is not properly designed so that, even if the control operates as designed, the control objective is not always met. A deficiency in *operation* exists when a properly designed control does not operate as designed or when the person performing the control does not possess the necessary authority or qualifications to perform the control effectively (AS2, ¶8).

Significant Deficiency

Not all control deficiencies are of equal severity. A *significant deficiency* is a control deficiency, or combination of control deficiencies, that adversely affects the entity's ability to initiate, authorize, record, process, or report external financial data reliably in accordance with generally accepted accounting principles such that there is more than a *remote likelihood* that a misstatement of the entity's annual or interim financial statements that is more than *inconsequential* will not be prevented or detected (AS2, ¶9).

Material Weakness

A control deficiency may be serious enough that it is to be considered not only a significant deficiency but also a *material weakness* in the system of internal control. A material weakness is a significant deficiency, or combination of significant deficiencies, that results in more than a *remote likelihood* that a *material* misstatement of the annual or interim financial statements will not be prevented or detected (AS2, ¶10).

Likelihood and Magnitude

According to the above definitions, in judging the significance of a control deficiency, management and the auditor must consider two dimensions of the control deficiency: *likelihood* and *magnitude*. The definitions of significant deficiency and material weakness both include the phrase "more than a remote likelihood." The term *remote* is to be interpreted using the guidance in FAS 5, *Accounting for Contingencies;* that is, the chance of the future event or events occurring is slight. Accordingly, the likelihood of an event is "more than remote" if it is either reasonably possible or probable. While this guidance is helpful, these concepts are clearly subjective and require the application of considerable professional judgment.

Determining the magnitude of a control deficiency is based on the "reasonable person" concept. "A misstatement is *inconsequential* if a reasonable person would conclude, after considering the possibility of further undetected misstatements, that the misstatement, either individually or when aggregated with other misstatements, would clearly be immaterial to the financial statements. If a reasonable person could not reach such a conclusion regarding a particular misstatement, that misstatement is *more than inconsequential*" (AS2, ¶9). Figure 7–1 represents how likelihood and magnitude relate to each other in the determination of whether a control deficiency rises to the level of a significant deficiency or a material weakness.

FIGURE 7–1	The Relationship of Likelihood and Magnitude in Determining the Materiality of a Control Deficiency

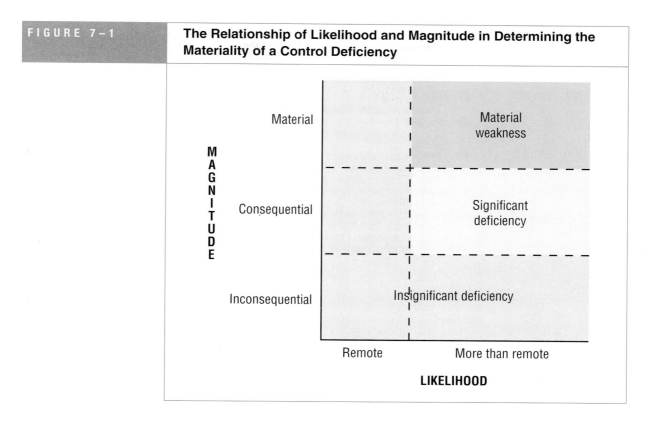

Later in the chapter we discuss how the auditor applies the concepts of likelihood and materiality in an audit of internal control over financial reporting.

Management's Assessment Process

[LO 5]   In order to issue a report on the effectiveness of internal control, management needs to first design and implement an effective system of internal control over financial reporting and then develop an ongoing assessment process. For most companies, this has proved a difficult and costly process involving a substantial amount of work by the entities' personnel. In many cases, third-party consultants have also been involved. It should be noted that an audit of internal control over financial reporting involves performing steps that closely parallel the elements included in management's assessment process. However, the entity's auditor cannot participate in performing management's assessment of internal control. Table 7–1 lists the elements that would typically be found in management's assessment process.

The first element in the process requires management to determine which controls should be tested, including controls over all relevant assertions related to significant accounts and disclosures in the financial statements. Table 7–2 presents a list of controls that would typically be included for testing. The second element requires management to evaluate

TABLE 7–1	**Elements in Management's Assessment Process for the Effectiveness of Internal Control**

Management's assessment process should include each of the following elements:

- Determining which controls should be tested, including controls over all relevant assertions related to all significant accounts and disclosures in the financial statements.
- Evaluating the likelihood that failure of the control could result in a misstatement, the magnitude of such a misstatement, and the degree to which other controls, if effective, achieve the same control objectives.
- Determining the locations or business units to include in the evaluation for a company with multiple locations or business units.
- Evaluating the *design* effectiveness of controls.
- Evaluating the *operating* effectiveness of controls based on procedures sufficient to assess their operating effectiveness.
- Determining the deficiencies in internal control over financial reporting that are of such a magnitude and likelihood of occurrence that they constitute significant deficiencies or material weaknesses.
- Communicating findings to the auditor and to others, if applicable.
- Evaluating whether findings are reasonable and support management's assessment.

the likelihood that failure of the control could result in a misstatement, as well as the magnitude of such a misstatement. Thus, management must make judgments about the amount of misstatement that could occur if the control was not designed properly or was not operating effectively.

The third element requires management to decide which locations or business units to include in the assessment. For small entities, or entities that have a few large business units, the decision as to which units to include may be simple. In such cases, a relatively small number of locations or business units will encompass a large portion of the entity's operations and financial position. However, some entities have numerous similar-size, diversified operations where a large number of locations or business units will need to be included.

The next two elements involve management's evaluation of the design and operating effectiveness of controls. Evaluating the design effectiveness of controls involves determining whether a necessary control is missing or an existing control is not properly designed. Testing the operating effectiveness

TABLE 7–2	**Controls Typically Included for Testing**

- Controls over initiating, authorizing, recording, processing, and reporting significant accounts and disclosures and related assertions embodied in the financial statements.
- Controls over the selection and application of accounting policies that are in conformity with generally accepted accounting principles.
- Antifraud programs and controls.
- Controls, including IT general controls, on which other controls are dependent.
- Controls over significant nonroutine and nonsystematic transactions, such as accounts involving judgments and estimates.
- Company level controls, including (1) the control environment and (2) controls over the period-end financial reporting process (e.g., controls over procedures used to enter transaction totals into the general ledger; to initiate, authorize, record, and process journal entries in the general ledger; and to record recurring and nonrecurring adjustments to the financial statements).

of controls includes control testing by internal audit or others under the direction of management, using a service organization's reports, inspection of evidence of the application of controls, or testing by means of an ongoing self-assessment process. When these two elements are completed, management must determine whether any of the identified control deficiencies alone or in combination will result in a misstatement of such a likelihood or magnitude that the deficiencies constitute a significant deficiency or material weakness.

The last two elements involve communication of the findings to the auditor and others, such as the board of directors or audit committee. Last, management must evaluate whether the results of its assessment support an assertion that internal control over financial reporting is effective.

Management's process involves special consideration of three topics. These topics must also be considered by the auditor during the audit of internal control over financial reporting. The three topics are

- Multiple locations and business units.
- Service organizations.
- Safeguarding assets.

The first *Advanced Module* at the end of the chapter discusses each of these topics in detail.

Management's Documentation

[LO 6] Management must develop sufficient documentation to support its assessment of the effectiveness of internal control. Such documentation should address each of the elements listed in Table 7–1. Management should document the design of controls over all relevant assertions related to all significant accounts and disclosures in the financial statements, including controls in all five components of internal control over financial reporting. The documentation should also address how significant transactions are initiated, authorized, recorded, processed, and reported, with sufficient information about the flow of transactions to identify the points at which material misstatements due to error or fraud could occur. Management should take particular care to document controls designed to prevent or detect fraud, controls over the period-end financial reporting process, and controls over safeguarding assets. Documentation should include a description of each control in place, the business processes to which each control relates, and the assertions addressed by each control. Finally, the results of management's testing and evaluation should be documented.

Documentation of internal control over financial reporting may take many forms, such as paper, electronic files, or other medium. It also includes a variety of information, such as policy manuals, process models, flowcharts, job descriptions, documents, and forms. Such documentation provides the foundation for appropriate communication concerning responsibilities for performing controls and for the entity's evaluation of and monitoring of the effective operation of controls. In fact, inadequate documentation of the design of controls over relevant assertions related to significant accounts and disclosures is considered a deficiency in the entity's internal control over financial reporting that normally will be at least a significant deficiency and may represent a material weakness.

Framework Used by Management to Conduct Its Assessment

🔊 [LO 7]   Management is required to base its assessment of the effectiveness of the entity's internal control over financial reporting on a suitable, recognized control framework established by a body of experts that follows due-process procedures. In the United States, most entities use the framework developed by COSO in the early 1990s (COSO *Internal Control—Integrated Framework*). Some may use the new COSO Enterprise Risk Management framework (*Enterprise Risk Management—Integrated Framework*), which subsumes and builds on the COSO internal control framework. Other suitable frameworks have been published in other countries.

As discussed in Chapter 6, the COSO framework identifies three primary objectives of internal control: reliable financial reporting, efficiency and effectiveness of operations, and compliance with laws and regulations. While the PCAOB focuses on the financial reporting objective, the controls that management designs and implements in the other two areas may help achieve objectives relating to financial reporting. Additionally, not all controls relevant to financial reporting are accounting controls. Therefore, all controls that could materially affect financial reporting, including controls that focus primarily on the effectiveness and efficiency of operations or compliance with laws and regulations and also have a material effect on the reliability of financial reporting, are a part of internal control over financial reporting.

Performing an Audit of Internal Control over Financial Reporting

🔊 [LO 8]   We now turn to how the auditor performs an audit of internal control over financial reporting. Remember: The overall goal is to obtain sufficient competent evidence about the design and operating effectiveness of controls over all relevant financial statement assertions relating to significant accounts and disclosures in the financial statements. The auditor does this by planning and performing the audit of internal control to obtain reasonable assurance that deficiencies rising to the level of a material weakness are identified.

The Audit Process   Figure 7–2 shows the steps involved in performing an audit of internal control. While Figure 7–2 suggests a sequential process, the audit of internal control over financial reporting involves an iterative process of gathering, updating, and analyzing information. The auditor may perform some of the procedures and evaluations described in Figure 7–2 while performing the internal control phase of the financial statement audit.

| FIGURE 7–2 | **Steps in the Audit of Internal Control over Financial Reporting** |

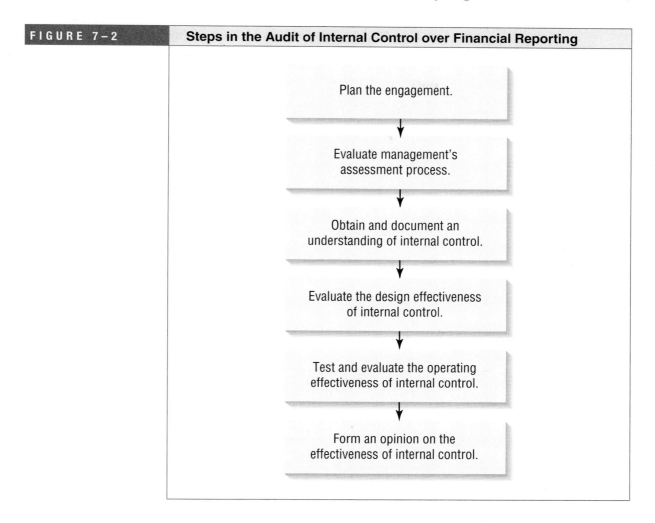

Plan the engagement.

Evaluate management's assessment process.

Obtain and document an understanding of internal control.

Evaluate the design effectiveness of internal control.

Test and evaluate the operating effectiveness of internal control.

Form an opinion on the effectiveness of internal control.

Planning the Engagement

The process for planning an audit of internal control over financial reporting is similar to planning a financial statement audit. In fact, because results from the two audits interrelate, the planning process should be integrated. Table 7–3 contains some of the factors that may affect the conduct of the audit of internal control. A number of these factors were discussed in Chapter 5.

Evaluating Management's Assessment Process

The auditor must evaluate management's process for assessing the effectiveness of the entity's internal control over financial reporting. The auditor's evaluation must cover each of the items listed in Table 7–1. The auditor should obtain an understanding of the results of procedures performed by internal auditors and third parties working under the direction of management. The auditor typically obtains his or her understanding of management's assessment process through inquiry of management and others. The auditor also must evaluate the adequacy of management's documentation of the assessment process (see items listed in "Management Documentation" section).

TABLE 7–3	**Factors That May Affect Planning an Audit of Internal Control over Financial Reporting**

- Knowledge of the company's internal control over financial reporting obtained during other engagements.
- Matters affecting the industry in which the company operates, such as financial reporting practices, economic conditions, laws and regulations, and technological changes.
- Matters relating to the company's business, including its organization, operating characteristics, capital structure, and distribution methods.
- The extent of recent changes in the company, its operations, or its internal control over financial reporting.
- Management's process for assessing the effectiveness of the company's internal control over financial reporting.
- Preliminary judgments about materiality, risk, and other factors relating to the determination of material weaknesses.
- Control deficiencies previously communicated to the audit committee or management.
- Legal or regulatory matters of which the company is aware.
- The type and extent of available evidence.
- The number of significant business locations or units.

Source: AS2, ¶39.

Obtaining an Understanding of Internal Control over Financial Reporting

Obtaining an understanding of internal control over financial reporting as part of an audit of internal control is similar to the process for understanding internal control described in Chapter 6, except that the understanding needed for an audit of internal control is more extensive. For example, understanding the internal control of a private company for purposes of planning a financial statement audit would *not* require an evaluation of the design of specific controls unless the auditor plans to rely on the client's controls. For a public company, the auditor must obtain an understanding of the design of controls related to each component of internal control discussed in Chapters 3 and 6, (i.e., control environment, risk assessment process, control procedures, information system and communication, and monitoring of controls). The procedures the auditor can perform to obtain an understanding of the design of specific controls include inquiring of appropriate management, supervisory, and staff personnel, inspecting company documents, observing the application of specific controls, and tracing transactions through the information system.

In addition, the auditor must apply procedures to identify, understand, and assess certain aspects of the client's system of internal control while developing an understanding of internal control over financial reporting. To gain this understanding, the auditor must

- Understand and assess company-level controls.
- Evaluate the effectiveness of the audit committee.
- Identify significant accounts.
- Identify relevant financial statement assertions.
- Identify significant processes and major classes of transactions.
- Understand the period-end financial reporting process.
- Perform walkthroughs.
- Identify controls to test.

TABLE 7–4	**Examples of Company-Level Controls**

- Controls within the control environment (e.g., tone at the top, the assignment of authority and responsibility, consistent policies and procedures, and companywide programs, such as codes of conduct and fraud prevention, that apply to all locations and business units);
- Management's risk assessment process;
- Centralized processing and controls, including shared service environments;
- Controls to monitor results of operations;
- Controls to monitor other controls, including activities of the internal audit function, the audit committee, and self-assessment programs;
- The period-end financial reporting process; and
- Board-approved policies that address significant business control and risk management practices.

Source: AS2, ¶53.

Company-Level Controls

Company-level controls can have a pervasive effect on the entity's ability to meet the COSO control criteria. For example, IT general controls over program development, program changes, computer operations, and access to programs and data help ensure that specific controls over the processing of transactions are operating effectively. If the IT general controls are not effective, the specific controls are probably unreliable. Further, many of the recent business frauds involved management override of specific controls. Company-level controls addressing management's ability to override specific controls (e.g., review of management-initiated transactions by the internal audit function) are thus of central importance. Table 7–4 contains a list of company-level controls.

The pervasiveness of company-level controls suggests that it may be appropriate for the auditor to test and evaluate them before evaluating the other aspects of internal control over financial reporting. However, testing company-level controls alone is not sufficient for the purpose of expressing an opinion on the effectiveness of an entity's internal control over financial reporting.

Evaluating the Effectiveness of the Audit Committee

The entity's audit committee plays an important role within the control environment and monitoring components of the COSO internal control framework. An effective audit committee helps set a positive "tone at the top." The entity's board of directors oversees and evaluates the performance and effectiveness of the audit committee (which is comprised of board members). However, the auditor should independently assess the effectiveness of the audit committee as part of understanding and evaluating the control environment and monitoring components of internal control. This can be a somewhat awkward area, because the audit committee is charged with hiring, compensating, and firing the auditor.

In evaluating the effectiveness of the audit committee, the auditor should focus on the independence of the audit committee members from management, the clarity with which the audit committee's responsibilities are articulated, and how well the audit committee and management understand those responsibilities. The auditor should also consider the audit committee's involvement and interaction with the internal audit function and with key members of financial management (e.g., chief financial officer and chief accounting officer). If an audit committee is not effective, the auditor should consider this at least a significant deficiency and a strong indicator of a material weakness.

Identifying Significant Accounts

In identifying significant accounts, the auditor must consider materiality. The same conceptual definition of materiality that applies to a financial statement audit (see Chapter 3) applies to identifying significant accounts, and includes both quantitative and qualitative considerations. The factors the auditor should evaluate when identifying significant accounts for an audit of internal control over financial reporting include nature, size, and composition of the account; susceptibility of loss due to errors or fraud; volume, complexity, and homogeneity of the individual transactions processed through the account; likelihood of significant contingent liabilities arising from the activities represented by the account; existence of related-party transactions in the account; and changes from the prior period in account characteristics (AS2, ¶65).

An account is defined as significant if there is more than a remote likelihood that the account could contain misstatements that individually, or when aggregated with others, might have a material effect on the financial statements (AS2, ¶61). Other accounts may be significant on a qualitative basis with reference to the expectations of a reasonable user. For example, in a financial statement audit, the auditor might not consider a fixed asset account to be particularly critical if it has a low volume of transactions each year and if inherent risk is assessed as low, even though the balance is material to the financial statements. Given the circumstances, the auditor might decide to perform only substantive procedures on the account balance. However, in an audit of internal control over financial reporting, such accounts are defined to be significant accounts because of their materiality to the financial statements.

Consider another example of qualitative considerations. The auditor of a financial institution might not consider trust accounts significant to the institution's financial statements for purposes of a financial statement audit, because such accounts are not included in the institution's balance sheet and the fee income generated by trust activities is not material. However, for purposes of the audit of internal control, the auditor may very well assess the activities of the trust department as significant in view of the contingent liabilities that could arise if the trust department failed to fulfill its fiduciary responsibilities (e.g., if investments were made that were not in accordance with stated investment policies).

Identifying Relevant Financial Statement Assertions

For each significant account, the auditor should determine the relevance of each of the financial statement assertions. *Relevant* assertions are those that have a meaningful bearing on whether the account is fairly stated. For example, valuation may not be relevant to the gross amount of the accounts receivable balance, but is relevant to the related allowance account. In determining whether a particular assertion is relevant to a significant account balance or disclosure, the auditor should evaluate the nature of the assertion, the volume of transactions or data related to the assertion, and the nature and complexity of the systems that process and control information supporting the assertion (AS2, ¶69).

Identifying Significant Processes and Major Classes of Transactions

The auditor should identify the significant processes over each major class of transactions affecting significant financial statement accounts. For example, consider an entity whose sales may be initiated by customers either through personal contact in a retail store or electronically through use of the Internet (e.g., EarthWear). These two types of sales would comprise two of the major classes of transactions within the sales process if they were both significant to the entity's financial statements.

The auditor should classify the major classes of transactions by transaction type: routine, nonroutine, and estimation. Routine transactions are recurring financial activities reflected in the accounting records in the normal course of business (e.g., sales, purchases, cash receipts, cash disbursements, and payroll), while nonroutine transactions are activities that occur only periodically (e.g., taking physical inventory and calculating depreciation expense). Estimation transactions are activities that involve management judgments or assumptions in formulating account balances in the absence of a precise means of measurement (e.g., determining the allowance for doubtful accounts, establishing warranty reserves, and assessing assets for impairment) (AS2, ¶72).

The auditor must understand relevant processing procedures involved in the flow of transactions, including those activities required to initiate, authorize, record, process, and report transactions. Examples of such activities for the revenue process include initially recording sales orders, preparing shipping documents and invoices, and updating the accounts receivable master file. Relevant processing procedures also include procedures for correcting and reprocessing previously rejected transactions and for correcting erroneous transactions through adjusting journal entries. For each significant business process (see Chapters 2 and 10), the auditor should

- Understand the flow of transactions.
- Identify the points within the process at which a misstatement related to each relevant financial statement assertion could arise.
- Identify the controls that management has implemented to address these potential misstatements.
- Identify the controls that management has implemented over the prevention or timely detection of unauthorized acquisition, use, or disposition of the company's assets (AS2, ¶74).

Understanding the Period–End Financial Reporting Process

The period-end financial reporting process is always a significant process because of its importance to financial statement reporting. The period-end financial reporting process controls include procedures used to enter transaction totals into the general ledger; initiate, authorize, record, and process journal entries in the general ledger; record recurring and nonrecurring adjustments to the annual and quarterly financial statements; and to draft annual and quarterly financial statements and related disclosures.

The auditor's evaluation of the period-end financial reporting process includes the inputs, procedures performed, and outputs of the processes the company uses to produce its annual and quarterly financial statements. The auditor should also consider the extent of IT involvement in each period-end financial reporting process element, who participates from management, the number of locations involved, types of adjusting entries, and the nature and extent of the oversight of the process by appropriate parties, including management, the board of directors, and the audit committee. The auditor's understanding of the entity's period-end financial reporting process and how it interrelates with the entity's other significant processes helps the auditor identify and test controls that are most relevant to financial statement risks. For example, it is not uncommon for entities to manually compile summary information for financial reporting purposes based on detailed financial information taken from accounting information systems. In some cases, entities use hundreds or even thousands of computer spreadsheets to build a "bridge" between the detailed data and the financial statements. Obviously, when data are entered and analyzed manually, there is an increased risk of input and processing errors that the auditor needs to address.

Performing Walkthroughs
AS2 requires that the auditor perform at least one walkthrough for each major class of transactions each year an audit of internal control is performed. To perform a walkthrough, the auditor traces a transaction from origination through the entity's information system until it is reflected in the entity's financial reports. It should encompass the entire process of initiating, authorizing, recording, processing, and reporting individual transactions and controls for each of the significant processes identified. Walkthroughs help the auditor in confirming his or her understanding of control design and transaction process flow, as well as in determining whether all points at which misstatements could occur have been identified, evaluating the effectiveness of the design of controls, and confirming whether controls have been placed in operation (AS2, ¶79).

In performing the walkthrough, the auditor should follow the process flow of actual transactions using the same documents and information technology that entity personnel use and make inquiries of relevant personnel involved in significant aspects of the process or controls. The auditor should question those personnel about their understanding of what is required by the controls and determine whether the processing procedures are performed as understood and on a timely basis. In addition, the auditor might ask relevant personnel to describe their understanding of the previous and succeeding processing or control activities. This helps corroborate responses from personnel in those control activities. Inquiries should include follow-up questions that can help identify abuse of controls or indicators of fraud. If there have been significant changes in the process flow of transactions during the period, the auditor should evaluate the nature of the changes and the effect on related accounts to determine whether to walk through transactions that were processed both before and after the change.

Identifying Controls to Test
Once the significant accounts, relevant assertions, and significant processes have been identified, the auditor identifies the controls to be tested. Identifying the controls to be tested is a subjective task that requires professional judgment. Table 7–5 provides a list of factors that the auditor should consider in deciding which controls to test. The auditor should evaluate whether to test preventive controls, detective controls, or a combination of both for relevant assertions related to significant accounts. For example, a monthly reconciliation (a detective control)

TABLE 7–5	**Factors to Evaluate When Identifying Controls to Test**

- Points at which errors or fraud could occur.
- The nature of the controls implemented by management.
- The significance of each control in achieving the objectives of the control criteria and whether more than one control achieves a particular objective or whether more than one control is necessary to achieve a particular objective.
- The risk that the controls might not be operating effectively. Factors that affect whether the control might not be operating effectively include the following:
  — Whether there have been changes in the volume or nature of transactions that might adversely affect control design or operating effectiveness.
  — Whether there have been changes in the design of controls.
  — The degree to which the control relies on the effectiveness of other controls (e.g., the control environment or IT general controls).
  — Whether there have been changes in key personnel who perform the control or monitor its performance.
  — Whether the control relies on performance by an individual or is automated; and
  — The complexity of the control.

Source: AS2, ¶83.

might detect an out-of-balance situation resulting from an unauthorized transaction being initiated due to an ineffective authorization procedure (a preventive control). When determining whether the detective control is effective, the auditor should evaluate whether the detective control is sufficient to achieve the control objective to which the preventive control relates.

Evaluting Design Effectiveness of Controls

Controls are effectively designed when they prevent or detect errors or fraud that could result in material misstatements in the financial statements. The auditor should determine whether the entity has controls to meet the objectives of the control criteria selected by management (e.g., COSO). This is accomplished by first identifying the controls that satisfy each of the entity's control objectives in each area and then determining whether the controls, if operating properly, would be likely to prevent or detect errors or fraud that could result in material misstatements in the financial statements (AS2, ¶88). Part of this process is to ensure a proper alignment between controls and the client's business and audit risks. Once key controls are identified, the auditor evaluates design effectiveness through inquiry, observation, walkthroughs, inspection of relevant documentation, and subjective evaluations of whether the controls are likely to prevent or detect errors or fraud that could result in misstatements assuming they are operated as prescribed by qualified persons. The procedures performed by the auditor to test and evaluate design effectiveness might in some cases also provide evidence about operating effectiveness.

Testing and Evaluating Operating Effectiveness of Controls

An auditor evaluates the operating effectiveness of a control by determining whether the control is operating as designed and whether the person performing the control possesses the necessary authority and qualifications to perform the control effectively. In testing the operating effectiveness of controls, the auditor needs to consider the scope (nature, timing, and extent) of testing.

Nature of Testing   Tests of controls for operating effectiveness include such procedures as inquiry of appropriate personnel, inspection of relevant documentation, observation of the entity's operations, and reperformance of the application of the control. In many instances, a combination of these procedures is necessary to ensure that the control is operating effectively.

As described in Chapter 5, inquiry is a procedure that seeks information of knowledgeable persons throughout the entity. It is used extensively throughout both the financial statement audit and the audit of internal control. Because inquiry alone does not provide sufficient evidence to support the operating effectiveness of a control, the auditor should perform additional tests of controls. For example, suppose an entity implements a control whereby its sales manager reviews and investigates a report listing invoices with unusually high or low gross margins. Inquiry of the sales manager as to whether he or she investigates discrepancies would not be sufficient evidence to ensure that the control is working effectively. The auditor should corroborate the sales manager's responses by performing other procedures, such as inspecting reports generated by the performance of the control and evaluating whether appropriate actions were taken.

The type of control often affects the nature of control testing the auditor can perform. For example, an entity may have a control that requires a signature (digital or otherwise) on a voucher package to indicate that the signer approved it. However, the presence of a signature does not necessarily mean that the person carefully reviewed the package before signing. As a result, the quality of the evidence regarding the effective operation of the control might not be sufficiently persuasive. In order to gain more persuasive evidence, the auditor should reperform the control by checking the voucher package for accuracy and completeness. The auditor might also inquire of the person responsible for approving voucher packages regarding what he or she looks for when approving packages and ask to see documentation of the errors that have been found and rectified in the recent past. This chapter's second *Advanced Module* offers a brief discussion of computer-assisted audit techniques available to the auditor in testing the operating effectiveness of controls.

Timing of Tests of Controls   The auditor must perform tests of controls over a period of time that is adequate to determine whether the significant controls are operating effectively as of the date in management's report. The period of time over which the auditor performs tests of controls will vary with the nature of the controls and the frequency with which they are applied. Some controls operate continuously (e.g., controls over the processing of routine sales transactions), while other controls operate only occasionally (e.g., monthly bank reconciliations). Routine transactions will typically involve routine processing controls, such as verification of data entry, edit checks and validation controls, completeness controls, and so forth. For nonroutine transactions, especially those involving estimation, the more critical controls are typically review and approval. In some cases, controls may operate after the "as of" date specified in management's report. For example, controls over a December 31 period-end financial reporting process normally operate in January of the following year.

In many instances, the auditor obtains evidence about the operating effectiveness of controls at an interim date. For example, the auditor might test controls over the revenue process for the first nine months of the year. The auditor will then need to determine what additional evidence is needed concerning the operating effectiveness of the controls for the remaining three-month period. In deciding what additional evidence is needed, the auditor considers the specific controls tested prior to the as of date and the results of those tests, the degree to which evidence about the operating effectiveness of those controls was obtained, the length of the remaining period, and the possibility that there have been significant changes in internal control subsequent to the interim date. For controls over significant nonroutine transactions, controls over accounts or processes with a high degree of subjectivity or judgment in measurement, or controls over the recording of period-end adjustments, the auditor should perform tests closer to the as of date.

If management implements changes to the entity's controls prior to the date specified in management's report to make them more effective or efficient, the auditor might not need to evaluate the controls that have been superseded. However, as discussed later, the auditor must communicate all identified significant deficiencies and material weaknesses to the audit committee in writing—including those that have been subsequently corrected through redesign or improved operating effectiveness.

Extent of Tests of Controls AS2 provides the following guidance on the extent of evidence:

> For each audit, the auditor must obtain sufficient evidence about whether the entity's internal control over financial reporting, including the controls for all internal control components, is operating effectively. This means that each year the auditor must obtain evidence about the effectiveness of controls for all relevant assertions related to all significant accounts and disclosures in the financial statements. The auditor also should vary from year to year the nature, extent, and timing of testing of controls to introduce unpredictability into the testing and respond to changes in circumstances. For example, each year the auditor might test the controls at a different interim period; increase or reduce the number and types of tests performed; or change the combination of procedures used (AS2, ¶104).

Because the auditor designs the audit procedures to provide a high level of assurance, the auditor should assess the following factors when deciding on the extent of testing:

- *Nature of the control.* Manual controls should be subjected to more extensive testing than automated controls in view of the greater variability inherent in controls involving people.
- *Frequency of operation.* Generally, the more frequently a manual control operates, the greater the number of operations of the control the auditor should test.
- *Importance of the control.* The more important the control, the more extensively it should be tested.

[LO 9] Special Consideration—Using the Work of Others AS2 requires the auditor to perform enough of the testing that his or her own work provides the *principal* evidence for the auditor's opinion (AS2, ¶108). However, a major consideration for the external auditor is how much of

EXHIBIT 7–1	An Example of an Auditor's Tests of a Daily Programmed Application Control and a Daily Information Technology–Dependent Manual Control

Bill Boyd is manager for Emets & Shinn, a large regional CPA firm. Emets & Shinn is the independent registered public accounting firm for Petheridge Packing Company (PPC). Boyd is planning the nature, timing, and extent of testing for cash and accounts receivable: two significant accounts for the audit of PPC's internal control over financial reporting. Based on discussions with PPC personnel and review of company documentation, the auditor learns that PPC had the following procedures in place over the entire period to account for cash received in the bank lockbox:

- The company receives from the bank an electronic file listing cash received from customers.
- The IT system applies cash received in the lockbox to individual customer accounts.
- Any cash received in the lockbox and not applied to a customer's account is listed on an exception report called the "unapplied cash exception report."

The application of cash to a customer's account is a *programmed application* control, while the review and follow-up of unapplied cash from the exception report is a *manual* control.

Boyd wants to determine whether misstatements in cash (primarily relating to the existence assertion) and accounts receivable (existence, valuation, and completeness) would be prevented or detected on a timely basis. In order to test these objectives, Boyd decides to test the two controls.

Nature, Timing, and Extent of Procedures

Objectives of Tests   To determine whether only appropriate cash items are posted to customers' accounts and matched to customer number, invoice number, amount, and so on, and that there is a listing of nonmatching cash items on the exception report. Boyd must test both the design and operating effectiveness of the controls.

Control 1

Test the programmed application control provided by the system in the daily reconciliation of lockbox receipts to customer accounts. Boyd decides to perform the following procedures to ensure the *design effectiveness* of this control:

1. Identified, through discussion with company personnel, the software used to receive the download from the banks and to process the transactions.

   Finding: Boyd learned that the company uses accounting software acquired from a reputable third-party supplier. The software consists of a number of modules. The client modifies the software only for upgrades supplied by the supplier.

2. Determined, through further discussion with company personnel, which cash module operates transactions relating to the lockbox and the posting of cash to the general ledger. The accounts receivable module posts the cash to individual customer accounts and produces the unapplied cash exception report, a standard report supplied with the package.

   Finding: Boyd found that this information was consistent with the supplier's documentation.

3. Identified, through discussions with company personnel and review of the supplier's documentation, the names, file sizes (in bytes), and locations of the executable files (programs) that operate the functionality under review.

   Finding: Boyd identified the compilation dates of these programs, which agreed with the original installation date of the application.

Test Results from Pervasive Controls   Michael Ta, the IT specialist for Emets & Shinn, evaluated and tested general computer controls, including program changes and logical access. Ta concluded that there were no unauthorized program changes and that data file access to the file downloaded from the banks and user access to the cash and accounts receivable modules were operating effectively. Boyd decided to perform the following tests of controls to ensure the *operating effectiveness* of the programmed control:

1. Boyd performed a walkthrough in July. Boyd concluded that it was sufficient to perform a walkthrough for only a single item.
2. During the walkthrough, Boyd performed and documented the following items:
   a. Selected one customer and agreed the amount billed to the customer to the cash received in the lockbox.
   b. Agreed the total of the lockbox report to the posting of cash receipts in the general ledger.
   c. Agreed the total of the cash receipt download from the bank to the lockbox report and supporting documentation.
   d. Selected one customer's remittance and agreed amount posted to the customer's account in the accounts receivable subsidiary ledger.

Based on the audit procedures, Boyd concluded that the automated control was operating effectively as of year-end.

Control 2

Test the manual control involving review and follow-up on the daily unapplied cash exception report.

Boyd decides to perform the following tests of controls to ensure the *operating effectiveness* of the control for the review and follow-up on the daily unapplied cash exception report.

1. Inquired of company personnel about the procedures in place to ensure that all unapplied items are resolved, the time frame in which such resolution takes place, and whether unapplied items are handled properly within the system.

   Findings: Boyd discussed these matters with the employee responsible for reviewing and resolving the daily unapplied cash exception reports. Boyd learned that items appearing on the daily unapplied cash exception report must be manually entered into the system. The employee typically performs the resolution procedures the next business day. In most cases, items that appear on the daily unapplied cash exception report relate to payments made by a customer who failed to reference an invoice number or purchase order number, or to underpayments of an invoice due to quantity or pricing discrepancies.

2. Observed entity personnel performing the control.

   Findings: Boyd observed the employee reviewing and resolving a daily unapplied cash exception report for one day. The day selected contained four exceptions: three related to payments made by a customer without an invoice number and one related to an underpayment due to a pricing discrepancy. For the pricing discrepancy, the employee determined through discussions with a sales person that the customer had been billed an incorrect price. The price break that the sales person had granted to the customer was not reflected on the customer's invoice. The employee resolved the pricing discrepancy, determined to which invoices the cash receipts pertained, and entered a correction into the system to properly apply cash to the customer's account and reduce accounts receivable and sales accounts for the amount of the price break.

3. Reperformed the control.

   Findings: Boyd selected 25 daily unapplied cash exception reports from the period January to September and reperformed the follow-up procedures that the employee performed. Boyd inspected the documents and sources of information used in the follow-up and determined that the transaction was properly corrected in the system. He also scanned other daily unapplied cash exception reports to determine that the control was performed throughout the period of intended reliance.

4. Follow-up tests: Because the tests were performed at an interim date, Boyd asked entity personnel about the procedures in place at year-end. The procedures had not changed from the interim period; therefore, Boyd observed that the controls were still in place by scanning daily unapplied cash exception reports to determine the control was performed on a timely basis during the period from September to year-end. No exceptions were noted.

Based on the audit procedures, Boyd concluded that the employee was clearing exceptions in a timely manner and that the control was operating effectively as of year-end.

---

the work performed by others (internal auditors or others working for management) can be relied on in adjusting the nature, timing, or extent of the auditor's work. For example, the auditor may determine that the client's internal audit function has performed control testing work relevant to the audit of internal control over financial reporting, and must decide the extent to which he or she should use that work in planning and conducting his or her own procedures. In determining the extent to which the auditor may use the work of others, the auditor should (1) evaluate the nature of the controls subjected to the work of others, (2) evaluate the competence and objectivity of the individuals who performed the work, and (3) test some of the work performed by others to evaluate the quality and effectiveness of their work. More detailed information on using the work of others is contained in the first *Advanced Module* at the end of the chapter.

An Example   Exhibit 7–1 presents a detailed example of an auditor's test of the design and operating effectiveness for a daily IT application control and a daily IT-dependent manual control.

Forming an
Opinion on the
Effectiveness of
Internal Control
over Financial
Reporting

The auditor should evaluate all evidence obtained before forming an opinion on internal control over financial reporting, including (1) the adequacy of the assessment performed by management, (2) the results of the auditor's evaluation of the design and tests of operating effectiveness of controls, (3) the negative results of substantive procedures performed during the financial statement audit, and (4) any identified control deficiencies. In addition, the auditor should review all reports issued during the year by the internal audit function that address controls related to financial reporting and evaluate any control deficiencies identified in those reports.

The auditor's report addresses both management's assessment and the effectiveness of internal control over financial reporting. The auditor may issue an unqualified opinion only when no material weaknesses are identified and when the scope of the auditor's work has been unrestricted.

The existence of a material weakness requires the auditor to express an *adverse* opinion on the effectiveness of internal control over financial reporting. The significance of the control deficiency, as discussed previously, is determined by the auditor's consideration of the likelihood and magnitude of the identified control deficiency. The auditor must evaluate identified control deficiencies and determine whether the deficiencies, individually or in combination, constitute significant deficiencies or material weaknesses. Note that the significance of a deficiency in internal control over financial reporting depends on the *potential* for a misstatement, not on whether a misstatement actually has occurred (AS2, ¶132). Table 7–6 contains factors that might affect the *likelihood* that a control deficiency could result in a misstatement in an account balance.

Factors that might affect the *magnitude* of a misstatement that could result from a deficiency in controls include (1) the financial statement amounts or total dollar amount of transactions exposed to the deficiency and (2) the volume of activity in the account balance or class of transactions exposed to the deficiency.

Some examples of control deficiencies that might constitute a significant deficiency or a material weakness include inadequate documentation of the design of controls and/or the absence of sufficient documented evidence to support management's assessment of the operating effectiveness of internal

TABLE 7–6	**Factors That Might Affect the Likelihood of a Control Deficiency (or a Combination of Deficiencies) Resulting in a Misstatement of an Account Balance or Disclosure**
	• The nature of the financial statement accounts, disclosures, and assertions involved.
	• The susceptibility of the related assets or liability to loss or fraud.
	• The subjectivity, complexity, or extent of judgment required to determine the amount involved.
	• The cause and frequency of known or detected exceptions for the operating effectiveness of a control.
	• The interaction or relationship of the control with other controls; that is, the interdependence or redundancy of the control.
	• The interaction of the deficiencies; that is, whether the deficiencies could affect the same financial statement accounts and assertions.
	• The possible future consequences of the deficiency.
	Source: AS2, ¶133.

EXHIBIT 7–2	An Example of a Significant Deficiency and Material Weakness— Reconciliations of Intercompany Accounts Are Not Performed on a Timely Basis

Scenario A. Significant Deficiency

Murray Company processes a significant number of routine intercompany transactions on a monthly basis. Individual intercompany transactions are not material and primarily relate to balance sheet activity; for example, cash transfers between business units to finance normal operations.

A formal management policy requires monthly reconciliation of intercompany accounts and confirmation of balances between business units. However, there is no process in place to ensure performance of these procedures. As a result, detailed reconciliations of intercompany accounts are not performed on a timely basis. Management does perform monthly procedures to investigate selected large-dollar intercompany account differences. In addition, management prepares a detailed monthly variance analysis of operating expenses to assess their reasonableness.

Based only on these facts, the auditor should determine that this control deficiency represents a significant deficiency for the following reasons: The magnitude of a financial statement misstatement resulting from this deficiency would reasonably be expected to be more than inconsequential, but less than material, because individual intercompany transactions are not material, and the compensating controls operating monthly should detect a material misstatement. Furthermore, the transactions are primarily restricted to balance sheet accounts. However, the compensating detective controls are designed only to detect material misstatements. The controls do not address the detection of misstatements that are more than inconsequential but less than material. Therefore, the likelihood that a misstatement could occur that was more than inconsequential, but less than material, is more than remote.

Scenario B. Material Weakness

Ragunandan Company processes a significant number of intercompany transactions on a monthly basis. Intercompany transactions relate to a wide range of activities, including transfers of inventory with intercompany profit between business units, allocation of research and development costs to business units, and corporate charges. Individual intercompany transactions are frequently material.

A formal management policy requires monthly reconciliation of intercompany accounts and confirmation of balances between business units. However, there is no process in place to ensure that these procedures are performed on a consistent basis. As a result, reconciliations of intercompany accounts are not performed on a timely basis, and differences in intercompany accounts are frequent and significant. Management does not perform any alternative controls to investigate significant intercompany account differences.

Based only on these facts, the auditor should determine that this deficiency represents a material weakness for the following reasons: The magnitude of a financial statement misstatement resulting from this deficiency would reasonably be expected to be material, because individual intercompany transactions are frequently material and relate to a wide range of activities. Additionally, actual unreconciled differences in intercompany accounts have been, and are, material. The likelihood of such a misstatement is more than remote because such misstatements have frequently occurred and compensating controls are not effective, either because they are not properly designed or are not operating effectively. Taken together, the magnitude and likelihood of misstatement of the financial statements resulting from this internal control deficiency meet the definition of a material weakness.

Source: Adapted from Example D-1 in AS2, ¶D3.

control. Additional examples of areas where control deficiencies are likely to be considered significant or material include controls over the selection and application of accounting policies, antifraud programs and controls, controls over nonroutine and nonsystematic transactions, and controls over the period-end financial reporting process (AS2, ¶139). Last, Table 7–7 shows particular circumstances that should be regarded as at least a significant deficiency and as a strong indicator of a material weakness.

Exhibit 7–2 presents two scenarios illustrating the process of assessing a control deficiency as either a significant deficiency or material weakness.

TABLE 7–7	Circumstances That Should Be Regarded as at Least a Significant Deficiency and as a Strong Indicator of a Material Weakness

- Restatement of previously issued financial statements to reflect the correction of a misstatement.
- Identification by the auditor of a material misstatement in financial statements in the current period that was not initially identified by the company's internal control over financial reporting.
- Oversight of the company's external financial reporting and internal control over financial reporting by the company's audit committee is ineffective.
- The internal audit function or the risk assessment function is ineffective at a company for which such a function needs to be effective for the company to have an effective monitoring or risk assessment component, such as for very large or highly complex companies.
- For complex entities in highly regulated industries, an ineffective regulatory compliance function. This relates solely to those aspects of the ineffective regulatory compliance function in which associated violations of laws and regulations could have a material effect on the reliability of financial reporting.
- Identification of fraud of any magnitude on the part of senior management.
- Significant deficiencies that have been communicated to management and the audit committee remain uncorrected after some reasonable period of time.
- An ineffective control environment.

Source: AS2, ¶140.

Written Representations

[LO 10]   In addition to the management representations obtained as part of a financial statement audit (see Chapter 17), the auditor also obtains written representations from management related to the audit of internal control over financial reporting. Table 7–8 presents the typical management representations made to the auditor related to the audit of internal control. Failure to obtain written representations from management, including management's refusal to furnish them, constitutes a limitation on the scope of the audit sufficient to preclude an unqualified opinion. While the required representations are typically drafted by the auditor, they are addressed to the auditor and are signed (and worded as if written) by the CEO and CFO.

Auditor Documentation Requirements

[LO 11]   AS2 requires that the auditor appropriately document the processes, procedures, judgments, and results relating to the audit of internal control. The auditor's documentation must include the auditor's understanding and evaluation of the design of each of the components of the entity's internal control over financial reporting. The auditor also documents the process used to determine, and the points at which misstatements could occur within, significant accounts, disclosures and major classes of transactions. The auditor must justify and document the extent to which he or she relied upon work performed by others. Finally, the auditor must describe the evaluation of any deficiencies discovered, as well as any other findings, that could result in a modification to the auditor's report (AS2, ¶159).

When an entity has effective internal control over financial reporting, the auditor should be able to perform sufficient testing of controls to assess

TABLE 7-8	**Written Representations Made by Management to the Auditor**

- Management is responsible for establishing and maintaining effective internal control over financial reporting.
- Management has performed an assessment of the effectiveness of the company's internal control over financial reporting and specifying the control criteria.
- Management did not rely on work performed by the auditor in forming its assessment of the effectiveness of internal control over financial reporting.
- Management's conclusion about the effectiveness of the entity's internal control over financial reporting based on the control criteria as of a specified date.
- Management has disclosed to the auditor all deficiencies in the design or operation of internal control over financial reporting identified as part of management's assessment and has identified all such deficiencies that it believes to be significant deficiencies or material weaknesses.
- Descriptions of any material fraud and any other fraud that, although not material, involves senior management or management or other employees who have a significant role in the company's internal control over financial reporting.
- Control deficiencies identified and communicated to the audit committee during previous engagements pursuant to paragraph 207 have (or have not) been resolved (and specifically identifying any that have not).
- Descriptions of any changes in internal control over financial reporting or other factors that might significantly affect internal control over financial reporting, including any corrective actions taken by management with regard to significant deficiencies and material weaknesses.

Source: AS2, ¶142.

control risk for all relevant assertions at a low level. These assessments have implications for the conduct of the financial statement audit (see Chapter 6). If, however, the auditor assesses control risk as other than low for certain assertions or significant accounts, the auditor should document the reasons for that conclusion.

Reporting on Internal Control over Financial Reporting

Management's Report �># [LO 12]

The Sarbanes-Oxley Act requires management of a public company to report on the effectiveness of internal control over financial reporting in the company's annual report. Management's description must include the following:

- A statement of management's responsibility for establishing and maintaining adequate internal control over financial reporting for the entity.
- A statement identifying the framework used by management to conduct the required assessment of the effectiveness of the company's internal control over financial reporting (e.g., the COSO internal control framework).
- An assessment of the effectiveness of the company's internal control over financial reporting as of the end of the company's most recent fiscal year, including an explicit statement as to whether that internal control over financial reporting is effective.
- A statement that the registered public accounting firm that audited the financial statements included in the annual report has issued an

attestation report on management's assessment of the company's internal control over financial reporting (AS2, ¶162).

The phrase "it is management's assessment that EarthWear Clothiers maintained effective internal control over financial reporting as of December 31, 2005," is an example of an appropriate way to state a direct conclusion about the effectiveness of the internal control. Other similar phrases also can be used.

Management cannot conclude that the company's internal control over financial reporting is effective if any material weaknesses are identified. Further, management is required to disclose all material weaknesses that exist as of the end of the most recent fiscal year. However, management might be able to accurately represent that internal control over financial reporting is effective as of the end of the company's most recent fiscal year even if one or more material weaknesses existed during the period. To make this representation, management must have changed the internal control over financial reporting to eliminate any material weaknesses sufficiently in advance of the as of date and must have satisfactorily tested the effectiveness of the modified controls over a sufficient period of time to determine whether internal control over financial reporting is effective as of the end of the fiscal year.

Exhibit 7–3 presents an example of a management report on internal control over financial reporting for EarthWear Clothiers.

The Auditor's Report
✸ [LO 13]

Once the auditor has completed the audit of internal control, he or she must issue an appropriate report to accompany management's assessment, published in the company's annual report. An overview of reporting on the audit of internal control over financial reporting is presented in this chapter. Additional detail is presented in Chapter 18.

Types of Reports Relating to the Audit of Internal Control

The auditor's report contains opinions on two separate items: (1) management's assessment of the effectiveness of internal control over financial reporting, and (2) the effectiveness of internal control over financial reporting based on the auditor's independent audit work. Similar to reports relating to the financial statement audit, the basic options for the opinions are unqualified, qualified, or adverse.

The auditor's opinion relating to management's assessment depends on whether the auditor agrees with management's conclusion regarding the effectiveness of internal control over financial reporting. If the auditor agrees, the opinion on management's assessment will be unqualified. If the auditor disagrees, the opinion will be adverse.

With respect to the auditor's opinion on the effectiveness of a client's internal control, an *unqualified* opinion signifies that the client's internal control is designed and operating effectively in all material respects. Significant deficiencies relate to possible financial statement errors that are less than material, and therefore do not require a departure from an unqualified opinion. A *qualified* opinion is issued under certain circumstances involving limitations on the scope of the auditor's work; however, serious

EXHIBIT 7–3	EarthWear's Management Report on the Financial Statements and Internal Control over Financial Reporting

To the Stockholders
EarthWear Clothiers, Inc.

Management of EarthWear Clothiers, Inc. (the "Company") is responsible for the preparation, consistency, integrity, and fair presentation of the consolidated financial statements. The consolidated financial statements have been prepared in accordance with accounting principles generally accepted in the United States of America applied on a consistent basis and, in management's opinion, are fairly presented. The financial statements include amounts that are based on management's informed judgments and best estimates.

Management has established and maintains comprehensive systems of internal control that provide reasonable assurance as to the consistency, integrity, and reliability of the preparation and presentation of financial statements; the safeguarding of assets; the effectiveness and efficiency of operations; and compliance with applicable laws and regulations. The concept of reasonable assurance is based upon the recognition that the cost of the controls should not exceed the benefit derived. Management monitors the systems of internal control and maintains an independent internal auditing program that assesses the effectiveness of internal control. Management assessed the Company's internal control over financial reporting for financial presentations in conformity with accounting principles generally accepted in the United States of America. This assessment was based on criteria for effective internal control over financial reporting established in *Internal Control—Integrated Framework,* issued by the Committee of Sponsoring Organizations of the Treadway Commission (the COSO Report). Based on this assessment, management believes that the Company maintained effective internal control over financial reporting for financial presentations in conformity with accounting principles generally accepted in the United States of America as of December 31, 2005.

The Board of Directors exercises its oversight role with respect to the Company's systems of internal control primarily through its Audit Committee, which is comprised solely of outside directors. The Committee oversees the Company's systems of internal control and financial reporting to assess whether their quality, integrity, and objectivity are sufficient to protect shareholders' investments.

The Company's consolidated financial statements have been audited by Willis & Adams LLP ("Willis & Adams"), independent auditors. As part of its audit, Willis & Adams considers the Company's internal control to plan the audit and determine the nature, timing, and extent of auditing procedures considered necessary to render its opinion as to the fair presentation, in all material respects, of the consolidated financial statements, which is based on independent audits made in accordance with the standards of the Public Company Accounting Oversight Board (United States). Management's assertion that the Company maintained effective internal control over financial reporting for financial presentations in conformity with accounting principles generally accepted in the United States of America has been audited by Willis & Adams. Management has made available to Willis & Adams all the Company's financial records and related data, and information concerning the Company's internal control over financial reporting, and believes that all representations made to Willis & Adams during its audits were valid and appropriate.

Calvin C. Rogers President and Chief Executive Officer	James C. Watts Senior Vice President and Chief Financial Officer

scope limitations require the auditor to *disclaim* an opinion. An *adverse* opinion is required if a material weakness is identified. Figure 7–3 illustrates the types of auditor's reports and the circumstances leading to each.

Elements of the Auditor's Report

The auditor's report on management's assessment of the effectiveness of internal control must include, among others, the following elements:

- A title that includes the word "independent."
- An identification of management's conclusion about the effectiveness of the company's internal control over financial

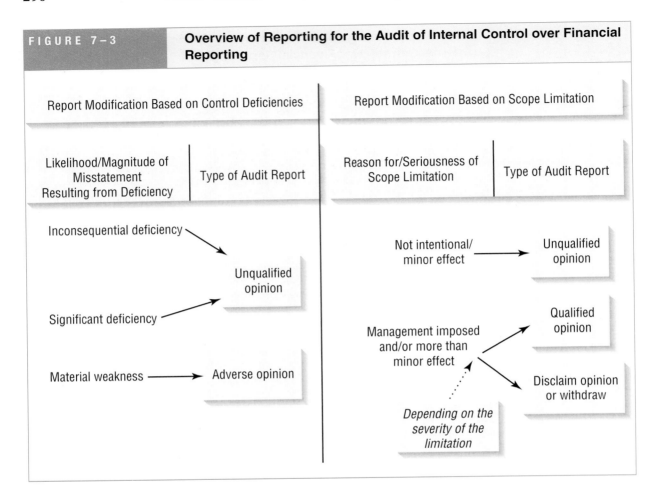

FIGURE 7–3   **Overview of Reporting for the Audit of Internal Control over Financial Reporting**

reporting, along with a statement that the assessment on which management's conclusion is based is the responsibility of management.

- A definition of internal control over financial reporting.
- A statement that the standards of the PCAOB require that the auditor plan and perform the audit to obtain reasonable assurance about whether effective internal control over financial reporting was maintained in all material respects.
- A statement that an audit includes obtaining an understanding of internal control over financial reporting, evaluating management's assessment, testing and evaluating the design and operating effectiveness of internal control, and performing such other procedures as the auditor considered necessary in the circumstances.
- A paragraph stating that, because of inherent limitations, internal control over financial reporting may not prevent or detect misstatements and that projections of any evaluation of effectiveness to future periods are subject to certain risks and uncertainties.

- The auditor's opinion on whether management's assessment of the effectiveness of the company's internal control over financial reporting as of the specified date is fairly stated, in all material respects, based on the control criteria.
- The auditor's opinion on whether the company maintained, in all material respects, effective internal control over financial reporting as of the specified date, based on the control criteria (AS2, ¶167).

The auditor may choose to issue separate reports on the company's financial statements and internal control over financial reporting or may issue a combined report. Under either approach, the date of the reports should be the same. The following sections explain the unqualified report, the adverse report for material weaknesses, and the qualified report and disclaimer of opinion for scope limitations.

Unqualified Report

Unqualified Report   An unqualified opinion on *management's assessment* signifies that the auditor agrees with the assessment in all material respects. Note that the auditor will issue an unqualified opinion if he or she agrees with the assessment, regardless of management's conclusion as to the effectiveness of internal control.

An unqualified opinion regarding the *effectiveness* of the client's internal control over financial reporting provides reasonable assurance that the client's controls are designed and operating effectively in all material respects as of the report date. The phrase "all material respects" means that the client's internal control over financial reporting is free of any material weakness. As depicted in Figure 7–3, an unqualified opinion can be issued even in the presence of significant deficiencies, which are not required to be publicly reported by management or by the auditor. Exhibit 7–4 presents an example of an auditor's unqualified report that is presented separately from the auditor's report on the financial statements. Note that the report includes an explanatory paragraph referring to the financial statement audit report. An example of a combined report is presented in Chapter 18.

Adverse Reports for a Material Weakness

Adverse Reports for a Material Weakness   The presence of a material weakness necessitates an adverse assessment by management and an adverse opinion by the auditor, unless management successfully corrects the material weakness prior to the end of the period and with sufficient time for management to reassess and for the auditor to retest the relevant controls. If management's assessment indicates that the company has not maintained effective internal control over financial reporting and the auditor agrees with this assessment, the auditor's report is unqualified with respect to management's assessment and adverse for the effectiveness of internal control. If management's report states that internal control over financial reporting was effective and the auditor disagrees, the auditor will issue an adverse opinion on both management's assessment and the effectiveness of internal control.

An adverse report includes a definition of a material weakness and a description of the particular material weakness identified in the client's system

EXHIBIT 7–4	**An Example of a Separate Report Giving an Unqualified Opinion on Management's Assessment of the Effectiveness of Internal Control over Financial Reporting and an Unqualified Opinion on the Effectiveness of Internal Control over Financial Reporting**

Report of Independent Registered Public Accounting Firm
[Introductory Paragraph]

We have audited management's assessment, included in the accompanying Management Report on the Financial Statements and Internal Control, that EarthWear Clothiers maintained effective internal control over financial reporting as of December 31, 2005, based on criteria established in *Internal Control—Integrated Framework*, issued by the Committee of Sponsoring Organizations of the Treadway Commission (COSO). EarthWear Clothiers' management is responsible for maintaining effective internal control over financial reporting and for its assessment of the effectiveness of internal control over financial reporting. Our responsibility is to express an opinion on management's assessment and an opinion on the effectiveness of the company's internal control over financial reporting based on our audit.

[Scope Paragraph]

We conducted our audit in accordance with the standards of the Public Company Accounting Oversight Board (United States). Those standards require that we plan and perform the audit to obtain reasonable assurance about whether effective internal control over financial reporting was maintained in all material respects. Our audit included obtaining an understanding of internal control over financial reporting, evaluating management's assessment, testing and evaluating the design and operating effectiveness of internal control, and performing such other procedures as we considered necessary in the circumstances. We believe that our audit provides a reasonable basis for our opinion.

[Definition Paragraph]

A company's internal control over financial reporting is a process designed to provide reasonable assurance regarding the reliability of financial reporting and the preparation of financial statements for external purposes in accordance with generally accepted accounting principles. A company's internal control over financial reporting includes those policies and procedures that (1) pertain to the maintenance of records that, in reasonable detail, accurately and fairly reflect the transactions and dispositions of the assets of the company; (2) provide reasonable assurance that transactions are recorded as necessary to permit preparation of financial statements in accordance with generally accepted accounting principles, and that receipts and expenditures of the company are being made only in accordance with authorizations of management and directors of the company; and (3) provide reasonable assurance regarding prevention or timely detection of unauthorized acquisition, use, or disposition of the company's assets that could have a material effect on the financial statements.

[Inherent Limitations Paragraph]

Because of its inherent limitations, internal control over financial reporting may not prevent or detect misstatements. Also, projections of any evaluation of effectiveness to future periods are subject to the risk that controls may become inadequate because of changes in conditions or that the degree of compliance with the policies or procedures may deteriorate.

[Opinion Paragraph]

In our opinion, management's assessment that EarthWear Clothiers maintained effective internal control over financial reporting as of December 31, 2005, is fairly stated, in all material respects, based on criteria established in *Internal Control—Integrated Framework,* issued by the Committee of Sponsoring Organizations of the Treadway Commission (COSO). Also in our opinion, EarthWear Clothiers maintained, in all material respects, effective internal control over financial reporting as of December 31, 2005, based on criteria established in *Internal Control—Integrated Framework*, issued by the Committee of Sponsoring Organizations of the Treadway Commission (COSO).

[Explanatory Paragraph]

We have also audited, in accordance with the standards of the Public Company Accounting Oversight Board (United States), the consolidated financial statements of EarthWear Clothiers, and our report dated February 15, 2006, expressed an unqualified opinion.

Willis & Adams
Boise, Idaho
February 15, 2006

EXHIBIT 7–5	An Example of a Report Expressing an Unqualified Opinion on Management's Assessment of the Effectiveness of Internal Control over Financial Reporting and an Adverse Opinion on the Effectiveness of Internal Control over Financial Reporting Because of the Existence of a Material Weakness

Report of Independent Registered Public Accounting Firm
[Standard Wording for the Introductory, Scope, Definition, and Inherent Limitations Paragraphs]
[Explanatory Paragraph]

A material weakness is a control deficiency, or combination of control deficiencies, that results in more than a remote likelihood that a material misstatement of the annual or interim financial statements will not be prevented or detected. The following material weakness has been identified and included in management's assessment. Treadron had an inadequate system for recording cash receipts, which could have prevented the Company from recording cash receipts on accounts receivable completely and properly. Therefore, cash received could have been diverted for unauthorized use, lost, or otherwise not properly recorded to accounts receivable. This material weakness was considered in determining the nature, timing, and extent of audit tests applied in our audit of the 2005 financial statements, and this report does not affect our report dated February 15, 2006, on those financial statements.

[Opinion Paragraph]

In our opinion, management's assessment that Treadron Company did not maintain effective internal control over financial reporting as of December 31, 2005, is fairly stated, in all material respects, based on criteria established in *Internal Control—Integrated Framework*, issued by the Committee of Sponsoring Organizations of the Treadway Commission (COSO). Also, in our opinion, because of the effect of the material weakness described above on the achievement of the objectives of the control criteria, Treadron Company has not maintained effective internal control over financial reporting as of December 31, 2005, based on criteria established in *Internal Control—Integrated Framework*, issued by the Committee of Sponsoring Organizations of the Treadway Commission (COSO).

Mortensen & Mortensen
Houston, Texas
February 15, 2006

of internal control, along with the auditor's opinion that the client has not maintained effective internal control over financial reporting as of the report date. Exhibit 7–5 presents sample paragraphs disclosing the required information. The paragraphs are excerpted from an audit opinion that is unqualified with respect to management's assertion and adverse with respect to the effectiveness of internal control.

It is possible for the auditor to issue an adverse opinion on internal control while at the same time issuing an unqualified opinion on the financial statement audit. Such a conclusion is reached when a client's internal control is not effective at preventing or detecting material errors, but the auditor concludes (based on substantive procedures) that the client's financial statements do not contain material misstatements.

Whether or not the auditor's opinion on the financial statements is affected by the adverse opinion on the effectiveness of internal control over financial reporting, the report on internal control over financial reporting (or the combined report) should indicate that the weakness was considered in determining the nature, timing, and extent of financial statement audit tests in the paragraph that describes the material weakness.

Qualified Report or Disclaimer for Scope Limitation

The auditor can express an unqualified opinion on management's assessment of internal control over financial reporting and an unqualified opinion on the effectiveness of internal control over financial reporting only if the auditor has been able to apply all the procedures necessary in the circumstances. If a limitation on the scope of the auditor's work occurs because of circumstances beyond the control of management or the auditor, the auditor should express a qualified opinion, disclaim an opinion, or withdraw from the engagement. The auditor's decision depends on his or her assessment of the importance of the omitted procedures to his or her ability to form an opinion on management's assessment and the effectiveness of the company's internal control. If the restrictions are imposed by management, the auditor generally should withdraw from the engagement or disclaim an opinion on management's assessment of internal control over financial reporting and the effectiveness of internal control over financial reporting.

Additional Required Communications in an Audit of Internal Control over Financial Reporting

[LO 14] The auditor has a number of communication responsibilities under AS2. The auditor must communicate in writing to management and the audit committee all significant deficiencies and material weaknesses identified during the audit. The written communication should be made prior to the issuance of the auditor's report on internal control over financial reporting. The auditor's communication should distinguish clearly between those matters considered to be significant deficiencies and those considered to be material weaknesses. If a significant deficiency or material weakness exists because the oversight by the company's audit committee is ineffective, the auditor must communicate that specific significant deficiency or material weakness in writing to the board of directors.

In addition, the auditor should communicate to management, in writing, all control deficiencies (deficiencies in internal control that are of a lesser magnitude than significant deficiencies—see Figure 7–1) identified during the audit and inform the audit committee when such a communication has been made. When making this communication, it is not necessary for the auditor to repeat information about such deficiencies that have been included in previously issued written communications, whether those communications were made by the auditor, internal auditors, or others within the organization. Furthermore, the auditor is not required to perform procedures sufficient to identify all control deficiencies; rather the auditor should communicate deficiencies in internal control over financial reporting of which he or she is aware.

The auditor's written communications should state that the communication is intended solely for the information and use of the board of directors, audit committee, management, and others within the organization. When there are requirements established by governmental authorities to furnish such reports, specific reference to such regulatory agencies may be made. These written communications also should include the definitions of control deficiencies, significant deficiencies, and material weaknesses and should clearly distinguish to which category the deficiencies being communicated belong. Because of the potential for misinterpretation of the limited degree of assurance associated with the auditor issuing a written report representing that no significant deficiencies were noted during an audit of internal control, the auditor should not make such representations.

When auditing internal control over financial reporting, the auditor may become aware of fraud or possible illegal acts. If the matter involves fraud, it must be brought to the attention of the appropriate level of management. If the fraud involves senior management, the auditor must communicate the matter directly to the audit committee. If the matter involves possible illegal acts, the auditor must assure himself or herself that the audit committee is adequately informed, unless the matter is clearly inconsequential. When timely communication is important, the auditor should communicate such matters during the course of the audit rather than at the end of the engagement. The decision to issue an interim communication should be determined based on the relative significance of the matters noted and the urgency of corrective follow-up action required.

Integrating the Audits of Internal Control and Financial Statements

[LO 15] The audits of internal control over financial reporting and of financial statements comprise what the PCAOB calls an "integrated audit." Both parts of the integrated audit must be performed by the same auditing firm, and the reports, if presented separately, must bear the same date. The audits are integrated because the results of each have implications for the other, and the audits can be performed more efficiently and effectively if done in an integrated fashion. The key point is not only does the control testing impact the planned substantive procedures but also the results of substantive procedures should be considered in the evaluation of controls—the integrated audit is an iterative process.

Effect of the Audit of Internal Control on the Financial Statement Audit

The integrated audit will in most cases lead to a reliance (as opposed to a substantive) audit strategy. As we discussed in Chapter 6, the results of controls testing have direct implications for the nature, timing, and extent of substantive procedures. If an auditor performs an integrated audit, the auditor will clearly have access to a large amount of information about the client's controls. This information can make the financial statement audit more efficient, because the auditor can rely on his or her tests of controls to reduce the extent of substantive procedures. In other words, the assurance bucket will be filled with a relatively high proportion of evidence obtained from tests of controls conducted as part of the audit of internal control. It can make the financial statement audit more effective, because information about control deficiencies helps the auditor target areas of higher risk of misstatement. If the auditor identifies a control deficiency during the audit of internal control over financial reporting, AS2 requires the auditor to determine the effect of the deficiency on the nature, timing, and extent of substantive procedures to be performed during the financial statement audit.

Regardless of the achieved level of control risk in connection with the audit of the financial statements, auditing standards require the auditor to perform some substantive procedures for all significant accounts and disclosures. These substantive procedures can consist of substantive analytical procedures or tests of details. AS2 specifically requires the auditor to perform substantive procedures to reconcile the financial statements to the accounting records and examine material adjustments made during the preparation of the financial statements. Consistent with our discussion of analytical procedures in Chapter 5, before relying on the results obtained from substantive analytical procedures, the auditor should test the effectiveness of controls over the information used as inputs or perform other procedures to support the reliability of the underlying information. When the risk of material misstatement is other than low, substantive analytical procedures alone usually are insufficient, and the auditor should plan and conduct additional substantive tests of details.

Effect of the Financial Statement Audit on the Audit of Internal Control

AS2 requires the auditor to evaluate the implications of the financial statement audit for the effectiveness of internal control over financial reporting. This evaluation includes:

- Misstatements detected.
- The auditor's risk evaluations in connection with the selection and application of substantive procedures, especially those related to fraud.
- Findings with respect to illegal acts and related party transactions.
- Indications of management bias in making accounting estimates and in selecting accounting principles.

Although misstatements detected during the financial statement audit will likely alter the auditor's judgment about the effectiveness of controls, the auditor cannot conclude that the absence of misstatements provides evidence that controls are effective (AS2, ¶157–158). In other words, misstatements are strong indicators of control deficiencies (see Table 7–7), but the PCAOB does not permit the absence of misstatements to be considered evidence that controls are effective. This latter requirement is primarily due to the fact that control deficiencies do not always result in misstatements and the PCAOB's desire that auditors test controls directly during the audit of internal control, and not reduce such tests by substituting substantive procedures performed as part of the financial statement audit.

Finally, keep in mind that the audit of internal control is intended to draw conclusions about the effectiveness of internal control over financial reporting as of a specific date. Thus, the testing performed as part of the audit of internal control may not address the entire period covered by the financial statements being audited. For example, a control over a significant account may have been modified late in the year. In such a situation, the auditor may test only the modified control for operating effectiveness. As another example, a material weakness may have existed during the period under audit but was corrected by the end of the period. Under either of these situations, for financial statement audit purposes the auditor would need to design additional tests of controls or additional substantive procedures for the period not covered by the new or corrected controls. Finally, if during the financial statement audit the auditor concludes that control risk is other than low for any relevant assertion related to a significant account, the auditor must document the effect of that conclusion on his or her opinion relating to the audit of internal control.

Advanced Module 1: Special Considerations for an Audit of Internal Control

The PCAOB specifies four areas that require special consideration by management and the auditor during an audit of internal control over financial reporting:

- Using the work of others.
- Multilocations and business units.
- Service organizations.
- Safeguarding assets.

Using the Work of Others

⚜ [LO 13]

As mentioned earlier, AS2 requires the auditor to perform enough of the testing that his or her own work provides the *principal* evidence for the auditor's opinion (AS2, ¶108). Thus, a major consideration for the external auditor is how much of the work performed by others can be relied on in adjusting the nature, timing, or extent of the auditor's work. To determine the extent to which the auditor may use the work of others, the auditor should

- Evaluate the nature of the controls subjected to the work of others.
- Evaluate the competence and objectivity of the individuals who performed the work.
- Test some of the work performed by others to evaluate the quality and effectiveness of their work.

Evaluating the Nature of the Controls Subjected to the Work of Others   In evaluating the nature of the controls tested by others, the auditor should consider the risk of material misstatement in the accounts and disclosures addressed by the control, the degree of judgment required to evaluate the operating effectiveness of the control, the pervasiveness of the control, and the potential for management override. As these factors increase in significance, the auditor should increase his or her own work on those controls and decrease reliance on the work of others. The auditor is not permitted to rely on the work of others in evaluating and testing the control environment.

Evaluating the Competence and Objectivity of Others   Chapter 5 discusses the use of internal auditors to assist the external auditor on a financial statement audit. Similar to the concepts discussed there, the extent

TABLE 7-9	Factors to Consider When Assessing the Competence and Objectivity of Others

Competence
- Their educational level and professional experience.
- Their professional certification and continuing education.
- Practices regarding the assignment of individuals to work areas.
- Supervision and review of their activities.
- Quality of the documentation of their work, including any reports or recommendations issued.
- Evaluation of their performance.

Objectivity
- The organizational status of the individuals responsible for the work of others in testing controls, including
  a. Whether the testing authority reports to an officer of sufficient status to ensure sufficient testing coverage and adequate consideration of, and action on, the findings and recommendations of the individuals performing the testing.
  b. Whether the testing authority has direct access and reports regularly to the board of directors or the audit committee.
  c. Whether the board of directors or the audit committee oversees employment decisions related to the testing authority.
- Policies to maintain the individuals' objectivity about the areas being tested, including
  a. Policies prohibiting individuals from testing controls in areas in which relatives are employed in important or internal control–sensitive positions.
  b. Policies prohibiting individuals from testing controls in areas to which they were recently assigned or are scheduled to be assigned upon completion of their controls testing responsibilities.

Source: AS2, ¶119–120.

to which the auditor uses the work of others depends on the competence and objectivity of the individuals performing the work. When evaluating the competence and objectivity of others, the auditor should consider the factors shown in Table 7–9.

Internal auditors are generally expected to have greater competence and objectivity than other company personnel, particularly if they follow the Institute of Internal Auditors' *International Standards for the Professional Practice of Internal Auditing* (see Chapter 21). If internal auditors have performed an extensive amount of relevant work and the auditor determines they possess a high degree of competence and objectivity, the auditor can rely on the results of their work to the extent possible while still providing the principal evidence for his or her opinion. A similar level of reliance by the auditor can result if the work of others is completed by a nonaffiliated public accounting firm working as a third party for management, if the firm meets AICPA or PCAOB quality control requirements.

Testing the Work of Others   The auditor should test some of the work of others to evaluate the quality and effectiveness of their work to the extent the results of such work is to be used by the auditor. The auditor's tests of others' work may be accomplished by (1) testing some of the controls that others tested or (2) testing similar controls not actually tested by others. In evaluating the quality and effectiveness of the work of others, the auditor should evaluate such factors as the scope of their work, the adequacy of their

TABLE 7–10	**Examples for Applying Guidance on the Use of the Work of Others**

Example 1. Controls over the Period-End Financial Reporting Process

Controls over the period-end financial reporting process address significant risks of misstatement of the accounts and disclosures in the annual and quarterly financial statements. These controls usually (1) require significant judgment to evaluate their operating effectiveness, (2) have a higher potential for management override, and (3) may affect accounts that require a high level of judgment or estimation.

Therefore, for controls over the period-end financial reporting process, the auditor might determine that he or she will perform more of the tests of those controls. Because of the nature of these controls, the auditor should use the work of others only if the degree of competence and objectivity of the others is high. Thus, the auditor might use the work of internal auditors to some extent but not the work of others within the company.

Example 2. Controls over the Calculation of Depreciation of Fixed Assets

Controls over the calculation of depreciation of fixed assets are usually not pervasive. Also, they normally involve a low degree of judgment in evaluating their operating effectiveness and can be subjected to objective testing. If these conditions describe the controls over the calculation of depreciation of fixed assets and if there is a low potential for management override, the auditor could determine that he or she could use the work of others to a large extent (perhaps entirely) so long as the degree of competence and objectivity of the individuals performing the test is at an appropriate level.

Source: AS2, ¶126, adapted.

work programs, the adequacy of the work performed (including evidence of supervision and review), the appropriateness of their conclusions, and the consistency of their reports with the work performed (AS2, ¶125).

Table 7–10 provides two examples of how the auditor might apply this guidance for using the work of others.

Testing Internal Control When a Company Has Multiple Locations or Business Units

❧ **[LO 16]**

A major issue faced by the auditor and management in performing an audit of internal control over financial reporting is to determine the locations or business units that should be subjected to testing. In making this decision, the auditor should evaluate the relative financial significance of the client's locations and the risk of material misstatement arising from them. Figure 7–4 presents a flowchart that provides guidance to the auditor and management in choosing which locations or business units to test. The assumption in this figure is that the entity has 150 locations or business units.

Locations or Business Units That Are Financially Significant

The auditor should first identify the locations or business units that are individually important. Because of the importance of financially significant locations or business units, the auditor should evaluate management's documentation of and perform tests of controls over all relevant assertions related to significant accounts and disclosures at each financially significant location or business unit. Generally, a relatively small number of locations or business units will encompass a large portion of a company's operations and financial position. In determining the scope at the individual locations or business units, the auditor should evaluate each entity's involvement, if any, with a central processing or shared service environment. Thus, in Figure 7–4, of the company's 150 locations or business units, only 15 are judged to be individually important.

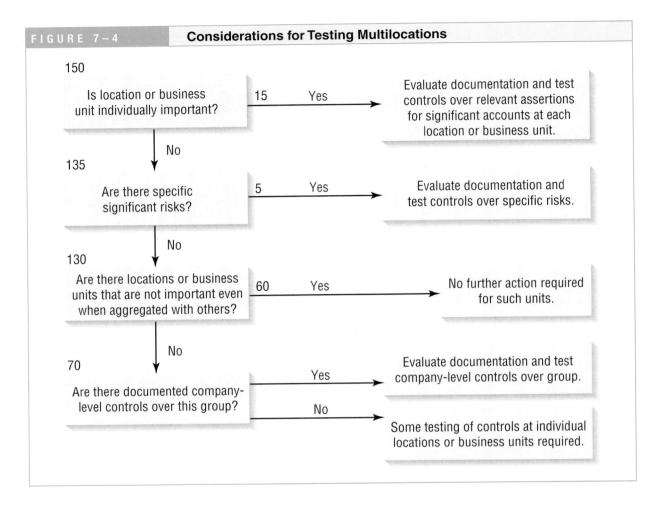

FIGURE 7-4   **Considerations for Testing Multilocations**

Locations or Business Units That Involve Specific Risks

For locations or business units that contain specific risks that, by themselves, could create a material misstatement, the auditor should evaluate their documentation of controls and test controls over the specific risks. The auditor does not need to test controls over all relevant assertions related to all significant accounts at these locations or business units. An example of a business unit that might involve a specific risk would be a business unit responsible for foreign exchange trading. While the relative financial significance of such transactions may be low, such a business unit could expose the company to the risk of material misstatement. In Figure 7–4, the company has five business units that have specific risk and therefore should be tested. This leaves 130 locations or business units remaining.

Locations or Business Units That Are Significant Only When Aggregated with Other Locations and Business Units

Next, the auditor should determine the other locations or business units that, when aggregated, represent a group with a level of financial significance that could create a material misstatement in the financial statements. In Figure 7–4,

70 locations or business units are financially significant in aggregate. For that group, the auditor should determine whether company-level controls are in place. Company-level controls are controls management has in place to provide assurance that appropriate controls exist throughout the organization. The auditor should perform tests of company-level controls to determine whether such controls are designed and operating effectively. However, testing company-level controls is not a substitute for the auditor's testing of controls over a large portion of the company's operations or financial position. A high level of financial significance of this group of business units could create a greater than remote risk of material misstatement of the financial statements. In such a case, the auditor might conclude that he or she needs to visit some or all of the business units in order to evaluate the operating effectiveness of such controls.

If management does not have company-level controls operating at these locations or business units, the auditor should determine the nature, timing, and extent of procedures to be performed at each location, business unit, or combination of locations and business units. Table 7–11 shows the factors that the auditor should evaluate when determining the locations or business units to visit and the controls to test.

Locations and Business Units That Do Not Require Testing No further work is necessary on the remaining locations or businesses, provided that they are not able to create, either individually or in the aggregate, a material misstatement in the financial statements. In Figure 7–4, there are 60 locations or business units that require no further actions.

Use of Service Organizations ❧ **[LO 17]**

Many companies use service organizations to process transactions. If the service organization's services make up part of a company's information system, then they are part of the information and communication component of the company's internal control over financial reporting. Management

TABLE 7–11	**Factors That the Auditor Should Evaluate When Determining the Locations or Business Units to Visit and the Controls to Test**

- The relative financial significance of each location or business unit.
- The risk of material misstatement arising from each location or business unit.
- The similarity of business operations and internal control over financial reporting at the various locations or business units.
- The degree of centralization of processes and financial reporting applications.
- The effectiveness of the control environment, particularly management's direct control over the exercise of authority delegated to others and its ability to effectively supervise activities at the various locations or business units. An ineffective control environment over locations or business units might constitute a material weakness.
- The nature and amount of transactions executed and related assets at the various locations or business units.
- The potential for material unrecognized obligations to exist at a location or business unit and the degree to which the location or business unit could create an obligation on the part of the company.
- Management's risk assessment process and analysis for excluding a location or business unit from its assessment of internal control over financial reporting.

Source: AS2, ¶B10.

should consider the activities of the service organization in making its assessment of internal control over financial reporting.

Management and the auditor should perform the following procedures with respect to the activities performed by the service organization: (1) obtain an understanding of the controls at the service organization that are relevant to the entity's internal control and the controls at the user organization over the activities of the service organization and (2) obtain evidence that the controls that are relevant to management's assessment and the auditor's opinion are operating effectively.

Evidence about the operating effectiveness of controls that are relevant to management's assessment and the auditor's opinion may be obtained by performing tests of the user organization's controls over the activities of the service organization, performing tests of controls at the service organization, or obtaining a service auditor's report on the design and operating effectiveness of controls placed in operation at the service organization. If a service auditor's report on controls placed in operation and tests of operating effectiveness is available, management and the auditor may evaluate whether this report provides sufficient evidence to support the assessment and opinion. Important factors that management and the auditor should consider include the time period covered by the tests of controls and its relation to the date of management's assessment, the scope of the examination, the controls tested and the way in which tested controls relate to the company's controls, the results of those tests of controls, and the service auditor's opinion on the operating effectiveness of the controls. In determining whether the service auditor's report provides sufficient evidence to support management's assessment and the auditor's opinion, management and the auditor should make inquiries concerning the service auditor's reputation, competence, and independence.

When a significant period of time has elapsed between the time period covered by the tests of controls in the service auditor's report and the date of management's assessment, additional procedures should be performed. For example, the auditor should inquire of management to determine whether it has identified any changes in the service organization's controls subsequent to the period covered by the service auditor's report. If changes have occurred, the auditor should determine whether management has performed procedures to evaluate the effect of such changes. The auditor should then determine whether to obtain additional evidence about the operating effectiveness of controls at the service organization. In making this decision, the auditor should consider the results of relevant procedures performed by management or the auditor, how much time has passed since the service auditor's report, the significance of the activities of the service organization, whether errors have been identified in the service organization's processing, and the nature and significance of any changes in the service organization's controls. As these factors increase in significance, the need for the auditor to obtain additional evidence increases.

If the auditor concludes that additional evidence about the operating effectiveness of controls at the service organization is required, the auditor should perform additional procedures. For example, the auditor might investigate whether management has taken actions to monitor or evaluate the quality of the service provider and evaluate the results of such actions. The auditor might also contact the service organization to obtain specific information, or request that a service auditor be engaged to perform procedures that will supply the necessary information. Finally, the auditor might even visit the service organization and perform such procedures firsthand. Based on the evidence obtained, management and the auditor should determine whether they have obtained sufficient evidence to obtain the reasonable assurance necessary for their assessment and opinion, respectively.

Safeguarding of Assets

[LO 18]

Safeguarding of assets is defined in AS2 as policies and procedures that "provide reasonable assurance regarding prevention or timely detection of unauthorized acquisition, use or disposition of the company's assets that could have a material effect on the financial statements." This definition is consistent with the definition in the COSO report. For example, a company could have safeguarding controls over inventory tags (preventive controls) and also perform timely periodic physical inventory counts (detective control) for its quarterly and annual financial reporting dates. Given that the definitions of material weakness and significant deficiency relate to the likelihood of misstatement of the financial statements, the failure of the inventory tag control will not result in a significant deficiency or material weakness if the physical inventory count prevents a misstatement of the financial statements. Therefore, the COSO definition indicates that although losses might occur, controls over financial reporting are effective if they provide reasonable assurance that those losses are properly reflected in the financial statements.

Advanced Module 2: Computer–Assisted Audit Techniques[1]

[LO 19]

Computer-assisted audit techniques (CAATs) generally assist the auditor in testing application controls. Many of these controls are embedded into the client's computer programs. Additionally, the auditor may need to use CAATs to execute substantive procedures when the information is maintained in machine-readable form. The following types of CAATs are discussed:

- Generalized audit software
- Custom audit software
- Test data

Other techniques (parallel simulation, integrated test facility, and concurrent auditing techniques) are discussed in advanced IT auditing books.[2]

---

[1]For more information on computer-assisted audit techniques, see American Institute of Certified Public Accountants, *Auditing with Computers* (Auditing Practice Release) (New York: AICPA, 1994).

[2]For example, see J. D. Warren, Jr., L. W. Edelson, X. L. Parker, and R. M. Thurun, *Handbook of IT Auditing* (Boston, MA: RIA Group/WG&L, 1998).

TABLE 7–12	Functions Performed by Generalized Audit Software	
	Function	*Description*
	File or database access	Reads and extracts data from a client's computer files or databases for further audit testing.
	Selection operators	Select from files or databases transactions that meet certain criteria.
	Arithmetic functions	Perform a variety of arithmetic calculations (addition, subtraction, and so on) on transactions, files, and databases.
	Statistical analyses	Provide functions supporting various types of audit sampling.
	Report generation	Prepares various types of documents and reports.

Generalized Audit Software

Generalized audit software (GAS) includes programs that allow the auditor to perform tests on computer files and databases. ACL, which is packaged with this book, is an example of a GAS program. GAS was developed so that auditors would be able to conduct similar computer-assisted audit techniques in different IT environments. For example, GAS permits an auditor to select and prepare accounts receivable confirmations from a variety of computer systems. This type of software provides a high-level computer language that allows the auditor to easily perform various functions on a client's computer files and databases. A sample of functions that can be performed by GAS is shown in Table 7–12.

The following steps are completed by the auditor in a typical GAS application. An accounts receivable application is used as an example.

1. Set the objectives of the application:
   - Test the mathematical accuracy of the accounts receivable subsidiary database.
   - Select for confirmation all accounts receivable customer accounts with balances greater than $10,000 plus a random sample of 50 accounts with balances less than $10,000.
   - Print out the confirmation and monthly statement for all selected customer accounts.
2. Design the application:
   - Identify the data structures used in the database.
   - Specify the format for the confirmation.
3. Code the instructions for the application:
   - Prepare the GAS specification sheets or enter the code directly into the GAS for the confirmation application.
4. Process the application:
   - Access the client's accounts receivable database with the GAS. Generally, a work file is extracted from the database for processing on the GAS.
5. Evaluate the results of the application:
   - Verify the output that tested the mathematical accuracy of the accounts receivable subsidiary ledger database.
   - Review the confirmations and monthly statements.
   - Mail confirmations and monthly statements to customers.

GAS offers several advantages: (1) it is easy to use, (2) limited IT expertise or programming skills are required, (3) the time required to develop the application is usually short, and (4) an entire population can be examined, eliminating the need for sampling in some instances. Among the disadvantages of GAS are that (1) it involves auditing *after* the client has processed the data rather than while the data is being processed, (2) it provides a limited ability to verify programming logic because its application is usually directed to testing client files or databases, and (3) it is limited to audit procedures that can be conducted on data available in electronic form.

Custom Audit Software

Custom audit software is generally written by auditors for specific audit tasks. Such programs are necessary when the entity's computer system is not compatible with the auditor's GAS or when the auditor wants to conduct some testing that may not be possible with the GAS. It may also be more efficient to prepare custom programs if they will be used in future audits of the entity or if they may be used on similar engagements. The major disadvantages of custom software are that (1) it is expensive to develop, (2) it may require a long development time, and (3) it may require extensive modification if the client changes its accounting application programs.

Inventory observation and testing provide a good example of where such a program might be useful. Suppose a client maintains computerized perpetual inventory records that are updated by the sales and purchasing systems. Further assume that the client conducts a physical inventory count once a year, at which time the perpetual records are corrected. At the time of the physical inventory count, the client's employees record the physical counts on special computer forms that are optically scanned to create a physical inventory file. The quantities on hand are priced using an approved price file. What results from this analysis is the inventory balance used for updating the perpetual records and the financial statements.

The auditors who observe the client's physical inventory count record the results on special computer forms that are optically scanned and used as input to the custom program. The custom program performs the following audit procedures: (1) traces the test counts into the client's perpetual inventory file and print out any exceptions; (2) performs a complete mathematical test, including extensions, footings, crossfootings, and use of approved prices; (3) summarizes the inventory by type; and (4) prints out items in excess of a predetermined amount for review.

Test Data

The auditor uses test data for testing the application controls in the client's computer programs. In using this method, the auditor first creates a set of simulated data (that is, test data) for processing. The data should include both valid and invalid data. After calculating the expected results of processing the test data, the auditor uses the client's computer and application programs to process the data. The valid data should be properly processed, while the invalid data should be identified as errors. The results of this processing are compared to the auditor's predetermined results. This technique can be used to check

- Data validation controls and error detection routines.
- Processing logic controls.

- Arithmetic calculations.
- The inclusion of transactions in records, files, and reports.

The objective of using the test data method is to ensure the accuracy of the computer processing of transactions.

The main advantage of the test data method is that it provides direct evidence on the effectiveness of the controls included in the client's application programs. However, the test data method has a number of potential disadvantages. First, it can be very time-consuming to create the test data. Second, the auditor may not be certain that all relevant conditions or controls are tested. The use of special computer programs called *test data generators* may help alleviate these potential disadvantages. Third, the auditor must be certain that the test data are processed using the client's regular production programs. This concern can be alleviated if the client's general controls for program changes, access, and library functions are reliable. Last, the auditor must be sure to remove the valid test data from the client's files.

KEY TERMS

Company-level controls. Controls that can have a pervasive effect on the entity's ability to meet the control criteria selected by management.

Control deficiency. A control whether by *design* or *operation* that does not allow management or employees, in the normal course of performing their assigned functions, to prevent or detect misstatements on a timely basis.

Internal control. A process designed by, or under the supervision of, the company's principal executive and principal financial officers, or persons performing similar functions, and effected by the company's board of directors, management, and other personnel, to provide reasonable assurance regarding the reliability of financial reporting and the preparation of financial statements for external purposes in accordance with generally accepted accounting principles.

Material weakness. A significant deficiency, or combination of significant deficiencies, that results in more than a *remote likelihood* that a *material* misstatement of the annual or interim financial statements will not be prevented or detected.

Relevant assertions. Assertions that have a meaningful bearing on whether the account is fairly stated.

Safeguarding of assets. Those policies and procedures that provide reasonable assurance regarding prevention or timely detection of unauthorized acquisition, use, or disposition of the company's assets that could have a material effect on the financial statements.

Significant account. An account that has more than a remote likelihood of containing misstatements that individually, or when aggregated with others, could have a material effect on the financial statements

Significant deficiency. A control deficiency, or combination of control deficiencies, that adversely affects the entity's ability to initiate, authorize, record, process, or report external financial data reliably in accordance with generally accepted accounting principles such that there is more than a *remote likelihood* that a misstatement of the entity's annual or interim financial statements that is more than *inconsequential* will not be prevented or detected.

Walkthrough. A transaction being traced by an auditor from origination through the entity's information system until it is reflected in the entity's financial reports. It encompasses the entire process of initiating, authorizing, recording, processing, and reporting individual transactions and controls for each of the significant processes identified.

www.mhhe.com/ messier4e	Visit the book's Online Learning Center for a multiple-choice quiz that will allow you to assess your understanding of chapter concepts.

REVIEW QUESTIONS

[LO1,2] 7-1 Briefly summarize management's and the auditor's basic responsibilities under Section 404 of the Sarbanes-Oxley Act of 2002.

[4] 7-2 Discuss how the terms *likelihood* and *magnitude* play a role in evaluating the significance of a control deficiency.

[5] 7-3 The first element in management's process for assessing the effectiveness of internal control is determining which controls should be tested. Identify the controls that would typically be tested by management.

[6] 7-4 Management must document its assessment of internal control. What would such documentation include?

[8] 7-5 List the steps in the auditor's process for an audit of internal control over financial reporting.

[8] 7-6 Describe how the auditor should identify the significant processes and major classes of transactions.

[8] 7-7 The period-end financial reporting process controls are always considered significant. What are those controls and what should the auditor's evaluation of those controls include?

[8] 7-8 A walkthrough involves tracing a transaction through the information system. What type of evidence does a walkthrough provide to the auditor?

[4,8] 7-9 AS2 indicates that certain circumstances should be regarded as at least significant deficiencies and as strong indicators of a material weakness. What are these circumstances, and why do you think the PCAOB assessed them as being of such importance?

[9] 7-10 How does the auditor evaluate the competence and objectivity of others who perform work for management?

[11] 7-11 What are the auditor's documentation requirements for an audit of internal control over financial reporting?

[13] 7-12 What are the types of reports that an auditor can issue for an audit of internal control over financial reporting? Briefly identify the circumstances justifying each type of report.

[16] 7-13 Describe how the auditor decides which locations or business units to test.

[17]   7-14   What should the auditor do when a significant period of time has elapsed between the service organization auditor's report and the date of management's assessment?

[19]   7-15   Distinguish between generalized and custom audit software. List the functions that can be performed by generalized audit software.

MULTIPLE-CHOICE QUESTIONS

[1,2]   7-16   The Sarbanes-Oxley Act of 2002 requires management to include a report on internal control in the entity's annual report. It also requires auditors to attest to management's internal control assertion. Which of the following statements concerning these requirements is false?

a. The auditor should evaluate whether internal controls are effective in accurately and fairly reflecting the firm's transactions.

b. Management's report should state its responsibility for establishing and maintaining an adequate internal control system.

c. Management should identify material weaknesses in its report.

d. The auditor should provide recommendations for improving internal control in the attestation report.

[4]   7-17   Which of the following statements concerning control deficiencies is true?

a. The auditor should communicate to management, in writing, all control deficiencies in internal control identified during the audit.

b. All significant deficiencies are material weaknesses.

c. All control deficiencies are significant deficiencies.

d. An auditor must immediately report material weaknesses and significant deficiencies discovered during an audit to the PCAOB.

[4]   7-18   A control deviation caused by an employee performing a control procedure that he or she is not authorized to perform is always considered a

a. Deficiency in design.

b. Deficiency in operation.

c. Significant deficiency.

d. Material weakness.

[4]   7-19   Which of the following is not a factor that might affect the *likelihood* that a control deficiency could result in a misstatement in an account balance?

a. The susceptibility of the related assets or liability to loss or fraud.

b. The interaction or relationship of the control with other controls.

c. The financial statement amounts exposed to the deficiency.

d. The nature of the financial statement accounts, disclosures, and assertions involved.

[4]   7-20   Significant deficiencies and material weaknesses must be communicated to an entity's audit committee because they represent

a. Materials fraud or illegal acts perpetrated by high-level management.

b. Disclosures of information that significantly contradict the auditor's going concern assumption.

    c. Significant deficiencies in the design or operation of internal control.

    d. Potential manipulation or falsification of accounting records.

[8]   7-21 Company-level controls can have a pervasive effect on the entity's ability to meet the control criteria. Which one of the following is not a company-level control?

    a. Controls to monitor results of operations.

    b. Management's risk assessment process.

    c. Controls to monitor the inventory taking process.

    d. The period-end financial reporting process.

[8]   7-22 Which of the following controls would most likely be tested during an interim period?

    a. Controls over nonroutine transactions.

    b. Controls over the period-end financial reporting process.

    c. Controls that operate on a continuous basis.

    d. Controls over transactions that involve a high degree of subjectivity.

[8]   7-23 Auditing Standard 2 requires an auditor to perform a walkthrough as part of the internal control audit. A walkthrough requires an auditor to

    a. Tour the organization's facilities and locations before beginning any audit work.

    b. Trace a transaction from every class of transaction from origination through the company's information system until it is reflected in the company's financial reports.

    c. Trace a transaction from every class of transaction from origination through the company's information system.

    d. Trace a transaction from each major class of transaction from origination through the company's information system until it is reflected in the company's financial reports.

[8]   7-24 Regarding the evaluation of whether controls over a large portion of a company's operations or financial position have been tested, the auditor should make his or her decision at the

    a. Individual significant account level.

    b. Overall company level.

    c. Subsidiary level.

    d. Individual financial statement level.

[8]   7-25 When auditors report on the effectiveness of internal control "as of" a specific date and obtain evidence about the operating effectiveness of controls at an interim date, which of the following items would be the least helpful in evaluating the additional evidence to gather for the remaining period?

    a. Any significant changes that occurred in internal control subsequent to the interim date.

    b. The length of the remaining period.

    c. The specific controls tested prior to the as of date and the results of those tests.

    d. The size of the sample used to test the control at the interim date.

[13] 7-26 If management makes an adverse assessment of internal control because of a material weakness (i.e., "internal control over financial

reporting is not effective") and the auditor agrees with the assessment, the auditor would issue

a. An adverse opinion.

b. An unqualified opinion on management's assessment and an adverse opinion on the operating effectiveness of internal control over financial reporting.

c. A disclaimer.

d. An adverse opinion on management's assessment and an unqualified opinion on the operating effectiveness of internal control over financial reporting.

[16] 7-27 In multilocation testing, if a location is not determined to be individually significant but may still present specific risks of a material misstatement, and if documented company-level controls exist, what work would the auditor do at that location?

a. Evaluate documentation and test controls over specific risks.

b. No further action required for such units.

c. Evaluate documentation and test company-level controls over this group.

d. Selectively test controls at that location.

[19] 7-28 Which of the following most likely represents a weakness in internal control of an IT system?

a. The systems analyst reviews output and controls the distribution of output from the IT department.

b. The accounts payable clerk prepares data for computer processing and enters the data into the computer.

c. The systems programmer designs the operating and control functions of programs and participates in testing operating systems.

d. The control clerk establishes control over data received by the IT department and reconciles control totals after processing.

[19] 7-29 A primary advantage of using generalized audit software packages to audit the financial statements of a client that uses an IT system is that the auditor may

a. Consider increasing the use of substantive tests of transactions in place of analytical procedures.

b. Substantiate the accuracy of data through self-checking digits and hash totals.

c. Reduce the level of required tests of controls to a relatively small amount.

d. Access information stored on computer files while having a limited understanding of the client's hardware and software features.

PROBLEMS

[8] 7-30 Following are three examples of controls for accounts that you have determined are significant for the audit of internal control over financial reporting. For each control, determine the nature, timing, and extent of testing of the design and operating effectiveness. Refer to Exhibit 7–1 for a way to format your answer.

Control 1. Monthly Manual Reconciliation: Through discussions with company personnel and review of company documentation, you find that company personnel reconcile the accounts receivable subsidiary ledger to the general ledger on a monthly basis. To determine whether misstatements in accounts receivable (existence, valuation, and completeness) would be detected on a timely basis, you decide to test the control provided by the monthly reconciliation process.

Control 2. Daily Manual Preventive Control: Through discussions with company personnel, you learn that company personnel make a cash disbursement only after they have matched the vendor invoice to the receiver and purchase order. To determine whether misstatements in cash (existence) and accounts payable (existence, valuation, and completeness) would be prevented on a timely basis, you decide to test the control over making a cash disbursement only after matching the invoice with the receiver and purchase.

Control 3. Programmed Preventive Control and Weekly Information Technology–Dependent Manual Detective Control: Through discussions with company personnel, you learn that the company's computer system performs a three-way match of the receiving report, purchase order, and invoice. If there are any exceptions, the system produces a list of unmatched items that employees review and follow up on weekly. The computer match is a programmed application control, and the review and follow-up of the unmatched items report is a manual detective control. To determine whether misstatements in cash (existence) and accounts payable–inventory (existence, valuation, and completeness) would be prevented or detected on a timely basis, you decide to test the programmed application control of matching the receiver, purchase order, and invoice, as well as the review and follow-up control over unmatched items.

[4,8] 7-31 Following are examples of control deficiencies that may represent significant deficiencies or material weaknesses. For each control deficiency, indicate whether it is a significant deficiency or material weakness. Justify your decision.

a. The company uses a standard sales contract for most transactions. Individual sales transactions are not material to the entity. Sales personnel are allowed to modify sales contract terms. The company's accounting function reviews significant or unusual modifications to the sales contract terms, but does not review changes in the standard shipping terms. The changes in the standard shipping terms could require a delay in the timing of revenue recognition. Management reviews gross margins on a monthly basis and investigates any significant or unusual relationships. In addition, management reviews the reasonableness of inventory levels at the end of each accounting period. The entity has experienced limited situations in which revenue has been inappropriately recorded in advance of shipment, but amounts have not been material.

b. The company has a standard sales contract, but sales personnel frequently modify the terms of the contract. The nature of the modifications can affect the timing and amount of revenue recognized. Individual sales transactions are frequently material to the entity, and the gross margin can vary significantly for each transaction. The company does not have procedures in place for the accounting function to regularly review modifications to sales contract terms. Although management reviews gross margins on a monthly basis, the significant differences in gross margins on individual transactions make it difficult for management to identify potential misstatements. Improper revenue recognition has occurred, and the amounts have been material.

c. The company has a standard sales contract, but sales personnel frequently modify the terms of the contract. Sales personnel frequently grant unauthorized and unrecorded sales discounts to customers without the knowledge of the accounting department. These amounts are deducted by customers in paying their invoices and are recorded as outstanding balances on the accounts receivable–aging. Although these amounts are individually insignificant, when added up they are material and have occurred regularly over the past few years.

[4,8]   **7-32**   Following are examples of control deficiencies that may represent significant deficiencies or material weaknesses. For each of the following scenarios, indicate whether the deficiency is a significant deficiency or material weakness. Justify your decision.

a. During its assessment of internal control over financial reporting, the management of Lorenz Corporation and its auditors identified the following control deficiencies that individually represent significant deficiencies:

- Inadequate segregation of duties over certain information system access controls.
- Several instances of transactions that were not properly recorded in subsidiary ledgers; transactions were not material, either individually or in the aggregate.
- A lack of timely reconciliations of the account balances affected by the improperly recorded transactions.

b. During its assessment of internal control over financial reporting, management of First Coast BankCorp and its auditors identified the following deficiencies that individually represent significant deficiencies: the design of controls over the estimation of credit losses (a critical accounting estimate); the operating effectiveness of controls for initiating, processing, and reviewing adjustments to the allowance for credit losses; and the operating effectiveness of controls designed to prevent and detect the improper recognition of interest income. In addition, during the past year, First Coast experienced a significant level of growth in the loan balances that were subjected to the controls governing credit loss estimation and revenue recognition, and further growth is expected in the upcoming year.

[4,13]   **7-33**   For each of the following independent situations, indicate the type of report on internal control over financial reporting you would issue. Justify your report choice.

a. Johnson Company's management does not have an adequate antifraud program or controls.

    b. Tap, Tap, & Associates completed the integrated audit of Maxim Corporation. It did not identify any control deficiencies during their audit.

    c. During the audit of Fritz, Inc., Boyd & Company discovered a material misstatement that was not discovered by Fritz's internal control system.

    d. Scoles Manufacturing Company does not have adequate controls over nonroutine sales transactions.

    e. Lee, Leis, & Monk (LL&M) performs the audit of Freedom Insurance Company. LL&M has determined that Freedom has an ineffective regulatory compliance function.

[4,13]　7-34　For each of the following independent situations, indicate the type of report on internal control over financial reporting you would issue. Justify your report choice.

    a. Hansen, Inc., has restated previously issued financial statements to reflect the correction of a misstatement.

    b. Shu & Han Engineering does not have effective oversight of the company's external financial reporting.

    c. Kim Semiconductor has an ineffective audit committee.

    d. The internal audit function at Smith Components, a very large manufacturing company, was ineffective. The company's auditor has determined that the internal audit function needed to be effective in order for the company to have an effective monitoring component.

    e. The auditors of Benron identified significant financial statement fraud by the company's chief financial officer.

    f. Conroy Trucking Company has an ineffective control environment.

    g. Edwards & Eddins, CPAs, communicated significant deficiencies to Waste Disposal's management and the audit committee for the last two years. At the end of the current year, these significant deficiencies remain uncorrected.

[4,13]　7-35　For each of the following independent situations, indicate the type of report on internal control over financial reporting you would issue. Justify your report choice.

    a. The auditor of Burns Security Systems has determined that management's process for assessing internal control over financial reporting is inadequate.

    b. The management's report on internal control over financial reporting issued by Graham Granary, Inc., includes disclosures about corrective actions taken by the company after the date of management's assessment and the company's plans to implement new controls.

    c. Meryll Company's management identified a material weakness prior to the as of date and implemented controls to correct it. Management believes that the new controls have been operating for a sufficient period of time to determine that they are designed and operating effectively. However, Meryll's auditor disagrees with the sufficiency of the time period for testing the operating effectiveness of the controls.

[4,13]　7-36　Assume that scenario *a* in Problem 7-33 is a material weakness. Prepare a draft of the auditor's report for an audit of internal control

over financial reporting. Assume that Lorenz's auditor is issuing a separate report on internal control.

[4,13] 7-37 Assume that scenario *b* in Problem 7-33 is a material weakness. Prepare a draft of the auditor's report for an audit of internal control over financial reporting. Assume that First Coast's auditor is issuing a combined report for the financial statement audit and audit of internal control.

[19] 7-38 Auditors use various audit techniques to gather evidence when a client's accounting information is processed using IT. Select the audit procedure from the following list and enter it in the appropriate place on the grid.

Audit procedure:
1. Test data method
2. Custom audit software
3. Auditing around the computer
4. Generalized audit software

Description of Audit Technique	Audit Technique
a. Program written by the auditor to perform a specific task for a particular client	
b. The auditor's auditing of the inputs and outputs of the system without verification of the processing of the data	
c. Processing fictitious and real data separately through the client's IT system	

[19] 7-39 Brown, CPA, is auditing the financial statements of Big Z Wholesaling, Inc., a continuing audit client, for the year ended January 31, 2005. On January 5, 2005, Brown observed the tagging and counting of Big Z's physical inventory and made appropriate test counts. These test counts have been recorded on a computer file. As in prior years, Big Z gave Brown two computer files. One file represents the perpetual inventory (first-in, first-out) records for the year ended January 31, 2005. The other file represents the January 5 physical inventory count.

Assume:
1. Brown issued an unqualified opinion on the prior year's financial statements.
2. All inventory is purchased for resale and located in a single warehouse.
3. Brown has appropriate computerized audit software.
4. The perpetual inventory file contains the following information in item number sequence:
   a. Beginning balances at February 1, 2004: item number, item description, total quantity, and price.
   b. For each item purchased during the year: date received, receiving report number, vendor item number, item description, quantity, and total dollar amount.

   c. For each item sold during the year: date shipped, invoice number, item number, item description, quantity, and dollar amount.
   d. For each item adjusted for physical inventory count differences: date, item number, item description, quantity, and dollar amount.
5. The physical inventory file contains the following information in item number sequence: tag number, item number, item description, and count quantity.

Required:
Describe the substantive auditing procedures Brown may consider performing with computerized audit software using Big Z's two computer files and Brown's computer file of test counts. The substantive auditing procedures described may indicate the reports to be printed out for Brown's follow-up by subsequent application of manual procedures. Do *not* describe subsequent manual auditing procedures.
   Group the procedures by those using (a) the perpetual inventory file and (b) the physical inventory and test count files.

INTERNET ASSIGNMENTS

[4,13] 7-40 Search the Internet (e.g., a company's website or sec.gov), and find an audit report for a company's audit of internal control over financial reporting. Determine whether the company used the combined or separate format.

[4,13] 7-41 Search the Internet (e.g., a company's website or sec.gov), and see if you can find an audit report for a company's audit of internal control over financial reporting that expresses an adverse opinion with respect to the effectiveness of internal control.

www.mhhe.com/ messier4e	Visit the book's Online Learning Center for problem material to be completed using the *ACL* software packaged with your new text.

Part IV

STATISTICAL AND NONSTATISTICAL SAMPLING TOOLS FOR AUDITING

LEARNING OBJECTIVES

Upon completion of this chapter you will

[1] Learn the definition of audit sampling.

[2] Understand basic sampling terminology.

[3] Learn the types of audit procedures that do and do not involve sampling.

[4] Learn the types of audit sampling.

[5] Learn the sampling requirements in auditing standards.

[6] Learn how to apply attribute sampling to tests of controls.

[7] Work through an example of attribute sampling.

[8] Learn how to apply nonstatistical sampling to tests of controls.

RELEVANT ACCOUNTING AND AUDITING PRONOUNCEMENTS

AICPA, *Audit Sampling* (Audit Guide) (New York: AICPA, 2001)

AU 311, Planning and Supervision

AU 312, Audit Risk and Materiality in Conducting an Audit

AU 319, Consideration of Internal Control in a Financial Statement Audit

AU 316, Consideration of Fraud in a Financial Statement Audit

AU 350, Audit Sampling

Audit Sampling: An Overview and Application to Tests of Controls

Major Phases of an Audit

Client acceptance/
continuance and establishing
engagement terms
(Chapter 5)

Preplanning
(Chapter 5)

Establish materiality
and assess risks
(Chapter 3)

Plan the audit
(Chapters 3 and 5)

Consider and audit
internal control
(Chapters 6 and 7)

Audit business processes
and related accounts
(e.g. revenue generation)
(Chapters 10–16)

Complete the audit
(Chapter 17)

Evaluate results and issue audit
report (Chapters 2 and 18)

In the next two chapters we examine how auditors apply sampling theory to gather evidence to confirm or disconfirm management's assertions. Sampling and statistics in general are topics that make many people feel uncomfortable. Before getting into technical audit sampling and statistical terms, we have found that it is useful for students to consider some of the basic concepts of sampling in a nontechnical context.

What If You Were an Apple Inspector?

Please imagine that you have just taken a job as an apple inspector for Best Apples, Inc.—a large apple grower. You are replacing a previous inspector who was recently fired for lack of due care, and your new employer has made it clear that you must meet high performance standards to make it through your probationary period. Best Apples owns and operates many apple orchards and sells its apples to major fruit processors (hereafter "buyers") whose products include fresh apples, apple sauce, and apple juice. Best Apple makes large shipments of apples to buyers on a daily basis during harvest season; each shipment contains approximately 1,500 bushels from various orchards. Each bushel contains 100 to 150 apples. The bushel indicates which orchard the apples came from. Your job is to manually inspect the quality of apples just prior to shipment. Obviously, there is neither the time nor need to inspect every apple, so you will examine a sample of apples.

Imagine it is your first day on the job; consider for a moment what information about the apples, your employer, or the buyer, you would like to know before you begin your inspections?

Among other things, before beginning your inspection, it would be useful to know the answers to the following questions:

- For what purpose will the current shipment be used (e.g., fresh apples, sauce, or juice)?
- The definition of a defect—what constitutes a bad apple?
- Tolerable defect percentage—what percentage of defective apples will the buyers accept in a shipment?
- What has Best Apple's historical defect percentage been?
- Have growing conditions (e.g., weather, pests) been normal this year?
- What happens if we send a shipment that contains an unacceptably high percentage of defects?
- Level of assurance or confidence—how confident do I need to be in my testing results?
- What quality controls and processes does Best Apples have in place?
- Are the defect percentages the same for all orchards?

Suppose you receive satisfactory answers to these questions and you begin your testing. The primary purpose of sampling is to draw inferences about the whole population based on the results of testing only a subset of the population. You draw a sample of 20 apples and find 1 defective apple. Projecting your sample defect rate to the total population suggests a shipment defect rate of 5 percent ($1/20$). While 5 percent is your best estimate based on your sample results, will you be positive that you have determined the correct defect rate for the entire shipment? The obvious answer is no, because there is a chance the shipment defect rate could be higher or lower than your sample rate of 5 percent. The uncertainty associated with sampling is known as *sampling risk*. Whenever inspectors or auditors test less than the entire population, there is a risk that the sample results will not be similar to what the results would be if the inspector were to test the entire population. In other words, sampling risk is the risk that the results of a sample are not representative of the population.

Sampling theory allows us to measure the risk associated with sampling. For example, if we knew a buyer would accept up to 10 percent defective apples in a shipment, we can compute the risk that the actual shipment defect rate is higher than 10 percent. For a sample of 20 apples with 1 defective apple there is approximately a 40 percent chance that the actual shipment defect rate exceeds the buyer's tolerable defect rate of 10 percent. Inspectors and auditors can reduce sampling risk by taking larger samples. In the extreme, if you tested 100 percent of the apples in shipment, then there would be no sampling risk because you would know with certainty the true shipment defect rate. While it would not be economical for you to inspect every apple, you could increase your sample size to reduce the risk that the shipment will contain an unacceptably high rate of defects. If you examine a sample of 100 apples and find 5 defects, sampling theory indicates that you would only face approximately a 6 percent chance that the true shipment defect rate exceeds the buyer's tolerable rate of 10 percent. So an important concept in audit sampling is that by increasing sample size, you can reduce uncertainty and risk.

The converse of sampling risk is *confidence level.* In other words, while both samples discussed above yielded a defect rate of 5 percent ($1/20$ and $5/100$), with the larger sample you can be approximately 94 percent confident (100 percent − 6 percent sampling risk) that the shipment is acceptable. The smaller sample only allows you to be 60 percent confident (100 percent − 40 percent sampling risk). We will continue to refer back to this apple inspector example as we introduce sampling terms and concepts in this chapter.

This chapter has two overall objectives: (1) to provide an introduction and overview of audit sampling and (2) to apply statistical and nonstatistical sampling techniques to tests of controls. Chapter 9 presents statistical and nonstatistical sampling techniques for substantive tests of account balances. 🌐

Introduction

In the early days of auditing, it was not unusual for the independent auditor to examine all of the records of the company being audited.[1] However, as companies grew in size and complexity, it became uneconomical to examine all of the accounting records and supporting documents. Auditors found it necessary to draw conclusions about the fairness of a company's

---

[1] See the introduction to the American Institute of Certified Public Accountant's *Audit Sampling* (AICPA Audit Guide) (New York: AICPA, 2001) for a discussion of the development of sampling in auditing.

financial statements based on an examination of a subset of the records and transactions. As a result, the auditor provides reasonable, not absolute, assurance (refer to the third standard of field work) that the financial statements are fairly presented. The justification for accepting some uncertainty is the trade-off between the cost of examining all of the data and the cost of making an incorrect decision based on a sample of the data. As noted in Chapter 2, this concept of reasonable assurance is addressed in the auditor's report.

Auditing standards recognize and permit both statistical and nonstatistical methods of audit sampling. Two recent studies report that nonstatistical methods are the most common in practice.[2] Later in the chapter we discuss some reasons why nonstatistical sampling has become more common in practice. Both nonstatistical and statistical methods are based on the same fundamental sampling theories. In fact, the steps and techniques used for these two sampling approaches are far more similar than they are different. To properly apply a nonstatistical sampling approach, it is necessary to understand the underlying statistical principles; thus, we cover statistical sampling before we discuss nonstatistical sampling.

Occasionally, students will ask if recent advances in technology have or will eliminate the need for audit sampling. Two advances have reduced the number of times auditors need to apply sampling techniques to gather audit evidence. First, companies have developed well-controlled, automated accounting systems that can process routine transactions with no or very few errors. Rather than rely on audit sampling to test routine transactions processed by these automated information systems, auditors test the processing software control configurations and general computer controls (e.g., restricted access, program change management) associated with the automated controls. Second, the advent of powerful audit software such as ACL allows auditors, in some situations, to download and examine electronic client data rather than sample.

While technology has reduced the number of situations where audit sampling is necessary, technology will never eliminate the need for auditors to rely on sampling to some degree because (1) many control processes require human involvement to operate effectively (e.g., reconciliations, review, and resolution of a system's generated exception reports), (2) many testing procedures require the auditor to physically examine an asset (e.g., inventory) or examine characteristics of a transaction or balance (e.g., terms in a contract), and (3) in many cases auditors are required to obtain and examine evidence from third parties (e.g., letters confirming accounts receivable balances from client customers). These situations require the auditor's "hands-on" attention. When the number of items or transactions in these populations is large, it is not economical for auditors to test 100 percent of the population; instead they use sampling to gather sufficient audit evidence.

---

[2]See N. Hitzig, "Audit Sampling: A Survey of Current Practice," *The CPA Journal* (July 1995), pp. 54–57; and W. F. Messier, Jr., S. J. Kachelmeier, and K. Jensen, "An Experimental Assessment of Recent Professional Developments in Nonstatistical Sampling Guidance," *Auditing: A Journal of Practice & Theory* (March 2001), pp. 81–96.

Definitions and Key Concepts

Audit Sampling

[LO 1]

Auditing standards define *audit sampling* as the application of an audit procedure to less than 100 percent of the items within an account balance or class of transactions for the purpose of evaluating some characteristic of the balance or class (AU 350.01). The fact that an audit involves sampling is expressed to users of the financial statements by the phrase "An audit includes examining, *on a test basis*" contained in the scope paragraph of the auditor's report.

Sampling Risk

[LO 2]

When sampling is used by an auditor, an element of uncertainty enters into the auditor's conclusions. This element of uncertainty, referred to as *sampling risk*, was discussed briefly under detection risk in Chapter 3 and in the apple inspector example at the beginning of this chapter. Sampling risk refers to the possibility that the sample drawn is not representative of the population and that, as a result, the auditor will reach an incorrect conclusion about the account balance or class of transactions based on the sample.

Due to sampling risk, the auditor faces the chance that sampling may lead to one of two possible types of decision errors: (1) deciding that the population tested is not acceptable when in reality it is and (2) deciding that the population tested is acceptable when in reality it is not. In statistical terms, these errors are known as Type I and Type II errors, respectively. More formally, Type I and Type II errors are defined as follows:

- **Risk of incorrect rejection (Type I).** In testing an internal control, this is the risk that the sample supports a conclusion that the control is not operating effectively when, in truth, it is operating effectively. When an auditor is evaluating the level of reliance that can be placed on a control in the context of a financial statement audit, this risk is also commonly referred to as the *risk of underreliance* or the *risk of assessing control risk too high.*

  In substantive testing, this is the risk that the sample supports the conclusion that the recorded account balance is materially misstated when it is actually not materially misstated.

- **Risk of incorrect acceptance (Type II).** In testing a control, this is the risk that the sample supports a conclusion that the control is operating effectively when, in truth, it is not operating effectively. When an auditor is evaluating the level of reliance that can be placed on a control in the context of a financial statement audit, this risk is also commonly referred to as the *risk of overreliance* or the *risk of assessing control risk too low.*

  In substantive testing, this is the risk that the sample supports the conclusion that the recorded account balance is not materially misstated when it is actually materially misstated.

The risk of incorrect rejection (a Type I decision error) relates to the *efficiency* of the audit. This type of decision error can result in the auditor conducting more audit work than necessary in order to reach the correct conclusion.

The risk of incorrect acceptance (a Type II decision error) relates to the *effectiveness* of the audit. This type of decision error can result in the auditor failing to detect a material misstatement in the financial statements. This can lead to litigation against the auditor by parties that rely on the financial statements. Because of the potentially severe consequences of a Type II decision error, auditors design their sampling applications to keep this risk to an acceptably low level. Auditors typically focus only on Type II decision errors in determining their sample sizes, because Type I decision errors affect efficiency and not effectiveness and because, by controlling for the risk of Type II errors, they also obtain relatively good coverage for the risk of Type I errors. For these reasons, in this chapter we do not address the potential implications on sampling applications of Type I errors.

Audit sampling can also involve *nonsampling risk*. Nonsampling risk is the risk of auditor error and arises from the possibility that the auditor may sample the wrong population to test an assertion, fail to detect a misstatement when applying an audit procedure, or misinterpret an audit result. While statistical sampling allows the auditor to quantify and control sampling risk, no sampling method allows the auditor to measure nonsampling risk. The uncertainty related to nonsampling risk can be controlled by adequate training, proper planning, and effective supervision.

Three Important Factors   In the preface to the chapter, we asked you to imagine that you were an apple inspector and we asked you to consider what information you would like to have before you began testing apples. While you would want answers to all the questions listed in the preface, you will find that three of the factors listed there are the most important inputs to determine sample sizes for all types of audit sampling. These three inputs are (1) desired level of assurance in the results (or confidence level), (2) acceptable defect rate (or tolerable misstatement), and (3) historical defect rate (or expected error).

Confidence Level   The first input, *confidence level*, is the complement of sampling risk. For example, as an apple inspector you have to accept some risk that the shipment defect percentage is higher than your sample defect percentage, and higher than the defect rate the buyer will tolerate. You would determine your acceptable level of sampling risk by considering the amount of reliance to be placed on your tests and the consequences of a decision error. The more the reliance placed on your inspection (versus other testing or quality control measures) and the more severe the consequences of a Type II decision error (e.g., the buyer will stop doing business with your company if you mistakenly accept and send a failed shipment), the less risk you will want to accept and the more confident you will want to be in your testing. Auditors, like inspectors, focus on both risk and confidence level. In statistical terminology, a confidence level represents the probability that a given interval includes the true but unknown measure of the characteristic of interest. For example, to place reliance on a control, an auditor may want to be 95 percent confident that the control operates effectively at least 97 percent of the time (or fails to operate no more than 3 percent of the time). Because risk is the complement of confidence level, auditors can either set confidence level or sampling risk. For example, the auditor may set sampling risk for a particular sampling application at 5 percent, which results in a confidence level of 95 percent. Confidence level and sampling risk are related to sample size: The larger the sample, the higher the confidence level and the lower the sampling risk.

Tolerable and Expected Error

Once the desired confidence level is established, the appropriate sample size is determined largely by how much tolerable error exceeds expected error. The smaller the difference between these two variables, the more precise the sampling results must be, and therefore the larger the sample size needed. For example, assume that during your interview for the apple inspector position you were told that the historical shipment defect rate has averaged 3 percent ± 2 percent and the buyers typically can accept up to 10 percent defective apples. However, as you are planning your sample on the first day of work, you learn that poor weather this year has resulted in an expected defect rate of 7 percent ± 3 percent. All else equal, the new information will require a larger sample size because now there is a smaller margin for error. This is because there is less room to accommodate sampling risk in the interval between 7 and 10 percent than there is in the interval between 3 and 10 percent. It doesn't matter which of the two factors causes a change in the difference between tolerable and expected error to be smaller; the critical factor is how large the difference is between the defect rate (or misstatement) that is expected and the defect rate (or misstatement) that can be tolerated.

In typical statistical sampling terminology, the term *precision* relates to how close a sample estimate is to the population characteristic being estimated, given a specified sampling risk. Thus, precision at the planning stage of an audit sampling application is the difference between the *expected* and the *tolerable* deviation rate or misstatement. Auditing standards use the term *allowance for sampling risk* to reflect the concept of precision in a sampling application. For example, if an auditor expected that a control would have a 2 percent deviation (failure) rate and he or she was willing to tolerate a deviation rate of 5 percent, the allowance for sampling risk would be 3 percent. Remember that in order to successfully apply audit sampling to gather audit evidence, auditors must be able to "tolerate" some deviations (for controls testing) or misstatement (for substantive testing) to provide an allowance for sampling risk. The only way to completely remove this risk is to test all the items in a population.

Audit Evidence Choices That Do and Do Not Involve Sampling
✵ [LO 3]

In assessing inherent risk or control risk, or in auditing an account balance or a class of transactions, the auditor seldom relies on a single test. Generally, the auditor applies a number of audit procedures in order to reach a conclusion. Some audit procedures involve sampling as defined by auditing standards, while others do not involve sampling. Table 8–1 indicates the types of evidence that are commonly gathered using audit sampling as well as types where sampling is generally not used.

TABLE 8–1	**Relationship between Evidence Types and Audit Sampling**	
	Type of Evidence	*Audit Sampling Commonly Used*
	Inspection of tangible assets	Yes
	Inspection of records or documents	Yes
	Reperformance	Yes
	Recalculation	Yes
	Confirmation	Yes
	Analytical procedures	No
	Scanning	No
	Inquiry	No
	Observation	No

We have already covered the types of evidence in earlier chapters, but here are some examples of typical sampling applications.

- **Inspection of tangible assets.** An auditor typically attends a client's year-end inventory count. Because the number of inventory items can be very large, the auditor may use audit sampling to select inventory items to physically inspect and count.

- **Inspection of records or documents.** A control may require that before a check is written to a vendor, the payables clerk must match an approved purchase order to an approved receiving report and indicate an acceptable match by initialing a copy of the check stapled to the other two documents. For large companies, this sort of control would be performed many times a day. The auditors can gather evidence on the effectiveness of the control by testing a sample of the documentation packages.

- **Reperformance.** As discussed in Chapter 7, to comply with rule 404 of the Sarbanes-Oxley Act of 2002, publicly traded clients must document and test controls over important assertions for significant accounts. In assessing the competence and objectivity of the client's work, the auditor may reperform a sample of the tests performed by the client.

- **Confirmation.** A common technique to gather evidence that accounts receivable balances exist and are accurately recorded is to send letters to customers asking them to confirm their balance. Rather than send a letter to all customers, the auditor can select a sample of customers.

Testing All Items with a Particular Characteristic

Table 8–1 indicates that sampling is commonly used to gather evidence of the first five types. It is also common for auditors to use other testing approaches instead of sampling or in combination with sampling to gather evidence. For example, when an account or class of transactions is made up of a few large items, the auditor may examine all the items in the account or class of transactions. Because the entire class or balance is subjected to a 100 percent examination, such an audit procedure does not involve sampling. More common than testing 100 percent of the items in an account balance or class of transactions is a technique in which the auditor tests all items with a particular characteristic of interest based on risk or monetary value. For example, if the auditor is aware of certain transactions that look unusual or present greater risk, the auditor should examine all these items rather than applying audit sampling.

Similarly, if a relatively small number of large transactions make up a relatively large percentage of an account or class of transactions, auditors will typically test all the transactions greater than a particular dollar amount. For example, the auditor may decide to audit all individual accounts receivable balances greater than a specified dollar amount (such as $100,000), because the 10 largest customers make up 70 percent of the total account balance. For the remaining 30 percent of the total account balance consisting of individual customer account balances less than $100,000, the auditor could apply audit sampling. Alternatively, the auditor could decide to apply substantive analytical procedures to the part of the total receivables balance consisting of individual customer accounts under $100,000, or may even decide to apply no audit procedures to this part of the total account because he or she deems that an acceptably low risk of material misstatement exists in this group. In these latter two instances, the auditor is not using sampling.

Testing Only One or a Few Items   Automated information systems process transactions consistently unless the system or programs are changed. When testing automated IT controls, the auditor may decide to adopt a strategy of testing one or a few of each type of transactions at a point in time. In conjunction with that test the auditor may test general controls over system and program changes to provide evidence that the automated controls have been operating over the audit period. This type of test of automated IT control does not involve audit sampling.

Types of Audit Sampling

Nonstatistical versus Statistical Sampling

❧ **[LO 4]**

There are two general approaches to audit sampling: *nonstatistical* and *statistical.* In nonstatistical (or judgmental) sampling, the auditor does not use statistical techniques to determine the sample size, select the sample, and/or measure sampling risk when evaluating results. Statistical sampling, on the other hand, uses the laws of probability to compute sample size and evaluate the sample results, thereby permitting the auditor to use the most efficient sample size and to quantify the sampling risk for the purpose of reaching a statistical conclusion about the population. Both approaches require the use of the auditor's professional judgment to plan, perform, and evaluate the sample evidence. The major advantages of statistical sampling are that it helps the auditor (1) design an efficient sample, (2) measure the sufficiency of evidence obtained, and (3) quantify sampling risk. The disadvantages of statistical sampling include additional costs of (1) training auditors in the proper use of sampling techniques, (2) designing and conducting the sampling application, and (3) lack of consistent application across audit teams due to the complexity of the underlying concepts.

With a nonstatistical sampling application, the auditor must rely on his or her professional judgment, in combination with audit firm guidance and knowledge of the underlying statistical sampling theories, to reach a conclusion about the audit test. Therefore, to properly apply nonstatistical sampling, auditors' judgment and their firm's sampling guidance must be grounded in statistical sampling theory. Thus, a disadvantage of nonstatistical sampling is that auditor judgment may diverge significantly from sampling theory resulting in testing that is not as effective as statistical sampling. Most firms manage this disadvantage by providing their auditors with nonstatistical sampling guidance and procedures that are easy to use, that encourage consistency in sampling applications across engagement teams, and that are grounded in sampling theory. Nonstatistical audit sampling can be simpler to use and more consistently applied than statistical sampling because some of the more difficult statistical decisions can be made by experts. The experts' decisions are then built into the audit firm's guidance and decision aids.

This chapter and Chapter 9 provide detailed coverage of both statistical and nonstatistical sampling. Even though nonstatistical sampling is very common in practice, we cover statistical sampling first because statistical theory provides the foundation for both sampling approaches.

Types of Statistical Sampling Techniques

Auditors use three major types of statistical sampling techniques: *attribute sampling*, *monetary-unit sampling*, and *classical variables sampling*.

Attribute Sampling

Attribute sampling is used to estimate the proportion of a population that possesses a specified characteristic. The most common use of attribute sampling is for tests of controls. In this case, the auditor wants to determine the deviation rate for a control implemented within the client's accounting system. For example, the auditor may want to estimate how often a credit check is not performed on customer orders before shipment. Measurement of the deviation rate provides evidence about whether the control is operating effectively to process accounting transactions properly and therefore provides support for the auditor's set level of control risk. Attribute sampling may also be used with a substantive test of transactions when such a test is conducted with a test of controls as a dual-purpose test.

Monetary-Unit Sampling

Monetary-unit sampling uses attribute sampling theory and techniques to estimate the dollar (or other currency) amount of misstatement for a class of transactions or an account balance. Variations of monetary-unit sampling are known as *probability-proportional-to-size sampling* and *cumulative monetary amount sampling*. Auditors use this sampling technique extensively because it has a number of advantages over classical variables sampling. Monetary-unit sampling builds upon attribute sampling theory to express a conclusion in dollar amounts.

Classical Variables Sampling   Classical variables sampling includes the sampling techniques typically taught in an undergraduate statistics class. While auditors sometimes use variables sampling to estimate the dollar value of a class of transactions or account balance, it is more frequently used to determine whether an account is materially misstated.

Regardless of the approach or type of sampling, auditing standards contain requirements that auditors must follow when planning, selecting a sample for, and performing and evaluating the audit sampling applications. We will refer to these requirements as we discuss the different approaches and types of audit sampling. Chapter 9 demonstrates the application of monetary-unit sampling and classical variables sampling to substantive tests of account balances.

The remainder of this chapter presents an application of statistical attribute sampling to tests of controls, followed by a discussion of nonstatistical sampling applied to tests of controls.

Attribute Sampling Applied to Tests of Controls

❋ [LO 5,6]   Attribute sampling is a statistical sampling method used to estimate the proportion of a characteristic in a population. In applying this technique to tests of controls, the auditor normally attempts to determine the operating effectiveness of a control in terms of deviations from a prescribed internal control.

In conducting a statistical sample for a test of controls, auditing standards (AU 350) require the auditor to properly plan, perform, and evaluate the sampling application and adequately document each phase of the sampling application in the papers. The following sections discuss the steps that are included in the three phases of an attribute-sampling application. The discussion utilizes examples from the revenue process. Table 8–2 lists the steps involved in the three phases of an attribute-sampling application.

Planning

Proper planning of an attribute-sampling application involves completing a number of important steps. Each of these steps, in turn, requires the use of professional judgment on the part of the auditor.

Step 1: Determine the Test Objectives   Auditing standards require that sampling applications be well planned and take into consideration the relationship of the sample to the objective(s) of the test. The objective of attribute sampling when used for tests of controls is to evaluate the operating effectiveness of the internal control for purposes of the internal control audit for public companies (see Chapter 7) or to determine the degree of reliance that can be placed on controls for a financial statement audit. Thus, the auditor assesses the deviation or error rate that exists for each control selected for testing. Audit sampling for tests of controls is generally appropriate when the application of the control leaves documentary evidence. For example, in most revenue processes, goods are billed after they are shipped. Therefore, no sales transaction should be recorded unless

TABLE 8-2	Steps in an Attribute-Sampling Application

Planning
1. Determine the test objectives.
2. Define the population characteristics:
   - Define the sampling population.
   - Define the sampling unit.
   - Define the control deviation conditions.
3. Determine the sample size, using the following inputs:
   - The desired confidence level or risk of incorrect acceptance.
   - The tolerable deviation rate.
   - The expected population deviation rate.

Performance
4. Select sample items.
5. Perform the auditing procedures:
   - Understand and analyze any deviations observed.

Evaluation
6. Calculate the sample deviation and the computed upper deviation rates.
7. Draw final conclusions.

a properly authorized shipping document is present. The auditor can test a sample of sales invoices for proper recording by examining the corresponding shipping documents.

Step 2: Define the Population Characteristics
To achieve the test objectives, the auditor must carefully consider the characteristics of the sampling population.

Define the Sampling Population.   All or a subset of the items that constitute the class of transactions (or account balance when not testing controls) make up the sampling population. The auditor must determine that the population from which the sample is selected is appropriate for the specific assertion, because sample results can be projected only to the population from which the sample was selected. For example, suppose the auditor is interested in examining the effectiveness of a control designed to ensure that all shipments to customers are billed by testing whether all shipments were, in fact, billed. If the auditor uses the population of sales invoices as the sampling population, he or she is not likely to detect goods shipped but not billed, because the population of sales invoices includes only sales that were billed. In this example, the correct sampling population for testing the completeness assertion would be the population of all shipped goods as documented by bills of lading.

There is a natural tendency to designate an entire class of transactions (or all the items in an account balance) as the population. However, the sample population should be restricted to the transactions and time period under the same system of controls that are relevant to the assertions being tested. For example, the auditor can define the population to be the period from the first day of the year to some interim date. The results of the sampling application in this case would apply only to the period tested.

However, the auditor must also consider whether to conduct additional tests in the remaining period under audit through year-end (see Chapter 5 for a discussion).

Once the population has been defined, the auditor must determine that the physical representation (referred to as the *frame*) of the population is complete typically by comparing the frame, an accounts receivable listing for example, to the general ledger. Because the auditor selects the sample from the frame, any conclusions relate only to that physical representation of the population. If the frame and the population differ, the auditor might draw the wrong conclusion about the population.

Define the Sampling Unit.   The individual members of the sampling population are called the sampling units. In the apple inspector example, the sampling unit is an individual apple. In auditing, a sampling unit may be a document, an entry, or a line item. Each sampling unit makes up one item in the population. The sampling unit should be defined in relation to the control being tested. For example, suppose the client has implemented a policy that when a customer order is received, the amount of the current sales transaction is compared to the available balance on the customer's approved line of credit. If the amount is less than the credit available, the sale is made. If the amount exceeds the credit limit, the sale is denied or is subjected to further management review before it is approved. In this case the sampling unit can be defined as the sales invoice packet that contains the customer order, sales order, bill of lading, and sales invoice. The sales order would show some indication that the credit department had approved the sale.

Define Control Deviation Conditions.   For tests of controls, a deviation is a departure from adequate performance of the internal control. It is important for the auditor to define carefully what is considered a deviation. Thinking back to the apple inspector example, before you begin your inspection, you need to know what constitutes a "bad" apple: Does it take a minor blemish or significant damage to conclude that an apple is defective? In the previous sales approval example, the control was to compare the sales amount to the available approved credit before the sale is approved. In this example, a deviation would be defined as a credit sale made without evidence of credit department approval.

Step 3: Determine the Sample Size   Considerable judgment is required in determining the appropriate values for the inputs that are used to compute sample size. The three key inputs to determining the sample are the same as those discussed earlier: the desired confidence level, tolerable deviation rate, and expected population deviation rate. Auditing standards require that auditors give adequate consideration to the appropriate value of these inputs. Because of the difficulty of making these input judgments, determining the sample size is typically the most difficult step of an audit sampling application.

Determine the Desired Confidence Level.   As discussed earlier in the chapter, the complement of the confidence level is the risk that the sample results will support a conclusion that the control is functioning effectively when in truth it is not (i.e., the risk of incorrect acceptance). In a financial statement audit, this can result in assessing control risk too low. This risk influences the effectiveness of the audit. If the auditor sets control risk too low and overrelies on the controls, the level of substantive procedures may be too low to detect material misstatements that may be present in the financial statement account. This is because when control risk decreases, the auditor increases detection risk to compensate (see discussion of the audit risk model in Chapter 3). Thus, if control risk is mistakenly set at a low level, detection risk will be set too high. This increases the risk that the auditor will fail to detect a material misstatement if one exists in the account.

In setting the desired confidence level and acceptable level of risk, the auditor considers the significance of the account and the importance of the assertion on which the control provides assurance, as well as the degree of reliance to be placed on the control. Generally, when the auditor has decided to rely on controls, the confidence level is set at 90 or 95 percent, meaning that the auditor is willing to accept a 10 or 5 percent risk of accepting the control as effective when in fact it is not. However, the auditor must remember that there is a direct relationship between the confidence level and sample size: The more confident the auditor would like to be (and the less risk he or she is willing to accept), the larger the sample size must be, all else equal. For example, in the illustration below the effect on the sample size is substantial (a 21 percent increase) when the desired confidence level increases from 90 to 95 percent.

Desired Confidence Level	Sample Size[3]
90%	77
95%	93

Thus, the auditor must balance effectiveness concerns with efficiency concerns when setting the desired confidence level and acceptable risk of incorrect acceptance.

Determine the Tolerable Deviation Rate.   The tolerable deviation rate is the maximum deviation rate from a prescribed control that the auditor is willing to accept and still consider the control effective (i.e., the control procedure would be relied on).

It can seem odd to students that auditors will actually "tolerate" any deviations in a control. There are two reasons auditors will tolerate deviations and still consider a control to be effective. The first reason is technical and relates to sampling risk. Remember that for an auditor (or an apple inspector) to use sampling to gather evidence, there must be some margin for error, because there is a risk that the sample deviation rate differs from the population deviation rate. Even if there are no deviations in a sample, there must still be an allowance (or upper confidence limit) for sampling

---

[3]The sample sizes assume a tolerable deviation rate of 5 percent, an expected population deviation rate of 1 percent, and a large population.

risk. Just as in the apple inspector example, the only way to know with certainty what the shipment defect rate actually is would be to inspect *all* the apples.

The second reason auditors are willing to tolerate some control deviations relates to the purpose and application of controls. To be effective, most controls do not need to operate 100 percent of the time so long as the times the control fails to operate are not predictable and the person(s) performing the control investigates processing exceptions observed during the proper application of the control. By way of analogy, suppose you have battery-operated smoke detectors in your apartment or house and one of the alarms starts to signal a low battery. The fact that a day or two passes between the removal of the old battery and installation of a new one doesn't render the system of controls ineffective for the entire period you have lived in the apartment or house. The risk of fire is pretty remote, even if there were no smoke detectors at all. Also, if one detector isn't working, you have other smoke detectors that will sound if smoke appears. Obviously, if all the smoke detectors are disabled for long periods of time, the system of fire detection is not effective and the risk of injury due to fire increases. Similarly, when a control fails to operate, it usually does not result in a monetary misstatement to the financial statements, because most transactions are properly input and processed (i.e., actual inherent risk is less than 100 percent) and there are other compensating controls or processes that might detect a misstatement should one occur. Furthermore, if the operator of the control investigates processing exceptions that are discovered, he or she can research the cause and potential implications of the exception(s) and take corrective actions if necessary.

To be effective, a control does need to operate effectively a reasonably high percentage of the time. Table 8–3 provides some examples of the relationship between the planned level of control risk and the tolerable deviation rate.

A low tolerable rate (such as 3 to 5 percent) is used when the auditor plans to place substantial reliance on the control and thus plans to assess control risk as low. A higher tolerable rate (6 to 10 percent) is used when the auditor plans a moderate level of control risk.

The tolerable deviation rate is *inversely* related to the sample size. The lower the tolerable deviation rate, the larger the sample size. Recall that in testing controls, the key determinant of sample size is the amount by which tolerable deviation rate exceeds the expected deviation rate. For example, assuming a desired confidence level of 95 percent, an expected population

TABLE 8–3	Suggested Tolerable Deviation Rates for Assessed Levels of Control Risk
Planned Assessed Level of Control Risk	*Tolerable Deviation Rate*
Low	3–5%
Moderate	6–10%
Slightly below maximum	11–20%
Maximum	Omit test

deviation rate of 0 percent, and a large population, the effect of tolerable deviation rate on sample size is:

Tolerable Deviation Rate	Sample Size
2%	149
6%	49
10%	29

Determine the Expected Population Deviation Rate.   The expected population deviation rate is the rate the auditor expects to exist in the population. Some level of deviation is commonly expected because the controls that auditors typically use sampling to test will be dependent on some human involvement (e.g., matching documents, credit approval, following up on system-generated exception reports), and humans are not perfect. The auditor can develop this expectation based on prior years' results or on a pilot sample. If the auditor believes that the expected population deviation rate exceeds the tolerable deviation rate, the statistical testing should not be performed because in such a situation no amount of sampling can reduce the population deviation rate below the tolerable rate. Instead, the auditor should perform additional substantive procedures rather than relying on the control.

The expected population deviation rate has a direct relationship to sample size: The larger the expected population deviation rate, the larger the sample size, all else equal. For example, assuming a desired confidence level of 95 percent, a tolerable deviation rate of 5 percent, and a large population, the effect of the expected population deviation rate on sample size is

Expected Population Deviation Rate	Sample Size
1%	93
1.5%	124
2%	181
3%	*

*Sample size is too large to be cost-effective for most audit applications.

The dramatic effect of expected population deviation rate on sample size highlights the importance of a good estimate of the expected deviation rate. It is perplexing to some that an estimate of the expected population deviation rate is required as an input to determine sample size—after all, isn't the whole purpose of testing a sample to estimate the deviation rate in the population? The reason an estimate is necessary relates back to the notion of precision, or by how much the tolerable deviation rate exceeds the estimated deviation rate, as discussed earlier in the chapter. Recall the apple inspector illustration where the buyer's tolerable defect rate was 10 percent and poor weather increased the expected defect rate from a historical rate of 3 percent ± 2 percent to 7 percent ± 3 percent. All else equal, the increase in expected defect rate will require a larger sample size, because there is now less room for sampling risk to be accommodated, and thus the sampling conclusion needs to be more precise. Just as the historical defect rate is an important input for apple inspection, a good estimate of the expected population deviation rate is very important for attribute sampling because the statistical sample size will be just large enough such that if the auditor observes the deviation rate she or he expects or lower, the sampling application will support a conclusion that the control is operating effectively. Similarly, if the auditor observes a higher deviation rate than the expected rate used in the sample size calculation, this usually means the sample results are unacceptable. As such, it is wise to be conservative when estimating the expected population deviation rate so that the sample size will be adequate even if the population deviation rate is larger than the auditor initially expected.

Population Size

Students and auditors are often surprised that the size of the population is not an important factor in determining sample size. The population size has little or no effect on the sample size, unless the population is relatively small, say less than 500 items. In fact, so long as the population is made up of similar items under the same system of controls, it doesn't matter if the population is 100,000 items, 1 million items, 100 million items, or more; the sample size is the same. Popular audit sampling programs, like ACL, completely ignore the effects of population size when computing sample size for attribute sampling. Because most of the populations auditors test are larger than a few hundred items, and because assuming large population sample size does not reduce the effectiveness of the sampling application, we ignore the effects of population size in this chapter. However, we have included a brief discussion of how sample sizes can be adjusted for smaller populations in the advanced module to this chapter.

Table 8–4 summarizes the effects of the four factors on the size of the sample to be selected.

Performance

After the sampling application has been planned, and auditor performs each of the following steps.

Sample Selection

Step 4: Select Sample Items   Auditing standards require that the sample items be selected in such a way that the sample can be expected to

TABLE 8–4	The Effect of Sample Selection Factors on Sample Size		
		Examples	
Factor	*Relationship to Sample Size*	*Change in Factor*	*Effect on Sample*
Desired confidence level	Direct	Lower	Decrease
		Higher	Increase
Tolerable deviation rate	Inverse	Lower	Increase
		Higher	Decrease
Expected population deviation rate	Direct	Lower	Decrease
		Higher	Increase
Population size	Decreases sample size only when population size is small (e.g., 500 or fewer items). Therefore, population size generally has no effect on sample size.		

represent the population. Thus, all items must have an equal opportunity to be selected. The following two selection methods are acceptable for attributes sampling.

Random-Number Selection.   The auditor may select a random sample using random numbers generated by a spreadsheet application or audit sampling software. Using this method of selection, every item in the population (such as a document or customer account) has the same probability of being selected as every other sampling unit in the population. Statistical sampling requires that the auditor be able to measure the probability of selecting the sampling units selected. Thus, random-number selection is used in many statistical sampling applications. Auditors typically use unrestricted random sampling without replacement for sampling applications. This means that once an item is selected, it is removed from the frame and cannot be selected a second time. Given the auditor's objectives, it seems sensible for an auditor to include an item only once in the sample. Generating a random sample using a spreadsheet program such as MS Excel or audit sampling software is easy and will be demonstrated later in the chapter.

Systematic Selection.   When using a systematic selection approach to select a sample, the auditor determines a sampling interval by dividing the sampling population by the sample size. A starting number is selected in the first interval, and then every *n*th item is selected. When a random starting point is used, systematic selection provides a sample where every sampling unit has an equal chance of being selected. For example, suppose the auditor wishes to select 100 items from a population of 15,000 items numbered 1 to 15,000. The sampling interval in this case is 150 (15,000 ÷ 100). The auditor chooses a random number in the first interval (i.e., between 1 and 150), say 125, and that item is selected for testing. The second item is 275 (125 + 150), the third item is 425, and so on. To avoid the possibility that a systematic sample will miss systematic deviations in the population (e.g., control deviations occurring every 300th unit or every Friday afternoon), the auditor can use several random starting points. In our example, after selecting 10 items, the auditor could use a new random start between the 10th and 11th interval to select the 11th item.

Step 5: Perform the Audit Procedures
After the sample items have been selected, the auditor conducts the planned audit procedures. Continuing the earlier example of testing the completeness of sales transactions, the auditor would examine the sales invoice packet for the presence of a shipping document to support each sales invoice. If the shipping document is present, the auditor considers the control properly applied. If the shipping document is not present, the sample item is considered a deviation from the control procedure.

   In conducting the audit procedures for tests of controls, the auditor may encounter the following situations:

- **Voided documents.** The auditor may occasionally select a voided document in a sample. If the transaction has been properly voided, it does not represent a deviation. The item should be replaced with a new sample item.

- ***Unused or inapplicable documents.*** Sometimes a selected item is not appropriate for the definition of the control. For example, the auditor may define a deviation for a purchase transaction as a vendor's bill not supported by a receiving report. If the auditor selects a telephone or utility bill, there will not be a receiving report to examine. In such a case, the absence of the receiving report would not be a deviation. The auditor would simply replace the item with another purchase transaction.

- ***Inability to examine a sample item.*** Auditing standards require that the auditor consider the effect of not being able to apply a planned audit procedure to a sample item. For most tests of controls, the auditor examines documents for evidence of the performance of the control. If the auditor is unable to examine a document or to use an alternative procedure to test whether the control was adequately performed, the sample item is a deviation for purposes of evaluating the sample results.

- ***Stopping the test before completion.*** If a large number of deviations are detected early in the tests of controls, the auditor should consider stopping the test as soon as it is clear that the results of the test will not support the planned assessed level of control risk. In such a case, for the audit of internal controls for public companies, the client would be informed, and the exceptions would be considered a control deficiency unless remediation and retesting are successful or there are other controls that adequately address the increased risk of misstatement. In the context of a financial statement audit, the auditor would rely on other internal controls or set control risk at the maximum for the audit assertion affected, and appropriately enhance the related substantive tests.

Whenever a deviation is observed in controls, the auditor should investigate the nature, cause, and consequence of the exception.

Understand and Analyze Deviations Observed.   The auditor should evaluate the qualitative aspects of the deviations identified. This involves two considerations. First, the nature of each deviation and its cause and consequences should be considered. For example, the auditor should determine if a deviation represents an unintentional error or a fraud and whether the deviation actually resulted in a monetary misstatement to the financial statements. The auditor should also attempt to determine whether a deviation resulted from a cause such as misunderstanding of instructions or carelessness. Understanding the nature and cause of a deviation helps the auditor better assess control risk and evaluate whether the deviation(s) represent control deficiencies. As noted in Chapter 7, AS 2 lists specific deficiencies that are indicative of significant deficiencies or material weaknesses (e.g., deviations indicate management fraud, deviation(s) resulted in monetary misstatements that are more than inconsequential). Second, the auditor should consider how the deviations may impact the other phases of the audit. For example, suppose that deviations found in a test of the revenue process resulted from improper granting of credit. As a result, the risk that the valuation assertion was not met for accounts receivable would increase, and the auditor would therefore increase substantive procedures for the allowance for uncollectible accounts.

After the audit procedures have been completed, the auditor proceeds with his or her evaluation of the sample results.

Evaluation

Step 6: Calculate the Sample Deviation and Computed Upper Deviation Rates
After completing the audit procedures, the auditor summarizes the deviations for each control tested and evaluates the results. Determining the sample results for an attribute-sampling application can be accomplished by the use of a computer program or attribute-sampling tables. The auditor calculates the sample deviation rate and the computed upper deviation rate. The sample deviation rate is simply the number of deviations found in the sample divided by the number of items in the sample. This calculation projects the sample results to the population and is required by auditing standards. For example, if 2 deviations were found in a sample of 50, the sample deviation rate would be 4 percent ($2 \div 50$). In attribute sampling, the sample deviation rate represents the auditor's best estimate of the population deviation rate. However, because this result is based on a sample, the auditor does not know the true population deviation rate and must consider an allowance for sampling risk.

In evaluating the results of testing a control, the auditor is normally concerned only with whether the true deviation rate exceeds the tolerable deviation rate. Because the auditor does not know the true deviation rate, he or she calculates a *computed upper deviation rate*. The computed upper deviation rate is the sum of the sample deviation rate and an appropriate allowance for sampling risk. This sum represents an upper limit on how high the population deviation rate might actually be, at a controlled level of sampling risk (e.g., 5 or 10 percent). In other words, there is only a 5 or 10 percent chance that the true population deviation rate exceeds the computed upper deviation rate. This is sometimes referred to as the *upper-limit approach*. We illustrate how to calculate the upper limit in the next section. The upper limit represents the upper one-sided confidence limit for the population deviation rate based on the sample size, the number of deviations, and the planned level of confidence. In evaluating the results of testing a control, the auditor is normally concerned only with whether the true deviation rate exceeds the tolerable deviation rate. Thus, the statistical test is one-tailed, because the auditor is generally concerned only with how *high* the population deviation rate might actually be. As long as the computed upper deviation rate is within the auditor's tolerable range, it doesn't matter how *low* the population deviation rate might be.

Step 7: Draw Final Conclusions
In drawing a conclusion about the statistical sampling application for tests of controls, the auditor compares the tolerable deviation rate to the computed upper deviation rate. If the computed upper deviation rate is less than the tolerable deviation rate, the

auditor can conclude that the controls can be relied upon. If the computed upper deviation rate exceeds the tolerable deviation rate, the auditor must conclude that the controls are not operating at an acceptable level. For an audit of internal control over financial reporting, the ineffective control would be considered a control deficiency unless the client remediates the control and both the client and the auditor retest to support the remediated control's effectiveness. For purposes of an audit of internal control the auditor must evaluate the likelihood and magnitude of a potential misstatement arising as a result of control deficiencies (see Chapter 7).

For a financial statement audit, the final conclusion about control risk for the accounting system being tested is based on the auditor's professional judgment of the sample results and other relevant tests of controls such as inquiry and observation. If the auditor concludes that the evidence supports the planned level of control risk, no modifications of the planned substantive procedures are necessary. On the other hand, if the planned level of control risk is not supported by the sample results and other tests of controls, the auditor should either (1) test other control procedures that could support the planned level of control risk or (2) increase the assessed level of control risk and modify the nature, extent, or timing of substantive procedures.

Table 8–5 shows the auditor's risks when evaluating sample evidence on the planned level of control risk. If the evidence supports the planned level of control risk and the internal control is reliable, the auditor has made a correct decision. Similarly, if the evidence does not support the planned level of control risk and the internal control is not reliable, a correct decision has been made. The other two combinations result in decision errors by the auditor. If the evidence supports the planned level of control risk and the internal control is not reliable, the auditor will have incorrectly accepted the control as effective and overrelied on internal control (Type II error). This results in the auditor establishing detection risk too high and leads to a lower level of evidence being gathered through substantive procedures. Thus, the auditor's risk of not detecting material misstatement is increased. This can lead to a lawsuit against the auditor. If the evidence does not support the planned level of control risk and the internal control is reliable (Type I error), the auditor will have incorrectly rejected the control and detection risk will have been set too low. Thus, a higher level of evidence will be gathered by substantive procedures, leading to overauditing and an inefficient audit.

TABLE 8–5	**The Auditor's Risks When Evaluating Sample Evidence on the Planned Level of Control Risk**	
	True State of Internal Control	
Auditor's Decision Based on Sample Evidence	*Reliable*	*Not Reliable*
Supports the planned level of control risk	Correct decision	Risk of incorrect acceptance (Type II)
Does not support the planned level of control risk	Risk of incorrect rejection (Type I)	Correct decision

An Example of an Attribute-Sampling Plan

[LO 7]   Calabro Paging Services, the company included in Discussion Case 3-32 in Chapter 3, will be used to demonstrate an attribute-sampling plan. Don Jones, senior-in-charge of the Calabro Paging Services audit, developed an understanding of Calabro's revenue process and has decided to rely on selected controls to reduce control risk below the maximum. Jones intends to test the entire year and has determined that the population is complete. The following subsections document Jones's sampling plan. Typically, a public accounting firm uses a formal working paper to document the steps in the sampling plan.

Determine the Test Objective (Step 1)

The objective of this test is to determine if Calabro's revenue process is functioning as documented. In particular, Jones wants to determine if the controls identified as reliable are operating effectively and thus allow control risk to be set below the maximum.

Define the Population Characteristics (Step 2)

Calabro's revenue transactions arise in the following manner:

> Subscribers may lease a pager from the company or purchase a pager and pay only an access fee for the company paging system. Each subscriber enters into a service contract with the company, which provides for the payment of the access fee and the purchase or lease of one or more pagers. The company's contracts with customers with large numbers of pagers are typically for three- to five-year terms, while contracts for smaller quantities are typically for one-year terms with annual renewal.

For this sampling application, Jones has decided to rely on three controls in Calabro's revenue process. The three control procedures and their definitions are as follows:

1. *Sales and service contracts are properly authorized for credit approval.* Calabro's credit department personnel check the creditworthiness of new customers and establish a credit limit based on that evaluation. For existing customers, the amount of the new sale or lease is added to the existing accounts receivable balance, and the total is compared to the customer's credit limit. If the amount is less than the credit limit, the transaction is processed. If the total is more than the credit limit, the transaction is subjected to review by the credit manager before the sale is approved. Therefore, a deviation in this test is defined as the failure of Calabro's credit department personnel to follow proper credit approval procedures for new and existing customers.

2. *Sales are not recorded without an approved sales and lease contract.* Calabro's revenue process contains a control that no revenue transactions are to be recorded unless an approved sales or lease contract is sent to the billing department. For this control, a deviation is defined as the absence of an approved sales or lease contract.

3. *Sales and lease contracts are properly priced.* Calabro's revenue process also includes a control that requires billing department

personnel to use an authorized price list for the sale of pagers. Access and lease fees are determined based on a fee structure that includes volume discounts for large unit subscribers. A deviation in this case is the use of an unauthorized price for a pager or an incorrect access or lease fee.

For the current test, Jones has decided to test the entire year. The physical representation of the population is the numeric file of sales and lease contracts maintained in the sales department. Based on a review of the client's procedures for completeness, Jones has determined that the frame is complete. The population of sales and lease transactions for the year contains 125,000 items that are numbered from 1 to 125,000.

The sampling unit for this test is defined as the sales or lease contract. Jones can perform all tests for the controls selected by examining this set of documents.

Determine the Sample Size (Step 3)

Table 8–6 shows Jones's decision for each of the parameters required to determine sample size. Jones decides to set the desired confidence level at 95 percent (i.e., the risk of incorrect acceptance is 5 percent), the tolerable deviation rate at 6 percent, and the expected population deviation rate at 1 percent for control 1. For control 1, Jones has planned a high confidence level (see Table 8–3). A similar strategy is followed for control 3. For control 2, Jones has planned a moderate confidence level because he plans to place less reliance on the control. In this sampling plan, the effect of the population size can be ignored because the population contains 125,000 transactions.

Tables 8–7 and 8–8 are used to determine the sample size for each of the controls. For control 1, Jones uses Table 8–7 to determine the sample size because the desired confidence level is 95 percent. Jones identifies the column for a 6 percent tolerable deviation rate and reads down that column until the row for a 1 percent expected population deviation rate is found. The sample size for control 1 is 78 items. For control 2, Jones uses Table 8–8 because the desired confidence level is 90 percent. Reading down the 8 percent tolerable deviation rate column until the 2 percent expected population

TABLE 8–6	The Auditor's Decisions for Sample Size			
		Control*		
Parameters		*1*	*2*	*3*
Desired confidence level		95%	90%	95%
Tolerable deviation rate		6%	8%	5%
Expected population deviation rate		1%	2%	1%
Sample size		78	48	93

*Control 1: Sales or lease contracts are properly authorized for credit approval.
Control 2: Sales are not recorded without an approved sales and lease contract.
Control 3: Sales and lease contracts are properly priced.

TABLE 8–7 — Statistical Sample Sizes for Attribute Sampling—95 Percent Desired Confidence Level (i.e., 5 Percent Risk of Incorrect Acceptance)

Expected Population Deviation Rate	Tolerable Deviation Rate										
	2%	3%	4%	5%	6%	7%	8%	9%	10%	15%	20%
0.00%	149(0)	99(0)	74(0)	59(0)	49(0)	42(0)	36(0)	32(0)	29(0)	19(0)	14(0)
.25	236(1)	157(1)	117(1)	93(1)	78(1)	66(1)	58(1)	51(1)	46(1)	30(1)	22(1)
.50	*	157(1)	117(1)	93(1)	78(1)	66(1)	58(1)	51(1)	46(1)	30(1)	22(1)
.75	*	208(2)	117(1)	93(1)	78(1)	66(1)	58(1)	51(1)	46(1)	30(1)	22(1)
1.00	*	*	156(2)	93(1)	78(1)	66(1)	58(1)	51(1)	46(1)	30(1)	22(1)
1.25	*	*	156(2)	124(2)	78(1)	66(1)	58(1)	51(1)	46(1)	30(1)	22(1)
1.50	*	*	192(3)	124(2)	103(2)	66(1)	58(1)	51(1)	46(1)	30(1)	22(1)
1.75	*	*	227(4)	153(3)	103(2)	88(2)	77(2)	51(1)	46(1)	30(1)	22(1)
2.00	*	*	*	181(4)	127(3)	88(2)	77(2)	68(2)	46(1)	30(1)	22(1)
2.25	*	*	*	208(5)	127(3)	88(2)	77(2)	68(2)	61(2)	30(1)	22(1)
2.50	*	*	*	*	150(4)	109(3)	77(2)	68(2)	61(2)	30(1)	22(1)
2.75	*	*	*	*	173(5)	109(3)	95(3)	68(2)	61(2)	30(1)	22(1)
3.00	*	*	*	*	195(6)	129(4)	95(3)	84(3)	61(2)	30(1)	22(1)
3.25	*	*	*	*	*	148(5)	112(4)	84(3)	61(2)	30(1)	22(1)
3.50	*	*	*	*	*	167(6)	112(4)	84(3)	76(3)	40(2)	22(1)
3.75	*	*	*	*	*	185(7)	129(5)	100(4)	76(3)	40(2)	22(1)
4.00	*	*	*	*	*	*	146(6)	100(4)	89(4)	40(2)	22(1)
5.00	*	*	*	*	*	*	*	158(8)	116(6)	40(2)	30(2)
6.00	*	*	*	*	*	*	*	*	179(11)	50(3)	30(2)
7.00	*	*	*	*	*	*	*	*	*	68(5)	37(3)

*Sample size is too large to be cost-effective for most audit applications. The number in parentheses represents the maximum number of deviations in a sample of that size that allows the auditor to conclude that the tolerable deviation rate is not exceeded.

TABLE 8–8 — Statistical Sample Sizes for Attribute Sampling—90 Percent Desired Confidence Level (i.e., 10 Percent Risk of Incorrect Acceptance)

Expected Population Deviation Rate	Tolerable Deviation Rate										
	2%	3%	4%	5%	6%	7%	8%	9%	10%	15%	20%
0.00%	114(0)	76(0)	57(0)	45(0)	38(0)	32(0)	28(0)	25(0)	22(0)	15(0)	11(0)
.25	194(1)	129(1)	96(1)	77(1)	64(1)	55(1)	48(1)	42(1)	38(1)	25(1)	18(1)
.50	194(1)	129(1)	96(1)	77(1)	64(1)	55(1)	48(1)	42(1)	38(1)	25(1)	18(1)
.75	265(2)	129(1)	96(1)	77(1)	64(1)	55(1)	48(1)	42(1)	38(1)	25(1)	18(1)
1.00	*	176(2)	96(1)	77(1)	64(1)	55(1)	48(1)	42(1)	38(1)	25(1)	18(1)
1.25	*	221(3)	132(2)	77(1)	64(1)	55(1)	48(1)	42(1)	38(1)	25(1)	18(1)
1.50	*	*	132(2)	105(2)	64(1)	55(1)	48(1)	42(1)	38(1)	25(1)	18(1)
1.75	*	*	166(3)	105(2)	88(2)	55(1)	48(1)	42(1)	38(1)	25(1)	18(1)
2.00	*	*	198(4)	132(3)	88(2)	75(2)	48(1)	42(1)	38(1)	25(1)	18(1)
2.25	*	*	*	132(3)	88(2)	75(2)	65(2)	42(1)	38(1)	25(1)	18(1)
2.50	*	*	*	158(4)	110(3)	75(2)	65(2)	58(2)	38(1)	25(1)	18(1)
2.75	*	*	*	209(6)	132(4)	94(3)	65(2)	58(2)	52(2)	25(1)	18(1)
3.00	*	*	*	*	132(4)	94(3)	65(2)	58(2)	52(2)	25(1)	18(1)
3.25	*	*	*	*	153(5)	113(4)	82(3)	58(2)	52(2)	25(1)	18(1)
3.50	*	*	*	*	194(7)	113(4)	82(3)	73(3)	52(2)	25(1)	18(1)
3.75	*	*	*	*	*	131(5)	98(4)	73(3)	52(2)	25(1)	18(1)
4.00	*	*	*	*	*	149(6)	98(4)	73(3)	65(3)	25(1)	18(1)
5.00	*	*	*	*	*	*	160(8)	115(6)	78(4)	34(2)	18(1)
6.00	*	*	*	*	*	*	*	182(11)	116(7)	43(3)	25(2)
7.00	*	*	*	*	*	*	*	*	199(14)	52(4)	25(2)

*Sample size is too large to be cost-effective for most audit applications. The number in parentheses represents the maximum number of deviations in a sample of that size that allows the auditor to conclude that the tolerable deviation rate is not exceeded.

deviation rate is found, Jones determines that the sample size is 48. Finally, the sample size for control 3 is 93. This is found by using Table 8–7 and reading down the 5 percent tolerable deviation rate column until the 1 percent expected deviation rate row is reached.

Auditors often establish one sample size for all controls tested within a business process. This is particularly true when all the tests of controls are to be conducted on the same sampling units. The auditor would use the largest sample size. Therefore, in this example, the sample size that would be used for testing the three controls would be 93. However, the sample sizes shown in Table 8–6 are used in the following example for illustrative purposes.

Significant areas of Tables 8–7 and 8–8 are covered by asterisks. The corresponding note at the bottom of the tables states, "Sample size is too large to be cost-effective for most audit applications." Another way to explain the cause of the asterisks is insufficient precision. Recall that to apply sampling there must be sufficient margin for error. When tolerable and estimated deviation rates are too close together, sample sizes will become too large to be practical or are simply not computable because there is insufficient allowance for sampling risk. Furthermore, in some instances where an asterisk appears in the tables, the expected population deviation rate is greater than the tolerable deviation rate; audit sampling obviously is not appropriate in such situations because there is no allowance for sampling risk.

Exhibit 8–1 shows the screen display from ACL™ for Windows software[4] for determining the sample size for control 3. The auditor opens a client workbook, chooses the sampling button on the menu and selects "calculate sample size." The size window is then displayed and the auditor enters the relevant data. Since this is attribute sampling, the auditor selects "record" for type of sampling. The auditor enters "95" for confidence, 125,000 for population size, and the upper error limit of 5 percent (i.e., tolerable deviation rate) and expected error rate of 1 percent (i.e., expected population deviation rate). This produces a sample size of 95 that is slightly larger than the amount determined using the tables. The ACL software produces an exact sample size calculation. If you have access to ACL, you may want to verify that ACL ignores population size when computing the sample size for attributes sampling. For example, what happens to the sample size if you enter a population size less than 95 in the example above (make sure you select "record" for the type of sampling)?

Select Sample Items (Step 4)

Exhibit 8–2 shows an example of the output from the random-number generator in ACL. The auditor chooses the tools button on the menu and selects "Generate Random Numbers." The random window is then displayed and the auditor enters the relevant data. The sample size of 95 is entered for "number." The seed is used to start the random-number process. If no value is entered into ACL, then ACL automatically creates a random seed. The

[4]This material is used with the permission of ACL Services Ltd. The authors are grateful to the company for allowing the use of this material.

EXHIBIT 8–1	**Sample Screens from ACL™ Software**

auditor then enters the range of the invoice number sequence (1 to 125,001).[5] The "unique" and "sorted" items should be checked so that each random number is unique and the output is produced in sequence. Using the random numbers generated, Jones selects the sample items. Alternatively, if auditors have the population data in electronic format, ACL or spreadsheet programs like MS Excel can randomly select the sample from the population.

Perform the Audit Procedures (Step 5)

Jones examines each of the sample items for the presence of a deviation. Thus, for control 1, Jones tests the 78 sales and lease contracts for proper credit authorization procedures by credit department personnel. The results of the audit procedures can be documented in a workpaper similar to the example shown in Exhibit 8–3. It should be noted that when multiple

---

[5]Each random number generated by ACL will be greater than or equal to the minimum value and less than the maximum value you specify. No random number will be equal to the maximum value. For this reason the maximum range is input as 125,001.

EXHIBIT 8-2

An Example of a Random Sample Drawn from ACL™

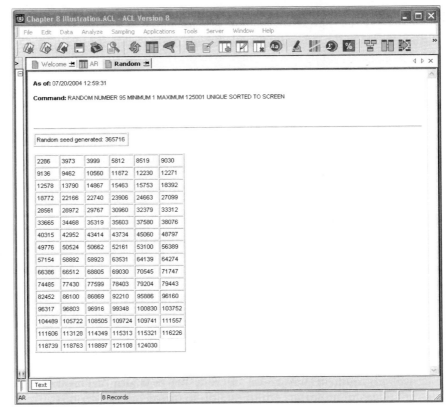

EXHIBIT 8–3	A Sample Working Paper for Recording the Results of Tests of Controls

CPS

B20
DLJ
2/3/06

CALABRO PAGING SERVICES
Controls Tested—Revenue Process
12/31/05

Sample Item	Sales Invoice Number	Control Procedure		
		1	2	3
1	35381	✓	✓	✓
2	82765	E	✓	✓
•			•	•
•			•	•
48	1347	✓	✓	•
49	1283	E		✓
•		•		✓
•		•		•
•		•		•
77	52140	✓		•
78	88878	✓		✓
•				✓
•				•
91	107409			✓
92	17080			✓
93	122891			✓
Number of deviations		2	0	0
Sample size		78	48	93
Sample deviation rate		2.6%	0%	0%
Computed upper deviation rate		8.2%	5.0%	3.3%
Tolerable deviation rate		6%	8%	5%
Auditor's decision		Does not support reliance	Supports reliance	Supports reliance

Tick Mark Legend
✓ = Sales or lease contract examined for proper performance of control procedure. No exception.
E = Control *not* performed properly.

controls are tested on one sampling unit, auditors often decide to test all controls for the full sample when such testing can be efficiently conducted. The choice of whether to test all controls for the full sample is a matter of risk management. The argument supporting this approach is that since the auditor is physically inspecting the documentation in the full sample, the auditor may want to reduce the risk that deficiencies go undetected in the documents examined for the full sample. The concern is that at some future date a litigation event may identify deviations in sample items 79 to 93 for control 1, and those deviations seem readily apparent to the courts based only on a cursory review of the documents. In legal terms, if the auditor failed to detect a deviation that a jury believes a professional auditor should have detected, then the risk that the auditor could be successfully sued for negligence increases. Chapter 20 covers auditor legal liability and the definitions of negligence.

Before calculating the sample results and drawing final conclusions on the sampling plan, Jones investigates the nature and cause of the exceptions. Jones also considers whether the deviations may impact the other phases of the audit. In the current example, two deviations were detected for control 1, which relates to proper authorization of credit. Jones's investigation indicates that both deviations had occurred when sales in excess of credit limits were made to existing customers. Further investigation disclosed that the sales manager instead of the credit manager had approved the sale. Jones now knows the nature and cause of the errors. The effect of the control deviations is likely to be an increase in the amount of audit work conducted on the allowance for uncollectible accounts.

Calculate the Sample Deviation and the Computed Upper Deviation Rates (Step 6)

Exhibit 8–3 shows the results of the tests of the three controls. Jones calculates the sample deviation rate and the computed upper deviation rate for each control tested. To determine the computed upper deviation rate, Jones uses either Table 8–9 or Table 8–10, depending on the desired confidence level for the test. Therefore, for control 1, Jones uses Table 8–9 in the following way: The column for the actual number of deviations found (2 deviations) is read down until the appropriate row for sample size is found. If the exact sample size is not found, the closest smaller sample size is used. This approach provides a conservative (larger) computed upper deviation rate. For control 1, the row for a sample size of 75 is used. The computed upper deviation rate for control 1 is 8.2 percent. Thus, for control 1, the sample deviation rate is 2.6 percent and the allowance for sampling risk is 5.6 percent (8.2 − 2.6). For control 2, Table 8–10 is used because the desired confidence level is 90 percent. In this case, no deviations were found, so the sample

TABLE 8–9	**Statistical Sample Results Evaluation Table (Computed Upper Deviation Rates) for Attribute Sampling—95 Percent Desired Confidence Level**

	Actual Number of Deviations Found										
Sample Size	*0*	*1*	*2*	*3*	*4*	*5*	*6*	*7*	*8*	*9*	*10*
25	11.3	17.6	*	*	*	*	*	*	*	*	*
30	9.5	14.9	19.6	*	*	*	*	*	*	*	*
35	8.3	12.9	17.0	*	*	*	*	*	*	*	*
40	7.3	11.4	15.0	18.3	*	*	*	*	*	*	*
45	6.5	10.2	13.4	16.4	19.2	*	*	*	*	*	*
50	5.9	9.2	12.1	14.8	17.4	19.9	*	*	*	*	*
55	5.4	8.4	11.1	13.5	15.9	18.2	*	*	*	*	*
60	4.9	7.7	10.2	12.5	14.7	16.8	18.8	*	*	*	*
65	4.6	7.1	9.4	11.5	13.6	15.5	17.4	19.3	*	*	*
70	4.2	6.6	8.8	10.8	12.6	14.5	16.3	18.0	19.7	*	*
75	4.0	6.2	8.2	10.1	11.8	13.6	15.2	16.9	18.5	20.0	*
80	3.7	5.8	7.7	9.5	11.1	12.7	14.3	15.9	17.4	18.9	*
90	3.3	5.2	6.9	8.4	9.9	11.4	12.8	14.2	15.5	16.8	18.2
100	3.0	4.7	6.2	7.6	9.0	10.3	11.5	12.8	14.0	15.2	16.4
125	2.4	3.8	5.0	6.1	7.2	8.3	9.3	10.3	11.3	12.3	13.2
150	2.0	3.2	4.2	5.1	6.0	6.9	7.8	8.6	9.5	10.3	11.1
200	1.5	2.4	3.2	3.9	4.6	5.2	5.9	6.5	7.2	7.8	8.4

*Over 20 percent.

| TABLE 8-10 | **Statistical Sample Results Evaluation Table (Computed Upper Deviation Rates) for Attribute Sampling—90 Percent Desired Confidence Level** |

	Actual Number of Deviations Found										
Sample Size	0	1	2	3	4	5	6	7	8	9	10
20	10.9	18.1	*	*	*	*	*	*	*	*	*
25	8.8	14.7	19.9	*	*	*	*	*	*	*	*
30	7.4	12.4	16.8	*	*	*	*	*	*	*	*
35	6.4	10.7	14.5	18.1	*	*	*	*	*	*	*
40	5.6	9.4	12.8	16.0	19.0	*	*	*	*	*	*
45	5.0	8.4	11.4	14.3	17.0	19.7	*	*	*	*	*
50	4.6	7.6	10.3	12.9	15.4	17.8	*	*	*	*	*
55	4.1	6.9	9.4	11.8	14.1	16.3	18.4	*	*	*	*
60	3.8	6.4	8.7	10.8	12.9	15.0	16.9	18.9	*	*	*
70	3.3	5.5	7.5	9.3	11.1	12.9	14.6	16.3	17.9	19.6	*
80	2.9	4.8	6.6	8.2	9.8	11.3	12.8	14.3	15.8	17.2	18.6
90	2.6	4.3	5.9	7.3	8.7	10.1	11.5	12.8	14.1	15.4	16.6
100	2.3	3.9	5.3	6.6	7.9	9.1	10.3	11.5	12.7	13.9	15.0
120	2.0	3.3	4.4	5.5	6.6	7.6	8.7	9.7	10.7	11.6	12.6
160	1.5	2.5	3.3	4.2	5.0	5.8	6.5	7.3	8.0	8.8	9.5
200	1.2	2.0	2.7	3.4	4.0	4.6	5.3	5.9	6.5	7.1	7.6

*Over 20 percent.

deviation rate is 0 percent and the upper computed deviation rate (and allowance for sampling risk) is 5 percent. No control deviations were found for control 3; therefore, the sample deviation rate is 0 percent. Table 8–9 shows a computed upper deviation rate (and allowance for sampling risk) of 3.3 percent.

Exhibit 8–4 shows the output from ACL. The auditor chooses the sampling button on the menu bar and selects "evaluate error." The evaluate window is then displayed and the auditor enters the relevant data: Confidence is 95 percent, sample size is 95, and 0 errors. The estimated limit error frequency (i.e., computed upper deviation rate) is 3.16 percent.

Draw Final Conclusions (Step 7)

The statistical conclusion about each control is made by comparing the tolerable deviation rate to the computed upper deviation rate. If the computed upper deviation rate is less than the tolerable deviation rate, the statistical tests indicate that the control is operating effectively or is reliable. If the computed upper deviation rate is greater than the tolerable deviation rate, the sample evidence does not support the reliability of the control. Exhibit 8–3 shows that the sample evidence does not support the operating effectiveness of control 1 (credit authorization) because the computed upper deviation rate (8.2 percent) exceeds the tolerable deviation rate (6 percent). In this case, the sample deviation rate was 2.6 percent and the allowance for sampling risk was 5.6 percent. The sample evidence supports the reliability of controls 2 and 3 because the computed upper deviation rate is less than the tolerable deviation rate. In this example, there appear to be no other

EXHIBIT 8–4

Evaluation Results from ACL™

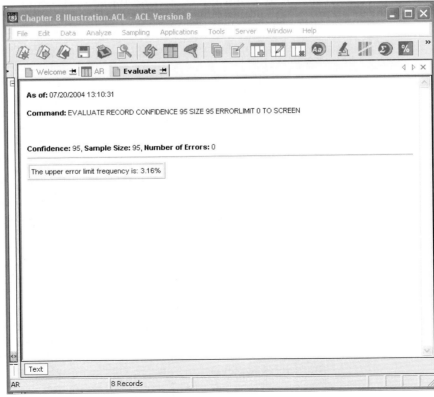

controls or other evidence to support the operating effectiveness of control 1. Thus, Jones increases both the assessed level of control risk and the substantive procedures related to the valuation assertion.

If Jones were performing tests of controls for the audit of internal control over financial reporting for a public company, he would conclude that controls 2 and 3 operate effectively and that the exceptions in control 1 represent a control deficiency. He would then need to evaluate the likelihood and magnitude of a potential misstatement arising as a result of the control deficiency.

Nonstatistical Sampling for Tests of Controls

[LO 8]   When conducting a nonstatistical sampling application for tests of controls, the auditor considers each of the steps shown in Table 8–2. The only differences between nonstatistical and statistical sampling occur in the following steps:

- Determining the sample size.
- Selecting the sample items.
- Calculating the computed upper deviation rate.

Determining the Sample Size

When a nonstatistical sampling application is used, the auditor should consider the desired confidence, the tolerable deviation rate, and the expected population deviation rate when determining sample size. However, the auditor is not required to use a statistical formula or table to determine sample size. Instead, guidance in audit firm policy and professional judgment are used to relate these factors and determine the appropriate sample size for the application; for example, an auditor might consider each of these factors and determine that a sample size of 30 is adequate.

A number of public accounting firms establish guidelines for nonstatistical sample sizes for tests of controls. Typically, accounting firms' nonstatistical guidelines are consistent with sampling theory and are designed to provide two primary benefits: (1) to simplify the judgments required by field auditors by having experts at firm headquarters make firmwide judgments and (2) to improve consistency in sampling applications within and across engagement teams. For example, a firm might establish guidelines as follows:

Desired Level of Controls Reliance	Sample Size
Low	15–20
Moderate	25–35
High	40–60

In developing nonstatistical sampling guidelines like those above, the firm's experts have decided what confidence levels achieve low, moderate, and high assurance (say 70–75, 80–85, and 90–95 percent confidence). The experts have decided reasonable levels of tolerable deviation rates (say 5 to 10 percent), and they have decided to base an initial sample on zero expected deviations. Following this guidance, if one or more deviations are found in the sample, the auditor needs to expand the sample or increase the assessed level of control risk.

Selecting the Sample Items

While random-sample or systematic-sample (with a random start) selection is required for statistical sampling, nonstatistical sampling allows the use of those selection methods as well as other selection methods such as haphazard sampling. When a haphazard selection approach is used, sampling units are selected without any conscious bias—that is, without a special reason for including or omitting items from the sample. This does not imply that the items are selected in a careless manner; rather, the sampling units are selected to represent the population. Haphazard selection may be useful for nonstatistical sampling, but it should not be used for statistical sampling because the auditor cannot measure the probability of an item being selected. When using audit sampling of any kind, the auditor should avoid distorting the sample by selecting only items that are unusual or large or items that are the first or last items in the frame, because the auditor needs a sample that represents the population in order to draw inferences about the population from the sample. This is not to say that selection of unusual, large or risky events, transactions, or balances should be avoided in other nonsampling audit procedures. To the contrary, the auditor should focus specific audit procedures on all such items and not turn the selection of these items over to chance (i.e., random or haphazard selection), which is required for audit sampling.

Calculating the Computed Upper Deviation Rate

With a nonstatistical sample, the auditor can calculate the sample deviation rate but cannot quantify the computed upper deviation rate and the sampling risk associated with the test. The AICPA Audit Guide *Audit Sampling* provides the following advice for considering sampling risk in a nonstatistical test of controls:

> It is generally appropriate for the auditor to assume that the sample results do not support the planned assessed level of control risk if the rate of deviation identified in the sample exceeds the expected population deviation rate used in designing the sample. In that case, there is likely to be an unacceptably high risk that the true deviation rate in the population exceeds the tolerable rate. If the auditor concludes that there is an unacceptably high risk that the true population deviation rate could exceed the tolerable rate, it might be practical to expand the test to sufficient additional items to reduce the risk to an acceptable level. Rather than testing additional items, however, it is generally more efficient to increase the auditor's assessed level of control risk to the level supported by the results of the original sample.[6]

Suppose an auditor planned a nonstatistical sampling application by setting the desired confidence level at high (i.e., 90 to 95 percent), the expected population deviation rate at 1.5 percent, and the tolerable deviation rate at 8 percent. Assume the auditor judgmentally determines to select a sample size of 50 items and makes the selections haphazardly. If the auditor detects no control deviations, the sample deviation rate is 0 percent. In this instance, the sample deviation rate (0 percent) is less than the expected population deviation rate (1.5 percent), and there is an acceptable risk that the true population deviation rate exceeds the tolerable deviation rate. If one control deviation is detected, the sample deviation rate is 2 percent.

---

[6]American Institute of Certified Public Accountants, *Audit Sampling* (Audit Guide), (New York: AICPA, 2001), p. 28.

Because the sample deviation rate is greater than the expected population deviation rate (1.5 percent), there is an unacceptably high risk that the true population deviation rate exceeds the tolerable deviation rate. Referring to the statistical evaluation table illustrates why the results of the nonstatistical sample are not likely to support the effectiveness of the control. Table 8–9 shows that if one deviation is found in a sample of 50 items, the computed upper deviation rate is 9.2 percent. This exceeds the tolerable deviation rate of 8 percent.

Students and auditors are sometimes confused by what causes a sampling approach to be "nonstatistical." An approach is nonstatistical if (1) judgment is used to determine the sample size, (2) a haphazard sample selection technique is used, and/or (3) the sample results are evaluated judgmentally. A nonstatistical approach can involve random selection and a judgmental evaluation. While haphazardly selected samples cannot be statistically evaluated, any randomly drawn sample can be statistically evaluated—even if the auditor labels the approach "nonstatistical" and even if the sample size was not statistically derived. This is an important point because it highlights the need for auditors to understand the key concepts of sampling theory even if they are using a nonstatistical approach. Remember, if an auditor randomly selects a sample and then evaluates the results judgmentally, the quality of his or her judgment can be evaluated against statistical theory by outside experts.

Advanced Module: Considering the Effect of the Population Size

The population size generally has little or no effect on the sample size. If the population contains more than 500 units, the effect on the sample size is negligible. The following examples assume a desired confidence of 90 percent, a tolerable deviation rate of 10 percent, and an expected population deviation rate of 1 percent.

Population Size	Sample Size
100	31
500	38
1,000	39
5,000	39

The attribute-sampling tables presented earlier in this chapter assume a large population. When the population size is smaller than 500, the sample size taken from the tables can be adjusted by using the finite population correction factor as follows:

$$\text{Finite population correction factor} = \sqrt{\frac{1 - n}{N}}$$

where

n = the sample size from the tables
N = the number of units in the population

For example, the sample size shown in the preceding table is 39 when population size is 1,000. If the population size were 100, the sample size of 39 could be adjusted as follows:

$$\text{Sample size} = \sqrt{\frac{1 - n}{N}}$$

$$= 39\sqrt{\frac{1 - 39}{100}} = 31$$

KEY TERMS

Allowance for sampling risk. The uncertainty that results from sampling; the difference between the expected mean of the population and the tolerable deviation or misstatement.

Attribute sampling. Sampling used to estimate the proportion of a population that possesses a specified characteristic.

Audit sampling. The application of an audit procedure to less than 100 percent of the items within an account or class of transactions for the purpose of evaluating some characteristic of the balance or class.

Classical variables sampling. The use of normal distribution theory to estimate the dollar amount of misstatement for a class of transactions or an account balance.

Desired confidence level. The probability that the true but unknown measure of the characteristic of interest is within specified limits.

Expected population deviation rate. The deviation rate that the auditor expects to exist in the population.

Monetary-unit sampling. Attribute-sampling techniques used to estimate the dollar amount of misstatement for a class of transactions or an account balance.

Nonsampling risk. The possibility that the auditor may use inappropriate audit procedures, fail to detect a misstatement when applying an audit procedure, or misinterpret an audit result.

Nonstatistical sampling. Audit sampling that relies on the auditor's judgment to select the sample and/or evaluate the results for the purpose of reaching a conclusion about the population.

Risk of incorrect acceptance. The risk that the sample supports the conclusion that the control is operating effectively when it is not or that the recorded account balance is not materially misstated when it is materially misstated.

Risk of incorrect rejection. The risk that the sample supports the conclusion that the control is not operating effectively when it actually is or that recorded account balance is materially misstated when it is not materially misstated.

Sampling risk. The possibility that the sample drawn is not representative of the population and that, as a result, the auditor reaches an incorrect conclusion about the reliability of the control, the account balance, or class of transactions based on the sample.

Sampling unit. The individual member of the population being sampled.
Statistical sampling. Sampling that uses the laws of probability to select and evaluate the results of an audit sample, thereby permitting the auditor to quantify the sampling risk for the purpose of reaching a conclusion about the population.
Tolerable deviation rate. The maximum deviation rate from a prescribed control that the auditor is willing to accept without altering the planned assessed level of control risk.

www.mhhe.com/ messier4e	Visit the book's Online Learning Center for a multiple-choice quiz that will allow you to assess your understanding of chapter concepts.

REVIEW QUESTIONS

[LO 1] 8-1 Define *audit sampling*. Why do auditors sample instead of examining every transaction?

[2] 8-2 Distinguish between Type I and Type II errors. What terms are used to describe these errors when the auditor is conducting tests of controls and substantive tests? What costs are potentially incurred by auditors when such decision errors occur?

[3] 8-3 List audit evidence choices that do not involve sampling.

[4] 8-4 Distinguish between nonstatistical and statistical sampling. What are the advantages and disadvantages of using statistical sampling?

[6,7] 8-5 Define *attribute sampling*. Why is this sampling technique appropriate for tests of controls?

[6,7,8] 8-6 After defining the population, the auditor must make what additional decisions concerning the population?

[7] 8-7 List the four factors that enter into the sample size decision. What is the relationship between sample size and each of these factors?

[6,7,8] 8-8 In performing certain audit procedures the auditor may encounter voided documents, inapplicable documents, or missing documents. How should each of these situations be handled within the attribute-sampling application?

[6,7,8] 8-9 The auditor should perform error analysis when deviations are found in a sampling application. What are the purposes of performing error analysis?

[8] 8-10 How should the results of a nonstatistical sample be evaluated in terms of considering sampling risk?

MULTIPLE-CHOICE QUESTIONS

[4] 8-11 An advantage of statistical sampling over nonstatistical sampling is that statistical sampling helps an auditor to
a. Eliminate the risk of nonsampling errors.
b. Reduce audit risk and materiality to a relatively low level.
c. Measure the sufficiency of the evidential matter obtained.
d. Minimize the failure to detect errors and fraud.

[4,6]   8-12   Samples to test internal controls are intended to provide a basis for an auditor to conclude whether

a. The controls are operating effectively.
b. The financial statements are materially misstated.
c. The risk of incorrect acceptance is too high.
d. Materiality for planning purposes is at a sufficiently low level.

[6,7]   8-13   To determine the sample size for a test of controls, an auditor should consider the tolerable deviation rate, the desired confidence level, and the

a. Expected population deviation rate.
b. Computed upper precision limit.
c. Risk of assessing control risk too high.
d. Risk of incorrect rejection.

[6,7]   8-14   Which of the following combinations results in a decrease in sample size in an attribute sample for a test of controls?

	Desired Confidence Level	Tolerable Deviation Rate	Expected Population Deviation Rate
a.	Decrease	Decrease	Increase
b.	Increase	Increase	Decrease
c.	Decrease	Increase	Decrease
d.	Decrease	Increase	Increase

Questions 8-15 and 8-16 are based on the following information:

An auditor desired to test credit approval on 10,000 sales invoices processed during the year. The auditor designed a statistical sample that would provide 1 percent risk of assessing control risk too low that not more than 7 percent of the sales invoices lacked approval. The auditor estimated from previous experience that about $2^1/_2$ percent of the sales invoices lacked approval. A sample of 200 invoices was examined, and 7 of them were lacking approval. The auditor then determined the computed upper deviation rate to be 8 percent.

[6,7]   8-15   In the evaluation of this sample, the auditor decided to increase the level of the preliminary assessment of control risk because the

a. Tolerable deviation rate (7 percent) was less than the computed upper deviation rate (8 percent).
b. Expected population deviation rate (7 percent) was more than the percentage of errors in the sample ($3^1/_2$ percent).
c. Computed upper deviation rate (8 percent) was more than the percentage of errors in the sample ($3^1/_2$ percent).
d. Expected population deviation rate ($2^1/_2$ percent) was less than the tolerable deviation rate (7 percent).

[6,7]   8-16   The allowance for sampling risk was

a. $5^1/_2$ percent.
b. $4^1/_2$ percent.
c. $3^1/_2$ percent.
d. 1 percent.

[2,6]   8-17   The following table depicts the auditor's estimated computed upper deviation rate compared with the tolerable deviation rate, and it also depicts the true population deviation rate compared with the tolerable deviation rate.

	True State of Population	
Auditor's Estimate Based on Sample Results	*Deviation Rate Is Less Than Tolerable Deviation Rate*	*Deviation Rate Exceeds Tolerable Deviation Rate*
Computed upper deviation rate is less than tolerable deviation rate.	I	III
Computed upper deviation rate exceeds tolerable deviation rate.	II	IV

As a result of tests of controls, the auditor assesses control risk higher than necessary and thereby increases substantive testing. This is illustrated by situation

a. I.

b. II.

c. III.

d. IV.

[6]   8-18   Which of the following statements is correct concerning statistical sampling in tests of controls?

a. Deviations from controls at a given rate usually result in misstatements at a higher rate.

b. As the population size doubles, the sample size should also double.

c. The qualitative aspects of deviations are *not* considered by the auditor.

d. There is an inverse relationship between the sample size and the tolerable deviation rate.

[2,6]   8-19   What is an auditor's evaluation of a statistical sample for attributes when a test of 50 documents results in three deviations if the tolerable deviation rate is 7 percent, the expected population deviation rate is 5 percent, and the allowance for sampling risk is 2 percent?

a. The planned assessed level of control risk should be modified because the tolerable deviation rate plus the allowance for sampling risk exceeds the expected population deviation rate.

b. The sample results should be accepted as support for the planned assessed level of control risk because the sample deviation rate plus the allowance for sampling risk exceeds the tolerable deviation rate.

c. The sample results should be accepted as support for the planned assessed level of control risk because the tolerable deviation rate less the allowance for sampling risk equals the expected population deviation rate.

d. The planned assessed level of control risk should be modified because the sample deviation rate plus the allowance for sampling risk exceeds the tolerable deviation rate.

[2,6]   8-20   As a result of sampling procedures applied as tests of controls, an auditor incorrectly assesses control risk lower than appropriate. The most likely explanation for this situation is that

a. The deviation rates of both the auditor's sample and the population exceed the tolerable deviation rate.

b. The deviation rates of both the auditor's sample and the population are less than the tolerable deviation rate.

c. The deviation rate in the auditor's sample is less than the tolerable deviation rate, but the deviation rate in the population exceeds the tolerable deviation rate.

d. The deviation rate in the auditor's sample exceeds the tolerable deviation rate, but the deviation rate in the population is less than the tolerable deviation rate.

PROBLEMS

[1]   8-21   Audit sampling is defined as applying an audit procedure to less than 100 percent of the population. The fact that an audit involves sampling is noted in the scope paragraph of the auditor's report, which contains the phrase "An audit includes examining, on a test basis." When an auditor uses sampling, an element of uncertainty enters into the auditor's conclusions.

Required:

a. Explain the auditor's justification for accepting the uncertainties that are inherent in the sampling process.

b. Discuss the uncertainties that collectively embody the concept of audit risk.

c. Discuss the nature of sampling risk and nonsampling risk. Include the effect of sampling risk on tests of controls.

[3]   8-22   Following is a list of audit procedures used as tests of controls in the revenue process.

1. Observing and evaluating segregation of duties.
2. Testing of whether sales invoices are supported by authorized customer orders and shipping documents.
3. Reviewing client's procedures for accounting for the numerical sequence of shipping documents.
4. Examining sales orders for proper credit approval.
5. Recomputing the information on copies of sales invoices.
6. Comparing the average days outstanding in accounts receivable with industry averages.

Required:

Indicate those audit procedures that do not involve sampling.

[6,7]   8-23   Following is a set of situations that may or may not involve sampling.

1. An auditor is examining loan receivables at a local bank. The population of loans contains two strata. One stratum is composed of 25 loans that are each greater than $1 million. The second stratum contains 450 loans that are less than $1 million. The auditor has decided to test all loans greater than $1 million and 15 loans less than $1 million.

2. Assume the same facts as number 1 except that the auditor decides to apply analytical procedures to the second strata of loans.
3. An auditor has haphazardly selected 30 sales invoices to be examined for proper pricing of the goods purchased by the customer.
4. The prepaid insurance account is made up of four policies that total $45,000. The audit has decided that this account is immaterial and decides that no policies will be examined.

Required:
Indicate which situations involve sampling and why.

[6,7] 8-24 Jenny Jacobs, CPA, is planning to use attribute sampling in order to determine the degree of reliance to be placed on an audit client's system of internal control over sales. Jacobs has begun to develop an outline of the main steps in the sampling plan as follows:
1. State the test objectives (for example, to test the reliability of internal controls over sales).
2. Define the population (the period covered by the test, the sampling unit, the completeness of the population).
3. Define the sampling unit (for example, client copies of sales invoices).

Required:
a. What are the remaining steps in the outline that Jacobs should include in the statistical test of sales invoices?
b. How does statistical methodology help the auditor develop a satisfactory sampling plan?

(AICPA, adapted)

[6] 8-25 Determine the sample size for each of the control procedures shown in the following table:

Parameters	Control Procedure			
	1	*2*	*3*	*4*
Risk of incorrect acceptance	5%	5%	10%	10%
Tolerable deviation rate	4%	5%	7%	8%
Expected population deviation rate	1%	2%	3%	4%
Sample size				

[6] 8-26 Using the sample sizes determined in Problem 8-25 and the number of deviations shown here, determine the sample deviation rate, the computed upper deviation rate, and the auditor's decision for each control procedure.

Results	Control Procedure			
	1	*2*	*3*	*4*
Number of deviations	0	5	4	3
Sample size				
Sample deviation rate				
Computed upper deviation rate				
Auditor's decision				

[6]   8-27   Determine the sample size for each of the control procedures shown in the following table:

Parameters	Control Procedure			
	1	2	3	4
Risk of incorrect acceptance	5%	5%	10%	10%
Tolerable deviation rate	6%	7%	4%	3%
Expected population deviation rate	2%	2%	1%	0%
Sample size				

[6]   8-28   Using the sample sizes determined in Problem 8-27 and the number of deviations shown here, determine the sample deviation rate, computed upper deviation rate, and the auditor's decision for each control procedure.

Results	Control Procedure			
	1	2	3	4
Number of deviations	4	2	2	0
Sample size				
Sample deviation rate				
Computed upper deviation rate				
Auditor's decision				

[8]   8-29   Calgari Clothing Company manufactures high-quality silk ties that are marketed under a number of copyrighted names. Winkle & Huss have been the company's auditors for five years. Lisa Austen, the senior-in-charge of the audit, has reviewed Calgari's controls over purchasing and inventory, and she determined that a number of controls can be relied upon to reduce control risk. Austen has decided to test two control procedures over purchases and inventory: (1) purchase orders are agreed to receiving reports and vendor's invoices for product, quantity, and price; and (2) inventory is transferred to raw material stores using an approved, prenumbered receiving report.

    Austen decided to use a nonstatistical sampling approach based on the following judgments for each control procedure and has judgmentally decided to use a sample size of 40 purchase orders for control 1 and 20 receiving reports for control 2.

Parameters	Control Procedure	
	1	2
Desired confidence	95%	90%
Tolerable deviation rate	7%	9%
Expected population deviation rate	3%	4%

After completing the examination of the sample items, Austen noted one deviation for each control procedure.

Required:

What conclusion should Austen reach about each control procedure? Justify your answer.

[8]   8-30   Nathan Matthews conducted a test of controls where the tolerable deviation rate was set at 5 percent and the expected population deviation rate was 3 percent. Using a sample size of 150, Matthews performed the planned test of controls. He found six deviations in the sample and he calculated the computed upper deviation rate to be 7 percent.

Required:

a. Based on the sample results, what is the allowance for sampling risk?

b. Assume that Matthews preliminarily assessed control risk as "low." Given the results above, the auditor could decide to do one of three things: (1) increase the sample size, (2) increase the preliminary assessment of control risk, or (3) not adjust the preliminary assessment of control risk. Describe how Matthews could justify each of those three actions.

[8]   8-31   Doug Iceberge, senior-in-charge of the audit of Fisher Industries, has decided to test the following two controls for Fisher's revenue process.

1. All sales invoices are supported by proper documentation, that is, a sales order and a shipping document.

2. All sales invoices are mathematically correct.
   Iceberge has decided to use a nonstatistical sampling approach based on the following judgments for each control and has judgmentally decided to use a sample size of 50 sales invoice packets.

	Control Procedure	
Parameters	1	2
Desired confidence level	95%	90%
Risk of assessing control risk too low	5%	10%
Tolerable deviation rate	6%	8%
Expected population deviation rate	3%	3%

After completing the examination of the 50 sample items, Iceberge noted one deviation for control 1 and two deviations for control 2.

Required:

What should Iceberge conclude about each control? Justify your answer.

DISCUSSION CASE

[2,5,6]   8-32   Baker, CPA, was engaged to audit Mill Company's financial statements for the year ended September 30. After studying Mill's internal control, Baker decided to obtain evidence about the effectiveness of both the design and the operation of the controls that may support

a low assessed level of control risk concerning Mill's shipping and billing functions. During the prior years' audits, Baker had used nonstatistical sampling, but for the current year Baker used a statistical sample in the tests of controls to eliminate the need for judgment.

Baker wanted to assess control risk at a low level, so a tolerable deviation rate of 20 percent was established. To estimate the population deviation rate and the computed upper deviation rate, Baker decided to apply a discovery sampling technique of attribute sampling that would use an expected population deviation rate of 3 percent for the 8,000 shipping documents and to defer consideration of the allowable risk of assessing control risk too low until the sample results were evaluated. Baker used the tolerable deviation rate, the population size, and the expected population deviation rate to determine that a sample size of 80 would be sufficient. When it was subsequently determined that the actual population was about 10,000 shipping documents, Baker increased the sample size to 100.

Baker's objective was to ascertain whether Mill's shipments had been properly billed. Baker took a sample of 100 invoices by selecting the first 25 invoices from the first month of each quarter. Baker then compared the invoices to the corresponding prenumbered shipping documents.

When Baker tested the sample, eight deviations were discovered. Additionally, one shipment that should have been billed at $10,443 was actually billed at $10,434. Baker considered this $9 to be immaterial and did not count it as an error.

In evaluating the sample results, Baker made the initial determination that a 5 percent risk of assessing control risk too low was desired and, using the appropriate statistical sampling table, determined that for eight observed deviations from a sample size of 100, the computed upper deviation rate was 14 percent. Baker then calculated the allowance for sampling risk to be 5 percent, the difference between the actual sample deviation rate (8 percent) and the expected error rate (3 percent). Baker reasoned that the actual sample deviation rate (8 percent) plus the allowance for sampling risk (5 percent) was less than the computed upper deviation rate (14 percent); therefore, the sample supported a low level of control risk.

Required:
Describe each incorrect assumption, statement, and inappropriate application of attribute sampling in Baker's procedures.

(AICPA, adapted)

CHAPTER 9

LEARNING OBJECTIVES

Upon completion of this chapter you will

[1] Understand the similarities and differences between audit sampling for tests of controls and substantive tests of details of account balances.

[2] Learn to apply monetary-unit sampling.

[3] Work through an extended example of monetary-unit sampling.

[4] Learn to apply nonstatistical sampling techniques.

[5] Learn to apply classical variables difference estimation.

[6] Work through an example of classical variables difference estimation.

RELEVANT ACCOUNTING AND AUDITING PRONOUNCEMENTS

AICPA, *Audit Sampling* (Audit Guide) (New York: AICPA, 2001)

AU 311, Planning and Supervision

AU 312, Audit Risk and Materiality in Conducting an Audit

AU 316, Consideration of Fraud in a Financial Statement Audit

AU 333, Management Representations

AU 350, Audit Sampling

AU 380, Communication with Audit Committees

Audit Sampling: An Application to Substantive Tests of Account Balances

Major Phases of an Audit

Client acceptance/
continuance and establishing
engagement terms
(Chapter 5)

|

Preplanning
(Chapter 5)

|

Establish materiality
and assess risks
(Chapter 3)

|

Plan the audit
(Chapters 3 and 5)

|

Consider and audit
internal control
(Chapters 6 and 7)

|

Audit business processes
and related accounts
(e.g. revenue generation)
(Chapters 10–16)

|

Complete the audit
(Chapter 17)

|

Evaluate results and issue audit
report (Chapters 2 and 18)

This chapter demonstrates the application of audit sampling to substantive tests of details of account balances. In Chapter 8, attribute sampling was used to determine whether controls were operating effectively and could therefore be relied on by the auditor to generate accurate accounting information. Thus, the objective of attribute sampling was to determine the reliability of the client's controls. In this chapter, the purpose of the sampling application is to determine if a financial statement account is fairly stated.

Two statistical sampling techniques, *monetary-unit sampling* and *classical variables sampling,* and nonstatistical sampling are demonstrated in this chapter. While both statistical sampling methods can provide sufficient, competent evidence monetary-unit sampling may be more practical for most audit applications. The chapter starts with an introduction of monetary-unit sampling and an extended example. Nonstatistical sampling is then covered. The *Advanced Module* contains a discussion and example of classical variables sampling.

Sampling for Substantive Tests of Details of Account Balances

[LO 1]   The basic statistical concepts discussed in Chapter 8 are also applicable for sampling approaches used to test account balances. Three important determinants of sample size are desired confidence level, tolerable misstatement, and estimated misstatement. Misstatements discovered in the audit sample must be projected to the population, and there must be an allowance for sampling risk.

In the preface to Chapter 8, we asked you to imagine that you were an apple inspector. We did this to illustrate some of the basic concepts of audit sampling before covering the technical details. Before we get into the details of audit sampling for substantive tests, we want you to use your developing professional judgment and understanding of sampling to evaluate the sampling results related to a test of the inventory balance provided below:

Book value of the inventory account balance	$3,000,000
Book value of items sampled	$ 100,000
Audited value of items sampled	$ 98,000
Total amount of overstatement observed in audit sample	$ 2,000

The purpose of audit sampling is to draw inferences about the entire population (the reported inventory account balance in the example above) from the results of a sample. Using just the information provided above, what is your best estimate of the misstatement in the inventory account balance? In Chapter 8 our best estimate of the population deviation rate for control testing was the sample deviation rate. Similarly, when using audit sampling to test account balances, we will want to project the misstatement observed in the sample to the population. In the example above, one method of misstatement projection is to compute the ratio of misstatement to the total dollars sampled: 2 percent ($2,000 ÷ $100,000). Applying this ratio to the entire account balance produces a *best estimate* or *projected misstatement* in the inventory account of $60,000 (2% × $3,000,000). If your best estimate is that the account is overstated by $60,000, do you believe the account is fairly stated? The answer to this question, like many questions in auditing is, "it depends." It depends in part on the amount of misstatement that can be tolerated for the inventory account. If the amount of misstatement that can be tolerated for this account is $50,000, then we cannot conclude that the account is fairly stated because our best estimate (or projected misstatement) is higher than the amount we can tolerate. What if tolerable misstatement was $110,000; would you conclude that the account is fairly stated? The answer is again, "it depends." Whenever sampling is used, the evaluation must include an allowance for sampling risk. When sampling is used to estimate monetary misstatement, an upper and lower confidence bound or misstatement limit must be established as an allowance for sampling risk. In the above example, the misstatement in the population could be $60,000, but it also might be higher or lower because the estimate is based on a sample. If tolerable misstatement is $110,000, and the upper limit on the account's possible misstatement is less than $110,000, then the account is considered fairly stated. The size of the upper limit on misstatement is largely dependent on the sample size, which is also directly related to the desired confidence level.

You may remember from your statistics courses using concepts such as "standard deviation" and a "normal distribution" (i.e., "Z scores") to compute *confidence limits* (which produce a *confidence interval*). This traditional statistical approach is used for classical variables sampling, which is covered in the *Advanced Module*. Before personal computers were commonly available, the mathematical complexity of classical variable sampling was problematic for auditors. In response, auditors developed an audit sampling approach for testing balances called monetary-unit sampling. Monetary-unit sampling is based on attribute-sampling concepts. While the computations involved in classical variables sampling can now easily be performed with a personal computer or handheld calculator, auditors have found that monetary-unit sampling provides other important advantages. For this reason, popular audit sampling software, such as ACL, include monetary-unit sampling but not classical variables sampling. However, MUS is not the best approach to use for all substantive tests of details; therefore, in this chapter we also cover nonstatistical sampling and classical variables sampling.

Monetary-Unit Sampling

[LO 2] Monetary-unit sampling (MUS) uses attribute-sampling theory to express a conclusion in dollar amounts rather than as a rate of occurrence. MUS is commonly used by auditors to test accounts such as accounts receivable, loans receivable, investment securities, and inventory. While MUS is based on attribute-sampling theory, the fact that MUS is designed to test monetary amounts (e.g., dollars, yen, pesos) rather than internal control effectiveness causes important differences in these techniques. The differences are driven by the characteristics of control deviations and monetary misstatements. In attribute sampling, the control either works or it does not. Thus, all items sampled are either correct or a deviation. Attributes sampling provides an estimate and upper limit on the percentage of the time that a control is failing. With MUS, the sampling item tested may be valid and posted to the correct account in the correct period, but the dollar amount may not be accurately recorded. For instance, an invoice for $2,565 might be entered into the accounting system as $2,655. In this case there is a misstatement, but the misstatement is only about 3.5 percent of the transaction. A direct application of attribute sampling to monetary items would treat all misstatements as deviations, or 100 percent misstatements. However, doing so would not result in a useful estimate of the monetary amount of the misstatement. MUS begins with attribute-sampling concepts as a foundation but takes into consideration misstatement amounts observed in each sampling unit when computing the best estimate of the population misstatement and formulating the confidence limits around this estimated misstatement.

To summarize, the basic underlying concepts of MUS are straightforward. MUS uses attribute-sampling theory to estimate the *percentage* of monetary units in a population that might be misstated and then multiplies this percentage by an estimate of *how much* the dollars are misstated. Keep these basic concepts in mind as you study MUS in this chapter.

MUS is designed primarily to test for *overstatement* errors. However, it can accommodate understatement errors if special considerations are made during the evaluation of the sample results. MUS is most appropriate for low-error-rate populations because it provides as effective a test as classical variables sampling does but has a more efficient sample size. Following are some advantages and disadvantages of MUS.

Advantages

- When the auditor expects no misstatements, MUS usually results in a smaller sample size than classical variables sampling.
- The calculation of the sample size and the evaluation of the sample results are *not* based on the variation (that is, the standard deviation) between items in the population. The standard deviation is required to compute the sample size for a classical variables sampling application because it relies on the central limit theorem.
- When applied using a probability-proportional-to-size sample selection procedure as outlined in this text, MUS automatically results in a stratified sample because sampled items are selected in proportion to their dollar amounts. Thus, larger dollar items have a higher probability of being selected. With classical variables sampling, the population must be stratified in order to focus on larger items.

Disadvantages

- The selection of zero or negative balances generally requires special design consideration. For example, if examining zero balances is important (searching for unrecorded liabilities in accounts payable), the auditor must test those items separately because such items will not be selected using a probability-proportional-to-size selection method. Alternatively, if an account such as accounts receivable contains credit balances, the auditor should segregate those items and test them separately.
- The general approach to MUS assumes that the audited amount of the sample item is not in error by more than 100 percent. If the auditor detects items that are in error by more than 100 percent, special adjustments will be necessary when calculating sample results. For example, suppose an accounts receivable account contains a debit balance book value of $1,500. If the auditor determines that the correct value for the account should be a credit balance of $3,000, the account will be in error by 300 percent. Such an item would require special consideration when the auditor projects the amount of misstatement.
- When more than one or two misstatements are detected using a MUS approach, the sample results calculations as shown in the textbook may overstate the allowance for sampling risk. This occurs because the methods used to determine the amount of misstatement

TABLE 9-1	**Steps in a Monetary-Unit Sampling Application**

Planning
1. Determine the test objectives.
2. Define the population characteristics:
   - Define the population.
   - Define the sampling unit.
   - Define a misstatement.
3. Determine the sample size, using the following inputs:
   - The desired confidence level or risk of incorrect acceptance.
   - The tolerable misstatement.
   - The expected population misstatement.
   - Population size.

Performance
4. Select sample items.
5. Perform the auditing procedures:
   - Understand and analyze any misstatements observed.

Evaluation
6. Calculate the projected misstatement and the upper limit on misstatement.
7. Draw final conclusions.

are very conservative. Thus, an auditor is more likely to reject an acceptable recorded book value and overaudit.[1]

Applying Monetary-Unit Sampling

In Chapter 8 the general considerations as to the use of sampling for substantive tests were discussed along with the steps in a sampling application. In conducting MUS for substantive tests of details of account balances, the auditor follows the same basic steps outlined in Chapter 8 for attribute sampling. Table 9–1 lists each step by the three phases in the sampling application. Again, the auditor is required to use substantial judgment and should adequately document the sampling application in the audit work papers.

Planning

Step 1: Determine the Test Objectives

Sampling may be used for substantive testing to (1) test the reasonableness of assertions about a financial statement amount (e.g., accuracy, existence) or (2) develop an estimate of some amount. The first use, which is the most frequent application of sampling as a substantive procedure in a financial statement audit, tests the assertion or hypothesis that a financial statement account is fairly stated. The second use is less frequent but is occasionally used to develop an estimate of an amount as part of a consulting engagement or in some cases to provide evidence on a client estimate (e.g., sales returns for a new product). The discussion in this chapter is limited to the use of audit

---

[1]There are alternative methods that overcome this disadvantage. However, these methods are more complex. See D. A. Leslie, A. D. Teitlebaum, and R. J. Anderson, *Dollar Unit Sampling: A Practical Guide for Auditors* (Toronto: Copp, Clark and Pitman, 1979), and W. L. Felix, Jr., R. A. Grimlund, F. J. Koster, and R. S. Roussey, "Arthur Andersen's New Monetary-Unit Sampling Approach," *Auditing: A Journal of Practice & Theory* (Fall 1990), pp. 1–16, for a discussion of alternative approaches.

sampling to test the assertion that an account or monetary population is fairly stated. The objective of MUS for substantive tests of details is to test the assertion that no material misstatements exist in an account balance, a class of transactions, or a disclosure component of the financial statements.

Step 2: Define the Population Characteristics
To achieve the test objectives, the auditor must carefully consider the characteristics of the sampling population.

Define the Population.   The auditor must define the population so that the selected sample is appropriate for the assertions being tested, because sample results can be projected only to the population from which the sample was selected. For example, if the auditor is concerned about understatements that result from omitted items (the completeness assertion), the sample cannot be drawn from a population of recorded transactions. In order to detect such understatements, the auditor should select the items from a population that includes the omitted items. For example, if the auditor is concerned about goods shipped but not billed, the population of shipping documents rather than sales invoices is the appropriate population for drawing the sample.

For MUS, the population is defined as the monetary value of an account balance, such as accounts receivable, investment securities, or inventory. As with attribute sampling, once the population has been defined, the auditor must determine that the physical representation, or *frame*, of the population is complete. For example, if the auditor is testing the accounts receivable account, he or she would foot the accounts receivable subsidiary ledger and agree the total to the general ledger account to verify the completeness of the frame. Because the auditor selects the sample from the frame, any conclusions about the population relate only to that frame, which is the physical representation of the population. If the frame and the intended sampling population differ, the auditor might very well draw an incorrect conclusion about the population.

Define the Sampling Unit.   With MUS, an individual dollar represents the sampling unit. In fact, this is where monetary-unit (or dollar-unit) sampling gets its name. For example, if the population to be sampled is the accounts receivable balance of $2.5 million, then there are 2.5 million sampling units in the population. However, because the accounts receivable balance is organized by customer or transaction (e.g., customer account or invoice number) and not individual dollars, the auditor does not audit the individual dollar but the account or transaction that contains the selected dollar. In other words, while the sampling unit is an individual dollar in a customer account (or invoice), the auditor can't very well audit a single dollar. Instead, the auditor will audit the entire account (or transaction) that contains the selected dollar. The account or transaction that contains the selected dollar is called the *logical unit*. In essence, by selecting a dollar contained in a customer account (or transaction), the auditor by extension selects the logical unit that contains the selected monetary unit to audit.

Define a Misstatement.   For MUS a misstatement is defined as the difference between monetary amounts in the client's records and amounts supported by audit evidence. A clear misstatement definition is important because definitions that are too narrow or too broad may result in inefficient or ineffective testing. For example, if an accounts receivable confirmation reports a difference between the customer records and the client's records, it would not be considered a misstatement if the difference is explainable and supportable by the circumstances, such as timing differences (e.g., the customer mistakenly confirms a balance as of January 31 when the confirmation letter requests the customer's balance as of the December 31 year-end) and other documentation supports the client's recorded value.

Step 3: Determine the Sample Size   Considerable judgment is required in determining the appropriate values for the inputs used to compute an MUS sample size. The following four factors must be considered.

Determine the Desired Confidence Level or Acceptable Risk of Incorrect Acceptance.   Confidence levels and the risk of incorrect acceptance are complements. If the auditor wants to be 95 percent confident in the sampling conclusion, then he or she must be willing to accept a 5 percent risk of incorrect acceptance. The risk of incorrect acceptance is the risk that the sample supports the conclusion that the recorded account balance is fairly stated when in fact it is not (a Type II error). This risk relates to the effectiveness of the audit. In determining an acceptable risk of incorrect acceptance, the auditor should consider the components of the audit risk model: the acceptable level of audit risk and the assessed levels of inherent and control risk. For practical purposes, the acceptable risk of incorrect acceptance is the same as detection risk (*DR*) after considering the assessed level of detection risk based on other substantive procedures such as substantive analytical procedures. If the auditor incorrectly accepts an account balance as being fairly stated when it is actually materially misstated, he or she will allow the issuance of financial statements that are not fairly presented. The users of those financial statements may then sue the auditor for damages that result from relying on those financial statements. There is an *inverse* relationship between the risk of incorrect acceptance and sample size. The lower the acceptable risk for incorrect acceptance, the larger the sample size must be. Finally, there is a *direct* relationship between the confidence level and sample size. The basic idea is fairly simple: To decrease risk or increase confidence, more work is required, which is reflected in a larger sample size.

Determine the Tolerable Misstatement.   Tolerable misstatement is the maximum amount by which the account can be misstated and still be acceptable to the auditor as being fairly presented. It will always be less than the overall materiality. In Chapter 3 we illustrated how the preliminary judgment about materiality and tolerable misstatement are determined. Remember from Chapter 3 that for an audit to be economically feasible, the auditor and users of the financial statements must tolerate some margin for misstatement (i.e., the auditor provides reasonable assurance that the financial statements are fair, not absolute assurance that the financial statements are error-free).

Sampling cannot be performed unless tolerable misstatement exceeds expected misstatement by a sufficient amount, because there must always be room for an allowance for sampling risk between the two measures. Tolerable misstatement is also inversely related to sample size—the lower the amount of tolerable misstatement, the more precise the test the auditor needs, and the larger the sample size must be.

Determine the Expected Misstatement.   The expected misstatement is the dollar amount of misstatement that the auditor believes exists in the population. The auditor can develop this expectation based on the assessment of inherent risk, prior years' results, a pilot sample, the results of related substantive procedures, or the results of tests of controls. As the expected misstatement approaches the tolerable misstatement, the auditor needs more precise information from the sample. Therefore, there is a direct relationship to sample size: The larger the expected misstatement, the larger the sample size must be.

Population Size.   Population size is directly related to sample size; however, because MUS populations are made up of individual dollars, populations tested with MUS are usually large, and as such, the effect of population size is typically not significant. In fact, when using the sample size table in Chapter 8 to determine MUS sample size (see example below), population size is not one of the inputs. We have included population size as a factor in this discussion because, for MUS, ACL does ask for population size as one of the inputs to determine sample size.

Table 9–2 summarizes the effects of the four factors on sample size.

TABLE 9–2   **The Effect of Sample Selection Factors on Sample Size**

		Examples	
Factor	*Relationship to Sample Size*	*Change in Factor*	*Effect on Sample*
Desired confidence level	Direct	Lower	Decrease
		Higher	Increase
Tolerable misstatement	Inverse	Lower	Increase
		Higher	Decrease
Expected misstatement	Direct	Lower	Decrease
		Higher	Increase
Population size	Direct	Lower	Decrease
		Higher	Increase

Computing
Sample Sizes
Using the
Attribute-
Sampling Tables

A monetary-unit sample size can be determined by using the attribute sample size tables shown in Chapter 8. The auditor first determines the desired confidence level and then converts the tolerable misstatement and the expected misstatement to percentages of the book value of the balance tested. For example, suppose the auditor has established a tolerable misstatement of $125,000 and an expected misstatement of $25,000 for an accounts receivable account with a book value of $2,500,000. The tolerable misstatement would be 5 percent ($125,000 ÷ $2,500,000), and the expected misstatement would be 1 percent ($25,000 ÷ $2,500,000). If the desired confidence level is 95 percent (for a risk of incorrect acceptance of 5 percent), the auditor would use Table 8–7 in Chapter 8. In this example, the sample size is 93. Be sure you can identify how the sample size was determined using Table 8–7 before moving on.

Computing
Sample Sizes
Using ACL

Software programs like ACL can also be used to determine sample size. Exhibit 9–1 shows the computation of sample size for the previous example using ACL software. To compute sample size, you open a workbook file (for sample size calculations, it can be any workbook file) and then select "calculate sample size" from the "sampling" menu. In the sample size dialogue box, select "monetary" for MUS. Enter the desired confidence level, which

EXHIBIT 9–1   **Sample Size Calculation Using ACL™ Software**

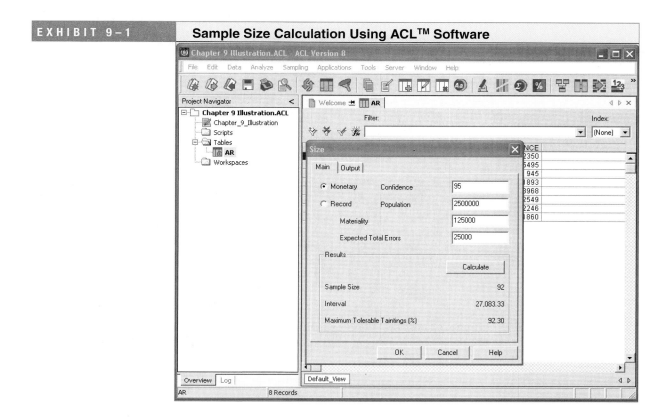

in our example is 95 percent. Enter the population, $2,500,000 in our example. Enter "materiality" or tolerable misstatement of $125,000, and finally "expected total errors" or expected misstatement of $25,000, and then hit the "calculate" button. Note that with ACL the auditor enters tolerable and expected misstatement in dollars rather than in percentage terms, like we did with attribute sampling in Chapter 8. The result is a sample size of 92, which is slightly smaller than the size determined using the tables. ACL software produces an exact sample size calculation.

While the underlying concepts and sample sizes produced by the attribute-sampling tables in Chapter 8 and ACL are similar, ACL uses a different approach to compute sample sizes. Rather than first solve for sample size and then compute the sampling interval (discussed in the next section), ACL first computes the sampling interval (i.e., the interval in Exhibit 9–1 is defined as every 27,083rd dollar) using factors based on the proportion of expected misstatement to tolerable misstatement. ACL then divides the population by the sampling interval to determine the sample size. Interested students may want to enter different population sizes into ACL while maintaining the same tolerable and estimated misstatements to see that the interval is not affected by population size but that the sample size is affected.

Performance

Step 4: Select Sample Items   In selecting the sample items, the auditor attempts to draw the sample in such a way that it accurately represents the population. The auditor selects a sample for MUS by using a systematic selection approach called *probability-proportionate-to-size selection,* often with the help of a computer program such as ACL. Probability proportionate-to-size sample selection uses an interval to select sample items. Keep in mind that MUS defines an individual dollar (or other monetary unit) as the sampling unit. The sampling interval can be determined by dividing the book value of the population by the sample size. Because the first sampling item is randomly selected within the first interval, each individual dollar in the population has an equal chance of being selected. Figure 9–1 provides an example of how probability-proportionate-to-size selection is applied.

In Figure 9–1, the total book value of the client's accounts receivable balance is $2,500,000, and the auditor determined a sample size of 93. The sampling interval will be $26,882 ($2,500,000 ÷ 93). To select a probability-proportionate-to-size sample, the auditor arranges the client's accounts receivable records in some order (e.g., by customer number or alphabetically) and then creates a column of cumulative dollars. In Figure 9–1, the customer records are arranged by customer number. The auditor obtains a random number between 1 and the size of the sampling interval ($26,882) by using computer software such as ACL or MS Excel. The random number becomes the first sample item selected, and then the sampling interval is added to determine the second sampling item and so on for every 26,882th dollar in the population. In the example illustrated in Figure 9–1, the random start is $3,977, and the customer account that contains the 3,977th dollar is selected for testing. In this case, Admington Hospital, with a balance of $15,495, is selected for testing. The auditor then begins to add the sampling

FIGURE 9–1	An Example of Probability-Proportionate-to-Size Selection

Customer Number and Name (Logical Unit)	Customer Balance	Cumulative Dollars	Sample Items (Random start $3,977, interval $26,882)		
1001 Ace Emergency Center	$ 2,350	$ 2,350			
1002 Admington Hospital	15,495	17,845	(1)	$	3,977
1003 Jess Base, Inc	945	18,780			
1004 Good Hospital Corp.	21,893	40,683	(2)		30,859
1005 Jen Mara Corp.	3,968	44,651			
1006 Axa Corporation	32,549	77,200	(3)		57,741
1007 Green River Mtg	2,246	79,446			
1008 Bead Hospital Centers	11,860	91,306	(4)		84,623
•	•	•			•
•	•	•			•
•	•	•			•
1213 Andrew Call Medical	0	2,472,032			•
1214 Lilly Health, Inc.	26,945	2,498,977	(93)		$2,477,121
1215 Jayne Ann Corp.	1,023	$2,500,000			
Total Accounts Receivable	$2,500,000				

interval, either manually or with the aid of a computer program, through the population and selects each logical unit that contains the computed amount.[2] Following this process, the second customer account selected would be Good Hospital Corp., which contains the 30,859th dollar ($3,977 + 26,882) and has a balance of $21,893. The third account would be Axa Corporation, which contains the 57,741th dollar (30,859 + 26,882), and so on until the entire population has been subjected to sampling and 93 units have been selected.

The advantage of using this approach to selecting the sample is that while each dollar in the population has an equal chance of being selected, logical units containing more dollars have a higher chance of being selected; hence the name, "probability-proportionate-to-size" sample selection. Note that all logical units with a book value larger than the sampling interval (such as Axa Corporation and Lilly Health, Inc.) are certain to be selected using this method. From an audit perspective, this approach guarantees that all individually significant accounts are examined and that, in general, the sample will be made up of larger accounts. This approach is particularly appropriate when the auditor is primarily concerned about overstatements and larger overstatements are expected to be found in larger logical units (such as with accounts receivable). If the auditor is primarily concerned about understatements or unrecorded amounts, other selection techniques (e.g., random or specific identification) should be used. Lets check your understanding. In the example in Figure 9–1, what is the probability that customer 1213, Andrew Call Medical, will be selected? The probability is zero, because the customer's balance is zero.

---

[2]The "sample records" command in ACL's sampling menu can also be used to select a probability-proportionate-to-size sample.

When the logical unit (a customer account in this example) exceeds the sampling interval, more than one sampling unit (dollar) may be selected from the same logical unit. If this happens, the logical unit is included only once when the sample results are evaluated. Thus, the number of logical units examined may be less than the computed sample size, which is another advantage of this selection technique.

Step 5: Perform the Audit Procedures
After the sample items have been selected, the auditor conducts the planned audit procedures on the logical units containing the selected sampling units. In some instances, the auditor may not be able to conduct the planned procedures on a particular logical unit (e.g., customer account). This may occur, for example, because a supporting document is missing. Unless other evidence is available, such items should be considered misstatements. The auditor must also be careful to conduct the audit procedures so as to avoid nonsampling errors caused by carelessness, poor supervision, or mistaken judgment. After all the audit procedures have been completed, the auditor evaluates the sample results.

Evaluation

The evaluation phase of the sampling application includes the following steps.

Step 6: Calculate the Projected Misstatement and the Upper Limit on Misstatement
The misstatements detected in the sample must be projected to the population. As mentioned earlier, an MUS application is designed primarily to test for overstatement errors. The projection of the errors to the population is referred to as the *projected misstatement* (ACL refers to this as the *most likely error*); it is comparable to the sample deviation rate or best estimate in Chapter 8. The auditor calculates an allowance for sampling risk and adds it to the projected misstatement. The total of the projected misstatement and the allowance for sampling risk is referred to as the *upper misstatement limit* (ACL refers to this as the *upper error limit*). These computations are somewhat involved, so rather than talk about them in abstract terms, we explain them using an example.

An Extended Example

❈ **[LO 3]**

An extended example is used to demonstrate the computation and evaluation of projected and upper misstatement limit (UML) of a monetary-unit sampling application. The following information relates to the audit of a client's accounts receivable balance:

Example Information

- Book value = $2,500,000
- Tolerable misstatement = $125,000
- Sample size = 93
- Desired confidence level (risk of incorrect acceptance) = 5%
- Expected amount of misstatement = $25,000
- Sampling interval = $26,882

The calculations of sample size and sampling interval were shown previously. Assume further that, based on the auditor's understanding of the business and previous experience auditing this account, the auditor is primarily concerned with overstatements.

Basic Precision

As you learned in Chapter 8 with attributes sampling, even when the auditor observes no control deviations, the allowance for sampling risk still results in a computed upper deviation limit. The same is true for MUS; if no misstatements are found in the sample, the projection or best estimate of the population misstatement would be zero dollars. However, even with zero projected misstatements, an allowance for sampling risk must be computed, which will result in an upper misstatement limit that is greater than zero. This allowance for sampling risk when no misstatements are observed is referred to as the *basic precision*. If the appropriate sample size was taken (i.e., 93 items in the previous example) and no misstatements were found, then the auditor would be guaranteed that the upper misstatement limit would be less than or equal to the tolerable misstatement used to design the sample.

For example, if the auditor finds no misstatements in auditing the client's accounts receivable, he or she will calculate the upper misstatement limit by going to Table 8–9 or 8–10 (depending on the desired confidence level) to locate the upper-limit factor associated with no misstatements and the related sample size. In the previous example, the sample size was 93 and the sampling interval was $26,882. Table 8–9 is the appropriate table, because the desired confidence level is 95 percent. Look down the zero misstatements column (Table 8–9 calls errors "Deviations") for the value that intersects with our sample size. Table 8–9 does not include a sample size of 93, so round up to 100.[3] The upper misstatement factor is 3.0. The upper misstatement limit (and basic precision) is thus $80,646 (3.0 × $26,882). The basic precision essentially assumes any undetected misstatements in the population are misstated by 100 percent. This is a very conservative but justifiable assumption given the high potential cost of underestimating the amount of misstatement in a client's financial statements.

In practice, auditors use firm-specific MUS guidance or software programs like ACL to determine MUS sample sizes and to evaluate MUS results. Although firms and software developers use different algorithms and assumptions in computing MUS misstatement limits, the underlying theory and ultimate conclusions are similar. Before demonstrating how to evaluate MUS results with ACL, we demonstrate how to manually complete the calculations using the evaluation tables in Chapter 8. Demonstrating the manual calculation will help you better understand output from packages like ACL.

---

[3]Actually, most MUS evaluation approaches, including the one used by ACL, use misstatement evaluation factors associated with a sample size of 100—regardless of the sample size actually used. We explain this convention after we compare the manually evaluated MUS results to ACL's evaluation.

Misstatements Detected

Assume that the auditor examined the 93 sample items selected from the client's accounts receivable account and detected the following misstatements:

Customer	Book Value	Audit Value	Difference	Tainting Factor (column 4 ÷ column 2)
Good Hospital	$21,893	$18,609	$ 3,284	.15
Marva Medical Supply	6,705	4,023	2,682	.40
Axa Corp.	32,549	30,049	2,500	Not applicable*
Learn Heart Centers	15,000	0	15,000	1.00

*Book value is greater than sampling interval.

Overstatement Misstatements Detected   If misstatements are found in the sample, the auditor needs to calculate a projected misstatement and an allowance for sampling risk. Because in an MUS sample each selected dollar "represents" a group of dollars in the population, the percentage of misstatement in the logical unit represents the percentage of misstatement in the sampling interval from which the dollar was selected. Three types of situations can occur with detected misstatements.

1. *The logical unit is equal to or greater than the sampling interval.* In this situation, the projected misstatement is equal to the actual misstatement detected in the logical unit. For example, the Axa Corporation account in Figure 9–1 contained a balance of $32,549, which is larger than the sampling interval of $26,882. In the example, the projected misstatement associated with this account would be $2,500, and no sampling risk is added. No allowance for sampling risk is necessary for these large accounts because all accounts larger than the sampling interval will automatically be selected by an MUS sampling approach. Since all the dollars in the large accounts are audited, there is no sampling risk associated with large accounts (logical units).

2. *The logical unit's book value is less than the sampling interval, and it is misstated by less than 100 percent.* This is the most common situation. The percentage of misstatement in the logical unit is referred to as the *tainting factor*. The tainting factor is calculated using the following formula:

$$\text{Tainting factor} = \frac{\text{Book value} - \text{Audit value}}{\text{Book value}}$$

For example, the Good Hospital Corp. account is overstated by $3,284. Thus, the tainting factor for the account would be .15 [(21,893 − 18,609) ÷ 21,893]. The projected misstatement for the interval containing this logical unit would be $4,032 (.15 × $26,882). The tainting factor associated with the interval containing the Marva Medical Supply account is .40 ($2,682 ÷ $6,705), and the projected misstatement for the interval is $10,753 (.40 × $26,882). An allowance for sampling risk would be added to these projected misstatements (illustrated below).

3. *The book value of the logical unit is less than the sampling interval, and it is 100 percent misstated.* Because the logical unit represents the group of dollars in the sampling interval, the sampling

interval is assumed to be 100 percent in error. In the above example, the audited value for Learn Heart Centers is $0. The projected error for the interval containing this logical unit is $26,882, which is determined by multiplying the percentage misstated (100 percent) by the size of the sampling interval ($26,882). An allowance for sampling risk would be added to this amount as illustrated below.

Compute the Upper Misstatement Limit

To compute the upper misstatement limit (UML), the auditor first computes basic precision and then ranks the detected misstatements based on the size of the tainting factor from the largest tainting factor to the smallest. Projected and upper misstatement limits are computed using the tainting factor and upper-limit factor from Table 8–9 or 8–10. Finally, misstatements detected in logical units greater than the sampling interval are added.

Customer Name	Tainting Factor	Sampling Interval	Projected Misstatement (columns 2 × 3)	95% Upper-Limit Increment (from Table 8–9)	Upper Misstatement (columns 2 × 3 × 5)
Basic Precision	1.0	$26,882	NA	3.0	$ 80,646
Learn Heart Centers	1.0	26,882	26,882	1.7 (4.7 − 3.0)	45,700
Marva Medical	.40	26,882	10,753	1.5 (6.2 − 4.7)	16,130
Good Hospital	.15	26,882	4,032	1.4 (7.6 − 6.2)	5,645
Add misstatements detected in logical units greater than the sampling interval:					
Axa Corp.	NA	26,882	NA	NA	2,500
			Upper Misstatement Limit		$150,621

NA, not applicable

The UML in this case is $150,621, and is calculated as follows. First, basic precision, $80,646, is computed by multiplying the sampling interval by the upper-limit factor from Table 8–9, ($26,882 × 3.0; the factor is based on a sample size of 100 and no misstatements). The $80,646 represents the sampling risk that exists even if no misstatements are observed in the sample. Remember, because we are basing our conclusions on a sample, we cannot be sure there are no misstatements in the population even if we find none in the sample.

Second, logical units where misstatements are detected, Learn Heart Centers, Marva Medical, and Good Hospital, are ranked according to the size of their tainting factor from largest to smallest.

Third, the projected misstatements for Learn Heart Centers, Marva Medical, and Good Hospital are calculated. Projected misstatement is computed by multiplying the sampling interval by the tainting factor (column 2 × column 3). This calculation is based on the assumption that the dollar selected for testing represents the sampling interval. In turn, it is assumed that the extent of misstatement in the logical unit that contains the sampled dollar represents the amount of misstatement in the sampling interval.

Next, for the intervals containing the Learn Heart Centers, Marva Medical and Good Hospital accounts, an allowance for sampling risk is added to the projected misstatement by multiplying the projected misstatement by the incremental change in the upper-limit factor for the confidence level used to design the sampling application. In this example, the desired confidence is 95 percent, so the upper-limit factors are taken from Table 8–9. For basic precision, the factor, 3.0, is taken directly from Table 8–9 because it is the first "layer" of the upper-limit calculation.

For the first misstatement observed, Learn Heart Centers, the upper-limit factor from Table 8–9 is 4.7 (sample size 100, 1 misstatement). However, the upper-limit factors in Table 8–9 are cumulative. In other words, the factor for 1 misstatement, 4.7, includes the sampling risk associated with zero misstatements (i.e., it includes the upper-limit factor 3.0 associated with zero misstatements). Since basic precision already includes the factor for zero misstatements, only the increase or *increment* is used for the first misstatement, and likewise for subsequent misstatements. The incremental change is calculated by simply subtracting the upper-limit factor for the current number of misstatements from the factor for the previous number of misstatements (i.e., $4.7 - 3.0 = 1.7$). Thus, for Good Hospital, the projected misstatement is $4,032, and the allowance for sampling risk is $1,613 ($5,645 − $4,032). The allowance for sampling risk for Marva Medical is $5,377 ($16,130 − $10,753).

Ranking the logical units by their tainting factors leads to an UML that is conservative because the largest tainting factor is multiplied by the largest incremental change in the upper-limit factor. This conservative approach means there is a higher risk that an acceptable account balance will be rejected by the auditor (see footnote 1).

Finally, misstatements detected in logical units that are greater than the sampling interval are added to the upper limit. As noted earlier, the reason misstatements from logical units greater than the sampling interval do not require projection or the consideration of sampling risk is because all accounts larger than the sampling interval will automatically be selected by a probability-proportionate-to-size sampling approach. Since all the dollars in the large accounts are audited, there is no sampling risk associated with large accounts (logical units). Thus, in the example above, the misstatement detected in Axa Corp.'s balance, $2,500 ($32,549 − $30,049) is simply added to the upper misstatement.

Step 7: Draw Final Conclusions   For this example, the final decision on whether the accounts receivable balance is materially misstated is made by comparing the tolerable misstatement to the UML. If the UML is less than or equal to the tolerable misstatement, the evidence supports the conclusion that the account balance is not materially misstated. In this case the UML of $150,621 is more than the tolerable misstatement of $125,000. Because the UML exceeds the tolerable misstatement of $125,000, the auditor has evidence that the accounts receivable account is materially misstated.

The auditor now has four options. First, the sample size can be increased. While this approach is possible in theory, it is not practical in many audit settings. Second, other substantive procedures can be performed. This approach might be followed if the auditor's qualitative analysis of the detected misstatements indicates that there is a systematic problem with the population. For example, the auditor might determine that three of the misstatements occurred in the pricing of one particular product line sold by the client. In this instance, he or she might design a substantive procedure that examines the pricing of all sales in that product line. Third, the auditor

TABLE 9–3	The Auditor's Risks When Evaluating a Financial Statement Account Based on Sample Evidence	
	True State of Financial Statement Account	
Auditor's Decision Based on Sample Evidence	*Not Materially Misstated*	*Materially Misstated*
Supports the fairness of the account balance	Correct decision	Risk of incorrect acceptance (Type II)
Does not support the fairness of the account balance	Risk of incorrect rejection (Type I)	Correct decision

can request that the client adjust the accounts receivable balance. In our example, the minimum adjustment would be $25,621 ($150,621 − $125,000). If the client adjusts the account by $25,621, the UML will be equal to or less than the tolerable misstatement at a 5 percent risk of incorrect acceptance. Finally, if the client refuses to adjust the account, the auditor would issue a qualified or adverse opinion (this action is rarely necessary).

Table 9–3 illustrates the risks auditors face when evaluating an account balance based on sample evidence. If the evidence supports the fairness of the account balance based on the sample evidence and the account is not materially misstated, the auditor has made a correct decision. If the evidence does not support the fairness of the account based on the sample evidence and the account is materially misstated, a correct decision has also been made. The other two combinations result in decision errors by the auditor. If the evidence supports the account as fairly stated when the account actually contains a material misstatement, the auditor will have incorrectly accepted the account (Type II error). Keep in mind, however, that the auditor almost never finds out the "true" account balance unless later events, such as lawsuits against the auditor for issuing a report on misleading financial statements, require an examination of the entire population. If the evidence does not support the fairness of the account when it is in reality not materially misstated (Type I error), the auditor will have incorrectly rejected the account. This can lead to overauditing and an inefficient audit.

Computing Projected Upper Misstatement Using ACL

Exhibit 9–2 shows the evaluation of the sample results using ACL software. The UML is calculated to be $152,744. To use ACL to evaluate sample results, open a workbook file (for sample evaluation calculations, it can be any workbook file) and then select "evaluate error" from the "sampling" menu. In the sample size dialogue box, select "monetary" for MUS. Enter the desired confidence level, which in our example is 95 percent. Enter the sampling interval, in our example $26,882. Enter book values followed by misstatement amount in the "errors" box. When using ACL, the order in which misstatements are input does not impact the results. In comparing the manually computed UML, $150,621 (illustrated earlier), to ACL's UML, we see that the upper limit on basic precision is identical, as are projected misstatements (to "most likely error") and the addition of misstatements from logical units greater than the sampling interval. However, ACL uses more precise upper-limit factors to create a more exact upper limit.

EXHIBIT 9–2

Sample Results with Overstatement Misstatements Using ACL™ Software

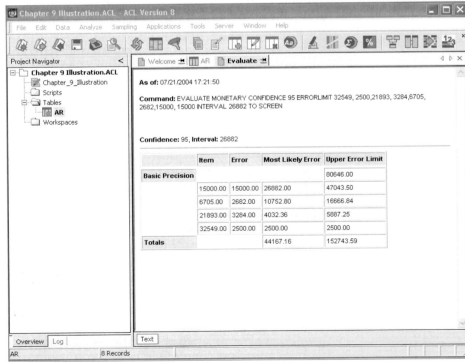

You should also be aware that alternative methods of calculating the upper limit on misstatement are available and used by some public accounting firms. These alternative methods will produce UMLs that are somewhat different from those shown here. For example, some of these methods correct for the overstatement of sampling risk.

Why Is Sample Size Not Used in Evaluating MUS Results?

Earlier (see footnote 3) we indicated that most MUS evaluation approaches use the misstatement factors and increments associated with a sample size of 100, regardless of the actual sample size used by the auditor. In other words, when we use Tables 8–9 and 8–10 to evaluate MUS results, the following factors will always be used:

Number of Errors	95% Desired Confidence Level[*]		90% Desired Confidence Level[†]	
	Misstatement Factor	Incremental Increase	Misstatement Factor	Incremental Increase
0	3.0		2.3	
1	4.7	1.7	3.9	1.6
2	6.2	1.5	5.3	1.4
3	7.6	1.4	6.6	1.3
4	9.0	1.4	7.9	1.3
•	•	•	•	•
•	•	•	•	•
•	•	•	•	•

[*]From Table 8–9.
[†]From Table 8–10.

Similarly, ACL uses the same underlying misstatement factors to compute most likely error and upper limit regardless of sample size. In fact, you will notice in Exhibit 9–2 that ACL doesn't even ask for sample or population size when evaluating MUS results. The reasons ACL uses the sampling interval (rather than sample size) as an input for evaluation purposes relate to (1) the development of MUS and (2) the sample selection process. While you do not need to understand the theoretical basis for MUS to apply it, we have found that some explanation into the underlying workings of MUS is helpful to students.

The Development of MUS.   MUS applies the theory of attribute sampling to monetary balances, which requires some assumptions and approximations. For example, one of the key assumptions is that the testing can be applied at the dollar-unit level. In reality, logical units (e.g., individual customer accounts or invoices) and not individual dollar units are audited. So while there are no "partial deficiencies" in attribute sampling, there are "partial misstatements" in MUS. Furthermore, in attribute sampling, there are no "individually significant" items (i.e., items tested that are larger than the sampling interval), while there are in MUS. The attribute-sampling evaluation approach needs to be tailored to handle these differences in population characteristics. Using the sampling interval instead of raw sample size as an input to the evaluation process is one way to account for individually significant items and partial misstatements (as opposed to all-or-nothing deviations).

The Sample Selection Process.   As mentioned previously, when an account (or other logical unit) is larger than the sampling interval, more than one dollar sampling unit will often be selected from that logical unit. Therefore, the number of logical units selected for audit will usually be less than the initial sample size. In some populations, the difference between the initial sample size and the actual number of logical units audited can be very significant. Thus, the raw sample size is not always very meaningful in MUS.

The sampling interval includes much of the information that is included in the sample size. For example, referring to Table 8–9, you will see that the basic precision misstatement factor (i.e., the upper-limit factor for zero errors) associated with a sample of 50 is 5.9, which is nearly double the factor associated with a sample size of 100 (3.0). What happens to the sampling interval if the sample size drops from 100 to 50? Assuming a sampling population of $2,500,000 for illustrative purposes, the interval doubles from $25,000 ($2,500,000 ÷ 100) to $50,000 ($2,500,000 ÷ 50). Because the sampling interval is used in MUS to compute the UML, a larger sampling interval (smaller sample size) will lead to a wider limit, similar to what would happen by doubling the basic precision misstatement factor in conjunction with a decrease in sample size from 100 to 50. Thus, the sample size information is also reflected in interval size, which is why the interval, and not sample size, can be used in the evaluation.

The developers of MUS made other assumptions based on statistical approximations. Over time, the approximations built into MUS have proved to be robust, effective, and efficient for audit sampling applications.

The Effect of Understatement Misstatements

The methodology used earlier for computing the UML is based on the auditor's assumption, at the time of planning the sampling application, that all errors in the population are overstatements. Recall that MUS is not particularly effective at detecting understatements because under an MUS approach the probability of selecting a smaller account is proportionately lower than the probability of selecting a larger account. Thus, an understated account is, by definition, less likely to be selected than an overstated account. In the extreme, an account could be 100 percent understated, in which case both the balance of the account and the probability of the account being selected for audit will be zero. When understatement errors are detected, different approaches can be used. When understatements are entered into ACL, ACL adjusts the total "most likely error" downward, but does not adjust the "upper-error limit." To demonstrate this approach, assume that the auditor detected the four overstatement misstatements shown in the previous example and that the following understatement misstatement was also detected.

Customer	Book Value	Audit Value	Difference	Tainting Factor (column 4 ÷ column 2)
Wayne County Medical	$2,000	$2,200	−200	−.10

Exhibit 9–3 shows the evaluation of the sample results, including the understatement misstatement, using ACL software. Note that the UML is still

EXHIBIT 9–3   **Sample Results with Under- and Overstatements Using ACL™ Software**

$152,744, but that "most likely error" is now reduced by the projected understatement −$2,688 (−.10 × $26,882).

Some auditors also adjust down the UML by the projected understatement to obtain a *net* upper misstatement limit.[4] This approach is followed when the auditor believes that the overall misstatement in the population is in the direction of overstatement. The understatements identified are used to adjust the UML.

Using the UML computed in Exhibit 9–3, the adjusted or net UML is $148,056 ($150,744 − $2,688). Using the previous decision rule, the auditor would still conclude that the account was materially misstated because the net UML of $148,056 is more than the tolerable misstatement of $125,000.

Nonstatistical Sampling for Tests of Account Balances[5]

⚘ [LO 4]   When conducting a nonstatistical sampling application for testing an account balance, the auditor considers each of the steps shown in Table 9–1. The sampling unit for nonstatistical sampling is normally a customer account, an individual transaction, or a line item on a transaction. When a nonstatistical sampling application is used, the following items need further explanation:

- Identifying individually significant items.
- Determining the sample size.
- Selecting sample items.
- Calculating the sample results.

Identifying
Individually
Significant Items

In many nonstatistical sampling applications, the auditor determines which items should be tested individually and which items should be subjected to sampling. The items that will be tested individually are items that may contain potential misstatements that individually exceed the tolerable misstatement. These items are tested 100 percent because the auditor is not willing to accept any sampling risk. For example, an auditor using nonstatistical sampling may be examining a client's accounts receivable balance in which 10 customer accounts are greater than tolerable misstatement. The auditor would test all 10 large accounts, and supposing that those 10 made up 40 percent of the account balance, the auditor would apply audit sampling to the remaining customer accounts making up the other 60 percent of the balance. Testing all individually significant items produces an emphasis on large item similar to probability-proportionate-to-size selection. Recall that probability-proportionate-to-size selection guarantees that all items greater than the sampling interval will be included in the sample.

---

[4]See Leslie et al., *Dollar Unit Sampling*. Alternative approaches are also used in practice. For example, if the direction of the errors in the population is unknown, a two-sided confidence interval can be constructed by separating the understatements and calculating a lower limit on misstatements. See A. D. Bailey, Jr., *Statistical Auditing: Review, Concepts, and Problems* (New York: Harcourt Brace Jovanovich, 1981), for a discussion of this approach.

[5]The approach presented here for nonstatistical sampling is based on the American Institute of Certified Public Accountants, *Audit Sampling* (Audit Guide) (New York: AICPA, 2001).

TABLE 9–4	**Assurance Factors for Nonstatistical Sampling**			
	Risk That Other Substantive Procedures Will Fail to Detect Material Misstatements			
Combined Assessment of Inherent and Control Risk	*Maximum*	*Slightly Below Maximum*	*Moderate*	*Low*
Maximum	3.0	2.7	2.3	2.0
Slightly below maximum	2.7	2.4	2.0	1.6
Moderate	2.3	2.1	1.6	1.2
Low	2.0	1.6	1.2	1.0

Risk that other substantive procedures will fail to detect a material misstatement:

Maximum: No other substantive procedures are performed to test the same assertion(s).

Slightly below maximum: Other substantive procedures that are performed to test the assertion(s) are expected to be slightly effective in detecting material misstatements in those assertion(s).

Moderate: Other substantive procedures that are performed to test the assertion(s) are expected to be moderately effective in detecting material misstatements in those assertion(s).

Low: Other substantive procedures that are performed to test the assertion(s) are expected to be highly effective in detecting material misstatements in those assertion(s).

Determining the Sample Size

When determining the sample size, the auditor should consider the variation in the population, the risk of incorrect acceptance, the tolerable and expected misstatements, and the population size. While an auditor may determine a nonstatistical sample size by using professional judgment, the following formula, based on the AICPA Audit Guide *Audit Sampling*, can be used:[6]

$$\text{Sample size} = \left(\frac{\text{Population book value}}{\text{Tolerable misstatement}} \right) \text{Assurance factor}$$

where "population book value" excludes the amount of items to be individually audited and "tolerable misstatement" represents the amount of materiality allocated to the account being audited. The assurance factor is determined by assessing inherent and control risk and the risk that other relevant substantive auditing procedures will fail to detect material misstatements. Table 9–4 contains the assurance factors for various combinations of these two assessments.

Selecting Sample Items

When any form of audit sampling is used to gather evidence, auditing standards require that the sample items be selected in such a way that the sample can be expected to represent the population. While some form of random-sample or systematic selection (e.g., probability proportionate to size) is required for statistical sampling, auditing standards allow the use of these selection methods, as well as other selection methods including haphazard sampling when using nonstatistical sampling. As discussed in Chapter 8, haphazard selection allows the auditor to "randomly" select items judgmentally (i.e., with no conscious biases or reasons for including or omitting items from the sample). This does not imply that the items are selected in a careless manner; rather, the sampling units are selected such that they will be

---

[6]This formula is based on the statistical theory underlying monetary-unit sampling.

representative of the population. The reason haphazard selection is not appropriate for statistical sampling is because humans are not very good at being truly random, no matter how hard we may try. For example, the first item on a report or computer screen may never be selected because it doesn't feel "random" to the auditor to select the very first item. Such biases mean that each item in the population did not have an equal chance of being selected.

Calculating the Sample Results

Auditing standards require that the auditor project the amount of misstatement found in the sample to the population. The AICPA Guide *Audit Sampling* describes two acceptable methods of projecting the amount of misstatement found in a nonstatistical sample.

The first method of projecting the sample results to the population is to apply the misstatement ratio observed in the sample to the population. For example, if the auditor finds misstatements of $1,500 in a sample totaling $15,000, the misstatement ratio in the sample is 10 percent (1,500 ÷ 15,000), and that ratio is applied to the population. If the total population is $200,000, then projected misstatement using the ratio approach will be $20,000 (10% × $200,000). This method of projection is often referred to as *ratio estimation,* and it is used with both nonstatistical sampling and classical variables statistical sampling (see the *Advanced Module* to this chapter).

The second method, referred to as *difference estimation,* projects the average misstatement of each item in the sample to all items in the population. For example, if the misstatements in a sample of 100 items total $300 and the population contains 10,000 items, the projected misstatement will be $30,000. This amount is determined by calculating the average misstatement in the sample of $3 ($300 ÷ 100 items) and multiplying it by the number of items in the population ($3 × 10,000 items).

These two methods of projecting misstatements give identical results if the sample includes the same proportion of items in the population as the proportion of the population's recorded amount included in the sample. If the proportions are different, the auditor chooses between the two methods on the basis of his or her understanding of the magnitude and distribution of misstatements in the population. If the auditor expects the amount of misstatement to relate closely to the size of the item, ratio estimation should be used. If the auditor expects the misstatements to be relatively constant for all items in the population, difference estimation should be used.

In evaluating the results of a nonstatistical sample, the auditor uses professional judgment and experience to draw a conclusion. If the sample is drawn haphazardly (versus randomly), the allowance for sampling risk cannot be statistically quantified within a specified level of confidence. The *Audit Sampling* guide provides the following direction. If the projected misstatement is close to or exceeds the tolerable misstatement, the auditor should conclude that there is an unacceptably high risk that the account is misstated. If the projected misstatement is considerably less than the tolerable misstatement, the auditor should compare the projected misstatement to the expected misstatement. If the projected misstatement is less than the expected misstatement, the auditor can conclude that there is an acceptably low sampling risk that the account is misstated. Conversely, if the projected misstatement significantly exceeds the expected misstatement, the auditor would generally conclude that there is an unacceptably high risk that the true misstatement exceeds the tolerable misstatement.

As noted in Chapter 8, students and auditors are sometimes unclear as to the factors that cause a sampling approach to be "nonstatistical." An approach is nonstatistical if (1) judgment is used to determine the sample size, (2) a haphazard sample selection technique is used, and/or (3) because the sample results are evaluated judgmentally. A nonstatistical approach can involve random selection and a judgmental evaluation. While haphazardly selected samples cannot be statistically evaluated, any randomly drawn sample *can* be statistically evaluated—even if the auditor labels the approach "nonstatistical" and even if the sample size was not statistically derived. This is an important point because it highlights the need for auditors to understand the key concepts of sampling theory *even if they are using a nonstatistical approach*. If an auditor randomly selects a sample and evaluates the results judgmentally, the quality of his or her judgment can be compared to statistical theory by an outside expert.

An Example of Nonstatistical Sampling

This example extends the example shown in Chapter 8 for the tests of controls of the revenue process for Calabro Paging Services. The senior-in-charge of the audit, Don Jones, has decided to design a *nonstatistical* sampling application to examine the accounts receivable balance of Calabro Paging Services at December 31, 2005. As of December 31, there were 11,800 accounts receivable accounts with a balance of $3,717,900 ($3,582,600 + $135,300 for the allowance for doubtful accounts), and the population is composed of the following strata:

Number and Size of Accounts	Book Value of Stratum
15 accounts > $25,000	$ 550,000
250 accounts > $3,000	850,500
11,535 accounts < $3,000	2,317,400

Jones has made the following decisions:

- Based on the results of the tests of controls, a low assessment is made for inherent and control risk.
- The tolerable misstatement allocated to accounts receivable is $40,000, and the expected misstatement is $15,000.
- There is a moderate risk that other auditing procedures will fail to detect material misstatements.
- All customer account balances greater than $25,000 are to be audited.

Based on these decisions, the sample size is determined as follows: First, individually significant items are deducted from the account balance, leaving a balance of $3,167,900 ($3,717,900 − $550,000) to be sampled. Second, the sample size for the remaining balance is determined using the AICPA's sample size formula:

$$\text{Sample size} = \left(\frac{\$3,167,900}{\$40,000} \right) 1.2 = 95$$

The assurance factor of 1.2 is determined by using Table 9–4 and a low assessment for inherent and control risk and a moderate risk that other auditing procedures will fail to detect material misstatements. The 95 sample items are divided between the two strata based on the recorded amount for each stratum. Accordingly, 26 of the 95 [($850,500 ÷ $3,167,900)95] are allocated to the stratum of accounts greater than $3,000 and 69 to the stratum of accounts less than $3,000. The total number of items tested is 110, composed of 15 individually significant accounts tested 100 percent and a sample of 95 items.

Jones mailed positive confirmations to each of the 110 accounts selected for testing. Either the confirmations were returned to Jones, or he was able to use alternative procedures to determine that the receivables were valid. Four customers indicated that their accounts were overstated, and Jones determined that the misstatements had resulted from unintentional errors by client personnel. The results of the sample are summarized as follows.

Stratum	Book Value of Stratum	Book Value of Sample	Audit Value of Sample	Amount of Overstatement
>$25,000	$ 550,000	$550,000	$549,500	$ 500
>$ 3,000	850,500	425,000	423,000	2,000
<$ 3,000	2,317,400	92,000	91,750	250

Based on analysis of the misstatements found, Jones concluded that the amount of misstatement in the population was likely to correlate to the total dollar amount of the items in the population and not to the number of items in the population. Thus, he decided to use ratio estimation (applying the ratio of misstatement in the sampling strata) to project his results. His projection of the misstatements follows:

Stratum	Amount of Misstatement	Ratio of Misstatements in Stratum Tested	Projected Misstatement
>$25,000	$ 500	100%	$ 500
>$ 3,000	2,000	$2,000 ÷ 425,000 × $850,500	4,002
<$ 3,000	250	$250 ÷ 92,000 × $2,317,400	6,298
Total projected misstatement			$10,800

The total projected misstatement is $10,800. Jones should conclude that there is an acceptably low risk that the true misstatement exceeds the tolerable misstatement because the projected misstatement of $10,800 is less than the expected misstatement of $15,000.

Before reaching a final conclusion on the fair presentation of Calabro's accounts receivable balance, Jones would consider the qualitative characteristics of the misstatements detected and the results of other auditing procedures. If these steps are successfully completed, Jones can conclude that the accounts receivable balance is fairly presented in conformity with GAAP.

The Rise and Fall of Statistical Audit Sampling

Nonstatistical audit sampling is very common in practice. In the 1970–1980s, statistical sampling was more common than it is today. In fact, many accounting firms developed proprietary statistical audit sampling software packages. Why did statistical sampling fall out of favor? We believe there were two primary reasons.

First, firms found that some auditors were overrelying on statistical sampling techniques to the exclusion of good judgment. As we discussed earlier, if the auditor can use knowledge and expertise to identify high-risk transactions or balances (e.g., large unusual items, transactions near period end, transactions in an area where material misstatements have been discovered in the past), then it is better to target those risky items and test 100 percent of them rather than to turn the selection procedure over to chance as is required by audit sampling, which is based on random-selection methods.

The second reason relates to poor linkage between the applied audit setting and traditional statistical sampling applications. In most scientific statistical applications, a high degree of confidence is required. However, in an audit context, sampling is often used to just top off the "assurance bucket" (see Chapter 5), which already contains evidence from risk assessment procedures, tests of controls, substantive analytical procedures, and other audit testing. Thus, in some instances, the auditors only needed a low or moderate level of confidence or assurance (e.g., 70 to 80 percent). Experienced auditors understood this intuitively but did not always have the knowledge to appropriately apply statistical sampling in an audit context. Thus, some of the audit firms simply moved to nonstatistical sampling with guidance based on judgment. With the increased scrutiny on audit firms in the last few years, the large firms have updated their nonstatistical sampling approaches to be more consistent with statistical theory.

Advanced Module: Classical Variables Sampling

[LO 5] Classical variables sampling uses normal distribution theory to evaluate the characteristics of a population based on sample data. This approach to audit sampling is similar to the techniques taught in college introductory statistics courses. While this is not a statistics book, we do want to discuss briefly how distribution theory is helpful for audit sampling. In Figure 9–2 you will see two normally distributed, bell-shaped curves that depict sampling distributions. The mean or average of the distributions is $10,000. Auditors most commonly use classical variables sampling to estimate the size of misstatement, so in our example let's say the $10,000 represents the size of the total misstatement in an account or population. The flatter, wider distribution in Figure 9–2 is based on a sample size of 50, and the taller, thinner distribution is based on a sample of size 200. Both sampling distributions are taken from the same underlying population.

The sampling distributions are formed by plotting the projected misstatements yielded by an infinite number of audit samples of the same size taken from the same underlying population. For example, the height of the flatter distribution at $9,000 represents the number (or percent) of times a sample of size 50 would return a projected misstatement of $9,000.

Rather than actually take an infinite number of samples of the same size to form a picture of the distribution, the distribution is modeled using the mathematical properties of the normal distribution. Thus, a sampling distribution is really a theoretical distribution that models how the means of

FIGURE 9–2	**Normally Distributed Sampling Distributions**

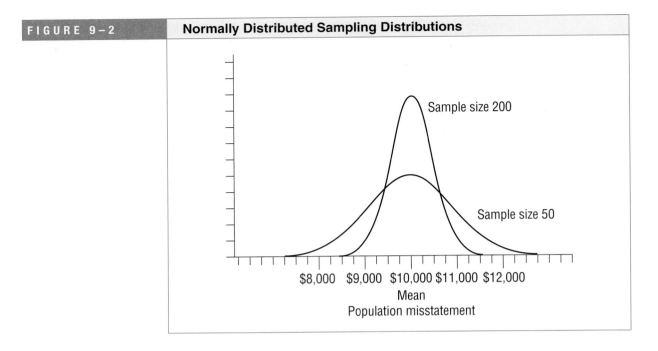

an infinite number of hypothetical samples of a given sample size would be distributed. A sampling distribution is useful because it allows us to estimate the probability of observing *any single* sample result. Two important features of sampling distributions are very useful for auditors:

- The mean of the sampling distribution will be equal to the true mean of the underlying population. Thus, Figure 9–2 tells us that the true misstatement in the population is $10,000.
- The area under the curve can be used to quantify likelihoods. For example, the standard error for the flatter curve is $1,000. If we look at the area covered by 2 standard errors above and 2 standard errors below the mean (i.e., the area under the curve between $8,000 and $12,000), we know that the area captures about 95% of all observed sample results. This is simply a mathematical property of a bell-shaped distribution.

Considering the first feature listed above, if auditors did actually take an infinite or even a very large number of samples of, say, size 50, they could determine with near certainty the amount of misstatement in an account. That seems easy enough—except that taking an infinite number or even 500 samples of size 50 is not economically practical. Instead, the auditor will only take one sample of size 50 and will use the results of that single sample to estimate the actual misstatement in the population. Given this audit approach, what information does distribution theory provide to an auditor that only takes one sample? It turns out that distribution theory can be very useful, even when the auditor is only drawing one sample, because the theory allows for an uncertain, but informed, prediction to be made about the underlying population.

Referring to the flatter distribution in Figure 9–2, which sampling outcome is more likely, a projected sample misstatement result of $10,000 or $12,000? The height of the curve in the middle indicates values around the mean of the distribution will be more commonly observed than values in the tails of the distribution. Because the most likely projected misstatement is one that is near the true misstatement, the auditor considers the observed projected sample misstatement as the best estimate of the true misstatement in the population. While the sample projection is the best estimate, the auditor understands there is uncertainty or sampling risk. Referring again to Figure 9–2, the most likely sample result is a projected misstatement at or near $10,000, but is it possible the auditor could draw a random sample of 50 that yields a projected misstatement of $8,000? Yes, due to sampling risk, it is possible to draw a nonrepresentative sample. However, observing a projected misstatement of $8,000 from a sample of 50 is not very likely given that the "true" population misstatement is $10,000. Now, consider the same question but with a sample size of 200 instead of 50. Could a sample of 200 produce a projected misstatement of $8,000? Again it is possible, but because the distribution for a sample of 200 is taller and tighter than the distribution for a sample of 50, it is much more unlikely that the auditor will get a projected misstatement result of $8,000 from a sample size of 200. The basic idea is simple: As the sample size increases, the results from the sample are increasingly likely to approximate the true population mean. In the extreme, if the sample size equaled the size of the population, the sample mean would exactly equal the true population mean.

Distribution theory allows auditors to quantify sampling risk through the use of *confidence bounds*, which are used to form what is commonly called a *confidence interval*. Referring to the flatter distribution in Figure 9–2, if the auditor wants to be 95 percent confident that his or her sample results include the true population misstatement, he or she would add and subtract 2 standard errors to and from the sample projected misstatement. For example, if the auditor takes a sample of 50 and computes a projected misstatement of $11,250, the auditor can be 95 percent confident that the interval between $9,250 and $13,250 ($11,250 ± $2,000) contains the true population misstatement. Thus, even though auditors do not know for sure which part of the actual sampling distribution their sample results come from (because they do not actually take an infinite number of samples to form the distribution), they use normal distribution theory to compute an interval of values that is likely to contain the true population value.

The computational complexity of calculating classical variables sampling results made it a difficult technique for auditors to use in the "olden days" before electronic calculators and personal computers were common on audit engagements. This complexity was one of the factors that led to the development of MUS. Today, the mathematical computations required by classical variables sampling are easily handled by computer software. However, because of the other advantages of MUS discussed earlier in the chapter, it continues to be an approach commonly used in practice.[7]

---

[7]Another important reason MUS was developed is that most accounting populations contain relatively little misstatement, and the estimators of potential misstatement involved in classical variables sampling are not very effective in populations with little misstatement.

Classical variables sampling can easily handle both overstatement and understatement errors. It is most appropriate for populations that contain a moderate to high rate of misstatement. Some applications of this sampling approach include auditing accounts receivable in which unapplied credits exist or a large amount of misstatement is expected, and inventory in which significant audit differences are expected between test counts and pricing tests. Following are some of the advantages and disadvantages of classical variables sampling.

Advantages

- When the auditor expects a large number of differences between book and audited values, classical variables sampling will normally result in a smaller sample size than monetary-unit sampling.
- Classical variables sampling techniques are effective for both overstatements and understatements. No special evaluation considerations are necessary if the sample data include both types of misstatements.
- The selection of zero balances generally does not require special sample design considerations because the sampling unit will be not an individual dollar but rather an account or a transaction, or a line item.

Disadvantages

- In order to determine the sample size, the auditor must estimate the standard deviation of the audited value or differences. However, the auditor may be able to develop a reasonably good estimate of the standard deviation by measuring the standard deviation of the book values using computer software, calculating the standard deviation from a pilot sample, or basing the estimate on prior years' audit results.
- If few misstatements are detected in the sample data, the true variance tends to be underestimated, and the resulting projection of the misstatements to the population is likely not to be reliable.

A number of classical variables sampling estimators are available to the auditor for projecting the sample results to the population. These include mean per unit, difference, ratio, and regression estimators. These estimators differ basically on the assumed relationship between the book value and the audit value. We demonstrated ratio estimation in the prior section on non-statistical sampling; in this section we present difference estimation.[8]

Applying Classical Variables Sampling

The discussion in this section focuses on the special features that apply to classical variables sampling. A detailed example is included to demonstrate the application of classical variables sampling.

[LO 6]   **Defining the Sampling Unit**   When an auditor uses classical variables sampling techniques, the sampling unit can be a customer account, an individual transaction, or a line item. For example, in auditing accounts

---

[8]See D. M. Roberts, *Statistical Auditing* (New York: AICPA, 1978), or Bailey, *Statistical Auditing*, for a discussion of the other classical variables sampling estimators.

receivable, the auditor can define the sampling unit to be a customer's account balance or an individual sales invoice included in the account balance.

Determining the Sample Size

The following formula can be used to determine the sample size for a classical variables sample:

$$\text{Sample size} = \left(\frac{\text{Population size} \times Z_{IA} \times SD}{\text{Tolerable misstatement} - \text{Estimated misstatement}} \right)^2$$

where

Z_{IA} = One-tailed Z value for the specified level of the risk of incorrect acceptance

SD = Estimated standard deviation

The risk of incorrect acceptance is the risk that the auditor will mistakenly accept a population as fairly stated when the true population misstatement is greater than tolerable misstatement. This risk is represented in one tail of the distribution, because the only time the auditor would incorrectly accept a population is if the sample projected misstatement came from the far left tail of the sampling distribution (i.e., the sample is nonrepresentative and yields a low misstatement). For the auditor to incorrectly accept a misstated account or group of transactions, the sample results would have to fall far enough to the left that even when the allowance for sampling risk (i.e., confidence bounds) is added, the upper limit is still below tolerable misstatement. If the audit sample yields a result anywhere on the distribution other than the extreme left tail, the auditor will add an allowance for sampling risk and appropriately reject the population.[9] Table 9–5 shows the Z values for various levels of each risk.

The following example demonstrates how to determine sample size using this formula. Assume that the auditor has decided to apply classical variables sampling to a client's accounts receivable account. Based on the results of testing internal controls over the revenue process, the auditor expects to find a moderate level of misstatement in accounts receivable due

TABLE 9–5

Z Values for Levels of Risk of Incorrect Acceptance

Risk of Incorrect Acceptance	Z Value
2.5%	1.96
5%	1.64
10%	1.28
15%	1.04
20%	.84

[9]The risk of incorrect rejection, Z_{IR}, can also be included in the sample size computation. If this risk is included in the formula, the Z_{IR} factor is added to Z_{IA} and the sample size will be larger. In practice, this risk is typically omitted because it affects efficiency and not effectiveness. When an account is incorrectly rejected due to a nonrepresentative sample, the auditor typically performs more work, which will provide evidence that the account is fairly stated. Auditors have determined that it is more costly to increase all sample sizes to control for the risk of incorrect acceptance than it is to simply perform additional procedures when they believe an account is rejected incorrectly.

mainly to improper pricing of products on sales invoices. The year-end balance for accounts receivable contains 5,500 customer accounts and has a book value of $5,500,000. The tolerable misstatement for accounts receivable has been established at $50,000, and the expected misstatement has been judged to be $20,000. The auditor sets the risk of incorrect acceptance at 2.5 percent. Based on the results of last year's audit work, the standard deviation is set at $31. Using these parameters, a sample size of 125 is calculated:

$$\text{Sample size} = \left(\frac{5,500 \times 1.96 \times \$31}{\$50,000 - \$20,000}\right)^2 = 125$$

In calculating the sample size, the Z values for the risk of incorrect acceptance is taken from Table 9–5. The Z value for a 2.5 percent risk of incorrect acceptance is 1.96.

Selecting the Sample   Sample selection for classical variables sampling normally relies on random-selection techniques. If the sampling unit is defined to be a customer account, the accounts to be examined can be selected randomly from the aged trial balance of accounts receivable. In this example, a random sample of 125 customer accounts is selected.

Calculating the Sample Results   The difference estimator is used to develop the sample projected misstatement. Continuing with the prior example, assume that the auditor has examined the 125 individual customer accounts receivable, and that 30 of these customer accounts contain misstatements. Table 9–6 presents the details of the 30 misstatements and the data necessary for calculating the sample results. The difference between the book value and the audited value is shown in the fifth column. The sixth column contains the square of each difference. The sum of these squared differences is needed to calculate the standard deviation.

The first calculation is that of the mean misstatement in an individual account, which is calculated as follows:

$$\text{Mean misstatement per sampling item} = \frac{\text{Total audit difference}}{\text{Sample size}}$$

$$= \frac{\$330.20}{125} = \$2.65$$

Thus, the average misstatement in a customer account based on the sample data is an overstatement of $2.65.

The mean misstatement must then be projected to the population. The projected mean misstatement for the population is an overstatement of $14,575, which is determined as follows:

$$\begin{array}{ccc} \text{Projected population} = & \text{Population size} & \times & \text{Mean misstatement} \\ \text{misstatement} & \text{(in sampling units)} & & \text{per sampling item} \end{array}$$

$$= \quad 5,500 \quad \times \quad \$2.65 = \$14,575$$

The projected population misstatement is the auditor's "best estimate" of the misstatement present in the account. Therefore, the best estimate or

TABLE 9-6		Summary of Misstatements Detected			
Sample Item Number	Account Number	Book Value	Audit Value	Audit Difference	(Audit Difference)²
1	3892	$ 1,221.92	$ 1,216.40	$ 5.52	$ 30.47
4	1982	2,219.25	2,201.34	17.91	320.77
8	893	1,212.00	1,204.34	7.66	58.68
9	25	5,201.51	5,190.21	17.11	292.75
13	1703	7,205.40	7,188.29	−11.00	121.00
19	4258	3,685.62	3,725.62	−40.00	1,600.00
22	765	58.30	50.64	7.66	58.65
34	1256	17,895.15	17,840.30	54.85	3,008.52
36	3241	542.95	525.98	16.97	287.98
45	895	895.24	823.70	71.54	5,117.97
47	187	10,478.60	10,526.40	−47.80	2,284.84
55	4316	95.00	90.00	5.00	25.00
57	2278	1,903.51	1,875.00	28.51	812.82
59	1843	185.23	200.25	−15.02	225.60
61	64	4,759.65	4,725.32	34.33	1,178.55
69	2371	2,549.61	2,540.26	9.35	87.42
70	1982	12,716.50	12,684.23	32.27	1,041.35
72	2350	361.45	375.50	14.05	197.40
75	349	11,279.40	11,250.40	29.00	841.00
87	2451	74.23	95.40	−21.17	448.17
88	3179	871.58	837.96	33.62	1,130.30
91	1839	571.13	590.00	−18.87	356.08
93	4080	9,467.24	9,504.50	−37.26	1,388.31
97	13	45.20	40.75	4.45	19.80
100	1162	524.90	515.15	9.75	95.06
101	985	7,429.09	7,356.21	72.88	5,311.49
108	304	12,119.60	12,043.60	76.00	5,776.00
110	1977	25.89	26.89	−1.00	1.00
115	1947	1,982.71	2,025.87	−43.16	1,862.79
118	1842	6,429.35	6,384.20	45.15	2,038.52
Total		$123,995.91	$123,665.71	$330.20	$36,018.32

point estimate of the accounts receivable balance is determined by subtracting the projected population misstatement from the book value of the account (because in our example the projected misstatement is an overstatement):

Accounts receivable = Book value − Projected population misstatement
   point estimate
$$= \$5,500,000 - \$14,575 = \$5,485,425$$

However, the auditor is relying on a sample, and the resulting uncertainty must be recognized by calculating an allowance for sampling risk. The allowance for sampling risk is represented by the confidence bound. To calculate the confidence bound, the auditor first calculates the standard deviation (*SD*), by using the following formula:

$$SD = \sqrt{\left[\frac{\text{Total squared audit differences} - (\text{Sample size} \times \text{Mean difference per sampling item}^2)}{\text{Sample size} - 1}\right]}$$

$$= \sqrt{\left[\frac{\$36,018.32 - (125 \times 2.65^2)}{124}\right]} = \$16.83$$

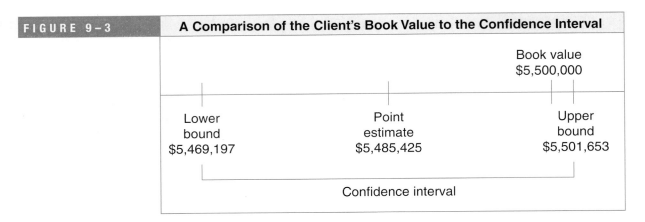

FIGURE 9-3   **A Comparison of the Client's Book Value to the Confidence Interval**

In our example, the standard deviation is $16.83. The confidence bound is then calculated using the following formula:

$$\text{Confidence bound} = \text{Population size} \times Z_{IA} \times \frac{SD}{\sqrt{(\text{Sample size})}}$$

$$= 5{,}500 \times 1.96 \times \frac{16.83}{\sqrt{125}} = \$16{,}228$$

In calculating the confidence bound, the auditor uses the Z value for the risk of incorrect acceptance.[10] In our example, the confidence bound is $16,228. The auditor then calculates a confidence interval as follows:

$$\text{Confidence interval} = \text{Population point estimate} \pm \text{Confidence bound}$$
$$= \$5{,}485{,}425 \pm \$16{,}228$$

where $5,469,197 is the lower limit and $5,501,653 is the upper limit. Based on the confidence interval, the auditor can accept the population as fairly stated and conclude that there is only a 2.5 percent risk that the true population value falls outside the confidence interval.

The auditor decides that the evidence supports or does not support the account balance by determining whether the recorded book value is included within the confidence interval. If the confidence interval includes the book value, the evidence supports the conclusion that the account is not materially misstated. If the book value is not included in the confidence interval, the evidence supports the conclusion that the account is materially misstated. In our example, the book value of $5,500,000 lies inside the precision interval, and the auditor can conclude the account is fairly stated. Figure 9-3 displays this result.

When the evidence indicates that the account may be materially misstated, the auditor must consider the same four options discussed under monetary-unit sampling: (1) increasing sample size, (2) performing additional substantive procedures, (3) adjusting the account, or (4) issue a qualified or adverse opinion.

---

[10]Note that the Z-value simply represents the number of standard errors the auditor would like to use in establishing the confidence bounds around the sample result. The sample mean ± 1 standard error results in about a 65 percent confidence interval, ± 2 standard errors results in about a 95 percent confidence interval, and + 3 standard errors in about a 99 percent confidence interval.

KEY TERMS

Allowance for sampling risk. The uncertainty that results from sampling; the difference between the expected mean of the population and the tolerable deviation or misstatement.

Audit sampling. The application of an audit procedure to less than 100 percent of the items within an account or class of transactions for the purpose of evaluating some characteristic of the balance or class.

Classical variables sampling. The use of normal distribution theory to estimate the dollar amount of misstatement for a class of transactions or an account balance.

Expected misstatement. The amount of misstatement that the auditor believes exists in the population.

Monetary-unit sampling. Attribute-sampling techniques used to estimate the dollar amount of misstatement for a class of transactions or an account balance.

Nonsampling risk. The possibility that the auditor may use inappropriate audit procedures, fail to detect a misstatement when applying an audit procedure, or misinterpret an audit result.

Nonstatistical sampling. Audit sampling that relies on the auditor's judgment to determine the sample size, select the sample, and/or evaluate the results for the purpose of reaching a conclusion about the population.

Risk of incorrect acceptance. The risk that the sample supports the conclusion that the recorded account balance is not materially misstated when it is materially misstated.

Risk of incorrect rejection. The risk that the sample supports the conclusion that the recorded account balance is materially misstated when it is not materially misstated.

Sampling risk. The possibility that the sample drawn is not representative of the population and that, as a result, the auditor reaches an incorrect conclusion about the account balance or class of transactions based on the sample.

Sampling unit. The individual member of the population being sampled.

Statistical sampling. Sampling that uses the laws of probability to select and evaluate the results of an audit sample, thereby permitting the auditor to quantify the sampling risk for the purpose of reaching a conclusion about the population.

Tolerable misstatement. The amount of the preliminary judgment about materiality that is allocated to a financial statement account.

Upper misstatement limit. The total of the projected misstatement plus the allowance for sampling risk.

Visit the book's Online Learning Center for a multiple-choice quiz that will allow you to assess your understanding of chapter concepts.

REVIEW QUESTIONS

[LO 1]   9-1   List the steps in a statistical sampling application for substantive testing.

[1]   9-2   How is the sampling unit defined when monetary-unit sampling is used for statistical sampling? How is the sampling unit defined when classical variables sampling is used?

[1]   9-3   How are the desired confidence level, the tolerable misstatement, and the expected misstatement related to sample size?

[2]   9-4   Identify the advantages and disadvantages of monetary-unit sampling.

[2,3]   9-5   How does the use of probability-proportional-to-size selection provide an increased chance of sampling larger items?

[2,3]   9-6   What is the decision rule for determining the acceptability of sample results when monetary-unit sampling is used?

[1,4]   9-7   How do changes in the variation of items in the population, the desired confidence level, and the tolerable and expected misstatements affect the sample size in a nonstatistical sampling application?

[4]   9-8   Describe the two methods suggested for projecting a nonstatistical sample result. How does an auditor determine which method should be used?

[5]   9-9   What are the advantages and disadvantages of classical variables sampling?

[5,6]   9-10   What is the decision rule for determining the acceptability of sample results when classical variables sampling is used?

MULTIPLE-CHOICE QUESTIONS

[1,5]   9-11   Which of the following sampling methods would be used to estimate a numeric measurement of a population, such as a dollar value?
a. Random sampling.
b. Numeric sampling.
c. Attribute sampling.
d. Variable sampling.

[1]   9-12   A number of factors influence the sample size for a substantive test of details of an account balance. All other factors being equal, which of the following would lead to a larger sample size?
a. Greater reliance on internal controls.
b. Greater reliance on analytical procedures.
c. Smaller expected frequency of misstatements.
d. Smaller amount of tolerable misstatement.

[1,2,4,5]   9-13   Which of the following sample planning factors would influence the sample size for a substantive test of details for a specific account?

	Expected Misstatement	Tolerable Misstatement
a.	No	No
b.	Yes	Yes
c.	No	Yes
d.	Yes	No

[1]   9-14   The risk of incorrect acceptance relates to the
a. Effectiveness of the audit.
b. Efficiency of the audit.
c. Preliminary estimates of materiality levels.
d. Allowable risk of tolerable misstatement.

[2,3]   9-15   Which of the following statements concerning monetary-unit sampling is correct?
a. The sampling distribution should approximate the normal distribution.
b. Overstated units have a lower probability of sample selection than units that are understated.
c. The auditor controls the risk of incorrect acceptance by specifying the risk level for the sampling plan.
d. The sampling interval is calculated by dividing the number of physical units in the population by the sample size.

[2,3]   9-16   In a probability-proportional-to-size sample with a sampling interval of $5,000, an auditor discovers that a selected account receivable with a recorded amount of $10,000 has an audit amount of $8,000. If this were the only error discovered by the auditor, the projected misstatement for this sample would be
a. $1,000.
b. $2,000.
c. $4,000.
d. $5,000.

[2,5]   9-17   An auditor is performing substantive procedures of pricing and extensions of perpetual inventory balances consisting of a large number of items. Past experience indicates that there may be numerous pricing and extension errors. Which of the following statistical sampling approaches is most appropriate?
a. Classical variables sampling.
b. Monetary-unit sampling.
c. Stop or go sampling.
d. Attribute sampling.

[1,2,5]   9-18   Which of the following statements concerning the auditor's use of statistical sampling is correct?
a. An auditor needs to estimate the dollar amount of the standard deviation of the population in order to use classical variables sampling.
b. An assumption of monetary-unit sampling is that the underlying accounting population is normally distributed.
c. A classical variables sample needs to be designed with special considerations to include negative balances in the sample.
d. The selection of zero balances usually does *not* require special sample design considerations when using monetary-unit sampling.

[1,5]   9-19   In estimation sampling for variables, which of the following must be known in order to estimate the appropriate sample size required to meet the auditor's needs in a given situation?
a. The qualitative aspects of misstatements.
b. The total dollar amount of the population.
c. The acceptable level of risk.
d. The estimated rate of misstatement in the population.

[2,5]   9-20   Which of the following would most likely be an advantage in using classical variables sampling rather than monetary-unit sampling?
a. An estimate of the standard deviation of the population's recorded amounts is *not* required.
b. The auditor rarely needs the assistance of a computer program to design an efficient sample.
c. Inclusion of zero and negative balances generally does *not* require special design considerations.
d. Any amount that is individually significant is automatically identified and selected.

PROBLEMS

[1,2,5]   9-21   Edwards has decided to use monetary-unit sampling (MUS) in the audit of a client's accounts receivable balance. Few, if any, misstatements of account balance overstatement are expected.

Required:
a. Identify the advantages of using monetary-unit sampling over classical variables sampling.
b. Calculate the sample size and the sampling interval Edwards should use for the following information:

Tolerable missstatement	$ 15,000
Expected misstatement	$ 6,000
Desired confidence level	95%
Recorded amount of accounts receivable	$300,000

c. Calculate the UML assuming that the following three misstatements were discovered in an MUS sample.

Misstatement Number	Book Value	Audit Value
1	$ 400	$ 320
2	500	0
3	3,000	2,500

(AICPA, adapted)

[2,3]   9-22   The firm of Le and Lysius was conducting the audit of Coomes Molding Corporation for the fiscal year ended October 31. Michelle Le, the partner in charge of the audit, decides that MUS is the appropriate sampling technique to use in order to audit Coomes's inventory account. The balance in the inventory at October 31 was $4,250,000. Michelle has established the following: risk of incorrect acceptance = 5% (i.e., the desired confidence level of 95%), tolerable misstatement = $212,500, and expected misstatement = $63,750.

Required:
a. Calculate the sample size and sampling interval.
b. Hon Zhu, staff accountant, performed the audit procedures listed in the inventory audit program for each sample item. Calculate the

upper limit on misstatement based on the following misstatements. What should Hon conclude about Coomes's inventory account?

Error Number	Book Value	Audit Value
1	$ 6,000	$ 2,000
2	24,000	20,000
3	140,000	65,000

[2,3] 9-23 McMullen and Mulligan, CPAs, were conducting the audit of Cusick Machine Tool Company for the year ended December 31. Jim Sigmund, senior-in-charge of the audit, plans to use MUS to audit Cusick's inventory account. The balance at December 31 was $9,000,000.

Required:

a. Based on the following information, compute the required MUS sample size:
Tolerable misstatement = $360,000
Expected misstatement = $90,000
Risk of incorrect acceptance = 5%

b. Nancy Van Pelt, staff accountant, used the sample items selected in part (a) and performed the audit procedures listed in the inventory audit program. She notes the following misstatements:

Misstatement Number	Book Value	Audit Value
1	$10,000	$7,500
2	9,000	6,000
3	60,000	0
4	800	640

Using this information, calculate the upper misstatement limit. What conclusion should Van Pelt make concerning the inventory?

c. Assume that, in addition to the four misstatements identified in part (b), Van Pelt had identified the following two understatements:

Misstatement Number	Book Value	Audit Value
5	$6,000	$6,500
6	750	800

Calculate the net projected population misstatement.

[4] 9-24 The progressive public accounting firm of Johnson and Johnson has decided to design a nonstatistical sample to examine the accounts receivable balance of Francisco Fragrances, Inc., at October 31. As of October 31, there were 1,500 accounts receivable accounts with a balance of $5.5 million. The accounts receivable population can be segregated into the following strata:

Number and Size of Accounts	Book Value of Stratum
10 accounts > $50,000	$ 750,000
440 accounts > $5,000	3,000,000
1,050 accounts < $5,000	1,750,000

Scott Judd, senior-in-charge of the audit, has made the following decisions:

- Based on the results of the tests of controls, a low assessment is made for inherent and control risk.
- There is a moderate risk that other substantive procedures will fail to detect material misstatements.
- The tolerable misstatement allocated to accounts receivable is $155,000, and the expected misstatement is $60,000.
- All the balances greater than $50,000 will be audited.

Required:
a. Using the formula included in the textbook, compute the suggested sample size for this test.
b. Judd confirmed the accounts receivable accounts selected and noted the following results:

Stratum	Book Value of Stratum	Book Value of Sample	Audit Value of Sample	Amount of Overstatement
> $50,000	$ 750,000	$750,000	$746,500	$ 3,500
> $ 5,000	3,000,000	910,000	894,750	15,250
< $ 5,000	1,750,000	70,000	68,450	1,550

What is the total projected misstatement? In projecting the misstatement, use ratio estimation. What conclusion should Judd make concerning the accounts receivable balance?

[5,6]   9-25   World-famous mining mogul Steve Wilsey hired the public accounting firm of Joe Paonessa Associates, P.C., to conduct an audit of his new acquisition, Cougar Goldust, Inc. The gold inventory was scheduled to be taken on November 30. The perpetual records show only the *weight* of the gold in various inventory bins. Paonessa has decided to use a variables sampling approach (difference estimation) to determine the correct weight of the gold on hand. (Note that the pricing of the inventory is straightforward because the market value on November 30 determines the price for balance sheet purposes.) There are 4,000 bins in the Cougar warehouse. The bins will serve as the sampling units. Paonessa wants to have a 5 percent risk of incorrect acceptance. The tolerable misstatement is set at 35,000 ounces, and the expected misstatement is 10,000 ounces. The perpetual record shows 700,000 ounces on hand.

Required:
[Note: Parts (a) and (b) are independent of each other.]
a. Compute the preliminary sample size. The estimated standard deviation is 25 ounces.
b. Assume that Paonessa examined a sample of 100 bins. The following information summarizes the results of the sample data gathered by Paonessa:

Difference Number	Recorded Weight	Audited Weight	Audit Difference	(Audit Difference)^2
1	445	440	5	25
2	174	170	4	16
•	•	•	•	•
•	•	•	•	•
•	•	•	•	•
29	217	215	2	4
30	96	97	(1)	1
Total	24,000	23,600	400	17,856

Compute the sample results and indicate what conclusion Paonessa should make concerning the inventory balance.

[5,6]   9-26   You are in charge of the audit of Hipp Supply Company for the year ended December 31. In prior years, your firm observed the inventory and tested compilation and pricing. Various misstatements were always found. About 10 percent of the dollar value of the inventory is usually tested.

This year you have established the tolerable misstatement to be $5,000. The client's book value is $97,500. The client has 960 inventory items, the number of which has been determined by examining inventory codes. Each item will be tagged with a prenumbered inventory tag numbered from 1 to 960. You plan to evaluate the results using classical variables sampling (difference estimation).

Assume you have selected a sample of 100 items randomly. For each sample item, audit tests are performed to make sure that the physical count is correct, the pricing is accurate, and the extensions of unit price and quantity are correct. The results are summarized as follows:

Inventory Tag Number	Book Value	Audit Value	Audit Difference	(Audit Difference)^2
6	$ 100	$ 100	$ 0	$ 0
42	85	85	0	0
46	120	120	0	0
51	420	450	30	900
55	18	18	0	0
56	10	10	0	0
•	•	•	•	•
•	•	•	•	•
•	•	•	•	•
851	25	25	0	0
854	152	150	2	4
857	85	85	0	0
862	76	86	10	100
Total	$10,147	$9,666	$481	$8,895

There were 50 differences, making up the net difference of $481. The recorded total of the client's inventory sheets is $97,500.

Required:
Determine the results of the audit tests using a desired confidence level of 90 percent. Indicate whether the evidence supports the fair presentation of the inventory account.

DISCUSSION CASES

[1,2,5]   9-27   Mead, CPA, was engaged to audit Jiffy Company's financial statements for the year ended August 31. Mead is applying sampling procedures.

During the prior years' audits Mead used classical variables sampling in performing tests of controls on Jiffy's accounts receivable. For the current year Mead decided to use monetary-unit sampling (MUS) in confirming accounts receivable because MUS uses each account in the population as a separate sampling unit. Mead expected to discover many overstatements but presumed that the MUS sample would still be smaller than the corresponding size for classical variables sampling.

Mead reasoned that the MUS sample would automatically result in a stratified sample because each account would have an equal chance of being selected for confirmation. Additionally, the selection of negative (credit) balances would be facilitated without special considerations.

Mead computed the sample size using the risk of incorrect acceptance, the total recorded book amount of the receivables, and the number of misstated accounts allowed. Mead divided the total recorded book amount of the receivables by the sample size to determine the sampling interval. Mead then calculated the standard deviation of the dollar amounts of the accounts selected for evaluation of the receivables.

Mead's calculated sample size was 60, and the sampling interval was determined to be $10,000. However, only 58 different accounts were selected because two accounts were so large that the sampling interval caused each of them to be selected twice. Mead proceeded to send confirmation requests to 55 of the 58 customers. Three selected accounts each had insignificant recorded balances under $20. Mead ignored these three small accounts and substituted the three largest accounts that had not been selected in the sample. Each of these accounts had a balance in excess of $7,000, so Mead sent confirmation requests to those customers.

The confirmation process revealed two differences. One account with an audited amount of $3,000 had been recorded at $4,000. Mead projected this to be a $1,000 misstatement. Another account with an audited amount of $2,000 had been recorded at $1,900. Mead did not count the $100 difference because the purpose of the test was to detect overstatements.

In evaluating the sample results, Mead determined that the accounts receivable balance was not overstated because the projected misstatement was less than the allowance for sampling risk.

Required:
Describe each incorrect assumption, statement, and inappropriate application of sampling in Mead's procedures.

(AICPA, adapted)

[LO 1,4]   9-28   Doug Stevens, CPA, is interested in testing the fairness of the ending inventory balance at an audit client, Morris Co. Doug has relatively little experience using statistical sampling methods and, quite frankly, doesn't like to turn anything over to random chance—especially the selection of items to test. Doug used a judgmental method of selecting items for testing. The method involves testing the inventory-item balances that he deems most risky or most likely to be misstated. Doug identified items to test based on size of balance, findings from prior years, age of inventory, description, and professional judgment.

He selected 26 items with a total book value of $720,000. In his "sample," he found a combined $80,000 in overstatement errors. The book value of inventory on the client's records is $1,090,000. Overall materiality for the engagement is $500,000. Doug's policy is to use 50 percent or less of overall materiality as tolerable error for any one account.

Required:
a. What is your opinion of Doug's method of selecting his "sample"?
b. Evaluate Doug's results. Does he have sufficient evidence to conclude the balance is fairly stated?

ACL

www.mhhe.com/ messier4e | Visit the book's Online Learning Center for problem material to be completed using the *ACL* software packaged with your new text.

AUDITING BUSINESS PROCESSES

407

CHAPTER 10

LEARNING OBJECTIVES

Upon completion of this chapter you will

[1] Understand why knowledge of an entity's revenue recognition policies is important to the audit.

[2] Understand the revenue process.

[3] Identify the types of transactions in the revenue process and the financial statement accounts affected.

[4] Identify and describe the types of documents and records used in the revenue process.

[5] Understand the functions in the revenue process.

[6] Know the appropriate segregation of duties for the revenue process.

[7] Identify and evaluate inherent risks relevant to the revenue process and related accounts.

[8] Assess control risk for a revenue process.

[9] Identify key internal controls and develop relevant tests of controls for revenue, cash receipts, and sales returns transactions.

[10] Relate the assessment of control risk to substantive testing.

[11] Identify substantive analytical procedures used to audit accounts receivable and revenue-related accounts.

[12] Identify tests of details of transactions used to audit accounts receivable and revenue-related accounts.

[13] Identify tests of details of account balances and disclosures used to audit accounts receivable and revenue-related accounts.

[14] Describe the confirmation process and how confirmations are used to obtain evidence about accounts receivable.

[15] Learn how to audit other types of receivables.

[16] Evaluate the audit findings and reach a final conclusion on accounts receivable and revenue-related accounts.

RELEVANT ACCOUNTING AND AUDITING PRONOUNCEMENTS

AICPA, Audit Guide, *Auditing Revenue in Certain Industries*

SEC Staff Accounting Bulletin No. 101, Revenue Recognition in Financial Statements

FASB Statement of Financial Accounting Concepts No. 5, Recognition and Measurement in Financial Statements of Business Enterprises (CON5)

FASB Statement of Financial Accounting Concepts No. 6, Elements of Financial Statements (CON6)

FAS 57, Related Parties Disclosures

AU 312, Audit Risk and Materiality in Conducting an Audit

AU 316, Consideration of Fraud in a Financial Statement Audit

AU 319, Consideration of Internal Control in a Financial Statement Audit

AU 322, The Auditor's Consideration of the Internal Audit Function in an Audit of Financial Statements

AU 329, Analytical Procedures

AU 330, The Confirmation Process

AU 339, Audit Documentation

AU 342, Auditing Accounting Estimates

AICPA Auditing Standards Board, Exposure Draft, "Understanding the Entity and Its Environment and Assessing the Risks of Material Misstatement"

AICPA Auditing Standards Board, Exposure Draft, "Audit Evidence"

AICPA Auditing Standards Board, Exposure Draft, "Performing Audit Procedures in Response to Assessed Risks and Evaluating the Audit Evidence Obtained."

Auditing the Revenue Process

Auditors generally divide an entity's information system into business processes or transaction cycles. Using this approach, the auditor is able to gather evidence by examining the processing of related transactions from their origin to their ultimate disposition in accounting journals and ledgers. We first introduced the concept of viewing business from a process perspective in Chapter 2. Figure 10–1 summarizes a model of business centering on business processes or transaction cycles. As the figure shows, the five basic processes are (1) the revenue process, (2) the purchasing process, (3) the human resource management process, (4) the inventory management process, and (5) the financing process. Auditors divide the financial statement components into business processes or cycles in order to manage the audit better.

In this chapter, the concepts and techniques learned in the previous chapters are applied to determine the risk of material misstatement (i.e., setting the level of inherent risk and control risk) for the revenue process and related accounts. The revenue process focuses on the sale of goods and services to customers. For virtually all entities, the revenue and purchasing processes represent the two major business processes that affect the financial statements.

The chapter starts by reviewing the basic concepts related to revenue recognition. An overview of the revenue process is then presented as an aid in providing you with an understanding of the process. This is followed by a discussion of the specific factors that affect the assessment of inherent risk for the revenue process and the auditor's assessment of control risk. While the main focus of this chapter is auditing the revenue process for a financial statement audit, the concepts covered for setting control risk are applicable to an audit of internal control over financial reporting for public companies under the Sarbanes-Oxley Act of 2002. The remainder of the chapter discusses the substantive procedures the auditor conducts to reach the appropriate level of detection risk for the accounts affected by the revenue process. While the main emphasis is on accounts receivable, the discussion also covers the allowance for uncollectible accounts, bad-debt expense, and sales returns and allowances. Because the cash account is affected by other business processes, it is covered separately in Chapter 16.

FIGURE 10–1	An Overview of Business

Revenue Recognition

[LO 1] Revenue recognition is reviewed at the beginning of this chapter because knowledge of this underlying concept is fundamental to auditing the revenue process. Additionally, revenue must be recognized in conformity with GAAP in order for an auditor to issue an unqualified opinion. A revenue-producing transaction generally consists of the sale of a product or the rendering of a service. FASB Statement of Financial Accounting Concepts No. 6, "Elements of Financial Statements" (CON6), defines revenues as

> inflows or other enhancements of assets of an entity or settlements of its liabilities (or a combination of both) from delivery or producing goods, rendering services, or other activities that constitute the entity's major or central operations. (para. 78)

Revenues are measured by the exchange value of the goods and services provided. In general, the entity receives cash or claims to cash for the goods or services provided. Claims to cash are usually referred to as trade accounts receivable. FASB Statement of Financial Accounting Concepts No. 5, "Recognition and Measurement in Financial Statements of Business Enterprises" (CON5, para. 83), requires that before revenue is recognized (recorded), it must be *realized* and *earned*. Revenue is realized when a product or service is exchanged for cash, a promise to pay cash, or other assets that can be converted into cash. Revenue is earned when an entity has substantially completed the earning process, which generally means a product has been delivered or a service has been provided.

The SEC in SAB No. 101 provides the following criteria for revenue recognition:

- Persuasive evidence of an arrangement exists.
- Delivery has occurred or services have been rendered.
- The seller's price to the buyer is fixed or determinable.
- Collectibility is reasonably assured.

Revenue recognition continues to pose a significant audit risk to auditors and has resulted in questions about the integrity of the financial reporting process. In fact, the auditing standard on fraud states that the auditor should ordinarily presume that there is a risk of material misstatement due to fraud relating to revenue recognition (AU 316.41). The auditor should be alert for the following issues related to revenue recognition:

- Side agreements are arrangements that are used to alter the terms and conditions of recorded sales in order to entice customers to accept delivery of goods and services.
- Channel stuffing (also known as *trade loading*) is a marketing practice that suppliers sometimes use to boost sales by inducing distributors to buy substantially more inventory than they can promptly resell (see Exhibit 10–1).

For most entities, this revenue recognition process occurs over a short period of time, but in certain industries, such as construction or defense, the revenue recognition process may extend over a period of years.

EXHIBIT 10-1	**Revenue Recognition Leads to Restating Reported Earnings**

Lucent Technologies, Inc., the once high-flying telecommunications equipment maker, restated its earnings downward for the 2000 fiscal year, which ended on September 30, by $679 million. The restatement included $199 million in credits offered to customers by sales teams, $28 million from the recognition of the sale of a system that had been incompletely shipped, and $452 million in equipment sales to distributors that were not utilized or passed on to customers. It appears that a strong push by the CEO, Richard McGinn, to meet revenue forecasts may have led Lucent sales personnel to promise customers credits and to "stuff" the distribution channel. Lucent's board of directors fired Mr. McGinn and numerous stockholder lawsuits have been filed against the company.

   Lucent is not the only company that has restated earnings due to revenue recognition issues. A study by the Financial Executives International found that there were 464 restatements over the period 1998–2000. That's higher than the prior 10 years combined. The most frequent cause of the restatements was improper revenue-recognition practices.

Sources: Lucent News Release, "Lucent Technologies Reports Results of Operational and Financial Review," December 21, 2000 (www.lucent.com); D. K. Berman, M. Schroeder, and S. Young, "SEC Probes Lucent Accounting Practices," *The Wall Street Journal* (February 9, 2001), pp. A3, A5; D. K. Berman and R. Blumenstein, "Behind Lucent's Woes: All-Out Revenue Goal and Pressure to Meet It," *The Wall Street Journal* (March 29, 2001), pp. A1, A8; J. Weil, "Restatements of Earnings Have Multiplied," *The Wall Street Journal* (June 7, 2001).

   An entity's revenue recognition policies affect how transactions are processed and how they are accounted for in the financial statements. Thus, an auditor must understand an entity's revenue recognition policies in order to audit the revenue process.

Overview of the Revenue Process

[LO 2]   In this section an overview of the revenue process for Earth-Wear Clothiers, Inc., is presented, beginning with an order from a customer, proceeding to the exchange of goods or services for a promise to pay, and ending with the receipt of cash. Exhibit 10–2 describes Earth-Wear's revenue process. Figure 10–2 presents the flowchart of EarthWear's revenue process, which will provide a framework for discussing controls and tests of controls in more detail. The discussion of the revenue process in this chapter can be applied equally well to manufacturing, wholesale, and service organizations. It should be kept in mind, however, that an accounting system must be tailored to meet the specific needs of an entity. Therefore, the reader should concentrate on understanding the basic concepts presented so that they can be applied to specific revenue systems. Problem 10-26 presents an example of a document flowchart for a revenue process that is basically a manual system. If the reader has limited knowledge of information technology (IT), this flowchart provides a simpler example of a revenue process.

   The reader should also notice that the revenue process shown in Figure 10–2 interacts with the inventory management process. Many accounting systems integrate the revenue, purchasing, human resources, and inventory processes. The flowcharts used in this text to represent those processes show the points where the processes interact with one another. As

EXHIBIT 10–2	**Description of EarthWear's Revenue Process**

EarthWear EarthWear provides 24-hour toll-free telephone numbers that may be called seven days a week (except Christmas Day) to place orders. Telephone calls are answered by the company's sales representatives, who use online computer terminals to enter customer orders and to retrieve information about product characteristics and availability. The company's sales representatives enter orders into an online order entry and inventory control system. Customers using the company's Internet site complete a computer screen that requests information on product code, size, color, and so forth. When the customer finishes shopping for products, he or she enters delivery and credit card information into a computer-based form. EarthWear provides assurance through CPA *WebTrust* that the website has been evaluated and tested to meet *WebTrust* Principles and Criteria.

Computer order processing is performed each night on a batch basis, at which time shipping tickets are printed with bar codes for optical scanning. Inventory is picked based on the location of individual products rather than orders, followed by computerized sorting and transporting of goods to multiple packing stations and shipping zones. The computerized inventory control system also handles items that customers return. Orders are generally shipped by United Parcel Service (UPS) at various tiered rates, depending upon the total dollar value of each customer's order. Other expedited delivery services are available for additional charges.

With the exception of sales to groups and companies for corporate incentive programs, customers pay in cash (in stores) or with credit cards. EarthWear's major bank is reimbursed directly by credit card companies, usually within three days. Group and corporate accounts are granted credit by the credit department. When group or corporate orders are received from new customers, the credit department performs a credit check following corporate policies. A credit authorization form is completed with the credit limit entered into the customer database. When a group or corporate order is received from an existing customer, the order is entered, and the data validation program performs a credit check by comparing the sum of the existing order and the customer's balance to the customer's credit limit.

entities use more advanced IT technology, it is becoming easier to integrate the information flow among the various accounting processes.

We now discuss the following topics related to the revenue process:

- Types of transactions and financial statement accounts affected.
- Types of documents and records.
- The major functions.
- The key segregation of duties.

Types of Transactions and Financial Statement Accounts Affected

[LO 3]

Three types of transactions are typically processed by the revenue process:

- The sale of goods or rendering of a service for cash or credit.
- The receipt of cash from the customer in payment for the goods or services.
- The return of goods by the customer for credit or cash.

The key controls involved in each of these transactions are discussed later in the chapter. For some entities, other types of transactions that may occur as part of the revenue process include scrap sales, intercompany sales, and related-party sales. Although such transactions are not covered specifically in this textbook, the auditor should be aware of how these transactions are processed and their related controls when they represent material amounts in the financial statements.

The revenue process affects numerous accounts in the financial statements. The most significant accounts affected by each type of transaction are as follows:

Type of Transaction	Account Affected
Sales transactions	Trade accounts receivable
	Sales
	Allowance for uncollectible accounts
	Bad-debt expense
Cash receipts transactions	Cash
	Trade accounts receivable
	Cash discounts
Sales return and allowance transactions	Sales returns
	Sales allowances
	Trade accounts receivable

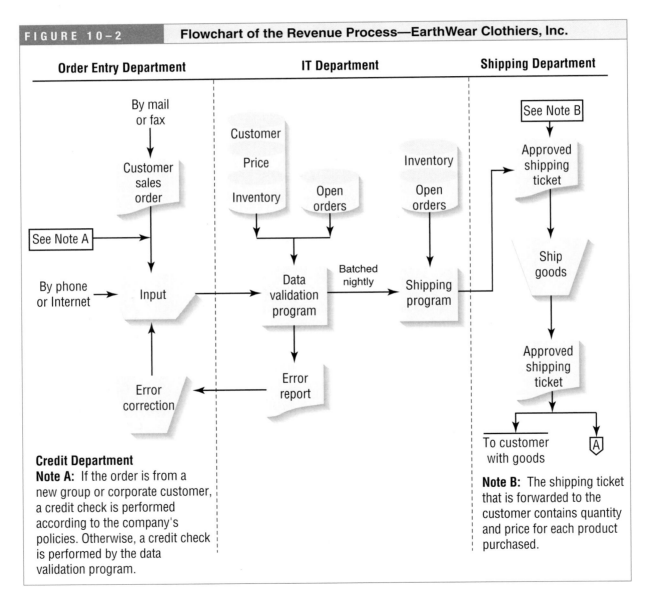

FIGURE 10–2   **Flowchart of the Revenue Process—EarthWear Clothiers, Inc.**

Credit Department
Note A: If the order is from a new group or corporate customer, a credit check is performed according to the company's policies. Otherwise, a credit check is performed by the data validation program.

Note B: The shipping ticket that is forwarded to the customer contains quantity and price for each product purchased.

FIGURE 10–2 **Flowchart of the Revenue Process—EarthWear Clothiers, Inc. *(continued)***

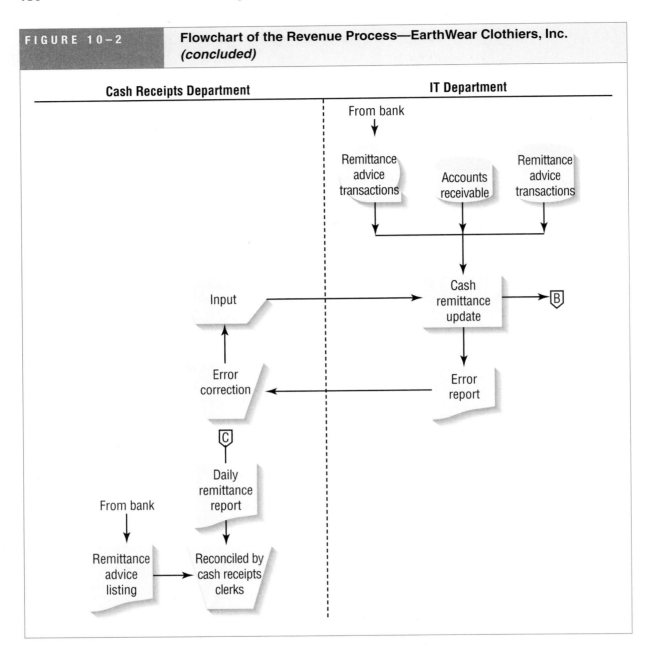

FIGURE 10–2   **Flowchart of the Revenue Process—EarthWear Clothiers, Inc.** *(concluded)*

Types of
Documents
and Records
    ✣ **[LO 4]**

Table 10–1 lists the more important documents and records that are normally contained in the revenue process. Each of these items is discussed briefly. The reader should keep in mind that in advanced IT systems some of these documents and records may exist for only a short period of time or may be maintained only in machine-readable form.

Customer Sales Order   This document contains the details of the type and quantity of products or services ordered by the customer. Customer

TABLE 10–1	Documents and Records Included in the Revenue Process
	Customer sales order.
	Credit approval form.
	Open-order report.
	Shipping document.
	Sales invoice.
	Sales journal.
	Customer statement.
	Accounts receivable subsidiary ledger.
	Aged trial balance of accounts receivable.
	Remittance advice.
	Cash receipts journal.
	Credit memorandum.
	Write-off authorization.

sales orders may be prepared and forwarded by a salesperson, mailed or faxed, or received by telephone or over the Internet. In the EarthWear example (Figure 10–2), order entry personnel enter the mailed or faxed information from customer sales orders into the revenue system. Phone or Internet sales are entered directly into the data validation program.

Credit Approval Form
When a customer purchases products on credit from the client for the first time, the client should have a formal procedure for investigating the creditworthiness of the customer. The result of this procedure should be documented on some type of credit approval form. When the customer plans to purchase additional products in the future, this procedure should be used to establish the customer's credit limit. The amount of the credit limit should be documented on the approval form. When credit limits are included in the client's customer files, the approval forms represent the source documents authorizing the amounts contained in the information system. EarthWear follows such a policy for its group and corporate customers (see Exhibit 10–2).

Open-Order Report
This is a report of all customer orders for which processing has not been completed. In the typical revenue process, once a customer's order has been accepted, the order is entered into the system. After the goods have been shipped and billed, the order should be noted as filled. This report should be reviewed daily or weekly, and old orders should be investigated to determine if any goods have been shipped but not billed or to determine why orders have not been filled. Figure 10–2 shows that EarthWear has an open-order file. Note C indicates that an open-order report is prepared weekly and reviewed by billing department personnel for long overdue orders.

Shipping Document
A shipping document must be prepared anytime goods are shipped to a customer. This document generally serves as a *bill of lading* and contains information on the type of product shipped, the quantity shipped, and other relevant information. In some revenue systems, the

shipping document and bill of lading are separate documents. A copy of the shipping document is sent to the customer, while another copy of the shipping document is used to initiate the billing process. Figure 10–2 shows that EarthWear follows a similar process using a shipping ticket.

Sales Invoice   This document is used to bill the customer. The sales invoice contains information on the type of product or service, the quantity, the price, and the terms of trade. The original sales invoice is usually forwarded to the customer, and copies are distributed to other departments within the organization. The sales invoice is typically the source document that signals the recognition of revenue. The majority of EarthWear's sales are made to customers using credit cards, and they do not receive a bill directly from the company. However, the shipping ticket that accompanies the goods contains the quantity and prices for products purchased. That amount shows up on the customer's credit card statement.

Sales Journal   Once a sales invoice has been issued, the sale needs to be recorded in the accounting records. The sales journal is used to record the necessary information for each sales transaction. Depending on the complexity of the entity's operation, the sales journal may contain information classified by type of sale (for example, product line, intercompany sales, related parties). The sales journal contains columns for debiting accounts receivable and crediting the various sales accounts. EarthWear maintains such a journal.

Customer Statement   This document is usually mailed to a customer monthly. It contains the details of all sales, cash receipts, and credit memorandum transactions processed through the customer's account for the period. EarthWear prepares monthly statements only for group or corporate customers who have accounts receivable with the company.

Accounts Receivable Subsidiary Ledger   The accounts receivable subsidiary ledger contains an account and the details of transactions with each customer. A transaction recorded in the sales journal and cash receipts journal is posted to the appropriate customer's account in the accounts receivable subsidiary ledger. For IT systems such as EarthWear's, this information is maintained in the accounts receivable file (see Figure 10–2).

Aged Trial Balance of Accounts Receivable   This report, which is normally prepared weekly or monthly, summarizes all the customer balances in the accounts receivable subsidiary ledger. Customers' balances are reported in categories (such as less than 30 days, 30–60 days, 60–90 days, more than 90 days old) based on the time expired since the date of the sales invoice. The aged trial balance of accounts receivable is used to monitor the collection of receivables and to ensure that the details of the accounts receivable subsidiary ledger agree with the general ledger control account. The auditor uses this report for conducting much of the substantive audit work in accounts receivable. EarthWear prepares an aged trial balance of accounts receivable for group and corporate customers.

Remittance Advice

This document is usually mailed with the customer's bill and returned with the customer's payment for goods or services. A remittance advice contains information regarding which invoices are being paid by the customer. Many entities use turnaround documents, where a portion of the sales invoice serves as a remittance advice that is returned with the customer's payment. EarthWear receives remittance advices from group and corporate customers after the payment has been processed by the company's bank. Payments from credit card companies are also made directly to the bank, and a remittance advice listing is forwarded to EarthWear.

Cash Receipts Journal

This journal is used to record the entity's cash receipts. The cash receipts journal contains columns for debiting cash, crediting accounts receivable, and crediting other accounts such as scrap sales or interest income. EarthWear maintains such a journal.

Credit Memorandum

This document is used to record credits for the return of goods in a customer's account or to record allowances that will be issued to the customer. Its form is generally similar to that of a sales invoice, and it may be processed through the system in the same way as a sales invoice. Exhibit 10–3 describes how EarthWear handles goods returned from customers. The process of customer returns is not shown in the revenue flowchart (Figure 10–2).

Write-Off Authorization

This document authorizes the write-off of an uncollectible account. It is normally initiated in the credit department, with final approval for the write-off coming from the treasurer. Depending on the entity's accounting system, this type of transaction may be processed separately or as part of the normal stream of sales transactions. EarthWear has negligible bad debts because most sales are made by credit card. Any bad debts related to group or corporate sales are written off by the credit department after approval by the treasurer.

EXHIBIT 10–3	**Description of EarthWear Clothiers' Process for Handling Customer Returns**

In order to receive credit for returned goods, customers must mail the goods to EarthWear's receiving department. There the goods are inspected, and a receiving document, which also serves as a credit memorandum, is prepared. Credit memoranda are entered into the revenue process along with the normal batching of customer orders. The customer receives either a replacement product, a cash refund, or a credit to his or her credit card.

The returned goods are placed back into inventory if they are not defective or damaged. If the goods are defective or damaged they are listed as "seconds" and sold at reduced prices. The inventory records are updated to reflect either the original cost or the reduced price.

TABLE 10-2	**Functions in the Revenue Process**	
	Order entry	Acceptance of customer orders for goods and services into the system in accordance with management criteria.
	Credit authorization	Appropriate approval of customer orders for creditworthiness.
	Shipping	Shipping of goods that has been authorized.
	Billing	Issuance of sales invoices to customers for goods shipped or services provided; also, processing of billing adjustments for allowances, discounts, and returns.
	Cash receipts	Processing of the receipt of cash from customers.
	Accounts receivable	Recording of all sales invoices, collections, and credit memoranda in individual customer accounts.
	General ledger	Proper accumulation, classification, and summarization of revenues, collections, and receivables in the financial statement accounts.

The Major
Functions

≋ [LO 5]

The principal objective of the revenue process is selling the entity's goods or services at prices and terms that are consistent with management's policies. Table 10–2 summarizes the functions that normally take place in a typical revenue process.

Order Entry   The initial function in the revenue process is the entry of new sales orders into the system. It is important that sales or services be consistent with management's authorization criteria before entry into the revenue process. In most entities, there is a separate order entry department (see Figure 10–2).

Credit Authorization   The credit authorization function must determine that the customer is able to pay for the goods or services. Failure to perform this function properly may result in bad-debt losses. In many entities, customers have preset credit limits. The credit authorization function must ensure that the credit limit is not exceeded without additional authorization. Where credit limits are programmed into the information system, a sale that causes a customer's balance to exceed the authorized credit limit should not be processed. The system should also generate an exception report or review by the credit function prior to further processing. Periodically, each customer's credit limits should be reviewed to ensure that the amount is consistent with the customer's ability to pay.

The credit authorization function also has responsibility for monitoring customer payments. An aged trial balance of accounts receivable should be prepared and reviewed by the credit function. Payment should be requested from customers who are delinquent in paying for goods or services. The credit function is usually responsible for preparing a report of customer accounts that may require write-off as bad debts. However, the final approval for writing off an account should come from an officer of the company who is not responsible for credit or collections. If the authorization for bad-debt write-off is part of the credit function, it is possible for credit personnel who have access to cash receipts to conceal misappropriation of cash by writing off customers' balances. In many organizations, the treasurer approves the write-off of customer accounts because this individual is responsible for cash management activities and the treasurer's department is usually separate from the credit function. In some entities, the accounts written off are turned over to a collection agency for continuing collection efforts. By following this procedure, an entity discourages the use of fictitious bad-debt write-offs to conceal the misappropriation of cash. Most entities have a separate credit department.

Shipping
Goods should not be shipped, nor should services be provided, without proper authorization. The main control that authorizes shipment of goods or performance of services is payment or proper credit approval for the transaction. The shipping function must also ensure that customer orders are filled with the correct product and quantities. To ensure timely billing of customers, completed orders must be promptly forwarded to the billing function. The shipping function is normally completed within a separate shipping department.

Billing
The main responsibility of the billing function is to ensure that all goods shipped and all services provided are billed at authorized prices and terms. The entity's controls should prevent goods from being shipped to customers who are not being billed. In an IT system, an open-order report should be prepared and reviewed for orders that have not been filled on a timely basis. In other systems, all prenumbered shipping documents should be accounted for and matched to their related sales invoices. Any open or unmatched transactions should be investigated by billing department or sales department personnel.

The billing function is also responsible for handling goods returned for credit. The key control here is that a credit memorandum should not be issued unless the goods have been returned. A receiving document should first be issued by the receiving department to acknowledge receipt of the returned goods.

Cash Receipts
The collection function must ensure that all cash collections are properly identified and promptly deposited intact at the bank. Many companies use a lockbox system, in which customers' payments are sent directly to the entity's bank. The bank then forwards a file of cash receipts transactions and remittance advices to the entity. In situations where payments are sent directly to the entity, the checks should be restrictively endorsed and a "prelisting" or control listing prepared. All checks should be deposited daily.

Accounts Receivable
The accounts receivable function is responsible for ensuring that all billings, adjustments, and cash collections are properly recorded in customers' accounts receivable records. Any entries in customers' accounts should be made from authorized source documents such as sales invoices, remittance advices, and credit memoranda. In an IT system, the entries to the customers' accounts receivable records may be made directly as part of the normal processing of these transactions. The use of control totals and daily activity reports provides the control for ensuring that all transactions are properly recorded. The accounts receivable function is

TABLE 10–3	Key Segregation of Duties in the Revenue Process and Possible Errors or Fraud
Segregation of Duties	*Possible Errors or Fraud Resulting from Conflicts of Duties*
The credit function should be segregated from the billing function.	If one individual has the ability to grant credit to a customer and also has responsibility for billing that customer, it is possible for sales to be made to customers who are not creditworthy. This can result in bad debts.
The shipping function should be segregated from the billing function.	If one individual who is responsible for shipping goods is also involved in the billing function, it is possible for unauthorized shipments to be made and for the usual billing procedures to be circumvented. This can result in unrecorded sales transactions and theft of goods.
The accounts receivable function should be segregated from the general ledger function.	If one individual is responsible for the accounts receivable records and also for the general ledger, it is possible for that individual to conceal unauthorized shipments. This can result in unrecorded sales transactions and theft of goods.
The cash receipts function should be segregated from the accounts receivable function.	If one individual has access to both the cash receipts and the accounts receivable records, it is possible for cash to be diverted and the shortage of cash in the accounting records to be covered. This can result in theft of the entity's cash.

normally performed within the billing department or a separate accounts receivable department.

General Ledger   The main objective of the general ledger function in terms of a revenue process is to ensure that all revenues, collections, and receivables are properly accumulated, classified, and summarized in the accounts. In an IT system, the use of control or summary totals ensures that this function is performed correctly. One important function is the reconciliation of the accounts receivable subsidiary ledger to the general ledger control account. The general ledger function is also normally responsible for mailing the monthly customer account statements.

Key Segregation of Duties

One of the most important controls in any accounting system is proper segregation of duties. This is particularly important in the revenue process because of the potential for theft and fraud. Therefore, individuals involved

TABLE 10–4	Segregation of Duties for Revenue and Accounts Receivable Functions by Department					
	Department					
Revenue and Accounts Receivable Functions	*Order Entry*	*Credit*	*Shipping*	*Accounts Receivable*	*Cash Receipts*	*IT*
Receiving and preparing customer order	X					
Approving credit		X				
Shipping goods to customer and completing shipping document			X			
Preparing customer invoice				X		X
Updating accounts receivable records for sales				X		X
Receiving customer's remittance					X	
Updating accounts receivable for remittances				X		X
Preparing accounts receivable aged trial balance				X		X

[LO 6]   in the order entry, credit, shipping, or billing functions should not have access to the accounts receivable records, the general ledger, or any cash receipts activities. If IT is used extensively in the revenue application, there should be proper segregation of duties in the IT department. Table 10–3 contains some of the key segregation of duties for the revenue process, as well as examples of possible errors or fraud that can result from conflicts in duties.

Table 10–4 shows the proper segregation of duties for individual revenue functions across the various departments that process revenue transactions.

Inherent Risk Assessment

[LO 7]   In examining the revenue process, the auditor should consider the inherent risk factors that may affect both the revenue and cash receipts transactions and the financial statement accounts affected by those transactions. The assessment of the potential effects of inherent risk factors is one of the inputs for the risk of material misstatement. Chapter 3 pointed out the three conditions (incentive/pressure, opportunity, and attitude) that are generally present when fraud occurs. Four specific inherent risk factors that may affect the revenue process are the following:

- Industry-related factors.
- The complexity and contentiousness of revenue recognition issues.
- The difficulty of auditing transactions and account balances.
- Misstatements detected in prior audits.

Industry-Related Factors

Factors such as the profitability and health of the industry in which an entity operates, the level of competition within the industry, and the industry's rate of technological change affect the potential for misstatements in the revenue process. For example, if the industry is experiencing a lack of demand for its products, the entity may be faced with a declining sales volume, which can lead to operating losses and poor cash flow. Similarly, competition within the industry can affect the entity's pricing policies, credit terms, and product warranties. If such industry-related factors are present, management may engage in activities that can result in misstatements.

The level of governmental regulation within the industry may also affect sales activity. While all industries are regulated by legislation restricting unfair trade practices such as price fixing, a number of industries are more highly regulated. For example, banks and insurance companies are subject to both state and federal laws that may limit an entity's operations. The products developed and sold by pharmaceutical companies are regulated by the Food and Drug Administration. Finally, most states have consumer protection legislation that may affect product warranties, returns, financing, and product liability. Industry-related factors directly impact the auditor's assessment of inherent risk for assertions such as authorization and accuracy.

The Complexity and Contentiousness of Revenue Recognition Issues

For most entities the recognition of revenue is not a major problem because revenue is recognized when a product is shipped or a service is provided. However, for some entities the recognition of revenue may involve complex calculations.[1] Examples include recognition of revenue on long-term construction contracts, long-term service contracts, lease contracts, and installment sales. There may be disputes between the auditor and management over when revenue, expenses, and related profits should be recognized. In such circumstances, the auditor should assess the risk of material misstatement to be high. Revenue recognition may also have a significant impact on the cutoff and accuracy assertions.

The Difficulty of Auditing Transactions and Account Balances

Accounts that are difficult to audit can pose inherent risk problems for the auditor. In addition to the issues related to revenue recognition discussed previously, the allowance for uncollectible accounts can be difficult to audit because of the subjectivity involved in determining its proper value. Thus, the estimation of this account directly affects the valuation of receivables on the financial statements. The risk of a material misstatement in the estimate of the allowance is also a function of factors such as the complexity of the customer base and the reliability of the data available to test the allowance account. For example, the only evidence available to determine the collectibility of a customer's account may be past payment history or a credit agency report. Such evidence is not as reliable as payments by the customer. The audit considerations for the allowance for uncollectible accounts are discussed later in this chapter.

Misstatements Detected in Prior Audits

As previously discussed, the presence of misstatements in previous audits is a good indicator that misstatements are likely to be present during the current audit. With a continuing engagement, the auditor has the results of prior years' audits to help in assessing the potential for misstatements in the revenue process.

Control Risk Assessment

[LO 8]   The concepts involved in control risk assessment were discussed in Chapter 6. The following sections apply the approach outlined there to the revenue process. For discussion purposes, it is assumed that the auditor has decided to follow a reliance strategy. Figure 10–3 summarizes the three steps for setting control risk when a reliance strategy is being followed. Each of these steps is briefly reviewed within the context of the revenue process.

---

[1]See American Institute of Certified Public Accountants, *Auditing Revenue in Certain Industries,* Audit Guide (New York: AICPA, 2001), for an overall discussion of the complexities of revenue recognition and, in particular, of the software and high-technology industries.

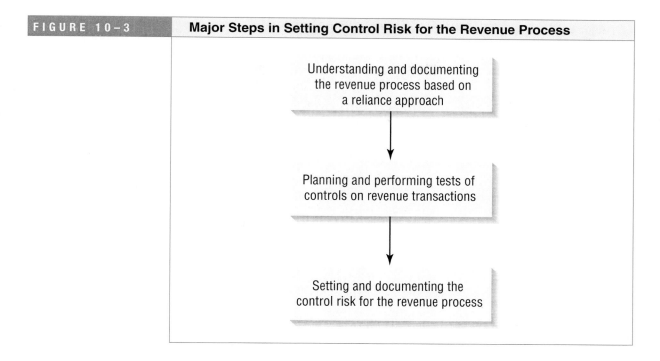

FIGURE 10–3   **Major Steps in Setting Control Risk for the Revenue Process**

Understanding and documenting
the revenue process based on
a reliance approach

↓

Planning and performing tests of
controls on revenue transactions

↓

Setting and documenting the
control risk for the revenue process

Understanding and Documenting Internal Control

In order to assess the control risk for the revenue process, the auditor must understand the five components of internal control.

Control Environment   Table 6–5 in Chapter 6 listed the factors that are important in understanding the control environment (e.g. integrity and ethical values, commitment to competence, etc). Because these factors have a pervasive effect on all accounting applications, understanding the control environment is generally completed on an overall entity basis. The auditor should, however, consider how the various control environment factors may affect the individual accounting applications. In the remaining discussion of the revenue process, it is assumed that the control environment factors, including general IT controls, are reliable.

The Entity's Risk Assessment Process   The auditor must understand how management considers risks that are relevant to the revenue process, estimates their significance, assesses the likelihood of their occurrence, and decides what actions to take to address those risks. Some of these risks include a new or revamped information system, rapid growth, and new technology. Each of these factors can represent a serious risk to an entity's internal controls over the revenue process.

Control Procedures   When a reliance strategy is adopted for the revenue process, the auditor needs to understand the controls that exist to ensure that management's objectives are being met. More specifically, the auditor identifies what controls ensure that the assertions for transactions and events are being met. The auditor's understanding of the revenue process can be documented using procedures manuals, narrative descriptions, internal control questionnaires, and flowcharts.

Information Systems and Communication

For each major class of transactions in the revenue process, the auditor needs to obtain the following knowledge:

- The process by which sales, cash receipts, and credit memoranda transactions are initiated.
- The accounting records, supporting documents, and accounts that are involved in processing sales, cash receipts, and sales returns and allowances transactions.
- The flow of each type of transaction from initiation to inclusion in the financial statements, including computer processing of the data.
- The process used to prepare estimates for accounts such as the allowance for uncollectible accounts and sales returns.

The auditor typically develops an understanding of an accounting (information) system such as the revenue process by conducting a transaction walkthrough. This involves the auditor's "walking" a transaction through the accounting system and documenting the various functions that process it. In the case of a continuing audit, the auditor has the prior years' systems documentation to assist in the walkthrough, although the possibility of changes in the system must be considered. If the system has been changed substantially, or the audit is for a new client, the auditor should prepare new documentation of the system.

Monitoring of Controls

The auditor needs to understand the client's monitoring of controls in the revenue process. This includes understanding how management assesses the design and operation of controls in the revenue process. It also involves understanding how supervisory personnel within the system review the personnel who perform the controls and evaluate the performance of the entity's IT function, as well as the effectiveness of controls.

Planning and Performing Tests of Controls

In performing this step, the auditor systematically examines the client's revenue process to identify relevant controls that help to prevent, or detect and correct, material misstatements. Because these controls are relied upon in order to set control risk below the maximum, the auditor conducts tests of controls to ensure that the controls in the revenue process operate effectively. Audit procedures used to test controls in the revenue process include inquiry of client personnel, inspection of documents and records, observation of the operation of the control, walkthroughs, and reperformance by the auditor of the control procedures.

Subsequent sections examine tests of controls for each major type of transaction in the revenue process more specifically. Chapter 8 presented sampling approaches to conducting tests of controls.

Setting and
Documenting
the Control Risk

Once the tests of controls in the revenue process have been completed, the auditor sets the level of control risk. If the results of the tests of controls support the planned level of control risk, the auditor conducts the planned level of substantive procedures for the related account balances. If the results of the tests of controls do not support the planned level of control risk, the auditor sets control risk at a level higher than planned. Additional substantive procedures in the accounts affected by the revenue process must then be conducted.

The auditor should document both the *achieved level* of control risk and the *basis* for his or her conclusion. The level of control risk for the revenue process can be set using either quantitative amounts or qualitative terms such as "low," "medium," and "high." The documentation of the achieved level of control risk for the revenue process would include documentation of the accounting system such as the flowchart included in Figure 10–2, the results of the tests of controls, and a memorandum indicating the overall conclusions about control risk.

Control Procedures and Tests of Controls—
Revenue Transactions

[LO 9] *EarthWear* Table 10–5 presents the assertions about transactions and events that were discussed in Chapters 4 and 6. Table 10–6 summarizes the assertions, possible misstatements, control procedures, and selected tests of controls for revenue transactions. Most of these controls exist within EarthWear's revenue process (Figure 10–2).

The auditor's decision process on planning and performing tests of controls involves considering the assertions and the possible misstatements that can occur if internal control does not operate effectively. The auditor evaluates the client's accounting system to determine the controls that will prevent or detect such misstatements. When controls are present and the auditor decides to rely on them, they must be tested to evaluate their effectiveness. For example, suppose the auditor's evaluation of the entity's

TABLE 10–5	Assertions about Classes of Transactions and Events for the Period under Audit

Occurrence. All revenue and cash receipt transactions and events that have been recorded have occurred and pertain to the entity.
Completeness. All revenue and cash receipt transactions and events that should have been recorded have been recorded.
Authorization. All revenue and cash receipt transactions and events are properly authorized.
Accuracy. Amounts and other data relating to recorded revenue and cash receipt transactions and events have been recorded appropriately.
Cutoff. All revenue and cash receipt transactions and events have been recorded in the correct accounting period.
Classification. All revenue and cash receipt transactions and events have been recorded in the proper accounts.

TABLE 10–6	Summary of Assertions, Possible Misstatements, Control Procedures, and Tests of Controls for Revenue Transactions		
Assertion	*Possible Misstatement*	*Control Procedure*	*Test of Controls*
Occurrence	Fictitious revenue Revenue recorded, goods not shipped, or services not performed	Segregation of duties	Observation and evaluation of proper segregation of duties.
		Sales recorded only with approved customer order and shipping document	Testing of a sample of sales invoices for the presence of authorized customer order and shipping document; if IT application, examination of application controls.
		Accounting for numerical sequences of sales invoices	Review and testing of client procedures for accounting for numerical sequence of sales invoices; if IT application, examination of application controls.
		Monthly customer statements; complaints handled independently	Review and testing of client procedures for mailing and handling complaints about monthly statements.
Completeness	Goods shipped or services performed, revenue not recorded	Accounting for numerical sequences of shipping documents and sales invoices	Review and testing of client's procedures for accounting for numerical sequence of shipping documents and sales invoices; if IT application, examination of application controls.
		Shipping documents matched to sales invoices	Tracing of a sample of shipping documents to their respective sales invoices and to the sales journal.
		Sales invoices reconciled to daily sales report	Testing of a sample of daily reconciliations.
		An open-order file that is maintained currently and reviewed periodically	Examination of the open-order file for unfilled orders.
Authorization	Goods shipped or services performed for a customer who is a bad credit risk	Proper procedures for authorizing credit and shipment of goods	Review of client's procedures for granting credit. Examination of sales orders for evidence of proper credit approval; if IT application, examination of application controls for credit limits.
	Shipments made or services performed at unauthorized prices or on unauthorized terms	Authorized price list and specified terms of trade	Comparison of prices and terms on sales invoices to authorized price list and terms of trade; if IT application, examination of application controls for authorized prices and terms.
Accuracy	Revenue transaction recorded at an incorrect dollar amount	Authorized price list and specified terms of trade	Same as above.
		Each sales invoice agreed to shipping document and customer order for product type and quantity; mathematical accuracy of sales invoice verified	Examination of sales invoice for evidence that client personnel verified mathematical accuracy. Recomputation of the information on a sample of sales invoices; if IT application, examination of application controls and consideration of use of computer-assisted audit techniques.
	Revenue transactions not posted correctly to the sales journal or customers' accounts in accounts receivable subsidiary ledger	Sales invoices reconciled to daily sales report Daily postings to sales journal reconciled with posting to subsidiary ledger	Examination of reconciliation of sales invoices to daily sales report. Examination of reconciliation of entries to sales journal with entries to subsidiary ledger.

(continued)

TABLE 10–6	Summary of Assertions, Possible Misstatements, Control Procedures, and Tests of Controls for Revenue Transactions (*concluded*)		
Assertion	*Possible Misstatement*	*Control Procedure*	*Test of Controls*
	Amounts from sales journal not posted correctly to general journal	Subsidiary ledger reconciled to general ledger control account	Review of reconciliation of subsidiary ledger to general ledger control account.
		Monthly customer statements with independent review of complaints	Review and testing of client procedures for mailing and handling complaints related to monthly statements.
Cutoff	Revenue transactions recorded in the wrong period	All shipping documents forwarded to the billing function daily	Comparison of the dates on sales invoices with the dates of the relevant shipping documents.
		Daily billing of goods shipped	Comparison of the dates on sales invoices with the dates they were recorded in the sales journal.
Classification	Revenue transaction not properly classified	Chart of accounts	Review of sales journal and general ledger for proper classification.
		Proper codes for different types of products or services	Examination of sales invoices for proper classification; if IT application, testing of application controls for proper codes.

revenue process indicates that monthly statements are mailed to customers by the accounts receivable department with complaints being handled by the billing department. This control is intended to prevent the recording of fictitious sales transactions. The auditor can review and test the client's procedures for mailing customer statements and handling complaints. If no exceptions or an immaterial number are noted, the auditor has evidence that the control is operating effectively.

Each of the assertions shown in Table 10–6 for revenue transactions is discussed mainly in terms of control procedures and tests of controls. The column for test of controls includes both manual tests and computer-assisted audit techniques. The choice of which type of test of controls is appropriate for a particular assertion will be a function of the following:

- The volume of transactions or data.
- The nature and complexity of the systems by which the entity processes and controls information.
- The nature of the available evidence, including audit evidence in electronic form.

The following sections also include a discussion of control procedures and tests of controls that are relevant for EarthWear's revenue process.

Occurrence of Revenue Transactions

Auditors are concerned about the occurrence assertion for revenue transactions because clients are more likely to overstate sales than to understate them. The auditor is concerned about two major types of material misstatements: sales to fictitious customers and recording of revenue when goods have not been shipped or services have not been performed. In other words, the auditor needs assurance that all recorded revenue transactions are *valid*. The controls shown in Table 10–6 are designed to reduce the risk that revenue is recorded before goods are shipped or services are performed. The major control for preventing fictitious sales is proper segregation of duties between the shipping function and the order entry and billing functions. If these functions are not properly segregated, unauthorized shipments can be made to fictitious customers by circumvention of normal billing control procedures. Requiring an approved customer sales order and shipping document before revenue is recognized also minimizes the recording of fictitious sales in a client's records. Accounting for the numerical sequence of sales invoices can be accomplished manually or by computer. The use of monthly customer statements also reduces the risk of revenue being recorded before goods are shipped or services are performed because customers are unlikely to recognize an obligation to pay in such a circumstance. Figure 10–2 shows that EarthWear's revenue process includes these control procedures where applicable.

For each of the controls shown, a corresponding test of control is indicated. For example, the auditor can observe and evaluate the segregation of duties. The auditor can also examine a sample of sales invoices for the presence of an authorized customer order and shipping document for each one. In an IT environment, such as EarthWear's revenue process, the auditor can test the application controls to ensure that revenue is recorded only after an approved customer order has been entered and the goods shipped.

Completeness of Revenue Transactions

The major misstatement that concerns both management and the auditor is that goods are shipped or services are performed and no revenue is recognized. Failure to recognize revenue means that the customer may not be billed for goods or services and the client does not receive payment. Control procedures that ensure that the completeness assertion is being met include accounting for the numerical sequence of shipping documents and sales invoices, matching shipping documents with sales invoices, reconciling the sales invoices to the daily sales report, and maintaining and reviewing the open-order file. For example, EarthWear (Figure 10–2) reconciles the batch totals of orders entered and provides a reconciliation of the daily shipping listing and the daily sales report. Additionally, the open-order file is reviewed periodically with follow-up on any order older than some predetermined date.

Tests of controls for these control procedures are listed in Table 10–6. For example, in a manual system, the auditor could select a sample of bills of lading and trace each one to its respective sales invoice and to the sales journal. If all bills of lading in the sample were matched to sales invoices and included in the sales journal, the auditor would have evidence that all goods shipped are being billed. The auditor could also use a generalized audit software package to print the items in the open-order file that are older than the client's predetermined time frame for completing a transaction. These transactions would then be investigated to determine why the sales were not completed.

Authorization of Revenue Transactions

Possible misstatements due to improper authorization include shipping goods to or performing services for customers who are bad credit risks and making sales at unauthorized prices or terms. As discussed earlier in this chapter, management should establish procedures for authorizing credit, prices, and terms. Additionally, no goods should be shipped without a properly authorized sales order. Table 10–6 lists a number of tests of controls for this assertion. In a computerized revenue process such as EarthWear's, the auditor may need to review the application controls and use computer-assisted audit techniques (CAATs) to test the proper authorization of revenue transactions.

Accuracy of Revenue Transactions

Accuracy is an important assertion because revenue transactions that are not processed accurately result in misstatements that directly affect the amounts reported in the financial statements. Again, the presence of an authorized price list and terms of trade reduces the risk of inaccuracies. There should also be controls that ensure proper verification of the information contained on the sales invoice, including type of goods and quantities shipped, prices, and terms. The sales invoice should also be verified for mathematical accuracy before being sent to the customer. In a manual system, the sales invoice may contain the initials of the client personnel who verified the mathematical accuracy. In an IT application such as EarthWear's, most of these controls would be programmed. For example, the price list is maintained in a master file. However, the client still needs controls to ensure that the authorized price list is updated promptly and that only authorized changes are made to the master file. The auditor can verify the application controls by using CAATs.

The accuracy assertion also includes the possibility that transactions are not properly summarized from source documents or posted properly from journals to the subsidiary and general ledgers. In the revenue process, control totals should be utilized to reconcile sales invoices to the daily sales report, and the daily recordings in the sales journal should be reconciled with the posting to the accounts receivable subsidiary ledger. The accounts receivable subsidiary ledger should periodically be reconciled to the general ledger control account. In a properly designed computerized revenue system, such controls are programmed and reconciled by the control groups in the IT Department and the user departments. The auditor can examine and test the application controls and various reconciliations. The use of monthly customer statements may also identify posting errors.

Cutoff of Revenue Transactions

If the client does not have adequate controls to ensure that revenue transactions are recorded on a timely basis, sales may be recorded in the wrong accounting period. The client should require that all shipping documents be forwarded to the billing function daily. The auditor can test this control by comparing the date on a bill of lading with the date on the respective sales invoice and the date the sales invoice was recorded in the sales journal. In EarthWear's revenue process, the shipping department forwards the approved shipping order to the billing department for entry into the billing program. In such a system, sales should be billed and recorded within one or two days of shipment.

Classification
of Revenue
Transactions

The use of a chart of accounts and proper codes for recording transactions should provide adequate assurance about this assertion. The auditor can review the sales journal and general ledger for proper classification, and can test sales invoices for proper classification by examining programmed controls to ensure that sales invoices are coded by type of product or service.

Control Procedures and Tests of Controls— Cash Receipts Transactions

✳ **[LO 9]**   Table 10–7 summarizes the assertions, possible misstatements, control procedures, and selected tests of controls for cash receipts transactions. In assessing the control risk for cash receipts transactions, the auditor follows the same decision process as described for revenue transactions. Each of the assertions shown in Table 10–7 is discussed with an emphasis on the control procedures and tests of controls.

Occurrence of
Cash Receipts
Transactions

The possible misstatement that concerns the auditor when considering the occurrence assertion is that cash receipts are recorded but not deposited in the client's bank account. In order to commit such a fraud, an employee needs access to both the cash receipts and the accounts receivable records; segregation of duties normally prevents this type of defalcation. Thus, proper segregation of duties between the cash receipts function and the accounts receivable function is one control procedure that can prevent such misstatements. Another very strong control that prevents such misstatements is the use of a lockbox system, such as the system used by EarthWear (Figure 10–2). With a lockbox system, the customers' cash receipts are mailed directly to the client's bank, thereby preventing the client's employees from having access to cash. The cash is deposited in the client's account, and the bank forwards the remittance advices and a file of the cash receipts transactions to the client for processing. Finally, preparation of monthly bank reconciliations that are independently reviewed reduces the possibility that cash receipts will be recorded but not deposited. Table 10–7 lists the tests of controls the auditor could conduct to assess the effectiveness of the client's controls over the occurrence assertion.

Completeness of
Cash Receipts
Transactions

A major misstatement related to the completeness assertion is that cash or checks are stolen or lost before being recorded in the cash receipts records. Proper segregation of duties and a lockbox system are strong controls for ensuring that this assertion is met. When a lockbox system is not used, checks should be restrictively endorsed when received, and a daily cash listing should be prepared. An additional control is reconciliation of the daily cash receipts with the amounts posted to customers' accounts in the accounts receivable subsidiary ledger. An example of this control is shown in EarthWear's system, where the total of the remittance advices is reconciled with the daily remittance report by the cash receipts department.

   In terms of tests of controls, the controls conducted for the occurrence assertion also provide some evidence about completeness. In addition, the

TABLE 10–7		Summary of Assertions, Possible Misstatements, Control Procedures, and Tests of Controls for Cash Receipts Transactions	
Assertion	*Possible Misstatement*	*Control Procedure*	*Test of Controls*
Occurrence	Cash receipts recorded but not received or deposited	Segregation of duties	Observation and evaluation of proper segregation of duties.
		Use of lockbox system	Inquiry of management about lockbox policy.
		Monthly bank reconciliations prepared and independently reviewed	Review of monthly bank reconciliation for indication of independent review.
Completeness	Cash receipts stolen or lost before recording	Same control procedures as above	Same tests of controls as above.
		Checks restrictively endorsed when received and daily cash list prepared	Observation of the endorsement of checks.
		Daily cash receipts reconciled with posting to accounts receivable subsidiary ledger	Testing of the reconciliation of daily cash receipts with posting to accounts receivable subsidiary ledger.
		Customer statements prepared on a regular basis; complaints handled independently	Inquiry of client personnel about handling of monthly statements and examination of resolution of complaints.
Authorization	Cash discounts not properly taken	Procedures specifying policies for cash discounts	Testing of a sample of cash receipts transactions for proper cash discounts.
Accuracy	Cash receipts recorded at incorrect amount	Daily remittance report reconciled to control listing of remittance advices	Review and testing of reconciliation.
		Monthly bank statement reconciled and independently reviewed	Examination of monthly bank reconciliation for independent review.
Cutoff	Cash receipts recorded in wrong period	Use of a lockbox system or a control procedure to deposit cash receipts daily	Examination of cash receipts for daily deposit.
	Cash receipts posted to wrong customer account	Daily remittance report reconciled daily with postings to cash receipts journal and accounts receivable subsidiary ledger	Review and testing of reconciliation; if IT application, testing of application controls for posting.
		Monthly customer statements with independent review of complaints	Review and testing of client procedures for mailing statements and handling complaints from customers.
	Cash receipts not properly posted to general ledger accounts	Monthly cash receipts journal agreed to general ledger posting	Review of posting from cash receipts journal to the general ledger.
		Accounts receivable subsidiary ledger reconciled to general ledger control account	Examination of reconciliation of accounts receivable subsidiary ledger to general ledger control account.
Classification	Cash receipts recorded in wrong financial statement account	Chart of accounts	Tracing of cash receipts from listing to cash receipts journal for proper classification.
			Review of cash receipts journal for unusual items.

auditor can observe the client's personnel endorsing the checks and preparing the cash listing. The reconciliation of the daily cash receipts with the postings to the accounts receivable subsidiary ledger can be tested by the auditor on a sample basis.

When the client does not have adequate segregation of duties or if collusion is suspected, the possibility of defalcation is increased. An employee who has access to both the cash receipts and the accounts receivable records has the ability to steal cash and manipulate the accounting records to hide the misstatement. This is sometimes referred to as *lapping*. When lapping is used, the perpetrator covers the cash shortage by applying cash from one customer's account against another customer's account. For example, suppose customer 1 has a balance of $5,000 and mails a check for $3,000 as payment on the account. A client's employee who has access to both the cash receipts and the accounts receivable records can convert the $3,000 payment to his or her personal use. The theft of the cash can be covered in the following way: The $3,000 payment is not reflected in the customer's account. When a payment is subsequently received from customer 2, the payment is deposited in the client's cash account but applied to customer 1's accounts receivable account. Now the shortage of cash is reflected in customer 2's accounts receivable account. The client employee who stole the cash keeps hiding the theft by shifting the $3,000 difference from one customer's accounts receivable account to another's. If cash is stolen *before* it is recorded as just described, the fraud is difficult and time-consuming for the auditor to detect. If the auditor suspects that this has occurred, the individual cash receipts have to be traced to the customers' accounts receivable accounts to ensure that each cash receipt has been posted to the correct account. If a cash receipt is posted to a different account, this may indicate that someone is applying cash to different accounts to cover a cash shortage. However, if duties are not properly segregated, that person may also be able to hide the theft through use of a credit memorandum, bad-debt write-off, or no recognition of the revenue transaction. For example, the employee could issue a credit memorandum for $3,000 against the customer's accounts receivable account to cover the $3,000 difference.

Authorization of Cash Discounts

Terms of trade generally include discounts for payment within a specified period as a way of encouraging customers to pay on time. Controls in the accounting system should ensure that management's policies concerning cash discounts are followed. For example, the client may establish terms of trade of 2/10, net/30 days. Customers paying within 10 days are then entitled to a 2 percent discount. When the cash is received, client personnel should check to be sure that the customer is complying with the payment terms. The auditor can test this control by examining a sample of cash receipts transactions to determine if the client's cash discount policies are being followed.

Accuracy of Cash Transactions

There are several reasons why cash receipts might be recorded at an incorrect amount. For example, the wrong amount could be recorded from the remittance advice, or the receipt could be incorrectly processed during data entry. The controls listed in Table 10–7 provide reasonable assurance that such errors would be detected and corrected. The corresponding tests of controls involve examining and testing the various reconciliations that take place in this part of the revenue process.

The other major misstatements that can occur for the accuracy assertion are cash receipts being posted to the wrong customer account or the wrong general ledger account. This last misstatement should not be confused with the misstatement discussed under the classification assertion. For the classification assertion, the misstatement results from the wrong financial statement accounts being credited in the cash receipts journal. The misstatement related to the accuracy assertion involves posting to the accounts receivable subsidiary ledger or from the totals in the cash receipts journal to the general ledger accounts.

The use of monthly customer statements provides a check on posting to the correct customer account because a customer who has made a payment and whose monthly statement does not reflect it will complain to the client. The other controls mainly involve the use of various reconciliations that ensure that cash receipts transactions are properly summarized and posted to the general ledger. Tests of controls that may be used by the auditor are presented for each control procedure shown in Table 10–7.

| Cutoff of Cash Receipts Transactions | If the client uses a lockbox system or if cash is deposited daily in the client's bank, there is a small possibility of cash being recorded in the wrong period. Generally, the auditor has little concern with this type of misstatement because most entities use such control procedures. |

| Classification of Cash Receipts | The auditor seldom has major concerns about cash receipts being recorded in the wrong financial statement account. The major control for preventing cash from being recorded in the wrong account is a chart of accounts. The auditor's concern is with applying appropriate account codes to the individual cash receipts, especially cash receipts from unusual sources such as scrap sales, notes receivable, and proceeds from sales of equipment. The auditor can trace a sample of remittance advices to the cash receipts journal to ensure proper classification. The cash receipts journal can also be reviewed for unusual items. |

Control Procedures and Tests of Controls— Sales Returns and Allowances Transactions

[LO 9] For most entities, sales returns and allowances transactions are few and do not represent a material amount in the financial statements. As a result, this text does not cover them in as much detail as revenue or cash receipts transactions. However, credit memoranda that are used to process sales returns and allowances transactions can also be used to cover an unauthorized shipment of goods or conceal a misappropriation of cash.

Two important controls should be present regarding the processing of credit memoranda. First, each credit memorandum should be approved by someone other than the individual who initiated it. This provides proper segregation of duties between access to the customer's record and authorization for issuing a credit memorandum. Second, a credit for returned goods should be supported by a receiving document indicating that the goods have been returned. The auditor can perform tests of controls on credit memoranda by examining a sample of credit memoranda for proper approval and the presence of the respective receiving documents. For a credit memorandum issued for a reason other than a return of goods, approval by an appropriate individual is the critical control. See Exhibit 10–3 for a discussion of the control procedures used by EarthWear to control sales returns.

For entities with few or immaterial sales returns and allowances transactions, the auditor may decide only to gain an understanding of how such transactions are processed and not to conduct tests of controls. Substantive analytical procedures (discussed later in this chapter) can then be used to provide sufficient evidence on the fairness of the sales returns and allowances account.

Relating the Assessed Level of Control Risk to Substantive Procedures

[LO 10]   The results of the auditor's testing of internal control for the revenue process directly impact detection risk and therefore the level of substantive procedures that will be required for the accounts affected by this process. This includes balance sheet accounts such as accounts receivable, allowance for uncollectible accounts, and cash, as well as income statement accounts such as sales, bad-debt expense, and sales returns and allowances.

When the results of testing controls support the planned level of control risk, the auditor can conduct substantive procedures of these accounts at the planned level. If the results of testing controls indicate that the control risk can be further reduced, the auditor can increase the detection risk. This might lead to a reduction in the amount or the mix of the substantive procedures. For example, if the tests of controls indicate that control risk is lower than planned, the auditor might plan to perform more substantive analytical procedures and fewer tests of details of account balances. However, if the results of the tests of controls do not support the planned level of control risk, the detection risk will have to be set lower. This normally leads to an increase in the amount of substantive procedures. For example, if controls for the occurrence assertion are weaker than planned for revenue transactions, the auditor might increase the number of accounts receivable confirmations mailed to customers.

Auditing Accounts Receivable and Related Accounts

The auditor uses substantive procedures to detect material misstatements in accounts receivable and related accounts.

As discussed in Chapter 5, there are two categories of substantive procedures: (1) substantive analytical procedures and (2) tests of details of classes of transactions, account balances, and disclosures. Substantive analytical procedures are used to examine plausible relationships among accounts receivable and related accounts. Tests of details focus on transactions, account balances, or disclosures. In the revenue process, tests of details of

TABLE 10–8	**Management Assertions about Account Balances and Disclosures for Accounts Receivable and Related Accounts**

Assertions about account balances at the period end:
- **Existence.** Recorded accounts receivable and related accounts exist.
- **Rights and obligations.** The entity holds or controls the rights to accounts receivable and related accounts, and any liabilities related to those accounts are the obligations of the entity.
- **Completeness.** All accounts receivable and related accounts that should have been recorded have been recorded.
- **Valuation and allocation.** Accounts receivable and related accounts are included in the financial statements at appropriate amounts, and any resulting valuation or allocation adjustments are appropriately recorded.

Assertions about presentation and disclosure:
- **Occurrence and rights and obligations.** All disclosed events, transactions, and other matters relating to accounts receivable and related accounts have occurred and pertain to the entity.
- **Completeness.** All disclosures relating to accounts receivable and related accounts that should have been included in the financial statements have been included.
- **Classification and understandability.** Financial information relating to accounts receivable and related accounts is appropriately presented and described, and disclosures are clearly expressed.
- **Accuracy and valuation.** Financial and other information relating to accounts receivable and related accounts are disclosed fairly and at appropriate amounts.

transactions (also called *substantive tests of transactions*) focus mainly on the sales and cash receipts transactions. Tests of details of account balances concentrate on the detailed amounts or estimates that make up the ending balance for accounts receivable and related accounts. Tests of details of disclosures are concerned with the presentation and disclosures related to accounts receivable and related accounts.

Table 10–5 presented the assertions for revenue and cash receipt transactions and events. Table 10–8 lists the assertions for account balances and disclosure as they apply to accounts receivable and related accounts. The reader should note that the auditor may test assertions related to transactions (substantive tests of transactions) in conjunction with testing internal control. If the tests of controls indicate that the controls are not operating effectively, the auditor may need to test transactions at the date the account balance is tested.

Substantive Analytical Procedures

✂ [LO 11]   Substantive analytical procedures are useful audit tests for examining the fairness of accounts such as sales, accounts receivable, allowance for uncollectible accounts, bad-debt expense, and sales returns and allowances because such tests provide sufficient evidence at low cost. Table 10–9 lists substantive analytical procedures that are useful in auditing accounts receivable and related accounts either at the planning stage or as an overall review.

For example, a comparison of gross profit percentage to previous years' or industry data may provide valuable evidence on unrecorded revenue (an understatement) or fictitious revenue (an overstatement) and related accounts receivable when this ratio is significantly higher or lower than previous years' or industry data. This ratio may also provide information on changes in pricing policies.

TABLE 10-9	Substantive Analytical Procedures for Accounts Receivable and Related Accounts

Substantive Analytical Procedure	Possible Misstatement Detected
Revenue	
Comparison of gross profit percentage by product line with previous years' and industry data.	Unrecorded (understated) revenue.
Comparison of reported revenue to budgeted revenue.	Fictitious (overstated) revenue.
Analysis of the ratio of sales in the last month or week to total sales for the quarter or year.*	Changes in pricing policies.
Comparison of revenues recorded daily for periods shortly before and after the end of the audit period for unusual fluctuations such as an increase just before and a decrease just after the end of the period.*	Product-pricing problems.
Comparison of details of units shipped with revenues and production records and consideration of whether revenues are reasonable compared to levels of production and average sales price.*	
Comparison of the number of weeks of inventory in distribution channels with prior periods for unusual increases that may indicate channel stuffing.*	
Comparison of percentages and trends of sales into the distributor channel with industry and competitors' sales trends, if known.*	
Accounts Receivable, Allowance for Uncollectible Accounts, and Bad-Debt Expense	
Comparison of receivables turnover and days outstanding in accounts receivable to previous years' and/or industry data.	Under- or overstatement of allowance for uncollectible accounts and bad-debt expense.
Comparison of aging categories on aged trial balance of accounts receivable to previous years.	
Comparison of bad-debt expense as a percentage of revenue to previous years' and/or industry data.	
Comparison of the allowance for uncollectible accounts as a percentage of accounts receivable or credit sales to previous years' and/or industry data.	
Examination of large customer accounts individually and comparison to previous year.	
Sales Returns and Allowances and Sales Commissions	
Comparison of sales returns as a percentage of revenue to previous years' or industry data.	Under- or overstatement of sales returns.
Comparison of sales discounts as a percentage of revenue to previous years' and/or industry data.	Under- or overstatement of sales discounts.
Estimation of sales commission expense by multiplying net revenue by average commission rate and comparison of recorded sales commission expense.	Under- or overstatement of sales commission expense and related accrual.

*Analytical procedures suggest in the AICPA's *Auditing Revenue in Certain Industries,* Audit Guide (New York: AICPA, 2001).

The five ratios shown under the "Accounts Receivable" subheading in Table 10–9 provide evidence on whether accounts receivable properly reflect net realizable value. Each ratio aids the auditor in assessing the fairness of the allowance for uncollectible accounts, which in turn affects the fairness of accounts receivable and bad-debt expense. The days outstanding in accounts receivable ratio for EarthWear provides a good example of a substantive analytical procedure that provides strong evidential support for the accurate valuation of accounts receivable. The days outstanding in accounts receivable ratio is 4.91 and 4.94 days for 2004 and 2005, suggesting that EarthWear collects its accounts receivable quickly. This result is consistent with the majority of the company's sales being made with credit cards. EarthWear is reimbursed in three to five days by its credit card providers.

Given this result, EarthWear's auditors may do no further audit work on accounts receivable.

Last, comparing the ratio of sales returns or sales discounts to revenue with previous years' and industry data provides the auditor with evidence on whether all sales returns or sales discounts have been recorded. The auditor can also estimate sales commission expense by multiplying the average commission rate by net sales and comparing that amount with recorded commission expense. In many situations, the auditor may be able to accept the sales returns, sales discounts, and sales commission expense as fairly presented without conducting any additional substantive tests if such substantive analytical procedures produce results that are consistent with the auditor's expectations.

Tests of Details of Classes of Transactions, Account Balances, and Disclosures

[LO 12] Table 10–10 presents the assertions for accounts receivable, allowance for uncollectible accounts, and bad-debt expense along with related tests of transactions, account balances, and disclosures.

Tests of details of transactions (substantive tests of transactions) are tests conducted to detect monetary misstatements in the individual transactions processed through all accounting applications. Often the auditor conducts substantive tests of transactions at the same time as tests of controls. Additionally, it is often difficult to distinguish a substantive test of transactions from a test of controls because the specific audit procedure may both test the operation of a control procedure and test for monetary misstatement. Table 10–10 presents a substantive test of transactions for each assertion for revenue transactions. Normally, most of these tests are conducted as tests of controls. However, if the controls are not operating effectively or if the auditor did not rely on those controls, substantive tests of transactions may be necessary for the auditor to reach an appropriate level of evidence. The cutoff assertion is the one that is most often conducted as a substantive procedure.

[LO 13] Table 10–10 also presents the assertions for account balances and disclosures. For each assertion, one or more tests of details are presented. In the following subsection, we discuss how the auditor approaches the audit of each important assertion for accounts receivable and related accounts. We begin with the completeness assertion for the accounts receivable balance because the auditor must establish that the detailed records that support the account to be audited agree with the general ledger account.

Completeness

The auditor's concern with completeness is whether all accounts receivable have been included in the accounts receivable subsidiary ledger and the general ledger accounts receivable account. The reconciliation of the aged trial balance to the general ledger account should detect an omission of a receivable from *either* the accounts receivable subsidiary ledger

TABLE 10–10	Summary of Assertions and Related Tests of Transactions, Account Balances and Disclosures—Accounts Receivable, Allowance for Uncollectible Accounts, and Bad-Debt Expense

Assertions about Classes of Transactions	Substantive Tests of Transaction*
Occurrence	For a sample of sales transactions recorded in the sales journal, tracing of the sales invoices back to customer orders and shipping documents.
Completeness	Tracing of a sample of shipping documents to the details of the sales invoices and to the sales journal and customers' accounts receivable subsidiary ledger.
Authorization and accuracy	Comparison of prices and terms on a sample of sales invoices with authorized price list and terms of trade.
Cutoff	Comparison of the dates on a sample of sales invoices with the dates of shipment and with the dates they were recorded in the sales journal.
Classification	Examine a sample of sales invoices for proper classification into revenue accounts.

Assertions about Account Balances	Tests of Details of Account Balances
Existence	Confirmation of selected accounts receivable. Performance of alternative procedures for accounts receivable confirmation exceptions and nonresponses.
Rights and obligations	Review of bank confirmations for any liens on receivables. Inquiry of management, review of any loan agreements, and review of board of directors' minutes for any indication that the accounts receivable have been sold.
Completeness	Obtaining of aged trial balance of accounts receivable and agreeing total to general ledger control accounts. Review results of testing the completeness assertion for assessing control risk; tracing of shipping documents into sales journal and to accounts receivable subsidiary ledger if such testing was not performed as a test of controls.
Valuation and allocation	Examination of the results of confirmations of selected accounts receivable. Examination of the adequacy of the allowance for uncollectible accounts.

Assertions about Presentation and Disclosure	Tests of Details of Disclosures
Occurrence, and rights and obligations	Determine whether any receivables have been pledged, assigned, or discounted. Determine if such items require disclosure.
Completeness	Complete financial reporting checklist to ensure that all financial statement disclosures related to accounts receivable and related accounts have been disclosed.
Classification and understandability	Review of aged trial balance for material credits, long-term receivables, and nontrade receivables. Determine whether such items require separate disclosure on the balance sheet. Read footnotes to ensure that required disclosures are understandable.
Accuracy and valuation	Read footnotes and other information to ensure that the information is accurate and properly presented at the appropriate amounts.

*Each of these substantive tests of transactions could be conducted as a test of controls or a dual-purpose test. Of these six assertions, the cutoff assertion is the one that is mostly to be conducted as a substantive procedure.

or the general ledger account. If the client's accounting system contains proper control totals and reconciliations, such errors should be detected and corrected by the relevant control procedures for accuracy and completeness. For example, in EarthWear's revenue process (Figure 10–2), control totals exist for daily shipping and billing. Personnel in the billing department would be responsible for reconciling the two totals. If such control procedures do not exist in a client's accounting system, or if they are not operating effectively, the auditor will have to trace a sample of shipping documents to sales invoices, the sales journal, and the accounts receivable subsidiary ledger to ensure that the transactions were included in the accounting records.

This process followed by the auditor is to agree the accounts receivable subsidiary ledger of customer accounts to the general ledger accounts receivable (control) account. This is typically accomplished by obtaining a copy of the aged trial balance of accounts receivable and comparing the total balance with the general ledger accounts receivable account balance. Exhibit 10–4 presents an aged trial balance of accounts receivable working paper for Calabro Paging Services (see Problem 3-32). An aged trial balance of the subsidiary ledger is used because the auditor will need this type of data to examine the allowance for uncollectible accounts.

The auditor must also have assurance that the detail making up the aged trial balance is accurate. This can be accomplished in a number of ways. One approach involves mainly manual audit procedures. First, the aged trial balance is footed and crossfooted. *Footing* and *crossfooting* mean that each column of the trial balance is added, and the column totals are then added to ensure that they agree with the total balance for the account. Then a sample of customer accounts included in the aged trial balance is

---

EXHIBIT 10–4	Example of an Aged Trial Balance of Accounts Receivable Working Paper

CP5

	CALABRO PAGING SERVICES Aged Trial Balance—Accounts Receivable 12/31/05				E10 DLJ 2/15/2006
Customer Name	*Total*	*<30 Days*	*30–60 Days*	*60–90 Days*	*>90 Days*
Abbott Construction	$ 10,945¥	$ 9,542	$ 1,403		
Acton Labs	9,705		5,205	$ 4,500	
•	•	•	•	•	•
•	•	•	•	•	•
•	•	•	•	•	•
Wright Industries	29,875¥	18,875	11,000		
Zorcon, Inc.	4,340				$ 4,340
Total	$3,717,900	$2,044,895	$1,301,215	$260,253	$111,537
	F T/B	F	F	F	F

F = Footed.
T/B = Agreed to trial balance.
¥ = Customer account traced to subsidiary ledger; agreed to total and proper aging tested.

selected for testing. For each selected customer account, the auditor traces the customer's balance back to the subsidiary ledger detail and verifies the total amount and the amounts included in each column for proper aging. A second approach involves the use of computer-assisted audit techniques. If the general controls over IT are adequate, the auditor can use a generalized audit software package to examine the accuracy of the aged trial balance generated by the client's accounting system.

Cutoff

The cutoff assertion attempts to determine whether all revenue transactions and related accounts receivable are recorded in the proper period. In some instances, the auditor can obtain enough assurance about the cutoff assertion for sales by conducting tests of controls. However, in most cases, cutoff tests are conducted as substantive tests of transactions. Additionally, sales cutoff is coordinated with inventory cutoff because the shipment of goods normally indicates that the earnings process is complete. The auditor wants assurance that if goods have been shipped in the current period, the resulting sale has been recorded, and also that if the sales have been recorded, the corresponding inventory has been removed from the accounting records. In addition, the auditor needs to determine if there is proper cutoff for sales returns.

If there is not a proper cutoff of revenue transactions, both revenue and accounts receivable will be misstated for the current and following years. In most instances, errors related to sales cutoff are unintentional and are due to delays in recognizing the shipment of goods or the recognition of the sale. In other instances, the client may intentionally fail to recognize revenue transactions in the current period or may recognize sales from the next period in the current period (see Exhibit 10–5 and Problem 10-32). The first situation can occur by the revenue transactions not being recorded in the sales journal until the next period. For example, sales that take place on the last two days of the current year are recorded as sales in the next year by delaying entry until the current-year sales journal is closed. The second situation is generally accomplished by leaving the sales journal "open" and recognizing sales from the first few days of the next period as current-period sales.

The client's accounting system should have controls that ensure timely recording of revenue transactions. The results of tests of controls, if performed, should provide evidence of the cutoff assertion. Additionally, the client should have end-of-period control procedures for ensuring a proper sales cutoff between accounting periods.

The test of sales cutoff is straightforward. The auditor first identifies the number of the last shipping document issued in the current period. Then a sample of sales invoices and their related shipping documents is selected for a few days just prior to, and subsequent to, the end of the period. Assuming that sales are recorded at the time of shipment (FOB–shipping point), sales invoices representing goods shipped prior to year-end should be recorded in the current period, and invoices for goods shipped subsequent to year-end should be recorded as sales in the next period. Any transaction recorded in the wrong period should be corrected by the client. For example, suppose the last shipping document issued in the current period

EXHIBIT 10–5	**Sunbeam Corporation Restates Financial Results**

Sunbeam Corporation restated its financial results for 1996, 1997, and the first quarter of 1998 based on an extensive audit by its audit committee and two public accounting firms. The special audit found that the previously issued financial statements overstated the loss for 1996, overstated profits for 1997, and understated the loss for the first quarter of 1998. Sunbeam reported that, for certain periods, revenue was incorrectly recognized in the wrong period, partly because of the company's "bill and hold" practice of billing customers in the current period for products that were delivered in a later period. The company also booked a significant amount of sales that were made to customers under such liberal terms that they did not constitute valid sales at all, but rather appeared to be consignments or guaranteed sales. In 1997 revenue was restated from $1,186 million to $1,073 million, and earnings were reduced from $123.1 million to $52.3 million. The reporting of these financial irregularities led to the resignation of Sunbeam's CEO, Al Dunlap.

In 2001, the SEC sued five ex-executives of Sunbeam and Andersen LLP agreed to pay $110 million to settle an accounting-fraud lawsuit over its audit work for Sunbeam.

Sources: J. R. Liang, "Dangerous Games: Did "Chainsaw Al" Dunlap Manufacture Sunbeam's Earnings Last Year?" *Barron's* (June 8, 1998), pp. 17–19; M. Brannigan, "Sunbeam Audit to Repudiate '97 Turnaround," *The Wall Street Journal* (October 20, 1998), p. A3; "Sunbeam to Restate Financial Results; Discloses Adjustments for 1996, 1997, and First Quarter 1998," *The PointCast Network* (October 20, 1998); N. Harris, "Andersen to Pay $110 Million to Settle Sunbeam Account-Fraud Lawsuit," *The Wall Street Journal* (May 2, 2001), A3; and J. Weil, "Five Sunbeam Ex-Executives Sued by SEC," *The Wall Street Journal* (May 16, 2001), A3.

was numbered 10,540. None of the recorded revenue transactions sampled from a few days prior to year-end should have related shipping document numbers higher than 10,540, and none of the sampled revenue transactions recorded in the first few days of the subsequent period should have related shipping document numbers lower than 10,540. In a computerized system such tests are still necessary because a delay in entering data may occur, or management may manipulate the recognition of the transactions.

The processing of sales returns may differ across entities. When sales returns are not material, or if they occur irregularly, the entity may recognize a sales return at the time the goods are returned. However, for entities like EarthWear, sales returns may represent a material amount or may occur regularly. In this instance, the client may estimate an allowance for sales returns. When sales returns represent a material amount, the auditor needs to test for proper cutoff.

Substantive analytical procedures may be used to test cutoff for sales returns. The ratio of sales returns to sales may indicate to the auditor that sales returns are consistent with expectations and therefore that the sales returns cutoff is adequate. If the auditor decides to conduct more detailed tests, the receiving documents used to acknowledge receipt of the returned goods must be examined. Using procedures similar to those for testing sales cutoff, the auditor selects a sample of receiving documents for a few days prior to and subsequent to the end of the period. The receiving documents are traced to the related credit memoranda. Sales returns recorded in the wrong period should be corrected, if material.

Existence

The existence of accounts receivable is one of the more important assertions because the auditor wants assurance that this account balance is not overstated through the inclusion of fictitious customer accounts or amounts. The major audit procedure for testing the existence assertion for accounts receivable is confirmation of customers' account balances. If a customer does not respond to the auditor's confirmation request, additional audit procedures may be necessary. The confirmation process is discussed later in this chapter.

Rights and Obligations

The auditor must determine whether the accounts receivable are owned by the entity because accounts receivable that have been sold should not be included in the entity's financial statements. For most audit engagements, this does not represent a problem because the client owns all the receivables. However, in some instances a client may sell its accounts receivable. The auditor can detect such an action by reviewing bank confirmations, cash receipts for payments from organizations that factor accounts receivable, or corporate minutes for authorization of the sale or assignment of receivables.

Valuation and Allocation

The major valuation issue related to accounts receivable is concerned with the net realizable value of accounts receivable. The auditor is concerned with determining that the allowance for uncollectible accounts, and thus bad-debt expense, is fairly stated. The allowance for uncollectible accounts is affected by internal factors such as the client's credit-granting and cash collection policies and external factors such as the state of the economy, conditions in the client's industry, and the financial strength of the client's customers.

In verifying the adequacy of the allowance for uncollectible accounts, the auditor starts by assessing the client's policies for granting credit and collecting cash. If the client establishes strict standards for granting credit, the likelihood of a large number of bad debts is reduced. Generally, the auditor assesses the adequacy of the allowance account by first examining the aged trial balance for amounts that have been outstanding for a long time. The probability of collecting these accounts can be assessed by discussing them with the credit manager, examining the customers' financial statements, obtaining credit reports (such as from Dun & Bradstreet), or reviewing the customers' communications with the client related to payment.

The second step in assessing the adequacy of the allowance account involves examining the client's prior experience with bad debts. The problem with examining only delinquent accounts is that no consideration is given to accounts that are current but that may result in bad debts. By maintaining good statistics on bad debts, the client can determine what percentage of each aging category will become uncollectible. The auditor can test these percentages for reasonableness. Following is an example of how this approach would work.

Suppose Calabro Paging Services developed the following historical data on bad debts:

Aging Category	Percentage as Bad Debts
<30 days	.001
30–60 days	.025
60–90 days	.14
>90 days	.55

The allowance for uncollectible accounts can be determined in the following manner, using the data from Exhibit 10–4:

<30 days	30–60 days	60–90 days	>90 days	Total
$2,044,895	$1,301,215	$260,253	$111,537	$3,717,900
× .001	× .025	× .14	× .55	
$ 2,045	$ 32,530	$ 36,435	$ 61,345	$ 132,355

The balance in the allowance for doubtful accounts on Calabro's general ledger is $135,300 and appears reasonable, given the auditor's calculation of $132,355. While determining the proper amount for the allowance for uncollectible accounts may seem relatively straightforward, considerable judgment on the part of the auditor is involved. As mentioned, the auditor must evaluate the collectibility of individual problem accounts and consider whether the historically derived percentages are reasonable, given the current economic and industry conditions.

Classification and Understandability

The major issues related to the presentation and disclosure assertion about classification are (1) identifying and reclassifying any material credits contained in accounts receivable, (2) segregating short-term and long-term receivables, and (3) ensuring that different types of receivables are properly classified. In many entities, when a customer pays in advance or a credit is issued, the amount is credited to the customer's accounts receivable account. The auditor should determine the amount of such credits and, if material, reclassify them as either a deposit or another type of liability. The second issue requires that the auditor identify and separate short-term receivables from long-term receivables. Long-term receivables should not be included with trade accounts receivable. The auditor must also ensure that nontrade receivables are properly separated from trade accounts receivable. For example, receivables from officers, employees, or related parties should not be included with trade accounts receivable because users might be misled if such receivables are combined.

Other Presentation and Disclosure Assertions

Disclosure is important for accounts receivable and related accounts. While management is responsible for the financial statements, the auditor must ensure that all necessary disclosures are made. Most public accounting firms use some type of financial statement reporting checklist to ensure that all necessary disclosures are made for each account (completeness). Table 10–11 presents examples of disclosure items for the revenue process and related

TABLE 10–11	Examples of Disclosure Items for the Revenue Process and Related Accounts

Revenue recognition basis.
Revenues recognized under the percentage-of-completion method.
Long-term sales contracts.
Revenues by reportable segment of the business.
Revenues and receivables from related parties.
Receivables by type (trade, officer, employee, affiliate, and so on).
Short- and long-term receivables.
Pledged or discounted receivables.

EXHIBIT 10–6	Sample Disclosures for Revenue Recognition and Related-Party Transactions

Revenue Recognition
Sales are recognized when the company's products are shipped. Sales to customers with whom the company has reciprocal purchase agreements are accounted for in the same manner as inter-company transactions and are eliminated in the financial statements.

Related-Party Transactions
The company's chairman of the board is also chairman of the board of Dayco Industries. Net sales to Dayco were $990,000 and $1,244,000 for the two years ended 2005 and 2004. Accounts receivable from Dayco were $243,000 and $489,000 at December 31, 2005 and 2004, respectively. The company believes that the terms of sale were substantially the same as those available to unrelated parties for similar products.

financial statement accounts. Exhibit 10–6 presents two examples of common disclosures for revenue-related accounts. The first disclosure relates to the basis for recognizing revenue. This disclosure is normally included in a footnote that describes significant accounting policies. The second example presents disclosure of related-party transactions. Disclosures about related-party transactions normally discuss the nature of the transactions, the amounts, and whether the transactions were similar in terms to those for unrelated parties.

The Confirmation Process—Accounts Receivable

⚜ **[LO 14]**   Confirmation is the process of obtaining and evaluating a direct communication provided by a third party in response to an auditor's request for information about a particular item affecting financial statement assertions (AU 330). Confirmation of accounts receivable is considered a generally accepted auditing procedure (AU 330.34), and therefore auditors normally request confirmation of accounts receivable during an audit.[2] However,

---

[2]See D. K. McConnell, Jr., and G. Y. Banks, "A Common Peer Review Problem," *Journal of Accountancy* (June 1998), pp. 39–44, for a discussion of deficiencies identified by the AICPA's practice-monitoring division in the use of accounts receivable confirmations by auditors.

auditing standards allow the auditor to omit confirming accounts receivable in the following circumstances:

- The accounts receivable are immaterial to the financial statements.
- The use of confirmations would not be effective as an audit procedure. (This might occur if, based on prior experience, the auditor determines that the response rate might be low or the responses might not be reliable.)
- The auditor's assessment of inherent risk and control risk is low, and evidence gathered from other substantive tests is sufficient to reduce audit risk to an acceptably low level.

Because of the importance of accounts receivable confirmations, the auditor should document completely the decision not to gather such evidence.

Confirmations can address more than one assertion. However, confirmations normally provide different levels of assurance for different assertions. Accounts receivable confirmations are generally a good source of evidence for testing the existence assertion. If the customer confirms the amount owed to the client, the auditor has competent evidence that the account receivable is valid.[3] Accounts receivable confirmations may also provide evidence on the cutoff, completeness, and valuation and allocation assertions. For example, a customer's confirmation of the dollar amount owed provides some evidence on the valuation and allocation assertion.

A number of factors affect the reliability of accounts receivable confirmations. The auditor should consider each of the following factors when using confirmations to test accounts receivable:

- The type of confirmation request.
- Prior experience with the client or similar engagements.
- The intended respondent.

The types of confirmations are discussed in the next section. The auditor should consider prior experience with the client in terms of confirmation response rates, misstatements identified, and the accuracy of returned confirmations when assessing the reliability of accounts receivable confirmations. For example, if response rates were low in prior audits, the auditor might consider obtaining evidence using alternative procedures. The intended respondents to accounts receivable confirmations may vary from individuals with little accounting knowledge to large corporations with highly qualified accounting personnel. The auditor should consider each respondent's competence, knowledge, ability, and objectivity when assessing the reliability of confirmation requests. For example, if an auditor is confirming accounts receivable for a small retail organization, it is possible that the respondents may not have the knowledge or ability to respond appropriately to the confirmation request. On the other hand, if confirmations are sent to medium-size or large corporations with well-controlled accounts payable

---

[3]Research has shown that accounts receivable confirmations are not always a reliable source of evidence. See P. Caster, "An Empirical Study of Accounts Receivable Confirmations as Audit Evidence," *Auditing: A Journal of Practice and Theory* (Fall 1990), pp. 75–91, and P. Caster, "The Role of Confirmations as Audit Evidence," *Journal of Accountancy* (February 1992), pp. 73–76, for a discussion of these findings.

systems, the information received in response to such confirmation requests is likely to be reliable. However, some large organizations and government agencies do not respond to confirmations because it may be difficult to accumulate the necessary data since they are on a voucher system. Such nonresponses must be tested using procedures discussed later in the chapter.

Types of Confirmations

There are two types of confirmations: *positive* and *negative*. A positive accounts receivable confirmation requests that customers indicate whether they agree with the amount due to the client stated in the confirmation. Thus, a response is required regardless of whether the customer believes the amount is correct or incorrect. Sometimes an auditor will use a "blank" form of positive confirmation, in which the request requires the customer to provide the amount owed to the client. Positive confirmations are generally used when an account's individual balances are large or if errors are anticipated because the control risk has been judged to be high. Exhibit 10–7 presents an example of a positive confirmation request.

EXHIBIT 10–7   **Example of a Positive Confirmation Request**

CALABRO PAGING SERVICES

Wright Industries
8440 S.W. 97 Boulevard
Starke, FL 32690

Dear Customers:

Please examine the accompanying statement carefully and either confirm its correctness or report any differences to our auditors

Abbott & Johnson, LLP
P.O. Box 669
Tampa, FL 32691

who are auditing our financial statements.
   Your prompt attention to this request will be appreciated. An envelope is enclosed for your reply. Please do not send your payments to the auditors.

Sincerely,
Jan Rodriguez
Controller, Calabro Paging Services

Confirmation:

The balance receivable from us for $29,875 as of December 31, 2005, is correct except as noted below:

_____

_____

_____

Wright Industries

Date_____ By _____

EXHIBIT 10–8	**Example of a Negative Confirmation Request**

CALABRO PAGING SERVICES

Zorcon, Inc.
P.O. Box 1429
Melrose, FL 32692-1429

Dear Customers:

Please examine the accompanying statement carefully. If it does NOT agree with your records, please report any differences directly to our auditors

Abbott & Johnson, LLP
P.O. Box 669
Tampa, FL 32691

who are auditing our financial statements.
   Your prompt attention to this request will be appreciated. An envelope is enclosed for your reply. Please do not send your payments to the auditors.

Sincerely,
Jan Rodriguez
Controller, Calabro Paging Services

A negative confirmation requests that customers respond only when they disagree with the amount due to the client. An example of a negative confirmation request is shown in Exhibit 10–8. Negative confirmation requests are used when there are many accounts with small balances, control risk is assessed to be low, and the auditor believes that the customers will devote adequate attention to the confirmation. On many audit engagements, a combination of positive and negative confirmations is used to test accounts receivable because of materiality considerations and a mix of customers. For example, positive confirmations may be sent to selected large-dollar customer accounts and negative confirmations sent to a sample of small-dollar customer accounts.

Because positive accounts receivable confirmations require that customers respond to the auditor, any amounts for which responses are not received must be verified by the auditor using alternative procedures. Negative accounts receivable confirmations require a response only when the information about the customer's balance is incorrect. Therefore, a nonresponse to a negative confirmation request is generally assumed to represent a valid accounts receivable. This can be a major drawback to the use of negative confirmations.

The accuracy of the accounts receivable confirmation request can generally be improved if a copy of the customer's monthly statement is enclosed with the confirmation request.

Timing

Accounts receivable may be confirmed at an interim date or at year-end. Such considerations were discussed in Chapter 6. The confirmation request should be sent soon after the end of the accounting period in order to max-imize the response rate. Sending the confirmations at the end of the ac-counting period reduces the chance of timing differences arising due to processing of purchases and cash disbursements by the customers.

Confirmation Procedures

The auditor must maintain control over the accounts receivable confirma-tions so as to minimize the possibility that direct communication between the customers and the auditor is biased by interception or alteration of the receivable confirmation by the client. For control purposes, the auditor should mail the confirmations outside the client's facilities. Direct mailing from the public accounting firm's office generally provides the best control. To ensure that any confirmations that are undeliverable by the post office are returned to the auditors and not the client, the confirmations should be mailed in envelopes with the public accounting firm's address listed as the return address. The envelope used by customers for returning the confir-mation response should also be addressed to the public accounting firm.[4] The fact that undeliverable confirmations are returned directly to the audi-tor also provides some assurance that fictitious customers are identified.

The auditor should maintain a record of the confirmations mailed and those returned. When positive confirmations are used, the auditor gener-ally follows up with second, and possibly third, requests to customers who do not reply, in an attempt to increase the response rate to the confirma-tion requests. In some cases, a customer may respond using electronic me-dia (such as e-mail or fax) or orally. In such situations the auditor should verify the source and contents of the communication. For example, a fax response may be verified by a telephone call to the respondent, and an oral response can be verified by requesting a written communication from the respondent.

Each confirmation exception (that is, difference between the recorded balance and the balance confirmed by the customer) should be carefully ex-amined by the auditor to determine the reason for the difference. In many cases, exceptions result from what are referred to as *timing differences*. Such differences occur because of delays in recording transactions in either the client's or the customer's records. For example, the client may ship goods to a customer on the last day of the period and record it as a current-period sale. The customer will probably receive and record the goods as a purchase in the next period. Such situations are not errors and result only because of a delay in recording the transaction. Payment for goods by a customer at the end of the period can result in a timing difference if the customer pre-pares and records the check in the current period but the client receives and records the check in the following period. Again, the difference in the con-firmed amount results from a timing difference. Table 10–12 presents some examples of exceptions and their potential causes.

The need to maintain control over accounts receivable confirmations and responses does not preclude the use of internal auditors in the confirmation

---

[4]R. H. Ashton and R. E. Hylas, "The Return of 'Problem' Confirmation Requests by the US Postal Service," *The Accounting Review* (October 1980), pp. 275–285, shows that the U.S. Postal Service does an excellent job of returning undeliverable confirmations to the return address.

TABLE 10–12	**Examples of Exceptions to Confirmation Requests**

Type of Difference	Potential Cause
Goods not received by customer	Timing difference.
	Goods delivered to wrong customer.
	Invoice sent to wrong customer.
	Fictitious sale.
Payment not recorded in client's records	Timing difference.
	Payment applied to wrong customer account.
	Cash misappropriated.
Goods returned for credit by customer	Timing difference.
Processing error	Incorrect quantity or price.
	Recording error.
Amount in dispute	Price of goods in dispute.
	Goods do not meet specifications.
	Goods damaged in transit.

process. For example, internal auditors may confirm accounts receivable as part of their normal duties, or they may directly assist the auditor in performing accounts receivable confirmations as part of the annual audit (AU 322). If internal auditors are used in this capacity, their work should be supervised, reviewed, evaluated, and tested by the independent auditor.

Alternative Procedures

When the auditor does not receive responses to positive confirmations, he or she must apply alternative procedures to determine the existence and valuation of the accounts receivable. Auditors normally send second and third requests; they also perform the following alternative audit procedures:

- Examination of subsequent cash receipts.
- Examination of customer orders, shipping documents, and duplicate sales invoices.
- Examination of other client documentation.

Examination of subsequent cash receipts involves checking the accounts receivable subsidiary ledger for payments of the specific sales invoices included in the customers' accounts receivable balances that were outstanding at the date of the confirmation. If the client has strong controls for recording cash receipts, the auditor may stop at this point. If the client's controls are weak, the auditor may extend the testing by tracing the payment in the subsidiary ledger to the cash receipts journal and to the bank statement. If the customer has paid for the goods, the auditor has strong evidence concerning the existence and valuation of the accounts receivable.

If a customer has not paid the accounts receivable, the auditor can examine the underlying documentation that supports the revenue transaction. This documentation includes the original customer order, shipping document, and duplicate sales invoice. If this documentation indicates that the customer ordered the goods and the goods were shipped, then the auditor would have evidence supporting the validity of the accounts receivable. Last, the auditor may need to examine other correspondence between the client and the customer to obtain adequate evidence on the validity and valuation of the accounts receivable.

Auditing Other Receivables

❈ **[LO 15]**   Up to this point the discussion has concentrated on trade accounts receivable. Most entities, however, have other types of receivables that are reported on the balance sheet. Some examples include

- Receivables from officers and employees.
- Receivables from related parties.
- Notes receivable.

The auditor's concern with satisfying the assertions for these receivables is similar to that for trade accounts receivable. Typically, each of these types of receivables is confirmed and evaluated for collectibility. The transactions that result in receivables from related parties are examined to determine if they were at "arm's length." Notes receivable would also be confirmed and examined for repayment terms and whether interest income has been properly recognized.

Evaluating the Audit Findings—Accounts Receivable and Related Accounts

❈ **[LO 16]**   When the auditor has completed the planned substantive procedures, the likely misstatement (the projected misstatement plus an allowance for sampling risk) for accounts receivable is determined using either statistical or nonstatistical sampling techniques. The likely misstatement is then compared to the tolerable misstatement. If the likely misstatement is less than the tolerable misstatement, the auditor may accept the account as fairly presented. Conversely, if the likely misstatement exceeds the tolerable misstatement, the auditor may conclude that the account is not fairly presented. For example, in Chapter 3 a tolerable misstatement for EarthWear was $885,000. Suppose that, after completing the substantive procedures, EarthWear's auditor determines that the likely misstatement is $250,000. In this case, the auditor may conclude that EarthWear's accounts receivable are not materially misstated. However, if the likely misstatement is $940,000, the auditor's conclusion will be that the account is materially misstated.

The auditor should also analyze the misstatements discovered through substantive procedures. In some instances, these misstatements may provide additional evidence on control risk. By identifying the causes of the misstatements, the auditor may determine that the original assessment of control risk was too low. For example, the auditor may lower his or her evaluation of the effectiveness of the control for granting credit (that is, may increase control risk) based on a large number of misstatements detected during tests of the allowance for uncollectible accounts. This may impact the auditor's assessment of audit risk.

If the auditor concludes that audit risk is unacceptably high, additional audit procedures should be performed, the client should adjust the related financial statement accounts to an acceptable level, or a qualified report should be issued. In the previous example, in which EarthWear's auditor determined that the likely misstatement was $940,000, additional audit procedures might be required. Such audit procedures would typically be directed at the *systematic* errors detected by the substantive procedures. For example, if the substantive tests of transactions indicated that sales invoices were priced incorrectly, the auditor's additional audit procedures would focus on determining the extent of pricing misstatements. Alternatively, the auditor could conclude that accounts receivable are fairly presented if EarthWear's management adjusts the financial statements by $55,000 or more ($940,000 − $885,000). This would result in the likely misstatement being equal to or less than the tolerable misstatement of $885,000.

In summary, the final decision about accounts receivable and the related accounts is based on whether sufficient competent evidence has been obtained from the substantive tests conducted.

KEY TERMS

Analytical procedures. Evaluations of financial information made by a study of plausible relationships among both financial and nonfinancial data.

Application controls. Controls that apply to the processing of specific computer applications and are part of the computer programs used in the accounting system.

Assertions. Expressed or implied representations by management that are reflected in the financial statement components.

Confirmation. The process of obtaining and evaluating direct communication from a third party in response to a request for information about a particular item affecting financial statement assertions.

General controls. Controls that relate to the overall information processing environment and have a pervasive effect on the entity's computer operations.

Lapping. The process of covering a cash shortage by applying cash from one customer's accounts receivable against another customer's accounts receivable.

Negative confirmation. A confirmation request to which the recipient responds only if the amount or information stated is incorrect.

Positive confirmation. A confirmation request to which the recipient responds whether or not he or she agrees with the amount or information stated.

Reliance strategy. The auditor's decision to rely on the entity's controls, test those controls, and reduce the direct tests of the financial statement accounts.

Tests of controls. Procedures that evaluate the effectiveness of the design and operation of internal controls.

Tests of details of account balances and disclosures. Tests that concentrate on the details of amounts contained in an account balance and in disclosures.

Tests of details of transactions. Tests to detect errors or fraud in individual transactions.

REVIEW QUESTIONS

[LO 1]   10-1   Accounting standards require that revenue must be earned and realized before it can be recognized. Discuss what is meant by the terms *earned* and *realized*.

[5,6]   10-2   Describe the credit function's duties for monitoring customer payments and handling bad debts.

[6]   10-3   When a client does not adequately segregate duties, the possibility of cash being stolen before it is recorded is increased. If the auditor suspects that this type of defalcation is possible, what type of audit procedures can he or she use to test this possibility?

[7]   10-4   The auditor needs to understand how selected inherent risk factors affect the transactions processed by the revenue process. Discuss the potential effect that industry-related factors and misstatements detected in prior periods have on the inherent risk assessment of the revenue process.

[8]   10-5   In understanding the accounting system in the revenue process, the auditor typically performs a walkthrough to gain knowledge of the system. What knowledge should the auditor try to obtain about the accounting system?

[9]   10-6   What are the two major controls for sales returns and allowances transactions?

[11]   10-7   List four analytical procedures that can be used to test revenue-related accounts. What potential misstatements are indicated by each of these analytical procedures?

[13]   10-8   Describe how the auditor verifies the accuracy of the aged trial balance.

[14]   10-9   List and discuss the three factors mentioned in the chapter that may affect the reliability of confirmations of accounts receivable.

[14]   10-10   Distinguish between positive and negative confirmations. Under what circumstances would positive confirmations be more appropriate than negative confirmations?

[15]   10-11   Identify three other types of receivables the auditor should examine. What audit procedures would typically be used to audit other receivables?

MULTIPLE-CHOICE QUESTIONS

[2,6]   10-12   For the control procedures to be effective, employees maintaining the accounts receivable subsidiary ledger should *not* also approve
a. Employee overtime wages.
b. Credit granted to customers.
c. Write-offs of customer accounts.
d. Cash disbursements.

[2,8]   10-13   When evaluating internal control of an entity that processes revenue transactions on the Internet, an auditor would be most concerned about the
    a. Lack of sales invoice documents as an audit trail.
    b. Potential for computer disruptions in recording sales.
    c. Inability to establish test data.
    d. Frequency of archiving and data retention.

[2,9]   10-14   The completeness of IT-generated sales figures can be tested by comparing the number of items listed on the daily sales report with the number of items billed on the actual invoices. This process uses
    a. Check digits.
    b. Control totals.
    c. Validity tests.
    d. Process-tracing data.

[2,9]   10-15   Which of the following controls is most likely to help ensure that all credit revenue transactions of an entity are recorded?
    a. The billing department supervisor sends a copy of each approved sales order to the credit department for comparison to the customer's authorized credit limit and current account balance.
    b. The accounting department supervisor independently reconciles the accounts receivable subsidiary ledger to the accounts receivable control account each month.
    c. The accounting department supervisor controls the mailing of monthly statements to customers and investigates any differences reported by customers.
    d. The billing department supervisor matches prenumbered shipping documents with entries in the sales journal.

[2,6,9]   10-16   Which of the following internal controls would be most likely to deter the lapping of collections from customers?
    a. Independent internal verification of dates of entry in the cash receipts journal with dates of daily cash summaries.
    b. Authorization of write-offs of uncollectible accounts by a supervisor independent of the credit approval function.
    c. Segregation of duties between receiving cash and posting the accounts receivable ledger.
    d. Supervisory comparison of the daily cash summary with the sum of the cash receipts journal entries.

[2,9]   10-17   Smith Corporation has numerous customers. A customer file is kept on disk. Each customer file contains a name, an address, a credit limit, and an account balance. The auditor wishes to test this file to determine whether credit limits are being exceeded. The best procedure for the auditor to follow would be to
    a. Develop test data that would cause some account balances to exceed the credit limit and determine if the system properly detects such situations.
    b. Develop a program to compare credit limits with account balances and print out the details of any account with a balance exceeding its credit limit.
    c. Request a printout of all account balances so that they can be manually checked against the credit limits.

     d. Request a printout of a sample of account balances so that they can be individually checked against the respective credit limits.

[2,9]   10-18   Cash receipts from sales on account have been misappropriated. Which of the following acts would conceal this defalcation and be *least* likely to be detected by an auditor?
     a. Understating the sales journal.
     b. Overstating the accounts receivable control account.
     c. Overstating the accounts receivable subsidiary ledger.
     d. Understating the cash receipts journal.

[13]   10-19   Which of the following is most likely to be detected by an auditor's review of a client's sales cutoff?
     a. Unrecorded sales for the year.
     b. Lapping of year-end accounts receivable.
     c. Excessive sales discounts.
     d. Unauthorized goods returned for credit.

[13,14]   10-20   Negative confirmation of accounts receivable is less effective than positive confirmation of accounts receivable because
     a. A majority of recipients usually lack the willingness to respond objectively.
     b. Some recipients may report incorrect balances that require extensive follow-up.
     c. The auditor cannot infer that all nonrespondents have verified their account information.
     d. Negative confirmations do not produce evidence that is statistically quantifiable.

[13,14]   10-21   The negative request form of accounts receivable confirmation is useful particularly when

	The Assessed Level of Control Risk Relating to Receivables Is	The Number of Small Balances Is	Consideration by the Recipient Is
a.	Low	High	Likely
b.	Low	Low	Unlikely
c.	High	Low	Likely
d.	High	High	Likely

[13,14]   10-22   An auditor should perform alternative procedures to substantiate the existence of accounts receivable when
     a. No reply to a positive confirmation request is received.
     b. No reply to a negative confirmation request is received.
     c. The collectibility of the receivables is in doubt.
     d. Pledging of the receivables is probable.

[13,16]   10-23   In evaluating the adequacy of the allowance for doubtful accounts, an auditor most likely reviews the entity's aging of receivables to support management's financial statement assertion of
     a. Existence.
     b. Valuation and allocation.
     c. Completeness.
     d. Rights and obligations.

PROBLEMS

[1] 10-24 For each of the following situations based on SAB No. 101, indicate how and/or when the client should recognize the revenue. Justify your decision.

1. Your client, Thomson Telecom, maintains an inventory of telecommunications equipment. Bayone Telephone Company placed an order for 10 new transformers valued at $5 million and Thomson delivered them just prior to December 31. Thompson's normal business practice for this class of customer is to enter into a written sales agreement that requires the signatures of all the authorized representatives of Thomson and its customer before the contract is binding. However, Bayone has not signed the sales agreement because it is awaiting the requisite approval by the legal department. Bayone's purchasing department has orally agreed to the contract and the purchasing manager has assured you that the contract will be approved the first week of next year.

2. Best Products is a retailer of appliances that offers "layaway" sales to its customers twice a year. Best retains the merchandise, sets it aside in its inventory, and collects a cash deposit from the customer. The customer signs an installment note at the time the initial deposit is received, but no payments are due until 30 days after delivery.

3. Dave's Discount Stores is a discount retailer who generates revenue from the sale of membership fees it charges customers to shop at its stores. The membership arrangement requires the customer to pay the entire membership fee (usually $48) at the beginning of the arrangement. However, the customer can unilaterally cancel the membership arrangement and receive a refund of the unused portion. Dave's estimates that 35 percent of the customers will cancel their memberships before the end of the contract.

[2,4,5,6,9] 10-25 Taylor, CPA, has been engaged to audit the financial statements of Johnson's Coat Outlet, Inc., a medium-size mail-order retail store that sells a wide variety of coats to the public.

Required:
Prepare the "Shipments" segment of Taylor's internal control questionnaire. Each question should elicit either a yes or no response. Do *not* prepare questions relating to cash receipts, sales returns and allowances, billing, inventory control, or other segments. Use the following format:

Questions	Yes	No

(AICPA, adapted)

[2,6,9] 10-26 The flowchart on the following page depicts activities relating to the sales, shipping, billing, and collection processes used by Newton Hardware, Inc.

Required:
Identify the weaknesses in internal control relating to the activities of (a) the warehouse clerk, (b) bookkeeper A, and (c) the collections clerk. Do not identify weaknesses relating to the sales clerk or book-keepers B and C. Do not discuss recommendations concerning the correction of these weaknesses.

(AICPA, adapted)

[2,6,9] 10-27   The Art Appreciation Society operates a museum for the benefit and enjoyment of the community. During the hours the museum is open to the public, two clerks who are positioned at the entrance collect a five-dollar admission fee from each nonmember patron. Members of the Art Appreciation Society are permitted to enter free of charge upon presentation of their membership cards.

At the end of each day one of the clerks delivers the proceeds to the treasurer. The treasurer counts the cash in the presence of the clerk and places it in a safe. Each Friday afternoon the treasurer and one of the clerks deliver all cash held in the safe to the bank and receive an authenticated deposit slip, which provides the basis for the weekly entry in the cash receipts journal.

The board of directors of the Art Appreciation Society has identified a need to improve the internal control system over cash admission fees. The board has determined that the cost of installing turnstiles or sales booths or otherwise altering the physical layout of the museum would greatly exceed any benefits that might be derived. However, the board has agreed that the sale of admission tickets must be an integral part of its improvement efforts.

Smith has been asked by the board of directors of the Art Appreciation Society to review the internal control over cash admission fees and suggest improvements.

Required:

Indicate weaknesses in the existing internal control system over cash admission fees, which Smith should identify, and recommend one improvement for each of the weaknesses identified. Organize your answer as indicated in the following example:

Weakness	Recommendation
1. There is no basis for establishing the documentation of the number of paying patrons.	1. Prenumbered admission tickets should be issued upon payment of the admission fee.

(AICPA, adapted)

[11,12,13,16] 10-28   Assertions are expressed or implied representations by management that are reflected in the financial statement components. The auditor performs audit procedures to gather evidence to test those assertions.

Required:

Your client is All's Fair Appliance Company, an appliance wholesaler. Select the most appropriate audit procedure from the following list and enter the number in the appropriate place on the grid. (An audit procedure may be selected once, more than once, or not at all.)

Audit Procedure:

1. Review of bank confirmations and loan agreements.
2. Review of drafts of the financial statements.
3. Selection of a sample of revenue transactions and determination that they have been included in the sales journal and accounts receivable subsidiary ledger.
4. Selection of a sample of shipping documents for a few days before and after year-end.
5. Confirmation of accounts receivable.
6. Review of aging of accounts receivable with the credit manager.

Assertion	Audit Procedure
a. Ensure that the entity has legal title to accounts receivable (rights and obligations).	
b. Confirm that recorded accounts receivable include all amounts owed to the client (completeness).	
c. Verify that all accounts receivable are recorded in the correct period (cutoff).	
d. Confirm that the allowance for uncollectible accounts is properly stated (valuation and allocation).	
e. Confirm that recorded accounts receivable are valid (existence).	

[13,14]   10-29   Adam Signoff-On, CPA, was auditing Defense Industries, Inc. Signoff-On sent positive accounts receivable confirmations to a number of Defense's government customers. He received a number of returned confirmations marked "We do not confirm balances because we are on a voucher system."

Required:

List three audit procedures that Signoff-On might use to ensure the validity of these accounts.

[13,14,16]   10-30   The "Accounts Receivable—Confirmation Statistics" working paper on the next page was prepared by an audit assistant during the calendar year 2005 audit of Lewis County Water Company, Inc., a continuing audit client. The engagement supervisor is reviewing the working papers.

Required:

Describe the deficiencies in the working paper that the engagement supervisor should discover. Assume that the accounts were selected for confirmation on the basis of a sample that was properly planned and documented on the working paper.

(AICPA, adapted)

[13,16]   10-31   During the year Strang Corporation began to encounter cash-flow difficulties, and a cursory review by management revealed receivable collection problems. Strang's management engaged Stanley, CPA, to perform a special investigation. Stanley studied the billing and collection process and noted the following:

- The accounting department employs one bookkeeper, who receives and opens all incoming mail. This bookkeeper is also responsible for depositing receipts, filing remittance advices on a daily basis, recording receipts in the cash receipts journal, and posting receipts in the individual customer accounts and the general ledger accounts. There are no cash sales. The bookkeeper prepares and controls the mailing of monthly statements to customers.
- The concentration of functions and the receivable collection problems caused Stanley to suspect that a systematic defalcation of

LEWIS COUNTY WATER CO., INC.
Accounts Receivable—Confirmation Statistics
12/31/05

| Index | B-3 |

	Accounts		Dollars	
	Number	*Percent*	*Amount*	*Percent*
Confirmation requests sent:				
Positives..	54	2.7%	$ 260,000	13.0%
Negatives..	140	7.0	20,000	10.0
Total sent..	194	9.7	$ 280,000	23.0
Accounts selected/client asked us not to confirm...............	6	0.3		
Total selected for testing...	200	10.0		
Total accounts receivable at 12/31/05, confirm date...........	2,000	100.0	$2,000,000✓★	100.0
Results:				
Replies received through 2/25/06:				
Positives—no exception...	44**C**	2.2	$ 180,000	9.0
Negatives—did not reply or replied "no exception".............	120**C**	6.0	16,000	0.8
Total confirmed without exception.......................................	164	8.2	$ 196,000	9.8
Differences reported and resolved, no adjustment:				
Positives..	6ϕ	0.3	$ 30,000	1.5
Negatives...	12	0.6	2,000	0.1
Total...	18‡	0.9	$ 32,000	1.6
Differences found to be potential adjustments:				
Positives..	2**CX**	0.1	$ 10,000	0.5
Negatives...	8**CX**	0.4	2,000	0.1
Total .6% adjustment, immaterial.......................................	10	0.5	$ 12,000	0.6
Accounts selected/client asked us not to confirm...............	6	0.3		

Tick Mark Legend
✓ = Agreed to accounts receivable subsidiary ledger.
★ = Agreed to general ledger and lead schedule.
ϕ = Includes one related-party transaction.
C = Confirmed without exception, W/P B-4.
CX = Confirmed with exception, W/P *B-5*.

Conclusion: The potential adjustment of $12,000, or .6%, is below the materiality threshold; therefore, the accounts receivable balance is fairly stated.

customers' payments through a delayed posting of remittances (lapping of accounts receivable) is present. Stanley was surprised to find that no customers complained about receiving erroneous monthly statements.

Required:
Identify the procedures Stanley should perform to determine whether lapping exists. *Do not discuss deficiencies in the internal control system.*

(AICPA, adapted)

[13,16]   10-32   You are engaged to audit the Ferrick Corporation for the year ended January 31, 2005. Only merchandise shipped by the Ferrick Corporation to customers up to and including January 30, 2005, has been

eliminated from inventory. The inventory as determined by physical inventory count has been recorded on the books by the company's controller. No perpetual inventory records are maintained. All sales are made on an FOB–shipping point basis. You are to assume that all purchase invoices have been correctly recorded.

The following lists of sales invoices are entered in the sales journal for the months of January 2005 and February 2005, respectively.

	Sales Invoice Amount	Sales Invoice Date	Cost of Merchandise Sold	Date Shipped
January 2005				
a.	$ 3,000	Jan. 21	$2,000	Jan. 31
b.	2,000	Jan. 31	800	Dec. 13
c.	1,000	Jan. 29	600	Jan. 30
d.	4,000	Jan. 31	2,400	Feb. 3
e.	10,000	Jan. 30	5,600	Jan. 29*
February 2005				
f.	$6,000	Jan. 31	$4,000	Jan. 30
g.	4,000	Feb. 2	2,300	Feb. 2
h.	8,000	Feb. 3	5,500	Jan. 31

*Shipped to consignee.

Required:
You are to ensure that there is proper cutoff of sales and inventory. If an item is not properly recorded, prepare the necessary adjusting entries.

DISCUSSION CASES

[1]   10-33   SEC Accounting and Auditing Enforcement Release (AAER) No. 108 specifies certain conditions or criteria that a bill and hold transaction of a public company should meet in order to qualify for revenue recognition. The AAER also specifies certain factors that should be considered in evaluating whether a bill and hold transaction meets the requirements for revenue recognition. AAER No. 108 states that a "bill and hold" transaction should meet the following conditions:
1. The risks of ownership must have passed to the buyer.
2. The customer must have made a fixed commitment to purchase the goods, preferably reflected in written documentation.
3. The buyer, not the seller, must request that the transaction be on a bill and hold basis. The buyer must have a substantial business purpose for ordering the goods on a bill and hold basis.
4. There must be a fixed schedule for delivery of the goods. The date for delivery must be reasonable and must be consistent with the buyer's business purpose (e.g., storage periods are customary in the industry).
5. The seller must not have retained any specific performance obligations such that the earning process is not complete.

6. The ordered goods must have been segregated from the seller's inventory and not be subject to being used to fill other orders.
7. The equipment must be complete and ready for shipment.

Required:
Identify and discuss the reliability of the types of evidence an auditor would need to determine whether each condition cited above was met for a bill and hold transaction.

[15,16] 10-34 Friendly Furniture, Inc., a manufacturer of fine hardwood furniture, is a publicly held SEC-registered company with a December 31 year-end. During May, Friendly had a flood due to heavy rains at its major manufacturing facility that damaged about $525,000 of furniture. Friendly is insured for the property loss at replacement value and carries business interruption insurance for lost production. The company anticipates that the total insurance proceeds will exceed the carrying value of the destroyed furniture and the cost of repairing the facility will be in the range of $700,000 to $1.75 million. The company believes that the insurance carrier will advance approximately 50 percent of the expected proceeds sometime during July. The company has resumed its operations to about one-half of normal capacity and expects to operate at full capacity by September. The company does not expect to file a formal insurance claim until then because it expects that the entire cost of the business interruption will not be known until September. Friendly expects to receive the proceeds of the settlement from the insurance carrier during its fourth quarter.

The company is in the process of making a stock offering and will file a registration statement with the SEC at the end of July, in which it will present stub period financial statements covering the six-month period through June 30. Based on the minimum amount of the expected proceeds, Friendly would like to recognize a receivable for the insurance proceeds and to report a gain in its financial statements for the period ended June 30. The company would also like to allocate a portion of the expected proceeds to cost of products sold.

Required:
a. How much of the expected proceeds from insurance coverage, if any, should Friendly include in its June 30 financial statements? Justify your answer with relevant accounting pronouncements.
b. Assuming that Friendly records a receivable from the insurance company at June 30 for the proceeds, what type of audit evidence would the auditor gather to support the amount recorded?

INTERNET ASSIGNMENTS

10-35 Visit the website of a catalog retailer similar to EarthWear Clothiers and determine how it processes sales transactions, recognizes revenue, and reserves for returns.

10-36   Visit the SEC's website (www.sec.gov) and identify a company that has been recently cited for revenue recognition problems. Prepare a memo summarizing the revenue recognition issues for the company.

www.mhhe.com/
messier4e

Visit the book's Online Learning Center for problem material to be completed using the *ACL* software packaged with your new text.

LEARNING OBJECTIVES

Upon completion of this chapter you will

[1] Understand why knowledge of an entity's expense and liability recognition policies is important to the audit.

[2] Develop an understanding of the purchasing process.

[3] Identify the types of transactions in the purchasing process and the financial statement accounts affected.

[4] Identify and describe the types of documents and records used in the purchasing process.

[5] Understand the functions in the purchasing process.

[6] Know the appropriate segregation of duties for the purchasing process.

[7] Identify and evaluate inherent risks relevant to the purchasing process and related accounts.

[8] Assess control risk for a purchasing process.

[9] Identify key internal controls and develop relevant tests of controls for purchasing, cash disbursements, and purchase return transactions.

[10] Relate the assessment of control risk to substantive testing.

[11] Identify substantive analytical procedures used to audit accounts payable and accrued expenses.

[12] Identify tests of details of transactions used to audit accounts payable and accrued expenses.

[13] Identify tests of details of account balances and disclosures used to audit accounts payable and accrued expenses.

[14] Describe how confirmations are used to obtain evidence about accounts payable.

[15] Evaluate the audit findings and reach a final conclusion on accounts payable and accrued expenses.

RELEVANT ACCOUNTING AND AUDITING PRONOUNCEMENTS

FASB Statement of Financial Accounting Concepts No. 5, Recognition and Measurement in Financial Statements of Business Enterprises (CON5)

FASB Statement of Financial Accounting Concepts No. 6, Elements of Financial Statements (CON6)

AU 312, Audit Risk and Materiality in Conducting an Audit

AU 316, Consideration of Fraud in a Financial Statement Audit

AU 319, Consideration of Internal Control in a Financial Statement Audit

AU 329, Analytical Procedures

AU 330, The Confirmation Process

AU 339, Audit Documentation

AU 342, Auditing Accounting Estimates

AICPA Auditing Standards Board, Exposure Draft, "Understanding the Entity and Its Environment and Assessing the Risks of Material Misstatement"

AICPA Auditing Standards Board, Exposure Draft, "Audit Evidence"

AICPA Auditing Standards Board, Exposure Draft, "Performing Audit Procedures in Response to Assessed Risks and Evaluating the Audit Evidence Obtained"

Auditing the Purchasing Process

Major Phases of an Audit

Client acceptance/
continuance
and establishing
engagement terms
(Chapter 5)

Preplanning
(Chapter 5)

Establish materiality
and assess risks
(Chapter 3)

Plan the audit
(Chapters 3 and 5)

Consider and audit
internal control
(Chapters 6 and 7)

Audit business processes
and related accounts
(e.g., revenue generation)
(Chapters 10–16)

Complete the audit
(Chapter 17)

Evaluate results and issue audit
report (Chapters 2 and 18)

The second major business process focuses on the purchase of and payment for goods and services from outside vendors. The acquisition of goods and services includes the purchase of raw materials, supplies, manufacturing equipment, furniture, and fixtures and payment for repairs and maintenance, utilities, and professional services. This process does not include hiring and paying employees or the internal allocation of costs within an entity. Chapter 12 covers the human resource management process.

This chapter begins by reviewing expense and liability recognition concepts with particular emphasis on the categories of expenses. The framework developed in Chapter 10 on the revenue process is used to present the auditor's consideration of internal control. This framework starts with an overview of the purchasing process, including the types of transactions, the documents and records involved, and the functions included in the process. Inherent risk factors that relate directly to the purchasing process are covered next. Assessment of control risk is then presented, followed by a discussion of control procedures and tests of controls. The last sections of the chapter cover the audit of accounts payable and accrued expenses, the major liability accounts affected by the process. Auditing the expense accounts affected by the purchasing process is covered in Chapter 15. While the main focus of this chapter is auditing the purchasing process for a financial statement audit, the concepts covered for setting control risk are applicable to an audit of internal control over financial reporting for public companies under the Sarbanes-Oxley Act of 2002.

Expense and Liability Recognition

[LO 1]   Many transactions processed through a typical purchasing process involve the recognition of an expense and its corresponding liability. As a result, the auditor should understand the basic underlying concepts of expense and liability recognition in order to audit the purchasing process. FASB Concept Statement No. 6, "Elements of Financial Statements" (CON6), defines expenses and liabilities as follows:

> Expenses are outflows or other using up of assets or incurrences of liabilities (or a combination of both) from delivering or producing goods, rendering services, or carrying out other activities that constitute the entity's ongoing major or central operations. (para. 85)
>
> Liabilities are probable future sacrifices of economic benefits arising from present obligations of a particular entity to transfer assets or provide services to other entities in the future as a result of past transactions or events. (para. 35)

An entity's expense recognition policies and the type of expenses involved affect how the transactions are recorded and accounted for in the financial statements. FASB Statement of Financial Accounting Concepts No. 5, "Recognition and Measurement in Financial Statements of Business Enterprises" (CON5), indicates that expenses can be classified into three categories.

1. Certain expenses can be matched directly with specific transactions or events and are recognized upon recognition of revenue. These types of expenses are referred to as *product costs* and include expenses such as cost of goods sold.
2. Many expenses are recognized during the period in which cash is spent or liabilities incurred for goods and services that are used up at that time or shortly thereafter. Such expenses cannot be directly related to specific transactions and are assumed to provide no future benefit. These expenses are referred to as *period costs*. Examples of such expenses include administrative salaries and rent expense.
3. Some expenses are allocated by systematic and rational procedures to the periods during which the related assets are expected to provide benefits. Depreciation of plant and equipment is an example of such an expense.

In general, the liabilities normally incurred as part of the purchasing process are trade accounts payable. Other incurred expenses are accrued as liabilities at the end of each accounting period. Most expenses recognized are product or period costs.

Overview of the Purchasing Process

[LO 2]   A purchase transaction usually begins with a purchase requisition being generated by a department or support function. The purchasing department prepares a purchase order for the purchase of goods or services from a vendor. When the goods are received or the services have been rendered, the

EXHIBIT 11–1	**Description of EarthWear's Purchasing System**

The major purchasing activity for EarthWear involves the purchase of clothing and other products that are styled and quality crafted by the company's design department. All goods are produced by independent manufacturers, except for most of EarthWear's soft luggage. The company purchases merchandise from more than 200 domestic and foreign manufacturers. For many major suppliers, goods are ordered and paid for through the company's electronic data interchange (EDI) system. The computerized inventory control system handles the receipt of shipments from manufacturers, permitting faster access to newly arrived merchandise.

Purchases of other goods and services are made in accordance with EarthWear's purchasing authorization policies. Company personnel complete a purchase requisition, which is forwarded to the purchasing department for processing. Purchasing agents obtain competitive bids and enter the information into the purchase order program. A copy of the purchase order is sent to the vendor. Goods are received at the receiving department, where the information is agreed to the purchase order (receiving report). The receiving report is forwarded to the accounts payable department, which matches the receiving report to the purchase order and vendor invoice. The accounts payable department prepares a voucher packet and enters the information into the accounts payable program.

When payment is due on a vendor invoice, the accounts payable program generates a cash disbursement report that is reviewed by the accounts payable department. Items approved for payment are entered into the cash disbursement program, and a check is printed. The checks are sent to the cashier's department for mailing. Final approval for electronic funds transfer for EDI transactions is made by the accounts payable department.

entity records a liability to the vendor. Finally, the entity pays the vendor. Exhibit 11–1 describes EarthWear's purchasing system.

EarthWear Figure 11–1 presents the flowchart for EarthWear's purchasing system, which serves as a framework for discussing control procedures and tests of controls. As mentioned previously, accounting applications are tailored to meet the specific needs of the client. The reader should focus on the basic concepts so that they can be applied to the specific purchasing processes encountered. The following topics related to the purchasing process are covered:

- Types of transactions and financial statement accounts affected.
- Types of documents and records.
- The major functions.
- The key segregation of duties.

Types of Transactions and Financial Statement Accounts Affected
[LO 3]

Three types of transactions are processed through the purchasing process:

- Purchase of goods and services for cash or credit.
- Payment of the liabilities arising from such purchases.
- Return of goods to suppliers for cash or credit.

The first type is a purchase transaction that includes acquiring goods and services. The second type is a cash disbursement transaction that involves paying the liabilities that result from purchasing goods and services. The final type is a purchase return transaction, in which goods previously purchased are returned to a supplier for cash or credit.

The purchasing process affects many accounts in the financial statements. The more common accounts affected by each type of transaction are

Type of Transaction	Account Affected
Purchase transaction	Accounts payable
	Inventory
	Purchases or cost of goods sold
	Various asset and expense accounts
Cash disbursement transaction	Cash
	Accounts payable
	Cash discounts
	Various asset and expense accounts
Purchase return transaction	Purchase returns
	Purchase allowances
	Accounts payable
	Various asset and expense accounts

FIGURE 11–1	**Flowchart of the Purchasing Process—EarthWear Clothiers, Inc.**

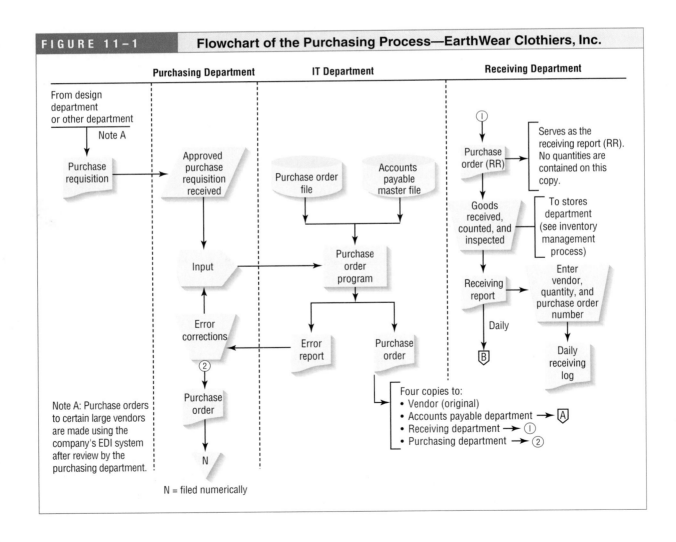

FIGURE 11-1	Flowchart of the Purchasing Process—EarthWear Clothiers, Inc. (concluded)

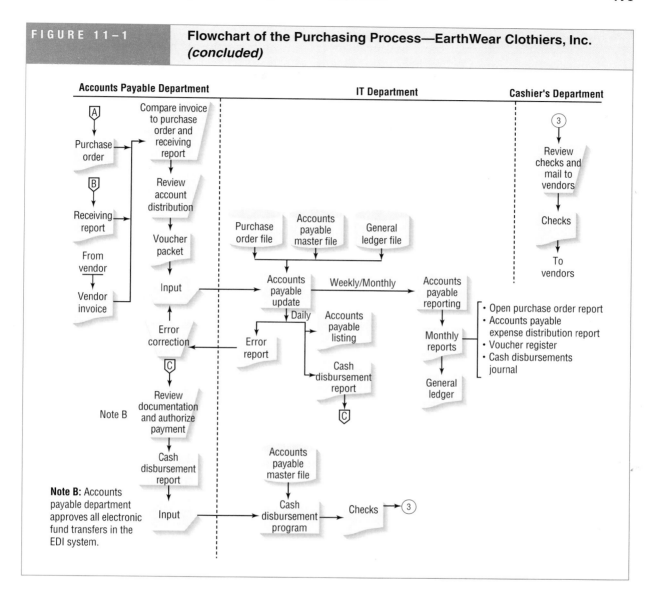

Types of Documents and Records

Table 11–1 lists the important documents and records that are normally involved in the purchasing process. Each of these items is briefly discussed here. The use of an advanced IT system may affect the form of the documents and the auditor's approach to testing the purchasing process.

[LO 4]   **Purchase Requisition**   This document requests goods or services for an authorized individual or department within the entity. Examples of such requests include an order for supplies from an office supervisor and an order for newspaper advertising space from a marketing manager. In EarthWear's purchasing system, the design department would generate purchase requisitions to acquire goods for sale.

TABLE 11-1	**Documents and Records Involved in the Purchasing Process**
	Purchase requisition.
	Purchase order.
	Receiving report.
	Vendor invoice.
	Voucher.
	Voucher register/purchases journal.
	Accounts payable subsidiary ledger.
	Vendor statement.
	Check.
	Cash disbursements journal/check register.

Purchase Order   This document includes the description, quality, and quantity of, and other information on, the goods or services being purchased. The purchase order also indicates who approved the acquisition and represents the authorization to purchase the goods or services. The purchase order may be mailed, faxed, or placed by telephone with the supplier or vendor. At EarthWear some purchase orders may be generated by the design department, reviewed by a purchasing agent, and then sent to a vendor using the company's EDI system.

Receiving Report   This document records the receipt of goods. Normally, the receiving report is a copy of the purchase order with the quantities omitted. This procedure encourages receiving department personnel to make an adequate, independent count of the goods received. Receiving department personnel record the date, description, quantity, and other information on this document. In some instances, the quality of the goods is determined by receiving department personnel. In other cases, an inspection department determines whether the goods meet the required specifications. The receiving report is important because receiving goods is generally the event that leads to recognition of the liability by the entity.

Vendor Invoice   This document is the bill from the vendor. The vendor invoice includes the description and quantity of the goods shipped or services provided, the price including freight, the terms of trade including cash discounts, and the date billed.

Voucher   This document is frequently used by entities to control payment for acquired goods and services. This document serves as the basis for recording a vendor's invoice in the voucher register or purchases journal. In many purchasing systems, such as EarthWear's, the voucher is attached to the purchase requisition, purchase order, receiving report, and vendor invoice to create a *voucher packet*. The voucher packet thus contains all the relevant documentation supporting a purchase transaction.

Voucher Register/Purchases Journal   A voucher register is used to record the vouchers for goods and services. The voucher register contains numerous columns for recording the account classifications for the goods or services, including a column for recording credits to accounts payable, and columns for recording debits to asset accounts such as inventory and expense accounts such as repairs and maintenance. The voucher register also contains columns for miscellaneous debits and credits. Some entities use a purchases journal instead of a voucher register. With a purchases journal, either vouchers or vendors' invoices may be used to record the liability. The major difference between a voucher register and a purchases journal is in the way individual vouchers or vendor invoices are summarized. When a voucher register is used, the details of accounts payable are normally represented by a list of unpaid vouchers. With a purchases journal, subsidiary records are normally maintained by the vendor in much the same manner as an accounts receivable subsidiary ledger. However, with computerization of accounts payable records, such distinctions are disappearing. By assigning a vendor number to each voucher, the voucher register can be sorted by vendor to produce a subsidiary ledger for accounts payable.

Accounts Payable Subsidiary Ledger   When a purchases journal is utilized, this subsidiary ledger records the transactions with, and the balance owed to, a vendor. When a voucher register system is used, the subsidiary ledger is a listing of the unpaid vouchers. The total in the subsidiary ledger should equal the balance in the general ledger accounts payable account.

Vendor Statement   This statement is sent monthly by the vendor to indicate the beginning balance, current-period purchases and payments, and the ending balance. The vendor's statement represents the purchase activity recorded on the vendor's records. It may differ from the client's records because of errors or, more often, timing differences due to delays in shipping goods or recording cash receipts. The client verifies the accuracy of its records by comparing vendor statements with the accounts payable records.

Check   This document, signed by an authorized individual, pays for goods or services. Again, in some advanced IT systems, goods and services may be paid for through electronic transfer of funds.

Cash Disbursements Journal/Check Register   This journal records disbursements made by check. It is sometimes referred to as a *check register*. The cash disbursements journal contains columns for recording credits to cash and debits to accounts payable and cash discounts. Columns may also record miscellaneous debits and credits. Payments recorded in the cash disbursements journal are also recorded in the voucher register or in the accounts payable subsidiary ledger, depending on which system is used by the entity.

The Major Functions

[LO 5]

The principal business objectives of the purchasing process are acquiring goods and services at the lowest cost consistent with quality and service requirements and effectively using cash resources to pay for those goods and services. Table 11–2 lists the functions that are normally part of the purchasing process.

TABLE 11–2	**Functions of the Purchasing Process**
Requisitioning	Initiation and approval of requests for goods and services by authorized individuals consistent with management criteria.
Purchasing	Approval of purchase orders and proper execution as to price, quantity, quality, and vendor.
Receiving	Receipt of properly authorized goods or services.
Invoice processing	Processing of vendor invoices for goods and services received; also, processing of adjustments for allowances, discounts, and returns.
Disbursements	Processing of payment to vendors.
Accounts payable	Recording of all vendor invoices, cash disbursements, and adjustments in individual vendor accounts.
General ledger	Proper accumulation, classification, and summarization of purchases, cash disbursements, and payables in the general ledger.

Requisitioning

The initial function in the purchasing process is a request for goods or services by an authorized individual from any department or functional area within the entity (see Figure 11–1). The important issue is that the request meets the authorization procedures implemented by the entity. One frequent organizational control is the establishment of authorization dollar limits for different levels of employees and executives. For example, department supervisors may be authorized to acquire goods or services up to $1,000, department managers up to $5,000, and divisional heads up to $25,000, while any expenditure greater than $100,000 requires approval by the board of directors.

Purchasing

The purchasing function executes properly authorized purchase orders. This function is normally performed by a purchasing department (see Figure 11–1), which is headed by a purchasing manager (or agent) and has one or more buyers responsible for specific goods or services. The purchasing function ensures that goods and services are acquired in appropriate quantities and at the lowest price consistent with quality standards and delivery schedules. Using multiple vendors and requiring competitive bidding are two ways the purchasing function can achieve its objectives.

Receiving

The receiving function is responsible for receiving, counting, and inspecting goods received from vendors. The personnel in the receiving department complete a receiving report that is forwarded to the accounts payable function.

Invoice Processing

The accounts payable department (see Figure 11–1) processes invoices to ensure that all goods and services received are recorded as assets or expenses and that the corresponding liability is recognized. This function involves matching purchase orders to receiving reports and vendor invoices as to terms, quantities, prices, and extensions. The invoice-processing function also compares the account distributions with established account classifications.

The invoice-processing function is also responsible for purchased goods returned to vendors. Appropriate records and control procedures must document the return of the goods and initiate any charges back to the vendor.

Disbursements The disbursement function is responsible for preparing and signing checks for paying vendors. Adequate supporting documentation must verify that the disbursement is for a legitimate business purpose, that the transaction was properly authorized, and that the account distribution is appropriate. To reduce the possibility that the invoice will be paid twice, all documentation (such as purchase order, receiving report, and vendor invoice) should be marked "CANCELED" or "PAID" by the cashier's department. Finally, the checks should be mailed to the vendor by the cashier's department or treasurer.

If IT is used to prepare checks, adequate user controls must ensure that only authorized transactions are submitted for payment. Adequate control totals should also be used to agree the amount of payables submitted with the amount of cash disbursed. Checks over a specified limit should be reviewed. For example, in EarthWear's system (see Figure 11–1), the accounts payable department matches the purchase order to the receiving report and the vendor's invoice. The voucher is then input into the accounts payable program. When the vouchers are due for payment, they are printed out on a cash disbursement report. Accounts payable personnel review the items to be paid and input them into the cash disbursement program. The checks are forwarded to the cashier's department for review and mailing to vendors. If a signature plate is used for signing checks, it must be properly controlled within the cashier's department or by the treasurer.

Accounts Payable The accounts payable department (see Figure 11–1) is also responsible for ensuring that all vendor invoices, cash disbursements, and adjustments are recorded in the accounts payable records. In IT systems, these entries may be made directly as part of the normal processing of purchase, cash disbursement, or returns and allowances transactions. Proper use of control totals and daily activity reports provides controls for proper recording.

General Ledger The main objective of the general ledger function for the purchasing process is to ensure that all purchases, cash disbursements, and payables are properly accumulated, classified, and summarized in the accounts. In an IT system, such as at EarthWear, the use of control or summary totals ensures that this function is performed correctly. The accounting department is normally responsible for this function.

The Key Segregation of Duties

    [LO 6]

As discussed in previous chapters, proper segregation of duties is one of the most important control procedures in any accounting system. Duties should be assigned so that no one individual can control all phases of processing a transaction in a way that permits errors or fraud to go undetected. Because of the potential for theft and fraud in the purchasing process, individuals responsible for requisitioning, purchasing, and receiving should be segregated from the invoice-processing, accounts payable, and general ledger functions. If IT is used extensively in the purchasing application, there should be proper segregation of duties in the IT department. Table 11–3 shows the key segregation of duties for the purchasing process and examples of possible errors or fraud that can result from conflicts in duties.

TABLE 11–3	Key Segregation of Duties in the Purchasing Process and Possible Errors or Fraud
Segregation of Duties	*Possible Errors or Fraud Resulting from Conflicts of Duties*
The purchasing function should be segregated from the requisitioning and receiving functions.	If one individual is responsible for the requisition, purchasing, and receiving functions, fictitious or unauthorized purchases can be made. This can result in the theft of goods and possibly payment for unauthorized purchases.
The invoice-processing function should be segregated from the accounts payable function.	If one individual is responsible for the invoice-processing and the accounts payable functions, purchase transactions can be processed at the wrong price or terms, or a cash disbursement can be processed for goods or services not received. This can result in overpayment for goods and services or the theft of cash.
The disbursement function should be segregated from the accounts payable function.	If one individual is responsible for the disbursement function and also has access to the accounts payable records, unauthorized checks supported by fictitious documents can be issued, and unauthorized transactions can be recorded. This can result in theft of the entity's cash.
The accounts payable function should be segregated from the general ledger function.	If one individual is responsible for the accounts payable records and also for the general ledger, that individual can conceal any defalcation that would normally be detected by reconciling subsidiary records with the general ledger control account.

TABLE 11–4	Segregation of Duties for Purchasing and Accounts Payable Functions by Department				
	Department				
Purchasing and Accounts Payable Function	Purchasing	Receiving	Accounts Payable	Cashier's	IT
Preparation and approval of purchase order	X				
Receipt, counting, and inspection of purchased materials		X			
Receipt of vendor invoices and matching them with supporting documents			X		
Coding (or checking) of account distributions			X		
Updating of accounts payable records			X		X
Preparation of vendor checks					X
Signing and mailing of vendor checks				X	
Preparation of voucher register					X
Reconciliation of voucher register to general ledger			X		

Table 11–4 shows the proper segregation of duties for purchasing and accounts payable functions across the various departments that process purchase transactions.

Inherent Risk Assessment

[LO 7]   At the beginning of the audit of the purchasing process and its related accounts, the auditor should consider the relevant inherent risk factors that may impact the transactions processed and the financial statement accounts. The following factors taken from Chapter 3 should be considered by the auditor in assessing the inherent risk for the purchasing process.

Industry-Related Factors

When auditing the purchasing process, the auditor must consider two important industry-related factors in assessing inherent risk: whether the supply of raw materials is adequate and how volatile raw material prices are. If the entity deals with many vendors and prices tend to be relatively stable, there is less risk that the entity's operations will be affected by raw material shortages or that production costs will be difficult to control.

Some industries, however, are subject to such industry-related factors. For example, in the high-technology sector, there have been situations in which an entity has depended on a single vendor to supply a critical component, such as a specialized computer chip. When the vendor has been unable to provide the component, the entity has suffered production shortages and shipping delays that have significantly affected financial performance. Other industries that produce basic commodities such as oil, coal, and precious metals can find their financial results significantly affected by swings in the prices of their products. Additionally, industries that use commodities such as oil as raw materials may be subject to both shortages and price instability. The auditor needs to assess the effects of such industry-related inherent risk factors in terms of assertions such as valuation.

Misstatements Detected in Prior Audits

Generally, the purchasing process and its related accounts are not difficult to audit and do not result in contentious accounting issues. However, auditing research has shown that the purchasing process and its related accounts are likely to contain material misstatements.[1] The auditor's previous experience with the entity's purchasing process should be reviewed as a starting point for determining the inherent risk.

Control Risk Assessment

[LO 8]   The discussion of control risk assessment follows the framework outlined in Chapter 6 on internal control and Chapter 10 on the revenue process. Again it is assumed that the auditor has decided to follow a reliance strategy. Figure 11–2 summarizes the major steps involved in setting control risk for the purchasing cycle.

Understanding and Documenting Internal Control

In order to set control risk for the purchasing process, the auditor must understand the five components of internal control.

Control Environment   Table 6–5 in Chapter 6 lists factors that affect the control environment. Two factors are particularly important when the auditor considers the control environment and the purchasing process: the entity's organizational structure and its methods of assigning authority and responsibility. The entity's organizational structure for purchasing may impact the auditor's assessment of control risk because control procedures are implemented within an organizational structure. Authority and responsibility for purchasing are usually granted via procedures that limit the amount of purchases that can be made by various levels of authority within the

---

[1]For example, see A. Eilifsen and W. F. Messier, Jr., "Auditor Detection of Misstatements: A Review and Integration of Empirical Research," *Journal of Accounting Literature* 2000 (19), pp. 1–43, for a detailed review of audit research studies that have examined sources of accounting errors.

FIGURE 11–2   **Major Steps in Setting Control Risk for the Purchasing Process**

Understanding and documenting the purchasing process based on a reliance approach

↓

Planning and performing tests of controls on purchase transactions

↓

Setting and documenting the control risk for the purchasing process

entity. The remaining discussions of the purchasing process assume that the control environment factors are reliable.

The Entity's Risk Assessment Process   The auditor must understand how management weighs the risks that are relevant to the purchasing process, estimates their significance, assesses the likelihood of their occurrence, and decides what actions to take to address those risks. Some of these risks include a new or revamped information system, rapid growth, and new technology. Each of these factors can represent a serious risk to an entity's internal control system over purchases.

Control Procedures   When a reliance strategy is adopted for the purchasing process, the auditor needs to understand the controls that exist to ensure that management's objectives are being met. More specifically, the auditor identifies the controls that assure the auditor that the assertions are being met.

Information Systems and Communication   For each major class of transactions in the purchasing process, the auditor again needs to obtain the following information:

- How purchase, cash disbursements, and purchase return transactions are initiated.
- The accounting records, supporting documents, and accounts that are involved in processing purchases, cash disbursements, and purchase return transactions.
- The flow of each type of transaction from initiation to inclusion in the financial statements, including computer processing of the data.
- The process used to estimate accrued liabilities.

The auditor develops an understanding of the purchasing process by conducting a transaction walkthrough. In the case of a continuing audit, the auditor has the prior years' documentation of the process to assist in the walkthrough, although the possibility of changes in the system must be considered. If the system has been changed substantially or the audit is for a new client, the auditor should prepare new documentation of the system.

Monitoring of Controls The auditor needs to understand the client's monitoring processes over the purchasing process, including how management assesses the design and operation of controls. It also involves understanding how supervisory personnel within the process review the personnel who perform the controls and evaluating the performance of the entity's IT system.

The auditor can document the purchasing process using procedures manuals, narrative descriptions, internal control questionnaires, and flowcharts.

Planning and Performing Tests of Controls

The auditor systematically analyzes the purchasing process in order to identify controls that ensure that material misstatements are either prevented or detected and corrected. The controls can be relied upon by the auditor to reduce the control risk. For example, the client may have formal procedures for authorizing the acquisition of goods and services. The auditor may decide to rely on these controls to reduce the control risk for the authorization assertion. Tests of controls would then be necessary to verify that this control is operating effectively. The auditor would examine a sample of purchase transactions to determine if the acquisition of the goods or services is consistent with the entity's authorization policy.

Setting and Documenting Control Risk

After the controls are tested, the auditor sets the level of control risk. When tests of controls support the planned level of control risk, no modifications are normally necessary to the planned level of detection risk, and the auditor may proceed with the planned substantive procedures. When the tests of controls do not support the planned level of control risk, the auditor must set a higher level of control risk. This results in a lower level of detection risk and leads to more substantive procedures than originally planned.

As discussed earlier, the auditor should establish and document the achieved level of control risk. Documentation of the control risk for the purchasing process might include a flowchart, the results of tests of controls, and a memorandum indicating the auditor's overall conclusion about the control risk.

Control Procedures and Tests of Controls— Purchase Transactions

[LO 9] Table 11–5 presents the assertions about transactions and events, while Table 11–6 summarizes the assertions and possible misstatements for purchase transactions. The table also includes key control procedures designed to prevent the possible misstatements and examples of tests of controls that can test the effectiveness of the control procedures. Most of these controls exist within EarthWear's purchasing process (see Figure 11–1). The

TABLE 11–5	Assertions about Classes of Transactions and Events for the Period under Audit

- **Occurrence.** All purchase and cash disbursement transactions and events that have been recorded have occurred and pertain to the entity.
- **Completeness.** All purchase and cash disbursement transactions and events that should have been recorded have been recorded.
- **Authorization.** All purchase and cash disbursement transactions and events are properly authorized.
- **Accuracy.** Amounts and other data relating to recorded purchase and cash disbursement transactions and events have been recorded appropriately.
- **Cutoff.** Purchase and cash disbursement transactions and events have been recorded in the correct accounting period.
- **Classification.** Purchase and cash disbursement transactions and events have been recorded in the proper accounts.

following sections also discuss control procedures and tests of controls that are relevant for EarthWear's purchasing process.

Occurrence of Purchase Transactions

The auditor's concern in testing the occurrence of purchase transactions is that fictitious or nonexistent purchases may have been recorded in the client's records. If fraudulent transactions are recorded, assets or expenses will be overstated. A liability will also be recorded and a resulting payment made, usually to the individual who initiated the fictitious purchase transactions. Proper segregation of duties is the major control for preventing fictitious purchases. The critical segregation of duties is the separation of the requisitioning and purchasing functions from the accounts payable and disbursement functions. If one individual can both process a purchase order and gain access to the accounting records, there is an increased risk that fictitious purchase transactions will be recorded.

The other control procedures shown in Table 11–6 also reduce the risk of purchase transactions being recorded without the goods or services being received. Even with proper segregation of duties, no purchase transaction should be recorded without an approved purchase order and a receiving report. The presence of an approved purchase order ensures that the purchase was authorized, and the presence of a receiving report indicates that the goods were received. In an IT environment, such as EarthWear's, the auditor can test the application controls to ensure that purchases are recorded only after an approved purchase order has been entered and the goods received. Accounting for the numerical sequence of receiving reports and vouchers can be accomplished either manually or by the computer. This control prevents the recording of fictitious purchase transactions through the use of receiving documents or vouchers that are numbered outside the sequence of properly authorized documents. Cancellation of all supporting documents ensures that a purchase transaction is not recorded and paid for a second time.

Completeness of Purchase Transactions

If the client fails to record a purchase that has been made, assets or expenses will be understated, and the corresponding accounts payable will also be understated. Controls that ensure that the completeness assertion is being met include accounting for the numerical sequences of purchase

TABLE 11-6	**Summary of Assertions, Possible Misstatements, Control Procedures, and Tests of Controls for Purchase Transactions**

Assertion	Possible Misstatement	Control Procedure	Test of Controls
Occurrence	Purchase recorded, goods or services not ordered or received	Segregation of duties	Observe and evaluate proper segregation of duties.
		Purchase not recorded without approved purchase order and receiving report	Test a sample of vouchers for the presence of an authorized purchase order and receiving report; if IT application, examine application controls.
		Accounting for numerical sequence of receiving reports and vouchers	Review and test client procedures for accounting for numerical sequence of receiving reports and vouchers; if IT application, examine application controls.
		Cancellation of documents	Examine paid vouchers and supporting documents for indication of cancellation.
Completeness	Purchases made but not recorded	Accounting for numerical sequence of purchase orders, receiving reports, and vouchers	Review client's procedures for accounting for numerical sequence of purchase orders, receiving reports, and vouchers; if IT application, examine application controls.
		Receiving reports matched to vendor invoices and entered in the purchases journal	Trace a sample of receiving reports to their respective vendor invoices and vouchers. Trace a sample of vouchers to the purchases journal.
Authorization	Purchase of goods or services not authorized	Approval of acquisitions consistent with the client's authorization dollar limits	Review client's dollar limits authorization for acquisitions.
		Approved purchase requisition and purchase order	Examine purchase requisitions or purchase orders for proper approval; if IT is used for automatic ordering, examine application controls.
	Purchase of goods or services at unauthorized prices or on unauthorized terms	Competitive bidding procedures followed	Review client's competitive bidding procedures.
Accuracy	Vendor invoice improperly priced or incorrectly calculated	Mathematical accuracy of vendor invoice verified	Recompute the mathematical accuracy of vendor invoice.
		Purchase order agreed to receiving report and vendor's invoice for product, quantity, and price	Agree the information on a sample of voucher packets for product, quantity, and price.
	Purchase transactions not posted to the purchases journal or the accounts payable subsidiary records	Vouchers reconciled to daily accounts payable listing	Examine reconciliation of vouchers to daily accounts payable report; if IT application, examine application controls.
	Amounts from purchases journal not posted correctly to the general ledger	Daily postings to purchases journal reconciled with postings to accounts payable subsidiary records	Examine reconciliation of entries in purchases journal with entries to accounts payable subsidiary records; if IT application, examine application controls.
		Voucher register or accounts payable subsidiary records reconciled to general ledger control account	Review reconciliation of subsidiary records to general ledger control account; if IT application, examine application controls.
		Vouchers reconciled to daily accounts payable listing	Test a sample of daily reconciliations.

(continued)

TABLE 11-6		Summary of Assertions, Possible Misstatements, Control Procedures, and Tests of Controls for Purchase Transactions *(concluded)*	
Assertion	*Possible Misstatement*	*Control Procedure*	*Test of Controls*
Cutoff	Purchase transactions recorded in the wrong period	All receiving reports forwarded to the accounts payable department daily Existence of procedures that require recording the purchases as soon as possible after goods or services are received	Compare the dates on receiving reports with the dates on the relevant vouchers. Compare the dates on vouchers with the dates they were recorded in the purchases journal.
Classification	Purchase transaction not properly classified	Chart of accounts Independent approval and review of accounts charged for acquisitions	Review purchases journal and general ledger for reasonableness. Examine a sample of vouchers for proper classification.

Note: Receiving reports are used to acknowledge the receipt of tangible goods such as raw materials, office supplies, and equipment. For services such as utilities and advertising, receiving reports are not used.

orders, receiving reports, and vouchers; matching receiving reports with vendor invoices; and reconciling vouchers to the daily accounts payable report. For example, EarthWear uses control totals to reconcile the daily number of vouchers processed with the daily accounts payable listing.

Tests of controls for these control procedures are listed in Table 11–6. For example, the auditor can trace a sample of receiving reports to their corresponding vendor invoices and vouchers. The vouchers can then be traced to the voucher register to ensure that each voucher was recorded. Again, these tests can be performed either manually or with CAATs. If each receiving report is matched to a vendor invoice and voucher and the voucher was included in the voucher register, the auditor has a high level of assurance as to the completeness assertion.

The auditor's concern with the completeness assertion also arises when the accounts payable and accrued expenses accounts are audited at year-end. If the client has strong controls for the completeness assertion, the auditor can reduce the scope of the search for unrecorded liabilities at year-end. This issue is discussed in more detail later in this chapter.

Authorization of Purchase Transactions

Possible misstatements due to improper authorization include the purchase of unauthorized goods and services and the purchase of goods or services at unauthorized prices or terms. The primary control to prevent these misstatements is the use of an authorization schedule or table that stipulates the amount that different levels of employees are authorized to purchase. Tests of controls include examination of purchase requisitions and purchase orders for proper approval consistent with the authorization table. If the client uses a sophisticated production system that reorders goods automatically, the auditor should examine and test the programmed controls. Competitive bidding procedures should be followed to ensure that goods and services are acquired at competitive prices and on competitive terms.

Accuracy of Purchase Transactions	A possible misstatement for the accuracy assertion is that purchase transactions may be recorded at incorrect amounts due to improper pricing or erroneous calculations. The purchase order should contain the expected price for the goods or services being purchased, based on price quotes obtained by the purchasing agents or prices contained in catalogs or published price lists. If the goods or services are purchased under a contract, the price should be stipulated in the contract. For example, an accounts payable clerk should compare the purchase order with the receiving report and vendor invoice (see Figure 11–1) and investigate significant differences in quantities, prices, and freight charges. The accounts payable clerk also checks the mathematical accuracy of the vendor invoice. The auditor's test of controls for this assertion involves reperforming the accounts payable clerk's duties on a sample of voucher packets.

The accuracy assertion is also concerned with proper posting of information to the purchases journal, accounts payable subsidiary records, and general ledger. Control totals should be used to reconcile vouchers to the daily accounts payable listing, or else the daily postings to the purchases journal should be reconciled to the accounts payable subsidiary records. In addition, the voucher register or accounts payable subsidiary ledger should be reconciled to the general ledger control account. If these control procedures are performed manually, the auditor can review and examine the reconciliations prepared by the client's personnel. In an IT application, such controls would be programmed and reconciled by the control groups in the IT and accounts payable departments. The auditor can examine the programmed controls and review the reconciliations.

Cutoff of Purchase Transactions	The client should have controls to ensure that purchase transactions are recorded promptly and in the proper period. For example, the client's procedures should require that all receiving reports be forwarded to the accounts payable department daily. There should also be a requirement in the accounts payable department that receiving reports be matched on a timely basis with the original purchase order and the related vendor invoice. In EarthWear's system, the receiving department forwards the receiving report to the accounts payable department daily. Within the accounts payable department, the vendor invoices are matched immediately with the original purchase orders and the receiving reports. The auditor can test these control procedures by comparing the date on the receiving report with the date on the voucher. There should seldom be a long period between the two dates. The auditor also wants to ensure that the vouchers are recorded in the accounting records in the correct period. This can be tested by comparing the dates on vouchers with the dates the vouchers were recorded in the voucher register.

Classification of Purchase Transactions	Proper classification of purchase transactions is an important assertion for the purchasing process. If purchase transactions are not properly classified, asset and expense accounts will be misstated. Two main controls are used for ensuring that purchase transactions are properly classified. First, the client should use a chart of accounts. Second, there should be independent

approval and review of the general ledger accounts charged for the acquisition. A typical procedure is for the department or function that orders the goods or services to indicate which general ledger account to charge. Accounts payable department personnel then review the account distribution for reasonableness (see Figure 11–1). A test of controls for this assertion involves examining a sample of voucher packets for proper classification.

Control Procedures and Tests of Controls— Cash Disbursement Transactions

[LO 9]   Table 11–7 summarizes the assertions and possible misstatements for cash disbursement transactions. The table also includes key internal controls related to each assertion and examples of tests of controls that can assess control risk.

Occurrence of Cash Disbursement Transactions

For the occurrence assertion, the auditor is concerned with a misstatement caused by a cash disbursement being recorded in the client's records when no payment has actually been made. A number of possibilities exist for the cause of this misstatement. For example, a check may be lost or stolen before it is mailed. The primary control procedures used to prevent such misstatements include proper segregation of duties, independent reconciliation and review of vendor statements, and monthly bank reconciliations. In the purchasing system shown in Figure 11–1, checks are distributed by the cashier's department, which is independent of the accounts payable department (the department authorizing the payment).

Table 11–7 lists tests of controls that the auditor can use to verify the effectiveness of the client's controls. For example, the auditor can observe and evaluate the client's segregation of duties and review the client's procedures for reconciling vendor statements and monthly bank statements.

Completeness of Cash Disbursement Transactions

The major misstatement related to the completeness assertion is that a cash disbursement is made but not recorded in the client's records. In addition to the control procedures used for the occurrence assertion, accounting for the numerical sequence of checks and reconciliation of the daily cash disbursements with postings to the accounts payable subsidiary records (see Figure 11–1) helps to ensure that all issued checks are recorded. The auditor's tests of controls may include reviewing and testing the client's procedures for accounting for the sequence of checks and reviewing the client's reconciliation procedures.

Authorization of Cash Disbursement Transactions

Proper segregation of duties reduces the likelihood that unauthorized cash disbursements are made. It is important that an individual who approves a purchase not have direct access to the cash disbursement for it. Additionally, the individuals in the accounts payable department who initiate payment should not have access to the checks after they are prepared. In EarthWear's purchasing process, the purchasing department functions are segregated from those of the accounts payable and cashier's departments.

TABLE 11–7	**Summary of Assertions, Possible Misstatements, Control Procedures, and Tests of Controls for Cash Disbursement Transactions**		
Assertion	*Possible Misstatement*	*Control Procedure*	*Test of Controls*
Occurrence	Cash disbursement recorded but not made	Segregation of duties	Observe and evaluate proper segregation of duties.
		Vendor statements independently reviewed and reconciled to accounts payable records	Review client's procedures for reconciling vendor statements.
		Monthly bank reconciliations prepared and reviewed	Review monthly bank reconciliations for indication of independent review.
Completeness	Cash disbursement made but not recorded	Same as above	Same as above.
		Accounting for the numerical sequence of checks	Review and test client's procedures for numerical sequence of checks; if IT application, test application controls.
		Daily cash disbursements reconciled to postings to accounts payable subsidiary records	Review procedures for reconciling daily cash disbursements with postings to accounts payable subsidiary records; if IT application, test application controls.
Authorization	Cash disbursement not authorized	Segregation of duties	Evaluate segregation of duties.
		Checks prepared only after all source documents have been independently approved	Examine indication of approval on voucher packet.
Accuracy	Cash disbursement recorded at incorrect amount	Daily cash disbursements report reconciled to checks issued	Review reconciliation.
		Vendor statements reconciled to accounts payable records and independently reviewed	Review reconciliation.
		Monthly bank statements reconciled and independently reviewed	Review monthly bank reconciliations.
	Cash disbursement posted to the wrong vendor account	Vendor statements reconciled and independently reviewed	Review reconciliation.
	Cash disbursements journal not summarized properly or not properly posted to general ledger accounts	Monthly cash disbursements journal agreed to general ledger postings	Review postings from cash disbursements journal to the general ledger.
		Accounts payable subsidiary records reconciled to general ledger control account	Review reconciliation.
Cutoff	Cash disbursement recorded in wrong period	Daily reconciliation of checks issued with postings to the cash disbursements journal and accounts payable subsidiary records	Review daily reconciliations.
Classification	Cash disbursement charged to wrong account	Chart of accounts	Review cash disbursements journal for reasonableness of account distribution.
		Independent approval and review of general ledger account on voucher packet	Review general ledger account code on voucher packet for reasonableness.

Checks are forwarded directly from the IT department to the cashier's department for mailing to the vendors. The other major control over unauthorized cash disbursements is that checks are not prepared unless all source documents (purchase requisition, purchase order, receiving report, and vendor's invoice) are included in the voucher packet and approved. For EarthWear's purchasing process, a complete voucher packet must be present in order to record the liability and authorize payment.

Accuracy of Cash Disbursement Transactions

The potential misstatement related to the accuracy assertion is that the payment amount is recorded incorrectly. To detect such errors, the client's personnel should reconcile the total of the checks issued on a particular day with the daily cash disbursements report. The client's control procedures should require monthly reconciliation of vendor statements to the accounts payable records. Monthly bank reconciliations also provide controls for detecting misstatements caused by cash disbursements being made in incorrect amounts. Each of these reconciliations should be independently reviewed by the client's personnel. The auditor's test of controls involves reviewing the various reconciliations.

Two other possible misstatements are of concern with the accuracy assertion: (1) cash disbursements are posted to the wrong vendor accounts and (2) the cash disbursements journal is not summarized properly or the wrong general ledger account is posted. The reconciliation of vendors' monthly statements is an effective control procedure for detecting payments posted to the wrong vendor accounts. Agreement of the monthly cash disbursements journal to general ledger postings and reconciliation of the accounts payable subsidiary records to the general ledger control account are effective control procedures for preventing summarization and posting errors (see Figure 11–1). The auditor's tests of controls would include checking postings to the general ledger and reviewing the various reconciliations.

Cutoff of Cash Disbursement Transactions

The client should establish procedures to ensure that when a check is prepared, it is recorded on a timely basis in the cash disbursements journal and the accounts payable subsidiary records. As shown in Figure 11–1, when a check is prepared, it is simultaneously recorded in the accounting records by the application programs that control transaction processing. The auditor's tests of controls include reviewing the reconciliation of checks with postings to the cash disbursements journal and accounts payable subsidiary records. The auditor also tests cash disbursements before and after year-end to ensure transactions are recorded in the proper period.

Classification of Cash Disbursement Transactions

The auditor's concern with proper classification is that a cash disbursement may be charged to the wrong general ledger account. In most purchasing systems, purchases are usually recorded through the voucher register or purchases journal. Thus, the only entries into the cash disbursements journal are debits to accounts payable and credits to cash. If these procedures are followed, proper classification of cash disbursements is not a major concern.

Sometimes a client pays for goods and services directly from the cash disbursements journal without recording the purchase transaction in the purchases journal. If a client does pay for goods and services directly from the cash disbursements journal, controls must be present to ensure proper classification. The use of a chart of accounts, as well as independent approval and review of the account code on the voucher packet, should provide an adequate control. The auditor can review the cash disbursements journal for reasonableness of account distribution as well as the account codes on a sample of voucher packets.

Control Procedures and Tests of Controls— Purchase Return Transactions

✼ [LO 9]

The number and magnitude of purchase return transactions are not material for most entities. However, because of the possibility of manipulation the auditor should, at a minimum, inquire about how the client controls purchase return transactions. When goods are returned to a vendor, the client usually prepares a document (sometimes called a debit memo) that reduces the amount of the vendor's accounts payable. This document is processed through the purchasing process in a manner similar to the processing of a vendor invoice.

Because purchase returns are often few in number and not material, the auditor normally does not test controls of these transactions. Substantive analytical procedures are usually performed to test the reasonableness of purchase returns. For example, comparison of purchase returns as a percentage of revenue to prior years' and industry data may disclose any material misstatement in this account.

Relating the Assessed Level of Control Risk to Substantive Procedures

✼ [LO 10]

The decision process followed by the auditor is similar to that discussed in Chapter 10 for the revenue process. If the results of the tests of controls support the achieved level of control risk, the auditor conducts substantive procedures at the planned level. If the results indicate that the control risk can be reduced further, the auditor can increase the detection risk, which will reduce the nature, timing, and extent of substantive procedures needed. However, if the results of the tests of controls do not support the planned level of control risk, the detection risk has to be set lower and substantive procedures increased.

The main accounts affected by the auditor's achieved control risk for the purchasing process include accounts payable, accrued expenses, and most of the expense accounts in the income statement. Additionally, the tests of controls over purchase transactions affect the assessment of detection risk for other business processes. For example, purchase transactions for the acquisition of inventory and property, plant, and equipment are subject to the controls included in the purchasing process. If those controls are reliable, the auditor may be able to increase the detection risk for the affected financial statement accounts and therefore reduce the number of substantive procedures needed.

Auditing Accounts Payable and Accrued Expenses

The assessments of inherent risk and control risk for the purchasing process are used to determine the level of detection risk for conducting substantive procedures for accounts payable and accrued expenses. Accounts payable generally represent normal recurring trade obligations. Accrued expenses represent expenses that have been incurred during the period but that have not been billed or paid for as of the end of the period; these include accruals for taxes, interest, royalties, and professional fees. A number of accrued expenses are also related to payroll. Because there is little difference between accounts payable and accrued expenses, they are covered together in this section.

Substantive analytical procedures and tests of details of classes of transactions, account balances, and disclosures are used to test accounts payable and accrued expenses. Substantive analytical procedures are used to examine plausible relationships among accounts payable and accrued expenses. Tests of details focus on transactions, account balances, or disclosures. In the purchasing process, tests of details of transactions (also called *substantive tests of transactions*) focus mainly on the purchases and cash disbursement transactions. Tests of details of account balances concentrate on the detailed amounts or estimates that make up the ending balance for accounts payable and accrued expenses. Tests of details of disclosures are concerned with the presentation and disclosures related to accounts payable and accrued expenses.

Table 11–7 presents the assertions for purchases and cash disbursement transactions and events; Table 11–8 lists the assertions for account balances and disclosures as they apply to accounts payable and accrued expenses. The reader should note that the auditor may test assertions related to transactions (substantive tests of transactions) in conjunction with testing internal controls. If the tests of controls indicate that the controls are not operating effectively, the auditor may need to test transactions at the date the account balance is tested.

TABLE 11–8	Management Assertions about Account Balances, and Disclosures for Accounts Payable and Accrued Expenses

Assertions about Account Balances at the Period End:
- **Existence.** Accounts payable and accrued expenses are valid liabilities.
- **Rights and obligations.** Accounts payable and accrued expenses are the obligations of the entity.
- **Completeness.** All accounts payable and accrued expenses have been recorded.
- **Valuation and allocation.** Accounts payable and accrued expenses are included in the financial statements at appropriate amounts, and any resulting valuation or allocation adjustments are appropriately recorded.

Assertions about Presentation and Disclosure:
- **Occurrence and rights and obligations.** All disclosed events, transactions, and other matters relating to accounts payable and accrued expenses have occurred and pertain to the entity.
- **Completeness.** All disclosures relating to accounts payable and accrued expenses that should have been included in the financial statements have been included.
- **Classification and understandability.** Financial information relating to accounts payable and accrued expenses is appropriately presented and described, and disclosures are clearly expressed.
- **Accuracy and valuation.** Financial and other information relating to accounts payable and accrued expenses are disclosed fairly and at appropriate amounts.

TABLE 11-9	Substantive Analytical Procedures for Auditing Accounts Payable and Accrued Expenses
Substantive Analytical Procedure	*Possible Misstatement Detected*
Compare payables turnover and days outstanding in accounts payable to previous years' and industry data.	Under- or overstatement of liabilities and expenses.
Compare current-year balances in accounts payable and accruals with prior years' balances.	Under- or overstatement of liabilities and expenses.
Compare amounts owed to individual vendors in the current year's accounts payable listing to amounts owed in prior years.	Under- or overstatement of liabilities and expenses.
Compare purchase returns and allowances as a percentage of revenue or cost of sales to prior years' and industry data.	Under- or overstatement of purchase returns.

Substantive Analytical Procedures

✼ [LO 11]   Substantive analytical procedures can be useful substantive procedures for examining the reasonableness of accounts payable and accrued expenses. Substantive analytical procedures can effectively identify accounts payable and accrual accounts that are misstated, as well as provide evidence regarding the fairness of the recorded accounts. Table 11–9 contains some examples of substantive analytical procedures that can be used in the auditing of accounts payable and accrued expenses.

Tests of Details of Classes of Transactions, Account Balances, and Disclosures

✼ [LO 12,13]   Table 11–8 presents the assertions for accounts payable and accrued expenses. The intended purpose of tests of details of transactions is to detect monetary misstatements in the individual transactions processed through the purchasing application. As previously mentioned, tests of details of transactions are often conducted in conjunction with tests of controls. Table 11–10 presents examples of tests of details of transactions, account balances, and disclosures for assertions related to accounts payable and accrued expenses. The discussion that follows focuses on tests of details of account balances of accounts payable and accrued expenses. We begin with the completeness assertion for the accounts payable balance because the auditor must establish that the detailed records agree to the general ledger.

Completeness   The completeness of accounts payable is first determined by obtaining a listing of accounts payable, footing the listing, and agreeing it to the general ledger control account. The items included on this listing are the unpaid individual vouchers (when a voucher system is used) or the balance in the individual vendor accounts in the subsidiary records (when a purchases journal is used). Exhibit 11–2 presents an example of the accounts payable listing for EarthWear in which the information is summarized by vendor from the accounts payable subsidiary ledger. Selected vouchers or vendor accounts are traced to the supporting documents or subsidiary accounts payable records to verify the accuracy of the details making up the listing.

TABLE 11–10	Summary of Assertions and Related Tests of Transactions, Account Balances, and Disclosures—Accounts Payable and Accrued Expenses

Assertions about Classes of Transactions	Substantive Tests of Transaction*
Occurrence	Test a sample of vouchers for the presence of an authorized purchase order and receiving report.
Completeness	Tracing of a sample of vouchers to the purchases journal.
Authorization	Test a sample of purchase requisition for proper authorization.
Accuracy	Recompute the mathematical accuracy of a sample of vendors' invoices.
Cutoff	Compare dates on a sample of vouchers with the dates transactions were recorded in the purchases journal.
	Test transactions around year-end to determine if they are recorded in the proper period.
Classification	Verify classification of charges for a sample of purchases transactions.

Assertions about Account Balances	Tests of Details of Account Balances
Existence	Vouch selected amounts from the accounts payable listing and schedules for accruals to voucher packets or other supporting documentation.
	Obtain selected vendors' statements and reconcile to vendor accounts.
	Confirmation of selected accounts payable.[†]
Rights and obligations	Review voucher packets for presence of purchase requisition, purchase order, receiving report, and vendor invoice.
Completeness	Obtain listing of accounts payable and agree total to general ledger.[†]
	Search for unrecorded liabilities by inquiring of management and examining post-balance sheet transactions.
	Obtain selected vendors' statements and reconcile to vendor accounts.
	Confirmation of selected accounts payable.[†]
Valuation and allocation	Obtain listing of accounts payable and account analysis schedules for accruals; foot listing and schedules and agree totals to general ledger.[†]
	Trace selected items from the accounts payable listing to the subsidiary records[†] and voucher packets.
	Review results of confirmations of selected accounts payable.
	Obtain selected vendors' statements and reconcile to vendor accounts.

Assertions about Presentation and Disclosure	Tests of Details of Disclosures
Occurrence and rights and obligations	Inquire about accounts payable and accrued expenses to ensure that they are properly disclosed.
Completeness	Complete financial reporting checklist to ensure that all financial statement disclosures related to accounts payable and accrued expenses have been disclosed.
Classification and understandability	Review of listing of accounts payable for material debits, long-term payables, and nontrade payables. Determine whether such items require separate disclosure on the balance sheet.
	Read footnotes to ensure that required disclosures are understandable.
Accuracy and valuation	Read footnotes and other information to ensure that the information is accurate and properly presented at the appropriate amounts.

* These tests of details of transactions are commonly conducted as a dual-purpose test (i.e., in conjunction with tests of controls).
[†] These tests can be conducted manually or using CAATs.

| EXHIBIT 11–2 | **Example of an Accounts Payable Listing Working Paper** |

N10
DLJ
2/14/2006

EarthWear

EARTHWEAR CLOTHIERS
Accounts Payable Listing
12/31/05

Vendor Name	Amount Due
Aarhus Industries	$ 52,758†V
Anderson Clothes, Inc.	237,344V
.	
.	
.	
.	
Washington Mfg., Inc.	122,465†V
Zantec Bros.	7,750
Total	$62,509,740
	F T/B

F = Footed.
† = Traced to accounts payable subsidiary records.
V = Voucher packets examined for transaction validity. No exceptions.
T/B = Agreed to trial balance.

For example, the tick mark next to the balance for Aarhus Industries indicates that the auditor has verified the account by tracing the balance to the accounts payable subsidiary records.

For accrued expense accounts, the auditor obtains a detailed account analysis schedule. For example, Exhibit 11–3 shows an account analysis schedule for accrued real estate taxes. The credits to the accrual account represent the recognition of real estate taxes owed at the end of each month. This amount should agree to the amount of real estate taxes expense shown in the income statement. The debits to the account are payments. This schedule is footed and agreed to the accrued real estate taxes account in the general ledger.

The second major test of the completeness assertion is for accounts payable and accruals concerned with unrecorded liabilities. Therefore, auditors frequently conduct extensive tests to ensure that all liabilities are recorded. Such tests are commonly referred to as a *search for unrecorded liabilities*. The following audit procedures may be used as part of the search for unrecorded liabilities:

1. Ask management about control procedures used to identify unrecorded liabilities and accruals at the end of an accounting period.
2. Obtain copies of vendors' monthly statements and reconcile the amounts to the client's accounts payable records.
3. Confirm vendor accounts, including accounts with small or zero balances.

EXHIBIT 11-3	Account Analysis for the Accrued Real Estate Taxes Account Working Paper

N21
DLJ
2/5/2006

EarthWear

EARTHWEAR CLOTHIERS

Analysis of Accrued Real Estate Taxes

12/31/05

Cash disbursements for real estate tax payments	233,911Γ	Beginning balance	$ 22,333‡
		12 monthly accruals for real estate taxes	235,245
		Ending balance	$ 23,667L✔
			F

F = Footed.
‡ = Agreed to prior year's working papers.
✔ = Amount of real estate taxes accrued appears reasonable.
Γ = Payments traced to real estate tax bills and cash disbursements journal.
L = Agreed to general ledger.

4. Vouch large-dollar items from the purchases journal and cash disbursements journal for a limited time after year-end; examine the date on each receiving report or vendor invoice to determine if the liability relates to the current audit period.

5. Examine the files of unmatched purchase orders, receiving reports, and vendor invoices for any unrecorded liabilities.

Existence

The auditor's major concern with the existence assertion is whether the recorded liabilities are valid obligations of the entity. To verify the validity of liabilities, the auditor can vouch a sample of the items included on the listing of accounts payable, or the accrued account analysis, to voucher packets or other supporting documents. If adequate source documents are present, the auditor has evidence that the amounts represent valid liabilities (see Exhibit 11-2). In some circumstances, the auditor may obtain copies of the monthly vendor statements or send confirmation requests to vendors to test the validity of the liabilities. Confirmation of accounts payable is discussed later in this chapter.

Cutoff

The cutoff assertion attempts to determine whether all purchase transactions and related accounts payable are recorded in the proper period. On most audits, purchase cutoff is coordinated with the client's physical inventory count. Proper cutoff should also be determined for purchase return transactions.

The client should have control procedures to ensure that a proper purchase cutoff takes place. The auditor can test purchase cutoff by first obtaining the number of the last receiving report issued in the current period. A sample of voucher packets is selected for a few days before and after year-end. The receiving reports contained in the voucher packets are examined to determine if the receipt of the goods is consistent with the recording of the liability. For example, suppose that the last receiving report issued by Earth-Wear in 2005 was number 15,755. A voucher packet recorded in the voucher register or accounts payable in 2005 should have a receiving report numbered 15,755 or less. If the auditor finds a voucher packet recorded in 2005 with a receiving report number higher than 15,755, the liability has been recorded in the wrong period. Accounts payable for 2005 should be adjusted and the amount included as a liability in the next period. For voucher packets recorded in 2006, the receiving reports should be numbered 15,756 or higher. If the auditor finds a voucher packet with a receiving report with a number less than 15,756, the liability belongs in the 2005 accounts payable.

Purchase returns seldom represent a material amount in the financial statements. If the client has adequate control procedures for processing purchase return transactions, the auditor can use substantive analytical procedures to satisfy the cutoff assertion for purchase returns. For example, the prior-year and current-year amounts for purchase returns as a percentage of revenue or cost of sales can be compared. If the results of the substantive analytical procedures are consistent with the auditor's expectation, no further audit work may be necessary.

Rights and Obligations

Generally, there is little risk related to this assertion because clients seldom have an incentive to record liabilities that are not obligations of the entity. Review of the voucher packets for adequate supporting documents relating liabilities to the client provides sufficient evidence to support this assertion.

Valuation

The valuation of individual accounts payable is generally not a difficult assertion to test. Accounts payable are recorded at either the gross amount of the invoice or the net of the cash discount if the entity normally takes a cash discount. The tests of details of account balances noted in Table 11–10 normally provide sufficient evidence as to the proper valuation of accounts payable.

The valuation of accruals depends on the type and nature of the accrued expenses. Most accruals are relatively easy to value, and proper valuation can be tested by examining the underlying source documents. Real estate taxes and interest are examples of accruals that are generally easy to value. In the first case, real estate appraisals or bills usually serve as the basis for the accrual amount (see Exhibit 11–3). In the second case, the amount of interest accrued relates directly to the amount of debt and the interest rate stipulated in the loan agreement. Other accruals, however, may require the auditor to verify the client's estimates. Auditing standards (AU 342) provide the auditor with guidance in auditing client's estimates. Examples of such estimates include accruals for vacation pay, pension expense, warranty expense, and income taxes.

Classification and Understandability

The major issues related to the presentation and disclosure assertion about classification are (1) identifying and reclassifying any material debits contained in accounts payable, (2) segregating short-term and long-term payables, and (3) ensuring that different types of payables are properly classified. Proper classification can usually be verified by reviewing the

TABLE 11-11	Examples of Disclosure Items for Purchasing Process and Related Accounts
	Payables by type (trade, officers, employees, affiliates, and so on).
	Short- and long-term payables.
	Long-term purchase contracts, including any unusual or adverse purchase commitments.
	Purchases from and payables to related parties.
	Dependence on a single vendor or a small number of vendors.
	Costs by reportable segment of the business.

EXHIBIT 11-4	A Sample Disclosure for Purchase Commitments
	The company has various agreements that provide for the purchase at market prices of wood chips, bark, and other residual fiber from trees.
	The company also has an agreement to purchase at market prices through 2007 the entire production of an unbleached kraft paper–making machine at Johnson Forest Products Company. The capacity of this machine is estimated to be 30,000 tons a year.

accounts payable listing and the general ledger accounts payable account. If material debits are present, they should be reclassified as receivables or as deposits if the amount will be used for future purchases. Any long-term payables should be identified and reclassified to the long-term liability section of the balance sheet. Also, if payables to officers, employees, or related parties are material, they should not be included with the trade accounts payable. The auditor should also ensure that accrued expenses are properly classified.

Other Presentation Disclosure Assertions

Even though management is responsible for the financial statements, the auditor must ensure that all necessary financial statement disclosures are made for accounts payable and accrued expenses. Again, a reporting checklist is a useful tool. Table 11–11 presents examples of items that should be disclosed for accounts payable and accrued expenses.

Two disclosures are particularly important. The auditor must ensure that all related-party purchase transactions have been identified. If material, such purchase transactions should be disclosed. The other major disclosure issue is purchase commitments. When the client has entered into a formal long-term purchase contract, adequate disclosure of the terms of the contract should be provided in a footnote. Exhibit 11–4 provides a sample disclosure for a purchase commitment.

Accounts Payable Confirmations

❧ **[LO 14]**   Chapter 10 discussed the confirmation process in general and accounts receivable confirmations specifically. This section expands that discussion to include confirmation of accounts payable. Accounts payable confirmations are used less frequently by auditors than accounts receivable confirmations

EXHIBIT 11–5	Example of an Accounts Payable Confirmation Request

EARTHWEAR CLOTHIERS

EarthWear

January 7, 2006

Zantec Bros.
P.O. Box 1469
Macon, GA 35792

Gentlemen:

Our auditors, Willis & Adams, are conducting an audit of our financial statements as of December 31, 2005. Please confirm to them the amount of our accounts payable. Additionally, please provide the following information as of that date:

1. An itemized statement of our account.
2. A list of any notes payable to you including any discounted notes. Please include the original dates and amounts, due dates, and amounts still outstanding.
3. A list of any consigned inventory held by us.

Sincerely,

Sally Jones
Controller, EarthWear Clothiers

Willis & Adams
P. O. Box 4080
Boise, Idaho 79443-4080

We confirm that EarthWear Clothiers' accounts payable balance at December 31, 2005, is _____.

Signature _____   Position _____

because the auditor can test accounts payable by examining vendor invoices and monthly vendor statements. These documents originate from sources external to the client, so this evidence is viewed as reliable. However, if the client has weak internal control, vendor statements may not be available to examine. In such a case, confirmations may be used as a main source of evidence.

While accounts payable confirmations provide evidence on a number of assertions, they primarily test the completeness assertion. If the client has strong control procedures for ensuring that liabilities are recorded, the auditor focuses on confirmation of large-dollar accounts. However, if the auditor has concerns about liabilities not being recorded, regular vendors with small or zero balances and a sample of other accounts may be confirmed in addition to large-dollar accounts. Small- and zero-balance accounts are confirmed because the client may owe such vendors for purchases but the amounts may not be recorded in the client's accounting records.

When confirming accounts payable, auditors generally use a form of positive confirmation referred to as a *blank or zero-balance* confirmation. This type of positive confirmation does not state the balance owed. Instead, the confirmation requests that the recipient fill in the amount or furnish other information. Exhibit 11–5 presents an example of an accounts payable confirmation request. Note that the confirmation requests the balance owed and a detailed statement of the account. The confirmation also requests additional information on notes payable and consigned inventory.

Generally, accounts payable confirmations are mailed at year-end rather than at an interim date because of the auditor's concerns about unrecorded liabilities. The selection and mailing of accounts payable confirmations should be controlled using the procedures outlined in Chapter 10. When accounts payable confirmations are received, the amounts provided by the vendors must be reconciled with the client's records. Differences are often due to the same types of timing differences noted in Chapter 10 for accounts receivable confirmations. The two major timing differences are due to inventory in transit to the client and cash paid by the client but not yet received by the vendor. Any inconsistencies not due to timing differences normally result in adjustments to the client's records.

Evaluating the Audit Findings—Accounts Payable and Related Accounts

[LO 15]   As discussed in previous chapters, when the auditor has completed the planned substantive procedures, all identified misstatements should be aggregated, including known misstatements detected by the auditor and projected misstatements plus an allowance for sampling risk. The likely misstatement is then compared to tolerable misstatement. If the likely misstatement is less than the tolerable misstatement, the auditor has evidence that the account is fairly presented. Conversely, if the likely misstatement exceeds the tolerable misstatement, the auditor should conclude that the account is not fairly presented.

For example, in Chapter 3, EarthWear's tolerable misstatement was $885,000. Exhibit 3–5 showed that Willis & Adams detected a misstatement in recording inventory that amounted to a $227,450 understatement of accounts payable. Because this misstatement ($227,450) is less than the tolerable misstatement of $885,000, Willis & Adams can conclude that the audit evidence supports fair presentation. However, if the misstatement was greater than the tolerable misstatement, the evidence would not support fair presentation. In this case, the auditor would have two choices: adjust the accounts to reduce the misstatement to an amount less than the tolerable misstatement or qualify the audit report.

The auditor should again analyze the misstatements discovered through the application of substantive procedures because these misstatements may provide additional evidence as to the control risk. For example, if most misstatements identified indicate that accounts payable are not properly valued, the auditor may reassess the control procedures used by the client for ensuring proper valuation. If the auditor concludes that the audit risk is unacceptably high, additional audit procedures should be performed, or the auditor must be satisfied that the client has adjusted the related financial statement accounts to an acceptable level. If the client does not adjust the accounts, the auditor should qualify the audit report.

KEY TERMS

Analytical procedures. Evaluations of financial information made by a study of plausible relationships among both financial and nonfinancial data.

Application controls. Controls that apply to the processing of specific computer applications and are part of the computer programs used in the accounting system.

Assertions. Expressed or implied representations by management that are reflected in the financial statement components.

Blank or zero-balance confirmation. A confirmation request on which the recipient fills in the amount or furnishes the information requested.

Confirmation. The process of obtaining and evaluating direct communication from a third party in response to a request for information about a particular item affecting financial statement assertions.

General controls. Controls that relate to the overall information-processing environment and have a pervasive effect on the entity's computer operations.

Positive confirmation. A confirmation request to which the recipient responds whether or not he or she agrees with the amount or information stated.

Reliance strategy. The auditor's decision to rely on the entity's controls, test those controls, and reduce the direct tests of the financial statement accounts.

Tests of controls. Procedures that evaluate the effectiveness of the design and operation of internal controls.

Tests of details of account balances and disclosures. Tests that concentrate on the details of amounts contained in an account balance and related footnotes.

Tests of details of transactions. Tests to detect errors or fraud in individual transactions.

www.mhhe.com/ messier4e	Visit the book's Online Learning Center for a multiple-choice quiz that will allow you to assess your understanding of chapter concepts.

REVIEW QUESTIONS

[LO 1]   11-1   Distinguish among the three categories of expenses. Provide an example of each type of expense.

[2,3]   11-2   What major types of transactions occur in the purchasing process? What financial statement accounts are affected by each type of transaction?

[4]   11-3   Briefly describe each of the following documents or records: purchase requisition, purchase order, receiving report, vendor invoice, and voucher. Why would an entity combine all documents related to a purchase transaction into a "voucher packet"?

[5,6] 11-4 List the key segregation of duties in the purchasing process. What errors or fraud can occur if such duties are not segregated?

[7] 11-5 List two inherent risk factors that directly affect the purchasing process. Why should auditors be concerned about issues such as the supply of raw materials and the volatility of prices?

[9] 11-6 What control procedures typically ensure that the occurrence, authorization, and completeness assertions are met for a purchase transaction? What tests of controls are performed for each of these assertions?

[9] 11-7 Identify two tests of controls that could be performed using computer-assisted audit techniques (CAATs) for purchase transactions.

[11] 11-8 List two substantive analytical procedures that can test accounts payable. What potential errors or fraud can be identified by each analytical procedure?

[13] 11-9 List the procedures an auditor might use to search for unrecorded liabilities.

[13] 11-10 Identify four possible disclosure issues related to the purchasing process and related accounts.

[14] 11-11 What are the differences between accounts receivable and accounts payable confirmations?

MULTIPLE-CHOICE QUESTIONS

[2,4,9] 11-12 In a properly designed accounts payable system, a voucher is prepared after the invoice, purchase order, requisition, and receiving report are verified. The next step in the system is
a. Cancellation of the supporting documents.
b. Entry of the check amount in the check register.
c. Entering of the voucher into the voucher register.
d. Approval of the voucher for payment.

[2,4,9] 11-13 When goods are received, the receiving clerk should match the goods with
a. The purchase order and the requisition form.
b. The vendor invoice and the receiving report.
c. The vendor shipping document and the purchase order.
d. The receiving report and the vendor shipping document.

[2,4,9] 11-14 Internal control is strengthened when the quantity of merchandise ordered is omitted from the copy of the purchase order sent to the
a. Department that initiated the requisition.
b. Receiving department.
c. Purchasing agent.
d. Accounts payable department.

[5,6,9] 11-15 Which of the following control procedures is *not* usually performed in the accounts payable department?
a. Matching the vendor's invoice with the related receiving report.
b. Approving vouchers for payment by having an authorized employee sign the vouchers.
c. Indicating the asset and expense accounts to be debited.
d. Accounting for unused prenumbered purchase orders and receiving reports.

[5,6,9]   11-16   In a properly designed purchasing process, the same employee most likely would match vendors' invoices with receiving reports and also
a. Post the detailed accounts payable records.
b. Recompute the calculations on vendors' invoices.
c. Reconcile the accounts payroll ledger.
d. Cancel vendors' invoices after payment.

[5,6,9]   11-17   For effective internal control purposes, which of the following individuals should be responsible for mailing signed checks?
a. Receptionist.
b. Treasurer.
c. Accounts payable clerk.
d. Payroll clerk.

[4,9,13]   11-18   To determine whether accounts payable are complete, an auditor performs a test to verify that all merchandise received is recorded. The population of documents for this test consists of all
a. Vendor invoices.
b. Purchase orders.
c. Receiving reports.
d. Canceled checks.

[9,13]   11-19   Which of the following audit procedures is best for identifying unrecorded trade accounts payable?
a. Examination of unusual relationships between monthly accounts payable balances and recorded cash payments.
b. Reconciliation of vendors' statements to the file of receiving reports to identify items received just prior to the balance sheet date.
c. Investigation of payables recorded just prior to and just subsequent to the balance sheet date to determine whether they are supported by receiving reports.
d. Review of cash disbursements recorded subsequent to the balance sheet date to determine whether the related payables apply to the prior period.

[9,13]   11-20   Purchase cutoff procedures should be designed to test whether all inventory
a. Purchased and received before the end of the year was paid for.
b. Ordered before the end of the year was received.
c. Purchased and received before the end of the year was recorded.
d. Owned by the company is in the possession of the company at the end of the year.

[13]   11-21   Which of the following procedures is *least* likely to be performed before the balance sheet date?
a. Test of internal control over cash.
b. Confirmation of receivables.
c. Search for unrecorded liabilities.
d. Observation of inventory.

[14]   11-22   When using confirmations to provide evidence about the completeness assertion for accounts payable, the appropriate population most likely would be
a. Vendors with whom the entity has previously done business.
b. Amounts recorded in the accounts payable subsidiary ledger.

   c. Payees of checks drawn in the month after year-end.

   d. Invoices filed in the entity's open invoice file.

PROBLEMS

[2,5,6,9]   **11-23**   Katz, CPA, has been engaged to audit the financial statements of Sommer Manufacturing, Inc. Sommer is a medium-size entity that produces a wide variety of household goods. All acquisitions of materials are processed through the purchasing, receiving, accounts payable, and treasurer functions.

Required:

Prepare the "Purchases" segment of the internal control questionnaire to be used in evaluating Sommer's internal control system. Each question should elicit either a yes or no response. Do *not* prepare the receiving, accounts payable, or treasurer segments of the internal control questionnaire. Do *not* discuss the internal controls over purchases. Use the following format:

Questions	Yes	No

(AICPA, adapted)

[2,4,5,6,9]   **11-24**   The flowchart on the following page depicts the activities relating to the purchasing, receiving, and accounts payable departments of Model Company, Inc.

Required:

Based only on the flowchart, describe the control procedures that most likely would provide reasonable assurance that specific assertions regarding purchases and accounts payable will be achieved. Do *not* describe weaknesses in internal control.

(AICPA, adapted)

[2,5,6,9]   **11-25**   In 2005 Kida Company purchased more than $10 million worth of office equipment under its "special" ordering system, with individual orders ranging from $5,000 to $30,000. "Special" orders entail low-volume items that have been included in an authorized user's budget. Department heads include in their annual budget requests the types of equipment and their estimated cost. The budget, which limits the types and dollar amounts of office equipment a department head can requisition, is approved at the beginning of the year by the board of directors. Department heads prepare purchase requisition forms for equipment and forward them to the purchasing department. Kida's "special" ordering system functions as follows:

- *Purchasing:* Upon receiving a purchase requisition, one of five buyers verifies that the person requesting the equipment is a department head. The buyer selects the appropriate vendor by searching

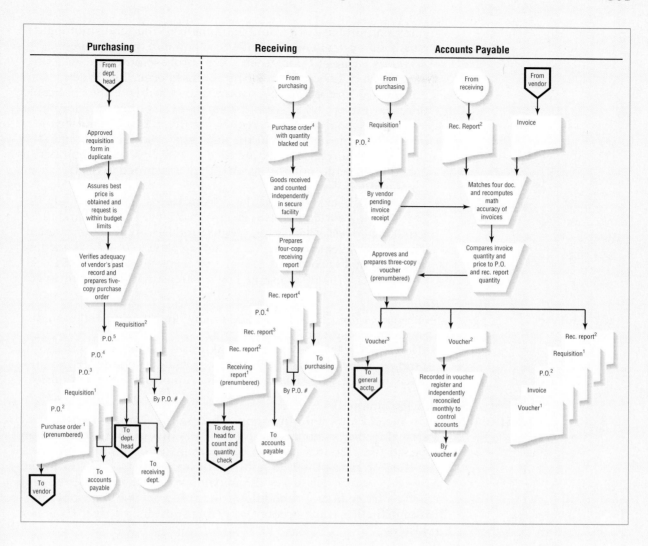

the various vendor catalogs on file. The buyer then phones the vendor, requests a price quotation, and gives the vendor a verbal order. A prenumbered purchase order is processed with the original sent to the vendor, a copy to the department head, a copy to receiving, a copy to accounts payable, and a copy filed in the open requisition file. When the buyer is orally informed by the receiving department that the item has been received, the buyer transfers the purchase order from the unfilled file to the filled file. Once a month the buyer reviews the unfilled file to follow up on and expedite open orders.

• *Receiving:* The receiving department receives a copy of the purchase order. When equipment is received, the receiving clerk stamps the purchase order with the date received and, if applicable, in red pen prints any differences between the quantity shown on the purchase order and the quantity received. The receiving clerk forwards the stamped purchase order and equipment to the requisitioning department head and orally notifies the purchasing department.

- *Accounts payable:* Upon receiving a purchase order, the accounts payable clerk files it in the open purchase order file. When a vendor invoice is received, the invoice is matched with the applicable purchase order, and a payable is set up by debiting the equipment account of the department requesting the items. Unpaid invoices are filed by due date, and at the due date a check is prepared. The invoice and purchase order are filed by purchase order number in a paid invoice file, and the check is then forwarded to the treasurer for signature.
- *Treasurer:* Checks received daily from the accounts payable department are sorted into two groups: those over $10,000 and those $10,000 and less. Checks for $10,000 and less are machine-signed. The cashier keeps the key and signature plate to the check-signing machine and records all use of the check-signing machine. All checks over $10,000 are signed by the treasurer or the controller.

Required:

a. Prepare a flowchart of Kida Company's purchasing and cash disbursements system.

b. Describe the internal control weaknesses relating to purchases of and payments for "special" orders of Kida Company for the purchasing, receiving, accounts payable, and treasurer functions.

(AICPA, adapted)

[11,12,13,14]   11-26   Coltrane, CPA, is auditing Jang Wholesaling Company's financial statements and is about to perform substantive audit procedures on Jang's trade accounts payable balances. After obtaining an understanding of Jang's internal control for accounts payable, Coltrane assessed control risk below the maximum. Coltrane requested and received from Jang a schedule of the trade accounts payable prepared using the trade accounts payable subsidiary ledger (voucher register).

Required:

Describe the substantive audit procedures Coltrane should apply to Jang's trade accounts payable balances. Do *not* include procedures that would be applied only in the audit of related-party payables, amounts withheld from employees, and accrued expenses such as pensions and interest.

(AICPA, adapted)

[13,14]   11-27   In obtaining evidence in support of financial statement assertions, the auditor develops specific audit procedures to access those assertions.

Required:

Your client is All's Fair Appliance Company, an appliance wholesaler. Select the most appropriate audit procedure from the list below and enter the number in the appropriate place on the grid. (An audit procedure may be selected once, more than once, or not at all.)

Audit Procedure:

1. Compare selected amounts from the accounts payable listing with the voucher and supporting documents.
2. Review drafts of the financial statements.
3. Search for unrecorded liabilities.
4. Select a sample of receiving documents for a few days before and after year-end.
5. Confirm accounts payable.
6. Obtain a listing of the accounts payable and agree total to general ledger control account.

Specific Assertion	Audit Procedure
a. Determine whether all accounts payable are properly valued. (valuation)	
b. Verify that recorded accounts payable include all amounts owed to vendors. (completeness)	
c. Verify that all accounts payable are recorded in the correct period. (cutoff)	
d. Determine whether accounts payable have been properly accumulated from the journal to the general ledger. (valuation)	
e. Determine whether recorded accounts payable are valid. (occurrence)	

[11,12,13,14] 11-28 Taylor, CPA, is auditing Rex Wholesaling for the year ended December 31, 2005. Taylor has reviewed internal control relating to the purchasing, receiving, trade accounts payable, and cash disbursement processes and has decided not to test controls. Based on substantive analytical procedures, Taylor believes that the trade accounts payable balance on the balance sheet as of December 31, 2005, may be understated.

Taylor has requested and obtained a client-prepared trade accounts payable schedule listing the total amount owed to each vendor.

Required:

What additional substantive audit procedures should Taylor apply in examining the trade accounts payable?

(AICPA, adapted)

DISCUSSION CASE

[13,14] 11-29 Mincin, CPA, is the auditor of the Raleigh Corporation. Mincin is considering the audit work to be performed in the accounts payable area for the current year's engagement. The prior year's working papers show that confirmation requests were mailed to 100 of Raleigh's 1,000 suppliers. The selected suppliers were based on Mincin's sample, which was designed to select accounts with large-dollar balances. A substantial number of hours was spent by Raleigh and Mincin in resolving relatively minor differences between the confirmation replies and Raleigh's accounting records. Alternative audit procedures were used for suppliers who did not respond to the confirmation requests.

Required:

a. Discuss the accounts payable audit objectives that Mincin must consider in determining the audit procedures to be followed.

b. Discuss situations in which Mincin should use accounts payable confirmations, and discuss whether Mincin is required to use them.

c. Discuss why the use of large-dollar balances as the basis for selecting accounts payable for confirmation might not be the most efficient approach, and indicate what more efficient procedures could select accounts payable for confirmation.

(AICPA, adapted)

INTERNET ASSIGNMENTS

11-30   Visit the website of a catalog retailer similar to EarthWear Clothiers, and determine how it processes purchase transactions and recognizes expenses. Note that you may have to examine the entity's annual report and 10k.

11-31   Visit the SEC's website (www.sec.gov), and identify a company that has been recently cited for financial reporting problems related to the recognition of expenses. Prepare a memo summarizing the expense issues for the company.

www.mhhe.com/ messier4e	Visit the book's Online Learning Center for problem material to be completed using the *ACL* software packaged with your new text.

LEARNING OBJECTIVES

Upon completion of this chapter you will

[1] Develop an understanding of the human resource management process.

[2] Identify the types of transactions in the human resource management process and the financial statement accounts affected.

[3] Identify and describe the types of documents and records used in the payroll application.

[4] Understand the functions in the human resource management process.

[5] Know the appropriate segregation of duties for the human resource management process.

[6] Identify and evaluate inherent risks relevant to the human resource management process.

[7] Assess control risk for a human resource management process.

[8] Identify key internal controls and develop relevant tests of controls for payroll transactions.

[9] Relate the assessment of control risk to substantive procedures.

[10] Identify substantive analytical procedures used to audit payroll expense and payroll-related accrued expenses.

[11] Identify tests of details of transactions used to audit payroll expense and payroll-related accrued expenses.

[12] Identify tests of details of account balances and disclosures used to audit payroll expense and payroll-related accrued expenses.

[13] Evaluate the audit findings and reach a final conclusion on payroll expense and payroll-related accrued expenses.

RELEVANT ACCOUNTING AND AUDITING PRONOUNCEMENTS

FASB Statement of Financial Accounting Standards No. 87, Employer's Accounting for Pensions (FAS 87)

FASB Statement of Financial Accounting Standards No. 106, Employer's Accounting for Postretirement Benefits Other Than Pensions (FAS 106)

AU 312, Audit Risk and Materiality in Conducting an Audit

AU 316, Consideration of Fraud as a Financial Statement Audit

AU 319, Consideration of Internal Control in a Financial Statement Audit

AU 329, Analytical Procedures

AU 339, Audit Documentation

AICPA Auditing Standards Board, Exposure Draft, "Understanding the Entity and Its Environment and Assessing the Risks of Material Misstatement"

AICPA Auditing Standards Board, Exposure Draft, "Audit Evidence"

AICPA Auditing Standards Board, Exposure Draft, "Performing Audit Procedures in Response to Assessed Risks and Evaluating the Audit Evidence Obtained"

Auditing the Human Resource Management Process

Major Phases of an Audit

Client acceptance/
continuance
and establishing
engagement terms
(Chapter 5)

Preplanning
(Chapter 5)

Establish materiality
and assess risks
(Chapter 3)

Plan the audit
(Chapters 3 and 5)

Consider and audit
internal control
(Chapters 6 and 7))

Audit business processes
and related accounts
(e.g., revenue generation)
(Chapters 10–16)

Complete the audit
(Chapter 17)

Evaluate results and issue audit
report (Chapters 2 and 18)

Compensation and related employee benefit costs represent major expenses for most entities. As a result, organizations tend to have strong control procedures for processing payroll transactions. Additionally, because of the routine nature of these transactions, an entity's payroll system is normally computerized, or an outside service bureau is contracted to process the payroll.

This chapter starts with an overview of the human resource management process and then discusses the three components of the audit risk model. Then the inherent risks that affect the human resource management process are addressed. This is followed by a discussion of the auditor's control risk assessment. While the main focus of this chapter is auditing the human resource management process for a financial statement audit, the concepts covered for setting control risk are applicable to an audit of internal control over financial reporting for public companies under the Sarbanes-Oxley Act of 2002. Last, the chapter covers substantive procedures for detection risk for payroll and related accounts.

Overview of the Human Resource Management Process

[LO 1]   The human resource process starts with the establishment of sound policies for hiring, training, evaluating, counseling, promoting, compensating, and taking remedial actions for employees. Once an individual has been hired as an employee, the main transaction that affects the financial statement accounts is a payroll (payment) transaction. A payroll transaction usually begins with an employee performing some job and recording the time spent on a time card. The time card is approved by a supervisor before being forwarded to the payroll department. The data are then reviewed and sent to the IT department for processing. Finally, payment is made directly to the employee or deposited in the employee's bank account.

EarthWear   Figure 12–1 presents a flowchart of EarthWear's payroll system that serves as a framework for discussing control procedures and tests of controls. Although the description of EarthWear's payroll system is fairly typical, the reader should focus on the basic concepts so that they can be applied to the specific payroll systems encountered. The following topics related to the human resource management process are covered:

- Types of transactions and financial statement accounts affected.
- Types of documents and records.
- The major functions.
- The key segregation of duties.

Types of Transactions and Financial Statement Accounts Affected

Two main types of transactions are processed through the human resource management process:

- Payments to employees for services rendered.
- Accrual and payment of payroll-related liabilities arising from employees' services, including liabilities for Social Security and unemployment taxes.

[LO 2]   The discussion of internal control focuses on payments to employees, including a description of how such transactions are processed and the key control procedures that should be present to ensure that no material misstatements occur. The audit of payroll-related accruals is discussed later in the chapter.

The financial statement accounts that are generally affected by the two types of payroll-related transactions are

Type of Transaction	Account Affected
Payroll transaction	Cash.
	Inventory.
	Direct and indirect labor expense accounts.
	Various payroll-related liability and expense accounts.
Accrued payroll liability transactions	Cash.
	Various accruals (such as payroll taxes and pension costs).

FIGURE 12-1	Flowchart of the Human Resource Management Process—EarthWear Clothiers

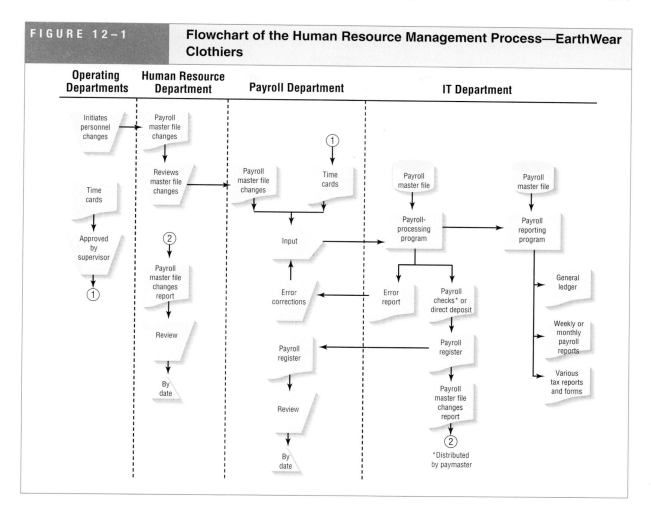

Types of Documents and Records 🕮 [LO 3]

Table 12–1 lists the important documents and records that are normally involved in the payroll application. Each of these items is briefly discussed here. The use of an advanced IT system may affect the form of the documents and the auditor's approach to testing the payroll application.

Personnel Records, Including Wage-Rate or Salary Authorizations

Personnel records contain information on each employee's work history, including hiring date, wage rate or salary, payroll deduction authorization forms, wage-rate and salary adjustment authorizations, performance evaluations, and termination notice, if applicable. Personnel records are normally maintained in the human resources department.

W-4 and Other Deduction Authorization Forms

The employee must authorize deductions from his or her pay. The organization should

TABLE 12–1	**Documents and Records Involved in the Payroll Application**
	Personnel records, including wage-rate or salary authorizations. W-4 and other deduction authorization forms. Time card. Payroll check/direct deposit records. Payroll register. Payroll master file. Payroll master file changes report. Periodic payroll reports. Various tax reports and forms.

therefore use authorization forms to document such deductions. For example, the employee must complete a W-4 form to authorize the withholding of federal and state income tax. Similar forms should be used for deductions for medical insurance, retirement contributions, and other benefits.

Time Card   This document records the hours worked by the employee, including the time the employee has started and stopped work. In some cases the employee fills in the time worked; in other cases a time clock records the time.

Payroll Check/Direct Deposit Records   These records indicate the amount paid to the employee for services rendered. The amount paid is the gross pay less any deductions. In many cases, the employee's pay is directly deposited into the individual's bank account and the company produces a listing of employees' payments that were sent to their bank accounts.

Payroll Register   This document, which is also referred to as the *payroll journal*, summarizes all payroll payments issued to employees. A payroll register normally indicates employees' gross pay, deductions, and net pay. In a computerized environment, the details for this document are maintained in the payroll master file.

Payroll Master File   This computer file maintains all the entity's records related to payroll, including information on each employee such as name, Social Security number, pay rate, and authorized deductions.

Payroll Master File Changes Report   This report contains a record of the changes made to the payroll master file. The human resource department reviews this report to ensure that all authorized changes have been properly made.

Periodic Payroll Reports   At the end of each week or month, a number of summary payroll reports may be prepared. The type of reports prepared depends on the type of organization. A manufacturing entity might have a payroll expense report that showed the allocation of direct labor to various products. EarthWear Clothiers reports a summary of payroll by various job classifications and departments. Department heads use this report to monitor payroll expense variances.

Various Tax Reports and Forms

Most companies are required to prepare various payroll tax reports for both the federal and state governments. Unemployment compensation forms must also be completed periodically. Additionally, an entity must provide each employee with a W-2 form at the end of the year. Compensation paid to a consultant or independent contractor must be reported on a 1099 form.

The Major Functions

[LO 4]

The principal objectives of the human resource management process are to (1) record production and other types of payroll costs in the accounts, (2) ensure that payroll costs are for legitimate entity activities, and (3) accrue liabilities for salaries and wages, payroll taxes, and various employee benefit programs. Table 12–2 lists the functions that are normally part of the payroll application.

Personnel

The personnel function is responsible for managing the human resource needs of the organization. This includes hiring and terminating employees, setting wage rates and salaries, and establishing and monitoring employee benefit programs. Most large organizations centralize these activities in a human resource department. However, in a small organization, these activities may be combined with the duties of selected operating and administrative personnel. In such organizations, control over human resource activities may not be as strong as when such activities are centralized. The human resource department maintains employees' personnel records. The human resource department may also be responsible for defining job requirements and descriptions, administering union contracts, and developing performance criteria and employee evaluation procedures.

Supervision

Supervisors within operating and supporting departments are responsible for reviewing and approving employees' attendance and time information. When time cards or other documents are used to record an employee's time worked and job classification, the supervisor approves

TABLE 12–2	Functions in the Payroll Application
Personnel	Authorization of hiring, firing, wage-rate and salary adjustments, salaries, and payroll deductions.
Supervision	Review and approval of employees' attendance and time information; monitoring of employee scheduling, productivity, and payroll cost variances.
Timekeeping	Processing of employees' attendance and time information and coding of account distribution.
Payroll processing	Computation of gross pay, deductions, and net pay; recording and summarization of payments and verification of account distribution.
Disbursement	Payment of employees' compensation and benefits.
General ledger	Proper accumulation, classification, and summarization of payroll in the general ledger.

this information before processing by the payroll function. Additionally, supervisors should monitor labor productivity and labor cost variances. Standardized labor performance measures, such as standard productivity and wage rates, improve the monitoring of payroll costs. Labor cost variances should be investigated by supervisory personnel and communicated to upper-level management. When employees are not required to complete time cards or job classification documents, the entity needs to have control procedures to notify the timekeeping or payroll-processing function about employees' absences and changes in employees' job classifications. This might be accomplished by having the supervisor submit a periodic attendance and job classification report.

Timekeeping   The timekeeping function prepares employees' time information for payroll processing. When payroll cost distribution is determined at the operating department level, the timekeeping function reviews this information before processing. Otherwise, the timekeeping function should be responsible for coding the payroll costs to appropriate accounts. In some organizations, a separate timekeeping department handles these functions. At EarthWear (see Figure 12–1), the operating and supporting departments are responsible for the timekeeping function.

Payroll Processing   The payroll-processing function is responsible for computing gross pay, deductions, and net pay. This function is also responsible for recording and summarizing payments and verifying account distribution. When IT is used to process payroll, as at EarthWear, the entity must have strong application controls to ensure proper payroll processing.

Disbursement   The disbursement function is responsible for paying employees for services and benefits. In particular, this function oversees the preparation and distribution of payroll checks. Check preparation normally occurs in the IT department. Therefore, it is necessary to have control procedures over access to blank checks and check signature plates. Checks are normally distributed by a paymaster, who is typically a member of the treasurer's department. When payments are directly deposited in employees' bank accounts, strong IT application controls are necessary.

General Ledger   The general ledger function for the human resource management process is responsible for properly accumulating, classifying, and summarizing payroll and benefit transactions in the general ledger. When IT is used to process payroll transactions, control totals can help ensure that this function is performed properly. This function is normally performed by the general accounting department.

The Key Segregation of Duties

As discussed in prior chapters, proper segregation of duties is one of the most important control procedures in any accounting system. Duties should be assigned to individuals in such a way that no one individual can control all phases of processing a transaction, thus permitting misstatements to go

TABLE 12–3   **Key Segregation of Duties in the Human Resource Management Process and Possible Errors or Fraud**

Segregation of Duties	Possible Errors or Fraud Resulting from Conflicts of Duties
The supervision function should be segregated from the personnel records and payroll-processing functions.	If one individual is responsible for the supervision, personnel records, and payroll-processing functions, fictitious employees can appear on the payroll records or unauthorized payments can be made. This can result in unauthorized payments to existing employees or payments to fictitious employees.
The disbursement function should be segregated from the personnel records, supervision, and payroll-processing functions.	If one individual is responsible for the disbursement function and also has the authority to hire and fire employees, approve time reports, or prepare payroll checks, unauthorized payroll checks can be issued.
The payroll-processing function should be segregated from the general ledger function.	If one individual is responsible for processing payroll transactions and also for the general ledger, that individual can conceal any defalcation that would normally be detected by independent review of accounting entries made to the general ledger.

TABLE 12–4   **Segregation of Duties for Payroll Functions by Department**

Payroll Function	Operating or Supporting	Human Resource	Timekeeping	Payroll	IT	Treasurer
			Department			
Initiation of wage or salary changes	X					
Initiation of employee hiring and firing	X					
Approval of wage or salary changes		X				
Updating of personnel records		X				
Updating of payroll records		X				
Approval of time cards and job classification	X					
Review of time data and payroll distribution			X			
Preparation of payroll				X	X	
Preparation and signing of payroll checks					X	
Distribution of payroll checks						X
Updating of general ledger for payroll activity					X	
Comparison of monthly departmental payroll expense to budget	X					
Calculation and recording of payroll taxes				X		

[LO 5] undetected. Individuals responsible for supervision and timekeeping should be segregated from the personnel, payroll-processing, and general ledger functions. If IT is used extensively in the payroll application, duties should be properly segregated in the IT department. Table 12–3 contains some of the key segregation of duties for the human resource management process and examples of possible errors or fraud that can result from conflicts in duties.

Table 12–4 shows more detailed segregation of duties for individual payroll functions across the various departments that are involved in processing payroll transactions.

Inherent Risk Assessment

[LO 6] Generally, few inherent risk factors directly affect the human resource management process and its related accounts for non-officers. Some factors the auditor might consider are the effect of economic conditions on payroll

EXHIBIT 12–1	**Executive Compensation Abuses at Tyco**

Tyco International Ltd.'s Dennis Kozlowski looms large as a rogue CEO. for the ages. His $6,000 shower curtain and vodka-spewing, full-size ice replica of Michelangelo's David will not be soon forgotten. In essence, prosecutors accused Kozlowski and former Chief Financial Officer Mark Swartz of running a criminal enterprise within Tyco's executive suite. The two were hit with 38 felony counts for pilfering $170 million directly from the company and for pocketing an additional $430 million through tainted sales of stock. Ironically, both Kozlowski and Swartz were former auditors; Kozlowski has become the personification of the widespread irrational exuberance of the late 1990s. Kozlowski handpicked some of the members of the compensation committee, and the changes worked to his benefit as his total compensation rose from $8.8 million in 1997 to $67 million in 1998 to $170 million in 1999. But it appears that Kozlowski believed that he deserved more money than he was making. The more he was paid as a reward for Tyco's soaring stock price, the more he spent on luxuries—and the more he allegedly stole. During these years, Kozlowski was secretly selling lots of stock—$280 million worth, according to the Manhattan DA's indictment of Kozlowski.

Kozlowski also ran up a $242 million tab at Tyco under a loan program designed to finance the purchase of company stock. Rather than use the money to buy Tyco stock, he used it to purchase fine art and antiques, a yacht, and a Nantucket estate. The loans were forms of compensation, but characterizing the compensation as a loan provided significant tax and accounting benefits to the executive and the corporation. Tyco's board approved some, but not all, of the forms of compensation Kozlowski had tapped into.

When Congress learned of the level of abuse in corporate loans, it was shocked. In the Sarbanes-Oxley Act of 2002, Congress forbid public companies to make or even arrange new loans to executives or to modify or renew old ones. The penalties for a violation are up to 20 years in jail and fines reaching $5 million for executives and $25 million for companies.

Sources: Ashlea Ebeling, "The Lending Game," *Forbes* (May 10, 2004), and Anthony Bianco, William Symonds, Nanette Byrnes, and David Polek, "The Rise and Fall of Dennis Kozlowski," *Business Week* (December 12, 2002).

costs, the supply of skilled workers, and the frequency of employee turnover. Additionally, the presence of labor contracts and legislation such as the Occupational Safety and Health Act may also affect the auditor's assessment of inherent risk. Because the payroll system and its related accounts generally contain few inherent risks, the auditor is normally able to set the inherent risk as low. However, inherent risk associated with officer compensation is frequently not set at low because, as illustrated in Exhibit 12–1, officers may have motive and opportunity to take advantage of their high-ranking offices in the form of excessive compensation.

Control Risk Assessment

[LO 7]   The discussion of control risk assessment follows the framework outlined in previous chapters. However, the discussion is not as thorough as the discussion of the revenue or purchasing processes because it is assumed that the reader has now developed a reasonable understanding of the decision process followed by the auditor when setting control risk. Figure 12–2 summarizes the three major steps involved in setting control risk for the human resource management process.

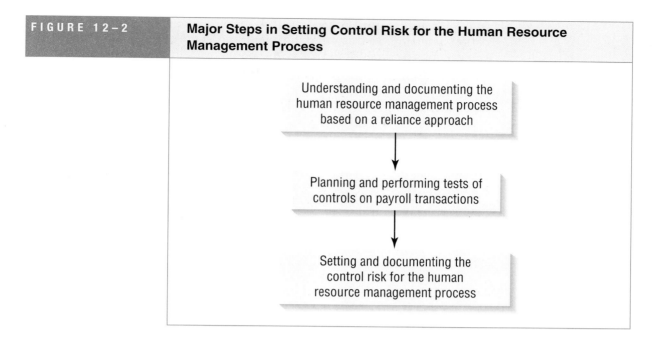

FIGURE 12–2   **Major Steps in Setting Control Risk for the Human Resource Management Process**

Understanding and Documenting Internal Control

The level of understanding of the five internal control components should be similar to that obtained for the other processes. The auditor's under-standing of the human resources management process is normally gained by conducting a walkthrough of the system to gather evidence about the various functions that are involved in processing the transactions through the system. For an ongoing audit, this process merely involves updating prior years' documentation of the payroll system by noting any changes that have occurred. For a new engagement, or if the system has undergone ma-jor changes, more time and effort are needed to document the understand-ing of internal control. The auditor's understanding of internal control for the payroll system should be documented in the working papers using flow-charts, internal control questionnaires, and memoranda.

Because the control environment pervasively affects all accounting ap-plications, including the payroll system, two factors shown in Table 6–5 in Chapter 6 should be considered. First, the entity's organizational structure, its personnel practices, and its methods of assigning authority and respon-sibility must be examined. The proper organizational structure for process-ing payroll transactions was discussed in the previous section. Second, the entity should have sound policies for hiring, training, promoting, and com-pensating employees. These policies should include specific authority and responsibility for hiring and firing employees, for setting wage rates and making salary changes, and for establishing benefits.

Planning and Performing Tests of Controls

When a reliance strategy is followed, the auditor must identify the control procedures that ensure that material misstatements are either prevented or detected and corrected. For example, the client may have formal procedures for classifying payroll costs in appropriate accounts. The auditor may decide to rely on this control procedure to reduce the control risk for the classification assertion. In this case, the client's procedures for classifying payroll transactions by types of payroll costs should be examined by the auditor.

Setting and Documenting the Control Risk

After the tests of controls are completed, the auditor sets the level of control risk and documents that assessment. The documentation supporting the achieved level of control risk for the payroll system might include a flowchart, the results of tests of controls, and a memorandum indicating the overall conclusion about control risk.

Control Procedures and Tests of Controls— Payroll Transactions

[LO 8]

Table 12–5 summarizes the assertions and possible misstatements for payroll transactions. The table also includes key control procedures for each assertion and examples of tests of controls that can test the effectiveness of the control procedures. The discussion that follows focuses only on the most important assertions for the payroll system. EarthWear's payroll system contains all of the relevant control procedures.

Occurrence of Payroll Transactions

The auditor wants assurance that payments for payroll-related services are being made to valid employees for time actually worked. Thus, the client needs control procedures that prevent payments to fictitious employees and to valid employees who have not worked. Controls must also ensure that payroll payments stop once an employee is terminated. Proper segregation of duties provides the main control against payments to fictitious employees. As noted in Table 12–4, proper segregation of duties among operating and supporting departments, the human resources department, and the payroll department minimizes the possibility of fictitious employees existing within the system. The maintenance of adequate personnel files should also prevent such misstatements.

The human resources department approves the termination of an employee and ensures that he or she is removed from the master payroll file. Required completion and approval of a time card also prevent payments to terminated employees. Proper review and approval of time cards by supervisors should prevent valid employees from being paid for work not performed.

Finally, when payroll transactions are processed by an IT system, a payroll check should not be prepared unless the employee transaction has a valid employee number. Review and observation are the main tests of controls the auditor uses to examine the control procedures shown in Table 12–5.

Authorization of Payroll Transactions

As in the discussion of the authorization assertion for other accounting applications, there are key authorization points within the payroll system. The client should have authorization procedures for hiring and terminating employees, setting pay rates, making withholdings, awarding benefits, and issuing payroll checks. For example, the department supervisor should approve the amount of time reported by an employee on his or her time card. Similarly, hiring and termination of employees and changes in pay

TABLE 12-5	Summary of Assertions, Possible Misstatements, Control Procedures, and Tests of Controls for Payroll Transactions		
Assertion	*Possible Misstatement*	*Control Procedure*	*Test of Controls*
Occurrence	Payments made to fictitious employees	Segregation of duties	Observe and evaluate proper segregation of duties.
	Payments made to terminated employees	Adequate personnel files	Review and test personnel files.
	Payments made to valid employees who have not worked	Initiation of changes in employment status, wages or salaries, and benefits made by operating departments reported to the office of human resources	Review and test client's procedures for changing employees' records; if IT application, examine application controls.
		Time clocks used to record time	Observe employees' use of time clock.
		Time cards approved by supervisors	Inspect time cards presented for approval by supervisor.
		Only employees with valid employee numbers paid	Review and test client's procedures for entering and removing employee numbers from the payroll master file; if IT application, examine application controls.
		Use of payroll budgets with review by department supervisors	Review client's budgeting procedures.
Completeness	Employee services provided but not recorded	Prenumbered time cards accounted for by client personnel	Check numerical sequence of time cards; if IT application, examine application controls.
Authorization	Unauthorized payments made to employees	Authorization procedures for	Review and test authorization procedures for each point of authorization in the payroll cycle; if IT application, examine application controls.
	Payments made to employees at a rate in excess of authorized amount or for unauthorized employee benefits	• Hiring and terminating employees • Time worked • Wage, salary, and commission rates • Withholdings • Benefits • Issuing payroll check	
Accuracy	Employee compensation and payroll deductions computed incorrectly	Verification of payroll amounts and benefit calculations	Review and test client's verification procedures; if IT application, examine application controls.
		Review of payroll register for unusual amounts	If IT-prepared, use computer-assisted audit techniques to test computer program logic for calculating amounts.
		Use of payroll budgets with review by department supervisors	Review client's budgeting procedures.
	Payroll transactions not posted correctly to the payroll journal	Changes to master payroll file verified through "before and after" reports	Examine reconciliation of "before and after" reports to payroll master file; if IT application, examine application controls.
	Amounts from payroll journal not posted correctly to general ledger	Payroll master file (payroll register) reconciled to general ledger payroll accounts	Review reconciliation of payroll master file to general ledger payroll accounts; if IT application, examine application controls.
Cutoff	Payroll transactions recorded in the wrong period	Notices of additions, terminations, and changes to salaries, wages, and deductions reported promptly to the payroll processing function, after which the changes are updated promptly on the master payroll file	Review and test client's procedures for changes to master payroll file; if IT application, examine application controls.

(continued)

TABLE 12–5	Summary of Assertions, Possible Misstatements, Control Procedures, and Tests of Controls for Payroll Transactions *(concluded)*		
Assertion	*Possible Misstatement*	*Control Procedure*	*Test of Controls*
		All time cards forwarded to the payroll department weekly	Review and test procedures for processing time cards.
		Procedures that require recording payroll liabilities as soon as possible after they are incurred	Review and test procedures for recording payroll liabilities.
Classification	Payroll transactions not properly classified	Chart of accounts	Review chart of accounts.
		Independent approval and review of accounts charged for payroll	Review and test procedures for classifying payroll costs.
		Use of payroll budgets with review by department supervisors	Review client's budgeting procedures.

rates should be authorized by the human resource department consistent with union contracts or corporate policies. Last, a payroll check should not be issued unless an employee's time card has been approved and that employee has a valid employee number on the payroll master file.

Accuracy of Payroll Transactions

The main concern related to the accuracy assertion is that an employee's gross pay and payroll deductions may be incorrectly computed. For example, an employee may be paid at a higher rate than authorized or payroll deductions may be incorrectly computed. The client should maintain verification procedures to ensure correct payroll and benefit calculations. The auditor can review the client's verification procedures as a test of control. When IT is used to prepare the payroll, the auditor can use computer-assisted audit techniques (CAATs) to test the program logic for proper calculations. In a manual system, or if a service bureau is used, the auditor can recompute the payroll calculations for a sample of payroll transactions.

Classification of Payroll Transactions

Because classification is an important assertion for payroll transactions, control procedures must ensure that the appropriate payroll accounts are charged. If payroll expense is charged to the wrong accounts, the financial statements may be misstated. For example, if payroll expense is not properly classified between direct and indirect labor, inventory and cost of goods sold may not be valued properly. The use of an adequate chart of accounts is one control procedure that helps to prevent misclassification. Additionally, the timekeeping function should review the payroll categories assigned by the operating departments. Budgets that compare actual payroll costs to budgeted payroll costs by each category of labor also provide a control over proper classification of payroll. The auditor can review and test the client's control procedures for classifying payroll costs.

Relating the Assessed Level of Control Risk to Substantive Procedures

[LO 9] If the results of the tests of controls for the payroll system support the planned level of control risk, the auditor conducts substantive procedures of payroll-related accounts at the assessed level. EarthWear, for example, has a strong set of control procedures for processing payroll transactions. If the auditor's tests of EarthWear's controls indicate that the controls are operating effectively, then no adjustment of detection risk is necessary. However, if the results of the control tests do not support the planned level of control risk for EarthWear's payroll system, the detection risk will have to be set lower. This would require that the nature and extent of substantive testing of payroll-related accounts be increased.

Auditing Payroll-Related Accounts

Two categories of substantive procedures for auditing payroll expense and payroll-related liabilities are discussed here: (1) substantive analytical procedures and (2) tests of details of classes of transactions, account balances, and disclosures. Table 12–6 presents the assertions for classes of transactions, events, account balances, and disclosures as they apply to payroll expense and payroll-related liabilities, which are often called *accrued payroll expenses*. You should note that the auditor may test assertions related to transactions (substantive tests of transactions) in conjunction with testing

TABLE 12–6	**Assertions about Classes of Transactions, Events, Account Balances, and Disclosures for Payroll Expense and Payroll-Related Accruals**

Assertions about Classes of Transactions and Events:
- **Occurrence.** Payroll transactions and events are valid.
- **Completeness.** All payroll transactions and events have been recorded.
- **Authorization.** All payroll transactions and events are properly authorized.
- **Accuracy.** Payroll transactions have been properly computed, and payroll expense has been properly accumulated from journals and ledgers.
- **Cutoff.** Payroll expense and related accruals are recorded in the correct accounting period.
- **Classification.** Payroll expense and related accruals have been recorded in the proper accounts.

Assertions about Account Balances at the Period End:
- **Existence.** Payroll expense is a valid expense and related accruals are valid liabilities.
- **Rights and obligations.** The payroll-related accruals are the obligations of the entity.
- **Completeness.** All payroll expense and related accruals have been recorded.
- **Valuation and allocation.** Payroll expense and related accruals are included in the financial statements at appropriate amounts, and any resulting valuation or allocation adjustments are appropriately recorded.

Assertions about Presentation and Disclosure:
- **Occurrence and rights and obligations.** All disclosed events, transactions, and other matters relating to payroll expense and related accruals have occurred and pertain to the entity.
- **Completeness.** All disclosures relating to payroll expense and related accruals that should have been included in the financial statements have been included.
- **Classification and understandability.** Financial information relating to payroll expense and related accruals is appropriately presented and described, and disclosures are clearly expressed.
- **Accuracy and valuation.** Financial and other information relating to payroll expense and related accruals are disclosed fairly and at appropriate amounts.

TABLE 12–7	Substantive Analytical Procedures for Auditing Payroll Accounts and Payroll-Related Accruals
Substantive Analytical Procedure	*Possible Misstatement Detected*
Payroll Expense Accounts	
Compare current-year balances in the various payroll expense accounts with prior years' balances after adjustment for pay changes and number of employees.	Over- or understatement of payroll expense.
Compare payroll costs as a percentage of sales with prior years' and industry data.	Over- or understatement of payroll expense.
Compare labor utilization rates and statistics with industry data.	Over- or understatement of payroll expense.
Compare budgeted payroll expenses with actual payroll expenses.	Over- or understatement of payroll expense.
Estimate sales commissions by applying commission formulas to recorded sales totals.	Over- or understatement of sales commissions.
Payroll-Related Accrual Accounts	
Compare current-year balances in payroll-related accrual accounts with prior years' balances after adjusting for changes in conditions.	Over- or understatement of accrued liabilities.
Test reasonableness of accrual balances.	Over- or understatement of accrued liabilities.

the internal controls. If the tests of controls indicate that the controls are not operating effectively, the auditor may need to test transactions at the date the account balance is tested.

Substantive Analytical Procedures

[LO 10]   Substantive analytical procedures can be useful substantive tests for examining the reasonableness of payroll expenses and payroll-related accrual accounts. When utilized as part of planning, preliminary analytical procedures can effectively identify payroll expense accounts and accrual accounts that may be misstated. Table 12–7 shows examples of substantive analytical procedures that can be used for auditing payroll. Two examples will help demonstrate their application in practice. First, the auditor can compare budgeted payroll costs with actual payroll costs. Variances due to quantity and wage differences should show up in the client's cost-accounting system (on weekly or monthly reports). If the variances are immaterial, the auditor has some evidence that payroll costs are reasonable. If the variances are material, the auditor should investigate the potential causes of the differences. This substantive analytical procedure also helps the auditor to determine the proper valuation of inventory when standard costs are used to value inventory. Second, the auditor can test the reasonableness of certain accrual balances. For example, if accrued wages represent payroll for two days, the auditor can multiply the total weekly payroll by 40 percent (2 days ÷ 5 days). If the auditor's calculation is close to the accrued amount, no further audit work may be required on the accrued wages account.

Tests of Details of Classes of Transactions, Account Balances, and Disclosures

[LO 11,12]   Table 12–6 presents the assertions for payroll expense and payroll-related liabilities. The intended purpose of tests of details of transactions is to detect monetary misstatements in the individual transactions processed through the payroll application. As previously mentioned, tests of details of transactions

TABLE 12–8	Examples of Payroll Tests of Transactions, Account Balances, and Disclosures

Assertions about Classes of Transactions	Substantive Tests of Transaction
Occurrence	Trace a sample of payroll checks to the master employee list to verify validity.*
Completeness	Tracing of a sample of time cards to the payroll register.*
Authorization	Test a sample of payroll checks for the presence of an authorized time card.*
Accuracy	Recompute the mathematical accuracy of a sample of payroll checks: CAATS may be used to test the logic of the computer programs for proper calculation of gross pay, deductions, and net pay.
Cutoff	Trace a sample of time cards before and after period end to the appropriate weekly payroll report, and trace the weekly payroll report to the general ledger to verify payroll transactions are recorded in the proper period.*
Classification	Examine a sample of payroll checks for proper classification into expense accounts.*

Assertions about Account Balances at Period End	Tests of Details of Account Balances
Existence	Vouch selected amounts from the account analysis schedules for the accruals to supporting documentation (payroll tax returns, corporate benefit policies, etc.).
Rights and obligations	Review supporting documentation to determine that the entity is legally obligated to pay the liability. Test a sample of bank reconciliations for the payroll bank account (see Chapter 16).
Completeness	Search for unrecorded liabilities (see Chapter 11). Use CAATs to foot weekly payroll reports and reconcile the total to the general ledger (payroll expense and related accruals).
Valuation and allocation	Obtain an account analysis schedule for accrued payroll liabilities; foot schedules and agree total to general ledger. Compare amounts accrued to supporting documentation, such as payroll tax returns.

Assertions about Presentation and Disclosure	Tests of Details of Disclosures
Occurrence, and rights and obligations	Inquire about accruals to ensure that they are properly disclosed.
Completeness	Complete financial reporting checklist to ensure that all financial statement disclosures related to payroll expense and related accruals have been made.
Classification and understandability	Review accrued payroll liabilities for proper classification between short-term and long-term liabilities. Read footnotes to ensure that required disclosures are understandable.
Accuracy and valuation	Review benefit contracts for proper disclosure of pension and postretirement benefits. Read footnotes and other information to ensure that the information is accurate and properly presented at the appropriate amounts.

* These tests of details of transactions are commonly conducted as dual-purpose tests (i.e., in conjunction with tests of controls).

are often conducted in conjunction with tests of controls. Table 12–8 presents examples of tests of details of transactions, account balances, and disclosures for assertions related to payroll. The discussion that follows focuses on tests of details of account balances of payroll expense and accrued payroll liabilities.

EXHIBIT 12–2	**Questionable Salary Payments at Lincoln Savings and Loan**

One of the most notorious cases noted during the savings-and-loan debacle was Lincoln Savings and Loan. In 1978 Charles Keating, Jr., founded American Continental Corporation (ACC), which acquired Lincoln six years later. In 1989 the Federal Home Loan Bank Board seized control of Lincoln Savings and Loan. The closing of Lincoln cost U.S. taxpayers approximately $2 billion. Exercising his ownership powers over Lincoln, Keating installed his son, Charles Keating III, as chairman of the board at an annual salary of $1 million. An examination report on ACC indicated that "funds sent by Lincoln to ACC were being used by ACC to fund treasury stock transactions [and] pay debt service, consulting fees, and exorbitant management salaries." The report estimated that $34 million had been expended on "Keating family benefits."

Source: The People, Plaintiff and Respondent, v. *Charles H. Keating, Jr., Defendant and Appellant* (31 Cal., App. 4th 1688, 1993).

Payroll Expense Accounts

Payroll transactions affect many expense accounts, including direct and indirect manufacturing expense, general and administrative salaries, sales salaries, commissions, and payroll tax expenses. Some companies account for such expenses by product line or division. In addition, fringe benefits such as medical and life insurance may be paid at least partly by the organization. If the entity's internal control is reliable, the auditor generally does not need to conduct detailed tests of these payroll expense accounts. On such audits, sufficient evidence can be gathered through an understanding of internal control, tests of controls, tests of details of transactions, and substantive analytical procedures. Additional testing is necessary only when control weaknesses exist or when the other types of audit tests indicate that material misstatements may be present.

Several payroll expense accounts may still be examined even when control risk is low. For example, it is common to verify the compensation paid to officers of the company because information on executive salaries and bonuses is needed for the 10K form, proxy statements, and the federal tax return. Limits may also be placed on officers' salaries and bonuses as part of lending agreements. If such limits are exceeded, the entity may be in default on the debt. Officers' compensation is also examined because as noted earlier officers are in a position to override the control procedures and pay themselves more than they are authorized to receive (see Exhibit 12–2). Officers' compensation expense can be verified by comparing the amounts shown in the payroll records with the amounts authorized in either board of directors' minutes or employment contracts and by using CAATS to search for other cash payments made to the officer, his or her family, or related parties.

Accrued Payroll Liabilities

An entity incurs a number of payroll-related liabilities. In addition to these accrued expenses, the entity also withholds various amounts from an employee's pay. These withholdings include payroll taxes (federal and state income taxes and FICA), medical and life insurance premiums, pension, and other miscellaneous deductions. Some examples of accrued payroll liabilities include

- Accrued wages and salaries.
- Accrued payroll taxes.
- Accrued commissions.
- Accrued bonuses.
- Accrued benefits such as vacation and sick pay.

In auditing accrued payroll liabilities, the auditor is concerned mainly with five audit assertions: *existence, completeness, valuation, cutoff,* and the *presentation and disclosure completeness* assertion. When control risk is low or the amounts in the accounts are relatively small, the auditor can verify accrued payroll liabilities using substantive analytical procedures. For example, the auditor can compare the prior year's balance in each accrual with the current year's balance after considering changing conditions.

For accrued payroll liability accounts for which the control risk is high or whose amounts are material, the auditor can obtain a detailed account analysis schedule. For example, Exhibit 12–3 shows an account analysis schedule for EarthWear's accrued payroll taxes. The credits to the account represent the recognition of payroll tax expense at the end of each pay period. These amounts can be traced to the various payroll tax returns or other documentation filed by the entity and should agree with the amount of payroll tax expense included in the income statement. The debits to the account represent payments made to relevant government agencies. These payments can be verified by tracing the amounts to the cash disbursements journal.

EXHIBIT 12–3	**Account Analysis for Accrued Payroll Taxes Account**

N25
DLJ
2/15/06

EARTHWEAR CLOTHIERS
Analysis of Accrued Payroll Taxes
12/31/05

Disbursements for payment of payroll taxes	$253,275£	Beginning balance	$216,950φ
		Weekly accruals for payroll tax expense	253,540✔
		Ending balance	$217,215λL
			F

F = Footed.
φ = Traced to prior year's working papers.
L = Agreed to general ledger.
✔ = Traced three weeks' (2/15, 4/20, and 9/30) payroll expense accruals to weekly payroll records.
£ = Traced three payments of payroll taxes to the cash disbursements journal.
λ = Recomputed amount of unpaid payroll taxes for two weeks at the end of December 2005.

An interesting aspect of this type of accrual account is that it periodically "clears out" the accrued amount. For example, if the client has to make payments for payroll taxes to the government on the 15th of each month, the accrued payroll taxes account will have a zero balance after the payment. Thus, at the end of any month, the accrued payroll taxes account should contain only an accrual for payroll taxes since the last payment (approximately two weeks). In many organizations, these costs are broken down into the various types of payroll taxes (employer's FICA and federal and state unemployment taxes).

Cutoff

The auditor also wants to determine whether all payroll-related liabilities are recorded in the proper period. An examination of supporting documentation for the accruals provides evidence on the proper period for recording the expense or liability. For example, an examination of the client's unemployment tax invoices should allow the auditor to determine if a proper accrual for unemployment tax has been made in the current period.

Existence and Valuation

The existence and valuation assertions can generally be tested at the same time. The auditor's concerns are whether the recorded liabilities are valid obligations of the entity and whether they are included in the financial statements at the appropriate amount. To verify the existence and valuation of an accrued payroll liability, the auditor can generally trace the amounts included on the account analysis working paper to supporting documentation such as payroll tax reports. If adequate documentation is present, the auditor has evidence that the amount represents a valid liability. The auditor can usually verify the accuracy of the amounts by recalculating the figures.

Completeness

The auditor wants to make sure that all payroll-related liabilities are recorded. The auditor should be aware of the normal payroll-related taxes that are paid by the entity and therefore should be able to determine if accruals have been made for payroll taxes such as Social Security taxes and unemployment insurance. In some instances, the auditor's search for unrecorded liabilities, which was discussed in Chapter 11, may provide evidence that all payroll-related liabilities are recorded.

Presentation and Disclosure Completeness Assertion

The auditor must ensure that all necessary financial statement disclosures for the human resource management process are made. Table 12–9 presents examples of items that should be disclosed.

Three accounting standards require substantial disclosure. FASB Nos. 87, 106, and 132 require detailed disclosures of pension costs and postretirement benefits. Although discussion of the audit of these items is beyond the scope of this text, the reader should be aware that such disclosures are important to the fairness of the financial statements. Profit-sharing plans and deferred compensation arrangements also require disclosure in the footnotes.

TABLE 12–9	Sample Disclosure Items for the Human Resource Management Process
	Pension disclosures required by FASB No. 87, 132.
	Postretirement benefit disclosures required by FASB No. 106, 132.
	Profit-sharing plans.
	Deferred compensation arrangements.

Evaluating the Audit Findings—Payroll-Related Accounts

[LO 13]   When the auditor has completed the planned substantive procedures of the payroll-related accounts, all of the identified misstatements should be aggregated. The likely misstatement is compared to the tolerable misstatement allocated to the payroll-related accounts. If the likely misstatement is less than the tolerable misstatement, the auditor may accept the accounts as fairly presented. Conversely, if the likely misstatement exceeds the tolerable misstatement, the auditor should conclude that the accounts are not fairly presented.

For example, in Chapter 3 tolerable misstatement was $885,000. Exhibit 3–5 showed that Willis & Adams detected a misstatement in recording payroll expense and bonuses that amounted to a $215,000 understatement of accrued liabilities. Because this misstatement is less than the tolerable misstatement of $885,000, Willis & Adams can conclude that the audit evidence supports fair presentation. However, if the misstatement was greater than the tolerable misstatement, the evidence would not support fair presentation. In this case the auditor would have two choices: adjust the accounts to reduce the misstatement to an amount less than the tolerable misstatement or qualify the audit report.

The auditor should again analyze the misstatements discovered through the application of substantive procedures because these misstatements may provide additional evidence on the control risk for the payroll system. If the auditor concludes that the audit risk is unacceptably high, additional audit procedures should be performed, or the auditor must be satisfied that the client has adjusted the payroll-related financial statement accounts to an acceptable level. For example, suppose the auditor's substantive analytical procedures indicate that commissions expense is overstated. The auditor might perform detailed computations of commissions expense or request that the client adjust the account by the amount of the estimated misstatement.

KEY TERMS

Analytical procedures. Evaluations of financial information made by a study of plausible relationships among both financial and nonfinancial data.

Application controls. Controls that apply to the processing of specific computer applications and are part of the computer programs used in the accounting system.

Assertions. Expressed or implied representations by management that are reflected in the financial statement components.

General controls. Controls that relate to the overall information-processing environment and have a pervasive effect on the entity's computer operations.

Reliance strategy. The auditor's decision to rely on the entity's controls, test those controls, and reduce the direct tests of the financial statement accounts.

Tests of controls. Procedures that evaluate the effectiveness of the design and operation of internal controls.

Tests of details of account balances and disclosures. Tests that concentrate on the details of amounts contained in an account balance and disclosures.

Tests of details of transactions. Tests to detect errors or fraud in individual transactions.

www.mhhe.com/ messier4e	Visit the book's Online Learning Center for a multiple-choice quiz that will allow you to assess your understanding of chapter concepts.

REVIEW QUESTIONS

[LO 1]   12-1   Why is the payroll system of most entities computerized?

[2]   12-2   What are the major types of transactions that occur in the payroll system? What financial statement accounts are affected by each of these types of transactions?

[3]   12-3   Briefly describe each of the following documents or records: payroll register, payroll master file, and payroll master file changes report.

[4]   12-4   What duties are performed within the personnel, timekeeping, and payroll-processing functions?

[5]   12-5   List the key segregation of duties in the human resource management process. What errors or fraud can occur if such duties are not segregated?

[7,8]   12-6   Discuss the two control environment factors that an auditor should consider when examining the human resource management process.

[8]   12-7   What are the key authorization points in a payroll system?

[8]   12-8   Why is it important for the client to establish control procedures over the classification of payroll transactions?

[6]   12-9   List the inherent risk factors that affect the human resource management process.

[8,11]   12-10   Identify two tests of controls or tests of details of transactions that can be performed using CAATs for payroll transactions.

[10]   12-11   List two substantive analytical procedures that can be used to test payroll expense accounts and payroll-related liabilities.

[12]   12-12   Discuss how an auditor would audit the accrued payroll taxes account.

[12]   12-13   Identify three possible disclosure issues for payroll expense and payroll-related liabilities.

MULTIPLE-CHOICE QUESTIONS

[3,8]   12-14   Matthews Corporation has changed from a system of recording time worked on clock cards to a computerized payroll system in which employees record time in and out with magnetic cards. The IT system automatically updates all payroll records. Because of this change,
   a. A generalized computer audit program must be used.
   b. Part of the audit trail is altered.
   c. The potential for payroll-related fraud is diminished.
   d. Transactions must be processed in batches.

[3,5,8]   12-15   Which of the following procedures would most likely be considered a weakness in an entity's internal controls over payroll?
   a. A voucher for the amount of the payroll is prepared in the general accounting department based on the payroll department's payroll summary.
   b. Payroll checks are prepared by the payroll department and signed by the treasurer.
   c. The employee who distributes payroll checks returns unclaimed payroll checks to the payroll department.
   d. The personnel department sends employees' termination notices to the payroll department.

[4,5,8]   12-16   In meeting the control objective of safeguarding of assets, which department should be responsible for the following?

	Distribution of Paychecks	Custody of Unclaimed Paychecks
a.	Treasurer	Treasurer
b.	Payroll	Treasurer
c.	Treasurer	Payroll
d.	Payroll	Payroll

[5]   12-17   For an appropriate segregation of duties, journalizing and posting summary payroll transactions should be assigned to
   a. The treasurer's department.
   b. General accounting.
   c. Payroll accounting.
   d. The timekeeping department.

[5]   12-18   The purpose of segregating the duties of hiring personnel and distributing payroll checks is to separate the
   a. Human resource function from the controllership function.
   b. Administrative controls from the internal accounting controls.
   c. Authorization of transactions from the custody-related assets.
   d. Operational responsibility from the record-keeping responsibility.

[8]   12-19   An auditor who is testing IT controls in a payroll system would most likely use test data that contain conditions such as

a. Deductions *not* authorized by employees.

b. Overtime *not* approved by supervisors.

c. Time cards with invalid job numbers.

d. Payroll checks with unauthorized signatures.

[8]   12-20   In a computerized payroll system environment, an auditor would be *least* likely to use test data to test controls related to

a. Missing employee numbers.

b. Proper approval of overtime by supervisors.

c. Time cards with invalid job numbers.

d. Agreement of hours per clock cards with hours on time cards.

[8]   12-21   If a control total was computed on each of the following data items, which would best be identified as a hash total for a payroll IT application?

a. Total debits and total credits.

b. Net pay.

c. Department numbers.

d. Hours worked.

[8]   12-22   Effective control procedures over the payroll function may include

a. Reconciliation of totals on job time cards with job reports by employees responsible for those specific jobs.

b. Verification of agreement of job time cards with employee clock card hours by a payroll department employee.

c. Preparation of payroll transaction journal entries by an employee who reports to the supervisor of the personnel department.

d. Custody of rate authorization records by the supervisor of the payroll department.

[9,12]   12-23   An auditor is most likely to perform substantive tests of details on payroll transactions and balances when

a. Cutoff tests indicate a substantial amount of accrued payroll expense.

b. The level of control risk relative to payroll transactions is set at low.

c. Substantive analytical procedures indicate unusual fluctuations in recurring payroll entries.

d. Accrued payroll expense consists primarily of unpaid commissions.

PROBLEMS

[4,5,8]   12-24   Brownstein, CPA, has been engaged to audit the financial statements of Young Computer Outlets, Inc., a new client. Young is a privately owned chain of retail stores that sells a variety of computer software and video products. Young uses an in-house payroll department at its corporate headquarters to compute payroll data and to prepare and distribute payroll checks to its 300 salaried employees.

Brownstein is preparing an internal control questionnaire to assist in obtaining an understanding of Young's internal control and in setting control risk.

Required:
Prepare a "Payroll" segment of Brownstein's internal control questionnaire that would assist in obtaining an understanding of Young's internal control and in setting control risk. Do *not* prepare questions relating to cash payroll, IT applications, or payments based on hourly rates, piecework, commissions, employee benefits (pensions, health care, vacations, and so on), or payroll tax accruals other than withholdings. Use the following format:

Internal Control Question	Yes	No
Are paychecks prenumbered and accounted for?		

(AICPA, adapted)

[5,7,8]   12-25   A CPA's audit documentation (working papers) contains a narrative description of a *segment* of the Croyden Factory, Inc., payroll system and an accompanying flowchart as follows.

Narrative
The internal control system with respect to the personnel department functions well and is *not* included in the accompanying flowchart.

At the beginning of each workweek, payroll clerk 1 reviews the payroll department files to determine the employment status of factory employees and then prepares time cards and distributes them as each individual arrives at work. This payroll clerk, who is also responsible for custody of the signature stamp machine, verifies the identity of each payee before delivering signed checks to the foreman.

At the end of each workweek, the foreman distributes the payroll checks for the preceding workweek. Concurrent with this activity, the foreman reviews the current week's employee time cards, notes the regular and overtime hours worked on a summary form, and initials the time cards. The foreman then delivers all time cards and unclaimed payroll checks to payroll clerk 2.

Required:
a. Based on the narrative and the flowchart on the next page, what are the weaknesses in internal control?
b. Based on the narrative and the accompanying flowchart, what inquiries should be made to clarify possible additional weaknesses in internal control? Do *not* discuss the internal control system of the personnel department.

(AICPA, adapted)

[10,11,12]   12-26   McCarthy, CPA, was engaged to audit the financial statements of Kent Company, a continuing audit client. McCarthy is about to audit Kent's payroll transactions. Kent uses an in-house payroll department to process payroll data and to prepare and distribute payroll checks.

During the planning process, McCarthy determined that the inherent risk of overstatement of payroll expense is high. In addition, McCarthy obtained an understanding of internal control and set the control risk for payroll-related assertions at the maximum level.

Croyden, Inc., Factory Payroll System

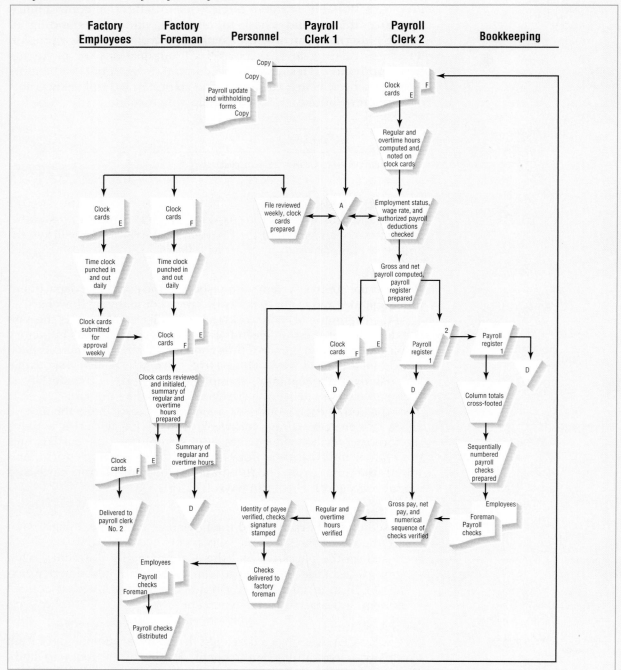

Required:
Describe the audit procedures McCarthy should consider performing in the audit of Kent's payroll transactions to address the risk of overstatement. Do *not* discuss Kent's internal control.

(AICPA, adapted)

[10,11,12]   12-27   James, who was engaged to examine the financial statements of Talbert Corporation, is about to audit payroll. Talbert uses a computer service center to process weekly payroll as follows.

Each Monday Talbert's payroll clerk inserts data in appropriate spaces on the preprinted service center–prepared input form and sends it to the service center via messenger. The service center extracts new permanent data from the input form and updates its master files. The weekly payroll data are then processed. The weekly payroll register and payroll checks are printed and delivered by messenger to Talbert on Thursday.

Part of the sample selected for audit by James includes the following input form and payroll register:

Required:

a. Describe how James should verify the information in the payroll input form shown.

b. Describe (but do not perform) the procedures that James should follow in examining the November 24, 2005, payroll register shown.

(AICPA, adapted)

TALBERT CORPORATION
Payroll Input
Week Ending Friday, November 24, 2005

| | | Employee Data—Permanent File | | | Current Week's Payroll Data | | | | |
| | | | | | Hours | | Special Deductions | | |
	Name	Social Security Number	W-4 Information	Hourly Rate	Regular	Overtime	Bonds	Union	Other
A.	Bell	999-99-9991	M-1	$10.00	35	5	$18.75		
B.	Carioso	999-99-9992	M-2	10.00	35	4			
C.	Deng	999-99-9993	S-1	10.00	35	6	18.75	$4.00	
D.	Ellis	999-99-9994	S-1	10.00	35	2		4.00	$50.00
E.	Flaherty	999-99-9995	M-4	10.00	35	1		4.00	
F.	Gillis	999-99-9996	M-4	10.00	35			4.00	
G.	Hua	999-99-9997	M-1	7.00	35	2	18.75	4.00	
H.	Jones	999-99-9998	M-2	7.00	35			4.00	25.00
I.	King	999-99-9999	S-1	7.00	35	4		4.00	
	New Employee:								
J.	Smith	999-99-9990	M-3	7.00	35				

TALBERT CORPORATION
Payroll Register
November 24, 2005

Employee	Social Security Number	Hours Regular	Hours Overtime	Payroll Regular	Payroll Overtime	Gross Payroll	FICA	Federal	State	Other Withheld	Net Pay	Check Number
A. Bell	999-99-9991	35	5	$ 350.00	$ 75.00	$ 425.00	$ 26.05	$ 76.00	$ 27.40	$ 18.75	$ 276.80	1499
B. Carioso	999-99-9992	35	4	350.00	60.00	410.00	25.13	65.00	23.60		296.27	1500
C. Deng	999-99-9993	35	6	350.00	90.00	440.00	26.97	100.90	28.60	22.75	260.78	1501
D. Ellis	999-99-9994	35	2	350.00	30.00	380.00	23.29	80.50	21.70	54.00	200.51	1502
E. Flaherty	999-99-9995	35	1	350.00	15.00	365.00	22.37	43.50	15.90	4.00	279.23	1503
F. Gillis	999-99-9996	35		350.00		350.00	21.46	41.40	15.00	4.00	268.14	1504
G. Hua	999-99-9997	35	2	245.00	21.00	266.00	16.31	34.80	10.90	22.75	181.24	1505
H. Jones	999-99-9998	35		245.00		245.00	15.02	26.40	8.70	29.00	165.88	1506
I. King	999-99-9999	35	4	245.00	42.00	287.00	17.59	49.40	12.20	4.00	203.81	1507
J. Smith	999-99-9990	35		245.00		245.00	15.02	23.00	7.80		199.18	1508
Total		350	24	$3,080.00	$333.00	$3,413.00	$209.21	$540.90	$171.80	$159.25	$2,331.84	

DISCUSSION CASES

[7,8,9]   12-28   Service Corporation hired an independent computer programmer to develop a simplified payroll application for its newly purchased computer. The programmer developed an online database micro-computer system that minimized the level of knowledge required of the operator. It was based on typing answers to input cues that appeared on the terminal's viewing screen, examples of which follow:

A. Access routine:
  1. Operator access number to payroll file?
  2. Are there new employees?
B. New employee routine:
  1. Employee name?
  2. Employee number?
  3. Social Security number?
  4. Rate per hour?
  5. Single or married?
  6. Number of dependents?
  7. Account distribution?
C. Current payroll routine:
  1. Employee number?
  2. Regular hours worked?
  3. Overtime hours worked?
  4. Total employees this payroll period?

The independent auditor is attempting to verify that certain input validation (edit) checks exist to ensure that errors resulting from omissions, invalid entries, or other inaccuracies are detected during the typing of answers to the input cues.

Required:
a. Discuss the various types of input validation (edit) controls that the independent auditor would expect to find in the IT system.
b. Describe the assurances provided by each identified validation check.

(AICPA, adapted)

[6,10,12]   12-29   Executive compensation ballooned in the 1990s, and as highlighted in Exhibit 12–1, there were notable compensation abuses. The most popular form of executive compensation in the 1990s was company stock (or options to purchase stock). Designers of these compensation plans argue that by compensating officers with stock, the officers will take actions in the best interest of the shareholders. Critics claim executive compensation is often too high in proportion to average salaries at companies and that the compensation levels motivate officers to take selfish actions.

Required:
a. Research executive compensation of some well-known companies. (You can find executive compensation in SEC filings on EDGAR at www.sec.gov or on a variety of Internet sites, such as eComp www.ecomponline.com). Use your best judgment to

compute the proportion of executive compensation to average salary (i.e., are executives earning 5 times, or 10 times, or 100 times the average employee). In your opinion, are the executives worth it?

b. In your opinion, what are the costs and benefits associated with compensating executives with stock or options to purchase stock?

c. What do you believe are the most effective audit procedures to use to test for executive compensation abuse or fraud? Please explain why.

INTERNET ASSIGNMENT

[11,12]   12-30   Using an Internet browser, search for information on labor costs in the retail catalog industry (for example, labor costs as a percentage of sales).

www.mhhe.com/ messier4e	Visit the book's Online Learning Center for problem material to be completed using the *ACL* software packaged with your new text.

CHAPTER 13

LEARNING OBJECTIVES

Upon completion of this chapter you will

[1] Develop an understanding of the inventory management process.

[2] Identify and describe the types of documents and records used in the inventory management process.

[3] Understand the functions in the inventory management process.

[4] Know the appropriate segregation of duties for the inventory management process.

[5] Identify and evaluate inherent risks relevant to the inventory management process.

[6] Assess control risk for the inventory system.

[7] Identify key internal controls and develop relevant tests of controls for inventory transactions.

[8] Relate the assessment of control risk to substantive procedures.

[9] Identify substantive analytical procedures used to audit inventory and related accounts.

[10] Know how to audit standard costs.

[11] Know how to observe physical inventory.

[12] Identify tests of details of transactions used to audit inventory and related accounts.

[13] Identify tests of details of account balances used to audit inventory and related accounts.

[14] Evaluate the audit findings and reach a final conclusion on inventory and related accounts.

RELEVANT ACCOUNTING AND AUDITING PRONOUNCEMENTS

FASB Statement of Financial Accounting Concepts No. 5, Recognition and Measurement in Financial Statements of Business Enterprises (CON5)

FASB Statement of Financial Accounting Concepts No. 6, Elements of Financial Statements (CON6)

AU 312, Audit Risk and Materiality in Conducting an Audit

AU 316, Consideration of Fraud in a Financial Statement Audit

AU 319, Consideration of Internal Control in a Financial Statement Audit

AU 329, Analytical Procedures

AU 330, The Confirmation Process

AU 331, Receivables and Inventory

AU 336, Using the Work of a Specialist

AU 339, Audit Documentation

AU 342, Auditing Accounting Estimates

AICPA Auditing Standards Board, Exposure Draft, "Understanding the Entity and Its Environment and Assessing the Risks of Material Misstatement"

AICPA Auditing Standards Board, Exposure Draft, "Audit Evidence"

AICPA Auditing Standards Board, Exposure Draft, "Performing Audit Procedures in Response to Assessed Risks and Evaluating the Audit Evidence Obtained"

Auditing the Inventory Management Process

Major Phases of an Audit

Client acceptance/
continuance
and establishing
engagement terms
(Chapter 5)

Preplanning
(Chapter 5)

Establish materiality
and assess risks
(Chapter 3)

Plan the audit
(Chapters 3 and 5)

Consider and audit
internal control
(Chapters 6 and 7)

Audit business processes
and related accounts
(e.g., revenue generation)
(Chapters 10–16)

Complete the audit
(Chapter 17)

Evaluate results and issue audit
report (Chapters 2 and 18)

For most manufacturing, wholesale, and merchandising (retail) entities, inventory is a major component of the balance sheet. Inventory also represents one of the most complex parts of the audit. For example, while determining the quantity of inventory on hand is usually an easy audit step to complete, assigning costs to value those quantities is more difficult. Additionally, there may be other troublesome valuation issues related to inventory such as obsolescence and lower-of-cost-or-market value.

The complexity of auditing inventory may also be affected by the degree of processing required to manufacture products. In a merchandising business, products are purchased directly from vendors with little or no additional processing by the entity before sale. In such cases, verifying inventory is relatively straightforward. On the other hand, determining a proper inventory value may be more difficult when the production process involves numerous steps. The presentation in this chapter mainly discusses inventory in terms of a merchandising company. However, the audit approach followed for merchandising entities is easily adapted to other types of inventory processes.

The coverage of the inventory management process follows the three components of the audit risk model. An overview of the inventory management process is presented first, followed by discussion of inherent risk factors and control risk assessment. While the main focus of this chapter is auditing the inventory management process for a financial statement audit, the concepts covered for setting control risk are applicable to an audit of internal control over financial reporting for public companies under the Sarbanes-Oxley Act of 2002. The last part of the chapter discusses the substantive procedures for inventory with particular emphasis on auditing standard costs and observing physical inventory.

Overview of the Inventory Management Process

[LO 1]   The inventory management process is affected by the control procedures previously discussed for the revenue, purchasing, and payroll processes. Figure 13–1 shows how each of these processes interacts with the inventory management process. The acquisition of and payment for inventory are controlled via the purchasing process. The cost of both direct and indirect labor assigned to inventory is controlled through the payroll process. Last, finished goods are sold and accounted for as part of the revenue process. Thus, the "cradle-to-grave" cycle for inventory begins when goods are purchased and stored and ends when the finished goods are shipped to customers.

Exhibit 13–1 describes EarthWear's inventory system, while Figure 13–2 flowcharts the system. This description and flowchart provide a framework for discussing the control procedures and tests of controls for the inventory management process in more detail. However, because of differences in products and their subsequent processing, the inventory system usually differs from one entity to the next. The reader should concentrate on understanding the basic concepts of internal control. The following topics related to the inventory management process are discussed:

- Types of documents and records.
- The major functions.
- The key segregation of duties.

Types of Documents and Records

Table 13–1 lists the more important documents and records that are normally involved in the inventory system. Not all of these documents are presented in Figure 13–2. They are discussed here to give the reader information on documents and records that might exist in an inventory management process of a

FIGURE 13–1	The Relationship of the Inventory Management Process to Other Accounting Processes

EXHIBIT 13–1	Description of EarthWear's Inventory System

EarthWear Clothing and other products sold by EarthWear are developed by the company's design department. All goods are produced by independent manufacturers, except for most of EarthWear's soft luggage. The company purchases merchandise from more than 200 domestic and foreign manufacturers. For many major suppliers, goods are ordered and paid for through the company's electronic data interchange (EDI) system. The computerized inventory control system handles the receipt of shipments from manufacturers. Goods are received at the receiving department, where the information is agreed to the purchase order (receiving report) and entered into the inventory control system.

The company's sales representatives enter orders into an online order entry and inventory control system; customers using the company's Internet site complete a computer screen that enters the orders. Computer processing of orders is performed each night on a batch basis, at which time shipping tickets are printed with bar codes for optical scanning. Inventory is picked based on the location of individual products rather than orders, followed by computerized sorting and transporting of goods to multiple packing stations and shipping zones.

⚹ **[LO 2]** manufacturing company. The reader should keep in mind that in an advanced IT system some of these documents and records may exist for only a short time or only in machine-readable form.

Production Schedule

A production schedule is normally prepared periodically based on the expected demand for the entity's products. The expected demand may be based on the current backlog of orders or on sales forecasts from the sales or marketing department. In EarthWear's system, this schedule is prepared by the design department. Production schedules determine the quantity of goods needed and the time at which they must be ready in order to meet the production scheduling. Many organizations use material requirements planning or just-in-time inventory programs to assist with production planning. Production schedules give the auditor information on the planned level of operating activity.

Receiving Report

The receiving report records the receipt of goods from vendors. This document was discussed as part of the purchasing process. It is reconsidered in the inventory management process because a copy of this document accompanies the goods to the inventory department and is used to update the client's perpetual inventory records. Note in

TABLE 13–1	Documents and Records Included in the Inventory Management Process

Production schedule.
Receiving report.
Materials requisition.
Inventory master file.
Production data information.
Cost accumulation and variance report.
Inventory status report.
Shipping order.

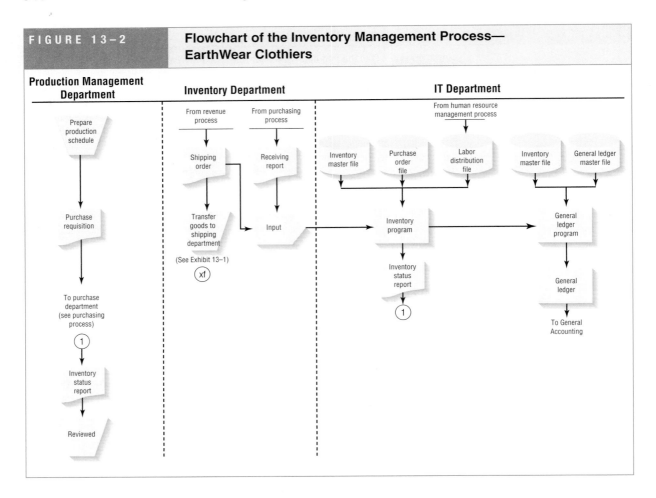

FIGURE 13-2   **Flowchart of the Inventory Management Process—EarthWear Clothiers**

Figure 13–2 that the data from the receiving report are input into the inventory program to update the inventory master file, which contains the information on the client's perpetual records.

Materials Requisition   Materials requisitions are normally used by manufacturing companies to track materials during the production process. Materials requisitions are normally prepared by department personnel as needed for production purposes. For example, the materials requisition is the document that authorizes the release of raw materials from the raw materials department. A copy of the materials requisition may be maintained in the raw materials department, and another copy may accompany the goods to the production departments.

Inventory Master File   The inventory master file contains all the important information related to the entity's inventory, including the perpetual inventory records. In sophisticated inventory systems such as EarthWear's, the inventory master file also contains information on the costs used to value inventory. In a manufacturing company, it would not be unusual for the inventory master file to contain the standard costs used to value the inventory at various stages of production.

Production Data Information

In a manufacturing company, production information about the transfer of goods and related cost accumulation at each stage of production should be reported. This information updates the entity's perpetual inventory system. It is also used as input to generate the cost accumulation and variance reports that are produced by the inventory system.

Cost Accumulation and Variance Report

Most inventory control systems in a manufacturing setting produce reports similar to a cost accumulation and variance report. Material, labor, and overhead costs are charged to inventory as part of the manufacturing process. The cost accumulation report summarizes the various costs charged to departments and products. The variance reports present the results of inventory processing in terms of actual costs versus standard or budgeted costs. The cost accounting and manufacturing departments review these reports for appropriate charges.

Inventory Status Report

The inventory status report shows the type and amount of products on hand. Such a report is basically a summary of the perpetual inventory records. This report can also be used to determine the status of goods in process. In sophisticated inventory systems, this type of information can be accessed directly through computer terminals or PCs.

Shipping Order

This document was discussed as part of the revenue process. It is reconsidered here because a copy of this document is used to remove goods from the client's perpetual inventory records. Note in Figure 13–2 that the inventory master file is updated when open orders are processed and a shipping order is generated.

The Major Functions

Table 13–2 summarizes the functions that normally take place in a typical inventory management process.

TABLE 13–2	Functions in the Inventory Management Process
Inventory management	Authorization of production activity and maintenance of inventory at appropriate levels; issuance of purchase requisitions to the purchasing department (see Chapter 11 on the purchasing process).
Raw materials stores	Custody of raw materials and issuance of raw materials to manufacturing departments.
Manufacturing	Production of goods.
Finished goods stores	Custody of finished goods and issuance of goods to the shipping department (see Chapter 10 on the revenue process).
Cost accounting	Maintenance of the costs of manufacturing and inventory in cost records.
General ledger	Proper accumulation, classification, and summarization of inventory and related costs in the general ledger.

[LO 3] **Inventory Management**   At EarthWear, the inventory management function is performed by the design department. This department is responsible for maintaining inventory at appropriate levels. It issues purchase requisitions to the purchasing department and thus represents the point at which the inventory management process integrates with the purchasing process. In a manufacturing company, a production management department would be responsible for managing inventory through planning and scheduling manufacturing activities.

Raw Materials Stores   In a manufacturing company, this function is responsible for the receipt, custody, and issuance of raw materials. When goods are received from vendors, they are transferred from the receiving department to the raw materials stores department. Once goods arrive in the raw materials storage area, they must be safeguarded against pilferage or unauthorized use. Finally, when goods are requested for production through the issuance of a materials requisition, this function issues the goods to the appropriate manufacturing department.

Manufacturing   The manufacturing function is responsible for producing the product. From an auditing perspective, there must be adequate control over the physical flow of the goods and proper accumulation of the costs attached to inventory. The manner in which costs are accumulated varies substantially from one entity to another. Entities may produce goods using a job order cost system, a process cost system, or some combination of both.

Finished Goods Stores   This function is responsible for the storage of and control over finished goods. When goods are completed by the manufacturing function, they are transferred to finished goods stores. Again, there must be adequate safeguards against pilferage or unauthorized use. When goods are ordered by a customer, a shipping order is produced by the revenue process and forwarded to the finished goods stores department. The goods are then transferred to the shipping department for shipment to

TABLE 13–3	Key Segregation of Duties in the Inventory Management Process and Possible Errors or Fraud
Segregation of Duties	*Possible Errors or Fraud Resulting from Conflicts of Duties*
The inventory management function should be segregated from the cost-accounting function.	If the individual responsible for inventory management also has access to the cost-accounting records, production and inventory costs can be manipulated. This may lead to an over- or understatement of inventory and net income.
The inventory stores function should be segregated from the cost-accounting function.	If one individual is responsible for both controlling and accounting for inventory, unauthorized shipments can be made or theft of goods can be covered up.
The cost-accounting function should be segregated from the general ledger function.	If one individual is responsible for the inventory records and also for the general ledger, it is possible for that individual to conceal unauthorized shipments. This can result in the theft of goods, leading to an overstatement of inventory.
The responsibility for supervising physical inventory should be separated from the inventory management and inventory stores functions.	If the individual responsible for production management or inventory stores function is also responsible for the physical inventory, it is possible that inventory shortages can be covered up through the adjustment of the inventory records to the physical inventory, resulting in an overstatement of inventory.

TABLE 13–4	**Segregation of Duties for Inventory Functions by Department**				
	Department				
Inventory Function	*Inventory Management*	*Raw Materials Stores*	*Finished Goods Stores*	*Cost Accounting*	*IT*
Preparation of production schedules	X				
Issuance of materials requisitions that accompany goods to the manufacturing department		X			
Updating of cost records with materials, labor, and overhead usage				X	X
Updating of inventory records				X	X
Release of goods to the shipping department			X		
Approval and issuance of purchase requisitions	X				

the customer. Because EarthWear is a merchandising company, it maintains only finished goods (see Figure 13–2).

Cost Accounting   This function is responsible for ensuring that costs are properly attached to inventory as goods are processed through the manufacturing function. Cost accounting reviews the cost accumulation and variance reports after such data are processed into the accounting records.

General Ledger   The main objective of the general ledger function is to ensure that all inventory and costs of production are properly accumulated, classified, and summarized in the general ledger accounts. In an IT system, control or summary totals ensure that this function is performed correctly. One important control performed by the general ledger function is the reconciliation of the perpetual inventory records to the general ledger inventory accounts.

The Key
Segregation
of Duties

※ [LO 4]

Segregation of duties is a particularly important control in the inventory management process because of the potential for theft and fraud. Therefore, individuals involved in the inventory management and inventory stores functions should not have access to the inventory records, the cost-accounting records, or the general ledger. When the inventory system is highly computerized, there should be proper segregation of duties within the IT department. Table 13–3 shows the key segregation of duties for the inventory management process and examples of possible errors or fraud that can result from conflicts in duties. Table 13–4 shows the proper segregation of duties for individual inventory functions across the various departments that control inventory processing.

Inherent Risk Assessment

※ [LO 5]   In examining the inventory management process, the auditor needs to consider the inherent risk factors that may affect the transactions processed by the system and the financial statement accounts affected by those transactions. The auditor should consider industry-related factors and operating and engagement characteristics (see Chapter 3) when assessing the possibility of a material misstatement.

EXHIBIT 13–2	**Digital Cameras Sink Polaroid**

Polaroid, the once high-flying company, filed for Chapter 11 bankruptcy in October 2001 after it was unable to meet payments on its heavy debt load. In August, the company's auditors, KPMG LLP, raised issue with the company's ability to continue as a going concern. The company, founded by Edward H. Land, was once one of the world's leading photography companies. Its main product was instant color film that developed when exposed to light. However, since 1995, Polaroid had faced stiff competition from one-hour photo shops and, more recently, from digital cameras. Polaroid was unable to restructure its debt or find a buyer for the company prior to seeking bankruptcy protection. In the years immediately before and after the bankruptcy, Polaroid recorded write-offs of tens of millions of dollars for obsolete inventory.

Sources: J. Bandler, "Polaroid Sustains Latest Setback as Auditor Questions Its Future," *The Wall Street Journal* (August 10, 2001), and J. Bandler and M. Pacelle, "Polaroid is Using Chapter 11 to Seek Buyer," *The Wall Street Journal* (October 15, 2001).

Industry-Related Factors

A number of industry factors may indicate the presence of material misstatements in inventory. For example, if industry competition is intense, there may be problems with the proper valuation of inventory in terms of lower-of-cost-or-market values. Technology changes in certain industries may also promote material misstatement due to obsolescence (see Exhibit 13–2).

Engagement and Operating Characteristics

A number of engagement and operating characteristics are important to the assessment of inherent risk for inventory. First, the type of product sold by the client can increase the potential for defalcation. For example, products that are small and of high value, such as jewelry, are more susceptible to theft than large products are. Second, inventory is often difficult to audit, and its valuation may result in disagreements with the client. Finally, the auditor must be alert to possible related-party transactions for acquiring raw materials and selling finished product. For example, the client may purchase raw materials from a company controlled by the chief executive officer at prices in excess of market value. In such a case, the value of inventory will be overstated, and cash will have been misappropriated from the entity.

Audit research has also shown that there is a relatively high risk that inventory contains material misstatements.[1] In fact, some of the most notorious accounting frauds in history have involved inventory manipulations. For example, in the 1990s fraudsters at *Phar-Mor,* a discount store retail chain, recorded a debit to a fraud holding account rather than to cost of goods sold when inventory was sold. Then just before year-end, Phar-Mor accountants emptied the contents of the fraud holding account and allocated it to stores as fictitious inventory (see the *Advanced Module* in Chapter 20 for a detailed description of the Phar-Mor fraud and related trial). Exhibit 13–3 describes the inventory fraud at Centennial Technologies, Inc.

Prior-year misstatements are good indicators of potential misstatements in the current year; thus, auditors should carefully consider if misstatements

---

[1]A. Eilifsen and W. F. Messier, Jr., "Auditor Detection of Misstatements: A Review and Integration of Empirical Research," *Journal of Accounting Literature* 2000 (19), pp. 1–43.

EXHIBIT 13–3	Inventory Scams at Centennial Technologies

Background

Centennial Technologies designed, manufactured, and marketed an extensive line of PC cards: rugged, lightweight, credit card–sized devices inserted into a dedicated slot in a broad range of electronic equipment that contain microprocessors, such as portable computers, telecommunications equipment, and manufacturing equipment. The company's customer list included companies such as Digital Equipment Corporation, Philips Electronics, Sharp Electronics Corporation, and Xerox Corporation.

Emanuel Pinez was the CEO of technology highflier Centennial Technologies, Inc., in the mid-1990s. In 1996, Centennial's surging stock graduated to the New York Stock Exchange just two years after going public. It finished 1996 as the best-performing stock on the big board, up a stunning 451 percent. Just before the fraud was uncovered, analysts still had "strong buy" recommendations outstanding.

Pinez had an impressive resume, but it turns out much of it was false. After the scandal broke, investors and the auditors learned what Pinez's wife knew, that he was a "pathological liar." For example, as a young man he claimed to set a world record in an international swimming competition across the English Channel. The reports were published, and Pinez was hailed briefly as a national hero—until the truth came out that there was no such competition or record. Pinez constantly made aggressive estimates regarding Centennial's growth, and in 1996 he began telling investors that Centennial was negotiating an order worth more than $300 million with AT&T (no such deal ever took place or apparently even existed). At about the same time as Pinez was touting the pending sale to AT&T, he was boosting inventory and profits with a variety of accounting scams.

PCMCIA Card Scam

Centennial's growth attracted several sophisticated institutional investors, such as Oppenheimer Funds Inc. and Fidelity Investments. Some investors started to crave a firsthand look at Centennial's operations. One investor sent an analyst to meet with Pinez and tour the headquarters in Billerica, Massachusetts. Although the analyst noticed some computer equipment in the administrative offices, he was somewhat surprised that there was none in Pinez's office. During a tour of Centennial's manufacturing facilities, he saw "a room full of people banging on cards with rubber mallets. I had a bad feeling." He returned to his firm and "dumped the Centennial shares immediately."

In truth, Pinez had enlisted a handful of employees in the company's Billerica manufacturing plant to assemble fake memory cards by simply welding the casings together and leaving out a critical silicon computer chip. These fake cards made their way into inventory and sales. Most of the sales of these cards are alleged to have gone to other companies controlled by Pinez.

Flash 98 Scam

In the fourth quarter of 1996 Centennial began shipping a new product called "Flash 1998." It was a miniature memory card for notebook computers. Sales for fiscal year 1996 amounted to about $2 million. The company told the auditors that it wanted to keep the details of the card relatively quiet for a few more months for competitive reasons. Pinez indicated that due to design advances developed by Centennial's research and development team, these new cards had an extremely low production cost, about 10 cents, with a sales price of a whopping $500. It turns out there was no such product. All sales were to one company, BBC. The company was run by a close personal friend of Pinez. To fool the auditors into thinking an actual sale took place, Pinez wired $1 million of his own personal funds to a third company, St. Jude Management Corp., which then paid Centennial on behalf of BBC for its Flash 98 purchases. The explanation provided for this rather unconventional form of payment was a "financial agreement" between St. Jude and BBC. Even though the check was from St. Jude Management, the $1 million payment was considered reasonable evidence supporting the sale. After the fraud was uncovered, the auditors, Coopers & Lybrand, claimed that the Flash 98 scam was a "unique" fraud because it appeared that a product was going out and cash was coming in.

Aftermath

From his prison cell, Pinez denied any wrongdoing and indicated that his actions were undertaken to benefit the company. Pinez attributed his problems to the scrutiny that inevitably comes with success: "You get lightning when you're very high."

Sources: M. Beasley, F. Buckless, S. Glover, and D. Prawitt. "Auditing Cases: An Interactive Learning Approach," 2d ed. Prentice Hall, 2003, and J. Auerbach, "How Centennial Technologies, a Hot Stock, Cooled," *Wall Street Journal* (April 11, 1997).

found in the prior years' audit may be present in the current inventory and plan the audit accordingly.

Control Risk Assessment

[LO 6]   The auditor may follow a substantive strategy when auditing inventory and cost of goods sold. When this is done, the auditor places no reliance on the control procedures in the inventory management process and sets the level of control risk at the maximum. The auditor then relies on substantive procedures to determine the fairness of inventory. Such a strategy may be appropriate when internal control is not adequate.

In many cases, however, the auditor can rely on internal control for inventory. This normally occurs when the client has an integrated cost-accounting/inventory management system. For discussion purposes, it is assumed that the auditor has decided to follow a reliance strategy. Figure 13–3 summarizes the three steps for setting the control risk following this strategy. Each of these steps is only briefly reviewed within the context of the inventory management process because the reader should thoroughly understand the control risk setting process followed by auditors.

Understanding and Documenting Internal Control

In order to set the control risk for the inventory management process, the auditor must understand the five internal control components. Two points should be mentioned. First, if the client uses sophisticated IT techniques for monitoring the flow of goods and accumulating costs, the auditor will need to evaluate both the general IT controls and the inventory application controls. Second, the auditor will need a thorough understanding of the process used by the client to value inventory.

FIGURE 13–3	Major Steps in Setting the Control Risk in the Inventory Management Process

Understanding and documenting the inventory management process based on a reliance strategy

↓

Planning and performing tests of controls on inventory transactions

↓

Setting and documenting the control risk for the inventory management process

Planning and
Performing Tests
of Controls

In performing this step, the auditor again must identify the relevant control procedures within the client's inventory system that ensure that material misstatements are either prevented or detected and corrected. Audit procedures used to test the client's control procedures in the inventory management process are discussed in subsequent sections.

Setting and
Documenting
the Control Risk

Once the controls in the inventory system have been tested, the auditor sets the level of control risk. The auditor should document the achieved level of control risk using either quantitative amounts or qualitative terms. The documentation supporting the achieved level of control risk for the inventory management process might include a flowchart such as the one shown in Figure 13–2, the results of the tests of controls, and a memorandum indicating the overall conclusions about control risk.

Control Procedures and Tests of Controls— Inventory Transactions

≋ **[LO 7]**   Table 13–5 provides a summary of the possible misstatements, control procedures, and selected tests of controls for inventory transactions. The discussion includes control procedures that are present in a manufacturing setting. Because EarthWear is a retailer, the controls over the production process are not relevant. A number of control procedures in the revenue and purchasing processes provide assurance for selected assertions for inventory. The discussion that follows is limited to the more important assertions.

Occurrence
of Inventory
Transactions

The auditor's main concern is that all recorded inventory exists. The major control procedure for preventing fictitious inventory transactions from being recorded is proper segregation of duties, in which the inventory management and inventory stores functions are separated from the departments responsible for inventory and cost-accounting records. This control prevents operating personnel from having access to both inventory and the perpetual inventory records. Additionally, prenumbered documents to handle the receipt, transfer, and withdrawal of inventory may prevent the recording of fictitious inventory in the accounting records.

The auditor should also be concerned that goods may be stolen. The auditor's concern about theft of goods varies depending upon the type of product sold or manufactured by the client. Products that are large or cumbersome may be difficult to steal. However, some products that are small and of high value, such as jewelry or computer memory chips, may be susceptible to theft. The client should maintain physical safeguards over inventory that are consistent with the susceptibility and value of the goods.

Review and observation are the main tests of controls used by the auditor to test the control procedures shown in Table 13–5. For example, the auditor can observe and evaluate the employees' segregation of duties. The auditor can also review and test the client's procedures for the transfer of raw materials from the receiving department and their issuance to the manufacturing departments.

TABLE 13–5	Summary of Assertions, Possible Misstatements, Control Procedures, and Tests of Controls for Inventory Transactions		
Assertion	*Possible Misstatement*	*Control Procedure*	*Test of Controls*
Occurrence	Fictitious inventory	Segregation of duties	Observe and evaluate proper segregation of duties.
		Inventory transferred to inventory department using an approved, prenumbered receiving report	Review and test procedures for the transfer of inventory.
		Inventory transferred to manufacturing using prenumbered materials requisitions	Review and test procedures for issuing materials to manufacturing departments.
		Accounting for numerical sequence of materials requisitions	Review and test client procedures for accounting for numerical sequence of materials requisitions.
	Inventory recorded but not on hand due to theft	Physical safeguards over inventory	Observe the physical safeguards over inventory.
Completeness	Inventory received but not recorded	The same as the control procedures for completeness in the purchasing process (see Table 11–6)	The same as the tests of controls performed on the control procedures in the purchasing process (see Table 11–6).
	Consigned goods not properly accounted for	Procedures to include goods out on consignment and exclude goods held on consignment	Review and test client's procedures for consignment goods.
Authorization	Unauthorized production activity, resulting in excess levels of inventory	Preparation and review of authorized purchase or production schedules	Review authorized production schedules.
	Inventory obsolescence	Use of material requirements planning and/or just-in-time inventory systems	Review and test procedures for developing inventory levels and procedures used to control them.
		Review of inventory levels by design department	
Accuracy	Inventory quantities recorded incorrectly	Periodic or annual comparison of goods on hand with amounts shown in perpetual inventory records	Review and test procedures for taking physical inventory.
	Inventory and cost of goods sold not properly costed	Standard costs that are reviewed by management	Review and test procedures used to develop standard costs.
		Review of cost accumulation and variance reports	Review and test cost accumulation and variance reports.
	Inventory obsolescence	Inventory management personnel review inventory for obsolete, slow-moving, or excess quantities	Review and test procedures for identifying obsolete, slow-moving, or excess quantities.
	Inventory transactions not posted to the perpetual inventory records	Perpetual inventory records reconciled to general ledger control account monthly	Review the reconciliation of perpetual inventory to general ledger control account.
	Amounts for inventory from purchases journal not posted correctly to the general ledger inventory account		
Cutoff	Inventory transactions recorded in the wrong period	All receiving reports processed daily by the IT department to record the receipt of inventory	Review and test procedures for processing inventory included on receiving reports into the perpetual records.
		All shipping documents processed daily to record the shipment of finished goods	Review and test procedures for removing inventory from perpetual records based on shipment of goods.
Classification	Inventory transactions not properly classified among raw materials, work in process, and finished goods	Materials requisitions and production data forms used to process goods through manufacturing	Review the procedures and forms used to classify inventory.

Completeness of Inventory Transactions

The control procedures for the completeness assertion relate to recording inventory that has been received. Typically, the control procedures for this assertion are contained within the purchasing process. These control procedures and the related tests of controls were presented in Table 11–6 in Chapter 11. For example, in some instances, additional control procedures may be used in the raw materials stores department to ensure that the goods are recorded in the perpetual inventory records. This might include comparing a summary of the receiving reports to the inventory status report.

If goods are consigned, the client must have control procedures to ensure that goods held on consignment by other parties are included in inventory and goods held on consignment for others are excluded from inventory. The auditor can review the client's procedures for including or excluding consigned goods.

Authorization of Inventory Transactions

The control procedures for the purchase of materials were discussed in Chapter 11 on the purchasing process. The auditor's concern with authorization in the inventory system is with unauthorized purchase or production activity that may lead to excess levels of certain types of finished goods. If such goods can quickly become obsolete, ending inventory may be overstated. The preparation and review of authorized purchase schedules by EarthWear's design department should prevent such misstatements. The use of some type of inventory-planning system, such as a material requirements planning system or a just-in-time inventory system, may also limit unauthorized production.

Accuracy of Inventory Transactions

Accuracy is an important assertion because inventory transactions that are not properly recorded result in misstatements that directly affect the amounts reported in the financial statements for cost of goods sold and inventory. The accurate processing of inventory purchase transactions involves applying the correct price to the actual quantity received. Similarly, when inventory is shipped, accurate processing requires that the actual number of items shipped be removed from inventory and that the proper cost be recorded to cost of goods sold. The use of a perpetual inventory system in conjunction with a periodic or annual physical inventory count should result in the proper quantities of inventory being shown in the client's perpetual inventory records. EarthWear maintains the purchase cost of its products in its master inventory file. Many manufacturing companies use standard costing systems to value their inventory. Standard costs should approximate actual costs, and the presence of large variances is one signal that the inventory may not be costed at an appropriate value. Auditing the client's physical inventory and standard costs is discussed in more detail later in the chapter.

Accurate valuation also considers inventory obsolescence. Inventory management personnel should periodically review inventory on hand for obsolete, slow-moving, or excess inventory. Such inventory should be written down to its fair market value. The auditor can review the client's procedures for identifying obsolete, slow-moving, or excess inventory. EarthWear's design department closely monitors its products to identify any end-of-season merchandise or overstocks, which are then sold at liquidation prices through special catalog inserts.

Classification
of Inventory
Transactions

Classification is not an important assertion for EarthWear because all goods are finished and ready for sale. However, in a manufacturing company, the client must have control procedures to ensure that inventory is properly classified as raw materials, work in process, or finished goods. This can usually be accomplished by determining which departments in the manufacturing process are included in raw materials, work in process, and finished goods inventory. Thus, by knowing which manufacturing department holds the inventory, the client is able to classify it by type.

Relating the Assessed Level of Control Risk to Substantive Procedures

[LO 8]   The same judgment process is followed in setting control risk in the inventory management process that was used with other processes. For example, EarthWear has strong controls over the processing of inventory transactions. The auditor can rely on those controls if tests of controls indicate that the controls are operating effectively. If the results of the tests of controls for the inventory system do not support the planned level of control risk, the auditor would set control risk higher and set detection risk lower. This would lead to increased substantive procedures.

TABLE 13–6	Assertions about Classes of Transactions, Events, Account Balances, and Disclosures for Inventory

Assertions about Classes of Transactions and Events:
- **Occurrence.** Inventory transactions and events are valid.
- **Completeness.** All inventory transactions and events have been recorded.
- **Authorization.** All inventory transactions and events are properly authorized.
- **Accuracy.** Inventory transactions have been properly computed, and ending inventory and related revenue and cost of good sold have been properly accumulated from journals and ledgers.
- **Cutoff.** Inventory receipts and shipments are recorded in the correct accounting period.
- **Classification.** Inventory is recorded in the proper accounts (e.g., raw materials, work in process, or finished goods).

Assertions about Account Balances at the Period End:
- **Existence.** Inventory recorded on the books and records actually exists.
- **Rights and obligations.** The entity has the legal right (i.e., ownership) to the recorded inventory.
- **Completeness.** All inventory is recorded.
- **Valuation and allocation.** Inventory is properly recorded in accordance with GAAP (e.g., lower of cost or market).

Assertions about Presentation and Disclosure:
- **Occurrence and rights and obligations.** All disclosed events, transactions, and other matters relating to inventory have occurred and pertain to the entity.
- **Completeness.** All disclosures relating to inventory that should have been included in the financial statements have been included.
- **Classification and understandability.** Financial information relating to inventory is appropriately presented and described, and disclosures are clearly expressed.
- **Accuracy and valuation.** Financial and other information relating to inventory are disclosed fairly and at appropriate amounts.

Auditing Inventory

The discussion of the audit of inventory follows the process outlined in prior chapters. Two categories of substantive procedures are discussed: substantive analytical procedures and tests of details of classes of transactions, account balances, and disclosures. Table 13–6 presents the assertions for classes of transactions, events, account balances, and disclosures as they apply to inventory. You should note that the auditor may test assertions related to transactions (substantive tests of transactions) in conjunction with testing the internal controls. If the tests of controls indicate that the controls are not operating effectively, the auditor may need to test transactions at the date the account balance is tested.

Substantive Analytical Procedures

☞ **[LO 9]** Substantive analytical procedures are useful audit tests for examining the reasonableness of inventory and cost of goods sold. When performed as part of audit planning, preliminary analytical procedures can effectively identify whether the inventory and cost of goods sold accounts contain material misstatements. Final analytical procedures are useful as an overall review for inventory and related accounts to identify obsolete, slow-moving, and excess inventory. Substantive analytical procedures are useful for testing the valuation assertion for inventory. Such tests can also identify problems with improper inclusion or exclusion of costs in overhead. Table 13–7 lists substantive analytical procedures that are useful in auditing inventory and related accounts at either the planning stage or as an overall review.

For example, the inventory turnover ratio (cost of goods sold ÷ inventory) can be compared over time or to an industry average. A high inventory turnover ratio normally indicates efficient inventory policies, while a low ratio may indicate the presence of slow-moving or obsolete inventory. The gross profit percentage can also be compared to previous years' or industry data and may provide valuable evidence on unrecorded inventory (an understatement) or fictitious inventory (an overstatement). This ratio may also provide information on the proper valuation of inventory. For example, a small or negative gross profit margin may indicate issues related to the

TABLE 13–7	Substantive Analytical Procedures for Inventory and Related Accounts
Substantive Analytical Procedure	*Possible Misstatement Detected*
Compare raw material, finished goods, and total inventory turnover to previous years' and industry averages.	Obsolete, slow-moving, or excess inventory
Compare days outstanding in inventory to previous years' and industry average.	Obsolete, slow-moving, or excess inventory
Compare gross profit percentage by product line with previous years' and industry data.	Unrecorded or fictitious inventory
Compare actual cost of goods sold to budgeted amounts.	Over- or understated inventory
Compare current-year standard costs with prior years' after considering current conditions.	Over- or understated inventory
Compare actual manufacturing overhead costs with budgeted or standard manufacturing overhead costs.	Inclusion or exclusion of overhead costs

lower-of-cost-or-market valuation of inventory. It is important that the auditor use sufficiently disaggregated analytical procedures in order to identify unusual patterns like the one illustrated in Figure 5–4, in Chapter 5.

Prior to presenting the tests of account balances for inventory, this chapter discusses two significant audit procedures: auditing standard costs and observing physical inventory.

Auditing Standard Costs

꙰ [LO 10]   Many manufacturing entities use a standard cost system to measure performance and to value inventory. If a standard cost system is integrated with the general accounting records, cost accumulation and variance reports are direct outputs of the client's inventory-accounting system.

For accuracy and proper valuation, standard costs should approximate actual costs. To test the standard costs, the auditor should first review the client's policies and procedures for constructing standard costs. Once the policies and procedures are understood, the auditor normally tests the component cost buildup for a representative sample of standard product costs.

Three components make up the cost of producing a product: materials, labor, and overhead. For discussion purposes, suppose that Calabro Paging Services (see Problem 3-32) assembles five types of pagers. Assume further that all parts used in the pagers are purchased from outside vendors. The process followed in auditing the three components that make up the standard costs for a type of pager follows.

Materials

Determining the materials costs requires testing the quantity and type of materials included in the product and the price of the materials. The quantity and type of materials are tested by reviewing the engineering specifications for the product. For example, in the case of pagers, the auditor can obtain a set of engineering specifications that includes a blueprint and a list of materials needed to manufacture a particular pager. The auditor can compare the list of materials with the standard cost documentation used to support the cost accumulation. The prices used on the standard cost documentation can be traced to vendors' invoices as a test of actual costs.

Labor

The determination of labor costs requires evidence about the type and amount of labor needed for production and the labor rate. Following our example, the amount of labor necessary to assemble a pager can be tested by reviewing engineering estimates, which may be based on time-and-motion studies or on historical information. The labor rates for each type of labor necessary to assemble a pager can be tested by examining a schedule of authorized wages. Labor costs included in inventory are often tested in conjunction with payroll expense.

Overhead

The auditor tests overhead costs by reviewing the client's method of overhead allocation for reasonableness, compliance with GAAP, and consistency. The auditor can examine the costs included in overhead to be sure that such costs can appropriately be assigned to the product. The inclusion or exclusion of such costs should be consistent from one period to the next. Using the pager example, the auditor would obtain a listing of expense accounts used to make up the overhead pool of costs. The auditor can compare the actual costs for the period to the budgeted costs. The auditor can also compare the costs included in the current year's listing with those in the prior year's listing.

Observing Physical Inventory

[LO 11]   The auditor's observation of inventory is a generally accepted auditing procedure (AU 331). However, the auditor is not required to observe all inventory, but only inventory that is material. Internal auditors may also observe physical inventory. The primary reason for observing the client's physical inventory is to establish the *existence* of the inventory. The observation of the physical inventory also provides evidence on the *rights and obligations* and *valuation* assertions. Based on the physical inventory count, the client compiles the physical inventory. While the form of compilation may differ among entities, it normally contains a list of the items by type and quantity, the assigned cost for each item, the inventory value for each item, and a total for the inventory.

Prior to the physical count of inventory, the auditor should be familiar with the inventory locations, the major items in inventory, and the client's instructions for counting inventory. During the observation of the physical inventory count, the auditor should do the following:

- Ensure that no production is scheduled. Or, if production is scheduled, ensure that proper controls are established for movement between departments in order to prevent double counting.
- Ensure that there is no movement of goods during the inventory count. If movement is necessary, the auditor and client personnel must ensure that the goods are not double counted and that all goods are counted.
- Make sure that the client's count teams are following the inventory count instructions. If the count teams are not following the instructions, the auditor should notify the client representative in charge of the area.
- Ensure that inventory tags are issued sequentially to individual departments. For many inventory counts, the goods are marked with multicopy inventory tags. The count teams record the type and quantity of inventory on each tag, and one copy of each tag is then used to compile the inventory. If the client uses another method of counting inventory, such as detailed inventory listings or handheld computers, the auditor should obtain copies of the listings or files prior to the start of the inventory count.
- Perform test counts and record a sample of counts in the working papers. This information will be used to test the accuracy and completeness of the client's inventory compilation.
- Obtain tag control information for testing the client's inventory compilation. Tag control information includes documentation of the numerical sequence of all inventory tags and accounting for all used and unused inventory tags. If inventory listings are used by the

client, copies of the listings will accomplish the objective of documenting the entire inventory count.

- Obtain cutoff information, including the number of the last shipping and receiving documents issued on the date of the physical inventory count.
- Observe the condition of the inventory for items that may be obsolete, slow moving, or carried in excess quantities.
- Inquire about goods held on consignment for others or held on a "bill-and-hold" basis. Such items should not be included in the client's inventory. The auditor must also inquire about goods held on consignment for the client. These goods should be included in the inventory count.

If these audit procedures are followed, the auditor has reasonable assurance that a proper inventory count has been taken.

Tests of Details of Classes of Transactions, Account Balances, and Disclosures

[LO 12]   Table 13–6 presents the assertions for inventory. The intended purpose of tests of details of transactions is to detect monetary misstatements in the inventory account. The auditor may conduct tests of details of transactions specifically for inventory. However, because the inventory management process interacts with the revenue, purchasing, and human resource management processes, transactions involving the receipt of goods, shipment of goods, and assignment of labor costs are normally tested as part of those processes. For example, receiving department personnel prepare a receiving report that includes the quantity and type of goods received. The receiving report and vendor invoice are then used to record the accounts payable. If the auditor intends to obtain substantive evidence on the perpetual inventory records, the tests of receipt and shipment of goods can be extended by tracing the transactions into the perpetual inventory records. For example, the receiving report is generally used by the client to record the goods in the perpetual inventory records or inventory master file (see Figure 13–2). The auditor can perform a test of detail of transactions by tracing a sample of receiving reports into the perpetual inventory records. Labor costs can also be traced to individual inventory transactions and into the cost-accounting records.

As previously mentioned, tests of details of transactions are often conducted in conjunction with tests of controls. Table 13–8 presents examples of tests of details of transactions, account balances, and disclosures for assertions related to inventory. The discussion that follows focuses primarily on tests of details of account balances of inventory.

[LO 13]   Table 13–8 summarizes the tests of the inventory account balance for each assertion. Accuracy is discussed first because the auditor must establish that the detailed records that support the inventory account agree with the general ledger account.

Accuracy   Testing the accuracy of inventory requires obtaining a copy of the compilation of the physical inventory that shows inventory quantities and prices.

TABLE 13-8	Examples of Inventory Tests of Transactions, Account Balances, and Disclosures

Assertions about Classes of Transactions	Substantive Tests of Transaction*
Occurrence	Vouch a sample of inventory additions (i.e., purchases) to receiving reports and purchase requisitions.
Completeness	Trace a sample of receiving reports to the inventory records (i.e., master file, status report).
Authorization	Test a sample of inventory shipments to ensure there is an approved shipping ticket and customer sales.
Accuracy	Recompute the mathematical accuracy of a sample of inventory transactions (i.e., price × quantity).
	Audit standard costs or other methods used to price inventory (see discussion in the chapter for the audit procedures used to audit standard costs).
	Trace costs used to price goods in the inventory compilation to standard costs or vendors' invoices.
Cutoff	Trace a sample of time cards before and after period end to the appropriate weekly inventory report, and trace the weekly inventory report to the general ledger to verify inventory transactions are recorded in the proper period.
Classification	Examine a sample of inventory checks for proper classification into expense accounts.

Assertions about Account Balances at Period End	Tests of Details of Account Balances
Existence	Observe count of physical inventory (see discussion in chapter for proper inventory observation procedures)
Rights and obligations	Verify that inventory held on consignment for others is not included in inventory.
	Verify that "bill-and-hold" goods are not included in inventory.
Completeness	Trace test counts and tag control information to the inventory compilation
Valuation and allocation	Obtain a copy of the inventory compilation and agree totals to general ledger.
	Trace test counts and tag control information to the inventory compilation.
	Test mathematical accuracy of extensions and foot the inventory compilation.
	Inquire of management concerning obsolete, slow-moving, or excess inventory.
	Review book-to-physical adjustment for possible misstatements (see Table 13–9).

Assertions about Presentation and Disclosure	Tests of Details of Disclosures
Occurrence, and rights and obligations	Inquire of management and review any loan agreements and board of directors' minutes for any indication that inventory has been pledged or assigned.
	Inquire of management about issues related to warranty obligations.
Completeness	Complete financial reporting checklist to ensure that all financial statement disclosures related to inventory are made.
Classification and understandability	Review inventory compilation for proper classification among raw materials, work in process, and finished goods.
	Read footnotes to ensure that required disclosures are understandable.
Accuracy and valuation	Determine if the cost method is accurately disclosed (e.g., LIFO).
	Inquire of management about issues related to LIFO liquidations.
	Read footnotes and other information to ensure that the information is accurate and properly presented at the appropriate amounts.

* Many of these tests of details of transactions are commonly conducted as dual-purpose tests (i.e., in conjunction with tests of controls).

The inventory compilation is footed, and the mathematical extensions of quantity multiplied by price are tested. Additionally, test counts made by the auditor during the physical inventory and tag control information are traced into the compilation.

Many times the client has adjusted the general ledger inventory balance to agree to the physical inventory amounts (referred to as *book-to-physical adjustment*) before the auditor begins the substantive tests of account balances. If the client has made the book-to-physical adjustment, the totals from the compilation for inventory should agree with the general ledger.

When the client maintains a perpetual inventory system, the totals from the inventory compilation should also be agreed to these records. The auditor can use computer-assisted audit techniques to accomplish these audit steps. For example, the auditor can use a generalized or custom audit software package to trace costs used to price goods in the inventory compilation to standard cost files. The extensions and footing can also be tested at the same time.

Cutoff

In testing the cutoff assertion for inventory, the auditor attempts to determine whether all sales of finished goods and purchases of raw materials are recorded in the proper period. For sales cutoff, the auditor can examine a sample of shipping documents for a few days before and after year-end for recording of inventory shipments in the proper period. For purchases cutoff, the auditor can examine a sample of receiving documents for a few days before and after year-end for recording of inventory purchases in the proper period. Chapters 10 and 11 discuss sales and purchases cutoff.

Existence

Existence is one of the more important assertions for the inventory account. The observation of the physical inventory is the primary audit step used to verify this assertion. If the auditor is satisfied with the client's physical inventory count, the auditor has sufficient, competent evidence on the existence of recorded inventory.

Completeness

The auditor must determine whether all inventory has been included in the inventory compilation and the general ledger inventory account. The tests related to the observation of the physical inventory count provide assurance that all goods on hand are included in inventory. Tracing test counts and tag control information into the inventory compilation provide assurance that the inventory counted during the physical inventory observation is included in the compilation. In some cases, inventory is held on consignment by others or is stored in public warehouses (AU 331). The auditor normally confirms or physically observes such inventory.

Rights and Obligations

The auditor must determine whether the recorded inventory is actually owned by the entity. Two issues related to ownership can arise. First, the auditor must be sure that the inventory on hand belongs to the client. If the client holds inventory on consignment, such inventory should not be included in the physical inventory. Second, in some industries, goods are sold on a "bill-and-hold" basis. In such cases, the goods are treated as a sale but the client holds the goods until the customer needs them. Again, the auditor must be certain that such goods are segregated and not counted at the time of the physical inventory.

Valuation and Allocation

A number of important valuation issues are related to inventory. The first issue relates to the costs used to value the inventory items included in the compilation. When the client, such as EarthWear, purchases inventory, valuation of the inventory can normally be accomplished by vouching the costs to vendors' invoices. When the client uses standard costs, the auditor audits the standard costs as discussed previously. The second valuation issue relates to the lower-of-cost-or-market tests for inventory. The auditor normally performs such tests on large-dollar items or on the client's various product lines. At EarthWear, the auditors would likely perform the lower-of-cost-or-market test on merchandise noted by management for liquidation. A third valuation issue relates to obsolete, slow-moving, or excess inventory. The auditor should ask management about such issues. When these issues exist, the inventory should be written down to its current market value. Finally, the auditor should investigate any large adjustments between the amount of inventory shown in the general ledger account and the amount determined from the physical inventory count (book-to-physical adjustments) for possible misstatements. Table 13–9 presents a list of items that may lead to book-to-physical differences.

Classification and Understandability

The presentation and disclosure assertion of classification of inventory for EarthWear is not an issue because the company sells only finished products. However, in a manufacturing company, the auditor must determine that inventory is properly classified as raw materials, work in process, or finished goods. In most manufacturing companies, proper classification can be achieved by determining which manufacturing processing department has control of the inventory on the date of the physical count. For example, if inventory tags are used to count inventory and they are assigned numerically to departments, classification can be verified at the physical inventory. The auditor can ensure that each department is using the assigned tags. The tag control information by department can be compared to the information on the inventory compilation to ensure that it is properly classified among raw materials, work in process, and finished goods.

Other Presentation and Disclosure Assertions

Several important disclosure issues are related to inventory. Table 13–10 presents some examples of disclosure items for inventory and related accounts. For example, management must disclose the cost method, such as LIFO or FIFO, used to value inventory. Management must also disclose the components (raw materials, work in process, and finished goods) of inventory either

TABLE 13–9	**Possible Causes of Book-to-Physical Differences**
	Inventory cutoff errors.
	Unreported scrap or spoilage.
	Pilferage or theft.

TABLE 13–10	**Examples of Disclosure Items for Inventory and Related Accounts**

Cost method (FIFO, LIFO, retail method).
Components of inventory.
Long-term purchase contracts.
Consigned inventory.
Purchases from related parties.
LIFO liquidations.
Pledged or assigned inventory.
Disclosure of unusual losses from write-downs of inventory or losses on long-term purchase commitments.
Warranty obligations.

EXHIBIT 13–4	**EarthWear's Financial Statement Disclosure for Inventory**

Inventory is stated at the last-in, first-out (LIFO) cost, which is lower than market. If the first-in, first-out method of accounting for inventory had been used, inventory would have been approximately $10.8 million and $13.6 million higher than reported at December 31, 2005 and 2004, respectively.

on the face of the balance sheet or in the footnotes. Finally, if the entity uses LIFO to value inventory and there is a material LIFO liquidation, footnote disclosure is normally required. Exhibit 13–4 presents EarthWear's financial statement disclosure for inventory. Note that the company uses LIFO to value inventory, and it discloses the approximate inventory value if FIFO had been used.

Evaluating the Audit Findings—Inventory

✑ [LO 14]   When the auditor has completed the planned substantive tests of the inventory account, all of the identified misstatements should be aggregated. The likely misstatement is compared to the tolerable misstatement allocated to the inventory account. If the likely misstatement is less than the tolerable misstatement, the auditor may accept the inventory account as fairly presented. Conversely, if the likely misstatement exceeds the tolerable misstatement, the auditor should conclude that the inventory account is not fairly presented.

For example, in Chapter 3, tolerable misstatement was $885,000. Exhibit 3–5 showed that Willis & Adams detected two misstatements in inventory: one that resulted in an overstatement of inventory by $312,500 based on a projection of a sample and one misstatement that understated inventory by $227,450 due to inventory in transit. Because neither of these misstatements is greater than the tolerable misstatement, Willis & Adams can conclude that the audit evidence supports fair presentation. However, if these misstatements, either individually or net, had been greater than the tolerable misstatement, the evidence would not support fair presentation. In this case the auditor would have two choices: adjust the accounts to reduce the misstatement to an amount less than the tolerable misstatement or qualify the audit report.

The auditor should again analyze the misstatements discovered through the application of substantive procedures, because these misstatements may provide additional evidence on the control risk for the inventory management process. If the auditor concludes that the audit risk is unacceptably high, additional audit procedures should be performed, or the auditor must be satisfied that the client has adjusted the related financial statement accounts to an acceptable level.

KEY TERMS

Analytical procedures. Evaluations of financial information made by a study of plausible relationships among both financial and nonfinancial data.

Application controls. Controls that apply to the processing of specific computer applications and are part of the computer programs used in the accounting system.

Assertions. Expressed or implied representations by management that are reflected in the financial statement components.

Computer-assisted audit techniques. Computer programs that allow auditors to test computer files and databases.

General controls. Controls that relate to the overall information-processing environment and have a pervasive effect on the entity's computer operations.

Reliance strategy. The auditor's decision to rely on the entity's controls, test those controls, and reduce the direct tests of the financial statement accounts.

Tests of controls. Procedures that evaluate the effectiveness of the design and operation of internal controls.

Tests of details of account balances and disclosures. Tests that concentrate on the details of amounts contained in an account balance and disclosures.

Tests of details of transactions. Tests to detect errors or fraud in individual transactions.

www.mhhe.com/ messier4e	Visit the book's Online Learning Center for a multiple-choice quiz that will allow you to assess your understanding of chapter concepts.

REVIEW QUESTIONS

[LO 1]   13-1   Why does inventory represent one of the more complex parts of the audit?

[1]   13-2   How does the inventory management process relate to the revenue, purchasing, and payroll processes?

[2]   13-3   Briefly describe each of the following documents or records: production schedule, materials requisition, inventory master file, production data information, and cost accumulation and variance reports.

[3]   13-4   What duties are performed within the inventory management, stores, and cost-accounting functions?

[4]   13-5   List the key segregation of duties in the inventory management process. What errors or fraud can occur if such segregation of duties is not present?

[5]   13-6   List the inherent risk factors that affect the inventory management process.

[6]   13-7   List the major steps in setting control risk in the inventory management process.

[7]   13-8   What control procedures can a client use to prevent unauthorized inventory production?

[9]   13-9   List three substantive analytical procedures that can test the fairness of inventory and related accounts.

[10]   13-10   Describe how an auditor audits standard costs.

[11]   13-11   List the procedures the auditor should perform during the count of the client's physical inventory.

[13]   13-12   What are some possible causes of book-to-physical inventory differences?

[13]   13-13   List five items for inventory and related accounts that may require disclosure.

MULTIPLE-CHOICE QUESTIONS

[1,3]   13-14   The objectives of internal control for an inventory management process are to provide assurance that transactions are properly executed and recorded and that
a. Independent internal verification of activity reports is established.
b. Transfers to the finished goods department are documented by a completed production report and a quality control report.
c. Production orders are prenumbered and signed by a supervisor.
d. Custody of work in process and finished goods is properly maintained.

[2,7]   13-15   Which of the following control procedures would be most likely to assist in reducing the control risk related to the occurrence of manufacturing transactions?
a. Perpetual inventory records are independently compared with goods on hand.
b. Forms used for direct materials requisitions are prenumbered and accounted for.
c. Finished goods are stored in locked limited-access warehouses.
d. Subsidiary ledgers are periodically reconciled with inventory control accounts.

[4,7]   13-16   Which of the following would most likely be an internal control procedure designed to detect errors and fraud concerning the custody of inventory?
a. Periodic reconciliation of work in process with job cost sheets.
b. Segregation of functions between general accounting and cost accounting.
c. Independent comparisons of finished goods records with counts of goods on hand.
d. Approval of inventory journal entries by the storekeeper.

[4,7]   13-17   Independent internal verification of inventory occurs when employ-ees who

    a. Issue raw materials obtain materials requisitions for each issue and prepare daily totals of materials issued.

    b. Compare records of goods on hand with physical quantities do *not* maintain the records or have custody of the inventory.

    c. Obtain receipts for the transfer of completed work to finished goods prepare a completed production report.

    d. Are independent of issuing production orders update records from completed job cost sheets and production cost reports on a timely basis.

[7]   13-18   An auditor's tests of controls over the issuance of raw materials to production would most likely include

    a. Reconciliation of raw materials and work-in-process perpetual inventory records to general ledger balances.

    b. Inquiry of the custodian about the procedures followed when de-fective materials are received from vendors.

    c. Observation that raw materials are stored in secure areas and that storeroom security is supervised by a responsible individual.

    d. Examination of materials requisitions and reperformance of client controls designed to process and record issuances.

[7]   13-19   Which of the following internal control procedures is most likely to address the completeness assertion for inventory?

    a. The work-in-process account is periodically reconciled with sub-sidiary records.

    b. Employees responsible for custody of finished goods do *not* per-form the receiving function.

    c. Receiving reports are prenumbered and periodically reconciled.

    d. There is a separation of duties between payroll department and inventory accounting personnel.

[8,11,13]   13-20   A client maintains perpetual inventory records in both quantities and dollars. If the level of control risk were set at high, an auditor would probably

    a. Insist that the client perform physical counts of inventory items several times during the year.

    b. Apply gross profit tests to ascertain the reasonableness of the physical counts.

    c. Increase the extent of tests of controls of the inventory system.

    d. Request that the client schedule the physical inventory count at the end of the year.

[11]   13-21   After accounting for a sequence of inventory tags, an auditor traces a sample of tags to the physical inventory listing to obtain evidence that all items

    a. Included in the listing have been counted.

    b. Represented by inventory tags are included in the listing.

    c. Included in the listing are represented by inventory tags.

    d. Represented by inventory tags are bona fide.

[11,13]   13-22   When auditing merchandise inventory at year-end, the auditor per-forms a purchase cutoff test to obtain evidence that

    a. All goods purchased before year-end are received before the phys-ical inventory count.

b. No goods held on consignment for customers are included in the inventory balance.

c. No goods observed during the physical count are pledged or sold.

d. All goods owned at year-end are included in the inventory balance.

[11,13]   13-23   Inquiries of warehouse personnel concerning possibly obsolete or slow-moving inventory items provide assurance about management's assertion of

a. Completeness.

b. Existence.

c. Presentation.

d. Valuation.

[11,13]   13-24   Periodic or cycle counts of selected inventory items are made at various times during the year rather than via a single inventory count at year-end. Which of the following is necessary if the auditor plans to observe inventory at interim dates?

a. Complete recounts are performed by independent teams.

b. Perpetual inventory records are maintained.

c. Unit cost records are integrated with production-accounting records.

d. Inventory balances are rarely at low levels.

[13]   13-25   An auditor using audit software would probably be *least* interested in which of the following fields in a computerized perpetual inventory file?

a. Economic order quantity.

b. Warehouse location.

c. Date of last purchase.

d. Quantity sold.

[13]   13-26   Which of the following audit procedures would probably provide the most reliable evidence concerning the entity's assertion of rights and obligations related to inventory?

a. Tracing of test counts noted during the entity's physical count to the entity's summarization of quantities.

b. Inspection of agreements to determine whether any inventory is pledged as collateral or subject to any liens.

c. Selection of the last few shipping advices used before the physical count and determination of whether the shipments were recorded as sales.

d. Inspection of the open-purchase-order file for significant commitments that should be considered for disclosure.

PROBLEMS

[1,3,7]   13-27   Yardley, CPA, prepared the flowchart on page 564, which portrays the raw materials purchasing function of one of Yardley's clients, a medium-size manufacturing company, from the preparation of initial documents through the vouching of invoices for payment. The flowchart represents a portion of the work performed on the audit engagement to evaluate internal control.

Required:
Identify and explain the control weaknesses evident from the flow-chart. Include the internal control weaknesses resulting from activities performed or not performed. All documents are prenumbered.

(AICPA, adapted)

[1,6,11,13]   13-28   Rasch is the partner-in-charge of the audit of Bonner Distributing Corporation, a wholesaler that owns one warehouse containing 80 percent of its inventory. Rasch is reviewing the working papers that were prepared to support the firm's opinion on Bonner's financial statements, and Rasch wants to be certain that essential audit tests are well documented.

Required:
a. What evidence should Rasch find in the working papers to support the fact that the audit was adequately planned and the assistants were properly supervised?
b. What substantive tests should Rasch expect to find in the working papers to document management's assertion about completeness as it relates to the inventory quantities at the end of the year?

(AICPA, adapted)

[11]   13-29   Abbott Corporation does not conduct a complete annual physical count of purchased parts and supplies in its principal warehouse but instead uses statistical sampling to estimate the year-end inventory. Abbott maintains a perpetual inventory record of parts and supplies and believes that statistical sampling is highly effective in determining inventory values and is sufficiently reliable to make a physical count of each item of inventory unnecessary.

Required:
a. Identify the audit procedures that should be used by the independent auditor that change, or are in addition to, normal required audit procedures when a client utilizes statistical sampling to determine inventory value and does not conduct a 100 percent annual physical count of inventory items.
b. List at least 10 normal audit procedures that should be performed to verify physical quantities whenever a client conducts a periodic physical count of all, or part, of its inventory.

(AICPA, adapted)

[11,13]   13-30   Kachelmeier, CPA, is auditing the financial statements of Big Z Wholesaling, Inc., a continuing audit client, for the year ended January 31, 2005. On January 5, 2005, Kachelmeier observed the tagging and counting of Big Z's physical inventory and made appropriate test counts. These test counts have been recorded on a computer file. As in prior years, Big Z gave Kachelmeier two computer files. One file represents the perpetual inventory (FIFO) records for the year ended January 31, 2005. The other file represents the January 5 physical inventory count.

Medium-Sized Manufacturing Company
Flowchart of Raw Materials Purchasing Function

Date _____
Prepared by _____
Approved by _____

Manufacturing Division

Accounts Payable

Stores   **Purchasing Office**   **Receiving Room**   **Controller's Division**

EXPLANATORY NOTES

A • Prepare purchase requisition (3 copies) as needed.
B • Prepare purchase order (6 copies).
C • Attach purchase requisition to purchase order.
D • Merchandise is received and counted, and receiving report (3 copies) is prepared based on count and purchase order.
E • Match purchase order, purchase requisition, receiving report, and invoice.
F • Prepare voucher after comparing data on purchase order, invoice, and receiving report.
G • To cash disbursements in controller's division for payment.

Assume that:

1. Kachelmeier issued an unqualified opinion on the prior year's financial statements.
2. All inventory is purchased for resale and located in a single warehouse.
3. Kachelmeier has appropriate computerized audit software.
4. The perpetual inventory file contains the following information in item number sequence:
   - Beginning balances at February 1, 2004: item number, item description, total quantity, and price.
   - For each item purchased during the year: date received, receiving report number, vendor item number, item description, quantity, and total dollar amount.
   - For each item sold during the year: date shipped, invoice number, item number, item description, quantity, and dollar amount.
   - For each item adjusted for physical inventory count differences: date, item number, item description, quantity, and dollar amount.
5. The physical inventory file contains the following information in item number sequence: tag number, item number, item description, and quantity.

Required:

Describe the substantive auditing procedures Kachelmeier may consider performing with computerized audit software using Big Z's two computer files and Kachelmeier's computer file of test counts. The substantive auditing procedures described may indicate the reports to be printed out for Kachelmeier's follow-up by subsequent application of manual procedures. Group the procedures by those using (a) the perpetual inventory file and (b) the physical inventory and test count files. Do *not* describe subsequent manual auditing procedures.

(AICPA, adapted)

[11,13]   13-31   An auditor is examining the financial statements of a wholesale cosmetics distributor with an inventory consisting of thousands of individual items. The distributor keeps its inventory in its own distribution center and in two public warehouses. An inventory computer file is maintained on a computer disk, and at the end of each business day the file is updated. Each record of the inventory file contains the following data:

- Item number.
- Location of item.
- Description of item.
- Quantity on hand.
- Cost per item.
- Date of last purchase.
- Date of last sale.
- Quantity sold during year.

The auditor plans to observe the distributor's physical count of inventory as of a given date. The auditor will have available a computer tape of the data on the inventory file on the date of the physical count and a generalized audit software package.

Required:

The auditor is planning to perform basic inventory-auditing procedures. Identify the basic inventory-auditing procedures and describe how the use of the generalized audit software package and the tape of the inventory file data might help the auditor perform such auditing procedures. Organize your answer as follows:

Basic Inventory-Auditing Procedure	How a Generalized Audit Software Package and Tape of the Inventory File Data Might Be Helpful
1. Observation of the physical count, making and recording test counts where applicable	1. By determining which items are to be test counted by selecting a random sample of a representative number of items from the inventory file as of the date of the physical count

(AICPA, adapted)

[13]   13-32   In obtaining evidential matter in support of financial statement assertions, the auditor develops specific audit procedures to address those assertions.

Required:

Your client is Hillmart, a retail department store that purchases all goods directly from wholesalers or manufacturers. Select the most appropriate audit procedure from the list below and enter the number in the appropriate place on the grid. (An audit procedure may be selected once, more than once, or not at all.)

Audit Procedure:

1. Examine current vendor price lists.
2. Review drafts of the financial statements.
3. Select a sample of items during the physical inventory count and determine that they have been included on count sheets.
4. Select a sample of recorded items and examine supporting vendor invoices and contracts.
5. Select a sample of recorded items on count sheets during the physical inventory count and determine that items are on hand.
6. Review loan agreements and minutes of board of directors' meetings.

Specific Assertion	Audit Procedure
a. Ensure that the entity has legal title to inventory (rights and obligations).	
b. Ensure that recorded inventory quantities include all products on hand (completeness).	
c. Verify that inventory has been reduced, when appropriate, to replacement cost or net realizable value (valuation).	
d. Verify that the cost of inventory has been properly determined (accuracy).	
e. Verify that the major categories of inventory and their bases of valuation are adequately reported in the financial statements (completeness and accuracy and valuation for presentation and disclosure).	

DISCUSSION CASE

[9,11,13,14]   13-33   The following discussion case extends Discussion Case 6-32 in Chapter 6.

Harris decided that the easiest way to make the Fabricator Division appear more profitable was through manipulating the inventory, which was the largest asset on the books. Harris found that by increasing inventory by 2 percent, income could be increased by 5 percent. With the weakness in inventory control, he felt it would be easy to overstate inventory. Employees count the goods using count sheets, and Harris was able to add two fictitious sheets during the physical inventory, even though the auditors were present and were observing the inventory. A significant amount of inventory was stored in racks that filled the warehouse. Because of their height and the difficulty of test counting them, Harris was able to cover an overstatement of inventory in the upper racks.

After the count was completed, Harris added four additional count sheets that added $350,000, or 8.6 percent, to the stated inventory. Harris notified the auditors of the "omission" of the sheets and convinced them that they represented overlooked legitimate inventory.

The auditors traced the items on these additional sheets to purchase invoices to verify their existence and approved the addition of the $350,000 to the inventory. They did not notify management about the added sheets. In addition, Harris altered other count sheets before sending them to the auditors by changing unit designations (for example, six engine blocks became six "motors"), raising counts, and adding fictitious line items to completed count sheets. These other fictitious changes added an additional $175,000 to the inflated inventory. None of them was detected by the auditors.

Required:

a. What audit procedures did the auditors apparently not follow that should have detected Harris's fraudulent increase of inventory?

b. What implications would there be to an auditor of failure to detect material fraud as described here?

c. What responsibility did the auditors have to discuss their concerns with the client's audit committee?

(Used with the permission of PricewaterhouseCoopers LLP Foundation.)

INTERNET ASSIGNMENTS

[9,13]   13-34   Using an Internet browser, search for information on inventory turnover and merchandise liquidations in the retail catalog industry.

[7,9,13,14]   13-35   Visit the SEC's website (www.sec.gov) and identify a company that has been recently cited for financial reporting problems related to inventory. Prepare a memo summarizing the inventory issues for the company.

ACL

www.mhhe.com/ messier4e	Visit the book's Online Learning Center for problem material to be completed using the *ACL* software packaged with your new text.

CHAPTER 14

LEARNING OBJECTIVES

Upon completion of this chapter you will

[1] Identify the various types of prepaid expenses, deferred charges, and intangible assets.

[2] Understand the auditor's approach to auditing prepaid insurance.

[3] Develop an understanding of the property management process.

[4] Identify the types of transactions in the property management process.

[5] Identify and evaluate inherent risks for property, plant, and equipment.

[6] Assess control risk for property, plant, and equipment.

[7] Know the appropriate segregation of duties for property, plant, and equipment.

[8] Identify substantive analytical procedures used to audit property, plant, and equipment.

[9] Identify tests of details of account balances and disclosures used to audit property, plant, and equipment.

[10] Evaluate the audit findings and reach a final conclusion on property, plant, and equipment.

RELEVANT ACCOUNTING AND AUDITING PRONOUNCEMENTS

FASB Statement of Financial Accounting Concepts No. 6, Elements of Financial Statements (CON6)

FASB Statement of Financial Accounting Standards No. 13, Accounting for Leases (FAS 13)

FASB Statement of Financial Accounting Standards No. 34, Capitalization of Interest Cost (FAS 34)

AU 312, Audit Risk and Materiality in Conducting an Audit

AU 316, Consideration of Fraud in a Financial Statement Audit

AU 319, Consideration of Internal Control in a Financial Statement Audit

AU 329, Analytical Procedures

AU 339, Audit Documentation

AU 342, Auditing Accounting Estimates

AICPA Auditing Standards Board, Exposure Draft, "Understanding the Entity and Its Environment and Assessing the Risks of Material Misstatement"

AICPA Auditing Standards Board, Exposure Draft, "Audit Evidence"

AICPA Auditing Standards Board, Exposure Draft, "Performing Audit Procedures in Response to Assessed Risks and Evaluating the Audit Evidence Obtained"

Auditing Financing Process: Prepaid Expenses and Property, Plant, and Equipment

Major Phases of an Audit

Client acceptance/
continuance
and establishing
engagement terms
(Chapter 5)

Preplanning
(Chapter 5)

Establish materiality
and assess risks
(Chapter 3)

Plan the audit
(Chapters 3 and 5)

Consider and audit
internal control
(Chapters 6 and 7)

Audit business processes
and related accounts
(e.g., revenue generation)
(Chapters 10–16)

Complete the audit
(Chapter 17)

Evaluate results and issue audit
report (Chapters 2 and 18)

This chapter examines the audit of selected asset accounts. Two categories of asset accounts, prepaid expenses and property, plant, and equipment, are used as examples. While the audit approach taken for each category is similar, differences exist between these two categories of asset accounts. For example, while transactions for both categories are subject to the control procedures in the purchasing process, property, plant, and equipment transactions are likely to be subject to additional control procedures because of their complexity or materiality. Additionally, prepaid expenses are normally classified as current assets, while property, plant, and equipment are classified as noncurrent assets.

Auditing Prepaid Expenses

[LO 1]   For many entities, accounts receivable and inventory represent the major current assets included in the financial statements. Also included in most financial statements are accounts that are referred to as *other assets*. When such assets provide economic benefit for less than a year, they are classified as current assets and are called *prepaid expenses*. Examples of prepaid expenses include

- Prepaid insurance.
- Prepaid rent.
- Prepaid interest.

Assets providing economic benefit for longer than a year are classified as *deferred charges* or *intangible assets*. Following are examples of deferred charges and intangible assets:

- Organization costs.
- Debt issuance costs.
- Copyrights.
- Trademarks.
- Trade names.
- Licenses.
- Patents.
- Franchises.
- Goodwill.
- Computer software development costs.

One major difference between asset accounts such as accounts receivable or inventory and prepaid expenses is the materiality of the account balances. On many engagements, prepaid expenses, deferred charges, and intangible assets are not highly material. As a result, substantive analytical procedures may be used extensively to verify these account balances.

Inherent Risk Assessment—Prepaid Expenses

The inherent risk for prepaid expenses such as prepaid insurance would generally be assessed as low because these accounts do not involve any complex or contentious accounting issues. Moreover, misstatements that may have been detected in prior audits would generally be immaterial in amount.

Deferred charges and intangible assets, on the other hand, may present serious inherent risk considerations. For example, the valuation and estimation of lives of patents, franchises, and goodwill involve considerable judgment and may lead to disagreements between the auditor and client. In such a situation, the auditor may assess the inherent risk as high.

Control Risk Assessment—Prepaid Expenses

Prepaid expenses, deferred charges, and intangible asset transactions are typically processed through the purchasing process. The remaining discussion focuses on the prepaid insurance account because it is encountered on virtually all engagements. Part of the auditor's assessment of control risk for prepaid insurance transactions is based on the effectiveness of the control procedures in the purchasing process. For example, the control procedures in the purchasing process should ensure that new insurance policies are properly authorized and recorded.

Additional control procedures may be used to control insurance transactions and information. For example, an *insurance register* may be maintained as a separate record of all insurance policies in force. The insurance register contains important information such as the coverage and expiration date of each policy. This register should be reviewed periodically by an independent person to verify that the entity has insurance coverage consistent with its needs.

The entity also needs to maintain controls over the systematic allocation of prepaid insurance to insurance expense. At the end of each month, client personnel should prepare a journal entry to recognize the expired portion of prepaid insurance. In some cases entities use estimated amounts when recording these journal entries during the year. At the end of the year, the prepaid insurance account is adjusted to reflect the actual amount of unexpired insurance.

Substantive Procedures—Prepaid Insurance

❧ **[LO 2]** On many audits the auditor can gather sufficient, competent evidence on prepaid insurance by performing substantive analytical procedures. Tests of details of transactions, if performed at all, are conducted as part of testing the purchasing process. Detailed tests of balances of the prepaid insurance balance are typically necessary only when misstatements are expected.

Substantive Analytical Procedures

Because there are generally few transactions in the prepaid insurance account and because the amount reported in the financial statements for prepaid insurance is usually immaterial, substantive analytical procedures are effective for verifying the account balance. The following substantive analytical procedures are commonly used to test prepaid insurance:

- Comparing the current-year balance in prepaid insurance and insurance expense with the prior year's balances after considering any changes in operations.
- Computing the ratio of insurance expense to assets or sales and comparing it with the prior year's ratio.

Tests of Details of the Prepaid Insurance Account

Tests of details of balances for prepaid insurance and insurance expense may be necessary when the auditor suspects misstatements based on prior years' audits or when substantive analytical procedures indicate that the account balance may be misstated. The auditor begins testing the prepaid

EXHIBIT 14-1	Example of an Account Analysis Working Paper for Prepaid Insurance

G10
DLJ
2/15/06

EarthWear

EARTHWEAR CLOTHIERS
Analysis of Prepaid Insurance
12/31/05

Insurance Company	Policy Number	Coverage	Term	Premium	Beginning Balance 1/1/05	Additions	Expense	Ending Balance 12/31/05
Babcock, Inc.**C**	46-2074	Liability Umbrella Policy	1/15/05 1/15/06	$55,000	$ 2,100	$55,000**V**	$ 54,800	$ 2,300ψ
Evans & Smith**C**	47801-X7	Fire & Casualty	3/30/05 3/30/06	33,600	7,500	33,600**V**	32,700	8,400ψ
Nat'l Insurance**C**	8945-X7	Key Executive Term Life Insurance	8/31/05 8/31/06	15,000	11,250	15,000**V**	15,000	11,250ψ
Total					$20,850¶	$103,600	$102,500**L**	$21,950**LF**
					F	**F**	**F**	**F**

F = Footed and crossfooted.
C = Information agreed to insurance company confirmation.
L = Agreed to general ledger.
¶ = Agreed to prior year's working papers.
V = Agreed to insurance company invoice.
ψ = Amount recomputed by auditor.

Reconciliation of insurance expense accounts:

Merchandise overhead insurance expense	$ 69,700**L**
General and administrative overhead insurance expense	32,800**L**
Total	$102,500

insurance account balance by obtaining a schedule from the client that contains a detailed analysis of the policies included in the prepaid insurance account.

EarthWear Exhibit 14–1 presents a prepaid insurance schedule for EarthWear Clothiers. The accuracy and completeness of this schedule is tested by footing it and tracing the ending balance to the prepaid insurance account in the general ledger. The auditor's work then focuses on testing the existence, completeness, rights and obligations, valuation, and disclosure-classification assertions. The cutoff assertion for prepaid insurance is normally tested as part of the search for unrecorded liabilities, and no footnote disclosures are generally necessary for prepaid insurance. These steps, along with other audit work, are shown in Exhibit 14–1.

Existence and Completeness   The auditor can test the existence and completeness of insurance policies included in the account analysis by sending a confirmation to the entity's insurance brokers, requesting information on each policy's number, coverage, expiration date, and premiums. This is an effective and efficient way of obtaining evidence on these two assertions. An alternative approach is examination of the underlying supporting documents such as the insurance bills and policies. This may be done on a test basis for the policies listed on the schedule. The auditor can also test completeness by comparing the detailed policies in the current year's insurance register with the policies included in the prior year's insurance register.

Rights and Obligations

The beneficiary of the policy can be tested by requesting such information on the confirmations sent to the insurance brokers or by examining the insurance policies. If the beneficiary is someone other than the client, the auditor may have evidence of an unrecorded liability or evidence that another party has a claim against the insured assets.

Valuation

The auditor is concerned with whether the unexpired portion of prepaid insurance, and thus insurance expense, is properly valued. This is easily tested by recomputing the unexpired portion of insurance after considering the premium paid and the term of the policy. By verifying the unexpired portion of prepaid insurance, the auditor also verifies the total amount of insurance expense. This is shown in Exhibit 14–1.

Classification

The auditor's concern with classification is that the different types of insurance are properly allocated to the various insurance expense accounts. Normally, an examination of the insurance policy's coverage indicates the nature of the insurance. For example, a fire insurance policy on the main manufacturing and administrative facilities should be charged both to the manufacturing overhead insurance expense account and to the general and administrative insurance expense account. Note in Exhibit 14–1 that the various insurance accounts included in the general ledger are reconciled to total insurance expense. One final procedure that the auditor should perform is asking the client or its insurance broker about the adequacy of the entity's insurance coverage.

Auditing the Property Management Process

[LO 3]   For most entities, property, plant, and equipment represent a material amount in the financial statements. When the audit is an ongoing engagement, the auditor is able to focus his or her efforts on the current year's activity because the assets acquired in earlier years were subjected to audit procedures at the time of acquisition. On the other hand, for a new engagement, the auditor has to verify the assets that make up the beginning balances in the client's property, plant, and equipment accounts.

The size of the entity may also affect the auditor's approach. If the client is relatively small with few asset acquisitions during the period, it is generally more cost-effective for the auditor to follow a substantive strategy. Following this strategy, the auditor conducts substantive analytical procedures and direct tests of the account balances. Large entities, on the other hand, are likely to have formal procedures for budgeting for and purchasing capital assets. While routine purchases might be processed through the purchasing process, as described in Chapter 11, acquisition or construction of specialized assets may be subject to different requisition and authorization procedures. When

FIGURE 14–1	Flowchart of the Property Management Process—EarthWear Clothiers

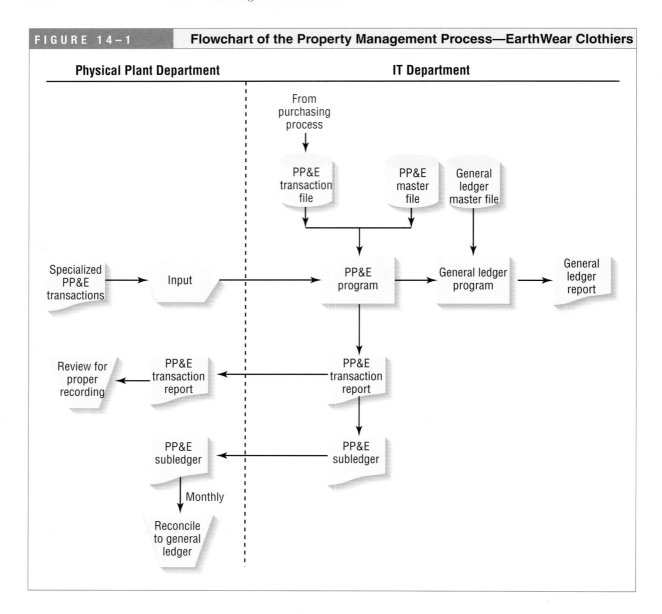

the entity has a formal control system over the property management process, the auditor may follow a reliance strategy and test controls.

Types of Transactions

[LO 4]

Four types of property, plant, and equipment transactions may occur:

- Acquisition of capital assets for cash or other nonmonetary considerations.
- Disposition of capital assets through sale, exchange, retirement, or abandonment.
- Depreciation of capital assets over their useful economic life.
- Leasing of capital assets.

Overview of
the Property
Management
Process

 Larger entities generally use some type of computer-based system to process property, plant, and equipment transactions, maintain subsidiary records, and produce required reports. Figure 14–1 presents a flowchart of EarthWear's accounting system for the property management process. Transactions are periodically entered both from the purchasing process and through direct input into the system. The property, plant, and equipment master file is then updated, and a number of reports are produced. The periodic report for property, plant, and equipment transactions is reviewed for proper recording by the physical plant department. The property, plant, and equipment subsidiary ledger is a record of all capital assets owned by the entity. It contains information on the cost of the asset, the date acquired, the method of depreciation, and accumulated depreciation. The subsidiary ledger also includes the calculation of depreciation expense for both financial statement and income tax purposes. The general ledger is posted to reflect the new property, plant, and equipment transactions and depreciation expense. The subsidiary ledger should be reconciled to the general ledger control account monthly.

Inherent Risk Assessment—Property Management Process

[LO 5] The assessment of inherent risk for the purchasing process provides a starting point for assessing inherent risk for property, plant, and equipment. The following three inherent risk factors classified as operating characteristics require consideration by the auditor:

- Complex accounting issues.
- Difficult-to-audit transactions.
- Misstatements detected in prior audits.

Complex
Accounting Issues

A number of different types of property, plant, and equipment transactions involve complex accounting issues. Lease accounting, self-constructed assets, and capitalized interest are examples of such issues. For example, in the case of a lease transaction the auditor must evaluate the client's decision either to capitalize the lease or to treat it as an operating lease. Because of the complexity of the capitalization decision and the subjectivity involved in assessing the capitalization criteria, it is not uncommon for such transactions to be accounted for incorrectly by the client. For example, EarthWear leases store and office space that is accounted for as operating leases. Willis & Adams must be sure that these leases do not qualify as capital leases.

Difficult-to-Audit
Transactions

The vast majority of property, plant, and equipment transactions are relatively easy to audit. When assets are purchased directly from vendors, most assertions can be tested by examining the source documents. However, transactions involving donated assets, nonmonetary exchanges, and

| EXHIBIT 14-2 | **WorldCom Overstates PP&E and Net Income** |

WorldCom started as a mom-and-pop long-distance company in 1983. But in the 1990s, it matured into a powerhouse. In 1997 it shocked the industry with an unsolicited bid to take over MCI, a company more than three times its size. In 1998 *CFO Magazine* named WorldCom's CFO, Scott Sullivan, one of the country's best CFOs. At age 37 he was earning $19.3 million a year. In 1999 WorldCom founder Bernie Ebbers moved the company to Clinton, Mississippi, his old college town, and everything changed. The stock price went through the roof. However, by early 2001, overexuberance for the telecom market had created a glut of companies like WorldCom, and earnings started to fall.

In March 2002, Cynthia Cooper, a WorldCom vice president and head of internal audit was informed by a worried executive in the wireless division that corporate accounting had taken $400 million out of his reserve account and used it to boost WorldCom's income. When Cooper went to the auditors Arthur Andersen to inquire about the maneuver, she was told matter-of-factly that it was not a problem. When she didn't relent, Sullivan angrily told Cooper that everything was fine and she should back off. He was furious at her, according to a person involved in the matter. Says Cooper, "When someone is hostile, my instinct is to find out why."

As the weeks went on, Cooper directed her team members to widen their net. Having watched the Enron implosion and Andersen's role in it, she was worried they could not necessarily rely on the accounting firm's audits. So the internal auditors decided to reaudit some areas. She and her team began working late into the night, keeping their project secret. In late May, Cooper and her group discovered a gaping hole in the books. In public reports, the company had classified billions of dollars as property, plant, and equipment in 2001, meaning the costs could be stretched out over a number of years into the future. However, these expenditures were for regular fees WorldCom paid to local telephone companies to complete calls and therefore were operating costs, which should be expensed in full each year. It was as if an ordinary person had paid his or her phone bills but written down the payments as if he or she were building a phone tower in his or her backyard. The trick allowed WorldCom to turn a $662 million loss into a $2.4 billion profit in 2001.

Internal audit began looking for ways to somehow justify what it had found in the books. Finally, the internal auditors confronted WorldCom's controller, David Myers, who admitted the accounting could not be justified. Cooper told the audit committee that the company accountants had understated expenses and overstated income. Sullivan was provided the opportunity to present his side of the story, but he could not convince them regarding the propriety of the accounting. Within days, the company fired its famed chief financial officer, Scott Sullivan, and told the world that it had inflated its profits by $3.8 billion—the number has since grown to over $9 billion.

Source: Amanda Ripley, "The Night Detective (Persons of the Year)," *Time* (December 30, 2002–January 6, 2003), p. 36.

self-constructed assets are more difficult to audit. For example, it may be difficult to verify the trade-in value of an asset exchanged or to properly audit the cost accumulation of self-constructed assets. The presence of these types of transactions should lead to a higher inherent risk assessment. It is certainly worth noting that one of the largest accounting frauds in history, WorldCom, involved the improper capitalization of operating expenses as property, plant, and equipment to overstate income. See Exhibit 14–2 for a more detailed description of the company, the fraud, and how the fraud was uncovered.

| Misstatements Detected in Prior Audits | If the auditor has detected misstatements in prior audits, the assessment of inherent risk should be set higher than if few or no misstatements have been found in the past.[1] For example, in prior years the auditor may have found numerous client misstatements in accumulating costs for valuing capital assets. Unless the client has established new control procedures over cost accumulation, the auditor should also expect to find misstatements during the current year's audit and therefore set inherent risk as high. |

Control Risk Assessment—Property Management Process

⚹ [LO 6] Although the auditor generally follows a substantive strategy when auditing property management process, an understanding of internal control is still required. The presentation that follows focuses on the major assertions, key control procedures, and tests of controls that relate directly to the property management process. Other control procedures related to the property management process were discussed as part of the purchasing process. Important examples of segregation of duties are also presented.

| Occurrence and Authorization | The control procedures for the occurrence and authorization assertions are normally part of the purchasing process. Purchase requisitions are initiated in relevant departments and authorized at the appropriate level within the entity. However, large capital asset transactions may be subject to control procedures outside the purchasing process. For example, highly specialized technical equipment is likely to be purchased only after passing through a specific capital-budgeting process, which might require that purchase of equipment meet predefined internal rate-of-return criteria. The purchase of equipment may also require that highly skilled engineers approve the technical specifications for the equipment. For such transactions, the auditor may need to examine more than the vendor's invoice to test validity. A review of additional documentation, such as capital-budgeting documents and engineering specifications, may be needed. |

Most entities have some type of authorization table for approving capital asset transactions. The client should have control procedures to ensure that the authorization to purchase capital assets is consistent with the authorization table. For example, the control procedures should specify dollar limits at each managerial level to ensure that larger projects are brought to the attention of higher levels of management for approval before commitments are made. Lease transactions should be subject to similar control procedures. The entity also needs to have control procedures for authorizing the sale or other disposition of capital assets. This should include a level of authorization above the department initiating the disposition. Control procedures should also identify assets that are no longer used in operations

---

[1]Research has shown that property, plant, and equipment accounts frequently contain misstatements. See A. Eilifsen and W. F. Messier, Jr., "Auditor Detection of Misstatements: A Review and Integration of Empirical Research," *Journal of Accounting Literature* 2000 (19), pp. 1–43, for a review of the audit research studies that have indicated that property, plant, and equipment accounts are likely to contain misstatements.

because they may require different accounting treatment. Finally, all major maintenance or improvement transactions should be properly authorized by an appropriate level of management.

Completeness

Most entities use some type of IT software to maintain detailed property records (see Figure 14–1). The detailed property, plant, and equipment subsidiary ledger usually includes the following information for each capital asset:

- Description, location, and ID number.
- Date of acquisition and installed cost.
- Depreciation methods for book and tax purposes, salvage value, and estimated useful life.

The control procedures used in the purchasing process for ensuring completeness provide some assurance that all capital asset transactions are recorded in the property, plant, and equipment subsidiary ledger and general ledger. One procedure that helps to ensure that this assertion is met is periodic reconciliation of the property, plant, and equipment subsidiary ledger to the general ledger control accounts. Figure 14–1 shows this control procedure as it is performed by EarthWear's physical plant department.

Another control procedure that an entity may use to ensure that all capital assets are recorded is periodic comparison of the detailed records in the subsidiary ledger with the existing capital assets. This may be done in a number of ways. The client may take a complete physical examination of property, plant, and equipment on a periodic or rotating basis and compare the physical assets to the property, plant, and equipment subsidiary ledger. Alternatively, the physical examination may be limited to major capital assets or assets that are subject to loss. In both instances the entity's internal auditors may test the reliability of the subsidiary ledger. Larger entities

TABLE 14–1	Key Segregation of Duties and Possible Errors or Fraud—Property Management Process
Segregation of Duties	*Possible Errors or Fraud Resulting from Conflicts of Duties*
The initiation function should be segregated from the final approval function.	If one individual is responsible for initiating a capital asset transaction and also has final approval, fictitious or unauthorized purchases of assets can occur. This can result in purchases of unnecessary assets, assets that do not meet the company's quality control standards, or illegal payments to suppliers or contractors.
The property, plant, and equipment records function should be segregated from the general ledger function.	If one individual is responsible for the property, plant, and equipment records and also for the general ledger functions, that individual can conceal any defalcation that would normally be detected by reconciling subsidiary records with the general ledger control account.
The property, plant, and equipment records function should be segregated from the custodial function.	If one individual is responsible for the property, plant, and equipment records and also has custodial responsibility for the related assets, tools and equipment can be stolen, and the theft can be concealed by adjustment of the accounting records.
If a periodic physical inventory of property, plant, and equipment is taken, the individual responsible for the inventory should be independent of the custodial and record-keeping functions.	If the individual who is responsible for the periodic physical inventory of property, plant, and equipment is also responsible for the custodial and record-keeping functions, theft of the entity's capital assets can be concealed.

sometimes employ outside specialists to physically examine property, plant, and equipment.

Segregation of Duties

❧ [LO 7]

The existence of adequate segregation of duties for the property management process depends on the volume and significance of the transactions processed. For example, if an entity purchases large quantities of machinery and equipment, or if it has large capital projects under construction, it will likely have a formal control system. On the other hand, if an entity has few capital asset purchases, it will generally not have a formal control system over such transactions. Table 14–1 shows the key segregation of duties for the property management process and examples of possible errors or fraud that can result from conflicts in duties.

Substantive Procedures—Property, Plant, and Equipment

As mentioned earlier, when the number of transactions is limited or efficiency is a consideration, auditors often follow a substantive strategy when auditing property, plant, and equipment. Therefore, a detailed discussion of the substantive procedures for property, plant, and equipment is provided next. The discussion focuses on substantive analytical procedures and tests of details of transactions, account balances, and disclosures.

Substantive Analytical Procedures—Property, Plant, and Equipment

❧ [LO 8] The following substantive analytical procedures can be used in the audit of property, plant, and equipment:

- Compare prior-year balances in property, plant, and equipment and depreciation expense with current-year balances after consideration of any changes in conditions or asset composition.
- Compute the ratio of depreciation expense to the related property, plant, and equipment accounts and compare to prior years' ratios.
- Compute the ratio of repairs and maintenance expense to the related property, plant, and equipment accounts and compare to prior years' ratios.
- Compute the ratio of insurance expense to the related property, plant, and equipment accounts and compare to prior years' ratios.
- Review capital budgets and compare the amounts spent with amounts budgeted.

For example, the auditor can calculate the ratio of depreciation expense to the related property, plant, and equipment accounts and compare it to prior years' ratios. If the ratio is less than prior years' and few assets have been disposed of, the auditor might conclude that depreciation has not been taken on some assets included in the account.

Tests of Details of Transactions, Account Balances, and Disclosures—Property, Plant, and Equipment

[LO 9]   Table 14–2 summarizes the substantive tests for the property, plant, and equipment accounts for each assertion relating to transactions and balances. The discussion that follows focuses on the major audit procedures conducted by the auditor. Completeness is discussed first because the auditor must establish that the detailed property, plant, and equipment records agree with the general ledger account.

Completeness

The auditor verifies the accuracy of property, plant, and equipment by obtaining a lead schedule and detailed schedules for additions and dispositions

TABLE 14–2	Examples of Tests of Transactions and Account Balances for Property, Plant, and Equipment (PP&E)
Assertions about Classes of Transactions	**Substantive Tests of Transaction***
Occurrence	Vouch significant additions and dispositions to vendor invoices or other supporting documentation.
	Review lease agreements to ensure that lease transactions are accounted for properly.
Completeness	Trace a sample of purchase requisitions to loading dock reports and to the PP&E records (i.e., transaction and master file).
Authorization	Vouch a sample of PP&E additions to documentation indicating proper authorization.
Accuracy	For assets written off, test amounts charged against income and accumulated depreciation.
Cutoff	Examine the purchases and sales of capital assets for a few days before and after year-end.
Classification	Vouch transactions included in repairs and maintenance for items that should be capitalized.
	Review lease transactions for proper classification between operating and capital leases.
Assertions about Account Balances at Period End	**Tests of Details of Account Balances**
Existence	Verify the existence of major additions by physically examining the capital asset.
Rights and obligations	Examine or confirm deeds or title documents for proof of ownership.
Completeness	Obtain a lead schedule of property, plant, and equipment; foot schedule and agree totals to the general ledger.
	Obtain detailed schedules for additions and dispositions of property, plant, and equipment; foot schedule; agree amounts to totals shown on lead schedule.
	Physically examine a sample of capital assets and trace them into the property, plant, and equipment subsidiary ledger.
Valuation and allocation	Evaluate fixed assets for significant write-offs or impairments by performing procedures such as
	• Identify the event or change in circumstance indicating that the carrying value of the asset may not be recoverable.
	• Verify impairment loss by determining the sum of expected future cash flows and comparing that sum to the carrying value.
	• Examine client documentation supporting impairment of write-off.
	Test depreciation calculations for a sample of capital assets.

* These tests of details of transactions are commonly conducted as dual-purpose tests (i.e., in conjunction with tests of controls).

of assets. This lead schedule is footed, and the individual accounts are agreed to the general ledger. The detailed schedules are also tested for accuracy. Exhibit 14–3 presents a lead schedule for EarthWear's property, plant, and equipment.

The auditor has some assurance about the completeness assertion from the control procedures in the purchasing process and, if present, the additional control procedures discussed previously in this chapter. If the auditor still has concerns about the completeness assertion, he or she can physically examine a sample of assets and trace them into the property, plant, and equipment subsidiary ledger. If the assets are included in the subsidiary ledger, the auditor has sufficient evidence supporting the completeness assertion.

Cutoff

On most engagements, cutoff is tested as part of the audit work in accounts payable and accrued expenses. By examining a sample of vendor invoices from a few days before and after year-end, the auditor can determine if capital asset transactions are recorded in the proper period. Inquiry of client personnel and a review of lease transactions for the same period can provide evidence on proper cutoff for leases.

Classification

First, the classification of a transaction into the correct property, plant, and equipment account is normally examined as part of the testing of the purchasing process. The auditor's tests of controls and substantive tests of transactions provide evidence as to the effectiveness of the control procedures for this assertion.

Second, the auditor should examine selected expense accounts such as repairs and maintenance to determine if any capital assets have been incorrectly recorded in these accounts. An account analysis of transactions included in the repairs and maintenance account is obtained, and selected transactions are vouched to supporting documents. In examining the supporting documents, the auditor must determine if the transactions are truly expense items or whether it would be more appropriate to capitalize the costs. For example, the auditor may examine an invoice from a plumbing contractor that shows that the water pipe system for a building has been replaced during the current period. If the amount of this transaction was material and improved the building, it should not be expensed as a repair but rather should be capitalized as a building improvement.

Last, the auditor should examine each material lease agreement to verify that the lease is properly classified as an operating or capital lease.

Existence

To test validity, the auditor obtains a listing of all major additions and vouches them to supporting documents such as vendors' invoices. If the purchase was properly authorized and the asset has been received and placed in service, the transaction is valid. In addition, the auditor may want to verify that assets recorded as capital assets actually exist. For major acquisitions, the auditor may physically examine the capital asset.

Similarly, disposition of assets must be properly authorized, and the supporting documentation such as sales receipts should indicate how the disposal took place. Generally, the auditor obtains a schedule of all major

EXHIBIT 14–3

An Example of a Lead Schedule for Property, Plant, and Equipment

EarthWear

K Lead
JLJ
1/15/06

EARTHWEAR CLOTHIERS
Lead Sheet—Property, Plant, and Equipment
12/31/05

Account	W/P Ref.	Cost				Accumulated Depreciation			
		Beginning Balance	Additions	Deletions	Ending Balance	Beginning Balance	Additions	Deletions	Ending Balance
Land	K10	$ 6,593,000L	$2,112,852	$1,786,852	$ 6,919,000				
Buildings	K20	60,211,250L	6,112,600	2,324,950	63,998,900	$23,638,300L	$ 3,411,493	$ 653,788	$26,396,005
Fixtures, Computers, and Equipment	K30	114,342,050L	19,791,763	1,634,988	132,498,825	51,162,450L	8,285,360	1,533,398	57,914,462
Leasehold Improvements	K40	2,894,100L	780,115	664,595	3,009,620	$ 1,455,500L	413,952	194,019	1,675,433
Totals		$184,040,400F	$28,797,330	$ 6,411,385	$206,426,345	$76,266,250F	$12,110,805	$2,381,155	$85,985,900
		F	F	F	F	F	F	F	F

F = Footed and crossfooted.
L = Agreed to general ledger.
¶ = Agreed to prior year's working papers.

dispositions and verifies that the asset was removed from the property, plant, and equipment records. If the disposition is the result of a sale or exchange, the auditor would verify the cash receipt for the sale of the asset or documentation that another asset was received in exchange.

The auditor must also ascertain the validity of lease transactions by examining the lease agreements entered into by the entity. If the lease agreement is properly authorized and the asset is placed in service, the evidence supports the validity of the recorded asset.

Rights and Obligations

The auditor can test for rights or ownership by examining the vendor's invoices or other supporting documents. In some instances, the auditor may examine or confirm property deeds or title documents for proof of ownership.

Valuation and Allocation

Capital assets are valued at acquisition cost plus any costs necessary to make the asset operational. The auditor tests the recorded cost of new assets by examining the vendor invoices and other supporting documents used by the client to establish the recorded value of the assets. If the client has material self-constructed assets, the auditor conducts detailed audit work on the construction-in-process account. This includes ensuring that interest is properly capitalized as a cost of the asset (see FASB No. 34, Capitalization of Interest Cost).

FASB No. 144, Accounting for the Impairment or Disposal of Long-Lived Assets, requires that long-lived assets be reviewed for impairment whenever events or changes in circumstances indicate that the assets' carrying amount may not be recoverable. In reviewing for recoverability, the entity should estimate future (undiscounted) cash flows from use and eventual disposition of the assets. If the sum of those future cash flows is less than the assets' carrying amount, the assets should be written down and a loss recognized. The standards provide guidance and illustrations on how to estimate future cash flows, but obviously this area requires substantial judgment and expertise. Typically, the auditor gathers assurance on the valuation of property, plant, and equipment through a variety of procedures (e.g., understanding of the business and industry and current events that may lead to impairment, tests of controls over the client's impairment evaluation, inquiry and observation regarding the condition and usefulness of long-lived assets, and tests of details of balances, such as those described in Table 14–2).

The other valuation issue the auditor must address is the recognition of depreciation expense. If the client uses a computer to process and account for capital assets, the auditor may be able to use computer-assisted audit techniques to verify the calculation of depreciation for various assets. Alternatively, the auditor may recompute the depreciation expense for a sample of capital assets. In making this calculation, the auditor considers the reasonableness of the estimated life of the asset, the depreciation methods used for book and tax purposes, and any expected salvage value.

Disclosure Issues

Table 14–3 shows a number of important items that may require disclosure as part of the audit of property, plant, and equipment. Some of these disclosures are made in the "summary of significant accounting policies" footnote, while other items may be disclosed in separate footnotes. Exhibit 14–4

TABLE 14-3	Examples of Disclosure Items—Property, Plant, and Equipment
	Classes of capital assets and valuation bases.
	Depreciation methods and useful lives for financial reporting and tax purposes.
	Nonoperating assets.
	Construction or purchase commitments.
	Liens and mortgages.
	Acquisition or disposal of major operating facilities.
	Capitalized and other lease arrangements.

EXHIBIT 14-4	Sample Disclosure of Nonoperating Property
	In March 2005 the company decided to temporarily idle the Southern Alabama Mill. The decision was made in response to adverse industry conditions, mainly reduced selling prices and increased raw material costs. In September 2005 it was further determined that because of continued deterioration of selling prices and the level of expenditures required to meet environmental restrictions, the Southern Alabama Mill would not resume operations. The assets of the mill cannot be sold for their historical cost, and in the third quarter the company recorded a $15.6 million loss on the mill.

is a sample disclosure for an entity's decision to discontinue operations at one of its operating facilities.

Evaluating the Audit Findings—Property, Plant, and Equipment

⚛ [LO 10] The process for evaluating the audit findings for property, plant, and equipment is the same as was discussed in previous chapters. The auditor aggregates the likely misstatements and compares this amount to the tolerable misstatement. If the likely misstatement is less than the tolerable misstatement, the evidence indicates that the property, plant, and equipment accounts are not materially misstated. This is the case with EarthWear. No misstatements were detected for property, plant, and equipment (see Exhibit 3–5). However, if the likely misstatement was greater than the tolerable misstatement, the auditor would either require adjustment of the accounts or issue a qualified audit report.

KEY TERMS

Analytical procedures. Evaluations of financial information made by a study of plausible relationships among both financial and nonfinancial data.
Application controls. Controls that apply to the processing of specific computer applications and are part of the computer programs used in the accounting system.
Assertions. Expressed or implied representations by management that are reflected in the financial statement components.

Computer-assisted audit techniques. Computer programs that allow auditors to test computer files and databases.

General controls. Controls that relate to the overall information processing environment and have a pervasive effect on the entity's computer operations.

Reliance strategy. The auditor's decision to rely on the entity's controls, test those controls, and reduce the direct tests of the financial statement accounts.

Tests of controls. Procedures that evaluate the effectiveness of the design and operation of internal controls.

Tests of details of account balances and disclosures. Tests that concentrate on the details of amounts contained in an account balance and diclosures.

Tests of details of transactions. Tests to detect errors or fraud in individual transactions.

www.mhhe.com/ messier4e	Visit the book's Online Learning Center for a multiple-choice quiz that will allow you to assess your understanding of chapter concepts.

REVIEW QUESTIONS

[LO 1]   14-1   Distinguish between prepaid expenses and deferred charges, and intangible assets. Give three examples of each of these "other assets."

[1,2]   14-2   Prepaid expenses are generally assessed to have a low inherent risk. Why would deferred charges and intangible assets present serious inherent risk consideration?

[2]   14-3   How does the purchasing process affect prepaid insurance and property, plant, and equipment transactions?

[2]   14-4   Identify two substantive analytical procedures that can be used to audit prepaid insurance.

[2]   14-5   Confirmation is a useful audit procedure for verifying information related to prepaid insurance. What type of information would be requested from an entity's insurance broker?

[4]   14-6   List four types of property, plant, and equipment transactions.

[5]   14-7   Describe three factors that the auditor should consider in assessing the inherent risk for the property management process.

[6]   14-8   What is a typical control over authorization of capital asset transactions?

[7]   14-9   What is the key segregation of duties for the property management process? What errors or fraud can occur if such segregation of duties is not present?

[8]   14-10   Identify three substantive analytical procedures that can be used to audit property, plant, and equipment.

[9]   14-11   What procedures would an auditor use to verify the completeness, rights and obligations, and valuation assertions for property, plant, and equipment?

MULTIPLE-CHOICE QUESTIONS

[2]   14-12   When auditing prepaid insurance, an auditor discovers that the original insurance policy on plant equipment is not available for inspection. The policy's absence most likely indicates the possibility of a(n)

a. Insurance premium due but not recorded.

b. Deficiency in the coinsurance provision.

c. Lien on the plant equipment.

d. Understatement of insurance expense.

[3,6] 14-13 Which of the following internal controls is most likely to justify a reduction of control risk concerning plant and equipment acquisitions?

a. Periodic physical inspection of plant and equipment by the internal audit staff.

b. Comparison of current-year plant and equipment account balances with prior-year actual balances.

c. Review of prenumbered purchase orders to detect unrecorded trade-ins.

d. Approval of periodic depreciation entries by a supervisor independent of the accounting department.

[3,6] 14-14 To strengthen control over the custody of heavy mobile equipment, the client would most likely institute a policy requiring a periodic

a. Increase in insurance coverage.

b. Inspection of equipment and reconciliation with accounting records.

c. Verification of liens, pledges, and collateralizations.

d. Accounting for work orders.

[3,6] 14-15 A weakness in control over recording retirement of equipment may cause an auditor to

a. Trace additions to the "other assets" account to search for equipment that is still on hand but no longer being used.

b. Select certain items of equipment from the accounting records and locate them in the plant.

c. Inspect certain items of equipment in the plant and trace those items to the accounting records.

d. Review the subsidiary ledger to ascertain whether depreciation was taken on each item of equipment during the year.

[3,6,7] 14-16 Which of the following procedures is most likely to prevent the improper disposition of equipment?

a. Separation of duties between those authorized to dispose of equipment and those authorized to approve removal work orders.

b. The use of serial numbers to identify equipment that could be sold.

c. Periodic comparison of removal work orders to authorizing documentation.

d. Periodic analysis of the scrap sales and the repairs and maintenance accounts.

[3,6] 14-17 Property acquisitions that are misclassified as maintenance expense would most likely be detected by an internal control system that provides for

a. Investigation of variances within a formal budgeting system.

b. Review and approval of the monthly depreciation entry by the plant supervisor.

c. Segregation of duties of employees in the accounts payable department.

d. Examination by the internal auditor of vendor invoices and canceled checks for property acquisitions.

[3,6,9] 14-18 When there are few property and equipment transactions during the year, the continuing auditor usually

a. Completely reviews the related control procedures and tests the control procedures being relied upon.

b. Completely reviews the related control procedures and performs substantive analytical procedures to verify current-year additions to property and equipment.

c. Develops a preliminary understanding of internal control and performs a thorough examination of the balances at the beginning of the year.

d. Develops a preliminary understanding of internal control and performs extensive tests of current-year property and equipment transactions.

[3,6,9] 14-19 Which of the following control procedures would most likely allow for a reduction in the scope of the auditor's tests of depreciation expense?

a. Review and approval of the periodic equipment depreciation entry by a supervisor who does not actively participate in its preparation.

b. Comparison of equipment account balances for the current year with the current-year budget and prior-year actual balances.

c. Review of the miscellaneous income account for salvage credits and scrap sales of partially depreciated equipment.

d. Authorization of payment of vendor's invoices by a designated employee who is independent of the equipment-receiving function.

[6,8,9] 14-20 When there are numerous property and equipment transactions during the year, an auditor who plans to set the control risk at a low level usually performs

a. Substantive analytical procedures for property and equipment balances at the end of the year.

b. Tests of controls and extensive tests of property and equipment balances at the end of the year.

c. Substantive analytical procedures for current-year property and equipment transactions.

d. Tests of controls and limited tests of current-year property and equipment transactions.

[9] 14-21 An auditor analyzes repairs and maintenance accounts primarily to obtain evidence in support of the assertion that all

a. Noncapitalizable expenditures for repairs and maintenance have been properly charged to expense.

b. Expenditures for property and equipment have *not* been charged to expense.

c. Noncapitalizable expenditures for repairs and maintenance have been recorded in the proper period.

d. Expenditures for property and equipment have been recorded in the proper period.

[9] 14-22 Which of the following combinations of procedures would an auditor be most likely to perform to obtain evidence about fixed-asset additions?

a. Inspecting documents and physically examining assets.

b. Recomputing calculations and obtaining written management representations.
c. Observing operating activities and comparing balances to prior-period balances.
d. Confirming ownership and corroborating transactions through inquiries of client personnel.

PROBLEMS

[1,2] 14-23 Natherson, CPA, is engaged to audit the financial statements of Lewis Lumber for the year ended December 31, 2005. Natherson obtained and documented an understanding of internal control relating to the purchasing process and set control risk at the maximum level. Natherson requested and obtained from Lewis a schedule analyzing prepaid insurance as of December 31, 2005, and sent confirmation requests to Lewis's insurance broker.

Required:
a. Identify two substantive analytical procedures that Natherson could use to verify prepaid insurance.
b. What substantive audit procedures should Natherson conduct on the schedule of prepaid insurance?

[1,2] 14-24 Taylor, CPA, has been engaged to audit the financial statements of Palmer Company, a continuing audit client. Taylor is about to perform substantive audit procedures on Palmer's goodwill (excess of cost over fair value of net assets purchased) that was acquired in prior years' business combinations. An industry slowdown has occurred recently, and the operations purchased have not met profit expectations.

During the planning process, Taylor determined that there was a high risk that material misstatements in the assertions related to goodwill could occur. Taylor obtained an understanding of internal control and set the control risk at the maximum level for the assertions related to goodwill.

Required:
a. Describe the substantive audit procedures Taylor should consider performing in auditing Palmer's goodwill. Do *not* discuss Palmer's control system.
b. Describe the two significant assertions that Taylor would be most concerned with relative to Palmer's goodwill. Do *not* describe more than two.

(AICPA, adapted)

[6,7] 14-25 Nakamura, CPA, has accepted an engagement to audit the financial statements of Grant Manufacturing Company, a new client. Grant has an adequate control environment and a reasonable segregation of duties. Nakamura is about to set the control risk for the assertions related to Grant's property and equipment.

Required:
Describe the key internal controls related to Grant's property, equipment, and related transactions (additions, transfers, major

maintenance and repairs, retirements, and dispositions) that Naka-mura may consider in setting the control risk.

(AICPA, adapted)

[4,6,9,10] 14-26 Gonzales, CPA, is the auditor for a manufacturing company with a balance sheet that includes the entry "Property, plant, and equipment." Gonzales has been asked by the company's management if audit adjustments or reclassifications are required for the following material items that have been included in or excluded from "Property, plant, and equipment":

1. A tract of land was acquired during the year. The land is to be the future site of the client's new headquarters, which will be constructed next year. Commissions were paid to the real estate agent used to acquire the land, and expenditures were made to relocate the previous owner's equipment. These commissions and expenditures were expensed and are excluded from "Property, plant, and equipment."
2. Clearing costs were incurred to ready the land for construction. These costs were included in "Property, plant, and equipment."
3. During the land-clearing process, timber and gravel were recovered and sold. The proceeds from the sale were recorded as other income and are excluded from "Property, plant, and equipment."
4. A group of machines was purchased under a royalty agreement that provides royalty payments based on units of production from the machines. The costs of the machines, freight costs, unloading charges, and royalty payments were capitalized and are included in "Property, plant, and equipment."

Required:

a. Describe the general characteristics of assets, such as land, buildings, improvements, machinery, equipment, fixtures, and so on, that should normally be classified as "Property, plant, and equipment," and identify assertions in connection with the examination of "Property, plant, and equipment." Do not discuss specific audit procedures.
b. Indicate whether each of the items numbered 1 to 4 requires one or more audit adjustments or reclassifications, and explain why such adjustments or reclassifications are required or not required. Organize your answer as follows:

Item Number	Is Auditing Adjustment or Reclassification Required? (Yes or No)	Reasons Why Audit Adjustments or Reclassifications Are Required or Not Required

(AICPA, adapted)

[8,9] 14-27 To support financial statement assertions, an auditor develops specific substantive procedures to satisfy or address each assertion.

Required:

Items (a) through (c) represent assertions for the property and equipment accounts. Select the most appropriate audit procedure from the following list and enter the number in the appropriate place on the grid. (An audit procedure may be selected once or not at all.)

Audit Procedure

1. Trace opening balances in the summary schedules to the prior year's audit working papers.
2. Review the provision for depreciation expense and determine that depreciable lives and methods used in the current year are consistent with those used in the prior year.
3. Determine that the responsibility for maintaining the property and equipment records is segregated from the responsibility for custody of property and equipment.
4. Examine deeds and title insurance certificates.
5. Perform cutoff tests to verify that property and equipment additions are recorded in the proper period.
6. Determine that property and equipment are adequately insured.
7. Physically examine all major property and equipment additions.

Specific Assertion	Audit Procedure
a. Verify that the entity has the legal right to property and equipment acquired during the year (rights and obligations).	
b. Verify that recorded property and equipment represent assets that actually exist at the balance sheet date (existence).	
c. Verify that net property and equipment are properly valued at the balance sheet date (valuation and allocation).	

(AICPA, adapted)

[8,9] 14-28 Pierce, an independent auditor, was engaged to examine the financial statements of Wong Construction, Inc., for the year ended December 31, 2005. Wong's financial statements reflect a substantial amount of mobile construction equipment used in the firm's operations. The equipment is accounted for in a subsidiary ledger. Pierce developed an understanding of internal control and set the control risk at moderate.

Required:

Identify the substantive audit procedures Pierce should utilize in examining mobile construction equipment and related depreciation in Wong's financial statements.

(AICPA, adapted)

DISCUSSION CASE

[9,10] 14-29 On January 15, 2005, Leno, Inc., which has a March 31 year-end, entered into a transaction to sell the land and building that contained its manufacturing operations for a total selling price of $19,750,000. The book value of the land and the building was $3,420,000. The final closing was not expected to occur until sometime between July 2006 and March 2007.

On March 15, 2005, Leno, Inc., received an irrevocable letter of credit, issued by a major bank, for $5,000,000, which represented more than 25 percent of the sales price. Leno, Inc., would collect the $5,000,000 and would keep the money even if the buyer decided not to complete the transaction. The letter of credit had an option for an extension for up to one year for a total period of two years. At closing, the entire selling price was to be paid in cash.

Leno, Inc., was going to continue its manufacturing operations in the building and would continue to be responsible for all normal occupancy costs until final closing, when it would move to another location. After the sale, the building would be torn down and replaced by a large office building complex.

Required:

a. Based on relevant accounting pronouncements, how should Leno, Inc., account for the transaction at March 31, 2005?

b. What additional types of evidence should the auditor examine prior to recognizing any gain on the transaction?

INTERNET ASSIGNMENTS

[3,4,9] 14-30 Visit the website of another catalog retailer similar to EarthWear Clothiers, and determine what useful lives and depreciation methods are used for property, plant, and equipment. Compare those methods to EarthWear, and, if different, consider the implications for using competitor data for preliminary or substantive analytical procedures. Note that you may have to examine the entity's annual report and 10K.

[3,4,10] 14-31 Visit the SEC's website (www.sec.gov) and identify a company that has been recently cited for problems related to property, plant, and equipment or lease accounting (e.g., Xerox Corporation). Prepare a memo summarizing the property, plant, and equipment or lease accounting issues for the company.

www.mhhe.com/ messier4e	Visit the book's Online Learning Center for problem material to be completed using the *ACL* software packaged with your new text.

LEARNING OBJECTIVES

Upon completion of this chapter you will

[1] Understand the types and features of long-term debt.

[2] Assess control risk for long-term debt.

[3] Identify key control procedures for long-term debt.

[4] Know how to conduct substantive audit procedures for long-term debt.

[5] Understand the types of stockholders' equity transactions.

[6] Assess control risk for stockholders' equity.

[7] Identify key control procedures for stockholders' equity.

[8] Know the appropriate segregation of duties for stockholders' equity.

[9] Know how to conduct substantive audit procedures for capital stock.

[10] Know how to conduct substantive audit procedures for dividends.

[11] Know how to conduct substantive audit procedures for retained earnings.

[12] Know how to conduct substantive audit procedures for income statement accounts.

RELEVANT ACCOUNTING AND AUDITING PRONOUNCEMENTS

FASB Statement of Financial Accounting Concepts No. 5, Recognition and Measurement in Financial Statements of Business Enterprises (CON5)

FASB Statement of Financial Accounting Concepts No. 6, Elements of Financial Statements (CON6)

AU 312, Audit Risk and Materiality in Conducting an Audit

AU 316, Consideration of Fraud in a Financial Statement Audit

AU 319, Consideration of Internal Control in a Financial Statement Audit

AU 328, Auditing Fair Value Measurements and Disclosures

AU 329, Analytical Procedures

AU 330, The Confirmation Process

AU 339, Audit Documentation

AU 420, Consistency of Application of Generally Accepted Accounting Procedures

AICPA Auditing Standards Board, Exposure Draft, "Understanding the Entity and Its Environment and Assessing the Risks of Material Misstatement"

AICPA Auditing Standards Board, Exposure Draft, "Audit Evidence"

AICPA Auditing Standards Board, Exposure Draft, "Performing Audit Procedures in Response to Assessed Risks and Evaluating the Audit Evidence Obtained"

Auditing Financing Process: Long-Term Liabilities, Stockholders' Equity, and Income Statement Accounts

Major Phases of an Audit

Client acceptance/
continuance
and establishing
engagement terms
(Chapter 5)

Preplanning
(Chapter 5)

Establish materiality
and assess risks
(Chapter 3)

Plan the audit
(Chapters 3 and 5)

Consider and audit
internal control
(Chapters 6 and 7)

Audit business processes
and related accounts
(e.g., revenue generation)
(Chapters 10–16)

Complete the audit
(Chapter 17)

Evaluate results and issue audit
report (Chapters 2 and 18)

This chapter presents the audit of long-term liabilities, stockholders' equity, and income statement accounts. Long-term debt and equity are the major sources of financing for most entities. A substantive audit strategy is normally followed when these financial statement accounts are audited, because although the number of transactions is few, each transaction is usually material.

The discussion of auditing the income statement focuses on how the auditor's work on internal control provides evidence on income statement accounts and how most income statement accounts are audited when their related balance sheet accounts are audited. While the main focus of this chapter is auditing the long-term liabilities, stockholder's equity, and income statement accounts for a financial statement audit, the concepts covered for setting control risk are applicable to an audit of internal control over financial reporting for public companies under the Sarbanes-Oxley Act of 2002. Last, the audit of selected income statement accounts is presented. 🌐

Auditing Long-Term Debt

[LO 1] Common types of long-term debt financing include notes, bonds, and mortgages. More sophisticated types of debt financing include collateralized mortgage obligations, repurchase and reverse repurchase agreements, interest-rate swaps, financial futures, derivatives (see Exhibit 15–1), and myriad other financial instruments. Accounting and auditing for such sophisticated debt instruments can be complex and is beyond the scope of this text (see AU 328). Capitalized lease obligations also represent a form of long-term debt. To simplify the presentation of the audit of long-term debt, the discussion focuses on notes and bonds, including the audit of interest payable and interest expense.

Long-term debt may have a number of features that can affect the audit procedures used. For example, debt may be convertible into stock, or it may be combined with warrants, options, or rights that can be exchanged for equity. Debt may be callable under certain conditions, or it may require the establishment of a sinking fund to ensure that the debt can be repaid. Last, debt may be either unsecured or secured by assets of the entity.

The auditor's consideration of long-term debt, however, is no different than for any other financial statement account. The auditor must be assured that the amounts shown on the balance sheet for the various types of long-term debt are not materially misstated. This assurance extends to the proper recognition of interest expense in the financial statements.

The approach to the audit of long-term debt varies depending on the frequency of the entity's financing activities. For entities that engage in frequent financing activities, the auditor may follow a reliance strategy under which internal control is formally evaluated and tests of controls are performed in order to set control risk. However, for the vast majority of entities, it is more efficient for the auditor to follow a substantive

EXHIBIT 15–1	**Derivatives Lead to Losses at Orange County and Major Corporations**

Derivatives are contracts that are written between two parties and have a value that is derived from the value of an underlying asset, such as currencies, equities, commodities, or interest rates, or from stock market or other indicators. While derivatives can be used wisely by management to manage risk, in some instances derivatives have actually increased risk.

In 1994 highly leveraged interest-rate derivatives caused a $1.7 billion loss in the Orange County Investment Pool—money managed for the county and its cities, school districts, and other agencies. The loss occurred because the county's treasurer, Robert L. Citron, leveraged the pool's $7.6 billion to almost $20 billion and "bet" that interest rates would decline or remain steady. When the Federal Reserve Bank raised interest rates, Orange County's derivatives unraveled.

Losses on derivatives have also occurred for Procter & Gamble and Gibson Greeting Cards. Both companies entered into derivatives with Bankers Trust. Procter & Gamble announced losses in excess of $150 million and sued Bankers Trust over the transactions. Gibson had an estimated loss of $20 million but settled with Bankers Trust for $6.2 million.

Sources: Carol J. Loomis, "Untangling the Derivatives Mess," *Fortune* (March 20, 1995), pp. 50–68; and R. H. D. Molvar and J. F. Green, "The Question of Derivatives," *Journal of Accountancy* (March 1995), pp. 55–61.

strategy and perform a detailed audit of long-term debt and the related interest accounts.

Control Risk Assessment—Long-Term Debt

[LO 2] When a substantive strategy is followed, the auditor needs a sufficient understanding of the entity's internal control system over debt to be able to anticipate the types of misstatements that may occur and thus plan the substantive procedures. The following discussion of control risk assessment for long-term debt focuses on the general types of control procedures that should be present to minimize the likelihood of material misstatement. The assertions that are of primary concern to the auditor are occurrence, authorization, completeness, valuation, and disclosure-classification. Proper segregation of duties is important for ensuring the propriety of long-term debt.

Assertions and Related Control Procedures

Following are some of the more common controls that should be present for the important assertions for long-term debt.

[LO 3]

Occurrence and Authorization The entity should have controls to ensure that any long-term borrowing is properly initiated by authorized individuals. First, adequate documentation must verify that a note or bond was properly authorized. The presence of adequate documentation, such as a properly signed lending agreement, allows the auditor to determine if the transaction was properly executed. Second, any significant debt commitments should be approved by the board of directors or by executives who have been delegated this authority. Entities that engage in recurring borrowing activities should have both general and specific controls. The board of directors should establish general controls to guide the entity's financing activities. The specific controls for borrowing and repayment may be delegated to an executive, such as the chief financial officer. When the chief financial officer or similar executive is responsible for both executing and accounting for long-term debt transactions, another executive body, such as the finance committee of the board of directors, should provide overall review and approval in the minutes. If the client has proper controls for issuing debt transactions, it is generally easy for the auditor to test those transactions for occurrence (validity) and authorization at the end of the period.

Completeness The client should maintain adequate detailed records of long-term debt transactions to ensure that all borrowings and repayments of principal and interest are recorded. One approach to handling detailed debt transactions is to maintain a subsidiary ledger that contains information about all the long-term debt owed by the client. The debt amount recorded in the subsidiary ledger should be reconciled to the general ledger control account regularly.

Valuation Note and bond transactions are recorded in the accounting records at their face value plus or minus any premium or discount. Premium or discount should be amortized using the effective interest method to calculate interest expense. Sometimes an entity incurs issuing costs such as underwriter's fees, legal fees, and accounting fees. Such costs should be recorded as deferred charges and amortized over the life of the debt. Valuation issues for sophisticated financing investments are far more complex. Although the client should have control procedures to ensure that long-term debt is properly valued, the client may ask the auditor to assist with recording the debt properly.

Disclosure–Classification   Controls should ensure that notes and bonds are properly classified in the financial statements. The major issue is to properly classify as a short-term liability the portion of long-term debt that is due in the next year.

One final issue related to the control risk for long-term debt is that the client should have adequate custodial procedures for any unissued notes or bonds to safeguard against loss from theft. Procedures should provide for periodic inspections by an individual independent of both the custodial and accounting responsibilities for long-term debt.

Substantive Procedures of Long-Term Debt

[LO 4]   A substantive strategy for auditing long-term debt involves examining any new debt agreements, determining the status of prior debt agreements, and confirming balances and other relevant information with outside parties.

Substantive analytical procedures are useful in auditing interest expense because of the direct relationship between the stated interest rate and the amount of long-term debt. For example, the auditor could estimate interest expense by multiplying the 12 monthly balances for long-term debt by the average interest rate. The reasonableness of interest expense could then be assessed by comparing this estimate to the interest expense amount recorded in the general ledger. If the two amounts are not materially different, the auditor can conclude that interest expense is fairly stated. If the estimated amount of interest expense is materially higher than the recorded amount, the auditor might conclude that the client has failed to record a portion of interest expense. On the other hand, if the recorded amount of interest expense is materially higher than the estimated amount, the client may have failed to record debt. Refer to Chapter 5 for an example of the use of a substantive analytical procedure to test the relationship between EarthWear's short-term line of credit and related interest expense.

Table 15–1 provides examples of tests of transactions and account balances for long-term debt for key assertions. The following discussion delineates the general approach to auditing long-term debt.

The auditor generally begins the audit of long-term debt by obtaining an analysis schedule for notes payable, bonds payable, and accrued interest payable. Exhibit 15–2 presents an example of such a schedule. Because EarthWear does not have long-term debt, the example in Exhibit 15–2 is based on Calabro Paging Services (see Problem 3-32). If there are numerous transactions during the year, this schedule may include only the debt outstanding at the end of the period. Note that this schedule includes a considerable amount

TABLE 15–1	**Examples of Tests of Transactions and Account Balances for Long-Term Debt**

Assertions about Classes of Transactions	Substantive Tests of Transaction*
Occurrence	Examine copies of new note or bond agreements. Examine board of directors' minutes for approval of new lending agreements.
Completeness	Trace large cash receipts and payments to source documents and general ledger (see Chapters 11 and 16). Review interest expense for payments to debt holders not listed on the debt analysis schedule. Review notes paid or renewed after the balance sheet date to determine if there are unrecorded liabilities at year-end. Evaluate lease contracts to determine if leases are properly accounted for as an operating or capital lease.
Authorization	Examine board minutes for evidence of proper authorization of notes or bonds.
Accuracy	Test a sample of receipts and payments
Cutoff	Review debt activity for a few days before and after year-end to determine if the transactions are included in the proper period.
Classification	Examine the due dates on notes or bonds for proper classification between current and long-term debt.

Assertions about Account Balances at Period End	Tests of Details of Account Balances
Existence	Confirm notes or bonds directly with creditors (in many instances, creditors are banks, insurance companies, or trustees representing the creditors).
Rights and obligations	Examine copies of note and bond agreements.
Completeness	Obtain an analysis of notes payable, bonds payable, and accrued interest payable; foot schedule and agree totals to the general ledger. Obtain a standard bank confirmation that requests specific information on notes from banks (see Chapter 16 for further discussion of bank confirmations). Confirm notes or bonds with creditors. Inquire of management regarding the existence of "off-balance sheet" activities. Review board meeting minutes for debt-related activity
Valuation and allocation	Examine new debt agreements to ensure that they were recorded at the proper value. Confirm the outstanding balance for notes or bonds and the last date on which interest has been paid. Recompute accrued interest payable. Verify computation of the amortization of premium or discount.

* These tests of details of transactions are commonly conducted as dual-purpose tests (i.e., in conjunction with tests of controls).

of information on each debt transaction, including the payee, date due, interest rate, original amount, collateral, and paid and accrued interest.

Exhibit 15–2 also indicates the audit procedures performed on the details of the debt schedule. The most important assertions are tested as follows: Each debt instrument is confirmed with the debtholders and includes a request to verify the amount owed and last date on which interest has been paid. Confirmation of the debt and accrued interest provides evidence on the existence, completeness, and valuation assertions. If the client's debt

P10
DLJ
1/27/06

CALABRO PAGING SERVICES

Schedule of Long-Term Debt and Accrued Interest Payable

12/31/05

Payee	Due Date	Face Amount	Security	Long-Term Debt				Accrued Interest Payable			
				Beginning Balance	Additions	Payments	Ending Balance	Beginning Balance	Expenses	Paid	Ending Balance
First National Bank— Line of credit	11/1/08	$ 7,000,000	All assetsC	$ 200,000	$900,000	$300,000γ	$ 800,000	$ 1,875	$ 22,000λ	$ 22,815	$ 1,560
8.75% lease obligation Patriot Insurance Co.	12/15/07	$ 2,000,000	Communications equipmentC	238,637		48,230γ	190,407	5,470	31,541λ	34,461	4,550
7% bonds payable— All American Insurance	6/30/10	$10,000,000	Land and buildingsC	3,100,000		200,000γ	2,900,000	36,850	224,602λ	219,820	41,632
Total				$3,538,637	$900,000	$548,230	$3,890,407L	$44,195	$284,643L	$281,096	$47,742L
				F	F	F	F	F	F	F	F
				Less current portion of long-term debt			424,061✓				
							$6,466,346				

L = Agreed to general ledger.
γ = Traced payments to cash disbursements journal.
λ = Recomputed interest expense.
C = Agreed all information to confirmation.
F = Footed.
✓ = Tested amount of current portion of long-term debt.

598

EXHIBIT 15-3	**Sample Disclosure of Restrictive Loan Covenants**

The 7 percent bond agreement contains provisions (1) limiting funded debt, security interests, and other indebtedness, (2) requiring the maintenance of defined working capital and tangible net worth, and (3) imposing restrictions on the payment of cash dividends. The company was in compliance with, or received a waiver regarding, each of the agreements during the year ended 2005. Under the terms of these agreements, $825,000 of retained earnings was available for payment of cash dividends at December 31, 2005.

is guaranteed by another party, a confirmation should be sent to the guarantor to confirm the guarantee.

The auditor also examines the due dates for the debt to ensure proper classification between current and long-term liabilities. Last, the auditor examines the debt agreements for any restrictive covenants that require disclosure in the footnotes. Examples of such covenants include restrictions on the payment of dividends or the issuance of additional debt or equity, and the maintenance of certain financial ratios. Exhibit 15–3 is an example of the disclosure of restrictive covenants.

Auditing Stockholders' Equity

[LO 5] For most entities, stockholders' equity includes common stock, preferred stock, paid-in capital, and retained earnings. In recent years, numerous financial instruments have been developed that contain both debt and equity characteristics and affect the audit of stockholders' equity. Myriad stock options and compensation plans also impact the audit of stockholders' equity. A discussion of these complex equity instruments and stock option plans is beyond the scope of this text.

Following are the three major types of transactions that occur in stockholders' equity:

- ***Issuance of stock.*** This includes transactions such as sale of stock for cash; the exchange of stock for assets, services, or convertible debt; and issuance of stock for stock splits.
- ***Repurchase of stock.*** This includes the reacquisition of stock (referred to as *treasury stock*) and the retirement of stock.
- ***Payment of dividends.*** This includes the payment of cash dividends or issuance of stock dividends.

Control Risk Assessment—Stockholders' Equity

[LO 6] A substantive strategy is most often used to audit stockholders' equity because the number of transactions is usually small. Although control risk can then be set at the maximum, the auditor must still understand the types of controls that are in place to prevent the misstatement of equity transactions.

Many large entities, such as publicly traded companies, use an independent *registrar, transfer agent,* and *dividend-disbursing agent* to process and record equity transactions. The registrar is responsible for ensuring that all stock issued complies with the corporate charter and for maintaining the control totals for total shares outstanding. The transfer agent is responsible for preparing stock certificates and maintaining adequate stockholders' records. The dividend-disbursing agent prepares and mails dividend checks to the stockholders of record. When an entity uses an independent registrar, transfer agent, and dividend-disbursing agent, the auditor may be able to obtain sufficient evidence by confirming the relevant information with those parties.

If an entity uses its own employees to perform the stock transfer and dividend disbursement functions, the auditor needs to perform more detailed testing of the stock-related records and transactions that occurred during the period. The following assertions, control procedures, and segregation of duties are relevant when client personnel transfer stock and disburse dividends.

Assertions and Related Control Procedures ✣ [LO 7]

Following are the major assertions for stockholders' equity:

- Verify that stock and dividend transactions comply with the corporate charter (occurrence).
- Verify that all stock and dividend transactions have been properly posted and summarized in the accounting records (accuracy).
- Verify that stock and dividend transactions have been properly approved (authorization).
- Verify that stock and dividend transactions have been properly valued (valuation).

Occurrence   One of the entity's officers, such as the corporate secretary or legal counsel, should ensure that every stock or dividend transaction complies with the corporate charter or any regulatory requirement that affects the entity. This individual should also maintain the stockholders' ledger, which contains the name of each stockholder and the number of shares held by that shareholder.

Accuracy   The control procedures for this assertion include reconciliation of the stockholders' records with the number of shares outstanding and reconciliation of dividends paid with the total shares outstanding on the dividend record date.

Authorization   For most entities, the board of directors or stockholders approve stock and dividend transactions. The authorization is normally documented in the minutes of the board of directors' meetings. The auditor can examine the board of directors' minutes for proper authorization.

Valuation   Stock issuances, stock repurchases, and dividends should be recorded by the treasurer's department at an amount that conforms to GAAP. The auditor can recompute the recording of the stock and dividend transactions.

Segregation
of Duties

    ✸ **[LO 8]**

If the entity has enough personnel, the following segregation of duties should be maintained:

- The individuals responsible for issuing, transferring, and canceling stock certificates should not have any accounting responsibilities.
- The individual responsible for maintaining the detailed stockholders' records should be independent of the maintenance of the general ledger control accounts.
- The individual responsible for maintaining the detailed stockholders' records should not also process cash receipts or disbursements.
- Appropriate segregation of duties should be established among the preparation, recording, signing, and mailing of dividend checks.

Auditing Capital-Stock Accounts

    ✸ **[LO 9]**

The capital-stock accounts include common stock, preferred stock, and paid-in capital. When auditing the capital-stock accounts, the auditor is normally concerned with the occurrence, completeness, valuation, and completeness of disclosures assertions. The auditor begins the audit of capital stock by obtaining a schedule of all activity in the accounts for the current period. The beginning balance is agreed to the prior year's working papers, and the ending balance is agreed to the general ledger. The majority of the auditor's work then focuses on the current-period activity in each account.

Occurrence and
Completeness

All valid capital-stock transactions are approved by the board of directors. Therefore, the auditor can test the occurrence of capital-stock transactions by tracing the transactions recorded in the current year to the board of directors' minutes. When an independent registrar and transfer agent are used by the entity, the auditor confirms the total number of shares outstanding at the end of the period. If the amount of shares listed as outstanding on the confirmation reconciles to the general ledger capital-stock accounts, the auditor has evidence that the total number of shares outstanding at the end of the year is correct.

    If the entity does not use outside agents, it will maintain a stock register and/or a stock certificate book. The auditor may perform the following tests:

- Trace the transfers of shares between stockholders to the stock register and/or stock certificate book (accuracy and completeness).
- Foot the shares outstanding in the stock register and/or stock certificate book and agree them to total shares outstanding in the general ledger capital-stock accounts (completeness).
- Examine any canceled stock certificates (occurrence).
- Account for and inspect any unissued stock certificates in the stock certificate book (completeness).

Valuation

When capital stock is issued for cash, the assessment of proper valuation is straightforward. The par, or stated, value for the shares issued is assigned to the respective capital-stock account, while the difference between the price and par, or stated, value is allocated to paid-in capital. The auditor can recompute the values assigned to each transaction. The proceeds from the sale of stock are normally traced to the cash receipts records.

TABLE 15–2	Examples of Disclosure Items for Stockholders' Equity
	Number of shares authorized, issued, and outstanding for each class of stock. Call privileges, prices, and dates for preferred stock. Preferred-stock sinking funds. Stock option or purchase plans. Restrictions on retained earnings and dividends. Any completed or pending transactions (such as stock dividends or splits) that may affect stockholders' equity.

The valuation issue is more complex when capital stock is issued in exchange for assets or services, for a merger or acquisition, for convertible securities, or for a stock dividend. For example, when a stock dividend is declared and the number of shares issued is less than 20 percent of the shares outstanding, the dividend is recorded at fair market value. The fair market value of the stock dividend is charged to retained earnings and credited to common stock and paid-in capital. To test valuation, the auditor can recompute the stock dividend and trace the entries into the general ledger.

Completeness of Disclosures

A number of important disclosures are frequently necessary for stockholders' equity. Table 15–2 contains examples of stockholders' equity disclosures. The normal sources of this information include the corporate charter, minutes of the board of directors' meetings, and contractual agreements.

Auditing Dividends

[LO 10]   Generally, all dividends that are declared and paid will be audited because of concerns with violations of corporate bylaws or debt covenants. When the entity uses an independent dividend-disbursing agent, the auditor can confirm the amount disbursed to the agent by the entity. This amount is agreed with the amount authorized by the board of directors. The auditor can recompute the dividend amount by multiplying the number of shares outstanding on the record date by the amount of the per share dividend approved by the board of directors. This amount should agree to the amount disbursed to shareholders and accrued at year-end. If the auditor is concerned about the client's controls over dividend disbursements, he or she may test the payee names and amounts on the individual canceled checks with the stock register or stock certificate book. The auditor also reviews the entity's compliance with any agreements that restrict the payments of dividends.

Auditing Retained Earnings

[LO 11]   Under normal circumstances, retained earnings are affected by the current year's income or loss, as well as dividends paid. However, certain accounting standards require that some transactions be included in retained earnings. Prior-period adjustments, correction of errors, valuation accounts for marketable securities and foreign currency translation, and changes in appropriations of retained earnings are examples of such transactions.

The auditor begins the audit of retained earnings by obtaining a schedule of the account activity for the period. The beginning balance is agreed to the prior year's working papers and financial statements. Net income or loss can be traced to the income statement. The amounts for any cash or stock dividends can be verified as described earlier. If there are any prior-period adjustments, the auditor must be certain that the transactions satisfy the requirements of the relevant accounting standards. Any new appropriations or changes in existing appropriations should be traced to the contractual agreements that required the appropriations. Last, the auditor must make sure that all necessary disclosures related to retained earnings are made in the footnotes. For example, many debt agreements restrict the amount of retained earnings that is available for payment as dividends (see Exhibit 15–3).

Auditing Income Statement Accounts

⍟ [LO 12]   In auditing income statement accounts, the auditor must be satisfied that the revenue and expense accounts are not materially misstated and that they are accounted for in accordance with GAAP. The income statement is viewed as an important source of information by various users of the financial statements. For example, creditors or potential creditors look to an entity's profitability as one indicator of the entity's ability to repay debt. Potential investors look to the income statement when deciding whether to purchase the entity's stock. Finally, vendors may examine the entity's earnings potential in order to assess whether the entity will be able to pay for goods or services purchased on credit.

The audit of the revenue and expense accounts depends on the extent of work conducted by the auditor on the entity's control system and balance sheet accounts. For example, the likelihood of material misstatement in the various revenue and expense accounts is a function of the entity's controls. The level of control risk established for the different business processes directly affects the extent of testing that the auditor requires to audit the income statement accounts.

Auditing the income statement includes consideration of the results of audit work conducted in other parts of the audit and completion of additional substantive procedures on selected income statement accounts, including the following:

- The results of testing controls for the various business processes.
- The results of the detailed tests of balance sheet accounts and the related income statement accounts.
- Performance of substantive analytical procedures on income statement accounts.
- Detailed tests of selected income statement accounts.

Assessing Control Risk for Business Processes

In previous chapters, the auditor's approach to setting the control risk for various business processes was discussed. If the control risk is set at the maximum, the auditor does not rely on controls but conducts extensive substantive procedures. When a reliance strategy is followed, the auditor conducts tests of controls and substantive tests of transactions to determine if the client's controls are operating effectively. If the controls operate effectively, the auditor may reduce the control risk below the maximum.

To better understand the effect of a reduced control risk assessment on the audit of the revenue and expense accounts, consider the income statement accounts affected by the revenue and purchasing business processes. For example, a reduced control risk assessment for the revenue process provides evidence that the sales, accounts receivable, allowance for uncollectible accounts, and sales returns and allowances accounts are not materially misstated. Similarly, a reduced control risk assessment for the purchasing process provides evidence that financial statement accounts such as inventory; property, plant, and equipment; accounts payable; and most expense accounts are not materially misstated. The important point here is that the auditor already has reliable evidence on the accounts included in the income statement. The findings for the purchasing process are particularly relevant, since proper controls provide evidence on most of the expense accounts. This allows the auditor to do considerably fewer substantive procedures for these income statement accounts.

Direct Tests of Balance Sheet Accounts

Income statement accounts are normally audited in the course of auditing the related balance sheet accounts. Table 15–3 lists balance sheet accounts and the related income statement accounts that are verified in this manner. For example, when the allowance for uncollectible accounts is audited, bad-debt expense is also tested. Similarly, when auditing notes receivable, the auditor can test interest income.

Substantive Analytical Procedures

Substantive analytical procedures can be used extensively to test the revenue and expense accounts. One type of substantive analytical procedure involves comparing the current year's dollar amount for each revenue and expense account with the prior year's balances. Any account that deviates from the prior year's by more than a predetermined amount should be investigated. An alternative to this type of substantive analytical procedure involves calculating the ratio of individual expense accounts to net sales and comparing these percentages across years. The auditor can also compare these percentages to industry averages. Individual expense accounts that are judged by the auditor to be out of line are investigated further. While these types of substantive analytical procedures are common, it is important that substantive analytical procedures designed to provide evidence regarding the fairness of revenue or other income statement accounts be conducted at a sufficiently disaggregated (i.e., monthly or weekly data versus annual data, by business segment or product) level to detect potential misstatements. As

TABLE 15–3	Examples of Income Statement Accounts Audited in Conjunction with the Balance Sheet Account
Balance Sheet Account Audited	*Related Income Statement Account Audited*
Accounts receivable/allowance for uncollectible accounts	Bad-debt expense
Notes receivable/investments/accrued interest receivable	Interest income
Property, plant, and equipment/accumulated depreciation	Depreciation expense, gain/losses on sales or retirements of assets
Prepaid insurance	Insurance expense
Long-term debt/accrued interest payable	Interest expense

noted in Chapter 5, even relatively small percentage misstatements in large income statement accounts are often material, thus the need for precise substantive analytical procedures.

Substantive analytical procedures can also be used to provide evidence of *specific* revenue or expense accounts. For example, the auditor can test sales commissions by using the client's commission schedule and multiplying commission rates by eligible sales. This estimate can be compared to the recorded commission expense. Other examples might include overall reasonableness tests for interest and depreciation expense.

Tests of Selected Account Balances

Even though the auditor has gathered considerable evidence about revenue and expense accounts based on the audit procedures just discussed, the auditor may want to examine some accounts further. For these accounts, the auditor typically analyzes in detail the transactions included in each account. The auditor verifies the transactions by examining (vouching) the supporting documentation. Accounts examined in this manner are generally accounts that are not directly affected by a business process, accounts that may contain sensitive information or unusual transactions, or accounts for which detailed information is needed for the tax return or other schedules included with the financial statements. Some examples of such accounts include legal and audit expense, travel and entertainment, charity expense, other income and expenses, and any account containing related-party transactions. Exhibit 15–4 presents an account analysis for EarthWear's legal and

---

EXHIBIT 15–4	**Example of an Account Analysis Working Paper**

T20
SAA
2/4/06

EarthWear

EARTHWEAR CLOTHIERS
Analysis of Legal and Audit Expense
12/31/05

Date	Payee	Amount	Explanation
Feb. 1	Katz & Fritz	$ 28,500.00**V**	For services related to a patent infringement suit by Gough Mfg. Co. Lawsuit was dismissed.
April 10	Willis & Adams	950,000.00**V**	Annual audit fee.
Oct. 1	Katz & Fritz	26,200.00**V**	Legal fee for patent infringement suit against Wershant, Inc.
Oct. 20	Smoothe, Sylk, Fiels, Goode & Associates	2,100.00**V**	Legal services for a purchase contract with McDonald Merchandise, Inc.
		$1,006,800.00	
		F T/B	

Tick Mark Legend
 V = Examined payees' bills for amount and description.
 F = Footed.
T/B = Agreed to trial balance.
Conclusion: Based on the audit work performed, EarthWear's legal and audit expense account is not materially misstated.

audit expense. In auditing this account, the auditor vouches the transactions to the attorneys' invoices. The auditor should examine the invoice not only for the amount but also for information on potential uncertainties, such as lawsuits against the client.

KEY TERMS

Analytical procedures. Evaluations of financial information made by a study of plausible relationships among both financial and nonfinancial data.

Assertions. Expressed or implied representations by management that are reflected in the financial statement components.

Confirmation. The process of obtaining and evaluating direct communication from a third party in response to a request for information about a particular item affecting financial statement assertions.

Reliance strategy. The auditor's decision to rely on the entity's controls, test those controls, and reduce the direct tests of the financial statement accounts.

Tests of controls. Procedures that evaluate the effectiveness of the design and operation of internal controls.

Tests of details of account balances and disclosures. Tests that concentrate on the details of amounts contained in an account balance and disclosures.

www.mhhe.com/ messier4e	Visit the book's Online Learning Center for a multiple-choice quiz that will allow you to assess your understanding of chapter concepts.

REVIEW QUESTIONS

[LO 1,4,5,9] 15-1 Why does the auditor generally follow a substantive strategy when auditing long-term debt and capital accounts?

[2,3] 15-2 What are the most important assertions for long-term debt? What documents would normally contain the authorization to issue long-term debt?

[4] 15-3 Describe how substantive analytical procedures may be used to test interest expense.

[4] 15-4 Confirmations of long-term debt provide evidence about which assertions?

[5] 15-5 What are the functions of the registrar, the transfer agent, and the dividend-disbursing agent?

[8] 15-6 What is the major segregation of duties that should be maintained when the client does not use a registrar or transfer agent and sufficient personnel are available to perform the stock transactions?

[9] 15-7 List two common disclosures for stockholders' equity and why such disclosures are necessary.

[10,11] 15-8 What approach would the auditor follow to audit dividends and retained earnings?

[12]   15-9   List three substantive analytical procedures that the auditor might use in auditing the income statement.

[12]   15-10   Why would the auditor do an account analysis and vouch selected transactions in income statement accounts such as legal expense, travel and entertainment, and other income/expenses?

MULTIPLE-CHOICE QUESTIONS

[3]   15-11   Which of the following questions would an auditor most likely include on an control questionnaire for notes payable?

    a. Are assets that collateralize notes payable critically needed for the entity's continued existence?

    b. Are two or more authorized signatures required on checks that repay notes payable?

    c. Are the proceeds from notes payable used to purchase noncurrent assets?

    d. Are direct borrowings on notes payable authorized by the board of directors?

[4]   15-12   An auditor's purpose in reviewing the renewal of a note payable shortly after the balance sheet date is most likely to obtain evidence concerning management's assertions about

    a. Existence.

    b. Presentation and disclosure-classification.

    c. Completeness.

    d. Valuation and allocation.

[4]   15-13   An auditor's program to examine long-term debt would most likely include steps that require

    a. Comparing the carrying amount of the debt to its year-end market value.

    b. Correlating the interest expense recorded for the period with the outstanding debt.

    c. Verifying the existence of the holders of the debt by direct confirmation.

    d. Inspecting the accounts payable subsidiary ledger for unrecorded long-term debt.

[4]   15-14   The auditor can best verify a client's bond sinking fund transactions and year-end balance sheet by

    a. Confirmation of retired bonds with individual holders.

    b. Confirmation with the bond trustee.

    c. Recomputation of interest expense, interest payable, and amortization of bond discount or premium.

    d. Examination and count of the bonds retired during the year.

[7,8,9]   15-15   When a client company does *not* maintain its own stock records, the auditor should obtain written confirmation from the transfer agent and registrar concerning

    a. Restrictions on the payment of dividends.

    b. The number of shares issued and outstanding.

    c. Guarantees of preferred stock liquidation value.

    d. The number of shares subject to agreements to repurchase.

[7,8]   15-16   The primary responsibility of a bank acting as a registrar of capital stock is to

a. Ascertain that dividends declared do not exceed the statutory amount allowable in the state of incorporation.

b. Account for stock certificates by comparing the total shares outstanding to the total in the shareholders' subsidiary ledger.

c. Act as an independent third party between the board of directors and outside investors concerning mergers, acquisitions, and the sale of treasury stock.

d. Verify that stock has been issued in accordance with the authorization of the board of directors and the articles of incorporation.

[9]   15-17   An auditor should trace corporate stock issuances and treasury stock transactions to the

a. Numbered stock certificates.

b. Articles of incorporation.

c. Transfer agent's records.

d. Minutes of the board of directors.

[9]   15-18   Although the quantity and content of audit working papers vary with each particular engagement, an auditor's permanent files most likely include

a. Schedules that support the current year's adjusting entries.

b. Prior years' accounts receivable confirmations that were classified as exceptions.

c. Documentation indicating that the audit work was adequately planned and supervised.

d. Analyses of capital stock and other owners' equity accounts.

[12]   15-19   An auditor compares 2005 revenues and expenses with those of the prior year and investigates all changes exceeding 10 percent. By this procedure the auditor would be most likely to learn that

a. Fourth-quarter payroll taxes were *not* paid.

b. The client changed its capitalization policy for small tools in 2005.

c. An increase in property tax rates has *not* been recognized in the client's accrual.

d. The 2005 provision for uncollectible accounts is inadequate because of worsening economic conditions.

[12]   15-20   Which of the following comparisons would be most useful to an auditor in evaluating the results of an entity's operations?

a. Prior-year accounts payable to current-year accounts payable.

b. Prior-year payroll expense to budgeted current-year payroll expense.

c. Current-year revenue to budgeted current-year revenue.

d. Current-year warranty expense to current-year contingent liabilities.

PROBLEMS

[4]   15-21   Maslovskaya, CPA, has been engaged to examine the financial statements of Broadwall Corporation for the year ended December 31, 2005. During the year, Broadwall obtained a long-term loan from a local bank pursuant to a financing agreement that provided that

1. The loan was to be secured by the company's inventory and accounts receivable.

2. The company was not to pay dividends without permission from the bank.

3. Monthly installment payments were to commence July 1, 2005.

In addition, during the year the company borrowed various short-term amounts from the president of the company, including substantial amounts just prior to year-end.

Required:

a. For purposes of the audit of the financial statements of Broadwall Corporation, what procedures should Maslovskaya employ in examining the described loans?

b. What financial statement disclosures should Maslovskaya expect to find with respect to the loans from the president?

(AICPA, adapted)

[4] 15-22 Erik Rekdahl, senior-in-charge, is auditing Koonce Katfood, Inc.'s, long-term debt for the year ended July 31, 2005. Long-term debt is composed of two bond issues, which are due in 10 and 15 years, respectively. The debt is held by two insurance companies. Rekdahl has examined the bond indentures for each issue. The indentures provide that if Koonce fails to comply with the covenants of the indentures, the debt becomes payable immediately. Rekdahl identified the following covenants when reviewing the bond indentures:

1. "The debtor company shall endeavor to maintain a working capital ratio of 2 to 1 at all times, and in any fiscal year following a failure to maintain said ratio, the company shall restrict compensation of officers to a total of $650,000. Officers include the chairperson of the board and the president."

2. "The debtor company shall keep all property that is security for these debt agreements insured against loss by fire to the extent of 100 percent of its actual value. Policies of insurance comprising this protection shall be filed with the trustee."

3. "The company is required to restrict 40 percent of retained earnings from availability for paying dividends."

4. "A sinking fund shall be established with the First Morgan Bank of Austin, and semiannual payments of $500,000 shall be deposited in the fund. The bank may, at its discretion, purchase bonds from either issue."

Required:

a. Provide any audit steps that Rekdahl should conduct to determine if the company is in compliance with the bond indentures.

b. List any reporting requirements that the financial statements or footnotes should recognize.

(AICPA, adapted)

[4] 15-23 The long-term debt working paper on page **611** (indexed K-1) was prepared by client personnel and audited by Andy Fogelman, an audit assistant, during the calendar year 2005 audit of American Widgets, Inc., a continuing audit client. The engagement supervisor is reviewing the working paper thoroughly.

Required:

Identify the deficiencies in the working paper that the engagement supervisor should discover.

(AICPA, adapted)

[8,9]   15-24   Lee, CPA, the continuing auditor of Wu, Inc., is beginning to audit the common stock and treasury stock accounts. Lee has decided to design substantive procedures without relying on the company's internal control system.

Wu has no par and no stated-value common stock, and it acts as its own registrar and transfer agent. During the past year Wu both issued and reacquired shares of its own common stock, some of which the company still owned at year-end. Additional common stock transactions occurred among the shareholders during the year.

Common stock transactions can be traced to individual shareholders' accounts in a subsidiary ledger and to a stock certificate book. The company has not paid any cash or stock dividends. There are no other classes of stock, stock rights, warrants, or option plans.

Required:

What substantive audit procedures should Lee apply in examining the common stock and treasury stock accounts?

(AICPA, adapted)

DISCUSSION CASE

[4]   15-25   On September 10, Melinda Johnson was auditing the financial statements of a new audit client, Mother Earth Foods, a health-food chain that has a June 30 year-end. The company is privately held and has just gone through a leveraged buyout with long-term financing that includes various restrictive covenants.

In order to obtain debt financing, companies often have to agree to certain conditions, some of which may restrict the way in which they conduct their business. If the borrower fails to comply with the stated conditions, it may be considered in default, which would give the lender the right to accelerate the due date of the debt, add other restrictions, waive the default for a stated period, or revise the covenants. Usually there is a grace period during which the borrower can cure the default.

Johnson believes that it is possible that at August 31 Mother Earth was in violation of the debt covenant restrictions, which became effective on that date. The debt covenants require the company to maintain a certain receivable turnover rate. Johnson is not certain, however, because the accounting records, including period-end cutoffs for sales and purchases, have not been well maintained. Nevertheless, Mother Earth's executives assure Johnson that if they were in violation, the company will be able to obtain a waiver or modification of the covenant.

	Prepared By	Initials	Date
	Prepared By	AF	1/22/06
	Approved By		

AMERICAN WIDGETS, INC.
Working Paper
December 31, 2005

Lender	Interest Rate	Payment Terms	Collateral	Balance 12/31/04	2005 Borrowings	2005 Reductions	Balance 12/31/05	Interest Paid to	Accrued Interest Payable 12/31/05	Comments
First Commercial Bank φ	12%	Interest only on 25th of month, principal due in full 1/1/09; no prepayment penalty	Inventories	$ 50,000✓	$300,000A 1/31/05	$ 100,000❋ 6/30/05	$ 250,000CX	12/25/05	$2,500NR	Dividend of $80,000 paid 9/2/05 (W/P N-3) violates a provision of the debt agreement, which thereby permits lender to demand immediate payment; lender has refused to waive this violation.
Lender's Capital Corporation φ	Prime plus 1%	Interest only on last day of month, principal due in full 3/5/07	2nd mortgage on Park Street Building	100,000✓	50,000A 2/29/05	—	200,000C	12/31/05	—	Prime rate was 8% to 9% during the year.
Gigantic Building & Loan Association φ	12%	$5,000 principal plus Interest due on 5th of month, due in full 12/31/14	1st mortgage on Park Street Building	720,000✓	—	60,000θ	660,000C	12/5/05	5,642R	Reclassification entry for current portion proposed (see RJE-3).
J. Lott, majority stockholder φ	0%	Due in full 12/31/08	Unsecured	300,000✓	—	100,000N 12/31/05	200,000C	—	—	Borrowed additional $100,000 from J. Lott on 1/7/06
				$1,170,000✓	$350,000	$ 260,000	$1,310,000T/B		$8,142T/B	
				F	F	F	F		F	

Interest costs from long-term debt
Interest expense for year	$ 281,333T/B
Average loan balance outstanding	$1,406,667R

Five-year maturities (for disclosure purposes)
Year-end	
12/31/06	$ 60,000
12/31/07	260,000
12/31/08	260,000
12/31/09	310,000
12/31/10	60,000
Thereafter	360,000
	$1,310,000
	F

Tick Mark Legend
C = Confirmed without exception, W/P K-2.
F = Readded, foots correctly.
CX = Confirmed with exception, W/P K-3.
NR = Does not recompute correctly.
A = Agreed to loan agreement, validated bank deposit ticket, and board of directors' authorization, W/P W-7.
θ = Agreed to canceled checks and lender's monthly statements.
N = Agreed to cash disbursements journal and canceled check dated 12/31/05, clearing 1/8/06.
T/B = Traced to working trial balance.
✓ = Agreed to 12/31/04 working papers.
φ = Agreed interest rate, term, and collateral to copy of note and loan agreement.
❋ = Agreed to canceled check and board of directors' authorization, W/P W-7.

Conclusions: Long-term debt, accrued interest payable, and interest expense are correct and complete at 12/31/05.

Required:

a. Discuss the audit procedures that Johnson would conduct to determine if Mother Earth violated the debt covenants. How would Johnson determine whether Mother Earth would be able to obtain a waiver, assuming that the company was in violation of the debt covenants?

b. Based on the case scenario, should Mother Earth continue to classify this debt as noncurrent? Justify your answer.

INTERNET ASSIGNMENT

[6,7,8,11]   15-26 Enron Corporation was once a high-flying energy trading company. Numerous financial analysts had complained that Enron's financial statements were "indecipherable." In October 2001, Enron reduced shareholders' equity by $1.2 billion because it decided to "unwind some transactions with limited partnerships with which it had done business." Questions have been raised about Enron's accounting for these transactions.

Required:

Use the Internet to obtain information about Enron's earnings restatement. Sources of information on this issue can be found at websites for Enron, the SEC, and various news providers (*The Wall Street Journal*). Prepare a memo summarizing the issues related to Enron's accounting. Consider why Enron's auditors (Andersen) might have allowed the company to account for those transactions in that manner.

| www.mhhe.com/ messier4e | Visit the book's Online Learning Center for problem material to be completed using the *ACL* software packaged with your new text. |

CHAPTER 16

LEARNING OBJECTIVES

Upon completion of this chapter you will

[1] Understand the relationship of the various business processes to cash.

[2] Know the different types of bank accounts.

[3] Identify tests of details of transactions used to audit cash.

[4] Identify tests of details of account balances used to audit cash.

[5] Know how to audit a bank reconciliation.

[6] Understand fraud-related audit procedures for cash.

[7] Understand why clients invest in securities of other entities.

[8] Identify key controls for investments.

[9] Know the appropriate segregation of duties for investments.

[10] Identify tests of details of account balances used to audit investments.

RELEVANT ACCOUNTING AND AUDITING PRONOUNCEMENTS

FASB Statement of Financial Accounting Standards No. 95, Statement of Cash Flows (FAS 95)

FASB Statement of Financial Accounting Standards No. 115, Accounting for Certain Investments in Debt and Equity Securities (FAS 115)

AU 312, Audit Risk and Materiality in Conducting an Audit

AU 316, Consideration of Fraud in a Financial Statement Audit

AU 319, Consideration of Internal Control in a Financial Statement Audit

AU 328, Auditing Fair Value Measurements and Disclosures

AU 329, Analytical Procedures

AU 330, The Confirmation Process

AU 332, Auditing Investments

AU 339, Audit Documentation

AICPA Auditing Standards Board, Exposure Draft, "Understanding the Entity and Its Environment and Assessing the Risks of Material Misstatement"

AICPA Auditing Standards Board, Exposure Draft, "Audit Evidence"

AICPA Auditing Standards Board, Exposure Draft, "Performing Audit Procedures in Response to Assessed Risks and Evaluating the Audit Evidence Obtained"

Auditing Financing Process: Cash and Investments

Major Phases of an Audit

Client acceptance/
continuance and establishing
engagement terms
(Chapter 5)

Preplanning
(Chapter 5)

Establish materiality
and assess risks
(Chapter 3)

Plan the audit
(Chapters 3 and 5)

Consider and audit
internal control
(Chapters 6 and 7)

Audit business processes
and related accounts
(e.g., revenue generation)
(Chapters 10–16)

Complete the audit
(Chapter 17)

Evaluate results and issue audit
report (Chapters 2 and 18)

This chapter covers the audit of cash and investments. These are the last accounts studied in this text because each of the other business processes interacts with cash. Additionally, the evidence gathered during the audit of other business processes affects the type and amount of evidence required to audit cash.

Proper management of cash and investments is essential to every entity. The principal goal of cash management is to ensure that sufficient cash is available to meet the entity's needs. Achieving this goal requires good forecasting of cash receipts and disbursements. By using sound cash-forecasting techniques, management can plan for (1) investing excess cash and (2) borrowing at favorable interest rates when cash is required. Because cash and investments are so liquid, they normally represent critical audit areas.

Cash and the Effect of Other Business Processes

[LO 1] The line item "cash" reported in the financial statements represents currency on hand and cash on deposit in bank accounts, including certificates of deposit, time deposits, and savings accounts. Frequently, certain "cash equivalents" are combined with cash for presentation in the financial statements. FASB Statement of Financial Accounting Standards No. 95, "Statement of Cash Flows" (FAS 95), defines *cash equivalents* as short-term, highly liquid investments that are readily convertible to cash or so near their maturity that there is little risk of change in their value (para. 8). Examples of such financial instruments include Treasury bills, commercial paper, and money market funds.

Because virtually all accounting transactions pass through the cash account as part of their "cradle-to-grave" cycle, cash is affected in one way or another by all of the entity's business processes. Figure 16–1 shows the effect each major business process has on the cash account. Although the main source of cash receipts is the revenue process, other sources of cash include (1) the sale of property, plant, and equipment and (2) the proceeds from issuing long-term debt or capital stock. The main sources of disbursements from cash are the purchasing and human resource management processes. Generally, large payments from the purchasing process are for acquisitions of inventory and property, plant, and equipment. Payments on long-term debt and repurchase of stock are other types of cash disbursements.

Because of the close relationship of cash to the revenue and purchasing processes, control issues were discussed in Chapters 10 and 11, respectively. Table 10–6 summarized the assertions, possible misstatements, control procedures, and tests of controls for cash receipt transactions. A similar

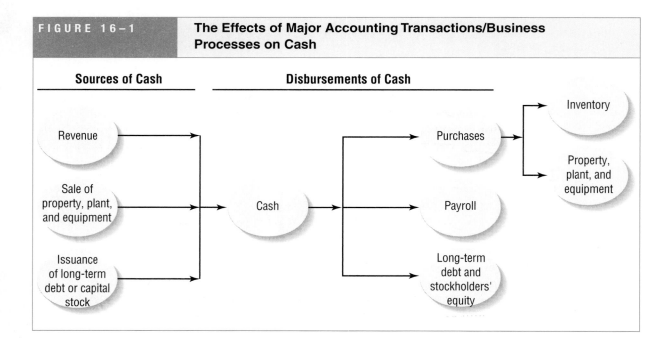

| FIGURE 16–1 | The Effects of Major Accounting Transactions/Business Processes on Cash |

Sources of Cash   **Disbursements of Cash**

Revenue

Sale of property, plant, and equipment

Issuance of long-term debt or capital stock

Cash

Purchases

Payroll

Long-term debt and stockholders' equity

Inventory

Property, plant, and equipment

summary was provided for cash disbursement transactions in Table 11–7. A discussion of control risk for cash receipt and disbursement transactions will not be repeated in this chapter. However, the auditor's assessment of the control risk for transactions processed through the revenue and purchasing processes strongly affects the nature and extent of testing for the ending cash balance. For example, if the control risk is below the maximum for both of these processes, the auditor can reduce the substantive testing of the cash balances. The reader should review the assessment of control risk for cash receipt and cash disbursement transactions.

Types of Bank Accounts

[LO 2]   As mentioned, cash management is an important function in all organizations. In order to maximize its cash position, an entity implements procedures for accelerating the collection of cash receipts and properly delaying the payment of cash disbursements. Such procedures allow the entity to earn interest on excess cash or to reduce the cost of cash borrowings.

In spite of the sophisticated nature of cash management, the entity's management must still be concerned with the control and safekeeping of cash. Using different types of bank accounts aids in controlling the entity's cash. The following types of bank accounts are typically used:

- General cash account.
- Imprest cash accounts.
- Branch accounts.

It is important to understand each of the different types of bank accounts used. While the audit approach to each type of account is similar, the extent of testing varies from one account to the next. Each type of bank account is briefly discussed.

General Cash Account

The general cash account is the principal cash account for most entities. The major source of cash receipts for this account is the revenue process, and the major sources of cash disbursements are the purchasing and human resource management processes. This cash account may also be used for receipts and disbursements from other bank accounts maintained by the entity. For many small entities, this is the only cash account maintained.

Imprest Cash Accounts

An imprest bank account contains a stipulated amount of money, and the account is used for limited purposes. Imprest accounts are frequently used for disbursing payroll and dividend checks. In the case of payroll, a separate bank account containing a minimum balance is established for disbursing payroll. Disbursement may be by check or direct deposit. Prior to the disbursement of payroll, a check is drawn or a cash transfer is made from the general cash account to the payroll account for the amount of the net payroll. The payroll is then drawn on this imprest account. Thus, the payroll account serves as a clearing account for payroll payments and facilitates the disbursement of cash while also maintaining adequate control over cash.

Use of imprest accounts also minimizes the time required to reconcile the general cash account.

Branch Accounts

Companies that operate branches in multiple locations may maintain separate accounts at local banks. This allows each branch to pay local expenses and to maintain a banking relationship in the local community. Branch cash accounts can be operated in a number of ways. In some cases, the branch accounts are nothing more than imprest accounts for branch payments in which a minimum balance is maintained. The branch submits periodic cash reports to headquarters, and the branch account receives a check or transfer from the general cash account. In other cases, the branch account functions as a general cash account by recording both cash receipts and cash disbursements.

For proper control, the branch should be required to submit periodic cash reports to headquarters, and the entity's management should carefully monitor the cash balances in the branch accounts.

Substantive Analytical Procedures—Cash

Because of its residual nature, cash does not have a predictable relationship with other financial statement accounts. As a result, the auditor's use of substantive analytical procedures for auditing cash is limited to comparisons with prior years' cash balances and to budgeted amounts. This limited use of substantive analytical procedures is normally offset by (1) extensive tests of controls and/or substantive tests of transactions for cash receipts and cash disbursements or (2) extensive tests of the entity's bank reconciliations.

Substantive Tests of Details of Transactions and Balances

[LO 3,4]   Table 16–1 contains examples of substantive tests of transactions for both cash receipts and cash disbursements. By testing both cash receipts and disbursements, the auditor obtains important evidence about the relevant assertions for the cash account. On most audits, the substantive tests of transactions for cash receipts and cash disbursements are conducted together with the tests of controls for the revenue and purchasing processes, respectively.

The Effects of Controls

The reliability of the client's controls over cash receipts and cash disbursements affects the nature and extent of the auditor's tests of details. The preceding chapters discussed a number of important controls for both cash receipts and disbursements. For example, incoming checks are to be restrictively endorsed (stamped "For deposit only" to the company's bank account), and daily cash receipts are to be reconciled with postings to the accounts receivable subsidiary ledger. The effective operation of these controls provides strong evidence that the completeness assertion is being met. Similarly, outgoing checks are to be signed only when all documents included in the voucher packet have been independently approved. The

TABLE 16–1	Examples of Tests of Details of Transactions for Cash Receipts and Disbursements	
	Substantive Tests of Transactions*	
Assertions about Classes of Transactions	*Cash Receipts*	*Cash Disbursements*
Occurrence	Trace a sample of entries in the cash receipts journal to remittance advices, daily deposit slips, and bank statement.	Trace a sample of entries from the cash disbursements journal to canceled checks, voucher packet, and bank statement.
Completeness	Trace a sample of remittance advices to cash receipts journal and, if necessary, to deposit slips.	Trace a sample of canceled checks to the cash disbursements journal.
Authorization	For a sample of days, examine the signature on the deposit slip and the check endorsements for proper authorization.	Examine a sample of canceled checks for authorized signature and proper endorsement.
Accuracy	For a sample of daily deposits, foot the remittance advices and entries on the deposit slip and agree to the cash receipts journal and bank statement. For a sample of weeks, foot the cash receipts journal and agree posting to the general ledger.	For a sample of voucher packets, agree amounts in purchase order, receiving report, invoice, canceled check, and disbursement journal. For a sample of weeks, foot the cash disbursements journal and agree posting to the general ledger.
Cutoff	Compare the dates for recording a sample of cash receipts transactions in the cash receipts journal with the dates the cash was deposited in the bank (note any significant delays). Observe cash on hand for the last day of the year, and trace deposits to cash receipts journal and cutoff bank statement	Compare the dates for a sample of checks with the dates the checks cleared the bank (note any significant delays). Record the last check issued on the last day of the year, and trace to cash disbursements journal.
Classification	Examine a sample of remittance advices for proper account classification	Examine a sample of canceled checks for proper account classification.

* These tests of details of transactions are commonly conducted as dual-purpose tests (i.e., in conjunction with tests of controls).

effective operation of this control procedure provides the auditor with evidence on the authorization assertion.

A major control that directly affects the audit of cash is the completion of a monthly bank reconciliation by client personnel who are independent of the handling and recording of cash receipts and cash disbursements. Such bank reconciliations ensure that the client's books reflect the same balance as the bank's after reconciling items have been considered. Control can be improved further if an independent party such as the internal auditor reviews the bank reconciliation.

If the client has good bank reconciliation procedures that are promptly performed, the auditor may be able to reduce the audit work on the ending cash balance.

Balance-Related Assertions

Table 16–2 summarizes the assertions and tests of details of account balances for cash accounts. The rights and obligations assertion is not included in Table 16–2 because it is seldom important to the audit of the cash balance. The major audit procedures for each cash account involve tests of the bank reconciliation. The approach to auditing a bank reconciliation is

TABLE 16-2	Examples of Tests of Details of Balances for Cash	
Assertions about Account Balances at Period End		**Tests of Details Account Balances**
Existence		Test bank reconciliation for each account:
		• Foot the reconciliation and the outstanding check listing.
Completeness		• Trace balances per book to the general ledger.
Valuation and Allocation		• Obtain standard bank confirmation and trace balance per bank to the bank reconciliation.
		• Obtain cutoff bank statement.
		• Trace deposits in transit, outstanding checks, and other reconciling items to cutoff bank statement.
		If control risk is high or if fraud is suspected:
		• Perform extended bank reconciliation procedures.
		• Perform a proof of cash.
		• Test for kiting.

basically the same regardless of the type of bank account being examined. However, the type and extent of the audit work are more detailed for the general cash account because it normally represents a material amount and because of the large amount of activity in the account.

Auditing the General Cash Account

[LO 5]

Table 16–2 shows that the main source of evidence for the existence, completeness, and valuation assertions is the audit work completed on the bank reconciliation. To audit a cash account, the auditor should obtain the following documents:

- A copy of the bank reconciliation.
- A standard form to confirm account balance information with financial institutions (referred to as a *standard bank confirmation*).
- A cutoff bank statement.

Bank Reconciliation Working Paper   Exhibit 16–1 provides an example of a bank reconciliation working paper for EarthWear's general cash account. Note that the difference between the cash balance showed in Exhibit 16–1 and the balance in cash on the financial statements is represented by cash equivalents (Treasury bills and commercial paper). On most audits, the auditor obtains a copy of the bank reconciliation prepared by the client's personnel. The working paper reconciles the balance per the bank with the balance per the books. The major reconciling items are deposits in transit, outstanding checks, and other adjustments, such as bank service charges and any check returned because the customer did not have sufficient cash (NSF check) in its account to cover payment of the check.

Standard Bank Confirmation Form   The auditor generally confirms the account balance information with every bank or financial institution that maintains an account for the client. The American Institute of Certified Public Accountants, American Bankers Association, and Bank Administration Institute have agreed on a standard format for confirming such

EXHIBIT 16-1	**Example of a Bank Reconciliation Working Paper**

C10
DLJ
1/14/06

EarthWear

EARTHWEAR CLOTHIERS
Bank Reconciliation
12/31/05
General Cash Account

Balance per bank: **C11**		$1,854,890**C**
Add:		
Deposits in transit:		
12/30/05	$156,940 ✓	
12/31/05	340,875 ✓	497,815
Deduct:		
Outstanding checks:		
#1243	$ 121,843 ɸ	
#1244	232,784 ɸ	
#1247	30,431 ɸ	
#1250	64,407 ɸ	
#1251	123,250 ɸ	(572,715)
Balance per books, unadjusted		1,779,990
Adjustments to books:		
Bank service charges	$ 250 ✓	
NSF check	7,400 ✓	(7,650)
Balance per books, adjusted		$1,772,340**L**
		F

F = Footed.
C = Traced balance to bank confirmation.
L = Agreed to cash lead schedule and general ledger.
✓ = Traced amount to cutoff bank statement.
ɸ = Examined canceled check for proper payee, amount, and endorsement.

Note: The controller has signed for the return of the cutoff bank statement.

---

information.[1] Exhibit 16–2 contains a completed copy of the confirmation form, which is titled "Standard Form to Confirm Account Balance Information with Financial Institutions." This form is also used to obtain information about any loans the client may have with the bank.

Note that the confirmation form does not require bank personnel to conduct a comprehensive, detailed search of the bank's records beyond the account information requested on the confirmation. However, it does request that bank personnel indicate any other deposits or loans that come to their attention while completing the confirmation. As a result, this confirmation

---

[1]See D. P. Sauter, "Bank Confirmation Form Receives Facelift," *Journal of Accountancy* (March 1991), pp. 82–89, for additional discussion of the new standard form for confirming bank accounts.

EXHIBIT 16–2	Example of a Completed Standard Bank Confirmation Form

**STANDARD FORM TO CONFIRM ACCOUNT
BALANCE INFORMATION WITH FINANCIAL INSTITUTIONS**

C11
DLJ
1/14/06

EarthWear

___EarthWear Clothiers___
CUSTOMER NAME

We have provided to our accountants the following information as of

the close of business on _____ December 31, _____, 2005 regarding our deposit and loan balances. Please confirm the accuracy of the information, noting any exceptions to the information provided. If the balances have been left blank, please complete this form by furnishing the balance in the appropriate space below.° Although we do not request or expect you to conduct a comprehensive, detailed search of your records, if during the process of completing this confirmation additional information about other deposit and loan accounts we may have with you comes to your attention, please include such information below. Please use the enclosed envelope to return the form directly to our accountants.

Financial
Institution's
Name and
Address

[   ]
First National Bank
P.O.   Box 1947
Boise, Idaho 79443

[   ]

1. At the close of business on the date listed above, our records indicated the following deposit balance(s):

ACCOUNT NAME	ACCOUNT NO.	INTEREST RATE	BALANCE°
General Account	04-78925	None	$ 1,854,890.00 to C10
Payroll Account	01-04354	None	$ 5,000.00 to C20

2. We were directly liable to the financial institution for loans at the close of business on the date listed above as follows:

ACCOUNT NO./ DESCRIPTION	BALANCE°	DATE DUE	INTEREST RATE	DATE THROUGH WHICH INTEREST IS PAID	DESCRIPTION OF COLLATERAL

Sally Jones   _12/31/05_
(Customer's Authorized Signature)   (Date)

The information presented above by the customer is in agreement with our records. Although we have not conducted a comprehensive, detailed search of our records, no other deposit or loan accounts have come to our attention except as noted below.   _J J Hammer_   _1/5/06_

(Financial Institution Authorized Signature)   (Date)

___Branch Manager___
(Title)

EXCEPTIONS AND/OR COMMENTS

Please return this form directly to our accountants:

Willis & Adams
P.O. Box 4080
Boise, Idaho 79443-4080

°Ordinarily, balances are intentionally left blank if they are not available at the time the form is prepared.

Approved 1990 by American Bankers Association, American Institute of Certified Public Accountants, and Bank Administration Institute. Additional forms available from AICPA — Order Department, P.O. Box 1003, NY, NY 10106-1003.

request cannot be relied upon to identify *all* information about a client's bank deposits or loans. If the auditor believes that additional information is needed about a client's arrangements with a financial institution, a separate confirmation letter signed by the client should be sent to the official at the financial institution who is responsible for the client's accounts. Details regarding lines of credit and compensating balances are examples of information that might be confirmed in this manner. This issue is discussed later in this chapter.

Cutoff Bank Statement   A major step in auditing a bank reconciliation is verifying the propriety of the reconciling items such as deposits in transit and outstanding checks. The auditor obtains a cutoff bank statement to test the reconciling items included in the bank reconciliation. A cutoff bank statement normally covers the 7- to 10-day period after the date on which the bank account is reconciled. Any reconciling item should have cleared the client's bank account during the 7- to 10-day period. The auditor obtains this cutoff bank statement by having the client request that the bank send the statement, including canceled checks, directly to the auditor.

Tests of the Bank Reconciliation   The auditor uses the following audit procedures to test the bank reconciliation:

1. *Test the mathematical accuracy of the bank reconciliation working paper and agree the balance per the books to the general ledger.* In Exhibit 16–1, the working paper has been footed and the balance per the books as shown on the reconciliation has been agreed to the general ledger.

2. *Agree the bank balance on the bank reconciliation with the balance shown on the standard bank confirmation.* The bank confirmation shown in Exhibit 16–2 has been prepared so that it corresponds to the bank reconciliation in Exhibit 16–1. The $1,854,890 shown on the bank reconciliation has been agreed to the $1,854,890 balance shown on the bank confirmation in Exhibit 16–2.

3. *Trace the deposits in transit on the bank reconciliation to the cutoff bank statement.* Any deposit in transit shown on the bank reconciliation should be listed as a deposit shortly after the end of the period. The tick mark next to the deposits in transit shown in Exhibit 16–1 indicates that the deposits were traced by the auditor to the cutoff bank statement.

4. *Compare the outstanding checks on the bank reconciliation working paper with the canceled checks contained in the cutoff bank statement for proper payee, amount, and endorsement.* The auditor should also ensure that no checks dated prior to December 31 are included with the cutoff bank statement that are not included as outstanding checks on the bank reconciliation. The tick mark next to the outstanding checks shown in Exhibit 16–1 indicates that the checks were traced by the auditor to the cutoff bank statement and that the canceled checks were examined for propriety.

5. *Agree any charges included on the bank statement to the bank reconciliation.* In some cases, these charges may result in an adjustment to the client's books. For example, the bank service charges of $250 and the NSF check for $7,400 received from a customer shown in Exhibit 16–1 require adjustment of the client's records.

6. *Agree the adjusted book balance to the cash account lead schedule.* The adjusted book balance would be part of the amount included in the financial statements for cash.

Fraud-Related Audit Procedures

✂ [LO 6]

If the client does not have adequate control procedures over cash or the auditor suspects that some type of fraud or defalcation involving cash has occurred, it may be necessary to extend the normal cash audit procedures. Although many types of fraud, such as forgery or collusion, are difficult to detect, auditing standards (AU 316) indicate that the auditor has a responsibility to plan and perform the audit to obtain reasonable assurance about whether the financial statements are free of material misstatement, whether caused by error or fraud.

Three audit procedures that auditors typically use to detect fraudulent activities in the cash accounts are

- Extended bank reconciliation procedures.
- Proof of cash.
- Tests for kiting.

Extended Bank Reconciliation Procedures In some instances, the year-end bank reconciliation can be used to cover cash defalcations. This is usually accomplished by manipulating the reconciling items in the bank reconciliation. For example, suppose a client employee was able to steal $5,000 from the client. The client's cash balance at the bank would then be $5,000 less than reported on the client's books. The employee could "hide" the $5,000 shortage in the bank reconciliation by including a fictitious deposit in transit. Thus, the typical approach to searching for possible fraud is to extend the bank reconciliation procedures to examine the disposition of the reconciling items included on the prior months' reconciliations and the reconciling items included in the current bank reconciliation.

For example, assume that the auditor suspected that some type of fraud had been committed. The auditor would examine the November and December bank reconciliations by ensuring that all reconciling items had been properly handled. For deposits in transit on the November bank reconciliation, the auditor would trace the deposits to the November cash receipts journal to verify that they were recorded. The deposits would also be traced to the December bank statement to verify that they were deposited in the bank. Checks listed as outstanding on the November bank reconciliation would be traced to the November cash disbursements journal, and the canceled checks returned with the December bank statement would be examined for propriety. Other reconciling items such as bank charges, NSF checks, and collections of notes by the bank would be similarly traced to the accounting records for proper treatment. The auditor

EXHIBIT 16–3	Example of a Proof of Cash

DP5

CALABRO PAGING SERVICES
Proof of Cash—General Cash Account
12/31/05

	11/30/05	December Receipts	December Disbursements	12/31/05
Balance per bank	$513,324	$457,822φ	$453,387φ	$517,759F
Deposits in transit:				
11/30/05	114,240	(114,240)		
12/31/05		116,437		116,437
Outstanding checks:				
11/30/05	(117,385)		(117,385)	
12/31/05			115,312	(115,312)
Collection of note receivable ν	(7,500)	7,500		
Balance per books, unadjusted	502,679	467,519γ	451,314μ	518,884F
Adjustments to books:				
Bank charges			125	(125)ε
NSF checks		(5,250)		(5,250)ε
Balance per books, adjusted	$502,679	$462,269	$451,439	$513,509FL
	F	F	F	F

F = Footed and crossfooted.
L = Agreed to general ledger.
φ = Traced to December bank statement.
γ = Agreed to December cash receipts journal.
μ = Agreed to December cash disbursements journal.
ν = Traced to November bank statement and December cash receipts journal.
ε = Traced to cutoff bank statement.

would examine the reconciling items included on the December bank reconciliation in a similar fashion to ensure that such items were not being used to cover a cash defalcation. Further investigation would be required for any reconciling items not properly accounted for. The client's management should be informed if the auditor detects any fraudulent transactions.

Proof of Cash   A proof of cash is used to reconcile the cash receipts and disbursements recorded on the client's books with the cash deposited into and disbursed from the client's bank account for a specific time period. Exhibit 16–3 presents an example of a proof of cash for Calabro Paging Services (Problem 3-32) for one month, although on some audits a proof of cash is performed for the entire period under audit. Because the proof contains four columns, a proof of cash is commonly referred to as a *four-column proof of cash*. The four columns include

- A bank reconciliation for the beginning of the period.
- A reconciliation of the cash deposited in the bank with the cash receipts recorded in the cash receipts journal.
- A reconciliation of the cash disbursed through the bank account with the cash disbursements recorded in the cash disbursements journal.
- A bank reconciliation for the end of the period.

The primary purposes of the proof of cash are (1) to ensure that all cash receipts recorded in the client's cash receipts journal were deposited in the client's bank account, (2) to ensure that all cash disbursements recorded in the client's cash disbursements journal have cleared the client's bank account, and (3) to ensure that no bank transactions have been omitted from the client's accounting records. The reader should note that a proof of cash will *not* detect a theft of cash when the cash was stolen *before* being recorded in the client's books. If the auditor suspects that cash was stolen before being recorded in the client's books, the audit procedures discussed under the completeness assertion for cash receipt transactions in Chapter 10 should be performed.

Tests for Kiting   When cash has been stolen by an employee, it is possible to cover the cash shortage by following a practice known as *kiting*. This involves an employee covering the cash shortage by transferring money from one bank account to another and recording the transactions improperly on the client's books. Concealing the cash shortage can be accomplished by preparing a check on one account before year-end but not recording it as a cash disbursement in the account until the next period. The check is deposited in a second account before year-end and recorded as a cash receipt in the current period. The deposit must occur close enough to year-end that it will not clear the first bank account before the end of the year.

One approach that auditors commonly use to test for kiting is the preparation of an *interbank transfer schedule* such as the one shown in Exhibit 16–4. This exhibit provides six examples of the types of cash transfers an auditor might encounter. For example, transfer 2 is an example of a proper cash transfer. A check was drawn on account 1 and recorded as a cash disbursement on December 30. It was recorded as a cash receipt in account 2 on December 30 and deposited in that account on December 31. The check cleared account 1 on January 2. The auditor would examine this transfer by tracing the check to the cash disbursements journal, the cash receipts journal, and the December 31 bank reconciliation. Because the check cleared the bank on January 2, it should be listed as an outstanding check on the December 31 bank reconciliation for account 1. The reader will also notice that transfers 1, 3, and 6 are proper transfers.

Transfer 4 represents an example of kiting. A check was written on account 1 before year-end, but the disbursement was not recorded in the disbursements journal until after year-end (January 2). The check was deposited in account 2 and recorded as a cash receipt before year-end. Thus, the cash shortage in account 2 is covered by a cash deposit from account 1, and cash is overstated by $10,000. Transfer 5 represents a different type of impropriety that would also require additional work on the part of the auditor.

EXHIBIT 16-4	Example of an Interbank Transfer Schedule				
		Account 1 **Disbursement Dates**		**Account 2** **Receipt and Deposit Dates**	
Transfer Number*	Amount	Per Client Books	Per Bank Statement	Per Client Books	Per Bank Statement
1	$15,000	12/28	12/30	12/28	12/29
2	7,500	12/30	1/2	12/30	12/31
3	8,400	12/31	1/2	12/31	1/2
4	10,000	1/2	1/2	12/30	12/31
5	3,000	1/3	1/3	1/3	12/30
6	17,300	1/2	1/4	1/2	1/2

*Explanation for each transfer in determining proper cash cutoff at 12/31/05:

1. The transfer was made on December 28 and recorded on the books as both a receipt and a disbursement on the same date. The check written was deposited on December 28 in the receiving bank account and credited on the bank statement the next day. The check cleared account 1 on December 30. All dates are in the same accounting period, so there are no questions as to the propriety of the cutoff.
2. This transfer is proper. However, the transfer check should appear as an *outstanding check* on the reconciliation of account 1.
3. Transfer 3 is also proper. In this example, the transfer should appear as a *deposit in transit* on the reconciliation of account 2 and as an outstanding check on the reconciliation of account 1.
4. This transfer represents kiting because the receipt was recorded on the books in the period prior to that in which the corresponding disbursement was recorded. Cash is overstated by $10,000.
5. Transfer 5 is also improper. In this case a deposit was made in the receiving bank in one period without the receipt being made in the books until the subsequent period. Unless this matter is explained on the reconciliation for the receiving bank, the transfer was apparently made to temporarily cover a shortage in that account. While the shortage will become apparent in the accounts as soon as the transfer is recorded in the following period, it will be covered by an unrecorded deposit on the balance sheet date.
6. This transfer is proper.

In some instances an interbank transfer schedule is used even though control procedures are adequate and no fraud is suspected. When a client maintains many cash accounts, cash transfers may be inadvertently mishandled. The use of an interbank transfer schedule provides the auditor with evidence on the proper cutoff for cash transactions.

Auditing a Payroll or Branch Imprest Account

The audit of any imprest cash account such as payroll or a branch account follows the same basic audit steps discussed under the audit of the general cash account. The auditor obtains a bank reconciliation, along with a standard bank confirmation and a cutoff bank statement. However, the audit testing is less extensive for two reasons. First, the imprest balance in the account is generally not material. An imprest payroll or branch account may contain a balance of only $1,000. Second, the types of disbursements from the account are homogeneous. The checks are for similar types of transactions and for relatively small amounts. For example, there may be a limit on the size of an individual payroll check.

Auditing a Petty Cash Fund

Most entities maintain a petty cash fund for paying certain types of expenses or transactions. Although the balance in the fund is not material, there is a potential for defalcation because a client's employee may be able to process numerous fraudulent transactions through the fund over the course of a year. Auditors seldom perform substantive procedures on the petty cash fund, except when fraud is suspected. However, the auditor may document the controls over the petty cash fund, especially for smaller clients.

Controls   A petty cash fund should be maintained on an imprest basis by an *independent* custodian. While it is preferable for the custodian not to be involved in any cash functions, this is not possible for many clients. When the petty cash custodian does have other cash-related functions to perform, another supervisory person such as the controller should review the petty cash activity.

Prenumbered petty cash vouchers should be used for withdrawing cash from the fund, and a limit should be placed on the size of reimbursements made from petty cash. Periodically, the petty cash fund is reimbursed from the general cash account for the amount of the vouchers in the fund. Accounts payable clerks should review the vouchers for propriety before replenishing the petty cash fund. Finally, someone independent of the cash functions should conduct surprise counts of the petty cash fund.

Audit Tests   The first step is for the auditor to gain an understanding of the client's controls over petty cash. The adequacy of the client's controls determines the nature and extent of the auditor's work. The audit of petty cash focuses on both the transactions processed through the fund during the period and the balance in the fund. The auditor may select a sample of petty cash reimbursements and examine the propriety of the items paid for by the fund. This may be done as part of the auditor's tests of controls or tests of details of transactions for the cash disbursement functions. The auditor tests the balance in the petty cash fund by counting it. When the count is conducted, the total of cash in the fund plus the vouchers should equal the imprest balance. This count may be done at an interim date or at year-end.

Disclosure Issues for Cash

The auditor must consider a number of important financial statement disclosures when auditing cash. Some of the more common disclosure issues are shown in Table 16–3. The auditor's review of the minutes of board of directors' meetings, line-of-credit arrangements, loan agreements, and similar documents is the primary source of the information for the financial statement disclosures. In addition, the auditor typically confirms items such as compensating balances required under a bank line of credit.

Exhibit 16–5 illustrates a letter for confirmation of compensating balances, while Exhibit 16–6 presents an example of footnote disclosures for compensating balances.

TABLE 16–3	Examples of Disclosure Items for Cash
	Accounting policy for defining cash and cash equivalents.
	Any restrictions on cash such as a sinking fund requirement for funds allocated by the entity's board of directors for special purposes.
	Contractual obligations to maintain compensating balances.
	Cash balances restricted by foreign exchange controls.
	Letters of credit.

EXHIBIT 16–5	Illustrative Letter for Confirmation of Compensating Balances

CALABRO PAGING SERVICES

December 31, 2005

Mr. Frank Lorchian
First National Bank
Tampa, FL 34201

Dear Mr. Lorchian:

In connection with an audit of the financial statements of Calabro Paging Services as of December 31, 2005, and for the year then ended, we have advised our independent auditors that as of the close of business on December 31, 2005, there were compensating balance arrangements as described in our agreement dated June 30, 2001. Withdrawal by Calabro Paging Services of the compensating balance was not legally restricted as of December 31, 2005. The terms of the compensating balance arrangements at December 31, 2005, were:

The company has been expected to maintain a compensating balance, as determined from your bank's ledger records without adjustment for estimated average uncollected funds, of 15% of its outstanding loans plus 10% of its unused line of credit.

The company was in compliance with, and there have been no changes in, the compensating balance arrangements during the year ended December 31, 2005, and subsequently through the date of this letter.

During the year ended December 31, 2005, and subsequently through the date of this letter, no compensating balances were maintained by the company at your bank on behalf of an affiliate, director, officer, or any other third party, and no third party maintained compensating balances at the bank on behalf of the company.

Please confirm whether the information about compensating balances presented above is correct by signing below and returning this letter directly to our independent auditors, Abbott & Johnson, LLP. P.O. Box 669, Tampa, FL 32691.

Sincerely,

Calabro Paging Services

BY: _____
        Jan Rodriguez, Controller

Dear Abbott & Johnson, LLP:

The above information regarding the compensating balance arrangement with this bank agrees with the records of this bank.

BY: _____   Vice President   Date: _____

EXHIBIT 16–6	Sample Disclosure of Compensating Balances

Lines of Credit:

On December 31, 2001, the company established a line of credit with a bank that provides for unsecured borrowings of $7,000,000 at the bank's prime rate (7% at December 31, 2005). At December 31, 2004 and 2005, $200,000 and $800,000, respectively, had been borrowed under this arrangement. Under the credit arrangement, the company is expected to maintain compensating balances equal to 5 percent of the borrowings in excess of $500,000. This requirement is generally met through normal operating cash balances, which are not restricted as to withdrawal.

Investments[2]

[LO 7]   Entities frequently invest in securities of other entities. Such investments might include equity securities such as common and preferred stock, debt securities such as notes and bonds, and hybrid securities such as convertible bonds and stocks. The accounting for such instruments is affected by factors such as the percentage of the other entity owned, the degree of influence exercised over the entity, the classification of the investment as a current or noncurrent asset, and myriad other factors. For example, FASB Statement of Financial Accounting Standards No. 115, "Accounting for Certain Investments in Debt and Equity Securities" (FAS 115), provides detailed guidance on how to account for investments in certain debt and equity securities.

The auditor's consideration of investments is no different than for any other financial statement account. That is, the auditor must be assured that the amounts shown on the balance sheet for the various types of investments are not materially misstated. This includes the proper recognition of interest income, dividends, and changes in value that must be included in the financial statements.

The auditor's approach to the audit of investments varies depending on the size of the investment and the amount of investment activity. For an entity that has a large investment portfolio, the auditor is likely to follow a reliance strategy in which internal control is formally evaluated and tests of controls are performed in order to set control risk below the maximum. However, for the vast majority of entities, it is more efficient for the auditor to follow a substantive strategy and perform a detailed audit of the investment securities at year-end.

Control Risk Assessment–Investments

[LO 8]   The discussion of investments that follows focuses on the general types of control procedures that should be present to minimize the likelihood of a material misstatement. Even when a substantive strategy is followed, the auditor must reasonably understand control over investments in order to anticipate the types of misstatements that may occur and plan the substantive procedures. The main assertions that concern the auditor are occurrence, authorization, completeness, accuracy, and classification. Proper segregation of duties is important in ensuring the propriety of investments and will be discussed briefly.

Assertions and Related Control Procedures

Following are some of the more common controls that should be present for each of the important assertions for investments.

Occurrence and Authorization
Controls must ensure that the purchase or sale of any investment is properly initiated by authorized individuals. First,

---

[2]See G. F. Patterson, Jr., "New Guidance on Auditing Investments," *Journal of Accountancy* (February 1997), pp. 65–67, for a discussion of auditing investments.

the client should have adequate documents to verify that a particular purchase or sale of a security was properly initiated and approved. The presence of adequate documentation allows the auditor to determine the validity of the transaction. Second, the commitment of resources to investment activities should be approved by the board of directors or by an executive who has been delegated this authority. An entity engaging in recurring investment activities should have both general and specific control procedures. The board of directors should establish general policies to guide the entity's investment activities, while the specific procedures for the purchase and sale of securities may be delegated to an individual executive, investment committee, or outside investment advisers. If the client has proper controls for initiating and authorizing securities transactions, it is generally easy for the auditor to verify security transactions at the end of the period.

Completeness

The client should maintain adequate controls to ensure that all securities transactions are recorded. One control for handling the detailed securities transactions is maintenance of a securities ledger that records all securities owned by the client. This subsidiary ledger should be reconciled to the general ledger control account regularly. Personnel responsible for investment activities should periodically review the securities owned to ensure that all dividends and interest have been received and recorded in the entity's records.

Accuracy and Classification

Some important accuracy and classification issues are related to investment securities. As mentioned previously, FAS 115 addresses accounting and reporting for investments in equity securities that have readily determinable fair values and for all investments in debt securities. The standard requires that those investments be classified in three categories and accounted for as follows:

- Debt securities that the entity has the positive intent and ability to hold to maturity are classified as *held-to-maturity securities* and reported at amortized cost.
- Debt and equity securities that are bought and held principally for the purpose of selling them in the near term are classified as *trading securities* and reported at fair value, with unrealized gains and losses included in earnings.
- Debt or equity securities not classified as either held-to-maturity or trading securities are classified as *available-for-sale securities* and are reported at fair value, with unrealized gains and losses excluded from earnings and reported in a separate component of shareholders' equity.

The client's controls should ensure that securities are properly classified and that appropriate prices are used to accurately value investments for financial statement.

One final issue related to the control risk for investments is that the client should have adequate custodial procedures to safeguard against theft. When securities are held by the client, they should be stored in a safe or safe-deposit box. Procedures should provide for periodic inspections by an

TABLE 16–4	Key Segregation of Duties for Investments and Possible Errors or Fraud
Segregation of Duties	*Possible Errors or Fraud Resulting from Conflicts of Duties*
The initiation function should be segregated from the final approval function.	If one individual is responsible for both the initiating and approving of securities transactions, fictitious transactions can be made or securities can be stolen.
The valuation-monitoring function should be segregated from the acquisition function.	If one individual is responsible for both acquiring and monitoring the valuation of securities, securities values can be improperly recorded or not reported to management.
Responsibility for maintaining the securities ledger should be separate from that of making entries in the general ledger.	If one individual is responsible for both the securities ledger and the general ledger entries, that individual can conceal any defalcation that would normally be detected by reconciliation of subsidiary records with general ledger control accounts.
Responsibility for custody of the securities should be separate from that of accounting for the securities.	If one individual has access both to securities and to the supporting accounting records, a theft of the securities can be concealed.

individual independent of both the custodial and accounting responsibilities for securities. If an independent custodian such as a broker maintains securities, the client needs to establish procedures for authorizing the transfer of securities. One approach would require dual authorization by appropriate management personnel.

Segregation of Duties

❧ **[LO 9]**

Only entities that engage in a significant number of investment activities are likely to have adequate segregation of duties. Table 16–4 contains some key segregation of duties for investments and examples of possible errors or fraud that can result from conflicts in duties.

Substantive Procedures for Testing Investments

❧ **[LO 10]**

As discussed earlier, it is generally more efficient to follow a substantive strategy for auditing investments. When the control risk is set at the maximum, the auditor conducts extensive substantive procedures to reach the planned level of detection risk. Additionally, because of the nature of the audit work, tests of details of transactions are seldom used as a source of evidence.

Substantive analytical procedures such as the following can test the overall reasonableness of investments:

- Comparison of the balances in the current year's investment accounts with prior years' balances after consideration of the effects of current-year operating and financing activities on cash and investments.

- Comparison of current-year interest and dividend income with the reported income for prior years and with the expected return on investments.

Auditing standards (AU 332) provide guidance concerning substantive auditing procedures the auditor can perform when gathering evidence related to assertions for investments. Table 16–5 summarizes the tests of the investment account for balance and presentation and disclosure assertions. The discussion of the investment account tests focuses on the more

TABLE 16–5	Examples of Tests of Transactions and Account Balances and Disclosures-Investments

Assertions about Account Balances at Period End	Test of Details of Account Balances
Existence Rights and obligations Completeness	Inspect securities if maintained by client or obtain confirmation from independent custodian. Examine brokers' advices for a sample of securities purchased during the year. Search for purchases of securities by examining transactions for a few days after year-end. Confirm securities held by independent custodian. Review and test securities information to determine if all interest and dividend income has been recorded.
Valuation and allocation	Review brokers' invoices for cost basis of securities purchased. Determine basis for valuing investments by tracing values to published quotations or marketable securities. Determine whether there has been any permanent impairment in the value of the cost basis of an individual security. Examine sales of securities to ensure proper recognition of realized gains or losses. Obtain a listing of investments by category (held-to-maturity, trading, and available-for-sale); foot listing and agree totals to securities register and general ledger.

Assertions about Presentation and Disclosure	Tests of Details of Disclosures
Occurrence, and rights and obligations	Determine whether any securities have been pledged as collateral by (1) asking management and (2) reviewing board of directors' minutes, loan agreements, and other documents.
Completeness	Determine that all disclosures required by FAS 115 have been made for investments (both debt and equity securities). Complete financial reporting checklist to ensure all financial statement disclosures related to investments are made.
Classification and understandability	Review and inquire of management of proper classification of investments. Read footnotes to ensure that required disclosures are understandable.
Accuracy and valuation	Read footnotes and other information to ensure that the information is accurate and properly presented at the appropriate amounts.

important assertions. The procedures shown for the other assertions should be familiar to the reader.

Existence

Auditing standards state that the auditor should perform one or more of the following audit procedures when gathering evidence for existence:

- Physical examination.
- Confirmation with the issuer.
- Confirmation with the custodian.
- Confirmation of unsettled transactions with the broker-dealer.
- Confirmation with the counterparty.
- Reading executed partnership or similar agreements.

If the client maintains custody of the securities, the auditor normally examines the securities. During the physical count, the auditor should note the name, class and description, serial number, maturity date, registration in the name of the client, interest rates or dividend payment dates, and other relevant information about the various securities. When the securities are held by an issuer or a custodian such as a broker or investment adviser, the auditor gathers sufficient, competent evidence for the existence assertion by confirming the existence of the securities. The information contained in the confirmation needs to be reconciled with the client's investment records.

Valuation and Allocation

When securities are initially purchased, they are recorded at their acquisition cost. The auditor can verify the purchase price of a security by examining a broker's invoice or similar document. Debt securities that are to be held to maturity should be valued at their amortized cost. The auditor should have verified the purchase price of the debt at the time of purchase, and the effective interest rate should be used to recognize the interest income, which the auditor can recompute. The fair value of most equity securities is available from securities exchanges registered with the Securities and Exchange Commission or on the over-the-counter market. The auditor can verify these values by tracing them to sources such as brokers, *The Wall Street Journal*, or other reliable financial literature.

The auditor must also determine if there has been any permanent decline in the value of an investment security. Auditing standards provide guidance for determining whether a decline in value below amortized cost is other than temporary. The following factors are cited as indicating other-than-temporary impairment of the investment:

- Fair value is significantly below cost.
- The decline in fair value is attributable to specific adverse conditions affecting a particular investment.
- The decline in fair value is attributable to specific conditions, such as conditions in an industry or in a geographic area.
- Management does not possess both the intent and the ability to hold the investment long enough to allow for any anticipated recovery in fair value.
- The decline in fair value has existed for an extended period.
- A debt security has been downgraded by a rating agency.
- The financial condition of the issuer has deteriorated.
- Dividends have been reduced or eliminated, or scheduled interest payments on debt securities have not been made.

If the investment value is determined to be permanently impaired, the security should be written down and a new carrying amount established. Last, the auditor should examine the sale of any security to ensure that proper values were used to record the sale and any realized gain or loss.

Disclosure Assertions

Two issues are important when the auditor examines the proper classification of investments. First, marketable securities need to be properly classified as held-to-maturity, trading, and available-for-sale because both the balance sheet and income statement are affected by misclassification. Second, the financial statement classification requires that all trading securities be reported as current assets. Held-to-maturity securities and individual available-for-sale securities should be classified as current or noncurrent assets based on whether management expects to convert them to cash within the next 12 months. If the security is expected to be converted to cash within 12 months, it should be classified as a current asset. The auditor should ask management about its plans for dispositing of securities.

Auditing standards also guide auditors in evaluating both management's intent with regard to an investment and the entity's ability to hold a debt security to maturity. In evaluating management's intent, the auditor should consider whether investment activities corroborate or conflict with management's stated intent. The auditor should examine evidence such as written and approved records of investment strategies, records of investment activities, instructions to portfolio managers, and minutes of meetings of the board of directors or the investment committee. In evaluating an entity's ability to hold a debt security to maturity, the auditor should consider factors such as the entity's financial position, working capital needs, operating results, debt agreements, guarantees, and other relevant contractual obligations, as well as laws and regulations. The auditor should also consider operating and cash flow projections or forecasts when considering the entity's ability to hold the debt security to maturity.

FAS 115 requires specific disclosures for securities. For example, the aggregate fair value and gross unrealized holding gains or losses on securities should be presented for securities classified as available-for-sale.

Most of the information necessary for such disclosures is developed as the other assertions are being tested. In addition, the amount of any securities pledged as collateral should be disclosed. Asking management and reviewing board of directors' minutes, loan agreements, and other documents would be the auditor's sources of such information.

KEY TERMS

Analytical procedures. Evaluations of financial information made by a study of plausible relationships among both financial and nonfinancial data.

Assertions. Expressed or implied representations by management that are reflected in the financial statement components.

Confirmation. The process of obtaining and evaluating direct communication from a third party in response to a request for information about a particular item affecting financial statement assertions.

Reliance strategy. The auditor's decision to rely on the entity's controls, test those controls, and reduce the direct tests of the financial statement accounts.

Tests of controls. Procedures that evaluate the effectiveness of the design and operation of internal controls.

Tests of details of account balance and disclosures. Tests that concentrate on the details of amounts contained in an account balance and disclosures.

www.mhhe.com/ messier4e	Visit the book's Online Learning Center for a multiple-choice quiz that will allow you to assess your understanding of chapter concepts.

REVIEW QUESTIONS

[LO 1]   16-1   How do the client's controls over cash receipts and disbursements affect the nature and extent of the auditor's substantive tests of cash balances?

[2]   16-2   Briefly describe each type of bank account. How does an imprest account help to improve control over cash?

[3]   16-3   Why are analytical procedures of limited use in the audit of the cash balance?

[4,5]   16-4   Explain why the standard bank confirmation form does *not* identify all information about a client's bank accounts or loans.

[4,5]   16-5   Why does an auditor obtain a cutoff bank statement when auditing a bank account? What information is examined on the canceled checks returned with the cutoff bank statement?

[6]   16-6   List three fraud-related audit procedures for cash.

[6]   16-7   What approach is used by the auditor to test for kiting?

[8,9]   16-8   What are the main transaction related assertions for investments? Identify the key segregation of investment-related duties and possible errors or fraud that can occur if this segregation is not present.

[10]   16-9   Briefly describe the valuation issues related to investments in debt and equity securities.

[10]   16-10   What two presentation classification issues are important for the audit of investments?

MULTIPLE-CHOICE QUESTIONS

Questions 16–11 and 16–12 relate to the following bank transfer schedule.

MILES COMPANY
Bank Transfer Schedule
December 31, 2005

Check Number	Bank Account		Amount	Date Disbursed per		Date Deposited per	
	From	To		Books	Bank	Books	Bank
2020	First National	Suburban	$32,000	12/31	1/5◆	12/31	1/3▲
2021	First National	Capital	21,000	12/31	1/4◆	12/31	1/3▲
3217	Second State	Suburban	6,700	1/3	1/5	1/3	1/6
0659	Midtown	Suburban	5,500	12/30	1/5◆	12/30	1/3▲

[4,6]   16-11   The tick mark ◆ most likely indicates that the amount was traced to the
         a. December cash disbursements journal.
         b. Outstanding check list of the applicable bank reconciliation.
         c. January cash disbursements journal.
         d. Year-end bank confirmations.

[4,6]   16-12   The tick mark ▲ most likely indicates that the amount was traced to the
         a. Deposits in transit of the applicable bank reconciliation.
         b. December cash receipts journal.
         c. January cash receipts journal.
         d. Year-end bank confirmations.

[5]   16-13   An auditor ordinarily sends a standard confirmation request to all banks with which the client has done business during the year under

audit, regardless of the year-end balance. A purpose of this procedure is to

a. Provide the data necessary to prepare a proof of cash.

b. Request that a cutoff bank statement and related checks be sent to the auditor.

c. Detect kiting activities that may otherwise *not* be discovered.

d. Seek information about loans from the banks.

[5]   16-14   The primary evidence regarding year-end bank balances is documented in the

a. Standard bank confirmations.

b. Outstanding check listing.

c. Interbank transfer schedule.

d. Bank deposit lead schedule.

[5]   16-15   On receiving the cutoff bank statement, the auditor should trace

a. Deposits in transit on the year-end bank reconciliation to deposits in the cash receipts journal.

b. Checks dated before year-end to outstanding checks listed on the year-end bank reconciliation.

c. Deposits listed on the cutoff statement to deposits in the cash receipts journal.

d. Checks dated after year-end to outstanding checks listed on the year-end bank reconciliation.

[6]   16-16   Which of the following cash transfers results in a misstatement of cash at December 31, 2005?

Bank Transfer Schedule

	Disbursement		Receipt	
Transfer	Recorded in Books	Paid by Bank	Recorded in Books	Received by Bank
a.	12/31/05	1/4/06	12/31/05	12/31/05
b.	1/4/06	1/5/06	12/31/05	1/4/06
c.	12/31/05	1/5/06	12/31/05	1/4/06
d.	1/4/06	1/11/06	1/4/06	1/4/06

[8,9]   16-17   Which of the following controls would most effectively ensure that the proper custody of assets in the investing process is maintained?

a. Direct access to securities in the safe-deposit box is limited to one corporate officer.

b. Personnel who post investment transactions to the general ledger are *not* permitted to update the investment subsidiary ledger.

c. Purchase and sale of investments are executed on the specific authorization of the board of directors.

d. The recorded balances in the investment subsidiary ledger are periodically compared with the contents of the safe-deposit box by independent personnel.

[10]   16-18   An auditor testing long-term investments would ordinarily use substantive analytical procedures to ascertain the reasonableness of the

a. Existence of unrealized gains or losses in the portfolio.

b. Completeness of recorded investment income.

c. Classification between current and noncurrent portfolios.

d. Valuation of marketable equity securities.

[10]   16-19   To establish the existence and rights of a long-term investment in the common stock of a publicly traded company, an auditor ordinarily performs a security count or

a.   Relies on the client's internal controls if the auditor has reasonable assurance that the control procedures are being applied as prescribed.

b.   Confirms the number of shares owned that are held by an independent custodian.

c.   Determines the market price per share at the balance sheet date from published quotations.

d.   Confirms the number of shares owned with the issuing company.

[10]   16-20   Which of the following is the most effective audit procedure for verifying dividends earned on investments in equity securities?

a.   Trace deposits of dividend checks to the cash receipts book.

b.   Reconcile amounts received with published dividend records.

c.   Compare the amounts received with prior-year dividends received.

d.   Recompute selected extensions and footings of dividend schedules and compare totals to the general ledger.

[10]   16-21   An auditor would most likely verify the interest earned on bond investments by

a.   Vouching the receipt and deposit of interest checks.

b.   Confirming the bond interest rate with the issuer of the bonds.

c.   Recomputing the interest earned on the basis of face amount, interest rate, and period held.

d.   Testing the controls over cash receipts.

PROBLEMS

[7,8,9]   16-22   Cassandra Corporation, a manufacturing company, periodically invests large sums in investment (debt and equity) securities. The investment policy is established by the investment committee of the board of directors, and the treasurer is responsible for carrying out the investment committee's directives. All securities are stored in a bank safe-deposit vault.

   The independent auditor's internal control questionnaire with respect to Cassandra's investments in debt and equity securities contains the following three questions:

*   Is investment policy established by the investment committee of the board of directors?
*   Is the treasurer solely responsible for carrying out the investment committee's directives?
*   Are all securities stored in a bank safe-deposit vault?

Required:

In addition to these three questions, what questions should the auditor's internal control questionnaire include with respect to the company's investments in debt and equity securities?

(AICPA, adapted)

[4,6]   16-23   Sevcik Company's auditor received, directly from the banks, confirmations and cutoff statements with related checks and deposit tickets for Sevcik's three general-purpose bank accounts. The auditor determined that the controls over cash are satisfactory and can be relied upon. The proper cutoff of external cash receipts and disbursements was established. No bank accounts were opened or closed during the year.

Required:

Prepare the audit program of substantive procedures to verify Sevcik's bank balances. Ignore any other cash accounts.

[5] 16-24 The following client-prepared bank reconciliation is being examined by Zachary Kallick, CPA, during the examination of the financial statements of Simmons Company.

Required:

Items (a) through (f) represent items an auditor would ordinarily find on a client-prepared bank reconciliation. The following list of audit procedures shows substantive auditing procedures. For each item, select one or more procedures, as indicated, that the auditor most likely would perform to gather evidence in support of that item. (The procedures on the list may be selected once, more than once, or not at all.)

SIMMONS COMPANY
Bank Reconciliation
1st National Bank of U.S. Bank Account
September 30, 2005

				Procedure(s)
a. Select 2 procedures	Balance per bank		$28,375	
b. Select 5 procedures	Deposits in transit:			
	9/29/05	$4,500		
	9/30/05	1,525	6,025	
			$34,400	
c. Select 5 procedures	Outstanding checks:			
	988 8/31/05	2,200		
	1281 9/26/05	675		
	1285 9/27/05	850		
	1289 9/29/05	2,500		
	1292 9/30/05	7,225	(13,450)	
			$20,950	
d. Select 1 procedure	Customer note collected by bank		(3,000)	
e. Select 2 procedures	Error:			
	Check 1282, written on 9/26/05 for $270, was erroneously charged by bank as $720; bank was notified on 10/2/05.		450	
f. Select 1 procedure	Balance per books		$18,400	

Assume that
- The client prepared the bank reconciliation on 10/2/05.
- The bank reconciliation is mathematically accurate.
- The auditor received a cutoff bank statement dated 10/7/05 directly from the bank on 10/11/05.

- The 9/30/05 deposit in transit, outstanding checks 1281, 1285, 1289, and 1292, and the correction of the error regarding check 1282 appear on the cutoff bank statement.
- The auditor set control risk concerning the financial statement assertions related to cash at the maximum.

Audit Procedure
1. Trace to cash receipts journal.
2. Trace to cash disbursements journal.
3. Compare to 9/30/05 general ledger.
4. Directly confirm with bank.
5. Inspect bank credit memo.
6. Inspect bank debit memo.
7. Ascertain reason for unusual delay.
8. Inspect supporting documents for reconciling item not appearing on cutoff statement.
9. Trace items on bank reconciliation to cutoff statement.
10. Trace items on the cutoff statement to bank reconciliation.

(AICPA, adapted)

[7,8,10]   16-25   The schedule on the following page was prepared by the controller of World Manufacturing, Inc., for use by the independent auditors during their examination of World's year-end financial statements. All procedures performed by the audit assistant were noted in the "Legend" section; the schedule was properly initialed, dated, and indexed and then submitted to a senior member of the audit staff for review. Internal control was reviewed and is considered to be satisfactory.

Required:
a. What information that is essential to the audit of debt and equity securities is missing from this schedule?
b. What essential audit procedures were not noted as having been performed by the audit assistant?

(AICPA, adapted)

[10]   16-26   Phung, CPA, has been engaged to audit the financial statements of Vernon Distributors, Inc., a continuing audit client, for the year ended September 30. After obtaining an understanding of Vernon's internal control system, Phung set control risk at the maximum level for all financial statement assertions concerning investments. Phung determined that Vernon is unable to exercise significant influence over any investee and none are related parties. Phung obtained from Vernon detailed analyses of its investments in domestic securities showing
- The classification among held-to-maturity, trading, and available-for-sale securities.
- A description of each security, including the interest rate and maturity date of bonds and the par value and dividend rate of stocks.
- A notation of the location of each security, either in the treasurer's safe or held by an independent custodian.
- The number of shares of stock or face value of bonds held at the beginning and end of the year.

WORLD MANUFACTURING, INC.
Marketable Securities
Year Ended December 31, 2005

Description of Security	%	Yr. Due	Serial No.	Face Value of Bonds	General Ledger 1/1	Purchased in 2005	Sold in 2005	Cost	General Ledger 12/31	12/31 Market	Pay Date(s)	Amt. Rec.	Accruals 12/31
Corp. Bonds													
A	6	12	21-7	10,000	9,400a				9,400	9,100	1/15 / 7/15	300b,d / 300b,d	275
D	4	08	73-0	30,000	27,500a				27,500	26,220	12/1	1,200b,d	100
G	9	13	16-4	5,000	4,000a				4,000	5,080	8/1	450b,d	188
Rc	5	10	08-2	70,000	66,000a		57,000b	66,000					
Sc	10	15	07-4	100,000		100,000e			100,000	101,250	7/1	5,000b,d	5,000
				100,000	106,900a	100,000	57,000	66,000	140,900	141,650		7,250	5,563
					a,f	f	f	f	f,g	f		f	f
Stocks													
P 1,000 shs. Common			1,044		7,500a				7,500	7,600	3/1 / 6/1 / 9/1 / 12/1	750b,d / 750b,d / 750b,d / 750b,d	250
U 50 shs. Common			8,530		9,700a				9,700	9,800	2/1 / 8/1	800b,d / 800b,d	667
					17,200				17,200	17,400		4,600	917
					a,f				f,g	f		f	f

Legends and comments relative to above schedule:

a = Beginning balances agreed to 2004 working papers.
b = Traced to cash receipts.
c = Board of directors' minutes examined—purchase and sales approved.
d = Agreed to 1099.
e = Confirmed by tracing to broker's advice.
f = Totals footed.
g = Agreed to general ledger.

641

- The beginning and ending balances at cost and at market, and the unamortized premium or discount on bonds.
- Additions to and sales from the portfolios for the year, including date, number of shares, face value of bonds, cost, proceeds, and realized gain or loss.
- Valuation allowances at the beginning and end of the year and changes therein.
- Accrued investment income for each investment at the beginning and end of the year, and income earned and collected during the year.

Phung then prepared the following partial audit program of substantive audit procedures:

1. Foot and crossfoot the analyses.
2. Trace the September 30 balances to the general ledger and financial statements.
3. Trace the beginning balances to the prior year's working papers.
4. Obtain positive confirmation of the investments held by any independent custodian as of the balance sheet date.
5. Determine that income from investments has been properly recorded as accrued or collected by reference to published sources, by computation, and by tracing to recorded amounts.
6. For investments in nonpublic entities, compare carrying value to information in the most recently available audited financial statements.
7. Determine that all transfers among held-to-maturity, trading, and available-for-sale securities have been properly authorized and recorded.
8. Determine that any other-than-temporary decline in the price of an investment has been properly recorded.

Required:

a. For procedures 4 to 8, identify the primary financial statement assertion relative to investments that would be addressed by each procedure.
b. Describe three additional substantive auditing procedures Phung should consider in auditing Vernon's investments.

(AICPA, adapted)

[10]   16-27   To support financial statement assertions, an auditor develops specific audit procedures to satisfy or accomplish each assertion.

Required:

Items (a) through (c) represent assertions for investments. Select the most appropriate procedure from the following list and enter the number in the appropriate place on the grid. (An audit procedure may be selected once or not at all.)

Audit Procedure

1. Trace opening balances in the subsidiary ledgers to the prior year's audit working papers.

2. Determine that employees who are authorized to sell investments do not have access to cash.
3. Examine supporting documents for a sample of investment transactions to verify that prenumbered documents are used.
4. Determine that any impairments in the price of investments have been properly recorded.
5. Verify that transfers from the current to the noncurrent investment portfolio have been properly recorded.
6. Obtain positive confirmations as of the balance sheet date of investments held by independent custodians.
7. Trace investment transactions to minutes of board of directors' meetings to determine that transactions were properly authorized.

Specific Assertion	Audit Procedure
a. Verify that investments are properly described and classified in the financial statements (presentation and disclosure-classification).	
b. Verify that recorded investments represent investments actually owned at the balance sheet date (rights and obligations).	
c. Verify that investments are properly valued at the lower of cost or market at the balance sheet date (valuation and allocation).	

(AICPA, adapted)

INTERNET ASSIGNMENT

[7,10] 16-28   Both Intel (www.intel.com) and Microsoft (www.microsoft.com) have large amounts of investment securities. Visit their home pages and review their financial statements for information on how they account for investment securities and the amounts of those securities.

www.mhhe.com/ messier4e	Visit the book's Online Learning Center for problem material to be completed using the *ACL* software packaged with your new text.

Part VI

COMPLETING THE AUDIT AND REPORTING RESPONSIBILITIES

17

Completing the Engagement

18

Reports on Audited Financial Statements and on Internal Control over Financial Reporting

CHAPTER 17

LEARNING OBJECTIVES

Upon completion of this chapter you will

[1] Understand the audit issues related to contingent liabilities.

[2] Know the audit procedures used to identify contingent liabilities.

[3] Understand the audit issues related to a legal letter.

[4] Understand why the auditor must be concerned with commitments.

[5] Know the types of subsequent events.

[6] Understand the effect of subsequent events on the dating of the audit report.

[7] Know the audit procedures used to identify subsequent events.

[8] Know the audit steps included in the auditor's final evidential evaluation process.

[9] Understand how to identify and assess entities with going-concern problems.

[10] Understand the auditor's communication with the audit committee and management and the matters that should be addressed.

[11] Know the auditor's responsibility for subsequent discovery of facts existing at the date of the auditor's report.

RELEVANT ACCOUNTING AND AUDITING PRONOUNCEMENTS

FAS 5, Accounting for Contingencies

AU 316, Consideration of Fraud in a Financial Statement Audit

AU 329, Analytical Procedures

AU 330, The Confirmation Process

AU 333, Client Representations

AU 337, Inquiry of a Client's Lawyer Concerning Litigation, Claims, and Assessments

AU 341, The Auditor's Consideration of an Entity's Ability to Continue as a Going Concern

AU 342, Auditing Accounting Estimates

AU 380, Communication with Audit Committees

AU 530, Dating of the Independent Auditor's Report

AU 560, Subsequent Events

AU 561, Subsequent Discovery of Facts Existing at the Date of the Auditor's Report

AICPA Auditing Standards Board, Exposure Draft, "Audit Evidence"

COSO, *Internal Control—Integrated Framework* (New York: AICPA, 1992)

PCAOB Auditing Standard No. 2, An Audit of Internal Control over Financial Reporting Performed in Conjunction with an Audit of Financial Statements (AS2)

PCAOB Auditing Standard No. 3, Audit Documentation (AS3)

Completing the Engagement

Major Phases of an Audit

Client acceptance/
continuance and establishing
engagement terms
(Chapter 5)

Preplanning
(Chapter 5)

Establish materiality
and assess risks
(Chapter 3)

Plan the audit
(Chapters 3 and 5)

Consider and audit
internal control
(Chapters 6 and 7)

Audit business processes
and related accounts
(e.g., revenue generation)
(Chapters 10–16)

Complete the audit
(Chapter 17)

Evaluate results and issue audit
report (Chapters 2 and 18)

Once the auditor has completed auditing the various business processes and their related financial statement accounts, the evidence is summarized and evaluated. In addition, before choosing the appropriate audit report the auditor considers a number of additional issues that may impact the financial statements. This chapter discusses the following topics:

- Review for contingent liabilities.
- Commitments.
- Review for subsequent events.
- Final evidential evaluation processes.
- Communications with the audit committee and management.
- Subsequent discovery of facts existing at the date of the auditor's report.

Review for Contingent Liabilities

[LO 1]   A *contingent liability* is defined as an existing condition, situation, or set of
circumstances involving uncertainty as to possible *loss* to an entity that will
ultimately be resolved when some future event occurs or fails to occur. FASB
No. 5, "Accounting for Contingencies" (FAS 5), states that when a contingent
liability exists, the likelihood that the future event will result in a loss or impairment of an asset or the incurrence of a liability can be classified into
three categories:

1. **Probable.** The future event is likely to occur.
2. **Reasonably possible.** The chance of the future event occurring is
   more than remote but less than likely.
3. **Remote.** The chance of the future event occurring is slight.

If the event is probable and the amount of the loss can be reasonably estimated, the loss is accrued by a charge to income. When the outcome of the
event is judged to be reasonably possible or the amount cannot be estimated, a disclosure of the contingency is made in the footnotes to the financial statements. Exhibit 17–1 presents an example of such disclosure
taken from a recent annual report. In general, loss contingencies that are
judged to be remote are not disclosed in the footnotes.

Examples of contingent liabilities include

- Pending or threatened litigation.
- Actual or possible claims and assessments.
- Income tax disputes.
- Product warranties or defects.
- Guarantees of obligations to others.
- Agreements to repurchase receivables that have been sold.

EXHIBIT 17–1	**Example of Footnote Disclosure for a Contingency**

On October 31, 2004, a class action complaint was filed by a stockholder against the company and certain of its officers and directors in the United States District Court ("the court"). Shortly thereafter, other stockholders filed similar class action complaints. On February 1, 2005, a consolidated amended class action complaint against the company and certain of its officers and directors was filed in the court. In their consolidated complaint, the plaintiffs seek to represent a class consisting generally of persons who purchased or otherwise acquired the company's common stock in the period from March 5, 2004, through August 14, 2004. These actions claim damages related to alleged material misstatements and omissions of fact and manipulative and deceptive acts in violation of federal securities laws and common-law fraud. In December 2006 a motion filed by the plaintiffs to certify a class of purchasers of the company's common stock was approved with limited exceptions, and a class period for certain claims was established from March 5, 2004, to August 14, 2004. Also in December 2006, in response to a motion by the company and individual defendants, claims of common-law fraud, deceit, and negligence, misrepresentation, and certain of the violations of the federal securities laws against certain of the individual defendants were dismissed. At this time, it is not possible to predict the outcome of the pending lawsuit or the potential financial impact on the company of an adverse decision.

Audit Procedures for Identifying Contingent Liabilities

※ [LO 2]

The auditor may identify contingent liabilities while conducting audit procedures directed at assertions related to specific business processes or financial statement accounts. Examples of such audit procedures include

1. Reading the minutes of meetings of the board of directors, committees of the board, and stockholders.
2. Reviewing contracts, loan agreements, leases, and correspondence from government agencies.
3. Reviewing income tax liability, tax returns, and IRS agents' reports.
4. Confirming or otherwise documenting guarantees and letters of credit obtained from financial institutions or other lending agencies.
5. Inspecting other documents for possible guarantees.

For example, the auditor normally reads the minutes of the board of directors' meetings for identification and approval of major transactions. Normally, the board of directors would discuss any material uncertainty that might exist for the entity. Similarly, the auditor examines the entity's income tax expense and accrued liability. The audit procedures for this account include determining if the IRS has audited the entity's prior year's tax returns. If so, the auditor should examine the IRS agents' report for any additional taxes assessed and determine whether the entity will contest the additional assessment.

In addition, near the completion of the engagement the auditor conducts *specific* audit procedures to identify contingent liabilities. Such procedures include

1. Inquiry of and discussion with management about its policies and procedures for identifying, evaluating, and accounting for contingent liabilities. Management has the responsibility for establishing policies and procedures to identify, evaluate, and account for contingencies. Large entities may implement such policies and procedures within their risk assessment process. The management of smaller entities, however, may rely on legal counsel and auditors to identify and account for contingencies.
2. Examining documents in the entity's records such as correspondence and invoices from attorneys for pending or threatened lawsuits. Chapter 15 presented an account analysis of legal expense. Even though the amount of the legal expense account may be immaterial, the auditor normally examines the transactions in the account. The purpose of this examination is to identify actual or potential litigation against the client. The account analysis can also be used to develop a list of attorneys who have been consulted by the entity.
3. Obtaining a legal letter that describes and evaluates any litigation, claims, or assessments. Legal letters are discussed in the next section.
4. Obtaining written representation from management that all litigation, asserted and unasserted claims, and assessments have been disclosed in accordance with FASB No. 5. This information is obtained in a representation letter (see the section in this chapter) furnished by the client.

TABLE 17–1	**Examples of Types of Litigation**

Breach of contract.
Patent infringement.
Product liability.
Violations of government legislation, including
    Securities laws.
    Antidiscrimination statutes based on race, sex, age, and other characteristics.
    Antitrust laws.
    Income tax regulations.
    Environmental protection laws.
    Foreign Corrupt Practices Act.
    Racketeer Influenced and Corrupt Organizations Act (RICO).

Legal Letters

[LO 3]

A letter of audit inquiry (referred to as a *legal letter*) sent to the client's attorneys is the primary means of obtaining or corroborating information about litigation, claims, and assessments.[1] Auditors typically analyze legal expense for the entire period and send a legal letter to each attorney who has been consulted by management. Auditors should be particularly careful with letters sent to the entity's general counsel and attorneys specializing in patent law or securities laws because the general counsel should be aware of major litigation, and patent infringement and securities laws are major sources of litigation. Additionally, a legal letter should be obtained from the entity's in-house counsel if such a position exists. Table 17–1 provides examples of types of litigation that the auditor may encounter.

The auditor should ask management to send a legal letter to the attorneys, requesting that they provide the following information:

- A list and evaluation of any pending or threatened litigation to which the attorney has devoted substantial attention. The list may be provided by the client.
- A list of unasserted claims and assessments considered by management to be probable of assertion and reasonably possible of unfavorable outcome.
- A request that the attorney describe and evaluate the outcome of each pending or threatened litigation. This should include the progress of the case, the action the entity plans to take, the likelihood of unfavorable outcome, and the amount or range of potential loss.
- A request for additions to the list provided by management or a statement that the list is complete.
- A request that the attorney comment on unasserted claims where his or her views differ from management's evaluation.
- A statement by management acknowledging an understanding of the attorney's professional responsibility involving unasserted claims and assessments.

---

[1]B. K. Behn and K. Pany, "Limitations of Lawyers' Letters," *The Journal of Accountancy* (February 1995), pp. 61–67.

- A request that the attorney indicate if his or her response is limited and the reasons for such limitations.
- A description of any materiality levels agreed upon for the purposes of the inquiry and response (AU 337).

 Exhibit 17–2 presents an example of a legal letter. Attorneys are generally willing to provide evidence on actual or pending litigation. However, they are sometimes reluctant to provide information on unasserted claims or assessments. An unasserted claim or assessment is one in which the injured party or potential claimant has not yet notified the entity

---

EXHIBIT 17–2	**Example of a Legal Letter**

EARTHWEAR CLOTHIERS

January 15, 2006

Leon, Leon & Dalton
958 S.W. 77th Avenue
Boise, Idaho 79443

Gentlemen:

In connection with an audit of our financial statements for the year ended December 31, 2005, please furnish our auditors, Willis & Adams, P.O. Box 4080, Boise, Idaho 79443-4080, with the information requested below concerning contingencies involving matters with respect to which you have devoted substantial attention on behalf of the company in the form of legal consultation or representation. For the purposes of your response to this letter, we believe that as to each contingency an amount in excess of $25,000 would be material, and in the aggregate $150,000. However, determination of materiality with respect to the overall financial statements cannot be made until our auditors complete their examination. Your response should include matters that existed at December 31, 2005, and during the period from that date to the date of completion of their examination, which is anticipated to be on or about February 15, 2006.

Regarding pending or threatened litigations, claims, and assessments, please include in your response (1) the nature of each matter; (2) the progress of each matter to date; (3) how the company is responding or intends to respond (for example, to contest the case vigorously or seek an out-of-court settlement); and (4) an evaluation of the likelihood of an unfavorable outcome and an estimate, if one can be made, of the amount or range of potential loss. Please furnish to our auditors such explanation, if any, that you consider necessary to supplement the foregoing information, including an explanation of the matters as to which your views may differ from those stated.

We understand that whenever, in the course of performing legal services for us with respect to a matter recognized to involve an unasserted possible claim or assessment that may call for financial statement disclosure, if you have formed a professional conclusion that we should disclose or consider disclosure concerning such possible claim or assessment, as a matter of professional responsibility to us, you will so advise us and will consult with us concerning the question of such disclosure and the applicable requirements of Statement of Financial Accounting Standards No. 5. Please specifically confirm to our auditors that our understanding is correct.

Please specifically identify the nature of and reasons for any limitation on your response.

Very truly yours,

Calvin J. Rogers
Chief Executive Officer
EarthWear Clothiers

of a possible claim or assessment. The following situation is an example of a possible unasserted claim. Suppose one of the entity's manufacturing facilities is destroyed by fire and a number of people are killed. Suppose further that a subsequent investigation shows that the client had failed to install proper fire safety equipment. The entity's fiscal year may end and the financial statements for the period that includes the fire may be released. Although the families of the employees have not yet initiated or threatened litigation, an unasserted claim may exist at the financial statement date. In this case, the entity's attorneys may be reluctant to provide the auditor with information about the unasserted claims because of client-attorney privilege. The attorneys may also be concerned that disclosing the unasserted claim in the financial statements may itself result in a lawsuit. This dilemma is generally solved by having the attorneys corroborate management's understanding of their professional responsibility involving unasserted claims and assessments. Refer to the third paragraph in the legal letter shown in Exhibit 17–2 for the manner in which the client requests the attorneys to communicate to the auditor. In general, disclosing an unasserted claim is not required unless it is probable that the claim will be asserted and there is a reasonable possibility that the outcome will prove to be unfavorable.

Attorneys may limit their responses to items to which they have given substantial attention. Attorneys may also be unable to respond to the outcome of a matter because the factors in the case do not allow them to reasonably estimate the likelihood of the outcome or to estimate the possible loss. Finally, refusal to furnish information in a legal letter is a limitation on the scope of the audit sufficient to preclude an unqualified opinion.

Commitments

[LO 4]   Companies often enter long-term commitments to purchase raw materials or to sell their products at a fixed price. The main purpose of entering into such a purchase or sales contract is to obtain a favorable pricing arrangement or to secure the availability of raw materials. Long-term commitments are usually identified through inquiry of client personnel during the audit of the revenue and purchasing processes. In most cases, such commitments are disclosed in a footnote to the financial statements. However, in certain instances the entity may have to recognize a loss on a long-term commitment even though there has been no exchange of goods.

For example, suppose that a client produces woolen cloth for use in women's suits and that the company has a December 31 year-end. Suppose further that the client enters a noncancelable contract on September 30, 2005, to purchase 1 million pounds of wool at $1.00 per pound with delivery on March 31, 2006. At year-end (December 31, 2005), the auditor compares the current market price of wool with the contract price. If the current price of wool is $1.00 or greater, only footnote disclosure of the commitment is necessary if it is material. However, if the price of wool is less than $1.00, a loss would be recognized at December 31, 2005. For example, if the current market price of wool is $.75 per pound, the client would recognize a $250,000 loss (1,000,000 pounds × $.25 per pound) at year-end.

Review for Subsequent Events for Audit of Financial Statements

[LO 5] Sometimes events or transactions that occur after the balance sheet date but before the issuance of the financial statements materially affect the financial statements. These events or transactions are referred to as *subsequent events* and require adjustment or disclosure in the financial statements (AU 560 and 561).

Two types of subsequent events require consideration by management and evaluation by the auditor:

1. Events that provide additional evidence about conditions that existed at the date of the balance sheet and affect the estimates that are part of the financial statement preparation process (a *Type I event*). Type I events require adjustment of the financial statements.

2. Events that provide evidence about conditions that did not exist at the date of the balance sheet but arose subsequent to that date (a *Type II event*). Type II events usually require financial statement disclosure. In some instances, where the effect of the event or transaction is so significant, pro forma financial statements may be required in order to prevent the financial statements from being misleading.

Examples of Type I events or conditions are (1) an uncollectible account receivable resulting from continued deterioration of a customer's financial condition leading to bankruptcy after the balance sheet date or (2) the settlement of a lawsuit after the balance sheet date for an amount different from the amount recorded in the year-end financial statements. Note that in both of these examples, additional evidence became available before the financial statements were issued that shed light on estimates previously made in the financial statements. Subsequent events affecting the realization of assets or the settlement of estimated liabilities normally require adjustment of the financial statements.

Examples of Type II events that result in disclosure include

- Purchase or disposal of a business by the entity.
- Sale of a capital stock or bond issue by the entity.
- Loss of the entity's manufacturing facility or assets resulting from a casualty such as a fire or flood.
- Losses on receivables caused by conditions such as a casualty arising subsequent to the balance sheet date.

In some instances, a Type II subsequent event may result in the auditor's adding an explanatory paragraph to the auditor's report to emphasize the event or transaction.

Figure 17–1 presents a diagram of the subsequent-events period for EarthWear. The period from the date of the financial statements (December 31, 2005) to the date of the auditor's report (February 15, 2006) is sometimes referred to as the *formal* subsequent-events period. During this time frame, the auditor actively conducts audit procedures related to the current-year audit. The period from the date of the auditor's report to the

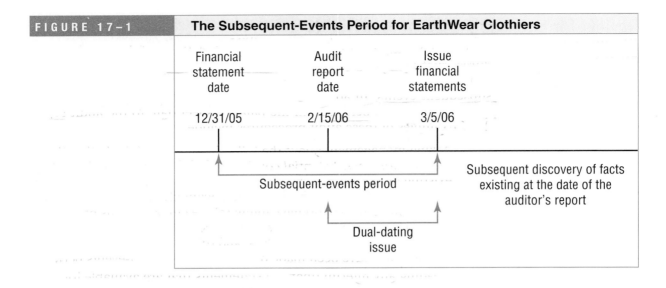

FIGURE 17–1   **The Subsequent-Events Period for EarthWear Clothiers**

issuance of the financial statements (March 5, 2006) is also part of the subsequent-events period, but the auditor is not responsible for making any inquiries or conducting any audit procedures after the date of the audit report. However, subsequent events may come to the auditor's attention during this period. If the subsequent event is Type I, the financial statements should be adjusted. Depending on the event and its circumstances, additional disclosure may be made in the footnotes. When the subsequent event is Type II, a footnote describing the event should be included with the financial statements.

Dual Dating

[LO 6]

When a subsequent event is recorded or disclosed in the financial statements after completion of the field work but before the issuance of the financial statements, the auditor must consider the dating of the auditor's report. For example, suppose that EarthWear notified Willis & Adams that the company had entered an agreement to purchase another catalog retailer company on March 1, 2006. Such an event is not indicative of conditions that existed at the balance sheet date and therefore would require only disclosure in the footnotes to the December 31, 2005, financial statements. Two methods are available for dating the audit report: Willis & Adams may (1) "dual date" the report, using wording such as "February 15, 2006, except for Note 10, as to which the date is March 1, 2006," or (2) use the date of the subsequent event. Dual dating is intended to limit the auditor's responsibility for events occurring subsequent to the completion of field work to the specific subsequent event referred to in the footnote. If the audit report is dated using only the March 1, 2006, date, the auditor's responsibility extends to that date. In this example, Willis & Adams's report would most likely be dual dated.

Figure 17–1 also includes the time period after the financial statements have been issued. This time period is discussed later in the chapter.

Audit Procedures
for Subsequent
Events

❧ [LO 7]

Some audit procedures for business processes and their related financial statement accounts are conducted before year-end, while others may be conducted during the subsequent-events period. Some of these audit procedures, such as testing proper sales and purchases cutoff, are applied to transactions *after* the balance sheet date. Such audit procedures may detect subsequent events. In addition, the auditor should conduct specific audit procedures for the period from the balance sheet date to the audit report date. Examples of these audit procedures include

- Asking management about the following matters: (a) whether there were or are any substantial contingent liabilities or commitments existing at the balance sheet date or at the date of inquiry; (b) whether there have been any significant changes in capital stock, long-term debt, or working capital; (c) the current status of any items in the financial statements that were accounted for based on preliminary or inconclusive data; and (d) whether any unusual adjustments have been made during the subsequent-events period.
- Reading any interim financial statements that are available for the period after year-end; they should be compared to the prior-period statements, and any unusual fluctuations should be investigated.
- Examining the books of original entry (such as sales journal, purchases journal, cash receipts and cash disbursements journals, and general ledger) for the subsequent-events period and investigating any unusual transactions.
- Reading the available minutes of meetings of stockholders, directors, or other committees for the subsequent-events period.
- Asking legal counsel about any litigation, claims, or assessments against the company.
- Obtaining a representation letter from management.

Review of Subsequent Events for Audit of Internal Control over Financial Reporting

Auditors of public companies are responsible for reporting any changes in internal control that might affect financial reporting between the end of the reporting period and the date of the auditor's report (AS2). The auditor's treatment of subsequent events relating to internal control is similar to the Type I and Type II treatments discussed above. In other words, the treatment depends on whether the change in control reveals information about a material weakness that existed as of the end of the reporting period or whether the event creates or reveals information about a new condition that did not exist as of the end of the reporting period. If the event reveals information about a material weakness that existed as of the end of the reporting period, the auditor should issue an adverse opinion on the effectiveness of internal control over financial reporting (and issue an adverse opinion on management's assessment of internal control over financial reporting if management's report does not appropriately assess the effect of the subsequent event; see Chapter 18). If the auditor is unable to determine the effect of the subsequent control event on the effectiveness of the company's internal control, the auditor should disclaim any opinion. If the event creates or reveals information about an internal control condition that did not exist as of the end of the reporting period and the information has a material effect on the company, the auditor should include an explanatory paragraph describing the event and its effects or directing the reader's attention to the event and its effects as disclosed in management's report.

Auditors of public companies are required to inquire of management whether there were any changes in internal control that might affect financial reporting between the end of the reporting period and the date of the auditor's report, and should obtain written representations regarding such changes. The public company auditor should also inquire about and examine, for this subsequent period, the following:

- Relevant internal audit reports (or similar functions, such as loan review in a financial institution) issued during the subsequent period.
- Independent auditor reports (if other than the primary auditor's) of significant deficiencies or material weaknesses.
- Regulatory agency reports on the company's internal control over financial reporting.
- Information about the effectiveness of the company's internal control over financial reporting obtained through other engagements (AS2).

Final Evidential Evaluation Processes

[LO 8]   In addition to the search for unrecorded liabilities and the review for subsequent events, the auditor conducts a number of audit steps before deciding on the appropriate audit report to issue for the entity. These include the following:

- Performance of final analytical procedures.
- Evaluation of the entity's ability to continue as a going concern.
- Obtaining a representation letter.
- Review of working papers.
- Final assessment of audit results.
- Evaluation of financial statement presentation and disclosure.
- Obtaining an independent review of the engagement.

Final Analytical Procedures

Auditing standards (AU 329) require that the auditor perform analytical procedures at the final review stage of the audit. The objective of conducting analytical procedures near the end of the engagement is to help the auditor assess the conclusions reached on the financial statement components and evaluate the overall financial statement presentation. These final analytical procedures may include recalculating some of the ratios discussed in the *Advanced Module* in Chapter 5 for planning the audit. However, more frequently, they involve reviewing the adequacy of the evidence gathered in response to unexpected fluctuations in the account balances identified during the planning of the audit and identifying any unusual or unexpected balances not previously considered. These final analytical procedures may indicate that more evidence is needed for certain account balances.

When the auditor performs final analytical procedures, it is a good time to consider the overall reasonableness of the financial statement amounts. In doing this analysis, the auditor should reexamine the client's business risks (refer to Chapter 3). For example, the auditor should consider the critical issues and significant industry business risks and whether such risks might impact the financial statements. The auditor should also assess the structure and profitability of the industry and how the client fits within the industry in terms of its profitability and solvency. In other words, the auditor should consider whether the financial statement amounts make sense given the auditor's knowledge of the client's business risks.

Going-Concern Considerations
❧ [LO 9]

Auditing standards (AU 341) indicate that the auditor has a responsibility to evaluate whether there is substantial doubt about an entity's ability to continue as a going concern for a reasonable period of time. A reasonable period of time is considered to be one year beyond the date of the financial statements being audited. While this assessment is made during the planning of the engagement, the auditor must also consider this issue near the end of the engagement.

Steps in the Going-Concern Evaluation
The auditor should follow three overall steps in making the going-concern evaluation:

1. Consider whether the results of audit procedures performed during the planning, performance, and completion of the audit indicate whether there is substantial doubt about the entity's ability to continue as a going concern for a reasonable period of time (one year).
2. If there is substantial doubt, the auditor should obtain information about management's plans to mitigate the going-concern problem and assess the likelihood that such plans can be implemented.
3. If the auditor concludes, after evaluating management's plans, that there is substantial doubt about the ability of the entity to continue as a going concern, he or she should consider the adequacy of the disclosures about the entity's ability to continue and include an explanatory paragraph in the audit report.

These steps are discussed next.

Identifying and Assessing Going-Concern Problems. Audit procedures are normally sufficient to identify conditions and events that indicate going-concern problems. Table 17–2 provides examples of audit procedures that may identify such conditions or events. Auditing standards identify four major categories of such conditions or events: *negative financial trends, other financial difficulties, internal problems,* and *external matters.*

TABLE 17–2	Normal Audit Procedures That May Identify Conditions and Events Indicating Going-Concern Problems
	Analytical procedures. Review of subsequent events. Tests for compliance with debt agreements. Reading of board of directors and other committee minutes. Inquiry of legal counsel. Confirmations with parties on arrangements to provide or maintain financial support.

TABLE 17–3	Financial Conditions and Ratios That Indicate Financial Distress
	Financial Conditions Recurring operating losses. Current-year deficit. Accumulated deficits. Negative net worth. Negative working capital. Negative cash flow. Negative income from operations. Inability to meet interest payments. **Ratios** Net worth/total liabilities. Working capital from operations/total liabilities. Current assets/current liabilities. Total long-term liabilities/total assets. Total liabilities/total assets. Net income before taxes/net sales.

Negative financial trends consist of poor results from operations and adverse financial ratios. Analytical procedures during the planning phase of the audit may be particularly helpful in identifying negative financial trends. Table 17–3 lists a number of important financial conditions and ratios that prior audit research[2] has shown to be good indicators of financial distress that can lead to a going-concern report. If the entity being evaluated meets a number of these financial conditions and also has adverse ratios, the auditor may conclude that the entity is not a going concern.

Conditions or events that may occur in the other three categories are shown in Table 17–4. Other financial difficulties are particularly important for the going-concern assessment. For example, if an entity has violated certain debt covenants or is in default on its debt, the debtholders may call for immediate payment. In such circumstances, the entity may be unable to meet its cash requirements and may have to seek bankruptcy protection or liquidation. Similarly, internal matters such as work stoppages may have

[2]J. Mutchler, "Auditor's Perceptions of the Going-Concern Opinion Decision," *Auditing: A Journal of Practice and Theory* (Spring 1984), pp. 17–30. J. Mutchler, "Empirical Evidence Regarding the Auditor's Going-Concern Opinion Decision," *Auditing: A Journal of Practice and Theory* (Fall 1986), pp. 148–63.

TABLE 17-4	**Other Conditions and Events Indicating a Problem with the Going-Concern Assumption**

Other Financial Difficulties
   Default on loans.
   Dividends in arrears.
   Restructuring of debt.
   Denial of trade credit by suppliers.
   No additional sources of financing.

Internal Matters
   Work stoppages.
   Uneconomic long-term commitments.
   Dependence on the success of one particular project.

External Matters
   Legal proceedings.
   Loss of a major customer or supplier.
   Loss of a key franchise, license, or patent.

severe consequences on the entity. In numerous recent instances strikes have caused entities to seek bankruptcy protection. Finally, external matters may cause an entity to cease being a going concern. For example, the loss of a single major customer has been known to cause a high-technology entity to face severe financial difficulties.

Consideration of Management's Plans.   Once conditions have been identified that indicate substantial doubt about the ability of the entity to continue, the auditor should consider management's plans for dealing with the adverse effects of the conditions or events. The auditor should consider the following actions by management:

- Plans to dispose of assets.
- Plans to borrow money or restructure debt.
- Plans to reduce or delay expenditures.
- Plans to increase ownership equity.

For example, management may attempt to sell assets to pay off debt or dispose of operations that are losing money. Management may negotiate with creditors in order to restructure debt or seek additional financing. Frequently, management will develop a plan to reduce wages or cut back the workforce. When evaluating management's plans, the auditor should perform audit procedures to obtain evidence about the elements of the plans and their likelihood of success. This will require examining the assumptions used by management in developing such plans. If the auditor concludes that there is substantial doubt about the entity's ability to continue as a going concern, the auditor will normally issue a modified auditor report similar to the one shown in Chapter 18 (Exhibit 18–3).

Representation Letter

During the course of the financial statement and internal control audits, management makes a number of representations to the auditor as part of the inquiries made to obtain sufficient competent evidence. Auditing standards

(AU 333, AS2) require that the auditor obtain a representation letter from management. The purpose of this letter is to corroborate oral representations made to the auditor and to document the continued appropriateness of such representations. The representation letter also reduces the possibility of misunderstanding concerning the responses provided by management to the auditor's inquiries.

For example, during the audit, the auditor may inquire about related parties and conduct specific audit procedures to identify related-party transactions. Even if the results of these audit procedures indicate that such transactions have been properly disclosed, the auditor should obtain written representations that management is not aware of any such transactions that have not been disclosed. In other instances, evidence may not be available to corroborate management's representations. For example, suppose that management indicates an intent to refinance a short-term obligation in the next period and reclassifies it as a long-term liability in the current financial statements. The auditor would obtain written representation from management to confirm that the obligations will be refinanced in the next period.

Exhibit 17–3 presents an example of a representation letter. Note the important types of information that management is asked to represent. The representation letter should be addressed to the auditor and generally given the same date as the auditor's report. Normally, the chief executive officer and chief financial officer sign the representation letter. Management's refusal to provide a representation letter results in a scope limitation that is sufficient to preclude an unqualified opinion and is ordinarily sufficient to cause an auditor to disclaim an opinion or withdraw from the engagement. In such cases, the auditor should also consider management's refusal when assessing whether he or she can rely on other management representations.

Working Paper Review[3]

All audit work should be reviewed by an audit team member senior to the person preparing the working papers. Thus, the senior-in-charge should conduct a detailed review of the working papers prepared by the staff and follow up on any unresolved problems or issues. In turn, the manager should review all working papers, although the extent of the manager's review may vary with how much the manager relies on the senior-in-charge. The engagement partner normally reviews working papers related to critical audit areas as well as working papers prepared by the manager. In reviewing the working papers, the reviewers must ensure that the working papers document that the audit was properly planned and supervised, that the evidence supports the assertions tested, and that the evidence is sufficient for the type of audit report issued.

Evaluating Financial Audit Results

In conjunction with the review of the working papers, the auditor must evaluate the results of the audit tests. In Chapter 7 we discussed evaluating the results of the audit of internal control over financial reporting. The evaluation of the results of the financial statement audit is concerned with two issues:

---

[3]See J. S. Rich, I. Solomon, and K. T. Trotman, "Multi-Auditor Judgment/Decision Making Research; A decade Later," *Journal of Accounting Literature* 14 (1997), pp. 86–126, for a discussion of practice and research on the audit review process.

EXHIBIT 17-3	**Example of a Representation Letter**

EARTHWEAR CLOTHIERS

February 15, 2006

Willis & Adams
P.O. Box 4080
Boise, Idaho 79443-4080

Gentlemen:

We are providing this letter in connection with your audits of our assertion about the effectiveness of internal control over financial reporting at December 31, 2005, and of the consolidated financial statements of EarthWear Clothiers as of December 31, 2005 and 2004, for the years then ended and for the purpose of expressing opinions on our internal control assessment, the effectiveness of EarthWear Clothiers internal control over financial reporting, and whether our consolidated financial statements present fairly, in all material respects, the financial position, results of operations, and cash flows of EarthWear Clothiers in conformity with accounting principles accepted in the United States of America. We confirm that we are responsible for the fair presentation in the consolidated financial statements of financial position, results of operations, and cash flows in conformity with generally accepted accounting principles.

Certain representations in this letter are described as being limited to matters that are material. Items are considered material, regardless of size, if they involve an omission or misstatement of accounting information that, in the light of surrounding circumstances, makes it probable that the judgment of a reasonable person relying on the information would have been changed or influenced by the omission or misstatement.

We confirm, to the best of our knowledge and belief, as of February 15, 2006, the following representations made to you during your audits.

1. The consolidated financial statements referred to above are fairly presented in conformity with accounting principles generally accepted in the United States of America, and include all disclosures necessary for such fair presentation and disclosures otherwise required to be included therein by laws and regulations to which the Company is subject.
2. We have made available to you all
    a. Financial records and related data.
    b. Minutes of the meetings of stockholders, directors, and committees of directors, or summaries of actions of recent meetings for which minutes have not yet been prepared.
3. There have been no communications from regulatory agencies concerning noncompliance with or deficiencies in financial reporting practices.
4. There are no material transactions, agreements, or accounts that have not been properly recorded in the accounting records underlying the financial statements.
5. The effects of the uncorrected financial statements misstatements summarized in the accompanying schedule are immaterial, both individually and in the aggregate, to the financial statements taken as a whole.
6. Receivables recorded in the financial statements represent valid claims against debtors for sales or other charges arising on or before the balance sheet date and have been appropriately reduced to their estimated net realizable value. Receivables classified as current do not include any material amounts which are collectible after one year.
7. Inventories recorded in the consolidated financial statements are stated at the lower of cost or market, cost being determined on the basis of LIFO, and due provision was made to reduce all slow-moving, obsolete, or unusable inventories to their estimated useful values. Inventory quantities at the balance sheet dates were determined from physical counts taken by competent employees at various times during the year. Liabilities for amounts unpaid are recorded for all items included in inventories at balance sheet dates and all quantities billed to customers at those dates are excluded from the inventory balances.
8. All liabilities of the Company of which we are aware are included in the financial statements at the balance sheet date. There are no other liabilities or gain or loss contingencies that are required to be accrued or disclosed by FASB Statement No. 5, *Accounting for Contingencies,* and no unasserted claims or assessments that our legal counsel has advised us are probable of assertion and required to be disclosed in accordance with that Statement.
9. We acknowledge our responsibility for establishing and maintaining comprehensive systems of internal control that provide reasonable assurance as to the consistency, integrity, and reliability of the preparation and presentation of financial statements; the safeguarding of assets; the effectiveness and efficiency of operations; and compliance with applicable laws and regulations.
10. We monitor the systems of internal control and maintain an independent internal auditing program that assesses the effectiveness of internal control. We did not use the Willis & Adams's procedures performed during the audits of internal control over financial reporting or the financial statements as part of the basis for our assessment of the effectiveness of internal control over financial reporting.

(continued)

EXHIBIT 17-3   **Example of a Representation Letter (*concluded*)**

11. We assessed the Company's internal control over financial reporting for financial presentations in conformity with accounting principles generally accepted in the United States of America. This assessment was based on criteria for effective internal control over financial reporting established in *Internal Control—Integrated Framework* issued by the Committee of Sponsoring Organizations of the Treadway Commission (the COSO Report). Based on this assessment, we believe that the Company maintained effective internal control over financial reporting for financial presentations in conformity with accounting principles generally accepted in the United States of America as of December 31, 2005.

12. There are no significant deficiencies, including material weaknesses, in the design or operation of internal controls that could adversely affect the Company's ability to record, process, summarize, and report financial data.

13. We acknowledge our responsibility for the design and implementation of programs and controls to prevent and detect fraud.

14. We have no knowledge of any fraud or suspected fraud affecting the entity involving:
    a. Management.
    b. Employees who have significant roles in internal control.
    c. Others that could have a material effect on the consolidated financial statements.

15. We have no knowledge of any allegations of fraud or suspected fraud affecting the entity received in communications from employees, former employees, analysts, regulators, short sellers, or others.

16. There have been no violations or possible violations of laws or regulations whose effects should be considered for disclosure in the consolidated financial statements or as a basis for recording a loss contingency.

17. The Company has no plans or intentions that may materially affect the carrying value or classification of assets and liabilities.

18. There have not been any changes, subsequent to the date being reported on, in internal control over financial reporting or other factors that might significantly affect internal control over financial reporting, including corrective actions with regard to significant deficiencies and material weaknesses.

19. All control deficiencies communicated to the audit committee during previous engagements have been resolved.

20. The following, if material, have been properly recorded or disclosed in the consolidated financial statements:
    a. Related-party transactions, including sales, purchases, loans, transfers, leasing arrangements, and guarantees, and amounts receivable from or payable to related parties (the term "related party" includes entities described in SAS No. 45, footnote 1).
    b. Guarantees, whether written or oral, under which the company is contingently liable.
    c. Significant estimates and material concentrations known to management that are required to be disclosed in accordance with the AICPA's Statement of Position 94-6, *Disclosure of Certain Significant Risks and Uncertainties*. (Significant estimates are estimates at the balance sheet date that could change materially within the next year. Concentrations refer to volumes of business, revenues, available sources of supply, or markets or geographic areas for which events could occur that would significantly disrupt normal finances within the next year.)

21. The Company has satisfactory title to all owned assets, and there are no liens or encumbrances on such assets, nor has any asset been pledged as collateral, except as disclosed in the consolidated financial statements.

22. The Company has complied with all aspects of contractual agreements that would have a material effect on the financial statements in the event of noncompliance.

23. The unaudited interim financial information has been prepared and presented in conformity with accounting principles generally accepted in the United States of America applicable to interim financial information and with Item 302(a) of Regulation S-K. The unaudited quarterly financial information for the year ended December 31, 2005, also has been prepared on a basis consistent with the corresponding interim periods in the year ended December 31, 2004, and, to the degree appropriate, with the consolidated financial statements for the years ended December 31, 2005, and December 31, 2004. The unaudited interim financial information for the three months ended December 31, 2005, and December 31, 2004, does not include any material amount of year-end adjustments that have not been disclosed or any material amounts that should have been included in earlier interim periods of the respective fiscal years.

24. Arrangements with financial institutions involving compensating balances or other arrangements involving restrictions on cash balances, line of credit, or similar arrangements have been properly disclosed.

25. We have fully disclosed to you all sales terms, including all rights of return of price adjustments and all warranty provisions.

To the best of our knowledge and belief, no events have occurred subsequent to the balance sheet date and through the date of this letter that would require adjustment to or disclosure in the aforementioned financial statements.

Calvin J. Rogers
Chief Executive Officer

James C. Watts
Chief Financial Officer

(1) the sufficiency of the audit evidence and (2) the effects of detected misstatements in the financial statements. In evaluating the audit evidence, the auditor determines whether there is sufficient evidence to support each relevant assertion. This evaluation considers evidence obtained to support the assessment of inherent and control risk, as well as the evidence gathered to reach the planned level of detection risk (substantive procedures). If this evaluation indicates that the evidence is not sufficient to meet the planned level of audit risk, the auditor may need to gather additional evidence. For example, if the final analytical procedures indicate that inventory may still contain material misstatements, the auditor should further test the inventory account balance.

Any misstatements detected during the audit process must be considered in terms of their effects on the financial statements. This involves performing the third step in applying materiality (refer to Chapter 3). In particular, the auditor must estimate the likely misstatements and compare the amount arrived at to the amount of materiality allocated to the relevant component of the financial statement. (*Likely misstatements* include both known and projected misstatements.) The auditor should also consider the effects of unadjusted misstatements on aggregated components of the financial statements such as assets, liabilities, equity, revenues, and expenses.

Exhibit 17–4 is the working paper introduced in Exhibit 3–5. As noted in Chapter 3, none of the errors detected is material in terms of the tolerable

EXHIBIT 17–4	Example Working Paper for Estimating Likely Misstatements

EarthWear

EARTHWEAR CLOTHIERS
Schedule of Proposed Adjusting Entries
12/31/05

Workpaper Ref.	Proposed Adjusting Entry	Assets	Liabilities	Equity	Revenues	Expenses
N10	Payroll expense					75,000
	Bonuses					140,000
	Accrued liabilities		215,000			
	To accrue payroll through 12/31 and recognize 2005 bonuses.					
F20	Cost of sales					
	Inventory	(312,500)				312,500
	To adjust ending inventory based on sample results.					
F22	Inventory	227,450				
	Accounts payable		227,450			
	To record inventory in transit at 12/31.					
R15	Accounts receivable	79,850				
	Sales				79,850	
	To record sales cutoff errors at 12/31.					
	Total	(5,200)	442,450		79,850	527,500

Tolerable misstatement = $885,000 (50 percent of preliminary materiality)
Conclusion: Based on the above analysis, the account balances for EarthWear Clothiers are fairly stated in accordance with GAAP.

misstatement ($885,000). Additionally, the overall effect of the misstatements is not material in terms of aggregated components of the financial statements. Even though the misstatements shown in Exhibit 17–4 are not material, it is common practice for the auditor to give those adjustments to the client in order to correct the books. It is normally expected that known misstatements will be corrected. However, the auditor would not necessarily require all proposed adjustments to be booked. If the likely misstatement for a particular account is greater than the tolerable misstatement, the account will require adjustment. Similarly, if the unadjusted misstatements affect the aggregated components of the financial statements, the auditor may find it necessary to adjust for these misstatements.

Evaluating Financial Statement Presentation and Disclosure

Either the client or the auditor normally prepares a draft of the financial statements, including footnotes. The auditor reviews the financial statements to ensure compliance with GAAP, proper presentation of accounts, and inclusion of all necessary disclosures. Most public accounting firms use some type of financial statement checklist to assist the auditor in this process.

Independent Partner Review

Most firms have a policy requiring a review by a concurring partner of the financial statements and audit report for publicly traded companies and those financial statements expected to be widely distributed.[4] The concurring partner is generally not associated with the details of the engagement and is expected to provide an independent review. The concurring partner should understand the audit approach, findings, and conclusions for critical audit areas and should review the audit report, financial statements, and footnotes for consistency.

Archiving and Retention

As discussed in Chapter 4, the events leading up to the Sarbanes-Oxley Act of 2002 focused the spotlight on the practice of archiving and retaining audit files (see Exhibit 4–3). The Sarbanes-Oxley Act of 2002 imposed new guidelines for audit file archiving and retention. The PCAOB's auditing standard, *Audit Documentation* (AS3), complies with the guidance under Sarbanes and requires that firms archive their public-company audit files (workpapers and other documentation) for retention within 45 days following the time the auditor grants permission to use the auditor's report in connection with the issuance of the company's financial statements. The Sarbanes-Oxley Act and PCAOB's documentation standard require that audit documentation be retained for seven years from the date of completion of the engagement, as indicated by the date of the auditor's report (or the date that field work is substantially completed), unless a longer period of time is required by law (e.g., pending or threatened lawsuit, investigation, or subpoena). Some states (e.g., New York and California) have adopted similar archiving and retention policies for all audits, including audits of nonpublic companies.

---

[4]See K. Epps and W. F. Messier, Jr., "Concurring Partner Review: Audit Firm Practices and SEC Enforcement Actions," working paper, Georgia State University, 2004.

All documents that "form the basis of the audit or review" are required to be retained. Sarbanes and the PCAOB documentation standard require that any document created, sent, or received, including documents that are inconsistent with a final conclusion, be included in the audit files for all significant matters. This includes any correspondence between engagement teams and national technical accounting or auditing experts in a public accounting firm's national office. Sarbanes and the PCAOB require such document retention to facilitate any subsequent investigations, proceedings, and litigation.

Communications with the Audit Committee and Management

[LO 10] Auditing standards (AU 380) require that the auditor communicate certain matters related to the conduct of the audit to those individuals responsible for oversight of the financial reporting process. This communication applies to (1) entities that have an audit committee or similar group, such as a finance committee or budget committee, and (2) all SEC engagements. The intent of this communication is to ensure that the audit committee or similar group receives additional information on the scope and results of the audit. The communication should address the following matters:

- The auditor's responsibility under GAAS.
- Significant accounting policies.
- Management judgments and accounting estimates.
- Significant audit adjustments.
- The auditor's judgments about the quality of the entity's accounting principles.
- Disagreements with management.
- Consultation with other accountants.
- Major issues discussed with management before the auditor was retained.
- Difficulties encountered during the audit.
- Fraud involving senior management and fraud that causes material misstatement of the financial statements.

This communication may be oral or written. If communicated orally, a memorandum of the communication should be included in the working papers. When the communication is in writing, the report should indicate that it is intended solely for the use of the audit committee, the board of directors, and, if applicable, management.

Audit of Internal Control over Financial Reporting

The auditor has a number of communications responsibilities with respect to the audit of internal control over financial reporting (AS2). The auditor must communicate in writing to management and the audit committee all significant deficiencies and material weaknesses identified during the audit. The written communication should be made prior to the issuance of the auditor's report on internal control over financial reporting. If a significant deficiency or material weakness exists because the oversight of the company's external financial reporting and internal control over financial reporting by the company's audit committee is ineffective, the auditor must communicate that specific significant deficiency or material weakness in writing to the board of directors. The auditor also must communicate, in writing, all control deficiencies identified (deficiencies in internal control that are of a lesser magnitude than significant deficiencies—see Chapter 7, for additional details regarding communication).[5]

In addition to the communications discussed above, the auditor normally prepares a *management letter*. The general intent of a management letter is to make recommendations to the client based on observations during the audit; the letter may include areas such as organizational structure and efficiency issues.

Subsequent Discovery of Facts Existing at the Date of the Auditor's Report

[LO 11] An auditor has no obligation to make any inquiries or conduct any audit procedures after the financial statements and audit report have been issued. However, facts may come to the auditor's attention after the issuance of the financial statements that might have affected the report had he or she known about them. In Figure 17–1, this would be events occurring after March 5, 2006. Auditing standards (AU 561) provide guidance for the auditor in those circumstances. While a number of situations may apply, the most common situation is where the previously issued financial statements contain material misstatements due to either unintentional or intentional actions by management. For example, the auditor may find out that a material amount of inventory was not included in the financial statements because of a computer error. Alternatively, the auditor may learn that management inflated inventory quantities and prices in an effort to increase reported profits. A number of such situations have arisen in recent years (see Exhibit 17–5). Events that occur after the issuance of the auditor's report, such as final settlements of litigation or additional information on accounting estimates becoming available, do not apply to this auditing standard.

When facts are encountered that may affect the auditor's previously issued report, the auditor should consult with his or her attorney because legal implications may be involved and actions taken by the auditor may involve confidential client-auditor communications. The auditor should determine whether the facts are reliable and whether they existed at the date of the audit report. The auditor should discuss the matter with an appropriate level of management and request cooperation in investigating the potential misstatement.

If the auditor determines that the previously issued financial statements are in error and the audit report is affected, he or she should request that the client issue an immediate revision to the financial statements and auditor's report. The reasons for the revisions should be described in the footnotes to the revised financial statements. If the effect on the financial

---

[5] AS2 also requires the auditor to communicate fraud or illegal acts to the appropriate level of management, or the audit committee if senior management is involved.

EXHIBIT 17–5	**Rite Aid Restates Earnings after Seven Month Investigation**

Rite Aid Corporation is the No. 3 drugstore chain, with approximately 77,000 full- and part-time associates serving customers in 30 states and the District of Columbia. Rite Aid operates approximately 3,400 stores with reported total sales of $14.491 billion at the end of its 2001 fiscal year. In 2000, after a seven-month investigation that involved the assistance of two accounting firms and cost $50 million, the company restated its profit for the prior two years by $1.1 billion. It reduced its 1999 net income by $566.2 million and its 1998 net income by $492.1 million. The restatement was the result of management actions ranging from manipulating costs to hiding depreciation expenses. The company reached a settlement with shareholders for $200 million.

Sources: D. Spurgeon and M. Maremont, "Rite Aid Posts Fiscal '00 Loss of $1.1 Billion," *The Wall Street Journal* (July 12, 2000), pp. A3, A6; M. Maremont, "Lawsuit Details Rite Aid's Accounting Woes," *The Wall Street Journal* (February 8, 2001), pp. C1, C14

statements cannot immediately be determined, the client should notify persons known to be relying on the financial statements and auditor's report. If the stock is publicly traded or subject to regulatory jurisdiction, the client should contact the SEC, stock exchanges, and other regulatory agencies.

If the client refuses to cooperate and make the necessary disclosures, the auditor should notify the board of directors and take the following steps, if possible:

1. Notify the client that the auditor's report must no longer be associated with the financial statements.
2. Notify any regulatory agencies having jurisdiction over the client that the auditor's report can no longer be relied upon.
3. Notify each person known to the auditor to be relying on the financial statements. Usually, notifying a regulatory agency such as the SEC is the only practical way of providing appropriate disclosure.

The practical outcome of these procedures is that the auditor has withdrawn his or her report on the previously issued financial statements. In notifying the client, regulatory agencies, and other persons relying on the auditor's report, the auditor should disclose the effect the information would have had on the auditor's report had it been known to the auditor.

KEY TERMS

Analytical procedures. Evaluations of financial information made by a study of plausible relationships among both financial and nonfinancial data.

Contingent liability. An existing condition, situation, or set of circumstances involving uncertainty as to possible loss to an entity that will ultimately be resolved when some future event occurs or fails to occur.

Dual dating. The auditor's report is dual dated when a subsequent event occurs after completion of field work but before the financial statements are issued.

Independent (concurring) partner review. A review by a concurring partner of the financial statements and audit report of a publicly traded company.

Legal letter. An audit inquiry sent to the client's attorneys in order to obtain or corroborate information about litigation, claims, and assessments.

Representation letter. A letter that corroborates oral representations made to the auditor by management and documents the continued appropriateness of such representations.

Subsequent event. An event or transaction that occurs after the balance sheet date but prior to the issuance of the financial statements and the auditor's reports that may materially affect the financial statements.

Working papers. The auditor's record of the work performed and the conclusions reached on the audit.

www.mhhe.com/ messier4e	Visit the book's Online Learning Center for a multiple-choice quiz that will allow you to assess your understanding of chapter concepts.

REVIEW QUESTIONS

[LO 1] 17-1 Define what is meant by *contingent liability*. What three categories are used to classify a contingent liability in FASB No. 5? Give four examples of a contingent liability.

[3] 17-2 What information does the auditor ask the attorney to provide on pending or threatened litigation? What is meant by an unasserted claim, and why are attorneys reluctant to provide information on unasserted claims in the legal letter?

[4] 17-3 Provide two examples of commitments. Under what conditions do such commitments result in the recognition of a loss in the financial statements?

[5] 17-4 What are the types of subsequent events relevant to financial statement audits and audits of internal control over financial reporting? Give one example of each type of subsequent event that might materially affect the financial statements and one example of each type for changes in internal control that might affect financial reporting.

[5,6] 17-5 Under what circumstances would the auditor dual date an audit report?

[8] 17-6 Are any analytical procedures required as part of the final overall review of the financial statements? What is the purpose of such analytical procedures?

[8] 17-7 Why does the auditor obtain a representation letter from management?

[8] 17-8 Describe the purposes of the concurring partner review.

[9] 17-9 List the three overall steps in the going-concern evaluation process.

[9] 17-10 What four major categories of events or conditions may indicate going-concern problems? Give two examples for each category.

[10]   17-11   What items should be included in the auditor's communication with an audit committee or similar group?

[11]   17-12   What types of events would generally require revision of the issued financial statements? What procedures should the auditor follow when the client refuses to cooperate and make the necessary disclosures?

MULTIPLE-CHOICE QUESTIONS

[1,2]   17-13   An auditor would be most likely to identify a contingent liability by obtaining a(n)
   a. Accounts payable confirmation.
   b. Transfer agent confirmation.
   c. Standard bank confirmation.
   d. Related-party transaction confirmation.

[3]   17-14   An auditor should request that an audit client send a letter of inquiry to those attorneys who have been consulted concerning litigation, claims, or assessments. The primary reason for this request is to provide
   a. The opinion of a specialist as to whether loss contingencies are possible, probable, or remote.
   b. A description of litigation, claims, and assessments that have a reasonable possibility of unfavorable outcome.
   c. An objective appraisal of management's policies and procedures adopted for identifying and evaluating legal matters.
   d. Corroboration of the information furnished by management concerning litigation, claims, and assessments.

[6]   17-15   An auditor issued an audit report that was dual dated for a subsequent event occurring after the completion of field work but before issuance of the auditor's report. The auditor's responsibility for events occurring subsequent to the completion of field work was
   a. Extended to subsequent events occurring through the date of issuance of the report.
   b. Extended to include all events occurring since the completion of field work.
   c. Limited to the specific event referenced.
   d. Limited to events occurring up to the date of the last subsequent event referenced.

[7]   17-16   Which of the following procedures would an auditor most likely perform to obtain evidence about the occurrence of any changes in internal control that might affect financial reporting between the end of the reporting period and the date of the auditor's report?
   a. Review of a fire insurance settlement during the subsequent period.
   b. Examine relevant internal audit reports issued during the subsequent period.
   c. Inquire of the entity's legal counsel concerning litigation, claims, and assessments arising after year-end.
   d. Confirm bank accounts established after year-end.

[8]   17-17   Final analytical procedures generally include
- a. Considering unusual or unexpected amount balances that were *not* previously identified.
- b. Testing transactions to corroborate management's financial statement assertions.
- c. Gathering evidence concerning account balances that have *not* changed from the prior year.
- d. Retesting control procedures that appeared to be ineffective during the assessment of control risk.

[8]   17-18   Auditing standards (AU 380) encourages which of the following conversations about financial reporting
- a. A conversation with only the audit committee to discuss matters pertaining to financial reporting.
- b. A conversation with only management to discuss matters pertaining to financial reporting.
- c. A conversation with both management and the audit committee to discuss matters pertaining to financial reporting.
- d. A conversation with the audit committee in which the committee reports on management's views on matters pertaining to financial reporting.

[8]   17-19   Which of the following audit procedures is most likely to assist an auditor in identifying conditions and events that may indicate substantial doubt about an entity's ability to continue as a going concern?
- a. Review compliance with the terms of debt agreements.
- b. Confirm accounts receivable from principal customers.
- c. Reconcile interest expense with outstanding debt.
- d. Confirm bank balances.

[10]   17-20   Which of the following matters is an auditor required to communicate to an entity's audit committee?

	Significant Audit Adjustments	Changes in Significant Accounting Policies
a.	Yes	Yes
b.	Yes	No
c.	No	Yes
d.	No	No

[11]   17-21   Which of the following events occurring after the issuance of an auditor's report would be most likely to cause the auditor to make further inquiries about the previously issued financial statements?
- a. A technological development that could affect the entity's future ability to continue as a going concern.
- b. The discovery of information regarding a contingency that existed before the financial statements were issued.
- c. The entity's sale of a subsidiary that accounts for 30 percent of the entity's consolidated sales.
- d. The final resolution of a lawsuit explained in a separate paragraph of the auditor's report.

PROBLEMS

[1,2,3] 17-22 During an audit engagement, Harper, CPA, has satisfactorily completed an examination of accounts payable and other liabilities and now plans to determine whether there are any loss contingencies arising from litigation, claims, or assessments.

Required:
What audit procedures should Harper follow with respect to the existence of loss contingencies arising from litigation, claims, and assessments? Do *not* discuss reporting requirements.

(AICPA, adapted)

[3] 17-23 Cole & Cole, CPAs, are auditing the financial statements of Consolidated Industries Company for the year ended December 31, 2005. On April 2, 2006, an inquiry letter to J. J. Young, Consolidated's outside attorney, was drafted to corroborate the information furnished to Cole by management concerning pending and threatened litigation, claims, and assessments, as well as unasserted claims and assessments. On May 6, 2006, C. R. Cao, Consolidated's chief financial officer, gave Cole a draft of the inquiry letter below for Cole's review before mailing it to Young.

May 6, 2006

J. J. Young, Attorney at Law
123 Main Street
Anytown, USA

Dear J. J. Young:

In connection with an audit of our financial statements at December 31, 2005, and for the year then ended, management of the company has prepared, and furnished to our auditors, Cole & Cole, CPAs, 456 Broadway, Anytown, USA, a description and evaluation of certain contingencies, including those set forth below involving matters with respect to which you have been engaged and to which you have devoted substantive attention on behalf of the company in the form of legal consultation or representation. Your response should include matters that existed at December 31, 2005. Because of the confidentiality of all these matters, your response may be limited.

In November 2005 an action was brought against the company by an outside salesman alleging breach of contract for sales commissions and pleading a second cause of action for an accounting with respect to claims for fees and commissions. The salesman's action claims damages of $300,000, but the company believes it has meritorious defenses to the claims. The possible exposure of the company to a successful judgment on behalf of the plaintiff is slight.

In July 2005 an action was brought against the company by Industrial Manufacturing Company ("Industrial") alleging patent infringement and seeking damages of $20 million. The action in U.S. District Court resulted in a decision on October 16, 2005, holding that the company had infringed seven Industrial patents and awarding damages of $14 million. The company vigorously denies these allegations and has filed an appeal with the U.S. Court of Appeals for the Federal Circuit. The appeal process is expected to take approximately two years, but there is some chance that Industrial may ultimately prevail.

Please furnish to our auditors such explanation, if any, that you consider necessary to supplement the foregoing information, including an explanation of those matters as to which your views may differ from those stated and an identification of the omission of any pending or threatened litigation, claims, and assessments or a statement that the list of such matters is complete. Your response may be quoted or referred to in the financial statements without further correspondence with you.

You also consulted on various other matters considered pending or threatened litigation. However, you may not comment on these matters because publicizing them may alert potential plaintiffs to the strengths of their cases. In addition, various other matters probable of assertion that have some chance of an unfavorable outcome, as of December 31, 2005, are unasserted claims and assessments.

C. R. Cao
Chief Financial Officer

Required
Describe the omissions, ambiguities, and inappropriate statements and terminology in Cao's letter.

(AICPA, adapted)

[5,7] 17-24 Namiki, CPA, is auditing the financial statements of Taylor Corporation for the year ended December 31, 2005. Namiki plans to complete the field work and sign the auditor's report about March 10, 2006. Namiki is concerned about events and transactions occurring after December 31, 2005, that may affect the 2005 financial statements.

Required:
a. What general types of subsequent events require Namiki's consideration and evaluation?
b. What auditing procedures should Namiki consider performing to gather evidence concerning subsequent events?

(AICPA, adapted)

[5,6,7] 17-25 For each of the following items, assume that Josh Feldstein, CPA, is expressing an opinion on Scornick Company's financial statements for the year ended December 31, 2005; that he completed field work on January 21, 2006; and that he now is preparing his opinion to accompany the financial statements. In each item a subsequent event is described. This event was disclosed to the CPA either in connection with his review of subsequent events or after the completion of field work. You are to indicate for each item the required accounting of the event. Each of the five items is independent of the other four and is to be considered separately.
1. A large account receivable from Agronowitz Company (material to financial statement presentation) was considered fully collectible at December 31, 2005. Agronowitz suffered a plant explosion on January 25, 2006. Because Agronowitz was uninsured, it is unlikely that the account will be paid.

2. The tax court ruled in favor of the company on January 25, 2006. Litigation involved deductions claimed on the 2002 and 2003 tax returns. In accrued taxes payable Scornick had provided for the full amount of the potential disallowances. The Internal Revenue Service will not appeal the tax court's ruling.

3. Scornick's Manufacturing Division, whose assets constituted 45 percent of Scornick's total assets at December 31, 2005, was sold on February 1, 2006. The new owner assumed the bonded indebtedness associated with this property.

4. On January 15, 2006, R. E. Fogler, a major investment adviser, issued a negative report on Scornick's long-term prospects. The market price of Scornick's common stock subsequently declined by 40 percent.

5. At its January 5, 2006, meeting, Scornick's board of directors voted to increase substantially the advertising budget for the coming year and authorized a change in advertising agencies.

[8] 17-26 Arenas, an assistant accountant with the firm of Better & Best, CPAs, is auditing the financial statements of Tech Consolidated Industries, Inc. The firm's audit program calls for the preparation of a written management representation letter.

Required:

a. In an audit of financial statements, in what circumstances is the auditor required to obtain a management representation letter? What are the purposes of obtaining the letter?

b. To whom should the representation letter be addressed, and when should it be dated? Who should sign the letter, and what would be the effect of his or her refusal to sign the letter?

c. In what respects may an auditor's other responsibilities be relieved by obtaining a management representation letter?

(AICPA, adapted)

[8] 17-27 During the examination of the annual financial statements of Amis Manufacturing, Inc., a nonpublic company, the company's president, R. Heinrich, and Luddy, the auditor, reviewed the matters that were to be included in a written representation letter. Upon receipt of the following client representation letter, Luddy contacted Heinrich to state that it was incomplete.

> To: E.K. Luddy, CPA
>
> In connection with your examination of the balance sheet of Amis Manufacturing, Inc., as of December 31, 2005, and the related statements of income, retained earnings, and cash flows for the year then ended, for the purpose of expressing an opinion as to whether the financial statements present fairly the financial position, results of operations, and cash flows of Amis Manufacturing, Inc., in conformity with generally accepted accounting principles, we confirm, to the best of our knowledge and belief, the following representations made to you during your examination. There were no
>
> - Plans or intentions that may materially affect the carrying value or classification of assets and liabilities.
> - Communications from regulatory agencies concerning noncompliance with, or deficiencies in, financial reporting practices.

- Agreements to repurchase assets previously sold.
- Violations or possible violations of laws or regulations whose effects should be considered for disclosure in the financial statements or as a basis for recording a loss contingency.
- Unasserted claims or assessments that our lawyer has advised are probable of assertion and must be disclosed in accordance with Statement of Financial Accounting Standards No. 5.
- Capital-stock repurchase options or agreements or capital stock reserved for options, warrants, conversions, or other requirements.
- Compensating balance or other arrangements involving restrictions on cash balances.

R. Heinrich, President
Amis Manufacturing, Inc.
March 14, 2006

Required:
Identify the other matters that Heinrich's representation letter should specifically confirm.

(AICPA, adapted)

[2,3,7,8,10]   17-28 Items 1 through 19 represent a series of unrelated statements, questions, excerpts, and comments taken from various parts of an auditor's working paper file. Below is a list of the likely sources of the statements, questions, excerpts, and comments. Select, as the best answer for each item, the most likely source. Select only one source for each item. A source may be selected once, more than once, or not at all.

1. During our audit we discovered evidence of the company's failure to safeguard inventory from loss, damage, and misappropriation.
2. The company considers the decline in value of equity securities classified as available-for-sale to be temporary.
3. Was the difference of opinion on the accrued pension liabilities that existed between the engagement personnel and the actuarial specialist resolved in accordance with firm policy and appropriately documented?
4. Our audit is designed to provide reasonable assurance of detecting misstatements that, in our judgment, could have a material effect on the financial statements taken as a whole. Consequently, our audit will not necessarily detect all misstatements that exist due to error, fraudulent financial reporting, or misappropriation of assets.
5. There have been no communications from regulatory agencies concerning noncompliance with or deficiencies in financial reporting practices.
6. Nothing came to our attention that caused us to believe that at October 31, 2005, there was any change in the capital stock, increase in long-term debt, or decrease in consolidated net current assets or stockholders' equity as compared with the amounts shown in the September 30, 2005, unaudited condensed consolidated balance sheet.
7. It is our opinion that the possible liability to the company in this proceeding is nominal in amount.

8. As discussed in Note 4 to the financial statements, the company experienced a net loss for the year ended July 31, 2005, and is currently in default under substantially all of its debt agreements. In addition, on September 25, 2005, the company filed a prenegotiated voluntary petition for relief under Chapter 11 of the U.S. Bankruptcy Code. These matters raise substantial doubt about the company's ability to continue as a going concern.

9. During the year under audit, we were advised that management consulted with Better & Best, CPAs. The purpose of this consultation was to obtain another CPA firm's opinion concerning the company's recognition of certain revenue that we believe should be deferred to future periods. Better & Best's opinion was consistent with our opinion, so management did not recognize the revenue in the current year.

10. The company believes that all material expenditures that have been deferred to future periods will be recoverable.

11. Our use of professional judgment and the assessment of audit risk and materiality for the purpose of our audit mean that matters may have existed that would have been assessed differently by you. We make no representation as to the sufficiency or appropriateness of the information in our working papers for your purposes.

12. Indicate in the space provided below whether this information agrees with your records. If there are exceptions, please provide any information that will assist the auditor in reconciling the difference.

13. Blank checks are maintained in an unlocked cabinet along with the check-signing machine. Blank checks and the check-signing machine should be locked in separate locations to prevent the embezzlement of funds.

14. The company has insufficient expertise and controls over the selection and application of accounting policies that are in conformity with GAAP.

15. The timetable set by management to complete our audit was unreasonable considering the failure of the company's personnel to complete schedules on a timely basis and delays in providing necessary information.

16. Several employees have disabled the antivirus detection software on their PCs because the software slows the processing of data and occasionally rings false alarms. The company should obtain antivirus software that runs continuously at all system entry points and that cannot be disabled by unauthorized personnel.

17. In connection with an audit of our financial statements, management has prepared, and furnished to our auditors, a description and evaluation of certain contingencies.

18. The company has no plans or intentions that may materially affect the carrying value or classification of assets and liabilities.

19. In planning the sampling application, was appropriate consideration given to the relationship of the sample to the assertion and to preliminary judgments about materiality levels?

List of Sources

A. Practitioner's report on management's assertion about an entity's compliance with specified requirements.

B. Auditor's communications on significant deficiencies and material weakness.

C. Audit inquiry letter to legal counsel.

D. Lawyer's response to audit inquiry letter.

E. Audit committee's communication to the auditor.

F. Auditor's communication to the audit committee (other than with respect to significant deficiencies and material weakness).

G. Report on the application of accounting principles.

H. Auditor's engagement letter.

I. Letter for underwriters.

J. Accounts receivable confirmation request.

K. Request for bank cutoff statement.

L. Explanatory paragraph of an auditor's report on financial statements.

M. Partner's engagement review notes.

N. Management representation letter.

O. Successor auditor's communication with predecessor auditor.

P. Predecessor auditor's communication with successor auditor.

DISCUSSION CASES

[1,2,3]   17-29   In February 2005, Ceramic Crucibles of America was notified by the state of Colorado that the state was investigating the company's Durango facility to determine if there were any violations of federal or state environmental laws. In formulating your opinion on the 2004 financial statements, you determined that, based primarily on management's representations, the investigation did not pose a serious threat to the company's financial well-being.

The company subsequently retained a local law firm to represent it in dealing with the state commission. At the end of 2005, you concluded that the action did not represent a severe threat. However, you have just received the attorney's letter, which is a little unsettling. It states:

> On January 31, 2006, the U.S. Environmental Protection Agency (EPA) listed the Durango site in Durango, Colorado, on the National Priorities List under the Comprehensive Environmental Response, Compensation, and Liability Act (Superfund). The site includes property adjoining the western boundary of Ceramic Crucibles' plant in Durango and includes parts of Ceramic Crucibles' property. The EPA has listed Ceramic Crucibles as one of the three "potentially responsible parties" ("PRPs") that may be liable for the costs of investigating and cleaning up the site. The EPA has authorized $400,000 for a "Remedial Investigation and Feasibility Study" of the site, but that study will not begin until sometime later in 2006. Thus, we do not deem it possible or appropriate at this time to evaluate this matter with regard to potential liability or cost to the company.

You immediately set up a meeting with Dave Buff, Ceramic Crucibles' vice president; Ron Bonner, the company's attorney; and

Margaret Osmond, an attorney who specializes in EPA-related issues. At the meeting you ascertain that

- Ceramic Crucibles bought the Durango facility from TW Industries in 1995.
- TW Industries had operated the facility as a manufacturer of ceramic tiles, and it had used lead extensively in incorporating color into the tile.
- The site has been placed on the National Priorities List ("the List") apparently because each state must have at least one site on the List. All sites on the List are rated on a composite score that reflects the relative extent of pollution. The Durango site has a rating of 8.3 compared to a rating of no less than 25 for the other sites on the List.
- The most severe lead pollution (based on toxicity) is in an area located on the other side of a levee behind Ceramic Crucibles' facilities. Although the area close to the building contains traces of lead pollution, the toxicity in this area is about 50 parts per million (ppm), compared to 19,000 ppm beyond the levee.
- Although Ceramic Crucibles used lead in coloring its crucibles until about 1997, the lead was locked into a ceramic glaze that met FDA requirements for appliances used in the preparation of food. Apparently, the acids used in determining the leaching properties of lead for EPA tests are stronger than that used by the FDA. Since 1997, Ceramic Crucibles has used leadfree mud in its crucibles.
- Affidavits taken from present and former employees of Ceramic Crucibles indicate that no wastewater has been discharged though the levee since Ceramic Crucibles acquired the property in 1995.
- The other PRPs and TW Industries are viable companies that should be in a position to meet their responsibilities resulting from any possible EPA action.

Materiality for purposes of evaluating a potential loss is $10 million to $13 million. This is based on the assumption that the loss would be deductible for income tax purposes. In that case, the loss would represent a reduction in stockholders' equity of 4.5 percent to 7.0 percent. Your best guess is that the company's exposure does not exceed that amount. Further, based on the financial strength of the company and its available lines of credit, you believe such an assessment would not result in financial distress to the company.

The creation of the Environmental Protection Agency (EPA) and that of the Comprehensive Environmental Response, Compensation, and Liability Act are a result of the increasing concern of Americans about pollution. An amendment to the act permits the EPA to perform the cleanup. As of the end of 2003, the EPA had a national priorities list of 27,000 sites thought to be severely damaged. The average cost of conducting remedial investigation and feasibility studies ranges from $750,000 to $1 million, and such studies may take as long as three years. Cleanup costs are usually another $10 million to $12 million. It is said that the current estimates that $100 billion will be spent to clean up nonfederal hazardous waste sites may be conservative.

The law requires the EPA to identify toxic waste sites and request records from PRPs. The PRPs are responsible for the cost of cleanup, but if they lack the funds, the EPA uses its funds for the cleanup. The EPA has spent $3.3 billion from its trust fund and collected only $65 million from polluters since the passage of the legislation.

Required:

a. How would this type of contingency be classified in the accounting literature, and how should it be accounted for?
b. Would the amount be material to the financial statements?
c. What additional evidence would you gather, and what kinds of representations should you require from the client?
d. Should the investigation affect your opinion on those financial statements?

[8] 17-30 Medical Products, Inc. (MPI), was created in 2003 and entered the optical equipment industry. Their made-to-order optical equipment requires large investments in research and development. To fund these needs, MPI made a public stock offering, which was completed in 2004. Although the offering was moderately successful, MPI's ambitious management is convinced that they must report a good profit this year (2005) to maintain the current market price of the stock. MPI's president recently stressed this point when he told his controller, Pam Adams, "If we don't make $1.25 million pretax this year, our stock will fall significantly."

Adams was pleased that even after adjustments for accrued vacation pay, 2005 pretax profit was $1.35 million. However, MPI's auditors, Hammer & Bammer (HB), proposed an additional adjustment for inventory valuation that would reduce this profit to $900,000. HB's proposed adjustment had been discussed during the 2004 audit.

An additional issue discussed in 2004 was MPI's failure to accrue executive vacation pay. At that time HB did not insist on the adjustment because the amount ($20,000) was not material to the 2004 results and because MPI agreed to begin accruing vacation pay in future years. The cumulative accrued executive vacation pay amounts to $300,000 and has been accrued at the end of 2005.

The inventory issue arose in 2003 when MPI purchased $450,000 of specialized computer components to be used with their optical scanners for a special order. The order was subsequently canceled, and HB proposed to write down this inventory in 2004. MPI explained, however, that the components could easily be sold without a loss during 2005, and no adjustment was made. However, the equipment was not sold by the end of 2005, and prospects for future sales were considered nonexistent. HB proposed a write-off of the entire $450,000 in 2005.

The audit partner, Johanna Schmidt, insisted that Adams make the inventory adjustment. Adams tried to convince her that there were other alternatives, but Schmidt was adamant. Adams knew the inventory was worthless, but she reminded Schmidt of the importance of this year's reported income. Adams continued her argument, "You can't take both the write-down and the vacation accrual in one year; it doesn't fairly present our performance this year. If you insist on taking that write-down, I'm taking back the accrual. Actually, that's a good idea because the executives are such workaholics, they don't take their vacations anyway."

As Adams calmed down, she said, "Johanna, let's be reasonable; we like you—and we want to continue our good working relationship with your firm into the future. But we won't have a future unless we put off this accrual for another year."

Required:

a. Should the inventory adjustment be taken in 2005?

b. Irrespective of your decision regarding the inventory adjustment, should the auditor insist on accrual of the executives' vacation pay?

c. Consider the conflict between Adams and Schmidt. Assuming that Schmidt believes the inventory adjustment and vacation pay accrual must be made and that she does not want to lose MPI as a client, what should she do?

INTERNET ASSIGNMENTS

[4]   17-31   A number of companies have reported accounting irregularities or fraud in recent years. Some of the companies reporting such fraud include Adelphia, Ahold, Cendant, Enron, Lucent, Sunbeam, Xerox, Waste Management, and WorldCom.

Required:

a. Use an Internet search engine to find information on two of the companies listed. Prepare a memorandum describing the accounting irregularity or fraud.

b. Extend your search to identify two additional companies that have recently reported an accounting irregularity or fraud. Prepare a memorandum describing the accounting irregularity or fraud.

[5]   17-32   It is unusual for an accounting firm to withdraw its opinion on a set of previously issued financial statements. Use an Internet search engine to find a recent example of a company whose public accounting firm has withdrawn its opinion.

| www.mhhe.com/ messier4e | Visit the book's Online Learning Center for problem material to be completed using the *ACL* software packaged with your new text. |

CHAPTER 18

LEARNING OBJECTIVES

Upon completion of this chapter you will

[1] Understand the standard unqualified financial statement audit report.

[2] Know the situations that result in modification to the standard unqualified financial statement audit report.

[3] Know the conditions that lead to a departure from the standard unqualified financial statement audit report.

[4] Know the other types of financial statement audit reports.

[5] Understand the effect of materiality on the auditor's choice of financial statement audit reports.

[6] Understand the situations that may cause different types of reports on comparative financial statements.

[7] Know the auditor's responsibility for other information in documents containing audited financial statements.

[8] Understand the auditor's reporting responsibility for financial statements prepared on a comprehensive basis other than GAAP.

[9] Understand the auditor's responsibility for reporting on specified elements, accounts, or items of a financial statement.

[10] Understand the auditor's reporting responsibility for compliance with contractual agreements or regulatory requirements related to financial statements.

[11] Understand the auditor's responsibility to evaluate and issue an opinion on management's assessment of the effectiveness of internal control over financial reporting.

[12] Understand the auditor's responsibility to issue an opinion on the effectiveness of a client's internal control over financial reporting as part of an integrated audit.

[13] Understand the unqualified report for the audit of internal control over financial reporting.

[14] Understand the conditions requiring modification of the auditor's opinion on the effectiveness of internal control and the types of reports available to the auditor under such conditions.

RELEVANT ACCOUNTING AND AUDITING PRONOUNCEMENTS

APB Opinion No. 20, "Accounting Changes" (APB 20)
FASB Statement of Financial Accounting Standards No. 5, "Accounting for Contingencies" (FAS 5)
AT 201, Agreed-Upon Procedures Engagements
AU 341, The Auditor's Consideration of an Entity's Ability to Continue as a Going Concern
AU 411, The Meaning of Present Fairly in Conformity with Generally Accepted Accounting Principles in the Independent Auditor's Report
AU 420, Consistency of Application of Generally Accepted Accounting Principles

AU 504, Association with Financial Statements
AU 508, Reports on Audited Financial Statements
AU 532, Restricting the Use of an Auditor's Report
AU 543, Part of Audit Performed by Other Independent Auditors
AU 550, Other Information in Documents Containing Audited Financial Statements
AU 623, Special Reports
PCAOB Auditing Standard 2: An Audit of Internal Control over Financial Reporting Performed in Conjunction with an Audit of Financial Statements (AS2)

Reports on Audited Financial Statements and on Internal Control over Financial Reporting

Major Phases of an Audit

Client acceptance/
continuance and establishing
engagement terms
(Chapter 5)

Preplanning
(Chapter 5)

Establish materiality
and assess risks
(Chapter 3)

Plan the audit
(Chapters 3 and 5)

Consider and audit
internal control
(Chapters 6 and 7)

Audit business processes
and related accounts
(e.g. revenue generation)
(Chapters 10–16)

Complete the audit
(Chapter 17)

Evaluate results and
issue audit report
(Chapters 2 and 18)

The fourth standard of reporting states that whenever the auditor is associated with financial statements, the report shall contain an opinion or, if an opinion cannot be issued, the reasons shall be disclosed in the report. An auditor is *associated* with financial statements when he or she has consented to the use of his or her name in a document such as an annual report. While other forms of services are covered by the term *association,* for the purposes of this chapter only audit-related engagements are considered.

The purpose of the fourth standard of reporting is to enable shareholders, bondholders, bankers, and other third parties who rely on the financial statements to determine the degree of responsibility taken by the auditor. To assist in accomplishing this goal, the auditing profession has adopted conventional wording for audit reports. This approach helps to prevent misunderstandings in the message being communicated by the auditor to the users of the financial statements. You are reminded that the financial statements are the representations of management and that the conformance of their presentation with GAAP is management's responsibility.

In addition to reporting on financial statements (see Chapter 2 for an overview), auditors must also perform and report on an audit of internal control over financial reporting for public-company clients. Chapter 7 discusses the nature of the audit of internal control and presents an overview of the auditor's reporting requirements. This chapter goes into greater depth regarding the auditor's reports with respect to the financial statement audit and the audit of internal control over financial reporting.

Reporting on the Financial Statement Audit: The Standard Unqualified Audit Report

[LO 1]   Chapter 2 presented the auditor's standard unqualified financial statement audit report. This report is issued when the auditor has gathered sufficient evidence, the audit was performed in accordance with GAAS, and the financial statements conform to GAAP. Exhibit 18–1 contains the auditor's standard unqualified audit report for a public company client. This report

EXHIBIT 18–1	The Auditor's Standard Unqualified Report—Comparative Financial Statements (with explanatory paragraph)
Title:	REPORT OF INDEPENDENT REGISTERED PUBLIC ACCOUNTING FIRM
Addressee:	*To the Stockholders of EarthWear Clothiers*
Introductory paragraph:	We have audited the consolidated balance sheets of EarthWear Clothiers as of December 31, 2005 and 2004, and the related consolidated statements of operations, stockholders' equity, and cash flows for each of the three years in the period ended December 31, 2005. These financial statements are the responsibility of the Company's management. Our responsibility is to express an opinion on these financial statements based on our audits.
Scope paragraph:	We conducted our audits in accordance with the standards of the Public Company Accounting Oversight Board (United States). Those standards require that we plan and perform the audit to obtain reasonable assurance about whether the financial statements are free of material misstatement. An audit includes examining, on a test basis, evidence supporting the amounts and disclosures in the financial statements. An audit also includes assessing the accounting principles used and significant estimates made by management, as well as evaluating the overall financial statement presentation. We believe that our audits provide a reasonable basis for our opinion.
Opinion paragraph:	In our opinion, the consolidated financial statements referred to above present fairly, in all material respects, the financial position of the Company as of December 31, 2005 and 2004, and the results of its operations and its cash flows for each of the three years in the period ended December 31, 2005, in conformity with U.S. generally accepted accounting principles.
Explanatory paragraph referring to the audit of internal control:	We also have audited, in accordance with the standards of the Public Company Accounting Oversight Board (United States), the effectiveness of EarthWear Clothiers' internal control over financial reporting as of December 31, 2005, based on criteria established in Internal Control—Integrated Framework issued by the Committee of Sponsoring Organizations of the Treadway Commission (COSO), and our report dated February 15, 2006 expressed an unqualified opinion on management's assessment that EarthWear Clothiers maintains effective internal control and an unqualified opinion that internal control was effective.
Name of auditor:	*Willis & Adams* *Boise, Idaho*
Date of report:	*February 15, 2006*

contains seven elements: (1) the report title, (2) the addressee, (3) the introductory paragraph, (4) the scope paragraph, (5) the opinion paragraph, (6) the name of the auditor, and (7) the audit report date. The EarthWear report refers to the standards of the PCAOB because EarthWear is a publicly traded company and is subject to public-company reporting requirements. The report presented in Exhibit 18–1 is a *separate report* on the financial statement audit, but you will note that, in addition to giving the auditor's opinion on EarthWear's *financial statements*, the report refers to the auditor's opinions relating to the *audit of internal control over financial reporting*. When the auditor's reports on the financial statement audit and on the audit of internal control are presented separately, the reports must be dated the same and each must include an explanatory paragraph referring to the opinion(s) expressed in the other report. The last section of this chapter addresses reporting on the audit of internal control.

Explanatory Language Added to the Standard Unqualified Financial Statement Audit Report

✎ [LO 2]   Chapter 2 presented five situations that may require the auditor to modify the wording or add an explanatory paragraph to the standard unqualified audit report:

1. Opinion based in part on the report of another auditor.
2. Going concern.
3. Auditor agreement with a departure from GAAP.
4. Lack of consistency.
5. Emphasis of a matter.

The first situation results in a modification of the wording for the three paragraphs included in the standard unqualified audit report. The other four situations lead to the addition of an explanatory paragraph that *follows* the opinion paragraph without any modifications to the wording of the introductory, scope, or opinion paragraphs. The audit reports that are issued for these situations are still unqualified opinions and are discussed in this section.

Opinion Based in Part on the Report of Another Auditor

On some audit engagements, parts of the audit may be completed by another public accounting firm. For example, in reporting on consolidated financial statements, one of the subsidiaries may be audited by other auditors. In such cases, the auditor for the parent company must be satisfied that he or she is the principal auditor. This is normally determined by the portion of the financial statements audited by the parent-company auditor in relation to the portion of the consolidated financial statements audited by the other independent auditors.

The principal auditor at this point must decide whether to refer to the other auditors in the report. The principal auditor must first assess the *professional reputation* and *independence* of the other auditors. If the principal auditor is satisfied as to the professional reputation and independence of the other auditors and their audit work, an opinion may be expressed without referring in the audit report to the work of the other auditors. In so doing, the auditor accepts full responsibility for the work done and conclusions drawn by the other auditors.

However, in most situations, when the subsidiary represents a material amount in the consolidated financial statements, the principal auditor refers to the other auditors. In referencing the other auditors, the principal auditor is sharing responsibility for the audit report.

The portion of the consolidated financial statements, (assets and revenues) audited by the other auditors is disclosed in the report. Exhibit 18–2 is an example of a report in which the principal auditor has referred to the other auditors. Generally, the other auditors are not referenced by name in the report. (For illustrative purposes only, the new wording is shown in italics.) Collins Company is a privately held company. Thus, the report indicates that the audit was conducted "in accordance with generally accepted auditing standards" and is titled "Independent Auditor's Report." If Collins

---

EXHIBIT 18–2	**Opinion Based in Part on the Report of Another Auditor**

Independent Auditor's Report

To the Stockholders
Collins Company

We have audited the consolidated balance sheets of Collins Company as of December 31, 2005 and 2004, and the related consolidated statements of income, retained earnings, and cash flows for the years then ended. These financial statements are the responsibility of the Company's management. Our responsibility is to express an opinion on these financial statements based on our audits. *We did not audit the financial statements of Furillo Company, a wholly owned subsidiary, whose statements reflect total assets of $25,450,000 and $23,750,000 as of December 31, 2005 and 2004, respectively, and total revenues of $42,781,000 and $40,553,000 for the years then ended. Those statements were audited by other auditors whose report has been furnished to us, and our opinion, insofar as it relates to the amounts included for Furillo Company, is based solely on the report of the other auditors.*

We conducted our audit in accordance with auditing standards generally accepted in the United States of America. Those standards require that we plan and perform the audit to obtain reasonable assurance about whether the financial statements are free of material misstatement. An audit includes consideration of internal control over financial reporting as a basis for designing audit procedures that are appropriate in the circumstances, but not for the purpose of expressing an opinion on the effectiveness of the Company's internal control over financial reporting. Accordingly, we express no such opinion. An audit also includes examining, on a test basis, evidence supporting the amounts and disclosures in the financial statements, assessing the accounting principles used and significant estimates made by management, as well as evaluating the overall financial statement presentation. We believe that our audit provides a reasonable basis for our opinion.

In our opinion, *based on our audits and the report of the other auditors*, the consolidated financial statements referred to above present fairly, in all material respects, the financial position of Collins Company as of December 31, 2005 and 2004, and the results of its operations and its cash flows for the years then ended in conformity with accounting principles generally accepted in the United States of America.

Agassi, Connors, Evert & Co.
February 12, 2006

were a public company, the report would be titled "Report of Independent Registered Public Accounting Firm" and would indicate that the audit was conducted "in accordance with the standards of the Public Company Accounting Oversight Board (United States)." Note also that this report expressly indicates that while internal control was considered for the purpose of designing financial statement audit procedures, no opinion is expressed on the effectiveness of internal control over financial reporting. Private companies can opt to have their audits done in accordance with PCAOB standards, in which case their audit reports would conform to PCAOB standards. The rest of the exhibits in the first part of this chapter represent audits of privately held companies. However, with the exceptions noted, the wording is similar for audits of public companies.

If the other auditors' report is other than a standard unqualified audit report, the principal auditor needs to determine the nature of the departure and its significance in relation to the *overall* financial statements. If the departure is not material, the principal auditor need not refer to the departure in his or her report. If the principal auditor assesses that the departure is material, it may be necessary to refer to the matter underlying the other auditor's qualified opinion.

Going Concern

A basic assumption that underlies financial reporting is that an entity will continue as a going concern. Auditing standards (AU 341) state that the auditor has a responsibility to evaluate whether there is substantial doubt about the entity's ability to continue as a going concern for a reasonable period of time, not to exceed one year beyond the date of the financial statements being audited.

When there is substantial doubt about an entity's ability to continue as a going concern, the auditor should consider the possible effects on the financial statements and the related disclosures. Additionally, the audit report should include an explanatory paragraph such as the one shown in Exhibit 18–3. The auditor may also disclaim an opinion on the entity. If the entity's disclosures with respect to the entity's ability to continue as a going concern are inadequate, a departure from GAAP exists, resulting in a qualified or an adverse opinion. If a client received a going-concern report in the prior period and the doubt regarding going concern is removed in the

EXHIBIT 18–3	**Unqualified Financial Statement Audit Report with an Explanatory Paragraph for Going-Concern Problems**

Independent Auditor's Report

[*Standard introductory, scope, and opinion paragraphs*]

The accompanying financial statements have been prepared assuming that the Company will continue as a going concern. As discussed in Note 6 to the financial statements, the Company has suffered recurring losses from operations and has a net capital deficiency that raises substantial doubt about its ability to continue as a going concern. Management's plans in regard to these matters are also described in Note 6. The financial statements do not include any adjustments that might result from the outcome of this uncertainty.

current period, the explanatory paragraph included with the prior year's audit report is not included with the auditor's report covering the comparative financial statements.

Auditor Agrees with a Departure from Promulgated Accounting Principles

The auditor's standard unqualified audit report states that the financial statements conform to GAAP. However, in unusual circumstances financial statements may be misleading if a promulgated accounting principle were followed. Rule 203 of the Code of Professional Conduct allows the auditor, in such circumstances, to issue an unqualified opinion. However, an explanatory paragraph should be added to the report. The explanatory paragraph should describe the departure, the approximate effects of the departure, if practicable, and the reasons that compliance with the accounting principle results in misleading financial statements. From a practical viewpoint, this situation seldom occurs.

Lack of Consistency

The auditor's standard unqualified audit report implies that the comparability of the financial statements is not affected by changes in accounting principles or that any such change is immaterial. Accounting Principles Board Opinion No. 20, "Accounting Changes," governs the accounting for changes in accounting principles. From the auditor's perspective, accounting changes can be categorized into changes that affect consistency and those that do not affect consistency.

Changes Affecting Consistency   If the change in accounting principle or in the method of its application materially affects the comparability of the financial statements, and the auditor concurs with the change, the auditor should discuss the change in an explanatory paragraph. Auditing standards (AU 420) refer to the following accounting changes as affecting comparability and requiring an explanatory paragraph:

1. *Change in accounting principle.* An example would be a change from straight-line depreciation to an accelerated method for depreciating equipment.
2. *Change in reporting entity.* An example would be the consolidation of a major subsidiary's financial statements with the parent company's financial statements in the previous year and accounting for the subsidiary on a cost or equity basis in the current year.
3. *Correction of an error in principle.* This refers to a situation in which a client has used an accounting principle that is not acceptable (for example, replacement cost for inventory) in prior years but changes to an acceptable accounting principle (such as FIFO) in the current year.

Exhibit 18–4 is an example of an unqualified opinion with an explanatory paragraph for an accounting change that results in a lack of consistency.

Changes Not Affecting Consistency   Other changes may affect comparability but not consistency. These include

1. *Change in accounting estimate.* A change in the service life of a depreciable asset is an example of a change in estimate.

EXHIBIT 18–4	**Unqualified Report with an Explanatory Paragraph for a Lack of Consistency**

Independent Auditor's Report

[*Standard wording for the introductory, scope, and opinion paragraphs*]

As discussed in Note 7 to the financial statements, the Company changed its method of computing depreciation in 2005.

2. ***Correction of an error that does not involve an accounting principle.*** An example would be a mathematical mistake in a previously issued financial statement.
3. ***Change in classification and reclassification.*** If an item was included in operating expenses last year and in administrative expenses in the current year, this would be a change in classification.
4. ***Change expected to have a material future effect.*** This would be a change in accounting principle that has an immaterial effect in the current year but is expected to have a material effect in future years.

Changes that do not affect consistency are normally disclosed in the footnotes to the financial statements but do not require an explanatory paragraph in the auditor's report.

Emphasis of a Matter

Under certain circumstances an auditor may want to emphasize a specific matter regarding the financial statements even though he or she intends to express an unqualified opinion. This information should be presented in an explanatory paragraph. Some examples of situations that might cause the auditor to add an explanatory paragraph are significant related-party transactions and important events occurring after the balance sheet date. When a client has a FAS No. 5 contingency that is properly disclosed in the client's financial statements or footnotes, auditing standards explicitly instruct the auditor *not* to emphasize the matter through explanatory language.

Departures from an Unqualified Financial Statement Audit Report

The fourth standard of reporting allows the auditor to assume differing degrees of responsibility on financial statements. The auditor can issue three types of audit reports that depart from the unqualified audit report. The conditions for issuing such reports are discussed next. Figure 18–1 reproduces the overview of audit reporting that was presented in Figure 2–2.

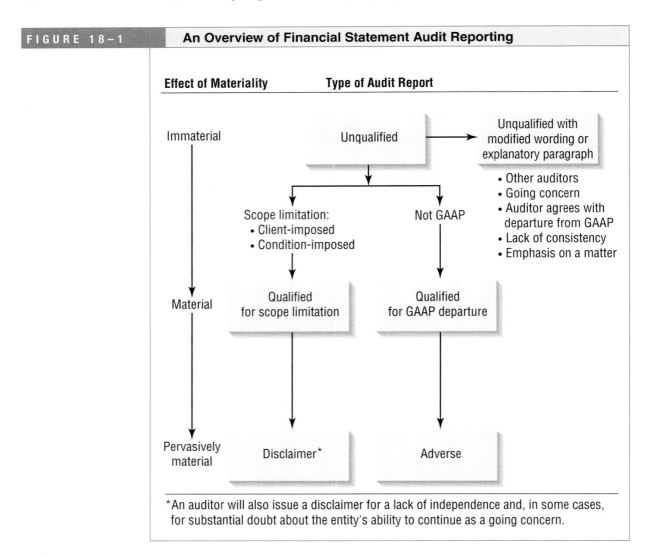

FIGURE 18–1 | **An Overview of Financial Statement Audit Reporting**

*An auditor will also issue a disclaimer for a lack of independence and, in some cases, for substantial doubt about the entity's ability to continue as a going concern.

Conditions for Departure

❀ [LO 3]

An auditor may be unable to express an unqualified opinion in three situations:

1. ***Scope limitation.*** A scope limitation results from an inability to collect sufficient competent evidence, such as when management prevents the auditor from conducting an audit procedure considered necessary.

2. ***Departure from GAAP.*** The financial statements are affected by a departure from GAAP.

3. ***Lack of independence of the auditor.*** The auditor must comply with the second general standard and the Code of Professional Conduct in order to issue an unqualified opinion.

Other Types of Financial Statement Audit Reports

❧ [LO 4]

The three types of reports other than unqualified are:

1. ***Qualified.*** The auditor's opinion is qualified because of either a scope limitation or a departure from GAAP, but overall the financial statements present fairly.
2. ***Disclaimer.*** The auditor disclaims an opinion on the financial statements either because there is insufficient competent evidence to form an opinion on the overall financial statements or because there is a lack of independence.
3. ***Adverse.*** The auditor's opinion states that the financial statements do not present fairly in conformity with GAAP because the departure materially affects the overall financial statements.

The choice of which audit report to issue depends on the condition and the materiality of the departure.

The Effect of Materiality on Financial Statement Audit Reporting

❧ [LO 5]

The concept of materiality plays a major role in the auditor's choice of audit reports. If the condition that might lead to the departure is judged by the auditor to be immaterial, a standard unqualified audit report can be issued. As the materiality of the condition increases, the auditor must judge the effect of the item on the *overall* financial statements.

When the auditor is faced with a scope limitation, the assessment of the omitted procedure(s) should consider the nature and magnitude of the potential effects of the item and its significance to the overall financial statements. If the potential effects relate to many items in the financial statements or if the effect of the item is so significant that the overall financial statements are affected, the auditor is more likely to issue a disclaimer than a qualified report. In other words, the *pervasiveness* of the item's effect on the financial statements determines whether the auditor should issue a qualified opinion or disclaim an opinion. For example, suppose an auditor is unable to perform certain audit procedures considered necessary in determining the fairness of a client's inventory balance. Assume further that inventory represents approximately 10 percent of total assets. In such a situation, the auditor would probably consider the item material, but not to the extent that the overall financial statements are not presented fairly, and would most likely issue a qualified opinion. However, if inventory represents a much larger percentage of total assets (such as 30 to 50 percent), the effect is highly material and would lead to the issuance of a disclaimer.

Judgments concerning the effects of a departure from GAAP are not much different. If the departure from GAAP is immaterial, the auditor should issue an unqualified opinion. If the departure from GAAP is material but the overall financial statements still present fairly, the auditor should issue a qualified opinion. If the departure is so pervasive that its effects are highly material, the auditor should issue an adverse opinion. For example, suppose that a client accounted for leased assets as operating leases when proper accounting required that the leases be capitalized. If a client had only one small piece of equipment that was treated in such a manner, the auditor would probably issue an unqualified opinion because the item would be immaterial. However, if the client had many leased assets that were accounted for as operating leases instead of capitalized leases, the auditor would normally issue a qualified or adverse opinion, depending on the pervasiveness of the problem.

Materiality is not a factor in considering an auditor's independence. When an auditor is not independent, a disclaimer should be issued.

Discussion of Conditions Requiring Other Types of Financial Statement Audit Reports

Scope Limitation

A scope limitation results from an inability to obtain sufficient competent evidence about some component of the financial statements. This occurs because the auditor is unable to apply all the audit procedures considered necessary. Such restrictions on the scope of the audit may be imposed by the client or by the circumstances of the engagement. Auditors should be particularly cautious when a client limits the scope of the engagement. In such a situation, the client may be trying to prevent the auditor from discovering material misstatements. Auditing standards suggest that when restrictions imposed by the client significantly limit the scope of the engagement, the auditor should consider disclaiming an opinion on the financial statements. However, if the auditor can overcome a scope limitation by performing alternative procedures, a standard unqualified audit report can be issued.

A number of these types of situations can occur on audit engagements. For example, auditing standards require that the auditor observe the physical inventory count (AU 331). However, circumstances may prevent the auditor from doing so. Suppose that the auditor is not engaged to conduct the audit until *after* year-end. In such a circumstance, the auditor may not be able to perform a number of audit procedures (like observing inventory). If such deficiencies in evidence cannot be overcome by other auditing procedures, the auditor will have to issue a qualified opinion or a disclaimer. Exhibit 18–5 is an example of a disclaimer of opinion due to this type of scope limitation.

EXHIBIT 18–5	**Disclaimer of Financial Statement Audit Opinion—Scope Limitation**

Independent Auditor's Report

We were engaged to audit the accompanying balance sheet of Kosar Company as of December 31, 2005 and 2004, and the related statements of income, retained earnings, and cash flows for the years then ended. These financial statements are the responsibility of the Company's management.

[Scope paragraph of standard report should be omitted.]

    We were unable to observe the taking of physical inventories stated in the accompanying financial statements at $4,550,000 as of December 31, 2005, and at $4,275,000 as of December 31, 2004, since those dates were prior to the time we were engaged as auditors for the Company. The Company's records do not permit the application of other auditing procedures regarding the existence of inventories.

    Since we did not observe physical inventories and we were not able to apply other auditing procedures to satisfy ourselves as to inventory quantities, the scope of our work was not sufficient to enable us to express, and we do not express, an opinion on these financial statements.

EXHIBIT 18–6	**Qualified Financial Statement Audit Report—Scope Limitation**

Independent Auditor's Report

[*Standard wording for the introductory paragraph*]

Except as discussed in the following paragraph, we conducted our audits in accordance with auditing standards generally accepted in the United States of America. Those standards require that . . . [*same wording as for the remainder of the standard scope paragraph*].

   We were unable to obtain audited financial statements supporting the Company's investment in a foreign affiliate stated at $12,500,000 and $11,700,000 at December 31, 2005 and 2004, respectively, or its equity in earnings of that affiliate of $1,200,000 and $1,050,000, which is included in net income for the years then ended as described in Note 10 to the financial statements; nor were we able to satisfy ourselves as to the carrying value of the investment in the foreign affiliate or the equity in its earnings by other auditing procedures.

   In our opinion, except for the effects of such adjustments, if any, as might have been determined to be necessary had we been able to examine evidence regarding the foreign affiliate and earnings, the financial statements referred to . . . [*same wording as for the remainder of the standard opinion paragraph*].

Another example occurs when a client requests that the auditor not confirm accounts receivable because of concerns about creating conflicts with customers over amounts owed. If the auditor is satisfied that the client's reasons for not confirming are legitimate and is unable to apply alternative audit procedures to determine fairness of the receivables, he or she would qualify the opinion or disclaim an opinion.

As a final example, the auditor may be unable to obtain audited financial statements for a long-term investment that is accounted for using the equity method. Exhibit 18–6 is an example of a qualified report for such a scope limitation.

Note that in all three examples the paragraph that explains the scope limitation is presented *before* the opinion or disclaimer paragraph.

Statements Not in Conformity with GAAP

If the financial statements are materially affected by an unacceptable departure from GAAP, the auditor should express a qualified or adverse opinion. Examples of these types of departures are an accounting principle that is not acceptable, inadequate disclosure, or a lack of justification for a change in accounting principle.

When the financial statements include an accounting principle that is not acceptable, the auditor should issue a qualified or adverse opinion, depending on materiality. When the auditor expresses a qualified opinion, a separate explanatory paragraph should be added to the report *before* the opinion paragraph. The explanatory paragraph should disclose the effects of the departure on the financial statements. Exhibit 18–7 is an example of a report that has been qualified because of the use of an unacceptable accounting principle.

If the departure's effect is so pervasive that the financial statements taken as a whole are not presented fairly, the auditor should issue an adverse opinion. When an adverse opinion is issued, the auditor should add an explanatory paragraph that *precedes* the opinion paragraph. The explanatory

| EXHIBIT 18–7 | Qualified Financial Statement Audit Report—Not in Conformity with Generally Accepted Accounting Principles |

Independent Auditor's Report

[Standard wording for the introductory and scope paragraphs]

The Company has excluded, from property and debt in the accompanying balance sheets, certain lease obligations that, in our opinion, should be capitalized in order to conform with generally accepted accounting principles. If these lease obligations were capitalized, property would be increased by $7,500,000 and $7,200,000, long-term debt by $6,900,000 and $6,600,000, and retained earnings by $1,420,000 and $1,290,000 as of December 31, 2005 and 2004, respectively. Additionally, net income would be increased by $250,000 and $220,000 and earnings per share would be increased by $.25 and $.22, respectively, for the years then ended.

In our opinion, except for the effects of not capitalizing certain lease obligations as discussed in the preceding paragraph, the financial statements referred to . . . *[same wording as for the remainder of the standard opinion paragraph]*.

paragraph should discuss the reasons for the adverse opinion and the effects of the departure on the financial statements. The opinion paragraph is modified to state that the financial statements *do not present fairly* in conformity with GAAP. Exhibit 18–8 is an example of an adverse report.

If a client fails to disclose information in the financial statements or footnotes as required by GAAP, the auditor should issue a qualified or

| EXHIBIT 18–8 | Adverse Financial Statement Audit Opinion—Not in Conformity with Generally Accepted Accounting Principles |

Independent Auditor's Report

[Standard wording for the introductory and scope paragraphs]

As discussed in Note 6 to the financial statements, the Company carries its property, plant, and equipment accounts at appraisal values and determines depreciation on the basis of such values. Generally accepted accounting principles require that property, plant, and equipment be stated at an amount not in excess of cost, reduced by depreciation based on such amount. Because of the departures from generally accepted accounting principles identified above, as of December 31, 2005 and 2004, respectively, inventories have been increased $1,500,000 and $1,340,000 by inclusion in manufacturing overhead of depreciation in excess of that based on cost; property, plant, and equipment, less accumulated depreciation, is carried at $13,475,000 and $12,950,000 in excess of an amount based on the cost to the Company. For the years ended December 31, 2005 and 2004, cost of goods sold has been increased $4,200,000 and $3,600,000, respectively, because of the effects of the depreciation accounting referred to above, resulting in a decrease in net income of $2,520,000 and $2,160,000, respectively.

In our opinion, because of the effects of the matters discussed in the preceding paragraph, the financial statements referred to above do not present fairly, in conformity with accounting principles generally accepted in the United States of America, the financial position of Morton Company as of December 31, 2005 and 2004, or the results of its operation or its cash flows for the years then ended.

EXHIBIT 18–9	**Qualified Financial Statement Audit Report—Inadequate Disclosure**

Independent Auditor's Report

We have audited the accompanying balance sheets of O'Dea Company as of December 31, 2005 and 2004, and the related statements of income and retained earnings for the years ended. These financial statements are the responsibility of the Company's management. Our responsibility is to express an opinion on these financial statements based on our audit.

[*Standard wording for the scope paragraph*]

The Company declined to present a statement of cash flows for the years ended December 31, 2005 and 2004. Presentation of such statement summarizing the Company's operating, investing, and financing activities is required by accounting principles generally accepted in the United States of America.

In our opinion, except that the omission of a statement of cash flows results in an incomplete presentation as explained in the preceding paragraph, the financial statements referred to . . . [*same wording as for the remainder of the standard opinion paragraph*].

---

adverse report, depending on the materiality of the omission. The auditor should provide the information in the report, if practicable, unless omission is allowed by auditing standards. One situation in which the auditor would *not* have to provide the information is where the client has declined to include a statement of cash flows. Auditing standards do not require that the auditor prepare a statement when one has been omitted by the client. Exhibit 18–9 is a qualified report for inadequate disclosure.

Auditor Not Independent

Much of the value that users of an auditor's report place on the report is based on the assumption of an unbiased relationship between the auditor and the client (see Chapter 19). There are few situations in which an auditor would be engaged to audit a client where independence between the two parties did not exist. It is possible that an auditor could be engaged by a client, believing that all members of the audit team were independent of the client. At the end of the engagement, it might come to the audit partner's attention that a member of the audit team had a financial interest in the client. This situation might jeopardize the audit firm's independence and result in the issuance of a report similar to the one shown in Exhibit 18–10.

If an auditor is not independent, a disclaimer of opinion should be issued. In the disclaimer, the auditor should *not* state the reasons for the lack

EXHIBIT 18–10	**Disclaimer of Financial Statement Audit Opinion When the Auditor Is Not Independent**

Accountant's Report

We are not independent with respect to Jordan Company, Inc., and the accompanying balance sheet as of December 31, 2005, and the related statements of earnings, retained earnings, and cash flows for the year then ended were not audited by us; accordingly, we do not express an opinion on them.

of independence nor describe any audit procedures performed. Note in Exhibit 18–11 that the title of the report does not contain the word *independent*. A title is not required for the disclaimer.

Special Reporting Issues

In addition to the types of audit reports just discussed, auditors often encounter a number of special reporting issues that affect the financial statement audit report. Three topics are covered in the remainder of this section of the chapter:

- Reports on comparative financial statements.
- Other information in documents containing audited financial statements.
- Special reports.

Reports on Comparative Financial Statements

※ [LO 6]   The fourth standard of reporting requires that the auditor either express an opinion on the financial statements taken as a whole or assert that an opinion cannot be expressed. When a client presents financial statements for the current period and one or more prior periods, the auditor must update the audit report on the financial statements presented on a comparative basis. For example, Exhibit 18–1 shows an unqualified standard audit report on EarthWear's comparative financial statements that covers the balance sheets for two years and statements of income, stockholders' equity, and cash flows for three years. Normally, the date of the auditor's report on the comparative statements is the date of the most recently completed audit.

During the current-year audit, the auditor should be alert for events that may affect prior-period financial statements. Three common situations are discussed.

Different Reports on Comparative Financial Statements

A number of situations may cause the auditor to express different reports on the comparative financial statements. One example is when the auditor expressed a standard unqualified opinion on prior years' financial statements but qualifies the current-year opinion. Exhibit 18–11 is an example of a report issued when a company decided not to capitalize certain lease obligations in the current year. In prior years, the company did not have capitalized lease obligations, so the financial statements for those years conformed to GAAP.

Another common situation occurs when the report on the current year is unqualified but prior-period financial statements were qualified or were disclaimed. Exhibit 18–12 is an example of a report issued when an auditor was hired subsequent to the observation of the physical inventory in the prior year and a disclaimer of opinion was issued for that period. In the current year, the auditor was able to conduct the audit without any scope limitation and issues an unqualified opinion.

EXHIBIT 18–11	**Comparative Report—Unqualified in Prior Years but Qualified in Current Year for Not Being in Conformity with Generally Accepted Accounting Principles**

Independent Auditor's Report

[*Standard wording for the introductory and scope paragraphs*]

The Company has excluded, from property and debt in the accompanying 2005 balance sheet, certain lease obligations that were entered into in 2005 which, in our opinion, should be capitalized in order to conform with accounting principles generally accepted in the United States of America. If these lease obligations were capitalized, property would be increased by $7,500,000, long-term debt by $6,900,000, and retained earnings by $1,420,000 as of December 31, 2005; net income would be increased by $250,000 and earnings per share would be increased by $.25, respectively, for the year then ended.

In our opinion, except for the effects on the 2005 financial statements of not capitalizing certain lease obligations as discussed in the preceding paragraph, the financial statements referred to . . . [*same wording as for the remainder of the standard opinion paragraph*].

A Change in Report on the Prior-Period Financial Statements

During the course of the current year's audit, the auditor may encounter circumstances or events that require updating the report issued on the prior-period financial statements. For example, the auditor may have issued a qualified or adverse opinion in the prior year because the client had not followed GAAP. If the client conforms to GAAP in the current year and restates the prior-period results, the auditor should express an unqualified opinion on the comparative financial statements. Exhibit 18–13 is an example of

EXHIBIT 18–12	**Comparative Report When the Prior Year Was Disclaimed for a Scope Limitation and the Current Year Received an Unqualified Opinion**

Independent Auditor's Report

[*Standard wording for the introductory paragraph*]

Except as explained in the following paragraph, we conducted our audits in accordance with auditing standards generally accepted in the United States of America . . . [*same wording as for the remainder of the standard scope paragraph*].

We did not observe the taking of the physical inventory as of December 31, 2003, since that date was prior to our appointment as auditors for the Company, and we were unable to satisfy ourselves regarding inventory quantities by means of other auditing procedures. Inventory amounts as of December 31, 2003, enter into the determination of net income and cash flows for the year ended December 31, 2004.

Because of the matter discussed in the preceding paragraph, the scope of our work was not sufficient to enable us to express, and we do not express, an opinion on the results of operations and cash flows for the year ended December 31, 2004.

In our opinion, the balance sheets of RUUD Rubber Company as of December 31, 2005 and 2004, and the related statements of income, retained earnings, and cash flows for the year ended December 31, 2005, present fairly, in all material respects, the financial position of RUUD Rubber Company as of December 31, 2005 and 2004, and the results of its operations and its cash flows for the year ended December 31, 2005, in conformity with accounting principles generally accepted in the United States of America.

EXHIBIT 18–13	Change in the Report on the Prior-Period Financial Statements

Independent Auditor's Report

[*Standard wording for the introductory and scope paragraphs*]

In our report dated March 1, 2005, we expressed an opinion that the 2004 financial statements did not fairly present financial position, results of operations, and cash flows in conformity with accounting principles generally accepted in the United States of America because of two departures from such principles: (1) the Company carried its property, plant, and equipment at appraisal values and provided for depreciation on the basis of such values, and (2) the Company did not provide for deferred income taxes with respect to differences between income for financial reporting purposes and taxable income. As described in Note 8, the Company has changed its method of accounting for these items and restated its 2004 financial statements to conform with accounting principles generally accepted in the United States of America. Accordingly, our present opinion on the 2004 financial statements, as presented herein, is different from that expressed in our previous report.

[*Standard wording for the opinion paragraph*]

such a report. Note that the paragraph that precedes the opinion paragraph contains the date of the previous report, the type of opinion previously issued, the reasons for the previous report being issued, and mention of the fact that the current report differs from the previously issued report. In this example, after the client conformed to GAAP in accounting for property, plant, and equipment and for deferred taxes and restated the prior-period financial statements, the auditor issued an unqualified report for both the current and prior years. Since the paragraph included in Exhibit 18–13 contains all the information required, a separate explanatory paragraph is not necessary.

Report by a Predecessor Auditor

When an entity has changed auditors, the predecessor auditor can reissue, at the request of the client, his or her report on the financial statements of the prior period, when those statements are presented on a comparative basis. In such a situation, the predecessor auditor must determine if the previously issued report is still appropriate, given the current circumstances. The predecessor auditor should do the following before reissuing the report:

1. Read the financial statements of the current period.
2. Compare the prior-period financial statements reported on with the current-year financial statements.
3. Obtain a letter of representations from the current-year or successor auditor.

The letter of representations should indicate whether the successor auditor discovered any material items that might affect, or require disclosure in, the financial statements reported on by the predecessor auditor. If the predecessor auditor is satisfied that the financial statements reported on should not be revised, the audit report is reissued using the date of the previous report.

In the event that the predecessor auditor becomes aware of circumstances or events that may affect the previously issued financial statements, he or she should make inquiries and perform any procedures considered necessary. For example, the successor auditor may discover errors indicating that the prior year's financial statements were materially misstated. If the financial statements are restated, the predecessor auditor should revise the report as necessary and dual date the reissued report.

If the prior-period financial statements have been audited but the predecessor auditor's report will not be included, the successor auditor should indicate in the introductory paragraph that the financial statements for the prior period were audited by other auditors and mention the date and the type of report issued by the predecessor auditor. If the predecessor's report was not standard, the successor auditor should describe the nature of and reasons for the explanatory paragraph added to the predecessor's report.

Other Information in Documents Containing Audited Financial Statements

[LO 7]   A client may publish documents such as annual reports and registration statements that contain other information in addition to the audited financial statements and the audit report. Auditing standards (AU 550) provide guidance for the auditor's consideration of other information contained in (1) annual reports of entities and (2) other documents to which the auditor devotes attention at the client's request.

The auditor has no responsibility beyond the financial information contained in the report, and he or she has no obligation to perform any audit procedures to corroborate the other information. However, the auditor is required to read the other information and consider whether such information is consistent with the information contained in the audited financial statements. For example, the audited financial statements may show a 10 percent increase in sales and a 5 percent increase in net income. If the president's letter that is included in the annual report states that sales were up 15 percent and net income increased by 12 percent, a material inconsistency would exist. The auditor would then have to determine whether the financial statements or the president's letter required revision. If the financial statements were correct, the auditor would request that the president change the other information. If the other information were not revised, the auditor should include an explanatory paragraph in the audit report, withhold the report, or withdraw from the engagement.

Special Reports Relating to Financial Statements

The first standard of reporting requires the auditor to report on whether the financial statements conform to GAAP. Auditors, however, are sometimes engaged to report on financial statements not prepared on the basis of GAAP. Auditors may also be engaged to report on parts of the financial statements or on a client's compliance with contractual agreements or regulatory requirements. Auditing standards (AU 623) provide the auditor with specific guidance for such engagements and cover the auditor's reporting responsibilities for the following situations:

- Financial statements prepared on a comprehensive basis of accounting other than GAAP (e.g., the cash basis of accounting).
- Specified elements, accounts, or items of a financial statement.
- Compliance with aspects of contractual agreements or regulatory requirements related to audited financial statements.

Financial Statements Prepared on a Comprehensive Basis of Accounting Other Than GAAP

A widely used type of special report is employed when an entity has prepared its financial statements on a comprehensive basis other than GAAP ("other comprehensive basis of accounting," or OCBOA). Auditing standards define OCBOA financial statements as including those prepared under the following bases:

- ***Regulatory basis.*** The basis used to comply with the requirements or financial reporting provisions of a governmental regulatory agency. An example would be when an insurance company reports in compliance with the rules of a state insurance commission.
- ***Tax basis.*** The basis the entity uses to file its income tax return. Real estate partnerships frequently use this basis for reporting to partners.
- ***Cash (or modified cash) basis.*** When the entity reports on revenues received and expenses paid. This may be modified to record depreciation or to accrue income taxes.

❧ [LO 8]

- ***A definite set of criteria having substantial support.*** Financial statements prepared on a price level–adjusted basis are an example of such a set of criteria.

Exhibit 18–14 is an example of a report on a set of financial statements prepared on a tax basis. Note that the introductory paragraph identifies the financial statements on which a report is being issued. It is important that these financial statements be titled so that they are not confused with financial statements prepared on a GAAP basis. In this case, the report covers a *statement of assets, liabilities, and capital—income tax basis* instead of a balance sheet and a *statement of revenues and expenses—income tax basis* instead of a statement of income or operations.

The scope paragraph is identical to that included in the standard unqualified audit report. The third paragraph discloses the basis used to prepare the financial statements and refers to a note in the financial statements that describes the basis in more detail. The opinion paragraph is a positive statement about the fairness of presentation in conformity with the OCBOA.

If the financial statements are prepared on a regulatory basis, the following paragraph is added (see AU 532) to restrict the distribution of the report to those parties within the entity and those involved in filing with the regulatory agency:

> This report is intended solely for the information and use of the board of directors and management of Great Atlantic Insurance Company and for filing with the Excelsior State Insurance Agency and should not be used by anyone other than these specified parties.

EXHIBIT 18—14	**Financial Statements Prepared on the Entity's Income Tax Basis**

Independent Auditor's Report

We have audited the accompanying statements of assets, liabilities, and capital—income tax basis of Patroon Partnership as of December 31, 2005 and 2004, and the related statements of revenue and expenses—income tax basis and of changes in partners' capital accounts—income tax basis for the years then ended. These financial statements are the responsibility of the Partnership's management. Our responsibility is to express an opinion on these financial statements based on our audits.

We conducted our audit in accordance with auditing standards generally accepted in the United States of America. Those standards require that we plan and perform the audit to obtain reasonable assurance about whether the financial statements are free of material misstatement. An audit includes consideration of internal control over financial reporting as a basis for designing audit procedures that are appropriate in the circumstances, but not for the purpose of expressing an opinion on the effectiveness of the Company's internal control over financial reporting. Accordingly, we express no such opinion. An audit also includes examining, on a test basis, evidence supporting the amounts and disclosures in the financial statements, assessing the accounting principles used and significant estimates made by management, as well as evaluating the overall financial statement presentation. We believe that our audit provides a reasonable basis for our opinion.

As described in Note 2, these financial statements were prepared on the basis of accounting the Partnership uses for income tax purposes, which is a comprehensive basis of accounting other than generally accepted accounting principles.

In our opinion, the financial statements referred to above present fairly, in all material respects, the assets, liabilities, and capital of Patroon Partnership as of December 31, 2005 and 2004, and its revenue and expenses and changes in partners' capital accounts for the years then ended, on the basis of accounting described in Note 2.

Specified Elements, Accounts, or Items of a Financial Statement

[LO 9]

In some situations an auditor may be engaged to audit only part (specified elements, accounts, or items) of the financial statements. Examples include a report on rentals, royalties, or profit participation or on the provision for income taxes. The basis of accounting for the elements, accounts, or items may be GAAP, OCBOA, or a basis of accounting prescribed by a contract or agreement.

An engagement to express an opinion on one or more specified elements, accounts, or items of a financial statement may be performed as a separate engagement or as part of an audit of financial statements. The only exception is when the auditor is engaged to report on the entity's net income or stockholders' equity. In this case, the auditor must audit the entire set of financial statements.

Generally, an audit of an element, account, or item is more extensive than if the same information were considered as part of an audit of the overall financial statements. Thus, materiality needs to be set in relation to the individual element, account, or item, and the auditor should consider how the item relates to other parts of the financial statements. For example, if the auditor is engaged to audit the entity's accounts receivable, other accounts such as sales and allowance for bad debts should also be considered.

Suppose an auditor is engaged to issue a special report on gross sales for the calculation of rent. The introductory paragraph states that this specific account was audited. Similar to the standard unqualified audit report, this paragraph states management's and the auditor's responsibilities. The scope paragraph differs from the standard report only in that it references the account being audited. The third paragraph expresses the auditor's opinion on the account. Finally, in the case when the specified element, account, or item is audited in compliance with the provisions of a contract or agreement, the auditor includes a paragraph limiting distribution of the report to the parties who are part of the contract.

Rather than auditing specified elements, accounts, or items, an auditor may be engaged to apply only *agreed-upon procedures*. Attestation standards (AT 201) provide the auditor with the necessary guidance for such engagements. An engagement to apply agreed-upon procedures is one in which the

EXHIBIT 18–15	Agreed-Upon Procedures Report in Connection with Claims of Creditors

Independent Auditor's Report on Applying Agreed-Upon Procedures

To the Trustee of Maxiscript Corporation:

We have performed the procedures described below, which were agreed to by the Trustee of Maxiscript Corporation, with respect to the claims of creditors to determine the validity of claims of Maxiscript Corporation as of May 31, 2005, as set forth in the accompanying Schedule A. Maxiscript Corporation is responsible for maintaining records of claims submitted by creditors of Maxiscript Corporation. This agreed-upon-procedures engagement was conducted in accordance with attestation standards established by the American Institute of Certified Public Accountants. The sufficiency of these procedures is solely the responsibility of the Trustee of Maxiscript Corporation. Consequently, we make no representation regarding the sufficiency of the procedures described below either for the purpose for which this report has been requested or for any other purpose.

The procedures and associated findings are as follows:

a. Compare the total of the trial balance of accounts payable at May 31, 2005, prepared by the company, to the balance in the Company's related general ledger account.

The total of the accounts payable trial balance agreed with the balance in the related general ledger account.

b. Compare the amounts for claims received from creditors as shown in claims documents provided by Maxiscript Corporation to the respective amounts shown in the trial balance of accounts payable. Using the data included in the claims documents and in Maxiscript's accounts payable detail records, reconcile any differences to the accounts payable trial balance.

All differences noted are presented in column 3 of Schedule A. Except for those amounts shown in column 4 of Schedule A, all such differences were reconciled.

c. Obtain the documentation submitted by the creditors in support of their claims and compare it to the following documentation in Maxiscript Corporation's files: invoices, receiving reports, and other evidence of receipt of goods or services.

No exceptions were found as a result of these comparisons.

We were not engaged to, and did not, perform an audit, the objective of which would be the expression of an opinion on the claims of the creditors set forth in accompanying Schedule A. Accordingly, we do not express such an opinion. Had we performed additional procedures, other matters might have come to our attention that would have been reported to you.

This report is intended solely for the information and use of the Trustee of Maxiscript Corporation and is not intended to be and should not be used by anyone other than this specified party.

auditor is engaged by a client to issue a *report of findings* based on specific procedures performed on the specific subject matter of specified elements, accounts, or items of a financial statement. The report does not express an opinion. On such engagements, standards require that the specified users take responsibility for the sufficiency of the agreed-upon procedures. The auditor can satisfy this requirement by performing one of the following or similar procedures:

1. Compare the procedures to be applied to the written requirements of the specified users.
2. Discuss the procedures to be applied with appropriate representatives of the users involved.
3. Review relevant contracts or correspondence from the specified users.

Exhibit 18–15 is an example of an agreed-upon procedures report. The report (1) identifies the specified users; (2) references the specified elements, accounts, or items of a financial statement and the character of the engagement; (3) lists the procedures performed and related findings; (4) disclaims an opinion; and (5) states restrictions on the use of the report.

Compliance Reports Related to Audited Financial Statements
❧ [LO 10]

An auditor may be asked to report on an entity's compliance with certain contractual agreements or regulatory requirements related to audited financial statements. For example, loan agreements may include covenants such as restrictions on dividends or maintenance of certain levels for selected financial ratios. Exhibit 18–16 is an example of a special report related to compliance with contractual provisions. Note that the auditor provides *negative assurance* as to compliance with the provisions of the loan agreement. Negative assurance consists of a statement that, after applying specified procedures, nothing came to the auditor's attention that

EXHIBIT 18–16	**Report on Compliance with Contractual Provisions Given in a Separate Report**

Independent Auditor's Report

We have audited, in accordance with auditing standards generally accepted in the United States of America, the balance sheet of Lynch Lumber Company as of December 31, 2005, and the related statement of income, retained earnings, and cash flows for the year then ended, and have issued our report thereon dated February 16, 2006.

In connection with our audit, nothing came to our attention that caused us to believe that the Company failed to comply with the terms, covenants, provisions, or conditions of sections 6.1 to 6.14, inclusive, of the indenture dated July 21, 2003, with First State Bank insofar as they relate to accounting matters. However, our audit was not directed primarily toward obtaining knowledge of such noncompliance.

This report is intended solely for the information and use of the board of directors and management of Lynch Lumber Company and First State Bank and is not intended to be and should not be used by anyone other than these specified parties.

indicated that the provisions of the loan agreement had not been complied with.

Reporting on the Audit of Internal Control over Financial Reporting

As discussed in Chapter 7, managements of public companies are required to implement and maintain internal control over financial reporting and annually test and evaluate its effectiveness. Management must then make a written assertion regarding the effectiveness of the company's internal control and engage an auditor to perform an integrated audit of the company's internal control and financial statements. An example of management's assessment of internal control is presented in Chapter 7 (see Exhibit 7–3). Once the auditor has completed the audit of internal control over financial reporting, he or she issues an appropriate report to accompany management's assessment.

The Auditor's Opinion on Management's Assessment

☞ **[LO 11]**

The auditor's report on the audit of internal control contains opinions on (1) management's assessment of the effectiveness of internal control over financial reporting and (2) the effectiveness of internal control (based on the auditor's independent audit work). The opinion on management's assessment is unqualified if the auditor agrees with management's conclusion. If the auditor disagrees, the opinion is adverse. The auditor should evaluate the following matters with respect to management's assessment (AS2, ¶166):

- Whether management has properly stated its responsibility for establishing and maintaining adequate internal control over financial reporting.
- Whether the framework used by management to conduct the evaluation is suitable.
- Whether management's assessment of the effectiveness of internal control over financial reporting is free of material misstatement.
- Whether management has expressed its assessment in an acceptable form. Management is required to state explicitly whether the company's internal control over financial reporting is effective; statements suggesting only negative assurance are not appropriate. For example, a statement by management that "nothing has come to management's attention to suggest that the company's internal control over financial reporting is less than effective" is not acceptable. Further, management is not permitted to conclude that the company's internal control over financial reporting is effective if there are one or more material weaknesses in the company's internal control over financial reporting as of the end of the reporting period.[1]

---

[1]See Chapter 7 for definitions of control deficiency, significant deficiency, and material weakness.

- Whether any material weaknesses identified in the company's internal control over financial reporting have been properly disclosed, including material weaknesses corrected during the period.

If the auditor is unable to conduct the necessary procedures to express an opinion on management's assessment, a qualified opinion may be expressed, or an opinion may be disclaimed, depending on the reason(s) and severity of the scope limitation.

The Auditor's Opinion on the Effectiveness of Internal Control over Financial Reporting

※ **[LO 12]**

After auditing the effectiveness of a client's internal control, an auditor issues an unqualified opinion if the client's internal control is designed and operating effectively in all material respects. Significant deficiencies do not require a departure from an unqualified opinion because they relate to possible financial statement misstatements that are less than material. If the scope of the auditor's work is limited, a qualified opinion or a disclaimer of opinion is issued on the effectiveness of internal control, depending on the severity of the circumstances and whether the scope limitation was intentionally imposed by management. If a material weakness is identified, the auditor issues an adverse opinion. Figure 18–2, which reproduces Figure 7–3, gives an

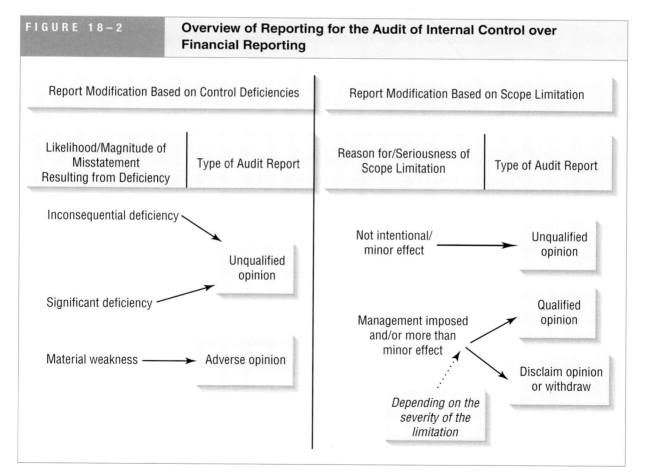

FIGURE 18–2 **Overview of Reporting for the Audit of Internal Control over Financial Reporting**

Report Modification Based on Control Deficiencies

Likelihood/Magnitude of Misstatement Resulting from Deficiency	Type of Audit Report
Inconsequential deficiency	Unqualified opinion
Significant deficiency	Unqualified opinion
Material weakness	Adverse opinion

Report Modification Based on Scope Limitation

Reason for/Seriousness of Scope Limitation	Type of Audit Report
Not intentional/minor effect	Unqualified opinion
Management imposed and/or more than minor effect	Qualified opinion
	Disclaim opinion or withdraw

Depending on the severity of the limitation

overview of the types of audit reports relating to the effectiveness of internal control over financial reporting.

Unqualified Report
✎ [LO 13]

An unqualified opinion on the effectiveness of the client's internal control over financial reporting is appropriate when a client's controls are designed and operating effectively in all material respects as of the report date. The phrase "in all material respects" means that the client's internal control over financial reporting is free of any material weakness. As depicted in Figure 18–2, an unqualified opinion can be issued even in the presence of significant deficiencies.

The auditor's report on the audit of internal control over financial reporting can be presented in a combined report along with the auditor's opinion on the client's financial statements, or the two reports can be presented separately. Under either approach, the date of the reports should be the same. When separate reports are issued, each report must refer to the other. Exhibit 18–1 presents a separate report on the *financial statement audit*. Note that the last paragraph refers to the audit of internal control over financial reporting and indicates that unqualified opinions were issued with respect to both management's assessment and the effectiveness of internal control. An example of a separate report on the *audit of internal control*, giving unqualified opinions on both management's assessment and the effectiveness of internal control, was presented in Chapter 7 (see Exhibit 7–4). Note that the last paragraph refers to the financial statement audit and indicates that an unqualified opinion was issued with respect to the client's financial statements.

▰EarthWear▰ Exhibit 18-17 presents a combined report for EarthWear Clothiers that gives an unqualified opinion on both the financial statement audit and the audit of internal control over financial reporting. When the auditor elects to issue a combined report, the report may address multiple reporting periods for the financial statements presented but will address only the end of the most recent fiscal year for management's assessment and for the effectiveness of internal control.

Modifications to the Unqualified Report on the Effectiveness of Internal Control
✎ [LO 14]

The auditor should modify the standard report if any of the following conditions exist.

- There is a material weakness in the company's internal control over financial reporting.
- There is a restriction on the scope of the engagement.
- The auditor decides to refer to the report of other auditors as the basis, in part, for the auditor's own report.
- A significant subsequent event has occurred since the date being reported on.
- There is other information contained in management's report on internal control.

Adverse Reports for a Material Weakness
Exhibit 7–5 in Chapter 7 presents a report where management's assessment indicates that the

EXHIBIT 18–17	**An Example of a Combined Report Expressing an Unqualified Opinion on Financial Statements, an Unqualified Opinion on Management's Assessment of the Effectiveness of Internal Control over Financial Reporting and an Unqualified Opinion on the Effectiveness of Internal Control over Financial Reporting**

Report of Independent Registered Public Accounting Firm

[*Introductory paragraph*]

We have audited the accompanying balance sheets of EarthWear Clothiers as of December 31, 2005 and 2004, and the related statements of income, stockholders' equity and comprehensive income, and cash flows for each of the years in the three-year period ended December 31, 2005. We also have audited management's assessment, included in the accompanying Management Report on the Financial Statements and Internal Control, that EarthWear Clothiers maintained effective internal control over financial reporting as of December 31, 2005, based on criteria established in *Internal Control—Integrated Framework* issued by the Committee of Sponsoring Organizations of the Treadway Commission (COSO). EarthWear Clothiers' management is responsible for these financial statements, for maintaining effective internal control over financial reporting, and for its assessment of the effectiveness of internal control over financial reporting. Our responsibility is to express an opinion on these financial statements, an opinion on management's assessment, and an opinion on the effectiveness of the company's internal control over financial reporting based on our audits.

[*Scope paragraph*]

We conducted our audits in accordance with the standards of the Public Company Accounting Oversight Board (United States). Those standards require that we plan and perform the audits to obtain reasonable assurance about whether the financial statements are free of material misstatement and whether effective internal control over financial reporting was maintained in all material respects. Our audit of financial statements included examining, on a test basis, evidence supporting the amounts and disclosures in the financial statements, assessing the accounting principles used and significant estimates made by management, and evaluating the overall financial statement presentation. Our audit of internal control over financial reporting included obtaining an understanding of internal control over financial reporting, evaluating management's assessment, testing and evaluating the design and operating effectiveness of internal control, and performing such other procedures as we considered necessary in the circumstances. We believe that our audits provide a reasonable basis for our opinions.

[*Definition paragraph*]

A company's internal control over financial reporting is a process designed to provide reasonable assurance regarding the reliability of financial reporting and the preparation of financial statements for external purposes in accordance with generally accepted accounting principles. A company's internal control over financial reporting includes those policies and procedures that (1) pertain to the maintenance of records that, in reasonable detail, accurately and fairly reflect the transactions and dispositions of the assets of the company; (2) provide reasonable assurance that transactions are recorded as necessary to permit preparation of financial statements in accordance with generally accepted accounting principles, and that receipts and expenditures of the company are being made only in accordance with authorizations of management and directors of the company; and (3) provide reasonable assurance regarding prevention or timely detection of unauthorized acquisition, use, or disposition of the company's assets that could have a material effect on the financial statements.

[*Inherent limitations paragraph*]

Because of its inherent limitations, internal control over financial reporting may not prevent or detect misstatements. Also, projections of any evaluation of effectiveness to future periods are subject to the risk that controls may become inadequate because of changes in conditions, or that the degree of compliance with the policies or procedures may deteriorate.

[*Opinion paragraph*]

In our opinion, the financial statements referred to above present fairly, in all material respects, the financial position of EarthWear Clothiers as of December 31, 2005 and 2004, and the results of its operations and its cash flows for each of the years in the three-year

(*continued*)

EXHIBIT 18–17	**(concluded)**

period ended December 31, 2005 in conformity with accounting principles generally accepted in the United States of America. Also in our opinion, management's assessment that EarthWear Clothiers maintained effective internal control over financial reporting as of December 31, 2005, is fairly stated, in all material respects, based on criteria established in *Internal Control—Integrated Framework* issued by the Committee of Sponsoring Organizations of the Treadway Commission (COSO). Furthermore, in our opinion, EarthWear Clothiers maintained, in all material respects, effective internal control over financial reporting as of December 31, 2005, based on criteria established in *Internal Control—Integrated Framework* issued by the Committee of Sponsoring Organizations of the Treadway Commission (COSO).

Willis & Adams
Boise, Idaho
February 15, 2006

company did not maintain effective internal control over financial reporting. In this circumstance, the auditor's report is unqualified with respect to management's assessment (because the auditor agreed with the negative assessment) and adverse for the effectiveness of internal control. If management's report states that internal control over financial reporting was effective and the auditor disagrees, the auditor will issue an adverse opinion on both management's assessment and the effectiveness of internal control (see Exhibit 18–18).

In some cases, the auditor's report on internal control over financial reporting might describe a material weakness that resulted in an adverse opinion on the effectiveness of internal control over financial reporting, while the report on the financial statement audit remains unqualified. Such a conclusion would be reached when a client's internal control is not sufficiently likely to prevent or detect material misstatements, but the auditor has collected sufficient competent evidence to conclude that the client's financial statements do not contain material misstatements. When the auditor's opinion on the financial statements is not affected by the adverse opinion on the effectiveness of internal control over financial reporting, the report on internal control over financial reporting (or the combined report) should include the following language in the paragraph that describes the material weakness:

> This material weakness was considered in determining the nature, timing, and extent of audit tests applied in our audit of the 2005 financial statements, and this report does not affect our report dated [*date of financial statement audit report*] on those financial statements.

Such disclosure is important to ensure that users of the auditor's report on the financial statements understand why the auditor issued an unqualified opinion on those statements.

Disclosure is also important when the auditor's opinion on the financial statements *is* affected by the adverse opinion on the effectiveness of internal control. In such a circumstance, the report on internal control over financial reporting (or the combined report) should similarly indicate that the material weakness was considered in determining the nature, timing, and extent of procedures performed as part of the financial statement audit.

EXHIBIT 18–18	**An Example of a Report Expressing an Adverse Opinion on Management's Assessment of the Effectiveness of Internal Control over Financial Reporting and an Adverse Opinion on the Effectiveness of Internal Control over Financial Reporting Because of the Existence of a Material Weakness**

Report of Independent Registered Public Accounting Firm

[Standard wording for the introductory, scope, definition, and inherent limitations paragraphs]

[Explanatory paragraph]

A material weakness is a control deficiency, or combination of control deficiencies, that results in more than a remote likelihood that a material misstatement of the annual or interim financial statements will not be prevented or detected. We have identified the following material weakness that has not been identified as a material weakness in management's assessment. *[Include a description of the material weakness and its effect on the achievement of the objectives of the control criteria.]* This material weakness was considered in determining the nature, timing, and extent of audit tests applied in our audit of the 2005 financial statements, and this report does not affect our report dated February 15, 2006, on those financial statements.

[Opinion paragraph]

In our opinion, because of the effect of the material weakness described above on the achievement of the objectives of the control criteria, management's assessment that GlobalCom maintained effective internal control over financial reporting as of December 31, 2005, is not fairly stated, in all material respects, based on criteria established in *Internal Control—Integrated Framework* issued by the Committee of Sponsoring Organizations of the Treadway Commission (COSO). Also, in our opinion, because of the effect of the material weakness described above on the achievement of the objectives of the control criteria, GlobalCom has not maintained effective internal control over financial reporting as of December 31, 2005, based on criteria established in *Internal Control—Integrated Framework* issued by the Committee of Sponsoring Organizations of the Treadway Commission (COSO).

Gambler & Hockster
Biloxi, MS
February 15, 2006

Qualified Report or Disclaimer for Scope Limitation   The auditor can express an unqualified opinion on the effectiveness of internal control over financial reporting only if the auditor has been able to apply all the procedures necessary in the circumstances. If the scope of the auditor's work is limited because of circumstances beyond the control of management or the auditor, the auditor should express a qualified opinion, disclaim an opinion, or withdraw from the engagement. The auditor's decision depends on an assessment of the importance of the omitted procedure(s) to his or her ability to form an opinion on the effectiveness of the company's internal control. If the restrictions are imposed by management, the auditor generally should withdraw from the engagement or disclaim an opinion on both management's assessment and the effectiveness of internal control over financial reporting.

An example of circumstances that may impose a restriction is if management identifies a material weakness prior to the end of the period and implements controls to correct it. If management believes the new controls have been operating for a sufficient period of time to determine that they are designed and operating effectively, management can express in its assessment the conclusion that internal control is effective as of the date specified. If the auditor has sufficient time to adequately evaluate and test the new controls and concludes that they were designed and operating effectively as of the end of the period, unqualified opinions can be issued on both management's assessment and on the effectiveness of internal control. If the auditor does not have sufficient time, the opinion is modified for a scope limitation. If the auditor disagrees with the sufficiency of the time period for testing the operating effectiveness of the control, the auditor should modify his or her opinions on both the effectiveness of internal control over financial reporting and management's assessment due to a scope limitation. Exhibit 18–19 presents a report in which the auditor qualified the opinions on management's assessment and the effectiveness of internal control.

The Auditor Decides to Refer to the Report of Other Auditors

As mentioned previously in this chapter in connection with the financial statement audit, on some engagements parts of the audit may be completed by another public accounting firm. In such circumstances, the auditor must decide whether to make reference in the report on internal control over financial reporting to work performed by the other auditor. The decision is based on factors similar to those considered by the auditor who uses the work and reports of other independent auditors when reporting on a company's financial statements. If the auditor decides to make reference to the report of the other auditor as a basis, in part, for his or her opinions, the auditor should refer to the report of the other auditor in describing the scope of the audit and in expressing the opinions (AS2, ¶183–185).

Subsequent Events   The auditor has a responsibility to report on any changes in internal control that might affect financial reporting between the end of the reporting period and the date of the auditor's report. Chapter 17 describes procedures the auditor might undertake to search for subsequent events affecting a client's financial statements and affecting the client's internal control over financial reporting. As noted in Chapter 17, the auditor's treatment of a subsequent event depends on whether the event reveals information about a material weakness that existed as of the end of the reporting period or whether the event creates or reveals information about a new condition that did not exist as of the end of the reporting period.

Management's Report Contains Additional Information   Management may include additional information in its report on internal control over financial reporting. For example, management may include disclosures about corrective actions taken by the company after the date of management's assessment, the company's plans to implement new controls, or a statement that management believes the cost of correcting a material weakness would exceed the benefits to be derived from implementing new

EXHIBIT 18–19	**An Example Report Expressing a Qualified Opinion on Management's Assessment of the Effectiveness of Internal Control over Financial Reporting and a Qualified Opinion on the Effectiveness of Internal Control over Financial Reporting Because of a Limitation on the Scope of the Audit**

Report of Independent Registered Public Accounting Firm

[*Standard wording for introductory paragraph*]

[*Scope paragraph*]

Except as described below, we conducted our audit in accordance the standards of the Public Company Accounting Oversight Board (United States). Those standards [*standard wording for the remainder of the scope paragraph*].

[*Explanatory paragraph that describes scope limitation*]

A material weakness is a control deficiency, or combination of control deficiencies, that results in more than a remote likelihood that a material misstatement of the annual or interim financial statements will not be prevented or detected. The following material weakness has been identified and included in management's assessment. Prior to December 20, 2005, Conquest Communications, Inc., had an inadequate system for recording cash receipts, which could have prevented the company from recording cash receipts on accounts receivable completely and properly. Therefore, cash received could have been diverted for unauthorized use, lost, or otherwise not properly recorded to accounts receivable. We believe this condition was a material weakness in the design or operation of the internal control of Conquest Communications, Inc., in effect prior to December 20, 2005. Although the company implemented a new cash receipts system on December 20, 2005, the system has not been in operation for a sufficient period of time to enable us to obtain sufficient evidence about its operating effectiveness.

[*Standard wording for definition and inherent limitations paragraphs*]

[*Opinion paragraph*]

In our opinion, except for the effect of matters we might have discovered had we been able to examine evidence about the effectiveness of the new cash receipts system, management's assessment that Conquest Communications, Inc., maintained effective internal control over financial reporting as of December 31, 2005, is fairly stated, in all material respects, based on criteria established in *Internal Control—Integrated Framework* issued by the Committee of Sponsoring Organizations of the Treadway Commission (COSO). Also, in our opinion, except for the effect of matters we might have discovered had we been able to examine evidence about the effectiveness of the new cash receipts system, Conquest Communications, Inc., maintained, in all material respects, effective internal control over financial reporting as of December 31, 2005, based on criteria established in *Internal Control—Integrated Framework* issued by the Committee of Sponsoring Organizations of the Treadway Commission (COSO).

[*Explanatory paragraph*]

We have also audited, in accordance with the standards of the Public Company Accounting Oversight Board (United States), the consolidated financial statements of Conquest Communications, Inc., and our report dated February 15, 2006, expressed an unqualified opinion.

D'Knote, Slikk & Associates
Denver, CO
February 15, 2006

controls. The auditor should disclaim an opinion on such information and include the following language as the last paragraph of the report:

> We do not express an opinion or any other form of assurance on management's statement referring to the costs and related benefits of implementing new controls.

If the auditor believes that the additional information contains a material misstatement of fact, he or she should discuss the matter with management. If the auditor concludes that management's additional information might not be correct, he or she should propose that management consult with the company's legal counsel. If the auditor concludes that a material misstatement of fact remains, he or she should notify management and the audit committee in writing. The auditor also should consider consulting the auditor's legal counsel about further actions to be taken, including the auditor's responsibility under the Securities Exchange Act of 1934 (AS2, ¶191–192).

KEY TERMS

Generally Accepted Auditing Standards. Measures of the quality of the auditor's performance.

Material weakness. A significant deficiency, or combination of significant deficiencies, that results in more than a remote likelihood that a material misstatement of the annual or interim financial statements will not be prevented or detected.

Materiality. The magnitude of an omission or misstatement of accounting information that, in light of surrounding circumstances, makes it probable that the judgment of a reasonable person relying on the information would have been changed or influenced.

Other comprehensive basis of accounting. Financial statements prepared under regulatory, tax, cash basis, or other definitive criteria having substantial support.

Reasonable assurance. A term that implies some risk that a material misstatement could be present in the financial statements without the auditor detecting it, even when the auditor has exercised due care.

Representation letter. A letter that corroborates oral representations made to the auditor by management and documents the continued appropriateness of such representations.

Scope limitation. A lack of evidence, such as an inability to conduct an audit procedure considered necessary.

Significant deficiency. A control deficiency, or combination of control deficiencies, that adversely affects the entity's ability to initiate, authorize, record, process, or report external financial data reliably in accordance with generally accepted accounting principles such that there is more than a remote likelihood that a misstatement of the entity's annual or interim financial statements that is more than inconsequential will not be prevented or detected.

www.mhhe.com/ messier4e	Visit the book's Online Learning Center for a multiple-choice quiz that will allow you to assess your understanding of chapter concepts.

REVIEW QUESTIONS

[LO 1]   18-1   Describe what is meant when an auditor is "associated with" a set of financial statements.

[2]   18-2   Distinguish between accounting changes that affect consistency and changes that do not.

[3] 18-3 Give examples of a client-imposed and a condition-imposed scope limitation. Why is a client-imposed limitation generally considered more serious?

[5] 18-4 How does the materiality of a condition that might lead to a departure from GAAP affect the auditor's choice of financial statement audit reports?

[6] 18-5 In 2004 your firm issued an unqualified report on Tosi Corporation. During 2005 Tosi entered its first lease transaction, which you have determined is material and meets the criteria for a capitalized lease. Tosi Corporation's management chooses to treat the transaction as an operating lease. What types of reports would you issue on the corporation's comparative financial statements for 2004 and 2005?

[7] 18-6 What are the auditor's responsibilities for other information included in an entity's annual report?

[7] 18-7 If the auditor determines that other information contained with the audited financial statements is incorrect and the client refuses to correct the other information, what actions can the auditor take?

[8,9,10] 18-8 List three examples of special reports.

[8] 18-9 List four bases for OCBOA financial statements. Why is it important that these financial statements be properly titled in the audit report?

[1,12] 18-10 Under what conditions might the auditor's opinions on management's assessment of internal control and on the effectiveness of internal control be different from each other?

[14] 18-11 Under what circumstances would an auditor give an adverse opinion on the effectiveness of a client's internal control over financial reporting?

[14] 18-12 Under what circumstances would an auditor disclaim an opinion on the effectiveness of a client's internal control over financial reporting?

[14] 18-13 Under what circumstances would an auditor qualify his or her opinion on the effectiveness of a client's internal control over financial reporting?

MULTIPLE-CHOICE QUESTIONS

[1,2] 18-14 In which of the following situations would an auditor ordinarily issue an unqualified financial statement audit opinion without an explanatory paragraph?
  a. The auditor wishes to emphasize that the entity had significant related-party transactions.
  b. The auditor decides to refer to the report of another auditor as a basis, in part, for the auditor's opinion.
  c. The entity issues financial statements that present financial position and results of operations but omits the statement of cash flows.
  d. The auditor has substantial doubt about the entity's ability to continue as a going concern, but the circumstances are fully disclosed in the financial statements.

[1,2]   18-15   An entity changed from the straight-line method to the declining balance method of depreciation for all newly acquired assets. This change has no material effect on the current year's financial statements but is reasonably certain to have a substantial effect in later years. If the change is disclosed in the notes to the financial statements, the auditor should issue a report with a(n)
  a. "Except for" qualified opinion.
  b. Explanatory paragraph.
  c. Unqualified opinion.
  d. Consistency modification.

[1,2]   18-16   An auditor includes a separate paragraph in an otherwise unmodified financial statement audit report to emphasize that the entity being reported upon had significant transactions with related parties. The inclusion of this separate paragraph
  a. Is appropriate and would *not* negate the unqualified opinion.
  b. Is considered an "except for" qualification of the opinion.
  c. Violates generally accepted auditing standards if this information is already disclosed in footnotes to the financial statements.
  d. Necessitates a revision of the opinion paragraph to include the phrase "with the foregoing explanation."

[3,4]   18-17   Eagle Company's financial statements contain a departure from generally accepted accounting principles because, due to unusual circumstances, the statements would otherwise be misleading. The auditor should express an opinion that is
  a. Unqualified but *not* mention the departure in the auditor's report.
  b. Unqualified and describe the departure in a separate paragraph.
  c. Qualified and describe the departure in a separate paragraph.
  d. Qualified or adverse, depending on materiality, and describe the departure in a separate paragraph.

[3,4]   18-18   Tech Company has disclosed an uncertainty due to pending litigation. The auditor's decision to issue a qualified opinion on Tech's financial statements would most likely be determined by the
  a. Lack of sufficient evidence.
  b. Inability to estimate the amount of loss.
  c. Entity's lack of experience with such litigation.
  d. Lack of insurance coverage for possible losses from such litigation.

[3,4]   18-19   In which of the following circumstances would an auditor usually choose between issuing a qualified opinion and issuing a disclaimer of opinion on a client's financial statements?
  a. Departure from generally accepted accounting principles.
  b. Inadequate disclosure of accounting policies.
  c. Inability to obtain sufficient competent evidence.
  d. Unreasonable justification for a change in accounting principle.

[3,4]   18-20   King, CPA, was engaged to audit the financial statements of Chang Company after its fiscal year had ended. King neither observed the inventory count nor confirmed the receivables by direct communication with debtors but was satisfied concerning both after applying alternative procedures. King's financial statement audit report most likely contained a(n)
  a. Qualified opinion.
  b. Disclaimer of opinion.

c. Unqualified opinion.

d. Unqualified opinion with an explanatory paragraph.

[6]   18-21   Comparative financial statements include the prior year's statements that were audited by a predecessor auditor whose report is not presented. If the predecessor's report was unqualified, the successor should

a. Express an opinion on the current year's statements alone and make no reference to the prior year's statements.

b. Indicate in the auditor's report that the predecessor auditor expressed an unqualified opinion.

c. Obtain a letter of representations from the predecessor concerning any matters that might affect the successor's opinion.

d. Request the predecessor auditor to reissue the prior year's report.

[6]   18-22   When reporting on comparative financial statements, which of the following circumstances should ordinarily cause the auditor to change the previously issued opinion on the prior year's financial statements?

a. The prior year's financial statements are restated following the purchase of another company in the current year.

b. A departure from generally accepted accounting principles caused an adverse opinion on the prior year's financial statements, and those statements have been properly restated.

c. A change in accounting principle causes the auditor to make a consistency modification in the current year's audit report.

d. A scope limitation caused a qualified opinion on the prior year's financial statements, but the current year's opinion is properly unqualified.

[7]   18-23   Which of the following best describes the auditor's responsibility for "other information" included in the annual report to stockholders that contains financial statements and the auditor's report?

a. The auditor has *no* obligation to read the "other information."

b. The auditor has *no* obligation to corroborate the "other information" but should read the "other information" to determine whether it is materially inconsistent with the financial statements.

c. The auditor should extend the examination to the extent necessary to verify the "other information."

d. The auditor must modify the auditor's report to state that the other information "is unaudited" or "is not covered by the auditor's report."

[8]   18-24   When reporting on financial statements prepared on the basis of accounting used for income tax purposes, the auditor should include in the report a paragraph that

a. Emphasizes that the financial statements are *not* intended to have been examined in accordance with generally accepted auditing standards.

b. Refers to the authoritative pronouncements that explain the income tax basis of accounting being used.

c. States that the income tax basis of accounting is a comprehensive basis of accounting other than generally accepted accounting principles.

d. Justifies the use of the income tax basis of accounting.

[9] 18-25 When an auditor is asked to express an opinion on the rental and royalty income of an entity, he or she may
  a. Not accept the engagement because to do so would be tantamount to agreeing to issue a piecemeal opinion.
  b. Not accept the engagement unless also engaged to audit the full financial statements of the entity.
  c. Accept the engagement provided the auditor's opinion is expressed in a special report.
  d. Accept the engagement provided distribution of the auditor's report is limited to the entity's management.

[14] 18-26 AnnaLisa, an auditor for N. M. Neal & Associates, is prevented by the management of Lileah Company from auditing controls over inventory. Lileah is a public company. Management explains that controls over inventory were recently implemented by a highly regarded public accounting firm that the company hired as a consultant and insists that it is a waste of time for AnnaLisa to evaluate these controls. Inventory is a material account, but procedures performed as part of the financial statement audit indicate the account is fairly stated. AnnaLisa found no material weaknesses in any other area of the client's internal control relating to financial reporting. What kind of report should AnnaLisa issue on the effectiveness of Lileah's internal control?
  a. An unqualified report.
  b. A qualified report.
  c. A disclaimer of opinion.
  d. An exculpatory opinion.

[14] 18-27 In auditing a public company audit client, Natalie, an auditor for N. M. Neal & Associates, identifies four deficiencies in internal control over financial reporting. Three of the deficiencies are highly unlikely to result in financial misstatements that are consequential in amount. One of the deficiencies is reasonably likely to result in misstatements that are more than consequential in amount. However, Natalie believes that this deficiency is highly unlikely to result in misstatements that would rise to the level of materiality. What type of audit report should Natalie issue?
  a. An unqualified report.
  b. A qualified report.
  c. A disclaimer of opinion.
  d. An exculpatory opinion.

[14] 18-28 In auditing internal control over financial reporting for a public company client, Emily finds that the company has a significant subsidiary located in a foreign country. Emily's accounting firm has no offices in that country, and the company has thus engaged another reputable firm to conduct the audit of internal control for that subsidiary. The other auditor's report indicates that there are no material weaknesses in the foreign subsidiary's internal control over financial reporting. What should Emily do?
  a. Disclaim an opinion because she cannot rely on the opinion of another auditor in dealing with a significant subsidiary.

b. Accept the other auditor's opinion and express an unqualified opinion, making no reference to the other auditor's report in her audit opinion.

c. Accept the other auditor's opinion after evaluating the auditor's work, and make reference to the other auditor's report in her audit opinion.

d. Qualify the opinion because she is unable to conduct the testing herself, and this constitutes a significant scope limitation.

PROBLEMS

[1,2,3,4,8]   18-29   For each of the following independent situations, indicate the reason for and the type of financial statement audit report that you would issue. Assume that each item is significant.

a. Barefield Corporation, a wholly owned subsidiary of Sandy, Inc., is audited by another CPA firm. As the auditor of Sandy, Inc., you have assured yourself of the other CPA firm's independence and professional reputation. However, you are unwilling to take complete responsibility for its audit work.

b. The management of Gough Corporation has decided to exclude the statement of cash flows from its financial statements because it believes that its bankers do not find the statement to be very useful.

c. You are auditing Diverse Carbon, a manufacturer of nerve gas for the military, for the year ended September 30, 2005. On September 1, 2005, one of its manufacturing plants caught fire, releasing nerve gas into the surrounding area. Two thousand people were killed and numerous others paralyzed. The company's legal counsel indicates that the company is liable, but the company does not want to disclose this information in the financial statements.

d. During your audit of Cuccia Coal Company, the controller, Tracy Tricks, refuses to allow you to confirm accounts receivable because she is concerned about complaints from her customers. You are unable to satisfy yourself about accounts receivable by other audit procedures.

e. On January 31, 2006, Takeda Toy Manufacturing hired your firm to audit the company's financial statements for the year 2005. You were unable to observe the client's inventory on December 31, 2005. However, you were able to satisfy yourself about the inventory balance using other auditing procedures.

f. Gelato Bros., Inc., leases its manufacturing facility from a partnership controlled by the chief executive officer and major shareholder of Gelato. Your review of the lease indicates that the rental terms are in excess of rental terms for similar buildings in the area. The company refuses to disclose this relationship in the footnotes.

g. Mitchell Manufacturing Company has used the double-declining balance method to depreciate its machinery. During the current year, management switched to the straight-line method because it felt that it better represented the utilization of the assets. You concur with its decision. All information is adequately disclosed in the financial statements.

[1,2,3,4,8]   18-30   For each of the following independent situations, indicate the reason for and the type of financial statement audit report that you would issue. Assume that each item is significant.

a.   International Mines, Inc., uses LIFO for valuing inventories held in the United States and FIFO for inventories produced and held in its foreign operations.

b.   HiTech Computers is suing your client, Super Software, for royalties over patent infringement. Super Software's outside legal counsel assures you that HiTech's case is without merit.

c.   In previous years, your client, Merc International, has consolidated its Panamanian subsidiary. Because of restrictions on repatriation of earnings placed on all foreign-owned corporations in Panama, Merc International has decided to account for the subsidiary on the equity basis in the current year.

d.   In prior years Worcester Wool Mills has used replacement cost to value its inventory of raw wool. During the current year Worcester changed to FIFO for valuing raw wool.

e.   Upon review of the recent history of the lives of its specialized automobiles, Gas Leak Technology changed the service lives for depreciation purposes on its autos from five years to three years. This change resulted in a material amount of additional depreciation expense.

f.   During the 2005 audit of Brannon Bakery Equipment, you found that a material amount of inventory had been excluded from the inventory amount shown in the 2004 financial statements. After discussing this problem with management, you become convinced that it was an unintentional oversight.

g.   Jay Johnson, CPA, holds 10 percent of the stock in Koenig Construction Company. The board of directors of Koenig asks Johnson to conduct its audit. Johnson completes the audit and determines that the financial statements present fairly in accordance with generally accepted accounting principles.

h.   Palatka Savings and Loan's financial condition has been deteriorating for the last five years. Most of its problems result from loans made to real estate developers in Saint Johns County. Your review of the loan portfolio indicates that there should be a major increase in the loan-loss reserve. Based on your calculations, the proposed write-down of the loans will put Palatka into violation of the state's capital requirements.

[2]   18-31   The CPA firm of May & Marty has audited the consolidated financial statements of BGI Corporation. May & Marty examined the parent company and all subsidiaries except for BGI-Western Corporation, which was audited by the CPA firm of Dey & Dee. BGI-Western constituted approximately 10 percent of the consolidated assets and 6 percent of the consolidated revenue.

Dey & Dee issued an unqualified opinion on the financial statements of BGI-Western. May & Marty will be issuing an unqualified opinion on the consolidated financial statements of BGI.

Required:

a. What procedures should May & Marty consider performing with respect to Dey & Dee's examination of BGI-Western's financial statements that will be appropriate whether or not reference is to be made to the other auditors?

b. Describe the various circumstances under which May & Marty could take responsibility for the work of Dey & Dee and make no reference to Dey & Dee's examination of BGI-Western in its own report on the consolidated financial statements of BGI.

(AICPA, adapted)

[2,3,4,6] 18-32 Devon, Inc., engaged Rao to examine its financial statements for the year ended December 31, 2005. The financial statements of Devon, Inc., for the year ended December 31, 2004, were examined by Jones, whose March 31, 2005, auditor's report expressed an unqualified opinion. The report of Jones is not presented with the 2005–2004 comparative financial statements.

Rao's working papers contain the following information that does not appear in footnotes to the 2005 financial statements as prepared by Devon, Inc.:

- One director appointed in 2005 was formerly a partner in Jones's accounting firm. Jones's firm provided financial consulting services to Devon during 2003 and 2002, for which Devon paid approximately $1,600 and $9,000, respectively.

- The company refused to capitalize certain lease obligations for equipment acquired in 2005. Capitalization of the leases in conformity with generally accepted accounting principles would have increased assets and liabilities by $312,000 and $387,000, respectively, decreased retained earnings as of December 31, 2005, by $75,000, and decreased net income and earnings per share by $75,000 and $.75, respectively, for the year then ended. Rao has concluded that the leases should have been capitalized.

- During the year, Devon changed its method of valuing inventory from the first-in, first-out method to the last-in, first-out method. This change was made because management believes LIFO more clearly reflects net income by providing a closer matching of current costs and current revenues. The change had the effect of reducing inventory at December 31, 2005, by $65,000 and net income and earnings per share by $38,000 and $.38, respectively, for the year then ended. The effect of the change on prior years was immaterial; accordingly, the change had no cumulative effect. Rao supports the company's position.

After completing the field work on February 28, 2006, Rao concludes that the expression of an adverse opinion is not warranted.

Required:

Prepare the body of Rao's report dated February 28, 2006, and addressed to the board of directors to accompany the 2005–2004 comparative financial statements. Rao is a public company.

(AICPA, adapted)

[8]   18-33   On March 12, 2006, Brown & Brown, CPAs, completed the audit of the financial statements of Modern Museum, Inc., for the year ended December 31, 2005. Modern Museum presents comparative financial statements on a modified cash basis. Assets, liabilities, fund balances, support, revenues, and expenses are recognized when cash is received or disbursed, except that Modern includes a provision for depreciation of buildings and equipment. Brown & Brown believes that Modern's three financial statements, prepared in accordance with a comprehensive basis of accounting other than generally accepted accounting principles, are adequate for Modern's needs and wishes to issue a special report on the financial statements. Brown & Brown has gathered sufficient competent evidence to be satisfied that the financial statements are fairly presented according to the modified cash basis. Brown & Brown audited Modern's 2004 financial statements and issued an auditor's special report expressing an unqualified opinion.

Required:
Draft the audit report to accompany Modern's comparative financial statements. Modern is a privately held company.

(AICPA, adapted)

[1,3,4,6]   18-34   For the year ended December 31, 2004, Friday & Co., CPAs ("Friday"), audited the financial statements of Kim Company and expressed an unqualified opinion on the balance sheet only. Friday did not observe the taking of the physical inventory as of December 31, 2003, because that date was prior to its appointment as auditor. Friday was unable to satisfy itself regarding inventory by means of other auditing procedures, so it did not express an opinion on the other basic financial statements that year.

For the year ended December 31, 2005, Friday expressed an unqualified opinion on all the basic financial statements and satisfied itself as to the consistent application of generally accepted accounting principles. The field work was completed on March 11, 2006; the partner-in-charge reviewed the working papers and signed the auditor's report on March 18, 2006. The report on the comparative financial statements for 2005 and 2004 was delivered to Kim on March 21, 2006.

Required:
Prepare Friday's audit report that was submitted to Kim's board of directors on the 2005 and 2004 comparative financial statements. Kim is a public company.

(AICPA, adapted)

[1,8]   18-35   The following auditors' report was drafted by a staff accountant of Nathan and Matthew, CPAs, at the completion of the audit of the comparative financial statements of Ocean Shore Partnership for the years ended December 31, 2005 and 2004. Ocean Shore is a privately held company that prepares its financial statements on the income tax basis of accounting. The report was submitted to the engagement partner, who reviewed matters thoroughly and properly concluded that an unqualified opinion should be expressed.

Auditors' Report

We have audited the accompanying statements of assets, liabilities, and capital—income tax basis of Ocean Shore Partnership as of December 31, 2005 and 2004, and the related statements of revenue and expenses—income tax basis and changes in partners' capital accounts—income tax basis for the years then ended.

We conducted our audits in accordance with standards established by the American Institute of Certified Public Accountants. Those standards require that we plan and perform the audit to obtain reasonable assurance about whether the financial statements are free of material misstatement. An audit includes examining, on a test basis, evidence supporting the amounts and disclosures in the financial statements. An audit also includes assessing the accounting principles used as well as evaluating the overall financial statement presentation.

As described in Note A, these financial statements were prepared on the basis of accounting the Partnership uses for income tax purposes. Accordingly, these financial statements are not designed for those who do not have access to the Partnership's tax returns.

In our opinion, the financial statements referred to above present fairly, in all material respects, the assets, liabilities, and capital of Ocean Shore Partnership as of December 31, 2005 and 2004, and its revenue and expenses and changes in partners' capital accounts for the years then ended, in conformity with generally accepted accounting principles applied on a consistent basis.

Nathan and Matthew, CPAs
April 3, 2006

Required:

Identify the errors and omissions in the auditors' report as drafted by the staff accountant. Group the errors and omissions by paragraph, where applicable. Do *not* redraft the report.

(AICPA, adapted)

DISCUSSION CASES

[2]   18-36   You are auditing the financial statements for your new client, Paper Packaging Corporation, a manufacturer of paper containers, for the year ended March 31, 2005. Paper Packaging's previous auditors had issued a going-concern opinion on the March 31, 2004, financial statements for the following reasons:

- Paper Packaging had defaulted on $10 million of unregistered debentures sold to three insurance companies, which were due in 2004, and the default constituted a possible violation of other debt agreements.

- The interest and principal payments due on the remainder of a 10-year credit agreement, which began in 2000, would exceed the cash flows generated from operations in recent years.

- The company had disposed of certain operating units. The proceeds from the sale were subject to possible adjustment through

arbitration proceedings, the outcome of which was uncertain at year-end.
- Various lawsuits were pending against the company.
- The company was in the midst of tax proceedings as a result of an examination of the company's federal income tax returns for a period of 12 years.

You find that the status of the above matters is as follows at year-end, March 31, 2005:
- The company is still in default on $4.6 million of the debentures due in 2004 but is trying to negotiate a settlement with remaining bondholders. A large number of bondholders have settled their claims at significantly less than par.
- The company has renegotiated the 2000 credit agreement, which provides for a two-year moratorium on principal payments and interest at 8 percent. It also limits net losses ($2.25 million for 2005) and requires a certain level of defined cumulative quarterly operating income to be maintained.
- The arbitration proceedings were resolved in 2005.
- The legal actions were settled in 2005.
- Most of the tax issues have been resolved, and, according to the company's legal counsel, those remaining will result in a net cash inflow to the company.

At year-end Paper Packaging had a cash balance of $5.5 million and expects to generate a net cash flow of $3.2 million in the upcoming fiscal year.

The following information about Paper Packaging's plans for its operations in fiscal year 2006 may also be useful in arriving at a decision.

	Fiscal Year 2006 Budget	Fiscal Year 2005 Actual	Fiscal Year 2005 Budget
Net revenues	$66.2	$60.9	$79.8
Gross margin	34.7	33.6	45.6
Operating expenses	27.9	34.7	31.4
Interest—net	5.1	6.0	5.7
Other income (expenses)—net	(.8)	2.1	—
Earnings before income taxes and extraordinary items	1.5	(5.1)	(.2)
Cash flows:			
Receipts	69.9	79.7	
Disbursements	66.7	96.9	
Excess/deficit	3.2	(22.8)	

Required:
a. What should you consider in deciding whether to discuss a going-concern uncertainty in your report?
b. How much influence should the report on the March 31, 2004, financial statements have on your decision?
c. Should your report for the year ended March 31, 2005, include a discussion of a going-concern uncertainty?

[13,14]   18-37   For each of the following independent situations relating to the audit of internal control, indicate the reason for and the type of audit report

you would issue regarding (1) management's assessment and (2) the effectiveness of the client's internal control over financial reporting.

a. During the audit of Wood Pharmaceuticals, you are surprised to find several control deficiencies in the company's internal control. You determine that there is more than a remote chance that any one of them could result in a misstatement that is more than inconsequential. Although the odds are extremely low that the deficiencies, singly or taken together, will result in a material misstatement of the company's financial statements, the large number of problems causes you concern. Management's written assessment concludes that the company's internal control was effective as of the report date.

b. You agreed to perform an audit for Rodriguez & Co., after the client's year-end. Due to time constraints, your audit firm could not complete a full audit of internal control. However, the evidence you did collect suggests that the company has exceptionally strong internal control over financial reporting. You seriously doubt that a material weakness would have been found if time had permitted a more thorough audit. Management's written assessment concludes that the company's internal control was effective as of the report date.

c. George & Diana Company's internal audit function identified a material weakness in the company's internal control over financial reporting. The client corrected this weakness about four months prior to the end of the annual reporting period. Management reassessed controls in the area and found them effective. After reevaluating and retesting the relevant controls, you believe the controls to have been effective for a sufficient period of time to provide adequate evidence that they were designed and operating effectively as of the end of the client's reporting period. However, the controls clearly were not effective for the first eight months of the reporting period. Management's written assessment concludes that the company's internal control was effective as of the report date.

d. You find no significant deficiencies or material weaknesses in the internal control over financial reporting of your audit client, Takamoto Building Co., but when considering the audit risk model, you still decide to set control risk at the maximum for purposes of the financial statement audit. Management's written assessment concludes that the company's internal control was effective as of the report date.

e. Reynolds' Distilleries identified what you agree is a material weakness and made an adverse assessment in its report on internal control. The company had not corrected the material weakness as of the end of the reporting period.

f. As part of the audit of internal control, you check with management for significant subsequent events. You identify an event that sheds light on a condition in existence prior to, and as of, the end of the reporting period. The condition is likely to significantly impact the effectiveness of the company's internal control over financial reporting. Unfortunately, you cannot determine the event's true impact on the client's system of internal control. Management's written assessment concludes that the company's internal control was effective as of the report date.

g. After auditing your client's internal controls, you conclude the system of internal control over financial reporting is well designed and operating effectively. Management's written assessment concludes that the company's internal control was effective as of the report date. However, you later conclude you cannot give the client a clean opinion on the financial statements due to a highly material misstatement you identified in performing substantive procedures.

h. Cindy & David Company's management identified a material weakness in the company's internal control over financial reporting during its assessment process. The client corrected this weakness about four months prior to the end of the annual reporting period. Management reassessed controls in the area, and believes they were effective as of the end of the reporting period. After reevaluating and retesting the relevant controls, you agree that the new controls are well designed, but since the controls over this particular area are applied only once at the end of each month (i.e., the controls have only operated three or four times since being corrected), you do not believe you have sufficient audit evidence to assess their operating effectiveness. Management's written assessment concludes that the company's internal control was effective as of the report date.

i. During the audit of internal control for Big Al & Larry Industries, you discover several control deficiencies. You determine that there is more than a remote chance that any one of them could result in a financial statement misstatement that is more than inconsequential. Although you do not believe that any of the deficiencies taken individually will result in a material misstatement, you believe there is a moderately low likelihood that, taken together, the deficiencies could produce a material misstatement. Management's written assessment concludes that the company's internal control was effective as of the report date.

[11,12,13,14] 18-38 The following audit report was drafted by a junior staff accountant of Meryll & Meryll, CPAs, at the completion of the audit of Douglas Company's internal control over financial reporting. Douglas is a public company and is thus subject to SEC reporting requirements. The report was submitted to the engagement partner, who reviewed matters thoroughly and properly concluded that there was a material weakness in the client's internal control over financial reporting. Douglas's management agreed and wrote an assessment indicating that the company's internal control was not effective as of the end of the reporting period. Sufficient, competent evidence was obtained during the financial statement audit to provide reasonable assurance that the overall financial statements present fairly in accordance with GAAP.

Required:
Identify the errors and omissions contained in the auditors' report as drafted by the staff accountant. Group the errors and omissions by paragraph, where applicable. Do *not* redraft the report.

Report of Independent Registered Public Accounting Firm

[*Introductory paragraph*]

We have audited management's assessment, included in the accompanying Management Report on the Financial Statements and Internal Control, that Douglas did not maintain effective internal control over financial reporting as of December 31, 2005, based on criteria established in *Enterprise Risk Management—Integrated Framework* issued by the Committee of Sponsoring Organizations of the Treadway Commission (COSO). Douglas's management is responsible for maintaining effective internal control over financial reporting and for its assessment of the effectiveness of internal control over financial reporting. Our responsibility is to express an opinion on management's assessment and an opinion on the effectiveness of the company's internal control over financial reporting based on our audit.

[*Scope paragraph*]

We conducted our audit in accordance with generally accepted auditing standards (United States). Those standards require that we plan and perform the audit to obtain assurance about whether effective internal control was maintained. Our audit included obtaining an understanding of internal control over financial reporting, evaluating management's assessment, testing and evaluating the operating effectiveness of internal control, and performing such other procedures as we considered necessary in the circumstances. We believe that our audit provides a reasonable basis for our opinion.

[*Definition paragraph*]

A company's internal control over financial reporting is a process designed to provide assurance regarding the reliability of financial reporting and the preparation of financial statements for external purposes in accordance with generally accepted auditing principles. A company's internal control over financial reporting includes those policies and procedures that (1) pertain to the maintenance of records that, in reasonable detail, accurately and fairly reflect the transactions and dispositions of the assets of the company; (2) provide assurance that transactions are recorded as necessary to permit preparation of financial statements in accordance with generally accepted auditing principles, and that receipts and expenditures of the company are being made only in accordance with authorizations of management and directors of the company; and (3) provide assurance regarding prevention or timely detection of unauthorized acquisition, use, or disposition of the company's assets that could have an inconsequential effect on the financial statements.

[*Inherent limitations paragraph*]

Because of its inherent limitations, internal control over financial reporting will prevent or detect misstatements. Also, projections of any evaluation of effectiveness to future periods are subject to the risk that controls may become inadequate because of changes in conditions, or that the degree of compliance with the policies or procedures may deteriorate.

[*Opinion paragraph*]

In our opinion, management's assessment that Douglas maintained ineffective internal control over financial reporting as of December 31, 2005, is fairly stated, in all material respects, based on criteria established in *Enterprise Risk Management—Integrated Framework* issued by the Committee of Sponsoring Organizations of the Treadway Commission (COSO). We therefore express an adverse opinion on management's assessment. Also in our opinion, Douglas maintained, in all material respects, effective internal control over financial reporting as of December 31, 2005, based on criteria established in *Enterprise Risk Management—Integrated Framework* issued by the Committee of Sponsoring Organizations of the Treadway Commission (COSO), except for one material weakness, which results in our issuing a qualified opinion on Douglas's internal control over financial reporting.

[*Explanatory paragraph*]

We have also audited, in accordance with generally accepted accounting standards (United States), the consolidated financial statements of Douglas, and our report dated February 15, 2006, expressed a qualified opinion.

Meryll & Meryll, CPAs
Mapleton, Arizona
March 11, 2006

PROFESSIONAL RESPONSIBILITIES

CHAPTER 19

LEARNING OBJECTIVES

Upon completion of this chapter you will

[1] Know the definitions and general importance of ethics and professionalism.

[2] Understand three basic theories of ethical behavior.

[3] Begin to understand how to deal with ethical dilemmas through an example situation.

[4] Understand the stages through which moral judgment develops in an individual.

[5] Be familiar with how professional ethics standards for auditors have developed over time and the entities involved.

[6] Understand the framework for the Code of Professional Conduct.

[7] Know the principles of professional conduct.

[8] Understand the framework for the Rules of Conduct.

[9] Be familiar with the rules of conduct that apply to independence, integrity, and objectivity.

[10] Know the basic differences between the SEC's independence rules for public company auditors and AICPA standards for audits of nonpublic entities.

[11] Be familiar with the rules of conduct that apply to general standards and accounting principles.

[12] Be familiar with the rules of conduct that apply to responsibilities to clients.

[13] Be familiar with the rules of conduct that apply to other responsibilities and practices.

[14] Understand the definition of a system of quality control and the AICPA's two-tiered quality peer review program.

[15] Know the elements of quality control and how a firm monitors its quality control system.

[16] Be familiar with the PCAOB inspection program for accounting firms that audit public companies

RELEVANT ACCOUNTING AND AUDITING PRONOUNCEMENTS

AICPA, Code of Professional Conduct (ET 50-500)
AU 161, The Relationship of Generally Accepted Auditing Standards to Quality Control Standards
ISB 1, Independence Discussion with Audit Committees
ISB 3, Employment with Audit Clients
QC 10, System of Quality Control for a CPA Firm's Accounting and Auditing Practice
QC 20, Monitoring a CPA Firm's Accounting and Auditing Practice

PCAOB AS No. 1, References in Auditors' Reports to the Standards of the Public Company Accounting Oversight Board
PR 100, Standards for Performing and Reporting on Quality Reviews
Securities and Exchange Commission Rule 2-01, Revision of the Commission's Auditor Independence Requirements

Professional Conduct, Independence, and Quality Control

PeopleSoft is a leading provider of software applications that assist companies in managing business activities. Ernst & Young LLP, a Big 4 public accounting firm, was PeopleSoft's auditor from 1994 to June 2000. Besides earning almost $1.7 million for auditing PeopleSoft's financial statements from 1994 to 1999, Ernst & Young allegedly entered into a variety of lucrative business arrangements with the company. On April 16, 2004, a federal court found, among other things, that Ernst & Young engaged in improper professional conduct, violated applicable professional ethics standards, and engaged in conduct that was both reckless and negligent. The court also found that a reasonable investor who knew of Ernst & Young's and PeopleSoft's mutual interests in the business success of their joint efforts "would make an objective and pragmatic assessment that Ernst & Young would not be objective in its audit of PeopleSoft."

The court reiterated the importance of auditor independence:

> Auditors have been characterized as "gatekeepers" to the public securities markets that are crucial for capital formation. The independent public accountant performing this special function owes ultimate allegiance to the corporation's creditors and stockholders, as well as to the investing public. This "public watchdog" function demands that the accountant maintain total independence from the client at all times and requires complete fidelity to the public trust.

The judge ordered Ernst & Young to (1) "disgorge" $1,686,500, the amount of its fees for auditing PeopleSoft for fiscal years 1994 through 1999, along with a significant amount of prejudgment interest on those fees, (2) retain an independent consultant to work with the firm to ensure that the firm's leadership implemented policies and procedures to remedy the professional ethics violations found and come into compliance with rules on auditor independence, and (3) refrain from accepting additional audit engagements for new public audit clients for a period of six months.[1] Of the three penalties, the sanction against accepting new clients was the most severe, as it had both significant reputation and revenue consequences.

In this chapter, we discuss the importance of ethical and professional conduct by auditors. We begin by defining ethics and professionalism and offering a general framework within which ethical issues can be evaluated. We then provide an overview of the nature of the principles, rules, and regulations governing public accountants' conduct, followed by a discussion of the specific rules and regulations accountants, and auditors

---

[1] For full details on the case and the source of the above quotes, see *Initial Decision Release No. 249, Administrative Proceeding, File No. 3-10933, United States of America before the Securities and Exchange Commission in the Matter of Ernst & Young LLP* (www.sec.gov/litigation/aljdec/id249bpm.htm).

in particular, must follow. Independence, arguably the most complicated and controversial aspect of auditor professionalism, is prominently highlighted in this discussion. Finally, we discuss how public accounting firms are monitored and inspected to help ensure quality audits and compliance with professional standards, regulations, and codes of conduct. 🌐

Ethics and Professional Conduct

Ethics and Professionalism Defined

❅ **[LO 1]**

Ethical conduct is the bedrock of modern civilization—it underpins the successful functioning of nearly every aspect of society, from daily family life to law, medicine, and business. *Ethics* refers to a system or code of conduct based on moral duties and obligations that indicate how an individual should behave in society. A sense for ethics guides individuals to value more than their own self-interest and to recognize and respect the interests of others as well. Our society would simply fall into chaos if people were devoid of ethics and moral sentiments. Imagine what it would be like if everyone ignored rules of the road, moral standards, obligations, and the rights and interests of others! Life in such a society would be, as the philosopher Hobbes might say, "solitary, poor, nasty, brutish, and short."

Ethical conduct is also the bedrock of modern professionalism. *Professionalism,* broadly defined, refers to the conduct, aims, or qualities that characterize or mark a profession or professional person.[2] All professions establish rules or codes of conduct that define ethical (professional) behavior for members of the profession. These rules are established so that (1) users of the professional services know what to expect when they purchase such services, (2) members of the profession know what behavior is acceptable, and (3) the profession can use the rules to monitor the actions of its members and apply discipline where appropriate. Consider the medical profession. When you see a doctor for a potentially serious medical condition, you as a user of this professional service have a valid and vital interest in expecting competent and honest behavior that is free from conflicts of interest. You expect, for example, that the doctor will prescribe the best medication for your condition, rather than one for which the doctor earns a commission. To better meet these expectations, the medical profession requires particular training and certifications, and has a code of professional conduct, the earliest form of which arguably is the Hippocratic oath, written in about 400 B.C.

Recall that in Chapter 1 we discussed the desired characteristics of a house inspector and concluded that competence, objectivity, and integrity are critical. We also discussed the role that auditors, as information inspectors, play in reducing information risk through *independent* verification of management assertions. To be a credible source of objective, independent assurance, the professional must have a solid reputation not only for competence but also for unquestioned character and integrity. The concepts of ethical behavior and professional conduct are clearly

---

[2]S. M. Mintz, *Cases in Accounting Ethics and Professionalism,* 3d ed. (New York: Irwin/McGraw-Hill, 1997), p. 4.

central to the success of the accounting profession. In fact, those who enter the accounting profession and engage in unethical conduct will inevitably harm themselves, others, and the profession. The most important concept you will read in this chapter is that of personal responsibility and integrity. As an accountant, auditor, manager, or businessperson you will face numerous difficult ethical issues, and you will experience pressures and temptations. Never forget that your most valuable assets as a professional are integrity and a good reputation. We encourage you to continually evaluate your choices and behavior and commit to a high level of integrity and ethical behavior as a student, professional, and member of society.

Given the importance of reputation, ethical behavior, and professionalism, the accounting profession has developed a *Code of Professional Conduct* that guides the behavior of accounting professionals. The profession's Code of Professional Conduct, together with related rules and regulations, is discussed later in this chapter, after we discuss a framework for considering ethical issues.

Theories of Ethical Behavior

❧ [LO 2]

When individuals are confronted with situations that have moral and ethical implications, they do not always agree on the issues at hand, which individuals or groups will be affected and how, or what solutions or courses of actions are available or appropriate for dealing with the situation. Such differences may be caused by differences in the individuals' concepts of fairness and different opinions about the right action to take in a particular situation. Some ethical choices are difficult simply due to the temptation or pressure to pursue one's self-interest, which can cloud judgment regarding what is right or wrong. Other choices are complicated by the sheer difficulty of sorting out the issues and deciphering what might be appropriate or inappropriate actions to take.

S. M. Mintz has suggested that there are three methods or theories of ethical behavior that can guide the analysis of ethical issues in accounting.[3] These theories are (1) *utilitarianism*, (2) a *rights-based approach*, and (3) a *justice-based approach*. No one approach is necessarily better than another. In fact, elements of each theory may be appropriate for resolving ethical dilemmas.

Utilitarian theory recognizes that decision making involves trade-offs between the benefits and burdens of alternative actions, and it focuses on the consequences of an action on the individuals affected. The theory proposes that the interests of all parties affected, not just one's self-interest, should be considered. From this perspective, an action conforms to the principle of utility only if that action will produce more pleasure or happiness (or prevent more pain or unhappiness) than any other possible action. The value of an action is determined solely by the consequences of the action on the welfare of individuals. This is why utilitarianism is sometimes also described as a "consequentialist" theory. One form of

---

[3]See S. M. Mintz, *Cases in Accounting Ethics and Professionalism*, 1997, for a more detailed discussion of each of these models.

utilitarianism holds that rules have a central position in moral judgment due to the adverse consequences that would likely arise if everyone chose to break them. This approach has significance for auditors, who are expected to follow the Code of Professional Conduct in carrying out their responsibilities. One disadvantage in applying the utilitarian theory to ethical dilemmas is that it is often difficult to measure the potential costs and benefits of the actions to be taken. It may also be difficult to balance the interests of all parties involved when those interests conflict with one another.

The theory of rights assumes that individuals have certain rights and other individuals have a duty to respect those rights. Thus, a decision maker who follows a theory of rights should undertake an action only if it does not violate the rights of *any* individual. An obvious disadvantage of the theory of rights is that it may be difficult or impossible to satisfy all rights of all affected parties, especially when those rights conflict. The theory of rights is important to auditors because of their public-interest responsibility. As the judge's ruling in this chapter's preface indicated, in conflicting situations, the rights of some individuals may not be satisfied in order that the primacy of the public-interest obligation of auditors be maintained. According to the concept known as the "moral point of view," auditors must be willing, at least sometimes, to put the interests of other stakeholders, such as investors and creditors, ahead of their own self-interests and those of the CPA firm. Thus, if a difference of opinion with top management exists over an accounting or reporting issue, the auditor should emphasize the interests of the investors and creditors in deciding what action to take, even if it means losing the client.

The theory of justice is concerned with issues such as equity, fairness, and impartiality. The theory of justice involves two basic principles.[4] The first principle posits that each person has a right to have the maximum degree of personal freedom that is still compatible with the liberty of others. The second principle asserts that social and economic actions should be to everyone's advantage and available to all. For example, someone in a position to accumulate wealth has a moral obligation to make sure that others are not treated unfairly as a result of his or her gains. Mintz indicates that decisions made within this theory should fairly and equitably distribute resources among those individuals or groups affected. There may be difficulty in trying to apply this theory in practice because the rights of one or more individuals or groups may be affected when a better distribution of benefits is provided to others. While none of these theories by itself can provide a perfect ethical framework, each can be useful in helping an auditor to solve dilemmas by providing an ethical perspective.

Example—An
Ethical Dilemma

Consider how an auditor might reason through the following simplified situation.

---

[4] *Theory of Justice* (The Belknap Press of Harvard University Press, 1971).

Sun City Savings and Loan Company

Pina, Johnson & Associates has recently been awarded the audit of Sun City Savings and Loan Company for the year ended December 31, 2005. Sun City Savings and Loan is now the largest client of the firm, and the fees from this engagement represent a significant portion of the firm's revenues. Upon accepting the Sun City engagement, the firm incurred additional costs by hiring several new employees and a new manager from a larger firm. In bidding on the engagement, Sam Johnson knew that the first-year fees would be just enough to cover the actual cost of the first year's audit, but he hoped that future audit fee increases and fees for other services might lead to a long-term, profitable engagement. Based on his discussions with the predecessor auditors, Johnson knew that there were possible problems with Sun City's loans because of the collateral used for security. Johnson was also concerned that there might be problems with loan-loss reserves due to the effects of the economic slowdown on the tourist industry in Sun City over the last two years. However, Johnson felt that these problems were manageable.

During the current year, the amount included in the loan-loss reserves account was $675,000, approximately the same as the figure for the prior year. The state's banking regulations require that an amount equal to 1.5 percent of the loans outstanding be included as a reserve against losses. The $675,000 was slightly above the statutory requirement. However, the audit staff identified two large loans, aggregating to $15 million, that appeared not to be collectible in full. The working papers disclosed that each loan had originated during the current year and that both had been in default for four months. Additionally, the collateral used to secure the loans was worth considerably less than the amount of the loans and was not in accordance with Sun City's loan policy procedures. Based on this information, the staff estimates that about 40 percent of the $15 million, or $6 million, will not be collected. The staff has also determined that these loans are to entities owned by Patricia Cabot, Sun City's CEO, and some of her business associates.

When Johnson met with Cabot to discuss the two delinquent loans, Cabot assured Johnson that the loans would be paid in full. She told Johnson that the loans had been properly made and that as soon as the economy picked up, payments would be made on the loans. She indicated that no additional reserves were needed and that if Johnson requires such adjustments, his firm might be replaced.

Johnson is concerned that if the loan-loss reserves are increased, Sun City's stock price may fall and hurt owners and investors. Further, if Johnson requires the adjustment, Pina, Johnson & Associates may lose Sun City as a client, his career goals will be damaged, and the firm may have to lay off professional and staff employees. Johnson believes there could be serious consequences to several different parties whatever decision he makes.

✖ **[LO 3]**   What ethical and professional concerns should Johnson consider in deciding on a course of action?

If Johnson follows a utilitarian approach, he will consider the consequences (benefits and costs) of his actions on all affected parties and whether any rules exist that might require a particular action. The benefits of requiring the increase in the reserve may be full and accurate disclosure of the facts as assessed by the audit team. Another benefit may arise from the time-honored convention of conservatism. Costs need to be assessed in terms of Sun City's stockholders, Cabot's reputation, and the situation of the public accounting firm. For example, Johnson might consider that if he requires an additional reserve amount for the loans, the price of Sun City's stock might decline and the stockholders would suffer losses. By forcing Sun City to increase the reserves, he might also damage Cabot's reputation if the loans are eventually paid. On the other hand, if Cabot is inappropriately using Sun

City's funds for personal gain, the stockholders are being harmed by her actions. Finally, Johnson might consider how the loss of Sun City as a client would affect his firm. If the client is lost, the newly hired personnel may need to be terminated. While Johnson knows that the reserve is in accordance with the state's statutory rule on loan losses, from a rules perspective he also knows that generally accepted accounting principles require that the loans be presented in the financial statements at net realizable value. Given the facts in this case and using a utilitarian approach, Johnson's conclusion as to whether the loan-loss reserves should be adjusted by the $6 million will be determined by the consequences of his actions on various interested parties. From a utilitarian perspective, Johnson should consider the aggregate interests of all parties involved, not just his self-interest. According to utilitarianism, Johnson should resolve the issue in a way that maximizes the benefits, or "utility" of the group, even if the resolution goes contrary to Johnson's self-interest.

The theory of rights requires that Johnson consider whose rights would be violated if he does not require an increase in the loan-loss reserves because, based on the evidence, generally accepted accounting principles would require an adjustment. The stockholders' right to fair and accurate information for decision-making purposes is being violated. If Cabot has entered into inappropriate loans at the expense of the stockholders, they will not have received accurate information about Sun City's profitability, liquidity, and so on. If Johnson does not require the adjustment and the loans eventually become uncollectible, the stockholders' rights will be violated and Johnson may be in violation of GAAS and other professional and even legal standards. Cabot, on the other hand, has no right to misappropriate funds or to report account balances incorrectly. Thus, under a rights approach, Johnson is likely to conclude that he has a duty to require the adjustment to the financial statements.

The theory of justice asserts that to be just, arrangements cannot be allowed to yield advantages for some at the expense of others. It focuses on the protection of those who may otherwise be at a disadvantage. This approach to ethical reasoning requires that Johnson consider the interests of the stockholders, Cabot, the depositors in the S&L, and the government, which is insuring the deposits. Johnson should avoid favoring the interests of any individual or group and should not select an action that will confer unfair advantages on some (e.g., the management of the S&L) at the expense of others (e.g., the public). The theory of justice also requires Johnson to carefully consider the interests of all parties involved. Integrity and objectivity require that Johnson not place his self-interest or that of the client ahead of the public interest. Given these ethical perspectives, and especially in view of the unique duty auditors have to the public, he must focus on Sun City's shareholders as members of the investing public. If he does not allow his self-interest to cloud his judgment, Johnson will require the client to book the $6 million adjustment for the delinquent loans, regardless of the consequences to himself or to his firm.

In this case, Johnson's professionalism is likely to be tested. While he realizes that the loan-loss reserves probably should be increased, he is also likely to be concerned about the possibility of losing this valuable client and the significant investment in new personnel that the firm has made. While it seems fairly clear what action should be taken (requiring the client to

TABLE 19–1	The Six Stages of Ethical Development

Level 1: Preconventional

At the preconventional level, the individual is concerned with self. Rules are imposed externally on the individual.

Stage I: The individual's actions are judged in terms of their physical consequences, such as avoidance of punishment.

Stage II: The individual is aware of others' needs, but satisfaction of the individual's own needs is the basic motivation for action.

Level 2: Conventional

At the conventional level, the individual is able to see situations from others' (such as family, peer group, or nation) points of view.

Stage III: The individual attempts to conform to group norms. The other's view of the situation is considered, and conflicts are resolved through the use of these norms.

Stage IV: The individual is concerned about order in society and its rules. The individual uses the laws and rules for guidance in conflict situations.

Level 3: Postconventional

At the postconventional level, society's laws and rules are questioned and redefined in terms of universal moral principles.

Stage V: The individual views social contracts and mutual obligations as important. Differences in conflict situations are resolved impartially and with consideration of everyone's interests.

Stage VI: The individual bases actions on universal moral and ethical principles (such as justice, equality, and dignity) that apply to all individuals and groups.

Source: Adapted from S. M. Mintz, *Cases in Accounting Ethics and Professionalism*, 3d ed. (New York: Irwin/McGraw-Hill, 1997), pp. 28–29.

adjust the reserve), the question becomes—as it so often does—does the auditor (Johnson) have the moral fortitude to do what is right?

Auditors frequently face such ethical dilemmas in their practice. It is important that auditors develop sound moral character so that they can respond appropriately in such situations. Mintz points out that auditors who possess certain "virtues" or traits of character are more capable of adhering to a moral point of view.[5] Examples of such virtues include honesty, integrity, impartiality, faithfulness, and trustworthiness. These are similar to the Principles of Professional Conduct discussed later in the chapter. The next section presents a model of moral development that can be used to demonstrate how Johnson's moral judgment should have developed to the point where he would require the S&L to provide additional reserves for the loans.

Development of Moral Judgment

[LO 4]

Substantial research[6] indicates that moral judgment develops over time and is a function of age, education, and complexity of experience. Lawrence Kohlberg[7] has proposed that moral development has six stages that can be divided into three levels of moral reasoning. Table 19–1 shows the six stages of Kohlberg's model. A *stage* refers to a mode or pattern of behaviors that characterizes some definable point in an individual's life. At the preconventional level, an individual is concerned with his or her own self-interest. Rules are imposed by others, and the individual is judged in terms of how well he or she

[5] S. M. Mintz, "Virtue, Ethics, and Accounting Education," *Issues in Accounting Education* (Fall 1995), pp. 24–31.

[6] See J. R. Rest, *Moral Development: Advances in Research and Theory* (New York: Praeger, 1986), for a detailed summary of this research.

[7] See L. Kohlberg, "Moral Stages and Moralization: The Cognitive Developmental Approach," in T. Lickona (ed.), *Moral Development and Behavior: Theory, Research, and Social Issues* (New York: Holt, Rinehart and Winston, 1976), for a complete discussion of the stages discussed here. Also see J. R. Rest, *Development in Judging Moral Issues* (Minneapolis: University of Minnesota Press 1979), for a revised view of the stages in moral development.

obeys. Young children are typically in this stage of moral development. At the conventional level, the individual is aware of others and the need to conform to group norms; he or she is concerned with order in society and relies on laws and rules for guidance. At the postconventional level, the individual recognizes society's laws and rules but resolves conflict situations impartially, using universal moral and ethical principles such as those discussed previously.

Referring back to the Sun City Savings and Loan case, if Johnson were at stage II in his moral development, he would go along with Cabot and would not increase the loan-loss reserves by $6 million. He would be concerned about losing the client and future revenues and therefore would most likely act in his own self-interest. Current research indicates that CPAs typically reason at stages III and IV.[8] At stage III, Johnson would be influenced by group norms, so his reasoning would likely be affected by the views of the members of his firm. At stage IV, the auditor's actions would be guided by strict adherence to the profession's technical standards and rules of conduct. If Johnson were at this stage, his reasoning would lead him to follow professional standards and increase the loan-loss reserve.

An Overview of Ethics and Professionalism in Public Accounting

A Tale of Two Companies

✣ [LO 5]

The first Kmart store opened in Garden City, Michigan, in March 1962. Kmart Corp. filed for Chapter 11 bankruptcy protection in January 2002, representing the largest retail bankruptcy ever in the United States. In May 2002, Kmart announced that it was restating its earnings for the first three quarters of the preceding fiscal year to reflect an additional $554 million in losses for a total 2001 loss of $2.4 billion. In January 2003, Kmart fired the last of 25 executives who pocketed a total of $28 million in loans that were forgiven before the company filed for bankruptcy. A month later, two former Kmart vice presidents, Enio Montini, Jr., and Joseph Hofmeister, were indicted for alleged crimes involving Kmart. On May 6, 2003, Kmart emerged from bankruptcy and currently operates out of more than 1,500 retail stores.

Arthur Andersen, originally founded in 1913 as Andersen, Delaney & Co., grew to become one of the five largest and most respected accounting firms in the world by the late 1990s, with about 85,000 employees. In fall 2001, it became clear that issues were arising in connection with the firm's audits of Enron Corp., and Andersen's Houston office undertook a massive shredding operation to destroy Enron-related documents in October and November 2001. The U.S. Justice Department indicted the firm in March 2002 on obstruction of justice charges relating to the shredding. Despite the fact that the Enron scandal was primarily centered in Texas, Andersen began to unravel quickly, losing over 400 of its publicly traded clients from all over the country by June 2002. The firm was convicted on a single count of obstruction of justice in June 2002, and the firm ceased to audit publicly held companies on August 31, 2002. Despite its strong financial condition

---

[8]See, for example, L. A. Ponemon, "Ethical Reasoning and Selection Socialization in Accounting," *Accounting, Organizations and Society* 17 (1992), pp. 239–58; and M. K. Shaub, "An Analysis of the Association of Traditional Demographic Variables with the Moral Reasoning of Auditing Students and Auditors," *Journal of Accounting Education* (Winter 1994), pp. 1–26.

as late as early 2002, the firm no longer provides accounting or auditing services and is essentially defunct.

Why was Kmart ultimately able to survive financial difficulties, questionable accounting practices, and federal indictments, while Arthur Andersen was not able to survive even though it was financially strong? The answer is that Kmart had physical assets and traded in physical goods, while Andersen's primary asset was its reputation for competence, professionalism, and integrity. That reputation was damaged prior to the Enron scandal by a string of questionable practices and audit failures (involving Sunbeam, Waste Management, the Baptist Foundation of Arizona, and others) and was finished off by the Enron scandal and indictment. The sudden death of one of the largest and formerly most respected public accounting firms was a serious wake-up call for the profession, and underscored the vital importance of ethical conduct and professionalism on the part of auditors.

Standards for Auditor Professionalism

This section provides an overview of the principles, rules, and regulations governing ethics and professionalism in public accounting. The topic is complicated by the fact that these rules and regulations were established over time by different professional and regulatory bodies and in some cases by legislation. Early in the history of the public accounting profession in the United States, nongovernmental associations took charge of setting standards and establishing codes of conduct for practicing accountants. In particular, the AICPA (and its predecessor, the American Association of Public Accountants) established auditing standards and a Code of Professional Conduct, mapping out the primary areas in which ethical conduct is expected of public accountants. The AICPA, being a private, nongovernmental association, only has the authority to require its *members* to comply with the code. However, state and federal courts have consistently held that all practicing CPAs, whether in public or private practice and whether or not a member of the AICPA, must follow professional ethical standards as laid out in the Code of Professional Conduct.

The SEC has legal authority to oversee the public accounting profession. Through much of its history, the SEC has allowed such private-sector entities as the Financial Accounting Standards Board and the Auditing Standards Board (or ASB, a standing committee within the AICPA) to set accounting and auditing standards, respectively. However, the SEC has not hesitated to exercise its considerable influence in the standard-setting process and has established standards of its own from time to time, some of which differ from those established by private-sector bodies.

The PCAOB adopted the professional standards established by the AICPA on an interim basis in 2003, including the Code of Professional Conduct. However, the PCAOB and the SEC have additional, more stringent *standards of professional conduct,* mostly in the key area of auditor independence, which must be followed by auditors of public companies. Because the Code of Professional Conduct provides the broadest map of the areas in which professionalism is expected from auditors, the code serves as the organizing framework for the following discussion. The chapter highlights the important ways in which SEC and PCAOB rules governing the conduct and independence of public-company auditors differ from AICPA rules and standards.

FIGURE 19–1   **Relevant Professional Standards for Audits of Private versus Public Companies**

Auditing Standards
ASB (AICPA)—GAAS

Standards of Professional Conduct
AICPA—Code of Professional Conduct
ISB—apply unless AICPA expressly disagrees

Auditing Standards
PCAOB—currently similar to ASB standards, with notable exceptions

Standards of Professional Conduct
PCAOB—Code of Professional Conduct (adopted from AICPA)
SEC—more stringent independence rules for public company audits
ISB—a cooperative effort between the AICPA and SEC; now defunct but standards apply

Private company audit

Public company audit

CPA (auditor)

Figure 19–1 summarizes the auditor's responsibilities with respect to auditing standards and standards of professional conduct for the audits of private and public companies. As the figure illustrates, in auditing a *privately held* entity a CPA must follow the auditing standards established by the AICPA's Auditing Standards Board and the independence and other standards of professional conduct established by the Code of Professional Conduct. In addition, the three standards and the three interpretations issued by the Independence Standards Board (ISB) during its short existence from 1997 to 2001 must generally be followed.[9]

In auditing a *publicly held* company, a CPA must follow the auditing standards of the PCAOB, currently very similar to those of the AICPA. A CPA

---

[9]The committee within the AICPA that is charged with setting, deleting, or modifying rules and interpretations and delivering ethics rulings in response to specific questions is known as the Professional Ethics Executive Committee (PEEC).

auditing a public company must follow the Code of Professional Conduct and also the more stringent independence requirements established by the SEC, ISB, and PCAOB.

The AICPA Code of Professional Conduct: A Comprehensive Framework for Auditors

[LO 6] The AICPA Code of Professional Conduct defines both ideal principles and minimum acceptable behavior for auditors. The code deals mainly with behavior and actions of *individual* auditors, though firms are also responsible for the conduct of their employees and partners. The AICPA bylaws provide a means by which the Institute can discipline individual members and member firms that do not comply with professional standards.

The AICPA Code of Professional Conduct consists of two sections:

- Principles of Professional Conduct (setting forth ideal attitudes and behaviors).
- Rules of Conduct (defining minimum standards).

The Principles of Professional Conduct provide the framework for the Rules of Conduct. Additional guidance for applying the Rules of Conduct is provided by

- Interpretations of Rules of Conduct.
- Rulings by the Professional Ethics Executive Committee.

The Interpretations of Rules of Conduct and Rulings are promulgated by the Professional Ethics Executive Committee to provide guidelines as to the scope and application of the Rules of Conduct. The interpretations and ethics rulings are enforceable, and an auditor who departs from such standards has the burden of justifying such departures.

The guidance provided by the Code of Professional Conduct starts at a conceptual level with the principles and progressively moves to general rules and detailed interpretations and then to specific rulings on individual cases. Figure 19–2 provides a pictorial representation of the four parts of the Code of Professional Conduct.

Principles of Professional Conduct

[LO 7] Six ethical principles provide a framework for the Code of Professional Conduct. The preamble to the Principles of Professional Conduct states the following:

> They [the principles] guide members in the performance of their professional responsibilities and express the basic tenets of ethical and professional conduct. The principles call for an unswerving commitment to honorable behavior, even at the sacrifice of personal advantage. (ET 51.02)

Table 19–2 presents the definition of each of the six principles. Note that the principles are stated at a conceptual level. Because they are conceptual ideals, these principles of ethical behavior are not specifically enforceable.

The first two principles address a CPA's responsibilities to exercise professional and moral judgment in a manner that serves the public interest.

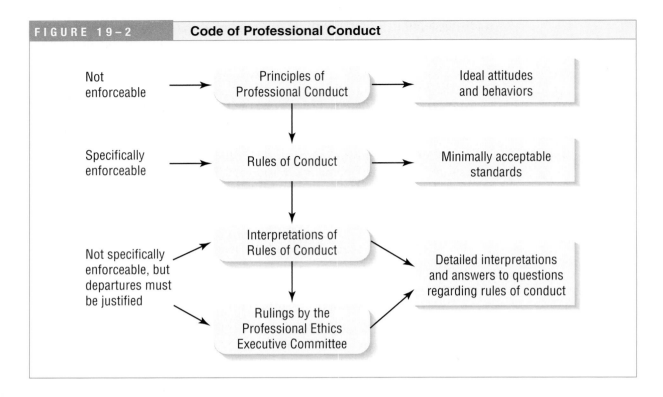

FIGURE 19–2   **Code of Professional Conduct**

These principles reinforce the conviction that the CPA's role in society is to serve the public.

As indicated by the third and fourth principles, the public relies on CPAs' integrity, objectivity, and independence in providing high-quality services. Integrity requires that a CPA be honest and candid, and honor both the form and the spirit of ethical standards. Thus, a CPA should make judgments that are consistent with the theories of rights and justice. When faced with an ethical dilemma, the CPA should ask, "What actions would an

TABLE 19–2   **Principles of Professional Conduct**

Responsibilities: In carrying out their responsibilities as professionals, members should exercise sensitive professional and moral judgments in all their activities.

The public interest: Members should accept the obligation to act in a way that will serve the public interest, honor the public trust, and demonstrate commitment to professionalism.

Integrity: To maintain and broaden public confidence, members should perform all professional responsibilities with the highest sense of integrity.

Objectivity and independence: A member should maintain objectivity and be free of conflicts of interest in discharging professional responsibilities. A member in public practice should be independent in fact and appearance when providing auditing and other attestation services.

Due care: A member should observe the profession's technical and ethical standards, strive continually to improve competence and the quality of services, and discharge professional responsibility to the best of the member's ability.

Scope and nature of services: A member in public practice should observe the Principles of the Code of Professional Conduct in determining the scope and nature of services to be provided.

individual with integrity take, given these facts and circumstances?" Objectivity and independence are hallmarks of the public accounting profession. The principle of objectivity requires the CPA to be impartial and free of conflicts of interest. Independence requires that the CPA avoid relationships that would impair his or her objectivity. When a CPA provides auditing- or attestation-related services, independence in both fact and appearance must be maintained.

The fifth principle, due care, requires that the CPA perform his or her professional responsibilities with competence and diligence. While the performance of professional services must take into account the interests of the client, the public's interest is more important when the two interests conflict. The last principle requires that the CPA determine that the services to be rendered are consistent with acceptable professional behavior for CPAs. This principle also requires that the CPA's firm have internal quality control procedures to ensure that services are delivered competently and that no conflict of interest exists.

Rules of Conduct
✖ [LO 8]

The Bylaws of the AICPA require that members adhere to the Rules of Conduct of the Code of Professional Conduct and that members be prepared to justify any departure from the rules. Table 19–3 provides an overview of the existing Rules of Conduct. As you can see in Table 19–3, the Rules of Conduct cover much of the same ground as the Principles of Professional Conduct, but are somewhat more specific. The rules are grouped and numbered in five categories:

- Independence, Integrity, and Objectivity (Section 100).
- General Standards and Accounting Principles (Section 200).
- Responsibilities to Clients (Section 300).
- Responsibilities to Colleagues (Section 400—no rules currently exist).
- Other Responsibilities and Practices (Section 500).

The rules contained in Section 100 of the Rules of Conduct cover issues relating to independence, integrity, and objectivity, including guidance relating to avoiding conflicts of interest and subordination of professional judgment. Section 200 deals with the accountant's responsibility to follow such general standards as competence and due professional care, to follow all applicable professional standards, and to adhere to generally accepted accounting principles when evaluating a client's financial statements. Section 300 covers the accountant's responsibilities to clients, covering such issues as confidentiality and contingent fees. Section 500 pertains to miscellaneous other responsibilities and practices, such as advertising, commissions, and referral fees. Section 400 is labeled "Responsibilities to Colleagues," but currently does not contain any rules because all of the 400-series rules were repealed in the 1970s under pressure from the U.S. Justice Department and the Federal Trade Commission, which contended that the rules were anticompetitive. Prior to their repeal, these rules prohibited advertising, encroaching upon other CPAs' clients, and offering employment to other CPAs' employees.

TABLE 19–3		Overview of AICPA Rules of Conduct
Rule No.	Rule Title	Text of the Rule*
101	Independence	A member in public practice shall be independent in the performance of professional services as required by standards promulgated by bodies designated by Council.
102	Integrity and objectivity	In the performance of any professional service, a member shall maintain objectivity and integrity, shall be free of conflicts of interest, and shall not knowingly misrepresent facts or subordinate his or her judgment to others.
201	General standards	A member shall comply with the following standards and with any interpretations thereof by bodies designated by Council. A. Professional competence. B. Due professional care. C. Planning and supervision. D. Sufficient relevant data.
202	Compliance with standards	A member who performs auditing, review, compilation, management consulting, tax, or other professional services shall comply with standards promulgated by bodies designated by Council.
203	Accounting principles	A member shall not (1) express an opinion . . . that the financial statements or other financial data of any entity are presented in conformity with generally accepted accounting principles or (2) state that he or she is not aware of any material modifications that should be made . . . in order for them to be in conformity with generally accepted accounting principles, if such statements or data contain any departure from an accounting principle . . . that has a material effect.
301	Confidential client information	A member in public practice shall not disclose any confidential client information without the specific consent of the client. . . . Members . . . shall not use to their own advantage or disclose any member's confidential client information that comes to their attention. . . .
302	Contingent fees	A member in public practice shall not (1) perform for a contingent fee any professional services for . . . a client for whom the member or the member's firm performs, an audit or review of a financial statement . . . or (2) prepare an original or amended tax return or claim for a tax refund for a contingent fee for any client.
501	Acts discreditable	A member shall not commit an act discreditable to the profession.
502	Advertising and other forms of solicitation	A member in public practice shall not seek to obtain clients by advertising or other forms of solicitation in a manner that is false, misleading, or deceptive. Solicitation by the use of coercion, overreaching, or harassing conduct is prohibited.
503	Commissions and referral fees	A member in public practice shall not for a commission recommend or refer to a client any product or service, or for a commission recommend or refer any product or service to be supplied by a client, or receive a commission, when the member or the member's firm also performs for that client an audit or review of a financial statement. . . . Any member who accepts a referral fee for recommending or referring any service of a CPA to any person or entity or who pays a referral fee to obtain a client shall disclose such acceptance or payment to the client.
505	Form of organization and name	A member may practice public accounting only in a form of organization permitted by law or regulation whose characteristics conform to resolutions of Council. A member shall not practice public accounting under a firm name that is misleading. Names of one or more past owners may be included in the firm name of a successor organization. A firm may not designate itself as "Members of the American Institute of Certified Public Accountants" unless all of its CPA owners are members of the Institute.

*Some of the longer rules have been excerpted or abridged. Refer to the full set of rules and interpretations at www.aicpa.org.

To offer some perspective, while the longer rules have been excerpted or abridged, much of the original text of the rules is included in Table 19–3. The "nitty-gritty" details in implementing the rules are found in the *Interpretations* of each rule. Table 19–4 lists the interpretations in effect for each Rule of Conduct in the code. For example, while Rule 101 relating to independence is comprised of only one brief sentence, the 13 interpretations of Rule 101 comprise over 25 pages of detail relating to financial or managerial interests that are, or are not, considered to compromise independence.

TABLE 19–4		Rules of Conduct and Related Interpretations
	Rules of Conduct	*Interpretations*
101	Independence	• Interpretation of Rule 101 (101-1) • Employment or association with attest clients (101-2) • Performance of nonattest services (101-3) • Honorary directorships and trusteeships of not-for-profit organizations (101-4) • Loans from financial institution clients and related terminology (101-5) • The effect of actual or threatened litigation on independence (101-6) • Effect on independence of financial interests in nonclients having investor or investee relationships with a member's client (101-8) • The effect on independence of relationships with entities included in the governmental financial statements (101-10) • Modified application of Rule 101 for certain engagements to issue restricted-use reports under the statements on standards for attestation engagements (101-11) • Independence and cooperative arrangements with clients (101-12) • The effect of alternative practice structures on the applicability of independence rules (101-14)
102	Integrity and objectivity	• Knowing misrepresentations in the preparation of financial statements or records (102-1) • Conflicts of interest (102-2) • Obligations of a member to his or her employer's external accountant (102-3) • Subordination of judgment by a member (102-4) • Applicability of Rule 102 to members performing educational services (102-5) • Professional services involving client advocacy (102-6)
201	General standards	• Competence (201-1)
202	Compliance with standards	• None
203	Accounting principles	• Departures from established accounting principles (203-1) • Status of FASB and GASB interpretations (203-2) • Responsibility of employees for the preparation of financial statements in conformity with GAAP (203-4)
301	Confidential client information	• Confidential information and the purchase, sale, or merger of a practice (301-3)
302	Contingent fees	• Contingent fees in tax matters (302-1)
501	Acts discreditable	• Retention of client's records (501-1) • Discrimination and harassment in employment practices (501-2) • Failure to follow standards and/or procedures or other requirements in governmental audits (501-3) • Negligence in the preparation of financial statements or records (501-4) • Failure to follow requirements of governmental bodies, commissions, or other regulatory agencies in performing attest or similar services (501-5) • Solicitation or disclosure of CPA examination questions and answers (501-6) • Failure to file tax return or pay tax liability (501-7)
502	Advertising and other forms of solicitation	• False, misleading, or deceptive acts in advertising or solicitation (502-2) • Engagements obtained through efforts of third parties (502-5)
503	Commissions and referral fees	• None
505	Form of organization and name	• Application of Rules of Conduct to members who own a separate business (505-2) • Application of Rule 505 to alternative practice structures (505-3)

Interpretations of the other rules tend to be significantly shorter and less involved. This is because independence has become the most complex and controversial area of auditor ethics and professionalism—not only has the AICPA established multiple pages of interpretations regarding independence, but the SEC and the now defunct Independence Standards Board (ISB) have also weighed in heavily on the independence issue. Differences between AICPA independence standards and the SEC independence regulations, which apply only to the audits of public companies, are discussed in the context of the AICPA Code of Professional Conduct.

TABLE 19–5	**Key Definitions Relating to the AICPA Rules of Conduct**

Attest engagement. An engagement that requires independence as defined in AICPA Professional Standards. Attest engagements include financial statement audits, reviews, and examinations of prospective financial information.

Attest engagement team. Individuals participating in the attest engagement, including those who perform concurring and second partner reviews. The attest engagement team includes all employees and contractors retained by the firm who participate in the attest engagement, regardless of their functional classification (for example, audit, tax, or management consulting services).

Client. Any person or entity, other than the member's employer, that engages a member or a member's firm to perform professional services.

Holding out. In general, any action initiated by a member that informs others of his or her status as a CPA or AICPA-accredited specialist constitutes holding out as a CPA. This would include, for example, any oral or written representation to another regarding CPA status, use of the CPA designation on business cards or letterhead, the display of a certificate evidencing a member's CPA designation, or listing as a CPA in local telephone directories.

Key position. A position in which an individual has primary responsibility for significant accounting functions, has primary responsibility for the preparation of the financial statements, or has the ability to exercise influence over the contents of the financial statements. Key positions include member of the board of directors, chief executive officer, president, chief financial officer, chief operating officer, general counsel, chief accounting officer, controller, director of internal audit, director of financial reporting, treasurer, or any equivalent position.

Member. A member, associate member, or international associate of the American Institute of Certified Public Accountants.

Partner. A proprietor, shareholder, equity or nonequity partner, or any individual who assumes the risks and benefits of firm ownership or who is otherwise held out by the firm to be the equivalent of any of the aforementioned.

Period of the professional engagement. The period for which a member either signs an initial engagement letter or other agreement to perform attest services or begins to perform an attest engagement for a client, whichever is earlier. The period lasts for the entire duration of the professional relationship (which could cover many periods) and ends with the formal or informal notification, either by the member or the client, of the termination of the professional relationship or by the issuance of a report, whichever is later. Accordingly, the period does not end with the issuance of a report and recommence with the beginning of the following year's attest engagement.

Practice of public accounting. The performance for a client, by a member or a member's firm, while holding out as CPA(s), of the professional services of accounting, tax, personal financial planning, litigation support services, and those professional services for which standards are promulgated by bodies designated by Council.

    However, a member or a member's firm, while holding out as CPA(s), is not considered to be in the practice of public accounting if the member or the member's firm does not perform, for any client, any of the professional services described in the preceding paragraph.

Professional services. All services performed by a member while holding out as a CPA.

Next we turn to an in-depth discussion of the *Rules of Conduct* and their most significant *interpretations*. Before proceeding, however, be sure you understand the definitions included in Table 19–5. These definitions are keys to understanding the rules and their respective interpretations.

Independence, Integrity, and Objectivity

[LO 9]   Section 100 of the AICPA Rules of Conduct currently contains two rules related to independence, integrity, and objectivity. SEC and ISB rules and standards relating to auditor independence are also discussed in this section to the extent that they differ in important ways.

Independence

If an auditor is not independent of his or her client, it is unlikely that a user of financial statements will place much reliance on the CPA's work. Rule 101 is a very general statement concerning auditor independence and relates only to attestation-related services, including audits.

> **Rule 101:** A member in public practice shall be independent in the performance of professional services as required by standards promulgated by bodies designated by Council. ✣

AICPA professional standards require a public accounting firm, including the firm's partners and professional employees, to be independent in accordance with AICPA Rule 101 whenever the firm performs an attest service for a client. Attest services include

- Financial statement audits.
- Financial statement reviews.
- Other attest services as defined in the Statements on Standards for Attestation Engagements (SSAEs).

Performing a compilation of a client's financial statements does not require independence, but an accountant or firm that lacks independence must explicitly indicate this fact in the compilation report. Likewise, independence is not required to perform other nonattest services (e.g., tax preparation, financial planning, or consulting services) if those services are the only services provided to a particular client.

Because of the difficulty that sometimes arises in defining independent relationships, numerous interpretations of Rule 101 have been issued. Table 19–4 lists the interpretations of Rule 101 that are currently in effect.

Table 19–6 presents Interpretation 101-1, a major interpretation related to independence. In reading Interpretation 101-1 it is important to consider the definition of a "covered member." The AICPA uses an engagement team approach to determine independence. Thus, a covered member includes

- An individual on the attest engagement team.
- An individual in a position to influence the attest engagement.
- A partner or manager who provides nonattest services to the attest client beginning once he or she provides 10 hours of nonattest services to the client within any fiscal year and ending on the later of the date (1) the firm signs the report on the financial statements for the fiscal year during which those services were provided or (2) he or she no longer expects to provide 10 or more hours of nonattest services to the attest client on a recurring basis.
- A partner in the office in which the lead attest engagement partner primarily practices in connection with the attest engagement.
- The firm, including the firm's employee benefit plans.
- An entity whose operating, financial, or accounting policies can be controlled (as defined by generally accepted accounting principles for consolidation purposes) by any of the individuals or entities described above or by two or more such individuals or entities if they act together.

Note that the independence rules apply to more than just the partner on the attest engagement. Every individual on the engagement team and others who may be in a position to influence the engagement must be independent

TABLE 19-6	Interpretation 101-1 (Interpretation of Rule 101)*

Independence Shall Be Considered to Be Impaired If:

A. During the period of the professional engagement a covered member
   1. Had or was committed to acquire any direct or material indirect financial interest in the client.
   2. Was a trustee of any trust or executor or administrator of any estate if such trust or estate had or was committed to acquire any direct or material indirect financial interest in the client.
   3. Had a joint closely held investment that was material to the covered member.
   4. Except as specifically permitted in interpretation 101-5, had any loan to or from the client, any officer or director of the client, or any individual owning 10 percent or more of the client's outstanding equity securities or other ownership interests.
B. During the period of the professional engagement, a partner or professional employee of the firm, his or her immediate family, or any group of such persons acting together owned more than 5 percent of a client's outstanding equity securities or other ownership interests.
C. During the period covered by the financial statements or during the period of the professional engagement, a firm, or partner or professional employee of the firm was simultaneously associated with the client as a(n)
   1. Director, officer, or employee, or in any capacity equivalent to that of a member of management;
   2. Promoter, underwriter, or voting trustee; or
   3. Trustee for any pension or profit-sharing trust of the client.

Application of the Independence Rules to Covered Members Formerly Employed by or Associated with a Client

An individual who was formerly employed by or associated with a client as a(n) officer, director, promoter, underwriter, voting trustee, or trustee for a pension or profit-sharing trust of the client would impair his or her firm's independence if the individual—
1. Participated on the attest engagement team or was an individual in a position to influence the attest engagement for the client when the attest engagement covers any period that includes his or her former employment or association with that client; or
2. Was otherwise a covered member with respect to the client unless the individual first dissociates from the client by—
   a. Terminating any relationships with the client described in interpretation 101-1.C;
   b. Disposing of any direct or material indirect financial interest in the client;
   c. Collecting or repaying any loans to or from the client, except for loans specifically permitted or grandfathered under interpretation 101-5;
   d. Ceasing to participate in all employee benefit plans sponsored by the client, unless the client is legally required to allow the individual to participate in the plan (for example, COBRA) and the individual pays 100 percent of the cost of participation on a current basis; and
   e. Liquidating or transferring all vested benefits in the client's defined benefit plans, defined contribution plans, deferred compensation plans, and other similar arrangements at the earliest date permitted under the plan. However, liquidation or transfer is not required if a penalty significant to the benefits is imposed upon liquidation or transfer.

Application of the Independence Rules to a Covered Member's Immediate Family

Except as stated in the following paragraph, a covered member's immediate family is subject to rule 101 [ET section 101.01], and its interpretations and rulings.
The exceptions are that independence would not be considered to be impaired solely as a result of the following:
1. An individual in a covered member's immediate family was employed by the client in a position other than a key position.
2. In connection with his or her employment, an individual in the immediate family of one of the following covered members participated in a retirement, savings, compensation, or similar plan that is a client, is sponsored by a client, or that invests in a client (provided such plan is normally offered to all employees in similar positions):
   a. A partner or manager who provides ten or more hours of non-attest services to the client; or
   b. Any partner in the office in which the lead attest engagement partner primarily practices in connection with the attest engagement.

For purposes of determining materiality under rule 101 the financial interests of the covered member and his or her immediate family should be aggregated.

Application of the Independence Rules to Close Relatives

Independence would be considered to be impaired if—
1. An individual participating on the attest engagement team has a close relative who had
   a. A key position with the client, or
   b. A financial interest in the client that
      (i) Was material to the close relative and of which the individual has knowledge; or
      (ii) Enabled the close relative to exercise significant influence over the client.
2. An individual in a position to influence the attest engagement or any partner in the office in which the lead attest engagement partner primarily practices in connection with the attest engagement has a close relative who had
   a. A key position with the client; or
   b. A financial interest in the client that
      (i) Was material to the close relative and of which the individual or partner has knowledge; and
      (ii) Enabled the close relative to exercise significant influence over the client.

TABLE 19–6	*(concluded)*

Grandfathered Employment Relationships

Employment relationships of a covered member's immediate family and close relatives with an existing attest client that impair independence under this interpretation and that existed as of November 2001, will not be deemed to impair independence provided such relationships were permitted under preexisting requirements of rule 101, and its interpretations and rulings.

Other Considerations

It is impossible to enumerate all circumstances in which the appearance of independence might be questioned. Members should consider whether personal and business relationships between the member and the client or an individual associated with the client would lead a reasonable person aware of all the relevant facts to conclude that there is an unacceptable threat to the member's and the firm's independence.

*Interpretation 101-1 has been excerpted and abridged. Refer to the full set of rules and interpretations at www.aicpa.org

with respect to the attest client. Other partners or managers of the CPA firm who are not on the attest engagement team must also generally be independent of the client if they provide *nonattest* services to that client (such as tax or consulting services), or even if a partner simply works in the same office as the attest engagement's lead partner. By this definition, a staff member of the CPA firm does not need to be independent of the attest client unless he or she performs work for the client or becomes a partner in the same office where the attest engagement's lead partner works.

The CPA firm itself must also be independent with respect to the client; for example, the CPA firm's benefit plan cannot invest in the firm's attest clients. Finally, any entity that can be controlled by any one or more of the parties listed above must also be independent of the attest client. For example, if two of the CPA firm's partners owned or otherwise controlled an investment trust, that trust must be independent of the CPA firm's attest client; otherwise, the independence of the CPA firm is considered impaired. Note that with few exceptions, the independence requirements under Rule 101 extend to the CPA's immediate family members (spouse, spousal equivalent, or dependents) and, in a few cases, to the CPA's close relatives (nondependent children, siblings, parents, etc.). The applicability of the independence requirements to family members and relatives is discussed later in this section.

While CPA firms are required to comply with Rule 101, most major CPA firms have their own firm-specific independence rules that are typically more stringent than the AICPA's standards. In addition, firms that audit public companies are required by AICPA and PCAOB standards to establish and maintain systems of quality control, a significant aspect of which is to ensure the firms' compliance with independence standards. Quality control requirements, the AICPA's peer review program, and the PCAOB's auditor inspection program are discussed later in this chapter.

Note that Interpretation 101-1 examines independence along two dimensions (*financial relationships* and *business relationships*) and considers the effects of family relationships on independence. A number of other interpretations of Rule 101 provide further explanations on such financial and business relationships.

Financial Relationships   Interpretation 101-1 prohibits members from any financial relationship with a client that may impair or give the appearance of impairing independence. This includes any *direct* or *material indirect* financial interest in the client. A direct financial interest results when a covered member (sometimes hereafter referred to as a CPA) has a financial interest in an attest client, such as ownership of stock or a loan to or from the client. With few exceptions (see below), direct financial interests by CPAs in attest clients impair independence. Interpretation 101-1 indicates that independence is considered impaired if, during the period of the engagement, *any* partner or professional employee of a CPA firm (covered member or not), his or her immediate family, or any group of such persons acting together own more than 5 percent of a client's outstanding equity securities or other ownership interests.

An indirect financial interest results when a CPA has a financial interest in an entity that is associated with an attest client. For example, an indirect financial interest is created if a CPA invests in a mutual fund that owns a client's shares. Indirect financial interests are generally permissible only if the amount involved is immaterial with respect to the covered member's income and wealth. Additional interpretations have been issued to clarify or provide exceptions to such financial interests.

Generally a loan to or from a client is considered to impair the member's independence (see Exhibit 19–1). However, there are situations in which a CPA is permitted to obtain loans from a financial institution that is a client. Interpretation 101-5 permits the following types of personal loans from a client that is a financial institution:

- Automobile loans and leases collateralized by the automobile.
- Loans fully collateralized by the surrender value of an insurance policy.

EXHIBIT 19–1   **ESM Government Securities, Inc.'s, Audit Partner Had "Loan" from Client**

ESM Government Securities, Inc., was a Fort Lauderdale brokerage firm that specialized in buying and selling debt securities issued by the federal government and its various agencies. Its main customers were small to moderate-size banks and municipalities. The major type of transaction engaged in by ESM was known as a "repo," in which a securities dealer sells a customer a large block of federal securities and simultaneously agrees to repurchase the securities at a later date at an agreed-upon price. A massive fraud was conducted at ESM by Ronnie Ewton and Alan Novick, who hid trading losses and other misappropriations from ESM's auditor, Alexander Grant. The trading losses incurred by ESM were transferred to an affiliated company. When the thefts and trading losses were finally tallied, there was a net deficit of $300 million for ESM.

Sadly, the audit partner, Jose Gomez, was aware of the fraud. Gomez was admitted as a partner to Alexander Grant in 1979. His major client was ESM Securities. Shortly after making partner, Gomez was informed by Novick that the company's 1977 and 1978 financial statements had been misstated. Novick was able to convince Gomez not to withdraw Alexander Grant's audit report on the assumption that ESM would recoup its losses. Novick was aware that Gomez was experiencing financial problems in spite of his salary as a partner. Over the course of the fraud (1977–1984), Gomez received approximately $200,000 in payments from Novick to relieve his financial problems.

See Chapter 20, Exhibit 20–12, for more information on ESM Government Securities, Inc. *In re Alexander Grant & Co. Litigation.*

- Loans fully collateralized by cash deposits at the same financial institution.
- Credit cards and cash advances where the aggregate outstanding balance is reduced to $10,000 or less by the payment due date.

Such loans must be made in accordance with the financial institution's *normal* lending procedures, terms, and requirements and must, at all times, be kept current as to all terms. *Normal lending procedures, terms, and requirements* are defined as lending procedures, terms, and requirements that are reasonably comparable to those relating to loans of a similar character given to other borrowers during the period in which the loan to the member is given, including (1) the amount of the loan in relationship to the value of the collateral pledged as security and the credit of the member or member's firm, (2) repayment terms, (3) the interest rate, including points, (4) closing costs, and (5) the general availability of such loans to the public.

A number of interesting issues arise when trying to apply the independence rules. For example, what happens when an audit client fails to pay a fee that is due to the auditor? If you think about it, unpaid fees might be considered a loan from the auditor to the client, which would constitute a direct financial interest! In fact, the rulings and interpretations of Rule 101 specify that if fees pertaining to services provided more than one year prior to the date of the audit report remain unpaid, the auditor's independence is impaired with respect to that client. However, unpaid fees from a client that is in bankruptcy do not impair the auditor's independence.

There may also be situations when financial interests of nonclients that are related in various ways to a client may affect a CPA's independence. Interpretation 101-8 specifically discusses two of these situations:

1. When a nonclient investee is material to a client investor, any direct or material indirect financial interest by a CPA in the nonclient investee impairs independence. If the nonclient investee is immaterial to the client investor, a CPA's material investment in the nonclient investee causes an impairment of independence.
2. When a client investee is material to a nonclient investor, any direct or material indirect financial interest of a CPA in the nonclient impairs independence. If the client investee is immaterial to the nonclient investor, and if a CPA's financial interest in the nonclient investor allows the CPA to exercise significant influence over the actions of the nonclient investor, the CPA's independence is considered impaired.

For example, suppose a CPA has a direct financial interest in a partnership that invests in a client. If the CPA serves, or acts, as a general partner in the partnership, independence is deemed to be impaired because he or she is considered to have a *direct* financial interest. If the CPA is a limited partner in the partnership, the CPA is considered to have an *indirect* financial interest in the client and independence is impaired only if the indirect financial interest is material to the CPA's net worth.

Business Relationships   Rule 101 (including relevant interpretations) essentially indicates that the independence of a CPA is impaired if the CPA performs a managerial or other significant role for a client's organization during the time period covered by an attest engagement. Such situations often arise when a former employee of the client becomes employed by the CPA firm or, more commonly, when a CPA takes a job with a former audit client. Interpretations of this rule, however, provide for certain exceptions.

For example, a former employee of an attest client cannot become a member of the attest engagement team or be placed in a position to influence the engagement for that client unless the subject of the attest engagement does not include any period of his or her former employment or association with the client. In addition, if a client employee joins the CPA firm and becomes a covered member with respect to the client, the CPA firm is not independent unless the former client employee first dissociates from the client, essentially by terminating noncomplying managerial and financial relationships with the client (see Table 19–7 for details).

Next, consider the situation that arises when a CPA goes to work for a client of his or her former CPA firm. This has been a controversial area, because several of the recent high-profile frauds unfortunately were facilitated by former auditors. Interpretation 101-2 indicates that a firm's independence will be considered to be impaired with respect to a client if a partner or professional employee leaves the firm and is subsequently employed by or associated with that client in a *key position* unless a number of conditions are met (see Table 19–5 for the definition of a key position). These conditions require that the CPA be completely disassociated from the CPA firm, and that the firm take steps to ensure that the engagement team exercises sufficient professional skepticism and is not unduly influenced by the former employee of the firm (see Table 19–7 for details). In fact, Interpretation 101-2 indicates that if a member of the attest engagement team or an individual in a position to influence the attest engagement even develops the *intention* to seek or discuss potential employment with, or has a job offer from, an attest client, independence is impaired with respect to the client unless the person promptly reports the situation to an appropriate person in the firm and removes himself or herself from the engagement until the offer is rejected or employment is no longer being sought. If another member of the engagement team (or other employee of the CPA firm) becomes aware that a member of the attest engagement team (or an individual in a position to influence the attest engagement) is considering employment with a client, the employee should notify an appropriate person in the firm so the firm can take steps to prevent the impairment of its independence.

Another situation can arise when a CPA is asked to serve as an *honorary* director or trustee for a not-for-profit client. It is not unusual for members of a CPA firm to be asked to lend the prestige of their names to a charitable, religious, civic, or similar organization and for their firm to provide accounting and auditing services to the not-for-profit organization. Interpretation 101-4 allows a member to serve as a director or trustee for a not-for-profit *client* "so long as his or her position is clearly honorary, and he or she cannot vote or otherwise participate in board or management functions." Any of the organization's documents that contain the member's name must identify the member's position as honorary.

TABLE 19–7	Interpretation 101-2—Employment or Association with Attest Clients

A firm's independence will be considered to be impaired with respect to a client if a partner or professional employee leaves the firm and is subsequently employed by or associated with that client in a key position unless all the following conditions are met:

1. Amounts due to the former partner or professional employee for his or her previous interest in the firm and for unfunded, vested retirement benefits are not material to the firm, and the underlying formula used to calculate the payments remains fixed during the payout period. Retirement benefits may also be adjusted for inflation and interest may be paid on amounts due.
2. The former partner or professional employee is not in a position to influence the accounting firm's operations or financial policies.
3. The former partner or professional employee does not participate or appear to participate in, and is not associated with, the firm, whether or not compensated for such participation or association, once employment or association with the client begins. An appearance of participation or association results from such actions as:
   - The individual provides consultation to the firm.
   - The firm provides the individual with an office and related amenities (for example, secretarial and telephone services).
   - The individual's name is included in the firm's office directory.
   - The individual's name is included as a member of the firm in other membership lists of business, professional, or civic organizations, unless the individual is clearly designated as retired.
4. The ongoing attest engagement team considers the appropriateness or necessity of modifying the engagement procedures to adjust for the risk that, by virtue of the former partner or professional employee's prior knowledge of the audit plan, audit effectiveness could be reduced.
5. The firm assesses whether existing attest engagement team members have the appropriate experience and stature to effectively deal with the former partner or professional employee and his or her work, when that person will have significant interaction with the attest engagement team.
6. The subsequent attest engagement is reviewed to determine whether the engagement team members maintained the appropriate level of skepticism when evaluating the representations and work of the former partner or professional employee, when the person joins the client in a key position within one year of disassociating from the firm and has significant interaction with the attest engagement team. The review should be performed by a professional with appropriate stature, expertise, and objectivity and should be tailored based on the position that the person assumed at the client, the position he or she held at the firm, the nature of the services he or she provided to the client, and other relevant facts and circumstances. Appropriate actions, as deemed necessary, should be taken based on the results of the review.

Responsible members within the firm should implement procedures for compliance with the preceding conditions when firm professionals are employed or associated with attest clients.

With respect to conditions 4, 5, and 6, the procedures adopted will depend on several factors, including whether the former partner or professional employee served as a member of the engagement team, the positions he or she held at the firm and has accepted at the client, the length of time that has elapsed since the professional left the firm, and the circumstances of his or her departure.

Considering Employment or Association with the Client

When a member of the attest engagement team or an individual in a position to influence the attest engagement intends to seek or discuss potential employment or association with an attest client, or is in receipt of a specific offer of employment from an attest client, independence will be impaired with respect to the client unless the person promptly reports such consideration or offer to an appropriate person in the firm, and removes himself or herself from the engagement until the employment offer is rejected or employment is no longer being sought. When a covered member becomes aware that a member of the attest engagement team or an individual in a position to influence the attest engagement is considering employment or association with a client, the covered member should notify an appropriate person in the firm.

The appropriate person should consider what additional procedures may be necessary to provide reasonable assurance that any work performed for the client by that person was performed with objectivity and integrity as required under rule 102 [ET section 102.01]. Additional procedures, such as reperformance of work already done, will depend on the nature of the engagement and the individual involved.

Provision of Nonaudit Services The AICPA Code of Professional Conduct restricts the types of nonaudit services that can be provided to attest clients. Interpretation 101-3 outlines these requirements and also binds member CPAs to follow the relevant requirements of other regulatory bodies where applicable. Thus, failure to comply with more restrictive provisions of other regulatory bodies also violates the Code of Professional Conduct. The Code permits CPAs to provide bookkeeping, systems implementation, internal audit outsourcing, and other services to attest clients subject to certain conditions and limits. For example, a CPA may assist an audit client in implementing a computer software package but may not "design" the financial information system by creating or changing the computer source code underlying the system. If the auditor makes any such modifications, the changes cannot be "more than insignificant." In addition, the Code indicates that CPAs may not perform appraisal, valuation, or actuarial services if the results of those services will have a material effect on the client's financial statements *and* the service involves considerable subjectivity. The SEC does not allow CPAs to provide the services discussed above to *public-company* attest clients under most circumstances. The SEC's more restrictive independence rules for audits of public companies, including restrictions on provision of nonattest services to audit clients, are discussed later in this chapter.

Interpretation 101-3 of the Code outlines general requirements for performing other professional services for attest clients:

1. The CPA should not perform management functions or make management decisions for the attest client. However, the CPA may provide advice, research materials, and recommendations to assist the client's management in performing its functions and making decisions.

2. The client must agree to perform the following functions in connection with the nonattest engagement:
   a. Make all management decisions and perform all management functions.
   b. Designate a competent employee, preferably within senior management, to oversee the services.
   c. Evaluate the adequacy and results of the services performed.
   d. Accept responsibility for the results of the services.
   e. Establish and maintain internal control, including monitoring ongoing activities.

3. Before performing nonattest services, the CPA should establish and document in writing his or her understanding with the client (board of directors, audit committee, or management, as appropriate in the circumstances) regarding the following:
   a. Objectives of the engagement.
   b. Services to be performed.
   c. Client's acceptance of its responsibilities.
   d. Member's responsibilities.
   e. Any limitations of the engagement.

Interpretation 101-3 offers the following examples of general activities that would be considered to impair a CPA's independence:

- Authorizing, executing, or consummating a transaction or otherwise exercising authority on behalf of a client.
- Preparing source documents, in electronic or other form, evidencing the occurrence of a transaction.
- Having custody of client assets.
- Supervising the client's employees in the performance of their normal recurring activities.
- Determining which recommendations of the member should be implemented.

- Reporting to the board of directors on behalf of management.
- Serving as a client's stock transfer or escrow agent, registrar, general counsel, or its equivalent.

So long as the CPA stays within the general guidelines listed above, which essentially revolve around the idea that the CPA should not act in a management or decision-making role when providing nonaudit services to attest clients, the AICPA does not strictly prohibit the provision of most types of professional services to attest clients.

For example, Interpretation 101-3 allows a CPA firm to provide outsourced internal audit services for a client for which the member also performs a professional service that requires independence (i.e., an audit or other attest service). Performing these extended audit services would not be considered to impair independence provided the member or his or her firm does not act or appear to act as either employee or management of the client. Thus, if a member provides assistance in the performance of an audit client's internal audit function, the member and client must understand that the *client* is responsible for

- Designating a competent individual or individuals, preferably within senior management, to be responsible for the internal audit function.
- Determining the scope, risk, and frequency of internal audit activities, including those to be performed by the member providing the extended audit services.
- Evaluating the findings and results arising from the internal audit activities, including those performed by the member providing the extended audit services.
- Evaluating the adequacy of the audit procedures performed and the findings resulting from the performance of those procedures by, among other things, obtaining reports from the member.

While the AICPA Code of Professional Ethics permits internal audit outsourcing, the SEC prohibits providing this and several other types of nonaudit professional services to a public-company audit client. The ways in which SEC (and ISB) independence rules differ for the audits of public companies are discussed next.

� [LO 10]   SEC Independence Requirements for Audits of Public Companies

The SEC's mission is to protect investors and maintain the integrity of the capital markets in which the securities of publicly traded companies are bought and sold. As part of its mission, the SEC has authority to establish standards relating to financial accounting, auditing, and the professional conduct of public accountants in the context of public-company accounting and auditing. The SEC has established standards that differ from those established by the AICPA, particularly in the area of auditor independence. The SEC's standards must be followed by auditors of public companies.

In this section we discuss the primary areas in which the SEC's independence rules differ from those of the AICPA Code of Professional Conduct. Until recently, the SEC's independence rules for auditors of public companies closely followed those of the AICPA. However, the SEC implemented more stringent rules in November 2000, which were further revised in January 2003, after Title II of the Sarbanes-Oxley Act required additional independence restrictions. You will better understand the reasoning behind the SEC's new auditor independence (and other) requirements if you keep in mind that they were in response to specific circumstances that came to light in the frauds of the early 2000s. For example, Arthur Andersen was earning more in consulting than in auditing fees at Enron, and David Duncan, Andersen's lead partner on the Enron engagement, was compensated partially based on the amount of nonaudit services he sold to the company. Further, several of Enron's employees in important accounting and finance positions were former Andersen auditors who had worked on the Enron audit engagement. Several of the SEC's independence revisions focus on these very issues. While most of the SEC's independence rules are very similar to the AICPA's, the recent changes resulted in some important differences relating to (1) provision of other professional services, (2) handling of human resource and compensation-related issues, and (3) certain required communications.[10] The major differences in these three areas are discussed next.

Provision of Other Professional Services.   The SEC's rules with respect to services provided by auditors are predicated on three basic principles of auditor objectivity and independence: an auditor should not audit his or her own work, an auditor should not function in the role of management, and an auditor should not serve in an advocacy role for his or her client. Consistent with these principles, the SEC prohibits several types of professional services by accounting firms for public-company audit clients, sometimes with the qualifier "unless it is reasonable to conclude that the results of these services will not be subject to audit procedures during an audit of the client's financial statements." Note that the rules do not limit the scope of nonaudit services provided by accounting firms to nonpublic companies or to public companies that are not audit clients. Additionally, accounting firms are expressly allowed to provide tax services to their audit clients.

The SEC specifies nine categories of nonaudit services that, with few exceptions, are considered to impair independence if provided to a public-company audit client:

- Bookkeeping or other services related to the accounting records or financial statements of the audit client.
- Financial information systems design and implementation.
- Appraisal or valuation services, fairness opinions, or contribution-in-kind reports.
- Actuarial services.
- Internal audit outsourcing services.
- Management functions or human resources.

---

[10]A number of other minor differences exist between AICPA and SEC independence rules, but this text focuses on only the major areas of divergence. For a thorough and detailed comparison of AICPA and SEC independence rules, see the document titled "AICPA and SEC Independence Rule Comparison" under the "Professional Ethics" link at www.aicpa.org.

- Broker or dealer, investment adviser, or investment banking services.
- Legal services.
- Expert services.

Consistent with the Sarbanes-Oxley Act, SEC regulations also prohibit any other service that the PCAOB determines impermissible. At this point, the PCAOB has not added any prohibited services to the list. While the first eight categories of services listed above were prohibited under pre-Sarbanes SEC independence rules ("expert services" is a newly added category), a number of exceptions to these prohibitions have been eliminated.

All audit and nonaudit services provided by a public company's auditor must be approved by the company's audit committee, either on a case-by-case basis or pursuant to preestablished policies and procedures. A company's audit committee is charged with overseeing the effectiveness of the company's internal and external audits. This rule essentially requires the audit committee to consider the possible effects of nonaudit services on the auditor's objectivity and on investors' perceptions of the auditor's independence from the company.

Human Resource and Compensation-Related Issues. SEC rules in this area are primarily concerned with the potential for audit partners to become "too close" to an engagement or a client over time and with potential threats to an auditor's objectivity resulting from employment and compensation arrangements that can create conflicts of interest. These rules can be summarized in three areas.

First, the lead and concurring partners on the engagement team for a public-company audit are prohibited from providing audit services to the company for more than five consecutive years. Once the partners "roll off" a client, a five-year "time-out" period is required before they can return to their former duties with that client. Audit partners other than the lead and concurring partners are prohibited from performing audit services for a particular client for more than seven consecutive years, with a two-year "time-out" period.

Second, if any individual with a "financial reporting oversight role" at a public company (subject to specified exceptions) was a member of the accounting firm's audit engagement team within a one-year "cooling-off" period, the accounting firm is prohibited from auditing the company's financial statements.[11]

Finally, the SEC does not consider an accounting firm to be independent from a public-company audit client if an audit partner receives compensation based on selling engagements to that client for services other than audit, review, and attest services. This applies not only to audits of domestic issuers but also to audits of foreign subsidiaries and affiliates of U.S. issuers.

---

[11]The *cooling-off period* is defined as the one-year period preceding the commencement of audit procedures for the period that included the date the engagement team member was first employed by the client company.

Required Communication.   New SEC rules also differ from those of the AICPA in requiring additional communication between auditors and their clients' audit committees and in requiring public-company audit clients to publicly report information regarding the fees paid to their auditors.

The auditor of a public company must report to the company's audit committee all "critical accounting policies" used by the company, all alternative treatments within GAAP for policies and procedures related to material items discussed with management, and other material written communications between the auditor and the company's management. In addition, the audit committee must be responsible for the appointment, compensation, and oversight of the external auditor's work. This is important, because it establishes the audit committee as the auditor's client, rather than management itself. Remember that management is ultimately responsible for a company's financial statements. Because the audit committee of a public company must be independent of management, setting up the audit committee as the point of contact for the auditor creates a healthier environment in which the auditor does not answer directly to or receive compensation from management.

Proxy statements and annual reports issued by public companies must contain disclosures regarding (1) audit fees, (2) audit-related fees, (3) tax fees, and (4) all other fees billed during the prior two fiscal years by the principal auditor of the company's financial statements. Details must also be provided on the nature of services provided in earning "other fees." The preapproval policies of the company's audit committee must also be disclosed. A purpose of this requirement is to make companies more sensitive to public perceptions of auditor independence and objectivity.

Independence Standards Board (ISB)

The ISB was created in 1997 as a joint effort of the AICPA and the SEC to address important issues arising at the time relating to audits of public companies. Without relinquishing its authority to set such standards, the SEC delegated the responsibility for setting and maintaining independence standards to the ISB. The board was housed within the SEC Practice Section of the AICPA. In 2000 the SEC issued its own comprehensive rule on auditor independence for the audits of public companies, and the ISB was disbanded in July 2001, when the SEC concluded that "the board's mission had been substantially fulfilled." During its brief tenure, the ISB issued three standards and three interpretations. Although the ISB is now defunct, its standards are recognized by the SEC, and they currently remain in effect for public-company audits. The AICPA Code of Professional Conduct also requires compliance with the ISB's standards unless it expressly indicates disagreement with particular provisions. Only the most significant provisions of the ISB standards and interpretations are described here.

ISB Standard No. 1, *Independence Discussions with Audit Committees*, requires discussion and written communication between the auditor and a public-company client's board of directors and audit committee. The auditor must disclose in writing to the board and audit committee any relationships between the auditor and the entity that could bear on auditor independence. The auditor must also confirm to the board that the CPA firm is independent with respect to the client, in accordance with SEC rules. The intended effect of this standard is to encourage boards of directors and audit committees to carefully consider auditor independence issues at least annually. ISB Standard No. 3, *Employment with Audit Clients,* deals with issues surrounding the employment of former audit personnel by client companies. The requirements of ISB Standard No. 3 are essentially included in Interpretation 101-2 (see Table 19–7). The other standard and interpretations issued by the ISB dealt with detailed issues that are beyond the scope of this text (e.g., assisting clients with implementation of FAS 133 on derivatives and dealing with certain implications of audits of mutual funds and related entities).

Effect of Family Relationships

The issues related to a CPA's financial or business interest in a client may extend to members of the CPA's family. Certain relationships between members of a CPA's family and a client are considered to affect the CPA's independence. This is an area where the AICPA's independence rules have been relaxed to recognize changing social factors such as dual-career families. A distinction is made in Interpretation 101-1 between a covered member's *immediate family* (spouse, spousal equivalent, or dependent) and *close relatives* (parent, sibling, or nondependent child). A covered member's immediate family is subject to Rule 101 and its interpretations and rulings. Table 19–6 contains two exceptions. For example, a covered member's spouse employed by a client would not impair independence if he or she were not employed in a key position.

Financial or business interests by close relatives such as nondependent children, brothers, sisters, parents, grandparents, parents-in-law, and their respective spouses do not normally impair independence. Interpretation 101-1 (Table 19–6) lists the situations where independence would be impaired by a close relative. The two major situations that can impair independence are

- A close relative has a financial interest in the client that is material to the close relative, and the CPA participating in the engagement is aware of the interest.
- An individual participating in the engagement has a close relative who could exercise significant influence over the financial or accounting policies of the client (key position).

For example, suppose a staff auditor's brother works as the controller for a client of the CPA firm. Because the accountant's brother exercises influence over significant accounting functions for the client, the auditor would not be allowed to participate in the audit of this client.

Effect of Actual or Threatened Litigation

Sometimes threatened or actual litigation between the client and the auditor can impair the auditor's independence. Such situations affect the CPA's independence when a possible adversarial relationship exists between the client and the CPA. Interpretation 101-6 cites three categories of litigation: (1) litigation between the client and the CPA, (2) litigation by shareholders, and (3) other third-party litigation where the CPA's independence may be impaired.

In order for a CPA to provide an opinion on a client's financial statements, the relationship between the client's management and the CPA must be one of "complete candor and full disclosure regarding all aspects of the client's business operations." When actual or threatened litigation exists between management and the CPA, complete candor may not be possible. The following criteria are offered as guidelines for assessing independence when actual or threatened litigation exists between the client and the CPA:

- The commencement of litigation by the present management alleging deficiencies in audit work for the client would be considered to impair independence.
- The commencement of litigation by the CPA against the present management alleging management fraud or deceit would be considered to impair independence.
- An expressed intention by the present management to commence litigation against the CPA alleging deficiencies in audit work would impair independence if the auditor concluded that it is probable that such a claim will be filed.

Litigation by client security holders or other third parties also may impair the auditor's independence under certain circumstances. For example, litigation may arise from a class action lawsuit by stockholders alleging that the client, its management, its officers, its directors, its underwriters, and its auditors were involved in the issuance of "false or misleading financial statements." Generally, such lawsuits do not alter the fundamental relationship between the CPA and the client. However, independence may be impaired if material client-auditor cross-claims are filed. For example, suppose that a class action suit is filed and the current client management intends to testify against the CPA, alleging that an improper audit was conducted. In such a situation, an adversarial relationship would exist and the CPA would no longer be independent. When this occurs, the CPA should either (1) withdraw from the engagement or (2) disclaim an opinion because of a lack of independence.

Other third-party litigation against the CPA may be commenced by lending institutions or by other creditors who rely on the client's financial statements that were opined on by the CPA. Normally, such lawsuits do not impair the CPA's independence unless the relationship between the CPA and the client is affected.

Integrity and Objectivity

Rule 102: In the performance of any professional service, a member shall maintain objectivity and integrity, shall be free of conflicts of interest, and shall not knowingly misrepresent facts or subordinate his or her judgment to others. ✷

This rule expands slightly on the principle from which it was developed and requires that a member maintain integrity and objectivity. There are a number of important interpretations of this rule. One interpretation (102-1) indicates that a member who knowingly makes or permits false and misleading entries in financial statements or records violates Rule 102. A second interpretation (102-2) states that a conflict of interest may occur if a member performs a professional service for a client or employer and the member of his or her firm has a relationship with another person, entity, product, or service that could be viewed as impairing the CPA's objectivity.

Two other interpretations relate mainly to members in industry. One interpretation (102-3) states that, in dealing with his or her employer's external accountants, a member must be candid and not knowingly misrepresent facts or knowingly fail to disclose material facts. In a related interpretation (102-4), if a member and his or her supervisor have a disagreement or dispute relating to the preparation of financial statements or the recording of transactions, the member must take steps to ensure that the situation does not result in a subordination of judgment. If the member concludes that the financial statements or records could be materially misstated, he or she should communicate those concerns to a higher level of management within the organization. If appropriate action is not taken, the member should consider whether to continue the relationship with the employer. The member should also consider whether any responsibility exists to communicate the problem to third parties, such as regulatory agencies or the employer's external accountants.

Educational services are professional services and therefore are subject to Rule 102 (Interpretation 102-5). Thus a member must maintain objectivity and integrity when performing such services. Finally, a member may be asked by a client to act as an advocate in performing tax or consulting services or in support of a client's position on an accounting or auditing issue (Interpretation 102-6). While a member may accept such an engagement, he or she must be sure that the requested service does not go beyond the bounds of sound professional practice and impair independence, integrity, and objectivity.

General Standards and Accounting Principles

[LO 11] This section of the Rules of Conduct contains two rules related to general standards and one rule related to accounting principles.

General Standards and Compliance with Standards

Rule 201: A member shall comply with the following standards and with any interpretations thereof by bodies designated by Council.

A. *Professional Competence.* Undertake only those professional services that the member or the member's firm can reasonably expect to be completed with professional competence.

B. *Due Professional Care.* Exercise due professional care in the performance of professional services.

C. *Planning and Supervision.* Adequately plan and supervise the performance of professional services.

D. *Sufficient Relevant Data.* Obtain sufficient relevant data to afford a reasonable basis for conclusions or recommendations in relation to any professional services performed.

Rule 201 captures much of what is contained in the 10 generally accepted auditing standards and makes it part of the Code. Interpretation 201-1 provides some additional clarification of "professional competence." In particular, when a CPA agrees to perform professional services, he or she is expected to have the necessary competence to complete those services according to professional standards. However, it is not necessary for the CPA to have all of the technical knowledge required to perform the engagement at the time the engagement commences. The CPA may conduct additional research or consult with other professionals during the conduct of the engagement. This need for additional information does not indicate a lack of competence on the part of the CPA.

> **Rule 202:** A member who performs auditing, review, compilation, management consulting, tax, or other professional services shall comply with standards promulgated by bodies designated by Council.

This rule is straightforward yet important because it requires that members of the AICPA comply with professional standards when performing professional services, whether or not they are practicing in public accounting.

Accounting Principles

While Rule 202 addresses compliance with standards for professional services, Rule 203 relates to compliance with accounting principles.

> **Rule 203:** A member shall not (1) express an opinion or state affirmatively that the financial statements or other financial data of any entity are presented in conformity with generally accepted accounting principles or (2) state that he or she is not aware of any material modifications that should be made to such statements or data in order for them to be in conformity with generally accepted accounting principles, if such statements or data contain any departure from an accounting principle promulgated by bodies designated by Council to establish such principles that has a material effect on the statements or data taken as a whole. If, however, the statements or data contain such a departure and the member can demonstrate that due to unusual circumstances the financial statements or data would otherwise have been misleading, the member can comply with the rule by describing the departure, its approximate effects, if practicable, and the reasons why compliance with the principle would result in a misleading statement. ✷

This rule was adopted to require compliance by CPAs with GAAP. Rule 203 and Interpretation 203-1 recognize that there may be unusual circumstances when applying GAAP may produce misleading financial statements, and a departure from GAAP may thus be justified. Some examples of circumstances that might require departure from GAAP are new legislation and the evolution of a new form of business transaction. An unusual degree of materiality and conflicting industry practices are examples of circumstances that would ordinarily *not* be considered unusual under Rule 203.

Interpretation 203-2 reiterates that the AICPA Council has designated the Financial Accounting Standards Board (FASB), the Governmental Accounting Standards Board (GASB), and the Federal Accounting Standards Advisory Board (FASAB) as the bodies authorized to establish accounting principles. For example, this interpretation defines GAAP to include FASB's Statements of Financial Accounting Standards, together with those Accounting Research Bulletins and Accounting Principles Board Opinions issued by predecessors of the FASB that have not been superseded. Interpretations by the FASB are recognized as authoritative when determining the existence of a departure from GAAP. Similar guidance issued by the GASB and FASAB would establish financial accounting principles for state and local governmental entities and federal government entities, respectively.

Interpretation 203-4, which relates mainly to members in industry, states that any representation regarding conformity with GAAP in a letter or other communication from a client to its auditor or others related to that entity's financial statements is subject to Rule 203. Thus, for example, if a member signs a representation letter indicating that the financial statements were in conformity with GAAP when in fact they were not, he or she has violated Rule 203.

Responsibilities to Clients

    ❧ **[LO 12]**   This section of the Rules of Conduct contains two rules related to a CPA's responsibilities to his or her clients.

Confidential
Client Information

> **Rule 301:** A member in public practice shall not disclose any confidential client information without the specific consent of the client.
>
>   This rule shall not be construed (1) to relieve a member of his or her professional obligations under rules 202 and 203, (2) to affect in any way the member's obligation to comply with a validly issued and enforceable subpoena or summons, or to prohibit a member's compliance with applicable laws and governmental regulations, (3) to prohibit review of a member's professional practice under AICPA or state CPA society or Board of Accountancy authorization, or (4) to preclude a member from initiating a complaint with, or responding to any inquiry made by, the professional ethics division or trial board of the Institute or a duly constituted investigative or disciplinary body of a state CPA society or Board of Accountancy.
>
>   Members of any of the bodies identified in (4) above and members involved with professional practice reviews identified in (3) above shall not use to their own advantage or disclose any member's confidential client information that comes to their attention in carrying out those activities. This prohibition shall not restrict members' exchange of information in connection with the investigative or disciplinary proceedings described in (4) above or the professional practice reviews described in (3) above. ❧

Rule 301 specifies four situations in which a CPA can disclose confidential information without the client's consent: (1) to meet disclosure requirements for GAAP and GAAS, (2) to comply with a valid and enforceable subpoena, (3) as required by an authorized peer review board or body, and (4) as part of an investigative or disciplinary proceeding.

Interpretation 301-3 specifically allows a review of a CPA's professional practice in conjunction with the purchase, sale, or merger of the practice. The CPA should take precautions that the prospective buyer does not disclose to outside parties any confidential client information. This can generally be accomplished through the use of a confidentiality agreement. Members who review a CPA's practice in connection with a prospective purchase or merger should not use that information to their advantage, nor should they disclose to others any confidential client information that comes to their attention.

Contingent Fees

Rule 302: A member in public practice shall not

(1) Perform for a contingent fee any professional services for, or receive such a fee from, a client for whom the member or the member's firm performs
    (a) an audit or review of financial statements; or
    (b) a compilation of a financial statement when the member expects, or reasonably might expect, that a third party will use the financial statement and the member's compilation report does not disclose a lack of independence; or
    (c) an examination of prospective financial information; or
(2) Prepare an original or amended tax return or claim for a tax refund for a contingent fee for any client.

The prohibition in (1) above applies during the period in which the member or member's firm is engaged to perform any of the services listed above and the period covered by any historical financial statements involved in any such listed services.

Except as stated in the next sentence, a contingent fee is a fee established for the performance of any service pursuant to an arrangement in which no fee will be charged unless a specific finding or result is attained, or in which the amount of the fee is otherwise dependent upon the finding or result of such service. Solely for purposes of this rule, fees are not regarded as being contingent if fixed by courts or other public authorities, or, in tax matters, if determined based on the results of judicial proceedings or the findings of governmental agencies.

A member's fees may vary depending, for example, on the complexity of the services rendered. ✘

If contingent fees were allowed for attestation-related services, users of those services might question the CPA's independence.

Other Responsibilities and Practices

✘ **[LO 13]**   This section contains four rules of conduct that relate to other aspects of the profession.

Acts Discreditable

Rule 501: A member shall not commit an act discreditable to the profession. ✘

This rule allows the AICPA to remove a member for committing acts that may affect the profession's reputation. So, for example, a CPA who is convicted of a serious crime could lose his or her membership in the AICPA. Seven interpretations have been issued that identify acts considered discreditable under Rule 501:

- Retention of client records (501-1).
- Discrimination and harassment in employment practices (501-2).
- Failure to follow standards and/or procedures or other requirements in government audits (501-3).
- Negligence in the preparation of financial statements or records (501-4).

- Failure to follow the requirements of government bodies, commissions, or other regulatory agencies in performing attest or similar services (501-5).
- Solicitation or disclosure of CPA examination questions and answers (501-6).
- Failure to file tax return or pay tax liability (501-7).

For example, a CPA may not retain a client's accounting or other records that were provided by the client as part of conducting the engagement even if there are fees still unpaid. If the CPA retains certain client records such as journals or ledgers, the client may be unable to continue operations. The CPA's working papers, on the other hand, are the property of the CPA. However, if the CPA's working papers contain information that is not reflected in the client's records and that would result in those records being incomplete, such information should be made available to the client upon request. If a CPA did not return a client's accounting records, that member would have committed a discreditable act under Rule 501. Similarly, a CPA commits a discreditable act if he or she discriminates in hiring, promotion, or salary practices on the basis of race, color, religion, sex, age, or national origin. A third example of a discreditable act would be when a CPA, by virtue of his or her negligence, makes or permits or directs another to make false or misleading entries in the financial statements or records of an entity. Last, a CPA who fails to file a tax return or pay the related tax liability would have committed a discreditable act.

Advertising and Other Forms of Solicitation

Rule 502: A member in public practice shall not seek to obtain clients by advertising or other forms of solicitation in a manner that is false, misleading, or deceptive. Solicitation by the use of coercion, over-reaching, or harassing conduct is prohibited. ✄

Interpretation 502-2 provides specific examples of activities that are prohibited by this rule. These include

- Creating false or unjustifiable expectations of favorable results.
- Implying an ability to influence any court, tribunal, regulatory agency, or similar body or official.
- Claiming that specific professional services in current or future periods will be performed for a stated fee, estimated fee, or fee range when it is likely at the time of representation that such fees will be substantially increased and the prospective client is not advised of that likelihood.
- Making any other representations that would be likely to cause a reasonable person to misunderstand or be deceived.

CPAs are often asked to provide professional services to clients or customers of third parties when those clients or customers have been obtained through advertising and/or solicitation. Interpretation 502-5 allows CPAs to render such services to clients or customers of third parties as long as all promotional efforts used to obtain such clients were conducted within the Code.

Commissions and Referral Fees

Rule 503:

A. *Prohibited commissions*

A member in public practice shall not for a commission recommend or refer to a client any product or service, or for a commission recommend or refer any product or service to be supplied by a client, or receive a commission, when a member or the member's firm also performs for that client

- an audit or review of financial statements; or
- a compilation of a financial statement when the member expects, or reasonably might expect, that a third party will use the financial statement and the member's compilation report does not disclose a lack of independence; or
- an examination of prospective financial information.

This prohibition applies during the period in which the member is engaged to perform any of the services listed above and the period covered by any historical financial statements involved in the listed services.

B. *Disclosure of permitted commissions*

A member in public practice who is not prohibited by this rule from performing services for or receiving a commission and who is paid or expects to be paid a commission shall disclose that fact to any person or entity to whom the member recommends or refers a product or service to which the commission relates.

C. *Referral fees*

Any member who accepts a referral fee for recommending or referring any service of a CPA to any person or entity or who pays a referral fee to obtain a client shall disclose such acceptance or payment to the client. ✖

Many professions, including doctors and lawyers, have been permitted to use referral fees. However, commissions and referral fees are prohibited for CPAs. The current rule does not allow commissions or referral fees in situations where the CPA's independence and objectivity are a focal point of attestation-related services.

Form of Organization and Name

Rule 505: A member may practice public accounting only in a form of organization permitted by law or regulation whose characteristics conform to resolutions of Council.

A member shall not practice public accounting under a firm name that is misleading. Names of one or more past partners may be included in the firm name of a successor organization.

A firm may not designate itself as "Members of the American Institute of Certified Public Accountants" unless all of its CPA owners are members of the Institute. ✖

This rule requires that the form of a CPA's public accounting practice conform to law or regulations whose characteristics conform to AICPA resolutions. In recent years, virtually all states have passed laws that allow CPAs to practice as limited liability partnerships. Rule 505 also prohibits firms from operating under names that may mislead the public.

Interpretation 505-2 states that a CPA in the practice of public accounting may own an interest in a separate business that performs for clients any of the professional services of accounting, tax, personal financial planning, litigation support services, and those services for which standards have been promulgated by the Council. Such a member must observe all of the Rules of Conduct.

A resolution by the AICPA Council requires, among other things, that CPAs own a majority of the financial interests in a firm engaged in attest services. In recent years, alternative practice structures have evolved under which, for example, CPA firms were purchased by other entities and (1) the majority of the financial interests in the attest firm was owned by CPAs and (2) all or substantially all of the revenues were paid to another entity in return for services and the lease of employees, equipment, and office space. If the CPAs who own the attest firm remain financially responsible, under applicable state law or regulation the member is considered to be in compliance with the financial interests provision of the resolution.

Disciplinary Actions

The AICPA has a number of avenues by which members can be disciplined for violating the Code of Professional Conduct. For violations that are not sufficient to warrant formal actions, the Professional Ethics Executive Committee can direct a member to take remedial or corrective actions. If the member rejects the committee's recommendation, the committee can refer the case to a hearing panel of the Trial Board. Membership in the AICPA can be suspended or terminated without a hearing if the member has been convicted of certain criminal offenses (such as a crime punishable by imprisonment for more than one year or filing a false income tax return on a client's behalf) or if the member's CPA certificate is suspended or revoked by a government agency. A member may also be expelled or suspended for up to two years by the Trial Board for violating any rule of the Code of Professional Conduct. For more information on the AICPA's disciplinary processes, the reader should refer to the AICPA Bylaws. Of course, the SEC and the PCAOB also have several options for pursuing disciplinary actions against auditors. These are briefly discussed in Chapter 20 in the context of auditor legal liability.

Don't Lose Sight of the Forest for the Trees

As you can see from the preceding discussion, professional conduct and auditor independence are complicated subjects, involving a great deal of technical detail. A sense for the depth of detail involved is essential. However, we encourage you not to lose sight of the big picture. The primary purpose of professional ethics rules is to establish a minimum level of professionalism to help auditors remain independent of their clients and objective and honest in their judgments. The essence of even the mind-numbingly detailed independence requirements is that independence in fact and appearance is critical to the CPA's reputation and the value she or he provides to society. Unfortunately, even practicing auditors can get so lost in the detail of the specific requirements that they sometimes lose sight of the fundamental principles on which the rules are based. If you pursue a career in accounting, you should at least occasionally step back and review the fundamental principles of the Code of Professional Conduct, which involve appropriate professional and moral judgments in all you do, an obligation to honor the public trust, and a commitment to perform professional responsibilities with the highest sense of integrity.

Quality Control Standards

[LO 14]   CPA firms are required to implement policies and procedures to monitor the firms' practices and ensure that professional standards are being followed. In 1977 the AICPA started a voluntary peer review program, and by January 1988 had approved mandatory quality peer reviews. The program is structured in two tiers: one for firms that have public-company audit clients and one for (usually smaller) firms that audit only private companies. The purpose of the quality peer review program is to ensure that firms comply with relevant quality control standards.

In 2004, the PCAOB assumed the AICPA's responsibilities relating to firms that audit public clients and instituted a mandatory quality inspection program for those firms. However, the AICPA continues to administer a two-tiered quality review system in order to enable firms to meet their state licensing, federal regulatory, and AICPA membership requirements and to serve firms that audit only privately held clients. The two tiers of quality reviews are offered through (1) the AICPA Center for Public Company Audit Firms Peer Review Program and (2) the AICPA Peer Review Program (designed for firms that audit only private companies). All AICPA member firms subject to PCAOB inspections are required to join the Center, whose peer review program is designed to review and evaluate those portions of a firm's accounting and auditing practice that are not subject to inspection by the PCAOB. The Center's program is nationally administered by a peer review committee made up of firms that are also subject to PCAOB inspection. Firms that are not subject to PCAOB inspection may choose to join the Center or may opt for the AICPA Peer Review Program.

Statement on Quality Control Standards (SQCS) No. 2, "System of Quality Control for a CPA Firm's Accounting and Auditing Practice" (QC 10), gives CPA firms professional guidance in establishing a system of quality control. SQCS No. 2 applies only to auditing and accounting practice (audit, attest, and review services). While not required, it is recommended that the guidance in this statement be applied to other services such as tax services and consulting services.

System of Quality Control

A firm's system of quality control encompasses its organizational structure and the policies and procedures established to provide the firm with reasonable assurance of conforming with professional standards (QC 10.03). A firm's system of quality control, however, has to be tailored to its size, the nature of its practice, its organization, and cost-benefit considerations. For a sole practitioner or small firm, a system of quality control is likely to be much less formal than one for a national or international firm. For example, a sole practitioner with three professional staff members may use a simple checklist and conduct periodic informal discussions to monitor his or her firm's compliance with professional standards. On the other hand, a large international CPA firm may develop involved in-house procedures and assign full- or part-time staff to oversee and ensure compliance with the firm's quality control system.

Elements of Quality Control

ꤶ [LO 15]

SQCS No. 2 identifies the following five elements of quality control:

- Independence, integrity, and objectivity.
- Personnel management.
- Acceptance and continuance of clients and engagements.
- Engagement performance.
- Monitoring.

TABLE 19-8	Elements of Quality Control

- *Independence, Integrity, and Objectivity:* Policies and procedures should be established to provide the firm with reasonable assurance that personnel maintain independence (in fact and in appearance) in all required circumstances, perform all professional responsibilities with integrity, and maintain objectivity in discharging professional responsibilities.
- *Personnel Management:* Policies and procedures should be established for hiring, assigning personnel to engagements, professional development, and advancement activities that provide reasonable assurance that
  a. Those hired possess the appropriate characteristics to enable them to perform competently.
  b. Work is assigned to personnel having the degree of technical training and proficiency required in the circumstances.
  c. Personnel participate in general and engagement-specific continuing professional education and participate in professional development activities that enable them to fulfill responsibilities assigned, and fulfill applicable continuing professional education requirements of the AICPA and regulatory agencies.
- *Acceptance and Continuance of Clients and Engagements:* Policies and procedures should be established for deciding whether to accept or continue a client relationship and whether to perform a specific engagement for that client. Such procedures should provide the firm with reasonable assurance that the likelihood of association with a client whose management lacks integrity is minimized.
- *Engagement Performance:* Policies and procedures should be established to provide the firm with reasonable assurance that the work performed by engagement personnel meets applicable professional standards, regulatory requirements, and the firm's standards of quality.
- *Monitoring:* Policies and procedures should be established to provide the firm with reasonable assurance that the policies and procedures established by the firm for each of the other elements of quality control are suitably designed and are being applied effectively.

Table 19–8 defines each of the elements. It should be apparent from the definitions that these elements are interrelated. For example, personnel management encompasses criteria for professional development, hiring, advancement, and assignment of the firm's personnel to engagements, which affect policies and procedures developed to meet quality control objectives. It is important for a firm to develop a system of quality control that takes each of these elements into account and to ensure that members of the firm understand the firm's quality control policies and procedures. While not required, communication of the firm's quality control system should be in writing, with the extent of documentation varying with the size of the firm. A firm's quality control policies and the Code of Professional Ethics should be covered in the firm's training programs.

Table 19–9 provides some selected examples of the types of policies or procedures a firm can implement to comply with a sound system of quality control.

Monitoring Quality Control

Quality control standards require consistent monitoring of (1) the relevance of and compliance with the firm's policies and procedures, (2) the adequacy of the firm's guidance materials and practice aids, and (3) the effectiveness of professional development programs (QC 20). Firms should implement monitoring procedures to identify and communicate circumstances that may necessitate changes and improvements to the firm's system of quality control. Procedures for monitoring include:

- Inspection procedures.
- Pre- and postcompletion review of selected engagements.
- Analysis and assessment of
  — New professional pronouncements.
  — Results of independence confirmations.
  — Continuing professional education and other professional development activities undertaken by firm personnel.

TABLE 19–9	Selected Quality Control Policies and Procedures

Independence, Integrity, and Objectivity
- Inform personnel of the firm's independence policies and procedures and advise them that they are expected to be familiar with these policies and procedures.
- Obtain from personnel annual, written representations stating that they are familiar with the policies and procedures and that prohibited investments are not held and were not held during the period.

Personnel Management
- Plan for the firm's personnel needs at all levels and establish quantified hiring objectives based on current clientele, anticipated growth, personnel turnover, individual advancement, and retirement.
- Identify the attributes to be sought in hirees, such as intelligence, integrity, honesty, motivation, and aptitude for the profession.

Acceptance and Continuance of Clients
- Establish procedures for evaluating prospective clients such as (1) obtaining and review of available financial information regarding the prospective clients and (2) inquiry of third parties about any information regarding the prospective client and its management.
- Designate an individual or group, at appropriate management levels, to evaluate the information obtained and to make the acceptance decision.

Engagement Performance
- Provide adequate supervision at all organizational levels, considering the training, ability, and experience of the personnel assigned.
- Develop guidelines for review of working papers and for documentation of the review process.

Monitoring
- Determine the inspection procedures necessary to provide reasonable assurance that the firm's other quality control policies and procedures are operating effectively.
- Inspect practice units, functions, or departments.

- Decisions related to acceptance and continuance of client relationships and engagements.
- Interviews of firm personnel.
- Determination of any corrective actions to be taken and improvements to be made in the quality control system.
- Communication to appropriate firm personnel of any weaknesses identified in the quality control system or in the level of understanding or compliance therewith.
- Follow-up by appropriate firm personnel to ensure that any necessary modifications are promptly made to the quality control policies and procedures.

The AICPA requires member firms to have their practices reviewed by peer firms approximately every three years. For example, Deloitte may engage PricewaterhouseCoopers to conduct its review.

PCAOB Inspections of Registered Public Accounting Firms
‰ [LO 16]

In addition to the AICPA peer review programs discussed above, the PCAOB conducts regular inspections of public accounting firms that are required to register with the board. These inspections review selected audit and quarterly review engagements and evaluate the sufficiency of the quality control system of registered firms. The purpose of these inspections is to ensure that registered firms, in connection with their audits of public companies, comply with the Sarbanes-Oxley Act, PCAOB rules, SEC rules, and professional standards.

The PCAOB conducts special inspections on an ad hoc basis when it has specific cause, but the frequency with which regular inspections are conducted is established by law. Registered firms that issue more than

100 audit reports for public companies per year are subject to an annual inspection, while those firms that regularly issue more than 1 but less than 100 audit reports in a year must be inspected at least once every three years.

Should a PCAOB inspection find that a firm, or anyone associated with it, may be in violation of legislation, accounting regulations, any professional standard, or even the firm's own quality control policies, then the PCAOB can conduct a special investigation into the possible violation. Following an investigation, the board will issue a draft report, at which time the firm has 30 days to respond to any accusations. At the end of this period, the board then issues a final report outlining the violations; however, assuming such violations do not involve fraud, the firm is granted a 12-month period in which to take necessary corrective action. If sufficient action is taken, the PCAOB does not publicly reveal the firm's violations—otherwise, public disciplinary action ensues against responsible parties.

Mandatory inspections apply to all firms that audit public U.S. companies. However, if the accounting firm is not based in the United States, there may be some exceptions to the inspection requirements. For instance, at the PCAOB's discretion, the board may rely (at least in part) on foreign authorities to conduct inspections.

KEY TERMS

Close relative. A parent, sibling, or nondependent child.

Covered member. A member that is
   a. An individual on the attest engagement team.
   b. An individual in a position to influence the attest engagement.
   c. A partner or manager who provides nonattest services to the attest client beginning once he or she provides 10 hours of nonattest services to the client within any fiscal year and ending on the later of the date (i) the firm signs the report on the financial statements for the fiscal year during which those services were provided or (ii) he or she no longer expects to provide 10 or more hours of nonattest services to the attest client on a recurring basis.
   d. A partner in the office in which the lead attest engagement partner primarily practices in connection with the attest engagement.
   e. The firm, including the firm's employee benefit plans.
   f. An entity whose operating, financial, or accounting policies can be controlled (as defined by generally accepted accounting principles for consolidation purposes) by any of the individuals or entities described in (*a*) through (*e*) or by two or more such individuals or entities if they act together.

Ethics. A system or code of conduct based on moral duties and obligations that indicates how an individual should behave.

Generally accepted auditing standards. Measures of the quality of the auditor's performance.

Immediate family. A spouse, spousal equivalent, or dependent (whether or not related).

Key position. A position in which an individual

    a. Has primary responsibility for significant accounting functions that support material components of the financial statements.

    b. Has primary responsibility for the preparation of the financial statements.

    c. Has the ability to exercise influence over the contents of the financial statements, including when the individual is a member of the board of directors or similar governing body, chief executive officer, president, chief financial officer, chief operating officer, general counsel, chief accounting officer, controller, director of internal audit, director of financial reporting, treasurer, or any equivalent position.

For purposes of attest engagements not involving a client's financial statements, a key position is one in which an individual is primarily responsible for, or able to influence, the subject matter of the attest engagement, as described above.

Professionalism. The conduct, aims, or qualities that characterize or mark a profession or professional person.

www.mhhe.com/ messier4e	Visit the book's Online Learning Center for a multiple-choice quiz that will allow you to assess your understanding of chapter concepts.

REVIEW QUESTIONS

[LO 2]   **19-1**   Briefly describe the three theories of ethical behavior that can be used to analyze ethical issues in accounting.

[4]   **19-2**   Identify the six stages of ethical development. What level of development would typically be attained by a professional such as an auditor?

[5]   **19-3**   Why are companies like Kmart able to continue in business after experiencing federal indictments, convictions of top executives, and bankruptcy, while accounting firms, like the once highly respected, financially strong accounting firm Arthur Andersen, can be destroyed by a single federal indictment?

[5]   **19-4**   What entities are involved in establishing standards and rules for the professional conduct of public accountants? Who establishes such standards for auditors of public versus private companies?

[6]   **19-5**   What are the two major sections of the Code of Professional Conduct? What additional guidance is provided for applying the Rules of Conduct?

[7]   **19-6**   Describe the six Principles of Professional Conduct.

[8]   **19-7**   What are the five major sections of the Rules of Conduct? Define the practice of public accounting as used in the Rules of Conduct.

[9]   **19-8**   What types of personal loans from a financial institution are allowed by the Rules of Conduct? What is meant by *normal lending procedures, terms, and requirements* within this context?

[10]   **19-9**   Summarize the major differences between the AICPA's Code of Professional Ethics independence rules and the SEC's independence rules for auditors of public companies. Briefly describe why the SEC's requirements diverged from those of the AICPA in the early 2000s.

[12] 19-10 Generally a CPA is not allowed to disclose confidential client information without the consent of the client. Identify four circumstances in which confidential client information can be disclosed under the Rules of Conduct without the client's permission.

[13] 19-11 Give three examples of acts that are considered discreditable under the Rules of Conduct.

[13] 19-12 A CPA is allowed to advertise as long as the advertising is not false, misleading, or deceptive. Provide three examples of advertising that might be considered false, misleading, or deceptive. Why are such acts of concern to the profession?

[14,15] 19-13 What is the purpose of a CPA firm's establishing a system of quality control? List the five elements of quality control and provide one example of a policy or procedure that can be used to fulfill each element.

[5,16] 19-14 Briefly describe the responsibility of the PCAOB with respect to standards for the professional conduct of auditors of public companies, and explain how it came to have that role. What is the role of the PCAOB inspection process in carrying out the board's responsibilities?

MULTIPLE-CHOICE QUESTIONS

[1,2,5] 19-15 Which of the following statements best explains why the public accounting profession has found it essential to promulgate ethical standards and to establish means for ensuring their observance?
a. Vigorous enforcement of an established code of ethics is the best way to prevent unscrupulous acts.
b. Ethical standards that emphasize excellence in performance over material rewards establish a reputation for competence and character.
c. A distinguishing mark of a profession is its acceptance of responsibility to the public.
d. A requirement for a profession is to establish ethical standards that primarily stress responsibility to clients and colleagues.

[10] 19-16 All of the following nonaudit services are identified by the SEC as generally impairing an auditor's independence except
a. Information systems design and implementation.
b. Human resource services.
c. Management functions.
d. Valuations and appraisals for tax purposes.
e. All of the above are seen by the SEC as impairing independence.

[10] 19-17 Under the SEC's rules regarding independence, which of the following must a client disclose?
a. Only fees for the external audit.
b. Only fees for internal and external audit services provided by the audit firm.

c. Fees for the external audit, audit-related fees, tax fees, and fees for other nonaudit services performed by the audit firm.

d. Only fees for systems implementation and design, and nonaudit services performed by the audit firm.

[6]   19-18   The AICPA Code of Professional Conduct contains both general ethical principles that are aspirational in character and also a

a. List of violations that would cause the automatic suspension of a CPA's license.

b. Set of specific, mandatory rules describing minimum levels of conduct a CPA must maintain.

c. Description of a CPA's procedures for responding to an inquiry from a trial board.

d. List of specific crimes that would be considered as acts discreditable to the profession.

[9]   19-19   In which of the following situations would a CPA's independence be considered impaired according to the Code of Professional Conduct?

1. The CPA maintains a checking account that is fully insured by a government deposit insurance agency at an audit-client financial institution.

2. The CPA has a direct financial interest in an audit client, but the interest is maintained in a blind trust.

3. The CPA owns a commercial building and leases it to an audit client. The rental income is material to the CPA.

a. 1 and 2.
b. 2 and 3.
c. 1 and 3.
d. 1, 2, and 3.

[9]   19-20   A client company has not paid its 2005 audit fees. According to the AICPA Code of Professional Conduct, for the auditor to be considered independent with respect to the 2006 audit, the 2005 audit fees must be paid before the

a. 2005 report is issued.
b. 2006 field work is started.
c. 2006 report is issued.
d. 2007 field work is started.

[9]   19-21   Which of the following legal situations would be considered to impair the auditor's independence?

a. An expressed intention by the present management to commence litigation against the auditor, alleging deficiencies in audit work for the client, although the auditor considers that there is only a remote possibility that such a claim will be filed.

b. Actual litigation by the auditor against the client for an amount *not* material to the auditor or to the financial statements of the client arising out of disputes as to billings for management advisory services.

c. Actual litigation by the auditor against the present management, alleging management fraud or deceit.

d. Actual litigation by the client against the auditor for an amount *not* material to the auditor or to the financial statements of the client arising out of a dispute as to billings for tax services.

[9,11,12,13]   19-22   A violation of the profession's ethical standards is *least* likely to occur when a CPA

    a. Purchases another CPA's accounting practice and bases the price on a percentage of the fees accruing from clients over a three-year period.

    b. Receives a percentage of the amounts invested by the CPA's audit clients in a tax shelter with the clients' knowledge and approval.

    c. Has a public accounting practice and also is president and sole stockholder of a corporation that engages in data processing services for the public.

    d. Forms an association—*not* a partnership—with two other sole practitioners and calls the association "Adams, Betts & Associates."

[11]   19-23   After beginning an audit of a new client, Larkin, CPA, discovers that the firm's professional competence for the engagement is lacking. Larkin informs management of the situation and recommends another CPA, and management engages the other CPA. Under these circumstances,

    a. Larkin's lack of competence should be construed to be a violation of generally accepted auditing standards.

    b. Larkin may request compensation from the client for any professional services rendered to it in connection with the audit.

    c. Larkin's request for a commission from the other CPA is permitted because a more competent audit can now be performed.

    d. Larkin may be indebted to the other CPA because the other CPA can collect from the client only the amount the client originally agreed to pay Larkin.

[9,11]   19-24   Green, CPA, is asked to render an opinion on the application of accounting principles by an entity that is audited by another CPA. Green may

    a. Not accept such an engagement because to do so would be considered unethical.

    b. Not accept such an engagement because Green would lack the necessary information on which to base an opinion without conducting an audit.

    c. Accept the engagement but should form an independent opinion without consulting with the continuing CPA.

    d. Accept the engagement but should consult with the continuing CPA to ascertain all the available facts relevant to forming a professional judgment.

[12]   19-25   Without the consent of the client, a CPA should *not* disclose confidential client information contained in working papers to a

    a. Voluntary quality control review board.

    b. CPA firm that has purchased the CPA's accounting practice.

    c. Federal court that has issued a valid subpoena.

    d. Disciplinary body created under state statute.

[14]   19-26   One of a CPA firm's basic objectives is to provide professional services that conform with professional standards. Reasonable assurance of achieving this basic objective is provided through

    a. A system of quality control.

    b. A system of peer review.

        c. Continuing professional education.

        d. Compliance with generally accepted reporting standards.

[15]   19-27   In connection with the element of personnel management, a CPA firm's system of quality control should ordinarily provide that all personnel

        a. Have the knowledge required to enable them to fulfill the responsibilities assigned to them.

        b. Meet the profession's independence rules.

        c. Seek assistance from persons having appropriate levels of knowledge, judgment, and authority.

        d. Demonstrate compliance with peer review directives.

PROBLEMS

[10]   19-28   Dean Wareham, an audit manager, is preparing a proposal for a publicly held company in the manufacturing industry. The potential client is growing rapidly and introducing many new products, yet still has a manual accounting system. The company also has never undertaken any tax planning activities and feels that it pays a higher percentage of its income in taxes than its competitors. Additionally, it is concerned that its monitoring activities are inadequate because it does not have an internal audit department. Dean knows that the SEC recently passed new rules regarding auditor independence.

Required:

1. Prepare a summary of nonaudit services that Dean can include in his proposal that do not violate the SEC's independence rules.

2. How would your answer to part 1 differ if the potential client were not publicly held? In other words, what additional nonaudit services could Dean include in his proposal? What conditions would have to be met in order for the firm to provide the additional services?

[9]   19-29   Each of the following situations involves a possible violation of the AICPA's Code of Professional Conduct. Indicate whether each situation violates the Code. If it violates the Code, indicate which rule is violated and explain why.

        a. Julia Roberto, a sole practitioner, has provided extensive advisory services for her audit client, Leather Ltd. She has interpreted financial statements, provided forecasts and other analyses, counseled on potential expansion plans, and counseled on banking relationships. Leather is a privately held entity.

        b. Steve Rackwill, CPA, has been asked by his audit client, Petry Plumbing Supply, to help implement a new control system. Rackwill will arrange interviews for Petry's hiring of new personnel and instruct and oversee the training of current client personnel. Petry Plumbing is a privately held company.

        c. Bob Lanzotti is the partner-in-charge of the audit of Fleet Mobile Homes, Inc. Over the years, he has become a golfing buddy of Fleet's CEO, Jim Harris. During the current year Lanzotti and Harris jointly purchased an exclusive vacation home in North

Carolina. The vacation home represents more than 10 percent of Lanzotti's personal wealth.

d. Kraemeer & Kraemeer recently won the audit of Garvin Clothiers, a large manufacturer of women's clothing. Jock Kraemeer had a substantial investment in Garvin prior to bidding on the engagement. In anticipation of winning the engagement, Kraemeer placed his shares of Garvin stock in a blind trust.

e. Zeker & Associates audits a condominium association in which the parents of a member of the firm own a unit. The unit is material to the parents' net worth, and the member participates in the engagement.

f. Jimmy Saad, a sole practitioner, audited Dallas Conduit, Inc.'s financial statements for the year ended June 30, 2005, and was issued stock by the client as payment of the audit fee. Saad disposed of the stock before commencing field work planning for the audit of the June 30, 2006, financial statements.

g. Dip-It Paint Corporation requires an audit for the current year. However, Dip-It has not paid Allen & Allen the fees due for tax-related services performed two years ago. Dip-It issued Allen & Allen a note for the unpaid fees, and Allen & Allen proceeded with the audit services.

[9]   **19-30**   The questions that follow are based on Rule 101 of the AICPA Code of Professional Conduct as it relates to independence and family relationships. Check "yes" if the situation violates the rule, "no" if it does not.

Situation	Yes	No
a. A partner's dependent parent is a 5% limited partner in a firm client. Does the parent's direct financial interest in the client impair the firm's independence?		
b. A shareholder assigned to a firm's New York office is married to the president of a client for which the firm's Connecticut office performs audit services. If the shareholder does not perform services out of or for the Connecticut office, cannot exercise significant influence over the engagement, and has no involvement with the engagement, such as consulting on accounting or auditing issues, is the firm's independence impaired?		
c. A managerial employee's father retired from his position as a review client's chief operating officer. On his retirement, he acquired a 10% interest in the client, which is material to his net worth. If the managerial employee participates in the review engagement, is the firm's independence impaired?		
d. An individual with a managerial position has a brother who owns a 60% interest in an audit client, which is material to the brother's net worth. If the managerial employee participates in the audit engagement, is the firm's independence impaired?		

[9,11,12,13]   **19-31**   Each of the following situations involves a possible violation by a member in industry of the AICPA's Code of Professional Conduct. For each situation, indicate whether it violates the Code. If it violates the Code, indicate which rule is violated and explain why.

a. Jack Jackson is a CPA and controller of Acme Trucking Company. Acme's external auditors have asked Jackson to sign the management representation letter. Jackson has signed the management representation letter, even though he knows that full disclosures have not been made to Acme's external auditors.

b. Mary McDermott, CPA, is employed in the internal audit department of the United Fund of America. The United Fund raises money from individuals and distributes it to other organizations. McDermott has audited Children's Charities, an organization that receives funds from United Fund.

c. Janet Jett, CPA, formerly worked for Delta Disk Drive, Inc. She is currently interviewing for a new position with Maxiscribe, Inc., another manufacturer of disk drives. Jett has agreed to provide confidential information about Delta's trade secrets if she is hired by Maxiscribe.

d. Brian Thorough, CPA, is currently employed as controller of Trans-Louisiana Oil Company. He has discovered that Trans-Louisiana has been illegally paying state environmental employees so that they will not charge Trans-Louisiana with dumping highly toxic chemicals into the bayous. Thorough discloses this information to the state attorney general.

e. Jill Burnett, CPA, was hired by Cooper Corporation to supervise its accounting department in preparing financial statements and presenting them to senior management. Due to considerable time incurred on other financial activities, Burnett was unable to supervise the accounting staff adequately. It is later discovered that Cooper's financial statements contain false and misleading information.

[9,11]   19-32   Savage, CPA, has been asked by a nonpublic company audit client to perform a nonrecurring engagement involving implementing an IT information and control system. The client requests that, in setting up the new system and during the period prior to conversion to the new system, Savage

- Counsel on potential expansion of business activity plans.
- Search for and interview new personnel.
- Hire new personnel.
- Train personnel.

In addition, the client requests that, during the three months subsequent to the conversion, Savage

- Supervise the operation of the new system.
- Monitor client-prepared source documents and make changes in basic IT-generated data as Savage may deem necessary without the concurrence of the client.

Savage responds that he may perform some of the services requested but not all of them.

Required:

a. Which of these services may Savage perform, and which of them may Savage not perform?

b. Before undertaking this engagement, Savage should inform the client of all significant matters related to the engagement. What are these significant matters?

c. If Savage adds to his staff an individual who specializes in developing computer systems, what degree of knowledge must Savage possess in order to supervise the specialist's activities?

(AICPA, adapted)

DISCUSSION CASES

[3,11,12,13] **19-33** Refer back to the hypothetical Sun City Savings and Loan case presented in this chapter, and consider each of the following independent situations:

a. Suppose that Pina, Johnson & Associates also audited one of the entities who had received one of the large loans that are in dispute. Sam Johnson is not involved with auditing that entity. Is it ethical for Johnson to seek information on the financial condition of that entity from the auditors in his firm? What are the rights of the affected parties in this instance, and what are the costs and benefits of using such information?

b. Suppose that Johnson has determined that one of the entities that owes a disputed loan is being investigated for violating environmental laws and may be sued to the point of bankruptcy by the Environmental Protection Agency. Can Johnson use this information in deciding on the proper loan-loss reserve? What are the ethical considerations?

[9,13] **19-34** Schoeck, CPA, is considering leaving a position at a major public accounting firm to join the staff of a local financial institution that does write-up work, tax preparation and planning, and financial planning.

Required:

a. Are the Rules of Conduct applied differently to CPAs that work for a local financial institution that is not CPA-owned, as compared to a major public accounting firm?

b. Do you think the rules should be applied differently to CPAs depending on the type of entity they work for?

[10] **19-35** For each of the following scenarios, please indicate whether or not independence-related SEC rules are being violated, assuming that the audit client is a *public company*. Briefly explain why or why not.

a. Adrian Reynolds now works as a junior member of the accounting team at Swiss Precision Tooling, a publicly traded manufacturing company. Three months ago, he worked as a staff auditor for Crowther & Sutherland, a local accounting firm, where he worked on the Swiss Precision Tooling audit team. Crowther & Sutherland is still the auditor for Swiss Precision Tooling.

b. Susana Millar finished working for Bircham, Dyson & Bell in August 2003. During that time, she was a concurring partner on the Unigate Dairies assignment (the engagement period on this audit ended in April 2004). In February 2005, Susana took up a position as controller of Unigate Dairies. Bircham, Dyson & Bell is still the dairy's auditor and plans to finish its current audit assignment in March 2005 (19 months after Susana left the firm).

c. Janay Butler, a senior auditor, is aware that under SEC rules her accounting firm should not conduct appraisal or valuation services for a public-company audit client. However, her manager has requested that she appraise some specific large inventory items to verify a public client's estimates, which are relied upon by others.

d. Greg Larsen has been working five full years as the lead partner on the audit of a subsidiary of Comet Electrical Co., the publicly held parent company. The subsidiary makes up 30 percent of Comet's annual revenue. Beginning this year, Greg's CPA firm will also conduct the parent company's audit. Greg will work on the audit of the parent company, but not as lead partner. Can Greg continue to work as lead partner on the subsidiary? Can he work as a nonlead partner on the parent-company audit?

e. Heath & Associates, CPAs, is the auditor of Halifax Investments, Inc., a public company. Heath makes most of its money by selling nonaudit services to its audit clients, but it ensures every service it provides for Halifax is in accordance with SEC rules and is preapproved by the company's audit committee. Last year, it billed the following to Halifax: audit fees $0.8 million, tax fees $2.3 million, and other fees $5.2 million. No services prohibited by the SEC were provided by Heath to Halifax, and the fee figures are appropriately disclosed in Halifax's financial statements.

INTERNET ASSIGNMENTS

[6,7,8]   19-36   Visit the AICPA's website (www.aicpa.org). Find Section 100 of the Code of Professional Ethics. Research the relevant rules, interpretations, and ethics rulings to answer the following questions:

a. Would independence be considered impaired if a member joined a trade association that is a client of the firm?

b. A member provides extensive advisory services for a client. In that connection, the member attends board meetings; interprets financial statements, forecasts, and other analyses; and counsels on potential expansion plans and on banking relationships. Would independence be considered impaired under these circumstances?

c. If a member signs or cosigns checks issued by a debtor corporation for a creditors' committee in control of the debtor corporation, which will continue to operate under its existing management, would independence be impaired with respect to the debtor corporation?

d. A member has been designated to serve as an executor or trustee of the estate of an individual who owns the majority of a client's stock. Would independence be considered impaired with respect to the client?

e. A member serves as a director or officer of a United Way or similar fund-raising organization. Certain local charities receive funds from the organization. Would independence be considered impaired with respect to such charities?

f. A member owns shares in a nonregulated mutual investment fund that holds shares of stock in a client. Would independence be considered impaired with respect to the client whose stock is held by the fund?

g. A client of the member's firm has not paid fees for previously rendered professional services. Would independence be considered impaired for the current year?

www.mhhe.com/ messier4e	Visit the book's Online Learning Center for problem material to be completed using the *ACL* software packaged with your new text.

CHAPTER 20

LEARNING OBJECTIVES

Upon completion of this chapter you will

[1] Understand the four general stages in the audit-related dispute process.

[2] Know the definitions of key legal terms.

[3] Know the auditor's liability to clients under common law.

[4] Understand the auditor's liability to third parties under common law.

[5] Understand the auditor's legal liability under the Securities Act of 1933.

[6] Understand the auditor's legal liability under the Securities Exchange Act of 1934.

[7] Know how the Private Securities Litigation Reform Act of 1995 and the Securities Litigation Uniform Standards Act of 1998 relieve some of the auditor's legal liability.

[8] Understand the auditor's legal liability under the Sarbanes-Oxley Act of 2002.

[9] Know how the SEC and PCAOB can sanction an auditor or audit firm.

[10] Understand how the Foreign Corrupt Practices Act can result in legal liability for auditors.

[11] Understand how the Racketeer Influenced and Corrupt Organizations Act can affect the auditor's legal liability.

[12] Know how an auditor can be held criminally liable for various federal and state laws.

[13] Know and understand the various approaches that the public accounting profession and firms can take to minimize legal liability.

RELEVANT ACCOUNTING AND AUDITING PRONOUNCEMENTS

AICPA, Code of Professional Conduct (ET 50-500)
AU 316, Consideration of Fraud in a Financial Statement Audit
AU 317, Illegal Acts

AU 325, Communication of Internal Control–Related Matters Noted in an Audit
AU 380, Communications with Audit Committees

Legal Liability

Chapter 1 presented an economic view of auditing, and we provided a house inspector analogy to illustrate the concepts. The auditor (or inspector) adds value to the principal-agent relationship by providing an objective, independent opinion on the quality of the information reported. However, what prevents the auditor from cooperating with management and issuing an unqualified report on a set of financial statements that are materially misstated? The main deterrent is the threat of legal liability. If a client or third party suffers a loss from such fraudulent behavior, the auditor's personal wealth and professional reputation may be affected by litigation.

This chapter discusses auditors' legal liability. The chapter starts by presenting an overview of legal liability that includes the stages of the auditor dispute process and briefly discusses the types of legal liability an auditor may encounter. Auditors' liability under common law to clients and third parties is discussed first. Statutory liability for both civil and criminal complaints is presented next. The last section discusses a number of actions that auditors can undertake to minimize their exposure to legal liability. The *Advanced Module* provides an in-depth look at the Phar-Mor trial, an actual auditor-liability case, and includes courtroom strategies and quotes based on trial transcripts. 🌍

www.mhhe.com/
messier4e

A number of legal cases discussed in this chapter are described in detail on the book's website.

Introduction

In the current legal environment, auditors can be held liable for a number of types of actions. In this chapter we discuss the types of claims that can be brought against auditors, the types of plaintiffs that typically sue auditors, what must be proved to sue auditors successfully, and the defenses available to the auditor. Before discussing the details of the various legal theories, we provide a brief historical perspective and broad overview.

Historical Perspective

Although auditors have always been liable to clients and certain third parties, claims against auditors were relatively uncommon before the 1970s. In fact, the number of claims against auditors in the last decade is nearly double the number of all claims previously brought.[1] In addition to the increasing number of claims, the severity of the claims has also risen dramatically. After the U.S. economy slumped in the early 1970s, numerous business failures led to a dramatic increase in the number of lawsuits filed against auditors under the federal Securities Exchange Act of 1934. After the economic recession in the early 1980s it became more common for banks to sue auditors to recover loan losses. The recession of 1990–1992 led to another upsurge in litigation culminating with a settlement related to the savings and loan debacle against Ernst & Young in excess of $400 million.

While some of the lawsuits brought against auditors were certainly legitimate, the 1980s and 1990s also found the profession expending enormous time and effort defending against weak claims. Experts estimate that during this time it took large firms an average of over three years and $3.7 million to defend against a single weak claim under federal securities laws. "Practice protection costs" (e.g., litigation costs and the cost of professional liability insurance) soared and quickly became the second largest cost to public accounting firms behind the cost of human resources. The profession pushed for litigation reform, and in the 1990s Congress passed litigation reform acts that provided some limits to auditor liability and made it more difficult to sue auditors successfully. However, Congress refocused attention on auditor performance, duties, and legal liability in the Sarbanes-Oxley Act of 2002, after the capital markets were shaken by the massive high-profile accounting frauds at Enron and WorldCom and by the conviction of Arthur Andersen on obstruction of justice in connection with the Enron investigation.

Overview
[LO 1]

In her monograph, Professor Zoe-Vonna Palmrose discusses the four general stages in the initiation and disposition of audit-related disputes: (1) the occurrence of events that result in losses for users of the financial statements, (2) the investigation by plaintiff attorneys before filing suit to link the user losses with allegations of material omissions or misstatements of financial statements, (3) the legal process that commences with the filing of the suit,

---

[1]Approximately 4,000 claims are currently being asserted against accounting firms in the United States each year, whereas in the late 1960s the number of such claims did not exceed a few hundred per year. See Chapter 11 in Goldwasser, Arnold, and Eickemeyer, *Accountants' Liability* (Practising Law Institute, 2003) for additional information on the magnitude and severity of claims.

TABLE 20–1	Definition of Key Legal Terms
Privity	Absent a contractual or fiduciary relationship, the accountant does not owe a duty of care to an injured party.
Breach of contract	Occurs when the client or auditor fails to meet the terms and obligations established in the contract, which is normally finalized in the engagement letter. Third parties may have privity or near privity of contract.
Tort	A wrongful act other than a breach of contract for which civil action may be taken.
Ordinary negligence	An absence of reasonable or due care in the conduct of an engagement. Due care is evaluated in terms of what other professional accountants would have done under similar circumstances.
Gross negligence	An extreme, flagrant, or reckless departure from professional standards of due care. This is also referred to as *constructive fraud.*
Fraud	Actions taken with the knowledge and intent to deceive.
Criminal law	Statutory law which defines the duties citizens owe to society and prescribes penalties for violations.
Civil law	All law which is not criminal.
Class action	Lawsuit filed by one or more individuals on behalf of all persons who may have invested on the basis of the same false and misleading information.

and (4) the final resolution of the dispute.[2] The first stage, the loss-generating events, includes events that result in losses, such as client bankruptcy, financial distress, fraudulent financial reporting, and misappropriation of assets. The second stage, pre-suit investigation, may involve investigation activities by plaintiffs and their attorneys before initiating legal proceedings. For example, a board of directors may hire a public accounting firm other than their external auditors to investigate potential fraud (see Exhibit 1–3). The legal process makes up the third stage. The stage involves activities such as filing of complaints, discovery, trial preparation, and the trial. The last stage involves the resolution of the dispute, which may include a summary judgment, a settlement to avoid or discontinue litigation, or a court decision on appeal after a trial.

[LO 2]   Auditors can be sued by clients, investors, creditors, and the government for failure to perform professional services adequately. Auditors can be held liable under two classes of law:

1. **Common law.** Case law developed over time by judges who issue legal opinions when deciding a case (the legal principles announced in these cases become precedent for judges deciding similar cases in the future).

2. **Statutory law.** Written law enacted by the legislative branch of federal and state governments that establishes certain courses of conduct that must be adhered to by covered parties.

It is important to understand the differences between these two broad legal categories. Table 20–1 defines key legal terms, and Table 20–2 summarizes the auditor's liability by type of liability and actions resulting in liability.

Typical civil actions under common law allege that the auditor did not properly perform the audit. For example, under common law, an auditor can be held liable to clients for breach of contract, negligence, gross negligence, and fraud. The auditor's liability to third parties (e.g., investors and creditors)

---

[2]See Chapter 2 in Z. Palmrose, *Empirical Research in Auditor Litigation: Considerations and Data,* Studies in Accounting Research #33 (Sarasota, FL: American Accounting Association, 1999), for a detailed discussion of the four stages of the process. This monograph contains detailed data on over 1,000 auditor-related lawsuits. It is an excellent source of data for both teaching and research.

TABLE 20–2	Summary of Types of Liability and Auditors' Actions Resulting in Liability
Type of Liability	*Auditors' Actions Resulting in Liability*
Common law—clients	Breach of contract Negligence Gross negligence/constructive fraud Fraud
Common law—third parties	Negligence Gross negligence/constructive fraud Fraud
Federal statutory law—civil liability*	Negligence Gross negligence/constructive fraud Fraud
Federal statutory law—criminal liability*	Willful violation of federal statutes

*Auditors may also be civilly and criminally liable under state statutes. Coverage of liability under specific state statutes is beyond the scope of this book.

under common law is complicated by the fact that legal precedent differs by jurisdiction. Most common-law cases are decided in state courts, but there are circumstances where common-law cases can be decided in federal court. In other words, the outcome of a common-law case depends on the location where the case is tried. Some jurisdictions follow a common-law doctrine that provides a very narrow interpretation of auditors' liability to third parties, while others follow a more liberal interpretation.

Under statutory law an auditor can be held civilly or criminally liable. A civil claim can result in fines and sanctions but not incarceration. While there are federal and state statutes, in this text we focus only on federal laws. Federal statutes such as the Securities Act of 1933, the Securities Exchange Act of 1934, and the Sarbanes-Oxley Act of 2002 (and related SEC rulings) represent sources of legal action against auditors. Auditors are liable mainly for gross negligence and fraud under these statutes; however, some parts of the acts have been used to hold auditors liable for ordinary negligence. While under certain circumstances an auditor can be held criminally liable under statutory law, there have been relatively few instances of major criminal actions against auditors.

The remainder of the chapter is organized according to the four types of liability faced by auditors outlined in Table 20–2:

- Common law—clients.
- Common law—third parties.
- Federal statutory law—civil liability (clients and third parties).
- Federal statutory law—criminal liability (government).

Common Law–Clients

[LO 3]   Common law does not require that the public accountant guarantee his or her work product. It does, however, require that the auditor perform professional services with *due care*. This requires that the auditor perform his or her professional services with the same degree of skill, knowledge, and judgment possessed by other members of the profession. When an auditor fails to carry out contractual arrangements with the client, he or she may be held liable for breach of contract or negligence. Under common law, the auditor is also liable to the client for gross negligence and fraud.

Breach of Contract

Breach-of-contract liability is based on the auditor's failing to complete the services agreed to in the contract with the client. As discussed in Chapter 5, an engagement letter should establish the responsibilities for both the public accounting firm and the client. In performing an audit, the auditor's obligation is to examine the client's financial statements and issue the appropriate opinion in accordance with professional standards. The contract between the client and the auditor stipulates the amount of fees to be charged for the designated professional services, and deadlines for completing the services are normally indicated or implied in the contract. If the client breaches its obligations under the engagement letter, the auditor is excused from his or her contractual obligations. If the auditor discontinues an audit without adequate cause, he or she may be liable for economic injury suffered by the client (see Exhibit 20–1). Similarly, other issues (such as timely delivery of

---

EXHIBIT 20–1 | **Deloitte & Touche's Withdrawal from Medtrans Audit Upheld**

Medtrans, an ambulance service provider, retained Deloitte & Touche to audit its financial statements. Medtrans needed capital and sought $10 million in financing from an outside investor. Medtrans gave the potential investor *unaudited* financial statements showing profits of $1.9 million. Deloitte & Touche was in the process of completing its audit during Medtrans's negotiations with the outside investor. Deloitte & Touche proposed adjustments that resulted in Medtrans's financial statements showing a $500,000 loss. Prior to Deloitte & Touche proposing the adjustments, the company's CFO resigned after indicating that he could not sign the management representation letter. When presented with the proposed adjustments, Medtrans's CEO threatened to get a court order forcing Deloitte & Touche to complete the audit. Deloitte withdrew from the engagement. Medtrans retained two other CPA firms, both of which were either discharged or withdrew. A third firm issued an unqualified audit report that contained the adjustments proposed by Deloitte & Touche.

Medtrans alleged that Deloitte & Touche's wrongful withdrawal resulted in the company's failure to complete the financing, and that the subsequent sale of the company was for significantly less than its true value. At trial Medtrans asserted that, under California law, a CPA firm could not, under any circumstances, withdraw from an engagement if it unduly jeopardized the interest of the client. Deloitte & Touche argued that the approved California jury instructions on the duration of a professional's duty were contrary to professional standards, which authorize the auditor to resign. The jury in this case ruled in favor of Medtrans and awarded the company nearly $10 million.

In March 1998 the California Court of Appeals reversed the decision, holding that judges should instruct juries about the profession's standards. The court held that an auditor, by auditing financial statements, assumes a public responsibility that transcends any employment relationship with the client. This decision is significant because it held that an accountant's duty of care can be based on professional standards rather than rules of law that are contrary to professional standards.

Sources: National Medical Transportation Network v. Deloitte & Touche, 98 D.A.R., 2850, March 23, 1998, and "Court Rules on Importance of GAAP and GAAS," Journal of Accountancy (June 1998), p. 24.

the audit report or failure to detect a material defalcation) can lead to litigation by the client against the auditor.

Negligence

A tort is a wrongful act other than a breach of contract for which civil action may be taken. If an engagement is performed without due care, the public accountant may be held liable for an actionable tort in negligence. Liability for negligence represents a deviation from a standard of behavior that is consistent with that of a "reasonable person." When an individual such as a public accountant possesses special skills and knowledge, ordinary reasonable care is not sufficient. An oft-cited quote from Cooley's *Torts*[3] indicates the responsibility of those offering special skills:

> In all those employments where particular skill is requisite, if one offers his services, he is understood as holding himself out to the public as possessing the degree of skill commonly possessed by others in the same employment, and if his pretensions are unfounded, he commits a species of fraud upon every man who employs him in reliance on his public profession. But no man, whether skilled or unskilled, undertakes that the task he assumes shall be performed successfully, and without fault or error; he undertakes for good faith and integrity, but not for infallibility, and he is liable to his employer for negligence, bad faith, or dishonesty, but not for losses consequent upon mere errors of judgment.

Thus, a CPA has the duty to conduct an engagement using the same degree of care that would be used by an ordinary, prudent member of the public accounting profession. To recover against an auditor in a negligence case, the client must prove the following:

1. A duty owed to the client to conform to a required standard of care.
2. Failure to act in accordance with that duty.
3. A causal connection between the auditor's negligence and the client's damage.
4. Actual loss or damage to the client.

Suits by clients against auditors often allege that the auditors did not detect some type of fraud or defalcation. Auditors' defense against client negligence claims includes the following:

1. No duty was owed.
2. The client was negligent (contributory negligence, comparative negligence, or management fraud).
3. The auditor's work was performed in accordance with professional standards.
4. The client suffered no loss.
5. Any loss was caused by other events.
6. The claim is invalid because the statute of limitations has expired (statute limitations vary from jurisdiction to jurisdiction).

The client can generally prove the existence of a duty of care based on the engagement contract. However, the auditor may be able to argue successfully

---

[3]D. Haggard, *Cooley on Torts*, 4th ed., p. 472.

that the client's loss was due to the client's negligence. Some states permit a defense of contributory negligence as a complete bar to recovery by a client. However, most states follow the view of comparative negligence because it is not as harsh as an all-or-nothing approach. Under the comparative negligence view, the jury is permitted to assess the relative fault of the parties. For example, if a client's system of internal control is deficient because the client failed to provide adequate training or personnel, any recovery by the client against the auditor is reduced in proportion to the fault of the client. When top management of the client has engaged in fraud, the auditor may be able to attribute the fraud to the client and prevent recovery for a negligently performed audit. This defense has been used successfully by auditors, including in the well-known *Cenco, Inc.* v. *Seidman & Seidman,* which was a case that involved such circumstances. Exhibit 20–2 presents a summary of the case. In this instance, the client (new management) alleged that Seidman & Seidman was negligent for not having uncovered the prior management's fraudulent actions. The court ruled that, considering management's involvement in the fraud, the CPA firm had not been negligent.

Another well-known case that alleged negligence by an accountant is the *1136 Tenants' Corp.* v. *Max Rothenberg & Co.,* which relates to unaudited financial statements and the CPA's failure to communicate suspicious circumstances to the client. Exhibit 20–3 presents a summary of the case. The *1136 Tenants'* case established a duty on the part of a CPA doing work on unaudited financial statements to communicate to the client any circumstances that give reason to believe that fraud may exist. One outcome of this case was the establishment of Statements on Standards for Accounting and Review Services, which prescribe procedures that CPAs should follow when performing

EXHIBIT 20–2	*Cenco, Inc.* v. *Seidman & Seidman* (1982)

Between 1970 and 1975, managerial employees of Cenco, Inc., engaged in a massive fraud. The fraud began in the company's Medical/Health Division and eventually spread to Cenco's top management. By the time the fraud was made public, the chairman and president, plus a number of other top managers, were involved in the fraud. A number of the board of directors were not involved in the fraud, but there was evidence that they had been negligent in allowing the fraud to continue. Seidman & Seidman was Cenco's auditor throughout the period of the fraud.

The fraud involved primarily the inflating of inventories in the Medical/Health Division above their fair market value. This increased the apparent value of Cenco as well as its stock price. Thus, the fraud did not involve stealing from the company. Rather, the fraudsters had devised ways to steal from outsiders (e.g., creditors and insurers) to the benefit of existing shareholders.

Cenco's new management filed breach-of-contract, negligence, and fraud claims against Seidman & Seidman, and a trial date was set. One day before the start of the trial, Seidman & Seidman offered to pay $3.5 million to settle the class action suit, but Cenco turned the offer down. Prior to submitting the case to the jury, the trial judge granted a directed verdict in favor of Seidman & Seidman on the claim that the CPA firm had aided and abetted the fraud. The case went to the jury on the three remaining counts of breach of contract, negligence, and fraud. The jury found that Seidman & Seidman was innocent on all counts. The verdict was appealed by Cenco. The U.S. Court of Appeals upheld the lower court and found that Seidman & Seidman had not been responsible for any liability for breach of contract, negligence, or fraud. The court held that the auditors of a corporation could use the fraud of corporate managers as a defense to claims against the auditor by the corporation.

EXHIBIT 20-3	***1136 Tenants' Corp. v. Max Rothenberg & Co.* (1967)**

Jerome Riker was a powerful New York City businessman with extensive business interests in the real estate industry. During the early 1960s, Riker diverted money from a number of trust funds of cooperatives that he managed for use in a personal real estate investment.

One of the cooperatives that was involved in the embezzlement was the 1136 Tenants' Corporation. Riker had misappropriated approximately $130,000 of the cooperative's funds. When the cooperative was unable to recover the funds from Riker, it filed a civil suit against the public accounting firm, Max Rothenberg & Company, which had prepared the annual financial statements and tax return. The plaintiffs alleged that the accounting firm should have discovered the embezzlement of funds by Riker.

One issue that arose during the trial was the contractual agreement between the public accounting firm and the 1136 Tenants' Corporation. There was no written engagement letter, only an oral agreement between one of the firm's partners and Riker. The cooperative alleged that the firm had been retained to do an audit, while the firm alleged that it had been retained only to prepare the tax return and perform "write-up" services. Another issue was the fact that the firm had identified some missing invoices and had not investigated these items further. The working papers detailed $44,000 of expenses for which no supporting documentation could be located. These were fictitious expenses used by Riker to extract funds from the cooperative.

The court ruled that even if the firm had agreed to provide only write-up services, it had an obligation to notify the tenants about the suspicious nature of the missing invoices. Damaging to the firm's defense was the admission by one of its partners that the engagement had been more extensive than that called for by a normal write-up engagement. The income statement also included a line item labeled "audit." The court ruled in favor of the tenants and awarded them damages of more than $230,000. The decision was upheld upon appeal by the New York appellate court. The size of the judgment was far in excess of the fee of $600 paid to the firm.

This court decision resulted in two significant changes in the profession:

- It reinforced the need by firms to have *written* engagement letters.
- It led to the issuance by the AICPA of Statements on Standards for Accounting and Review Services.

engagements such as compilations and reviews (discussed in Chapter 21). However, the outcome of legal cases that have resulted from actions taken for compilation and review services has not removed public accountants from potential liability. For example, in *Robert Woller & Co.* v. *Fidelity Bank,* the court held the firm liable for problems in a company resulting from internal control weaknesses, even though SSARS No. 1 states that a review engagement does not contemplate a study and evaluation of internal control.

Fraud

An auditor can be held liable to clients for fraud when he or she acted with knowledge and intent to deceive. Generally, however, actions alleging fraud result from lawsuits by third parties and thus are discussed in more detail in the next section.

Common Law—Third Parties

☀ [LO 4]   Under common law, auditors can be held liable to third parties for negligence, gross negligence, and fraud. This area of liability is very complex, and court rulings are not always consistent across federal and state judicial jurisdictions.

Negligence

When an auditor fails to conduct an engagement with due care, he or she can be held liable for *ordinary negligence* to third parties (plaintiffs) under common law. To prevail in a suit alleging negligence, the third party must prove all of the following:

1. The auditor had a duty to the plaintiff to exercise due care.
2. The auditor breached that duty and was negligent in not following professional standards.
3. The auditor's breach of due care was the direct cause of the third party's injury (e.g., the financial statements were misleading and the third party relied on the financial statements).
4. The third party suffered an actual loss as a result.

The main difficulty faced by third parties in proving negligence against an auditor is showing that the auditor's duty to exercise due care extended to them. Over time, four common-law standards have evolved for determining the types of third parties that can successfully sue auditors for ordinary negligence. The four legal standards are *privity, near privity, foreseen third parties or (restatement standard),* and *reasonably foreseeable third parties.* The doctrine that will be applied in deciding a case depends on the precedents established in the location where the case is decided.

Privity   The most restrictive view under common law is that auditors have no liability to third parties who do not have a privity relationship with the auditor. Privity means that a contract or specific agreement exists between two parties. Third parties to a contract between an auditor and a client, such as investors or creditors of the client, typically lack privity because they were not directly involved in the agreement between the auditor and the client and thus cannot successfully sue the auditor, even if negligent. The landmark decision in this area, *Ultramares* v. *Touche, et al.,* held that the auditor was not liable to third parties who relied on a negligently prepared audit report. Exhibit 20–4 provides a summary of the Ultramares case. The rationale for this finding by the New York Court of Appeals is summarized in a famous quote by Judge Benjamin Cardozo:

> If a liability for negligence exists, a thoughtless slip or blunder, the failure to detect a theft or forgery beneath the cover of deceptive entries, may expose accountants to a liability in an indeterminate amount for an indeterminate time to an indeterminate class. The hazards of a business on these terms are so extreme as to enkindle doubt whether a flaw may not exist in the implication of a duty that exposes to these circumstances.

The privity standard does not apply under the *Ultramares* doctrine when the auditor is charged with fraud. Furthermore, while Judge Cardozo followed a strict privity doctrine in the *Ultramares* case, he opened the door for third parties without privity to sue if the negligence was so great as to constitute gross negligence or constructive fraud.

Near Privity   While the *Ultramares* decision held to a strict privity standard, a number of subsequent court decisions in other states have moved away from the strict privity standard over time. In 1985 the New York Court

EXHIBIT 20-4	***Ultramares. v. Touche, et al.* (1931)**

Fred Stern & Company imported and sold rubber during the 1920s. This industry required extensive working capital, and the company used borrowings from banks for its financing activities. In 1924 Stern requested a $100,000 loan from Ultramares Corporation. Before deciding to make the loan, Ultramares requested that Stern provide an audited balance sheet. Touche, Niven & Company had just issued an unqualified audit report on the December 31, 1923, balance sheet.

Stern's management asked Touche to provide 32 serially numbered copies of the audit report. Touche had audited Stern for three years and knew that the audit reports were being used by Stern to obtain external debt financing. Touche, however, did not know which specific banks or finance companies would be given the reports. The balance sheet showed assets of $2.5 million. Ultramares provided the $100,000 loan and two additional loans totaling $65,000. In addition, Stern obtained bank loans of approximately $300,000 by providing the December 31, 1923, balance sheet audited by Touche.

In 1925 the company declared bankruptcy. It came to light during the trial that Stern had already been bankrupt in 1923 and that false accounting record entries had concealed the company's problems. Ultramares alleged that Touche had been both negligent and fraudulent in its audit of Stern.

The jury in the case dismissed the fraud charges against Touche but ruled that Touche had been negligent and awarded approximately $186,000 in damages. The trial judge overturned the jury's verdict on the grounds that Ultramares had not been in privity with Touche. The appellate division of the New York Supreme Court voted 3 to 2 in favor of Ultramares, ruling that the judge had inappropriately overruled the jury verdict. Touche's attorneys appealed the decision to the court of appeals, which ruled unanimously in favor of Touche, therefore upholding the privity doctrine. The quote included in the text by Judge Cardozo, the chief justice of the court of appeals, summarizes the decision.

of Appeals expanded the privity standard in the case of *Credit Alliance* v. *Arthur Andersen & Co.* to include third parties whose relationship with the accountant approaches privity. In this lawsuit, Credit Alliance alleged that the auditor had known that the plaintiff was the client's principal lender and had frequently communicated with the plaintiff regarding the audited financial statements. The court upheld the lender's claim that Arthur Andersen had known that Credit Alliance was relying on the financial statements prior to extending credit. The court also ruled that there had been direct communication between the lender and the auditor regarding the client. The Credit Alliance case lists the following tests that must be satisfied for holding auditors liable for negligence to third parties: (1) the accountant must be aware that the financial statements are to be used for a particular purpose or purposes, (2) in the furtherance of which a known party or parties was intended to rely, and (3) there must have been some conduct on the part of the accountants linking them to that party or parties, which provides evidence of the accountants' understanding of intended reliance.

In a 1992 case, *Security Pacific Business Credit, Inc.* v. *Peat Marwick Main & Co.,* the New York Court of Appeals ruled in favor of Peat Marwick because the plaintiff's reliance was based on one telephone call to the firm's audit partner. Based on this case, it appears that a critical test established in the *Credit Alliance* case is the third test, the requirement that the third party be known to the auditor and that the auditor has directly conveyed the audit report or acted to induce reliance on the audit report. Most parties who are not in actual privity of contract with the auditors will not likely meet the demanding near privity standard, since the auditor will not have communicated directly with the plaintiff.

Foreseen Third Party or Restatement Standard   The approach followed by the vast majority of states (and federal courts located within those states) expands the class of third parties that can successfully sue an auditor for negligence beyond near privity to a person or limited group of persons whose reliance is actually *foreseen,* even if the specific person or group is unknown to the auditor. In essence, the courts in these jurisdictions have reexamined the notion of *caveat emptor* ("buyer beware") and substituted the concept of public responsibility. Among the reasons that have been advanced by the courts for extending the near privity standard are (1) the increased liability of other professionals to nonprivity users of their services, (2) the lack of fairness of imposing the burden of economic loss on innocent financial statement users, (3) the assumption that expanded liability will cause auditors to improve their auditing procedures, (4) the ability of auditors to obtain insurance against the increased risks, and (5) the ability of the auditors to pass the increased audit costs and insurance premiums on to their clients.

In 1968 a federal district court decision, *Rusch Factors, Inc.* v. *Levin,* applied Section 552 of the Restatement (Second) of the Law of Torts to an accountant's third-party liability suit. The case is described in Exhibit 20–5. Basically, a company engaged Levin to audit the financial statements for the purpose of obtaining financing from Rusch Factors. The statements portrayed the company as solvent. The plaintiff made a large loan to the company, which subsequently went bankrupt. The federal district court found the public accounting firm negligent, relying on Section 552 of the Restatement in reaching its decision.

The Restatement is a compendium of common law prepared by legal scholars and presents an alternative view to the traditional *Ultramares* rule. Section 552 states the following:

1. One who, in the course of his business, profession, or employment, or in a transaction in which he has a pecuniary interest, supplies false information for the guidance of others in their business transactions,

---

EXHIBIT 20–5	***Rusch Factors, Inc.* v. *Levin* (1968)**

In this case, the plaintiff, Rusch Factors, Inc., had requested audited financial statements as a prerequisite for providing a loan to a Rhode Island corporation. Levin audited the financial statements, which showed the company to be solvent when it was actually insolvent. Rusch Factors loaned the corporation $337,000 based on the audited financial statements. When the company went into receivership, Rusch Factors sued Levin for a loss of $121,000.

The federal district court, sitting in Rhode Island, denied Levin's motion to dismiss for a lack of privity. In finding Levin liable for negligence, the court concluded that the *Ultramares* doctrine was inappropriate and relied heavily on the Restatement (Second) of the Law of Torts. The court stated that the auditor had known that his certification was to be used and relied upon by Rusch Factors, and therefore he could be held liable for financial misrepresentations relied upon by *foreseen and limited classes of persons.*

is subject to liability for pecuniary loss caused to them by their justifiable reliance upon the information, if he fails to exercise reasonable care or competence in obtaining or communicating the information.

2. Except as stated in subsection (3), the liability stated in subsection (1) is limited to loss suffered (a) by the person or one of the persons for whose benefit and guidance he intends to supply the information, or knows that the recipient intends to supply it; and (b) through reliance upon it in a transaction which he intends the information to influence, or knows that the recipient so intends, or in a substantially similar transaction.

3. The liability of one who is under a public duty to give the information extends to loss suffered by any of the class of persons for whose benefit the duty is created, in any of the transactions in which it is intended to protect them.

The Restatement broadens the auditor's liability beyond those with near privity to a small group of persons and classes who are or should be foreseen by the auditor as relying on the financial information. However, because the language of the Restatement is general, it is subject to different interpretations. The following examples abstracted from the Restatement help illustrate the possibilities for auditor liability.

Example 1

> Cornelius Manufacturing Co. is negotiating for a $1,000,000 loan from the First National Bank of Sun City. The bank requires that Cornelius Manufacturing provide audited financial statements. Cornelius engages the public accounting firm of Cantbe & Mustbe (C&M) to conduct the audit, informing them that the audit is for the express purpose of obtaining credit from the First National Bank of Sun City. C&M accepts the engagement with the understanding that the financial statements are for the bank's use. The First National Bank of Sun City goes into bankruptcy, and Cornelius submits the audited financial statements to Waldo National Bank without communicating with C&M. Waldo National Bank lends Cornelius the $1,000,000. The financial statements materially overstate the financial resources of Cornelius, and Waldo National Bank suffers a loss on the loan. In this example, the Restatement indicates that C&M is not liable to Waldo National Bank because Waldo was *not* a foreseen third party.

Example 2

> The same facts apply as in Example 1, except that Cornelius says nothing to C&M about supplying the financial statements to the First National Bank of Sun City; Cornelius merely tells C&M that the company expects to negotiate a bank loan and is considering going to the First National Bank of Sun City. In this instance, the Restatement indicates that C&M would be liable to Waldo National Bank because Waldo was a foreseen third party.

Example 3

> The same facts apply as in Example 2, except that Cornelius informs C&M that the company is planning on negotiating a bank loan without mentioning a specific bank. Again, under the Restatement, C&M would be liable to Waldo National Bank because Waldo was a foreseen third party.

Subsequent to *Rusch Factors,* a number of federal and state courts have followed the approach outlined in the Restatement.

Reasonably Foreseeable Third Parties   The courts of three jurisdictions (Mississippi, New Jersey, and Wisconsin) have used a more expansive view of auditors' liability to third parties: *reasonably foreseeable third parties.* In the precedent-setting case in this area, *H. Rosenblum, Inc.* v. *Adler,* the New Jersey Supreme Court ruled that Touche Ross & Co. was responsible for damages incurred by all reasonably foreseeable third parties who had relied on the financial statements. Exhibit 20–6 provides more details on this case.[4]

Another important case that followed this approach was *Citizens State Bank* v. *Timm, Schmidt & Company* (1983). In this case, the bank sued the public accounting firm after relying on financial statements for one of its

EXHIBIT 20–6	*H. Rosenblum, Inc.* v. *Adler* (1983)

The Rosenblum family agreed to sell its retail catalog showroom business, H. Rosenblum, Inc., to Giant Stores in exchange for Giant common stock. The Rosenblums relied on Giant's 1971 and 1972 financial statements, which had been audited by Touche Ross & Co. A year later, it was revealed that Giant Stores' financial statements contained material misstatements. Giant Stores filed for bankruptcy, and the company's stock became worthless. The Rosenblums sued Touche, alleging negligence. Touche did not know the Rosenblums and had not known that the financial statements would be relied on during merger negotiations.

The lower courts in this case did not allow the Rosenblums' claims against Touche, on the grounds that the Rosenblums did not meet either the *Ultramares* privity test or the Restatement (Second) of the Law of Torts' "foreseen third parties" test. The New Jersey Supreme Court overturned the lower courts' decisions. The court held that the auditor had "a duty to all those whom the auditor should reasonably foresee as recipient from the company of the statements for its proper business purposes, provided that the recipients rely on the statements." Thus the court concluded that auditors should be liable to all reasonably foreseeable third parties who rely on the financial statements. The court indicated that the auditor's function had expanded from one of a watchdog for management to that of an independent evaluator of the adequacy and fairness of the financial statements presented by management to third parties. The court also cited the accountant's ability to obtain insurance against third-party claims.

---

[4]While the precedent set by the *Rosenblum* case in New Jersey has been followed by other states, subsequent legislation in New Jersey (1995) overturned *Rosenblum* and restricts auditor liability to the near privity standard. Recent court cases in New Jersey have upheld the near privity standard (e.g., *E. Dickerson & Sons, Inc.* v. *Ernst & Young, 2003*).

debtors that had been audited by Timm, Schmidt & Company. The Wisconsin court extended the scope of third parties to include all reasonably foreseeable users. The court used a number of the reasons just cited for extending auditors' liability beyond privity. The following quote from this case demonstrates the court's thoughts.

> If relying third parties, such as creditors, are not allowed to recover, the cost of credit to the general public will increase because creditors will either have to absorb the cost of bad loans made in reliance on faulty information or hire independent accountants to verify the information received. Accountants may spread the risk through the use of liability insurance.

One difficulty with this approach is that public accounting firms may not be able to secure sufficient liability insurance, or the cost of such insurance may be exorbitant.

Since 1987 no state high court has adopted the foreseeability approach to accountant liability, while a large number have approved or adopted one of the narrower standards.[5] For example, in the 1992 *Bily* v. *Arthur Young & Co.* the California Supreme Court expressly rejected the foreseeablity approach in favor of the Restatement standard. The court gave a number of reasons for rejecting the foreseeablity approach, including the foreseeability rule exposes auditors to potential liability in excess to their proportionate share and that sophisticated plaintiffs have other ways to protect themselves from the risk of inaccurate financial statements (i.e., they can negotiate improved terms or hire their own auditor).

However, in *Murphy* v. *BDO Seidman, LLP,* 2003, the California Court of Appeals ruled that "grapevine plaintiffs," who alleged indirect reliance based on what others (e.g., stockholders and stockbrokers) told them about the financial statements, had legal claims for negligence against the auditors so long as the auditor would have reasonably foreseen that stockholders or stockbrokers would tell other people of the content of the financial statements and that the other people would rely upon the misrepresentations in purchasing the corporate stock. The court ruled that nothing in the *Bily* decision precludes indirect reliance.

Auditor Defenses   The defenses presented under liability to clients above are also available to auditors sued by third parties for negligence under common law. In addition, depending on the jurisdiction, the auditor can argue that the third party does not qualify as a foreseen party or does not have near privity.

Fraud

If an auditor has acted with knowledge and intent to deceive a third party, he or she can be held liable for fraud. As noted earlier, common-law liability for fraud is not limited to persons in privity of contract with the auditor. The plaintiff (third party) must prove (1) a false representation by the accountant, (2) knowledge or belief by the accountant that the representation was

---

[5]See Chapter 4 in Goldwasser, Arnold, and Eickemeyer, *Accountants' Liability* (Practising Law Institute, 2003).

false, (3) that the accountant intended to induce the third party to rely on the false representation, (4) that the third party relied on the false representation, and (5) that the third party suffered damages. Courts have held that fraudulent intent may be established by proof that the accountant acted with knowledge of the false representation (referred to as *scienter*).

However, liability for fraud is not limited only to cases where the auditor was *knowingly* deceitful. Some courts have interpreted gross negligence as an instance of fraud (also referred to as *constructive fraud*). *Gross negligence* is defined to be an extreme, flagrant, or reckless deviation from professional standards of due care. An important case in this area is *State Street Trust Co.* v. *Ernst* (1938). In this case, the auditors issued an unqualified opinion on their client's financial statements, knowing that State Street Trust Company was making a loan based on those financial statements. A month later, the auditors sent a letter to the client indicating that receivables had been overstated. The auditors, however, did not communicate this information to State Street Trust Company, and the client subsequently went bankrupt. The New York court ruled that the auditor's actions appeared to be gross negligence and that "reckless disregard of consequences may take the place of deliberate intention."

The 1996 *Phar-Mor* case (discussed in the *Advanced Module* to this chapter) is another example of how auditors were found guilty of fraud under both common and statutory law, even though the plaintiffs acknowledged that the auditors had no intent to deceive. Instead, the plaintiff successfully argued reckless disregard for the truth which gives rise to an inference of fraud (i.e., gross negligence or constructive fraud). Thus, plaintiffs that are barred from suing for ordinary negligence, because they are not in privity or not forseen users, can opt to sue the auditor for fraud because to be found guilty under a fraud charge, the plaintiffs need only prove gross negligence.

In recent cases (e.g., *Houbigant, Inc.* v. *Deloitte & Touche LLP*, 2003, and *Reisman* v. *KPMG Peat Marwick LLP*, 2003) courts ruled that to be found guilty of fraud, the plaintiffs must only prove that the auditor was aware that its misrepresentations might reasonably be relied upon by the plaintiff, not that the auditor *intended* to induce the detrimental reliance. In the *Houbigant* decision the court referred to the recent audit failures in its decision:

> [I]t should be sufficient that the complaint contains some rational basis for inferring that the alleged misrepresentation was knowingly made. Indeed, to require anything beyond that would be particularly undesirable at this time, when it has been widely acknowledged that our society is experiencing a proliferation of frauds perpetrated by officers of large corporations . . . unchecked by the "impartial" auditors they hired.

Damages under Common Law

Plaintiffs who are awarded damages for a negligence or gross negligence claim against an auditor are eligible for compensatory damages, which means they are awarded damages to return them to a position equivalent to where they would have been in the absence of the auditor's negligence. Punitive damages are awarded to punish outrageous conduct and may be awarded when the auditor is found guilty of fraud or constructive fraud. Punitive damages are not permitted under federal statutory law, which provides plaintiffs incentive to file fraud charges under common law (often in addition to statutory fraud charges). However, The Securities Litigation Uniform Standards Act of 1998 (discussed below) forces certain fraud charges to be brought in federal court under statutory law.

Where the damages to the plaintiff can be apportioned between contributing parties, the auditor is only liable for his or her share of the total damages. If apportionment is not possible, some states follow the principle of *joint and several liability*. Joint and several liability means that the auditor can be responsible for the entire loss even if other parties contributed to the loss. Some courts have ruled that joint and several liability is inconsistent with the comparative fault concept, and some state legislatures have abolished joint and several liability in favor of a proportionate fault approach (i.e., if the auditor is found to be 30 percent at fault, he or she is only liable for 30 percent of the damages awarded).

Statutory Liability

Various statutes have been passed at both the federal and state levels that are intended to protect the public from malfeasance in the marketplace. While not aimed directly at auditors, these statutes do raise the potential for legal liability. The discussion in this chapter is limited to the major federal statutes.

The Securities Act of 1933, the Securities Exchange Act of 1934, and the Sarbanes-Oxley Act of 2002 are the three major statutes that provide sources of liability for auditors. On the other hand, the Private Securities Litigation Reform Act of 1995 and the Securities Litigation Uniform Standards Act of 1998 provide some protection for auditors, and others, from securities litigation. The Foreign Corrupt Practices Act and RICO are two other statutes that have the potential of imposing liability on auditors. The reader should also note that most states have securities laws and RICO statutes.

Securities Act of 1933
≈ [LO 5]

The Securities Act of 1933 generally regulates the disclosure of information in a registration statement for a *new* public offering of securities, whereas the Securities Exchange Act of 1934 regulates trading of securities *after* they are issued. The SEC's "S-forms" (e.g., S-1, S-2) are filed in connection with registration of securities under the 1933 act. Common forms filed under the 1934 act include the 10-K (annual report), 10-Q (quarterly reports) and the 8-K (material events).While a number of sections of the Securities Act of 1933 may subject auditors to liability, Section 11 imposes a liability on issuers and others, including auditors, for losses suffered by third parties when false or misleading information is included in a registration statement. Section 11 states:

(a) *Persons possessing cause of action; persons liable.* In case any part of the registration statement, when such part became effective, contained an untrue statement of a material fact or omitted to state a material fact required to be stated therein or necessary to make the statements therein not misleading, any person acquiring such security (unless it is proved that at the time of such acquisition he knew of such untruth or omission) may, either at law or in equity, in any court of competent jurisdiction, sue—

(4) every accountant . . . who has with his consent been named as having prepared or certified any part of the registration statement. . . .

In contrast to the situation under common law, the plaintiff does not have to prove negligence or fraud, reliance on the auditor's opinion, a causal relationship, or a contractual relationship; the plaintiff need only prove that a loss was suffered by investing in the registered security and that the audited financial statements contained a material omission or misstatement. The misstatement can be the result of mere ordinary negligence. Section 11 is more favorable for plaintiffs than is common law because the burden of proof is shifted to the *auditor* to prove that he or she was not negligent. In other words, the auditor is presumed to have been negligent unless he or she can prove otherwise. The extremely plaintiff-friendly legal standards under the 1933 act reflects the fact that audited financial statements are typically more crucial for purchase decisions for new public offerings because few other credible sources of information are typically available for new issues.

One defense available to the auditor sued under Section 11 is that of "due diligence." That is, the auditor must have made a reasonable investigation of the facts supporting or contradicting the information included in the registration statement. Such an investigation should be similar to one that a prudent person would make under similar circumstances. A leading case under Section 11 is *Escott* v. *BarChris Construction Corp.,* in which the court held that the auditor's actions for events subsequent to the audited balance sheet had not been conducted with due diligence. In this instance, the senior auditor reviewing subsequent events had not spent sufficient time on this important task and had accepted glib answers to key questions. The court determined that there had been sufficient danger signals that further investigation was necessary. The *Escott* v. *BarChris Construction Corp.* case is also of interest because of the court's ruling on certain accounting matters and its determination of materiality. A detailed summary of this case is provided on the book's website (www.mhhe.com/ messier4e).

A more recent and significant case under Section 11 and other sections of the 1933 act was *Bernstein* v. *Crazy Eddie, Inc.* Crazy Eddie, Inc., made a number of public offerings of securities. Then the founder and president of the company resigned, and the successor management team discovered that the financial statements issued by the company during the public offering were fraudulent. The company's financial statements had been misstated through inflated inventory and improper transactions by the founder and his family. The court ruled against the auditors, indicating that the plaintiffs did not have to prove fraud or gross negligence. They had to prove only that the misstated information was material. Exhibit 20–7 describes the case.

Other important cases tried under the Securities Act of 1933 are Continental Vending (*United States* v. *Simon*) and National Student Marketing (*United States* v. *Natelli*). Both cases resulted in criminal proceedings against the auditor, and are described on the book's website (www.mhhe.com/ messier4e).

EXHIBIT 20–7	*Bernstein* v. *Crazy Eddie, Inc.* (1989)

Eddie Antar was the founder of and major shareholder in Crazy Eddie. The company made several public offerings of securities, including the sale of shares held by Eddie Antar and his family. The prospectuses and financial statements from 1984 through 1987 erroneously gave the impression that Crazy Eddie was a rapidly growing firm. When Mr. Antar resigned his position as president, the successor management discovered that the financial statements issued prior to and included in the public offerings had been materially misstated. In particular, there was an estimated inventory shortage of $65 million, and the company's net worth was now only $7 million.

The financial statements had been misstated by a number of schemes. Net income and inventory had been inflated through improper financial reporting practices. First, inventory marked for return to manufacturers had been included as inventory merchandise. Second, certain consignments had been treated as sales. Last, there had been related inventory sales to the founder and members of his family that were later resold to others. The company had also overstated per-store sales figures. All of these actions appear to have been taken to support the price of Crazy Eddie stock and to directly benefit Mr. Antar and his family. The discovery of the extent of the problems was complicated by the fact that certain documents had been altered or destroyed prior to the new management's assuming control.

The plaintiffs in this case were purchasers of the company's stock prior to the disclosure of the fraudulent financial statements. They sued the public accounting firm, the board of directors, and others, alleging that the accounting firm had violated GAAS and GAAP by failing to uncover the company's fraudulent and fictitious activities. The plaintiffs were able to show that the certified financial statements in the registration statements and prospectuses had been false and misleading in violation of Sections 11 and 12 of the Securities Act of 1933.

The court ruled against the public accounting firm and upheld the plaintiffs' Section 11 and 12 claims. The court held that the plaintiffs did not have to prove fraud or gross negligence, only that any material misstatement in the registration statements was misleading.

Securities Exchange Act of 1934

✻ [LO 6]

This statute is concerned primarily with ongoing reporting by companies whose securities are listed and traded on a stock exchange or that meet certain other statutory requirements. Typical reporting requirements under the 1934 act include the quarterly filing of a 10Q Form, the annual filing of a 10K Form, and the periodic filing of an 8K Form whenever a significant event takes place affecting the entity. While a number of sections of this statute may have liability consequences for the auditor, two sections are particularly important: Section 18 and Section 10(b), including Rule 10b-5.

Section 18 imposes liability on any person who makes a material false or misleading statement in documents filed with the Securities and Exchange Commission (SEC). The auditor's liability can be limited if the auditor can show that he or she "acted in good faith and had no knowledge that such statement was false or misleading." However, a number of cases have limited the auditor's good-faith defense when the auditor's action has been judged to be grossly negligent.

Perhaps the greatest source of liability for auditors under the 1934 act is Section 10(b) and the related Rule 10b-5. Section 10(b) provides for a wide scope of liability. Rule 10b-5 amplifies Section 10(b) and states that it is

unlawful for any person, directly or indirectly, by the use of any means or instrumentality of interstate commerce, or of the mails, or of any facility of any national securities exchange,

  a. To employ any device, scheme, or artifice to defraud,

b. To make any untrue statement of a material fact or to omit to state a material fact necessary in order to make the statement made, in the light of the circumstances under which they were made, not misleading, or

c. To engage in any act, practice, or course of business which operates or would operate as a fraud or deceit upon any person, in connection with the purchase or sale of any security.

Once a plaintiff has established that he or she can sue under Rule 10b-5, the following elements must be proved:

1. A material, factual misrepresentation or omission.
2. Reliance by the plaintiff on the financial statements.
3. Damages suffered as a result of reliance on the financial statements.
4. Scienter.

The first element can include materially misleading information or the omission of material information. The fourth element, *scienter*, is defined as intent to deceive, manipulate, or defraud. However, some courts have ruled that gross negligence or reckless behavior is sufficient to satisfy the fourth element.

A number of important cases have used Section 10(b) and Rule 10b-5 as a basis for actions against auditors. In *Herzfeld* v. *Laventhol, Krekstein, Horwath & Horwath* (1974), the U.S. district court allowed recovery by an investor. The investor had purchased securities from the client prior to an audit conducted by Laventhol. After the audit, the client offered to refund all investments made prior to the audit. The plaintiff declined the refund based on the audited financial statements and lost his investment when the company went bankrupt a year later. The plaintiff sued, claiming that the financial statements had been false and misleading because profits from the sale of properties were reported in the income statement even though there was some uncertainty about the collectibility of the related receivables. Laventhol's opinion was qualified "subject to" the collectibility of the receivables. The court held that the disclosure of the qualification footnote had been inadequate and that Laventhol was liable "because of their active participation in the preparation and issuance of false and materially misleading accounting reports upon which Herzfeld relied to his damage."

In *Ernst & Ernst* v. *Hochfelder*, which is described in more detail in Exhibit 20–8, the president of a brokerage firm, Leston Nay, induced brokerage customers to invest in high-yield accounts that he personally managed. The accounts were fictitious, and he used the funds for his own purposes. Nay was able to conceal this scheme by having a rule that only he was to open mail addressed to him. The defrauded customers sued Ernst & Ernst, arguing that they, as auditors, should have been aware of the mail rule and that such knowledge would have led to discovery of the fraud. Ernst & Ernst argued that Rule 10b-5 did not encompass negligent behavior. The U.S. Supreme Court ruled that an action under Rule 10b-5 may not be maintained by showing that the defendant was negligent; the rule requires that scienter, or intent to deceive, be present. Unfortunately, the Supreme Court did not decide whether reckless behavior was sufficient for liability under Section 10(b) or Rule 10b-5. However, a number of subsequent decisions by lower courts have recognized that reckless behavior or

EXHIBIT 20-8	***Ernst & Ernst* v. *Hochfelder et al.* (1976)**

Leston Nay was the president and principal owner of First Securities Company of Chicago, a small brokerage firm. Nay induced brokerage customers to invest in a high-yield escrow syndicate that loaned money to companies experiencing working capital shortages. The investors were promised above-average returns on their investments. Nay converted his investors' money to his personal use. The fraud became public when Nay committed suicide after concluding that he could no longer conceal the scheme from some of his investors.

The investors eventually sued Ernst & Ernst, the public accounting firm that had audited First Securities Company, alleging that the firm had aided and abetted Nay's fraud by failing to detect Nay's "mail rule." Nay had forbidden anyone to open mail addressed directly to him. He had used this tactic to conceal the existence of the escrow syndicate from First Securities and the auditors. The investors charged Ernst & Ernst with negligence.

The civil lawsuit against Ernst & Ernst charged violation of Section 10(b) and Rule 10b-5 of the Securities Exchange Act of 1934. The federal district court dismissed the lawsuit, contending that there was no substantive evidence that the firm had been negligent in auditing First Securities. The court of appeals reversed the lower court's decision and ordered a trial. Ernst & Ernst appealed the court of appeals' decision to the U.S. Supreme Court. The Court held that an action under Rule 10b-5 could not be maintained by simply showing that the defendant had been negligent. The plaintiff had to prove that the defendant had acted with *scienter,* a manipulative intent to deceive. The Court, however, did not decide whether "reckless behavior" would be considered equivalent to scienter and thus violate Rule 10b-5. Lower-court decisions have found that reckless behavior can be used to maintain an action against an auditor under Section 10(b).

gross negligence by the auditor satisfies the scienter requirement of Rule 10b-5. Reckless conduct is behavior that represents an extreme departure from standards of ordinary care, that is, failure to see the obvious or a disregard for the truth.

Prior to 1994, courts frequently held that an auditor who was not liable as a primary violator of Section 10(b) and Rule 10b-5 could still be held liable *aiding and abetting* if the auditor had knowledge and had substantially assisted in the primary violation. In 1994 the Supreme Court held in *Central Bank* v. *First Interstate Bank* that there is no aiding and abetting liability under Section 10(b). However, as a result of the numerous accounting frauds disclosed in the last few years, bills have been introduced in Congress to restore aiding and abetting liability in private damage actions.

The issue of what is necessary to establish primary liability under Section 10(b) can be significant in determining when an individual accountant may be held liable. This is an issue in the litigation arising out of the Enron-Andersen collapse. While Andersen as a firm clearly made statements that permit Section 10(b) claims, stating primary liability claims against most of the individual Andersen defendants has proved difficult for plaintiffs. See Exhibit 20–9 (see page 804) for more information on the Enron-Andersen litigation.

The proper measure of damages in most Section 10(b) and Rule 10b-5 cases is the out-of-pocket loss suffered by the plaintiff. The out-of-pocket loss is the difference between what the plaintiff paid or received for the securities and what he or she would have paid or received had there been no wrongful conduct by the auditor. Punitive damages are not permitted in a Section 10(b) or Rule 10b-5 action, although, as noted earlier, such damages can sometimes be recovered in a concurrent common-law fraud action.

In the wake of the Enron and Worldcom accounting frauds, the Sarbanes-Oxley Act lengthened the statute of limitations for actions under Section 10(b) and Rule 10b-5 based on claims of "fraud, deceit, manipulation, or contrivance in contravention of a regulatory requirement concerning the securities laws." The Sarbanes-Oxley Act provides that any action shall be brought no later than two years from discovery and within five years from when the fraudulent conduct occurred. This provision was the only portion of Sarbanes-Oxley that specifically affected private securities fraud actions. The prior statute of limitations was one and three years, respectively.

The *Advanced Module* to this chapter covers a legal case that fell under the Securities Exchange Act of 1934: *Phar-Mor*. The book's website (www.mhhe.com/messier4e) describes two other recent cases: Continental Vending and Mini-Scribe.

Private Securities Litigation Reform Act of 1995[6] and the Securities Litigation Uniform Standards Act of 1998

⚭ [LO 7]

Prior to the passage of the Private Securities Litigation Reform Act of 1995, auditors sued under federal statutory law were held to the legal doctrine of *joint and several liability*, which holds each defendant fully liable for all assessed damages, regardless of the extent to which he or she contributed to the injury. This legislation provides, in general, for *proportionate liability*, where each defendant is liable solely for the portion of the damages that corresponds to the percentage of responsibility of that defendant. The act also raises the pleading requirement at the beginning of a case. For example, no longer can plaintiffs plead a general claim of fraud and then use discovery proceedings to conduct a "fishing expedition" in the auditors' workpapers and files in search for actionable conduct. Rather, the Act requires that misrepresentation claims state the time, place, and contents of the allegedly false representations, the identity of the person making them, and what he or she obtained as a result of the fraud. This may discourage "deep-pockets" lawsuits where plaintiffs hope to pressure defendants to settle out of court because the legal costs to fight the lawsuit may be greater than the costs to settle.

In response to concerns that plaintiff lawyers would attempt to circumvent the Private Securities Litigation Reform Act of 1995 by bringing class action suits involving nationally traded securities to state court, Congress passed the Securities Litigation Uniform Standards Act of 1998. The purpose of the Uniform Standards Act was to "prevent plaintiffs from seeking to evade the protections that Federal law provides against abusive litigation by filing suit in State, rather than Federal Court." The primary federal protections to which the Act refers are proportionate liability, disallowed punitive damages, and higher filing standards. As a result of the Uniform Standards Act, most large class actions against auditors alleging securities fraud must now be brought in federal court. The Uniform Standards Act defines a "covered class action" to include any lawsuit or group of lawsuits

---

[6]See R. R. King and R. Schwartz, "The Private Securities Litigation Reform Act of 1995: A Discussion of Three Provisions," *Accounting Horizons* (March 1997), pp. 92–106, for a detailed discussion of this statute.

where damages are sought on behalf of more than 50 persons. Thus, smaller class actions lawsuits can still be pursued in state court. In an attempt to circumvent the Uniform Standards Act, attorneys brought a number of Enron-related lawsuits in Texas state court with each suit filed on behalf of fewer than 50 persons.[7]

Sarbanes-Oxley Act of 2002

⬝ [LO 8]

The Sarbanes-Oxley Act of 2002 is considered the most sweeping securities law since the 1933 and 1934 Acts. Its main objectives are to restore investor confidence in the securities markets and to deter future corporate frauds. The Act does include sections directly addressing legal liability, but the other aspects of the Act (e.g., the creation of the PCAOB, stricter independence rules, audits of internal controls, and increased reporting responsibilities) are more important to auditors' performance and create new federal laws that the auditor must comply with. The creation of the PCAOB is the single most significant aspect of the legislation, ending decades of self-regulation by the accounting profession. While the Sarbanes-Oxley Act and PCAOB standards and enforcement actions only relate to public company auditors, state boards of accountancy may very well adopt or refer to the PCAOB rules in carrying out their regulatory functions for all public accountants.

Although Congress created and passed the Sarbanes-Oxley Act, as is customary with similar legislation, Congress did not develop the detailed accounting and securities rules and regulations needed to execute the Act's provisions. Instead, the Act delegates substantial authority and responsibility to the SEC to create the detailed rules and regulations. For example, Section 302 of the Sarbanes-Oxley Act directed the SEC to create rules requiring CEO and CFO certification of periodic financial reports within 30 days of the legislation's signing, which the SEC did in August 2002.[8]

The Act does not prohibit the SEC from extending the rules beyond what is required by the Act. For instance, Section 802 stipulates that audit firms must retain their audit documentation for a period of five years, while the SEC's final ruling extends the period to seven years. Failure to retain audit documentation can result in fines and imprisonment for up to 10 years.

Some of the most important provisions of the Sarbanes-Oxley Act are aimed at increasing the responsibility of corporate officers and directors for the reliability of their company's financial statements. Congress understood that the primary culprits in corporate fraud are dishonest officers and directors. Sections 302 and 906 of the Act require the chief executive and chief financial officers of each public company to certify personally, among other things, the fairness of the financial information and the company's compliance with the 1934 Act in each annual or quarterly report filed with the SEC.

---

[7]As a result of the discovery of numerous accounting frauds in 2001–2003, bills have been introduced in Congress that would restore joint and several liability in securities fraud cases. While none of these provisions was enacted as part of the Sarbanes-Oxley Act, future efforts to return to joint and several liability are likely.

[8]U.S. Securities Exchange Commission, "Final Rule: Certification of Disclosure in Companies' Quarterly and Annual Reports" (Release No. 33-8124, August 2002).

Rather than address the various legal liability aspects of the Act in this section, we discuss them in the pertinent sections which follow because most of the legal liability legislation in the Sarbanes-Oxley Act represents enhancements or revisions to existing laws.

SEC and PCAOB Sanctions

⚇ [LO 9]

Rule 2(e) of the Rules of Practice empowers the SEC to suspend for any person the privilege of appearing and practicing before it if that person

1. Has been convicted of a misdemeanor involving moral turpitude.
2. Has been convicted of a felony.
3. Has had his or her license to practice as an accountant suspended or revoked.
4. Has been permanently enjoined from violating provisions of the federal securities laws.
5. Has been found by the commission in an administrative proceeding or by a court of competent jurisdiction to have violated provisions of the federal securities laws.

This sanction can be applied not only to an individual auditor but also to an entire accounting firm. If a firm is suspended or barred from practice before the SEC, the impact on the firm's clients can be severe. For example, if a firm is suspended, its clients may not be able to file their reports with the SEC on a timely basis. Typically, if a firm is faced with suspension, it will work out some type of consent agreement in which the firm does not admit guilt but agrees to lesser sanctions. These sanctions may include not taking on new SEC clients for a specified period and subjecting the firm to special reviews to ensure that the alleged problems have been corrected. For example as noted in the preface to Chapter 19, in 2004 Ernst & Young was sanctioned by the SEC for violating independence standards during the audit of PeopleSoft for the years 1994–1999. The sanctions included fines and a six-month suspension from accepting new SEC registrant audit clients.

The SEC can also impose fines, such as the $7 million fine imposed in 2001 upon Arthur Andersen in connection with audits of Waste Management. The Waste Management case was particularly egregious because Andersen agreed to a plan to cover up Waste Management's financial misstatements by reversing them over a period of years rather than correcting them immediately. It also followed on the heels of other Andersen audit failures at Sunbeam Corporation and the Baptist Foundation, and was a foreshadowing of the Enron and Worldcom failures disclosed within a year of the fine.

A study of SEC sanctions imposed on auditors for their association with fraudulently misstated financial statements found that the most common problems cited were the auditor's failure to gather sufficient audit evidence, properly apply GAAP, exercise due professional care and an appropriate level of professional skepticism, and properly tailor audit procedures to address inherent risk.[9]

---

[9]M. Beasley, J. Carcello, and D. Hermanson, "Lessons from Fraud-Related SEC Cases: Top 10 Audit Deficiencies," *Journal of Accountancy* (April 2001).

The Sarbanes-Oxley Act grants the PCAOB broad investigative and disciplinary authority over registered public accounting firms and persons associated with such firms. As directed by the Act, the board adopted rules relating to investigations and adjudications in September 2003. Under the adopted rules, the PCAOB may conduct investigations concerning any acts or practices involving auditors of publicly traded firms that may "violate any provision of the Act, the rules of the Board, the provisions of the securities laws relating to the preparation and issuance of audit reports and the obligations and liabilities of accountants with respect thereto, including the rules of the SEC issued under the Act, or professional standards."

When violations are detected, the board has the authority to impose sanctions. The sanctions can include revoking a firm's registration, barring a person from participating in audits of public companies, monetary penalties and requirements for remedial measures, such as training, new quality control procedures, and the appointment of an independent monitor. The PCOAB's rules, disciplinary decisions, and sanctions are subject to the approval of the SEC.

Foreign Corrupt Practices Act

❧ [LO 10]

The Foreign Corrupt Practices Act (FCPA) was passed by Congress in 1977 in response to the discovery of bribery and other misconduct on the part of more than 300 American companies. The Act was codified in 1988 as an amendment to the Securities Exchange Act of 1934. As a result, an auditor may be subject to administrative proceedings, civil liability, and civil penalties under the FCPA. The FCPA prohibits corporate officers from knowingly participating in bribing foreign officials to obtain or retain business. The FCPA also imposes record-keeping and internal control requirements on public companies. Basically, corporations must keep their books, records, and accounts in sufficient detail to accurately reflect transactions. Companies are also required to develop and maintain adequate systems of internal control. To comply with the provisions of the FCPA, many corporations have established codes of conduct that prohibit bribery. Compliance with corporate codes of conduct should be checked by the audit committee and the internal auditors. The external auditor may detect activities that violate the FCPA; such violations should be communicated to management immediately. Guidance for such reporting can be found in AU 325 Communication of Internal Control–Related Matters in an Audit, and AU 380 Communications with Audit Committees. These standards were covered in Chapters 6 and 17, respectively.

Racketeer Influenced and Corrupt Organizations Act

❧ [LO 11]

Although the Racketeer Influenced and Corrupt Organizations Act (RICO) was enacted by Congress in 1970 to combat the infiltration of legitimate businesses by organized crime, it has been used against auditors. RICO provides civil and criminal sanctions for certain types of illegal acts. A major factor in bringing an action under RICO is that the law provides for treble damages in civil RICO cases. Racketeering activity includes a long list of federal and state crimes, with mail fraud and wire fraud the most common acts alleged against auditors. For example, the federal mail fraud statute provides that

> Whoever, having devised or intending to devise any scheme or artifice to defraud, or for obtaining money or property by means of false or fraudulent pretenses, representations, or promises . . . for the purpose of executing such scheme or artifice or attempting to do so, places in any post office or authorized depository for mail matter, any matter or thing whatever to be sent or delivered by the Postal Service, or takes or receives therefrom, any such matter or thing, or knowingly causes to be delivered by mail according to the direction thereon, or at the place at which it is directed to be delivered by the person to whom it is addressed, any such matter or thing, shall be fined not more than $1,000 or imprisoned not more than five years, or both.

The wire fraud statute is similar, except that it relates to the use of wire, radio, or television communication to perpetrate the fraud.

Generally, a single instance of racketeering activity is not sufficient to establish a pattern of racketeering. In a recent case, *Reves* v. *Ernst & Young* (1993), the Supreme Court established an "operations and management test" for auditors that requires that the plaintiff prove that the accounting firm participated in the operation or management of the client's business. A number of lower courts have followed the Supreme Court and dismissed similar RICO claims against auditors.[10] The significance of the *Reves* v. *Ernst & Young* case is that auditors are less likely to settle out of court in RICO cases merely to avoid the possibility of treble damages. A description of this case is presented on the book's website (www.mhhe.com/messier4e).

Prior to the Private Securities Litigation Reform Act of 1995, securities fraud was an offense under RICO. The reform act eliminated securities fraud as an offense in civil suits under RICO unless the auditor is criminally convicted of the fraud. Thus, experts believe that after the reform act, Section 10(b) and Rule 10b-5 violations will almost never be grounds for a civil damage claim against an auditor under RICO.[11] As a result of the wave of massive accounting frauds disclosed in 2000–2002, a bill was introduced in Congress to restore securities fraud as a basis for a civil RICO damage claim. However, this bill was not passed, and the Sarbanes-Oxley Act of 2002 did not restore securities fraud as a basis for a civil RICO damage claim.

Criminal Liability

[LO 8,12] Auditors can be held criminally liable under the laws discussed in the previous sections. In addition, auditors can be held criminally liable for various federal and state laws, such as banking and insurance regulations. Criminal prosecutions require that some form of criminal intent be present. However, many of the laws described in this chapter contain provisions for criminal penalties to be levied if an auditor's actions reflect gross negligence. In a famous quote from *United States* v. *Benjamin*, the Court stated that an auditor would be held criminally liable if he "deliberately closed his eyes to facts he had a duty to see . . . or recklessly stated as facts things of which he was ignorant."

---

[10]*Journal of Accountancey* (May 1993), p. 24; *Journal of Accountancy* (October 1994), pp. 119–22.

[11]See Chapter 5 in Goldwasser, Arnold, and Eickemeyer, *Accountants' Liability* (Practising Law Institute, 2003).

A number of significant cases against auditors have resulted in criminal prosecution, with auditors being given large fines and serving time in prison. Included among these cases are Continental Vending (*United States* v. *Simon*), National Student Marketing (*United States* v. *Natelli*), Equity Funding (*United States* v. *Weiner*), and ESM Government Securities, Inc. (*In re Alexander Grant & Co. Litigation*). Note that in addition to criminal prosecution of the auditors, the auditors' firms were civilly liable for violating various statutes and paid large sums to settle the cases. These cases are described on the book's website (www.mhhe.com/messier4e).

Of course, the most damaging criminal conviction against an audit firm came in June 2002, when Arthur Andersen was found guilty ofone count of obstruction of justice in the Enron investigation (see Exhibit 20–9).

Numerous sections of the Sarbanes-Oxley Act include criminal provisions, the Act enhances prosecutorial tools available in major fraud cases by expanding statutory prohibitions against fraud and obstruction of justice,

---

EXHIBIT 20–9   **Enron Corp. and Arthur Andersen LLP**

Enron Corporation, based in Houston, Texas, was formed as a result of the 1985 merger of Houston Natural Gas and InterNorth Inc. In its early years, Enron was a traditional natural gas pipeline company, delivering natural gas to businesses and utilities. However, changes in the government regulations of electrical power markets opened the door for change. Enron transformed itself into a market maker for numerous different energy-related commodities. Enron's stock price surged during the late 1990s, moving Enron into the spotlight of U.S. business. It became the seventh largest company in the United States and was praised for being one of America's most innovative companies.

In 2001, after showing profits for the previous several years, Enron reported a third quarter loss of $618 million and a $1.2 billion reduction in owner's equity related to off-balance sheet partnerships. The news resulted in a sharp drop in Enron's stock price and a formal SEC inquiry. On November 8, 2001, Enron announced that it had overstated profits by $586 million, erasing almost all its profits from the past five years, collapsing the stock price, and diminishing the confidence of its clients. Within a month of this announcement, Enron filed for Chapter 11 bankruptcy. At the time, Enron was the one of the largest corporate bankruptcies in history.

The Enron collapse involved many players, including company executives, investment bankers, financial analysts, and accountants. Enron's auditor Arthur Andersen, one of the largest national accounting firms at the time, quickly became the source of public scrutiny.

The government's investigation of Enron's accounting practices revealed a number of accounting improprieties, including misuse of special-purpose entities (SPE) to sell off underperforming assets at a profit. Because of undisclosed Enron guarantees related to the transactions, most of these "sales" were really schemes to overstate "paper" gains and understate liabilities.

Fueled by a public uproar, the government began criminal proceedings. The Justice Department accused top Andersen officials of directing employees to alter and/or shred Enron-related documents after it knew about the SEC investigation. In June 2002, Andersen was found guilty of one count of obstruction of justice, fined $500,000, and sentenced to five years' probation. However, the criminal indictment in itself so severely harmed Andersen's reputation that clients fled and the firm essentially liquidated within months.

In 2004 Andrew Fastow, Enron's former CFO and principal player in the company's accounting schemes, pleaded guilty to two counts of conspiracy, agreed serve the maximum 10-year sentence, and became the highest-ranking Enron executive to cooperate with the government.

increasing criminal penalties for traditional fraud and cover-up crimes, and strengthening sentencing guidelines applicable to large-scale financial frauds. The Act adds a new securities fraud offense and increases authorized penalties for securities and financial reporting fraud (e.g., up to 25 years in prison). It is expected that the Act's increased penalties will result in longer prison terms because of the corresponding changes in the federal sentencing guidelines.

The Sarbanes-Oxley Act increases penalties for impeding official investigations, and because most frauds are discovered by employees rather than external auditors, the Act strengthens the legal protections accorded whistleblowers. It is common for employers to retaliate against informants by demoting or firing them. The Act makes it a felony punishable by 10-year imprisonment to retaliate against anyone who voluntarily comes forward to report suspected violations of any federal laws.

As we noted in the last chapter, individual ethics and integrity cannot be legislated. As such, the Sarbanes-Oxley Act will not be a cure-all for corporate reform. Greed, mismanagement, conflicts of interest, and professional failures will never completely disappear. However, most observers in the legal and accounting professions generally believe that the reforms imposed by the Sarbanes-Oxley Act were needed, will contribute to improved governance, and will send a signal that society does not tolerate widespread deceit in financial reporting.

Approaches to Minimizing Legal Liability

[LO 13]   Everyone involved with the public accounting profession has an interest in minimizing auditors' exposure to legal liability. Lawsuits against public accountants not only result in direct financial effects such as large settlement costs but also impact the profession and society in other ways. For example, many public accounting firms have seen their costs of defending such lawsuits, including management time and their insurance premiums, increase dramatically in recent years. The firms have also suffered significant blows to their reputations through the negative publicity arising from litigation. To reduce practice risk, many public accounting firms adopt client acceptance strategies that may avoid entire industries. Some small to medium-size public accounting firms are limiting or abandoning their audit practices. A number of steps can be taken by the profession and by individual firms to minimize legal liability.

At the Profession Level

The public accounting profession, through the AICPA, PCAOB, state boards of accountancy, and state societies, can do a number of things to reduce its exposure to legal liability. These include

- ***Establishing stronger auditing and attestation standards.*** While adherence to auditing standards (and GAAP) is a minimum defense against lawsuits, the profession should strive to issue standards that require the best form of practice. This includes revising standards to address practice problems that are revealed through litigation.

- *Continually updating the Code of Professional Conduct and sanctioning members who do not comply with it.* The profession should continually revise the Code of Professional Conduct to reflect acceptable practices that meet users' needs. Recent changes to the auditor independence rules are an example of the types of changes needed. Unfortunately, the most significant changes to the independence rules were forced on the profession by the SEC and the Sarbanes-Oxley Act. The profession needs to take the lead in maintaining an appropriately strong code of Professional Conduct. Members who do not comply with the code should be sanctioned to demonstrate the profession's willingness to discipline members who act unprofessionally. The PCAOB is expected to be vigilant in investigating and punishing unethical and unprofessional conduct by auditors of publicly traded companies.

- *Educating users.* In recent years, the profession has undertaken a number of actions to close the "expectation gap," including revision of a number of important auditing standards. These revisions clarified auditors' responsibilities for issues such as errors and fraud, illegal acts, going-concern evaluation, and internal control evaluations. The wording in the auditor's report was also revised so as to better communicate to users what an audit entails. The profession needs an ongoing program to educate the public about auditors' activities.

At the Firm Level

Individual public accounting firms can also take steps to avoid litigation. These include

- *Instituting sound quality control and review procedures.* A system of quality control and review can give the firm reasonable assurance of conforming with professional standards. Chapter 19 provided detailed coverage of quality control and review.

- *Ensuring that members of the firm are independent.* Members of the firm must be independent in both fact and appearance. A review of legal cases indicates that on numerous occasions auditors did not maintain a sufficiently high level of "professional skepticism" and accepted a client's responses without investigating the facts adequately.

- *Following sound client acceptance and retention procedures.* Auditors need to be very careful in accepting new clients. If a client is known to lack integrity, the likelihood increases that its management will take actions that are detrimental to user groups, including management fraud.

- *Being alert to risk factors that may result in lawsuits.* A number of important risk factors seem to lead to litigation. These include the presence of management fraud, the commission of illegal acts, insolvency, disagreements between auditors and management, first-year audits, and acquisition audits. For example, when management fraud occurs, auditors are usually subject to litigation, and such cases are more costly to resolve. Some audit deficiencies have also been noted in the litigation against public accounting firms. These include incomplete client acceptance or retention procedures, unrealistic risk assessments given the client's circumstances, staff that is inadequately trained to audit specialized industries, inadequate documentation of difficult decisions, insufficient partner and manager participation in resolving key issues, and excessive reliance on management representations.

- ***Performing and documenting work diligently.*** A quality audit involves following relevant professional standards and includes (1) planning properly, (2) understanding the client's internal control adequately, (3) obtaining sufficient competent evidence as to financial assertions, (4) having experienced personnel review the work done, and (5) issuing an appropriate audit report.

The threat of legal liability serves to prevent or limit inappropriate behavior on the part of auditors. However, auditors cannot be expected to ensure the accuracy of either financial statements or the financial health of a business entity. The auditor's responsibility is to provide reasonable assurance that there are no material misstatements in the financial statements.

Advanced Module: A View of an Accounting Fraud and Litigation from inside the Courtroom

What the Jury Heard in the Phar-Mor Case[12]

In the Phar-Mor case, several members of top management confessed to, and were convicted of, financial statement fraud. Certain of Phar-Mor's creditors and investors subsequently brought suit against Phar-Mor's independent auditor, Coopers & Lybrand, alleging the firm was reckless in performing its audits. A jury found the audit firm liable for fraud. While this module can only contain a very small portion of what the jury heard in the five-month trial, we identify the most important points presented to the jury through a careful review of the trial transcripts and selected interviews with attorneys who were in the courtroom on a daily basis. Unless otherwise noted, all facts and statements are based on actual trial transcripts.

Background   The $500 million accounting fraud at Phar-Mor, Inc., led to the bankruptcy of one of the largest private companies in the United States in 1992. As a result of the company's fraud and subsequent failure, charges were filed against both Phar-Mor's management and the company's auditors. Phar-Mor's former management was collectively fined just over $1 million, and two former members of Phar-Mor management received prison sentences. The company's former auditors, Coopers & Lybrand LLP (Coopers),

---

[12]Adapted with permission from, "Finding Auditors Liable for Fraud: What the Jury Heard in the Phar-Mor Case," David Cottrell and Steven Glover, *CPA Journal* (July 1997).

faced claims of more than $1 billion, although final settlements were a small fraction of that amount. Even though neither Phar-Mor's management, the plaintiffs' attorneys, nor anyone else associated with the case ever alleged the auditors *knowingly* participated in the Phar-Mor fraud, on February 14, 1996, a jury found Coopers liable under a fraud claim. The crux of this fraud charge was that Coopers made representations recklessly without regard to whether they were true or false, which legally enabled plaintiffs to sue the auditors for fraud under statutory and common law.

Between 1985 and 1992, Phar-Mor grew from 15 to 310 stores in 32 states, posting sales of more than $3 billion. By seemingly all standards, Phar-Mor was a rising star touted by some retail experts as the next Wal-Mart. However, in summer 1992, the illusion of Phar-Mor's success came to an abrupt end— the company's executives had cooked the books. The magnitude of the collusive management fraud at the company was almost inconceivable. The fraud was carefully carried out over several years by individuals at several organizational layers, including the president, CFO, COO, vice president of marketing, director of accounting, controller, and a host of others.

Investors and creditors filed suit against Coopers under Section 10(b) of the Federal Securities Exchange Act of 1934 and under Pennsylvania state common law. To prevail against auditors on a claim filed under Section 10(b), a plaintiff must prove by a preponderance of the evidence that the auditors acted knowingly or with reckless disregard for the truth. While the burden of proof under the federal law is substantial, the burden of proof is even higher under Pennsylvania state common law. The judge in the Phar-Mor case ruled the plaintiffs were not primary beneficiaries under Pennsylvania law, meaning the plaintiffs were required to prove by clear and convincing evidence that either (1) the auditor knew the financial statements were misrepresented or (2) the auditor issued an audit opinion recklessly.

Courtroom Strategies

The Defense.   Attorneys for Coopers continually impressed upon the jury that the fraud was perpetrated by Phar-Mor's management, not by the auditor. They clearly illustrated that the fraud was a collusive effort by multiple individuals within upper management at Phar-Mor, which continually worked to hide evidence from the auditors. The auditors were portrayed as victims of the fraud team at Phar-Mor that would, and did, do whatever it took to cover up the fraud. The perpetrators lied, forged documents, and carefully "scrubbed" everything the auditors saw to hide any indications of malfeasance. The fraud team included several former auditors, including auditors who had worked for Coopers on prior Phar-Mor audits.

After the verdict was rendered against the auditors, Coopers' attorney said, "The jury [rightly] saw that a corporate fraud had been committed, but it mistakenly blamed the outside auditor for not uncovering something no one but the perpetrators could have known about." He added, "It . . . effectively turns outside auditors into insurers against crooked management."

The Plaintiffs.   The plaintiffs opened their case by acknowledging that the incidence of management fraud does not, by itself, prove there was an audit failure. Moreover, they did not allege that Coopers knowingly participated in the Phar-Mor fraud; nor did they allege Coopers was liable just because it did not find the fraud. Rather, the plaintiffs alleged that Coopers made fraudulent representations in its audit opinions. The two key alleged misrepresentations were Coopers' statements that its audits of Phar-Mor were performed in accordance with generally accepted auditing standards (GAAS) and the audited statements of Phar-Mor were in conformity with generally accepted accounting principles (GAAP). The following quotes from plaintiff attorneys' statements to the jury illustrate the plaintiffs' strategy:

> [W]e invested in Phar-Mor on the basis of the financials of Phar-Mor, with the clean opinions of Coopers & Lybrand. We've now lost our investment, and it's a very simple case. We just want our money back. . . . [I]f Coopers can demonstrate to you that they performed a GAAS audit in the relevant time periods, then you should find for them. But if you find based upon the testimony of our experts and our witnesses that Coopers never, ever conducted a GAAS audit . . . then I submit you should ultimately find for [plaintiffs]. (Ed Klett, attorney for Westinghouse)

> So the question, ladies and gentlemen, is not whether Coopers could have discovered the fraud. The question is whether Coopers falsely and misleadingly stated that it conducted a GAAS audit and falsely and misleadingly told [plaintiffs] that Phar-Mor's worthless financial statements were fairly presented. And the answer to that question is yes. (Sarah Wolff, attorney for Sears)

After the verdict, plaintiffs' attorney Sarah Wolff indicated that the Phar-Mor case could prove to be a model for getting a jury to find that a respected accounting firm behaved "recklessly." The key to proving reckless behavior is that it is sufficient to achieve a guilty verdict on fraud charges.

In addition, throughout the five-month trial, the plaintiffs continually emphasized the following facts in their effort to convince the jury that the auditors were motivated to overlook any problems that might have been apparent to a diligent auditor:

- The fraud went on for a period of three to six years and, therefore, should have become apparent to a diligent auditor.
- Coopers was aware that Phar-Mor's accountants never provided the auditors with requested documents or data without first carefully reviewing them.
- Greg Finnerty, the partner-in-charge of the Phar-Mor audit, had previously been criticized for exceeding audit cost budgets and, therefore, was under pressure to carefully control audit costs.
- Mickey Monus, Phar-Mor's president, was viewed by Finnerty as a "constant source of new business" and thus a boon to his personal career at Coopers.

The areas where the plaintiffs alleged the auditors were reckless and did not perform an audit in accordance with professional auditing standards centered around accounting for inventory and corresponding effects on both the balance sheet and income statement. The plaintiffs' allegations centered on the four major issues detailed below.

The Price Test Fact Pattern
Inventory at Phar-Mor increased rapidly from $11 million in 1989 to $36 million in 1990 and $153 million in 1991.

Phar-Mor did not keep perpetual inventory records but made periodic counts and used the retail method for valuing inventory. Phar-Mor contracted with an outside firm to physically count and provide the retail price of each item in inventory twice per year. Phar-Mor would then apply a "cost complement" to determine the cost of inventory. Phar-Mor's initial strategy was to mark all merchandise up 20 percent, resulting in a gross margin of 16.7 percent and a corresponding cost complement of 83.3 percent. However, to be competitive, Phar-Mor lowered the margins on certain "price-sensitive" items to get customers in the door. As a result, Phar-Mor's overall budgeted gross margin fell to 15.5 percent, resulting in a cost complement of 84.5 percent.

Coopers identified inventory valuation as a high-risk area in its workpapers. Coopers annually observed the company's physical inventory count at four stores and selected from 25 to 30 items per store on which to perform price testing. Sample items were determined by the attending auditor using a "haphazard" sample selection approach (see Chapters 8 and 9 for a discussion of audit sampling techniques). Purchase invoices were examined for the items selected, and an overall gross margin for the sample was determined. In the years 1988 through 1991, Coopers' sample gross margins averaged from 16.1 to 17.7 percent. Coopers explained that the difference between the expected 15.5 percent gross margin and the sample gross margin resulted because the sample taken did not include very many price-sensitive items, and therefore the sample gross margin was higher than Phar-Mor's overall margin. Coopers concluded the difference noted was reasonable and not unexpected given Phar-Mor's approach to valuing inventory.

After a store had a physical inventory, a gross profit schedule was prepared by Phar-Mor accountants. These schedules compared gross margins based on the physical inventory with the general ledger for the current and prior years. Coopers tested a sample of these gross profit schedules each year. After the fraud was uncovered, it was determined that Phar-Mor's actual margins were much lower than the budgeted 15.5 percent, because the price-sensitive items made up a relatively large percentage of sales. Beginning in 1989, when Phar-Mor's management saw that the fiscal gross profit reports were coming in below historical levels, it started changing the gross margin reports reviewed by the auditor. Management continued to alter the gross profit reports from that time until the fraud was uncovered in 1992.

Plaintiffs' Allegations.   The plaintiffs argued that if Coopers had employed a more extensive and representative price test, it would have known what Phar-Mor's gross margins actually were, no matter what the fraud team was doing to the gross profit reports. Plaintiffs alleged the way the auditors conducted their price test and the way they interpreted the results were woefully inadequate and unreliable due to the small sample size and acknowledged lack of representativeness of the sample to the whole population of Phar-Mor merchandise.

> [T]he attitudes of the people involved in this were simply that even though there was clear recognition in the work papers that this test was so flawed that it was virtually worthless, did not produce anything to them that they could use in their audit, yet they still concluded year after year that everything was reasonable,

and that defies my imagination. I don't understand how that conclusion can come from their own recognition of that, the test was so severely flawed. Also, they gave consideration to doing a better price test, but in fact never made any attempt to do so because in each of the four years they did the same exact kind of test, year after year after year, even though they knew the test produced unreliable results. (Charles Drott, expert witness)

The plaintiffs also pointed to Coopers' workpapers where the auditors had indicated that even a .5 percent misstatement in gross margin would result in a material misstatement in net profits. Plaintiffs argued the auditors recklessly ignored the sample results indicating a material misstatement. The plaintiffs also argued the gross profit schedules could not be used to independently test the cost complement, because the calculated profit margin and ending inventory were a function of the standard cost complement that was applied to the retail inventory balance derived from the physical inventory.

So, what we have here is a daisy chain . . . the price test is the basis for the gross margin test. The price test is reasonable because the gross margins are reasonable. But, the only reason the gross margins are reasonable is because they are based on the price test. It keeps ping-ponging back and forth. And the problem is, none of this was tested. (Sarah Wolff, attorney)

Defense Response.   Coopers explained to the jury that the price test was simply a reasonableness analysis intended to provide limited assurance that Phar-Mor was properly applying its methodology for pricing and costing inventory.

It was a valid test, it still is a valid test after reviewing it time and time again. And the staff person suggesting we drop it was just not . . . right. And throughout the whole time that we audited Phar-Mor, we continued to do the price test. It was a valid test, and it still is. (Greg Finnerty, partner)

Coopers pointed out that some differences are always expected in reasonableness analyses and that those differences do not usually represent actual misstatements. Coopers also explained that it performed a number of other procedures that compensated for the weaknesses in the price tests. The primary testing was performed on Phar-Mor's gross profit reports. Coopers recalculated percentages and traced inventory balances back to the physical inventory report submitted by the independent count firm for a sample of gross profit schedules.

Inventory Compilations Fact Pattern
After the outside inventory service submitted a report of its physical count, Phar-Mor accountants would prepare an inventory compilation packet. The package included the physical counts, retail pricing, Phar-Mor's calculations of inventory at cost, and cost of goods sold. Based on the compilation, a series of journal entries were prepared and recorded in the general ledger. Each year, the auditors randomly selected one compilation packet for extensive testing and 14 other packets for limited testing. The auditors reviewed journal entries for reasonableness for all 15 packets.

The court-appointed fraud examiners determined that many of Phar-Mor's inventory compilation packets contained fraudulent journal entries. The entries were often large, even-dollar amounts, did not have journal entry numbers, had no explanations or supporting documentation, and contained suspicious account names like "Accounts Receivable Inventory Contra" or "Cookies." Phar-Mor's fraud team used these entries to inflate inventory and earnings. Based on the physical count and results of the compilation, an appropriate entry was made to reduce (credit) inventory. However, rather than record the offsetting debit to cost of goods sold, a debit entry was recorded to a "fraud holding" account. The fraudulent holding accounts accumulated the fraudulent entries during the year. At year-end, to avoid auditor detection, the holding accounts were emptied by allocating a portion back to the individual stores as inventory or some other asset.

Plaintiffs' Allegations.   The plaintiffs alleged that some of the compilations reviewed by the auditors contained fraudulent entries. Plaintiffs' experts claimed Coopers should have noticed these unusual entries.

> Coopers' audit work in this inventory compilation area, because of its failure to investigate all of these fraudulent entries which were obvious, suspicious entries on their face, their failure to do this is a failure, in my opinion, that is reckless professional conduct, meaning that it is an extreme departure from the standard of care. They had the entries in front of them, and they chose to do nothing whatsoever to investigate. Had they done so, they would have found the fraud right then and there. (Charles Drott, expert witness)

Defense Response.   Coopers was able to prove, using the firm's workpapers, that none of the compilations selected by the auditors for extensive review over the years contained fraudulent entries. While Coopers did retain an entire copy of the extensively tested compilation packet in its workpapers, it retained only notes of key information from the packets subjected to limited testing.

In preparation for the trial, the packets that had been subjected to limited testing were pulled from Phar-Mor's files, many of them containing fraudulent journal entries. However, evidence suggested these compilations were altered after Coopers had initially reviewed them. For example, in many cases, even the "key information" Coopers had noted in its workpapers no longer agreed to the file copies. Mark Kirsten, who had been a staff and senior auditor on the Phar-Mor engagement, testified why he believed the compilations retrieved from Phar-Mor's files were altered after Coopers performed its audit work:

> I never saw this entry or any other fraudulent entries. When we got these packages, we got them from John Anderson who was part of this fraud. And I refuse to agree that John Anderson walked into my audit room, and we are poring over these for a couple days at a time, and says, here, if you happen to turn to the third page, you are going to find a fraudulent entry that has no support. That's unimaginable. (Mark Kirsten, staff auditor)

General Ledger Fact Pattern   A monthly operating general ledger (GL) was prepared and printed for each store and for corporate headquarters. The plaintiffs argued that the fraud could have been uncovered not only by examining the journal entries proposed on the inventory compilations but also by simply scanning the GL. Because the fraud team was aware that zero-balance accounts typically draw little attention from the auditor, it recorded numerous "blowout" entries in the last monthly corporate GL to empty the fraudulent holding accounts that had accumulated the fraud during the year. The holding accounts were emptied by allocating a portion, usually in equal-dollar amounts, back to the individual Phar-Mor retail stores as inventory or other assets. These entries were typically very large. For example, in 1991, an entry labeled "Accrued Inventory" for $9,999,999.99 was made.

Plaintiffs' Allegations. The plaintiffs pointed out that scanning the GL, which was a recognized procedure in Coopers' audit manual and training materials, would certainly and easily have uncovered the fraud. Further, plaintiffs pointed to Coopers' inventory audit program for Phar-Mor that included procedures requiring the examination of large and unusual entries.

The plaintiffs repeatedly played a video clip of one of the chief perpetrators of the Phar-Mor fraud, the former CFO, saying that if Coopers had asked for the backup to any one of the fraudulent journal entries, "It [the fraud] would have been all over."

Defense Response. Coopers' audit program did include a step to obtain selected nonstandard adjusting journal entries so that any large and unusual items could be further examined. The step was signed off by staff auditors without further explanation. Coopers' witnesses testified that the fact that the step was signed off indicated that either the step was performed or was considered not necessary. Trial testimony indicated that auditors had asked Phar-Mor accountants if there were any large and unusual adjusting entries and the auditors were told there were none.

While Coopers was aware of the operating GLs, the auditors worked primarily with the consolidated GL, which combined all the operating GLs and included only ending balances and not transaction detail. In the consolidated GL, the fraud holding accounts were either completely absent or had zero balances.

Roll-Forward Fact Pattern
Because the physical inventories were completed during the fiscal year, it was necessary to roll forward or account for the inventory purchase and sales transactions between the inventory count date and the balance sheet date. Coopers' roll-forward examinations always revealed a large increase in the ending book inventory balance. Phar-Mor explained to the auditors that the inventory "spike" was due to two factors. First, inventory levels at the physical count date were always lower than normal because a store would reduce inventory shipments in the weeks prior to the physical inventory to prepare for the physical count. Second, since the fiscal year-end was June 30, there was always a buildup of inventory to handle the big July 4 holiday demand. The drop-off in inventory just after fiscal year-end was attributed mainly to the large amounts of inventory sold over July 4. While the client's explanation did account for a portion of the spike, investigations performed subsequent to the discovery of the fraud indicate that a large portion of the spike was attributable to the fraud.

Plaintiffs' Allegations.   Plaintiffs claimed the spike was a prominent red flag that Coopers recklessly overlooked.

> [T]his is simply showing a sharp spike upward at fiscal year-end . . . and subsequent to the fiscal year . . . the inventory levels drop off. Now, that is a very interesting red flag. If I were an auditor, I'd certainly want to know why the inventories increase sharply, reaching its crest right at the fiscal year-end date. In other words, when the financial statements were prepared, and why they drop off again after fiscal year-end, just two weeks later, as a matter of fact, and go down that much. It's what I call the spike. Clearly the spike, in my opinion, was caused in large part by the actual fraud at Phar-Mor, because if you recall, these fraudulent entries, these blow-out entries that I described, were these very large journal entries that were adding false inventory to each of the stores, and it was done at fiscal year-end. (Charles Drott, expert witness)

Defense Response.   When asked if the spike would cause an experienced retail auditor to be suspicious about inventory at Phar-Mor, the Phar-Mor audit partner responded:

> Well, no, it wouldn't. But, let me give you an example. At Christmastime, it's the same concept. There is a tremendous spike in inventory of retailers at Christmastime, and then after that, after Christmas, sales go down. That is, you are going to see a natural decline in the inventory levels of a retailer after Christmas. So, it so happens in this analysis, this has to do with the year-end of Phar-Mor, June 30. (Greg Finnerty, partner)

Coopers elected not to test specific purchases or sales transactions during the roll-forward period. Rather, it relied on its tests of the gross profit schedules both before and after year-end, which suggested the controls over purchases and sales were functioning properly. Unfortunately, as discussed previously, the Phar-Mor fraud team was falsifying the gross profit reports.

What Can Be Learned?

First, auditors should remember that plaintiffs in a lawsuit can successfully replace allegations of *knowing intent* ("scienter") with assertions of *reckless conduct* to prevail in a lawsuit against auditors where the legal standard requires evidence of auditor fraud. Second, in the clear light of hindsight, audit weaknesses can be taken out of context and magnified in the jury's mind so that honest judgment calls or even mistakes may be made to appear as reckless misconduct. The final settlement amounts were not publicly disclosed, but Coopers reported that it was a small fraction of the amount filed by plaintiffs.

KEY TERMS

Due professional care. A legal standard requiring that the auditor perform his or her professional services with the same degree of skill, knowledge, and judgment possessed by other members of the profession.

Engagement letter. A letter that formalizes the contract between the auditor and the client and outlines the responsibilities of both parties.

Generally Accepted Auditing Standards. Measures of the quality of the auditor's performance.

Gross negligence. An extreme, flagrant, or reckless departure from professional standards of due care.

Ordinary negligence. An absence of reasonable or due care in the conduct of an engagement.

Privity. A party's contractual or fiduciary relationship with the accountant.

Professional skepticism. An attitude that includes a questioning mind and a critical assessment of audit evidence. The auditor should not assume that management is either honest or dishonest.

Reasonable assurance. A term that implies some risk that a material misstatement could be present in the financial statements without the auditor detecting it.

Tort. A wrongful act other than a breach of contract for which civil action may be taken.

---

www.mhhe.com/ messier4e

Visit the book's Online Learning Center for a multiple-choice quiz that will allow you to assess your understanding of chapter concepts.

REVIEW QUESTIONS

[LO 1] 20-1 Briefly describe the four stages of the auditor dispute process.

[2] 20-2 What is meant by *proportionate liability?* Contrast this legal doctrine with the doctrine of *joint and several liability.*

[3] 20-3 For what types of actions are auditors liable to a client under common law? Why would the client prefer to sue the auditor for a tort action rather than for a breach of contract?

[3] 20-4 What elements must a client prove to maintain an action against an auditor for negligence?

[4] 20-5 Distinguish among the three standards that have evolved for defining auditors' liability to third parties under common law. Why is this area of auditors' liability so complex?

[5,6] 20-6 Distinguish between the Securities Act of 1933 and the Securities Exchange Act of 1934. Why is it easier for a plaintiff to sue an auditor under the Securities Act of 1933?

[6] 20-7 What elements must a plaintiff prove in order to win action under Rule 10b-5 of the Securities Exchange Act of 1934? What was the significance of the outcome of the *Ernst & Ernst* v. *Hochfelder* case for auditors' liability?

[7] 20-8 What were the most significant components of the Private Securities Litigation Reform Act of 1995 and the Securities Litigation Uniform Standards Act of 1998?

[8] 20-9 In what ways does the Sarbanes-Oxley Act of 2002 change criminal liability for auditors of public companies?

[9] 20-10 What types of sanctions can the SEC and the PCAOB impose on auditors.

[11]   20-11   Briefly describe the Racketeer Influenced and Corrupt Organizations Act and why plaintiffs seek to sue auditors under this statute.

[12]   20-12   What actions can result in an auditor being held criminally liable under statutes and regulations?

[13]   20-13   Identify steps that can be taken at the professional level and the individual level to minimize legal liability against auditors.

MULTIPLE-CHOICE QUESTIONS

[2,3,4]   20-14   Cable Corporation orally engaged Drake & Company, CPAs, to audit its financial statements. Cable's management informed Drake that it suspected the accounts receivable were materially overstated. Though the financial statements Drake audited included a materially overstated accounts receivable balance, Drake issued an unqualified opinion. Cable used the financial statements to obtain a loan to expand its operations. Cable defaulted on the loan and incurred a substantial loss.

   If Cable sues Drake for negligence in failing to discover the overstatement, Drake's best defense would be that Drake did *not*
   a. Have privity of contract with Cable.
   b. Sign an engagement letter.
   c. Perform the audit recklessly or with an intent to deceive.
   d. Violate generally accepted auditing standards in performing the audit.

[3]   20-15   Which of the following best describes whether a CPA has met the required standard of care in auditing a client's financial statements?
   a. Whether the client's expectations are met with regard to the accuracy of audited financial statements.
   b. Whether the statements conform to generally accepted accounting principles.
   c. Whether the CPA conducted the audit with the same skill and care expected of an ordinarily prudent CPA under the circumstances.
   d. Whether the audit was conducted to investigate and discover all acts of fraud.

[3,4]   20-16   Sun Corporation approved a merger plan with Cord Corporation. One of the determining factors in approving the merger was the financial statements of Cord, which had been audited by Frank & Company, CPAs. Sun had engaged Frank to audit Cord's financial statements. While performing the audit, Frank failed to discover fraud that later caused Sun to suffer substantial losses. For Frank to be liable under common-law negligence, Sun at a *minimum* must prove that Frank
   a. Knew of the fraud.
   b. Failed to exercise due care.
   c. Was grossly negligent.
   d. Acted with scienter.

[4]   20-17   Brown & Company, CPAs, issued an unqualified opinion on the financial statements of its client King Corporation. Based on the strength of King's financial statements, Safe Bank loaned King

$500,000. Brown was unaware that Safe would receive a copy of the financial statements or that they would be used by King in obtaining a loan. King defaulted on the loan.

If Safe commences an action for negligence against Brown and Brown is able to prove that it conducted the audit in conformity with GAAS, Brown will

a. Be liable to Safe, because Safe relied on the financial statements.

b. Be liable to Safe, because the Statute of Frauds has been satisfied.

c. Not be liable to Safe, because there is a conclusive presumption that following GAAS is the equivalent of acting reasonably and with due care.

d. Not be liable to Safe, because there was a lack of privity of contract.

[5]   20-18   How does the Securities Act of 1933, which imposes civil liability on auditors for misrepresentations or omissions of material facts in a registration statement, expand auditors' liability to purchasers of securities beyond that of common law?

a. Purchasers have to prove only that a loss was caused by reliance on audited financial statements.

b. Privity with purchasers is *not* a necessary element of proof.

c. Purchasers have to prove either fraud or gross negligence as a basis for recovery.

d. Auditors are held to a standard of care described as "professional skepticism."

[5]   20-19   To be successful in a civil action under Section 11 of the Securities Act of 1933 concerning liability for a misleading registration statement, the plaintiff must prove

	Defendant's Intent to Deceive	Plaintiff's Reliance on the Registration Statement
a.	Yes	Yes
b.	Yes	No
c.	No	Yes
d.	No	No

Questions 20-20 and 20-21 are based on the following information:

Dart Corporation engaged Jay Associates, CPAs, to assist in a public stock offering. Jay audited Dart's financial statements and gave an unqualified opinion, despite knowing that the financial statements contained misstatements. Jay's opinion was included in Dart's registration statement. Hansen purchased shares in the offering and suffered a loss when the stock declined in value after the misstatements became known.

[5]   20-20   In a suit against Jay and Dart under the Section 11 liability provisions of the Securities Act of 1933, Hansen must prove that

a. Jay knew of the misstatements.

b. Jay was negligent.

c. The misstatements contained in Dart's financial statements were material.

    d. The unqualified opinion contained in the registration statement
       was relied on by Hansen.

[5]   20-21   If Hansen succeeds in the Section 11 suit against Dart, Hansen will
                  be entitled to
                  a. Damages of three times the original public offering price.
                  b. Rescind the transaction.
                  c. Monetary damages only.
                  d. Damages, but only if the shares were resold before the suit was
                     started.

[6]   20-22   Fritz Corporation engaged Hay Associates, CPAs, to assist in a pub-
                  lic stock offering. Hay audited Fritz's financial statements and gave
                  an unqualified opinion, despite knowing that the financial state-
                  ments contained misstatements. Hay's opinion was included in
                  Fritz's registration statement. Samson purchased shares in the of-
                  fering and suffered a loss when the stock declined in value after the
                  misstatements became known.

                  In a suit against Hay under the antifraud provisions of Section
                  10(b) and Rule 10b-5 of the Securities Exchange Act of 1934, Sam-
                  son must prove all of the following *except* that
                  a. Samson was an intended user of the false registration statement.
                  b. Samson relied on the false registration statement.
                  c. The transaction involved some form of interstate commerce.
                  d. Hay acted with intentional disregard of the truth.

[7]   20-23   Under the Private Securities Litigation Reform Act of 1995, Baker,
                  CPA, reported certain uncorrected illegal acts to Supermart's board
                  of directors. Baker believed that failure to take remedial action
                  would warrant a qualified audit opinion because the illegal acts had
                  a material effect on Supermart's financial statements. Supermart
                  failed to take appropriate remedial action and the board of directors
                  refused to inform the SEC that it had received such notification
                  from Baker. Under these circumstances, Baker is required to
                  a. Resign from the audit engagement within 10 business days.
                  b. Deliver a report concerning the illegal acts to the SEC within one
                     business day.
                  c. Notify the stockholders that the financial statements are materi-
                     ally misstated.
                  d. Withhold an audit opinion until Supermart takes appropriate re-
                     medial action.

[8]   20-24   Which of the following is not a provision of the Sarbanes-Oxley Act
                  of 2002?
                  a. A requirement to retain audit working papers for at least five years.
                  b. It is a criminal offense to take any harmful action in retaliation
                     against anyone who voluntarily comes forward to report a sus-
                     pected accounting or securities fraud.
                  c. Broad investigative and disciplinary authority over registered
                     public accounting firms is granted to the Public Company Ac-
                     counting Oversight Board.
                  d. The statute of limitations for actions under Section 10(b) and
                     Rule 10b-5 was reduced to one year from the discovery of fraud
                     and five years after the fraud occurred.

[10]   20-25   Which of the following is a provision of the Foreign Corrupt Practices Act?

    a. It is a criminal offense for an auditor to fail to detect and report a bribe paid by an American business entity to a foreign official for the purpose of obtaining business.

    b. The auditor's detection of illegal acts committed by officials of the auditor's publicly held client in conjunction with foreign officials should be reported to the Enforcement Division of the Securities and Exchange Commission.

    c. If the auditor of a publicly held company concludes that the effects on the financial statements of a bribe given to a foreign official are *not* susceptible of reasonable estimation, the auditor's report should be modified.

    d. Every publicly held company must devise, document, and maintain a system of internal accounting controls sufficient to provide reasonable assurance that internal control objectives are met.

PROBLEMS

[2,3,4]   20-26   Becker, Inc., purchased the assets of Bell Corporation. A condition of the purchase agreement was that Bell retain a CPA to audit its financial statements. The purpose of the audit was to determine whether the unaudited financial statements furnished to Becker fairly presented Bell's financial position. Bell retained Salam & Company, CPAs, to perform the audit.

While performing the audit, Salam discovered that Bell's bookkeeper had embezzled $500. Salam had some evidence of other embezzlements by the bookkeeper. However, Salam decided that the $500 was immaterial and that the other suspected embezzlements did not require further investigation. Salam did not discuss the matter with Bell's management. Unknown to Salam, the bookkeeper had, in fact, embezzled large sums of cash from Bell. In addition, the accounts receivable were significantly overstated. Salam did not detect the overstatement because of Salam's failure to follow its audit program.

Despite the foregoing, Salam issued an unqualified opinion on Bell's financial statements and furnished a copy of the audited financial statements to Becker. Unknown to Salam, Becker required financing to purchase Bell's assets and furnished a copy of Bell's audited financial statements to City Bank to obtain approval of the loan. Based on Bell's audited financial statements, City loaned Becker $600,000.

Becker paid Bell $750,000 to purchase Bell's assets. Within six months, Becker began experiencing financial difficulties resulting from the undiscovered embezzlements and overstated accounts receivable. Becker later defaulted on the City loan.

City has commenced a lawsuit against Salam based on the following causes of action:

- Constructive fraud
- Negligence

Required:

In separate paragraphs, discuss whether City is likely to prevail on the causes of action it has raised. Set forth reasons for each conclusion.

(AICPA, adapted)

[3,4,5,6]   **20-27**   Astor Electronics, Inc., markets a wide variety of computer-related products throughout the United States. Astor's officers decided to raise $1 million by selling shares of Astor's common stock in an exempt offering under Regulation D of the Securities Act of 1933. In connection with the offering, Astor engaged Apple & Company, CPAs, to audit Astor's financial statements. The audited financial statements, including Apple's unqualified opinion, were included in the offering memorandum given to prospective purchasers of Astor's stock. Apple was aware that Astor intended to include the statements in the offering materials.

Astor's financial statements reported certain inventory items at a cost of $930,000 when in fact they had a fair market value of less than $100,000 because of technological obsolescence. Apple accepted the assurances of Astor's controller that cost was the appropriate valuation, despite the fact that Apple was aware of ongoing sales of the products at prices substantially less than cost. All of this was thoroughly documented in Apple's working papers.

Musk purchased 10,000 shares of Astor's common stock in the Regulation D offering at a total price of $300,000. In deciding to make the purchase, Musk had reviewed the audited financial statements of Astor that accompanied the other offering materials and had been impressed by Astor's apparent financial strength.

Shortly after the stock offering was completed, Astor's management discovered that the audited financial statements reflected the materially overstated valuation of the company's inventory. Astor advised its shareholders of the problem.

Upon receiving notice from Astor of the overstated inventory amount, Musk became very upset because the stock value was now substantially less than what it would have been had the financial statements been accurate. In fact, the stock was worth only about $200,000.

Musk has commenced an action against Apple, alleging that Apple is liable to Musk based on the following causes of action:

- Common-law fraud.
- Negligence.
- A violation of Section 10(b) and Rule 10b-5 of the Securities Exchange Act of 1934.

During the litigation Apple has refused to give to Musk its working papers pertaining to the Astor audit, claiming that these constitute privileged communications. The state in which the actions have been commenced has no accountants' privileged communication statute.

The state law applicable to this action follows the *Ultramares* decision with respect to accountants' liability to third parties for negligence or fraud. Apple has also asserted that the actions should be dismissed because of the absence of any contractual relationship between Apple and Musk, that is, a lack of privity.

Required:
Answer the following, setting forth your reasons for any conclusions stated.
a. Will Apple be required to give Musk its working papers?
b. What elements must be established by Musk to support a cause of action based on negligence?
c. What elements must be established by Musk to support a cause of action based on a Rule 10b-5 violation?
d. Is Apple's assertion regarding lack of privity correct with regard to Musk's causes of action for negligence and fraud?

(AICPA, adapted)

[5,6]   20-28   Butler Manufacturing Corporation planned to raise capital for a plant expansion by borrowing from banks and making several stock offerings. Butler engaged Meng, CPA, to audit its December 31, 2005, financial statements. Butler told Meng that the financial statements would be given to certain named banks and included in the prospectuses for the stock offerings.

In performing the audit, Meng did not confirm accounts receivable and, as a result, failed to discover a material overstatement of accounts receivable. Also, Meng was aware of a pending class action product liability lawsuit that was not disclosed in Butler's financial statements. Despite being advised by Butler's legal counsel that Butler's potential liability under the lawsuit would result in material losses, Meng issued an unqualified opinion on Butler's financial statements.

In May 2006 Union Bank, one of the named banks, relied on the financial statements and Meng's opinion in giving Butler a $500,000 loan.

Butler raised an additional $16,450,000 through the following stock offerings, which were sold completely:

- *June 2006:* Butler made a $450,000 unregistered offering of Class B nonvoting common stock under Rule 504 of Regulation D of the Securities Act of 1933. This offering was sold over two years to 30 nonaccredited investors and 20 accredited investors by general solicitation. The SEC was notified eight days after the first sale of this offering.
- *September 2006:* Butler made a $10,000,000 unregistered offering of Class A voting common stock under Rule 506 of Regulation D of the Securities Act of 1933. This offering was sold over two years to 200 accredited investors and 30 nonaccredited investors through a private placement. The SEC was notified 14 days after the first sale of this offering.
- *November 2006:* Butler made a $6,000,000 unregistered offering of preferred stock under Rule 505 of Regulation D of the Securities Act of 1933. This offering was sold during a one-year period to

40 nonaccredited investors by private placement. The SEC was notified 18 days after the first sale of this offering.

Shortly after obtaining the Union loan, Butler began experiencing financial problems but was able to stay in business because of the money raised by the offerings. Then Butler was found liable in the product liability suit. This resulted in a judgment Butler could not pay. Butler also defaulted on the Union loan and was involuntarily petitioned into bankruptcy. This caused Union to sustain a loss and Butler's stockholders to lose their investments. As a result,

- The SEC claimed that all three of Butler's offerings had been made improperly and had not been exempt from registration.
- Union sued Meng for negligence and common-law fraud.
- The stockholders who purchased Butler's stock through the offerings sued Meng, alleging fraud under Section 10(b) and Rule 10b-5 of the Securities Exchange Act of 1934.

These transactions took place in a jurisdiction providing for accountants' liability for negligence to known and intended users of financial statements.

Required:
Answer the following questions and give the reasons for your conclusions:
a. Will Union be successful in its suit against Meng for
    1. Negligence?
    2. Common-law fraud?
b. Will the stockholders who purchased Butler's stock through the 2004 offerings succeed against Meng under the antifraud provisions of Section 10(b) and Rule 10b-5 of the Securities Exchange Act of 1934?

(AICPA, adapted)

[5,6]   20-29 Sleek Corporation is a public corporation whose stock is traded on a national securities exchange. Sleek hired Garson Associates, CPAs, to audit Sleek's financial statements. Sleek needed the audit to obtain bank loans and to offer public stock so that it could expand.

Before the engagement, Fred Hedge, Sleek's president, told Garson's managing partner that the audited financial statements would be submitted to Sleek's banks to obtain the necessary loans.

During the course of the audit, Garson's managing partner found that Hedge and other Sleek officers had embezzled substantial amounts of money from the corporation. These embezzlements threatened Sleek's financial stability. When these findings were brought to Hedge's attention, Hedge promised that the money would be repaid and begged that the audit not disclose the embezzlements.

Hedge also told Garson's managing partner that several friends and relatives of Sleek's officers had been advised about the projected business expansion and proposed stock offering and had purchased significant amounts of Sleek's stock based on this information.

Garson submitted an unqualified opinion on Sleek's financial statements, which did not include adjustments for or disclosures about the embezzlements and insider stock transactions. The financial statements and audit report were submitted to Sleek's regular banks, including Knox Bank. Knox, relying on the financial statements and Garson's report, gave Sleek a $2 million loan.

Sleek's audited financial statements were also incorporated into a registration statement prepared under the provisions of the Securities Act of 1933. The registration statement was filed with the SEC in conjunction with Sleek's public offering of 100,000 shares of its common stock at $100 per share.

An SEC investigation of Sleek disclosed the embezzlements and the insider trading. Trading in Sleek's stock was suspended, and Sleek defaulted on the Knox loan.

As a result, the following legal actions were taken:

- Knox sued Garson.
- The general-public purchasers of Sleek's stock offering sued Garson.

Required:
Answer the following questions and give the reasons for your conclusions.
a. Would Knox recover from Garson for fraud?
b. Would the general-public purchasers of Sleek's stock offerings recover from Garson
  1. Under the liability provisions of Section 11 of the Securities Act of 1933?
  2. Under the antifraud provisions of Rule 10b-5 of the Securities Exchange Act of 1934?

(AICPA, adapted)

DISCUSSION CASES

[4,5,6] 20-30 Conan Doyle & Associates (CD&A), CPAs, served as the auditors for Lestrad Corporation and Watson Corporation, publicly held companies traded on NASDAQ. Watson recently acquired Lestrad Corporation in a merger that involved swapping 1.75 shares of Watson for 1 share of Lestrad. In connection with that merger, CD&A issued an unqualified report on the financial statements and participated in the preparation of the pro forma unaudited financial statements contained in the combined prospectus and proxy statement circulated to obtain shareholder approval of the merger and to register the shares to be issued in connection with the merger. Watson prepared a Form 8K and Form 10K in connection with the merger. Shortly thereafter, financial disaster beset the merged company, resulting in large losses to the shareholders and creditors. A class action suit on behalf of shareholders and creditors has been filed against Watson and its management. In addition, it names CD&A as a codefendant, challenging the fairness, accuracy, and truthfulness of the financial statements.

Required:

Discuss the various bases of CD&A's potential civil liability to the shareholders and creditors of Watson as a result of issuing an unqualified report on the audited financial statements of Watson and Lestrad and having participated in preparing the unaudited financial statements required in connection with the merger under

(a) State common law.

(b) The federal securities acts.

(AICPA, adapted)

[8]   20-31   Critics of the Sarbanes-Oxley Act of 2002 do not believe the Act will be effective at deterring accounting frauds because it primarily relies on specifying new crimes and higher penalties (i.e., increasing the maximum fine and prison terms). Critics argue that if corporate executives are not deterred by the prospect of 5 or 10 years in prison (pre-Sarbanes penalties), the threat of imprisonment will have little or no practical effect no matter what the maximum is raised to. Thus, critics conclude that the Act was more of an expression of political outrage than good policy.

Proponents of the Act believe the new crimes, increased penalties, and the other provisions in the Act will be effective at significantly reducing corporate accounting frauds.

Required:

Provide arguments for both sides of the debate and formulate your own opinion.

| www.mhhe.com/ messier4e | Visit the book's Online Learning Center for problem material to be completed using the *ACL* software packaged with your new text. |

Part VIII

ASSURANCE, ATTESTATION, AND INTERNAL AUDITING SERVICES

21

Assurance, Attestation, and Internal Auditing Services

CHAPTER 21

LEARNING OBJECTIVES

Upon completion of this chapter you will

[1] Know the definition of assurance services.

[2] Be familiar with the types of assurance services.

[3] Know the definition of an attestation engagement.

[4] Know the types of attestation engagements.

[5] Be familiar with the 11 attestation standards and how they compare to the 10 generally accepted auditing standards.

[6] Understand an attestation engagement that reports on an entity's internal control over financial reporting.

[7] Understand an attestation engagement that reports on an entity's financial forecasts and projections.

[8] Be familiar with accounting and review services.

[9] Understand the role of, standards pertaining to, and services provided by internal auditors

[10] Understand CPA *Trust Services* and know the *Trust Services* Principles and Criteria.

[11] Understand the assurance process for *WebTrust*.

[12] Understand the assurance process for SysTrust.

[13] Understand CPA PrimePlus (formerly ElderCare) assurance service.

RELEVANT ACCOUNTING AND AUDITING PRONOUNCEMENTS

Committee of Sponsoring Organizations of the Treadway Commission, *Internal Control—Integrated Framework* (New York: AICPA, 1992)

AU 319, Consideration of Internal Control in a Financial Statement Audit

AU 325, Communication of Internal Control–Related Matters Noted in an Audit

Attestation Standards: Revision and Recodification (SSAE No. 10, Chapters 1–7)

Codification of Statements on Standards for Accounting and Review Services (AR 100–600)

Professional Practices Framework of the Institute of Internal Auditors

Assurance, Attestation, and Internal Auditing Services

In recent years, external auditors have been asked to perform a variety of services beyond the audit of historical financial statements. However, auditors found it difficult to provide such services within the bounds of auditing standards. In 1986, the AICPA developed *attestation standards.* The attestation standards are broader in scope than auditing standards so that they can be applied to the array of services being requested of the accounting profession. In 2001, the Auditing Standards Board completed a substantial revision and recodification of the attestation standards. The PCAOB adopted the AICPA attestation standards on an interim basis in April 2003.

The profession aggressively sought to expand the opportunities for auditor services in the late 1990's. The AICPA Special Committee on Assurance Services ("the Elliott Committee") issued a report in 1996 that led to the AICPA establishing a program to promote assurance services.[1]

This chapter first provides an overview of assurance services. An *Advanced Module* offers a detailed presentation of three specific types of services. Attest services and standards are presented next. The reader should note that many of the assurance services are conducted as attestation engagements. The chapter also covers other types of accounting services offered by CPAs. The last part of the chapter discusses the services and standards relating to internal auditing. 🐾

---

[1]See the AICPA's home page (www.aicpa.org) for more information about the AICPA's Assurance Service Program.

Assurance Services

[LO 1]   Figure 21–1 reproduces Figure 1–2, which presents the relationship of assurance services to attest and auditing. As discussed in Chapter 1, assurance services include attestation and auditing services. The AICPA Special Committee on Assurance Services has defined assurance services as follows:

> **Assurance services** are independent professional services that improve the quality of information, or its context, for decision makers.

This definition captures a number of important concepts. First, the definition focuses on decision making. Making good decisions requires quality information, which can be financial or nonfinancial. Figure 21–2, adapted from the Elliott Committee's report, presents a model for decision making and the role of information in decision-making activities. Information is critical in this decision model. For example, the Elliott Committee points out that three types of information enter into the problem definition stage of the decision model: (1) environmental information, (2) process monitoring and diagnostic information, and (3) outcome feedback information. An assurance service engagement can help the decision maker search through this information in order to identify which pieces of information are relevant for the required decision. The second concept relates to improving the quality of information or its context. In the decision model shown in Figure 21–2, an assurance service engagement can improve quality by increasing confidence in the information's reliability and relevance. Context can be improved via the format in which information is presented.

The third important concept in the definition of assurance services is independence. As with the earlier discussions of financial statement auditing,

FIGURE 21–1   **The Relationship between Assurance Services, Attest, and Auditing**

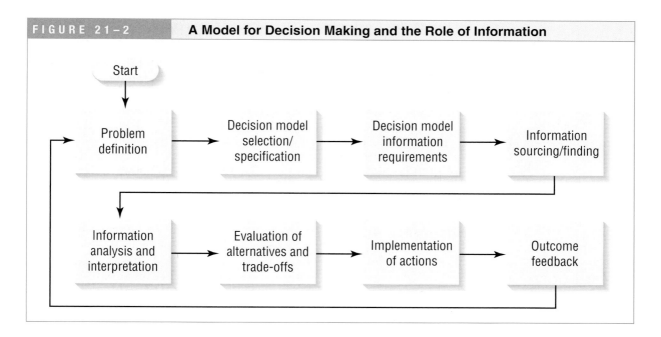

FIGURE 21–2   **A Model for Decision Making and the Role of Information**

independence is the hallmark of the profession. The last concept is professional services, which encompasses the application of professional judgment. The practitioner applies professional judgment to the information that is the subject of the assurance service. In summary, assurance services can capture information, improve its quality, and enhance its usefulness for decision makers.

Types of Assurance Services

≋ [LO 2]

The AICPA, through its Assurance Services Executive Committee, identified and developed six general categories of assurance services.

- ***Risk assessment***—assurance that an entity's profile of business risks is comprehensive and evaluation of whether the entity has appropriate systems in place to effectively manage those risks.
- ***Business performance measurement***—assurance that an entity's performance measurement system contains relevant and reliable measures for assessing the degree to which the entity's goals and objectives are achieved or how its performance compares to that of competitors.
- ***Information system reliability***—assurance that an entity's internal information systems provide reliable information for operating and financial decisions.
- ***Electronic commerce***—assurance that systems and tools used in electronic commerce provide appropriate data integrity, security, privacy, and reliability.
- ***Health care performance measurement***—assurance about the effectiveness of health care services provided by HMOs, hospitals, doctors, and other providers.

- **PrimePlus**—assurance that specified goals regarding the elderly are being met by various caregivers.

Seven other areas where assurance services might be appropriate include corporate policy compliance, outsourced internal auditing, trading partner accountability, mergers and acquisitions, ISO 9000 certification, investment managers' compliance with Association of Investment Management and Research Performance Presentation Standards, and World Wide Web assertions. These proposed services should give the reader a sense of the wide variety of opportunities that exist for practitioners to provide assurance services to their existing and new clients. To give you a better understanding of the nature of such services, this chapter's *Advanced Module* offers a detailed presentation of three specific types of nonaudit attestation services developed by the AICPA over the last several years (WebTrust, SysTrust, and PrimePlus services).

Attest Engagements[2]

[LO 3]   Chapter 1 of SSAE No. 10 defines an attest engagement as follows:

> **Attest** services occur when a practitioner is engaged to issue or does issue a report on subject matter, or an assertion about subject matter, that is the responsibility of another party.

In this definition, *practitioner* refers to a certified public accountant in the practice of public accounting. Because attestation engagements are attest engagements other than audits, the attestation standards use *practitioner* instead of *auditor*. *Subject matter* of an attest engagement may take many forms, including historical or prospective performance information, analyses (e.g., break-even analysis), systems and processes (e.g., internal control), and behavior (e.g., compliance with laws and regulations). The term *assertion* here refers to any declaration, or set of related declarations, about whether the subject matter is based on or in conformity with the criteria selected. An example of an assertion by management would be "Gregorio's Restaurants maintains effective internal control over financial reporting."

Typically, an attestation engagement involves three parties: a user or users; a party responsible for the subject matter or the assertion, such as management; and a CPA. Figure 21–3 depicts the relationship among the three parties to an attestation engagement. Note the direction of the arrows in this figure. The responsible party is responsible for the subject matter or assertion to the user and acknowledges that responsibility to the CPA. The CPA expresses a conclusion to the user on the subject matter or assertion. In some cases, the engagement may involve only two parties because the user and the responsible party are the same.

The practitioner should use an attestation risk model to meet the standards of field work in an attestation engagement. Attestation risk is defined in a manner similar to audit risk and is composed of the same three components

---

[2]See J. M. Marino and C. E. Landes, "A New Look at the Attestation Standards," *Journal of Accountancy* (July 2001), pp. 41–45, for a discussion of the revisions made to the SSAEs in 2001.

| FIGURE 21-3 | **The Three-Party Relationship in an Attest Engagement** |

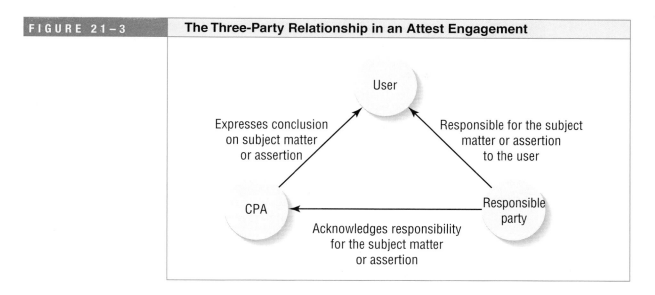

(inherent risk, control risk, and detection risk) as the audit risk model discussed in Chapter 3. The attestation risk should be set consistent with the type of engagement being performed.

Types of Attest Engagements

✳ [LO 4]

Attestation standards generally provide for three types of engagements: *examination, review,* and *agreed-upon procedures.* The AICPA's Statements on Standards for Attestation Engagements (SSAE) provide additional guidance on these types of engagements. The PCAOB adopted the SSAEs on an interim basis in April 2003.

Examination

In an examination, the practitioner expresses an opinion that (a) the subject matter is based on (or in conformity with) the criteria in all material respects or (b) the assertion is presented (or fairly stated), in all material respects, based on the criteria. Such an opinion may be for general or limited distribution. If distribution is limited, the opinion must state the limitations on the use of the report. Because an examination engagement provides the highest level of assurance on an assertion, the practitioner must gather sufficient evidence to limit the attestation risk to a low level, and express positive assurance.

Review

In a review engagement, the practitioner expresses negative assurance. That is, the accountant indicates that no information came to his or her attention indicating that (a) the subject matter is not based on (or in conformity with) the criteria in all material respects or (b) the assertion is not presented (or fairly stated), in all material respects, based on the criteria. Distribution of a review report can also be either general or limited. A review engagement should provide sufficient evidence to limit the attestation risk to a moderate level.

TABLE 21–1	Overview of Attestation Engagements			
Type of Engagement	*Level of Assurance*	*Attestation Risk*	*Type of Report*	*Report Distribution*
Examination	High	Low	Opinion	General or limited
Review	Moderate	Moderate	Negative assurance	General or limited
Agreed-upon procedures	Variable	Variable	Summary of findings	Limited

Agreed–Upon Procedures   An agreed-upon procedures engagement is one in which a practitioner is engaged by a client to issue a report of findings based on specific procedures performed on the subject matter. The level of assurance provided by such an engagement depends on the nature and scope of the procedures agreed upon with the specified parties. Thus, the attestation risk is a function of the intended level of assurance. Distribution of the report based on such an engagement is *limited* to the specified users. The report on an agreed-upon procedures engagement summarizes findings resulting from the application of the agreed-upon procedures.

Table 21–1 provides an overview of the types of attestation engagements.

Attestation Standards

[LO 5]   Table 21–2 lists the 11 attestation standards and the 10 generally accepted auditing standards for comparative purposes.

General Standards   There are five general standards for attestation engagements. All but the second and third general standards have counterparts in generally accepted auditing standards. The second standard requires that the practitioner have adequate knowledge of the subject matter. Such a requirement can be met by the CPA through education and practical experience. The CPA may also use a specialist to help meet this knowledge requirement.

The third standard is particularly important because it stipulates that the practitioner shall perform the engagement only if he or she has reason to believe that the subject matter is capable of evaluation against criteria that are suitable and available to users. *Criteria* are standards or benchmarks used to measure and present the subject matter and against which the practitioner evaluates the subject matter. Criteria can be established or developed by the client, the responsible party, industry associations, or other groups that do not follow due process procedures. For example, criteria can be issued by bodies designated under the AICPA's Code of Professional Conduct. With respect to attestation engagements for reporting on internal control for privately held companies, the practitioner can use criteria from AU 319, which are based on the Committee of Sponsoring Organizations of the Treadway Commission's document *Internal Control—Integrated Framework* (the COSO Report). Criteria can be made available to users publicly, by inclusion in the presentation of the subject matter or assertion, or by inclusion in the practitioner's report. The criteria can also be such that they are available to only specified parties.

TABLE 21–2	Attestation Standards Compared with Generally Accepted Auditing Standards

Attestation Standards	*Generally Accepted Auditing Standards*
General Standards	
1. The engagement shall be performed by a practitioner having adequate technical training and proficiency in the attest function.	1. The audit is to be performed by a person or persons having adequate technical training and proficiency as an auditor.
2. The engagement shall be performed by a practitioner having adequate knowledge in the subject matter.	
3. The practitioner shall perform an engagement only if he or she has reason to believe that the subject matter is capable of evaluation against criteria that are suitable and available to users.	
4. In all matters relating to the engagement, an independence in mental attitude shall be maintained by the practitioner.	2. In all matters relating to the assignment, an independence in mental attitude is to be maintained by the auditor or auditors.
5. Due professional care shall be exercised in the planning and performance of the engagement.	3. Due professional care is to be exercised in the planning and performance of the audit and the preparation of the report.
Standards of Field Work	
1. The work shall be adequately planned and assistants, if any, shall be properly supervised.	1. The work is to be adequately planned and assistants, if any, are to be properly supervised.
	2. A sufficient understanding of internal control is to be obtained to plan the audit and to determine the nature, timing, and extent of tests to be performed.
2. Sufficient evidence shall be obtained to provide a reasonable basis for the conclusion that is expressed in the report.	3. Sufficient competent evidence is to be obtained through inspection, observation, inquiries, and confirmations to afford a reasonable basis for an opinion regarding the financial statements under audit.
Standards of Reporting	
1. The report shall identify the subject matter or the assertion being reported on and state the character of the engagement.	
2. The report shall state the practitioner's conclusion about the subject matter or the assertion in relation to the criteria against which the subject matter was evaluated.	1. The report shall state whether the financial statements are presented in accordance with generally accepted accounting principles.
	2. The report shall identify those circumstances in which such principles have not been consistently observed in the current period in relation to the preceding period.
	3. Informative disclosures in the financial statements are to be regarded as reasonably adequate unless otherwise stated in the report.
3. The report shall state all of the practitioner's significant reservations about the engagement, the subject matter, and, if applicable, the assertion related thereto.	4. The report shall contain either an expression of opinion regarding the financial statements, taken as a whole, or an assertion to the effect that an opinion cannot be expressed. When an overall opinion cannot be expressed, the reasons therefore should be stated. In all cases where an auditor's name is associated with financial statements, the report should contain a clear-cut indication of the character of the auditor's work, if any, and the degree of responsibility the auditor is taking.
4. The report shall state that the use of the report is restricted to specified parties under the following circumstances:	
• When the criteria used to evaluate the subject matter are determined by the practitioner to be appropriate only for a limited number of parties who either participated in their establishment or can be presumed to have an adequate understanding of the criteria.	
• When the criteria used to evaluate the subject matter are available only to specified parties.	
• When reporting on subject matter and a written assertion has not been provided by the responsible party.	
• When the report is on an attest engagement to apply agreed-upon procedures to the subject matter.	

Standards of
Field Work

The only difference in the standards of field work between the attestation standards and generally accepted auditing standards is that the attestation standards do not require an understanding of internal control. Given the varied nature of services that can be performed under the attestation standards, such a requirement would be prohibitively restrictive. The approach to field work for an attestation engagement should involve proper planning and supervision, and sufficient evidence must be gathered to provide a reasonable basis for the practitioner's conclusion about the subject matter or assertion.

Standards of
Reporting

Reporting standards for attestation engagements differ in a number of respects from those of generally accepted auditing standards. First, in view of the wide variety of possible services, the attestation standards do not contain anything about consistent application of GAAP or informative disclosures. However, they do require that the report identify the subject matter or assertion and the type of engagement being performed. The reporting standards also require that the practitioner state any significant reservation about the engagement or presentation of the assertion. The fourth standard of reporting lists four situations where the use of the report is restricted to specified parties, for example, when the attest engagement involves the application of agreed-upon procedures.

Reporting on an Entity's Internal Control over Financial Reporting

[LO 6]   In recent years, accountants have increasingly been asked to provide reports on the effectiveness of an entity's internal control. Impetus was given for such reporting when Congress passed the Federal Deposit Insurance Corporation Act of 1991, which requires that the management of large financial institutions issue a report on the effectiveness of the institution's internal control. The Act also requires that these institutions engage accountants to attest to management's report. As discussed in Chapter 7, the Sarbanes-Oxley Act of 2002 imposed similar requirements on all publicly held companies. While an audit of internal control is not required of privately held companies, some such companies may engage an accounting firm to provide attestation services relating to internal control.

The practitioner should obtain from the responsible party a written assertion about the effectiveness of internal control. The responsible party may present the written assertion in either (1) a separate report that will accompany the practitioner's report or (2) a representation letter to the practitioner. When management's assertion does not accompany the practitioner's report, the first paragraph of the report should also contain a statement of management's assertion.

Conditions for
Conducting an
Engagement

In order for the practitioner to examine management's assertions about the effectiveness of internal control in an attestation engagement, the following conditions are necessary:

- Management of the entity accepts responsibility for the effectiveness of the entity's internal control.

- The responsible party evaluates the effectiveness of the entity's internal control using suitable criteria (referred to as *control criteria*).
- Sufficient competent evidence exists or could be developed to support the responsible party's evaluation.
- Management provides to the practitioner its written assertion based on control criteria referred to in its report.

Criteria issued by the AICPA, regulatory agencies, and other bodies of experts that follow due process qualify as control criteria. For example, management may use the criteria provided in AU 319–Consideration of Internal Control in a Financial Statement Audit, which is based on the control criteria included in the COSO Report.

A practitioner is allowed to perform either of two types of attestation engagements for reporting on internal control: (1) examination or (2) agreed-upon procedures. The standard specifically prohibits the practitioner from accepting an engagement to *review* and report on management's assertion relating to internal control.

Examination Engagement

The practitioner's objective in an engagement to examine management's assertion about the effectiveness of the entity's internal control is to express an opinion on (1) the effectiveness of the entity's internal control, in all material respects, based on the control criteria or (2) whether the responsible party's assertion about the effectiveness of internal control is fairly stated, in all material respects, based on the control criteria. An examination engagement is conducted similarly to the audit of internal control required of public companies, as described in Chapters 7 and 18.

While examining the entity's internal control, the practitioner may encounter control deficiencies. Attestation standards rely on auditing standards (AU 325–Communication of Internal Control–Related Matters Noted in an Audit) to distinguish between reportable conditions and material weaknesses.[3] In general, a material weakness will preclude the practitioner from concluding that the entity has effective internal control. If the practitioner identifies any reportable conditions, they should be communicated to the audit committee.

Finally, the practitioner should obtain written representations from management, similar to those listed in Exhibit 7–8 in Chapter 7. If management refuses to provide written representations, a scope limitation exists.

---

[3]The PCAOB adopted the terms *significant deficiency* and *material weakness* in connection with the audit of internal control over financial reporting for public companies (see Chapter 7 for definitions of these terms). The AICPA and PCAOB definitions of *material weakness* are similar to each other. However, the AICPA definition of a *reportable condition* is somewhat different from the PCAOB definition of a *significant deficiency*. AICPA standards define a *reportable condition* as a deficiency in the "design or operation of internal control that could adversely affect the entity's ability to initiate, record, process, and report financial data consistent with the assertions of management in the financial statements" (AT Section 501). At the writing of this book, the AICPA has issued an exposure draft (*Reporting on an Entity's Internal Control over Financial Reporting*) proposing that the wording of the AICPA attestation standards be made consistent with PCAOB standards.

Reporting on
Management's
Assertion about
Internal Control

The practitioner's report should include (1) a title that includes the word *independent*, (2) an identification of the subject matter (internal control over financial reporting), (3) a statement that the responsible party is responsible for maintaining effective internal control over financial reporting, (4) a statement that the practitioner's responsibility is to express an opinion based on his or her examination, (5) a statement that the examination was conducted in accordance with standards established by the AICPA, (6) a statement that the practitioner believes the examination provides a reasonable basis for his or her opinion, and (7) a paragraph stating that, because of the inherent limitations of any internal control, errors or fraud may occur and not be detected. The practitioner's report should contain an opinion on whether the entity has maintained, in all material respects, effective internal control over financial reporting as of the specified date, based on control criteria. When the report is subject to limited distribution, the practitioner's report should contain a statement limiting the use of the report. Again, these reporting requirements are similar to those for reporting on the audit of internal control over financial reporting.

Financial Forecasts and Projections

[LO 7]   Auditors have been asked to provide assurance with respect to prospective financial statements. Attestation standards (Chapter 3, SSAE No. 10) provide guidance for practitioners providing such services. The practitioner's involvement may include (1) assembling or assisting the client in assembling prospective financial statements or (2) reporting on prospective financial statements. In either of these situations, the practitioner can *examine*, apply *agreed-upon procedures*, or *compile* the prospective financial statements if such statements are expected to be used by a third party.

Types of
Prospective
Financial
Statements

Prospective financial statements contain financial information made up of either financial forecasts or financial projections. *Financial forecasts* are prospective financial statements that present an entity's *expected* financial position, results of operations, and cash flows. They are based on assumptions reflecting conditions the responsible party *expects to exist* and the course of action it *expects to take*. *Financial projections* are prospective financial statements that present, *given one or more hypothetical assumptions,* an entity's expected financial position, results of operations, and cash flows. These assumptions may not reflect the most likely or expected conditions. The primary difference between the two is that the financial projection is based on hypothetical assumptions and is intended to respond to a question, such as "What would happen if . . . ?" A financial projection is sometimes prepared to present one or more possible courses of action for evaluation.

Prospective financial statements are for either general use or limited use. *General use* of prospective financial statements refers to the use of the statements by persons with whom the responsible party is not negotiating directly. An example would be an offering statement containing prospective financial statements for an entity's debt or equity securities. Because the

TABLE 21–3	**Minimum Presentation Guidelines for Prospective Financial Information**

Sales or gross revenues.
Gross profit or cost of sales.
Unusual or infrequently occurring items.
Provision for income taxes.
Discontinued operations or extraordinary items.
Income from continuing operations.
Net income.
Basic and fully diluted earnings per share.
Significant changes in financial position.
A description of what the responsible party intends the prospective financial statements to present, a statement that the assumptions are based on information about circumstances and conditions existing at the time the prospective information was prepared, and a caveat that the prospective results may not be achieved.
Summary of significant assumptions.
Summary of significant accounting policies.

intended users cannot question the responsible party, the only appropriate basis of presentation is the *expected results.* Therefore, only a financial *forecast* is appropriate for general use.

Limited use of prospective financial statements refers to use of the statements by the responsible party alone or by the responsible party and third parties with whom the responsible party is directly negotiating. Examples of limited use include negotiations for a bank loan, submission to a regulatory agency, or use solely within the entity. In such cases, the third parties can question the responsible party about the prospective financial information and can agree on the assumed conditions on which it is based. Thus, any type of prospective financial statement is appropriate for limited use.

While the responsible party is responsible for presentation of prospective financial statements, other parties, such as accountants, may assist in meeting the presentation guidelines specified in the attestation standards. Prospective financial statements should preferably be in the same format as the historical financial statements; however, they may be limited to the items shown in Table 21–3. A presentation that omits any item in Table 21–3 is referred to as a *partial* presentation.

Examination of Prospective Financial Statements

An examination of prospective financial statements involves four steps: (1) evaluating the preparation of the prospective financial statements, (2) evaluating the support underlying the assumptions, (3) evaluating the presentation of the prospective financial statements for conformity with SSAE No. 10, and (4) issuing an examination report. The accountant should be independent, have adequate technical training and proficiency to examine prospective financial statements, and obtain sufficient evidence to issue an examination report. Exhibits 21–1 and 21–2 present examples of the standard examination report for a forecast and a projection, respectively. The only major difference between the two reports is the paragraph limiting distribution of the projection to specified users.

EXHIBIT 21–1	**Example of a Standard Examination Report on a Forecast**

Independent Accountant's Report

We have examined the accompanying forecasted balance sheet, statements of income, retained earnings, and cash flows of Panatta Company as of December 31, 2005, and for the year then ending. Panatta Company's management is responsible for the forecast. Our responsibility is to express an opinion on the forecast based on our examination.

Our examination was made in accordance with attestation standards established by the American Institute of Certified Public Accountants and, accordingly, included such procedures as we considered necessary to evaluate both the assumptions used by management and the preparation and presentation of the forecast. We believe that our examination provides a reasonable basis for our opinion.

In our opinion, the accompanying forecast is presented in conformity with guidelines for presentation of a forecast established by the American Institute of Certified Public Accountants, and the underlying assumptions provide a reasonable basis for management's forecast. However, there will usually be differences between the forecasted and actual results, because events and circumstances frequently do not occur as expected, and those differences may be material. We have no responsibility to update this report for events and circumstances occurring after the date of this report.

The following circumstances may require a departure from the standard examination report:

- Departure from SSAE No. 10 presentation guidelines.
- Unreasonable assumptions.
- Scope limitation.

EXHIBIT 21–2	**Example of a Standard Examination Report on a Projection**

Independent Accountant's Report

We have examined the accompanying projected balance sheet, statements of income, retained earnings, and cash flows of Hansen Company as of December 31, 2005, and for the year then ending. Hansen Company's management is responsible for the projection, which was prepared for the Panama City National Bank for the purpose of negotiating a loan to expand Hansen Company's plant. Our responsibility is to express an opinion on the projection based on our examination.

Our examination was made in accordance with attestation standards established by the American Institute of Certified Public Accountants and, accordingly, included such procedures as we considered necessary to evaluate both the assumptions used by management and the preparation and presentation of the projection. We believe that our examination provides a reasonable basis for our opinion.

In our opinion, the accompanying projection is presented in conformity with guidelines for presentation of a projection established by the American Institute of Certified Public Accountants, and the underlying assumptions provide a reasonable basis for management's projection, assuming the granting of the requested loan for the purpose of expanding Hansen Company's plant as described in the summary of significant assumptions. However, even if the loan is granted and the plant is expanded, there will usually be differences between the projected and actual results, because events and circumstances frequently do not occur as expected, and those differences may be material. We have no responsibility to update this report for events and circumstances occurring after the date of this report.

The accompanying projection and this report are intended solely for the information and use of Hansen Company and Panama City National Bank and are not intended to be and should not be used by anyone other than these parties.

The presence of such events can result in a report that is either qualified or adverse. A disclaimer may also be issued.

Agreed-Upon Procedures for Prospective Financial Statements

An agreed-upon procedures engagement is significantly more limited in scope than is an examination. An accountant may perform an agreed-upon procedures attestation engagement for prospective financial statements provided that attestation standards are complied with and

1. The practitioner and the specified users agree upon the procedures performed or to be performed by the practitioner.
2. The specified users take responsibility for the sufficiency of the agreed-upon procedures for their purposes.
3. The prospective financial statements include a summary of significant assumptions.
4. The prospective financial statements to which the procedures are to be applied are subject to reasonably consistent evaluation against criteria that are suitable and available to the specified parties.
5. Criteria to be used to determine findings are agreed upon between the practitioner and the specified users.

The accountant must satisfy the requirement that the specified users take full responsibility for the sufficiency of the procedures to be performed by the accountant by doing at least one of the following:

- Comparing the procedures to be applied to the written requirements of the specified users.
- Discussing the procedures to be applied with an appropriate representative of the specified users.
- Reviewing relevant contracts with or correspondence from the specified users.

Exhibit 21–3 presents an example of a report on the use of agreed-upon procedures. Use of an agreed-upon procedures report is always explicitly restricted to the users specified in the report.

Compilation of Prospective Financial Statements

A practitioner can perform a compilation of prospective financial information. A compilation of prospective financial statements involves

- Assembling, to the extent necessary, the prospective financial statements based on the responsible party's assumptions.
- Performing the required compilation procedures, which include reading the prospective financial statements with their summaries of significant assumptions and accounting policies and considering whether they appear to be (1) presented in conformity with the attestation standards shown in Table 21–2 and (2) not obviously inappropriate.
- Issuing a compilation report.

A practitioner should *not* issue a compilation report on prospective financial statements that exclude disclosure of the *summary of significant*

EXHIBIT 21-3	**Example of an Agreed-Upon Procedures Report for a Forecast**

Independent Accountant's Report on Applying Agreed-Upon Procedures

Board of Directors—Donnay Corporation
Board of Directors—Clinkton Company

At your request, we have performed certain agreed-upon procedures, as enumerated below, with respect to the forecasted balance sheet, and the related forecasted statements of income, retained earnings, and cash flows of Matlin Company, a subsidiary of Clinkton Company, as of December 31, 2005, and for the year then ending. These procedures, which were agreed to by the boards of directors of Donnay Corporation and Clinkton Company, were performed solely to assist you in evaluating the forecast in connection with the sale of Matlin Company to Clinkton Company.

This agreed-upon procedures engagement was conducted in accordance with attestation standards established by the American Institute of Certified Public Accountants. The sufficiency of these procedures is solely the responsibility of the specified users of the report. Consequently, we make no representation regarding the sufficiency of the procedures described below either for the purpose for which this report has been requested or for any other purpose.

The procedures and associated findings are as follows:

a. With respect to forecasted rental income, we compared the assumptions about expected demand for rental of the housing units to demand for similar housing units at similar rental prices in the city area in which Matlin Company's housing units are located.

No exceptions were found as a result of this comparison.

b. We tested the forecast for mathematical accuracy.

The forecast was mathematically accurate.

We were not engaged to and did not conduct an examination, the objective of which would be the expression of an opinion on the accompanying prospective financial statements. Accordingly, we do not express an opinion on whether the prospective financial statements are presented in conformity with AICPA presentation guidelines or on whether the underlying assumptions provide a reasonable basis for the presentation. Had we performed additional procedures, other matters might have come to our attention that would have been reported to you. Furthermore, there will usually be differences between the forecasted and actual results, because events and circumstances frequently do not occur as expected, and those differences may be material. We have no responsibility to update this report for events and circumstances occurring after the date of this report.

This report is intended solely for the use of the boards of directors of Donnay Corporation and Clinkton Company and is not intended to be nor should be used by anyone other than these parties.

EXHIBIT 21-4	**Example of Standard Compilation Report for a Forecast**

Independent Accountant's Report

We have compiled the accompanying forecasted balance sheet, statements of income, retained earnings, and cash flows of Lumatta Company as of December 31, 2005, and for the year then ending, in accordance with attestation standards established by the American Institute of Certified Public Accountants.

A compilation is limited to presenting in the form of a forecast information that is the representation of management and does not include evaluation of the support for the assumptions underlying the forecast. We have not examined the forecast and, accordingly, do not express an opinion or any other form of assurance on the accompanying statements or assumptions. Furthermore, there will usually be differences between the forecasted and actual results, because events and circumstances frequently do not occur as expected, and those differences may be material. We have no responsibility to update this report for events and circumstances occurring after the date of this report.

assumptions. Exhibit 21–4 provides an example of a compilation report for a forecast. Note that the report explicitly indicates that the accountant does not offer assurance when providing a compilation service.

Accounting and Review Services

æ **[LO 8]** Many nonpublic businesses do not need an audit of their financial statements. This typically occurs because the entity is small and the owner is involved in the day-to-day operations, there are no debts or regulations requiring an audit, or an audit may be too costly for the entity. However, these same entities may employ a CPA to assist with preparing their financial statements, tax returns, or other financial documents.

Until 1977 there was relatively little guidance on how to perform or report on engagements involving *unaudited* financial statements. As discussed in Chapter 20, the *1136 Tenants'* case involved auditors' liability for unaudited financial statements. One outcome of this case was the establishment of the Accounting and Review Services Committee by the AICPA. This committee was designated by the AICPA to issue Statements on Standards for Accounting and Review Services (SSARS) in connection with unaudited financial statements.

SSARS provide for two types of services: *compilation* of financial statements and *review* of financial statements. A compilation differs significantly from a review. The work done on a compilation provides no assurance about the fair presentation of the financial statements. A review, on the other hand, provides the accountant with a reasonable basis for expressing limited assurance that no material modifications should be made to the financial statements. This can be compared to an audit, in which the auditor provides an opinion about whether the financial statements present fairly the financial position and results of operations of the entity. Figure 21–4 compares the assurance provided by an audit with the assurances provided by a review and a compilation.

Compilations and reviews specifically apply to engagements for which the output of the service is a set of financial statements. An accountant may provide other types of services, such as preparing a working trial balance, assisting in adjusting the account books, consulting on accounting, tax, and similar matters, preparing tax returns, and providing various manual or automated bookkeeping or data processing services, without having to comply with the standards for compilations and reviews.

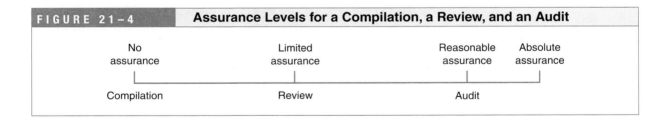

FIGURE 21–4	Assurance Levels for a Compilation, a Review, and an Audit

No assurance	Limited assurance	Reasonable assurance	Absolute assurance
Compilation	Review	Audit	

Compilation of Financial Statements

A *compilation* is defined as presenting, in the form of financial statements, information that is the representation of management or owners without undertaking to express any assurance on the statements. In conducting a compilation, the accountant must have the following knowledge about the entity:

- The accounting principles and practices of the industry in which the entity operates.
- A general understanding of the nature of the entity's business transactions, the form of its accounting records, and the stated qualifications of its accounting personnel.
- The accounting basis on which the financial statements are to be presented and the form and content of the financial statements.

Note that the accountant is not required to conduct any inquiries or to perform any procedures to verify or corroborate any information supplied by the client. However, the accountant should read the compiled financial statements to determine whether they are in appropriate form and free from obvious errors, such as mathematical or clerical mistakes or mistakes in the application of accounting principles. Because this service is usually provided to small companies that have few accounting personnel, the accountant is normally heavily involved with preparing the financial statements.

There are three forms of compilation reports:

- Compilation with full disclosure.
- Compilation that omits substantially all disclosures.
- Compilation when the accountant is not independent.

The report should be dated as of the completion of the compilation. Additionally, each page of the financial statements should be marked with a notation such as "See Accountant's Compilation Report."

Compilation with Full Disclosure

When the entity presents a set of financial statements that contain all necessary financial disclosures required by generally accepted accounting principles or another comprehensive basis of accounting, the accountant can issue what might be referred to as a standard compilation report. Exhibit 21–5 is an example of such a report.

EXHIBIT 21–5	**Example of a Compilation Report with Full Disclosure**

We have compiled the accompanying balance sheet of Learn Medical Services as of December 31, 2005, and the related statements of income, retained earnings, and cash flows for the year then ended, in accordance with Statements on Standards for Accounting and Review Services issued by the American Institute of Certified Public Accountants.

A compilation is limited to presenting in the form of financial statements information that is the representation of management. We have not audited or reviewed the accompanying financial statements and accordingly do not express an opinion or any other form of assurance on them.

EXHIBIT 21–6	**Example of a Compilation Report That Omits Substantially All Disclosures**

We have compiled the accompanying balance sheet of Loisel Company as of December 31, 2005, and the related statements of income, retained earnings, and cash flows for the year then ended, in accordance with Statements on Standards for Accounting and Review Services issued by the American Institute of Certified Public Accountants.

A compilation is limited to presenting, in the form of financial statements, information that is the representation of management. We have not audited or reviewed the accompanying financial statements and accordingly do not express an opinion or any other form of assurance on them.

Management has elected to omit substantially all of the disclosures required by generally accepted accounting principles. If the omitted disclosures were included in the financial statements, they might influence the user's conclusions about the company's financial position, results of operations, and cash flows. Accordingly, these financial statements are not designed for those who are not informed about the matters.

Compilation That Omits Substantially All Disclosures

Sometimes an entity may request that the accountant compile financial statements without making all the necessary disclosures. Many times this request is made to minimize the cost of the engagement. The accountant can compile such financial statements so long as the omission is clearly indicated in the report and the client's intent is not to mislead the user. Exhibit 21–6 is an example of a compilation report in which financial disclosures have been omitted.

Compilation When the Accountant Is Not Independent

An accountant can perform a compilation engagement even though he or she is not independent of the entity. This is allowed by the Code of Professional Conduct. If the accountant is not independent, the lack of independence must be disclosed in the report. However, the reasons for the lack of independence should not be described. This requirement prevents the accountant from trying to minimize the lack of independence by "explaining away" the circumstances. The following sentence is added as the last paragraph of the report when the accountant is not independent: "We are not independent with respect to Learn Medical Services."

Review of Financial Statements

A *review* is defined as the performance of inquiry and analytical procedures to provide the accountant with a reasonable basis for expressing *limited assurance* that *no material modifications* should be made to the statements in order for them to conform to generally accepted accounting principles or another comprehensive basis of accounting. In conducting a review, the accountant's work involves the following:

- Obtaining knowledge of the accounting principles and practices of the industry in which the entity operates and an understanding of the entity's business.
- Obtaining a general understanding of the entity's organization, its operating characteristics, and the nature of its assets, liabilities,

TABLE 21–4	**Examples of Inquiries Made during a Review Engagement**

1. Inquiries concerning the client's accounting principles and practices.
2. Inquiries concerning the client's procedures for recording, classifying, and summarizing accounting transactions.
3. Inquiries concerning actions taken at stockholders', board of directors', and other committee meetings.
4. Inquiries of persons responsible for the financial statements concerning
   Whether the statements are in accordance with GAAP.
   Changes in the client's business activities or accounting principles.
   Any exceptions concerning other analytical procedures.
   Subsequent events having a material effect on the statements.

revenues, and expenses (this would include general knowledge of the entity's production, distribution, and compensation methods, types of products and services, operating locations, and material transactions with related parties).

- Asking the entity's personnel about some of the items noted in Table 21–4.
- Performing analytical procedures to identify relationships and individual items that appear to be unusual (the process followed for conducting analytical procedures is similar to the one described for audits in Chapter 5).
- Reading the financial statements to determine if they conform to GAAP.
- Obtaining reports from other accountants, if any, who have audited or reviewed the financial statements or significant components thereof.
- Obtaining a representation letter from management (generally, the chief executive officer and chief financial officer should sign the representation letter).

Note that a review engagement does not require the accountant to obtain an understanding of internal control, test accounting records by performing detailed tests, or corroborate inquiries, as would normally be done on an audit. However, if while conducting the review the accountant becomes aware of information that is incorrect, incomplete, or misleading, he or she should perform any additional procedures necessary to provide limited assurance that no material modifications to the financial statements are required.

Review Report

A standard review report assumes that the financial statements are in accordance with generally accepted accounting principles or another comprehensive basis of accounting. This includes all necessary disclosures. The review report should be dated as of the completion of the accountant's inquiry and analytical procedures. Additionally, each page of the financial statements should contain a notation such as "See Accountant's Review Report." Exhibit 21–7 is an example of the standard review report.

EXHIBIT 21-7	**Example of a Standard Review Report**

We have reviewed the accompanying balance sheet of Sierra Company as of December 31, 2005, and the related statements of income, retained earnings, and cash flows for the year then ended, in accordance with Statements on Standards for Accounting and Review Services issued by the American Institute of Certified Public Accountants. All information included in these financial statements is the representation of the management of Sierra Company.

A review consists principally of inquiries of company personnel and analytical procedures applied to financial data. It is substantially less in scope than an audit in accordance with generally accepted auditing standards, the objective of which is the expression of an opinion regarding the financial statements taken as a whole. Accordingly, we do not express such an opinion.

Based on our review, we are not aware of any material modifications that should be made to the accompanying financial statements in order for them to be in conformity with generally accepted accounting principles.

Conditions That May Result in Modification of a Compilation or Review Report

When the accountant conducts a compilation or review, he or she may become aware of situations that require modification to the standard report. Two particular situations are (1) a departure from generally accepted accounting principles and (2) a going-concern uncertainty. If there is a departure from GAAP, the departure should be disclosed in a separate paragraph of the report. Exhibit 21–8 is an example of a review report modified for a departure from GAAP (italics indicate an added phrase).

If the accountant believes that there are questions concerning the continuing viability of the entity, the accountant should add the following paragraph after the standard three paragraphs:

> The accompanying financial statements have been prepared assuming that the company will continue as a going concern. As discussed in Note 7 to the financial statements, the company has suffered recurring losses from operations and has a net capital deficiency that raises substantial doubt about its ability to continue as a going concern. Management's plans in regard to these matters are also described in Note 7. The financial statements do not include any adjustments that might result from the outcome of this uncertainty.

The process the accountant follows in determining whether the entity is a going concern is similar to the process used for assessing going-concern issues during an audit, discussed in Chapter 17.

EXHIBIT 21-8	**Example of a Modified Review Report for a Departure from GAAP**

[*Same wording as in the first and second paragraphs of the standard review report*]

Based on our review, *with the exception of the matter described in the following paragraph,* we are not aware of any material modifications that should be made to the accompanying financial statements in order for them to be in conformity with generally accepted accounting principles.

As disclosed in Note 4 to the financial statements, generally accepted accounting principles require that inventory cost consist of material, labor, and overhead. Management has informed us that the inventory of finished goods and work in process is stated in the accompanying financial statements at material and labor cost only, and that the effects of this departure from generally accepted accounting principles on financial position, results of operations, and cash flows have not been determined.

Internal Auditing

[LO 9]   Up to this point, we have focused on nonaudit assurance and attestation services that are provided by public accountants. The remainder of the chapter focuses on the role of, standards pertaining to, and services provided by, internal auditors in recognition of their significance as a large and important assurance domain.

The largest financial statement fraud in the history of the United States may not have been discovered were it not for the persistent investigative efforts of Cynthia Cooper and her internal audit team (see Exhibit 14–2). Cynthia Cooper, the whistle-blower of the $9 billion WorldCom fraud, was head of internal audit at the communications giant at the time. According to the 2003 *Report of Investigation by the Special Investigative Committee of the Board of Directors of Worldcom, Inc.*, despite being ordered by the company's management to discontinue investigations in the areas where the fraud had been committed, Cooper's team aggressively pushed ahead and eventually uncovered the massive fraud.

After the Enron and WorldCom frauds, the Sarbanes-Oxley Act of 2002 placed increased emphasis on the importance of public companies' internal audit functions, and in August 2002 the New York Stock Exchange (NYSE) indicated that all companies wishing to trade on the exchange are required to have a viable internal audit function. The role of the internal auditor has clearly become increasingly crucial to effective corporate governance and to the success of large organizations.

Internal auditing can be a challenging and rewarding career path. Many public accountants who work as external auditors eventually become internal auditors, and many internal auditors eventually become executives within their organizations. These opportunities arise because internal auditors are in a unique position to understand the organization from a perspective that is both broad and deep.

Internal Auditing Defined

The Institute of Internal Auditors (IIA), which oversees and sets standards for internal auditing internationally, defines *internal auditing* as follows:

> Internal auditing is an independent, objective assurance and consulting activity designed to add value and improve an organization's operations. It helps an organization accomplish its objectives by bringing a systematic, disciplined approach to evaluate and improve the effectiveness of risk management, control, and governance processes.

This definition outlines the main goals of the profession and broadly states the methods whereby these goals may be achieved. The IIA has issued detailed and rigorous standards for the practice of internal auditing; however, there are several important differences between the internal and external auditing professions.

The Institute of Internal Auditors

Established in 1941, the IIA is an international professional association with world headquarters in Altamonte Springs, Florida. The IIA has over 93,000 members in internal auditing, risk management, governance, internal control, IT audit, education, and security. The Institute is the recognized authority, principal educator, and acknowledged leader in certification, research, and technological guidance for the internal auditing profession worldwide. The IIA offers not only the general Certified Internal Auditor (CIA) certification but also specialty certifications in areas including government accounting and financial services.

IIA Standards

In order to bridge the gap between a changing business environment and the guidance that was previously available, the IIA developed a *Professional Practices Framework*. This framework consists of three broad categories of guidance:

- Standards and Ethics (consisting of the Code of Ethics and the International Standards for the Professional Practice of Internal Auditing);
- Practice advisories; and
- Practice aids.

The first of these areas, standards and ethics, provides mandatory guidance for IIA members and consists of the *Code of Ethics* and the *International Standards for the Professional Practice of Internal Auditing*. The International Standards for the Professional Practice of Internal Auditing are in turn divided into three main areas: attribute standards, performance standards, and implementation standards.

Attribute standards define the expected attributes of organizations and the auditors conducting internal audit services, and *performance standards* outline criteria against which internal auditors can measure their performance. The standards in these two areas are similar in scope to the 10 generally accepted auditing standards applicable to external auditors. Table 21–5 presents the IIA's attribute and performance standards. Given the substantial variation in internal audit environments across the world, attribute and performance standards are necessarily general; however, the third category of IIA standards, known as *implementation standards*, are more detailed, focusing on direct applications to specific situations.

Code of Ethics

As with most reputable professions, internal auditors must follow guidelines promoting ethical conduct (see Chapter 19 for a discussion of the AICPA/PCAOB Code of Professional Conduct, which applies to external auditors). The IIA Code of Ethics is important for internal auditors because the reliability of their work depends on a reputation for high levels of objectivity and personal integrity. The Code of Ethics specifies four main principles of ethical conduct and some associated rules that underpin the expected conduct of IIA members: integrity, objectivity, confidentiality, and competency (see Tables 21–6 and 21–7).

Internal Auditors' Roles

Internal auditors are called "internal" because they work within an individual entity and report the results of their work to management or (ideally) to the entity's audit committee or board of directors. They are not typically

TABLE 21–5	International Standards for the Professional Practice of Internal Auditing

Standard	Definition
Attribute Standards	
1000—Purpose, authority, and responsibility	The purpose, authority, and responsibility of the internal audit activity should be formally defined in a charter, consistent with the Standards, and approved by the board.
1100—Independence and objectivity	The internal audit activity should be independent, and internal auditors should be objective in performing their work.
1200—Proficiency and due professional care	Engagements should be performed with proficiency and due professional care.
1300—Quality assurance and improvement program	The chief audit executive should develop and maintain a quality assurance and improvement program that covers all aspects of the internal audit activity and continuously monitors its effectiveness. This program includes periodic internal and external quality assessments and ongoing internal monitoring. Each part of the program should be designed to help the internal auditing activity add value and improve the organization's operations and to provide assurance that the internal audit activity is in conformity with the Standards and the Code of Ethics.
Performance Standards	
2000—Managing the internal audit activity	The chief audit executive should effectively manage the internal audit activity to ensure it adds value to the organization.
2100—Nature of work	The internal audit activity should evaluate and contribute to the improvement of risk management, control, and governance processes using a systematic and disciplined approach.
2200—Engagement planning	Internal auditors should develop and record a plan for each engagement, including the scope, objectives, timing and resource allocations.
2300—Performing the engagement	Internal auditors should identify, analyze, evaluate, and record sufficient information to achieve the engagement's objectives.
2400—Communicating results	Internal auditors should communicate the engagement results.
2500—Monitoring progress	The chief audit executive should establish and maintain a system to monitor the disposition of results communicated to management.
2600—Resolution of management's acceptance of risks	When the chief audit executive believes that senior management has accepted a level of residual risk that may be unacceptable to the organization, the chief audit executive should discuss the matter with senior management. If the decision regarding residual risk is not resolved, the chief audit executive and senior management should report the matter to the board for resolution.

TABLE 21–6	IIA Code of Ethics Principles

Principles	Definition
Integrity	The integrity of internal auditors establishes trust and thus provides the basis for reliance on their judgment.
Objectivity	Internal auditors exhibit the highest level of professional objectivity in gathering, evaluating, and communicating information about the activity or process being examined. Internal auditors make a balanced assessment of all the relevant circumstances and are not unduly influenced by their own interests or by others in forming judgments.
Confidentiality	Internal auditors respect the value and ownership of information they receive and do not disclose information without appropriate authority unless there is a legal or professional obligation to do so.
Competency	Internal auditors apply the knowledge, skills, and experience needed in the performance of internal auditing services.

TABLE 21–7	**IIA Rules of Conduct**

Principles	*Expectations*
Integrity	Internal auditors: 1.1. Shall perform their work with honesty, diligence, and responsibility. 1.2. Shall observe the law and make disclosures expected by the law and the profession. 1.3. Shall not knowingly be a party to any illegal activity, or engage in acts that are discreditable to the profession of internal auditing or to the organization. 1.4. Shall respect and contribute to the legitimate and ethical objectives of the organization.
Objectivity	Internal auditors: 2.1. Shall not participate in any activity or relationship that may impair or be presumed to impair their unbiased assessment. This participation includes those activities or relationships that may be in conflict with the interests of the organization. 2.2. Shall not accept anything that may impair or be presumed to impair their professional judgment. 2.3. Shall disclose all material facts known to them that, if not disclosed, may distort the reporting of activities under review.
Confidentiality	Internal auditors: 3.1. Shall be prudent in the use and protection of information acquired in the course of their duties. 3.2. Shall not use information for any personal gain or in any manner that would be contrary to the law or detrimental to the legitimate and ethical objectives of the organization.
Competency	Internal auditors: 4.1. Shall engage only in those services for which they have the necessary knowledge, skills, and experience. 4.2. Shall perform internal auditing services in accordance with the International Standards for the Professional Practice of Internal Auditing. 4.3. Shall continually improve their proficiency and the effectiveness and quality of their services.

expected to report to the public or to parties outside the entity. However, internal audit functions differ widely in how they are managed and staffed. Some entities have internal audit functions that are staffed entirely "in-house," while others are "co-sourced." When an organization co-sources its internal audit function the entity typically hires a public accounting firm to provide internal audit services in conjunction with the entity's own internal auditors, and this has become a significant source of revenue for many large accounting firms. Ideally an entity will have a chief audit executive (CAE), whose role is to oversee the internal audit function (whether in-house or co-sourced) and to help coordinate the work of the internal and external auditors. You will recall from Chapter 19, however, that SEC rules prohibit a public accounting firm from providing internal audit services to a financial statement audit client that is a public company.

The roles played by internal auditors fall into two primary categories—*assurance services* and *consulting services*.

> Assurance services involve the internal auditor's objective assessment of evidence to provide an independent opinion or conclusions regarding a process, system or other subject matter. The nature and scope of the assurance engagement are determined by the internal auditor. There are generally three parties involved in assurance services: (1) the person or group directly involved with the

process, system or other subject matter—the process owner, (2) the person or group making the assessment—the internal auditor, and (3) the person or group using the assessment—the user.

Consulting services are advisory in nature, and are generally performed at the specific request of an engagement client. The nature and scope of the consulting engagement are subject to agreement with the engagement client. Consulting services generally involve two parties: (1) the person or group offering the advice—the internal auditor, and (2) the person or group seeking and receiving the advice—the engagement client. When performing consulting services the internal auditor should maintain objectivity and not assume management responsibility.[4]

In general terms, an organization's internal audit function is most often used by management and the board of directors in the broad areas of evaluating risks, evaluating compliance, and performing financial and operational auditing. Through these activities, internal auditors contribute to effective *corporate governance* within an organization, which includes all management-administered policies and procedures to control risk and oversee operations within a company. Indeed, the IIA and other influential organizations, such as the NYSE, identify the internal audit function as one of the cornerstones of effective corporate governance.

Evaluating Risks and Controls
As outlined by IIA Standard 2110, internal auditors should be directly involved in an entity's risk management process. In fact, IIA standards require internal auditors to conduct an evaluation of the organization's risk management process. Although the internal auditor's industry expertise allows him or her to stay abreast of general industry risks, it is his or her specific experience within the organization that enables him or her to accurately gauge risks relating to the integrity of financial and operational information, the safeguarding of assets, and compliance with laws and regulations. Internal auditors are often asked to determine the sources of these risks, and may sometimes be called on to recommend approaches to manage identified risks. As we discussed in Chapter 7, Section 404 of the Sarbanes-Oxley Act requires public companies to implement and annually assess internal control over financial reporting. Internal auditors have long been involved in evaluating and enhancing their organizations' system of internal control over financial reporting and over other areas of the organization, and internal auditors often play a substantial role in ensuring compliance with these new requirements. By testing and assessing internal control, internal auditors also facilitate senior management's ability to provide the certifications required by Section 302 of the Sarbanes-Oxley Act—*Corporate Responsibility for Financial Reports*.

Reviewing Compliance
In many industries, compliance with relevant laws and regulations is an extremely complicated and important endeavour. For example, if a company fails to comply with the many requirements of

---

[4]*Introduction to the International Standards for the Professional Practice of Internal Auditing* (www.theiia.org).

the Occupational Safety and Health Act of 1970 (OSHA), the government can levy significant fines and penalties against the offending company. Many other governmental agencies have also issued rules and regulations that must be followed by businesses and other organizations. Such agencies include the Environmental Protection Agency (EPA) and the Food & Drug Administration (FDA), among many others. Internal auditors play an important role in helping management ensure that the organization complies with the laws, rules, and regulations that apply to the entity, as well as in ensuring that employees comply with organizational guidelines and rules.

Financial Auditing   Although the financial auditing performed by internal auditors involves many of the same concepts you have already studied in this text, it differs from the audits conducted by external auditors in several ways. For example, internal auditors do not generally audit periodic financial statements, but tend to focus on specific financial issues as directed by management. The nature of their audit report is also different. Because the intention of the audit may relate to either very general or very specific factors, it is impossible to require a standardized internal audit report. Consequently, internal audit reports are normally uniquely composed to fulfill the requirements of the particular assignment, as opposed to external audit reports which are quite standardized. Exhibit 21–9 describes a real-life situation where an organization's internal auditor uncovered a fraud while evaluating a specific financial area at the request of the organization's management.

Operational Auditing   Due to their unique position in an organization, internal auditors typically achieve a thorough understanding of how the organization operates, and internal auditors are thus able to provide various types of services to improve the entities in which they work. An auditor should be prepared to recognize when enhancements could be made to align current operations with the entity's objectives. Operational audits serve a wide variety of purposes. They are primarily conducted to identify the causes of problems or to enhance the efficiency or effectiveness of operations. In many organizations, internal auditors spend most of their time

---

EXHIBIT 21–9 | **Internal Financial Audit Uncovers Employee Fraud**

At a major research university, the internal audit team was called in to facilitate required budget cuts in the accounting department. The accounting department was understaffed and had only one staff member assigned to review procurement card transactions through the accounting office for staff and faculty. The internal auditor quickly identified some suspicious receipts that totalled $1,200. The investigation led to a single employee, and eventually over four van-loads of suspected unauthorized purchases were removed from the employee's home and personal vehicle. The fraud amounted to approximately $60,000 and led to the criminal prosecution of the suspect. The internal audit function saved the accounting department money immediately, but by identifying several weaknesses in the internal control system, it no doubt improved the efficiency and effectiveness of internal control for the entire university.

Source: Internal Auditor (June 2004), pp. 97–99.

performing operational audits. In fact, because they often spend relatively little of their time performing financial audits, the term *internal auditing* is often (incorrectly) used interchangeably with *operational auditing*.

**Internal Audit
Product Offerings**

In order to illustrate the diversity of services offered by internal auditors, refer to Figure 21–5, which shows how DuPont decided to deploy its internal audit resources. The figure illustrates two important points. First, the management of risk is the central focus of internal audit at DuPont. Risk management is important because a successful company must be able not only to deal with current problems but also to anticipate and prepare for other potential obstacles. Second, the wheel in Figure 21–5 is not static, but contains several ongoing and interdependent processes. A modern internal audit function must be adaptable and able to keep up with the changing demands of the modern business environment in large and complex organizations such as DuPont. Exhibit 21–10 offers a more detailed description of each of the product categories outlined in DuPont's "internal audit product wheel."

| FIGURE 21-5 | **DuPont's Uses of the Internal Audit Function** |

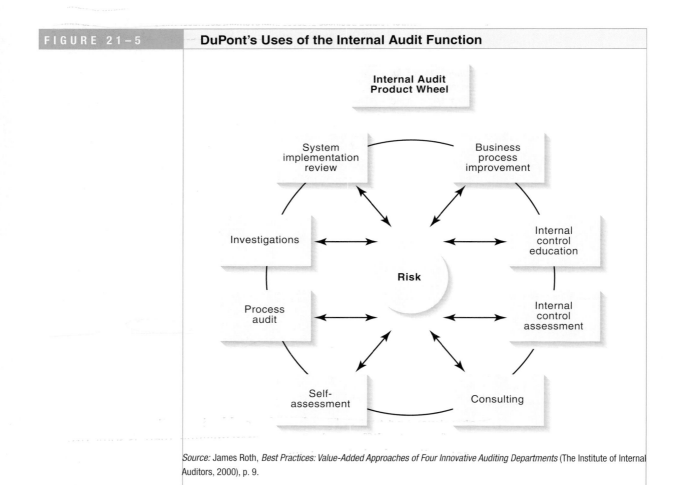

Source: James Roth, *Best Practices: Value-Added Approaches of Four Innovative Auditing Departments* (The Institute of Internal Auditors, 2000), p. 9.

EXHIBIT 21–10	Definitions of the Services Provided by DuPont's Internal Auditors

Process Audits Internal auditing undertakes comprehensive analyses and appraisals of all phases of business activities and provides management with appropriate recommendations concerning the activities reviewed. This product includes business process audits, which appraise the adequacy and efficiency of accounting, financial, and operating controls; information systems audits, which focus on technical IS audit activities, system implementation and application reviews; reviews of emerging technology; and new site reviews which occur in the early stages of start-up operations, joint ventures, or acquisitions to ensure that cost-effective internal control is in place.

Special Investigation This service provides the client with an independent review of facts and circumstances surrounding an event or series of events and presents recommendations to management for appropriate resolution/action. Investigations are often associated with known or suspected wrongdoing, waste, fraud, abuse of company assets, other business ethics violations, and/or serious mismanagement.

System Implementation Review System implementation reviews are conducted as part of the prevention quadrant of internal auditing's products. The System Implementation Review promotes the inclusion of cost-effective controls into systems prior to implementation and assures that the controls will operate as intended when implemented.

Business Process Improvement In limited circumstances, internal auditing may initiate or participate in internal control-related business process improvement activities. This product is used to identify and minimize control deficiencies in business processes and is designed to assist organizations in making process changes that result in strengthened internal control and optimal performance.

Internal Control Education This offering assists the client organization to reduce risk though an enhanced understanding of the business value of internal control and business ethics. Instructional sessions may be conducted by internal auditing or by the client with internal auditing support.

Internal Control Assessment This product provides the client with an overall opinion or assessment of the current state of internal control and future risks. Internal control assessments are conducted periodically on a corporate, regional, SBU, and functional basis. The COSO model serves as the methodology for conducting these assessments.

Consulting This is an internal auditing activity normally provided in response to a request from management. It is designed to provide expertise in the resolution of internal control issues. Consulting may involve answering questions, developing solutions to problems, recommending courses of action, and/or formulating an opinion. Consulting may also involve the review of proposed procedures for internal control content.

Self-Assessment Self-assessments are performed by the client based upon a framework and facilitation provided by internal auditing. Internal auditing will be an active participant in self-assessment activities, which involve an assessment of risk and control activities within the business and/or function under review.

Source: James Roth, *Best Practices: Value-Added Approaches of Four Innovative Auditing Departments* (The Institute of Internal Auditors, 2000), pp. 9–10.

Interactions between Internal and External Auditors

The objectives and types of work performed by internal and external auditors are often quite different, but as you may imagine, there is some overlap. External auditors do their work with the purpose of expressing an opinion as to whether the entity's financial statements are free of material misstatements. Because external auditors rely on the concept of materiality, they typically are not concerned with auditing a particular area in a great deal of depth—they gather evidence until they obtain reasonable assurance that no misstatements are present that would be considered significant in the context of the financial statements taken as a whole. They then report externally, outside of the organization being audited.

Internal auditors, on the other hand, assist management and the board of directors in evaluating and managing risk, assessing compliance with laws and regulations, assessing operational efficiency, and performing detailed financial audits of areas requiring particular attention. Because their objectives are often different from those of external auditors, the concept of materiality is usually quite different as well. For example, in auditing for employee fraud, the amounts involved are usually far from material in terms of the financial statements taken as a whole. However, internal auditors can reduce the incidence of employee fraud, saving money, and improving controls in the process.

Some of the work performed by internal auditors is directly relevant to the work of the independent auditor. For example, as discussed in Chapter 7, the external auditor can sometimes make use of controls-testing work performed by the internal auditor. Similarly, Chapter 5 briefly discusses the external auditor's use of work performed by the internal audit function in the context of the financial statement audit. Before relying on the work of internal auditors, the external auditor must evaluate the internal auditors' objectivity and competence. If the external auditor decides that some reliance is justified, the cost savings in terms of the reduction in the external audit fee can be significant.

Advanced Module: Examples of Assurance Services—Trust Services and PrimePlus Services

Trust Services

✵ [LO 10]

Electronic commerce involves individuals and organizations conducting business transactions without paper documents, using computer and telecommunications networks. This includes transactions under electronic data interchange (EDI), where formal contracts exist between the parties, and business over the Internet (World Wide Web), where the parties do not have a preexisting contractual relationship. Electronic commerce over the Internet has grown tremendously, as have the system requirements necessary to support this technology.

This growth in technology has also increased concerns by businesses and individuals. Businesses are concerned with such things as maintaining reliable, effective systems, while individuals worry about such things as the confidentiality of their information (such as credit card numbers). To respond to these concerns, the AICPA and the Canadian Institute of Chartered Accountants (CICA) developed *SysTrust* and *WebTrust*—two unique sets of principles by which CPAs could evaluate business systems and controls. In 2003, the AICPA and CICA combined the underlying principles of these two services into one common set of principles called Trust Services. The AICPA still offers SysTrust and WebTrust services, but these formerly separate services are now based on a common set of principles and criteria.

As seen in Table 21–8, Trust Services are built on five principles: security, availability, processing integrity, online privacy, and confidentiality.

TABLE 21–8	***Trust Services* Principles**

Security
> The system is protected against unauthorized access (both physical and logical).

Availability
> The system is available for operation and use as committed or agreed.

Processing Integrity
> System processing is complete, accurate, timely, and authorized.

Online Privacy
> Personal information obtained as a result of e-commerce is collected, used, disclosed, and retained as committed or agreed.

Confidentiality
> Information designated as confidential is protected as committed or agreed.

Complete Trust Services Principles and Criteria may be found online at www.aicpa.org/download/trust_services/final-Trust-Services.pdf.

These are broad principles that are nontechnical and easy to understand. Using these principles, CPAs can offer a wide variety of advisory and assurance services to their clients.

CPA WebTrust

[LO 11]

Three broad risks are associated with electronic commerce: business practices, transaction integrity, and information protection. Because commerce over the Internet may involve transactions between parties who do not know each other, how can a consumer know that the entity behind the Web page is "real"? How can the consumer be sure that the entity follows good business practices and that consumers will not be defrauded? Similarly, how can the consumer have assurance that electronic transactions will not be changed, lost, duplicated, or processed incorrectly? And how can the consumer be sure that private information will be protected? While setting up a Web page on the Internet is relatively easy, establishing strong security controls can be complex and costly. As a result of these risks, consumers have legitimate concerns about transaction integrity and confidentiality. An objective third party, such as a CPA, can provide assurance to customers about these risks. The WebTrust seal of assurance symbolizes to potential customers that a CPA has evaluated the website's business practices and controls to determine that they conform to the principles and criteria. Table 21–9 presents a WebTrust criterion and related disclosures for each of two principles for EarthWear Clothiers.

In order to obtain the WebTrust seal of assurance, an entity must meet all the Trust Services Principles as measured by the Trust Services Criteria and engage a CPA who is licensed by the AICPA to provide WebTrust service. Generally, this service will cover a period of three months or more. Once the seal is obtained, the entity can display it on its website provided the assurance examination is updated regularly and the entity informs the practitioner of any significant changes in its business policies, practices, processes, or controls. The entity's WebTrust seal will be managed by a trusted third-party service organization (the "seal manager"). If the entity receives an unqualified report, the practitioner notifies the seal manager that the seal can

TABLE 21–9	Selected *WebTrust* Criteria for EarthWear Clothiers

Processing Integrity

Criterion	Controls
1. The entity maintains controls to provide reasonable assurance that • Each order is checked for accuracy and completeness. • Positive acknowledgment is received from the customer before the order is processed.	• EarthWear's order entry system automatically checks each order for accuracy and completeness. • All customer order information is stored in a "shopping basket." When the customer has finished shopping, the contents of the shopping basket are displayed. The customer clicks "yes" to accept the order.

Confidentiality

Criterion	Controls
1. The entity maintains controls to protect transmissions of private customer information over the Internet from unintended recipients.	• Private customer information is protected during transmission by encryption technology. • EarthWear has registered its domain name and Internet IP address. The address is unique. • The company's Web page has a digital certificate that can be checked using features in a standard Web browser. • EarthWear's Webmaster updates and reviews the site daily to ensure that no improper content or links have been added.

be displayed on the entity's website and provides an expiration date. Unless update notification is received, the authorization to display the seal expires on the expiration date, and the seal manager will remove the seal's display authorization. The seal displayed at the website can be verified by clicking on the seal, which displays a special WebTrust digital certificate. Verisign, Inc., serves as the designated seal manager for the AICPA.

A WebTrust assurance engagement is performed as an examination under the attestation standards described in this chapter. In examining an entity's website, the practitioner would use guidance provided in SSAE No. 10 (Chapter 5) and the Committee of Sponsoring Organizations of the Treadway Commission's *Internal Control—Integrated Framework*. In such an examination, the practitioner expresses a positive opinion that the presentation of assertions conforms to the AICPA's Trust Services Principles and Criteria. Exhibit 21–11 presents EarthWear's management's assertions about its website. The report of management's assertions is signed by the president and CEO and the chief financial officer. Exhibit 21–12 contains a public accounting firm's unqualified report on those assertions. Note that because EarthWear is a publicly traded company and a WebTrust attestation service involves reporting on internal control, independence considerations prohibit the company's financial statement auditor, Willis & Adams, from providing a WebTrust attestation service to the company (see Chapter 19). Thus, EarthWear engaged another accounting firm, Felix & Waller, to provide the service. The first paragraph of the Felix & Waller report states that the assertions have been examined. The second paragraph states that management is responsible for the assertions while the accountant's responsibility is to express an opinion based on the examination. The third paragraph states the four steps that were undertaken to complete the examination of management's assertions. In particular, Felix & Waller (1) obtained an understanding of EarthWear's e-commerce business and information privacy practices and its controls over the processing of e-commerce

EXHIBIT 21-11	**Management's Assertions for EarthWear's Website**

EarthWear Clothiers, on its Website for electronic commerce (at www.mhhe.com/earthwear), asserts the following:

- We have maintained effective controls to provide reasonable assurance that customers' orders placed using e-commerce were completed and billed as agreed; and
- We have maintained effective controls to provide reasonable assurance that private customer information obtained as a result of e-commerce was protected from uses not related to our business during the period from December 16, 2005, through March 15, 2006, in conformity with the AICPA *WebTrust* Principles and Criteria.

Calvin J. Rogers   James C. Watts
President & CEO   Chief Financial Officer

transactions and the protection of related private customer information, (2) selectively tested transactions executed in accordance with the disclosed business and information privacy practices, (3) tested and evaluated the operating effectiveness of the controls, and (4) performed other procedures that it considered necessary. The opinion paragraph provides an unqualified opinion on EarthWear's management's assertions.

SysTrust
❧ [LO 12]

As more organizations become dependent on information technology to run their businesses and to interact with customers, suppliers, and business partners, it is critical that an entity's information systems operate effectively. The AICPA and CICA have identified this as an opportunity for CPAs and CAs to provide assurance on the information system by offering a service called SysTrust. The system components include its infrastructure, software, personnel, procedures, and data. SysTrust follows the Trust Services Principles and Criteria.

A SysTrust engagement is conducted under attestation standards. The CPA evaluates a system against the Trust Services Principles and Criteria and determines whether controls over the system exist. The CPA then performs tests to determine whether those controls were operating effectively during the specified period. In order for the entity to receive an unqualified opinion, the system must meet all of the Trust Services Principles and Criteria. The accountant's report would look similar to the WebTrust report shown in Exhibit 21–12, except that it would include management's assertions about the effectiveness of the controls over the system.

CPA PrimePlus[5] Services
❧ [LO 13]

The population in the United States and Canada is aging, and many older people have accumulated significant wealth. Additionally, individuals are living to ages at which they require some form of assisted living. For example, the U.S. Census Bureau estimates that in 2000, 16.6 million people in the United States were 75 years of age or older; and they controlled between $11 and $13 trillion in wealth. However, changing demographics show a

---

[5]Until recently, PrimePlus Services were known as ElderCare Services. Upon discussions with clients and CPAs, the AICPA found that the term "ElderCare" was not appealing. The AICPA and the CICA therefore decided to change the name from ElderCare to PrimePlus.

EXHIBIT 21–12	Accountant's WebTrust Attestation Report for EarthWear Website

To the Management of EarthWear Clothiers:

We have examined the assertion by the management of EarthWear Clothiers regarding the effectiveness of its controls over transaction integrity and information protection for e-commerce (at www.mhhe.com/earthwear) based on the AICPA/CICA Web Trust Criteria during the period from December 16, 2005, through March 15, 2006.

These e-commerce disclosures and controls are the responsibility of EarthWear Clothiers management. Our responsibility is to express an opinion based on our examination.

Our examination was conducted in accordance with attestation standards established by the American Institute of Certified Public Accountants, and, accordingly, included (1) obtaining an understanding of the EarthWear Clothier's e-commerce business and information privacy practices and its controls over the processing of e-commerce transactions and the protection of related private customer information, (2) selectively testing transactions executed in accordance with disclosed business and information privacy practices, (3) testing and evaluating the operating effectiveness of the controls, and (4) performing such other procedures as we considered necessary in the circumstances. We believe that our examination provides a reasonable basis for our opinion.

Because of inherent limitations in controls, errors or fraud may occur and not be detected. Furthermore, the projection of any conclusions, based on our findings, to future periods is subject to the risk that (1) changes made to the system or controls, (2) changes in processing requirements, or (3) changes required because of the passage of time, such as to accommodate dates in the year 2005, or (4) the degree of compliance with the policies or procedures may alter the validity of such conclusions.

In our opinion, during the period from December 16, 2005, to March 15, 2006, EarthWear Clothiers, in all material respects:

- maintained effective controls to provide reasonable assurance that customers' orders placed using e-commerce were completed and billed as agreed

- maintained effective controls to provide reasonable assurance that private customer information obtained as a result of e-commerce was protected from uses not related to the company's business

based on the AICPA/CICA WebTrust Criteria.

The CPA *WebTrust* Seal of assurance on EarthWear Clothiers' website for e-commerce constitutes a symbolic representation of the contents of this report and it is not intended, nor should it be construed, to update this report or provide any additional assurance.

This report does not include any representation as to the quality of the EarthWear Clothiers' goods or services nor their suitability for any customer's intended purpose.

Felix & Waller
Tucson, Arizona
April 3, 2006

more mobile younger generation. In many of these younger families, both spouses work outside the home, and they do not have time to care for elderly relatives. The CPA can bring another level of assurance or comfort to the elderly person and his or her family members.

PrimePlus Services are defined as

a unique, customizable package of services offered by Certified Public Accountants to assist the elderly in maintaining—for as long as possible—their lifestyle and financial independence. Practitioners who provide ElderCare/PrimePlus Services draw upon their strengths and competencies in a variety of areas, including cash flow planning and budgeting, pre- and post-retirement planning, insurance reviews and tax planning . . . the services included in each individual ElderCare/PrimePlus engagement will be based upon the needs and wants of each ElderCare/PrimePlus client as well as the skill set of the ElderCare/Prime-Plus practitioner (www.aicpa.org/assurance/eldercare).

The role of the practitioner is one of oversight. The practitioner acts in the place of the absent family members and relies on qualified specialists, employed by the client or the responsible family member, to provide the services outside the scope of the practitioner's expertise. The practitioner's role is to observe and report on how those service providers are meeting the needs of the client and the criteria for care established by the family members. It is likely that this service will be combined with traditional financial services, and the practitioner will establish strategic alliances with other professionals (such as elder law attorneys, geriatric care managers, and social workers or medical personnel). Based on research conducted by the AICPA, it appears that there is a demand for this type of service.

Practitioners can offer three types of PrimePlus services: (1) consulting/facilitating services, (2) direct services, and (3) assurance services.

Consulting/Facilitating Services   This type of service involves the practitioner consulting with the client or third party (the responsible individual) to establish the standards of care expected. This might include giving the third party a list of services that are available in the community. Consulting services might also include assisting the client or third party in selecting the care provider and level of care for each type of care required.

Direct Services   Direct services include practitioner services such as receiving, depositing, and accounting for the individual's income; paying bills and conducting routine financial transactions for the client; and supervising investments and accounting for the estate. These services might also include arranging for proper care, paying for it, and periodically ensuring that the care is being received at the appropriate level; arranging for transportation for the client; and supervising household items such as home maintenance and repairs.

Assurance Services   In this type of service the practitioner issues periodic reports about the quality of care provided to the elderly person. PrimePlus assurance services are conducted as agreed-upon procedures in attestation engagements as described in this chapter. This type of assurance service may involve the practitioner visiting the elderly person and inspecting documentation such as logs, diaries, or other evidence to support that the contracted services have been provided at the appropriate level of care.

The first step for a practitioner is to create an inventory of services available in his or her community for older clients and identify other professionals, such as doctors and geriatric care managers, who can help the practitioner provide services for older clients. For example, the practitioner may partner with a social worker to periodically assess the level of health care provided to the client. The practitioner then observes and reports how the service providers are meeting the needs of the client.

The second step in providing PrimePlus services is an engagement letter that is specifically tailored to the elderly individual. It should clearly identify the practitioner's responsibilities and duties on the engagement. Once the engagement is initiated, it must be properly staffed. While the practitioner will rely on other professionals to deliver services not in the practitioner's area of expertise, the practitioner or members of the practitioner's staff should be assigned tasks commensurate with their abilities.

The type of work that the practitioner performs on a PrimePlus engagement will vary depending upon the circumstances of the engagement. A typical PrimePlus engagement would include consulting services involving assisting the client or third party in selecting the care provider, and level of care, for each type of care required. The typical engagement would also include direct services such as depositing income and paying bills. The more difficult work involves assurance-related procedures such as visiting the client and inspecting logs, diaries, or other evidence to support that the services contracted have been provided appropriately. The engagement may require that the practitioner periodically report to family members.

KEY TERMS

Agreed-upon procedures. Specific procedures performed on the subject matter of an assertion while a practitioner is engaged by a client to issue a report of findings.

Assurance services. Independent professional services that improve the quality of information, or its context, for decision makers.

Attest. A service when a practitioner is engaged to issue or does issue a report on subject matter, or an assertion about subject matter, that is the responsibility of another party.

Auditing. A systematic process of (1) objectively obtaining and evaluating evidence regarding assertions about economic actions and events to ascertain the degree of correspondence between those assertions and established criteria and (2) communicating the results to interested users.

Compilation of financial statements. The presentation, in the form of financial statements, of information that is the representation of management or owners without undertaking to express any assurance on the statements.

Electronic (Internet) commerce. Business transactions between individuals and organizations that occur without paper documents, using computers and telecommunications networks.

Electronic data interchange. The transmission of business transactions over telecommunications networks.

Financial forecasts. Prospective financial statements that present an entity's expected financial position, results of operations, and cash flows.

Financial projections. Prospective financial statements that present, given one or more hypothetical assumptions, an entity's expected financial position, results of operations, and cash flows.

Internal auditing. An independent, objective assurance and consulting activity designed to add value and improve an organization's operations. It helps an organization accomplish its objectives by bringing a systematic, disciplined approach to evaluate and improve the effectiveness of risk management, control, and governance processes.

Reasonable assurance. A term that implies some risk that a material misstatement could be present in the financial statements without the auditor detecting it.

Review of financial statements. The performance of inquiry and analytical procedures that give the accountant a reasonable basis for expressing limited assurance that no material modifications should be made to the statements in order for them to conform to GAAP.

Risk assessment process. The process through which management of an entity identifies, plans for, and controls the possible threats to achieving the entity's objectives.

www.mhhe.com/ messier4e	Visit the book's Online Learning Center for a multiple-choice quiz that will allow you to assess your understanding of chapter concepts.

REVIEW QUESTIONS

[LO 1] 21-1 Define *assurance services*. Discuss why the definition focuses on decision making and information.

[3,4] 21-2 Define an attest engagement. List the two conditions that are necessary in order to perform an attest engagement.

[4] 21-3 What types of engagements can be provided under the attestation standards? Give two examples of attestation engagements.

[4] 21-4 How can the practitioner satisfy the requirement that specified users take responsibility for the adequacy of procedures performed on an agreed-upon procedures engagement?

[6] 21-5 What kind of entity might request an attestation report on internal control, and why?

[7] 21-6 What are the two types of prospective financial statements? How do they differ from each other?

[8] 21-7 What types of services can be performed under Statements on Standards for Accounting and Review Services?

[8] 21-8 What type of knowledge must an accountant possess about the entity in order to perform a compilation engagement? A review engagement?

[9] 21-9 Define corporate governance. Why do you think an effective internal audit function is referred to as one of the cornerstones of corporate governance?

[9] 21-10 Explain how internal auditors play a role in helping management comply with the requirements of the Sarbanes-Oxley Act of 2002.

[2] 21-11 The Elliott Committee developed six assurance services with significant market potential for CPA firms. What are these six services?

[10] 21-12 What are the risks of electronic commerce? What are the WebTrust Principles?

[10,12] 21-13 Describe the principles used in SysTrust to evaluate a system as reliable.

[13] 21-14 Why is PrimePlus potentially a major service for CPA firms? What types of PrimePlus services can a practitioner offer?

MULTIPLE–CHOICE QUESTIONS

[1,2] 21-15 An assurance report on information can provide assurance about the information's
a. Reliability.
b. Relevance.
c. Timeliness.
d. All of the above.

[3,4,] 21-16 Which of the following professional services would be considered an attest engagement?
a. A management consulting engagement to provide IT advice to a client.
b. An engagement to report on compliance with statutory requirements.
c. An income tax engagement to prepare federal and state tax returns.
d. Compilation of financial statements from a client's accounting records.

[7] 21-17 An accountant may accept an engagement to apply agreed-upon procedures to prospective financial statements, provided that
a. The prospective financial statements are also examined.
b. Responsibility for the adequacy of the procedures performed is taken by the accountant.
c. Negative assurance is expressed on the prospective financial statements taken as a whole.
d. Distribution of the report is restricted to the specified users.

[7] 21-18 Which of the following statements concerning prospective financial statements is correct?
a. Only a financial forecast would normally be appropriate for limited use.
b. Only a financial projection would normally be appropriate for general use.
c. Any type of prospective financial statement would normally be appropriate for limited use.
d. Any type of prospective financial statement would normally be appropriate for general use.

[8] 21-19 When compiling the financial statements of a nonpublic entity, an accountant should
a. Review agreements with financial institutions for restrictions on cash balances.
b. Understand the accounting principles and practices of the entity's industry.
c. Inquire of key personnel concerning related parties and subsequent events.
d. Perform ratio analyses of the financial data of comparable prior periods.

[8] 21-20 Which of the following statements is correct concerning both an engagement to compile and an engagement to review a nonpublic entity's financial statements?

a. The accountant does *not* contemplate obtaining an understanding of internal control.

b. The accountant must be independent in fact and appearance.

c. The accountant expresses *no* assurance on the financial statements.

d. The accountant should obtain a written management representation letter.

[8] 21-21 The standard report issued by an accountant after reviewing the financial statements of a nonpublic entity states that

a. A review includes assessing the accounting principles used and significant estimates made by management.

b. A review includes examining, on a test basis, evidence supporting the amounts and disclosures in the financial statements.

c. The accountant is *not* aware of any material modifications that should be made to the financial statements.

d. The accountant does *not* express an opinion or any other form of assurance on the financial statements.

[8] 21-22 Financial statements of a nonpublic entity that have been reviewed by an accountant should be accompanied by a report stating that

a. The scope of the inquiry and the analytical procedures performed by the accountant have *not* been restricted.

b. All information included in the financial statements is the representation of the management of the entity.

c. A review includes examining, on a test basis, evidence supporting the amounts and disclosures in the financial statements.

d. A review is greater in scope than a compilation, the objective of which is to present financial statements that are free of material misstatements.

[9] 21-23 The *general* accreditation granted by the Institute of Internal Auditors is known as the

a. CFE.

b. CGAP.

c. CFSA.

d. CIA.

[9] 21-24 Which of the following is *not* one of the general areas of the IIA's International Standards for the Professional Practice of Internal Auditing?

a. Performance standards.

b. Implementation standards.

c. Ethical standards.

d. Attribute standards.

[9] 21-25 The four principles of the IIA Code of Ethics are

a. Confidentiality, competency, objectivity, and integrity.

b. Objectivity, independence, compliance, and due diligence.

c. Honesty, integrity, independence, and competency.

d. Integrity, confidentiality, independence, and compliance.

[10]   21-26   Which of the following is not a Trust Services Principle?
a. Processing integrity.
b. Online privacy.
c. Digital certificate authorization.
d. Availability.

[12]   21-27   Which of the following assurances is *not* provided by an unqualified opinion on a SysTrust report?
a. There are procedures to protect the system against unauthorized physical access.
b. The financial statements created by the system are free of material misstatements.
c. The documented system availability objectives, policies, and standards have been communicated to authorized users.
d. Documented system processing integrity objectives, policies, and standards have been communicated to authorized users.

[13]   21-28   Which of the following reasons best explains why a practitioner should obtain an engagement letter for a PrimePlus engagement?
a. Attestation standards require that the practitioner use an engagement letter.
b. An engagement letter will specify the practitioner's responsibilities and duties on the engagement.
c. It will provide absolute protection for the practitioner in the event of a lawsuit by the client.
d. The practitioner will be able to shift the responsibility for non–assurance-related actions to others.

[13]   21-29   Which of the following is not a type of PrimePlus service?
a. Assurance services.
b. Consulting/facilitating services.
c. Direct services.
d. Systems design services.

PROBLEMS

[6]   21-30   You have audited the financial statements of the Orange Grove Savings and Loan for the year ended December 31, 2005. Orange Grove's management is required to provide a report about the effectiveness of Orange Grove's internal control over financial reporting under the Federal Deposit Insurance Corporation Act of 1991. You have been engaged to examine management's report, which will be presented in a separate report. Management uses the definition of internal control based on the internal control framework set forth in SAS No. 55 (the COSO framework).

Required:
a. Prepare a draft of the examination report on management's report on the effectiveness of the S&L's internal control. Assume that there are no material weaknesses.
b. Draft the same report, except assume that the S&L has a material weakness in its loan application procedures for ensuring the adequacy of collateral for loans.

[7]   21-31   Your client, Cheaney Rental Properties, has engaged you to perform a compilation of its forecasted financial statements for a loan with the National Bank of Rockwood.

Required:
a. Describe the steps an accountant should complete when conducting a compilation of prospective financial statements.
b. Prepare a standard compilation report for Cheaney Rental Properties.

[7]   21-32   You are the manager of the examination engagement of the financial projection of Honey's Health Foods as of December 31, 2005, and for the year then ended. The audit senior, Currie, has prepared the following draft of the examination report:

To the Board of Directors of Honey's Health Foods:

We have examined the accompanying projected balance sheet and statements of income, retained earnings, and cash flows of Honey's Health Foods as of December 31, 2005, and for the year then ending. Our examination was made in accordance with standards for an examination of a projection and accordingly included such procedures as we considered necessary to evaluate the assumptions used by management.

In our opinion, the accompanying forecast is presented in conformity with guidelines for presentation of a forecast established by the American Institute of Certified Public Accountants, and the underlying assumptions provide a reasonable basis for management's projection. However, there will usually be differences between the projected and actual results because events and circumstances frequently do not occur as expected, and those differences may be material.

Waller & Felix, CPAs

Required:
Identify the deficiencies in Currie's draft of the examination report. Group the deficiencies by paragraph.

[8]   21-33   The following report was drafted on October 25, 2005, by Major, CPA, at the completion of an engagement to compile the financial statements of Ajax Company for the year ended September 30, 2005. Ajax is a nonpublic entity in which Major's child has a material direct financial interest. Ajax decided to omit substantially all of the disclosures required by generally accepted accounting principles because the financial statements will be for management's use only. The statement of cash flows was also omitted because management does not believe it to be a useful financial statement.

To the Board of Directors of Ajax Company:

I have compiled the accompanying financial statements of Ajax Company as of September 30, 2005, and for the year then ended. I planned and performed the compilation to obtain limited assurance about whether the financial statements are free of material misstatements.

A compilation is limited to presenting information in the form of financial statements. It is substantially less in scope than an audit in accordance with generally accepted auditing standards, the objective of which is the expression of an opinion regarding the financial statements taken as a whole. I have not audited the accompanying financial statements and accordingly do not express any opinion on them.

Management has elected to omit substantially all of the disclosures required by generally accepted accounting principles. If the omitted disclosures were included in the financial statements, they might influence the user's conclusions about the company's financial position, results of operations, and changes in financial position.

I am not independent with respect to Ajax Company. This lack of independence is due to my child's ownership of a material direct financial interest in Ajax Company.

This report is intended solely for the information and use of the board of directors and management of Ajax Company and should not be used for any other purpose.

Major, CPA

Required:
Identify the deficiencies contained in Major's report on the compiled financial statements. Group the deficiencies by paragraph where applicable. Do *not* redraft the report.

(AICPA, adapted)

[8]   21-34   This question consists of 13 items pertaining to possible deficiencies in an accountant's review report. Select the *best* answer for each item. Indicate your answers in the space provided.

Jordan & Stone, CPAs, audited the financial statements of Tech Company, a nonpublic entity, for the year ended December 31, 2004, and expressed an unqualified opinion. For the year ended December 31, 2005, Tech issued comparative financial statements. Jordan & Stone reviewed Tech's 2005 financial statements, and Kent, an assistant on the engagement, drafted the following accountant's review report. Land, the engagement supervisor, decided not to reissue the prior year's auditors' report but instructed Kent to include a separate paragraph in the current year's review report describing the responsibility assumed for the prior year's audited financial statements. This is an appropriate reporting procedure.

Land reviewed Kent's draft and indicated in the supervisor's review notes (shown following the accountant's review report) that there were several deficiencies in Kent's draft.

Accountant's Review Report

We have reviewed and audited the accompanying balance sheets of Tech Company as of December 31, 2005 and 2004, and the related statements of income, retained earnings, and cash flows for the years then ended, in accordance with Statements on Standards for Accounting and Review Services issued by the American Institute of Certified Public Accountants and generally accepted auditing standards. All information included in these financial statements is the representation of the management of Tech Company.

A review consists principally of inquiries of company personnel and analytical procedures applied to financial data. It is substantially less in scope than an audit in accordance with generally accepted auditing standards, the objective of which is the expression of an opinion regarding the financial statements taken as a whole.

Based on our review, we are not aware of any material modifications that should be made to the accompanying financial statements. Because of the inherent limitations of a review engagement, this report is intended for the information of management and should not be used for any other purpose.

The financial statements for the year ended December 31, 2004, were audited by us, and our report was dated March 2, 2005. We have no responsibility for updating that report for events and circumstances occurring after that date.

Jordan and Stone, CPAs

March 1, 2006

Required:

Items 1 through 13 represent deficiencies noted by Land. For each deficiency, indicate whether Land is correct (C) or incorrect (I) in the criticism of Kent's draft.

Supervisor's Review Notes	C or I
1. There should be *no* reference to the prior year's audited financial statements in the first (introductory) paragraph.	
2. All the current-year basic financial statements are *not* properly identified in the first (introductory) paragraph.	
3. There should be *no* reference to the American Institute of Certified Public Accountants in the first (introductory) paragraph.	
4. The accountant's review and audit responsibilities should follow management's responsibilities in the first (introductory) paragraph.	
5. There should be *no* comparison of the scope of a review to an audit in the second (scope) paragraph.	
6. Negative assurance should be expressed on the current year's reviewed financial statements in the second (scope) paragraph.	
7. There should be a statement that *no* opinion is expressed on the current year's financial statements in the second (scope) paragraph.	
8. There should be a reference to "conformity with generally accepted accounting principles" in the third paragraph.	
9. There should be *no* restriction on the distribution of the accountant's review report in the third paragraph.	
10. There should be *no* reference to "material modifications" in the third paragraph.	
11. There should be an indication of the type of opinion expressed on the prior year's audited financial statements in the fourth (separate) paragraph.	
12. There should be an indication that *no* auditing procedures were performed after the date of the report on the prior year's financial statements in the fourth (separate) paragraph.	
13. There should be *no* reference to "updating the prior year's auditor's report for events and circumstances occurring after that date" in the fourth (separate) paragraph.	

(AICPA, adapted)

[10,11]   21-35   Rhett Corporation, a local sporting goods company, has asked your firm for assistance in setting up its website. Eric Rhett, the CEO, is concerned that potential customers will be reluctant to place orders over the Internet to a relatively unknown entity. He recently heard about companies finding ways to provide assurance to customers about secure websites, and Rhett has asked to meet with you about this issue.

Required:

Prepare answers to each of the following questions that may be asked by Rhett.

a. Why are customers reluctant to engage in e-commerce?

b. What type of assurance can your firm provide to his customers concerning the company's website?

c. What process will your firm follow in providing a WebTrust assurance service for Rhett's website?

[10,12]   21-36   Beachwood Sparks Company, a nonpublic company that supplies apparel to retail stores, recently has implemented a new information system. However, during system development and implementation, the company experienced a great deal of turnover in personnel involved with designing and implementing the system. Consequently, the company's board of directors is concerned about whether the system is reliable. It has heard of an assurance service called SysTrust, but would like to know more about it before discussing it with it's CPA firm.

Required:

a. What types of assurances does a SysTrust examination provide? What are the main principles underlying a reliable system that a SysTrust examination considers?

b. What special skills does a CPA undertaking a SysTrust examination require?

c. Beachwood's board of directors is wondering whether any of its constituents would be interested in the SysTrust report. For example, the company is interested in renewing its business interruption insurance, winning business from new retailers, and making itself attractive as a takeover target. Describe how an unqualified SysTrust report would benefit Beachwood from the point of view of the insurance company, potential customers, and potential buyers of the company. (Hint: Examine the SysTrust principles and underlying criteria perhaps by obtaining SysTrust documentation available on the AICPA website, www.aicpa.org, specifically considering which principles and criteria would be of interest to each of the three constituents.)

[13]   21-37   Mr. and Mrs. Greg Jun called your firm, Hillison & Reimer, in response to a brochure they received from Greg's elderly mother. The Juns reside in Ann Arbor, Michigan, while Greg's mother has retired to Tallahassee, Florida. In recent months, the Juns have become very concerned about Greg's mother and her ability to care for herself. On a number of occasions, Greg has received calls from his mother's friends expressing concern that she has not been eating properly and is not regularly taking her medicine for a heart condition.

Required:

a. Describe the PrimePlus service to the Juns, including the types of services that can be offered.

b. Because the Juns' concerns do not relate to areas of your expertise as a CPA, explain to them how you will be able to provide assurance on the care providers.

DISCUSSION CASE

[3,4,5]   21-38   The accounting profession is concerned about whether companies are in compliance with various federal and state environmental laws and regulations and whether they have reported environmental liabilities in their financial statements. *Environmental auditing* typically refers to the process of assessing compliance with environmental laws and regulations, as well as compliance with company policies and procedures. SSAE No. 10, Chapter 6, "Compliance Attestation," allows a practitioner to perform agreed-upon procedures to assist users in evaluating management's written assertions about (1) the entity's compliance with specified requirements, (2) the effectiveness of the entity's internal control over compliance, or (3) both.

Required:
a. Discuss how a practitioner would conduct an agreed-upon procedures engagement to evaluate an entity's written assertion that it was in compliance with its state's environmental laws and regulations.
b. Assume that this same entity maintained an internal control system that monitored the entity's compliance with its state's environmental laws and regulations. Discuss how a practitioner would evaluate the effectiveness of the entity's internal control over compliance.

INTERNET ASSIGNMENTS

[9]   21-39   The IIA maintains its own website containing useful information about the institute and the internal auditing profession in general. Visit the IIA's home page (www.theiia.org).

Required:
a. Follow the link to the official magazine of the IIA. What is the mission of this respected publication?
b. Although the IIA does not require that its members obtain CIA certification, it is becoming popular worldwide. What advantages are afforded to those who certify, according to the IIA's website? Who might benefit from the CIA designation?

[10,11,12]   21-40   The AICPA has developed an assurance service related to electronic commerce called CPA WebTrust. Visit the AICPA's home page (www.aicpa.org) and examine the CPA WebTrust seal.

Required:
a. List the assertions made by the management of the AICPA. Who "signed" the management report on assertions? What time period is covered by the report?
b. Examine the assurance report prepared by the AICPA's CPA firm. What is the name of the CPA firm?

[10,11,12]   21-41   EarthWear has a number of competitors that sell goods over the Internet. Visit the home page for any two of EarthWear's competitors. For example, visit the home page for Timberland (www.timberland.com), L. L. Bean (www.llbean.com), or Land's End (www.landsend.com).

Required:

a. Determine if any of the sites selected provides any type of assurance on its electronic commerce. Note that you may have to prepare to order a product before any assurances are presented on the site.

b. If any of the sites provides assurance on electronic commerce, compare the assurances provided with the Trust Services Principles and Criteria.

[13]   21-42   PrimePlus services may require that the practitioner prepare an inventory of services that are available in his or her community.

Required:

a. Search the Joint Commission on Accreditation of Healthcare Organizations' website (www.jcaho.org) to investigate the types of information that are available on health care organizations in your area.

b. Search the Internet to identify other resources and services that might be available in your area.

| www.mhhe.com/
messier4e | Visit the book's Online Learning Center for problem material to be completed using the *ACL* software packaged with your new text. |

Index

Note: Page numbers followed by *n* indicate material in numbered footnotes.